A General and Heraldic Dictionary of the Peerages of England, Ireland, and Scotland, Extinct, Dormant, and in Abeyance. England

Frederick Augustus Guelph

DUKE OF YORK & ALBANY, &c.

Last Extinct Peer of Royal Blood

London Published by Colburn & Bentley Oct.r 1 1831

)IC

AND,

e.

ɪE

ɪ,

EX

D

A

GENERAL AND HERALDIC

DICTIONARY

OF

THE PEERAGES

OF

ENGLAND, IRELAND, AND SCOTLAND,

Extinct, Dormant, and in Abeyance.

Loquimur de antiquitate Generis, et gloriâ Majorum.

By JOHN BURKE, Esq.,

AUTHOR OF A GENERAL AND HERALDIC DICTIONARY OF THE PEERAGE
AND BARONETAGE, &c. &c.

England.

LONDON:
HENRY COLBURN AND RICHARD BENTLEY,
NEW BURLINGTON STREET.
M.DCCC.XXXI.

LONDON:

HENRY BAYLIS, JOHNSON'S-COURT, FLEET-STREET.

THIS WORK

IS INSCRIBED TO THE MEMORY

OF

THEIR ROYAL HIGHNESSES

FREDERICK, DUKE OF YORK,

AND

EDWARD, DUKE OF KENT,

PRINCES OF THE ILLUSTRIOUS FAMILY OF GUELPH,

AND

Last Extinct Peers

OF

ROYAL BLOOD.

PREFACE.

WHEN I formed the resolution of writing upon Titles of Honour, it was my intention to begin with Extinct, Dormant, and Suspended Dignities; for out of these, I knew, had arisen the most eminent names in the modern roll of nobility, and I felt the great difficulty of rendering any thing like justice to the illustrious living, without the previous opportunity of commemorating the illustrious dead. I discovered, too, that much of the obscurity and unintelligibility of similar works could be traced to the absence of what might be termed an Introductory Volume—to the total want of the slightest information as to the origin of the subject. I had resolved therefore to commence with an Extinct and Dormant Peerage: but from such a course I was eventually diverted by those better versed in the doctrine of chances than myself. I was assured that the probabilities of success would become greatly augmented, could I first make my way in public favour by the production of a work wherein the great mass of the public were more immediately interested—by postponing the heroes of Cressy and Agincourt to those of Trafalgar and Waterloo. To that opinion, after some deliberation, but not without reluctance, I acceded—and my Dictionary of the Existing Peerage and Baronetage, now for the fourth time in the press, was the result.

From the admirable scheme of amalgamating the younger children of our nobility with the community at large, a GRADE in society has arisen amongst us, not to be found in any other country of Europe— a GRADE inferior to the NOBLE in nought beside the artificial importance attached to rank. In the antiquity of his family—in his education—his habits—his influence, the English gentleman stands hardly one step, if at all, below the English nobleman. Nay, there are few of his *order* that cannot boast an alliance with, or descent from, some ancient ennobled house; and it is in this point of view—in shewing the connecting link between the existing gentry of England, and her ancient nobility—that a work upon Extinct, Dormant, and Suspended Dignities, may be rendered in the highest degree interesting and valuable. How far I have succeeded, must rest entirely upon the judgment of my readers. I shall feel, however, greatly obliged by suggestions in extension or amendment of the design.

The Second Volume, comprising the Extinct and Dormant Peers of Scotland and Ireland, is in progress, and any information regarding their representatives will be most acceptable.

In conclusion, I have only to intreat forbearance towards the inaccuracies, which, despite of every effort, are inseparable from the First Edition of a work of this description.

J. B.

November, 1831.

NOTES EXPLANATORY.

ABEYANCE. On the death of a baron, whose dignity originated in a Writ of Summons, without issue male, the barony becomes vested in his daughters; if he leave an only daughter, she succeeds to the dignity, but if there be more daughters than one, the title falls into ABEYANCE amongst them, and continues in that state until all but one of the daughters, or the sole heir of only one daughter survives; in which case, the barony devolves on the surviving daughter, or on the heir of her body. The CROWN can, however, at any time, terminate an ABEYANCE in favor of one of the heirs.

AIDS PAYABLE TO THE KING. Among the ancient aids payable to the king, from the immediate tenants of the crown, (and likewise to inferior lords from their immediate tenants,) were these three, namely, to make his eldest son a knight; to marry his eldest daughter; and to ransom his person when made prisoner in war.

BULLS AND BRIEFS. Apostolical letters were of two description—one denominated *Briefs*, because comprised in a compendious way of writing, and sealed on wax only *Cum annullopiscatoris*, that is, with the impression of a signet ring. The other called BULLS, from the leaden *Bulla* hanging thereto. *Bulla*, amongst the antients, is supposed to have been a golden badge, which persons that triumphed over their enemies wore on their breasts like a medal; and it came afterwards to signify a deed, instrument, or writing, described on parchment, or vellum, with a piece of lead suspended thereto by a string. On this piece of lead, the heads of the two Apostles, *St. Peter and St. Paul*, were impressed from the papal seal, which being affixed to the pope's letters, the BULL was considered then to be complete.

CROWN LANDS AND REVENUE. These anciently comprised 1422 manors or lordships, in several counties, besides farms and lands in Middlesex, Shropshire, and Rutland, in the last of which, the king had also £150 of rent in white money —to which may be added the escheats and forfeitures. In short, the revenue of the king was so great, that ODERICUS VITALIS, says it was reported to be one thousand and sixty pounds sterling, thirty shillings, and one penny halfpenny, of the just rents and profits of England, every day of the year—besides gifts and pecuniary punishments.

DICTUM OF KENILWORTH. An edict or award between Henry III. and those barons who had been in arms against him. It was so called because made at Kenilworth Castle, in Warwickshire, (in the 51st year of that monarch). It provided that those involved in the rebellion should pay a compensation of five years' rent for the recovery of their estates. This celebrated statute is to be seen at large in a MS. copy in the Cottonian Library. It was proclaimed in the camp before Kenilworth, 31st October.

GENERAL SURVEY. The survey was begun in the year 1080, and finished in 1086. It was made by verdict or presentment of juries, or certain persons sworn in every hundred, wapentake, or county, before commissioners consisting of the greatest earls or bishops, who inquired into, and described, as well the possessions and customs of the king, as of his great men. They noted what and how much arable land, pasture, meadow, and wood every man had, with the extent and value in the time of EDWARD *the Confessor*, and at the period of making the survey. They also noted the mills and fisheries, and, in some counties, the number of freemen, socmen, villains, borders, servants, young cattle, sheep, hogs, working horses, &c. in every town and manor, and the name of the proprietor. Always setting down the king's name first, then the bishops, abbots, and all the great men that held of the king in capite. This survey was chiefly intended to afford the monarch a true statement of his own lands and demesnes, and also what were held by his tenants. All England, except Westmorland, Cumberland, and Northumberland, was described, with part of Wales, and the description or survey written in two books called the GREAT and LITTLE DOOMSDAY BOOKS, which were deposited in the Exchequer. The smaller book contains only Norfolk, Suffolk, and Essex. This survey being the highest record in the kingdom, was then, and is to this day, a decisive evidence in any controversy on which there may be occasion to consult it.

HOMAGE AND LIVERY. When the king's *tenant in capite* died, his lands were in the king's hands until the heir had done homage, and was of age. When the heir sued to have his estate out of the possession of the crown, his obtaining it was called LIVERY, and the profits received in the mean time by the king were denominated *primer seisin.* For this livery or relief the heir paid certain fees. By the laws of the CONQUEROR, the relief of an EARL was eight horses saddled and bridled, four helmets, four coats of mail, four shields, four spears, four swords, four chasers, and one palfrey saddled and bridled. That of a BARON, half as much, with a palfrey. That of a VAVASOR to his lord, his best horse, helmet, coat of mail, shield, spear, sword, or, in lieu of these, a hundred shillings. That of the countryman, his best beast; and of him that farmed his lands, a year's rent. These were afterwards turned into money.

KNIGHTS' FEE. An ancient law term, signifying so much land of inheritance as was esteemed sufficient to maintain a knight with suitable retinue, which in the time of HENRY III. was reckoned at £15 per annum; and, by stat. 1 Ed. II., such as had £20 per annum in fee, or for life, might be compelled to accept of knighthood. But this statute was repealed by the 16th Charles I. *Stow* says, that in the time of the *Conqueror* there were in England 60,211 knights' fees.

SCUTAGE. Escuage or Scutage, was a duty or service arising out of baronies and knights' fees. It denoted *Servitium Scuti*, the service of the shield; and was wont to be rendered thus: for every knight's fee, the service of one knight; for every half fee, the service of half a knight; and so in proportion. Baronies were charged in a similar manner, according to the number of knights' fees, whereof the barony by its original enfeoffment, consisted. The service of scutage was performed, either personally, in the king's army, or else by pecuniary commutation.

VAVASORS. The Vavasors in Lombardy, whence they appear originally to have come, were inferior to the *capitanei*, which comprehended dukes, marquisses, counts, &c.; but they were invested, either by the sovereign or lord, with some territory of feudal command, without any of these designations of nobility. So that vavasor meant a powerful description of vassal; *validus Vassallus.*

ABBREVIATIONS.

b. born.   *m.* married.   *d.* died.   *s. p.* sine prole.   *s.* succeeded.

CONTENTS.

ERRATA.

IN THE PRESS,

The Fourth Edition, revised and much enlarged, of

A GENERAL AND HERALDIC DICTIONARY

OF THE

PEERAGE AND BARONETAGE

OF THE

BRITISH EMPIRE.

Dedicated, by Permission, to HIS MOST GRACIOUS MAJESTY,

BY JOHN BURKE, ESQ.

This Work, which has undergone another very laborious revisal, will be found to comprise a great mass of new matter, and several curious documents long out of print, or never printed before.

The armorial bearings have been newly and splendidly engraved.

This popular work justly deserves to be considered as a History of the British Nobility. It is enriched by a variety of personal anecdotes, never before published, relative to many illustrious houses, in addition to numerous authentic details connected with their lineage, and communicated to the author by the noble inheritors of the titles. The Editor's attention having also been directed to collaterals, he has introduced all those who come within the most remote remaindership of family honours; and he has used more than ordinary care in tracing presumptive heirs. To the Baronetcies of Scotland and Ireland, appertaining to more than 200 ancient families, whose lineage is given exclusively in this Work, the utmost attention has also been paid.

" The work which Mr. Burke has just given to the public, is equally well planned and well executed. The author justly observes in the preface, that the grand object in a work of reference is the facility afforded to the reader, of finding any information he may want. Mr. Burke's arrangement is excellently adapted to this purpose. Great ability is also shewn in the condensation of all the requisite matter, which, owing to the clear and beautiful mode of printing and engraving, is justly entitled to be called a cheap one, not only in comparison with the tedious and expensive works on the same subject, but in reference to the quantity of reading it contains, and the superior style of its execution."—*Examiner.*

Also preparing for publication,

A DICTIONARY OF THE COMMONERS OF ENGLAND,

QUALIFIED BY LANDED PROPERTY

TO

BECOME COUNTY MEMBERS OF PARLIAMENT,

BUT UNDISTINGUISHED BY AN HEREDITARY TITLE OF HONOUR.

BY JOHN BURKE, ESQ.

Author of the " General and Heraldic Dictionary of the Peerage and Baronetage."

This original work has been undertaken by Mr. Burke as a sequel to his very popular Dictionary of the Peerage and Baronetage of the United Kingdom, and upon an exactly similar plan; so that when completed, the two publications will embrace the entire of the Peerage, Baronetage, and Gentry of the empire.

Communications for the Author, in answer to the circular letters transmitted to the parties interested, are requested to be addressed, free of expense, to the Publishers.

PEERAGES OF ENGLAND,

EXTINCT, DORMANT, AND IN ABEYANCE..

ABRINCIS—EARLS OF CHESTER.

Created by WILLIAM the *Conqueror*, Anno 1070.

Lineage.

Upon the detention, a prisoner in Flanders, of GHERBOD, a Fleming who first held the Earldom of Chester, that dignity was conferred by the CONQUEROR, upon (his sister's son)

HUGH DE ABRINCIS, surnamed LUPUS, and called by the Welch, *Vras*, or "the Fat." "Which Hugh," says Dugdale, "being a person of great note at that time amongst the Norman nobility, and an expert soldier, was, for that respect, chiefly placed so near those unconquered *Britains*, the better to restrain their bold incursions : for it was, ' consilio prudentum,' by the advice of his council, that King William thus advanced him to that government; his power being, also, not ordinary; having royal jurisdiction within the precincts of his earldom—which honor he received *to hold as freely by the sword as the King himself held England by the crown.* But, though the time of his advancement was not till the year 1070, certain it is, that he came into England with the conqueror, and thereupon had a grant of Whitby, in Yorkshire, which lordship he soon afterwards disposed of to William de Percy, his associate in that famous expedition." In the contest between WILLIAM RUFUS, and his brother ROBERT CURTHOSE, this powerful nobleman sided with the former, and remained faithful to him during the whole of his reign. He was subsequently in the confidence of Henry the First, and one of that monarch's chief councillors. " In his youth and flourishing age," continueth the author above quoted, " he was a great lover of worldly pleasures and secular pomp : profuse in giving, and much delighted with interludes, jesters, horses, dogs, and other like vanities ; having a large attendance of such persons, of all sorts, as were disposed to those sports : but he had also in his family both clerks and soldiers, who were men of great honor, the venerable Anselme (Abbot of Bec, and afterwards Archbishop of Canterbury) being his confessor ; nay, so devout he grew before his death,

that sickness hanging long upon him, he caused himself to be shorn a monk in the abbey of St. Werburge, where, within three days after, he died, Anno 1101." His lordship m. Ermentrude, daughter of Hugh de Claremont, Earl of Bevois, in France, by whom he had an only son,

RICHARD, his successor.

Of his illegitimate issue, were Ottiwell, tutor to those children of King Henry the First, who perished at sea. Robert, originally a Monk in the Abbey of St. Ebrulf in Normandy, and afterwards Abbot of St. Edmundsbury in Suffolk, and Geva,* the wife of Geffery Riddell, to whom the Earl gave Drayton Basset, in Staffordshire.

That this powerful nobleman enjoyed immense wealth in England is evident, from the many lordships he held at the general survey; for, besides the whole of Cheshire, excepting the small part which at that time belonged to the bishop, he had nine lordships in Berkshire, two in Devonshire, seven in Yorkshire, six in Wiltshire, ten in Dorsetshire, four in Somersetshire, thirty-two in Suffolk, twelve in Norfolk, one in Hampshire, five in Oxfordshire, three in Buckinghamshire, four in Gloucestershire, two in Huntingdonshire, four in Nottinghamshire, one in Warwickshire, and twenty-two in Leicestershire. It appears too, by the charter of foundation to the Abbey of St. Werburge, at Chester, that several eminent persons held the rank of Baron under him. The charter runs thus :—" Hæc sunt itaque dona data Abbatiæ S. Werburge, quæ omnia ego Comes HUGO et RICHARDUS filius meus et Ermentrudis Comitissa, et mei Barones, et mei homines dedimus, &c.," which *Barones et Homines* mentioned therein, were the following:—

---

* The legitimacy of this lady is maintained from the circumstance of her father having bestowed upon her the Manor of Drayton, in free marriage, which the lawyers say could not be granted to a bastard ; but had she been legitimate, she would surely have succeeded to the earldom before her aunt.

1. William Malbanc.
2. Robert, son of Hugo.
3. Hugo, son of Norman.
4. Richard de Vernun.
5. Richard de Rullos.
6. Ranulph Venator.
7. Hugo de Mara.
8. Ranulph, son of Ermiwin.
9. Robert de Fremous.
10. Walkelinus, nephew of Walter de Vernon.
11. Seward.
12. Gislebert de Venables.
13. Gaufridus de Sartes.
14. Richard de Mesnilwarin.
15. Walter de Vernun.

The charter concludes—" Et ut hæc omnia essent rata et stabilia inperpetuum, ego Comes Hugo et mei Barones confirmavimus, (&c) ita quod singuli nostrum propriâ manu, in testimonium posteris signum in modum Crucis facerent :"—and is signed by the EARL himself,

Richard—his son.
Hervey, Bishop of Bangor.
Ranulph de Meschines, his nephew, who eventually inherited the earldom.
Roger Bigod.
Alan de Perci.
William Constabular.
Ranulph Dapifer.
William Malbanc.
Robert Fitz-Hugh.
Hugh Fitz-Norman.
Hamo de Masci.
Bigod de Loges.

Those barons, be it remembered, were each of them men of great individual power, and large territorial possessions. Hugh Lupus, Earl of Chester, was succeeded by his only son (then but seven years of age),

RICHARD DE ABRINCIS, as second earl. This nobleman, after he had attained maturity, attached himself faithfully to King Henry I., and never subsequently swerved in his allegiance. His lordship espoused Maud, daughter of Stephen, Earl of Blois, by Adela, daughter of William the Conqueror, but had no issue—himself and his countess being soon afterwards amongst the victims of the memorable shipwreck, (Dec., 1119,) wherein the king's two sons, WILLIAM and RICHARD, with their tutor Ottiwell, the earl's bastard brother, Geffery Riddell, his sister Geva's husband, and many others of the nobility perished. This melancholy event is thus recorded by *Ordericus.*

" The master of the ship was Thomas, son of Stephen, who came to King Henry the First, then in Normandy, and ready to take shipping for England, and offered him a mark of gold, desiring that as Stephen, his father, had transported the conqueror when he fought against King Harold, and was his constant mariner in all his passages between England and Normandy, so that he himself likewise might now have the transportation of King Henry and all his attendants, as it were, in fee; for he had a very good vessel, called ' Candida Navis,' or ' the White Ship,' well furnished for that purpose. The king thanked him: but withal told him, he

had already made choice of another ship, which he would not change; yet, he would commend him to his two sons, William and Richard, with many others of his nobility; whereat the mariners much rejoiced, and desired the prince to bestow some wine upon them to drink. He gave them ' tres modios vini,' three hogsheads of wine, wherewith they made themselves sufficiently drunk. There were almost three hundred in this unfortunate ship, besides the young gallants who were to be transported; as well as fifty skilful oars or galleymen, who, had they not been intoxicated, would have been fully able to manage her; but having neither the power to govern themselves nor the vessel, they suffered her to split upon a rock, and so all were drowned, except one Berolde, a butcher of Roan, who was taken up the next morning by some fishermen, after a cold frosty night's shipwreck; and with much ado recovered, and lived twenty years after."

Upon the demise thus of RICHARD DE ABRINCIS, second Earl of Chester, the male line of the family becoming extinct, the earldom passed to the deceased nobleman's first cousin, RANULPH DE MESCHINES, son of Ralph de Meschines, by Maud de Abrincis, sister of Earl Hugh Lupus—(see Meschines, Earls of Chester).

ARMS—az. a wolf's head erased, ar.

AIREMINE—BARONESS BELASYSE OF OSGODBY.

Created by Letters Patent, 25th of March, 1674.

Lineage.

SIR WILLIAM AIREMINE, Bart., of Osgodby, in the county of Lincoln, m. Arme, daughter and co-heiress of Sir Robert Crane, Baronet, of Chillington, in the county of Suffolk, and left two daughters, his co-heirs, of whom the elder,

SUSAN AIREMINE, m. first, the Honorable Sir Henry Belasyse, son and heir of John, Baron Belasyse, of Warlaby, and had a son,

> HENRY BELASYSE, who s. to the title of Belasyse of Warlaby, upon the decease of his grandfather, his father, Sir Henry, dying previously—(see Belasyse of Warlaby).

LADY BELASYSE m. secondly, —— Fortrey, Esq., of Chequers, but had no issue. Her ladyship was created a peeress for life, by King Charles II. by letters patent dated 25th of March, 1674, as BARONESS BELASYSE OF OSGODBY. She d. 6th March, 1712-13, when the dignity EXPIRED.

ALAN, surnamed FERGAUNT, EARL OF RICHMOND.

(See De Dreaux, Earls of Richmond.)

ALBINI—EARLS OF ARUNDEL.

By feudal tenure of ARUNDEL CASTLE, in the County of Sussex, A. D. 1139.

Lineage.

WILLIAM DE ALBINI, surnamed *Pincerna,* son of Roger de Albini, and elder brother of Nigel de Albini, whose posterity assumed, and attained such eminence under the name of MOWBRAY, accompanied the conqueror into England, and acquired extensive territorial possessions by royal grants in the county of Norfolk and other shires. Of which grants was the lordship of Bokenham, to be holden by the service of being BUTLER to the Kings of England on the day of their coronation, and in consequence we find this William styled in divers charters, "*Pincerna Henrici Regis Ang{iorum.*" Amongst the numerous persons despoiled of their lands by those grants, was one EDWYNE, a Dane, who appealing to the Conqueror, told him, that neither before nor after the conquest, had himself or the other ejected Danes, acted or conspired against him; which complaint induced the king to institute an immediate inquiry throughout the realm, and to order that all those who had lived peaceably, should have restitution of their lands, to enjoy as freely as they had done before, and thenceforward to be called *Drenges.* Edwyne could however recover only a portion of his property, but he was soon afterwards sent into Normandy for the king's illegitimate daughter, whom the monarch bestowed upon his (Edwyne's) son *Ascour;* and thus the protection of the Dane was secured during the remainder of his life.

William de Albini founded the Abbey of Wymundham in Norfolk, and gave to the monks of Rochester, the tithes of his manor of Elham; as also one carucate of land in Achestede, with a wood called Acholte. He likewise bestowed upon the Abbey of St. Stephen at Caen, in Normandie, all his lands lying in Staveil, which grant he made in the presence of King Henry and his barons. He m. Maude, daughter of Roger Bigot, with whom he obtained ten knights' fees in Norfolk—and had issue,

William.

Nigel.

Oliver.

Oliva, m. to Raphe de Haya, a feudal baron of great power.

At the obsequies of Maude, William de Albini gave to the monks of Wymundham, the manor of Hapesburg, in pure alms, and made livery thereof to the said monks by a cross of silver, in which, (says Dugdale,) was placed certain venerable reliques, viz. " part of the wood of the Cross whereon our Lord was crucified; part of the manger wherein he was laid at his birth; and part of the sepulchre of the blessed Virgin; as also a gold ring, and a silver chalice, for retaining the holy eucharist, admirably wrought in form of a sphere: unto which pious donation his three sons were witnesses, with several other persons." The exact time of the decease of this great feudal baron is not ascertained, but it is known that he was buried before the high altar in the Abbey of Wymundham, and that the monks were in the constant habit of praying for his soul, by the name of " William de Albini the king's butler." He was *s.* by his eldest son,

WILLIAM DE ALBINI, surnamed " William with the strong hand," from the following circumstance, as related by Dugdale—

" It happened that the Queen of France, being then a widow, and a very beautiful woman, became much in love with a knight of that country, who was a comely person, and in the flower of his youth:

and because she thought that no man excelled him in valour, she caused a tournament to be proclaimed throughout her dominions, promising to reward those who should exercise themselves therein, according to their respective demerits; and concluding that if the person whom she so well affected, should act his part better than others in those military exercises, she might marry him without any dishonour to herself. Hereupon divers gallant men, from forrain parts hasting to Paris, amongst others came this our William de Albini, bravely accoutred; and in the tournament excelled all others, overcoming many, and wounding one mortally with his lance, which being observed by the queen shee became exceedingly enamoured of him, and forthwith invited him to a costly banquet, and afterwards bestowing certain jewels upon him, offered him marriage; but having plighted his troth to the Queen of England, then a widow, he refused her, whereat she grew so much discontented, that she consulted with her maids how she might take away his life; and in pursuance of that designe, inticed him into a garden, where there was a secret cave, and in it a fierce lion, unto which she descended by divers steps, under colour of shewing him the beast; and when she told him of his fierceness, he answered, that it was a womanish and not a manly quality to be afraid thereof. But having him there, by the advantage of a folding door, thrust him in to the lion; being therefore in this danger, he rolled his mantle about his arm, and putting his hand into the mouth of the beast, pulled out his tongue by the root; which done, he followed the queen to her palace, and gave it to one of her maids to present her. Returning thereupon to England, with the fame of this glorious exploit; he was forthwith advanced to the EARLEDOME OF ARUNDEL, and for his arms the LION given him." He subsequently obtained the hand of the Queen Adelisa, relict of King Henry I., and daughter of GODFREY, DUKE OF LORRAINE, which Adeliza, had the CASTLE OF ARUNDEL in dowry from the deceased monarch, and thus her new lord became its feudal earl. His lordship was one of those who solicited the Empress Maude to come into England, and received her and her brother ROBERT, EARL OF GLOUCESTER, at the Port of Arundel, in August 1139, and in three years afterwards (1142), in the report made of King Stephen's taking William de Mandevil at St. Albans, it is stated—" that before he could be laid hold on, he underwent a sharp skirmish with the king's party, wherein the Earl of Arundell, though a stout and expert souldier, was unhorsed in the midst of the water by Walkeline de Oxeai, and almost drowned." In 1150, his lordship wrote himself EARL OF CHICHESTER, but we find him styled again EARL OF ARUNDEL, upon a very memorable occasion—namely, the reconciliation of Henry Duke of Normandy, (afterwards Henry II.) and King Stephen at the siege of Wallingford Castle in 1152. " It was scarce possible," says Rapin, " for the armies to part without fighting. Accordingly the two leaders were preparing for battle with equal ardour, when by the prudent advice of the EARL OF ARUNDEL, who was on the king's side, they were prevented from coming to blows." A truce and peace followed this interference of the earl's, which led to the subsequent accession of Henry after Stephen's decease, in whose favour the earl stood so high, that he not only obtained for himself and his heirs, the castle and honour of Arundel, but a confirmation of the Earldom of SUSSEX, of which county he was really EARL, by a grant of the *Tertium Denarium* of the pleas of that shire. In 1164, we find the Earl of Arundel deputed with Gilbert Foliot, Bishop of London, to remonstrate with Lewis, King of France, upon affording an asylum to Thomas à Becket within his dominions, and on the failure of that mission, dispatched with the Archbishop of York, the Bishops of Winchester, London, Chichester, and Exeter—Wido Rufus, Richard de Invecestre, John de Oxford (Priests)—Hugh de Gundeville, Bernard de St. Valery, and Henry Fitzgerald, to lay the whole affair of Becket at the foot of the pontifical throne. Upon this occasion the Earl of Arundel is said to have addressed the Pope—"Sir, we being illiterate, are ignorant what the bishops have expressed; but we are not to be instructed to what purpose we are sent. We come not to do any thing contumeliously in the presence of so great a person, to whose authority the whole world doth stoop; but we are to declare, in the presence of this whole court, how great a devotion our king hath borne, and doth bear to your holyness; and that if he could have found out any persons more great and noble to have signified the same, than these now sent, he would have employed them on this errand." Upon levying the aid for the marriage of the king's daughter—12th of Henry II., the knights' fees of the honour of Arundel were certified to be ninety-seven, and those in Norfolk belonging to the earl, forty-two. In 1173, we find the Earl of Arundel commanding in conjunction with William Earl of Mandeville, the king's army in Normandy, and compelling the French monarch to abandon Verneuil after a long siege, and in the next year, with Richard de Lucy, Justice of England, defeating Robert Earl of Leicester, then in rebellion at St. Edmundsbury. This potent nobleman, after founding and endowing several religious houses, departed this life at Waverley, in Surrey, on the 3d of October 1176, and was buried in the Abbey of Wymundham. His lordship left four sons and three daughters, viz.—

1. William.
2. Godfrey.
3. ———
4. ———
1. Alice, m. to John Earl of Ewe.
2. Oliva.
3. Agatha.

He was s. by his eldest son,

WILLIAM DE ALBINI, second earl, who had a grant from the crown, 23rd Henry II., of the earldom of Sussex, and in the 1st of Richard I., had a confirmation from that prince, of the castle and honour of Arundel, as also of the *Tertium Denarium* of the county of Sussex. In five years afterwards we find this nobleman paying eighty-four pounds, ten shillings, for his scutage for King Richard's redemption, and the next year one hundred pounds, for his relief for his lands in Norfolk. His lordship was at Runnimede at the signing of the great charters, but upon the king's side; he subsequently, however, swore to obey the determination of the twenty-five barons, chosen to enforce the execution of those charters. In 1218, the earl embarked in the Crusade, and was at the celebrated siege of Damieta, but died in returning, anno 1222. His lordship m. Maude, daughter and heiress of James de Sancto Sidonio, and widow of Roger, Earl of Clare, by whom he left issue.

WILLIAM, } successors to the earldom.
HUGH, }
Isabel, m. to JOHN FITZALAN, Baron of Clun and Oswestry.
Mabel, m. to Robert de Tateshall.
Nicolaa, m. to Roger de Somery.
Cecilia, m. to Roger de Montalt.
Colet, m. to

The earl was s. by his elder son,

WILLIAM DE ALBINI, third earl, who m. Mabel, second of the four sisters and co-heiresses of Ranulph, Earl of Chester, with whom he obtained landed property to the amount of £500. per annum. Dying, however, issueless in the eighteenth year of Henry III., his honours devolved upon his only brother (then in minority),

HUGH DE ALBINI, fourth earl. This nobleman gave two thousand and five hundred marks fine to the king for the possession of all the lands and castles which descended to him from his brother, and those which he inherited from his uncle, *Ranulph*, EARL OF CHESTER. At the nuptials of King Henry III. we find the Earl of Warren serving the king with the royal cup in the place of this earl, by reason he was then but a youth, and not knighted. His lordship m. Isabel, daughter of William, Earl of Warren and Surrey, but dying in 1243, s. p., this branch of the great house of Albini expired, while its large possessions devolved upon the earl's sisters as co-heiresses—thus,

Mabel Tateshall, had the castle and manor of Buckenham.
Isabel Fitzallan, had the castle and manor of Arundel, &c., which conveyed the earldom to her husband.
Nichola de Somery, had the manor of Barwe, in the county of Leicester.
Cecilie de Montalt, had the castle of Rising, in the county of Norfolk.

The earl had another sister, Colet, to whom her uncle, Ranulph, Earl of Chester, gave thirty pounds towards her marriage portion, which gift was confirmed by King Henry III.

ARMS—Gu. a lion rampant or, armed and langued az.

ALDEBURGH — BARONS ALDEBURGH.

By Writ of Summons, dated 8th January, 1371, 44 Edward III.

Lineage.

WILLIAM DE ALDEBURGH was summoned

to parliament as a BARON, from 8th January, 1371, to 8th August, 1386, in which latter year his lordship died, and was s. by his only son,

WILLIAM DE ALDEBURGH, second baron, but never summoned to parliament. This nobleman dying without issue, the BARONY OF ALDEBURGH fell into ABEYANCE, at his lordship's decease, between his two sisters.

ALLINGTON — BARONS ALLINGTON OF WYMONDLEY.

By Letters Patent, dated 5th Dec., 1682.

Lineage.

WILLIAM ALLINGTON, Esq., high sheriff of the counties of Cambridge and Huntington, in the reign of Edward IV., said to derive from Sir Hildebrand de Alington, under-marshal to William the Conqueror, at Hastings, m. Elizabeth, only daughter and heiress of John de Argentine, fifth Baron Argentine, and acquired by her the manor of Wymondeley, in the county of Hertford, held in grand serjeanty, by service of presenting the first cup at the coronation of the kings of England; which service was claimed and allowed at the coronation of King James II., and has ever since been performed by the lords of that manor. From this William Allington and Elizabeth his wife lineally descended

SIR GILES ALLINGTON, who m. Mary, only daughter and heiress of Sir Richard Gardiner, Knt., and had several children, of whom three of the younger sons, George, John, and Richard, were the founders of families. Sir Giles was s. by his eldest son,

GILES ALLINGTON, Esq., of Horseheath, in the county of Cambridge; high sheriff of that shire in the 22d of Henry VIII., and of Huntingdon in the 37th of the same monarch. Mr. Allington appears to have attended King Henry VIII. as master of the ordnance at the siege of Bulloigne, by the inscription of a clock which he brought from that siege, and affixed over the offices at Horseheath Hall, in which was the alarum-bell of the garrison of Bulloigne. He died in 1586, and from him lineally descended

WILLIAM ALLINGTON, Esq., of Horseheath Hall, who was elevated to the peerage of Ireland, as BARON ALLINGTON, of Killard, on the 28th July, 1642. His lordship m. Elizabeth, daughter of Sir Lionel Tallemache, Bart., of Helmingham, in the county of Norfolk, by whom he had, with five sons, three daughters; viz.

    Elizabeth m. to Charles Lord Seymour, of Troubridge.

    Catherine m. to Sir John Jacob, Bart., of Gamlinghay, in the county of Cambridge.

    Diana d. unmarried.

Lord Allington was s. by his second, but eldest surviving son,

WILLIAM ALLINGTON, second baron, who was created a peer of England on the 5th of December, 1682, by the title of BARON ALLINGTON, of Wymondley, in the county of Herts. His lordship m., first, Catherine, second daughter of Henry Lord Stanhope, son of Philip, second earl of Chesterfield, by whom

he had no issue. He m., secondly, Joanna, daughter of Baptist, Lord Campden, and had a daughter, Joanna, who m. Scroope, Lord Howe. Lord Allington, m., thirdly, Diana, daughter of William Russell, first duke of Bedford, by whom he had one surviving son, Giles, and two daughters; viz.

    Diana m. to Sir George Warburton, Bart., of Arley, in the county of Chester, and d. in 1705.

    Catherine m. to Sir Nathaniel Napier, Bart., of Middlemersh Hall, in the county of Dorset.

His lordship d. in 1684, and was succeeded by his son,

GILES ALLINGTON, third baron of the Irish creation, and second of the English. This nobleman dying in his tenth year, anno 1691, the English peerage expired, while that of Ireland reverted to his uncle,

The HON. HILDEBRAND ALLINGTON, son of the first lord, as fourth baron; but his lordship did not inherit the fortune. William, the second lord, having devised his estates, the most extensive in the county of Cambridge, to his widow during the minority of his children, with a power of granting leases to raise portions for his daughters, that lady, in consequence of an error in the will, found herself possessed of the power of leasing ad infinitum, and she accordingly made a lease of the whole to Henry Bromley, Esq., afterwards Lord Montford, ancestor of the present lord, for 999 years; to whom, subsequently, Hildebrand, Lord Allington, also disposed of the small interest then remaining to him in the estates. His lordship dying s. p. in 1722, the Irish barony of ALLINGTON OF KILLARD, likewise became EXTINCT.

ARMS—Sa. a bend ingrailed betw. six billets as.

AMORIE—BARONS D'AMORIE.

By Writ of Summons, dated 20th Nov., 1317.
2 Edward II.

Lineage.

GILBERT DE AUMARI, in the 15th Henry II., gave fifteen marks for livery of his lands at Winford, in the county of Somerset; after this Gilbert came another,

GILBERT D'AMORIE, who in the 22nd Ed. I. was in the expedition made into Gascony. This Gilbert had three sons, viz :—

1. ROGER (Sir), of whom presently.
2. NICHOLAS, who in the 6th Ed. II. obtained a charter of Free Warren, in all his demesne lands within the manors of Bokenhall, and Blechesdon, in the county of Oxford, and Thornebergh in the county of Bucks. He was s. by his son,

    SIR RICHARD D'AMORIE, who was summoned to Parliament as a BARON, from 20th Edw. II. to 4th Edw. III. This nobleman was in the wars of Scotland in 1320, and in three years afterwards, being at the time steward of the king's household, had command to besiege the Castle of Walingford, then in possession of the rebellious lords. His lordship died in 1330, leaving issue

RICHARD, second baron, but never summoned to parliament. His lordship who was engaged in the Flemish and French wars, from 1341 to 1347, d. without issue in 1375, when this BARONY EXPIRED, but the estates devolved upon his sisters,

ELIZABETH, m. to Sir John Chandos, K. G.

ELEANOR, m. to Roger Colyng.

MARGARET, whose only child, Isabel, m. Sir John Annesley, Knight.

3. RICHARD (Sir), continued the male line, after the extinction of his elder brothers, and from him sprang the family of DAMER, EARLS OF DORCHESTER, now represented by the Earl of Portarlington and his brothers.

The eldest son,

SIR ROGER D'AMORIE, was summoned to parliament as a BARON, from 20th Nov., 1317, to 15th May, 1321. This nobleman obtained in 13th Edward II., from the crown, confirmed by the parliament then held at York, the Manors of Sandall, in Yorkshire, Haighton, in the county of Oxford, and Faukeshall, in Surrey, as likewise one hundred marks per annum to be paid out of the exchequer. His lordship was engaged in the wars of Scotland, and was governor at different times of Knaresborough Castle, the Castle of Gloucester, and St. Briavel's Castle. He was also warden of the forest of Dene. He joined, however, in the confederacy against the Spencers, and enrolling himself under the banner of Thomas, Earl of Lancaster, marched on Burton-upon-Trent, and thence to Tutbury Castle, in the county of Stafford, where falling ill, he died in 1322; and was buried in the priory at Ware, in Hertfordshire. His lordship m. Elizabeth, third sister and co-heir of Gilbert de Clare, Earl of Gloucester, (who had been previously twice a widow, first of John de Burgh, Earl of Ulster, and secondly, of Theobald de Verdon, she was also niece of King Edward II.). By this lady he had issue, two daughters, his coheirs, viz.

Elizabeth, m. to John, Lord Bardolph, by whom she had

WILLIAM, Lord Bardolph, whose son

THOMAS, Lord Bardolph, being attainted, the BARONIES OF BARDOLPH AND D'AMORIE, fell under the attainder and EXPIRED in 1404.

Eleanor, m. to John de Raleigh, progenitor of the celebrated Sir Walter Raleigh.

Upon the decease of Lord D'Amorie, orders were given to seize all his lands as an enemy and rebel, and to make livery of them to Elizabeth de Burgh, his widow. This lady died in the 34th Edward III., leaving. Dugdale says, Elizabeth Lady Bardolph, then above thirty years of age; Nicolas calls this Elizabeth the only daughter and heir of Roger, Lord D'Amorie; as such, she of course inherited the Barony of Damorie, and it EXPIRED as stated above, with that of Bardolph; but Banks mentions the other daughter, who if Sir Walter Raleigh sprang from her, left descendants, amongst some of whom

6

the BARONY OF D'AMORIE, may yet be in ABEYANCE.

ARMS. Barry of six, nebulée, az. and gu., a bend as.

ANNESLEY—EARLS OF ANGLESEY.

By Letters Patent, dated 20th April, 1661.

Lineage.

The ancient family of ANNESLEY, derived their surname from the town of Annesley, in the county of Nottingham, which was possessed in 1079, by

RICHARD DE ANNESLEY, from whom lineally descended

SIR JOHN ANNESLEY, Knight of Hedynton, in the county of Oxford, member of parliament for the county of Nottingham, temp. Edward III. and Richard II. This gentleman m. Isabel, daughter and heir of Margaret, third sister and co-heir of Sir John Chandos, K.G., Baron of St. Saviour le Viscount, in Normandy, whereby becoming interested in that barony, he cited Thomas de Caterton, who had been governor of the castle of St. Saviour le Viscount, into the Court of Chivalry, to appear before the Lord High Constable of England and others, at Westminster, on 7th May, 1380, to answer his delivering up to the French the said castle of St. Saviour's, a third part whereof being Sir John's property, in right of his wife. And the said Thomas, endeavouring to avoid the challenge by frivolous exceptions, John, Duke of Lancaster, third son of King Edward III., swore, that if he did not perform what he ought to do therein, according to the law of arms, he should be drawn to the gallows as a traitor. The combat took place in the March following, in the Palace Yard of Westminster, and "Caterton," says Barnes, in his History of Edward III., "was a mighty man of valour, of a large stature, and far overtopped the knight, being also of great expectation in such matters. But, however, whether justice, or chance, or valour, only decided the business, the knight prevailed, and Caterton, the day after the combat (as some say,) died of his wounds, though, considering the laws attending duels in such cases, I rather incline to FABIAN, who affirms he was drawn to Tyburn, and there hanged for the treason, whereof being vanquished he was proved guilty." The king taking into consideration the damage done to this Sir John Annesley, was pleased, 26th May, 1385, to grant to him, and Isabel his wife, for their lives, an annuity of £40. per annum out of the exchequer. He was s. by his son,

THOMAS ANNESLEY, of Annesley, in the county of Nottingham, member of parliament for that Shire, temp. Richard II., from whom descended,

ROBERT ANNESLEY, of Newport-Pagnel, in the county of Bucks, who died in the first year of Queen Mary. And we pass to his great grandson,

SIR FRANCIS ANNESLEY, Knight, of Newport-Pagnel, who was created a BARONET OF IRELAND, upon the institution of that order by King James I. And filling the offices in the Irish government of *Vice Treasurer* and *Secretary of State*, he was elevated to the peerage of that kingdom, by letters patent, dated 8th February, 1628, as BARON MOUNT NORRIS, of Mount Norris, in the county of Armagh, having been created the year previously VISCOUNT VALENTIA, in the county of Kerry, to hold immediately after the death of Henry Power, the then Viscount Valentia, in case the said Henry died without male issue, which dignity he accordingly enjoyed upon the decease of that nobleman. In the 19th of James I. Sir Francis, then one of the principal Secretaries of State, was in commission with the Lord Deputy, the Lord Chancellor, and the Archbishop of Armagh; to inquire into the clerical affairs of Ireland. During the lieutenancy of the Earl of Strafford, his lordship was, however, committed to prison, and sentenced to lose his head, by a most extraordinary stretch of power, which proceeding afterwards constituted the 5th article of the impeachment of Lord Strafford. The charge against Lord Mountnorris, upon which he was tried and condemned by a council of war, was thus set forth by the Lord Deputy himself :—" That within three or four days, or thereabouts, after the end of the parliament, it being mentioned at the Lord Chancellor's table, that after we, the Lord Deputy, had dissolved the parliament, being sitting down in the presence-chamber, one of our servants, in moving a stool, happened to hurt our foot, then indisposed through an accession of gout; that one then present, at the Lord Chancellor's table, said to the Lord Mountnorris, being there likewise, that it was Annesley, his lordship's kinsman, and one of our, the Lord Deputy and general's gentlemen ushers, had done it: whereupon the Lord Mountnorris then publicly, and in a scornful, contemptuous manner, answered, ' *Perhaps it was done in revenge of that public affront which my Lord Deputy had done him formerly; but he has a brother that would not take such a revenge;*'" which public affront the Lord Deputy thus explains :—" That his said kinsman, (being one of the horse troop commanded by us, the Lord Deputy,) in the time of exercising the said troop, was out of order on horseback, to the disturbance of the rest, then in exercising; for which we, the Lord Deputy, in a mild manner, reproving, as soon as we turned aside from him, we observed him to laugh and jeer us for our just reproof of him; which we disliking, returned to him, and laying a small cane (which we then carried) on his shoulders (yet without any blow or stroke then given him therewith), told him, that, if he did serve us so any more, we would lay him over the pate." And the Lord Deputy draws his inference thus against Lord Mountnorris :—" We conceive offence to contain an incitement to revenge in these words, ' *but he has a brother that would not take such a revenge;*' which incitement might have given encouragement to that brother, being then and now in this kingdom, and lieutenant of the said Lord Mountnorris's foot company." Upon this frivolous accusation Lord Mountnorris was found guilty, and adjudged " to be imprisoned, to stand from henceforth deprived from all the places, with the entertainments due thereunto, which he holds now in the army, to be disarmed, to be ba-

nished the army, and disabled from ever bearing office therein hereafter; and, lastly, to be shot to death, or to lose his head, at the pleasure of the general. Given at his Majesty's Castle of Dublin, 12th day of December, 1635." Although the extremity of this iniquitous sentence was not put into execution, his lordship was deprived, in conformity with it, of all his offices, and confined in the Castle of Dublin for nearly a year and a half. He lived, however, to witness the disgrace and public execution of his persecutor, the Earl of Strafford Lord Mountnorris, who became Viscount Valentia, m., first, Dorothy, daughter of Sir John Philips, of Picton Castle, in the county of Pembroke, by whom he had, with other issue,

ARTHUR, his successor.

John, m. Charity, daughter of Henry Warren, Esq., of Grange Begg, in the county of Kildare.

Anne, m. to George Cook, Esq., of Pebmarsh, in the county of Essex.

His lordship espoused, secondly, Jane, daughter of Sir John Stanhope, Knt., sister of Philip, Earl of Chesterfield, and widow of Sir Peter Courtene, Bart., of Adlington, in the county of Worcester, by whom he had surviving issue :

Francis, of Cloghmaghericalt, afterwards Castle Wellan, in the county of Down, who m. Debora, daughter of Doctor Henry Jones, Bishop of Meath, and widow of John Boudler, Esq., of Dublin, and was s. by his son,

Francis, member of the Irish parliament for Downpatrick, and of the English for Westbury, m. Elisabeth, daughter of Sir John Martin of London, by whom, with several other children, he had

WILLIAM, who was elevated to the peerage of Ireland, as *Baron Annesley*, of Castle Wellan, and VISCOUNT GLERAWLEY.

Catharine, m. to Sir Randolph Beresford, Bart. of Colerain.

The Viscount d. in 1660, and was s. by his eldest son, ARTHUR ANNESLEY, second Viscount Valentia. This nobleman was appointed in the life-time of his father (anno 1645), first of the three commissioners then nominated by parliament, to govern the kingdom of Ireland. And a little before the restoration, in the year 1660, being President of the Council, he evinced, according to Lord Clarendon, a strong disposition towards the exiled monarch, for which, and his subsequent adhesion to the restored government, he was sworn of the Privy Council, and created, 20th April, 1661, a peer of England, by the titles of *Baron Annesley* of Newport-Pagnel in the County of Bucks, and EARL OF ANGLESEY.

His lordship subsequently held the office of Privy Seal. He was a person of learning—a distinguished statesman, and an able political writer. The earl m. Elisabeth, one of the daughters and coheirs of Sir James Altham, Knight of Oxey, in the county of Herts, one of the Barons of the Exchequer, by whom he had five sons and five daughters, viz.

1. JAMES, Lord Annesley.

2. ALTHAM, who was created an Irish Peer,

7

A

14th February, 1680, by the title of BARON ALTHAM, with limitation to his younger brothers. His lordship, *m.* first, Alice, daughter and sole heiress of Charles Leigh, Esq., of Leighton Buzzard, in the county of Bedford, and grand-daughter of Thomas, first Lord Leigh, but had no issue. He espoused, secondly, ———, and dying in 1699, was *s.* by his only son,

    JAMES GEORGE, second Lord Altham, at whose decease, in infancy, the dignity reverted to his uncle,

The Hon. and very Rev.

    RICHARD ANNESLEY, (3) Dean of Exeter, as third Lord Altham, who *d.* in 1701, the year in which he succeeded to the peerage, and was *s.* by his son,

        ARTHUR, fourth Lord Altham, who *m.* Mary, illegitimate daughter of John Sheffield, Duke of Buckingham, but dying, as supposed, issueless, in 1727, the title devolved upon his brother,

        RICHARD, fifth Lord Altham, of whom hereafter, as sixth EARL OF ANGLESEY.

3. RICHARD, in holy orders, Dean of Exeter, who inherited, as stated above, the BARONY OF ALTHAM, upon the decease of his nephew.

4. Arthur.

5. Charles.

1. Dorothy, *m.* to Richard Power, Earl of Tyrone.

2. Elizabeth, *m.* to the Honorable Alexander Macdonnell, second son of the Earl of Antrim.

3. Frances, *m.* first, to Francis Windham, Esq., of Felbridge, and secondly, to Sir John Thompson, of Haversham, Bucks, Bart., afterwards Lord Haversham.

4. Philippa, *m.* first, to Charles, Lord Mohun, and secondly, to Thomas Coward, Esq., of the county of Somerset, serjeant at law.

5. Anne, *m.* to — Baker, Esq.

His lordship *d.* 6th April, 1686, and was *s.* by his eldest son,

JAMES ANNESLEY, second Earl of Anglesey, who *m.* Lady Elizabeth Manners, daughter of John, Earl of Rutland, and had issue,

    JAMES, Lord Annesley,   Successively Earls of
    JOHN,   Anglesey.
    ARTHUR,

    Elizabeth, *m.* to Robert Gayer, Esq., of Stoke Poges, in the county of Bucks.

His lordship *d.* in 1690, and was *s.* by his eldest son,

JAMES ANNESLEY, third Earl of Anglesey. This nobleman *m.* 28th October, 1699, Lady Catherine Darnley, natural daughter of King James II., by Catherine, daughter of Sir Charles Sedley, Bart., by whom he had an only daughter and heiress,

    Catherine, who *m.* William Phipps, Esq., son of Sir Constantine Phipps, Knight, Lord Chancellor of Ireland, and had issue,

CONSTANTINE PHIPPS, created Baron Mulgrave, in the peerage of Ireland. A dignity inherited by his lordship's son HENRY, present Earl of Mulgrave.

His lordship *d.* 18th January, 1701-2, and having no male issue, the honours devolved upon his brother,

JOHN ANNESLEY, fourth Earl of Anglesey, who, in the year 1710, was constituted Vice Treasurer, Receiver General, and Paymaster of the Forces in Ireland, and sworn of the privy council. His lordship *m.* in 1706, Lady Henrietta Stanley, eldest daughter and co-heir of William, Earl of Derby, by whom he had an only daughter, Elizabeth, who *d.* in infancy. The earl *d.* 18th Sept., 1710, and was *s.* by his only surviving brother,

ARTHUR ANNESLEY, fifth Earl of Anglesey. Upon the death of Queen Anne, this nobleman was chosen by King George I. to be one of the lords justices, until his Majesty's arrival from Hanover; after which he was sworn of the privy council. He was afterwards joint treasurer of Ireland, and treasurer at war. His lordship was also high steward of the University of Cambridge, which seat of learning he represented in three successive parliaments while a commoner. He *m.* Mary, daughter of John Thompson, Lord Haversham, but dying without issue, the honours were assumed by his kinsman,

RICHARD ANNESLEY, fifth Lord Altham, as sixth Earl of Anglesey (revert to issue of Arthur, second Viscount Valentia and first Earl of Anglesey). Soon after the assumption of the dignity by this Earl Richard, a claimant to the honours arose in Mr. James Annesley, who asserted himself to be the son of Arthur, fourth Lord Altham, by Mary, his wife, and a publication entitled, "The Adventures of an Unfortunate Young Nobleman," sets forth his case in a very curious and interesting narrative. In that statement it is alleged that Mr. Annesley is the true and lawful son and heir of Arthur, Lord Altham, and that he had been kidnapped and transported by his uncle Richard, to make room for his own accession to the honours and estates of the family. Mr. Annesley did more, however, to establish his legitimacy. He commenced a suit at law for the recovery of his property from his uncle, and after a trial in the Court of Exchequer in Ireland, James Annesley, against Richard, called Earl of Anglesey, commenced 11th November, 1743, and continued by adjournment daily to the 25th of the same month, he obtained a VERDICT. But he does not appear to have made any effort for the peerage, for Richard survived the issue of the suit eighteen years, and was always esteemed Earl of Anglesey. The conduct of this nobleman to Miss Simpson, a lady whom he married, was quite as atrocious, as the alleged expatriation of his nephew.

"In the year 1727, (says Jacob, in his peerage,) the Honourable Richard Annesley, the youngest son of Richard, Lord Altham, Dean of Exeter, who had been an ensign in the army, but struck off the half-pay in the year 1715, and then destitute of any fortune or subsistence whatever, being at Dublin, and passing as a bachelor, made his addresses to Miss Anne Simpson, the only daughter of Mr. John Simpson, a wealthy and reputable citizen, she at that time being no more than fourteen or fifteen years of age. After many solicitations (her mother, and most careful guardian having died some time before) he at length prevailed on her to be privately married to him, without the knowledge or consent of her father, who was highly displeased with her on that account. But Arthur, Lord Altham, elder brother of the said Richard, having interposed his good offices for a reconciliation, they were again, at the requisition of her father, and of the said Lord Altham, who insisted upon it, married in a public manner, by the Rev. Henry Daniel, then Curate of St. Catharine's, by a licence taken out of the Consistorial Court of the diocese of Dublin. Mr. Simpson, her father, thereupon was not only reconciled to them, and took his said daughter and her husband into his favour and family, but gave the said Richard a considerable portion with her, and supported them for some years after their marriage, suitable to their rank, which was attended with an extraordinary expence, on account of the said Richard's having by the death of his elder brother, which happened soon after his marriage, assumed the title of Lord Altham, and from the time of the said marriage, they lived publicly together as man and wife, under the denomination of Lord and Lady Altham, and as such were universally deemed, reputed and received, and treated by all their acquaintances. In the year 1729, Nicholas Simpson, a relation of her father, filed his bill in Chancery against the said Richard Lord Altham, and Anne, Lady Altham, his wife, to be relieved against a promissory note, perfected by the said Nicholas to them or one of them; to which bill they put in a joint answer, taken upon honor, by the name and style of Richard, Lord Altham, and Anne, Baroness Altham, his wife; wherein the said Richard acknowledged his marriage with the said Anne, which bill and answer are upon record in that Court.

"On the death of Mr. Simpson, Lady Altham's father, in the year 1730, he bequeathed legacies to her ladyship and Lord Altham, as his daughter and son-in-law, and Lord Altham received the property so devised. In seven years afterwards Arthur, Earl of Anglesey, dying without issue, Richard, Lord Altham, assumed *that* dignity, and as such, with his lady, was presented to the Duke of Devonshire, then lord lieutenant of Ireland, and both were acknowledged at the Irish court as Earl and Countess of Anglesey. Up to this period his lordship appears to have lived in great harmony with his countess, and to have taken great care of the education of his three daughters; but having soon after formed a criminal connection with one Julian Donovan, the daughter of Richard Donovan, a person who kept an unlicensed ale-house in the village of Camolin, near his lordship's residence, he thenceforward began to treat the countess and her children with great indifference and neglect, and was at length, by the contrivance of the said Julian Donovan, and the wicked arts of one John Jans, a surgeon, her confederate, prevailed upon, not only to treat them with great cruelty, and totally to aban-

don her and his hapless children to absolute want, but to break open her escrutoire, and rob her of all her writings, particularly of a deed of provision for her and her said daughter, which had been delivered into her own custody some time before by her brother, John Simpson. But happily for her and her unfortunate children, the original draft of the deed, as settled by Sir Simon Bradstreet, hath been since acknowledged, and due execution of the said deed proved by the witnesses. In the year 1741 the countess instituted a suit in the Ecclesiastical court, for cruelty and adultery against the earl, and she then obtained an order against his lordship for an interim alimony of four pounds a week, until a full sentence should be pronounced; and further, that the said earl should pay her costs to that time, and her future costs in the cause. The said earl having been served with a monition to obey the said order, and having declined to perform the same, sentence of excommunication was pronounced against him; and having still continued in obstinacy, he was, after all due forms had been used, declared an excommunicated person, and so remained till his death. Application was made to the lord chancellor for a writ *de excommunicato capiendo*, to take the said earl into custody, but the chancellor refusing to grant it on account of the privilege of peerage, the countess eventually gained nothing by the suit; and her sole support, and that of her children, from thenceforward to her death, which happened in August, 1765, was derived from a pension of £200. a year upon the Irish establishment. Here it is to be observed, that the Earl of Anglesey having tried in vain to get up a case of adultery against the countess, at length attempted to defend himself in the Consistorial court, by alleging that, at the period of his union with the countess, he had then a wife living in England, named Anne Phrust.

"From this period the earl lived entirely with Juliana Donovan, to whom he was married in 1752, at Camolin Park, by the Rev. Laurence Neale, although it appears that the countess was then alive, and lived for thirteen years after, being four years longer than his lordship."

By his unhappy lady the earl had surviving issue,

Dorothea, m. to — Dubois, Esq.

Caroline, m. to — Green, }

Elizabeth, m. to — Green, } brothers.

By Juliana Donovan he had ARTHUR, and other children.

His lordship d. on the 4th February, 1761, when the legitimacy of his son was contested by the heir at law, John Annesley, Esq., of Ballysack, who petitioned the Irish parliament to be admitted to the honours of the family. The matter excited great public interest, and was pending in the Irish House of Lords nearly four years, when their lordships came to a decision establishing the marriage with Miss Donovan, and confirming the rights of her son,

ARTHUR, as Baron Mountnorris, Baron Altham, and Viscount Valentia, and as a Baronet of Ireland—and his lordship took his seat accordingly when he came of age, anno 1765, in the House of Lords. He then applied for his writ to the English House of Peers, as Earl of Anglesey, but then the decision as to his legitimacy and the marriage of his mother, was against him, and the writ was denied. He continued to sit in the Irish parliament however as Viscount Valentia (his case being again investigated, and his right confirmed), and was created, in 1793, EARL OF MOUNT-NORRIS, in the peerage of Ireland—dignities now borne by his lordship's son and successor, George, present EARL OF MOUNTNORRIS.

Upon the decease of Richard, EARL OF ANGLESEY, therefore, in 1761, the EARLDOM OF ANGLESEY is deemed to have expired—and the dignity has since been conferred upon another family.

ARMS.—Paly of six ar. and az. a bend gules.

ANSON — BARON ANSON, OF SOBERTON, IN THE COUNTY OF SOUTHAMPTON.

By Letters Patent, dated 13th June, 1747.

The ANSONS have been seated in the county of Stafford for several generations: formerly at Dunston; but since the time of James I. at Shugborough, a manor purchased in that monarch's reign, by WILLIAM ANSON, Esq., whose descendant,

WILLIAM ANSON, Esq., of Shugborough, m. Isabella, daughter and co-heiress of Charles Carrier, Esq., of Wirksworth, in the county of Derby, and had issue,

> THOMAS, who dying s. p., left his estates to his nephew, George Adams, Esq., with an injunction that he should assume the name and arms of ANSON.
>
> GEORGE, of whom presently.
>
> Janetta, m. to Sambroke Adams, Esq., of Sambroke, in the county of Salop, and had issue,
>
>> GEORGE, who succeeded to the estates of both his uncles, and assumed by sign manual, 30th April, 1773, the surname and arms of ANSON. Mr. Anson m. in 1763, the Hon. Mary Vernon, daughter of George, first Lord Vernon, and was s. by his eldest son,
>>
>>> THOMAS ANSON, Esq., who was created, on 17th February, 1806, Baron Soberton and VISCOUNT ANSON. His lordship m. in 1794, Anne Margaret, daughter of Thomas Wenman Coke, Esq., of Holkham, and dying in 1818, was s. by his eldest son, Thomas William, present VISCOUNT ANSON.

Mr. Anson's younger son,

GEORGE ANSON, Esq., so celebrated as a naval commander, and immortalised as a circumnavigator, was elevated to the peerage as a reward for his useful and gallant services, on 13th June, 1747, in the dignity of BARON ANSON, of Soberton, in the county of Southampton. The achievements of this great captain are too ample for detail in a work of this description, and in reality belong to another branch of literature. His voyage to the South Seas—his perils—his capture of the rich Manilla ship, and his eventual arrival at home, have been published by authority. The month preceding his advancement to the peerage, Vice

10

Admiral Anson, then in command of a squadron, captured a large fleet of French merchantmen, bound to the West Indies, with almost the entire convoy of men of war that conducted it. Lord Anson, after passing through the usual gradations, was made Vice Admiral of England. He was also a lord of the Admiralty. His lordship m. Lady Elizabeth York, daughter of Philip, first Earl of Hardwick, but dying without issue, in 1762, the BARONY OF ANSON became EXTINCT, while his estates devolved upon his nephew, GEORGE ADAMS, Esq. (refer to children of William Anson, Esq.).

ARMS.—Quarterly, first and fourth ar., three bends ingrailed gules, second and third sa., a bend between three half spears, ar. *ariel*

AP-ADAM—BARONS DE AP-ADAM.

By Writ of Summons, dated 6th February, 1299, 27 Edward I.

Lineage.

JOHN DE AP-ADAM having married, in the 19th year of king Edward I., Elizabeth, daughter and heiress of John de Gurnai, Lord of Beverstan, in the county of Gloucester, obtained considerable landed property in that shire by the alliance, and, in five years afterwards, an accession of estates in Somersetshire, upon the decease of the lady's mother, Olivia. This John had a royal charter, in the 21st of Edward I., for a weekly market and a yearly fair to be holden at Beverstan, and another charter, in the 26th of the same monarch, for a weekly market and annual fair to be holden at his manor of Netherwere. In this latter year he was engaged in the Scottish wars; and again, in eight years subsequently. He was summoned to parliament from the 25th of Edward I. to the 2d of Edward II. inclusive. His lordship died about the year 1309, leaving in minority a son and heir,

THOMAS AP-ADAM, whose wardship *Ralph de Montherner* obtained, in consideration of six thousand marks. This Thomas arrived at maturity in the 18th of Edward II., and had livery of his lands upon doing homage; but of this gentleman and family nothing further is recorded than the sale, by his lordship, of his castle of Beverstan and manor of Overe, in the county of Gloucester, in the 4th year of Edward III., to Thomas de Berkley and Margaret his wife.

ARMS—Ar. on a cross gu., five mullets or.

ARCHDEKNE — BARONS ARCHDEKNE.

By Writ of Summons, dated 15th May, 1321.

Lineage.

THOMAS LE ARCHDEKNE, of Shepestall, in the county of Cornwall, petitioned the king, in parliament, 35th Edward I., soliciting that an investigation might be instituted touching the seizure of his lands for neglect of service in the wars of Scotland, whereas neither himself nor his ancestors had ever been bound to perform such service, and praying for the restitution of the said lands. In the 6th of Edward II. this Thomas Le Archdekne was governor of Tintaget Castle, in the county of

Cornwall, and, in twelve years afterwards, a commissioner with Ralph Lord Basset, of Drayton, and Arnold de Durefort, to receive all such persons, in the duchy of Aquitaine, into protection as should submit to the king's authority,. He was summoned to parliament, as BARON ARCHDEKNE, from the 15th May, 1321, to 13th Sept., 1394; and, dying, was s. by his son,

JOHN LE ARCHDEKNE, second baron—summoned to parliament on the 25th February, 1394; but not subsequently. This nobleman distinguished himself in the expedition to Flanders, in the 13th of Edward III., and, two years afterwards, was in Scotland, in the train of William de Many. In the next year we find him serving under Oliver de Ingham in the wars of Gascony; and, in the 19th of Edward III., upon the great expedition then made into France, he had summons to fit himself with horse and arms, so that he might be in readiness against the Feast of St. Lawrence to attend the king upon that enterprise. Again, in the 29th of the same monarch, Lord Archdekne attended Henry Duke of Lancaster upon another expedition against France. His lordship m. Cecilie, daughter and heiress of Sir John Fitzstephen, Knt., of Haccombe, and was succeeded by his son,

WARINE LE ARCHDEKNE, third baron, who m. Elisabeth, one of the sisters and coheiresses of John Talbot, of Richard's Castle, and had issue—

    Alianore, m. to Walter de Lucie, by whom she had,
        William, who d. s. p.
        Alianore, m. to Thomas Hopton.
        Maud, m. to Thomas Vaux.
    Philippa, m. to Hugh Courtenay.
    Margaret, m. to Thomas Arundel.

At the decease of Lord Archdekne, the barony fell into ABEYANCE, and so continues amongst the representatives of his daughters.

Arms—Ar. three chevronels sa.

ARCHER—BARONS ARCHER, OF UMBERSLADE, IN THE COUNTY OF WARWICK.

Created by Letters Patent, dated 14th July, 1747.

Lineage.

ROBERT L'ARCHER, son of Fulbert L'Archer, who came into England with the Conqueror, obtained considerable grants from king Henry I., whose tutor he had been, and acquired the lands of Omberslade, in the county of Warwick, as a marriage portion with his wife Sebit, daughter of Henry de Villiers, sewer to William de Newburgh, Earl of Warwick, all which possessions were confirmed by Henry II. to his son,

WILLIAM L'ARCHER, whose son,

JOHN L'ARCHER, being champion to Thomas Earl of Warwick, obtained special charter from that nobleman, granting to himself and his heirs the privilege of hunting and hawking every where within the territory of Taneworth, except the park, and of exercising all other liberties belonging to the earl within Monkspath and Omberslade, paying to the said Earl and his heirs twelve broadarrow heads and a couple of capons yearly, at

Whitsuntide, as an acknowledgment. This John d. in the 35th Henry III., leaving four sons and two daughters. The three younger sons appear to have been churchmen. Thomas, the second, was prior of St. John's of Jerusalem, in England, temp. Edward II. The eldest son,

JOHN ARCHER, purchased of William de Olenhale the manor of Monkspath, adjoining Omberslade. This John m. Margery, daughter of Sir William Tracey, of Todington, in the county of Gloucester, and was s. by his eldest son,

JOHN ARCHER, who m. Isabel, daughter of Ralph Erscote, Esq., of Erscote, in the county of Warwick, by whom he had two sons and two daughters; and, dying in the 23d of Edward III., was succeeded by the elder son,

THOMAS ARCHER. This gentleman m. Margaret, daugter and co-heiress of John Malley, Esq., of Malley, in the county of Salop, and had issue—

    Thomas, his successor.
    Gilbert, who, writing himself of Taneworth, had license from the crown, in the 16th Rich. II., to give to the prior and convent of Kenilworth one messuage, with divers lands at Hitchenden, in the county of Buckingham.
    Joane, m. to William Shelly, Esq.

This Thomas Archer's will is dated " Thursday next after the Feast of St. Thomas the Martyr, 1372," and he was succeeded in that year by his elder son,

THOMAS ARCHER, one of the gallant soldiers of the martial reign of Edward III. In 1373 he had a command in the army of John of Gaunt, and fell into the hands of the French and Burgundians in a rencounter at Ouchy le Chasteau, near Soissons, on the 20th October, in that year, being surprised when foraging with Sir Matthew Redmayn, Sir Thomas Spencer, Sir Hugh Brudenel, Sir John Bourchier, and several other knights and esquires. In the 49th of Edward III. we again find him in France under Thomas Beauchamp, Earl of Warwick, from whom he received a pension for his services, dated at Worcester "20 Martii, 1 Rich. II.;" in the 21st of which latter reign he received a special pardon dated 8th June, for all manner of transgressions, and for whatever he had acted contrary to his allegiance, &c. in behalf of Thomas, late Duke of Gloucester, Richard, late Earl of Arundel, and Thomas, Earl of Warwick; after which, in the same year, he was in commission for assessing and collecting a fifteenth and tenth, then granted to the king in parliament. This Thomas Archer m. Agnes, daughter of Sir Walter Cokesey, of Cokesey, in the county of Worcester, and grand-daughter of Hugh Cokesey and of Dionis his wife, one of the four sisters and co-heiresses of Edmund le Boteler, by whom he had three sons. He died, after being bedridden for three years, in the 84th year of his age, on the Feast of Pentecost, in 1425, and was s. by his second but eldest surviving son,

RICHARD ARCHER, who was one of the persons of note in the county of Warwick summoned in the 7th of Henry V. to serve the king in person for the defence of the realm, being, according to the writ, " one that did bear ancient arms from his ancestors." This gentleman m. first, Alice, daughter of William Hugford, Esq., of Hugford and Middleton, in the county of Salop, sister and heiress of her brother, William Hugford, and widow of Sir Thomas Lucy, Knt., of Charlecote, by whom he had one son,

    JOHN, who m. in the 26th Henry VI., Christian, widow of Henry Sewal, of London, and only daughter and heiress of Ralph Blacklow, of the same city, and of his wife Joan, only daughter and heiress of Thomas Coke, alias Malling, of West Malling, Kent, by whom he had an only son, JOHN. King Henry VI. by his letters patent dated 12th May, in the eighth year of his reign, retained this John Archer, Esq., by his factors or attorneys, to convey in ships all manner of provisions for victualling the town and fortress of Calais. Mr. Archer fell in battle in 1463, on the side of the Earl of Warwick, against King Edward IV. His widow remarried in the 3rd of Edward IV., Henry Beech, Esq.

RICHARD ARCHER, m. secondly, Margaret, relict of Thomas Newport, Esq., of Ercall, in Shropshire, ancestor of the Earls of Bradford, and thirdly, Joane, daughter and heiress of William Ley, of Stotford, in the county of Stafford. In the 7th of Henry VI. Mr. Archer had summons to attend the king in France, to be present at his coronation there; Sir Ralph Bruce, Knt., Sir Edward Dodingfell, and Nicholas Burdett, with others of the county of Warwick, being also summoned. In the 19th of the same monarch, he served the office of sheriff for the county of Salop, and the next year, that of sheriff for the county of Stafford, in which shire he resided at Stotford. He d. in the 85th year of his age, anno 1471, when his large estates in the counties of Salop, Stafford and Bedford, devolved upon his grandson,

JOHN ARCHER, Esq., b. in 1449, m. Alice, daughter of Sir Baldwin Mountfort, Knt., of Coltshill, in the county of Warwick, and dying at Omberslade, 4th December, 1519, was s. by his only son,

JOHN ARCHER, Esq., who m. Margaret, daughter of Humphrey Strafford, Esq., of Bletherwick in the county of Northampton, by whom he had four sons and a daughter. He d. in a year after his father, and was s. by his eldest son,

RICHARD ARCHER, Esq., Eschaetor of the county of Warwick, in the 22nd of Henry VIII. and justice of the peace for that shire. This gentleman m. Maud, second daughter of Nicholas Delamere, Esq., of Little Hereford, in the county of Hereford, and co-heiress with her sister Susan, wife of John Dansey, Esq., of her brother Edmund Delamere, Esq., and had issue,

    Humphrey, b. in 1527.
    Miles, b. in 1530.
    Edward, b. in 1533, d. unm.
    Francis, b. in 1534.
    Anne, b. in 1526.
    Winifrede, b. in 1535.

In the 32nd of Henry VIII. Mr. Archer was appointed steward of the manor of Knole, in the county of Warwick, being then, as recited in the letters patent, one of the esquires of the king's

12

body, and in two years afterwards, he was commanded to take the muster of all able men, as well horsemen as foot, that he could furnish both of the king's tenants, inhabiting upon farms whereof he had the stewardship; as also his own servants and tenants dwelling on his own lands, &c. He d. 5th October, 1544, and was s. by his eldest son,

HUMPHREY ARCHER, Esq., who married in the 4th of Edward VI. (6th October) Anne, daughter of Sir Robert Townshend, Knt., chief justice of the marches of Wales and Chester, and granddaughter of Sir Roger Townshend, of Reynham, in the county of Norfolk, one of the justices of the court of common pleas, ancestor of the Viscounts Townshend, by whom he had surviving issue,

    ANDREW, his successor.
    John, m. Eleanor, daughter and heiress of Richard Frewin, Esq., of Handley, in the county of Worcester.
    Bridget, m. to John Bancroft, Esq., of Hanbury, in the county of Worcester.
    Margery, m. to John Colles, Esq., of Hatfield, in the county of Hertford.
    Elizabeth, m. to John Hereford, Esq., of Sufton, in the county of Hertford.

Mr. Archer d. at Omberslade, 24th October, 1562, and was s. by his eldest son,

ANDREW ARCHER, Esq., who extended his territorial possessions by the purchase of large estates in the reigns of Queen Elizabeth, and King James I. In the 7th year of which latter reign, he was sheriff of the county of Warwick. He m. in 1580, Margaret, daughter of Simon Raleigh, Esq., of Farnborough, in the county of Warwick, and had issue,

    Thomas, who d. in his 24th year, before his father, unmarried.
    SIMON, successor to the estates.
    Richard, m. Mary, daughter and sole heiress of Rowland Bull, Esq., of Neithropp, in the county of Oxford (with whom he acquired that estate), and had a son, Rowland.

Mr. Archer d. 23rd of April, 1629, and was s. by his eldest surviving son,

SIR SIMON ARCHER, Knt., sheriff of Warwickshire, in the 3rd year of King Charles I. and member for Tamworth, in the parliament which assembled on the 30th April, 1640. This gentleman was distinguished as a man of letters and an antiquary, and Sir William Dugdale acknowledges himself greatly indebted to him in compiling his antiquities of Warwickshire. Sir Simon m. Anne, daughter of Sir John Ferrers, Knt., of Tamworth Castle, in the county of Warwick, by whom he had surviving issue,

    Thomas, his successor.
    Anne, m. to Philip Young, Esq., of Keneton, in the county of Salop.
    Elizabeth.
    Penelope, m. to Erasmus de Ligne, Esq., of Harlaxton, in the county of Lincoln.

Sir Simon Archer was s. at his decease, by his son,

THOMAS ARCHER, Esq., who, at the commencement of the civil wars, was a colonel in the parliament army, and raised a troop of horse at his own expense; but, so soon as he discovered the designs of the parliamentarians, he threw up his commission, and emigrating, remained abroad until the restoration of the monarchy when he represented the city of Warwick in parliament. He m. Anne, daughter of Richard Leigh, Esq., of London, and had issue,

    ANDREW, his successor.

    Thomas, groom-porter to Queen Anne, and to
      Kings George I. and II. d. s. p. in 1743.

    Leigh, d. unm.

    Elizabeth, m. to Sir Herbert Croft, Bart., of
      Croft Castle, in the county of Hereford.

    Frances, m. to Sir Francis Rous, Bart., of
      Rous-Lench, in the county of Worcester.

Mr. Archer d. in 1685, and was s. by his eldest son,

ANDREW ARCHER, Esq., M.P. for the county of Warwick in the reigns of William and Mary, Queen Anne, and King George I., and one of the commissioners appointed in 1711 to inquire into the numbers and quality of the forces in Her Majesty's pay in Portugal, and to examine the accounts relating to the said forces, and to the garrisons of Portmahon and Gibraltar. Mr. Archer m. Elizabeth, daughter of Sir Samuel Dashwood, Lord Mayor of London in 1702, and had issue,

    THOMAS, his successor.

    Henry, M.P. for Warwick, m. Lady Elizabeth
      Montagu, sister of George, Earl of Halifax,
      and d. in 1768.

    Anne.

    Elizabeth.

    Sarah.

    Diana, m. to Thomas Chaplin, Esq., of Blank-
      ney Hall, in the county of Lincoln.

Mr. Archer d. at Umberslade, which he had rebuilt, on the 31st of December, 1741, and was s. by his elder son,

THOMAS ARCHER, Esq., M.P. for Warwick, and subsequently for Bamber, who was elevated to the peerage on the 14th July, 1747, by the title of BARON ARCHER, OF UMBERSLADE, IN THE COUNTY OF WARWICK. His lordship m. Catharine, daughter and co-heiress of Sir Thomas Tipping, Baronet, of Wheetfield, in the county of Oxford, and Anne, 'his wife, daughter and heiress of Thomas Cheke, Esq., by his wife, Letitia, daughter and eventually sole heiress of Edward Russell (brother of William, first Duke of Bedford) and sister and heiress of Edward Russell, Earl of Orford, by whom he had issue,

    ANDREW, his successor, M.P. for Coventry.

    Catharine, m. 11th August, 1750, to Other,
      4th Earl of Plymouth.

    Anne, m. 15th March, 1756, to Edward Garth
      Tournour, Esq., of Shillingley Park, in the
      county of Sussex; created subsequently
      Earl of Winterton, in Ireland.

His lordship d. in 1768, and was s. by his only son,

ANDREW ARCHER, second baron. This nobleman m. in 1761, Sarah, elder daughter of James West, Esq., M.P. for Alscot in the county of Warwick, by whom he had three daughters, his co-heirs, viz.

    Catharine, m. first, to Other-Lewis, 4th Earl of
      Plymouth, by whom she had, with other issue,
      Other-Hickman, 5th Earl.

    She espoused, secondly, William Pitt, first

Earl Amherst, by whom she was mother of the present earl.

    Catharine, m. to —— Musgrave, Esq.

    ——, m. to —— Howard, Esq., of Corby.

His lordship d. in 1778, when the title EXPIRED in default of an heir male.

ARMS—Az. three arrows or.

ARGENTINE—BARONS DE ARGENTINE.

By Writ of Summons, dated 26 January, 1297, 25 Ed. 1.

Lineage.

REGINALD DE ARGENTEON, left a widow, Maud, who had license to marry again in the 5th year of Stephen, upon giving a composition to the king for her dowry. This Reginald d. before the year 1139, and was s. by his son,

REGINALD DE ARGENTEON, who was sheriff of the counties of Cambridge and Huntingdon, from the 5th to the 9th years of Richard I., and in the next year executed the duties of the same office for the counties of Hertford and Essex, for one half of the year. This feudal lord adhering to the insurrectionary barons, had letters of safe conduct in the 17th year of John, to come to the king in order to treat for peace; nothing effectual however resulted from the mission: but in the 1st of Henry III., making his own composition, orders were given to the sheriff of Cambridgeshire, to restore to him all his lands in that county. He d. about the year 1223, and was s. by his son,

RICHARD DE ARGENTINE, who being sheriff for the counties of Essex and Hertford, in the 8th of Henry III., was constituted governor of the Castle of Hertford. He was likewise sheriff of the counties of Cambridge and Huntingdon, and subsequently (11th Henry III.) one of the stewards of the king's household. In the 14th of Henry III., this Richard being, (in the words of M. Paris,) a noble knight and valiant in arms, went on a pilgrimage to the holy land, and dying there in the year 1246, was s. by his son,

GILES DE ARGENTINE, a knight also of great valour, who, in the 16th of Henry III., being with the king in an expedition made that year into Wales, fell into the hands of the enemy in a sharp conflict near Montgomerie. In ten years afterwards this feudal lord had summons with other important personages to attend the king with horse and arms into Gascony, and the next year he was appointed governor of Windsor Castle; but soon after we find him joining the rebel barons, at the battle of Lewes (wherein the king was taken prisoner), and elected by them one of the nine counsellors to assume the government of the kingdom. The barons being however defeated at the subsequent battle of Evesham, his lordship's lands and those of his son Reginald were sequestered. He d. in the 11th of Edward I., seised of the manor of Great Wymondeley in the county of Cambridge, holden by grand Serjeantie, viz.—" to serve the king upon the day of his coronation with a silver cup," and was s. by his son (then in minority),

REGINALD DE ARGENTINE, who doing homage, had livery of all his father's lands in the counties of Cambridge, Norfolk, Suffolk, and Hertford. This nobleman was summoned to parliament in the 25th Edward I., 26th January, 1297. His lordship m. Lora, daughter of Robert de Vere, Earl of Oxford, and dying in 1307, was s. by his son,

JOHN DE ARGENTINE, second baron, who had livery of his father's lands, but was never summoned to parliament. This nobleman m. first Joane ——, and had issue,

Joane, who m. John le Botiller.
Elizabeth, m. William le Botiller.
Dionyse.

which ladies inherited as co-heiresses the property of their mother. His lordship m. secondly ——, and dying in the 19th year of Edward II., was s. by his only son, then but six months old,

JOHN DE ARGENTINE, third baron, who received the honour of knighthood in the 4th of Edward III., but was never summoned to parliament. He m. Margaret ——, and had issue,

William, his successor.
Maud, m. to Eudo or Ivo Fitz-Warren.
Joane, m. to Sir Barth Naunton.
Elizabeth, m. to Sir Baldwin St. George.

He was s. at his decease by his only son,

WILLIAM DE ARGENTINE, 4th baron, but never summoned to parliament; who was s. by his only son,

JOHN DE ARGENTINE, 5th baron, but not summoned to parliament. With this nobleman the male line of the Argentines ceased, and the manor of Wymondeley was carried by his only daughter and heiress Elizabeth into the family of Allington, upon her marriage with William Allington, Esq., ancestor of the Lords Allington. This manor of Wimley or Wymondeley, is said to have fallen to the Argentines by marriage, with the heiress of Fits Tees, who derived themselves from David D'Argenton, a Norman, who came over with William the Conqueror.

ARMS—Gu. three covered cups, Ar.

Note: "Of this family," says Dugdale, "was Reginald de Argentine, who in 21 Henry III., being a knight-templar, was standard bearer of the Christian army, in a great battel against the Turks near Antioch, in the holy land, and carried it till his hands and legs being broken, he was there slain. So likewise was Sir Giles Argentine, Knt., slain in Scotland at the battel of Bannoksburne, near Strivelin, in 7th of Edward II. It is said, that the king himself being in that fatal battel, and seeing the danger, by the advice of this Sir Giles (who being then lately come from the wars of Henry de Luxemburgh, the Emperour, and reputed a stout warriour) fled to Dunbar; and that this Sir Giles saying he was not wont to fly, returned to the English host, and was slain."

ARUNDEL—BARONS ARUNDEL OF TRERICE.

By Letters Patent, dated 23rd March, 1664.

Lineage.

RANDELL ARUNDEL, m. Elizabeth, daughter and heiress of John Steward, and left a son,

RALPH ARUNDEL, living in the 31st of Edward III., who m. Jane, daughter and heiress of

Michael Trerice, by whom he had two sons, Nicholas and Thomas, and a daughter Jane, m. to Robert Trevanion. The elder son,

NICHOLAS ARUNDEL, m. Elizabeth, daughter of John Pellocer, and sister and co-heiress of Martin Pellocer, and was s. by his son,

SIR JOHN ARUNDEL, of Trerice, in the county of Cornwall, who m. Joan, daughter and heiress of John Durant, and was s. by his elder son,

NICHOLAS ARUNDEL, who m. Jane, daughter of Edward St. John, Esq., by whom he had four sons and four daughters. He was s. by his eldest son,

SIR JOHN ARUNDEL, Knt., Sheriff of Cornwall in 1471. "This gentleman being forewarned," says Carew in his survey of Cornwall, "that he should be slain on the sands, forsook his house at Elford, as too maritime, and removed to Trerice, his more inland habitation in the same county; but he did not escape his fate, for being sheriff of Cornwall in that year, and the Earl of Oxford surprising Mount Michael, for the house of Lancaster, he had the king's commands, by his office, to endeavour the reducing of it, and lost his life in a skirmish on the sands thereabouts. Sir John Arundel, m. first, Margaret, daughter of Sir Hugh Courtenay, Knt., by whom he had two sons, who d. young; and secondly, Anne, daughter of Sir Walter Moyle, Knt., by whom he had also two sons, and was s. by the elder,

SIR JOHN ARUNDEL, Sheriff of Cornwall, anno 1524. This gentleman, m. Joan, daughter of Thomas Greenvil, Esq., and was s. by his only son,

JOHN ARUNDEL, Esq., who received the honour of knighthood at the battle of Spurs. This gallant person, who was Vice Admiral to Kings Henry VII. and VIII., acquired great renown by the defeat and capture of Duncan Campbell, the Scottish pirate, in a sea fight. Sir John Arundel, m. first, Mary, daughter and co-heiress of John Bevil, of Garnache, in the county of Cornwall, by whom he had a son Roger, and three daughters: namely,

Elizabeth, m. to Robert Tridenham, Esq.
Catherine, m. to Richard Prideux, Esq., of Thewborough.
Jane, m. to William Wall, Esq.

Sir John, m. secondly, Julian, daughter of James Erisey, and widow of —— Gurlyn, by whom he had issue,

John, who became his heir.
Margaret, m. to Robert Breket, Esq.
Grace, m. to John Nance, Esq.
Margery, m. to John Dunham, Esq.
Mary.
Jane.

He was s. by his only surviving son,

JOHN ARUNDEL, Esq., who m. first Catherine, daughter and co-heiress of John Cosworth, Esq., by whom he had four daughters: viz.

Mary, m. to Oliver Dynham, Esq.
Dorothy, m. to Edward Cosworth, Esq.
Julian, m. to Richard Carew, Esq., of Anthony, in the county of Cornwall.
Alice, m. to Henry Somaster, Esq., of Painsford.

Mr. Arundel, m. secondly, Gertrude, daughter of Robert Dennis, Esq., of Holcomb, by whom he had two sons, John and Thomas, and two daughters,

Anne, m. to William Carnfew, Esq., of Bucclesly, and Catherine, m. to John St. Aubyn, Esq. He d. in 1580, and was s. by his elder son,

JOHN ARUNDEL, Esq., of Trerice, M.P. for the county of Cornwall, temp. Queen Elizabeth and King James I., and for Tregony in the reign of King Charles I. At the breaking out of the civil war, this eminent person, with his four sons, espoused the cause of royalty, and took up arms for the king. Of these sons, two, John and William, lost their lives in the service of their unfortunate master, while their gallant father hurled defiance to the rebels from the battlements of Pendennis, and maintained his position there, to the very end of those unhappy conflicts, although besieged both by sea and land, being as Lord Clarendon relates, then nearly fourscore years of age, and of one of the best estates and interests in the County of Cornwall. Whitlock states, that on the 31st of August, 1646, letters came to the parliament, of the surrender of Pendennis Castle, and in it were Colonel Arundel, the governor, four knights, five colonels, and divers others of quality. That they had store of arms, but little provision. Colonel Arundel m. Mary, daughter of George Carey, Esq., of Clovelley, in the county of Devon, by whom he had four sons and two daughters; viz. Richard, John, William, Francis, Agnes, and Mary. The latter was m. first, to —— Trevanion, Esq., and secondly, to Sir John Arundel of Langherne. He was s. at his decease by his eldest son,

RICHARD ARUNDEL, Esq., member in the two last parliaments of King Charles I., for Lestwithiel, and in his military capacity, attached to the personal staff of that unhappy prince. This gallant officer had a command in the battle of Kineton, in the County of Warwick, where he displayed the hereditary valour of his family, and he was subsequently actively engaged during the whole of the civil wars, in which disastrous contest he was despoiled of the entire of his landed property. On the re-establishment of the monarchy, however, that was restored to him, and in consideration of the devotedness of his father, his brothers, and himself, to the royal cause, he was elevated to the peerage by letters patent, dated 23rd March, 1654, as BARON ARUNDEL OF TRERICE in the county of Cornwall. His lordship m. Gertrude, daughter of Sir James Bagg, Knt., of Saltham, in the county of Devon, and widow of Sir Nicholas Slanning, Knt., of Bickley, and was s., at his decease in 1688, by his only surviving child,

JOHN ARUNDEL, second baron; this nobleman m. first, Margaret, daughter and sole heiress of Sir John Acland, Knt., of Columb-John in the county of Devon, by whom he had issue,

     JOHN, his successor.

     Gertrude, m. first, to Sir Peter Whitcomb of   Essex; and secondly, to Sir Bennet Hoskins.

His lordship m. secondly, Barbara, daughter of Sir Henry Slingsby of Scriven, in the county of York, Baronet—and relict of Sir Richard Maleverer of Aleston-Maleverer in the same shire, by whom he had an only son,

     Richard, M.P., m. 2nd September, 1732, Frances,   daughter of John, second Duke of Rutland.

Lord Arundel d. 27th of September, 1697, and was s. by his elder son,

JOHN ARUNDEL, third Baron, who m. Elisabeth, daughter of the Right Rev. William Beaw, D.D., Lord Bishop of Landaff, and dying 24th of September, 1706, was s. by his only surviving child,

JOHN ARUNDEL, fourth Baron. This nobleman m. in 1722, Elizabeth, daughter of Sir William Wentworth, of Ashby Puerorum in the county of Lincoln, and sister of Thomas, Earl of Strafford, by whom, who d. in 1750, he had no issue. His lordship d. in 1768, when the barony EXPIRED.

ARMS—Quarterly i. first and fourth, sa. six swallows close, three, two, and one arg. second and third sa. three Chevronels of the second.   *Jtrice*

ASTLEY—BARONS ASTLEY.

By Writ of Summons, dated 23rd June, 1295,
23 Edward I.

Lineage.

THIS noble family derived its surname from the Manor of ASTLEY (or Estley, as formerly written), in the county of Warwick, which with other estates in that shire, belonged to the Astleys so far back as the reign of Henry I.

PHILIP DE ESTLEY—grandson of the first possessor, was certified, upon the assessment of the aid towards the marriage portion of King Henry the Second's daughter, to hold three knights' fees of William Earl of Warwick, *de veteri Foeffumento*—by the service " of laying hands on the earl's stirrop when he did get upon, or alight from horseback." This feudal baron was s. by his son,

THOMAS DE ASTLEY, who holding certain lands of the Honour of Leicester, became a kind of bailiff to Simon de Montfort, Earl of Leicester, " as may be seen," says Dugdale, " by a fine of fourscore marks and a palfrey, to the king, in 9th John, to be discharged of the profits required of him for that earl's lands, during the time he had to do with them." In the 19th of King John, this Thomas Astley payed a hundred marks to the crown, to be excused going beyond the sea: Dugdale supposes, in an expedition to Ireland. In the 17th of the same reign, he was committed prisoner to Bedford Castle, and had his lands seised for his participation in the rebellion of the barons; but returning to his allegiance, he was reinstated in his territorial possessions, in the 1st year of Henry III.; and in two years afterwards, he was constituted a commissioner for restoring to the crown all the demesnes of which King John was possessed at the beginning of his wars with the barons, &c. This feudal lord m. Maud, one of the sisters and coheirs of Roger de Camvill of Creeke in the county of Northampton, and was s. by his son,

WALTER DE ASTLEY. This nobleman had been concerned in the rebellion of the barons against John. He was s. by his son,

SIR THOMAS DE ASTLEY, Knt., who was constituted in the 26th of Henry III., one of the king's justices for the gaol delivery at Warwick, and again in the next year, when he paid to the king £15. for his relief. In the 39nd of Henry III., this Sir Thomas de Astley was sent with several other persons of rank and power, into Gascoigne: but we afterwards find him, 47th Henry III., a leader amongst the rebellious barons, who seized upon the revenues of the crown in the counties of Warwick and Leicester; and when the king submitted to the PROVISIONS OF OXFORD, the following year, he was nominated CUSTOS PACIS for Leicestershire. Sir Thomas fell, however, soon after (49th Henry III., 1964,) with Montford Earl of Leicester, and other insurrectionary nobles, at the battle of Evesham, when his estates, valued at £151. 16. 11. per annum, being confiscated, were conferred upon Warine de Bassingburne, but the king compassionating his widow and children, reserved to them out of those estates, certain lands, valued at £34. 18. 1. per annum, subject to one mark yearly to the said Warine and his heirs. Sir Thomas de Astley, m. first, Joane, daughter of Ernald de Bois, a person of great power in the county of Leicester—and had issue,

ANDREW—his successor.

Isabel, m. to William de Bermingham, (son and heir of Robert de Bermingham, one of the companions in arms of Strongbow, Earl of Pembroke, in his expedition into Ireland, temp. Henry II.) and left a son, PETER DE BERMINGHAM, who was summoned to Parliament, in Ireland, as BARON ATHENRY, in the reigns of John and Henry III., and from his lordship descended twenty-one successive Barons of Athenry, when the dignity merged in the extinct Earldom of Louth.

Sir Thomas m. secondly, Editha, daughter of Peter Constable, Esq., of Melton Constable, in the county of Norfolk, and sister of Sir Ralph Constable, Knt., by whom he had three sons and a daughter, of whom,

THOMAS, settled at Hill Morton, but dying s. p. his estates devolved upon his brother,

RALPH ASTLEY, from whom the extinct Barons Astley of Reading derived, and Sir Jacob Astley, Bart., of Hill Morton, in the county of Warwick, and of Melton Constable in the county of Norfolk, descends. (See Burke's Dictionary of the Peerage and Baronetage.)

After the decease of Sir Thomas de Astley, his eldest son,

THOMAS DE ASTLEY, by virtue of the decree called, Dictum de Kenilworth, was put into possession of his father's estates—paying as a compensation to Warine de Bassingbourne, three hundred and twenty marks, sterling, to raise which sum he sold his manor of Little Copston, to the monks of Combe. He was subsequently engaged in the Scottish wars of King Edward I., and participated in the victory of Falkirk. Thomas de Astley was summoned to parliament as BARON ASTLEY, from 23rd of June, 1295, to 3rd November, 1306, and was s. at his decease by his son,

NICHOLAS DE ASTLEY, second Lord Astley, summoned to parliament, from 4th July, 1309, to 11th July, 1309. His lordship and his brother Sir Giles de Astley attending King Edward II. into Scotland, were taken prisoners at Bannocksburn.

The period of this nobleman's decease is not ascertained, but having outlived his brother above mentioned, and, dying issueless, the title and estates devolved upon his nephew (Sir Giles de Astley's son and heir by Alice, second daughter and coheiress of Sir Thomas Wolvey, Knt.),

THOMAS DE ASTLEY, third Lord Astley, summoned to parliament, from 25th February, 1342, to 10th March, 1349. This nobleman founded a chantry in the parish church of Astley, in the 11th year of Edward III., and afterwards obtaining permission to change his chantry priests into a dean and secular canons, he erected a fair and beautiful collegiate church in the form of a cross, with a tall spire, covered with lead, and dedicated it to the assumption of the blessed Virgin. His lordship m. Elizabeth, daughter of Guy de Beauchamp, Earl of Warwick, and left issue,

William, (Sir) his successor.

Thomas, (Sir) M.P. for the county of Warwick, m. Elizabeth, daughter of Richard, son of Sir William Harecourt, Knt., from which union the ASTLEYS of Patstrull, in the county of Stafford, lineally derive. Of which family was JOHN DE ASTLEY, memorable for fighting a duel on horseback, upon the 29th August, 1438, with Peter de Massel, a Frenchman, in the street St. Antoine, at Paris, before Charles VII. King of France, where having pierced his antagonist through the head, he had the helmet, by agreement of the vanquished, to present to his lady. He subsequently fought Sir Philip Boyle, an Arragonian knight, in Smithfield, in the City of London, in the presence of King Henry VI., and his court, which combat, we are told, was gallantly performed on foot, with battle axes, spears, swords, and daggers, and at its conclusion, that John de Astley was knighted by the king, and rewarded with a pension of one hundred marks for his life. "Yea," (says Dugdale,) "so famous did Sir John de Astley grow for his valour, that he was elected a knight of the garter, and bore for his arms the coats of *Astley* and *Harecourt*, quarterly, with a *label of three points ermine.*"

Giles, ancestor of the Astleys of Wolvey.

Thomas, third Lord Astley, was s. at his decease by. his eldest son,

WILLIAM DE ASTLEY, fourth Lord Astley, but never summoned to parliament. This nobleman was included in several commissions during the reigns of Henry IV. and Henry VI. His lordship m. Catherine, daughter of William, Lord Willoughby de Eresby, by whom he left an only daughter,

JOANE, m. first, to Thomas Raleigh, Esq., of Farnborough, in the county of Warwick, by whom she had no issue, and secondly, to Reginald, Lord Grey de Ruthyn (being his lordship's second wife), by whom she had three sons, and a daughter: viz.

Edward, of whom presently,

John de Grey, of Barwell, in the county of Leicester.

Robert de Grey, of Enville and Whittington, in the county of Stafford.

Eleanor, m. to William Lucy, Esq., of
Charlecote, in the county of Warwick.

EDWARD DE GREY, the eldest son, marrying Elizabeth, only daughter and heiress
of Henry, son and heir of William, Lord
Ferrars, of Groby, by Isabel, second daughter and co-heiress of Thomas Mowbray,
Duke of Norfolk, was summoned to parliament in 1446, as LORD FERRARS, of
Groby, which barony, and that of ASTLEY,
descended regularly to Henry Grey, third
marquess of Dorset, K.G. who was created
DUKE OF SUFFOLK, 10th October, 1551,
and became forfeited upon the decapitation and attainder of his grace in 1554.

ARMS—Az. a cinquefoil ermine.

ASTLEY — BARONS ASTLEY, OF READING.

By Letters Patent, dated 4th November, 1664,
20 Charles I.

Lineage.

THE HON. RALPH DE ASTLEY, a younger
son of Thomas, Lord Astley, of Astley, in the
county of Warwick, by his second wife, Editha,
daughter of Peter Constable, Esq., of Melton-Constable, in the county of Norfolk, and sister and co-
heiress of Sir Robert Constable, Knt., of the same
place, was lineal ancestor of

JOHN ASTLEY, Esq., of Hill-Morton and
Melton-Constable, who m. Frances, daughter and
heiress of John Cheyney, Esq., of Sittingborne, in
the county of Kent, and was s. by his only surviving son,

ISAAC ASTLEY, Esq. This gentleman m.
Mary, daughter of Edward Waldegrave, Esq., of
Borley, in the county of Essex, and had two sons—

Thomas, ancestor of the Astleys (Baronets) of
Hill-Morton, in the county of Warwick, and

SIR JACOB ASTLEY, Knt., a distinguished
captain under the royal banner during the civil
wars; governor of Oxford and Reading, and pre-
eminently conspicuous at the battles of Edgehill,
Brentford, and Newbury; who for his gallant and
faithful services was raised to the peerage by letters
patent, dated 4th Nov., 1664, as LORD ASTLEY, of
READING, in the COUNTY OF BUCKS. His lordship
m. Agnes Imple, a German lady, and had issue—

ISAAC, his successor.

Thomas,
Henry, } all d. issueless.
Bernard,
Edward,

Elizabeth, m. to (her cousin) Sir Edward Astley,
Knt., and left SIR JACOB ASTLEY, Knt., who
inherited, upon the decease of his uncle, Sir
Isaac Astley, Bart., s. p., in 1659, the estates
of Hill-Morton and Melton-Constable, and
succeeded to the entailed property of Lord
Astley.

Of Jacob Lord Astley, Clarendon says—" He was
an honest, brave, plain man; as fit for the military
posts he held as Christendom yielded; and was ge-

nerally esteemed very discerning, and prompt in
giving orders, as occasion required; and most cheerful and present in action. An enemy to long
speeches, as usually made in council; he himself using only few, but very pertinent words." His
lordship died in 1651, and was succeeded by his
eldest son,

ISAAC ASTLEY, second lord, who m. Anne,
fourth daughter of Sir Francis Stydolfe, Knt., o
Norbury, in the county of Surrey, and had issue—

JACOB, his successor.

Francis died s. p.

His lordship d. in 1662, and was s. by his elder
son,

JACOB ASTLEY, third lord. His lordship m.
Frances, daughter and co-heiress of Sir Richard Stydolfe, of Norbury, son of Sir Francis, but had no
issue. Lord Astley d. in 1688, when the barony of
Astley of Reading EXPIRED.

ARMS—Az. a cinquefoil ern. within a bordure
engrailed or.

ATON—BARONS DE ATON.

By Writ of Summons, dated 30th December, 1324.
18 Edward II.

Lineage.

The paternal surname of this family arose from
the feudal barony of ATON, in the county of York,
of which its members were lords from the conquest;
for we find that

GILBERT, SON OF LAGI, assumed the surname
of ATON so far back as the reign of king Henry I.
from those lands; but the importance of the family
was founded by the marriage of this Gilbert de
Aton's great-grandson,

GILBERT DE ATON, with Margerie, daughter and heiress of WARINE DE VESCI, a younger
son of William de Vesci, Lord of Alnwick, in the
county of Northumberland, through which alliance
the ATONS inherited, eventually, the extensive possessions of the great barons de Vesci: thus—

EUSTACE DE VESCI, one of the twenty-five barons appointed to enforce the observance of
MAGNA CHARTA, elder brother of the above
WARINE, succeeded his father, m. Margaret,
daughter of William and sister of Alexander,
kings of Scotland; and, dying about 1216,
was s. himself by his son,

WILLIAM DE VESCI, to whom s., in 1253,
his son,

JOHN DE VESCI, who had summons
to parliament, as a baron, in 1264,
but dying s.p., was s. by his brother,

WILLIAM DE VESCI, summoned to parliament
in the reign of Edward I., and one of the competitors for the Scottish throne in the same
era. He d. about the year 1297, without legitimate issue, when the BARONY EXPIRED; but
the estates devolved upon his natural son,

WILLIAM DE VESCI, who was summoned
to parliament in 1313; but dying in two
years afterwards, s.p., that BARONY also
EXPIRED, while the estates reverted to
the great-grandson of the above Gilbert
de Aton and Margerie de Vesci, his wife.

Gilbert de Aton d. in the 19th of Henry III., and was s. by his son,

WILLIAM DE ATON, who was succeeded by his son,

SIR GILBERT DE ATON, one of the Knights of the Bath, created by PRINCE EDWARD, in the 34th of Edward I. Sir Gilbert dying s. p., was s. by his brother,

WILLIAM DE ATON, whose son and heir,

GILERT DE ATON, inherited, in the 9th of Edward II., the estates of the BARONS DE VESCI, as deduced above. This Gilbert had command, the year before, to fit himself with horse and arms, and to be at NEWCASTLE-UPON-TYNE on the feast-day of the Blessed Virgin, to restrain the hostilities of the Scots. In the 13th of Edward II., he was in the expedition to Scotland; and in the 17th of the same monarch, he confirmed (in consideration of receiving 700 marks sterling) as heir of William de Vesci, to Henry Lord Percie, the castle and lands of Alnwick, which Anthony Beke, Bishop of Durham and Patriarch of Jerusalem, has sold to the said Henry, although but confided to the bishop by William Lord de Vesci in trust for his bastard son, the last William de Vesci. In the following year (30th Dec. 1324) Gilbert de Aton was summoned to parliament as a baron of the realm, and he was so summoned during the remainder of his life. His lordship died in 1342, and was s. by his son,

WILLIAM DE ATON, second BARON ATON, who had summons to parliament on the 8th of January, 1371. His lordship married Isabel, daughter of William Lord Percy, by whom he had an only son, who predeceased him, and three daughters, his co-heiresses, namely—

- Anastasia, m. to Sir Edward de St. John, and left a daughter and heiress, Margaret de St. John, who m. Thomas de Bromflete, king's Butler, temp. Richard II. (See Bromflete.)
- Katherine, m. to Sir Ralph de Eure.
- Elizabeth, m. first, to William Playtz, and, secondly, to John Conyers, Esq., of Stockburne, in the county of Durham.

William Lord Aton was engaged in the French wars of king Edward III. He was sheriff of Yorkshire in the 42d of that monarch, and governor of the Castle of York, and again in the 43d and 46th of the same reign. His lordship d. —— when his estates were divided amongst his daughters, and the BARONY fell into ABEYANCE, as it still continues.

ARMS—Or, three bars az. on a canton gu., a cross patonce ar.

ALDITHELEY, OR AUDLEY — BARONS AUDLEY, OF HE-LEIGH.

By Writ of Summons, dated 15th May, 1321, 14th Edward II.

Lineage.

"That this family of Alditheley, vulgarly called Audley," says Dugdale, "came to be great and eminent, the ensuing discourse will sufficiently manifest: but that the rise thereof was no higher than King John's time; and that the first who assumed this surname was a branch of that ancient

and noble family of VERDON, whose chief seat was at Alton Castle, in the northern part of Staffordshire, I am very inclinable to believe; partly by reason that Henry had the inheritance of Alditheley given him by Nicholas de Verdon, who died in the 16th Henry III., or near that time; and partly for that he bore for his arms the same ordinary as Verdon did, viz. Fretté, but distinguished with a large canton in the dexter part of the shield, and thereon a cross paté; so that probably the ancestor of this Henry first seated himself at Alditheley: for that there hath been an antient mansion there, the large moat, northwards from the parish-church there (somewhat less than a furlong, and upon the chief part of a fair ascent), do sufficiently manifest."

HENRY DE ALDITHELEY, to whom Dugdale alludes above, being in great favour with Ranulph, Earl of Chester and Lincoln, (the most powerful subject of England in his time,) obtained from that nobleman a grant of Newhall in Cheshire, with manors in Staffordshire, and other parts—and for his adhesion to King John, in that monarch's struggle with the insurrectionary barons, a royal grant of the lordship of Storton, in Warwickshire, part of the possessions of Roger de Summerville. In the four first years of King Henry III., he executed the office of sheriff for the counties of Salop and Stafford, as deputy for his patron, the great Earl Ranulph—in the fourth year of which service the men of Staffordshire were required to aid him in fortifying the king's castle of Shrewardine, in the county of Salop. In the 10th of Henry III. this Henry de Alditheley was appointed governor of the castles of Carmarthen and Cardigan, and made sheriff the next year of the counties of Salop and Stafford and constable of the castles of Salop and Bridgenorth, which sheriffalty he held for five years. Upon his retirement from office he had special license to build a castle upon his own land, called Radcliff, in Shropshire, afterwards designated REDCASTLE, from the colour of the high rock upon which it was founded: and in the same year he had a confirmation of all such lands, whereof he was then possessed, as well those granted to him by Ranulph, Earl of Chester, and Nicholas de Verdon, as those in Ireland, given him by Hugh de Laci, EARL OF ULSTER, whose constable he was in that province. He subsequently obtained divers other territorial grants from the crown, but, notwithstanding, when Richard Mareschal, EARL OF PEMBROKE, rebelled, and made an incursion into Wales, the king, Henry III., thought it prudent to secure the persons of this Henry, and all the other barons-marchers. He was afterwards, however, constituted governor of Shrewsbury, in place of John de Laci, Earl of Lincoln, and on the death of John, Earl of Chester, governor of the castle of Chester, and also of that of Beeston, then called the "Castle on the Rock," and soon after made governor of Newcastle-under-Lyne. This powerful feudal baron m. Bertred, daughter of Ralph de Meisnilwarin of Cheshire, and had a son JAMES, and a daughter Emme, who m. Griffin ap Madoc, Lord of Bromefield, a person of great power in Wales. He d. in 1236, having founded and endowed the Abbey of Hilton, near to his castle at Heleigh,

18

in Staffordshire, for Cistercian monks, and was s. by his son,

JAMES DE ALDITHELEY, a great favorite of Richard, Earl of Cornwall, at whose coronation as king of Almaigne he assisted. This nobleman had livery of his lands in the 31st of Henry III., and was constituted in two years afterwards constable of Newcastle-under-Lyne. Being one of the lords-marchers he was actively employed for some years against the Welsh, and was appointed governor of the castles of Salop and Bridgenorth, and sheriff for the counties of Salop and Stafford. In the 47th of Henry III. he was made justice of Ireland; and in the same year, upon the misunderstanding between the king and the barons, regarding the *provisions of Oxford*, being referred to the arbitration of the monarch of France, he was one of the noblemen who undertook for the king therein. The next year we find him with Roger de Mortimer and the other barons-marchers, giving battle to *Lewelin*, Prince of Wales, and afterwards joining the Earl of Gloucester at Evesham in rescuing the king, who had become captive to the Earl of Leicester at the battle of Lewes. In the 52nd of Henry III. his lordship performed a pilgrimage to the shrine of St. James in Galicia, and the following year embarked in the Crusade. His death, occasioned by breaking his neck, occurred soon afterwards (1271). He had a daughter, Joan, who m. John, son of Robert de Beauchamp, to whose child, prior to its birth, the said John being then deceased, his lordship was appointed guardian. He had also five sons, the youngest of whom, Hugh, is supposed to have been the Hugh Alditheley, who had summons to parliament 15th May, 1321, and whose son became Earl of Gloucester. His lordship was s. by his eldest son,

JAMES DE ALDITHELEY, who d. s. p. in 1272, and was s. by his brother,

HENRY DE ALDITHELEY, between whom and John D'Eivill, who had m. Maud, widow of his deceased brother, a covenant was made in the 3rd of Edward I., conveying on the part of Henry a considerable landed dowry to the said Maud. He d. issueless in 1275, and was s. by his brother,

WILLIAM DE ALDITHELEY, who, attaining majority in a year after his accession, had livery of all his lands, save a reasonable dowry to Dulcia, the widow of his deceased brother Henry. In the 10th of Edward I. the king, by his precept to the barons of his exchequer, acknowledging that he was indebted to James de Alditheley, father of this William, in the sum of one thousand two hundred and eighty-eight pounds, five shillings, and ten pence, upon the surplusage of his account since he was justice of Ireland, commanded them to discharge the said William of two hundred and thirty pounds, fourteen shillings, and ten pence, a debt due by James to the exchequer upon another account. In this year (1275) William de Alditheley fell in an engagement with the Welsh, wherein several other brave warriors were slain, and the king lost fourteen banners. Dying without issue, he was s. by his brother,

NICHOLAS DE ALDITHLEY, who doing homage, had livery of his lands, and then paid £10 for his relief of the tenth part of the Barony of Wiche-Malbanc. In the 22nd of Edward I. this feudal lord received command to attend the king at Portsmouth, upon the 1st of September, well fitted with horse and arms, and thence to accompany the monarch into Gascoigne; which service he performed. In three years afterwards, 26th January, 1297, he had summons to parliament amongst the other barons of the realm, and was likewise in the expedition to Scotland, with the Earls of Warren and Warwick, and participated in the victory obtained at Dunbar. His lordship m. Catherine, daughter and coheiress of John Giffard of Brimesfield, by Maud, widow of William de Longespe, and daughter of Walter de Clifford; and dying in 1299, was s. by his eldest son, then in his tenth year,

THOMAS DE ALDITHELEY, who m. Eve, daughter and heiress of John, Lord Clavering, but dying s. p. in 1307, the inheritance devolved upon his brother,

NICHOLAS DE ALDITHELEY, who had summons to parliament from 8th January, 1313, (6th Edward II.) to 25th August, 1318, (12th Edward II.) His lordship m. Joane, widow of Henry Lacy, Earl of Lincoln, and sister and coheiress of William Martin—Baron Martin, (by writ, 23rd June, 1295; which barony fell into abeyance between the descendants of the said Joane and her sister, Eleanore, the other coheiress, wife of Philip de Columbers,) and was s. at his decease, in 1319, by his son,

JAMES DE AUDLEY—LORD AUDLEY—one of the most celebrated warriors of the martial reign of King Edward the III. His lordship was but three years of age at the decease of his father, when his castle of Heleigh, and divers other estates were committed to the guardianship of Ralph de Camoys, while he was himself confided in ward to Roger Mortimer, Earl of March. At the early age of twenty-three, we find him governor of Berwick-upon-Tweed, and receiving orders to attend King Edward the III. in his expedition into France, with twenty men at arms, and twenty archers. In the next year (17th Edward III.), his lordship did homage for lands inherited through his aunt Eleanore de Columbers, and then served the king with twenty men at arms and twenty archers, in his wars in France. In the 19th of Edward the III., he had command to attend the monarch in person, and to serve him with all his retinue, for the defence of the realm against the French, at the king's proper cost. In two years afterwards, he was again in France, and his lordship had the honour of being one of the Original Knights of the Garter,* upon

* ORIGINAL KNIGHTS OF THE GARTER. Camden gives the following list of those noble persons, who are designated founders of the order. EDWARD III., KING OF ENGLAND, EDWARD, PRINCE OF WALES, Henry, Duke of Lancaster, Thomas, Earl of Warwick, Ralph, Earl of Stafford, William Montacute, Earl of Salisbury, Roger Mortimer, Earl of March, Capdall de Buche, John L'Isle, Bartholomew Burghwash, John Beauchamp, John de Mohun, Hugh Courtenay, Thomas Holland, John Grey, Robert Fitz-Simon, Miles Stapleton,

the institution of that illustrious order. From this period, Lord Audley was pre-eminently distinguished as a soldier upon the French soil, until the glorious conflict of Poictiers placed his military renown upon the highest elevation. Of his lordship's conduct in this celebrated battle, *Froissard* gives the following account.

"The Lord James Audley, went not from the Prince of a great season, but when he saw that they should needs fight, he said to the prince, 'Sir, I have served always truly my lord, your father, and you also, and shall do as long as I live. I say this, because I made once a vow, that the first battel that either the king your father, or any of his children should be at, how that I would be one of the first setters on, or else to die in the pain; thereof I require your grace, as in reward for my service that ever I did to the king your father, or to you, that you would give me license to depart from you, and to set myself there, as I may accomplish my vow.' The prince accorded to his desire, and said, '*Sir James, God give you this day that grace to be the best knight of all other*;' and so took him by the hand. Then the knight departed from the prince, and went to the foremost front of all the battel, all onely accompanied with four esquires, who promised not to fail him. This lord James was a right sage and a valiant knight; and by him was much of the host ordained and governed the day before.

"The Lord James Audley, with his four esquires, was in the front of the battel, and there did marvels in arms; and, by great prowess, he came and fought with *Sir Arnold Dondraher*, under his own banner, and there they fought long together, and Sir Arnold was there sore handled." Froissard goes on to say, "that his lordship continuing to combat in his advanced position, he was sore hurt in the body, and in the visage; as long as his breath served him, he fought. At last, at the end of the battel, his four esquires took and brought him out of the field, and laid him under a hedge to refresh him, and they unarmed him, and bound up his wounds as well as they could.

"As soon as the Earl of Warwick (continues the same authority,) and Lord Cobham were departed, the prince demanded regarding the Lord Audley; some answered, 'He is sore hurt, and lieth in a litter here beside.'—'*By my faith*, (said the prince,) *of his hurts I am right sorry; go, and know if he may be brought hither, else I will go and see him there as he is.*' Then two knights came to the Lord Audley, and said, 'Sir, the prince desireth greatly to see you.' 'Ah, Sir,' (said Lord Audley,) 'I thank the prince when he thought on so poor a a knight as I am.' Then he called eight of his servants, and caused them to bear him in his litter, to the place were the prince was.

"Then the prince took him in his arms and kissed him, and made him great cheer, and said, '*Sir James, I ought greatly to honor you, for by your*

valiance, you have this day achieved the grace and renown of us all; and ye are reputed for the most valiant of all other.' 'Ah, Sir,' (said the knight,) 'ye say as it pleaseth you; I would it were so: and if I have this day any thing avanced myself, to serve you and accomplish the vow that I made, it ought not to be reputed to my own prowess.' '*Sir James*, (said the prince,) *I, and all ours take you in this journey for the best doer in arms; and to the intent to furnish you the better to pursue the wars; I retain you for ever to be my knight, with five hundred marks of yearly revenues, the which I shall assign you of my heritage in England.*' 'Sir,' (said the knight,) 'God grant me to deserve the great goodness that ye shew me.' And so he took his leave of the prince, for he was right feeble; and so his servants brought him to his lodging.

"The Lord James Audley gave to his four esquires the five hundred marks revenue that the prince had given him.

"When the prince heard of this gift made by Sir James Audley to his four esquires, he thanked him for so doing, and gave him six hundred marks per annum more."

In confirmation of Froissard, it appears by the public records, that this eminent soldier had for his singular services at the battle of Poictiers, a grant from Edward the Black Prince, of an annuity of £400 during his life, and for one year after, to be received out of the coinage of the Stanneries in Cornwall, and the king's lands in that county. After this period, he continued to serve in the wars, with equal renown to himself and glory to his country. His lordship m., first, Joane, daughter of Roger Mortimer, Earl of March, and had issue,

NICHOLAS, his successor.

Joane, m. to Sir John Tuchet, grandson of which marriage, Sir John Tuchet, was summoned to parliament as Baron Audley, upon the extinction of the male line of the family. (See Tuchet, Barons Audley.)

Margaret, m. to Sir Roger Hillary.

The baron m., secondly, Isabel, daughter and coheiress of William Malbank, Baron of Wich-Malbank, by whom he had,

Rowland, } both of whom d. s. p.
Thomas, }

Margaret, m. to Fouke, son of Sir Fouke Fitz-Warine, Knt.

His lordship made his will in the 9th of Richard II., at Heleigh Castle, by which he bequeathed his body to be buried in the Quire of his Abbey at Hilton, before the high altar, in case he should depart this life in the marches; but if in Devon or Somersetshire, then in the Quire of the Fryers Preachers at Exeter, before the high altar there; and appointed that there should be about his corpse, five great tapers, and five morters of wax, burning on the day of his funeral, as also £40 sterling, then distributed to poor people, to pray for his soul. To Nicholas, his son, he gave £100 in money, and one dozen of silver vessels, with all the armour for his own body. To Fouke Fitz-Warine and Philip his uncle, all his other armour of plate and mail. To Margaret Hillary, his daughter, £10 in money; and to the monks of Hilton

Thomas Walle, Hugh Wristhesley, Niel Loring, John Chandos, JAMES DE AUDLEY, Otho Holland, Henry Ewe, Zanchet Dabridgecourt, William Paynel.

Abbey, to pray for his soul, £10. This great soldier *d.* at Heleigh, on the 1st of April, 1386, and was *s.* by his eldest son,

NICHOLAS AUDLEY, Lord Audley, who was summoned to parliament from the 17th December, 1387, to 12th September, 1390. His lordship, *m.* Elizabeth, daughter of Adelice de Beaumont, by whom he had no issue; he *d.* in 1392, and his half-brothers having pre-deceased him, issueless, the male line of this branch of the family of ALDITHELEY OR AUDLEY, expired, while the "Barony of Audley" devolved upon the grandson of his lordship's sister, Joane Tuchet, his other sister, Margaret Hillary, having also died without issue.

ARMS—Gules, a fret, or.

AUDLEY, OR DE ALDITHELEY—BARONS AUDLEY, AND SUBSEQUENTLY EARL OF GLOUCESTER.

Barony by Writ of Summons, 15th May, 1321, 14th Edward II.

HUGH DE ALDITHELEY, OR AUDLEY, brother it is presumed of Nicholas, Lord Audley, of Heleigh, was summoned to parliament as "Hugh de Audley, Seniori," on the 15th May, 1321, 14th Edward II. His lordship had been engaged during the reign of Edward I. in the king's service, and was called "Senior," to distinguish him from his son. Being concerned in the insurrection of Thomas, Earl of Lancaster, 16th of Edward II., the baron was committed a close prisoner to Wallingford Castle, but making his peace with the king he obtained his release, and suffered nothing further. His lordship sate in the parliament of the 11th and 14th of Edward II. He *m.* Isolda, widow of Walter Balim, and left two sons, by the elder of whom he was succeeded.

HUGH DE AUDLEY, who had been summoned to parliament in the life-time of his father as "HUGH DE AUDLEY, JUNIORI," from 20th November, 1317, to 15th May, 1321, and after that nobleman's decease as "HUGH DE AUDLIE," from 3rd December, 1326, 20th Edward II., to 10th Edward III. His lordship *m.* Margaret, sister and co-heiress of Gilbert de Clare, Earl of Gloucester, and widow of Piers Gaveston, by whom he left an only daughter and heiress,

> Margaret, who *m.* Ralph, Lord Stafford, and carried the barony of Audley into that family : it expired upon the attainder of Edward, Duke of Buckingham, with that nobleman's other honours, in 1521.

Hugh, Lord Audley, was created Earl of Gloucester, 23rd April, 1337, and under that title a further account of his lordship will be found. He *d.* in 1347.

AUDLEY—BARON AUDLEY, OF WALDEN.

Created by Letters Patent, 29th November, 1538, 30th Henry VIII.

Lineage.

THOMAS AUDLEY, an eminent lawyer in the reign of Henry VIII., but of what family neither Dugdale nor the other genealogists have been able to ascertain, having attracted royal favor by his zeal in the spoliation of religious houses, as speaker of the parliament which originated that measure, attained within a short period the highest honors which royalty could bestow. In the 22nd of Henry VIII. he was nominated attorney for the duchy of Lancaster, raised to the degree of sergeant-at-law, and appointed king's sergeant. In two years afterwards Mr. Sergeant Audley succeeded Sir Thomas More in the custody of the great seal, as lord keeper, when he received the honor of knighthood, and before the close of the year he was elevated to the dignity of LORD CHANCELLOR OF ENGLAND. In addition to those lucrative honors, Sir Thomas had a grant of the scite and precinct, with all the lands and plate thereunto belonging of the suppressed priory of *Christchurch*, " near Aldgate, in the city of London," where he erected a mansion-house for his residence. In the 30th of the same reign his lordship sate as high steward upon the trial of Henry Courtenay, Marquess of Exeter, for conspiring to raise Reginald Pole (the subsequently eminent Cardinal Pole) to the throne. And in that year he obtained a grant of the great *Abbey of Walden*, in Essex, in compensation, as he alleged, "for having in this world sustained great damage and infamy in serving the king." Having acquired this last possession he was raised to the peerage by letters patent, dated 20th November, 1538, as BARON AUDLEY OF WALDEN, and installed a knight of the most noble order of the garter. His lordship *m.* Elizabeth, daughter of Thomas Grey, Marquess of Dorset, and had two daughters, viz.

> Margaret, *m.* first to Lord Henry Dudley, son of John, Duke of Northumberland, who fell at St. Quinton in 1557, dying *s. p.;* and secondly to Thomas Howard, Duke of Norfolk, who was beheaded 2nd July, 1572, by whom her grace had issue—
>> THOMAS, summoned to parliament as LORD HOWARD OF WALDEN, and afterwards created EARL OF SUFFOLK, lord high treasurer temp. James I. and K.G. From this nobleman descend the Earls of Suffolk and Berkshire.
>> Henry, died young.
>> William, ancestor of the Earls of Carlisle.
>> Elizabeth, died unmarried.
>> Margaret, *m.* to Robert Sackville, second Earl of Dorset, ancestor of the Dukes of Dorset.
> The Duchess of Norfolk inherited the entire property of her father upon the decease of her sister.
> Mary, who died unmarried.

Lord Audley died 19th April, 1544, when the title *expired* in default of a male heir. He was succeeded in the custody of the seals by Sir Thomas Wriothesley. His lordship bequeathed by his last testament, his body to be buried in the tomb of his new chapel at Walden; and appointed that his executors should, upon the next new year's day after his decease, deliver a legacy of one hundred pounds to the king, "from whom he had received all his reputations and benefits." Of this nobleman Rapin says, "Chancellor Audley was a person of good sense. He served the reformers when he could without danger: but he was too much a courtier to insist upon what he judged reasonable, if the king was against it."

ARMS—Quarterly per pale indented or, and az. In the second and third an eagle displayed of the first, on a bend of the second a fret between two martlets of gold.

AVESNES—EARL OF CAMBRIDGE.

Creation of King Edward III.

Lineage.

In the year 1340,

JOHN DE AVESNES, of Hainault, uncle or brother of Philippa, King Edward the Third's consort, was created EARL OF CAMBRIDGE, but engaging afterwards in the interest of France he was deprived of the dignity. His lordship never had summons to parliament.

BADLESMERE—BARONS BADLESMERE.

By Writ of Summons, dated 26th October, 1309, 3rd Edward II.

Lineage.

The first mention of this family occurs in the 16th year of the reign of Henry II., when

BARTHOLOMEW DE BADLESMERE, had a law-suit with William de Cheney concerning a landed property in the county of Kent; and in the 22nd of the same king, we find this Bartholomew amerced twenty marks for trespassing in the royal forests. To Bartholomew succeeded,

WILLIAM DE BADLESMERE, who adhering to the cause of the barons was taken prisoner, with several others, in the castle of Rochester, towards the close of King John's reign, and did not obtain his freedom until the sixth year of Henry III. After this William, came

GILES DE BADLESMERE, who lost his life in a skirmish with the Welsh, in the 32nd year of Henry III., and after him,

GUNCELINE DE BADLESMERE, known first as a great rebel to Henry III., for which he was excommunicated by the Archbishop of Canterbury; but subsequently, returning to his allegiance, as Justice of Chester, in which office he continued until the 9th of Edward I. In the next year he was in the expedition made into Wales, and in the 25th of the same monarch, in that into Gascony. He d. in four years afterwards, seised of the manor of Badlesmere, which he held in capite of the crown, as of the barony of Crevequer, by the service of one knight's fee. He was s. by his son, then twenty-six years of age,

BARTHOLOMEW DE BADLESMERE, who in the life-time of his father, (22nd Edward II.) received command to attend the king at Portsmouth, upon the 1st day of September, with horse and arms to embark with him for Gascony, and in

22

the year that he succeeded to his paternal property was in the wars of Scotland. He was afterwards in the retinue of Robert de Clifford in the Welsh wars, and in the 1st year of Edward II., was appointed governor of the castle of Bristol. In two years afterwards he was summoned to parliament as Badlesmere, and had a grant from the king, through the especial influence of Gilbert de Clare, Earl of Gloucester and Hertford, and Henry de Laci, Earl of Lincoln, of the castle and manor of Chelham in Kent, for his own and his wife's life, which castle had been possessed by Alexander de Baliol in right of his wife Isabel, and ought to have escheated to the crown upon the decease of the said Alexander, by reason of the felony of John de Strabolgi, Earl of Athol, (Isabel's son and heir,) who was hanged. In the 5th of Edward II., Lord Badlesmere was constituted governor of the castle of Ledes, and obtained at the same time grants of divers extensive manors. In the next year but one, his lordship was deputed, with Otto de Grandison and others, ambassador to the court of Rome, and the next year, upon the death of Robert de Clifford, he obtained a grant of the custody of the castle of Skypton in Yorkshire, as of all other castles in that county, and Westmoreland, whereof the said Robert died possessed, to hold during the minority of Roger de Clifford, his son and heir.

His lordship was further indebted to the crown for numerous charters for fairs and marts throughout his extensive manors; and he held the high office of steward of the household for a great number of years; but notwithstanding his thus basking in the sunshine of royal favour, his allegiance was not trustworthy, for joining the banner of Thomas Earl of Lancaster, and other discontented nobles of that period, he went into Kent without the king's permission; where being well received, he put himself at the head of some soldiers from his castle at Ledes, and thence proceeded to Canterbury, with nineteen knights, having linen jackets under their surcoats, all his esquires being in plate armour, and thus repaired to the shrine of St. Thomas, to the great amazement of the good citizens. While Lord Badlesmere remained at Canterbury, John de Crumwell and his wife sought his lordship's aid, and pledging himself to afford it, he hasted to Oxford, where the barons of his party had been then assembled. In the mean time the king being apprised of the baron's proceedings despatched the queen to Ledes, and upon admission being denied to her, the castle was regularly invested by Adomere de Valence, Earl of Pembroke, and John de Britannia, Earl of Richmond, to whom it eventually surrendered, when Lord Badlesmere's wife, young son, and daughters, all falling into the hands of the besiegers, were sent prisoners to the Tower of London. The baron and his accomplices afterwards were pursued by Edmund, Earl of Kent, and John de Warren, Earl of Surrey, and being defeated and taken prisoners at the battle of Borough-bridge, his lordship was hanged, drawn, and quartered, at Canterbury, and his head set upon a pole at Burgate. At the time of the baron's execution, upwards of ninety lords, knights, and others concerned in the same insurrection, suffered a similar fate in various parts of the kingdom. Margaret, his lordship's widow, (one of the daughters and co-heiresses of Thomas, third son of Thomas, second son of Richard de Clare, Earl of Gloucester,) continued prisoner in the Tower, until, through the influence of William Lord Roos, of Hamlake, and others, she obtained her freedom. Whereupon betaking herself to the nunnery of *Minoresses*, without Aldgate, in the suburbs of London, she had two shillings a day for her maintenance, to be paid by the sheriff of Essex; she subsequently, however, obtained a large proportion of the deceased lord's manors for her dowry. By this lady, Lord Badlesmere left issue,

> GILES.
>
> Maud, *m.* to John de Vere, Earl of Oxford.
>
> Elizabeth, *m.* first to Edmund Mortimer, and secondly, to William Bohun, Earl of Northampton.
>
> Margaret, *m.* to Sir John Tibetot.
>
> Margery, *m.* to William, Lord Roos, of Hamlake.

His lordship had been summoned to parliament, from the 26th October, 1309, to 5th August, 1320. His unhappy fate occurred in 1322; but notwithstanding *that*, his son,

GILES DE BADLESMERE, second baron, found such favour from the king, that he had a special precept to the keeper of the wardrobe, in the Tower, to deliver unto him all his father's harneys, as well coat-armours as others. This nobleman doing homage in the 7th of Edward III., although not then at majority, had livery of his lands, and the next year attended the king in an expedition into Scotland, in which service he was engaged the three ensuing years. His lordship had summons to parliament from 22d January, 1336, to 18th August, 1337. He *m.* Elizabeth, daughter of William de Montacute, Earl of Salisbury; but dying without issue, in 1338, the BARONY OF BADLESMERE fell into *ABEYANCE between his sisters and co-heiresses, and it so continues amongst their descendants.

   ARMS—Ag. a fesse betw. two bars gamelles, gules.

BALIOL—BARONS BALIOL.

Feudal.

Lineage.

In the reign of WILLIAM RUFUS,

GUY DE BALIOL had a grant from the crown of the BARONY of BIWELD, in the county of Northumberland, and thus became its feudal lord. This Guy, although a benefactor to the church, and

---

* The barony of Badlesmere was assumed without any legal right by the deceased lord's eldest sister, Maud, Countess of Oxford, and the Earl, her husband, and was retained in that family until the demise of John de Vere, fourteenth earl, without male issue, in the reign of Henry VIII., when it was certified, 5th April, 1626, to have fallen into abeyance between that nobleman's four sisters.

within the see of Durham, was nevertheless interdicted hunting in any of the bishop's forests. He was *s.* by his son,

BARNARD DE BALIOL, a military commander of reputation, who participated in the victory achieved over the Scots, in 1138, at Northalerton, known in history as the "Battle of the Standard," but was afterwards taken prisoner, at Lincoln, with King Stephen. Upon the incursion of the Scots, in the 20th Henry II., Barnard de Baliol again took up arms, and joining Robert de Stuteville, proceeded to the relief of Alnwick Castle, and having surprised the besiegers, seized the king of Scots with his own hand, and sent him prisoner to the Castle of Richmond. In the course of this forced march to Alnwick, when, in consequence of a dense fog, a halt was recommended, Baliol exclaimed, "Let those stay that will, I am resolved to go forward, although none follow me, rather than dishonour myself by tarrying here." This feudal chief is supposed to have been the founder of the fortress upon the banks of the Teise, called "Barnard Castle." He was a munificent benefactor to the church, having, among other grants, bestowed lands upon the Abbey of St. Mary at York, and upon the monks at Riebault, for the health of his own soul, and that of his wife, AGNES DE PINCHENI. He was *s.* by his son,

EUSTACE DE BALIOL, who gave £100 for license to marry the widow of Robert Fitzpiers. This feudal lord had issue—

> HUGH, his successor.
>
> Henry, *m.* Lora, one of the co-heiresses of Christian, wife of William de Mandeville, Earl of Essex; and dying in the 30th of Henry III., his widow, the Lady Lauretta (as termed in the record), had livery of all the lands in Essex, Hertford, and Norfolk, which he held of her inheritance.
>
> Eustace, *m.* Helewise, daughter and heiress of Ralph de Levyngton, a baron of Northumberland, and his wife, Ada, who had been the widow of William de Furnivall. In the 45th Henry III. this Eustace was sheriff of Cumberland and governor of the castle of Carlisle. In nine years afterwards, assuming the cross, he attended Prince Edward to the Holy Land. Upon the decease of his wife, Eustace de Baliol appears to have had a great contest with her heirs-at-law regarding her inheritance in a moiety of the barony of BUROH; the heirs claiming immediate possession, while Eustace held, that, having had a child born alive by the deceased, he was entitled by the courtesy of England to a life-interest in the estate. The heirs seem, however, to have eventually prevailed. Eustace espoused, for his second wife, Agnes, second daughter of Joane de Perci, and granddaughter (maternally) of William de Bruere, a powerful feudal baron of that period.

Eustace de Baliol, Sen., was *s.* by his eldest son,

HUGH DE BALIOL, who was certified to hold the barony of Biwell of the crown by the service of five knights' fees, and to find thirty soldiers for the guard of Newcastle-upon-Tyne, as his progenitors had done from the time of Rufus. He held likewise the lordship of Hiche, in Essex, *in capite*, as an augmentation of his barony, by the gift of Henry II. From King John he obtained the lands of Richard de Unfranville, and of Robert de Meisnell, in the county of York, in consideration of his services in the Baronial War. In the 18th of that monarch's reign, he was joined with Philip de Hulcotes in defence of the northern border towards Scotland; and when the king of Scots had subjugated the whole of Northumberland for Lewis of France, those generals held out stoutly all the fortresses upon the line of the Teise, particularly *that* of Barnard Castle, where Eustace de Vesci (who had married the Scottish monarch's sister), coming with his royal brother-in-law to the siege, was slain. Hugh de Baliol was succeeded by his son,

JOHN DE BALIOL. This feudal lord *m.* Dervorguill, one of the three daughters and co-heirs of Alan of Galloway, a great baron of Scotland, by Margaret, eldest sister of John le Scot, the last Earl of Chester, and one of the heirs of David, sometime earl of Huntingdon, from which alliance arose the claim of the Baliols to the crown of Scotland. By this illustrious lady he acquired the Scottish barony of Galloway. In the 28th Henry III., when ways and means were required to discharge the debt incurred by the war in Gascony, John de Baliol was one of the committee of twelve chosen to report to parliament upon the subject; and the next year he paid thirty pounds for thirty knights' fees, which he held towards the levy in aid, for marrying the king's daughter. He was afterwards sheriff of Cumberland for six successive years, and governor of the castle of Carlisle. Subsequently he had a military summons to attend the king at Chester, to oppose the Welsh, and was sheriff of the counties of Nottingham and Derby for three years; at which time he had the *honour of Peverell* committed to his custody. In the baronial contest he adhered faithfully to the king, and fell into the hands of the Earl of Leicester, with his royal master, at the battle of Lewes, in 1264; but he appears to have effected his escape, and to have joined the other loyal barons in raising fresh troops for the captive monarch's redemption. This John Baliol was founder of the college that bears his name at Oxford. He *d.* in 1268, and was *s.* by his son (then twenty-eight years of age),

HUGH DE BALIOL, who *m.* Anne, daughter of William de Valence, Earl of Pembroke, but dying the next year without issue, was *s.* by his brother,

ALEXANDER DE BALIOL. The barony inherited by this feudal lord consisted of more than five-and-twenty extensive lordships. He *d.* in 1278, and was *s.* by his son,

· JOHN DE BALIOL, who *m.* Isabel, daughter of John de Warren, Earl of Surrey. This feudal nobleman was one of the chief competitors for the crown of Scotland, in the reign of Edward I., and was eventually declared king, by the decision of that monarch, to whose arbitration the claimants submitted their pretensions.

To elucidate Baliol's right to the Caledonian sceptre, it will be necessary to digress somewhat into the genealogy of the Scottish princes.

24

DAVID, *King of Scotland*, had an only son, HENRY, who pre-deceased him, leaving three sons, viz.—

1. MALCOLM, who ascended the throne as Malcolm IV., and was *s.* by his brother,

2. WILLIAM the Lion, who was *s.* by his son,
   ALEXANDER the Third. This prince espoused Margaret, daughter of Henry III. King of England, and sister of King Edward I. and had three children. viz.—

   Alexander, } both died in the life-time
   David,   } of their father, *s. p.*

   Margaret, *m.* in 1281, ERIC, KING OF NORWAY, and left an only daughter,

       MARGARET, who was acknowleged QUEEN OF SCOTS, but died in her passage from Norway, and with her terminated the lines of David's two sons, Malcolm and William.

3. DAVID, Earl of Huntingdon, in England, espoused Maud, daughter of Hugh, and sister and co-heiress of Ranulph, Earl of Chester, by whom he left issue at his decease in 1219,
   John, surnamed Le Scot, *s.* to the Earldom of Huntingdon, and became Earl of Chester, died *s. p.*
   Margaret, *m.* to Alan, of Galloway, and had two daughters, viz.—
       Dervorguill, *m.* to John de Baliol, grandfather of John de Baliol, of whom we are now immediately treating.
       Marjory, *m.* to John Comyn, and died *s. p.*
   Isabella, *m.* Robert Bruce, and had a son, ROBERT BRUCE, the celebrated claimant for the Scottish crown.
   Ada, *m.* Henry de Hastings, Lord Hastings, and left issue,
       HENRY, Lord Hastings, also a competitor for the Scottish throne.
       Margaret.
       Hillarie, *m.* to Sir William Harcourt, ancestor of the EARLS OF HARCOURT, recently extinct.

By this table, the claim of Baliol seems indisputable, his mother, who was then alive, having abdicated her right in his favour, but Bruce contended that he was himself one step of kindred nearer to David, Earl of Huntingdon, than Baliol, being that nobleman's grandson; and he met the question of seniority, by alleging, that he had to contest that point in reality with Baliol's mother, and that being a male, he ought to be preferred to a female, according to the law and usage of nations, of which he adduced divers precedents. Edward, decided, however, in favour of BALIOL, and the new king swore fealty to the English monarch, on 30th November, 1292, as his superior lord. In the oath he acknowledged the sovereignty of the King of England over Scotland, in very express and submissive terms; and he caused an authentic act of allegianse to be drawn up. Baliol's installation followed, and was performed at Scone, with the usual ceremonies, all the Scottish lords swearing fealty to him, save ROBERT BRUCE, who absented himself. Thus the English FEUDAL BARONY OF BALIOL, merged in the royal dignity of Scotland.

ARMS—Gu. an orle ar.

BALIOL—BARONS BALIOL.

By Writ of Summons, dated 26th September, 1300, 28 Edward I.

Lineage.

ALEXANDER BALIOL, brother of JOHN DE BALIOL, KING OF SCOTLAND, being in the retinue of that magnificent prelate, *Anthony Beke*, Bishop of Durham, and Patriarch of Jerusalem; in the expedition made by King Edward I. into Flanders, was restored to all his lands in Scotland, in the 25th of that monarch's reign—and was summoned to parliament as a BARON, from the 26th September, 1300, to the 3rd November, 1306. His lordship m. Isabell, daughter and heiress of Richard de Chilham, and widow of David de Strabolgi, Earl of Athol, by whom he obtained for life, the castle and manor of Chilham, in the county of Kent. Dying, however, without issue, the BARONY OF BALIOL became EXTINCT.

BARDOLF—BARONS BARDOLF.

By Writ of Summons, dated 6th February, 1299, 27 Edward I.

Lineage.

THE first of this family upon record, WILLIAM BARDULF, was sheriff of Norfolk and Suffolk, from the 16th to 21st of Henry II., inclusive, and after him came

THOMAS BARDULF, who, upon the scutage being levied of such barons as did not attend King Henry II. into Ireland, in the 18th of that monarch's reign, nor contribute men or money to that service, paid £25. for the scutage of those knights' fees which formerly belonged to Ralph Hanselyn, Baron of Shelford in the county of Nottingham, whose daughter and heiress, ROSH, he had married. This Thomas obtained from William, brother of King Henry II., the Lordship of Bradewell, to hold to himself and his heirs, by the service of one knight's fee. Three parts of which he bestowed upon his three daughters: viz. ——, wife of Robert de St. Remigio; ——, wife of William Bacun; and ——, wife of Baldwin de Thoni. Thomas Bardulf was s. by his son,

DOUN BARDOLF, who marrying Beatrix, daughter and heiress of William de Warren, acquired by her the Barony of Wirmegay, in the county of Norfolk. He d. in 1209, leaving his widow Beatrix surviving, who gave 3100 marks to the king, for livery of her father's lands, and a reasonable dowry from the lands belonging to her husband; as also that she might not be compelled to marry again, contrary to her inclination. Doun Bardolf was s. by his son,

WILLIAM BARDOLF, who in the 26th of Henry III., attended that monarch in person, in the expedition which he then made into France. In the next year, he had livery of the honor of Wirmegay,

which during his minority had been in the hands of Hubert de Burgh, Earl of Kent; and he subsequently obtained royal charters for markets and free warren throughout his different lordships and manors. In the 41st of the same monarch, he attended the king in his expedition into Wales, and was soon after constituted governor of Nottingham Castle. He was at the fatal battle of Lewes, under the royal banner, in 1264, and was there taken prisoner along with the king. He d. in the 4th of Edward I., anno 1275, and was s. by his son,

WILLIAM BARDOLF, who doing homage, had livery of his lands, lying in the counties of Leicester, Lincoln, Nottingham, Norfolk, and Sussex; and soon after obtained charters for fairs and markets to be holden at his different manors. He m. Julian, daughter of Hugh de Gurnay, and dying in 1292, was s. by his son,

HUGH BARDOLF, who in the 22d of Edward I., had summons with other eminent persons, to attend the king, to advise upon the affairs of the realm, and was subsequently summoned to parliament, as BARON BARDOLF, from the 6th of February, 1299, to the 2nd of June, 1302. He m. Isabel, daughter and heiress of Robert Aguillon,[*] by whom he had two sons, Thomas and William. His lordship, who was employed in the French and Scottish wars of this reign, d. in 1303, and was s. by his elder son,

SIR THOMAS BARDOLF, K.B., as second BARON BARDOLF. This nobleman was summoned to parliament, from 26th August, 1307, to 23rd October, 1330. In the latter of which years his lordship d., and was s. by his son,

JOHN BARDOLF, third BARON BARDOLF, summoned to parliament, from 22nd January, 1336, to the 1st June, 1363. His lordship m. Elizabeth, daughter and coheiress of Sir Roger D'Amorie, and, as Dugdale calls her, "that great woman," his wife, Elizabeth, by whom he acquired a considerable accession of landed property. This nobleman participated in the glories of the martial reign of Edward III., and attained the high dignity of BANNERET. He d. in 1371, and was s. by his son,

WILLIAM BARDOLF, fourth BARON BARDOLF—summoned to parliament, from 20th January, 1376, to 3rd September, 1385, as "William Bardolf of Wormegay." His lordship m. Agnes, daughter of Sir Michael Poynings, Knt. He served in the French and Irish wars: latterly under John of Gaunt, Duke of Lancaster, and dying in 1385, was s. by his son,

THOMAS BARDOLF, fifth BARON BARDOLF—summoned to parliament, from 12th September, 1390, to 25th August, 1404. This nobleman joining Henry, Earl of Northumberland, Thomas, Earl

---

[*] In Gibson's Camden's Britannia, it is stated, that Sir Robert Aguillon had a castle at the manor of Addington in Surrey, which was holden in fee, by the serjeantcy, to find in the king's kitchen, on the coronation day, a person to make a dainty dish, called, "Mapigernoun, or Dillegrout," and serve the same up to the king's table. This service has been regularly claimed by the lords of the said manor, and allowed at the respective coronations of the kings of England.—*Banks' Extinct Peerage.*

Marshal and Nottingham, and Richard Scroope, Archbishop of York, in their rebellion, temp. Henry IV., (for which the earl marshal and archbishop were beheaded at York,) he was forced, with the earl of Northumberland, to fly to France, but those lords returning in about three years afterwards, and again raising the standard of insurrection in Yorkshire, they were attacked by the sheriff and the power of the county at Bramham Moor, where sustaining a total defeat, the earl fell in the field, and Lord Bardolf died soon afterwards of his wounds. His lordship had married Avicia, daughter of Ralph, Lord Cromwell, and left two daughters, viz.

Anne, m. first, to Sir William Clifford, Knt., and secondly, to Reginald Lord Cobham.

Joane, m. to Sir William Phelip, K.G., (son of Sir John Phelip, Knt., of Donynton, in the county of Suffolk,) a valiant soldier in the French wars of King Henry V., to which monarch he was treasurer of the household, and at his decease had the chief direction of his funeral. Sir William is said to have been raised to the peerage by letters patent, as LORD BARDOLF, in the reign of Henry VI., but he was never summoned to parliament. By Joane Bardolf he left an only daughter and heiress,

Elizabeth, who m. John, Viscount Beaumont. (See that dignity.)

Thomas, the fifth and unfortunate Lord Bardolf, dying thus, and being afterwards attainted, his BARONY and large possessions became forfeited. The estates were divided between Thomas Beaufort, Duke of Exeter, the king's brother, Sir George Dunbar, Knt., and the queen: but the latter proportion, upon the petition of Sir William Clifford and his wife, and Sir William Phelip and his wife, to the king, was granted in reversion after the queen's decease, to those representatives of the attainted nobleman. Dugdale states, "that Lord Bardolf's remains were quartered, and the quarters disposed of, by being set upon the gates of London, York, Lenne, and Shrewsbury, while the head was placed upon one of the gates of Lincoln. His widow obtained permission, however, in a short time to remove and bury them."

ARMS—Az. three cinque foils, or.

BASSET — BARONS BASSET OF WELDEN.

By Writ of Summons, dated 6th February, 1299, 27th Edward I.

Lineage.

Few families in the early annals of England can boast of a more eminent progenitor, than the Bassets, and the descendants of few of the Anglo-Norman nobles attained a higher degree of power than those of,

RALPH BASSET, who[*] is said to have been raised by Henry I., from a lowly condition, to

large possessions, and to have been "exalted above earls and other eminent men," by that monarch. 'Tis true he was constituted JUSTICE of ENGLAND, and invested with the power of sitting in whatever court he pleased and where he might list for the administration of justice; but it is not equally certain that he was of so humble an origin, for we find his son Ralph, in the reign of Stephen, "abounding in wealth, and erecting a strong castle upon some part of his inheritance in Normandy." The son having such an heritable property would certainly indicate that the family was of importance in the dukedom, prior to the conquest of England; it is not of any consequence, however, for RALPH BASSET required none of the artificial aids of ancestry to attain distinction; he had within himself powers sufficient at any period to reach the goal of honour, but particularly in the rude age in which he lived. To his wisdom we are said to be indebted for many salutary laws, and among others for that of frank pledge. Like all the great men of his day, he was a most liberal benefactor to the church. He d. in 1120, leaving issue,

THURSTINE, who s. to the manor of Colston.

Thomas, ancestor of the Bassets of Haddington, from whom diverged the Wycombe Bassets.

Richard, of whom presently. This Richard is called the eldest son by Dugdale, and by others, the second.

Nicholas, who was overthrown under the banner of Stephen, fighting against the Empress Maud; and his son forfeited all the estates to Henry II.

Gilbert, of Little Rissington, in the county of Gloucester, ancestor of the Bassets of that place.

The third son,

RICHARD BASSET, succeeded his father as JUSTICE of ENGLAND, which high office he filled in the latter part of King Henry I.'s reign, and through the whole of King Stephen's. In the 5th year of the latter monarch, he was sheriff of Surrey, Cambridge, and Huntingdonshire, with Aleric de Vere; and he served the same office for Essex, Hertford, Buckingham, Bedford, Norfolk, Suffolk, Northampton, and Leicestershires. His lordship m. Maud, only daughter and heiress of Geoffrey Ridel, Lord of Witheringe, by Geva, daughter of Hugh Lupus, Earl of Chester, and had issue,

Geoffrey, who, from his mother, assumed the surname of "Ridel."

Ralph, of Drayton, in the county of Stafford (a lordship bestowed upon his mother by the Earl of Chester).

William, of Sapcoate.

He d. —— and was s. by his eldest son,

GEOFFREY RIDEL. This feudal lord married twice, and had issue by both wives, by the first, two sons: viz.

GEOFFREY, who obtained the principality of Blaye, in France.

Richard, of whom presently.

By the second, one son,

Hugh, from whom the present baronets RIDELL derive.

---

[*] De ignobili stirpe illustravit ac de pulvere (ut ita dicam,) extulit; datâque multiplici facultate super consules et illustres oppidanos exaltavit. —Ordericus Vitalis.

Geoffrey Ridel was *s.* at his decease by his eldest surviving son, who re-assuming his paternal surname, and seating himself at Welden, in Northamptonshire, became

RICHARD BASSET, *of Welden*, and was *s.* by his son,

RALPH BASSET, who, in the 2nd of Henry III., paid thirty marks for the fifteen knights' fees he then held, upon the levy of the first scutage for the king. He *d.* sometime before the year 1257, and was *s.* by his son,

RALPH BASSET, who had livery of his lands, upon doing homage in the 42nd Henry III. He was *s.* by his son,

RICHARD BASSET, who *d.* in 1275, and was *s.* by his son,

RALPH BASSET, who *d.* in 1294, and was *s.* by his son,

RICHARD BASSET, who was summoned to parliament, on the 6th of February, 1299, as " *Richarde Basset de Welden.*" In the 34th Edward I., his lordship was in the expedition made against the Scots, in the retinue of Ahmare de Valence, Earl of Pembroke, and being subsequently engaged in the same service, he was slain at the battle of Strevelyn. He was *s.* by his son, (then in minority, whose wardship was granted to Richard de Grey,)

RALPH BASSET, second baron, who making proof of his age, had livery of his lands in the 15th Edward II. His lordship *m.* Joane, daughter of John de la Pole, citizen of London, and had issue,

> Ralph, his successor.
> Eleanor, *m.* to Sir John Knyvett, Lord Chancellor of England.
> Joane, *m.* to Sir Thomas Aylesbury, Knt.

His lordship was *s.* at his decease by his son,

RALPH BASSET, third baron, but never summoned to parliament. This nobleman becoming a canon regular in the priory of Laund, his son and heir,

RALPH BASSET, doing his homage, had livery of all his father's lands, and dying in the 6th of Richard II., was *s.* by his son,

RICHARD BASSET, who died *s. p.* in the 10th of Henry IV., leaving his cousins,

Sons of Eleanor and Joane Basset, mentioned as above.	Sir John Aylesbury and John Knyvett.	Heirs to his extensive estates, but the barony appears to have existed with the baron who had been summoned to parliament only. Wherefore, though, is not very intelligible.

The male line of Sir John Aylesbury failed with his son Sir Thomas, who left two daughters, coheiresses : namely,

> Isabel, wife of Sir Thomas Chaworth, Knt.
> Eleanor, *m.* to Humphrey Stafford, of Grafton.

ARMS—Or. three piles, gu. within a bordure, Sa. Bessanter.

BASSET — BARONS BASSET, OF DRAYTON.

By Writ of Summons, dated 14th December, 1264, 48th Henry III.

Lineage.

In the 42nd year of King Henry III.

RALPH BASSET, Lord of Drayton, in the county of Stafford, great grandson of Richard Basset, Justice of England, and his wife Maud Ridel, had summons, (amongst other great men,) to attend the king at Chester, well furnished with horse and arms, to oppose the incursions of the Welsh. But in the 48th of the same monarch, having joined Simon Montford, Earl of Leicester, and the other rebellious barons, he was appointed the next year, after the defeat of the king's arms at Lewes, and capture of the king, governor for those lords of the castles of Salop and Bruges. He fell, however, before the close of the same year, at the battle of Evesham. It is said, that when the Earl of Leicester perceived the great force and order of the royal army, calculating upon defeat, he conjured Ralph Basset and Hugh Dispenser to retire, and reserve themselves for better times; but they bravely answered, " that if he perished, they would not desire to live." Lord Basset *m.* Margaret, daughter of Roger de Someri, Baron of Dudley, and widow of Urian St. Pierre, and had issue,

> RALPH, his successor.
> Maud, *m.* to John Lord Grey de Wilton.

Notwithstanding the death of Lord Basset, thus in arms against the king, his widow was so favoured by the monarch, as to have the chief of his estates settled upon her for life, but soon afterwards taking the veil, she passed her title in those lands to her son,

RALPH BASSET, second baron, who had summons to parliament, 23d June, 1295, as " *Radulphus Basset de Drayton.*" This nobleman was engaged in the French and Scottish wars of King Edward I. In the latter, as one of the retinue of Edmund, Earl of Lancaster, the king's brother. His lordship *m.* Joan,[a] daughter of John Grey, Justice of Chester, and had issue,

> RALPH, his successor.
> Margaret, *m.* Edmund, baron of Stafford, the great-grandson of which marriage, THOMAS, EARL OF STAFFORD, was one of the heirs to Ralph, last Lord Basset of Drayton.
> Maud, *m.* to William de Heres, the great-great-grand-daughter of which marriage, Alice, wife of Sir William Chaworth, Knt., was one of the heirs to Ralph, last Lord Basset of Drayton, of whom at conclusion.

His lordship *d.* in 1299, and was *s.* by his son,

RALPH BASSET, *third Lord Basset of Drayton*, summoned to parliament from 29th December, 1299, to 25th February, 1342. This nobleman was one of the eminent persons made knights of the bath with

---

[a] Dugdale, under Basset of Drayton, makes this lady as above, but under Grey, of Wilton, he calls her the daughter of Reginald Grey, the son of John.

Prince Edward, in the 34th of Edward I, and who attended the king that year into Scotland, but returning thence without leave, orders were issued to the sheriffs of Stafford, Nottingham, and Derbyshire, to seize his lands: he received, however, his pardon in the following year. His lordship was, for several years afterwards, in constant service in Scotland. In the 15th Edward II. he was joined in commission with John de Someri, to seize the castle of Kenilworth for the king, by reason of the forfeiture of Thomas, Earl of Lancaster, and in the same year was constituted steward of the Duchy of Acquitane. During his government there, Lord Basset was embroiled in a contest with the king of France, but being supported by his royal master, he bade defiance to the wrath of the French monarch. He did not remain long, however, in that government, but returning to England in the year but one afterwards, he was made constable of Dover Castle, and warden of the Cinque Ports. In the 1st and 7th of Edward III. he was again in the Scottish wars, and in the 8th of the same reign, he was appointed justice of North Wales. His lordship m. Joane, daughter of Thomas Beauchamp, Earl of Warwick, and had issue,

    RALPH, who m. Alice, daughter of Nicholas, Lord Audley, and dying before his father, anno 1323, left issue,

        RALPH, successor to his grandfather.

        Isabel,* m. to Sir Thomas Shirley, ancestor of the present EARL FERRARS.

Ralph, Lord Bassett, of Drayton, d. 25th February, 1343, and was s. by his grandson,

RALPH BASSET, 4th Lord Basset of Drayton, summoned to parliament from 35th December, 1357, to 6th December, 1389. This nobleman was distinguished in arms during the reigns of Edward III. and Richard II., and was honoured with the garter, in consequence of which, his achievement is still to be seen in one of the stalls of the chapel at Windsor. His lordship m. Joane, sister of John, Duke of Britanny, but had no issue. He d. 10th May, 1390, directing by his will, that his body should be buried at Lichfield, near the altar of St. Nicholas, and devising his estates, according to some authorities, to Sir Hugh Shirley, his nephew, son of his sister Isabel (see above), upon condition that he should assume the surname and arms of Basset, in failure of which proviso, those estates were then to pass to his cousin, Edmund, Lord Stafford. But the matter is differently represented by other authorities; it is certain, however, that great disputes arose after the decease of Lord Basset, between Humphrey, Earl of Stafford, and Sir Thomas Chaworth, Knt., regarding the lordship of Colston-Basset, in the county of Nottingham, but it does not appear that the Shirleys were engaged in it, nor did they take the name of Basset. Amongst other directions, Lord Basset orders in his will, that the person, whomsoever it should be, that should first adopt his surname and arms, should have the use of his great velvet bed during his life; and to the same person he also bequeathed four silver basons,

with two ewers, whereon his arms were graven, six silver dishes, two silver pots, and four chargers, all marked with his arms; as also a cup, with cover gilt, having one ring on the side thereof. His lordship constituted Walter Skyelaw, Bishop of Durham, Richard Scrope, Bishop of Chester, and Sir Richard Scrope, Knt., his executors. The BARONY OF BASSET has remained in abeyance since the decease of this nobleman, which can only be accounted for by the presumption, that Isabel, Lady Shirley, was not the legitimate daughter of his lordship's father, and the supposition becomes almost a certainty by the inquisitions taken after the baron's decease: according to the first, Thomas, Earl of Stafford, was found to be his cousin and next heir; and by the second, the same Thomas, Earl of Stafford, and Alice, the wife of Sir John Chaworth, were found his cousins and next heirs, without any mention whatever of his next relative, were she legitimate, Isabel, Lady Shirley.

ARMS—or, three piles gu. a canton erm.

BASSET — BARONS BASSET OF SAPCOATE.

By Writ of Summons, dated 14th December, 1264, 49 Henry III.

Lineage.

This branch of the BASSETS was founded by WILLIAM BASSET, one of the itinerant justices for Yorkshire, in the 21st Henry II., who settled at Sapcoate in Leicestershire, and was younger brother of Ralph Basset, Lord of Drayton, in the county of Stafford: as deputy to whom he executed the office of sheriff of Warwick and Leicestershire, in the 9th of the same monarch's reign. In the 10th he was sheriff of Leicestershire himself: from the 11th to half of the 16th years, inclusive, sheriff of both shires, and from the 23rd to the 30th, sheriff of Lincolnshire. To this William Basset succeeded his son,

SIMON BASSET, who m. in the 6th of Richard I., one of the daughters and co-heiresses of William Avenel, of Haddon, in the county of Derby, and was s. by his son,

RALPH BASSET. This feudal lord held the sheriffalty of Lincolnshire from the 25th to the 29th of Henry III., inclusive, and in four years after performed a pilgrimage to St. James in Gallicia. In the 42nd of the same monarch he received command to attend the king at Chester, to repel the incursions of the Welsh, and he was constituted in that year governor of Northampton Castle. But after the battle of Lewes, being summoned to the parliament, which the barons held in the king's name (49 Henry III.), he subsequently sided with Simon Montford, Earl of Leicester, and fell with that ambitious noble at the battle of Evesham on the 4th August, 1265. His lordship espoused Millisent, one of the daughters and co-heiresses of Robert de Chaucombe, and was s. by his son,

SIMON BASSET, second baron, who had summons in the 22nd of Edward I. to attend the king, wheresoever he should be, to advise touching the important affairs of the realm, and was shortly

---

* It is doubtful whether this lady was legitimate or not.

afterwards ordered to come to Portsmouth on the 1st of September, well equipped with horse arms, and to accompany the king into Gascony. His lordship was s. by his son,

RALPH BASSET, third Baron Basset of Sapcoate, who had summons to parliament from the 8th January, 1371, to 6th October, 1372. His lordship was one of the gallant soldiers of the martial reign of Edward III., and shared in the glories of Cressy. We find him, however, subsequently experiencing some of the vicissitudes of a soldier's fortune; for being again in France in the 46th of Edward III., under the command of the Duke of Lancaster, and sustaining great losses at Douchy and Rabymont, he was reproved by the king upon his return, which preceded that of the duke. His lordship m. first, Sybil, daughter of Sir Giles Astley, and had issue—

> Alice, who m. Sir Robert Moton, Knt., and carried into that family the estates of Sapcoate and Castle Bytham, (the latter came to the Bassets through the Colvilles,) which subsequently devolved upon the family of Pole, by the marriage of Elizabeth, daughter and co-heiress of Reginald Moton, with Ralph Pole of Radborne, and continued in that family until the beginning of the last century, when the greater part of them were alienated by sale.

Lord Basset, of Sapcoate, m. secondly, Alice, daughter of John Dirby, and had another daughter,

> Elizabeth, who m. Richard, Lord Grey, of Codnor, of which line Henry, last Lord Grey of Codnor, who d. in 1496, without legitimate male issue, bequeathed to his bastard son, *Richard Grey*, the manor of Ratcliffe-upon-Trent, in the county of Nottingham—and Elizabeth, the daughter and heiress of the said Richard, marrying Richard, third son of Sir Richard Sacheverel, that estate came in the course of descent also to the Pole family, now represented by Sacheverel Pole, Esq., of Radborne Hall, in the county of Derby.

His lordship d. in 1378, and the BARONY OF BASSET OF SAPCOATE, fell INTO ABEYANCE between his two daughters, and so continues amongst their descendants.

ARMS.—Ar. two bars undée sa.

Note—Dugdale disposes of Alice, the elder daughter and co-heiress of the last Lord Basset, of Sapcoate, differently. He marries her to Sir Laurence Dutton, Knt.; but the statement above, from Banks, appears the more probable.

BAVENT — BARONS BAVENT.

By Writ of Summons, dated 8th January, 1313, 6 Edward II.

Lineage.

In the 25th of Edward I.

ROBERT BAVENT was in the expedition made then into Gascony, and in the 30th of the same monarch he obtained a charter for a weekly market at Marom, in the county of Lincoln. In the 6th of Edward II. he was summoned to parliament as

BARON BAVENT. His lordship was s. at his decease by his son,

THOMAS BAVENT, second baron, but never summoned to parliament, who, in the 4th of Edward III., obtained license for a weekly market at Eaton-Bavent, in the county of Suffolk. His lordship was s. by his son,

PETER BAVENT, third baron, but not summoned to parliament. This nobleman d. in 1370, leaving two daughters and co-heiresses, viz.

Eleanor, } between whom the BARONY OF
Cecily, } BAVENT fell into ABEYANCE, and it so continues amongst their descendants, if there be any.

ARMS.—Ar. a chief indented sa.

BAYNING—VISCOUNTS BAYNING, OF SUDBURY.

By Letters Patent, dated 8th March, 1627, 3 Charles II.

Lineage.

SIR PAUL BAYNING, BART., (so created 24th September, 1612,) of Bentley-Parva, in the county of Essex, (son of Paul Bayning, Esq., one of the sheriffs of London, in the reign of Elizabeth, anno 1593,) was elevated to the peerage on the 27th February, 1627, in the dignity of BARON BAYNING, *of Horkesley-Bentley, in the county of Essex*, and advanced to the rank of VISCOUNT BAYNING, *of Sudbury, in the county of Suffolk*, on the 8th of March, in the same year. His lordship m. Anne, daughter of Sir Henry Glemham, of Glemham, in the county of Suffolk, Knt., and had issue—

> PAUL, his successor.
>
> Cecilia, m. Henry Viscount Newark, who succeeded his father, in 1643, in the earldom of Kingston, and was created MARQUESS OF DORCHESTER in the following year, by whom she had two surviving daughters; viz.—
>> Anne, m. to John, Lord Ros, afterwards earl of Rutland, a marriage dissolved by parliament in 1668.
>> Grace died unmarried in 1703.
>
> Anne, m. to Henry Murray, Esq., one of the grooms of the bedchamber to King Charles I. This lady was created VISCOUNTESS BAYNING, of Foxley. (See that dignity.)
>
> Mary, m. first, to William Viscount Grandison, and secondly, to Christopher, Earl of Anglesey.
>
> Elizabeth, m. to Francis Leonard, Lord Dacre.

The Viscount died "at his own house, in Mark-lane, within the city of London," on the 29th July, 1629, and was succeeded by his son,

PAUL BAYNING, second viscount, who m. Penelope, only daughter and heiress of Sir Robert Naunton, Knt., master of the court of ward and liveries, by whom he left two daughters; viz.—

> Anne, m. to Aubrey de Vere, Earl of Oxford.
>
> Penelope, m. to the Hon. John Herbert, youngest son of Philip, fourth earl of Pembroke, and first earl of Montgomery.

His lordship dying thus without male issue, all his honours EXPIRED, while his estates passed to daughters, as co-heiresses.

BEAUCHAMP—EARLS OF WARWICK.

Creation of William the Conqueror, and conveyed to the family of Beauchamp by Isabel de Mauduit, wife of William de Beauchamp, feudal Baron of Elmley.

Lineage.

Amongst the most eminent Norman families in the train of the Conqueror, was that of BEAUCHAMP, and amongst those that shared most liberally in the spoils of the conquest.

HUGH DE BEAUCHAMP, the companion in arms of the victorious Norman, who obtained grants to a very great extent from his triumphant chief, as he appears, at the general survey, to be possessed of large estates in Hertford, Buckingham, and Bedfordshires, was the founder of this illustrious house in England. This Hugh had issue—

Simon, who died *s. p.*

Payne, ancestor of the Beauchamps, of Bedford.

Walter, of whom presently.

Milo, of Eaton, in the county of Bedford.

Adeline, *m.* to Walter Espee, Lord of Kirkham and Helmesley, in the county of York.

The third son,

WALTER DE BEAUCHAMP, of Elmley Castle, in the county of Gloucester, having married Emeline, daughter and heiress of Urso de Abitot, constable of the Castle of Worcester, and hereditary sheriff of Worcestershire, (who was brother of Robert le Despenser, steward to the conqueror,) was invested with that sheriffalty by King Henry I., and obtained a grant from the same monarch (to whom he was steward) of all the lands belonging to Roger de Worcester, with a confirmation of certain lands given to him by Adeline, widow of his father-in-law, the said Urso. Walter de Beauchamp was *s.*, as well in his estates as in the royal stewardship, by his son,

WILLIAM DE BEAUCHAMP, who, for his zeal in the cause of the Empress Maud, was dispossessed of the Castle of Worcester by King Stephen, to which, and all his other honours and estates, however, he was restored by King Henry II.; and in that monarch's reign, besides the sheriffalty of Worcestershire, which he enjoyed by inheritance, he was sheriff of Warwickshire (2d Henry II.), sheriff of Gloucestershire (from the 3d to the 9th Henry II. inclusive), and sheriff of Herefordshire (from the 8th to the 16th Henry II. inclusive). Upon the levy of the assessment towards the marriage portion of one of King Henry's daughters, this powerful feudal lord certified his knight's fees to amount to fifteen. He *m.* Maud, daughter of William Lord Braose, of Gower, and was *s.*, at his decease, by his son,

WILLIAM DE BEAUCHAMP, who *m.* Joane, daughter of Sir Thomas Walerie; and dying before the 13th of King John's reign, was *s.* by his son (a minor, whose wardship and marriage Roger de Mortimer and Isabel, his wife, obtained for 3000 marks),

WALTER DE BEAUCHAMP. This feudal lord was appointed governor of Hanley Castle, in the county of Worcester, in the 17th of King John, and entrusted with the custody of the same shire in that turbulent year; but proving faithless to the king, and joining the insurrectionary barons, all his lands were seized by the crown, and himself excommunicated, a course of proceeding which extorted immediate submission to his temporal and spiritual lords; for we find him soon after making his peace with the king, and soliciting absolution from *Gualo*, the legate, which absolution he seems to have obtained, for, upon giving security to Henry III., who had just then succeeded to the throne, he had restitution of his castle at Worcester, with his hereditary sheriffalty. Walter de Beauchamp *m.* Bertha, daughter of William Lord Braose, by whom he had two sons, Walcheline and James. Of this nobleman we find further, that, being one of the *barons-marchers*, he gave security to the king for his faithful services (with the other lords-marchers), until peace should be fully settled in the realm; and for the better performance thereof, gave up James, his younger son, as a hostage. He *d.* in 1235, and was *s.* by his elder son,

WALCHELINE DE BEAUCHAMP, who *m.* Joane, daughter of Roger, Lord Mortimer, and dying in the same year as his father, was *s.* by an only son,

WILLIAM DE BEAUCHAMP, feudal Lord of Elmley. This nobleman attended King Henry III., in the 37th year of his reign, into Gascoigne, and in two years afterwards marched under the banner of Robert de Clare, Earl of Gloucester, against the Scots. In the 41st of the same reign he had summons (with other illustrious persons) to meet the king at Chester on the feast day of *St. Peter, at Vincula*, well fitted with horse and arms to oppose the incursions of Lewelline, Prince of Wales. In consideration of which services the king, at the request of the said Earl of Gloucester, respited the payment of certain moneys, due by him to the exchequer, until a further time. His lordship had several similar summonses in the same reign, the highest proof at that period of power, prowess, and loyalty. Lord Beauchamp *m.* Isabel, daughter of William Mauduit, of Hanslape, in the county of Bucks, heritable chamberlain of the exchequer, and sister and heiress of WILLIAM MAUDUIT, EARL OF WARWICK, (who inherited that dignity from his cousin, Margery de Newburgh, Countess of Warwick, in the year 1263,) which lady had, in *frank-marriage*, all her father's lands at Ledecumbe, with a proviso, that should those lands not amount to £90. a year, that sum should be made up elsewhere. His lordship made his will in 1268, the year in which he died, and bequeathed " to Walter, his son, signed with the cross, for a pilgrimage to the Holy Land, on the behalf of the testator (his father), and Isabel, his mother, two hundred marks. To Joane, his daughter, (who *m.* Bartholomew de Sudley,) a canopy sometime belonging to St. Wolstan, and a book of Lancelot, which he (the testator) lent them. To Isabel, his daughter, a silver cup. To Sibill, his daughter, towards her marriage, all the money due to him from his son William; and forty marks more, with the land which he bought in Bvtilamton; to enjoy until she should be married, and no longer. To Sarah, his daughter, (who s. Richard Talbot,) a hundred marks for her marriage portion. To William, his eldest son, the cup and hornes of St. Hugh; and to the countess, his wife, a ring, with a ruby in it. To Sir Roger de Mortimer, a ring; to Sir Bartholomew de Sudley, a ring. To the friers-minors of Worcester, forty shillings. To the friers-minors of Gloucester, one mark. To the hospital of St. Wolstan, at Worcester, one mark. To the hospital of St. Oswald there, ten shillings, &c.. &c. To the church of Salewark, a house and garden near the parsonage, to find a lamp continually burning therein, to the honor of God, the blessed Virgin, St. Katherine, and St. Margaret." Besides the daughters mentioned above, Lord Beauchamp left four sons, viz.

WILLIAM, of whom presently.

John, of Holt, in the county of Worcester.

Walter, of Powyke and Alcester.

Thomas, died s. p.

The eldest son,

WILLIAM DE BEAUCHAMP, inherited not only the feudal barony of Elmley from his father, but had previously derived from his mother the EARLDOM OF WARWICK, (originally possessed by the Newburghs,) and the barony of Hanslape (which had belonged to the Mauduits). This eminent nobleman was a distinguished captain in the Welsh and Scottish wars of King Edward I. "In the 23rd year of which reign, being in Wales with the king," as Dugdale relates, "he performed a notable exploit; namely, hearing that a great body of the Welsh were got together in a plain, betwixt two woods, and to secure themselves, had fastened their pikes to the ground, slopping towards their assailants, he marched thither with a choice company of cross-bow-men and archers, and in the night time encompassing them about, put betwixt every two horsemen, one cross-bow-man, which cross-bow-man, killing many of them that held the pikes, the horse charged in suddenly, and made a very great slaughter. This was done near Montgomery." His lordship m. Maud, widow of Girard de Furnival, and one of the four daughters and coheiresses of Richard Fitz-John, son of John Fitz-Geffery, chief justice of Ireland, by whom he had surviving issue—

GUY, his successor.

Isabel, m. to Peter Chaworth.

Maud, m. to —— Rithoo.

Margaret, m. to John Sudley.

Anne, ⎫ nuns at Shouldham, in the county
Amy, ⎬ of Norfolk, a monastery founded by
⎭ his lordship's maternal great grandfather.

William de Beauchamp, first Earl of Warwick of that family, d. in 1298, and was s. by his eldest son,

GUY DE BEAUCHAMP, second earl, so called in memory of his celebrated predecessor, the Saxon, GUY, EARL OF WARWICK. This nobleman acquired high military renown in the martial reign of Edward I., distinguishing himself at the battle of Falkirk, for which he was rewarded with extensive grants of lands in Scotland, at the siege of Caerlaverock,

and upon different occasions beside beyond the sea. In the reign of Edward II. he likewise played a very prominent part. In 1310 his lordship was in the commission appointed by parliament to draw up regulations for "the well governing of the kingdom and of the king's household," in consequence of the corrupt influence exercised at that period by Piers Gaveston, in the affairs of the realm, through the unbounded partiality of the king; and in two years afterwards, when that unhappy favorite fell into the hands of his enemies upon the surrender of Scarborough Castle, his lordship violently seized upon his person, and after a summary trial, caused him to be beheaded at Blacklow Hill, near Warwick. The earl's hostility to Gaveston is said to have been much increased by learning that the favorite had nicknamed him "the Black Dog of Ardenne." For this unwarrantable proceeding his lordship, and all others concerned therein, received within two years the royal pardon, but he is supposed to have eventually perished by poison, administered in revenge by the partisans of Gaveston. The earl m. Alice, relict of Thomas de Laybourne, daughter of Ralph de Toni, of Flamsted, in the county of Herts, and sister and heiress of Robert de Toni, by whom he had issue—

THOMAS, his successor, whose sponsors were, Thomas Plantagenet, Earl of Lancaster, and Henry his brother, and Thomas de Warrington, prior of Kenilworth.

John, a very eminent person in the reign of Edward III., being captain of Calais, admiral of the fleet, STANDARD BEARER at CRESSY, and one of the original knights of the Garter. He was summoned to parliament as a BARON, but dying s. p. the dignity expired.

Maud, m. to Geoffrey, Lord Say.

Emma, m. to Rowland Odingsels.

Isabel, m. to John Clinton.

Elizabeth, m. to Sir Thomas Astley, Knt.

Lucia, m. to Robert de Napton.

This great Earl of Warwick, was like most of the nobles of his time, a munificent benefactor to the church, having bestowed lands upon several religious houses, and founded a chantry of priests at his manor of Elmley. His will bears date, "at WARWICK CASTLE, on Munday next after the feast of St. James the Apostle, An. 1315," and by it he bequeaths to Alice his wife, a proportion of his plate, with a crystal cup, and half his bedding; as also, all the vestments and books belonging to his chappel; the other moiety of his beds, rings, and jewels, he gives to his daughters. To his son Thomas, his best coat of mail, helmet, and suit of harness; to his son John, his second coat of mail, &c., appointing that all the rest of his armour, bows, and other warlike provisions, should remain in Warwick Castle for his heir. His lordship, immediately before his death, obtained a grant from the king, that his executors should have the custody of his lands during the minority of his heir, accounting for the receipts to the exchequer at Michaelmas and Easter every year, provided that his castles of Elmley and Warwick, should not be disposed of, without a special license from the crown. But notwithstanding this grant, and a confirmation thereof, after the earl's death to John Hamelyn, and the other executors, the king soon afterwards passed the custody of those castles and lands, by new letters patent, to Hugh le Despencer, the elder, in satisfaction of a debt of £6,770. asserted to be due to Despencer by the crown. Alice, widow of the earl, had very extensive estates assigned her in dowry, in the November following the death of her husband, and in the next year she paid a fine of five hundred marks, for licence to marry William La Zouche, of Ashby, in the county of Leicester, to whom she was accordingly wedded. The earl d. at Warwick Castle, on the 12th of August, 1315, and was s. by his eldest son, then but two years of age,

THOMAS DE BEAUCHAMP, third earl, regarding whom we find the king (Edward II.) in two years subsequently soliciting a dispensation from the pope, to enable him to marry his cousin Catherine, daughter of Roger de Mortimer, Lord of Wigmore, under whose guardianship the young earl had been placed; an alliance eventually formed, when his lordship had completed his fifteenth year. In two years afterwards, the earl by special licence from the crown, was allowed to do homage, and to assume his hereditary offices of Sheriff of Worcestershire, and Chamberlain of the Exchequer. This nobleman sustained in the brilliant reign of Edward III., the high military renown of his illustrious progenitor, and became distinguished in arms almost from his boyhood. So early as the third year of that monarch, he commanded the left wing of the king's army at Wysonfosse, where Edward proposed to give the French battle, and from that period was the constant companion of the king, and his gallant son, in all their splendid campaigns. At Cressy, he had a principal command in the van of the English army, under the Prince of Wales, and at Poictiers, where Dugdale says he fought so long and so stoutly, that his hand was galled with the exercise of his sword and pole-axe: he personally took William de Meileun, Archbishop of Sens, prisoner, for whose ransom he obtained eight thousand marks. After these heroic achievements in France, the earl arrayed himself under the banner of the cross, and reaped fresh laurels on the plains of Palestine, whence upon his return he brought home the son of the King of Lithuania, whom he had christened at London by the name of Thomas, answering for the new convert himself at the baptismal font; for his lordship was not more distinguished by his valour than his piety, as his numerous and liberal donations to the church while living, and bequests at his decease, testify. This nobleman rebuilt the walls of Warwick Castle, which had been demolished in the time of the Manduits; adding strong gates, with fortified gateways, and embattled towers; he likewise founded the choir of the collegiate church of St. Mary, built a booth hall in the market place, and made the town of Warwick toll free. His lordship had issue, by the countess already mentioned, six sons, and nine daughters: viz.

    Guy, called by Dugdale, a " stout souldier," m. Philippa, daughter of Henry, Lord Fer-

rars, of Groby, and dying before his father, left three daughters: viz.

    Katherine, } nuns at Shouldham, in
    Elizabeth, } Norfolk.
    Margaret, }

THOMAS, inheritor of the honors.

Reynburne, who left an only daughter, Alianore, wife of John Knight of Hanslape, in the county of Bucks, by whom she left a daughter, Emma, who m. —— Forster, from whom the Forsters of Hanslape derived.

    John, }
    Roger, } all d. unm.
    Hierom, }

Maud,* m. to Roger de Clifford.

Philippa, m. to Hugh, Earl of Stafford.

Alice, m. to John, Lord Beauchamp, of Hacche, in the county of Somerset.

Joane, m. to Ralph, Lord Basset, of Drayton.

Isabel, m. first, to John, Lord Strange, of Blackmere, and secondly, to William Ufford, Earl Suffolk.

Margaret, m. to Guy de Montford, after whose decease, she took the veil at Shouldham.

Agnes, m. first, —— Cokesay, and afterwards —— Bardolf.

Juliana, d. unm.

Catharine took the veil at Wroxhall, in Warwickshire.

The earl was one of the original knights of the Garter. His lordship d. on the 13th November, 1369, of the plague at Calais, where he was then employed in his military capacity, and had just achieved a victory over the French; he was s. by his eldest son,

THOMAS, fourth Earl, K.G. who was appointed by parliament, governor of the young king, Richard II. in the third year of that monarch's reign, but did not long enjoy the office, for we find him in arms with Thomas, Duke of Gloucester, (the king's uncle,) long before the majority of Richard, constraining the assembling of parliament, for which proceeding, however, in several years afterwards, he was seised at a feast given to him by the king—tried and condemned to death—a sentence commuted by the king, at the instance of the Earl of Salisbury, to banishment to the Isle of Man, while his castle and manors of Warwick, with his other estates, were granted to Thomas Holland, Earl of Kent, to whom the custody of his son and heir, Richard Beauchamp, was also confided. From the Isle of Man, the Earl was brought back to the Tower of London, and imprisoned there during the remainder of King Richard's reign; but upon the accession of Henry IV. he was released, and re-instated in all his honors and possessions. His lordship m. Margaret, daughter of William, Lord Ferrars, of Groby, and had issue,

---

* Those ladies' portraitures are curiously drawn, and placed in the windows on the south side of the quire of the collegiate church at Warwick, in the habit of their time. Seven of them were married, and have their paternal armes upon their inner garments; and on their outer mantle, their husbands' armes; the picture of Isabel, who married twice, is twice drawn.—*Dugdale's Baronage.*

RICHARD, his successor, for whom King Richard II. and Richard Scrope, then Bishop of Coventry and Lichfield, (afterwards Archbishop of York,) stood sponsors.

Katherine, d. young.

Margaret, } nuns.
Katherine,

Elizabeth.

The Earl d. in 1401 and was s. by his son,

RICHARD DE BEAUCHAMP, fifth earl, b. 28th January, 1381. This nobleman was made a knight of the Bath at the coronation of King Henry IV., and at the coronation of the Queen in the following year, attained high reputation for the gallantry he had displayed in the lists. In the 4th year of the same monarch, he was pre-eminently distinguished against Owen Glendower, whose banner he captured, and put the rebel himself to flight; and about the same time, he won fresh laurels in the memorable battle of Shrewsbury, against the Percies, after which, he was made a knight of the most noble order of the Garter. Of his lordship's pilgrimage to the Holy Land, Dugdale gives the following account:—"In the 9th of Henry IV., obtaining licence to visit the Holy Land, he fitted himself with all necessaries for that journey, and passed the sea: in which voyage, visiting his cousin, the DUKE OF BARR, he was nobly received and entertained by him for eight days, who thence accompanied him to Paris; where being arrived, the King of France then wearing the crown, in reverence of that holy feast, made him to sit at his table, and at his departure, sent an herald to conduct him safely through that realm. Out of which, entering Lumbardy, he was met by another herald from Sir Pandulph Malacet, with a challenge to perform certain feats of arms with him at Verona, upon a day assigned, for the order of the Garter; and in the presence of Sir Galiot of Mantua; whereunto he gave his assent. And as soon as he had performed his pilgrimage at Rome, returned to Verona, where he and his challenger were first to just, next to fight with axes, afterwards with arming swords, and lastly with sharp daggers. At the day and place assigned for which exercises, came great resort of people, Sir Pandulph entering the lists with nine spears borne before him: but the act of spears being ended, they fell to it with axes; in which encounter Sir Pandulph received a sore wound on the shoulder, and had been utterly slain, but that Sir Galiot cried peace."

" When he came to Jerusalem, he had much respect shewed him by the patriarch's deputy, and having performed his offerings at the sepulchre of our Saviour, he set up his arms on the north side of the temple. While at Jerusalem, a noble person, called Baltredam, (the Soldan's lieutenant,) hearing that he was descended from the famous Sir Guy, of Warwick, whose story they had in books of their own language, invited him to his palace, and royally feasting him, 'presented him with three precious stones of great value,' besides divers cloaths of silk and gold given to his servants. Where this Baltredam told him privately, that he faithfully believed as he did, though he durst not discover himself; and rehearsed the articles of the creed. But on the morrow he

feasted Sir Baltredam's servants, and gave them scarlet, with other English cloath, which being shewed to Sir Baltredam, he returned again to him, and said, he would wear his livery, and be marshal of his hall. Whereupon he gave Sir Baltredam a gown of black peak, furred; and had much discourse with him, for he was skilful in sundry languages." At the coronation of King Henry V., in whose service, when Prince of Wales, his lordship had been engaged, the earl was constituted HIGH STEWARD OF ENGLAND for that solemnity, and in the next year, we find him actively engaged for the king against the Lollards. In the 3rd of Henry V. he was at Calais, and there his chivalric disposition led him into a rencounter with three French knights, the result of which Dugdale thus relates:—"which letters (challenges sent by the earl under fictitious names) were sent to the king's court at France, where three French knights received them, and promised their fellows to meet at a day and place assigned: whereof the first was a knight called Sir Gerard Herbaumes, who called himself *Le Chevalier Rouge*; the second, a famous knight, named Sir Hugh Launey, calling himself *Le Chevalier Blanc*; and the third a knight named Sir Collard Fines. Twelfday, in Christmas, being appointed for the time that they should meet, in a land called the *Parkhedge of Gynes*. On which day the Earl came into the field with his face covered, a plume of ostrich feathers upon his helm, and his horse trapped with the Lord of Toney's arms (one of his ancestors), viz. *argent a manch gules*: where, first encountering with the Chevalier Rouge, at the third course he unhorsed him, and so returned with closed visor, unknown to his pavilion, whence he sent to that knight a good courser. The next day he came into the field with his visor closed, a chaplet on his helm, and a plume of ostrich feathers aloft, his horse trapped with the arms of *Hanslap*, viz. *silver two bars gules*, where he met with the Blanc knight, with whom he encountered, smote off his visor thrice, broke his besagurs and other harneys, and returned victoriously to his pavilion, with all his own habiliments safe, and as yet not known to any: from whence he sent the Blanc knight a good courser. But the morrow after, viz. the last day of the justs, he came with his face open, and his helmet as the day before, save that the chaplet was rich with pearls and precious stones; and in his coat of arms, of *Guy* and *Beauchamp* quarterly; having the arms of *Toney* and *Hanslap* on his trappers; and said, ' *That as he had, in his own person, performed the service the two days before, so with God's grace he would the third.*' Whereupon, encountering with Sir Collard Fines, at every stroke he bore him backward to his horse; insomuch, as the Frenchman saying, ' that he himself was bound to his saddle;' he alighted and presently got up again, but all being ended, he returned to his pavilion, sent to Sir Collard Fines a fair courser, feasted all the people, gave to those three knights great rewards, and so rode to Calais with great honor." About this time the Earl attended the deputation of bishops and other learned persons, from England to the COUNCIL OF CONSTANCE, and during his stay there slew a great duke in justing.

In the next year, he was with King Henry at the siege of Caen, and upon the surrender of that place was appointed governor of its castle. His lordship continued actively engaged in military and diplomatic services, during the remainder of the reign of King Henry V., by whose will he was appointed governor to his infant son and successor, Henry VI., which charge having fulfilled with great wisdom and fidelity, his lordship was appointed, upon the death of John Plantagenet, Duke of Bedford, Regent of France, LIEUTENANT GENERAL of the whole REALM OF FRANCE, and DUCHY OF NORMANDY. The earl, who had been created EARL OF ALBEMARLE, for life, in 1417, died in the castle of Roan, in his French government, on the 30th of April, 1439—having by his will, ordered his body to be brought over to England, where it was afterwards deposited, under a stately monument,* appointed by the deceased lord, to be erected in the collegiate church of St. Mary, at Warwick. His lordship m. first, Elizabeth, daughter and heiress of Thomas, Lord Berkeley, Viscount Lisle, by whom he had three daughters, viz.

> Margaret, m. to John Talbot, Earl of Shrewsbury, (his lordship's second wife, by whom he had one son, John Talbot, Lord Viscount Lisle, of whom the Dudleys, Earls of Warwick, derived.)
>
> Allanor, m. first, to Thomas, Lord Roos, from whom the Dukes of Rutland derive; and secondly, to Edmund, Duke of Somerset.
>
> Elizabeth, m. to George Nevil, Lord Latimer.

The Earl m. secondly, Isabel, daughter, and eventually heiress of Thomas le Despencer, Earl of Gloucester, and widow of his uncle, Richard Beauchamp, Earl of Worcester, (for which marriage he obtained a papal dispensation,) and had a son and daughter—namely,

> HENRY, his successor, whose sponsors were Cardinal Beaufort, Humphrey, Earl of Stafford, and Joane, Lady Bergavenny.
>
> Anne, who m. Sir Richard Nevil, son and heir of Richard, Earl of Salisbury, and grandson of Ralph Nevil, first Earl of Westmoreland.

The Earl of Warwick was s. by his son,

---

* When his executors, pursuant to his will, erected this most magnificent tomb, (which yet remains in uncommon splendour,) inferior to none in England, unless that of Henry VII. in Westminster Abbey, they covenanted with John Borde, of Corfe, marbler, to make the same of fine and well-coloured marble, four feet and a half high, from the base, the base six inches thick, and eighteen broad; the uppermost stone of the base, nine feet long, four broad, and seven inches thick; and to have for the marble, carriage to Warwick, and work, £45. For marble to pave the chapel, workmanship, and carriage of every hundred of these stones, £2, in all £4. 13s. 4d. The charges of the chapel and tomb came to £2481. 4s. 7½d., a vast sum, when the price of an ox was thirteen shillings and fourpence, and a quarter of bread corn, three shillings and fourpence.—*Hutchins's Dorset.*

34

HENRY DE BEAUCHAMP, sixth earl, K.G. This nobleman, having, before he had completed his nineteenth year, tendered his services for the defence of the Duchy of Aquitaine, was created by charter, dated 2nd April, 1444, PREMIER EARL OF ENGLAND, and his lordship obtained, at the same time, permission for himself and his heirs male, to wear a golden coronet about his head, in the presence of the king and elsewhere. In three days after he was advanced to the dignity of DUKE OF WARWICK, with precedence immediately after the Duke of Norfolk, and before the Duke of Buckingham : which extraordinary mark of royal favour, so displeased the latter nobleman, that an act of parliament was subsequently passed to appease his jealousy, declaring that from the 2nd of December, then next ensuing, the two dukes should take place of each other, alternately year about, but with precedency of the first year to the Duke of Warwick. After which, his Grace of Warwick, had a grant in reversion upon the death of the Duke of Gloucester, of the Isles of Guernsey, Jersey, Serke, Erme, and Alderney, for the annual rent of a rose ; also the hundred and manor of Bristol, for £60. a year, with all the royal castles and manors in the Forest of Dene, for £100. per annum, and he was crowned by Henry himself, King of the Isle of Wight. His grace m. in the life-time of his father, when but ten years old, and then called Lord Despencer, Cicily, daughter of Richard Nevil, Earl of Salisbury, whose portion was four thousand seven hundred marks—by whom he left an only daughter,

> ANNE.

His grace d. in the 22nd year of his age, on the 11th June, 1445, when the dukedom (and the male line of this branch of the Beauchamps) expired, but his other honours devolved upon his daughter,

ANNE DE BEAUCHAMP, *Countess of Warwick*, then but two years old, who was committed to the guardianship first of Queen Margaret, and afterwards of William de la Pole, Duke of Suffolk. Her ladyship dying however in a few years afterwards, on the 3rd of January, 1449, the honours of the illustrious house of Beauchamp reverted to the young countess's aunt.

ANNE, wife of Richard Nevil, Earl of Salisbury, who then became Countess of Warwick, and her husband was subsequently created Earl of Warwick. —(See Nevil, Earl of Salisbury and Warwick), the celebrated KING-MAKER.

ARMS.—Gules, a fesse between six cross crosslets, or.

BEAUCHAMP — BARONS ST. AMAND.

By Writ of Summons, dated 25th March, 1313, 6 Edward II.

Lineage.

WALTER DE BEAUCHAMP, younger son of John, Lord Beauchamp, of Powyke, a military person of celebrity in the reigns of Henry IV. and Henry V., m. Elizabeth, daughter and co-heiress of Sir John Roche, Knt., and had issue,

WILLIAM, of whom presently.

Richard, Bishop of Salisbury, supposed to have been the first chancellor of the order of the Garter.

Elizabeth, m. to Sir Richard Dudley, and had a son and daughter, the latter of whom, Joane Dudley, became heiress to the former, and married Sir John Baynton, Knt., from which marriage through a long line of distinguished ancestors descended Edward Baynton Rolt, Esq., of Spy Park, in the county of Wilts, who was created a baronet in 1762, an honour NOW EXTINCT.

The elder son,

WILLIAM DE BEAUCHAMP, m. Elizabeth, eldest daughter and co-heiress of Gerard de Braybrooke, (grandson, and eventually heir of Almaric St. Amand, third and last Baron St. Amand of that family,) and was summoned to parliament in right of his wife, " as William de Beauchamp, Baron of St. Amand," from the 2nd January, 1449, (the barony had been forty-six years previously in abeyance,) to the 26th May, 1455. His lordship was soon afterwards, being then sewer to the king, constituted chamberlain of North Wales. He d. in 1457, and was s. by his only son,

RICHARD DE BEAUCHAMP, second Baron St. Amand, of the family of Beauchamp, attainted in the 1st of Richard III., but fully restored upon the accession of Henry VII. This nobleman was in the expedition made in the 8th of Henry VII., in aid of Maximilian the Emperor against the French. He died in 1508, and by his testament dated on the 12th June, in that year, he desires to be interred in the Black Friers' Church, near Ludgate, within the City of London, and for lack of issue by Dame Anne his wife, settles divers lordships in the counties of Wilts, Bedford, Berks, Huntingdon, and Hereford, upon his natural son by Mary Wroughton, Anthony St. Amand, and the heirs of his body. The BARONY at the decease of this nobleman, Nicolas, in his synopsis, presumes became vested in the descendants and representatives of Isabella, sister of Almaric St. Amand, second Baron St. Amand of that family, (Maud and Alianore, the sisters of Elizabeth Braybrooke, who brought the barony into the family of Beauchamp, the other co-heiresses of Gerard de Braybrooke having died issueless,) which Isabella married first, Richard Handlo, and secondly, Robert de Ildesle; but Mr. Nicolas observes further in a note, " that although no other issue is assigned to William Beauchamp, fourth Lord St. Amand, (or first of that family,) in either of the numerous pedigrees he had consulted, than his son Richard the last Baron, it is to be remarked, that in the will of the said Richard, Lord St. Amand, he bequeathes a cup to his niece Loverseye. This expression was probably used to describe his wife's niece; but it must be observed, that if he had a sister of the whole blood who left issue, the barony became vested in her and her descendants," upon the death of the last lord.

ARMS—Gules, a fesse between six martlets, or. within a bordure, ar.

BEAUCHAMP — BARON BEAUCHAMP, OF BLETSHO.

By Writ of Summons, dated 1st June, 1363, 37 Edward III.

Lineage.

ROGER DE BEAUCHAMP, one of the eminent warriors of the reign of Edward III., and grandson of Walter de Beauchamp, of Alcester, was summoned to parliament, as BARON BEAUCHAMP, OF BLETSHO, from the 1st of June, 1363, to the 20th October, 1379. In the 20th of Edward III., we first find this gallant person serving in France, and the next year the king confirming unto him and his wife, Sibel, the manor of Lydeard-Tregos, in the county of Wilts, granted to them by Peter de Grandison; which Sibel was eldest of the four sisters and co-heirs of Sir William de Patshul, Knt., and grand-daughter, maternally, of Mabel, eldest of the four sisters and co-heirs of Otto de Grandison. In the 28th of Edward III., Roger de Beaumont was captain of Calais; in the 33d of the same monarch he attended the king in his expedition into Gascoigne, and in the next year he obtained, in right of his wife, the manor of BLETNESHO, or BLETSHO, in the county of Bedford, which he made the chief place of his residence. In the 46th of Edward III., being still captain of Calais, his lordship had licence to transport his household goods and other necessaries thither without the payment of any custom upon the same, and in the next year he had a special commission to take care that the peace then made between King Edward and the Earl of Flanders should be preserved within the marches of Calais. In the 5th of Edward, being then CHAMBERLAIN OF THE HOUSEHOLD, Lord Beauchamp had a pension for life of 100 marks per annum, in consideration of his eminent services, out of the farm of the castle and town of Devizes, in Wiltshire. His lordship d. in 1379, and by his testament, which bears date two years previously, at London, 19th June, he bequeathes his body to be buried in the church of the friers' preachers (commonly called the Black Friers) within the city of London, near to the grave of Sibel his wife; and wills that, at his funeral, there should be placebo and dirige with note; as also, on the morrow after, two masses, one of our Lady, and another of requiem; and in regard that he was obliged to do service against the Infidels in the Holy Land, by the appointment of Walter de Beauchamp, his grandfather, to the expense of 200 marks, he desires that Roger, his son, when he arrive at maturity, shall assume the cross, and perform that duty. His lordship was succeeded by his son,

ROGER DE BEAUCHAMP, as second BARON BEAUCHAMP, of Bletsho; but this nobleman was never summoned to parliament. His lordship proving his age in the 7th of Rich. II., had livery of all his lands. In the 19th of the same reign, we find this nobleman attending the king into Ireland; but of his lordship nothing more is known than that he was succeeded by his son,

JOHN DE BEAUCHAMP, third baron, but never summoned to parliament. This nobleman doing homage in the 8th of Henry IV., had livery of his lands; but he died in six years afterwards, and was *s.* by his son,

JOHN DE BEAUCHAMP, fourth baron, then only two years old, at whose decease the title and estates passed to his only sister and heiress,

MARGARET DE BEAUCHAMP, who *m.* first, Sir Oliver St. John, Knt., and conveyed the BARONY OF BEAUCHAMP, OF BLETSHO, into that family; from which it was carried, by Anne St. John, of Bletsho—(see *Burke's Peerage and Baronetage*, article St. John)—into the family of William Lord Howard, son and heir of Charles, first Earl of Nottingham, whose daughter and heiress, Elizabeth, *m.* John Mordaunt, fifth Earl of Peterborough, and the barony of Beauchamp, of Bletsho, with that of Mordaunt, is now vested in his Grace the Duke of Gordon. Margaret de Beauchamp *m.* secondly, John Beaufort, Earl of Somerset, and by him was mother of Margaret Countess of Richmond, whose son ascended the British throne, as King Henry VII.

BEAUCHAMP — BARONS BEAUCHAMP, OF HACHE, IN THE COUNTY OF SOMERSET.

By Writ, 29th December, 1299, 28 Edward I.

Lineage.

The first of this Somersetshire family, of whom mention is made by Dugdale, is

ROBERT DE BEAUCHAMP, who, in the 3d of Henry II., accounted the king six pounds for a mark of gold, and, in the 9th of the same monarch, was sheriff of the counties of Somerset and Dorset. In three years afterwards, this Robert, upon the assessment of the aid for marrying the king's daughter, then levied, certified his knight's fees, *de veteri feoffamento,* to amount in number to seventeen, for which, in the 14th of Henry II., he paid seven pounds one shilling and eight-pence, that is, eight shillings and four-pence for each knight's fee. In the 22d of the same Henry, he again enjoyed the sheriffalty for the same counties, and continued in office for five years, and one half of the sixth year following. This feudal lord *d.* in 1226, leaving in minority, and in ward to Hubert de Burgh, his son and heir,

ROBERT DE BEAUCHAMP, who *d.* before 1251, and was *s.* by his son,

ROBERT DE BEAUCHAMP. Of this feudal baron nothing is known beyond his being engaged against the Welsh with Henry III., and his founding the priory of Frithelstoke, in the county of Devon. He was *s.* by his son,

JOHN DE BEAUCHAMP, who, in the 5th of Ed. I., was made governor of the castles of Kaermerdin and Cardigan. He *m.* Cicely, daughter and heiress of Maud de Kyme, daughter of William Ferrers, Earl of Derby, by her second husband, William de Vivonia, which William was son of Hugh de Vivonia, by Mabel, one of the co-heirs of William Mallet, a great baron, who *d.* temp. Hen. III. This John de Beauchamp was *s.* by his son,

36

JOHN DE BEAUCHAMP, who was summoned to parliament as a baron, by the style of " Io de Bello Campo de Somerset," on the 29th December, 1299, 28th of Edward I., and in the 34th of the same reign was one of the distinguished persons who received the honour of knighthood with Prince Edward, the king's eldest son, being in the expedition made into Scotland in that year. In the 8th of Edward II. his lordship was again in the Scottish wars; and in the 14th of the same king he succeeded to the very extensive landed possessions of his mother, comprising the manor of Sturminster-Marshal, in the county of Dorset, a moiety of the manor West Kington, in the county of Wilts, of the whole manor of Wadmersh, in the county of Surrey, of the manor of Bullingham, in the county of Cambridge, as also of the hamlets of Watweton and Widecombe. In two years afterwards Lord Beauchamp was made governor of the castle of Bridgewater. In the 7th of Edward III. he obtained licence to fortify his manor houses at Hacche, Estokes, and South Hainedon, and to embattle their walls. His lordship *d.* in 1336, up to which period he had regular summonses, and was *s.* by his son,

JOHN DE BEAUCHAMP, *second Lord Beauchamp, of Hacche,* summoned to parliament from 24th August, 1336, to 24th February, 1343. This nobleman participated in the glories of Edward the Third's reign, being constantly engaged in the French wars of that monarch. His lordship *d.* in 1343, and was *s.* by his son (then twelve years of age, and under the guardianship of Robert de Ferrers, and Reginald de Cobham),

JOHN DE BEAUCHAMP, third baron, summoned to parliament from 15th November, 1351, to 20th November, 1360. This nobleman was in the expedition made into Gascoigne, in the 33rd of Edward III., and of the retinue of Thomas de Beauchamp, Earl of Warwick, whose daughter Alice he had married. His lordship *d.* in 1360 without issue, when the BARONY OF BEAUCHAMP OF HACCHE fell into ABEYANCE between his two sisters and co-heiresses, and in that state it still continues amongst their descendants. Those ladies were—

Cecily, *m.* first, to Sir Roger de St. Maur, by whom she had a son, William, from whom the extant Dukes of Somerset, and Marquesses of Hertford, derive; and secondly, to Richard Turberville, of Bere Regis, in the county of Dorset, by whom she left a daughter, Juliana Turberville.

Eleanor, *m.* to —— Meriet, and left a son, John Meriet, whose daughter and heiress, Elizabeth, married also a St. Maur.

Upon the division of the estates, Cecily had for her share the manors of Hacche, Shipton, Beauchamp, Murifield, and one-third of the manor of Shipton Mallet, in the county of Somerset, with certain lands in Sturminster-Marshal, in the county of Dorset; the manors of Boultberry and Harberton, in Devonshire; the manor of Dourton, in Buckinghamshire; of Little Hawes, in Suffolk, and two parts of the manor of Selling, in Kent.

Arms.—Vaire az. and ar.

BEAUCHAMP — BARONS BEAUCHAMP, OF KYDDERMINSTER.

By Letters Patent, (the first Barony so created,) 10th October, 1387.

Lineage.

SIR JOHN DE BEAUCHAMP, Knt., of Holt, in the county of Worcester, (great grandson of William de Beauchamp, Lord of Elmley, and his wife, Isabel, daughter and heiress of William Mauduit, of Hanslope,—see Beauchamp, Earls of Warwick,) having participated in the high achievements of his distinguished family, during the martial reign of Edward III., obtained a grant, in the 11th of Richard II., of the manors and lands belonging to the priory of Deerhurst, in the county of Gloucester, being then steward of the king's household, and was elevated to the peerage by letters patent, dated 10th October, 1387, (the first barony* so conferred,) as LORD BEAUCHAMP, OF KYDDERMINSTER. An honour, however, which he did not long enjoy, for, in the same year, he was attainted of high treason along with Sir John Tresilian, chief justice of the King's Bench, and several others, by the parliament which the nobles forced the king to assemble, and beheaded upon Tower-hill, his sentence being so commuted from hanging and quartering (which latter punishment the chief justice underwent). Lord Beauchamp m. Joane, daughter and heiress of Robert le Fitzwith, and was s. by his only son (then but ten years of age, the lordship of Holt being committed, during his minority, to Thomas, Earl of Warwick),

JOHN DE BEAUCHAMP, second baron (the attainder being, we presume, repealed). This nobleman attended King Richard II. into Ireland, in the 22nd year of that monarch's reign, and executed the office of escheator of the county of Worcester, in the 8th of Henry IV. His lordship d. in 1420, leaving an only daughter and heiress, Margaret, who m. first, John Pauncefort, and secondly, John Wysham, when the BARONY OF BEAUCHAMP, OF KYDDERMINSTER, expired.

BEAUCHAMP — BARONS BEAUCHAMP, OF POWYKE.

By Letters Patent, dated 2d May, 1447,

Lineage.

WALTER DE BEAUCHAMP, a younger son of William de Beauchamp, Lord of Elmley, and his

---

* That the solemn investure of this John, and all other barons who were thenceforth created by patent, was performed by the king himself, by putting on a robe of scarlet, as also a mantle (with two gards on the left shoulder) and a hood, all furred with minever, there is no doubt; which form of creation continued until the 13th year of King James, that Sir James Hay (a Scotchman) was advanced to the dignity of a baron of this realm, by letters patent date Junii, by the title of Lord Hay, of Sauley, the lawyers then declaring that the delivery of the letters patent was sufficient without any ceremony.—DUGDALE.

---

wife Isabel, sister and heiress of William Mauduit, Earl of Warwick, (see Beauchamp, Earls of Warwick,) having purchased from Reginald Fitzherbert, a moiety of the manor of ALCESTER, in the county of Warwick, made that one of his principal seats, the other being at POWYKE, in the county of Gloucester. This Walter, who was a very eminent person at the period in which he lived, being signed with the cross for a pilgrimage to the Holy Land, had a legacy of 200 marks bequeathed to him by his father, for his better performance of that voyage. He was steward of the household to King Edward I., and attended that monarch to Flanders, and into Scotland, where he shared in the honours of Falkirk on the 22d July, 1298. In the 29th of the same reign he was one of the lords in the parliament of Lincoln, being then styled *Dominus de Alcester*, who signified to the pope, under their seals, the superiority of King Edward over the kingdom of Scotland. His lordship m. ALICE, daughter of —— Tony, " which marriage," says Dugdale, " in regard they were within the fourth degree of consanguinity, was after ratified by Godfrey, bishop of Worcester, and the children begot between them decreed legitimate by him who had authority so to do by the pope, in regard they knew nothing of that impediment at the time of the contract made," of which marriage there was surviving issue—

WALTER, successor to his father.

William, a military man of celebrity, who succeeded to part of the estates of his elder brother.

Giles, who inherited the lordship of Alcester, by the settlement of his eldest brother.

The eldest son,

WALTER DE BEAUCHAMP, succeeded his father in 1306, and was the next year in the expedition against the Scots. In 1317, soon after the death of Guy, Earl of Warwick, his kinsman, he had custody of all the lands belonging to Warwick Castle, together with the castle itself, during the minority of the young earl. In 1327 he had a special commission to execute the office of constable of England in a particular case; and dying in the following year, s. p. was s. by his brother,

WILLIAM DE BEAUCHAMP, a military officer of high reputation, who had attended Edward I. in several of his expeditions into Flanders and Scotland. In the 10th of that monarch he acted as sheriff of Worcestershire, which office was granted to him during the minority of the heir of his kinsman, Guy, Earl of Warwick. In the 14th of Edward II. he was appointed governor of St. Briavel Castle, in the county of Gloucester, and of the Forest of Dean, and was constituted, in the year following, one of the king's commissioners for the safe custody of the city of Worcester. Dying, however, without issue, his estates devolved upon his brother,

GILES DE BEAUCHAMP, who had already inherited, by the settlement of his eldest brother, the lordship of Alcester, the manor-house of which, called Beauchamp's Court, he had licence to fortify in the 14th of Edward III. with a wall of stone and lime, and to embattle it; and he obtained similar permission regarding his house at Fresh-Water, in the Isle of Wight, in the 16th year of the same reign. This Giles was *s.* by his son,

JOHN DE BEAUCHAMP, of whom little is mentioned save his founding a chantry in the parish church of Alcester, temp. Edward III., for one priest to celebrate divine service daily at the altar of All Saints, and his being in the expedition against France in the 3d of Richard II. This John de Beauchamp left two sons—

WILLIAM (Sir) his successor.

Walter (Sir), from whom the Beauchamps, Barons of St. Amand, derived, (see that dignity,)

and was *s.* by the elder,

SIR WILLIAM DE BEAUCHAMP, Knt., who in the 18th of Richard II., was made constable of the castle of Gloucester. In the 3rd of Henry IV., was appointed sheriff of Worcestershire, and upon the accession of Henry V., sheriff of Gloucestershire. He *m.* Catharine, daughter of Gerrard de Ufflete, and was *s.* by his son,

SIR JOHN BEAUCHAMP, Knt., who purchased from Thomas de Botreaux, the other moiety of the manor of Alcester, which had continued in that family for divers descents. In the 17th of Henry VI., this Sir John de Beauchamp, upon the death of Richard, Earl of Warwick, was constituted one of the commissioners for the guardianship of all his castles and lands, during the minority of Henry, the young earl. And in the 25th of the same monarch, 2nd May, 1447, he was elevated to the peerage, in consequence of the many good and acceptable services performed by him to that king, and to Henry V. his father, by the title of LORD BEAUCHAMP, BARON OF POWYKE, obtaining at the same time, a grant of £60. per annum, out of the fee-farm of the city of Gloucester, to himself and his heirs, for the better support of the honour. He was also constituted Justice of South Wales, with power to exercise that office personally or by deputy : and ere long (26th Henry VI.) was raised to the office of LORD TREASURER OF ENGLAND, and honoured with the garter. His lordship *d.* in 1478, and by his last testament, dated 9th April, 1475, bequeathed his body to sepulture in the church of the Dominican Friers, at Worcester, in a new chapel to be made on the north side of the quire, to which religious house, in consideration of his burial there, he gave twenty marks, to be bestowed in vestments and stuffs, besides an organ of his own : and appointed that a priest of that friery, should daily say mass at the altar within that chapel, before his tomb, after the order of a *trental* for his soul, as also for the souls of his father and mother, &c., his children and ancestors' souls, and, especially for the soul of *Sir John Fastolf, Knt., William Botreaux,* and all christian souls; taking by the week, for that mass so daily to be said, eightpence, for evermore. Which chapel and tomb, with his effigies in alabaster, he enjoined his executors to cause to be erected. Lord Beauchamp was *s.* by his only son, then forty years of age,

SIR RICHARD BEAUCHAMP, second LORD BEAUCHAMP, of *Powyke*, who *m.* Elizabeth, daughter of Sir Humphrey Stafford, Knt., (in the private chapel of his manor house, at Beauchamp's Court,

by virtue of a special licence from the Bishop of Worcester,) and had issue,

Elizabeth, *m.* to Sir Robert Willoughby, Lord Willoughby de Broke, and had an only son Edward, who pre-deceased his father, leaving by his wife Elizabeth, daughter of Richard Nevil, Lord Latimer, three daughters, of whom the eldest, Elizabeth, alone left issue ; which Elizabeth *m.* Sir Fulke Greville, second son of Sir Fulke Greville, of Melcote, in the county of Warwick, and from that union descends the extant Earls of Brooke and Warwick, and the Barons Willoughby de Broke.

Anne, *m.* to Richard Lygon, Esq., of Worcestershire, and from this marriage the present Earl Beauchamp derives. (See *Burke's Dictionary of the Peerage and Baronetage.*)

Margaret, *m.* to Richard Rede, Esq., of the county of Gloucester.

His lordship *d.* in 1496, and thus leaving no male issue, the BARONY OF BEAUCHAMP OF POWYKE EXPIRED, while the estates of the deceased lord devolved upon the above ladies as co-heiresses. Elizabeth, Lady Willoughby de Broke, having the manor of Alcester, and her sisters, Powyke and other lands in the county of Worcester.

BEAUCHAMP — EARL OF ALBEMARLE.

By Letters Patent, dated ——, 1417.
(See Beauchamp, fifth Earl of Warwick.)

BEAUFORT — EARL OF DORSET, AND DUKE OF EXETER.

By Letters Patent, dated 18th November, 1416.

Lineage.

This was a branch of the royal house of PLANTAGENET, springing from the celebrated

JOHN OF GAUNT, (fourth son of King Edward III., and so denominated from the place of his birth, Gaunt, anno 1340,) Earl of Richmond, Duke of Lancaster, and Duke of Aquitaine, K.G., who espoused, for his third wife, Katherine, daughter of Sir Paen Roet, Knt., King at Arms, and widow of Sir Hugh (or Otes) Swineford, but had the following issue by her before his marriage, who were legitimated by parliament, in the 20th Richard II., for all purposes, save accession to the crown.

John, Earl of Somerset, from whom descends the present ducal house of BEAUFORT.

Henry, Cardinal of St. Eusebius, and Bishop of Winchester.

Thomas, of whom presently.

Joane, *m.* first, to Sir Robert Ferrers, and secondly, to Ralph Nevill, Earl of Westmoreland.

The youngest son, (surnamed *Beaufort,* from the castle of Beaufort in France, part of the marriage portion of BLANCH OF ARTOIS, upon her marriage with Edward Crouchback, first Earl of Lancaster,)

SIR THOMAS BEAUFORT, having attained some eminence in the reign of Richard II., was appointed Admiral of the whole fleet to the northwards, in the 5th of Henry IV., and retained to serve the king in that command with three hundred men at arms, himself and one banneret, being part of the number. In the 10th of the same monarch he was made Captain of Calais, and in the next year, had another grant of the office of Admiral, both of the northern and western seas, for life. In which employments Sir Thomas deported himself with so much discretion, that he was soon afterwards (2nd Henry IV.) appointed LORD CHANCELLOR OF ENGLAND, with a pension of eight hundred marks per annum, over and above the ordinary fees and wages of that high office, to enjoy from the 31st day of January preceding, so long as he should hold the same. He obtained likewise a grant of some of the forfeited lands of Sir Robert Belknap, and in addition to the command of the northern and western seas, the Admiralship of Ireland, Acquitaine, and Picardy, with six tuns of wine yearly, from the port of Kingston upon Hull. In the 13th of Henry IV., he was elevated to the peerage, as EARL OF DORSET, and upon the accession of Henry V., being then LIEUTENANT of ACQUITAINE, he was retained to serve the king in that capacity for one half year, with two hundred and forty men at arms, and twelve hundred archers. In the second year of the new monarch, his lordship was one of the ambassadors to negotiate a marriage between his royal master, and Catherine, daughter of the King of France; and in the next year he had the honour of commanding the rear guard at the celebrated BATTLE OF AGINCOURT, "consisting of archers, and such as were armed with spears, halberds, and bills," and was constituted Lieutenant of Normandy. In the 4th of Henry V., his lordship was created DUKE OF EXETER *for life only*, in the parliament then held at London, having therewith a grant of a thousand pounds per annum out of the exchequer, and forty pounds per annum more payable from the City of Exeter. During the remainder of the martial reign of the gallant Henry V., at whose solemn funeral he assisted as a mourner, his grace continued constantly engaged upon the plains of Normandy, and reaped fresh laurels in each succeeding campaign. Upon the accession of the new monarch, (Henry VI.) the Duke's services in France were retained, with three bannerets, three knights, one hundred four score and two men at arms, and six hundred archers, and he obtained in the same year the office of Justice of North Wales. His grace m. Margaret, daughter and co-heiress of Sir Thomas Nevil, of Horneby, in the county of Lincoln, Knt., but had no issue. He d. on the 27th of December, 1426, when the EARLDOM OF DORSET, AND DUKEDOM OF EXETER EXPIRED, but his great landed possessions devolved upon his nephew, John, Duke of Somerset. In the last testament of this eminent person, dated 29th December, in the 5th of Henry VI., he ordains that as soon after his decease, (viz. the first day if possible, or the second or third at the furthest) a thousand masses should be solemnly sung for his soul, &c.; that no great cost should be incurred at his funeral, and that five tapers only in so many candlesticks should be placed round his remains. That as many poor men, as

he should be years of age at the time of his death, should carry a torch at his funeral, each of them having a gown or hood of white cloth, and as many pence as he himself had lived years; likewise the same number of poor women to be similarly attired and remunerated. Furthermore he bequeathed to each poor body coming to his funeral a penny; and he appoints, that at every anniversary of himself, and Margaret, his wife, that the Abbot of St. Edmundsbury, if present, should have six shillings and eight pence; the prior, if present, three shillings and four pence; and every monk there, at that time, twenty pence; giving to the monastery for the support of these anniversaries, four hundred marks. To Joane, his sister, Countess of Westmorland, he gives a book, called TRISTRAM, and to Thomas Swineford, a cup of silver gilt, with a cover. To the use of poor scholars in Queen's College OXON, he bequeaths one hundred pounds to be deposited in a chest, to the end that they might have some relief thereby, in loan, desiring that the borrowers, should in charity pray for his soul, &c., and upon the like terms he bequeaths one hundred pounds more, to be similarly placed to Trinity Hall, Cambridge. The deceased duke was a knight of the Garter.

BEAUFORT — EARLS AND DUKES OF SOMERSET.

Earldom	} by Letters Patent {	Anno 1397.
Dukedom		—— 1442.

Lineage.

In the 20th year of Richard II., the Lord Chancellor having declared in parliament, that the king had created

SIR JOHN BEAUFORT, Knt., eldest son of JOHN OF GAUNT, by Catharine Swineford, (see Beaufort, Duke of Exeter,) EARL OF SOMERSET, he was brought in between the Earl of Huntingdon, and the Earl Marshal, in a vesture of honour, his sword (with the pomel gilt) carried before him. When the charter of creation being publicly read, he was girt with the same sword; and having done homage, was placed between the Earl Marshal, and the Earl of Warwick. His lordship was advanced in the next year (also in open parliament) to the MARQUISATE OF DORSET, a dignity which he soon afterwards resigned; and was created on the day of his resignation, MARQUESS OF SOMERSET. He bore, however, subsequently, the former title, and as Marquess of Dorset, was made constable of Walingford Castle, and constable of Dover Castle, and Warden of the Cinque Ports. In the same year, his lordship had extensive grants from the crown, and was appointed admiral of the king's fleet, both to the north and west; but upon the accession of Henry IV., having been one of the accusers of Thomas de Woodstock, Duke of Gloucester, his right to the Marquisate of Dorset was declared void by parliament, and his only title then remaining was Earl of Somerset, by which, in the same year, he was constituted LORD CHAMBERLAIN OF ENGLAND. In the 4th of the new monarch, the commons in parliament, however, petitioned for his restitution to the Marquisate of Dorset; but the

Earl seemed unwilling to re-adopt the designation of MARQUESS, that being then so new a dignity in England. His lordship did at length though resume it, for we find him in a few years after appointed, as Marquess of Dorset, LORD HIGH ADMIRAL OF ENGLAND. The Marquess espoused Margaret, daughter of Thomas Holland, and sister and heiress of Thomas, both Earls of Kent, (who married after his decease, Thomas, Duke of Clarence,) and had issue,

> HENRY, who s. as second Earl of Somerset.
> John, successor to his brother.
> Edmund, who, in the 9th of Henry VI., was appointed, under the title of Lord Morteign, commander of the forces in France (but of him hereafter).
> Jane, m. to James I. King of Scotland.
> Margaret, m. to Thomas Courtenay, Earl of Devon.

His lordship who, amongst his other honours, was a KNIGHT OF THE GARTER, d. in 1410, and was s. by his eldest son,

HENRY BEAUFORT, second Earl of Somerset, god-son to King Henry IV., who, dying in his minority, was s. by his brother,

JOHN BEAUFORT, third Earl of Somerset, K.G., a distinguished military commander in the reigns of Henry V. and Henry VI. by the latter of whom he was created, in 1443, Earl of Kendal, and DUKE OF SOMERSET, by which title he was made lieutenant-general of Aquitaine, and of the whole realm of France, and Duchy of Normandy. His grace m. Margaret, daughter of Sir John Beauchamp, of Blesto, Knt., and heiress of John, her brother, (which lady m. after the duke's decease, Sir Leode Welles,) by whom he left an only daughter and heiress,

> MARGARET, who m. Edmund Tudor, surnamed of Hadham, Earl of Richmond, by whom she was mother of
>> HENRY, EARL OF RICHMOND, who ascended the throne as Henry VII.
> Her ladyship espoused, secondly, Sir Henry Stafford, Knt., and thirdly, Thomas, Lord Stanley, but had issue by neither. The virtues of this distinguished lady have been greatly celebrated, and Walpole mentions her in his catalogue of noble authors, as having written upon several occasions; and by her son's command and authority, "made the orders for great estates of ladies and noblewomen, for their precedence, attires, and wearing of harbes at funerals, over the chin and under the same."

John, Duke of Somerset, d. in 1444, when that dignity, and the Earldom of Kendal expired: but the Earldom of Somerset devolved upon his brother,

EDMUND BEAUFORT, Marquess of Dorset, as fourth Earl of Somerset. This nobleman had commanded in the 10th of Henry VI., one of the divisions of the Duke of Bedford's army in Normandy, and upon the death of that eminent general, was appointed joint commander, with Richard, Duke of York, of all the English forces in the duchy. He subsequently (15th Henry VI.) laid successful siege to Harfleur; and afterwards crossing the Somme, invested, with equal fortune, the Fort of Fulleville, when he formed a junction with Lord Talbot. In a few years following, he acquired an accession of renown by his relief of Calais, then invested by the Duke of Burgundy, and for his good services upon that occasion, was created on the 24th of August, 1441, EARL OF DORSET. His lordship continuing to distinguish himself in arms, was advanced, on the 24th of June, 1442, to the MARQUISATE OF DORSET, by which title he inherited the Earldom of Somerset at the decease of his brother in 1444, and the next year was constituted REGENT OF FRANCE. In three years afterwards (31st March, 1448) he was created DUKE OF SOMERSET. His grace was also a knight of the Garter, and LORD HIGH CONSTABLE. But the fortune of war veering soon after, and Caen falling into the hands of the French, the duke had to encounter a storm of unpopularity in England, to which he was recalled, with the hostility of Richard, Duke of York, and espousing the Lancastrian cause, in the lamentable war of the Roses, which about that period broke out, he fell in the first battle of St. Albans, in 1445. His grace had m. Alianore, one of the daughters and co-heiresses of Richard Beauchamp, Earl of Warwick, and had issue,

> HENRY, Earl of Morteign, his successor.
> Edmund, successor to his brother.
> John, slain at the battle of Tewkesbury.
> Alianore, m. first, to James Boteler, Earl of Wiltshire, and secondly, to Sir Robert Spencer, Knt.
> Joane, m. to the Lord Houth, of Ireland, and afterwards to Sir Richard Fry, Knt.
> Anne, m. to Sir William Paston, Knt.
> Margaret, m. to Humphrey, Earl of Stafford, and afterwards to Sir Richard Darell, Knt.
> Elizabeth, m. to Sir Henry Lewes, Knt.

The duke was s. by his eldest son,

HENRY BEAUFORT, second DUKE OF SOMERSET, a very distinguished personage in the York and Lancaster contest. His lordship, like his father, being a staunch Lancastrian, was constituted in the 36th of Henry VI., governor of the Isle of Wight, with the castle of Caresbroke, and in the following year appointed captain of Calais. He subsequently continued high in the confidence of his royal master, until the defeat sustained by the Lancastrians at Towton, on the 12th of March, 1461, when flying from the field with the unfortunate Henry, he is accused of abandoning the fallen monarch at Berwick, and of making his peace with the new king (Edward IV.) by the surrender of Bamburgh Castle. Certain it is, that he was taken into favour by that prince, and obtained a grant from him of a thousand marks per annum. In the next year however, upon the appearance of Margaret of Anjou, in the North, at the head of a considerable force, his grace resumed "the Red Rose," but falling into the hands of the Yorkists at Hexham, in 1463, he was beheaded the day after the battle; and attainted by parliament in the 5th of Edward IV. The duke had no legitimate issue, but left by Joane Hill, an illegitimate son, CHARLES SOMERSET, from whom the present ducal family of Somerset directly descends. His grace was s. by his brother,

EDMUND BEAUCHAMP, who after enduring a miserable exile with his brother John in France, was restored to the honours of his family, upon the temporary re-establishment of the Lancastrian power, in the 10th of Edward IV., when he is said to have been summoned to parliament as DUKE OF SOMERSET. His grace commanded the archers at the battle of BARNETFIELD in the next year, and upon the loss of that battle fled into Wales to the Earl of Pembroke; he was subsequently in command at Tewkesbury, where the ill fortune of the day was attributed to his defection. His grace fled the field, but he was soon overtaken, and paid the forfeit of his head (anno 1471). Dying without issue, all his honours EXPIRED, leaving ATTAINDERS out of the question, while his sisters or their representatives became his heirs.

ARMS.—Quarterly, France and England, a border Gobony, ar. and az.

BEAUMONT — BARONS AND VIS-COUNTS BEAUMONT.

By Writ of Summons, dated 4th March, 1309, 2nd Edward II., and by Letters Patent, 12th February, 1440.

Lineage.

The original descent of this noble family does not appear to have been clearly ascertained. Some authorities deduce it from Lewis, son of Charles, Earl of Anjou, a younger son of Lewis VIII., king of France; some from Lewis de Brenne, second son of John de Brenne, the last king of Jerusalem; and some from the Viscounts Beaumont,* of Normandy.

* Of these viscounts a perfect narrative cannot be pretended to be given; but what can be said we will venture to offer. It appears, then, that our King Henry I. had many natural sons and daughters; of the latter of which, one named Constance, is said, by Sandford, to have married Rosceline, Viscount Beaumont, in Normandy, and to have been endowed by her father with the manor of Ahrichecott, in the town of Suttanton, in Devonshire. Of this Viscountess Beaumont, Mr. Madox, in his Baronia Anglicana, has produced from the Pipe Rolls several payments of money in the 4th of Henry II., (who was her nephew,) which payments were made to a lady, styled only " Vicecomitissa," though afterwards " Vicecomitissa de Bellomonte." She had issue a son Richard, who succeeded to the viscounty, (and probably Odoard le Viscount, to whom King Henry II. gave the manor of Emildon, in Northumberland, might be one of her younger sons,) in which he was succeeded by Ralph, who, very likely, when the duchy of Normandy was lost by King John, sought refuge and relief in England. For, in the next reign, it appears that mention is made of William de Beaumont, and also of Godfrey, who, with Cecilia de Ferrers, his wife, levied a fine of the manor of Rokburn, in Northamptonshire, 6th Edward I. Why may not, then, one of these be father of the Lady Vesey and her brothers?—(Horneby's Remarks on Dugdale's Baronage.)

This note is taken from Bankes's Extinct Peerage.

Certain it is, however, that in the reign of Edward I., mention is made of Isabel de Beaumont, wife of John de Vesci; of Lewis, who, in 1294, was treasurer of the church of Salisbury, and afterwards Bishop of Durham; and of

HENRY DE BEAUMONT, who, attending the king, 30th Edward I., in his expedition against the Scots, obtained a precept to the collectors of the Fifteenth in Yorkshire for two hundred marks towards his support in those wars. In the first year of King Edward II. this Henry had a grant in fee of the manors of Folkynham, Edenham, and Barton-upon-Humber, and of all the knight's fees belonging to Gilbert de Gant, which Laura de Gant, his widow, held in dower, and in three years afterwards had a further grant of the Isle of Man, to hold for life, by the services which the lords thereof had usually performed to the kings of Scotland. In the preceding year he had been constituted governor of Roxborough Castle, and deputed, with Humphrey de Bohun, Earl of Hereford, and Robert de Clifford, to guard the marches. About this period he espoused Alice, daughter, and eventually heiress of Alexander Comin, Earl of Boghan, constable of Scotland, and, doing his homage, in the 6th of Edward II., had livery of her lands. In the 10th of the same monarch, Lord Beaumont, (he had been summoned to parliament as a BARON on the 4th March, 1309,) being then the king's lieutenant in the north, accompanying thither two cardinals who had come from Rome, partly to reconcile the king to the Earl of Lancaster, and partly to inthronise his lordship's brother, Lewis de Beaumont, in the bishopric of Durham, was attacked, near Darlington, by a band of robbers, headed by Gilbert de Middleton, and despoiled of all his treasure, horses, and every thing else of value, as were likewise his companions. His lordship and his brother were also made prisoners, the former being conveyed to the castle of Mitford, and the latter to that of Durham, there to remain until ransomed. From this period the baron continued to bask in the sunshine of royal favor, and to receive from the crown further augmentations to his territorial possessions, until the 16th of Edward II., when, being required to give his advice in council regarding a truce then meditated with the Scots, he declined contemptuously, observing, " that he would give none therein," which so irritated the king, that his lordship was ordered to depart the council, and he retired, saying, " he had rather begone than stay." He was in consequence committed, with the consent of the lords present, to prison, but soon after released upon the bail of Henry de Perci and Ralph de Nevile. He seems within a short time, however, again to enjoy the king's favor, for we find him in two years constituted one of the plenipotentiaries to treat of peace with France, and in two years subsequently nominated guardian to David, son and heir of David de Strabolgi, Earl of Athol, deceased, in consideration of the sum of one thousand pounds. His lordship after this time, entirely deserting his royal master, sided with the queen consort Isabella, and was the very person to deliver up the unhappy monarch to his enemies, upon his abortive attempt to fly beyond sea. The king, thereupon, was committed close prisoner to Berkeley Castle, where he was inhumanly murdered in 1327. For this act of treachery Lord Beaumont received a grant of the manor of Loughborough, part of the possessions of Hugh le Despenser, the attainted Earl of Winchester, and was summoned to parliament on the 22nd January, 1334, 7th Edward III., as EARL OF BOGHAN. His lordship, during the reign of Edward III., had many high and confidential employments, and took a prominent part in the affairs of Scotland, being at one time sent as constable of the king's army into that country for defence of the realm. The earl d. in 1340, leaving two children, namely,

JOHN, his heir.

Elizabeth, m. to Nicholas de Audley, son and heir of James, Lord Audley, of Heley.

His lordship inherited, upon the decease of his sister, Isabell, wife of John de Vesci, of Alnwick, in the county of Northumberland, (one of the most powerful barons of the north,) a lady of great eminence in her time, without issue, large possessions in the county of Lincoln, which, added to his own acquirements, placed him amongst the most wealthy nobles of the kingdom at the period of his death. He was s. by his son,

JOHN DE BEAUMONT, second BARON BEAUMONT, summoned to parliament 25th February, 1342, but never entitled Earl of Boghan. His lordship m. Lady Alianore Plantagenet, 5th daughter of Henry, Earl of Lancaster, and great grand-daughter of King Henry III., by whom he had an only child, Henry, born in Brabant, during her ladyship's attendance upon Philippa, queen consort of Edward III.; in consideration of which, Lord Beaumont obtained the king's special letters patent, declaring, "that, notwithstanding the said Henry was begotten and born in foreign parts, nevertheless, in regard it was by reason of his and his lady's attendance on the queen, he should be reputed a lawful heir, and inherit his lands in ENGLAND, as if he had been born there." This nobleman, like his father, was much engaged in the Scottish wars. His lordship d. in 1342, and was s. by his son,

HENRY DE BEAUMONT, third Baron, whose legitimacy, (owing to his being born beyond the sea,) was ratified by act of parliament, in the 25th Edward III. In the 34th of the same monarch, being then of full age, his lordship did homage and had livery of his lands, and was summoned to parliament from the 14th August, 1362, to the 24th February, 1368. He m. Margaret, daughter of John de Vere, Earl of Oxford, (which lady m. after his decease, Nicholas de Lorraine,) and dying in 1368, was s. by his only child, (placed, in the 47th Edward III., under the guardianship of William Lord Latimer),

JOHN DE BEAUMONT, fourth baron, who attaining maturity in the 6th Richard II., had livery of his lands, and in the same year with Henry de Spencer, Bishop of Norwich, was, in the English army, sent to oppose the adherents of Pope Clement VII. In four years afterwards, his lordship accompanied JOHN OF GAUNT, then called King of Castille and Leon, into Spain; but before the close of that year, he was expelled the court, as one of the king's evil advizers, by the great lords assembled at Harin-

gey Park. Soon afterwards, however, he made his peace, and had license to repair to Calais, in order to engage in a tournament, and he had then the honor of tilting with the Lord Chamberlain of the King of France. In the 12th Richard II., he was made Admiral of the king's fleets to the northwards, and one of the Wardens of the Marches towards Scotland; "whereupon he entered that country forty miles, spoyled the Market at Fowke, and brought many prisoners back." In the next year he had the castle of Cherburgh in France, committed to his custody, and about that time was specially enjoined to abstain from exercising any feats of arms with the French, without permission from Henry de Perci, Earl of Northumberland. In the 16th of the same reign, his lordship received a pension of £100. per annum for his services, and was constituted Constable of Dover Castle, and Warden of the Cinque Ports; and in the 19th, he was appointed one of the commissioners to negotiate a marriage between the King of England, and Isabell, daughter of the King of France. His lordship m. Katherine, daughter of Thomas de Everingham of Laxton, in the county of Nottingham, and had issue,

HENRY, his successor.

Thomas, ancestor of the Beaumonts of Stoughton Grange.

Richard.

The baron, who had been summoned to parliament from the 20th August, 1383, to the 13th November, 1393, and had the high honour of being a KNIGHT OF THE GARTER, died in 1396, and was s. by his eldest son,

HENRY DE BEAUMONT, fifth baron, who received the honor of knighthood at the coronation of King Henry IV.; and in the 11th of the same monarch's reign, was constituted one of the commissioners to treat of peace with France. His lordship m. Elizabeth, daughter of William, Lord Willoughby de Eresby, and had issue,

JOHN, his heir.

Henry, from whom the Beaumonts of Wednesbury, in the county of Stafford, descended.

Lord Beaumont, who had been summoned to parliament from 25th August, 1404, to the 22nd March, 1413, died in the latter year, and was s. by his eldest son,

JOHN DE BEAUMONT, sixth baron, a very distinguished personage in the reign of Henry VI., and high in that monarch's favour, under whom he enjoyed the most lucrative and honorable employments, and in whose service he eventually laid down his life. In the 14th of King Henry, his lordship obtained by letters patent, to himself and his heirs male, the Earldon of Boloine, being at that time upon his march for the relief of Calais, and in four years afterwards, 12th February, 1440, he was created VISCOUNT BEAUMONT, (being the first person dignified with such a title,) with precedency above all barons of the realm, and with a yearly fee of twenty marks, out of the revenues of the county of Lincoln. His lordship received, subsequently, a patent of precedency (23rd Henry VI.) above all viscounts thenceforth to be created; and in five years afterwards, was constituted LORD HIGH CHAMBERLAIN OF ENGLAND. The viscount finally lost his life at the battle of Northampton, fighting under the Lancastrian banner on the 10th July, 1459. His lordship was a KNIGHT OF THE GARTER, and had been summoned to parliament in the BARONY OF BEAUMONT, from 24th February, 1432, to 26th September, 1439. He had m. Elizabeth, only daughter and heiress of Sir William Phelip, Lord Bardolf, by whom he left,

WILLIAM, his successor.

Joane, m. to John, Lord Lovel, of Tichmersh, and dying before her brother, left a son, who succeeded as Lord Lovel, but died without issue, and two daughters, viz.

    1. Joane, m. to Sir Brian Stapleton, of Carlton, Knt., from which marriage, lineally descended,

       Gilbert Stapleton, Esq, who left one son and one daughter, out of a numerous family, that had issue, namely,

         Sir Miles Stapleton, Bart., who d. in 1707, an infant son and daughter having pre-deceased him.

         Anne, m. to Mark Errington, Esq., of Conteland, and left a son,

           Nicholas, who assumed the name of Stapleton, and marrying Mary Scroope, left at his decease, in 1715, an only surviving son,

             NICHOLAS STAPLETON, who m. first, Charlotte Eure, by whom he had four daughters; secondly, Mary Bagnell, but had no surviving issue; and thirdly, Winefred White, by whom he left an only surviving son,

               THOMAS STAPLETON, Esq. of Carlton, who claimed the BARONY OF BEAUMONT, but unsuccessfully, in 1798.

    2. Frideswide, m. to Sir Edward Norres, of Yattenden, Knight, and whose grandson, Henry Norres, was summoned to parliament, temp. Elizabeth, as Baron Norres, of Rycote, a barony now merged in the Earldom of Abingdon. Her ladyship had an only grand-daughter,

       Mary, sister of Lord Norres, who m. first, Sir George Carew, and secondly, Sir Arthur Champernoun, and left issue.

John, Viscount Beaumont, was s. by his only son,

WILLIAM DE BEAUMONT, second Viscount and seventh Baron, who inherited likewise large possessions from his mother, the heiress of the Bardolfs. This nobleman adhering faithfully to the Lancastrian interest, was made prisoner by the Yorkists at Towton field, in the 1st year of Edward IV., when he was attainted, and his large possessions bestowed upon Lord Hastings; from this period until the accession of King Henry VII., his lordship shared the fallen fortunes of his party, but rising with that event, he was restored to his honors and estates, by act of parliament, passed on the 7th November, in the 1st year of the new monarch's reign. The viscount m. first, Elizabeth, daughter of Richard Scrope, and niece of Lord Scrope, of Bolton; and secondly, Joane, daughter of Humphrey Stafford, Duke of Buckingham, but dying without issue in 1507, THE VISCOUNTCY EXPIRED, while THE BARONY OF BEAUMONT fell into ABEYANCE, and so continues, according to the decision upon the claims of Mr. Stapleton, in 1798, "Between the coheirs of William, Viscount Beaumont, (in whom it was vested by descent from his father, John, Lord Beaumont, who was summoned to and sat in parliament, 2nd Henry VI., as a baron in fee,) descended from his sister Joane, and that the petitioner Thomas Stapleton, Esq., was one of those coheirs."

ARMS—Az. a lion rampant semée de lis, or.

BEAUMONT—EARLS OF LEICESTER.

By Charter of Creation, dated anno 1103.

Lineage.

ROBERT DE BELLOMONT, OR BEAUMONT, (son of Roger, grandson of Turolf of Pont Audomere, by Wevia, sister to Gunnora, wife of Richard I., Duke of Normandy,) came into England with the Conqueror, and contributed mainly to the Norman triumph at Hastings. This Robert inherited the earldom of Mellent in Normandy, from his mother Adelina, daughter of Waleran, and sister of Hugh, (who took the habit of a monk in the abbey of Bec,) both Earls of Mellent. Of his conduct at Hastings, William Pictavensis thus speaks: "A certain Norman young soldier, son of Roger de Bellomont, nephew and heir to Hugh, Earl of Mellent, by Adelina his sister, making the first onset in that fight, did what deserveth lasting fame, boldly charging and breaking in upon the enemy, with that regiment which he commanded in the right wing of the army," for which gallant services he obtained sixty-four lordships in Warwickshire, sixteen in Leicestershire, seven in Wiltshire, three in Northamptonshire, and one in Gloucestershire, in all NINETY-ONE. His lordship did not however arrive at the dignity of the English peerage before the reign of Henry I., when that monarch created him EARL OF LEICESTER. The mode by which he attained this honour is thus stated by an ancient writer: "The CITY OF LEICESTER had then four lords, viz., the KING, the BISHOP OF LINCOLN, EARL SIMON, and YVO, the son of Hugh de Grentmesnel. This Earl of Mellent, by favour of the king, cunningly entering it on that side which belonged to Yvo, (then governor thereof, as also sheriff, and the king's farmer there,) subjecting it wholly to himself; and by this means, being made an EARL in England, exceeded all the nobles of the realm in riches and power." His lordship espoused Isabel, daughter of Hugh, Earl of Vermandois, and had issue,

    Walaren, who s. to the Earldom of Mellent.
    ROBERT, successor to the English Earldom.
    Hugh, surnamed Pauper, obtained the EARL-
      DOM OF BEDFORD from King Stephen,
      with the daughter of Milo de Beauchamp,
      upon the expulsion of the said Milo. Being
      a person (says Dugdale) remiss and negli-
      gent himself, he fell from the dignity of an
      earl, to the state of a knight; and in the
      end to miserable poverty.
With several daughters, of whom,
    Elisabeth, was concubine to Henry I., and
      afterwards wife of Gilbert Strongbow, Earl
      of Pembroke.
    Adeline, m. to Hugh de Montfort.
    ———— m. to Hugh de Novo Castello.
    ———— m. to William Lupellus, or Lovel.
This great earl is characterised as "the wisest of all men betwixt this and Jerusalem, in worldly affairs; famous for knowledge, plausible in speech, skilful in craft, discreetly provident, ingeniously subtile, excelling for prudence, profound in counsel, and of great wisdom." In the latter end of his days, he became a monk in the Abbey of Preaux, where he died in 1118, and was s. in the earldom of Leicester, by his second son,

    ROBERT, (called Bossu,) as second earl. This nobleman stoutly adhering to King Henry I. upon all occasions, was with that monarch at his decease in 1135, and he afterwards as staunchly supported the interests of his grandson, Henry II., upon whose accession to the throne, his lordship was constituted JUSTICE OF ENGLAND. He m. Amicia, daughter of Ralph de Waer, Earl of Norfolk, by whom he had a son, ROBERT, and two daughters; one, the wife of Simon, Earl of Huntingdon, the other, of William, Earl of Gloucester. The earl, who was a munificent benefactor to the church, and founder of several religious houses, d. in 1167, after having lived for fifteen years a canon regular in the Abbey of Leicester, and was s. by his son,

    ROBERT, (surnamed Blanchmaines, from having white hands,) as third earl, who adhering to Prince Henry, in the 19th of Henry II., in his rebellion, incurred the high displeasure of that monarch. The king commanding that his town of Leicester should be laid waste, it was besieged, and the greater part burnt; the inhabitants having permission for three hundred pounds to move whither they pleased. He was received however into royal favour in four years afterwards, (1177,) and had restoration of all his lands and castles, save the castle of Montsorel, in the county of Leicester, and Pacey, in Normandy; but surviving King Henry, he stood in such favour with Richard I., that those castles were likewise restored to him, and he was appointed to carry one of the swords of state at that monarch's coronation. His lordship m. Patro-

44

nil, daughter of Hugh de Grentesmesnil, with whom he had the whole honour of Hinkley, and STEWARDSHIP of England, and had issue,

    ROBERT FITZPARNEL, his successor.
    Roger, Bishop of St. Andrews, in Scotland.
    William, a leaper, founder of the hospital of
      St. Leonards, at Leicester.
    Amicia, m. to Simon de Montfort, who after
      the Earldom of Leicester expired, with the
      male line of the BEAUMONTS, was created
      Earl of Leicester, by King John (see Mont-
      ford, Earl of Leicester).
    Margaret, m. to Sayer de Quincy.
The earl d. in his return from Jerusalem, at Duras, in Greece, anno 1190, and was s. by his son,

    ROBERT, (surnamed Fits-parnel from his mother,) fourth earl, who in 1191, being at Messina, in his journey to the Holy Land, was invested into his father's earldom of Leicester, by King Richard, with the cincture of a sword. After which, whilst his royal master was detained in captivity by the Emperor, the King of France having invaded Normandy, and taken divers places, this earl coming to Roan, excited the inhabitants to so vigorous a defence, that the French monarch was obliged to retreat. Furthermore, it is related of him, that making a pilgrimage into the Holy Land, he there unhorsed, and slew the Soldan in a tournament, when returning into England, he d. in 1204, and was buried in the Abbey of Leicester, before the high altar, betwixt his mother and grandfather. His lordship had m. Lauretta, daughter of William, Lord Braose, of Brember, but having no issue, the EARLDOM OF LEICESTER became EXTINCT, while his great inheritance devolved upon his two sisters, as coheirs, which was divided between them, thus—

    SIMON DE MONTFORT, husband of Amicia,
      had one moiety of the earldom of Leicester,
      with the honour of Hinkley, and was
      CREATED EARL OF LEICESTER; he also
      enjoyed the stewardship of England, as in
      right of the said honor of Hinkley.
    SAYER DE QUINCEY, husband of Margaret,
      had the other moiety of the earldom of
      Leicester, and was shortly after created
      EARL OF WINCHESTER. (See that dignity).
ARMS.—Gu. a cinquefoil Erm. pierced of the field.

BEAUMONT—EARL OF BEDFORD.
(See Beaumont, Earl of Leicester.)

BEC OR BEKE—BARONS BEKE OF ERESBY.

By Writ of Summons, dated 23rd June, 1295.
23rd Edward I.

Lineage.

Amongst the companions in arms of the CONQUEROR, was,

WALTER BEC, who, although enjoying a fair inheritance in Normandy, embarked zealously in the enterprise against England, and obtained upon the triumph of his master a grant of the manor of Eresby, in the county of Lincoln, with other important lordships. This Walter m. Agnes, daughter and heiress of Hugh, the son of Pinco, (one of the chiefs in Duke William's army,) commonly called Hugh Dapifer, and had issue—

Hugh, who died *s. p.* in his return from the Holy Land.

Henry, being a person of weak understanding, his two next brothers shared with him the inheritance.

Walter, } participators with their brother
John, } Henry, in their father's lands.

Thomas inherited the church patronage of his father.

The eldest surviving son,

HENRY BEKE, inherited ERESBY, and other manors, and was *s.* by his son,

WALTER BEKE, who m. Eva, niece of Walter de Grey, Archbishop of York, and was *s.* by his son,

JOHN BEKE, who gave to King John a hundred pounds and four palfreys, for license to marry the widow of William Bardolph. This feudal lord was *s.* by his son,

HENRY BEKE, who m. Hawyse, sister of Thomas de Muleton, and obtained large estates; in the county of Lincoln thereby, as a gift from the said Thomas. To this feudal Baron of Eresby, *s.* his son,

WALTER BEKE, who left three sons, viz.—

JOHN, his successor in the lordship of Eresby.

ANTHONY, the celebrated BISHOP OF DURHAM, and PATRIARCH OF JERUSALEM. "This Anthony, (says Dugdale,) was signed with the cross in the 54th Henry III., in order to his going to the Holy Land with Prince Edward; and on the 3rd of Edward I., being then a clerk, was made constable of the Tower of London. Moreover, in anno 1283, being present at the translation of St. William, Archbishop of York, and at the whole charge of that great solemnity, (the king, queen, and many of the nobility being also there,) he was then consecrated BISHOP OF DURHAM, by William Wickwane, Archbishop of York, in the church of St. Peter, within that city. After which, anno 1294, (22nd Edward I. the king discerning his great losses in Gascoigne,) he was sent to Rodolph, King of Almaine, to make a league with him; and the same year, upon the arrival of the cardinals to treat of peace between King Edward and the King of France, he readily answered their proposals in the French tongue. Furthermore, in anno 1296, King Edward entered Scotland with a powerful army; he brought thither to him no less than five hundred horse, and a thousand foot, besides a multitude of Welsh and Irish. After which, the same year, being sent ambassador into that realm, he was solemnly met by the king and nobles; and after much dispute, brought them to such an accord, that they totally submitted themselves to the pleasure of King Edward. Also upon that rebellion, which again broke out there the next year following, (at which time they used great cruelties to the English,) he was again sent thither to inquire the truth, and to advertise the king thereof. And in the 26th of Edward I. was again sent into Scotland, with certain forces, at which time he assaulted the castle of Dulton, and took it. And lastly, in 33rd of Edward I. being with the Earl of Lincoln, and some other bishops, sent to Rome, to present divers vessels of pure gold from King Edward to the Pope, his Holyness taking especial notice of his courtly behaviour and magnanimity of spirit, advanced him to the title of PATRIARCH OF JERUSALEM."

"Amongst other works of this great prelate, (continues Dugdale,) he founded the collegiate churches of Chester and Langcester, as also the collegiate chappel at Bishops-Aukland, all in the county palatine of Durham. Moreover, it is reported that no man in all the realm, except the king, did equal him for habit, behaviour and military pomp, and that he was more versed in state affairs than in ecclesiastical duties; ever assisting the king most powerfully in his wars; having sometimes in Scotland, twenty-six standard bearers, and of his ordinary retinue, an hundred and forty knights; so that he was thought to be rather a temporal prince than a priest or bishop; and lastly, that he died on 3rd of March, 1310, and was buried above the HIGH ALTAR in his cathedral of Durham." This prelate was the first bishop that presumed to lie in the church, on account of the interment of the holy St. Cuthbert, and so superstitious were they in those days, that they dared not bring in the remains at the doors, but broke a hole in the wall, to convey them in at the end of the church, which breach is said to be still visible.

Thomas, Bishop of St. David's.

The eldest son,

JOHN BEKE, *s.* his father in the feudal lordship of Eresby, and was summoned to parliament as BARON BEKE, OF ERESBY, on the 23rd of June, 20th of September, and 2nd of November, 1295, and the 26th of August, 1296, having previously (4th of Edward I.) had license to make a castle of his manor house at Eresby. His lordship m. ————, and had issue,

WALTER, his successor.

Alice, m. to Sir William de Willoughby, Knt., and had issue,

ROBERT WILLOUGHBY, who inherited, at the decease of his grand uncle, Anthony Beke, Bishop of Durham, the great possessions of that eminent prelate, and was summoned to parliament, temp. Edward II. as LORD WILLOUGHBY DE ERESBY. (See that dignity in *Burke's Dictionary of the Peerage and Baronetage.*)

Margaret, m. to Sir Richard de Harcourt, Knt., ancestor of the Harcourts, Earls of Harcourt.

45

Mary, *d.* unm.

Lord Beke, *d.* in 1302, and was *s.* by his son,

WALTER, second baron, but never summoned to parliament; at whose decease without issue, the BARONY OF BEKE DE ERESBY fell into ABEYANCE, between his two sisters and co-heirs, the ladies Willoughby and Harcourt, and so continues amongst their descendants.

ARMS—Gules, a cross moline, ar.

BECHE—BARONS LA BECHE.

By Writ of Summons, dated 25th February, 1342, 16 Edward III.

Lineage.

Of this family, DE LA BECHE, of Aldworth, in the county of Bucks,

NICHOLAS DE LA BECHE was constituted Constable of the Tower of London in the 9th of Edward III., and had a grant from the crown, in two years afterwards, of the manor of Whitchurch, with other lands. About this period, too, he obtained license to encastellate his houses at De La Beche, Beaumys, and Watlyington. He was subsequently distinguished in the wars in Brittany, and was summoned to parliament, as a BARON, on the 25th of February, 1342. In 1343 his lordship became seneschal of Gascony, and the next year was constituted one of the commissioners to treat with Alphonsus, king of Castile, touching a marriage between the eldest son of that monarch and Joane, daughter of the king of England.

Lord De La Beche died in 1347, and leaving no issue, the BARONY expired, but the estates passed to the sisters of John de la Beche, who died nineteen years previously, and is supposed to have been the elder brother of the baron; consequently the co-heiresses were his lordship's sisters likewise. Of those ladies,

Joane, the elder, *m.* first, Sir Andrew Sackville, and secondly, Sir Thomas Langford.

———— *m.* Robert Danvers.

Arms—Vairée ar. and gules.

BELASYSE — BARONS FAUCONBERG, OF YARUM, IN THE COUNTY OF YORK. VISCOUNTS FAUCONBERG, OF HENKNOWLE, IN THE COUNTY OF DURHAM. EARLS OF FAUCONBERG.

Barony, Viscounty, Earldom,	by Letters Patent,	dated 25th May, 1627. dated 31st Jan., 1643. dated first, 9th April, 1689; second, 16th June, 1774.

Lineage.

This eminent Norman family deduced an uninterrupted descent from

BELASIUS, one of the commanders in the army of the Conqueror, distinguished for having sup-

pressed the adherents of Edgar Ethling, in the Isle of Ely, whence the spot where he had pitched his camp was named Belasius Hill, now known by the corrupted designation of Belsar's Hill. The son of this gallant soldier,

ROWLAND, marrying Elgiva, daughter and heiress of Ralph de Belasyse, of Belasyse, in the county of Durham, assumed, upon succeding to the inheritance of his wife, the surname of "Belasyse, of Belasyse," and his descendants ever afterwards adhered to the same designation, although the spelling has frequently varied. The great-grandson of this Rowland Belasyse,

SIR ROWLAND BELASYSE attained the honour of knighthood by his gallant bearing at the battle of Lewes, in the 48th of Henry III. Sir Rowland *m.* Mary, daughter and heiress of Henry Spring, Lord of Howton-le-Spring, in the bishopric of Durham, by whom he acquired a considerable accession of property, and was *s.* by his son,

SIR ROGER BELASYSE, who *m.* Joan, daughter of Sir Robert Harbottle, Knt., and had issue—

    ROBERT, his successor.

    John, *m.* to Mary, daughter of Robert Bertram, Esq.

    Elizabeth, *m.* to Thomas Madison, Esq., of Unthank Hall.

Sir Roger was *s.* by his elder son,

SIR ROBERT BELASYSE, from whom lineally descended,

WILLIAM BELASYSE, Esq., *of Belasyse*, who *m.* first, Cecily, daughter and heiress of William Hotton, Esq., and had issue—

    RICHARD, his successor.

    Anthony, LL.D., master in Chancery in 1545, when he was one of the four especially appointed to hear causes, and pass decrees in the Court of Chancery, in the absence of the lord chancellor, Sir Thomas Wriothesley. And in the reign of Edward VI., being written Anthony Belasis, Esq., was one of the king's council in the north. On the dissolution of the monasteries he obtained from the crown a grant of Newborough Abbey, in the county of York, which he afterwards gave to his nephew, Sir William Belasyse.

    Elizabeth, *m.* to William Clervaux, of Crofts, in the county of York.

    Margaret, *m.* to —— Minshull, Esq.

    Anne, *m.* to Anthony Smith, Esq., of Kalton.

Mr. Belasyse *m.* secondly, Jane, daughter of Thomas Tipping, Esq., but had no issue by that lady. He was *s.* by his son,

RICHARD BELASYSE, Esq., who was constituted constable of Durham for life, to officiate in person, or by deputy. He *m.* Margaret, daughter and heiress of Richard Errington, Esq., of Cockley, in the county of Northumberland, and dying in the 30th of Henry VIII., was *s.* by his son, (then in minority,)

SIR WILLIAM BELASYSE, Knt., who served the office of sheriff for Yorkshire in the 17th year of Elizabeth. He *m.* Margaret, daughter of Sir Nicholas Fairfax, of Malton, in the county of York, and dying at an advanced age, 13th April, 1604, was s. by his eldest son,

SIR HENRY BELASYSE, of Newborough, in the country of York, who, having received the honour of knighthood from King James I., at York, in his majesty's journey to London, 17th April, 1603, was created a BARONET upon the institution of that dignity, on the 29th June, 1611. Sir Henry m. Ursula, daughter of Sir Thomas Fairfax, of Denton, in the county of York, and had issue—

THOMAS, his successor.

Dorothy, m. to Sir Conyers Darcy, Knt., of Hornby.

Mary, m. to Sir William Lester, Knt., of Thornton, in the county of York.

He was s. at his decease by his son,

SIR THOMAS BELASYSE, second baronet, b. in 1557, and advanced to the peerage by the title of BARON FAUCONBERG, of Yarum, in the county of York, on the 25th May, 1627. His lordship, adhering faithfully to the fortunes of King Charles I., was created, on the 31st of January, 1642, VISCOUNT FAUCONBERG, of Henknowle, in the county palatine of Durham. His lordship was subsequently at the siege of York, and at the battle of Marston Moor, under the Duke of Newcastle, with whom he fled to the continent after that unfortunate defeat. He m. Barbara, daughter of Sir Henry Cholmondeley, Baronet, of Roxby, in the county of York, and had issue—

——, M.P. for the county of York; of whom Clarendon writes:—"Harry Belasis, with the Lord Fairfax, the two knights who served in parliament for Yorkshire, signed articles for a neutrality for that county, being nearly allied together, and of great kindness, till their several opinions and affections had divided them in this quarrel; the Lord Fairfax adhering to the parliament, and the other, with great courage and sobriety, to the king." Mr. Belasyse m. Grace, daughter and heiress of Sir Thomas Barron, of Smithells, in the county of Lancaster, and dying in the life-time of his father, left issue,

THOMAS, successor to his grandfather.

Henry, d. unmarried.

Rowland, (Sir) K.B., m. Anne, eldest daughter and sole heiress of J. Davenport, Esq., of Sutton, in the county of Chester, and dying in 1699, left

THOMAS, who s. as third Viscount Fauconberg.

Henry, d. unmarried.

John, died s. p.

Rowland, m. Frances, daughter of Christopher, Lord Teynham, by whom he had, with other issue,

Anthony, who m. Susannah, daughter of John Clarvet, Esq., and had issue—

ROWLAND, who s. as sixth viscount.

Charles, D.D., of Sorbonne, who s. as seventh viscount.

Thomas, m. Marie Louise de Maneville, and had five daughters.

Frances.

Barbara.

Grace, m. to George, Viscount Castletown, in Ireland.

Frances, m. to Sir Henry Jones, of Aston, in the county of Oxford, Knt., of which marriage there was an only daughter and heiress,

FRANCES, m. to Richard, Earl of Scarborough.

Arabella, m. to Sir William Frankland, Bart., of Thirklaby, in the county of York.

Barbara, m. first, to Walter Strickland, Esq., son of Sir Robert Strickland, of Sizergh, and secondly, to Sir Marmaduke Dalton, of Huxwell, Yorkshire.

John, created LORD BELASYSE, of Worlaby (see that dignity).

Margaret, m. to Sir Edward Osborn, of Kiveton.

Mary, m. to John, Lord Darcy, of Aston.

Barbara, m. to Sir Henry Slingsby, Bart., of Scriven, in the county of York, who was put to death under Cromwell's usurpation, and died, as he said on the scaffold, for being an honest man.

Ursula, m. to Sir Walter Vavasor, of Haslewood, Bart.

Frances, m. to Thomas Ingram, Esq., eldest son of Sir Arthur Ingram, of Temple Newsom, Yorkshire.

His lordship d. in 1652, and was s. by his grandson,

THOMAS BELASYSE, second viscount, who m. first, Mildred, daughter of Nicholas, Viscount Castleton, by whom he had no issue; and secondly, on the 19th of November, 1657, at Hampton Court, Mary, daughter of the protector Cromwell. Of this nobleman Lord Clarendon gives the following account:—" After Cromwell was declared protector, and in great power, he married his daughter to the Lord Fauconberg, the owner of a very great estate in Yorkshire, and descended of a family eminently loyal. There were many reasons to believe that this young gentleman, being then about three or four-and-twenty years of age, of great vigour and ambition, had many good purposes that he thought that alliance might qualify and enable him to perform. His marriage was celebrated at Whitehall (Wood has given the time at Hampton Court,) with all imaginable pomp and lustre. And it was observed, that, though it was performed in public, according to the rites and ceremonies then in use, they were presently afterwards, in private, married by ministers ordained by bishops, and according to the form in the book of Common Prayer, and this with the privity of Cromwell." In 1657, his lordship was made one of the council of state, and sent the next year, by his father-in-law, with a complimentary message to the court of Versailles. This was the only employment Lord Fauconberg had under the usurper; for, as the noble author before mentioned relates, "his domestic delights were lessened every day; he plainly discovered that his son Fauconberg's heart was set, upon an interest destructive to his, and grew to hate him perfectly." Of Lady Fauconberg, Burnet writes:—"She was a wise and worthy woman, more likely to have maintained the post (of protector) than either of her brothers; according to a saying that went of her, *that those who wore breeches deserved petticoats better ; but if those in petticoats had been in breeches, they would have held faster.*" That his lordship forwarded the restoration, is evident from his being appointed, by the restored monarch, in 1660, lord-lieutenant of the bishopric of Durham, and in the same year, lord-lieutenant and custos rotulorum of the North Riding of Yorkshire. He was soon afterwards accredited ambassador to the state of Venice and the princes of Italy, and nominated captain of the band of gentleman pensioners. In 1679, Lord Fauconberg was sworn of the privy council; and again, in 1689, upon the accession of King William and Queen Mary, when his lordship was created EARL FAUCONBERG, by letters patent, dated on the 9th of April, in that year. He d. on the 31st December, 1700, and leaving no issue, the EARLDOM EXPIRED, while his other honours reverted to his nephew (refer to Sir Rowland Belasyse, K.B., third son of the first lord),

THOMAS BELASYSE, Esq., as third Viscount Fauconberg. His lordship m. Bridget, daughter of Sir John Gage, of Firle, in the county of Sussex, Bart., and co-heiress of her mother, who was daughter of Thomas Middlesmore, Esq. of Egbaston, in the county of Warwick, by whom he had surviving issue,

THOMAS, his successor.
Rowland.
Mary, m. 9th April, 1721, to John Pitt, Esq. third son of Thomas Pitt, Esq., governor of Fort St. George.

And two other daughters, both of whom d. unmarried. His lordship d. 26th November, 1718, and was s. by his elder son,

THOMAS, fourth Viscount, who was created EARL FAUCONBERG, of Newborough, in the county of York, on the 15th June, 1756. His lordship m. in 1726, Catherine, daughter and heiress of John Betham, Esq., of Rowington, in the county of Warwick, and co-heiress of William Fowler, Esq., of St. Thomas, in the county of Stafford, by whom he had surviving issue,

HENRY, his successor.
Barbara, m. in 1752, to the Hon. George Barnewall, only brother of Henry Benedict, Viscount Kingsland.
Mary, m. in 1776, to Thomas Eyre, Esq., of Hassop, in the county of Derby.
Anna, m. in 1761, to the Hon. Francis Talbot, brother of George, fourteenth Earl of Shrewsbury.

His lordship, who conformed to the established church, died 4th February, 1774, and was s. by his son,

HENRY BELASYSE, second earl. His lordship m. first, in 1766, Charlotte, daughter of Sir Matthew Lamb, of Brocket Hall, in the county of

Hertford, Bart., and had four daughters, his co-heirs: viz.—

Charlotte, m. to Thomas Edward Wynn, Esq., third son of Colonel Glynn Wynn, who assumed the surname and arms of BELASYSE, in addition to his own.
Anne, m. to Sir George Wombwell, Bart.
Elizabeth, m. in 1789, to Bernard Howard, Esq., (present Duke of Norfolk,) from whom she was divorced in 1794, when she re-married the Earl of Lucan.
Harriot.

The earl m. secondly, Miss Chesshyre, but had no issue. He d. 23rd March, 1802, when the EARLDOM became EXTINCT, but the other honours devolved upon his kinsman (refer to descendants of the Hon. Henry Belasyse, eldest son of Sir Thomas Belasyse, the first Viscount).

ROWLAND BELASYSE, as 6th Viscount, who died s. p. in 1810, and was s. by his brother,

The REV. CHARLES BELASYSE, D.D., of the Roman Catholic Church, as seventh Viscount, at whose decease, in 1815, the Barony and Viscounty of Fauconberg, became EXTINCT.

ARMS.—Quarterly, first and fourth, ar. a Chev. gu. between three fleurs-de-lis, az.; second and third, ar. a pale ingrailed between two pallets plain, sa.

BELASYSE — BARONS BELASYSE, OF WORLABY, IN THE COUNTY OF LINCOLN.

By Letters Patent, dated 27th January, 1644, 20 Charles I.

Lineage.

THE HON. JOHN BELASYSE, second son of Thomas, first Viscount Fauconberg, having distinguished himself as one of the gallant leaders of the royal army during the civil wars, was elevated to the peerage on the 27th January, 1644, as LORD BELASYSE, *of Worlaby, in the county of Lincoln.* At the commencement of the rebellion, this eminent person arrayed six regiments of horse and foot under the royal banner, and had a principal command at the battles of Edge-Hill, Newbury, and Knaresby, and at the sieges of Reading and Bristol; and being appointed, subsequently, governor of York, and commander-in-chief of the king's forces in Yorkshire, he fought the battle of Selby with Lord Fairfax. His lordship being lieutenant-general of the counties of Lincoln, Nottingham, Derby, and Rutland, and governor of Newark, valiantly defended that garrison against the English and Scotch armies, until his majesty came in person, and ordered it to surrender; at which time he had also the honour of being general of the king's horse-guards. In all those arduous services, General Belasyse deported himself with distinguished courage and conduct, was frequently wounded, and thrice incarcerated in the Tower of London. At the restoration of the monarchy, his lordship was made lord lieutenant of the east riding of the county of York, governor of Hull, general of his majesty's forces in Africa, governor of Tangier, and captain of the king's guards of gentlemen pensioners. In the reign of King James II., Lord Belasyse was first lord of the treasury. His lordship m. first, Jane, daughter and sole heiress of Sir Robert Boteler, Knt., of Woodhall, in the county of Hertford, by whom he had issue—

> HENRY (Sir) K.B., who m. first, Rogersa, daughter and co-heir (with her sister Elizabeth, Duchess of Richmond and Lenox) of Richard Rogers, Esq., of Brianston, in the county of Dorset, by whom he had no issue; and secondly, Susan, daughter and co-heiress of Sir William Armine, of Osgodby, in the county of Lincoln, (which lady was created BARONESS BELASYSE, for her own life, after the decease of her husband,) by whom he left, at his decease in 1668, an only son,
>> HENRY, of whom presently, as second LORD BELASYSE.
> Mary, m. to Robert, Viscount Dunbar, of Scotland.

Lord Belasyse m. secondly, Anne, daughter and co-heiress of Sir Robert Crane, of Chilton, in the county of Suffolk; and thirdly, Anne, daughter of John, fifth Marquess of Winchester, by whom he had several children, of which the following alone survived infancy—

> Honora, m. to George Lord Abergavenny, and died s. p.
> Barbara, m. to Sir John Webb, Bart., of Oldstock, in the county of Wilts.
> Katherine, m. to John Talbot, Esq., of Longford.
> Isabella, m. to Thomas Stoner, Esq., of Stoner, in the county of Oxford, and died s. p. in 1706.

His lordship d. in 1689, and was s. by his grandson,

HENRY BELASYSE, second baron, who married Anne, daughter of Francis, son and heir of Robert Brudenel, Earl of Cardigan; but dying in 1692, without issue, the BARONY OF BELASYSE became EXTINCT, while the estates reverted to his lordship's aunts by the half blood, as co-heiresses.

Arms—Arg. a chevron gu. between three fleurs-delis, with due difference.

BENSON — BARON BINGLEY.

By Letters Patent, dated 21st July, 1713.

Lineage.

ROBERT BENSON, Esq., M.P. for the city of York, son of Robert Benson, Esq., of Wrenthorn, in the county of York, by Dorothy, daughter of Tobias Jenkins, Esq., having filled the offices of commissioner, and chancellor, and under treasurer of the exchequer, was elevated to the peerage, as BARON BINGLEY, on the 21st July, 1713. His lordship was subsequently ambassador to the court of Madrid. He m. Elisabeth, elder daughter of Heneage Finch, first Earl of Aylesford, and had an only daughter and heiress,

> HARRIOT, who m. George Fox Lane, Esq., M.P. for the city of York, who was created LORD BINGLEY, in 1772 (see that title).

His lordship d. 9th April, 1730, and thus leaving no male issue, the Barony of BINGLEY, became ex-

tinct, while one hundred thousand pounds, and seven thousand pounds a year, devolved upon his daughter, with the fine seat of Bramham Park, erected by the deceased lord.

Arms.—Arg. three trefoils in bend sa cotessed gules.

BENHALE—BARON BENHALE.

By Writ of Summons, 3rd April, 1360,
34 Edward III.

Lineage.

ROBERT DE BENHALE, a soldier of distinction in the expedition made into France, in the 10th year of Edward III., and again in two years afterwards, in the expedition made into Flanders, was summoned to parliament as BARON BENHALE, on the 3rd April, 1360, but never subsequently, and nothing further is known of his lordship, or his descendants.

BERKELEY — VISCOUNT BERKELEY, EARL OF NOTTINGHAM, AND MARQUESS OF BERKELEY.

Viscounty, Earldom, Marquisate,	by Letters Patent, dated	12th April, 1481, 28th June, 1483, 1488.

Lineage.

The family of Berkeley, established in England at the Norman conquest, was founded by a leading chief in the conqueror's army, named

ROGER, who is styled, in the 20th year of William's reign, " ROGERUS SENIOR DE BERKELE," from the possession of BERKELEY CASTLE, in the county of Gloucester. This Roger bestowed several churches upon the priory of Stanley, with the tithes and lands thereunto belonging, and being shorn a monk there, in 1091, restored the lordship of Shoteshore, which he had long detained from that convent. He was s. at his decease by his nephew,

WILLIAM DE BERKELEY, second feudal lord of Berkeley Castle, who was s. by his son,

ROGER DE BERKELEY. This nobleman, adhering to the Empress Maud, " underwent (says Dugdale,) a very hard fate, through the perfidiousness and cruelty of Walter, brother to Milo, Earl of Hereford, his seeming friend, (and kinsman by consanguinity,) being treacherously seized on, stripped naked, exposed to scorn, put into fetters, and thrice drawn by a rope about his neck, on a gallows, at his own castle gates, with threats, that if he would not deliver up that his castle to the earl, he should suffer a miserable death: and when he was, by this barbarous usage, almost dead, carried to prison, there to endure further tortures." This feudal baron was s. by his son,

ROGER DE BERKELEY, the last of the original family of Berkeley, of Berkeley Castle, whose daughter and heiress, Alice, at the instigation of King Henry II., espoused

MAURICE DE BERKELEY, (son of Robert Fitshardinge, upon whom had been conferred, for his attachment to the Empress Maud, the lordship of Berkeley and Berkeley Harness, the confiscated possessions of the above Roger, the adherent of King Stephen; but, to reconcile the parties, King Henry, who had restored to Roger his manor and castle of Dursley, caused an agreement to be concluded between them, that the heiress of the ousted lord should be given in marriage to the heir of the new baron; and thus passed the feudal castle of Berkeley to another chief,) which Robert de Berkeley became feudal Lord of Berkeley upon the decease of his brother Henry, and dying in 1189, left six sons, and was *s.* by the eldest,

ROBERT DE BERKELEY, who, in the turbulent times of King John, forfeited his castle and lands by his participation in the rebellious proceedings of the barons, but upon submission, and paying a fine of nine hundred and sixty-five pounds, and one mark, had all restored save the castle and town of Berkeley, in the first year of Henry III. This nobleman, who had been a munificent benefactor to the church, died *s. p.* in 1219, and was *s.* by his brother,

THOMAS DE BERKELEY, who, in the 8th of Henry III., upon giving his two nephews as pledges for his fidelity, had restitution of Berkeley Castle. His lordship *m.* Joane, daughter of Ralph de Somery, Lord of Campden, in the county of Gloucester, and niece of William Marshal, Earl of Pembroke, and dying in 1243, was *s.* by his eldest son,

MAURICE DE BERKELEY, who *d.* in 1281, and was *s.* by his son,

THOMAS DE BERKELEY, who was summoned to parliament as a BARON, from the 23rd June, 1295, to the 15th May, 1321. This nobleman was of great eminence in the reigns of Edward I. and Edward II., being in the French, Welsh, and Scottish wars of those periods, particularly at the celebrated siege of KAERLAVEROCK. He was involved, however, at the close of his life, in the treason of Thomas, Earl of Lancaster. His lordship *m.* Jane, daughter of William de Ferrars, Earl of Derby, and dying in 1321, was *s.* by his son,

MAURICE DE BERKELEY, second baron, from whom we pass to

THOMAS, *fifth Lord Berkeley,* who *m.* Margaret, daughter and heiress of Gerard Warren, Lord Lisle, by whom he left an only child,

Elizabeth,* *m.* to Richard Beauchamp, Earl of Warwick, and had three daughters, viz.

1. Margaret, *m.* to John Talbot, first Earl of Shrewsbury (his lordship's second wife).
2. Alianor, *m.* first, to Thomas, Lord Ross, and secondly, to Edward, Duke of Somerset.
3. Elizabeth, *m.* to George Nevill, Lord Latimer.

His lordship *d.* on the 13th July, 1416, and thus leaving no male issue, his nephew,

JAMES BERKELEY, became his heir; and inheriting, by virtue of a special entail and fine, the castle and lordship of BERKELEY, with other lordships in the said fine specified, was summoned to parliament from the 9th of October, 1421, to 23d May, 1461. His lordship *m.* first, ———, daughter of Humphrey Stafford, of Hooke, in the county of Dorset, by whom he had no issue; and secondly, Isabel, widow of Henry, son and heir of William, Lord Ferrers, of Groby, and second daughter and co-heir of Thomas Mowbray, first Duke of Norfolk, Earl Marshal of England, by Elizabeth, his wife, eldest sister and co-heiress of Thomas Fitz-Alan, Earl of Arundel, by whom he had issue,

WILLIAM, his successor.

Maurice, successor to the barony at the decease of his brother.

James, killed in France.

Thomas, from whom descended the Berkeleys of Worcestershire and Herefordshire.

Elizabeth, *m.* to Thomas Burdett, Esq., of Arrow, in the county of Warwick.

Isabel, *m.* to Thomas Trye, Esq., of Hardwick, in the county of Gloucester.

Alice, *m.* to Richard Arthur, Esq., of Clapham, in the county of Somerset.

His lordship *m.* thirdly, Joan, daughter of John Talbot, first Earl of Shrewsbury, which lady, after his decease, *m.* Edmund Hungerford, Esq. Lord Berkeley *d.* in 1463, and was *s.* by his eldest son,

SIR WILLIAM DE BERKELEY, Knt., Baron Berkeley, who had been, when a boy, in the retinue of Henry Beaufort, Cardinal Bishop of Winchester. This nobleman having a dispute with Thomas Talbot, Viscount Lisle, regarding some landed property, the contest ran so high, that they encountered with their respective followers at Wotton-under-Edge, in 1469, when Lord Lisle was mortally wounded by an arrow shot through his mouth. In the next year, when the Duke of Clarence and the Earl of Warwick took up arms against the king, we find Lord Berkeley commanded, with Maurice Berkeley, of Beverstone, to muster and array all fitting to bear arms in the county of Glou-

---

* According to the usual descents of baronies in fee, (says Mr. Nicolas, in a note to his Synopsis,) the BARONY of BERKELEY, created by writ of summons of the 23d Edward I. devolved on the said Elizabeth, daughter and heir of Thomas, Lord Berkeley, instead of the heir male; but whether this anomaly arose from an idea then prevailing, that the tenure of the CASTLE OF BERKELEY conferred the barony, or that the heir male had the greatest political influence, cannot now, perhaps, be ascertained; the inference which may be drawn from the relative situations of the husband of the said Elizabeth, who was one of the most powerful noblemen of the time, and that of James Berkeley, who succeeded to the Barony, is, that the tenure of BERKELEY CASTLE was then considered to confer the dignity of Baron on its possessor, and consequently,

that the said James was allowed that dignity as his right, rather than by favour of the crown. If, however, modern decisions may be applied to the subject, the Barony of Berkeley, created by the writ of the 23d Edward I. is now in ABEYANCE between the descendants and representatives of the three daughters and co-heirs of Elizabeth, Countess of Warwick, above mentioned; and the barony merged in the present Earldom of Berkeley, is the new one created by the writ of the 9th of Henry V. to James Berkeley.

cester; and so great a regard had King Edward IV. for his lordship, that he created him VISCOUNT BERKELEY, on the 21st of April, 1481, with a grant of one hundred marks per annum, payable out of the customs of the port of Bristol, for life. The viscount was advanced to the EARLDOM OF NOTTINGHAM, (a dignity enjoyed by his ancestors, the Mowbrays,) by King Richard III., on the 28th of June, 1483; but his lordship afterwards espousing the cause of the Earl of Richmond, upon the accession of that nobleman to the throne, as Henry VII., was constituted EARL MARSHAL OF ENGLAND, with limitation of that great office to the heirs male of his body; and created on the 28th of January, 1488-99, MARQUESS OF BERKELEY. His lordship m. first, Elizabeth, daughter of Reginald West, Lord de la Warre, from whom he was divorced without having issue; secondly, Jane, widow of Sir William Willoughby, Knt., and daughter of Sir Thomas Strangeways, Knt., by whom he had two sons, who died young; and thirdly, Anne, daughter of John Fiennes, Lord Dacre, but had no issue. The Marquess d. thus s. p. on the 14th of February, 1491-2, when all the honors acquired by himself became EXTINCT, while the barony and castle of Berkeley, with his lordship's other estates, should have devolved upon his brother Maurice, but for a settlement made by the deceased nobleman, who seems to have been offended with his brother for marrying lowly, of the CASTLE OF BERKELEY, upon King Henry VII. and the heirs male of that monarch's body, which castle and lands were thus alienated until the decease of King Edward VI., the last male descendant of Henry VII., when they returned to the house of Berkeley, and have since been enjoyed by that noble family.*

---

* The dispute between Viscount Lisle, and William Lord Berkeley, is thus mentioned by Dugdale:—"But it was not long after, ere this Viscount L'Isle arrived at his full age; and thirsting after the Castle of Berkeley, practised with one Thomas Holt, the keeper of Whitley Park, and one Maurice King, porter of the castle, to betray it into his hands; one Robert Veel, (the Viscount's engineer,) being likewise an active person in that design, giving bond to Maurice King in the summe of an hundred pounds, that as soon as the work should be accomplished, he should be made keeper of Wotton Park, with the fee of five marks per annum during his life. But this plot being discovered by Maurice King, so much perplexed the Viscount L'Isle, that he forthwith sent this Lord Berkeley a challenge, 'requiring him of knighthood and manhood, to appoint a day, and to meet him half way, to try their quarrel and title, to eschew the shedding of Christian blood; or to bring the same day the utmost of his power.' This letter of challenge, under the hand of that Viscount, was sent 19th Martii, 10th Edward IV., he being then not full twenty-two years of age, having seed out his livery upon the 14th July before; and his wife then with child of her first born. Unto which the Lord Berkeley returned this answer in writing: viz. 'that he would not bring the tenth man he could make; and bid him to meet on the morrow, at Nybley Green, by eight or nine of the

ARMS—gu. a chev. betw. ten crosses, pattée, six in chief, and four in base, ar.

BERKELEY—BARONS BERKELEY, OF STRATTON.

By Letters Patent, dated 19th May, 1658.

Lineage.

Descended from the BARONS BERKELEY, of BERKELEY CASTLE, was,

SIR RICHARD BERKELEY, Knt., of Stoke-Gifford, in the county of Gloucester, who died in 1514, leaving issue by his wife, Elizabeth, daughter of Sir Humphrey Coningsby, Knt., two sons; namely, Sir John Berkeley, of Stoke-Gifford, ancestor to Lord Botetort, and

SIR MAURICE BERKELEY, K.B., of Bruton, in the county of Somerset, standard-bearer to King Henry VIII. and Edward VI., and to Queen Elizabeth. Of this gentleman it is mentioned, that, in the first year of Queen Mary, riding casually on London, he met with Sir Thomas Wiat at Temple Bar, and persuading him to yield himself to the queen, Sir Thomas took his advice, and, mounting behind Sir Maurice, rode to the court. Sir Maurice Berkeley m. first, Catherine, daughter of William Blount, Lord Mountjoy, and had issue two sons, Henry and Edward, and four daughters, viz.—

> Gertrude, m. to Edward Horne, Esq.
> Elizabeth, m. to James Percival, of Weston Gordon, Esq., in the county of Somerset.
> Anne, m. to Nicholas Poynings, Esq., of Adderley.
> Frances, d. unmarried.

Sir Maurice m. secondly, Elizabeth, daughter of Anthony Sands, Esq., by whom he had two sons and a daughter. He was s. at his decease by his eldest son,

SIR HENRY BERKELEY, Knt., who was s. by his eldest son,

SIR MAURICE BERKELEY, who received the honour of knighthood from the Earl of Essex, while serving under that nobleman in the expedition to Calais, anno 1596. Sir Maurice m. Elizabeth, daughter of Sir Henry Killigrew, of Hanworth, in the county of Middlesex, and had issue, five sons and two daughters; viz.—

> 1. CHARLES, who received the honour of knighthood at Bewley, in 1623, and, being eminently loyal to King Charles I., was sworn of the privy council upon the restoration of the monarchy, and appointed first, comptroller, and then treasurer, of the household. Sir Charles m. Penelope, daughter of Sir William Godolphin, of Godolphin, in the county of Cornwall, Knt., and had issue—
>
>> Maurice, created a baronet 2d July, 1660, successor to the viscounty of Fitzhardinge, &c. at the decease of his father; but died s. p.

clock, which standeth (saith he) on the borders of the Livelode that thou keepest untruly from me.' Whereupon, they accordingly met, and the Viscount L'Isle's visor being up, he was slain by an arrow shot through his head."

CHARLES, who for his fidelity to King Charles II. during his majesty's exile, and other eminent services, was created a peer of Ireland, as *Baron Berkeley, of Rathdown*, and VISCOUNT FITZHARDINGE, with remainder to his father, and his issue male; and a peer of England, on the 17th March, 1664, by the titles of *Baron Botetort, of Langport, in the county of Somerset*, and Earl of Falmouth. His lordship *m.* Elizabeth, daughter of Colonel Hervey Bagot, second son of Sir Henry Bagot, Bart., of Blithfield, in the county of Stafford, by whom he had an only daughter—

> Mary, *m.* to Gilbert Cosyn Gerrard, Esq., eldest son of Sir Gilbert Gerrard, Bart., of Feskerton, in the county of Lincoln, from whom she was divorced in 1684, and *d.* in 1693.

Lord Falmouth fell in a naval engagement with the Dutch, 3d June, 1665, and his remains were honourably interred in Westminster Abbey. At the decease of his lordship, his English honours EXPIRED, while those of Ireland reverted, according to the patent, to his father, Sir Charles Berkeley.

William (Sir), governor of Portsmouth, and vice-admiral of the white, killed at sea in 1666.

John, who succeeded his eldest brother, as VISCOUNT FITZHARDINGE, was treasurer of the chamber, and one of the tellers of the exchequer, in the reign of Queen Anne. He *m.* ———, daughter of Sir Edward Villiers, and sister to the Earl of Jersey, governess to his royal highness William Duke of Gloucester, and had issue—

> Mary, *m.* to Walter Chetwynd, Esq., of Ingestre, in the county of Stafford, who was created, in 1717, Baron Rathdown and Viscount Chetwynd, with the remainder to the heirs male of his father.

> Frances, *m.* to Sir Thomas Clarges, Bart.

His lordship *d.* on the 19th of December, 1712, and thus leaving no male issue, the Irish *Barony of Berkeley*, and VISCOUNTY OF FITZHARDINGE, became EXTINCT.

Sir Charles Berkeley, upon the decease of his second son, Charles, Earl of Falmouth, succeeding to that nobleman's Irish honours, became *Baron Berkeley of Rathdown*, and VISCOUNT FITZHARDINGE, of the kingdom of Ireland; and dying 12th June, 1668, those honours descended to his eldest son, Sir Maurice Berkeley, Bart.

2. Henry (Sir).
3. Maurice (Sir).
4. William (Sir).

52

5. John (Sir), of whom presently.
1. Margaret.
2. Jane.

The youngest son,

SIR JOHN BERKELEY, having a command in the army raised to march against the Scots, in 1638, received the honour of knighthood from the King at Berwick, in the July of that year, and at the breaking out of the rebellion, appearing in arms for his sovereign, was one of those very good officers, (as Lord Clarendon calls them,) who were ordered, with the Marquess of Hertford, to form an army in the west. But, before entering upon that duty, (in 1642,) Sir John safely conducted a supply of arms and ammunition from the queen into Holland. Soon after this, being constituted commissary-general, he marched into Cornwall at the head of about one hundred and twenty horse, and not only secured the whole of that county, but made incursions into Devonshire; and being in joint commission with Sir Ralph Hopton, obtained divers triumphs over the insurgents of those western shires in the several battles of Bradock, Saltash, Launceston, and STRATTON, as also at Modbury, in the county of Devon; subsequently investing Exeter, he reduced that garrison, and gallantly repulsed the enemy's fleet, then at Topsham, under the command of the Earl of Warwick; when he was constituted governor of Exeter, and general of all his majesty's forces in Devon. Sir John Berkeley stood so high in the estimation of the queen, that her majesty selected the city under his protection as the place of her accouchement, and was delivered, at Exeter, of the Princess Henrietta Maria; and writing to the king on the 13th March, 1644, she says, "Farewell, my dear heart: behold the mark • which you desire to have, to know when I desire any thing in earnest. I pray begin to remember what I spoke to you concerning Jacke Berkeley, for master of the wards." Exeter subsequently surrendered to Sir Thomas Fairfax, but its governor obtained the most honourable terms for its inhabitants and garrison. Sir John Berkeley was afterwards employed with Mr. Ashburnham, in endeavouring to negociate terms for the unfortunate Charles; and in a statement which he has given of the affair, attributes the ruin of the king to his misplaced confidence, after his escape from Hampton Court, in Colonel Hammond, governor of the Isle of Wight, at the instigation of Ashburnham, by whom Rapin is of opinion that Charles was betrayed; but Clarendon considers Ashburnham faithful, but outwitted by Cromwell. During the usurpation, Sir John Berkeley remained in exile with the royal family, and after the death of Lord Byron, in 1652, was placed at the head of the Duke of York's family, having the management of all his receipts and disbursements. In a few years afterwards, he was elevated to the peerage by the exiled monarch, as BARON BERKELEY, of *Stratton, in the county of Somerset*, (one of the scenes of his former triumphs over the rebels,) by letters patent, dated at Brussels in Brabant, on the 19th of May, 1658, in the 10th year of his majesty's reign. Upon the restoration of the monarchy, his lordship was sworn of the privy council; and at the close of the year

1669, was constituted lord lieutenant of Ireland, where he landed in 1670, and continued in the government for two years, when his lordship was succeeded by the Earl of Essex. In 1675, he was accredited ambassador extraordinary to the court of Versailles, and died on the 26th of August, 1678. His lordship had m. Christian, daughter and heiress of Sir Andrew Riccard, president of the East India Company, and widow of Henry Rich, Lord Kensington, son and heir of Henry, Earl of Holland, by whom he had three sons, all of whom eventually succeeded to the title, and one daughter, Anne, m. to Sir Dudley Cullum, Bart., of Hawsted, in the county of Suffolk. Lord Berkeley was s. by his eldest son,

CHARLES BERKELEY, second baron, captain of the Tiger man-of-war, who d. at sea, unmarried, in the twenty-fourth year of his age, on the 21st September, 1682, and was s. by his brother,

JOHN BERKELEY, third baron, groom of the stole, and first gentleman of the bed-chamber to Prince George of Denmark, and in the reign of King William, one of the admirals of the fleet, and colonel of the second regiment of marines. His lordship m. Jane Martha, daughter of Sir John Temple, Knt., of East Sheen, in the county of Surrey, (who was married, after his lordship's decease, to William, Earl of Portland,) by whom he had no surviving issue. He d. on the 27th February, 1696, and was s. by his brother,

WILLIAM BERKELEY, fourth baron, who was constituted chancellor of the Duchy of Lancaster, and sworn of the privy council, to Queen Anne, on the 20th September, 1710. His lordship m. Frances, youngest daughter of Sir John Temple, (aforesaid,) and had issue,

> JOHN, his successor.
>
> William, Captain of the Tiger man-of-war, on board of which he died, on the 25th March, 1733, s. p.
>
> Charles, m. in 1745, Frances, daughter of Colonel John West, and dying in 1765, left two daughters,
>
>> Frances-Sophia.
>> Mary.
>
> Jane, d. unm. .
>
> Frances, m. first, to William, Lord Byron, and secondly, to Sir Thomas Hay, Bart., of Alderston, N.B.
>
> Barbara, m. in 1736, to John Trevanion, Esq., of Carhays, Cornwall, by whom she had a son, William, and two daughters.
>
> Anne, m. in 1737, to James Cocks, Esq., of Ryegate, in the county of Surrey, by whom she left, at her decease in 1739, a son, James.

His lordship d. on the 24th of March, 1740, and was s. by his eldest son,

JOHN BERKELEY, fifth baron, who was constituted, in 1743, captain of the yeomen of his majesty's guard, sworn of the privy council in 1752, and appointed captain of the band of gentlemen pensioners in 1745. His lordship was subsequently constable of the Tower of London, and lord lieutenant of the Tower Hamlets. He m., but dying s. p. in 1773, the BARONY OF BERKELEY, OF STRATTON, became EXTINCT.

ARMS—gu. a chev., erm, betw. ten crosses pattée, ar.

BERKELEY—BARON BOTETOURT.

By Writ of Summons, dated 10th March, 1308,
1 Edward II.

Lineage.

In the year 1763,

NARBONNE BERKELEY, Esq., only son and heir of John Symes Berkeley, Esq., by his second wife, Elizabeth, daughter and co-heiress of Walter Narbonne, Esq., of Calne, in the county of Wilts, claimed the BARONY OF BOTETOURT, which had been in abeyance from the decease of Joyce, Lady Burnell, s. p. in 1406, grand-daughter of John de Botetourt, (see Botetourt, Barons Botetourt,) and his right being established, he was summoned to parliament in that ancient dignity, on the 13th April, 1764. But dying without issue in 1776, it again fell into ABEYANCE, and so remained, until once more called out in favour of Henry Somerset, fifth Duke of Beaufort, son and heir of Charles, fourth duke, by Elizabeth, (who d. in 1799,) sister and sole heiress of the above mentioned Narbonne, the deceased lord. The BARONY OF BOTETOURT is now therefore merged in the DUKEDOM OF BEAUFORT.

BERKELEY—EARL OF FALMOUTH.

By Letters Patent, dated 17th of March, 1664.

Lineage.

CHARLES BERKELEY, Esq., second son of Sir Charles Berkeley, Knt., and nephew of John, first Lord Berkeley, of Stratton, standing high in the favour of King Charles II., was elevated by that monarch to the peerage of Ireland, as Baron Berkeley and Viscount Fitzhardinge, with remainder, in default of male issue, to his father, and his male descendants; and afterwards created, on the 17th of March, 1664, a peer of England, in the dignities of *Baron Botetort, of Langport, in the county of Somerset*, and EARL OF FALMOUTH. His lordship m. Elizabeth, daughter of Colonel Hervey Bagot, second son of Sir Henry Bagot, Bart., of Blithfield in the county of Stafford, by whom he had an only daughter,

> Mary, who m. Gilbert Cosyn Gerrard, Esq., eldest son of Sir Gilbert Gerrard, Bart., of Feskerton, in the county of Lincoln, from whom she was divorced in 1684, and d. in 1693.

Lord Falmouth fell in a bloody naval engagement with the Dutch, on the 3rd of June, 1665, and his remains were honorably interred in Westminster Abbey. Dying thus without male issue, his lordship's English honours EXPIRED, while those of Ireland reverted, according to the limitation of the patent, to his father, Sir Charles Berkeley, who then became Charles, second Viscount Fitzhardinge, of that realm.

ARMS—Gu. a chevr. betw. ten crosses formée, ar. a label of three points.

BERMINGHAM — BARONS BERM-INGHAM.

By Writ of Summons, dated in 1326,
1 Edward III.

Lineage.

This family assumed its surname from the town of BERMINGHAM, in Warwickshire, which

PETER DE BERMINGHAM, Steward to Gervase Paganell, Baron of Dudley, held of that nobleman in the 19th of Henry II., with no less than nine knights' fees, de veteri feoffamento, of which William, his father, had been enfeoffed in the reign of Henry I. This Peter had a castle at Bermingham, which stood scarcely a bow-shot from the church to the westward, and by a charter from the crown, held a weekly Thursday market there, by which charter he had the liberties of *Thol, Theam, Sock, Sack,* and *Infungethef,*[*] to him and his heirs for ever. This Peter was s. by his son,

WILLIAM DE BERMINGHAM, who having m. Isabell, daughter of Thomas de Estley (or Astley), a great feudal lord, and joining his father-in-law in rebellion, fell at the battle of Evesham, in the 49th of Henry III., and was s. by his son,

WILLIAM DE BERMINGHAM, who, in the 22nd of Edward I. was in the expedition made then into Gascony, and in three years afterwards, he accompanied the Earl of Lincoln, and Sir John de St. John, to the relief of Belgrade, then besieged by the Earl of Arras. But the English army forming into two divisions, that under General St. John, in which William de Bermingham immediately served, had the misfortune to encounter the whole force of the enemy, led by the Earl of Arras himself, and to be totally routed, numbers falling in the field, and numbers being made prisoners, of which latter was this William Bermingham; to whom s. at his decease, his son,

WILLIAM DE BERMINGHAM, who was s. by his son,

WILLIAM DE BERMINGHAM, who having filled several eminent employments during the reign of Edward II., was summoned to parliament as BARON BERMINGHAM, in the 1st year of Edward III. But (says Dugdale) never afterwards,[†] so that I shall not pursue the story of him nor his descendants any farther, than to observe, that his grandson,

SIR THOMAS DE BERMINGHAM, left issue one sole daughter and heiress, Elizabeth, m. to Thomas de la Roche, of which marriage there were two daughters, co-heiresses, viz.

Elena, m. first, to Edward, Lord Ferrars, of Chartley, and secondly, to Philip Chetwynd.

Elizabeth, m. to George Longvill, Esq., ancestor of Charles Longvill, Baron Grey of Ruthyn and Hastings.

ARMS.—Per pale indented or. and gules.

---

[*] *Toll, &c.*—a power of punishing offenders within his own bounds; a power of obliging all that live in his jurisdiction to plead in his courts: a cognizance of all courts: a power to punish natives for theft.

[†] The collateral male line of the Berminghams

54

BERTIE — DUKES OF ANCASTER AND KESTEVAN, IN THE COUNTY OF LINCOLN. MARQUESSES OF LINDSEY. EARLS OF LINDSEY. BARONS WILLOUGHBY DE ERESBY.

The Barony, by Writ of Summons, dated
26th July, 1313.

Earldom,	} by Letters Patent	{ dated 22nd Nov., 1626.
Marquisate,		{ dated 29th Dec., 1706.
Dukedom,		{ dated 16th July, 1715.

Lineage.

The family of LINDSEY came originally into England from Bertiland, in Prussia, with the Saxons, and obtained from one of our Saxon monarchs a castle and town in the county of Kent, which was denominated from them BERTIE-Stad, (Saxon-town,) now Bersted, near Maidstone.

It appears from an old manuscript in the Cotton Library, that

LEOPOLD DE BERTIE was constable of Dover Castle, temp. King Ethelred, but opposing strongly the government upon some occasion, his son and heir,

LEOPOLD DE BERTIE, upon succeeding to the inheritance, apprehensive of his safety in consequence of his father's proceedings, fled to Robert, King of France, and marrying a French woman, settled in that kingdom, where his posterity continued until the year 1154, when

PHILIP BERTIE, accompanying King Henry II. into England, was restored by that monarch to his ancient patrimony in Bersted. From this Philip lineally descended,

THOMAS BERTIE, Esq., of Bersted, captain of Hurst Castle in the Isle of Wight, temp. Henry VII., who m. ——, daughter of, —— Say, Esq., of the county of Salop, and left a son and heir,

RICHARD BERTIE, Esq., who espoused Katherine Willoughby, Baroness Willoughby de Eresby, in her own right, and Duchess of Suffolk, in right of her first husband, CHARLES BRANDON, DUKE OF SUFFOLK, and had issue,

PEREGRINE, his successor.

Susan, m. first, to Reginald Gray, Earl of Kent, and secondly, to Sir John Wingfield.

During the reign of Queen Mary, the Duchess of Suffolk, being a zealous supporter of the reformation, was obliged to retire, accompanied by Mr. Bertie, from England, and they subsequently encountered great privations and dangers upon the continent, until received under the protection of the King of Poland, and placed by that monarch in the earldom of Crozan in Sanogelia. Mr. Bertie

---

continued however much longer than the race of barons, and possessed the lordship of Birmingham, until the close of King Henry VIII.'s reign, when Edward Bermingham was "*odly*" wrested out of it, according to Dugdale, by John Dudley, afterwards Viscount Lisle, Earl of Warwick, and Duke of Northumberland. From this family sprung also the Berminghams, Earls of Louth in Ireland.

died in 1582, two years after her grace, and was s.
by his son,

PEREGRINE BERTIE, Baron Willoughby
de Eresby, who being born in the Duchy of
Cleves, was naturalised by patent, dated 2nd August, 1588, and declared by order of Queen Elizabeth, by the Lord Treasurer Burghley, the Lord
Chamberlain Sussex, and the Earl of Leicester,
in the Star Chamber, on the 11th November, 1588,
entitled to the ancient Barony of Willoughby—
just as those high personages were about to sit down
to dinner, when his lordship was placed by them
in his proper situation at table; and he took his seat
in parliament on the Monday following, next to
Lord Zouch, of Harringworth. His lordship was
deputed, in 1582, to attend, with the Earl of Leicester, and other nobles, upon the Duke of Anjou,
into Antwerp, and was sent in the same year to
Frederick, King of Denmark, with the ensigns of
the Order of the Garter. In the 29th of Elizabeth,
Lord Willoughby was employed at the siege of
Zutphen in the Netherlands, and in an encounter
with the forces of the garrison, overthrew General
George Cressiak, Commander-in-chief of the cavalry, and took him prisoner. His lordship, in the
next year, upon the retirement of the Earl of Leicester, was appointed Commander-in-chief of the
English Auxiliary Forces in the United Provinces,
and most valiantly defended Bergen-op-Zoam,
against the Prince of Parma. He subsequently
commanded an English army sent into France, in
aid of the King of Navarra. Of this nobleman,
Sir Robert Naunton, says, in his Fragmenta Regalia, " That he was one of the Queen's first swords-
men, and a great master of the art military." His
lordship m. Mary, daughter of John Vere, Earl of
Oxford, sister and heiress of the whole blood, to
Edward, seventeenth Earl of Oxford, and had issue,
five sons,

Robert, Peregrine, Henry, Vere, and Roger,
with a daughter, Catherine, who m. Sir Lewis Watson, of Rockingham Castle, in the county of Northampton, afterwards Lord Rockingham. Lord Willoughby died in 1601, and was s. by his eldest son,

ROBERT BERTIE, as 10th Baron Willoughby de
Eresby. This nobleman claimed the Earldom of Oxford, and the Baronies of Bulbec, Sandford and Badlesmere, with the office of Lord High Chamberlain
of England in right of his mother, but succeeded
in establishing his right to the chamberlainship
only : he was, however, created Earl of Lindsey,
on the 22nd November, 1626, and in four years after
elected a Knight of the Most Noble Order of the
Garter. In the 7th of Charles I., he was constituted Constable of England, for the trial of Lord
Rea, and David Ramsey. In the 11th of the same
reign, he was made Lord High Admiral; and in
1639, upon the Scots taking up arms, he was appointed
Governor of Berwick. His lordship was chosen
General of the King's Forces, at the breaking out
of the Civil War, and fell at the battle of Edge
Hill, in 1642. Lord Willoughby m. Elizabeth,
only child of Edward, first Lord Montague, of
Boughton, and grand-daughter, maternally, of Sir
John Jefferies, Lord Chief Baron of the Exchequer,
and had issue,

Montagu, his successor.

Roger (Sir), K.B., m. Miss Lawley, daughter
and heiress of Sir Edward Lawley, Knt., and
d. in 1654.

Robert, d. in 1602.

Peregrine, m. Anne, daughter of William
Harvey, Esq., of Eveden, in the county of
Lincoln, with whom he acquired that seat
and settled there. He left at his decease,
an only daughter and heiress, Elizabeth,
who m. William, Lord Widrington.

Francis, Captain of Horse, killed in the king's
service, in Ireland, anno 1641.

Robert, m. first, Alice, daughter of Richard
Barnard, Esq., and secondly, Elizabeth,
second daughter of Sir Thomas Bennet, of
Baberham, in the county of Cambridge.

Henry, Captain of Horse, killed at Newberry,
fighting under the royal banner.

Vere, and Edward, died unmarried.

Catherine, m. to Sir William Paston, Bart.,
of Oxnead, in the county of Norfolk.

Elizabeth, m. to Sir Miles Stapleton, of Carlton, in the county of York.

Sophia, m. first, to the Rev. John Hewit, D.D.,
beheaded for his loyalty to King Charles I.,
and secondly, to Sir A. Shipman, Knt.

His lordship was s. by his eldest son,

MONTAGU BERTIE, second earl, who commanded the king's royal regiment of guards, at Edge
Hill, and being near his gallant father, when that nobleman fell wounded into the hands of the enemy,
voluntarily surrendered himself to a commander of
the horse on the rebel side, in order to be in attendance upon his afflicted parent. Being afterwards
exchanged, he continued zealously to support the
royal cause—and at the head of the guards fought at
the three battles of Newberry, at Cropredy, at Lost-
withiel, and at the fatal fight of Naseby, where he
was wounded; nor did he forsake his royal master to
the very last; for being one of the Lords of the Bed-
chamber, and of the Privy Council, he attended
personally upon the unhappy monarch, until his
majesty put himself into the hands of the Scots.
After the foul murder of the king, Lord Lindsey
compounded for his estate, and lived in privacy
until the restoration of the monarchy, when he was
called to the privy council, and elected a Knight of
the Most Noble Order of the Garter. His lordship
had the honour and gratification too of officiating at
the coronation of King Charles II., as Lord High
Chamberlain of England. The earl m. first,
Martha, daughter of Sir William Cockain, of Rushton, in the county of Northampton, Knt., and widow of James Ramsay, Earl of Holderness, by whom
he had,

Robert, his successor.

Peregrine, m. Susan, daughter and co-heiress
of Sir Edward Monins, Bart., of Waldershare in the county of Kent, and had two
daughters,

Bridget, wife of John, Earl of Poulet.

Mary, m. first, to Anthony Henley, Esq.,
of the Grange, in the county of Southampton ; and secondly, to the Honorable Henry Bertie, third son of James,
Earl of Abingdon.

Vere, Justice of the Common Pleas, temp. Charles II., d. unmarried in 1680.

Charles, of Uffington, in the county of Lincoln, m. Mary, daughter of Peter Tryon, Esq., of Harringworth, in the county of Northampton, and widow of Sir Samuel Jones, by whom he had a son,

    Charles, m. Mary, daughter and heiress of John Narbonne, Esq., of Great Stukley, in the county of Huntingdon, and had,

        Charles, m. to Bathsheba, daughter of Doctor Mead, and had several children.

    Elizabeth, m. to Charles Mildmay, Lord Fitz-Walter.

Elizabeth, m. to Baptist Noel, Viscount Campden.

Bridget, m. to Thomas Osborne, Duke of Leeds.

Catherine, m. to Robert Dormer, Esq., of Dourton, in the county of Bucks.

The earl m. secondly, Bridget, daughter and sole heiress of Edward Wray, Esq., (third son of Sir W. Wray, of Glentworth, in the county of Lincoln, Bart.,) by Elizabeth, his wife, daughter and heiress of Francis, Lord Norreys and Earl of Berkshire, and had issue,

JAMES, who succeeded to the Barony of Norreys, of Rycote, in the county of Oxford, and was created Earl of Abingdon: his lordship is ancestor to the extant Earls of Abingdon.

Henry, m. Philadelphia, daughter of Sir Edward Norris, of Western, in the county of Oxford, d. in 1734.

Mary, m. to Chs. Dormer, Earl of Caernarvon. His lordship d. on the 25th July, 1666, and was s. by his eldest son,

ROBERT BERTIE, third earl. This nobleman m. first, Mary, second daughter and co-heir of John Massingherd, Esq., and had an only daughter, Arabella, m. to Thomas Savage, Earl of Rivers. He m. secondly, Elizabeth, daughter of Philip, Lord Wharton, by whom he had five sons, viz.

ROBERT, his successor, who was summoned to the house of peers, as Baron Willoughby;

Peregrine, vice-chamberlain of the household to Queen Anne, and one of the tellers of the exchequer, died s. p. in 1711.

Philip d. unmarried in 1728.

Morris d. unmarried.

Albemarle.

His lordship m. thirdly, Elisabeth, daughter of Thomas Pope, Earl of Down, in Ireland, by whom he had a son and daughter, who both died unmarried. The earl d. on the 8th May, 1701, and was s. by his eldest son,

ROBERT BERTIE, Lord Willoughby de Eresby, as fourth earl, who was created MARQUESS OF LINDSEY on 29th December, 1706; and upon the decease of Queen Anne, was appointed one of the lords justices until the arrival of King George I. His lordship was subsequently called to the privy council, appointed lord-lieutenant and custos-rotulorum of the county of Lincoln, and elevated, on the 30th July, 1715, to the DUKEDOM OF ANCASTER AND

KESTEVEN. His grace m. first, 30th July, 1678, Mary, daughter of Sir Richard Wynn, of Gwydier, in the county of Caernarvon, Bart., by whom he had issue—

PEREGRINE, his successor,

And three daughters, who all died unmarried. He m. secondly, Albinia, daughter of Major-General William Farrington, of Chisselhurst, in Kent, by whom he had,

Vere, M.P. for Boston, m., in 1736, to Miss Anne Casey, of Braunston, near Lincoln, and left, in 1768, two daughters, his coheirs; viz.—

    Albinia, m. 27th May, 1757, to the Hon. George Hobart, who succeeded his brother as third earl of Buckinghamshire.

    Louisa.

Montagu, Capt. R.N., m. Elizabeth, daughter of William Piers, Esq., M.P. for Wells, and left, in 1753, two daughters—

    Augusta, m., in 1758, to John Lord Burghersh, afterwards Earl of Westmoreland.

Robert, a general officer in the army. In 1756 his lordship happened to be on board the Ramillies (proceeding to join his regiment in Minorca), with Admiral Byng, in the engagement with the French fleet off that island, and gave a very clear and candid evidence in behalf of that unfortunate officer, at his trial in the January following. Lord Robert sate in parliament successively for Whitechurch, Hants, and Boston in Lincolnshire. He m. Chetwynd, daughter and heir of Montagu, Viscount Blundell, in Ireland.

Thomas, Capt. R.N., d. unmarried, 21st July, 1749.

Louisa, m., in 1736, to Thomas Bludworth, Esq., gentleman of the horse to the Prince of Wales, and one of the grooms of the bedchamber.

His grace d. 26th July, 1723, and was s. by his eldest son,

PEREGRINE BERTIE, second duke, who had been summoned to parliament, in the life-time of his father, as LORD WILLOUGHBY DE ERESBY. His grace was called to the privy council in 1724, and appointed in the same year lord-lieutenant and custos-rotulorum of the county and city of Lincoln. In 1734 he was constituted lord warden and justice in Eyre of all his majesty's parks, chases, forests, &c. north of the Trent. The duke espoused Jane, one of the four daughters and co-heirs of Sir John Brownlow, Bart., of Belton, in the county of Lincoln, by whom he had

PEREGRINE, his successor.

Brownlow, who s. as fifth duke.

Mary, m. to Samuel Greteheed, Esq., of Guy's-Cliffe, near Warwick, and d. in 1774.

Albinia, m. to John Beckford, Esq., and d. in 1754.

Jane, m. to Captain Matthews.

Carolina, m. to George Dewar, Esq., and d. in 1774.

His grace d. on the 1st January, 1742, and was s. by his eldest son,

PEREGRINE BERTIE, third duke, who m. first, 22nd May, 1735, Elizabeth, daughter and sole heiress of William Blundell, Esq., of Basingstoke, in the county of Southampton, and relict of Sir Charles Gunter Nichols, K.B., but had no issue. His grace, m. secondly, 27th November, 1750, Mary, daughter of Thomas Panton, Esq., by whom he had surviving issue,

    ROBERT, his successor.

    Priscilla-Barbara-Elizabeth, m. 23rd February, 1779, to Peter Burrell, Esq., of Beckenham, Kent, afterwards created a baronet, and elevated to the peerage, as BARON GWYDYR. (See Willoughby de Eresby—Burke's Dictionary of the Peerage and Baronetage.)

    Georgiana-Charlotte, m. to James, first Marquess Cholmondeley.

In 1745, on the breaking out of the rebellion in Scotland, his grace raised a regiment of foot for his majesty's service, and attained through the different gradations, the rank of general in the army, in 1772. At the coronation of King George III., the duke officiated as LORD GREAT CHAMBERLAIN OF ENGLAND. In 1766, he was appointed Master of the Horse; he was also Recorder of Lincoln. He d. on the 12th April, 1778, and was s. by his son,

ROBERT BERTIE, fourth duke, at whose decease, unmarried, 8th July, 1779, the BARONY OF WILLOUGHBY DE ERESBY fell into ABEYANCE between his grace's two sisters, but was called out by the crown, in the following year, in favour of the elder, and is now enjoyed by her ladyship's son and heir. The LORD GREAT CHAMBERLAINSHIP devolved jointly upon the two ladies; while his grace's other honours reverted to his uncle,

LORD BROWNLOW BERTIE, as fifth duke. This nobleman m. first, 6th November, 1762, Harriot, daughter and sole heiress of George Morton Pitt, Esq., of Twickenham, in the county of Middlesex, but her grace d. in the following year without issue. He m. secondly, 2nd January, 1769, Mary Anne, youngest daughter of Major Layard, by whom, (who d. 13th January, 1804,) he had an only daughter, MARY-ELIZABETH, m. 26th May, 1793, to Thomas, Viscount Milsington, now Earl of Portmore—and left at her decease, in 1797, an only son, BROWNLOW-CHARLES, who inherited the great personal estates of his grandfather, the Duke of Ancaster, but died at Rome, in 1818, of wounds received from a banditti. His grace d. in 1809, when the DUKEDOMS OF ANCASTER AND KESTAVEN, and the MARQUESITE AND EARLDOM OF LINDSEY, became EXTINCT.

ARMS—Ar., three battering rams, bar-ways, in pale, proper, armed and garnished azure.

The following quaint old ballad, was written to commemorate the sufferings of her Grace, the Duchess of Suffolk; and her husband, Mr. Bertie, during their exile, in the reign of Queen Mary. It is entitled, "The most rare and excellent history of the Duchess of Suffolk, and her husband Richard Bertie's calamities. To the tune of Queen Dido." Originally published in the reign of Queen Elizabeth.

" When God had taken, for our sin,
    That prudent prince, King Edward, away,
Then bloody Bonner did begin
    His raging malice to bewray;
All those that did God's word profess,
He persecuted more or less.

Thus while the Lord on us did low'r,
    Many in prison he did throw,
Tormenting them in Lollards' Tower,[*]
    Whereby they might the truth forego;
Then Cranmer, Ridley, and the rest,
Were burning in the fire that Christ profess'd.

Smithfield was then with faggots fill'd,
    And many places more beside;
At Coventry was Saunders kill'd,
    At Worcester eke good Hooper died;
And to escape this bloody day
Beyond sea many fled away.

Among the rest that sought relief,
    And for their faith in danger stood,
Lady Elizabeth was chief,
    King Henry's daughter of royal blood;
Who in the Tower did prisoner lie,
Looking each day when she should die.

The Dutchess of Suffolk seeing this,
    Whose life likewise the tyrant sought,
Who in the hopes of heavenly bliss,
    Within God's word her comfort wrought;
For fear of death was forc'd to fly,
And leave her house most secretly.

That for the love of God alone,
    Her lands and goods she left behind;
Seeking still that precious stone,
    The word and truth so rare to find;
She with her husband, nurse and child,
In poor array their sighs beguil'd.

Thus thro' London they pass'd along,
    Each one did take a several street;
And all along escaping wrong,
    At Billingsgate they all did meet;
Like people poor, in Gravesend barge,
They simply went with all their charge.

And all along from Gravesend town,
    With journey short, on foot they went;
Unto the sea-coast came they down,
    To pass the seas was their intent;
And God provided so that day,
That they took ship, and sail'd away.

And with a prosp'rous gale of wind
    In Flanders they did safe arrive;
This was to them great ease of mind,
    And from their hearts much woe did drive
And so, with thanks to God on high,
They took their way to Germany.

Thus as they travell'd still disguis'd,
    Upon the highway suddenly
By cruel thieves they were surpris'd,
    Assaulting their small company;
And all their treasure, and their store,
They took away, and beat them sore,

---

[*] There is a place so named, in the palace of the Archbishop of Canterbury at Lambeth.

The nurse, amidst of all their fright,
Laid down the child upon the ground;
She ran away out of their sight,
And never after that was found.
Then did the Dutchess make great moan,
With her good husband all alone.

The thieves had then their horses kill'd,
And all their money quite had took;
The pretty baby almost spoil'd,
Was by the nurse likewise forsook;
And they far from their friends did stand,
And succourless in a strange land.

The sky likewise began to scoul,
It hail'd and rain'd in piteous sort,
The way was long, and wond'rous foul;
Then may I now full well report,
Their grief and sorrow were not small,
When this unhappy chance did fall.

Sometimes the Dutchess bore the child,
As wet as ever she could be,
And when the lady, kind and mild,
Was weary, then the child bore he;
And thus they one another eas'd,
And with their fortunes seemed well pleas'd.

And after many a weary step,
All wet-shod both in dirt and mire;
After much grief their hearts yet leap,
For labour doth some rest require;
A town before them they did see,
But lodged there they could not be.

From house to house then they did go,
Seeking that night where they might lie;
But want of money was their woe,
And still their babe with cold did cry;
With cap and knee they court'sy make,
But none of them would pity take.

Lo! here a princess of great blood,
Doth pray a peasant for relief,
With tears bedewed as she stood,
Yet few or none regard her grief:
Her speech they could not understand,
But some gave money in her hand.

When all in vain her speech was spent,
And that they could not house-room get,
Into a church-porch* then they went,
To stand out of the rain and wet;
Then said the Dutchess to her dear,
" O, that we had some fire here!"

Then did her husband so provide,
That fire and coals they got with speed;
She sat down by the fire side,
To dress her daughter that had need;
And while she dress'd it in her lap,
Her husband made the infant pap.

Anon the sexton thither came,
And finding them there by the fire,
The drunken knave, all void of shame,
To drive them out was his desire;
And spurning out the noble dame
Her husband's wrath he did inflame.

And all in fury as he stood,
He wrung the church-keys from his hand,
And struck him so that all the blood
Ran down his head as he did stand;
Wherefore the sexton presently,
For aid and help aloud did cry.

Then came the officers in haste,
And took the Dutchess and her child;
And with her husband thus they past.
Like lambs beset with tigers wild;
And to the governor were brought,
Who understood them not in aught.

Then Master Birtle, brave and bold,
In Latin made a gallant speech,
Which all their mis'ries did unfold,
And their high favour did beseech.
With that, a doctor sitting by
Did know the Dutchess presently.

And thereupon arising straight,
With looks abased at the sight;
Unto them all that there did wait,
He thus broke forth in words aright :
" Behold! within your sight," quoth he,
" A princess of most high degree!"

With that the governor, and all the rest,
Were much amaz'd the same to here!
Who welcomed this new come guest,
With rev'rence great, and princely cheer!
And afterwards convey'd they were,
Unto their friend, Prince Casimir.

A son she had in Germany,
Peregrine Bertie call'd by name,
Surnam'd the good Lord Willoughby,
Of courage great, and worthy fame :
Her daughter young, that with her went,
Was afterwards Countess of Kent.

For when Queen Mary was deceas'd,
The Dutchess home return'd again;
Who was of sorrow quite releas'd
By Queen Elizabeth's happy reign;
Whose godly life and piety
We may praise continually.

BERTRAM — BARONS BERTRAM, OF MITFORD.

By Writ of Summons, dated 14th December, 1264,
49 Henry III.

Lineage.

In the reign of King Henry I.,
WILLIAM BERTRAM, with the approbation of
his wife and sons, founded the Augustinian Priory,
of BRINKBURNE, in the county of Northumberland, and was s. at his decease by his son,
ROGER BERTRAM, who, in the 12th of
Henry II., upon the assessment in aid of the marriage portion of the king's daughter, certified his
knight's fees to be six and a half; and, in the 18th

---

* Of St. Willebrode, at Wesel, in Germany, where
the Duchess fell in labour, and was delivered of a
son, called Peregrine, afterwards Lord Willoughby
de Eresby.

of the same monarch, paid six pounds, ten shillings, scutage for not going in person, nor sending soldiers, upon the expedition then made into Ireland. To this feudal lord succeeded his son and heir,

WILLIAM BERTRAM, who obtained a grant from the crown, in the 5th year of King John, of the manor of Felton, in Northumberland, with all the woods thereunto belonging. He m. Alice, sister of Robert de Umfravil, and died in or before the 7th year of the same reign, for at that time we find King John conferring the wardship of his lordship's son and heir, Roger, upon Peter de Brus, with the custody of his lands during the minority, in consideration of the sum of three hundred marks. To the possession of which lands succeeded, when at full age, the said

ROGER BERTRAM. This feudal lord being involved in the proceedings of the barons, in the 17th of King John, his castle and lands of Mitford were seized, and conferred upon Philip de Ulecotes: but afterwards making his peace, and Philip de Ulecotes not seeming willing to obey the king's mandate in restoring those lands, he was threatened with the immediate confiscation of his own territorial possessions, in the counties of York, Nottingham, and Durham. After this period Roger Bertram appears to have enjoyed the royal favour; and in the 13th of Henry III., when Alexander of Scotland was to meet the English monarch at York, he was one of the great northern barons who had command to attend him thither. He d. in 1241, and was s. by his son,

ROGER BERTRAM, who, in the 42nd of Henry III., had command, with other great barons of the north, to march into Scotland for the rescue of the young king of Scots, the king of England's son-in-law, out of the hands of his rebellious subjects: but, in the 48th of the same monarch, being in arms with the other rebellious barons, he was taken prisoner at NORTHAMPTON, and his castle of Mitford seized upon by the escheator of the crown, while he was himself committed to the custody of William de Valence. He must, however, have made his peace very soon afterwards, for we find him summoned to parliament as a BARON, in the next year, 14th December, 1264. His lordship had issue—

Roger, his successor.

Agnes, m. to Thomas Fitz-William, Lord of Elmeley and Sprotborough, in the county of York, and had issue—
WILLIAM FITZ-WILLIAM, who was succeeded by his son,
WILLIAM FITZ-WILLIAM, (from whom the extant Earls Fitz-William descend,) one of the co-heirs of the BARONY and estates at the decease of his cousin, AGNES BERTRAM.

Isabel, m. to —— Darcy, and had Norman Darcy, who was s. by his son,
PHILIP DARCY, one of the co-heirs of the BARONY and estates at the decease of his cousin, AGNES BERTRAM.

Christian, m. to ————, and had a son,
ELIAS DE PENULBURY, one of the co-

heirs to the BARONY and lands, at the decease of his cousin, AGNES BERTRAM.

Ada, m. to —— de Vere, and had a daughter, Isabel, whose son,
GILBERT DE ATON, was one of the co-heirs to the BARONY and lands, at the decease of his cousin, AGNES BERTRAM.

The baron was s. at his decease by his son,

ROGER BERTRAM, second baron, but never summoned to parliament. This nobleman d. in 1311, leaving an only daughter and heiress,

AGNES BERTRAM, at whose decease, without issue, the BARONY OF BERTRAM OF MITFORD, fell into ABEYANCE, between her ladyship's cousins and co-heirs, mentioned above, and so continues amongst their representatives.

Arms—As. an escutcheon or.

BIGOD—EARLS OF NORFOLK.

By creation of King Stephen, and also of King Henry II.

Lineage.

The first of this great family that settled in England, was

ROGER BIGOD, who in the Conqueror's time possessed six lordships in Essex, and a hundred and seventeen in Suffolk. This Roger adhering to the party that took up arms against William Rufus, in the first year of that monarch's reign, fortified the castle of Norwich, and wasted the country around. At the accession of Henry I. being a witness of the king's laws, and staunch in his interests, he obtained Framingham in Suffolk, as a gift from the crown. We find further of him, that he founded in 1103, the Abbey of Whetford, in Norfolk, and that he was buried there at his decease in four years after, leaving by Adeliza, a son and heir,

WILLIAM BIGOD, steward of the household to King Henry I., one of the unhappy persons who perished with the king's children and several of the nobility, in the memorable shipwreck which occurred in the 20th of that monarch's reign. This feudal lord leaving no issue, his great possessions devolved upon his brother,

HUGH BIGOD, also steward to King Henry I., who, being mainly instrumental in raising Stephen, Earl of Boloigne, to the throne, upon the decease of his royal master, was rewarded by the new king with the EARLDOM OF THE EAST ANGLES, commonly called NORFOLK, and by that designation we find him styled in 1140 (6th Stephen). His lordship remained faithful in his allegiance to King Stephen through the difficulties which afterwards beset that monarch, and gallantly defended the castle of Ipswich against the Empress Maud and her son, until obliged at length to surrender for want of timely relief. In the 19th Henry II., this powerful noble certified his knight's fees to be one hundred and twenty-five " de veteri feoffamento," and thirty-five " de Novo," upon the occasion of the assessment in aid of the marriage of the king's daughter: and he appears to have acquired at this period a considerable degree of royal favour; for we find him not only recreated EARL OF NORFOLK by charter, dated at Northampton, but by the same instrument obtaining a grant of the office of steward, to hold in as ample a manner as his father had done in the time of Henry I. Notwithstanding, however, these and other equally substantial marks of the king's liberality, the Earl of Norfolk arrayed himself under the banner of Robert, Earl of Leicester, in the insurrection incited by that nobleman in favour of the king's son, (whom Henry himself had crowned,) in the 19th of the monarch's reign; but his treason upon this occasion cost him the surrender of his strongest castles, and a fine of a thousand marks. After which he went into the Holy Land, with the Earl of Flanders, and died in 1177.

His lordship had married first, Julian, daughter of Alberic de Vere, by whom he had a son ROGER; and secondly, Gundred ——, who brought him two sons, Hugh and William. He was s. by his eldest son,

ROGER BIGOD, second earl, who, in the first year of Richard I., had a charter dated at Westminster, 27th November, reconstituting him EARL OF NORFOLK, and Steward of the Household, his lordship obtaining at the same time restitution of some manors, with grants of others, and confirmation of all his wide-spreading demesne. In the same year he was made one of the ambassadors from the English monarch to Philip of France, for obtaining aid towards the recovery of the Holy Land. But for the privilege of enjoying the Earldom of Norfolk, and that Hugh, his brother, should not have livery of any lands which were his father's, except by judgment of the king's court, and his peers, he paid no less than a thousand marks to the king. Upon the return of King Richard from his captivity, the Earl of Norfolk assisted at the great council held by the king at Nottingham; and at his second coronation, his lordship was one of the four earls that carried the silken canopy over the monarch's head. In the reign of King John, he was one of the barons that extorted the great CHARTERS OF FREEDOM from that prince, and was amongst the twenty-five lords appointed to enforce their fulfilment. His lordship m. Isabel, daughter of Hamelyn, Earl of Warren and Surrey, and had issue,

  HUGH, his successor.

  William, m. Margaret, daughter of Robert de Sutton, with whom he acquired considerable property.

  Thomas.

  Margery, m. to William de Hastings.

  Adelina, m. to Alberic de Vere, Earl of Oxford.

  Mary, m. to Ralph Fitz Robert, Lord of Middleham.

The earl d. in 1220, and was s. by his eldest son,

HUGH BIGOD, third earl, who m. Maud, eldest daughter of William Mareschal, Earl of Pembroke, and had issue,

  ROGER, his successor.

  Hugh, an eminent lawyer, appointed CHIEF JUSTICE OF ENGLAND, by the barons in 1257. He m. first, Joane, daughter of Robert Burnet, by whom he had issue,

    ROGER, successor to his uncle in the earldom.

    John.

He m. secondly, Joane, daughter of Nicholas Stuteville, and widow of —— Wake, but had no issue. His lordship fell under the baronial banner at the battle of Lewes.

Ralph, m. Berta, daughter of the Baron Furnival, and had a daughter,

  Isabel, who m. first, Gilbert, son of Walter de Lacy, Lord of Meath in Ireland; and secondly, John Fitz Geoffrey.

His lordship who was also one of the twenty-five barons appointed to enforce the observance of MAGNA CHARTA, d. in 1225, and was s. by his eldest son,

ROGER BIGOD, fourth earl, whose guardianship Alexander, King of Scotland, obtained, for five hundred marks. This nobleman attained high reputation in all martial and warlike exercises. Skilful and valiant alike in the tilting, and the battle field, he held a high rank amongst the chivalrous spirits of his day, and won many a trophy in court and camp. In the tournament held at Blithe, in Nottingham, (21st Henry III.,) which terminated in a conflict between the southern and northern lords, the Earl of Norfolk was pre-eminently distinguished, and in a few years afterwards he gained new laurels at the battle of Zantoigne. But the most remarkable event in his lordship's life was his personal dispute with King Henry III., as thus stated by Dugdale: "In the 39th Henry III., the Earl of Norfolk making a just apology for Robert de Ros, (a great baron of that age,) then charged with some crime, which endangered his life, he had very harsh language given him by the king, being openly called *traytor*: whereat, with a stern countenance he told him (the king) *that he lied; and, that he never was, nor would be a traytor*; adding, ' if you do nothing but what the law warranteth, you can do me no harm.'—' Yes,' quoth the king, ' I can thrash your corn, and sell it, and so humble you.' To which he replied, ' If you do so, I will send you the heads of your threshers.' But by the interposing of the lords then present, this heat soon passed over; so that (shortly after) he was, together with the Earl of Leicester, and some others, sent on an embassy to the King of France, to treat with him for restoring some rights, which he withheld from the king." His lordship was subsequently appointed by the barons, after their victory at Lewes, (48th Henry III.,) Governor of the Castle of Orford, in Suffolk. To this nobleman, by reason of his mother MAUD, being the eldest co-heiress of William Mareschal, Earl of Pembroke, the MARSHALSHIP OF ENGLAND, with the rights thereunto belonging, was assigned. His lordship espoused Isabel, sister of Alexander, King of Scotland, but dying issueless, all his honours and possessions devolved upon his nephew, (refer to Hugh, second son of the third earl,)

ROGER BIGOD, fifth Earl of Norfolk, and second Earl Marshal of this family. This nobleman took a distinguished part in the wars of King Edward I., having previously, however, in conjunction with the Earl of Hereford, compelled even that resolute monarch to ratify THE GREAT CHARTER, AND CHARTER OF THE FOREST. His lordship m. first, Aliva, daughter and heiress of Philip, Lord Basset, and widow of Hugh Despencer, slain at Evesham, and secondly, Joane, daughter of John de Anesine, Earl of Bayonne, but had no issue by neither. In the 20th of Edward I., the earl constituted that monarch his heir, and surrendered into his hands, the marshal's rod, upon condition that it should be returned, in the event of his having children, and that he should receive £1000. prompt, and £1000. a year for life. In consequence of which surrender, his lordship was re-created EARL OF NORFOLK, in 1302, with remainder to his heirs male, by his first wife, but dying without issue, as stated above, in five years afterwards, the EARLDOM became, according to the surrender, EXTINCT, in the BIGOD family : although his lordship left a brother,

JOHN BIGOD, his heir at law, whose right seems to have been annihilated in this very unjust and extraordinary manner—and so completely destroyed, that he did not even inherit any of the great estates of his ancestors.

ARMS—Gules, a lion passant, or.

BLOUNT—BARONS MONTJOY OF THURVESTON, IN THE COUNTY OF DERBY, AND EARL OF DEVONSHIRE.

Barony, by Charter, dated 20th June, 1465.
Earldom, by Letters Patent, dated 21st July, 1603.

Lineage.

BLOUND, Lord of Guisnes, in France, had three sons, who accompanied the Conqueror into England, one of whom returned into Normandy, while the other two,

SIR ROBERT and SIR WILLIAM, } remained, and participated, largely, in the spoils of conquest —Sir William obtaining several lordships in Lincolnshire, and

SIR ROBERT LE BLOUND, no less than thirteen lordships in the county of Suffolk, of which Ixworth was the head of the feudal barony. The great grandson and lineal descendant of this Sir Robert,

GILBERT LE BLOUND, Lord of Ixworth, m. Agnes de Lisle, and had two sons,

WILLIAM, who succeeded to the feudal barony, and marrying Cicely de Vere, had issue,

WILLIAM, Baron of Ixworth, standard-bearer to the army of the insurgent barons, under Simon Monfort, Earl of Leicester, and slain at the battle of Lewes, temp. Henry III., when leaving no issue, the male line of the Barons of Ixworth ceased, and his sisters became his co-heirs.

Agnes, m. to Sir William de Cricketot.
Rohese, m. to Robert de Valoines. } Co-heirs.

Stephen, m. Mary, only daughter and heiress of Sir William le Blound, of Saxlingham, in the county of Suffolk, (fourth, in a direct line, from Sir William, brother of Sir Robert,) and from this union sprang the

BLOUNTS, of which we are now about to treat, as well as the still existing families of the name in England.

WALTER BLOUNT, (descended from the said Stephen,) was made treasurer of Calais in the 39th of Henry VI., and had the same office confirmed to him upon the accession of King Edward IV. In the 4th year of which latter monarch's reign, he was constituted, by letters patent, dated 24th November, LORD TREASURER OF ENGLAND, and the next year, advanced, by charter, dated 20th June, to the peerage, by the title of BARON MONTJOY, of Thurveston, in the county of Derby. This nobleman became so staunch an adherent of the House of York, that he shared largely in the confiscated estates of the leading Lancastrians—particularly in those of Sir William Carey, Sir William Vaux, and Thomas Courtenay, Earl of Devon, obtaining thereby extensive territorial possessions in the counties of Devon, Cornwall and Worcester. He was also honoured with the GARTER. His lordship m. Anne, widow of Humphrey, Duke of Buckingham, and had several children, of whom the eldest son,

JOHN, died in the life-time of his father, leaving issue by Margaret, daughter and heiress of Sir Thomas Itchingham,

Edward, successor to his grandfather.
Elizabeth, m. to Andrews Windsor, who was summoned to parliament as BARON WINDSOR, in 1529.

His lordship d. in 1474, and was s. by his grandson,

EDWARD BLOUNT, second baron, who died the following year, having attained only the eighth year of his age, when his estates devolved upon his sister, but the Barony of Montjoy reverted to his uncle,

JOHN BLOUNT, third baron, who d. in 1485, leaving by his will, bearing date on the 6th October in that year, a chain of gold, with a gold lion set with diamonds, to his son, Rowland Blount, and to his daughter, Constantine, £100. for her marriage portion. His lordship was s. by his eldest son,

WILLIAM BLOUNT, fourth baron. This nobleman was called to the privy council, upon the accession of King Henry VII., and was constituted in the 1st year of Henry VIII., Master of the Mint in the Tower of London, as also throughout the whole realm of England, and the town of Calais. His lordship subscribed, in the latter reign, to the articles against Cardinal Wolsey, and the letter to Pope Clement the VIIth, regarding the King's divorce from Queen Catherine. He m. first, Elizabeth, daughter and heiress of Sir William Say, by whom he had an only daughter, Gertrude, m. to Henry Courtenay, Marquess of Exeter. His lordship m. secondly, Dorothy, daughter of Henry Keble, by whom he had a son, CHARLES, and thirdly, Alice ——. He d. in 1535, and was s. by his son,

CHARLES BLOUNT, fifth baron, who in the 36th Henry VIII., served in the rear-guard of the army then sent into France, and by his testament made at that time, ordained a stone to be laid over his grave, in case he should there be slain, with the following epitaph, as a memento to his children, to continue and keep themselves worthy of so much honour, as to be called forward to die in the cause of their king and country.

Willingly have I sought,
    And willingly have I found,
The fatal end that wrought
    Me hither, as duly bound.

Discharg'd I am of that I ought
    To my country by honest ownde ;
My soul departed Christ hath bought,
    The end of man is ground.

His lordship died in the following year, anno 1545, leaving issue by his wife Anne, daughter of Robert, Lord Willoughby de Broke, three sons, JAMES, Francis, and William, of whom the eldest,

JAMES BLOUNT, succeeded as sixth baron. This nobleman was one of the peers who sate in judgment upon Thomas, Duke of Norfolk, temp. Elizabeth. His lordship *m.* Catherine, daughter of Sir Thomas Wills, of the county of York, and had two sons, William and Charles. He *d.* in 1593, and was *s.* by the elder, ·

WILLIAM BLOUNT, seventh baron, who *d.* in 1594, *s. p.*, and was *s.* by his brother,

CHARLES BLOUNT, eighth baron. This nobleman, when a commoner, being a person of high military reputation, had a command in the fleet which defeated the famous Spanish Armada: and a few years afterwards succeeded the Earl of Sussex in the governorship of Portsmouth. In 1597, his lordship was constituted lieutenant of Ireland; and in two years after repulsed the Spaniards with great gallantry at Kinsale. Upon the accession of King James, he was reinvested with the same important office, and created by letters patent, dated 21st July, 1603, EARL OF DEVONSHIRE, being made at the same time a knight of the most noble order of the GARTER. The high public character of the earl was, however, considerably tarnished by one act of his private life, the seduction of Penelope, sister of the Earl of Essex, and wife of Robert, Lord Rich. By this lady he had several children ; and upon his return from Ireland, finding her divorced from her husband, he married her at Wanstead, in Essex, on the 26th of December, 1605, the ceremony being performed by his chaplain, William Laud, afterward Archbishop of Canterbury. Camden says, that this nobleman was so eminent for valour and learning, that in those respects, " he had no superior, and but few equals," and his secretary Moryson, writes, " that he was beautiful in person, as well as valiant ; and learned, as well as wise." His lordship *d.* on the 3rd April, 1606, and leaving no *legitimate* issue, all his honours became EXTINCT.

ARMS.—Barry nebulée of six or. and sa.

BLOUNT—BARONS MONTJOY, OF THURVESTON, IN THE COUNTY OF DERBY, AND EARLS OF NEWPORT.

Barony, } by Letters { ———— 1627.
Earldom, } Patent, { 3rd August, 1628.

Lineage.

MONTJOY BLOUNT, Esq., illegitimate son of Charles Blount, Earl of Devonshire, by Penelope,

daughter of Walter Devereux, first Earl of Essex, of that family—the divorced wife of Robert, Lord Rich, (whom the Earl of Devonshire subsequently married,)—was elevated to the peerage of Ireland, as LORD MONTJOY, OF MONTJOY FORT, by King James I., and created in the following reign, anno 1627, BARON MONTJOY *of Thurveston, in the county of Derby*, and EARL OF NEWPORT, on the 3rd August, 1628. His lordship *m.* Anne, daughter of John, LORD BUTLER, of Bramfield, and dying in 1665, was *s.* by his eldest son,

GEORGE BLOUNT, second earl, at whose decease, unmarried, in 1676, the honours devolved upon his brother,

CHARLES BLOUNT, third earl, who likewise died a bachelor, in the same year, and was *s.* by his only surviving brother,

HENRY BLOUNT, 4th earl. This nobleman *m.* Susanna, daughter of John Briscoe, Esq., and widow of Edmund Mortimer, Esq.: by dying *s. p.*, in 1681, all his honours EXPIRED.

ARMS—Barry nebulée of six or and sa.

BLOUNT—BARON BLOUNT.

By Writ of Summons, dated 25th January, 1340, 4 Edward III.

Lineage.

WILLIAM LE BLUND, OR BLOUNT, having *m.*, in the 2nd Edward III., Margery, one of the daughters and co-heiresses of Theobald de Verdon, obtained livery of the castle of Webbele, in the county of Hereford, with divers other lands and lordships, as her portion of the inheritance, and was summoned to parliament as a BARON, from the 25th January, 1330, to 18th August, 1337. His lordship had a command in the Scottish wars, in the 9th of Edward III. He *d.* in 1337, and leaving no issue, the BARONY OF BLOUNT EXPIRED, while his lordship's estates devolved upon his brother and heir, John Blount, of Sodington, in the county of Worcester, from whom descend the present Baronets (Blount) of Sodington.

ARMS—Barry, nebulée of six or. and sa.

BLOUNT—BARON BLOUNT.

By Writ of Summons, dated 3rd December, 1396, 20 Edward II.

Lineage.

THOMAS LE BLOUNT, descended from a younger branch of the great feudal baronial house of Blound, of Ixworth, (see Blount, Lords Mountjoy, and Earls of Devonshire,) was summoned to parliament as a BARON, from the 3rd December, 1396, to the 15th June, 1398. His lordship *m.* Julian, daughter of Thomas de Leiburn, and widow of John, Lord Bergavenny, but it does not appear that he had any issue. In the 20th of Edward II., Lord Blount being steward of the king's household, espoused the cause of the queen after the taking of Bristol, and the flight of the king into Wales. Of this nobleman or his descendants, nothing further

being known, it is presumed that the barony EX-
PIRED at his decease.

ARMS—Barry nebulée of six or and se.

BLOUNT—EARL OF DEVONSHIRE.

By Letters Patent, dated 21st July 1603.

Lineage.

See Courtenay, Earls of Devon.

BOHUN—BARONS BOHUN OF MID-
HURST.

By Writ of Summons, dated 1st June, 1363.
37th Edward III.

Lineage.

In addition to the illustrious house of Bohun,
Earls of Hereford, Essex, and Northampton, there
was another family of the same name, and probably
descended from the same source, whose chief seat
was at Midhurst, in the county of Sussex. In the
reign of King Henry III.

SAVARIE DE BOHUN held three knights' fees
in Ford and Midhurst, and had to wife, ——, sister
of John Fitz Geffrey, Justice of Ireland, by whom
he had issue,

FRANCO DE BOHUN, who m. Sibel, one of the
daughters of William de Ferrars, Earl of Derby, by
Sibel, his wife, daughter to William Marshal, Earl
of Pembroke, and sister and co-heiress of Anselm,
Earl of Pembroke, by whom he had a son and successor,

JOHN DE BOHUN, serjeant of the king's
Chapel, and *spigurnel*, that is, sealer of the writs,
temp. Edward I. In the twelfth year of which reign
he d., leaving with other children, his successor,

JAMES DE BOHUN, who m. one of the daughters
and co-heiresses of William de Braose, of Gower, and
was s. by his son,

JOHN DE BOHUN, who making proof of his
age, and doing homage, had livery of his lands in
the 16th Edward II. "This is he, (says Dugdale,)
who for his great services in Flanders, and elsewhere
beyond sea, in 14th Edward III., (when the king
first laid claim to the crown of France,) as also in
that famous expedition into France, 19th Edward III., (shortly after which, the king obtained
that glorious victory at Cressey, whereof our historians make ample mention,)· became afterwards
one of the BARONS of the realm, being summoned
to sit in parliament, in 37th, 38th, and 39th of that
king's reign." His lordship m. first, Isabel ——, by
whom he had two daughters, viz.

Joane, m. to John de L'Isle, of Gatcombe.
Eve.

The baron m. secondly, Cecely, daughter and heiress
of John Fillol, of Essex, and left a son and heir,

JOHN DE BOHUN, who attaining majority in
the 7th Richard II., and doing his homage, had
livery of his lands; but he does not appear ever to
have been summoned to parliament as a baron,
neither were his descendants considered as such.
He was s. by his son,

HUMPHREY DE BOHUN, whose son and successor,

JOHN DE BOHUN, left at his decease, in the
reign of Henry VII., two daughters, co-heiresses,
viz.

> Mary, m. to Sir David Owen, Knt., natural
> son of Owen Tudor, grandfather of King
> Henry VIIth, by whom she had—Henry,
> Jasper, Roger, and Anne.
> Ursula, m. to Robert Southwell, of the county
> of Suffolk.

ARMS.—Or, a cross, as. (in a field or.)

BOHUN — EARLS OF HEREFORD,
EARLS OF ESSEX, EARLS
OF NORTHAMPTON, AND
HIGH CONSTABLES OF
ENGLAND.

The first Earldom, by Charter of Creation,
28th April, 1199.
The second, by the same, of King Henry III.
The third, by the same, 17th March, 1337.

Lineage.

The founder of this family in England was,

HUMPHREY DE BOHUN, kinsman and companion in arms of William the Conqueror, generally
known as " *Humphrey with the Beard;*" by reason
that most of the Normans did at that period totally
shave their faces. Of this Humphrey little more is
ascertained than that he possessed the lordship of
Taterford, in Norfolk, and was s. by his son,

HUMPHREY DE BOHUN, surnamed the
GREAT, who by command of King William Rufus
espoused Maud, daughter of Edward de Saresbury,
(progenitor of the ancient Earls of Sarum,) by
whom he acquired large estates in the county of
Wilts, and had issue, Maud, and his successor,

HUMPHREY DE BOHUN, who was steward
and sewer to King Henry I. This feudal lord married Margery, daughter of Milo de Gloucester, Earl
of Hereford, Lord High Constable of England, and
sister and co-heiress of Mabel, last Earl of Hereford,
of that family. At the instigation of which Milo,
he espoused the cause of the Empress Maud and her
son, against King Stephen, and so faithfully maintained his allegiance, that the empress, by her especial charter, granted him the office of steward
and sewer, both in Normandy and England. In
the 20th of Henry II., this Humphrey accompanied
Richard de Lacy, (Justice of England,) into Scotland, with a powerful army, to waste that country;
and was one of the witnesses to the accord made by
William, King of Scots, and King Henry, as to the
subjection of that kingdom to the crown of England. He died on the 6th April, 1187, and was s.
by his son,

HUMPHREY DE BOHUN, who was EARL OF
HEREFORD, and CONSTABLE OF ENGLAND, in right
of his mother, if the Chronicles of Lanthony be correct. His lordship m. Margaret, daughter of Henry,
Earl of Huntingdon, sister of William, King of
Scots, and widow of Conale Petit, Earl of Britanny
and Richmond, and was s. by his son,

HENRY DE BOHUN, who in reality was the
first EARL OF HEREFORD, of this family, being so
created by charter of King John, dated 28th April,

63

1199; but the constableship he inherited from his father. His lordship taking part with the barons against King John, had his lands sequestered, but they were restored at the signing of MAGNA CHARTA, at Runnimede, the earl being one of the twenty-five lords, appointed there, to enforce the observance of the celebrated charters. His lordship was subsequently excommunicated by the pope, and he became a prisoner at the battle of Lincoln, in the 1st year of Henry III. He m. Maud, daughter of Geoffrey Fitz-Piers, Earl of Essex, and eventually, heiress of her brother, William de Mandeville, last Earl of Essex of that family, (see Mandeville, Earls of Essex,) by whom he acquired the *honour of Essex*, and other extensive lordships,—and had surviving issue, Humphrey, and Ralph, and a daughter Margery, who m. Waleran, Earl of Warwick. His lordship d. on the 1st January, 1290, and was s. by his son,

HUMPHREY DE BOHUN, as EARL OF HEREFORD, and possessing the honour of Essex, through his mother, was created EARL OF THAT COUNTY, by King Henry III., at whose marriage his lordship performed the office of marshal in the king's house, and in three years afterwards, anno 1239, was one of the godfathers at the font, for Edward, eldest son of the king, there being no less than nine sponsors on the occasion, viz., five temporal and four spiritual lords. In 1246, he signed with the rest of the English peers, a letter to the pope, remonstrating against the oppression of the Court of Rome, under which the kingdom at that period groaned, and threatening to free themselves, if not speedily redressed. In 1250, he took up the cross and proceeded to the Holy Land. In three years afterwards, his lordship was present, with other peers, when that formal curse was denounced in Westminster Hall, with *bell, book, and candle*, against the violators of Magna Charta; in which year, he founded the Church of the *Fryers Augustines*, in Broad-street, within the city of London. In the great contest between the king and his barons, this nobleman fought under the banner of the latter, at Evesham, where he was taken prisoner, but he did not long continue in bondage, for we find him soon after, again in favour, and receiving new grants from the crown. His lordship m. first, Maud, daughter of the Earl of Ewe, by whom he had issue,

> HUMPHREY, a very distinguished person amongst the rebellious barons, in the reign of Henry III. In the 47th of that monarch, he was excommunicated, with Simon de Montfort, Earl of Leicester, and others, for plundering divers churches, and committing sacrilege. He was afterwards one of the commanders at the battle of Lewes, where the king was made prisoner, and was constituted Governor of Goodrich, and Winchester Castles. In the year following, he commanded the infantry at the battle of Evesham, where he fell into the hands of the royalists, and was sent prisoner to Beeston Castle in Cheshire, where he soon afterwards died, leaving issue by his wife, Eleanor, daughter and co-heir of William de Breause, of Brecknock, and co-heir of her mother,

64

Eve, one of the five daughters and co-heirs of William Marshal, Earl of Pembroke.

> HUMPHREY, who succeeded his grandfather.
> Maud, m. to Anselm Mareschal.
> Alice, m. to —— Thony.
> ——, m. to —— Quincy.

HUPHREY DE BOHUN, Earl of Hereford, Earl of Essex, and Lord High Constable. This nobleman inheriting the high and daring spirit of his predecessors, often strenuously opposed the measures of the court, and was often therefore in disgrace, but appears at the close of his career to have regained royal favour, for we find him attending the king into Scotland, when that monarch, (Edward I.,) obtained a great victory near Roxborough. His lordship m. Maud, daughter of Ingelram de Fines, and third sister of William, Lord Fines, and dying in 1298, was s. by his son,

HUMPHREY DE BOHUN, as Earl of Hereford, Earl of Essex, and Lord High Constable. In the 30th Edward I., this nobleman gave and granted unto the king, by a formal conveyance, the inheritance of all his lands and lordships, as also, of his Earldoms of Hereford and Essex, and the Constableship of England, which upon his marriage with Elizabeth Plantagenet, widow of John, Earl of Holland, and daughter of the king, were regranted to him, and entailed upon his issue lawfully begotten by that lady; in default thereof, and from and after the death of himself and wife, then the lordship of Plassets, and certain other lordships in Essex, and elsewhere, together with the constableship, should remain wholly to the king and his heirs for ever. In the 34th of the same reign he had a grant, similarly entailed, of the whole territory of Anandale, in Scotland. After this, his lordship was in the wars of Scotland, and was taken prisoner, in the 7th Edward II., at the disastrous battle, (to the English) of Stryvelin. But he was exchanged for the wife of Robert Bruce, who had long been captive in England. From this period we find him constantly engaged in the service of the crown, until the fourteenth year of the king's reign, when Edward learning that the earl was raising forces in the marches of Wales, against Hugh de Spencer the younger, sent him a peremptory command to forbear, which his lordship not only refused obeying, but forthwith joined Thomas, Earl of Lancaster, in the great insurrection then incited by that nobleman, for the redress of certain grievances, and the banishment of the Spencers. In this proceeding, however, he eventually lost his life, being run through the body by a soldier at the battle of BOROUGHBRIDGE, in Yorkshire, where his party received so signal a defeat on the 16th March, 1321. The earl had issue, five surviving sons, and two surviving daughters, viz.

> JOHN,
> HUMPHREY,
> Edward,
> { successors primogeniturely to the honours. The eldest was made a Knight of the Bath in the 20th Edward II., having by special command of Prince Edward, the robes for that solemnity out of the royal wardrobe, as for an earl.

WILLIAM, a personage of great eminence in the turbulent times in which he lived: and one of the gallant heroes of CRESSEY. In the parliament held at London, in the 11th Edward III., upon the advancement of the Black Prince to the dukedom of Cornwall, he was created EARL OF NORTHAMPTON, (17th March, 1337,) and from that period, his lordship appears the constant companion in arms of the martial EDWARD, and his illustrious son. At Cressey, he was in the second battalia of the English army, and he was frequently engaged in the subsequent wars of France and Scotland. He was entrusted at different periods with the most important offices, such as ambassador to treat of peace with hostile powers, commissioner to levy troops, &c. &c., and he was finally honoured with the GARTER. His lordship m. Elizabeth, daughter of Bartholomew de Badlesmere, one of the co-heirs of her brother, Giles, and widow of Edmund de Mortimer, by whom he had an only son,

> HUMPHREY, second Earl of Northampton, of whom hereafter as successor to his uncle, in the earldoms of Hereford and Essex, and constableship of England.

He d. in 1360.

Alianore, m. to James Butler, Earl of Ormonde.

Margaret, m. to Hugh, son and heir of Hugh de Courtenay, first Earl of Devonshire.

The earl was s. by his eldest son,

SIR JOHN DE BOHUN, K.B. as Earl of Hereford, Earl of Essex, and Lord High Constable. This nobleman, who had served in the Scottish wars, being in an infirm state of health, was allowed in the 4th Edward III., to depute his brother Edward to execute the duties of constable. His lordship m. first, Lady Alice Fitz-alan, daughter of Edmund, Earl of Arundel, and secondly, Margaret, daughter of Ralph, Lord Basset of Drayton, but had no issue. He d. in 1335, when all his honours and estates devolved upon his next brother,

HUMPHREY DE BOHUN, Earl of Hereford, Earl of Essex, and Lord High Constable, K.G. This nobleman was one of the great lords who assisted, in the 15th of Edward III., at the celebrated feast and justs which the king then held at London in honour of the Countess of Salisbury, and, in the 20th of the same monarch, attended the king to the relief of Aguillon, then besieged by the French. His lordship never married, and dying in 1361, his honours and estates reverted to his nephew (see William, fourth son of the last earl but one),

HUMPHREY DE BOHUN, second earl of Northampton, then a minor, and under the guardianship of Richard Earl of Arundel. His lordship did not, however, long enjoy this great accumulation of wealth and honour, for he died in 1372, in the thirty-second year of his age, leaving, by his wife Joane, daughter of his late guardian, the Earl of Arundel, two daughters, his co-heirs; viz.

> Alianore, m. to Thomas of Woodstock, Duke of Gloucester, sixth son of King Edw. III.

Mary, m. to Henry, Earl of Derby, (son of John of Gaunt, Duke of Lancaster,) who afterwards ascended the throne as HENRY IV.

Upon the decease of this nobleman, the EARLDOM OF HEREFORD EXPIRED; but his son in-law, the Earl of Derby, was subsequently created (in 1397) DUKE OF HEREFORD, prior, of course, to his becoming KING OF ENGLAND, while the lordships of Essex and Northampton, and the CONSTABLESHIP, fell to his other son-in-law, the Duke of Gloucester, and the EARLDOMS of Essex and NORTHAMPTON BECAME EXTINCT.

Arms—AZ. a bend ar. between two cottises and six lions rampant or. *3 molets gu on the bend for N. hants*

BOLEYNE — VISCOUNT ROCHFORD, EARL OF WILTSHIRE, AND EARL OF ORMONDE.

Viscounty,	} by Letters Patent, {	18th June, 1525.
Earldoms,		8th Dec., 1529.

Lineage.

The family of Bullen, or Boleyne, is said to have been of ancient date in the county of Norfolk: we shall, however, begin with

SIR GEOFFREY BOLEYNE, who, settling in the city of London, attained great opulence as a mercer there, and had the honour of filling the Lord Mayor's chair in the year 1458, when he was made a knight bachelor. He m. Anne, eldest daughter and co-heiress of Thomas Lord Hoo and Hastings, by whom he had several children, of which the eldest son,

SIR WILLIAM BOLEYNE, settled at Brickling, in Norfolk, and m. Margaret, youngest daughter of Thomas Butler, seventh Earl of Ormonde, by whom, with other issue, he left, at his decease in 1505, a son and heir,

SIR THOMAS BOLEYNE. This gentleman took up arms in the 19th of Henry VII., with his father and other persons of rank, against the Cornish rebels; and in the beginning of the next reign, being one of the knights of the king's body, was constituted governor of the Castle of Norwich, jointly with Sir Henry Wyatt, Knt., master of the king's jewel-house. In the next year he was one of the ambassadors to the Emperor Maximilian, touching a war with France; and a few years afterwards was appointed sole constable of Norwich Castle. In the 11th of the same reign, being ambassador to France, he arranged the preliminaries for the famous interview between his royal master and Francis I., between Guisnes and Ardres. In three years afterwards he was ambassador to the court of Spain, and was advanced to the peerage on the 18th June, 1525, in the dignity of VISCOUNT ROCHFORD. In 1527 his lordship was one of the commissioners to invest the king of France with the order of the Garter. In 1529 he subscribed the articles then exhibited against Cardinal Woolsey; and upon the 8th of December, in the same year, being then a knight of the Garter, he was advanced to the EARLDOMS of WILTSHIRE and ORMONDE—the former to the heirs of his body, and the latter to heirs general. In the January following, his lordship was nominated lord privy-seal, soon after which he was again accredited to the court of Spain. The earl m. Elizabeth, daughter of Thomas Howard, Duke of Norfolk, and had issue,

> GEORGE, who was summoned to parliament in the life-time of his father, as VISCOUNT ROCHFORD. This nobleman was deputed by King Henry to announce his private marriage with his lordship's sister, Anne Boleyne, to the king of France, and to solicit that monarch's advice regarding its public avowal. In two years afterwards he was made constable of Dover Castle, and lord warden of the Cinque-Ports. Again the viscount was accredited to Versailles, in the 27th of his brother-in-law's reign, touching a projected union between the king's infant daughter, Elizabeth, and one of the sons of France. His lordship, who had risen with his sister, shared in the downfal of that unhappy lady—was committed to the Tower on the 2d of May, 1536, and arraigned and beheaded on the 17th of the same month. He m. Jane, daughter of Sir Henry Parker, (eldest son and heir of Henry, Lord Morley,) an infamous woman, who continued a lady of the bed-chamber to the three succeeding queens, but eventually shared the fate of Catherine Howard. His lordship had no issue. He was attainted soon after his execution.
>
> ANNE, created MARCHIONESS OF PEMBROKE on the 1st Sept. 1532, married in the following year to King Henry VIII., and thus became QUEEN CONSORT of ENGLAND. Beheaded in 1536, leaving an only child,
>
>> ELISABETH, who ascended the English throne, as QUEEN REGNANT, at the decease of her half-sister, Mary, on the 17th November, 1558.
>
> Mary, m. to William Carey, Esq., whose son and heir was created, in 1559, Baron Hunsdon, (see Carey, Lord Hunsdon).

The Earl of Wiltshire and Ormonde died in two years after his unhappy son and daughter, when the VISCOUNTY OF ROCHFORD and EARLDOM OF WILTSHIRE became EXTINCT, that of ORMONDE being to heirs general, fell into abeyance between the representatives of his daughters—"On the death of Queen Elizabeth," says Nicolas, "the only issue of Anne Boleyn, the eldest co-heir, became EXTINCT, when it is presumed that the abeyance, agreeable to the limitation, terminated, and consequently that dignity reverted to the representative of the other co-heir, the heir general of whom is the present Earl of Berkeley, and under the said limitation, must probably be considered as EARL OF ORMOND."

ARMS.—Ar. a chev. gules, betw. three bulls' heads, sa. armed or.

66

BOLEYNE—MARCHIONESS OF PEMBROKE.

By Letters Patent, dated 1st September, 1532.

Lineage.

This dignity was conferred by King Henry VIII. upon his unhappy Queen Anne Boleyne, prior to his marriage. For that unfortunate lady's family (see Boleyne, Earl of Wiltshire and Ormonde).

BONVILE—BARON BONVILE.

By Writ of Summons, dated 23rd September, 1449, 28th Henry VI.

Lineage.

In the 4th of Richard II.,

SIR WILLIAM DE BONVILE was constituted sheriff of the counties of Somerset and Dorset, which trust he also held the next ensuing year: and in the 13th of the same reign was sheriff of Devonshire. He d. in 1408, and was s. by his grandson,

SIR WILLIAM BONVILE, who, in the 5th of Henry V., in the expedition then made into France, was of the retinue of Thomas, Duke of Clarence, the king's brother. In the 1st year of Henry VI. Sir William was appointed sheriff of Devonshire, and being afterwards engaged in the French wars, wherein he deported himself with great valour, he was constituted seneschal of the duchy of Aquitaine, and had summons to parliament as a BARON, from 23rd September, 1449, to 30th July, 1460, under the title of LORD BONVILE, of Chuton. His lordship subsequently espousing the interests of the house of York, was one of those to whom the custody of King Henry VI. was committed after the battle of Northampton, but the tide of fortune turning, his lordship lost his head, with the Duke of Exeter and the Earl of Devon, after the second battle of St. Albans. Lord Bonvile had an only son,

> WILLIAM, who died before the baron, having m. Elizabeth de Harrington, daughter and heir of William, Lord Harrington, and leaving an only child,
>
>> WILLIAM, commonly called Lord Harrington, who m. Lady Catherine Nevil, daughter of Richard, Earl of Salisbury, and had an only daughter, CECILY. This William was slain at the battle of Wakefield, fighting under the banner of the house of York, in the 39th Henry VI.

Lord Bonvile was succeeded, at his decease, by his great grand-daughter, the above mentioned CECILY BONVILE, who married, first, Thomas Grey, Marquess of Dorset, and secondly, Henry Stafford, Earl of Wiltshire, but had issue by the former only. Through this union the BARONIES OF BONVILE AND HARRINGTON were conveyed to, and continued in the family of Grey, until the attainder of Henry Grey, Duke of Suffolk, (grandson of the said Thomas and Cecily,) in 1554, when, with his grace's other honours, those dignities EXPIRED.

ARMS.—Sa. six mullets ar. pierced gu.

BOOTH—BARONS DELAMERE, OF DUNHAM MASSIE, IN THE COUNTY OF CHESTER, AND EARLS OF WARRINGTON.

Barony, } by Letters Patent, { 20th April, 1661.
Earldom, } { 17th April, 1690.

Lineage.

The family of BOOTH was of great repute and honourable station in the counties of Lancaster and Chester for several centuries before it arrived to the dignity of the peerage.

ADAM DE BOOTHS, so called from his place of abode in Lancashire, was father of

WILLIAM DE BOOTHS, living in 1275, who m. Sibel, daughter of Sir Ralph de Bereton, Knt., and was s. by his son,

THOMAS DE BOOTHS, to whom s. his son,

JOHN DE BOUTHE, living temp. Edw. II., who m. Agnes, daughter and heiress of Sir Gilbert de Barton, and was s. by his son.

SIR THOMAS BOUTH, of Barton, called " Tomalin of the Boothes," m. Ellen, daughter of Thomas de Workesley, Esq., of Workesley, now Worsley, in the county of Lancaster, and had issue,

JOHN, his successor.

Henry—left a son, John.

Thomas—left a son, Robert.

Alice, m. first, to William Leigh, Esq., of Baguley, in the county of Chester, and secondly, to Thomas Duncalf, Esq., of Foxwist.

Catherine.

Margaret.

Anne, m. to Sir Edward Weever.

Sir Thomas was s. by his eldest son,

JOHN BOUTH, Esq., of Barton, who lived in the reigns of Richard II. and Henry IV., and m. first, Joan, daughter of Sir Henry Trafford, of Trafford, in the county of Lancaster, by whom he had issue,

THOMAS, who received the honour of knighthood in the 14th Henry VI. Sir Thomas m. a daughter of Sir George Carrington, Knt., and widow of —— Weever, and had issue,

Sir John Bouth, Knt., to whom King Hen. VII. granted an annuity of 10 marks sterling for his good services. Sir John fell at Flodden-Field in the 5th of Henry VIII., and his male line ceased with his great-grandson, JOHN, who left, at his decease, three daughters, co-heiresses.

Robert, of whom presently, as ancestor of the Lords Delamere.

William, Archbishop of York.

Richard, of Strickland, near Ipswich, in the county of Suffolk.

Roger, m. Catherine, daughter and heiress of Ralph Hatton, Esq., of Mollington, near Chester, and had issue,

Robert Booth, Esq., of Sawley, in the county of Derby.

Isabel, m. to Ralph Nevil, third earl of Westmoreland, and had issue,

Anne, who m. William Lord Coniers.

John, Bishop of Exeter, anno 1465; buried in the church of St. Clement Danes, London, in 1478.

Ralph, Archdeacon of York.

Margery, m. to John Byron, Esq., of Clayton, in the county of Lancaster.

Joan, m. first, to Thomas Sherborne, Esq., Stanhurst, in the county of Lancaster, and secondly, to Sir Thomas Sudworth, Knt.

Catherine, m. to Thomas Ratcliffe, Esq., of Wimmorley.

Alice, m. to Sir Robert Clifton, Knt., of Clifton, in the county of Nottingham.

Mr. Booth married a second wife, (but the lady's name is not known,) and left a son,

Laurence Booth, who was chancellor of the university of Cambridge, bishop of Durham, and afterwards archbishop of York. His lordship was appointed keeper of the privy-seal in the 35th of Henry VI., and LORD CHANCELLOR OF ENGLAND in the 19th of Edward IV. He d. in 1480.

The line Sir Thomas Bouth, the eldest son, terminating, as stated above, in co-heiresses, we proceed with the second son,

SIR ROBERT BOUTH, Knt., of Dunham Massie, in the county of Chester, which seat he acquired by his wife, Douce, daughter and co-heiress of Sir William Venables, of Bollen, in the same shire; which Sir William was son of Joane, daughter and heir of Hamon Fitton, who was grandson of John Fitton, of Bollen, by Cicelie his wife, eldest daughter and co-heir of Sir Hamon de Massie, the sixth and last Baron of Dunham Massie, one of the eight feudal lordships instituted by Hugh Lupus, Earl of Chester, in the time of the Conqueror. By this lady Sir Robert Bouth had no less than nine sons and five daughters. Of the former,

WILLIAM, the eldest, inherited the fortune.

Phillip, the youngest, m. ——, daughter and heiress of Sir William Hampton, of Wellington, Knt.

The daughters were,

Lucy, m. to William Chauntrell, Esq., of the Bache, near Chester.

Ellen, m. to Robert Leigh, Esq., of Adlington, in the county of Chester.

Alice, m. to Robert Hesketh, Esq., of Rufford, in the county of Lancaster, ancestor of the Baronets Hesketh.

Joan, m. to Hamond Massie, Esq., of Rixton, Lancashire.

Margery, m. to James Scarebrich, Esq.

Sir Robert and his eldest son had a grant of the office of sheriff of Cheshire for both their lives, and to the survivor of them, by patent, dated at Chester on the 8th of March, in the 21st of Henry VI., with all fees appertaining to the said office, and to execute its duties, either personally or by deputy. Sir Robert died on the 16th September, 1460, and was s. by his eldest son,

SIR WILLAM BOTHE, who m. Maud, daugh-

67

ter of John Dutton, Esq., of Dutton, in the county of Chester, by whom he had five sons and nine daughters, which daughters were,

> Douce, m. to Thomas Leigh, Esq., of West Hall, in the county of Chester.
>
> Anne, m. first, to John Leigh, Esq., of Booths, Cheshire, and secondly, to Geoffery Shakerly, of Shakerly, in the county of Lancaster.
>
> Ellen, m. to Sir John Leigh, of Baguley, in the county of Chester.
>
> Margery, m. John Hyde, Esq., of Haighton, Lancashire.
>
> Alice, m. to John Ashley, Esq., of Ashley, in the county of Chester.
>
> Elizabeth, m. to Thomas Fitton, Esq., of Pownall, Cheshire.
>
> Joane, m. to William Holt, Esq.
>
> Isabella.
>
> Catherine.

Sir William d. in 1476, and was s. by his eldest son,

GEORGE BOTHE, Esq. This gentleman m. Catherine, daughter and heiress of Robert Mountfort, Esq., of Bescote, in the county of Stafford, and of Monkspath, Warwickshire, by whom he acquired considerable estates in the counties of Salop, Stafford, Warwick, Leicester, Wilts, Somerset, Cornwall, and Hereford, and had issue,

> WILLIAM, his successor.
>
> Laurence.
>
> Roger.
>
> Alice, m. to William Massie, Esq., of Denfield, in the county of Chester.
>
> Ellen, m. first, to Thomas Vaudrey, Esq., and secondly, to —— Trafford, Esq., of Bridge-Trafford.

Mr. Bothe d. in 1483, and was s. by his eldest son,

SIR WILLIAM BOTHE, Knt., who m. first, Margaret, daughter and co-heir of Sir Thomas Ashton, of Ashton-under-Lyne, in the county of Lancaster, and of his wife Anne, daughter of Ralph, Lord Graystock, by which alliance a great accession of property came to the family of Bothe. He had issue of this marriage,

> George, his successor.
>
> John, m. to Margery, daughter of Sir Piers Dutton, of Dutton, in the county of Chester, and had two sons, William and Robert.

Sir William m. secondly, Ellen, daughter of Sir John Montgomery, of Trewly, in the county of Stafford, and had

> William, m. to ——, daughter of —— Smith, Esq., of the county of Leicester.
>
> Hammet, m. to ——, daughter of Humphrey Newton, Esq.
>
> Edward, m. to Mary, daughter and co-heir of Roger Knutsford, Esq., of Twemlow, in the county of Chester, from whom descended the Booths of Twemlow Hall, still extant.
>
> Henry, m. to ——, daughter of —— Bowdon, Esq., of the county of Chester.
>
> Andrew.

68.

> Jane, m. first, to Hugh, son and heir of Sir Piers Dutton, of Dutton, in the county of Chester, and secondly, to Thomas Holford, Esq., of Holford, in the same shire.
>
> Dorothy, m. to Edward, son and heir of Laurence Warren, Esq., of Pointon, in the county of Chester.
>
> Anne, m. to Sir William Brereton, of Brereton, Cheshire.

Sir William d. 9th November, in the 11th Hen. VIII., and was s. by his eldest son,

GEORGE BOTHE, Esq., who m. Elizabeth, daughter of Sir Thomas Boteler, of Beausey, near Warrington, and had issue,

> GEORGE, his successor.
>
> John, m. to Elizabeth, daughter of Joh Dutton, Esq., and left four sons,
>
>> William.
>>
>> Robert.
>>
>> Edmund.
>>
>> Henry.
>
> Robert, in holy orders, rector of Thornton-in-the-Moors, in the county of Chester.
>
> Ellen, m. to John Carrington, Esq., of Carrington.
>
> Anne, m. to William Massie, Esq., of Popington.
>
> Margaret, m. to Sir William Davenport, of Bromhall.
>
> Elizabeth, m. Richard Sutton, Esq., of Sutton, near Macclesfield.
>
> Dorothy, m. to Robert Talton, Esq., of Wilthenshaw.
>
> Alice, m. to Peter Daniel, Esq., of Over-Tabley.
>
> Cecilie, d. unmarried.

Mr. Bothe died in the 23d Henry VIII., and was s. by his eldest son,

GEORGE BOTHE, Esq., who left, at his decease in 1548, a son and three daughters, viz.

> WILLIAM, his successor.
>
> Elizabeth, m. to William Chauntrell, Esq., of the Bache, near Chester.
>
> Mary, m. to Randle Davenport, Esq., of Henbury, in the county of Chester.
>
> Anne, m. to —— Wentworth, Esq., of the county of York.

To this George Bothe, Queen Jane Seymour commanded a letter to be written, acquainting him with the birth of a son, (afterwards King Edward VI.,) bearing date, at Hampton Court, the very day of her delivery, October 12th, 29th Henry VIIL, in these words:—

BY THE QUEEN.

"Trusty and welbeloved, we grete youe well. And for asmuche as by the inestimable goodness and grace of Almighty God, we be delivered and brought in childbed of a prince, conceived in most lawful matrimonie between my Lord the King's Majestye and us, doubting not but that for the love and affection which ye beare unto us, and to the commyn wealth of this realme, the knowledge thereof shud be joyous and glad tidings unto youe, we have thought fit to certifie youe of the same. To thintent ye might not only rendre unto God condigne thanks and praise for soo great a benefit, but also pray for the long continuance and preservation of the same here in this fief, to the honor of God, joy and pleasor of my Lord the King, and us, and the universall weale, quiet, and tranquillyty of this hole realme. Gevyn under our signet, at my Lord's manor of Hampton-Cort, the xii. day of October.

" To our trusty and welbeloved,

" George Both', Esq."

Mr. Bothe had also the honour of a letter from King Henry himself, dated at Westminster, 16th February, in the 34th year of his reign, concerning forces to be raised to war against the Scotch. Mr. Bothe was s. by his son,

WILLIAM BOTHE, or BOUTHE, who, being then but three years old, was in ward to the king. He received the honour of knighthood in 1578. Sir William m. Elizabeth, daughter of Sir John Warburton, of Warburton and Arley, in the county of Chester, and had seven sons and six daughters. Of the former,

GEORGE succeeded his father.

John, m. to ——, daughter of —— Preistwich, of Hulme, near Manchester; and had several children.

Richard, m. ——, daughter and heiress of —— Massie, Esq., of Coghull.

The married daughters were,

Elizabeth, m. first, to William Basnet, Esq., of Eaton, in the county of Denbigh, and secondly, to —— Walsh, Esq., of ——, in Ireland.

Dorothy, m. to Ralph Bunnington, Esq., of Barrowcote, in the county of Derby.

Alice, m. to —— Panton, Esq.

Susan, m. first, to Sir Edward Warren, of Pointon, in the county of Chester, and secondly, to John Fetton, Esq., of the city of Chester.

Sir William d. on the 28th Nov., 1579, and was s. by his eldest son,

SIR GEORGE BOOTH, whose extensive estates were placed by Queen Elizabeth during his minority, under the guardianship of her favourite, Robert Dudley, Earl of Leicester. In the latter end of her majesty's reign, Sir George received the honour of knighthood, and upon the institution of the order of baronet, he was amongst the first raised to that dignity, on the 22d May, 1611. Sir George Booth, m. first, his second cousin, Jane, only daughter, and heiress of John Carrington, Esq., of Carrington, in the county of Chester. By whom he had no issue, nor did he live long with her, yet he inherited the lands of her father; the same being strictly so settled by that gentleman, before the marriage of his daughter, to descend to the family of Booth; in which settlement, among other provisions, is one particularly worthy of notice: " That if she, the said Jane, should, after marriage, be detected of incontinency, the estate should remain to the family of Booth." After the decease of this lady, Sir William m. Catharine, daughter of Chief Justice Anderson, of the Court of Common Pleas, and had several children, of whom,

WILLIAM, the eldest son, m. Vere, second daughter, and co-heir of Sir Thomas Egerton, Viscount Brackley, LORD CHANCELLOR

OF ENGLAND, and predeceasing his father, (26th April, 1636,) left issue,

GEORGE, of whom presently, as successor to the baronetcy.

Nathaniel, m. Anne, third daughter of Thomas Ravenscroft, Esq., of Bretton, in the county of Flint, whose line terminated with his great-grand-daughter, Hannah Vere Booth, in 1785.

Catherine, m. to Sir John Jackson, of Hickleton, in the county of York, baronet.

John, the youngest son, having actively espoused the cause of King Charles II., received the honour of knighthood after the restoration, anno 1660. Sir John m. Dorothy, daughter of Sir Anthony St. John, younger son of Oliver, Earl of Bolingbroke, and left several children at his decease, in 1678.

Alice, m. George Vernon, Esq., of Haslinton, in the county of Chester.

Susan, m. Sir William Brereton, of Handforth, in the county of Chester, baronet.

Elizabeth, m. to Richard, Lord Byron, (his lordship's second wife,) and died without issue.

Sir George Booth, who served the office of sheriff of Cheshire twice, and as often of Lancashire, d. on the 24th October, 1652, and was s. in his title and estates by his grandson (whose guardianship he had purchased from the crown for £4000.),

SIR GEORGE BOOTH, second baronet. This gentleman was committed prisoner to the Tower of London during the usurpation, for his zeal in the royal cause, and his efforts to restore the exiled prince. He had the pleasure eventually, however, of being chosen one of the twelve members deputed by the House of Commons, in May, 1660, to carry to that prince the recal of the house, in answer to his majesty's letters. And on Monday, 13th July, 1660, the House of Commons ordered, " that the sum of £10,000. be conferred on Sir George, as a mark of respect for his eminent services, and great sufferings in the public cause;" which order obtained the sanction of the House of Lords in the ensuing month. In addition to which honourable grant, the baronet was elevated to the peerage, by letters patent, dated 20th April, 1661, as BARON DELAMERE, of Dunham Massie, in the county of Chester. His lordship m. first, Lady Caroline Clinton, daughter, and co-heir of Theophilus, Earl of Lincoln, by whom he had an only daughter, Vere, who d. unmarried, in 1717, in the 74th year of her age. He m. secondly, Lady Elizabeth Grey, eldest daughter of Henry, Earl of Stamford, by whom he had seven sons and five daughters, of whom,

HENRY, succeeded to the title.

George, m. Lucy, daughter of the Right Hon. Robert Robartes, Viscount Bodmin, son and heir of John, Earl of Radnor, by whom he had an only son, Henry, who d. unmarried.

Robert, in holy orders, Archdeacon of Durham, in 1691, and Dean of Bristol, in 1708. This gentleman m. first, Ann, daughter of Sir Robert Booth, chief justice of the Court of

Common Pleas in Ireland, by whom he had a son, Henry, who died *s. p.* He *m.* secondly, Mary, daughter of Thomas Hales, Esq., of Howlets, in the county of Kent, and had five sons and four daughters, of whom,

NATHANIEL, the fourth, and only surviving, succeeded to the BARONY OF DELAMERE, but of him hereafter.

Mary, *m.* to Charles Thrupp, Esq., of the city of London.

Vere, *m.* to George Tyndale, Esq., of Bathford, Somersetshire, and had a son, George Booth Tyndale, Esq., Barrister at Law.

Elisabeth, *m.* to Edward, Earl of Conway.

Diana, *m.* to Sir Ralph Delavall, Bart., of Seaton-Delavall, in the county of Northumberland, and after his decease to Sir Edward Blacket, Bart., of Newby, in the county of York.

George, first Lord Delamere, *d.* on the 8th August, 1684, and was *s.* by his eldest surviving son,

HENRY BOOTH, second baron. This nobleman, who had been committed to the Tower prior to the death of King Charles II., was brought to trial, in the reign of King James, for high treason, before the Lord Chancellor Jeffreys, constituted high steward on the occasion, and a select number (27) of peers, but was most honourably acquitted. After which he lived in retirement until the revolution, when espousing the cause of the Prince of Orange, he was deputed with the Marquess of Halifax, and the Earl of Shrewsbury, upon the arrival of the prince at Windsor, 17th December, 1688, to bear a message to the fallen monarch, requiring that his majesty should remove from Whitehall. An office which his lordship executed so delicately that King James was afterwards heard to remark; "that the Lord Delamere, whom he had used ill, treated him with much more regard, than those to whom he had been kind, and from whom he might better have expected it." His lordship was afterwards sworn of the privy council, and appointed chancellor of the exchequer, an office which he held but one year; when, upon his retirement, he was advanced to the dignity of EARL OF WARRINGTON, by letters patent, dated 17th April, 1690. The earl *m.* Mary, daughter, and sole heiress of Sir James Langham, Bart., of Cottesbrooke, in the county of Northampton, by whom he had four sons and two daughters, which latter were,

Elizabeth, *m.* to Thomas Delves, Esq., son and heir apparent of Sir Thomas Delves, Bart., of Dodington, in the county of Chester, and died *s. p.* in 1697.

Mary, *m.* to the Hon. Russel Robartes, and had issue,

Henry, last Earl of Radnor of that family.

His lordship, who published a Vindication of his friend, Lord Russel, and other literary productions mentioned in Walpole's Catalogue, *d.* on the 2d January, 1693-4, and was *s.* by his second, but eldest surviving son,

GEORGE BOOTH, second Earl of Warrington. This nobleman *m.* Mary, eldest daughter, and coheiress of John Oldbury, Esq., of London, merchant, by whom he had an only daughter,

70

Mary, who *m.* in 1736, Henry Grey, fourth Earl of Stamford, and left,

HENRY, who *s.* to the Earldom of Stamford, upon the decease of his father, in 1768, and was created in 1796, Baron Delamere, and Earl of Warrington— (see those dignities in *Burke's Dictionary of the Peerage and Baronetage*).

His lordship *d.* on the 2d August, 1758, when his estates passed to his daughter, Mary, Countess of Stamford; the EARLDOM OF WARRINGTON EXPIRED, while the barony reverted to his cousin, (refer to the Very Reverend Dean Robert Booth, son of the first Lord Delamere).

NATHANIEL BOOTH, Esq., as fourth Baron Delamere. His lordship *m.* Margaret, daughter of Richard Jones, Esq., of Ramsbury Manor in the county of Wilts, by whom he had two sons, who both died young, and a daughter, Elisabeth, who *d.* unmarried, in 1765. Lord Delamere was appointed chairman of the committees of the House of Lords in 1765, and *d.* in 1770, when the BARONY OF DELAMERE became EXTINCT.

ARMS.—Three boars heads erect and erased sa.

BOTELER—BARONS BOTELER OF OVERSLEY AND WEMME.

By Writ of Summons, dated 26th August, 1296.
24 Edward I.

Lineage.

In the reign of the *First* HENRY,

RALPH BOTELER, so called, from holding the office of butler to Robert, Earl of Mellent and Leicester, seated himself at Oversley, in the county of Warwick, where he erected a strong castle, and at a mile distant, founded a monastery for Benedictine Monks, (anno 1140, and 5th Stephen). This Ralph was *s.* by his son,

ROBERT BOTELER, who was *s.* by his son,

RALPH BOTELER, one of the barons who took up arms against King John, and whose lands were seised in consequence; but making his peace he had restitution on paying 40 marks upon the accession of Henry III., in whose reign he was constituted a commissioner for collecting the *fifteenth* then levied in the counties of Warwick and Leicester. In the former of which shires he was likewise a justice of assize. He was *s.* at his decease by his son,

MAURICE BOTELER, one of the justices of assize for the county of Warwick, in the 13th and 16th of Henry III., and a commissioner for assessing and collecting the fourteenth part of all men's moveable goods, according to the form and order then appointed. This feudal lord filled the office of justice of assize for the same shire, a second and third time, and was repeatedly justice for the gaol delivery at Warwick, in the same king's reign. He was *s.* by his son,

RALPH BOTELER, who *m.* Maud, daughter and heiress of William Pantulf, by whom he acquired the great Lordship of Wemme, in the county of Salop. This feudal baron had divers summonses to attend the king, Henry III., in his wars with the Welsh, and adhering faithfully to that monarch, against Simon de Montfort, and the revolted barons, he was amply rewarded by grants of lands and money from the crown. He was *s.* at his decease by his son,

WILLIAM BOTELER, who, in the life-time of his father, had *m.* Ankaret, niece of James de Aldithley. He died, however, in a very few years after inheriting his paternal property, (anno 1283,) leaving three sons, John, Gawine, and William, and was *s.* by the eldest,

JOHN BOTELER, at whose decease in minority, anno 1296, the inheritance devolved upon his brother,

GAWINE BOTELER, who, dying issueless, was *s.* by his brother,

WILLIAM BOTELER, who, in the 24th Edward L., was in ward to Walter de Langton, Lord Treasurer of England, and Walter de Beauchamp, of Alcester, Steward of the King's Household. This feudal lord obtaining renown in the Scottish wars of the period, was summoned to parliament as a BARON, from 26th August, 1296, to the 10th October, 1325. His lordship *m.* first, Ankaret, daughter of Griffin, and had an only son, WILLIAM, his successor. He *m.* secondly, Ela, daughter, and co-heiress of Roger de Hardeburgh, by whom he had two sons, Edmund and Edward, who both died issueless, and four daughters, viz.

Ankaret, *m.* to John Le Strange, of Blackmere.
Ida, *m.* to Sir Fulke Pembrugge.
Alice, *m.* to Nicholas Langford.
Dionysa, *m.* to Hugh de Cokesey.

He *d.* in 1334, and was *s.* by his eldest son,

WILLIAM BOTELER, second Baron Boteler of Wemme, but never summoned to parliament. This nobleman *m.* Margaret, daughter of Richard Fits-Alan, Earl of Arundel, and dying in 1361, was *s.* by his son,

WILLIAM BOTELER, third Baron Boteler of Wemme, summoned to parliament from the 23rd February, 1368, to 6th April, 1369. His lordship *m.* Joane, elder sister and co-heir of John Lord Sudley, and dying in 1369, left an only daughter and heiress,

Elizabeth, who *m.* first, Sir Robert Ferrers, a younger son of Robert, second Baron Ferrers of Chartley, and conveyed to him the great lordship of Wemme, in the county of Salop, and the said Robert was summoned to parliament as "Robert Ferrers de Wemme, Chev." in the 49th Edward III. Elizabeth Boteler *m.* secondly, Sir John Say, and thirdly, Sir Thomas Molinton, who styled himself "Baron of Wemme," but was never summoned to parliament. Her ladyship had no issue by her second and third husbands, but by the first she left a son,

ROBERT FERRERS, who inherited the barony of Boteler, as well as that of Ferrers of Wemme, but was never summoned to parliament. His lordship *d.* in 1410, leaving two daughters, co-heiresses, viz.

Elizabeth, *m.* to John, son of Ralph, Lord Greystock.

Mary, *m.* to Robert Nevill, Earl of Westmoreland.

Between whose representatives those BARONIES are still in ABEYANCE.

Arms.—Gu. a Fesse componée or. and sa. betw. six crosses patée. arg.

BOTELER—BARON SUDLEY.

(See Sudley, Baron Sudley.)

BOTELER—BARONS BOTELER OF WERINGTON.

By Writ of Summons, dated 23rd June, 1295, 23 Edward I.

Lineage.

The first of this family who assumed the surname of BOTELER was

ROBERT LE BOTELER, from filling the office of boteler or butler to Ranulph de Gernons, Earl of Chester, and under that designation he founded an abbey for Cistercian monks in the year 1158. This Robert left a son Robert, but nothing further is known of the family until the time of King John, when

WILLIAM LE BOTELER was certified to hold eight knights' fees, in capite of the king, in the county of Lancaster. To this William succeeded another,

WILLIAM LE BOTELER, who, in the 43rd of Henry III., was constituted sheriff of the county of Lancaster, and governor of the castle there. But being involved with the turbulent barons of that period he appears subsequently to have lost his lands, until making his peace in the 49th of the same monarch, soon after the battle of Evesham, the sheriff of Lancashire had orders to restore them. In the early part of the next reign this William le Boteler had charters from the crown to hold markets and fairs upon some of his manors, and was summoned to parliament as a BARON, from the 23rd June, 1295, to 26th August, 1296. In the 34th of Edward I. his lordship was engaged in the Scottish war, having been previously upon military service in Gascony. He was *s.* at his decease by his son and heir,

JOHN LE BOTELER, who had summons to parliament in the 14th Edward II., but after this nobleman nothing further is known of the family.

Arms—Az, a bend betw. six garbs or.

BOTETOURT — BARONS BOTETOURT.

By Writ of Summons, dated 10th March, 1308, 1 Edward II.

Lineage.

JOHN DE BOTETOURT, governor of St. Briavel's Castle, in the county of Gloucester, and admiral of the king's fleet, in the reigns of Edward I. and Edward II., was summoned to parliament as a BARON by the latter monarch, from the 10th March, 1308, to the 13th September, 1324. His lordship *m.* Maud, sister and heiress of Otto,* son and heir of Beatrice de Beauchamp, widow of William de Munchensi of Edwardstone, by whom he had issue,

 THOMAS, who *m.* Joane, sister and heiress of John de Somery, Baron of Dudley, and dying before his father left an only son,

  JOHN, who *s.* his grandfather.

 John, of Beauchamp Otes, *m.* ——, and left a son,

  John, who *m.* Joane, daughter and heiress of John Gernon, and left an only daughter and heiress,

   JOANE, *m.* to Sir Robert Swynburne, Knt.

 Otto, of Mendlesham, *m.* ——, and had issue,

  John, who *m.* Catherine, daughter of Sir William Wayland, Knt., and had an only daughter and heiress,

   JOANE, *m.* to John, son and heir of Sir John Knyvet, Knt.

  Elizabeth, *m.* first, to William, Lord Latimer, and secondly, to Robert Ufford.

  Joane, contracted to Robert, son and heir of Robert Fitzwalter, Lord of Wodeham, in Essex.

Lord Botetourt, who was one of the eminent military characters of the reign of Edward I., took a leading part in the Scottish wars of that monarch, and was entrusted with the government of the strongest castles, the command of the fleet, and other duties of the highest importance. His lordship *d.* in 1324, and was *s.* by his grandson,

JOHN DE BOTETOURT, second baron, who had livery of his lands in the 14th Edward III., and in two years afterwards attended the king in the expedition made then into France, in the train of Thomas de Beauchamp, Earl of Warwick. From that period his lordship appears to have been constantly engaged in the French wars of his sovereign, and was summoned to parliament from 25th February, 1342, to the 3rd February, 1385. He *m.* Joyce, daughter of William, Lord Zouche of Har-

---

* In the time of Richard I. money coined in the east of Germany began to be of especial request in England, and for the purity thereof was called "EASTERLING MONEY," as all the inhabitants of those parts were called Easterlings; and shortly after some of that country, skilful in mint matters and allaies, were sent for into this realm, to bring the coin to perfection, which, since that time was called of them "STERLING" for "Easterling," which implied as much as good and lawful money of England. Of these Easterlings, Otho, a German, was the principal, and in old records is called "Otho Cuneator," who grew to such wealth, that Thomas, his son, surnamed Fitz-Otes, married one of the co-heirs of Beauchamp of Bedford, was Lord of Mendlesham in Suffolk, and "held in fee to make the coining stamps serving for all England." Which office, by his heir general, descended to this family of Botetourt, from which, by sale, the 3rd Edward III., it passed into that of Latimer.—Banks.

72

---

yngworth, (aunt and heir of Hugh de la Zouche of Richard's Castle,) and had issue,

 JOHN, who *m.* Maud, daughter of John, Lord Grey of Rotherfield, and predeceasing his father, left a son, John, who died before his grandfather, and a daughter, Joyce, who *m.* Sir Hugh Burnell, Knt., and died *s. p.*

 Maud, Abbess of Polesworth.

 Agnes, a nun at Elstow.

 Elizabeth, *m.* to Sir Baldwin Frevil, Knt., but died before co-habitation.

 Alice, *m.* to —— Kyriel, and had an only daughter and heiress, Joane, who *m.* John Wykes, and left two daughters, Agnes, who *d.* unmarried, and Joyce, *m.* to Hugh Stanley.

 Joyce, *m.* first, to Sir Baldwin Frevil, Knt., and secondly, to Sir Adam de Preshale, Knt., and had issue by the former,

  BALDWIN, who, dying before his mother, left by his wife, Joane, daughter of Sir Thomas Green, Knt.,

   BALDWIN, who *d.* young.

   Elizabeth, *m.* Thomas, second son of William, Lord Ferrers of Groby.

   Margaret, *m.* first, to Sir Hugh Willoughby, Knt., and secondly, to Sir Richard Bingham, Knt.

  Joyce, *m.* to Sir Roger Aston, Knt.

 Katherine, *m.* to Maurice de Berkeley of Stoke Gifford, in the county of Gloucester, and left an only son and heir,

  MAURICE DE BERKELEY, who *m.* Joan, daughter of Sir John Denham, Knt., and his great grandson,

   RICHARD BERKELEY, having married Elizabeth, daughter of Sir Humphrey Coningsby, Knt., left at his decease, in 1514, Sir Maurice Berkeley, Knt., from whom the BERKELEYS OF STRATTON descended, and an elder son,

    SIR JOHN BERKELEY of Stoke, who *m.* Isabel, daughter of Sir William Dennis, Knt., and whose great-great-great grandson,

     RICHARD BERKELEY, *d.* in 1671, left issue,

      George, *m.* to Jane, daughter of Viscount Fitzhardinge, and died *s. p* in 1685.

      John - Symes, *m.* to Elizabeth, daughter and co-heiress of William Norbonne, Esq., of Calne, in the county of Wilts, and dying in 1736, left a son and heir,

       NORBONNE, who was summoned to parliament as BARON BOTETOURT in 1765, and died s. p. in 1776.

Elizabeth, heiress to her brother, m. to Charles, Duke of Beaufort.

John, second Lord Botetourt, d. in 1385, leaving Joyce, Lady Burnell, his grand-daughter, his heiress; but that lady dying in 1406, the BARONY OF BOTE-TOURT then fell into ABEYANCE between his three surviving married daughters, and so continued amongst their descendants for more than three centuries and a half, when it was at length called out in favour of the representative of Katherine de Berkeley (see Berkeley, Baron Botetourt).

ARMS.—OR. a Saltier engr. sa.

BOURCHIER — BARONS FITZ-WARINE, EARLS OF BATH.

Barony, by Writ of Summons, dated 23rd June, 1299, 23 Edward I.

Earldom, by Letters Patent, dated 9th July, 1536.

Lineage.

SIR WILLIAM BOURCHIER, (third son of William BOURCHIER, EARL OF EWE, in Normandy, and Anne his wife, daughter and heiress of Thomas, of Woodstock, Duke of Gloucester, youngest son of King Edward III.,) having espoused Thomasine, daughter and heiress of Richard Hankford, Esq., by Elizabeth his wife, sister and heiress of Fulke Fitz-warine, seventh and last Baron Fitz-warine, of that family, who died s. p., in 1429, was summoned to parliament jure uxoris, as BARON FITZ-WARINE, from 2nd January, 1449, to 7th September, 1469. This nobleman, who was one of the foresters in the reign of Edward IV., had licence from that monarch to export, duty-free, a thousand woollen cloths of his own goods. His lordship appears to have married secondly, Catherine, widow of —— Stukeley, by whom he had a daughter, Elizabeth, to whom her mother bequeaths in her last will, dated in 1468, "a girdle of red tissue." Lord Fitz-warine d. about the year 1470, and was s. by his son,

SIR FULKE BOURCHIER, Knt., second Baron Fitz-warine, who was summoned to parliament on the 19th August, 1472. This nobleman m. Elizabeth, sister and heiress of John, Lord Dynham, and had issue,

JOHN, his successor.

Joane, m. to James, Lord Audley.

Elizabeth, m. first, to Sir Edward Stanhope, Knt., and secondly, to Sir Richard Page, Knt.

His lordship d. in 1479, and was s. by his son,

JOHN BOURCHIER, third Baron Fitz-warine, who, in the 6th of Henry VII., being of full age, had livery of his lands, and was summoned to parliament from the 12th August, 1492, to the 8th June, 1536. His lordship inherited likewise, the large

estates of his mother, the heiress of the Lords Dynham. This nobleman signed the celebrated letter to Pope Clement VII., in the 22nd Henry VIII., wherein the subscribing lords apprised his holiness of the frail tenure of his supremacy, should he refuse the pontifical assent to the divorce of the king from Queen Katherine. Lord Fitz-warine, was subsequently advanced, by Letters Patent, dated 9th July, 1536, to the EARLDOM OF BATH. His lordship m. Cecila, daughter of Giles, Lord D'Aubeney, and sister and heiress of Henry D'Aubeney, Earl of Bridgewater, and had, with other issue,

JOHN, his successor.

Elizabeth, m. to Edward Chichester, Esq.

Dorothy, m. to Sir John Fulford, Knt.

The earl d. 30th of April, 1539, leaving amongst other directions in his will, "that an honest secular priest should sing mass for the health of his soul, for the space of twenty years after his decease." His lordship was succeeded by his eldest son,

JOHN BOURCHIER, fourth Baron Fitz-warine, and second EARL OF BATH. This nobleman upon the decease of King Edward VI., being amongst the first to declare for Queen Mary, was constituted one of the commissioners for receiving the claims of those, who in respect of their tenures, were to perform service upon the day of her majesty's coronation. His lordship m. first, Elizabeth, daughter of Sir Walter Hungerford, Knt., by whom he had one daughter, Elizabeth. He m. secondly, Eleanor, daughter of George Manners, Lord Ros, and sister of Thomas, first Earl of Rutland, of that family, and had issue,

JOHN, Lord Fitz-warine, who d. in the lifetime of his father, leaving by his wife, Frances, daughter of Sir Thomas Kitson, Knt., of Hengrave, in the county of Suffolk, WILLIAM, who s. to the honors of his grandfather.

Henry.

George, (Sir) general of the army sent to suppress the rebellion in the province of Munster, in Ireland, anno 1580; m. Martha, daughter of William, Lord Howard, of Effingham, and had issue,

Sir Henry Bourchier, Knt., who s. as sixth EARL OF BATH.

Fulke.

Mary, m. to Hugh Wyot, of Exeter.

Cecilia, m. to Thomas Peyton, Customer of Plymouth.

The earl m. thirdly, Margaret, daughter and heiress of John Donington, Esq., and widow of Sir Richard Long, Knt., and of this marriage there were two daughters, viz.,

Susanna.

Bridget, wife of Thomas Price, Esq., of Vaynor, in the county of Montgomery.

His lordship d. in 1560, and was s. by his grandson,

WILLIAM BOURCHIER, fifth baron and third earl. This nobleman was in the expedition, 26th Elisabeth, to the Netherlands, in aid of the Dutch, under Robert, Earl of Leicester. His lordship m. Elizabeth, daughter of Francis Russell, Earl of Bedford, and had surviving issue,

EDWARD, who was made Knight of the Bath,

L   73 at the coronation of Henry, Prince of Wales, anno 1610.

Frances, d. unm.

The earl d. on the 19th July, 1623, and was s. by his son,

EDWARD, sixth BARON, and fourth EARL, who m. first, Dorothy, daughter of Oliver, Lord St. John, of Bletso, and sister of Oliver, Earl of Bolingbroke, by whom he had surviving issue,

    Elizabeth, m. to Basil, Earl of Denbigh, and died s. p.

    Dorothy, m. to Thomas, Lord Grey, of Groby, eldest son of Henry Grey, first Earl of Stamford, and had issue,

        Thomas, who s. his grandfather as Earl of Stamford, his father dying previously.

        Elizabeth, m. to Henry Benson, Esq.

        Anne, m. to James Grove, Esq., Serjeant at Law.

    Her ladyship m. secondly, Gustavus Mackworth, Esq., by whom she had

        Mary, m. ———.

    Anne, m. first, to James Cranfield, Earl of Middlesex, by whom she had a daughter,

        Elizabeth, m. to John, Lord Brackley, but died s. p.

    Lady Middlesex m. secondly, Sir Christopher Wrey, Bart. from whom the present Sir Bourchier Wrey descends, and who inherits the mansion of Tavistock, in the county of Devon, the chief seat of the Earl of Bath.

His lordship m. secondly, Anne, daughter of Sir Robert Lovet, Knt., of Liscombe in the county of Buckingham. The earl dying thus in 1636, without male issue, the BARONY OF FITZ-WARINE fell into ABEYANCE between his three daughters, and so continues among their descendants, of whom the present Sir Bourchier Wray, Bart., is one, while the EARLDOM OF BATH devolved upon (General, Sir George Bourchier's son,—refer to the third son of the second earl,) his cousin,

HENRY BOURCHIER, fifth Earl, who m. Rachael, daughter of Frances Fane, Earl of Westmoreland, but dying without issue on the 18th August, 1654, the EARLDOM OF BATH became EXTINCT.

ARMS.—Ar. a cross engrailed gu. betw. four water bougets sa. label of three points sa. charged with nine fleur-de-lis, or.

BOURCHIER — BARONS BERNERS.

By Writ of Summons, dated 26th May, 1455,
33 Henry VI.

Lineage.

SIR JOHN BOURCHIER, K.G. fourth son of William, Earl of Ewe, by Anne Plantagenet, daughter of Thomas of Woodstock, Duke of Gloucester, and grand-daughter of King Edward III., (see Bourchier, Earl of Essex,) having married Margery, daughter and heiress of Richard Berners, (commonly called Lord Berners,) of West Horsley, in the county of Surrey, was summoned to parliament, from the 26th May, 1455, to the 19th August, 1472, as " JOHN BOURCHIER DE BERNERS, CHE-

VALIER." This nobleman appears to have played a safe game between the houses of York and Lancaster, for we find him in the reign of Henry VI., arrayed at the battle of St. Albans, under the red rose, and in that of Edward IV., a staunch adherent of the white. In the first year of the latter king, Lord Berners was made constable of Windsor Castle, and warden of the forests and parks thereunto belonging, and his lordship attended Edward into the north in the following year, when he invested the Castle of Bamburg, and the other strong places in Northumberland, then holding out for the Lancastrians. His lordship died in 1474, leaving amongst other bequests in his last will, to the monks of the Abbey of St. Peter at Chartsey, where he ordered his remains to be interred, a cross of silver gilt; having a foot, whereon were the images of Mary and John; as also other jewels and ornaments, to the value of forty pounds, to the intent that they should pray for his soul, and the soul of Margery, his wife, and all their children's souls. The baron had issue—

    HUMPHREY, (Sir) slain at the battle of Barnetfield, fighting under the banner of King Edward IV., and left issue by his wife, Elizabeth, daughter and heiress of Sir Frederick Tilney, and widow of Sir Thomas Howard, Knt.

        JOHN, who s. his grandfather.

        Anne, m. to Thomas Fynes, Lord Dacre.

    Thomas, who joining Henry, Earl of Richmond, upon his march to Bosworth-field, participated in the victory that placed the diadem upon the head of Henry VII., and was afterwards in the twelfth year of that monarch, at the battle fought on Blackheath, with the cornish rebels.

    Elizabeth, m. to Robert, Lord Welles, and died s. p.

    Joanna, m. to Sir Henry Nevil, Knt.

His lordship was s. by his grandson,

JOHN BOURCHIER, second Baron BERNERS, summoned to parliament, from 14th October, 1495, to 9th November, 1529. This nobleman was captain of the pioneers, in the 5th Henry VIII., and the next year being made chancellor of the king's exchequer for life, he attended the Lady Mary, the king's sister into France, upon her marriage with Lewis XII. His lordship m. Catherine, daughter of John, Duke of Norfolk, by whom he had two daughters, viz.,

    Mary, the younger, who m. Alexander Unton, Esq., but dying s. p., the estates entirely devolved upon her eldest sister,

    Jane, m. to Edmund Knyvett, Esq., of Ashwelworth, serjeant porter to King Henry VIII., by whom she had a son,

        John Knyvet, of Plumstead, in the county of Norfolk, who m. Agnes, daughter of Sir John Harcourt, Knt., of Stanton Harcourt, in the county of Oxford, and dying before his mother, left a son,

            SIR THOMAS KNYVET, Knt, who d. in 1616 or 17, and from him sprang, through various descents, the two brothers,

1. Sir John Knyvet, who m. Mary, daughter of Sir Thomas Bedingfeld, and had several children, all of whom died issueless, except

Elizabeth, who m. Thomas Glemham, Esq., and left an only son,

Thomas, who died s. p., in 1710. In 1717, Catherine, a younger daughter than Elizabeth, claimed the Barony of Berners, and obtained it; but her ladyship dying without issue, in 1743, it again fell into Abeyance.

2. Thomas Knyvet, Esq., who m. Emme, daughter of Thomas Hayward, Esq., of Cranwise, in the county of Norfolk, and left a son,

John Knyvet, who m. Lucy, daughter and co-heiress of Charles Suckling, Esq., of Brakendale, Norfolk, and had several children of whom only two left issue, viz.—

Elizabeth, m. to Henry Wilson, Esq. and had,

Henry.
Knevit.
Harriot, m. to John Layton, Esq.

Lucy m. first, to Thos. Holt, Esq., and had a daughter, Elizabeth Anne. She m. secondly, John Field, Esq., and left two daughters, Lucy. Catherine.

Of Lord Berners, Dugdale concludes his account, thus:—"It is further observable of John, Lord Berners, that he was a person not a little eminent for his learning, and that thereupon, by the command of King Henry VIII., he translated the Chronicle of Sir John Froissart (canon treasurer of Chinay, clerk and servant to King Edward III., as also to Queen Philippa,) out of French into English. He likewise translated out of French, Spanish, and Italian, several other works, viz.—The Life of *Sir Arthur*, an Armorican knight; the famous exploits of Hugh of Bordeaux; *Marcus-Aurelius*, and the *Castle of Love*. He also composed a book of the Duties of the Inhabitants at Calais; and a comedy, intituled *Ite in Vineam*." His lordship is likewise noticed in Walpole's Catalogue of Noble Authors. By his will, he bequeaths to Humphrey Boucher, his son, his gown of damask-tawney, furred with jennets, and certain legacies to James and George, his other sons; but all these children were illegitimate. His lordship d. in 1532, when his only surviving daughter, the lady Joane Knyvet, had livery of his lands, but the Barony of Berners, appears to have lain dormant, until allowed to her ladyship's descendant, Katherine Knyvet, then the wife of Thomas Bokenham, Esq., in 1717; but upon this lady's decease, s. p. in 1743, it again became dormant, although it is presumed it devolved upon her ladyship's cousin, Mrs. Wilson. Robert Wilson, Esq., of Dedlington, and of Ashwellthorpe, in the county of Norfolk, that lady's grandson, presented a petition a few years ago to his majesty, praying that the abeyance might be terminated in his favour.

Arms.—Ar. a cross engrailed, gu. betw. four water bougets, sa.

BOURCHIER — BARONS BOURCHIER, EARLS OF ESSEX.

Barony, by Writ of Summons, dated 25th February, 1342.
Earldom, by Letters Patent, dated 30th June, 1461.

Lineage.

In the reign of King Edward II.,

SIR JOHN DE BURCER or BOURCHIER, Knt., one of the Justices of the Court of King's Bench, marrying Helen, daughter and heiress of Walter de Colchester, and niece maternally of Roger de Montchensy, acquired the manor of Stansted Hall in the county of Essex, and took up his abode there. Sir John had two sons, Robert and John, and was s. at his decease by the elder,

ROBERT DE BOURCHIER, who in the 4th Edward III., obtained a royal charter for holding a Court Leet at Halsted, and in the 10th of the same monarch, had permission to impark his woods there. In four years afterwards, this eminent person was constituted Lord Chancellor of England, with £500 a year above the customary fees, for his suitable maintenance; and in the next year he had licence to make a castle of his mansion-house at Halsted. Uniting the civic and military characters, his lordship was subsequently distinguished in arms, particularly in the glorious field of Cressy, where he was attached to the division of the army, under the immediate command of the Black Prince. He m. Margaret, daughter and sole heiress of Sir Thomas Prayers, of Sible-Hedingham, in the county of Essex, by Anne, daughter and heiress of Hugh de Essex, descended from a younger son of Henry de Essex, Baron of Raleigh, standard-bearer of England, and had issue—

John, his successor.

William, m. Eleanor, daughter and heiress of Sir John de Louvaine, and dying in 1366, left,

William, who was made constable of the Tower of London, and created Earl of Ewe, in Normandy, by Henry V. His lordship m. Anne

75

PLANTAGENET, widow of Edward, Earl of Stafford, and daughter, and eventually sole heiress of Thomas of Woodstock, Duke of Gloucester, son of King Edward III., and left at his decease four sons and a daughter, viz.—

> HENRY, EARL OF EWE, of whom hereafter as EARL OF ESSEX.
>
> Thomas, Bishop of Ely, and subsequently Archbishop of Canterbury.
>
> William, Lord Fitz-warine, see that dignity.
>
> John, Lord Berners, see that dignity.
>
> Anne, m. to John Mowbray, Duke of Norfolk.

Lord Bourchier, who had been summoned to parliament from 25th February, 1342, to 10th March, 1349, died in the latter year, and was s. by his elder son,

SIR JOHN BOURCHIER, Knt., as second Baron Bourchier: summoned to parliament from 16th July, 1381, to 30th September, 1399. This nobleman was engaged during the greater part of his life, in the French wars of Edward III., and Richard II., and was installed a KNIGHT OF THE GARTER, for his gallant services therein. In the 9th year of the latter king, his lordship was appointed chief governor of Flanders, and particularly of the town of Gaunt, at the express desire of the Flemings. Prior to his decease he obtained a special exemption, owing to age and infirmity, from parliamentary duties, and from attending councils. His lordship m. Elizabeth, daughter of Sir John Coggeshall, and dying in 1400, was s. by his only son,

BARTHOLOMEW BOURCHIER, third baron Bourchier, summoned to parliament from 9th Sept. 1400, to 26th Oct. 1409. This nobleman obtained, like his father, when he became old and infirm, an exemption from parliament and council, and from military service in Scotland and beyond the seas. His lordship m. first, Margaret, widow of Sir John de Sutton, but had no issue. He m. secondly, Idonea Lovey, widow, first, of Edmund, son of Sir John de Brooksburn, and afterwards of John Glevant, and dying, in 1409, left an only daughter,

ELIZABETH BOURCHIER, Baroness Bourchier, who m. first, SIR HUGH STAFFORD, Knt. who thereupon assumed the dignity of LORD BOURCHIER, but had summons to parliament (from the 21st Sept. 1411, to 22d March, 1414) as "Hugoni Stafford" only. His lordship d., however, s. p., and his widow remarried with Sir Lewis Robsart, K.G., standard-bearer to King Henry V., who assumed also the title of BOURCHIER, but was summoned, in like manner, in his own name only. He, likewise, died issueless, and upon the decease of Lady Bourchier, in 1432, the barony devolved upon her ladyship's cousin and next heir,

HENRY BOURCHIER, second earl of Ewe, in Normandy—(revert to William, second son of Robert, first Baron Bourchier)—who had summons to parliament in the 13th Henry VI., in his Norman dignity, but never subsequently under that title.

In the 25th Henry VI., 14th December, 1446, his lordship was advanced to the dignity of VISCOUNT BOURCHIER, and had summons accordingly; and in the 33d of the same monarch he was constituted LORD TREASURER OF ENGLAND. But, notwithstanding such sterling marks of royal favour, the lord treasurer forsook his royal master, and, espousing the interests of the Earls of March and Warwick, was reinvested with the treasurership by the former (his brother-in-law) upon his accession as Edward IV., and created, by letters patent, dated 30th June, 1461, EARL OF ESSEX. His lordship m. Isabel, daughter of Richard, Duke of York, Protector of England, (great-grandson of King Edward III.,) and sister of King Edward IV., by whom he had issue—

> WILLIAM, who m. Anne, daughter of Richard Widvile, Earl Rivers, and sister of Elizabeth, queen of King Edward IV.; and dying in the life-time of his father, left issue—
>
> > HENRY, successor to his grandfather.
> >
> > Cecily, m. to John Devereux, Lord Ferrers, of Chartley, and left a son,
> >
> > > SIR WILLIAM DEVEREUX, Lord Ferrers, of Chartley, from whom sprang the extinct house of DEVEREUX, EARLS OF ESSEX, and the extant family of Devereux, VISCOUNTS HEREFORD.
>
> HENRY (Sir), m. Elizabeth, daughter and heiress of Thomas, Lord Scales.
>
> Humphrey, m. Joane, niece and co-heiress of Ralph, Lord Cromwell.
>
> John (Sir), m. Elizabeth, niece and heiress of William, Lord Ferrers, of Groby.
>
> Thomas (Sir), m. Isabel, daughter and heiress of Sir John Barre, Knt., and widow of Humphrey Stafford, Earl of Devon.
>
> Edward (Sir), slain at the battle of Wakefield.
>
> Fulke, } both d. young.
> Isabel, }

This nobleman shared largely in the confiscated estates of the Lancastrians, particularly in those of the attainted Earls of Devon (Thomas Courtenay) and Wiltshire, and the Lord Roos. His lordship d. in 1483, and was s. by his grandson,

HENRY BOURCHIER, second earl of Essex, who had special livery, 9th Hen. VII., of the great estates which descended to him from the Earl of Essex, his grandfather—his father—Isabel, his grandmother—Anne, his mother, and Sir Thomas Bourchier, Knt, his uncle, to all of whom he was heir. This nobleman, who is represented to have been a person of singular valour and worth, was of the privy council of King Henry VII., and had a chief command at the battle of Blackheath, in the 12th of that monarch. Upon the accession of Henry VIII., his lordship was appointed captain of the king's horse-guard, then newly constituted as a body-guard to the monarch. The corps consisted of fifty horse, "trapped with cloth of gold, or goldsmith's work; whereof every one had his archer, a demi-lance, and courtrill." In the 5th of the same king, he attended his highness into France, as lieutenant-general of all the spears; and at the famous tournament which Henry held on the 19th and 20th of May, in the 8th year of his reign, in honour of his sister, Margaret, Queen of Scotland, the Earl of Essex, with the king himself, the Duke of Suffolk, and Nicholas Carew, Esq., answered all comers. In the 12th of Henry, his lordship again attended his sovereign into France, and swelled the pageantry of the monarch in his magnificent interview with FRANCIS I. upon the "*Field of the Cloth of Gold.*" The earl m. Mary, eldest daughter and co-heiress of Sir William Say, Knt., by whom he had an only daughter,

> ANNE, who m. Sir William Parr, Knt., (brother of Queen Katherine Parr,) but that marriage was disannulled by parliament in the 5th of Edward VI., and the issue thereof bastardised.

The earl died, in consequence of a fall from his horse, at his manor of Basse, in the county of Hereford, in 1539, when the EARLDOM OF ESSEX and the VISCOUNTY OF ESSEX EXPIRED; while the BARONY OF BOURCHIER devolved upon his only daughter, Anne Lady Parr; but that lady's issue being, as above stated, *illegitimated*, it passed, at her decease, to Walter Devereux, Baron Ferrers, of Chartley, son and heir of Cecily, the deceased earl's sister—(see descendants of William, eldest son of the first earl)—and united with the barony of Ferrers, until the decease, issueless, of Robert, eleventh Baron Ferrers, of Chartley, and Earl of Essex, in 1646, when it fell into ABEYANCE between his lordship's two sisters and co-heiresses, Frances, Marchioness of Hertford, and Dorothy, wife of Sir Henry Shirley, Bart.; and it so continues between Anne-Eliza, Duchess of Buckingham and Chandos, as heir-general of Frances, the elder co-heir, and the present Marquess Townshend, the representative of the junior.

Arms—Ar. a cross ingrailed gu. between four water bougets, sa.

BOURCHIER—BARON CROMWELL.

See *Cromwell, Baron Cromwell*, of TATSHALL.

BOYLE — COUNTESS OF GUILD-FORD.

By Letters Patent, dated 14th July, 1660.

Lineage.

LADY ELIZABETH FIELDING, daughter of William, first Earl of Denbigh, m. Lewis Boyle, Viscount Boyle, of Kynalmeaky, in the peerage of Ireland, (second son of the first Earl of Cork,) by whom she had no issue. His lordship fell at the battle of Liscarroll, in 1642, and her ladyship was advanced to the peerage of England *for life*, on the 14th July, 1660, as COUNTESS OF GUILDFORD; she died in 1673, when the dignity, of course, EXPIRED.

BOYLE — BARONS CLIFFORD, OF LANESBOROUGH, IN THE COUNTY OF YORK, EARLS OF BURLINGTON.

Barony,   } by Letters { dated 4th Nov., 1644.
Earldom, } Patent, { dated 20th March, 1664.

Lineage.

RICHARD BOYLE, second Earl of Cork, having married (5th July, 1635), Lady Elizabeth Clifford, only daughter and heiress of Henry, fifth and last Earl of Cumberland, of that family, was created a peer of England, by letters patent, dated 4th November, 1644, as BARON CLIFFORD, *of Lanesborough*, in the county of York, and advanced to the EARLDOM OF BURLINGTON on the 20th March, 1664, having been constituted, previously, LORD HIGH TREASURER OF IRELAND. His lordship was a zealous supporter of the royal cause during the civil wars, and one of the chief promoters of the restoration. His eldest son,

> CHARLES, Lord Viscount Dungarven, (who predeceased the earl,) was summoned to the English parliament by writ, in 1682, as Lord Clifford. His lordship m. first, Lady Jane Seymour, youngest daughter of William, Duke of Somerset, and first cousin of King Edward VI., by whom he had surviving issue—
>> CHARLES, successor to his grandfather.
>> Henry, one of the ministers of the crown, in the reigns of William and Mary, and King George I., created BARON CARLTON (see that dignity).
>> Elizabeth, m. to James, Earl of Barrymore.
>> Mary, m. in 1685, to James Douglas, Duke of Queensbury, afterwards created Duke of Dover.
>> Arabella, m. to Henry, Earl of Shelburne.
> His lordship m. secondly, Arethusa, daughter of George, Earl Berkeley, and had,
>> Arethusa, m. to James Vernon, Esq.

Richard, first earl of Burlington, d. 15th January, 1697, and was s. by his grandson,

CHARLES BOYLE, second earl of Burlington, (third earl of Cork,) lord high treasurer of Ireland. This nobleman (who was esteemed one of the most accomplished gentlemen in England,) m. Juliana, daughter and heiress of Henry Noel, Esq., of Luffenham, in the county of Rutland, and had issue—

> RICHARD, Lord Dungarven.
> Elizabeth, m. in 1719, to Sir Henry Arundel Bedingfeld, Bart.
> Juliana, m. in 1719, to Charles, Lord Bruce, son and heir of Thomas, Earl of Aylesbury, and died s. p. in 1739.
> Henrietta, m. in 1726, to Henry Boyle, Esq., of Castle Martyr, in the county of Cork, created Earl of Shannon.

His lordship d. 9th February, 1703, and was s. by his son,

RICHARD BOYLE, third Earl of Burlington, (fourth Earl of Cork,) lord high treasurer of Ireland, K.G. His lordship m. Lady Dorothy Savile, eldest daughter, and co-heir of William, Marquess of Halifax, by whom he had issue—

> Dorothy, b. in 1724, m. in 1741, to George, Earl Euston, and died s. p. in 1742.
> Juliana, b. in 1727, and d. in 1730.
> Charlotte Elizabeth, b. in 1731, m. in 1748, to William, Marquess of Hartington, son and heir of the Duke of Devonshire.

His lordship, who was distinguished by his patronage of the arts, and a very splendid and refined taste in architecture, d. 4th December, 1753, when the

EARLDOM OF BURLINGTON, and BARONY OF CLIFFORD, in the peerage of England expired, while the Irish honors devolved upon his kinsman, JOHN, fifth EARL OF ORRERY (see Earl of Cork, in extant peerage). The deceased nobleman's extensive estates, at Chiswick, in the county of Middlesex, and at Lismore, in the county of Waterford, with Burlington House, in London, passed with his lordship's only surviving daughter and heiress, Charlotte Elisabeth, Marchioness of Hartington, into the Devonshire family.

ARMS.—Per bend crenelle, ar. and gules.

BOYLE—BARON CARLTON.

By Letters Patent, dated 26th October, 1714.

Lineage.

The Right Honorable,

HENRY BOYLE, (third son of Charles, Lord Clifford, by his first wife, Lady Jane Seymour, daughter of William, Duke of Somerset,) representative in parliament for the University of Cambridge, and for the city of Westminster, was elevated to the peerage of England, on the 26th October, 1714, in the dignity of BARON CARLTON, and was constituted lord president of the council, on the 14th March, 1794. His lordship had previously filled the offices of chancellor of the exchequer, (1701,) and principal secretary of state, (1707). He was made HIGH TREASURER OF IRELAND in 1704, during the minority of Richard, Earl of Cork, and he was constituted one of the commissioners for the union with Scotland, in 1706. His lordship died unmarried, on the 14th March, 1794, when the BARONY OF CARLTON became EXTINCT.

BRADESTON — BARONS BRADESTON.

By Writ of Summons, dated 25th February, 1392, 16 Edward III.

Lineage.

The first person of this family, of whom anything memorable occurs, is

THOMAS DE BRADESTON, of Bradeston, in the county of Gloucester, the ancient seat of his predecessors, (all of whom were homagers to the castle of Berkeley, for their manors of Bradeston and Stinchcombe, which they held by knight's service,) who, in the 10th and 13th of Edward II., was engaged in the Scottish wars; but in the 15th of the same monarch, adhering to the Lord Berkeley against the favourite Spencer, his lands were seized by the crown: he was, however, the next year included in a general amnesty, and upon paying an hundred marks and renewing his oath of allegiance, had his property restored. He was afterwards constituted keeper of Kingswood Chase, near Bristol, and governor of Berkeley Castle; and subsequently taking part with the queen consort, Isabella, he was made one of the gentlemen of the privy chamber, at the accession of the young King

Edward III., and through the influence of the queen, obtained a grant of three considerable wardships. In the 4th of the new monarch, he was honoured with knighthood, by bathing, &c., having robes and all other things appertaining to that solemnity, allowed him from the king's wardrobe, as in the case of a banneret. In the next year, he was constituted provost of a certain part of Aquitain, and had a confirmation of a grant made to him by Queen Isabella, of the castle, Berton and Tyne, of Gloucester, for life, upon paying £1. and £10. yearly, into the exchequer. Sir Thomas was afterwards engaged in the Scottish wars, and had extensive grants of forfeited lands for his services, in Scotland, particularly those of Patric de Dunbar, Earl of March. In the 11th of Edward III., he had a grant of a ship, called The CHRISTMAS, taken in fight, from the French, by the merchants of Bristol; and, in the next year, was in the grand expeditions made into Flanders and Scotland, and for his good services, was made a KNIGHT BANNERET. Continuing actively engaged in foreign warfare, and acquiring fresh reputation each succeeding campaign, Sir Thomas de Bradeston was summoned to parliament as a BARON, on the 25th of February, 1342, and from that period until the 3rd April, 1360, during which interval his services were remunerated by extensive territorial grants, and by high and lucrative employments. This nobleman appears to have had one son, ROBERT, who predeceased him, leaving an only son, Thomas. Of Robert, the only thing memorable is, that having been taken prisoner in the 19th of Edward III., by the citizens of Pisa, in his journey to the Holy Land, the English monarch caused all the merchants of Pisa, as well as those of St. Luca, then in London, with their goods, to be seized, until he was released, twelve of the principal of whom were committed to the Tower, and not discharged until bail was given that young Bradeston should be forthwith enlarged. His lordship d. in 1360, and was s. by his grandson,

THOMAS DE BRADESTON, second Baron, but never summoned to parliament. This nobleman, like his predecessors, having a martial spirit, was in the expedition against France, in the 43rd of Edward III., before he had attained majority. He died, however, in five years afterwards, leaving an infant, only daughter and heiress,

ELIZABETH, who, in the reign of Richard II., made proof of her age, and had livery of her lands, being then the wife of Walter de la Pole, by whom she left a daughter and heiress,

——, who m. —— Ingoldsthorp, whose heir general espoused JOHN NEVIL, Marquess of Montagu, brother to the celebrated Richard Nevil, Earl of Warwick.

ARMS.—Ar. on a canton gu. a rose or barbed vert.

BRANDON—DUKES OF SUFFOLK.

By Letters Patent, dated 1st February, 1514.

Lineage.

SIR WILLIAM BRANDON, KNT. had, with

other issue, by his wife, Elizabeth, daughter of Sir Robert Wingfield, Knt., two sons, both zealous partisans of Henry of Richmond, in his contest with Richard III. The younger,

THOMAS, living to witness the accession of his patron to the crown, as Henry VII., was made one of the esquires of that king's body, and bore his buckler at the battle of STOKE. In consideration of which, and other services, he obtained the wardship of Richard Fenys, son and heir of William Fenys, Lord Say, with the benefit of his marriage; and before the termination of the same reign, was installed a KNIGHT of the most NOBLE order of the GARTER. Sir Thomas d. in the first year of Henry VIII., being then one of the knights of the king's body, and marshal of the court of common-pleas. He left no issue.

The elder son,

SIR WILLIAM BRANDON, standard-bearer at Bosworth, fell by the hand of King Richard in that celebrated field, leaving by his wife, Elizabeth, daughter and co-heir of Sir Henry Bruyn, Knt., a son and heir,

CHARLES BRANDON. "Which Charles," says Dugdale, "being a person comely of stature, high of courage, and conformity of disposition, to King Henry VIII., became so acceptable to him, especially in all his youthful exercises and pastimes, as that he soon attained great advancement, both in titles of honor, and otherwise." In the 1st of Henry he was made one of the esquires of the king's body, and chamberlain of the principality of North Wales, in the 4th he distinguished himself in a naval engagement off Brest, and the next year, attending the king upon the expedition of *Thereune and Tournay*, he was elevated to the peerage (5th March, 5th Henry VIII.) as VISCOUNT L'ISLE, and appointed commander of the advanced guard of the army: in which campaign he behaved so valiantly, that, in reward of his distinguished services, he was created, in the following February, (anno 1514,) DUKE OF SUFFOLK, and shortly afterwards, assisting at the coronation of the Lady Mary, (King Henry's sister,) then wife of Lewis XII. of France, at St. Dennis, he acquired so much renown by overthrowing the knight with whom he tilted at a princely tournament, celebrated upon the occasion, that he won the affections of the queen, who, upon the decease of her royal husband, which occurred soon after, bestowed upon him her hand; and having reconciled the kings of England and France to the union, he obtained from the former a grant in general tail, of all the lordships, manors, &c., which had previously belonged to Edmund de la Pole, Duke of Suffolk (who was beheaded and attainted in 1513). His grace made one of the retinue of his royal master at his magnificent interview with Francis I. upon "the field of the Cloth of Gold," between Guisnes and Ardres, in Picardy; and, in the next year, (15th Henry VIII.,) he led an army almost to the gates of Paris, to the great consternation of the good citizens, whose destruction was averted only by the recal of the general. In the 21st of Henry VIII. he was one of the peers who

subscribed the articles against Cardinal Wolsey, and, in the next year, the declaration to Pope Clement VII. regarding the king's divorce from Queen Katherine. His grace was afterwards constituted chief justice in Eyre of all the king's forests, and at the dissolution of the great monasteries he had a large proportion of the spoil. The duke was also a KNIGHT of the most NOBLE order of the GARTER. His grace married no less than four wives, first, Margaret, daughter of John Nevil, Marquess of Montagu, and widow of Sir John Mortimer, by whom he had no issue; secondly, Anne, daughter of Sir Anthony Browne, Knt., governor of Calais, by whom he had two daughters—

Anne, m. to Sir Edward Grey, Lord Powys.

Mary, m. to Thomas Stanley, Lord Monteagle.

His grace espoused, thirdly, the Lady Mary Tudor, second daughter of King Henry VII., and queen dowager of (Lewis XII., king of) France, by whom he had issue—

HENRY, created EARL OF LINCOLN in 1525, who predeceased the duke unmarried, when the EARLDOM of Lincoln expired.

Frances, m., first, to Henry Grey, third Marquess of Dorset, who was created DUKE OF SUFFOLK after the decease of his wife's half brother, Henry Brandon, (last duke of that family,) in 1551, but beheaded and attainted in three years afterwards. The issue of this marriage were—

LADY JANE GREY, the amiable but unfortunate aspirant to the crown at the decease of Edward VI.

Lady Catherine Grey, the unhappy wife of Edward Seymour, Earl of Hertford, d. a prisoner in the Tower in 1567.

Lady Mary Grey, m. to Martin Keys, Esq.

Her grace married, secondly, Adrian Stokes.

Eleanor, m. to Henry Clifford, Earl of Cumberland.

His grace m., fourthly, Catherine, Baroness Willoughby de Eresby, (only daughter and heiress of William, Lord Willoughby, who d. in 1525,) by whom he had two sons,

HENRY, his successor,

Charles.

Charles Brandon, DUKE OF SUFFOLK, d. on the 24th August, 1545, and was s. by his elder son,

HENRY BRANDON, second duke, who, with his brother Charles, died in minority, 14th July, 1551, at the residence of the Bishop of Lincoln at Bugden, in Huntingdonshire, of the sweating sickness, when the DUKEDOM OF SUFFOLK became EXTINCT. The patent of the VISCOUNTY OF L'ISLE was cancelled soon after its creation, owing to the refusal of Elizabeth Grey (only daughter and heiress of John Grey, Viscount L'Isle, at whose decease that dignity expired in the Grey family, in 1519,) to fulfil, on coming of age, her marriage contract with his grace, then Charles Brandon, Viscount L'Isle, the said patent being in reversion to his issue by that lady. Miss Grey afterwards married Henry Courtenay, second Earl of Devonshire, and d. issueless.

ARMS.—Barry of ten ar. and gu., over all a lion rampant or. crowned per pale ar.

NOTE.—In the 2nd of Elizabeth the extensive possessions of this celebrated Duke of Suffolk were shared amongst the descendants of Sir William Brandon, his grandfather, viz.—

Sir Henry Sidney, Knt., descended from John Sidney and Anna Brandon.

William Cavendish, Esq., from John Cavendish and Elizabeth Brandon.

Thomas Glenham, Esq., from ———— Glenham and Alianora Brandon.

Franis Kersey, Esq., son of John Kersey, by Margaret Lovel, daughter and heiress of Margaret Brandon, by her husband, Lovel, Esq.

Christian Darnell, widow.

Walter Ascough, Esq., and his son.

Henry Ascough.

John Tyre, Esq.

BRANDON—EARL OF LINCOLN.

See Brandon, Duke of Suffolk.

BRAY—BARONS BRAY.

By Writ of Summons, dated 3d November, 1529.
21 Henry VIII.

Lineage.

SIR REGINALD BRAY, Knight Banneret, and Knight of the Garter, (the first member of this family mentioned by Dugdale, as of note,) was in the service of Margaret, Countess of Richmond, at the accession of Richard III., and contributed his exertions to the elevation of her ladyship's son to the throne, as Henry VII. Sir Reginald d. without issue, and Margery, the only daughter of his brother John, became his heir, which Margery m. Sir William Sandys, afterwards Lord Sandys. Sir Reginald Bray had, however, another brother, whose son and heir,

SIR EDMUND BRAY, Knt., was summoned to parliament as a BARON, from the 3d November, 1529, to 8th June, 1536. His lordship m. Jane, daughter, and heiress of Richard Haliwell, (by his wife, Anne, daughter, and heiress of Sir John Norbury, Knt., grandson of Sir John Norbury, Knt., by Elizabeth, eldest sister, and co-heir of Ralph Boteler, Lord Sudley,) and had issue—

JOHN, his successor.

Anne, m. George Brooke, Lord Cobham.

Elizabeth, m. first, to Sir Ralph Vernon, and secondly, to Sir Richard Catesby.

Frediswide, m. to Sir Percival Hash.

Mary, m. to Robert Peckham, Esq.

Dorothy, m. first, to Edmund, Lord Chandos, and secondly, to William, Lord Knolles, K.G.

Frances, m. to Thomas Lifield, Esq., of Stoke D'Aubernon, Surrey, and left a daughter, and heiress,

Jane, who m. Thomas Vincent, Esq., lineal ancestor of the present Sir Francis Vincent, Bart., of Stoke D'Aubernon.

Lord Bray d. in 1539, and was s. by his son,

JOHN BRAY, second baron, summoned to parliament from the 3d November, 1545, to the 21st October, 1555. This nobleman was a commanding officer in the expedition made into France under the Earl of Hertford, in the 38th of Henry VIII.; and upon the insurrection in Norfolk, in the 2d of Edward VI., his lordship marched with the Marquess of Northampton for its suppression; and in three years afterwards he was appointed to attend the same nobleman upon his embassy into France, as bearer of the order of the garter to the French monarch. In the 4th year of Mary, he assisted at the siege of St. Quintius, in Picardy. His lordship m. Anne, daughter of Francis, Earl of Shrewsbury, but dying s. p. on the 18th November, 1557, his estates devolved upon his sisters, and the BARONY OF BRAY, fell into ABEYANCE, amongst these ladies, as it still continues with their descendants.

ARMS.—Ar. a chev. betw. three eagles legs erased à là quisé, sa.

BROMFLETE—BARON OF VESCY.

By Writ of Summons, dated 24th January, 1449,
27 Henry VI.

Lineage.

In the 11th year of Richard II.,

THOMAS DE BROMFLETE obtained a charter of free warren in all his demesne lands in the county of York, and marrying in two years afterwards, Margaret, daughter, and heiress of Sir John St. John, Knt., by Anastasia, daughter, and co-heir of William de Aton, Lord of Vesci, had livery of the lands of her inheritance. In the 19th of the same reign he was constituted the king's chief butler, and received the honor of knighthood. In the 2d of Henry V., Sir Thomas served the office of sheriff of Yorkshire, and was governor of the castle at York. He d. in the 9th of Henry VI., and was s. by his only surviving son,

SIR HENRY DE BROMFLETE, Knt., who had then livery of his lands, and was soon after constituted sheriff of the county of York, and governor of the castle there. In the 12th of Henry VI., Sir Henry was sent ambassador to the great council, holden at Basil, in Germany; having license to take with him, in gold, silver, jewels, and plate, to the value of £2000 sterling, and an assignation of £300 for every half year he should be detained upon the mission, beyond the first six months. In the 27th of the same reign, he was summoned to parliament by special writ, dated 24th January, (1449,) as "HENRICO BROMFLETE DE VESCI, CHEVALIER," in remainder to the heirs male of his body, being the first and only writ with such a limitation. His lordship had afterwards a specific dispensation from the duty of attending parliament, in consideration of his eminent services to King Henry V., in that monarch's wars of France and Normandy, for which he had never received any remuneration, and in consideration, likewise, of his advanced age. Lord Vesci d. on the 6th January, 1468, and leaving no male issue, the BARONY EXPIRED, according to the terms of the writ. A portion of his lordship's estates were devoted, by his will, to religious purposes, while the remainder devolved upon his only daughter,

> MARGARET DE BROMFLETE, who m. first, John Clifford, Lord Clifford, who fell at the battle of Towton, on the 1st of Henry IV., (see Clifford, Lords Clifford,) and secondly, Sir Lancelot Threlkeld, Knt., by whom she had three daughters, viz. :—
>> ——, m. to Thomas Dudley.
>> ——, m. to James Pickering.
>> Winifred, m. to William Pickering.

Henry Bromflete, Lord Vesey, was summoned to parliament altogether, from the 24th January, 1449, to the 26th February, 1466.

ARMS—Sa, a bend florée counter-florée, or.

BROOKE—BARONS COBHAM.

By Writ of Summons, dated 8th January, 1313,

6 Edward II.

Lineage.

This ancient barony came into the family of Brooke, with Joane, only daughter, and heiress of Sir Reginald Braybroke, and his wife, Joane de la Pole, grand-daughter and heiress of John Cobham, second and last Lord Cobham, of that family, (see Cobham, Barons Cobham,) which

JOANE BRAYBROKE espoused SIR THOMAS BROKE, Knt., and had issue,

SIR EDWARD BROOKE, Knt., who was summoned to parliament as "EDWARDO BROOKE DE COBHAM, CHEVALIER," from the 13th January, 1445, to the 30th July, 1460. (The barony of Cobham had lain dormant from the execution of Sir John Oldcastle, Lord Cobham, until the issue of the first of these summonses.) His lordship was a zealous supporter of the house of York, under whose banner he participated in the victory of St. Albans, in the 33d of Henry VI., and commanded the left wing of the Yorkshiremen at Northampton. He m. Elizabeth, daughter of James, Lord Audley, and dying in 1464, was s. by his son,

JOHN BROOKE, who was summoned to parliament as LORD COBHAM, from the 19th August, 1472, to the 16th January, 1497. This nobleman distinguished himself in arms in the reigns of Edward IV., and Henry VII. His lordship m. Margaret, daughter of Edward Nevil, Lord Abergavenny, and dying in 1506, was s. by his son,

THOMAS BROOKE, summoned to parliament, from 17th October, 1509, to 12th November, 1515. His lordship attended King Henry VIII. into France at the taking of Tournay. He m. thrice, but had issue by his first wife, Dorothy, daughter of Sir Henry Heyden, only, and dying in 1599, was s. by his eldest son,

GEORGE BROOKE, summoned to parliament, from 3d November, 1529, to 20th January, 1558. Upon the dissolution of the greater monasteries in the reign of Henry VIII., this nobleman obtained a grant in fee of the manor of Chettingdon, in Kent; as also of the college of Cobham, and in the 5th of Edward VI., on some apprehension of danger from the French, he was constituted lieutenant-general of those forces which were sent into the north for the purpose of fortifying some havens there. At the accession of Queen Mary he was committed to the Tower on suspicion of being implicated in the treason of Sir Thomas Wyat, but was soon afterwards liberated. His lordship m. Anne, daughter of Edmund, Lord Bray, and had issue, WILLIAM, his successor, with seven other sons, the fifth of whom, Henry, was ancestor of the Brookes, of Hekinton, and two daughters, namely—

> Elizabeth, m. to William Parr, Marquess of Northampton, (his lordship's second wife).
> Katherine, m. to John Jerningham, Esq.

Lord Cobham, who was a knight of the garter, d. at Cobham Hall, on the 29th September, 1558, and was s. by his eldest son,

WILLIAM BROOKE, summoned to parliament, from 1558 to 1596. This nobleman being lord warden of the cinque ports at the death of Queen Mary, was deputed to announce to the Spaniards, in the Netherlands, the accession of Elizabeth, and to acquaint them that her majesty had added to the commission, appointed to negotiate a peace at Cambray, William, Lord Howard, of Effingham. In the 14th of Elizabeth, his lordship being one of those committed to the Tower of London, for participating in the designs of the Duke of Norfolk, regarding that nobleman's marriage with Mary, Queen of Scots, made a discovery of all he knew of the affair, in the hope of obtaining his own pardon. The baron was subsequently employed upon two occasions to treat of peace with France. He was afterwards constable of Dover Castle, and warden of the cinque ports, lord chamberlain of the household, and a KNIGHT of the most NOBLE order of the GARTER. His lordship m. first, Dorothy, daughter of George, Lord Abergavenny, by Mary, daughter of Edward, Duke of Buckingham, by whom he had an only daughter,

> Frances, m. first, to Thomas Coppinger, Esq., of Kent, and secondly, to Edmund Beecher, Esq.

Lord Cobham, m. secondly, Frances, daughter of Sir John Newton, and had issue—

> Maximilian, who d. before his father, s. p.
> HENRY, successor to the title.
> George, executed and attainted in the reign of King James I. as a participator in "Raleigh's conspiracy," and left issue by his wife, Elizabeth, daughter of Thomas, Lord Borough,
>> WILLIAM, restored in blood, m. Penelope, daughter of Sir Moses Hill, Knt., and left two daughters,*
>>> ——, m. to Sir John Denham, Knt., the poet.
>>> Hill, m. to Sir William Boothley, Knt.
> William, (Sir,) killed in 1597.
> Elizabeth, m. to Robert, Earl of Salisbury.
> Frances, m. first, to John, Lord Stourton, and secondly, to Sir Edward Moore.
> Margaret, m. to Sir Thomas Sondes, Knt., and had,
>> FRANCES, m. to Sir Richard Levison, Knt., and left,
>>> SIR JOHN LEVISON, Knt., of Tren-

---

* To these ladies, notwithstanding the attainder, the king granted the precedency of a baron's daughters.

tham, Staffordshire, who had issue—

   Sir Richard Levison, K.B., died s. p.

   Frances, m. to Sir Thomas Gower, ancestor of the Marquess of Stafford.

   Christiana, m. to Sir Peter Temple, of Stowe, in the county of Bucks, whose grandson, Sir Richard Temple, was created in 1714, Baron Cobham, and in 1718, Viscount and Baron Cobham (see Temple, Lord Cobham, under the head of Buckingham, in *Burke's Dictionary of the Peerage and Baronetage*).

His lordship d. in 1596, and was s. by his eldest son, HENRY BROOKE, summoned to parliament on the 24th October, 1597. This nobleman was constituted by Queen Elizabeth, warden of the cinque ports; but in the reign of King James, being arraigned with his brother George for participation in the alleged treason of Sir Walter Raleigh, they were found guilty and condemned to death, but George Brooke alone suffered. His lordship was reprieved, yet nevertheless attainted, and left to drag on in misery, and the most wretched poverty, the remainder of an unhappy life in imprisonment, wherein he died in 1619. His wife was Frances, daughter of Charles Howard, Earl of Nottingham, but he had no issue. Under the attainder of this unfortunate nobleman the ancient BARONY OF COBHAM EXPIRED, although his nephew and heir William Cobham, (son of the beheaded and attainted George,) was restored in blood in 1610, but "not to enjoy the title of Lord Cobham without the king's especial grace," which was never conferred upon him.[*]

---

[*] The plot in which Henry, Lord Cobham, and his brother the Honourable George Brooke were involved, is known as the "Raleigh Conspiracy," and amongst the principal actors were the Lord Grey of Wilton, Sir George Carew, and other persons of eminence. Lord Cobham appears to have been not many degrees removed from a fool, but enjoying the favour of the Queen, he was a fitting tool in the hands of his more wily associates. Upon his trial he was dastardly to the most abject meanness. The mode of bringing the prisoners on the scaffold, and aggravating their sufferings, with momentary expectation of their catastrophe, before the pre-intended pardon was produced, was a piece of management and contrivance for which King James was by the sycophants of the court very highly extolled, but such a course was universally esteemed the pitiful policy of a weak contemptible mind.

On this occasion, however, says Sir Dudley Carleton, Cobham, who was now "to play his part," did much cozen the world, for he came to the scaffold with good assurance, and contempt of death. And in the short prayers he made, so outprayed the company which helped to pray with him, that a stander-by observed, "that he had a good mouth in a cry, but was nothing single."

ARMS.—Gules, a chevron ar. a lion rampant sa. crowned or.

BROOKE—BARON COBHAM.

By Letters Patent, dated 3rd January, 1645, 20 Charles I.

Lineage.

SIR JOHN BROOKE OF HEKINGTON, (son of the Honourable Henry Brooke, 5th son of George, fourth Lord Cobham of that family,) having eminently distinguished himself in the cause of King Charles I., was elevated to the peerage on the 3rd January, 1645, as LORD COBHAM, "to enjoy that title in as ample a manner as any of his ancestors had done," save that the remaindership was limited to heirs male. His lordship d. in 1651, s. p. when the barony EXPIRED.

ARMS.—Gu. a chevron ar. a lion rampant sa. crowned or.

BROTHERTON — EARL OF NORFOLK.

See Plantagenet, Earl of Norfolk.

BROWN—VISCOUNTS MONTACUTE OR MONTAGU.

By Letters Patent, dated 2d September, 1554.

Lineage.

SIR ANTHONY BROWN, who was made Knight of the Bath at the coronation of King Richard II., left two sons, the younger, Sir Stephen Brown, Lord Mayor of London, in 1439, imported during his mayoralty, large cargoes of rye from Prussia, in consequence of the scarcity of wheat, and distributed them amongst the poorer classes of the people. The elder son,

SIR ROBERT BROWN, was father of

SIR THOMAS BROWN, treasurer of the household to King Henry VI., who m. Eleanor, daughter and co-heiress of Sir Thomas Fits-Alan, and niece

---

After they were remanded (Sir Dudley says), and brought back on the scaffold, "they looked strange on one another, like men beheaded and met again in the other world." He is stated to have died in a state of filth, for want of apparel and linen; which was a singular judgment, that a man of near £7,000 a year, and a personal estate of £30,000, which should have escheated to the crown, but whereof the king was cheated, should die for want; as in such cases the king usually grants maintenance thereout, though not from the revenue of the crown. It is moreover asserted, that the lady Cobham, his wife, though very rich, would not even give him the crumbs from her table.

Thus the noble mansion of Cobham Hall, in Kent, with the surrounding estate, the ancient seat of the once illustrious and spreading branches of the Cobham family, fell to the crown; and were granted by James I., in the 10th of his reign, to his kinsman, Lodowick Stewart, Duke of Lenox, and afterwards of Richmond, from whom they at length descended through an heiress to the family of Bligh, Baron of Clifton in England, and Earls of Darnley in Ireland.

of John, Earl of Arundel, by whom he acquired the castle of Beechworth, in Surrey, and had, with other issue—

George (Sir) of Beechworth Castle, who, in the 1st Richard III., was amongst those ordered to be apprehended as adherents of the Duke of Buckingham. From this Sir George Brown descended,

SIR AMBROSE BROWN, Baronet of Beechworth, who m. Elizabeth, daughter and heiress of William Adair, Esq., of Saffron Waldron, and was s. by his son,

SIR ADAM BROWN, second baronet, whose only son AMBROSE, predeceasing him unmarried, the baronetcy and line terminated at his decease.

William, died s. p.

Anthony, of whom presently.

Robert, (Sir) m. Mary, daughter of Sir William Mallet, Knt., and left an only daughter and heiress Eleanor, m. first to Thomas Fogo, Esq., and secondly, to William Kempe, Esq., of Olantye, Kent.

Catherine, m. to Humphrey Sackvile, Esq., of Buckhurst, in the county of Sussex.

The third son,

ANTHONY BROWN, was appointed in the 1st year of Henry VII. standard-bearer, for the whole realm of England and elsewhere; and the next year, being one of the esquires of the king's body, was constituted governor of Queenborough Castle, Kent. At this period participating in the victory achieved over the Earl of Lincoln, and Lambert Simnell, at Newark, he received the honour of knighthood. Sir Anthony, m. Lucy, one of the daughters and co-heirs of JOHN NEVIL, MARQUESS OF MONTAGU, and widow of Sir Thomas Fitz-williams, of Aldwarke, in the county of York, and had issue—

ANTHONY, his successor.

Elizabeth, m. to Henry Somerset, Earl of Worcester.

Lucy, m. to Sir Thomas Clifford, Knt.

Sir Anthony was s. by his son,

SIR ANTHONY BROWN, who was with the Earl of Surrey, Lord High Admiral, at Southampton, in the 14th Henry VIII., when he convoyed the emperor from that port to Biscay; and after landing at Morlaix, in Britanny, was knighted for his gallantry in the assault, and winning of that town. In two years afterwards, being then an esquire of the household, he was one of the challengers in feats of arms held at Greenwich before the king; and the next year he was appointed Lieutenant of the Isle of Man, during the minority of the Earl of Derby. After this he was twice deputed on important occasions, ambassador to the court of France; and obtained in 30th of the same reign a grant of the office of master of the horse, with the annual fee of forty pounds: in which year he had also a grant of the house and scite of the late Monastery of Battle, in the county of Sussex. In the next year he was elected, with the Lord Chancellor Audley, a KNIGHT of the most NOBLE order of the GARTER. In the 30th of Henry, Sir Anthony was constituted standard-bearer to the king, and was nominated by his majesty one of the executors to his will. Sir Anthony Brown, m. Alice, daughter of Sir John Gage, K.G., and had, with other issue—

ANTHONY, his heir.

William, m. Anne, daughter and co-heiress of Hugh Hastings, Esq., by whom he acquired Elsing, in the county of Southampton.

Mary, m. to John Grey, second son of Thomas, Marquess of Dorset.

Mabel, m. to Gerald, Earl of Kildare.

Lucy, m. to Thomas Roper, Esq., of Eltham, in Kent.

Sir Anthony, d. 6th May, 1548, and was s. by his eldest son,

SIR ANTHONY BROWN, KNT., sheriff of Surrey and Sussex in the last year of King Edward VI., who was elevated to the peerage by Queen Mary, on the 2nd September, 1554, in the dignity of VISCOUNT MONTAGU, and immediately after deputed, by order of parliament, with Thomas Thurlby, Bishop of Ely, to the pope, for the purpose of reuniting the realm of England with the church of Rome. In the next year his lordship was installed a KNIGHT of the most NOBLE order of the GARTER; but upon the accession of Queen Elizabeth his name was left out of the privy council, and he voted soon after, in his place in parliament, with the Earl of Shrewsbury, against abolishing the pope's supremacy. Yet, according to Camden, he contrived to ingratiate himself with her majesty. "Queen Elizabeth," says that writer, "having experienced his loyalty, had great esteem for him, (though he was a stiff Romanist,) and paid him a visit some time before his death: for she was sensible that his regard for that religion was owing to his cradle and education, and proceeded rather from principle than faction, as some people's faith did." His lordship m., first, Jane, daughter of Robert Ratcliffe, Earl of Sussex, and had issue—

ANTHONY, who predeceased him on the 29th June, 1592, leaving by his wife, Mary, daughter of Sir William Dormer, Knt. of Ethorp, in the county of Bucks—

ANTHONY, who succeeded as second viscount.

John, m. Anne, daughter of —— Gifford, Esq., and had

Stanislaus, whose grandson, MARK-ANTHONY BROWN, inherited as ninth viscount.

George.

Dorothy, m. to Edward Lee, Esq., of Stanton Barry, in the county of Bucks.

Jane, m. to Sir George Englefield, Bart.

Catharine, m. to —— Tregasian, Esq.

Mary, m., first, to Henry Wriothesley, Earl of Southampton; secondly, to Sir Thomas Heneage, Knt.; and thirdly, to Sir William Harvey, Bart., created Lord Ross in Ireland, and Baron Kidbrook in England.

The viscount m., secondly, Magdalen, daughter of William, Lord Dacres of Gillesland, and had, with other issue—

George, (Sir,) of Wicham-Breux, in the county of Kent, m. Mary, daughter of Sir Robert

Tirwhitt, of Kettleby, in the county of Lincoln, Knt., and had

Henrietta, m. to Richard Harcourt, Esq.

His lordship d. on the 28th June, 1717. and was s. by his son,

> George, m. Eleanor, daughter of Sir Richard Blount, of Mapledurham, in the county of Oxford, Knt., and had two sons and a daughter.

Henry, of Kiddington, in the county of Oxford, m. Anne, daughter of Sir William Catesby, Knt., and had

> Peter, (Sir,) who was slain in the service of King Charles I., leaving two sons,
>
>> Henry, created a baronet in 1656, with remainder to his brother.
>>
>> Francis.

Elisabeth, m. to Sir Robert Dormer, afterwards Lord Dormer.

Mabel, m. to Sir Henry Capel, ancestor to the Earl of Essex. *and so Car s/e*

Jane, m. to Sir Francis Lacon of Willey, in the county of Salop, Knt.

His lordship, who was on the trial of Mary, Queen of Scots, d. on the 19th October, 1592, and was s. by his grandson,

ANTHONY BROWN, second viscount, who m. in February, 1591, Jane, daughter of Thomas Sackville, Earl of Dorset, Lord High Treasurer of England, and had issue—

Francis, his successor.

Mary, m., first, to William, Lord St. John of Basing ; and secondly, to William, second son of Thomas, Lord Arundel of Wardour.

Catherine, m. to William Tirwhitt, Esq., of Kettleby.

Anne, } became nuns abroad.
Lucy, }

Mary, m. to Robert, Lord Petre.

His lordship d. 23rd October, 1629, and was s. by his son,

FRANCIS BROWN, third viscount. This nobleman suffered considerably in the royal cause during the civil wars, but lived to hail the restoration of the monarchy. His lordship m. Elizabeth, youngest daughter of Henry Somerset, Marquess of Worcester, and had issue, Francis and Henry, successively viscounts, and Elizabeth, m. to Christopher Roper, fifth Lord Teynham. His lordship d. on the 2nd November, 1682, and was s. by his elder son,

FRANCIS BROWN, fourth viscount. This nobleman, who was a zealous catholic, was appointed lord-lieutenant of Sussex, by King James II., in 1687. His lordship m. Mary, daughter of William Herbert, Marquess of Powis, and widow of Robert Molineux, eldest son of Carryl, Viscount Molineux, but dying s. p. in 1708, his honors devolved upon his brother,

HENRY BROWN, fifth viscount, who m. Barbara, daughter of James Walsingham, Esq., of Chesterford, in the county of Essex, and had issue—

Anthony, his successor.

Mary, d. unmarried.

Elizabeth, a nun.

Barbara, m. to Ralph Salvin, Esq.

Catherine, m. to George Collingwood, Esq., of Northumberland.

Anne, m., to Anthony Kemp, Esq., of Slindon, in Sussex.

84

ANTHONY BROWN, sixth viscount. This nobleman m. Frances, sister of Sir Herbert Macworth, Bart., and widow of Alexander, Lord Halkerton, by whom he had issue—

George-Samuel, his successor.

Elizabeth Mary, m. in 1794, to William Stephen Poyntz, Esq., of Medgham, Berks.

His lordship d. in 1787, and was s. by his son,

GEORGE-SAMUEL BROWN, seventh viscount, who met an untimely fate, in a rash attempt to pass the waterfalls of Schauffhausen, accompanied by his friend, Mr. Sedley Burdet, in a small flat-bottomed boat, contrary to the advice, and even restriction of the local magistrate, who, knowing the certain result of so unprecedented an enterprise, had placed guards to intercept the daring travellers. They found means, however, to elude every precaution, and having pushed off, passed the first fall in security, but in attempting to clear the second they disappeared, and were never afterwards seen or heard of. It is presumed that the boat, impelled by the violence of the cataract, got jammed between the two rocks, and was thus destroyed. This melancholy event occurred in 1793, and about the same period his lordship's magnificent mansion at Coudray was accidentally burnt to the ground. His lordship dying unmarried the viscounty was supposed to devolve upon (the grandson of Stanislaus Brown, Esq., son and heir of John Brown, Esq., brother of Anthony, second viscount, and grandson of the first lord) his cousin,

MARK ANTHONY BROWN, Esq., as ninth Viscount Montagu, at whose decease, in 1797, without issue, the dignity became extinct.

Arms.—Sa. three lions passant in bend between two double cotizes ar.

BRUCE—BARON BRUCE, OF ANANDALE.

By Writ of Summons, dated 23rd June, 1295, 23 Edward 1st.

Lineage.

The illustrious family of Bruce, was founded in England, by

SIR ROBERT DE BRUS, a noble Norman, who accompanied the conqueror, and obtained no less than ninety-four lordships in the county of York, of which Skelton, manor and castle, was the chief, and the manors of Herts and Hertness, in the bishopric of Durham. This eminent person m. first, Agnes, daughter of Fulk Paganal, and had issue—

> Adam, who s. to the Yorkshire estates, and whose male line terminated with
>
>> Peter de Brus, in 1271, at whose decease, s. p., his great possessions reverted to his four sisters, as co-heiresses. viz.
>
> Margaret, m. to Robert de Roos.
>
> Agnes, m. to Walter Fauconberge.
>
> Lucy, m. to Marmeduke de Thweng.
>
> Laderine, m. to John de Bellew.

Sir Robert, m. secondly, Agnes Anand, a great Scottish heiress, by whom he acquired the Lordship of Anandale, in that kingdom, which, with Hert and Hertness, he bestowed upon his son by that lady,

ROBERT DE BRUS, of whom little is recorded, save some benefactions, which he bestowed upon the church. He was s. by his son,

WILLIAM DE BRUS, who is likewise unnoticed, except for his religious grants; he was living at the close of the twelfth century—and was s. at his decease by his son,

ROBERT DE BRUS, who m. Isabel, daughter of David, Earl of Huntingdon, niece of WILLIAM, KING OF SCOTLAND, and one of the sisters and co-heiresses of John, surnamed Scot, Earl of Huntingdon, and last Count Palatine, of Chester: and was s. by his son,

ROBERT DE BRUS, who, in the 34th of Henry III., was one of the justices of the court of Common Pleas, and in two years afterwards, doing homage, had livery of the great estates which he inherited from his mother. In the 39th of the same monarch, he was constituted sheriff of Cumberland, and governor of the castle of Carlisle. Adhering to the king against the turbulent barons, he shared the fortunes of his royal master, and rose again into power after the triumph of the royal arms, at Evesham, (49th Henry III.,) when he was reinstated in his governorship of the castle of Carlisle. Upon the demise of Alexander III., of Scotland, in 1296, this English feudal lord, preferred his claims to the Scottish throne, but the matter being referred to the arbitration of King Edward, of England, that monarch decided in favor of John Baliol, the grandson of David, Earl of Huntingdon, to whom, however, Brus refused to do homage, and thereupon resigned his lands in Anandale, to his eldest son ROBERT, but Robert also refusing fealty to the new king, the estates were transferred to his second son, another ROBERT, who complied with the condition. Robert de Brus, m. first, Isabel, daughter of Gilbert de Clare, Earl of Glocester, by whom he had a son, ROBERT the elder. He m. secondly, a daughter of the Earl of Carrick, and had the younger,

ROBERT DE BRUS, who did homage to Baliol, as stated above, and obtained, in consequence, the Lordship of Anandale. In the 22nd of Edward I., this feudal baron, had, with other great men, summons to repair to Portsmouth, upon the 1st day of September, well fitted with horse and arms, to attend the king upon an expedition, preparing at that period, against France: but dying in the same year, he was s. by his son,

ROBERT BRUCE, who was summoned as a BARON, to the English parliament, from the 23rd June, 1295, to 26th January, 1297, as "Robert de Brus, senior," to distinguish him from his brother Robert Bruce, Earl of Carrick. This nobleman adhering faithfully to King Edward I., was engaged several years in the Scottish wars. His lordship dying s. p. in 1304, the BARONY EXPIRED, while his lands devolved upon his brother,

ROBERT BRUCE, Earl of Carrick, who was crowned, KING OF SCOTLAND, at Scone,

on the 24th March, 1305, and obtained, subsequently, so much celebrity, as "THE BRUS OF BANNOCKBURN." He was succeeded upon the Scottish throne, by his son,

DAVID, who d. without issue, when the crown devolved upon his nephew, (the son of his sister and heiress, Margery, by Walter Stewart, Lord High Steward of Scotland).

ROBERT, first monarch of the HOUSE of STEWART.

ARMS.—Or. a saltier and chief gules.

BRUCE — EARLS OF AYLESBURY, BARONS BRUCE OF WHORLTON, IN THE COUNTY OF YORK.

Barony Earldom } By Letters Patent. { 13th July, 1640. 18th March, 1662.

Lineage.

THOMAS BRUCE, first Earl of Elgin in the peerage of Scotland, was created a peer of England on the 13th July, 1640, as BARON BRUCE OF WHORLTON, in the county of York, and dying in 1663, was s. by his only son,

ROBERT BRUCE, second Earl of Elgin, who was advanced in the peerage of England on the 18th March, 1662, to the dignities of Baron Bruce of Skelton, in the county of York, Viscount Bruce of Ampthill, in the county of Bedford, and EARL OF AYLESBURY. His lordship m. Diana, daughter of Henry, second Earl of Stamford, and dying in 1685, was s. by his only surviving son,

THOMAS BRUCE, third Earl of Elgin, and second Earl of Aylesbury, who m., first, in 1676, Elizabeth, daughter of Henry, Lord Beauchamp, and heiress of her brother, William, third Duke of Somerset, by whom he had issue—

CHARLES, his successor, who was summoned to parliament in 1711, as LORD BRUCE OF WHORLTON.

Elizabeth, m. to George Brudenell, third Earl of Cardigan, and had issue—

GEORGE, fourth Earl of Cardigan, m. Mary, daughter of John, Duke of Montagu, and, assuming the surname of Montagu, was advanced, at the decease of his father-in-law, to the Marquisate of Monthermer, and DUKEDOM OF MONTAGU. His grace d. in 1790, leaving one married daughter,

Elizabeth, Duchess of Buccleuch.

James, successor to his brother, as fifth Earl of Cardigan.

Robert, whose son inherited as sixth Earl of Cardigan,

THOMAS, who, upon succeeding his uncle, the Earl of Aylesbury, in the barony of BRUCE of Tottenham, assumed the surname of Bruce, and was subsequently created EARL OF AYLESBURY.

His lordship, who m., secondly, Charlotte, Countess of Sannu, and had an only daughter, Charlotte-Maria, wife of Prince Home, died in 1741, and was s. by his only surviving son,

GEORGE BRUCE, third Earl of Aylesbury, and fourth Earl of Elgin. This nobleman m. Anne, eldest daughter, and one of the co-heirs of William Savile, Marquess of Halifax, by whom he had issue—

    Robert, m. Francis, daughter of Sir William Blacket, Bart., and died before his father, issueless.

    Mary, m. to Henry Brydges, Duke of Chandos.

    Elizabeth, m., in 1732, to Hon. Benjamin Bathurst, son and heir of Allen, Lord Bathurst.

His lordship m., secondly, Juliana, second daughter of Charles Boyle, Earl of Burlington, but had no issue. He m., thirdly, in 1739, Caroline, only daughter of General John Campbell, and niece of the Duke of Argyll, by whom he had an only daughter,

    Mary, m. in 1757, to Charles, Duke of Richmond.

After the decease of his son the Earl of Aylesbury and Elgin obtained, by letters patent, dated 17th April, 1746, the English Barony of BRUCE OF TOTTENHAM, in the county of Wilts, in remainder to his nephew, the Hon. Thomas Brudenell. His lordship d. on the 10th of February, 1747, when his Scottish honors passed to his heirs general, (see Elgin, Burke's Peerage and Baronetage). The English BARONY OF TOTTENHAM as limited, and the EARLDOM OF AYLESBURY, with his lordship's other English honors, EXPIRED.

Arms.—Or. a saltier and chief gu. on a canton ar. a lion rampant sa.

BRUGES—EARL OF WINCHESTER.

By Creation in open Parliament, 13th Oct., 1472, 12 Edward IV.

Lineage.

LEWES DE BRUGES, Lord of Gruthuse, and Prince of Steenhuse, a Burgundian, having evinced the greatest sympathy for King Edward IV., during that monarch's exile, (when forced to fly by the Lancastrians in the tenth year of his reign,) at the court of his brother-in-law, Charles de Valois, Duke of Burgundy, was received in two years afterwards by Edward, then re-established monarch in his English dominions, with the highest honors, and as a testimony of the gratitude felt by the nation towards so staunch a friend, its sovereign, the House of Commons, in parliament assembled, besought the king, through their speaker, William Alyngton, to bestow upon the foreign prince some especial mark of royal favor. In compliance with which request Edward advanced him, on the 13th October, 1472, to the dignity of EARL OF WINCHESTER, in the parliament chamber, by cincture with a sword. And granted to the new peer for upholding the dignity the sum of £200. annually. In the November following his lordship obtained a patent of arms as Earl of Winchester, viz., " Azure dix mascles d'or, enorme d'une canton de armes de Angleterre; cestassavoir de gules, a une lipard passant d'or, armée d'azure," which were so depicted in colours in the roll, wherein his patent for them is recorded. But in the 15th of Henry VII. (which

was about twenty-seven years after,) both these grants were surrendered to the king, then at Calais, and upon each of their enrolments a vacat made, without having any reason assigned for the proceedings.

His lordship m. Margaret, daughter of Henry de Borselle, and had issue—

    JOHN, Lord of Gruthuse, father of REGINALD, who d. without issue male.

Arms.—Az. ten mascles, fourth, third, second, and first, or. on a canton, gules, a lion passant guardant of the second.

BRYAN—BARON BRYAN.

By Writ of Summons, dated 25th November, 1350, 24 Edward III.

Lineage.

In the 29th of Henry III.

GUY DE BRIAN, whose chief seat was in the marches of Wales, received command to assist the Earl of Gloucester against the Welsh: and in the 42nd of the same reign, he had a second military summons for a similar service. We find him subsequently, however, arrayed under the baronial banner, and constituted after the victory of his party, at Lewes, governor of the castles of KARDIGAN, and KERMERDYN, but he soon afterwards returned to his allegiance, and was one of the sureties—51st Henry III.—for Robert de Vere, Earl of Oxford, that that nobleman should thenceforward deport himself peaceably, and abide by the *dictum of Kenilworth*, for the redemption of his lands. This Guy de Brian, m. Eva, only daughter and heiress of Henry de Traci, and dying in the 35th Edward I., was s. by his son,

SIR GUY DE BRYAN, who, in the 4th Edward III., was constituted governor of the castle of Haverford, but he was afterwards found to be of unsound mind—when an agreement was made, that the Barony of " *Chastel Walwayn*," should at once come into possession of his son GUOYEN, upon his undertaking to provide for his two sisters* from the revenues thereof. This

GUOYEN DE BRYAN, thus invested with the Barony of Chastel-Walwyen, served in the Scottish wars, in the 11th of Edward III., and in consideration of his special services, had an annuity of £40. granted him by the king, out of the exchequer, for life. In the 15th of the same reign, he was made governor of St. Briavel's Castle, and warden of the forest of Dene, in the county of Gloucester; and from the 16th to the 20th, he was engaged in the French wars. He d. in 1350, and was s. by his son,

GUY DE BRYAN, who became a person of considerable note, at that period in which he lived. About the time of his father's death, he was standard-bearer to King Edward III., in the cele-

---

* Banks surmises, that those ladies were,

Ella, the wife of Robert Fitz-payne, and

Elizabeth, wife of Robert de Grey, who inherited a portion of the Fitz-payne estates, and assumed the surname of Fitz-payne. (See Fitz-payne.)

brated fight with the French at Calais, and deporting himself with great valour upon that occasion, he had a grant of two hundred marks per annum, out of the exchequer, for life. He was also constituted governor of St. Briavels Castle, and warden of the forest of Dene; and was summoned to parliament, as a BARON, from 25th November, 1350, to 6th December, 1369. In 1354, his lordship was one of the ambassadors to the court of Rome, to procure the papal ratification of a league, then made, between the. Kings of England and France; the next year, he attended King Edward in his expedition into France, when he was made a banneret, and be continued for several years subsequently, in the French wars. In 1361, he was again accredited upon a mission of importance, to the holy see, and being some years afterwards, once more engaged against the French, he was made admiral of the king's fleet—a command renewed to his lordship in the next year, (44th Edward III,) and he was soon after elected a KNIGHT of the GARTER. In the reign of Richard II., Lord Bryan also served against the French, and he was in the expedition made into Ireland, with Edward Mortimer, Earl of March. His lordship m. Elizabeth, daughter of William de Montacute, Earl of Salisbury, and widow of Hugh le Despenser, by whom, (with two younger sons, who d. issueless,) he had,

> GUY, who d. in the lifetime of his father, leaving issue,
>> PHILIPPA, m. first, to John Devereux, and secondly, to Sir Henry le Scrope, Knt., but died s. p.
>> ELIZABETH, m. to Sir Robert Lovell, Knt., and had an only daughter and heiress,
>>> MAUDE LOVELL, who m. first, John Fitzalan, Earl of Arundel, and had issue,
>>>> HUMPHREY, EARL OF ARUNDEL, died s. p.
>>> Her ladyship m. secondly, Sir Richard Stafford, and had a daughter,
>>>> AVICE, m. to James Butler, Earl of Ormond, and died issueless, in 1456.

His lordship d. in 1390, leaving his two grand-daughters, Philippa, then twelve, and Elizabeth, nine years of age, his co-heirs, between whom the BARONY OF BRYAN fell into ABEYANCE, and it became EXTINCT, at the decease of Avice, COUNTESS OF ORMOND, in 1456.

ARMS.—Or, three piles meeting in point, as.

BRYDGES — BARONS CHANDOS OF SUDELEY CASTLE, IN THE COUNTY OF GLOUCESTER, EARLS OF CAERNARVEN, DUKES OF CHANDOS.

Barony		8th April, 1554.
Earldom	by Letters Patent,	19th Oct., 1714.
Dukedom		30th April, 1729.

Lineage.

SIR SIMON DE BRUGGE, of the county of Hereford, supposed to have sprung from the old Counts de Rethel, in the province of Champagné, in France, having taken part against Henry III., lost by confiscation, a great proportion of his lands, which were conferred upon Roger, Lord Clifford. Sir Simon was father of another

SIMON DE BRUGGE, (commonly omitted in the printed pedigrees,) who m. the daughter of Walwyn, a family of distinction, in the county of Hereford, even to the present time—and had issue,

JOHN DE BRUGGE, M.P. for the county of Hereford, 16th Edward II., 1322, who left issue,

SIR BALDWIN BRUGGE, who m. Isabel, daughter and heiress, (or co-heiress,) of Sir Piers Grandison, (son of Sir William Grandison, by Sibel, daughter and co-heir of John, Lord Tregos,) and had three sons,

> THOMAS, his heir.
> John, (Sir) who was in the battle of Azincourt, 25th October, 1415, and the next year served the office of Sheriff for Herefordshire, at which period he bore for his arms, ar. on a cross sa. a leopard's face or., as since used, and has been borne by Simon de Brugge, one of the same family, who was sheriff of this county, in 1379. Sir John was also sheriff of Gloucestershire, in the 7th Henry V., and was returned to parliament by that county, the following year. He left at his decease, an only daughter and heiress,
>> Joanna, who m., Sir John Baskeville, of Erdisley, Herefordshire.
> Simon, of the Leye, in the county of Hereford, left a numerous posterity, of whom the chief branch was still living at the Leye, when Gregory King made his visitation of that county, in 1684. And hence descended Sir John Bridges, who was Lord Mayor of London, 19th Henry VIII., whose daughter Winifrede, m. first, Sir Richard Sackville, by whom she was mother of Thomas Sackville, Lord Buckhurst, and Earl of Dorset, the celebrated poet. Her ladyship espoused secondly, John Powlett, Marquess of Winchester.

Sir Baldwin Brugge was s. by his eldest son,

THOMAS BRUGGE, or BRUGES, who m. Alice, daughter and co-heiress of Sir Thomas Berkeley, of Coberley, in the county of Gloucester, by Elizabeth, sister and co-heiress of Sir John Chandos, (see that dignity,) and acquired the seat of Coberley, and other large estates, which descended down to George Brydges, sixth Lord Chandos, who d. in 1654. By this great heiress, Thomas Bruges had issue,

> GYLES, of whom presently.
> Edward, of Lone, in the county of Gloucester, who d. in 1436, leaving a daughter and heiress, married to John Throgmorton, Esq., ancestor to the Throgmortons of Totworth, in the county of Gloucester.

The elder son,

SIR GYLES BRUGES, was seated at Coberley, in the county of Gloucester, and in the 7th Henry V., (1419,) was amongst the persons of note, of that county, who had command to serve the king, in person, for the security of the realm, all those then required so to do, being such, (as the words of the writ impart,) "as did bear ancient arms, by descent, from their ancestors." In 1429, he was sheriff of Gloucestershire, and again in 1453. In the next year, Sir Gyles Bruges and William Whittinton, were returned members of parliament for that shire. He m. Catherine, daughter of James Clifford, Esq., of Frampton, in the county of Gloucester, and widow of Anselm Guise, Esq., of Elmore, by whom he had,

THOMAS, his successor,

Cicily, who m. first, Thomas Gates, Esq., and secondly, John Wellesborne, Esq.

Sir Gyles d. in 1466, and was s. by his son,

THOMAS BRUGES, Esq., of Coberley, who was returned to parliament by the county of Gloucester, in 1459, and by the county of Hereford, in 1472. He m. Florence, daughter of William Darell, Esq., of Littlecot, in Wilts (a family of great consideration, one of whom intermarried with the royal blood, and branched from those of Sessy, in Yorkshire, whose heiress carried that estate to the Dawneys, now Viscounts Downe. Another branch of the Darells settled, temp. Henry IV., at Cale-hill, in Kent, and still continues there). By this lady, Thomas Bruges, had issue,

GILES, his successor.

Henry, of Newberry, in the county of Berks, who m. ———, daughter of John Hunger-ford, Esq., and had a daughter, m. to Gifford, of Itchel House, Hants—and a son and heir,

SIR RICHARD BRIDGES, of Shefford, Berks, and of Ludgershall, Wilts, K.B. This gentleman m. Jane, daughter of Sir William Spencer, of Wormleighton, ancestor to the Duke of Marlborough, and had issue,

ANTHONY, of Great Shefford, whose heiress, Eleana, carried that estate to Sir George Browne, a son of Viscount Montague, by whom she had no issue.

Edmund, of Bradley, in the county of Somerset.

Elizabeth, m. to William Cassey, Esq., and subsequently to Walter Rowdon, Esq.

Elice, m. to Thomas Chicheley, of Wympull, in the county of Cambridge.

Eleanor, m. to Sir Thomas Pauncefoot, Knt.

The eldest son,

SIR GILES BRUGES, of Coberley, received the honour of knighthood, for his valour at the battle of Blackheath, 22nd June, 1497. He m. Isabel, daughter of Thomas Baynham, and had issue,

JOHN, of whom presently.

Thomas, of Cornbury, in Oxfordshire, and Keinsham Abbey, in Somersetshire. This gentleman was sheriff of Gloucestershire, in the 3rd of Edward VI., and of Berkshire and Oxfordshire, in the 3rd and 4th of Philip and Mary. In the reign of Queen Mary, he was an officer of the Tower, under his brother, Lord Chandos. He d. 14th November, 1559, leaving issue by Anne,

daughter and co-heiress of John Sidenham, Esq., of Orchard, in the county of Somerset,—Mary, m. to Rowland Arnold, Esq., of Higham, in the county of Gloucester. Ellen, m. to John Ashfield, Esq., and a son and heir,

HENRY BRYDGES, Esq., of Keinsham, who m. Anne, daughter of John Hungerford, Esq., of Downe Ampney, in the county of Gloucester, and was s. by his son,

SIR THOMAS BRYDGES, of Keinsham, whose son,

THOMAS BRYDGES, Esq., m. Philippa, daughter of Sir George Speke, K.B., and was s. by his son,

SIR THOMAS BRYDGES, of Keinsham, an eminent loyalist, who m. Anne, daughter and co-heiress of Sir Edward Rodney, of Stoke Rodney, in the county of Somerset, by whom he had with other issue,

1. HARRY BRYDGES, Esq., who inherited the estates, and m. Lady Diana Holles, daughter of John, second Earl of Clare, by whom he had a daughter, Arabelle, m. to John Mitchell, Esq., of Kingston Russel, in the county of Dorset. Mr. Brydges m. secondly, Miss Freeman, and had two more daughters; upon his decease, his estates devolved, by an entail, upon his nephew,

GEORGE RODNEY BRYDGES.

2. GEORGE-RODNEY BRYDGES, of Avington, Hants, m. Lady Anne Maria Brudenell, daughter of Robert, second Earl of Cardigan, and widow of Francis Talbot, eleventh Earl of Shrewsbury, who was killed in a duel by George, Duke of Buckingham, upon her account, by whom he had a son,

GEORGE RODNEY BRYDGES of Avington, who inherited the estates upon the decease of his uncle, Harry Brydges, as stated above. He was M.P. for the city of Winchester, from 1714 to 1751. This gentleman was found drowned, in the canal of his garden, at Avington, in the 72nd year of his age; leaving no issue, the greater part of his estates reverted to the Chandos branch of the family, but he devised a property at Alresford, in Hampshire, to George Brydges Rodney, afterwards Lord Rodney.

The elder son and heir of Sir Giles Bruges,

SIR JOHN BRUGES, was under age at his father's decease, and was in ward to King Henry VIII. He had an early ambition of military glory, and though very young, attended the king in his expedition into France, 1513, when Terouenne and Tournay were taken. He was likewise at the battle of Spurs, and for his valiant conduct in those engagements received the honor of knighthood. In the 10th of Henry VIII. Sir John covenanted to serve the king with one hundred archers under his command; and being one of the knights of the king's body, was in his train at Bulloign, at the interview at Sedingfield with the French king, attended by three servants and one horse keeper, according to the appointment then made. In 1537, he was constituted constable of Sudeley Castle, and in the same year was, amongst those of the court, summoned with the nobility and bishops to be present, on October 15th, at the christening of Prince Edward. In the year 1544, he passed the seas with the king, and for his gallant behaviour at the siege of Bulloign, was, on the surrender thereof, appointed deputy governor of the town; in which post he was continued by King Edward VI. He had also, in the first year of the reign of that king, a grant of divers manors in consideration of his services. In

1549, (3 Edward VI.,) Bulloign being besieged by the French, he had the command of the place as deputy governor, and successfully defended it against the French king in person, and an army flushed with the conquest of Newhaven, and other places. On the death of Edward VI., Sir John Bruges waited upon Queen Mary, assisted her against those who had usurped the government; and upon her majesty's entrance into London to the Tower, was one of the principal persons in her train; for which services he was then appointed governor of the Tower, and had a grant, at the same time, of the castle and manor of SUDELEY, in Gloucestershire. He was subsequently, Sunday, 8th April, 1554, elevated to the peerage in the dignity of BARON CHANDOS, of Sudeley, to him and the heirs male of his body, " in consideration not only of his nobility and loyalty, but of his probity, valour, and other virtues." Four days afterwards he attended Lady Jane Grey to the scaffold, and that unhappy lady presented him, (as related by some,) in testimony of his civilities to her, with her prayer book; but, according to others, it was a table book, with some Greek and Latin verses which she wrote in it, upon his lordship's begging her to write something that he might retain as a memorial of her. His last will bears date, 2d March, in the 2d and 3rd of Philip and Mary, and he d. 4th March following, (1556,) an adherent to the old religion. His lordship m. Elizabeth, daughter of Edmund, Lord Grey de Wilton, sister to the gallant soldier, William, Lord Grey de Wilton, and aunt to Arthur, Lord Grey de Wilton, the celebrated lord deputy of Ireland. By this lady he had seven sons and three daughters, of the latter, Catherine, m. Edward Sutton, Lord Dudley; Elizabeth, m. John Tracy, Esq., of Todington, in the county of Gloucester, and Mary wedded George Throgmorton, Esq., son of Sir George Throgmorton, of Coughton, in the county of Warwick—of the sons,

EDMUND, inherited the title.

Charles, who was of Wilton Castle, near Ross, in Herefordshire, became cup-bearer to King Philip, and was deputy lieutenant of the Tower to his father, John, Lord Chandos, when the warrant came for executing the Princess Elizabeth, which he refused to obey, until he should receive orders from the king and queen, and thereby was the means of saving her life; for the order being disowned at court a stop was put to the execution. Mr. Brydges lived to an advanced age, and was sheriff of Herefordshire, in the 39d of Elizabeth. He m. Jane, daughter of Sir Edward Carne, of Wenny, in the county of Glamorgan, Knt., and dying in 1619, was s. by his eldest son,

GILES BRYDGES, Esq., of Wilton Castle, who was created a baronet, 17th May, 1627. Sir Giles m. Mary, daughter of Sir James Scudamore, and was s. by his eldest son,

SIR JOHN BRYDGES, second baronet, who m. Mary, only daughter, and heir of James Pearle, Esq., of Dewsal and Anconbury, in the county of Hereford, and dying in 1651, was s. by his only son,

SIR JAMES BRYDGES, third baronet, of whom hereafter, as EIGHTH LORD CHANDOS.

Anthony, m. Catherine, daughter of Henry Fortescue, Esq., of Faulkbourn Hall, in Essex, of whose descendants hereafter, as claimants of the Barony of Chandos.

Lord Chandos was s. by his eldest son,

EDMUND BRUGES, second baron, who, influenced by the same desire of martial glory as his father, adopted early the profession of arms, and served under the Earl of Hertford, in the reign of King Henry VIII., and in 1547, behaving himself with great bravery in the famous battle of Musleborough, he was made a knight banneret by the Duke of Somerset, in the camp of Roxborough. In the reign of Queen Elisabeth he was elected a knight companion of the most noble order of the Garter, and installed at Windsor, 17th June, 1572. His lordship m. Dorothy, fifth daughter, and eventually co-heir of Edmund, Lord Bray, and dying 11th Sept., 1573, was s. by his elder son,

GILES BRUGES, third baron, who, in the lifetime of his father, represented the county of Gloucester in parliament. His lordship m. Lady Frances Clinton, daughter of Edward, first Earl of Lincoln, admiral of England, by whom he had two daughters, Elisabeth, who m. Sir John Kennedy, of Scotland, and Catherine, m. to Frances, Lord Russell, of Thornhaugh, afterwards Earl of Bedford. Those ladies were his heirs. His lordship d. 21st February, 1593-4, and was s. in the peerage by his brother,

WILLIAM BRUGES, fourth baron, who m. Mary, daughter of Sir Owen Hopton, lieutenant of the Tower, and dying in 1602, was s. by his elder son,

GREY BRUGES, fifth baron, K.B. This nobleman, from the magnificence of his style of living at his mansion, in Gloucestershire, and the splendour of his retinue when he came to court, acquired the title of KING OF COTSWOULD. He had an ample fortune, which he expended in the most generous and liberal manner. His house was open three days in the week to the gentry, and the poor were fed as constantly from the remnants of his entertainments. On the 8th November, 1617, Lord Chandos was appointed to receive and introduce the Muscovite ambassadors, who had brought rich and costly presents from their master to the king. His lordship m. Lady Anne Stanley, daughter and co-heir of Fernando, Earl of Derby, and dying 10th August, 1621, was s. by his elder son,

GEORGE BRUGES, sixth baron. This nobleman, who was but a year old at the decease of his father, became at the breaking out of the civil wars, in 1641, a stout supporter of the royal cause. At the battle of Newberry his lordship had three horses killed under him, which so far from damping his ardour, roused his valour to a higher pitch, for mounting a fourth charger, he renewed the attack, and was mainly instrumental in breaking the enemy's cavalry. In consideration of his splendid conduct in this action, Lord Chandos had an offer from

the king to be created Earl of Newberry, but he modestly declined, until it should please God to restore his majesty to the crown, an event which he did not survive to see: but, on the contrary, many severe mortifications and sufferings, and much mental adversity, as well as worldly oppression. When the parliamentarians triumphed, his lordship, besides having suffered imprisonment, paid at one time £3973 10s., and what was left him he generously bestowed in relieving the distressed clergy, and those who had suffered by the wars. Speaking of the surrender of Sudely Castle, Lord Clarendon says,—"Waller prosecuting his march towards Worcester, where his majesty then was, persuaded, rather than forced, the garrison of Sudeley Castle, the strong house of Lord Chandois, to deliver up that place to him. The lord of that castle was a young man of spirit and courage; and had for two years served the king very bravely at the head of a regiment of horse, which himself had raised at his own charge; but had lately, out of pure weariness of the fatigue, and having spent most of his money, and without any diminution of his affection, left the king, under pretence of travel; but making London in his way, he gave himself up to the pleasures of that place; which he enjoyed, without considering the issue of the war, or shewing any inclination to the parliament; nor did he in any degree contribute to the delivery of his house; which was at first imagined, because it was so ill, or not at all, defended. It was under the government of Sir William Morton, a gentleman of the long robe; (who, in the beginning of the war, cast off his gown, as many other gallant men of that profession of the law did, and served as lieutenant-colonel in the regiment of horse, under the Lord Chandois; and had given so frequent testimony of signal courage, in several actions, in which he had received many wounds, both by the pistol and the sword, that his mettle was never suspected, and his fidelity as little questioned; and after many years' imprisonment, sustained with great firmness and constancy, he lived to receive the reward of his merit, after the return of the king; who made him first, a serjeant at law, and afterwards a judge of the king's bench; where he sat many years, and discharged the office with much gravity and learning; and was terrible to those who chose to live by robbing on the highway.) He was unfortunate, though without fault, in the giving up that castle in so unseasonable a conjuncture; which was done by the faction and artifice of an officer within, who had found means to go out to Waller, and to acquaint him with the great wants of the garrison; which, indeed, had not plenty of anything: and so, by the mutiny of the soldiers, it was given up, and the governor made prisoner, and sent to the Tower, where he remained some years after the end of the war."

In the year, 1652, Lord Chandos had a difference with Colonel Henry Compton, grandson of Henry, Lord Compton, about a lady he recommended to the colonel, whose person and fortune were below few matches in the kingdom; which unhappily ended in a duel at Putney Heath, on the 13th May, when Colonel Compton fell. His lordship and his second, Lord Arundel, of Wardour, having been imprisoned more than a year, were at length arraigned in the upper bench, 17th May, 1654, and found guilty of manslaughter. He d. in the February of the following year of the small-pox, and was buried at Sudeley. His lordship m. first, Susan, daughter of Henry, Earl of Manchester, and had two daughters, Mary, m. to William Brownlow, Esq., of Humby, in the county of Limerick, and Elisabeth wedded first, to Edward, Lord Herbert, of Chesbury, secondly, to William, Earl of Inchiquin, and thirdly, to Charles, Lord Howard, of Escrick. Lord Chandos espoused secondly, Jane, daughter of John Savage, Earl Rivers, by whom he had with two other daughters that d. unmarried, Lucy, m. to Adam Loftus, Viscount Lisburn, in Ireland. His lordship dying thus, without male issue, the major part of his fortune passed under settlement to Jane, his last wife, who afterwards m. George Pitt, Esq., of Strathfieldsay, ancestor of the present Lord Rivers, and conveyed to that gentleman Sudeley Castle, and other lands of great value. The peerage devolved upon his lordship's brother,

WILLIAM BRUGES, seventh baron, who m. Susan, daughter and co-heir of Gerrot Keire, of London, merchant, but having no male issue, the title devolved at his decease, in 1676, upon his kinsman, (refer to Charles, second son of John, first Lord Chandos).

SIR JAMES BRYDGES, Bart., of Wilton Castle, as eighth Baron Chandos. This noble was accredited ambassador to Constantinople, in 1680, where he resided for some years in great honor and esteem. His lordship m. Elizabeth, eldest daughter, and co-heir of Sir Henry Bernard, Knt., an eminent Turkey merchant. By this lady he had no less than twenty-two children, of which number fifteen only were christened, and seven of those dying young, the remainder were,

JAMES, his successor.

Henry, in holy orders, of Addlestrop, in Gloucestershire, archdeacon and prebendary of Rochester, and rector of Agmondesham, Bucks. Mr. Brydges m. Annabella, daughter of Henry, and grand-daughter of Sir Robert Atkins, lord chief baron of the exchequer, by whom he had a large family.

Francis, receiver general of the duties on malt, died s. p.

Mary, m. to Theophilus Leigh, Esq., of Addlestrop, in the county of Gloucester.

Elizabeth, m. first, to Alexander Jacob, Esq., and secondly, to the Rev. Dr. Thomas Dawson, vicar of Windsor.

Emma, m. to Edmund Chamberlain, Esq., of Stow, in the county of Gloucester.

Anne, m. to Charles Walcote, Esq., of Walcote, in the county of Salop.

Catherine, m. first, to Brereton Bourchier, Esq., of Barnsley Court, in the county of Gloucester, and secondly, to Henry Perrot, Esq., of North Leigh, in the county of Oxford.

His lordship d. in 1714, and was s. by his eldest son,

JAMES BRYDGES, ninth baron, who, upon the accession of King George I., was created, by letters patent, dated 19th October, 1714, Viscount Wilton,

and EARL OF CARNARVON, with a collateral remainder to the issue male of his father; and in the November following, a patent passed the great seal, granting to his lordship and his two sons, John and Henry, the reversion of the office of clerk of the hanaper in chancery. In 1719, on the 30th April, his lordship was advanced to the Marquisate of Caernarvon, and DUKEDOM OF CHANDOS, and he acquired by his magnificence the appellation of the princely Chandos. He espoused first, 26th February, 1696-7, Mary, only surviving daughter of Sir Thomas Lake, of Cannons, in the county of Middlesex, by whom he had two surviving sons,

JOHN, Marquess of Caernarvon, m. in 1724, Lady Catharine Talmache, daughter of Lionel, Earl of Dysart, by whom he had issue—

Catharine, m. first, to Captain Lyon, of the horse guards, and secondly, to Edwin Francis Stanhope, Esq., and,

Jane, (a posthumous child,) m. to James Brydges, Esq., of Pinner. Lord Caernarvon d. 8th April, 1727.

HENRY, Marquess of Caernarvon, after the decease of his brother.

His grace m. secondly, Cassandra, daughter of Francis Willoughby, Esq., and sister of Thomas Willoughby, Lord Middleton; and thirdly, Lydia Catherine Van Hatten, widow of Sir Thomas Davall, Knt., but had no issue by either of these ladies. He d. at his noble seat of Cannons,* 9th August, 1744, and was s. by his only surviving son,

HENRY BRYDGES, second duke, who m., in 1728, Mary, eldest daughter and co-heir of Charles, Lord Bruce, only son and heir apparent of Thomas, Earl of Aylesbury, by whom he had issue,

---

* CANNONS.—This most splendid palace stood on the road leading to Edgeware. The fronts were all of freestone, and the pillars of marble, as were also the steps of the great stair-case. The gilding was executed by the famous Pargotti, and the hall painted by Paolucci. The apartments were most exquisitely finished, and most richly furnished. The gardens, avenues, and offices, were proportionably grand. At night there was a constant watch kept, who walked the rounds and proclaimed the hours. The duke also maintained a full choir, and had divine service performed with the best music, in a chapel that could hardly be exceeded in the beauty of its workmanship. But all this terminated with his life; for on his decease this magnificent mansion was disposed of piecemeal. The stone obelisks, with copper lamps, which formed the approach from the Edgeware road, were purchased for the Earl of Tilney, for his new building at Wanstead, in Essex, which has since experienced the fate of Cannons; the marble staircase was bought by the Earl of Chesterfield for his residence in May Fair. The ground and site whereon this magnificent edifice stood became the property of an opulent tradesman, who built thereon a neat habitation which still remains, after having passed into the hands of the well known Colonel O'Kelly of sporting celebrity.

91

JAMES, Marquess of Caernarvon.

Caroline, m. to John Leigh, Esq., of Addlestrop, in the county of Gloucester.

His grace espoused, secondly, Anne Jeffreys, and by her he had a daughter, Augusta-Anne, m. to Henry John Kearney, Esq. The duke m., thirdly, in 1767, Elizabeth, second daughter and co-heir of Sir John Major, Bart., of Worlingworth Hall, in the county of Suffolk, by whom he had no issue. He d. 28th November, 1771, and was s. by his son,

JAMES BRYDGES, third duke, b. 27th December, 1731. This nobleman, upon the accession of his majesty, King George III., was appointed one of the lords of his bed-chamber. In 1775, he was sworn of the privy council, and was afterwards constituted lord-steward of the household. His grace m., 22nd May, 1753, Mary, daughter and sole heiress of John Nicol, Esq., of Southgate, Middlesex, by whom he acquired Minchenden House at Southgate, together with the whole fortune of his father-in-law. By this lady, who d. in 1768, he had no issue. The duke espoused, secondly, 21st June, 1777, Anne-Eliza, daughter of Richard Gamon, Esq., and widow of Roger Hope Elletson, Esq., by whom he had one surviving daughter and heiress,

ANNE-ELIZA, who m., in 1796, RICHARD, Earl Temple, now DUKE OF BUCKINGHAM AND CHANDOS.

His grace d. without male issue 29th September, 1789, when all his honours became EXTINCT, but the BARONY OF CHANDOS, which was immediately claimed by the Rev. EDWARD TYMEWELL BRYDGES, M.A., of Wootton Court, in Kent, as next heir male of the body of Sir John Brydges, LORD CHANDOS, the first grantee, who d. in 1557. The first hearing of this celebrated cause took place before the Committee of Privileges of the House of Lords 1st June, 1790; the second 21st December, in the same year; the 3rd, 4th, 5th, 6th, and 7th, in 1794; the 8th and 9th in 1795; the 10th, 11th, 12th, and 13th, in 1802; thirteen other hearings in 1803; and at length, after a few more investigations, it was determined, 17th June, 1803, upon a division, in which the majority of the lords who then voted, (being only twenty-two,) resolved that the evidence was not sufficient.

The claimant deduced his descent from

The Hon.

ANTHONY BRUGES, or BRYDGES, third son of John, first Lord Chandos, who m. Catherine, daughter of Henry Fortescue, Esq., of Faulkbourn Hall, Essex, by whom he had issue,

ROBERT.

Elizabeth, m. to Robert Brayne.

Catherine, m. to Sir John Astley, Knt., of the palace at Maidstone, in Kent, Master of the Revels to King Charles I.

The son,

ROBERT BRYDGES, (as stated by the claimant,) resided at Maidstone, and died there in 1636, leaving a son, Edward, and a daughter, Anne, m. to William Best, of a good Kentish family. As Robert derived no inheritance from his father, he appears to have relied for support on the wealth acquired by his sister's marriage, which it must be supposed drew him to fix his residence at Maidstone, where, both in the register, and in legal proceedings, he has the addition of *Esquire* affixed to his name. His only son,

EDWARD BRIDGES, married a small heiress connected with the maritime commerce of a neighbouring town, moving in a far inferior sphere to his own ancestors, which seems to have highly offended the arrogant pride of Lady Astley, if we may judge by a singular letter, which was produced in evidence, and which was decyphered by the present Lord Chief Justice of England, (then Mr. Abbott). This Edward Brydges left one surviving son,

JOHN BRYDGES, b. in 1634, who removed to Canterbury, where he died at the age of sixty-five, having retrieved the fortunes of his branch of the family. By his first wife, of the name of Ackman, he had no surviving issue; by his second wife, whose maiden name was Young, he had four sons, John, Edward, Thomas, and Robert. The three last died without issue. The eldest son,

JOHN BRYDGES, was b. in 1660, and bred to the bar. He married in 1704, Jane, sole surviving daughter and heir of Edward Gibbon, Esq.,* of Westcliffe, near Dover, by Martha, daughter of Sir John Roberts, of Beaksbourne, in Kent. With this lady he acquired the seat and estate of Wootton, and by her he had issue,

John, } who both retired to, and spent their
Edward, } lives at Wootton Court.

Deborah, m. to Edward Tymewell, Esq., of Chegwell, in Essex.

Mr. Brydges died of a fever, in his thirty-second year, in July, 1712, and was s. by his elder son,

JOHN BRYDGES, Esq., of Wootton Court, b. in 1710, who spent his life in rural retirement at Wootton Court, and dying in 1780, unmarried, was s. by his brother,

EDWARD BRYDGES, Esq., of Wootton Court, who had retired in early life with his brother, to enjoy the tranquillity of a country life. He m. in 1747, Jemima, daughter and co-heir of William Egerton, L.L.D., prebendary of Canterbury, and his wife Anne, daughter of Sir Francis Head, Bart. (Dr. Egerton was grandson of John, second earl of Bridgewater.) By this lady he had, (with five daughters,) three sons, viz.

EDWARD TYMEWELL, b. in May, 1749.

Samuel Egerton, b. 30th November, 1789-3, created a BARONET, 27th December, 1814.

John William Head, b. in 1764, M.P., m. in 1812, Lady Isabella Anne Beresford, eldest daughter of George, first Marquess of Waterford, by whom he has one son, and two daughters.

Mr. Brydges d. a few months after his brother, and was s. by his elder son,

The Reverend

EDWARD TYMEWELL BRYDGES, the unsuccessful claimant for the BARONY OF CHANDOS. This Rev. gentleman, m. in 1785, Caroline, daughter of Richard Fairfield, Esq., of Berners-street, and

---

* This Edward Gibbon was elder brother of Matthew Gibbon, great grandfather of Edward Gibbon the historian.

died in October 1807, without surviving issue. He was s. by his next brother,

SIR SAMUEL EGERTON BRYDGES, Bart., of Wootton Court, who maintains his right, notwithstanding the decision against his brother, to the BARONY OF CHANDOS.*

---

* Having thus detailed the "CHANDOS PEERAGE," the claim to the revival of which occupied the House of Lords no less than thirteen years, we shall briefly state a circumstance to which the friends of the claimant attributed in some measure his discomfiture. Just at the close of the investigation, Mr. Brydges, in a moment of impatience, ill advised, and with a sort of indiscretion, not easily defended, printed and sent round to the lords a circular letter,† requesting their attendance in a tone which was construed to be either a reproach or a canvass. In itself, the letter was the most inoffensive and harmless of addresses, but the question was now approaching to a conclusion; and it was known that it would come to a vote; the opposition were therefore marshalling their forces, with great eagerness. A noble duke, (Norfolk,) moved that the letter was a breach of privilege; and stormy debates with closed doors ensued, after which the hostile resolution against the claim was carried. The claimant sunk under the blow, but lingered for four years, when he died issueless: his widow survived till 1824. The opposition to the claim was sustained, by an endeavour to rebut the claimant's documents by counter evidence; by disputing the identity of the Maidstone branch of the House of Bruges or Brydges altogether, and by a project of a counter descent. And this notwithstanding, the evidence of reputation was decisively established by the testimony of Lady Caroline Leigh, sister of the late Duke of Chandos, of his first cousin, Lady Catherine Stanhope, of the claimant's brother, and of the Rev. George Lefroy; while the regular armorial achievements, with the due mark of the *third* branch, as borne by the claimant's ancestors, (which were luckily still in existence,) were exhibited to the personal inspection of the committee.

---

† Copy of a circular letter from the Claimant to the Barony of Chandos, (printed in the Lords' Journal.)
      Wigmore Street, 20th May, 1803.

"My Lord,

"I have the honour of apprizing your lordship, that Thursday next, the 26th instant, is appointed for the final discussion of the committee of privileges upon my claim to the Chandos Peerage: and I have been compelled to take this liberty, that your lordship might not by any accidental omission of notice, be deprived of an opportunity of deciding upon a matter, not important merely to myself, but to the rights of your lordship's house of parliament, and to the just prerogative of the crown. I am not presuming to solicit any favour or partiality from your lordship. I address myself to your justice. I ask but for your lordship's candid consideration of the evidence which is recorded in your proceedings, and will survive for the information of posterity,

BULKELEY — BARON BULKELEY OF BEAUMARIS, IN THE ISLE OF WIGHT.

By Letters Patent, 14th May, 1784.

Lineage.

The ancient family of Bulkeley descended from,

ROBERT BULKELEY, Lord of the Manor of Bulkeley, in the county of Chester, temp. King John, whose son and successor,

WILLIAM BULKELEY, of *Bulkeley*, had five sons,

> ROBERT, his successor.
>
> Willcock, of Petty Hall, in the county of Chester, *m.* Mary, daughter of Hugh Venables, Baron of Kinderston, and had an only son,
>
>> WILLCOCK.
>
> Roger, of Orton Madock, Cheshire.
>
> Ralph, of Rudal Hall, in the same county, died *s. p.*
>
> David, from whom the Bulkeley's of Bickerton, in Cheshire, descended.

Mr. Bulkeley was *s.* by his eldest son,

ROBERT BULKELEY, of *Bulkeley*, whose son and successor,

WILLIAM BULKELEY, living at Bulkeley, in the year 1302, *m.* first, Maud, daughter of Sir John Davenport, Knt., and had issue,

> WILLIAM, of Bulkeley, whose line terminated with his grand-daughter, Alice Bulkeley, the wife of Thomas Holford, of Holford, in the county of Chester.
>
> Robert, of whom presently.
>
> Roger, of Norbury, in Cheshire, whence his descendants derived the surname of "Norbury."
>
> Thomas, *m.* Alice, daughter and co-heir of Matthew Alprahum, Esq., of Alprahum, by whom he acquired that seat, and settled there. He left an only daughter and heiress Helen, who *m.* Sir Thomas Arden, of Aldford, in the county of Chester.

Mr. Bulkeley *m.* secondly, Alice, daughter of Bryan St. Pierre, and had one son,

> RICHARD, to whom he gave the Manor of Prestland, in Cheshire, whence he assumed the surname of Prestland, which his descendants continued to bear.

Mr. Bulkeley's second son,

ROBERT BULKELEY, Esq., became seated at EATON, in Cheshire, and was sheriff of that county in 1341. He *m.* Isabel, daughter of Philip Egerton, Esq., of Malpas, in the same shire, and had a

---

when all the insinuations and prejudices that I have had to contend with, shall be utterly forgotten. It is upon the truth of that evidence, my lord, that I am anxious to rest my pretensions to character and the unsullied honour of my family.

"I have the honour to be, &c. &c.

"EDWARD TYMEWELL BRYDGES."

daughter, Cecily, *m.* to Thomas Weaver, Esq., and two sons, Robert and Richard. The elder,

    Robert, succeeded at Eaton, and served the office of sheriff of Cheshire, anno 1341, his father being then alive, and was *s.* by his elder son,

        John, living temp. Richard II., who was father of,

           Sir William Bulkeley, Knt., of Eaton, Chief Justice of Chester in the reign of Henry IV., who *m.* Margaret, daughter of Sir Richard Molyneux, of Sefton, and grand-daughter maternally, of Thomas, Earl of Derby, and had with other children,

                Thomas, his successor, at Eaton.

                Ralph, *m.* ——, daughter and heir of —— Vernon, of White-croft, Cheshire, and Parwick, in the county of Derby, by whom he acquired those lands, and from this union a numerous posterity descended.

                Thomas Bulkeley, the elder son, *s.* at Eaton, *m.* Jane, daughter of Sir Geoffrey Warburton, and had issue,

                    Thomas, whose son, Thomas, died *s. p.*

                    Robert, whose son, William, died *s. p.*

                    William, whose two sons, Robert and Richard, died *s. p.*

                    Joan, *m.* to Roger Puleston, Esq., of Kumbrall.

                    Elizabeth, *m.* to John Probisher, Esq., of Chirke, Flintshire.

RICHARD BULKELEY, the second son, *m.* in 1307, Agnes, daughter and co-heiress of Roger Cheadle, Esq., of Cheadle, in the county of Chester, and was *s.* by his son,

RICHARD BULKELEY, Esq., of Cheadle, who, in the reign of Henry VI., being constable of Beaumaris, prevented the Duke of York from landing there, in his return from Ireland. He *m.* Ellen, daughter of Guilliam ap Griffith, Esq., of Pentrie, and was *s.* by his eldest son,

ROWLAND BULKELEY, Esq., of Beaumaris, who *m.* Alice, daughter and heiress of William Beconsal, Esq., of Beconsal, in the county of Lancaster, by whom he had five sons and two daughters. He was *s.* at his decease, by his eldest son,

SIR RICHARD BULKELEY, Knt., chamberlain of North Wales, in 1534, who was *s.* by his son,

SIR RICHARD BULKELEY, M.P. for the county of Anglesey, in the reigns of Queens Mary and Elizabeth, *m.* first, Margaret, daughter of Sir John Savage, of Rock Savage, in the county of Chester, by whom he had issue, Richard, his successor, with five other sons and five daughters. He *m.* secondly, Anne, daughter of Thomas Needham, Esq., of Shenton, and had eight sons and two daughters—of whom

Launcelot was consecrated Archbishop of Dublin, in 1619, and sworn of the privy council. His grace *m.* Alice,[*] daughter of Rowland Bulkeley Esq., of Beaumaris, by whom he had two sons and two daughters; the elder, Richard, was created a baronet, in 1672, and dying in 1685, was *s.* by his son,

    Sir Richard, second baronet, at whose decease, *s. p.*, in 1710, the title ceased.

Sir Richard Bulkeley, was *s.* by his eldest son,

SIR RICHARD BULKELEY, Knt., of Beaumaris, who *m.* first, Catherine, daughter of Sir William Davenport, of Broomhall, in the county of Chester, by whom she had a son and daughter; and secondly, Mary, daughter of William, Lord Borough, of Gainsborough, in the county of Lincoln, and had,

    Richard. (Sir)

    Thomas, of whom presently.

    Eleanor, *m.* to Sir Thomas Porter.

    Margaret, *m.* to George Shellet, Esq., of Heath, in the county of York.

    Penelope, *m.* in 1614, to Sir Edwyn Sandys, of Worsburgh, son and heir of Sir Samuel Sandys, of Ombersley, in the county of Worcester, whose descendant was created, Lord Sandys, of Ombersley.

THOMAS BULKELEY, Esq., the younger son, was seated at Baron-Hill, near Beaumaris, and espousing, zealously, the cause of King Charles I., was created by that monarch, by patent, under the privy seal, dated at Oxford, 6th January, 1643, Viscount Bulkeley, of Cashel, in the peerage of Ireland. His lordship *m.* first, Blanch, daughter of Robert Coytmore, Esq., of Coytmore, in the county of Caernarvon, by whom he had issue,

    Richard, treacherously killed by Richard Cheadle, for which that person was executed at Conway.

    Robert, successor to his father.

    Thomas, of Dinas, in the county of Caernarvon, *m.* Jane, daughter and co-heiress of Griffith Jones, Esq., of Castlemarch.

    Henry, master of the household to King Charles II., and James II., *m.* Lady Sophia Stewart.

    Edwin, *d.* unm.

    Catherine, *m.* to Richard Wood, Esq., of Rosmore.

    Lumley, *m.* to Piers Lloyd, Esq., of Lisgway.

    Mary, *m.* to Sir Roger Mostyn, Baron of Mostyn, in the county of Flint (his 2nd wife).

    Penelope.

---

[*] The commissioners of government having published an order to prevent the killing of lambs, owing to the great decay and scarcity of sheep, upon the penalty of 10s. for each lamb, to be paid as well by the killer as the eater, she petitioned for license to eat lamb, by reason of her great age, and weakness of body: in consideration of which, her petition was granted, and she had a license, 17th March, 1652, to kill and dress so much as should be necessary for her own use and eating, not exceeding three lambs in the whole of that year.

The viscount, who m. secondly, Miss Cheadle, daughter of Mr. Cheadle, some time his lordship's steward, was s. at his decease, by his eldest surviving son,

ROBERT BULKELEY, second Viscount, member for the county of Anglesey, of the parliament which restored King Charles II. His lordship m. Sarah, daughter of Daniel Harvey, Esq. of Coombe, in the county of Surrey, and had issue,

> RICHARD, his successor.
> James, L.L.D., M.P. for Beaumaris.
> Thomas, M.P. for the county of Caernarvon.
> Elizabeth, m. to John Griffeth, Esq., of Glyn, in the county of Caernarvon.
> Catherine, m. to the Rev. Philip Atkinson, D.D.
> Penelope.
> Lumley.
> Martha, m. to Roger Price, Esq., of Rhinias.
> Eleanor, m. to Sir William Smith, Bart., of Vinhall.

The viscount d. 18th October, 1688, and was s. by his eldest son,

RICHARD BULKELEY, third Viscount, M.P. for the county of Anglesey. This nobleman m. first, Mary, eldest daughter of Sir Philip Egerton, Knt., of Egerton and Oulton, in the county of Chester, by whom he had a son,

> RICHARD.

His lordship m. secondly, Elizabeth, daughter of Henry White, Esq., of Hawthlin, in the county of Pembroke, but had no issue. He d., 9th August, 1704, and was s. by his son,

RICHARD BULKELEY, fourth Viscount, M.P. for the county of Anglesey, which honour, together with the constableship of Beaumaris Castle, and chamberlainship of North Wales, had been almost uninterruptedly in this family, from the reign of Elizabeth. His lordship m. Lady Bridget Bertie, eldest daughter of James, first Earl of Abingdon, and had issue,

> Richard, } successive Viscounts.
> James, }
> Eleanor-Mary, m. to George Hervey, Esq., of Tiddington, in the county of Oxford.
> Anne, m. to the Rev. William Bertie, D.D., brother of Willoughby, third Earl of Abingdon.
> Elizabeth, m. to William Price, of Eulace, Esq.

His lordship d. on the 4th June, 1724, and was s. by his elder son,

RICHARD BULKELEY, fifth Viscount, at whose decease, s. p., 15th March, 1738, the viscounty devolved upon his brother,

JAMES BULKELEY, sixth Viscount, constable of the castle of Beaumaris, and chamberlain of North Wales. His lordship m., 5th August, 1749, Emma, only daughter and heiress of Thomas Rowland, Esq., of Carew, in the island of Anglesey, and dying 23rd April, 1752, was s. by his only surviving child,

THOMAS-JAMES BULKELEY, seventh Viscount, who was created a peer of Great Britain, on the 11th May, 1784, as BARON BULKELEY, OF BEAUMARIS. His lordship m. 26th April, 1777, Elizabeth-Harriet, only daughter and heiress of Sir

George Warren, K.B., (upon which occasion, he assumed the surname of Warren, before that of Bulkeley,) but had no issue. He d. in 1822, when all his honours became EXTINCT.

ARMS.—sa., a chev. betw. three bull's head ar. armed or.

BULMER—BARON BULMER.

By Writ of Summons, dated 25th February, 1342.

Lineage.

In the reign of King Henry I.

ASCHITEL DE BULEMER, gave twelve oxgangs of land lying in Bramham, to the canons of Nostell, and was s. by

BERTRAM DE BULEMER, sheriff of Yorkshire in the times of King Stephen, and Henry II., and founder of the priory of Barton, in that county. To this Bertram s.

STEPHEN DE BULEMER, who, upon the aid being levied in the 12th Henry II., towards the marriage portion of that monarch's daughter, certified his knights fees to amount to the number of five, de veteri feoffamento; and one-and-a-half, and fourth part, de novo: for which, in two years afterwards, he paid six marks and a half. Stephen de Bulemer was s. by his son,

THOMAS DE BULEMER, who, in the 18th Henry II., paid a hundred shillings scutage for not joining the expedition then made into Ireland. He was s. by his son,

ROBERT DE BULEMER, who was s. by his son,

BERTRAM DE BULEMER. This feudal lord left an only daughter and heiress,

> Emme, who m. Geffrey de Nevill, and conveyed to the Nevills the Lordship of Branspeth, in the county of Durham, which had previously been the family seat of the Bulemers.

The male line of the original feudal house thus failing, the next of the name met with is,

JOHN DE BULEMER, who, in the 53d Henry III., m. Theophania, one of the three daughters, and co-heiress of Hugh de Morewyke, of Morewyke, in the county of Northumberland, whose son and heir,

RALPH DE BULMER, obtained a special charter from the crown, in the 4th Edward II., enabling him to hold his park at Riceberg, and keep dogs to hunt therein, and to have free warren in all his demesne lands. In the 9th of the same monarch, we find this Ralph doing homage, and having livery of the estates which descended to him upon the decease of his mother: in the next year he was in the wars of Scotland, and again, in two years afterwards. In the 20th Edward II., he was made deputy-governor of the castle of York, to William de Ros, of Hamlake, and upon the accession of King Edward III. was summoned to parliament as a BARON. In four years afterwards he had special license to make a castle of his manor-house of Milton, in the county of York, being the same year constituted sheriff of Yorkshire, and governor of the castle at York. His lordship participated again (the 8th Edward III.) in the wars of Scotland. He d. in 1357, and was s. by his son, then in his sixteenth year.

RALPH BULMER, who was placed under the

guardianship of the king's daughter, Isabel, and by her assigned to Ralph de Nevill. He had livery of his lands, upon attaining maturity, in the 36th Edward III., after which, 40th Edward III., he had license, together with William, a younger son of Ralph, Lord Nevill, of Raby, to travel into foreign parts, and he appears to have d. at the close of that year; leaving a son and heir, then but a year old.

RALPH BULMER, " whose descent," (says Dugdale,) " I shall not trace down farther, in regard that none of this family, after the before specified Ralph, who was summoned to parliament from the first till 23d Edward III., were barons of the realm." The male line of this branch of Bulmers continued, however, to the time of Philip and Mary, when it terminated with Sir Richard Bulmer, Knt.

ARMS.—Gu. a lion rampant, salient erminois.

BURGH—EARL OF KENT.

By Charter of Creation, 11th February, 1226.

Lineage.

The great and powerful family of BURGH, (at the head of which now stands the noble house of Clanricarde,) deduced its lineage from,

CHARLES, DUKE OF INGELHEIM, fifth son of the Emperor Charlemaign, whose grandson,

GODFREY, a distinguished soldier of the cross, was father of

BALDWIN, whose son,

BALDWIN, the second, was founder of the house of BLOIS, in France, and progenitor of the noble families of Burgh (Burke), and Vesey, in Ireland, through his son,

JOHN, EARL OF COMYN, and Baron of Tonsburgh, in Normandy, who being general of the king's forces, and governor of his chief towns, obtained the surname " DE 'BURGH." This nobleman had issue,

HARLOWEN, of whom presently.

Eustace, Baron of Tonsburgh.

Millicent, m. to Fulk, Earl of Anjou, who s. as King of Jerusalem, in 1131.

The eldest son,

HARLOWEN DE BURGH, espoused Arlotta, mother of William the Conqueror, and dying before his father, left issue.

ODO, Bishop of Bayeux, created Earl of Kent, (see Odo, Earl of Kent), and,

ROBERT, EARL OF MORETON, in Normandy, who participating with his brother, the Bishop of Bayeux, in the triumph of Hastings, was rewarded by his victorious kinsman, Duke William, with the EARLDOM OF CORNWALL, (anno 1088,) and grants of not less than seven hundred and ninety-three manors. This nobleman m. Maud, daughter of Roger de Montgomery, Earl of Shrewsbery, and had issue,

WILLIAM, his successor,

and three daughters, one of whom m. Andrew de Vetrel, another, Guy de Val, and the youngest, the Earl of Thoulouse, brother of Raymond, Count of St. Giles, who behaved so valiantly in the Jerusalem expedition. The period of the decease of Robert,

Earl of Moreton and Cornwall is not ascertained, but he appears to have been s. by his son,

WILLIAM DE MORETON, Earl of Cornwall, who, rebelling against King Henry II., died a prisoner, having had his eyes put out by order of that monarch, and his earldom of Cornwall transferred to Stephen of Blois, (see De Moreton, Earl of Cornwall). This unfortunate nobleman left two sons,

ADELME, from whom the extant house of CLANRICARDE, and the numerous families of De Burgh, Burgo, Burke, and Bourke, derive.

And,

JOHN DE BOURGH, whose son,

HUBERT DE BOURGH, became one of the most eminent and conspicuous nobles of his time; and as a subject was considered the greatest in Europe, during the reigns of King John and Henry III. " The first mention of this Hubert I find," says Dugdale, " is, that he was servant to King Richard I., as also to King John, being sent by the latter from Roan, in the first year of his reign, to treat of a marriage for him with a daughter to the king of Portugal; and had such great estimation from that king, that in the third of his reign, being lord-chamberlain of the household, he was constituted warden of the marches of Wales, and had a hundred soldiers to attend him in those parts." In the next year we find him employed on an embassy to Philip of France, to treat for the restitution of Normandy, then seized upon by that monarch—and for some years after engaged in the important duties of sheriff for the counties of Dorset, Somerset, Hereford, Berks, and Lincoln. At the period that the barons rose against King John, this even then powerful nobleman was seneschal of Poictou, and, taking part with his royal master, he was nominated one of the commissioners to treat with the insurrectionary lords at RUNNYMEDE, in which capacity he witnessed the signing of MAGNA CHARTA, and was advanced by the king, before he left the field, to the high station of JUSTICE OF ENGLAND. In ten days afterwards he was constituted sheriff of the counties of Kent and Surrey, and governor of the castle of Canterbury, and within a month made sheriff of Herefordshire, governor of the castle of Hereford, and governor of the castles of Norwich and Oxford. In the October following he obtained a grant of the lordship and hundred of Hoa in Kent, part of the possessions of Robert Bardolph, and was again constituted, on the 19th of the ensuing November, one of the commissioners upon the part of the king, to treat with Richard, Earl of Clare, and others, then deputed by the barons in the church of Erith, in Kent, touching a peace between the king and those turbulent nobles. He subsequently augmented his reputation by the gallant defence of Dover Castle against Lewis of France, when King John was compelled to fly to Winchester, and after the death of that monarch, by still faithfully holding the castle for the young king, Henry III., although the highest honours and rewards were tendered him personally by the French prince for its surrender. In the fourth year of the new king he succeeded William Mareschall, Earl of Pembroke, just then deceased, in the guardianship of young Henry, (at that time but fourteen years of age,) and in the government of the kingdom : and he suppressed in the next year a dangerous insurrection of the Londoners, begun by one *Constantine*, a chief man of the city, whom he caused to be hanged. His great power soon after, however, exciting the jealousy of the barons, the Earl of Chester, and others of the discontented party, signified to the king, that unless he forbore to require their castles, and to hearken to the counsels of this Hubert, who then assumed a higher deportment than any nobleman in the kingdom, they would all rise in rebellion against him ; but it does not appear that this cabal prevailed, for we find in the next year, when the king solemnised the festival of Christmas at Westminster, this Hubert, by especial royal appointment, proposing to the lords spiritual and temporal, then assembled, an aid " for vindicating the injuries done to the king and his subjects in the parts·beyond sea." And soon afterwards, having executed the office of sheriff for the counties of Norfolk and Suffolk, from the 1st to the 9th of Henry III. inclusive, and of the county of Kent, from the 3rd to the 11th of the same reign. he.was created, (on the 11th of February, 1226,) EARL OF KENT, with most extensive territorial grants from the crown. Within the year, too, he was constituted, by the advice of the peers of the whole realm, JUSTICE OF ENGLAND. His lordship afterwards, however, incurred the temporary displeasure of his royal master, as Dugdale thus states—" But before the end of this thirteenth year, (about Michaelmas,) the king having a rendezvous at Portsmouth, of the greatest army that had been seen in this realm, (it consisting of English, Irish, Scotch, and Welch,) designing therewith the recovery of what his father had lost in foreign parts ; and expecting all things in readiness, with ships for their transportation ; but finding not half so many as would suffice for that purpose : he wholly attributed the fault to this Hubert, and publicly calling him *Old Traytor*, told him, that he had taken five thousand marks as a bribe from the queen of France, and thereupon drawing out his sword, would have killed him on the spot, had not the Earl of Chester, and some others, prevented it, but displaced him from his office of Justice, whereupon he withdrew until the king grew better pacified, as, it seems, he soon was ; for the next ensuing year, when divers valiant knights, coming to the king out of Normandy, earnestly besought him to land forces in that country, assuring him that it might be easily recovered, this Hubert wholly dissuaded him from attempting it, and prevailed with him to make an expedition into Gascony and Poictou, where he succeeded so well, that, having little opposition, he freely received the homage of the inhabitants of those countries."

His lordship subsequently so fully re-established himself in royal favour, that he obtained permission, under certain circumstances, to execute the office of JUSTICE OF ENGLAND by deputy, and he soon afterwards had a grant of the office of JUSTICE OF IRELAND ; and was appointed governor of the Tower of London, castellan of Windsor, and warden of Windsor Forest. Here, however, he appears to have

reached the summit of his greatness, for, sharing the common fate of favorites, he was soon afterwards supplanted in the affections of the king, and exposed to the hostility of his enemies, so that, at one period, his life was saved only by his taking sanctuary in the church of Merton. He was afterwards dragged from before the altar of the chapel, at the Bishop of Norwich's manor-house in Essex, and conveyed prisoner, with his legs tied under the belly of his horse, by Sir Godfrey de Crawcombe, to the Tower of London ; " whereof," (says Dugdale,) " when they made relation to the king, who had sate long up to hear the news, he went merily to bed." " Howbeit," (continues the same authority,) " the next morning, Roger, Bishop of London, being told how they had dragged him from the chappel, went immediately to the king, and boldly rebuked him for thus violating the peace of holy church, saying, that if he did not forthwith free him of his bonds, and send him back to that chappel, whence he had been thus barbarously taken, he would pronounce the sentence of excommunication against all who had any hand therein. Whereupon the king, being thus made sensible of his fault, sent him back to the same chappel upon the 5th calend of October, but withall directed his precept to the sheriff of Essex and Hertfordshire, upon pain of death, to come himself in person, as also to bring with him the *posse comitatus*, and to encompass the chappel, so to the end he should not escape thence, nor receive any manner of food, which the sheriff accordingly did, making a great ditch, as well about the bishop's house as the chappel, resolving to stay there forty days." From this perilous situation the earl was relieved through the influence of his staunch friend, the Archbishop of Dublin, upon condition of expatriating himself, being conveyed, in the interim, again to the Tower. When the king, learning that the disgraced lord had deposited great treasure in the new temple of London, peremptorily demanded the same, but the Templars as peremptorily refused surrendering the property entrusted to them, without the consent of the owner, which latter being obtained " great store of plate, both of gold and silver, much money, and divers jewels of very great value," were seized, and deposited in the royal treasury. His lordship was subsequently committed close prisoner to the castle of Devizes, where, it is said, upon hearing of the death of his great enemy, the Earl of Chester, (5th November, 1233,) " he fetched a deep sigh, and exclaimed, *God have mercy on his soul ;* and calling for his psalter, stood devoutly before the cross, ceasing not before he had sung it all over, for the health of his soul." Soon after this the earl received a full and free pardon for his flight and outlawry, with a grant that his heirs should enjoy all the lands of his own inheritance, but as to such as he had otherwise acquired, " they should stand to the king's favour and kindness, and such terms as the king should think fit." Whereupon, relinquishing his title to the office of JUSTICE OF ENGLAND, and entering into obligation upon oath never again to claim it, he had restitution of numerous extensive lordships and manors. He did not, however, obtain his freedom, but was still closely confined at Devizes, from whence he eventually made his escape into Wales, and was ultimately pardoned, with the other English nobles who had joined Lewellyn, Prince of Wales, upon the conclusion of peace with that chieftain. Again, though, he incurred the displeasure of the king, in consequence of his daughter Margaret having wedded Richard, Earl of Gloucester, a minor, without license, but was pardoned upon clearing himself of all cognizance of the matter, and paying a fine. He was, however, again in disgrace, and again mulct, and so on until he was stript of almost all his splendid possessions.

His lordship m., first, Joane, daughter of William de Vernun, Earl of Devon, and widow of William de Brewer, with whom he acquired the whole Isle of Wight, and the lordship of Christ church in Hampshire, but by whom he had no issue. He m., secondly, Beatrix, daughter of William de Warren of Wirmgay, in the county of Norfolk, and widow of Dodo Bardolf; thirdly, Isabell, daughter and co-heiress of William, Earl of Gloucester, and widow of Geoffrey de Mandeville; and fourthly, Margaret, daughter of William, king of Scotland. By the last he is said to have had two sons, " but that," observes Mr. Banks," " appears by no means the fact, for had it so been the issue from them would have been nearer to the crown of Scotland than any of the competitors who preferred their claim thereto, temp. Edward I., inasmuch as the offspring from the daughter of William, king of Scotland, would have had a better pretension than Bruce or Baliol, who were only descended from the daughters of David, younger brother of the said William." His lordship had issue, however, two sons and two daughters, viz.

    John, (Sir) m. to Hawyse, daughter and heiress of William de Lanvalay, and left issue a son, John. This Sir John de Burgh never inherited the Earldom of Kent. He fought under the banner of the barons, at the battles of Lewes and Evesham, in the reign of Henry III. The period of his decease is not ascertained. His son and heir,

        JOHN, d. in the 8th Edward I., leaving the extensive manors and estates which he inherited from his father and mother, to three daughters, as co-heirs, viz. :—
        Hawyse, m. to Robert de Gretlly.
        Dervorgild, m. to Robert Fitz-Walter.
        Margerie, a nun at Chiksand, in the county of Bedford.
    Hubert, ancestor of the Barons Borough, of Gainsborough.
    Margaret, m. to Richard de Clare, Earl of Gloucester.
    Magotta, ——.

Hubert de Burgh, thus celebrated, as Earl of Kent, d. on the 4th March, 1243, and his remains were honorably interred within the church of the Friers preachers, (commonly called the Black-Friers,) in the city of London. With his lordship the EARLDOM OF KENT, in the family of Burgh, EXPIRED, which Collins accounts for in his parliamentary precedents, by the allegation that the patent by which the earldom was conferred, was, in remainder, to his heirs male by the Scottish princess only, and

that lady leaving no issue, the dignity of course ceased.

ARMS.—Gules, seven lozenges varry three, three and one.

BURGH — BARONS SOMERHILL, VISCOUNTS TUNBRIDGE, EARLS OF ST. ALBANS.

| Barony and Viscty. | By Letters | 3d April, 1624. |
| Earldom, | Patent, | 23d August, 1628. |

Lineage.

RICHARD BURKE, OR DE BURGH, fourth Earl of Clanricarde, in the peerage of Ireland, was created a peer of England, on 3d April, 1624, as *Baron Somerhill, and Viscount Tunbridge*, both in the county of Kent, and advanced to the EARLDOM OF ST. ALBANS, on the 23d August, 1628. His lordship m. Frances, daughter and heiress of Sir Francis Walsingham, and widow of Sir Philip Sydney, and of the unfortunate Earl of Essex, by whom he had issue,

    ULICK, his successor.
    Margaret, m. to the Hon. Edmond Butler, son of James, Earl of Ormonde.
    Honora, m. to John Paulett, Marquess of Winchester.

His lordship d. in 1636, and was s. by his son,
ULICK BURKE, OR DE BURGH, fifth Earl of Clanricarde, and second Earl of St. Albans, who was created Marquess of Clanricarde, in Ireland, on the 21st February, 1644. This nobleman, who was appointed lord lieutenant of Ireland, in 1650, took so distinguished a part against the rebels in the unhappy times of Charles I., that he was excepted from pardon for life or estate, in the act passed by Cromwell's parliament for the settlement of Ireland, 12th August, 1652. His lordship m. in December, 1622, Lady Anne Compton, then only daughter of William, Earl of Northampton, and by her had an only child,

    Margaret, who m. first, Charles, Viscount Muskerry, and had issue—
        CHARLES JAMES, who s. his grandfather, Donogh, Earl of Clancarty.
        Frances, d. unm.
    Her ladyship m. secondly, in 1676, Robert Villiers, called Viscount Purbeck, by whom she had an only son,
        John Villiers, who claimed the Earldom of Buckingham.
    She espoused thirdly, Robert Fielding, Esq. Her ladyship d. in 1698.

His lordship d. in 1657, when the Irish marquisate, and the English EARLDOM OF ST. ALBANS, with the minor English honors, became EXTINCT; his other dignities passed to his heir at law.

ARMS.—Or, a cross gu. in the dexter canton a lion, rampant, sa.

BURGH—BARONS BURGH, OR BOROUGH, OF GAINSBOROUGH, IN THE COUNTY OF LINCOLN.

By Writ of Summons, dated 1st September, 1487.
3 Henry VII.

Lineage.

This family sprang directly from HUBERT DE

BURGH, younger son of the celebrated HUBERT DE BURGH, EARL OF KENT, but it does not appear to have attained much importance until the reign of Edward IV., when,

SIR THOMAS DE BURGH, joined Sir William Stanley in rescuing that prince from Neville, Earl of Warwick, whose prisoner he was at the castle of Riddleham, but allowed the privilege of hunting for his recreation, upon one of which recreations his escape was effected. Sir Thomas fought afterwards under the banner of the same monarch, and shared with him in the fruits of the victory of Barnet-field. He m. Elizabeth, daughter and co-heiress of Sir Henry Percy, of Athol, Knt., son of Sir Thomas Percy, (second son of Henry, first Earl of Northumberland,) by his wife, Elizabeth, daughter and heiress of David Strabolgi, Earl of Athol, by which lady the Percys acquired the manor of Gainsborough, and thus it passed to the De Burghs. Sir Thomas de Burgh was s. by his son,

SIR THOMAS DE BURGH, who was created a knight of the garter by King Richard III., and was summoned to parliament, as BARON BOROUGH, OF GAINSBOROUGH, on the 1st September, 1487. His lordship m. Margaret, daughter of Thomas, Lord Roos, of Kendal, and widow of Sir Thomas Botreaux, by whom he had issue—

Edward, (Sir).

Thomas, ——.

Elizabeth, m. to Richard, Lord Fitz-Hugh.

Anne, ——.

The baron d. in 1496, and was s. by his son,

EDWARD DE BURGH, second baron, but never summoned to parliament, who m. Anne, daughter and heiress of Sir Thomas Cobham, of Starborough, and was s. by his son,

THOMAS DE BURGH, third baron, summoned to parliament from the 3d November, 1529, to the 8th September, 1552. This nobleman m. Anne, daughter of Sir Thomas Tirwhit, of Kirtilby, in the county of Lincoln, and dying in 1552, was s. by his son,

THOMAS DE BURGH, fourth baron, who m. Elizabeth, daughter of Sir David Owen, Knt., but the lady proving faithless, and having children by another person, his lordship obtained an act of parliament to bastardize those children. He m. secondly, Alice, daughter of ——, and had issue—

Henry, d. in the life-time of his father, s. p.

WILLIAM, successor to the title.

Dorothy, m. to Sir Anthony Nevill, Knt.

His lordship was s. by his son,

WILLIAM DE BURGH, fifth baron, one of the peers who sate in judgment upon the Duke of Norfolk, in the reign of Elizabeth. His lordship m. Katherine, daughter of Edward Clinton, Earl of Lincoln, and had issue,

THOMAS, his successor.

Henry, slain by Holcroft.

John, (Sir,) d. in 1594.*

---

* Sir John Bourgh—upon this gallant person, the following epitaph appears in Westminster Abbey:—
MS.

The celestial part is fled to Heaven,
And the earthly is laid in the ground:

Mary, m. to —— Bulkeley.

Elizabeth, m. to —— Rider.

Anne, m. to Sir Henry Ashley, Knt.

The baron was s. at his decease by his eldest son,

THOMAS BURGH, sixth baron, summoned to parliament from 11th January, 1563, to 24th October, 1597. This nobleman was sent in the 36th Elizabeth, upon an embassy into Scotland to incite King James against the Spanish faction there, and in four years afterwards succeeded Sir William Russell in the lieutenantcy of Ireland. His lordship m. ——, and had issue—

ROBERT, his successor.

Thomas, d. in minority, s. p.

Elizabeth, m. to George Brooke, fourth son of Lord Cobham, and had issue—

Sir William Brooke, K.B., who m. Penelope, daughter of Sir Moses Hill, of Hillsborough Castle, earl marshal of Ireland, and left a daughter,

HILL BROOKE, who m. first, the Hon. Mr. Wilmot, eldest son of Lord Wilmot; secondly, Sir William Boothby, from whom the present Sir William Boothby, Bart., descends: and thirdly, Edward Russell, brother of the Earl

---

Light substances ascend,
Whilst the heavy tend downwards.
If this church contain his body,
His fame fills the world,
And his spirit ranges the infinite space of Heaven.
The magnanimous and most illustrious,
JOHN BOURGH,
Son of the most noble, Lord William Bourgh,
(Descended from that most courageous Hero,
Hubert de Burgh, Earl of Kent,)
And of the most noble, Lady Catherine Clinton,
Daughter of Edmund Clinton, Earl of Lincoln,
Late admiral of England,
Renowned for his exploits, by sea and land;
Governor of Duisburgh.
He was twice knighted. First in Holland,
By his Excellency, the Earl of Leicester,
General of the English and Dutch forces;
Next by Henry IV., King of France,
On the victory of St. Andre.
Afterwards, he overcame, and brought to England,
A large Spanish Caracca ship,
Laden with precious stones, silver, gold, spices, &c.,
For which he was received, with the greatest
Honour and applause.
But unhappily, fighting the enemy,
Who fought with much courage,
He fell by an untimely death,
to the great grief of his men, and his country's loss;
In the 53rd year of his age, March 7th, 1594.
And here waits the trumpet's signal,
for the universal resurrection.
To keep up the remembrance of
so great a man,
this monument, in lieu of one more stately,
and more suitable to his high deserts and name,
is in the testimony of their love, erected,
by G. B. and M. P.

of Bedford, by whom she had several children.

Frances, *m.* to Francis Coppinger, Esq.

Anne, *m.* to Sir Drew Drury.

Catherine, *m.* to Thomas Knevit, Esq., and *d.* in 1640.

His lordship, who was a knight of the Garter, *d.* in 1597, and was *s.* by his elder son,

ROBERT BURGH, seventh baron, at whose decease unmarried in minority, (his brother having *d.* previously,) his estates devolved upon his sisters as co-heiresses, while the BARONY OF BOROUGH, OF GAINSBOROUGH, fell into ABEYANCE amongst those ladies, and so continues with their representatives.

ARMS.—Azure three fleur-de-lis ermine.

BURGHERSH — BARONS BURG-HERSH.

By Writ of Summons, dated 12th November, 1303, 32 Edward I.

Lineage.

In the 26th year of Edward I.

ROBERT DE BURGHERSH, had his commission renewed, as constable of Dover Castle, and lord warden of the Cinque Ports, and was summoned to parliament in six years afterwards, as BARON BURGHERSH; in which dignity he had summons from the 12th November, 1303, to the 13th June, 1305. His lordship *d.* in 1306, and was *s.* by his son,

STEPHEN DE BURGHERSH, second Baron, but never summoned to parliament; this nobleman had issue,

BARTHOLOMEW, his successor.

Henry, Bishop of Lincoln, temp., Edward II., and in the reign of Edward III., LORD TREASURER, and LORD CHANCELLOR. This distinguished prelate died at Ghent, in 1343, and his remains were brought over and interred in Lincoln Cathedral. A story subsequently circulated—that his lordship having incurred many a bitter curse, for despoiling his poorer tenantry of their grounds, to form a park at Tynghurst, appeared after his decease, to a certain person, (who had been one of his esquires,) in the habit of a keeper, with his bow, quiver of arrows, and a horn by his side, arrayed in a short green coat, and thus addressed him—"Thou knowest how I have offended God, and injured the poor, by my inclosure of this park: for this cause, therefore, am I enjoyned penance, to be the keeper of it, till it be laid open again. Go, therefore, to the canons of Lincoln, (my brethren,) and intreat them from me, to make a restitution to the poor, of what I thus wrongfully took from them." Whereupon having delivered the message to the canons, they sent one of their company, called William Batchelor, to see the desired restitution accomplished; who caused the banks and pales to be forthwith thrown down, and the ditches to be filled up.

Stephen de Burghersh, was *s.* by his elder son,

BARTHOLOMEW DE BURGHERSH, third Baron, who had summons to parliament, from 25th January, 1330, (4th Edward III.,) to 15th March, 1354, latterly with the addition of "Seniori." This nobleman was in the wars of Scotland and France, temp. Edward II., in the retinue of Bartholomew, Lord Badlesmere; but in the 15th of the same reign, joining Thomas, Earl of Lancaster, against the Spencers, he was taken prisoner with Lord Badlesmere, after the battle of Boroughbridge, upon the surrender of that nobleman's Castle of Leeds, in Kent, and sent to the Tower of London. He was restored, however, to his freedom and rank, on the arrival of Queen Isabel and Prince Edward, and constituted governor of Dover Castle, and warden of the Cinque Ports—trusts confirmed to him by King Edward III., in whose reign his lordship became still more highly distinguished, participating in the glories of CRESSY, and filling several important offices, such as lord chamberlain of the household, constable of the tower, &c. Lord Burghersh *m.* Elizabeth, daughter and co-heiress of Theobald de Verdon, a great Staffordshire Baron, by whom he had issue,

Henry, who *m.* Isabel, one of the sisters and co-heirs of Edmund de St. John, but died, *s. p.*

BARTHOLOMEW, his successor.

Joane.

His lordship *d.* in 1355, and was *s.* by his only surviving son,

BARTHOLOMEW DE BURGHERSH, fourth Baron, summoned to parliament, from 1st December, 1357, (31st Edward III.,) to 24th February, 1368. This nobleman was one of the most eminent warriors of the martial times of Edward III., having served in the immediate staff, (as we should now call it,) of the Black Prince, in the French wars, and attaining therein so much renown, as to be deemed worthy of one of the original garters, upon the institution of that order. In a few years afterwards, he journeyed into the Holy Land; and he was, subsequently, for several years, again in attendance upon his royal master, the Black Prince, during which period, he participated in the triumph of POYTIERS. His lordship *m.* first, Cecily, daughter and heiress of Richard de Weyland, by whom he had an only daughter, and, eventually, heiress,

Elizabeth, who *m.* Sir Edward le Despencer, K.G., and carried the Barony of Burghersh into the family of her husband. The great grand-daughter, and representative of this marriage,

Elizabeth Beauchamp, *m.* Edward, a younger son of Ralph Nevil, Earl of Westmoreland, and her great grand-daughter,

MARY, only daughter and heiress of Henry Nevil, last Lord Abergavenny and Despencer, espoused Sir Thomas Fane, Knt., whose son, Sir Francis Fane, K.B., was created in 1624, BARON BURGHERSH, and EARL OF WESTMORELAND, honours now enjoyed by his lordship's descendant, John Fane, tenth EARL OF WESTMORELAND, K.G.

Lord Burghersh *m.* secondly, Margaret, sister of Bartholomew, Lord Badlesmere, but had no issue. His lordship *d.*, in 1369; in which year, his last will and testament bears date, at London, 4th April. By this instrument, he directs, that his body be interred in the Chapel of Massingham, before the image of the blessed Virgin; that a *dirge* be there said, and in the morning a mass; and that a dole should be daily given to the poor of that place, at the discretion of his executors. To Sir Walter Pavely, (whom, with Lord Badlesmere, he had constituted executors,) he bequeathed a standing cup, gilt, with an L, upon the cover, as also his whole suit of arms for the justs, with his coat of mail and sword. Upon the demise of this nobleman, the last male representative of this branch of the family of Burghersh, the BARONY OF BURGHERSH, passed with his daughter, as stated above, into the family of Despencer, and the dignity is now vested, although not assumed, in Thomas Stapleton, present BARON LE DESPENCER.

ARMS.—Gu. a lion rampant, double quevée or.

Note.—Of this family was,

JOHN DE BURGHERSH, who *m.* Maud, one of the daughters and heiresses of Edmund Bacon, of ——, in the county of Essex, and left a son,

SIR JOHN DE BURGHERSH, Knt., who was in the expedition, made in the 47th Edward III., into Flanders. This Sir John *m.* Jamania, daughter of —— Hanham, of ——, in the county of Gloucester, and widow of Sir John Ralegh, Knt., by whom he left two daughters, his co-heirs, viz.

Margaret, *m.* first, to Sir John Grenveville, Knt., and secondly, to John Arundell, Esq., of the county of Cornwall.

Maud, *m.* to Thomas Chaucer, son of the celebrated poet, and dying in 1436 or 1437, left an only daughter,

Alice Chaucer, who *m.* William de la Pole, Duke of Suffolk, K.G., Lord Chancellor, and Lord High Admiral.

BURNELL—BARONS BURNELL.

By Writ of Summons, dated 19th Dec. 1311,
5 Edward II.

Lineage.

" That this family," says Dugdale, "hath been of great antiquity, here in England, an old Martyrologe (sometime belonging to the abbey of Buldewas, in the county of Salop), doth plainly demonstrate; for thereby appeareth that Sir Robert Burnell, Knt., died 15th Nov. 1067; Sir Philip, 14th Dec. 1107; Sir Roger, 5th Feb. 1140; Sir Hugh, 7th Jan. 1149; Sir Richard, 20th Jan. 1189; Sir Hugh, 12th May, 1242; and another Sir Robert, 6th Dec. 1249."

The next persons of the name upon record are,

WILLIAM BURNELL, who took part with the rebellious barons at the close of King Henry III.'s reign, and his brother,

ROBERT BURNELL, who, in the 54th of the same monarch, obtained a charter for a weekly market, and two fairs yearly, to be holden at his manor of ACTON-BURNELL, in the county of Salop; and before the end of the same year, we find him, amongst others, signed with the cross for a voyage to the Holy Land with Prince Edward. He was,

however, drowned, along with his above-mentioned brother, in 1289, when he was succeeded by his nephew, (the son of his brother Philip,)

PHILIP BURNELL, who was *s.* by his first cousin, (son of his uncle, Hugh Burnell,)

PHILIP BURNELL, who, in the 19th Edw. I., had a charter for free warren in all his demesne lands in the county of Salop, and in two years afterwards inherited estates in the counties of Southampton, Wilts, Berks, Stafford, Essex, and Surrey, from his uncle, Robert Burnell, bishop of Bath and Wells. This feudal lord *m.* Maud, daughter of Richard Fitz-Alan, Earl of Arundel, and had issue,

EDWARD, his successor.

Maud, *m.* first, to John Lovel, of Tichmarch, in the county of Northampton, by whom she had issue,

John Lovel, who was deprived of his inheritance by fine.

Maud *m.* secondly, John de Handlo, who was summoned to parliament, as BARON HANDLO, in 1342. (See that dignity.)

Philip Burnell *d.* in the 23d of Edward I., and was *s.* by his son,

EDWARD BURNELL, who, being in the wars of Scotland, had summons to parliament, as BARON BURNELL, from the 19th December, 1311, to the 24th October, 1314. His lorship *m.* Olivia, daughter of Hugh le Despenser; but dying without issue, in 1315, the barony EXPIRED; while his estates, save those held by his widow, in dower, devolved upon his only sister, MAUD, (mentioned above,) as sole heiress.

ARMS—Ar. a lion rampant sa. crowned, or. within a bordure, az.

BURNELL—BARONS BURNELL, OF HOLGATE, IN THE COUNTY OF SALOP.

By Writ of Summons, dated 25th Nov. 1350,
24 Edward III.

Lineage.

MAUD BURNELL, sister and sole heiress of Edward Lord Burnell, who *d.* in 1315, when his barony expired, espoused for her second husband John de Handlo, afterwards, summoned to parliament as LORD HANDLO, and had issue, two sons, viz.—

Richard, who *d.* in the life-time of his father, leaving a son,

Edmund de Handlo, who succeeded to the barony of Handlo, (see Handlo,)

And,

NICHOLAS DE HANDLO, who inherited, in the 22d Edward III., the estates of his mother, and assumed, in consequence, the surname of BURNELL; by which designation he was summoned to parliament, as BARON, on the 25th November, 1350. His lordship distinguished himself in arms, and participated in the glory acquired by his victorious sovereign upon the French soil. He *d.* on the 19th of January, 1383, and was *s.* by his son,

SIR HUGH BURNELL, Knt., as second *Baron Burnell*. This nobleman was constituted governor of the castle of Bridgenorth, in the county of Salop, in the 10th of Richard II.; but being denounced, in next year, as one of the favourites and evil counsellors of that unhappy prince, he was banished the court. He regained popular favour, however, so much within a few years, that upon the deposal of his royal master, he was one of the lords deputed to receive the unfortunate king's resignation of the crown and government, at the Tower of London. In the next reign we find Lord Burnell entrusted with the government of several strong castles on the Welch border. His lordship m. first, Joyce, daughter of John Botetourt, and grand-daughter and heiress of John, second Lord Botetourt, by whom he had no issue; but by a second wife he had an only son,

    EDWARD, who, dying in the life-time of his father, left, by his wife Alice, daughter of Thomas, Lord Strange, three daughters, viz.—

       Joyce, m. to Thomas Erdington, Esq., jun., and had,

          Sir Thomas Erdington, Knt.

       Margery, m. to Edmund, son of Sir Walter Hungerford, Knt., and had

          Thomas, father of Sir John Hungerford.

       Katherine, m. to Sir John Ratcliffe, whose son married the heiress of — Fitz-Walter.

Lord Burnell, who had been summoned to parliament from the 20th August, 1383, to the 21st October, 1490, died in the latter year; when his above-mentioned grand-daughters became his heirs, and the BARONY OF BURNELL fell into ABEYANCE amongst them, as it still continues with their representatives.

Arms.—Ar. a lion rampant sa. crowned or. within a bordure az.

NOTE.—As in the instance of this barony, it may appear rather strange that the issue of the second husband of Maud Burnell, by John Handlo, instead of her issue by her first husband, John Lovell, should come in for the barony, it may be necessary to observe, that, on the decease of her brother, Edward, Lord Burnell, without issue, the honour terminated with him, as she could not make herself heir to his lordship so as to take any thing by virtue of the record of his creation: wherefore, John Handlo being seised of the manors of Holgate, Acton-Burnell, &c. for life, in right of Maud, his wife, the remainder to Nicholas Handlo, (alias Burnell,) son of the said Maud and John, (by a fine in court,) the said NICHOLAS was summoned to parliament, amongst the barons of the realm, by reason of the fine aforesaid, and possession of the caput baroniæ, (Holgate, in the county of Salop,) and not John Lovel, who was heir to the said Maud by her first husband.—BANKS.

BUTLER—EARL OF WILTSHIRE.

By Letters Patent, dated 8th July, 1449.

Lineage.

JAMES BUTLER, son and heir of James, fourth Earl of Ormonde, in Ireland, by Joan, daughter of William Beauchamp, Lord Abergavenny, was elevated to the peerage of England, by letters patent, dated 8th July, 1449, as EARL OF WILTSHIRE, and

succeeded to the Irish honors, as fifth Earl of Ormonde, at the decease of his father, in 1452. This nobleman, who was a staunch adherent of the house of Lancaster, was made lieutenant of Ireland in the 30th Henry VI., and in three years afterwards LORD TREASURER OF ENGLAND. Shortly after this his lordship was with King Henry in the first battle of St. Albans, where the Yorkists prevailing, he fled, and cast his armour into a ditch. In the 38th of the same monarch he was reconstituted lord treasurer, and appointed keeper of the forest of Pederton, in the county of Somerset, and of Craneburne Chase, lying in the counties of Wilts and Dorset; being, at the same time, honoured with the Garter. His lordship participated this year in the triumph of his party at WAKEFIELD, where the Duke of York fell; but sharing also their defeat at MORTIMER CROSS, he fled the field: and pursuing a similar course after the unfortunate issue to the Lancastrians, of TOWTON-FIELD, he was taken prisoner by Richard Salkeld, Esq., and beheaded at Newcastle on the 1st May, 1461. His lordship d. without issue, and being attainted by parliament in the November following his execution; his EARLDOM OF WILTSHIRE EXPIRED, as should the Irish honors of the family, the deceased lord's brother and heir, John Butler, being also attainted for his Lancastrian principles, and being likewise engaged at the battle of Towton, but that the said John was restored in blood by King Edward IV., and thus enabled to inherit as sixth Earl of Ormonde. James, Earl of Ormonde and Wiltshire, m. thrice; first, Amy, daughter of John Fitz-Alan, Earl of Arundel; secondly, Amicea, daughter of Sir Richard Stafford, a great heiress, and thirdly, Eleanor, daughter of Edmund Beaufort, Duke of Somerset, but never had issue.

ARMS.—Or. a chief indented, az. a label of five points, ar.

BUTLER — BARON BUTLER, OF WESTON, IN THE COUNTY OF HUNTINGDON.

By Letters Patent, anno 1673.

Lineage.

LORD RICHARD BUTLER, second son of James, first Duke of Ormonde, was advanced to the peerage of Ireland, as EARL OF ARRAN, in 1662, and created a peer of England, by the title of BARON BUTLER, OF WESTON, in 1673. Upon his father's quitting Ireland in 1682, this nobleman was left deputy until his return, and performed great service against the mutinous garrison of Carrick-Fergus. His lordship distinguished himself also in the celebrated naval engagement with the Dutch in 1673. He m. first, Mary, daughter of James Stuart, Duke of Richmond and Lenox, but had no issue. He espoused secondly, Dorothy, daughter of John Ferrars, Esq., of Tamworth Castle, in the county of Warwick, by whom he had an only surviving daughter,

    Charlotte, m. to Charles, Lord Cornwallis.

He d. in 1685, when leaving no male issue, all his HONORS EXPIRED, but were revived in the person of his nephew, the Hon. Charles Butler, (see Butler, Baron Butler, of Weston).

ARMS.—Or. a chief, indented as.

BUTLER — BARON BUTLER, OF WESTON, IN THE COUNTY OF HUNTINGDON.

By Letters Patent, dated 23d January, 1693.

Lineage.

The Honorable

CHARLES BUTLER, second son of the celebrated Thomas, Earl of Ossory (by courtesy), and Lord Butler, of Moorpark, by writ, eldest son of James, Duke of Ormonde, was elevated to the peerage of Ireland on the 23d January, 1693, as *Baron Cloghgrenan, Viscount Tullough,* and EARL OF ARRAN, and created at the same time a peer of England, by the title of BARON BUTLER, of Weston, in the county of Huntingdon. This nobleman was one of the Lords of the bedchamber, and colonel of horse, in the reign of King William; governor of Dover Castle, and deputy-warden of the Cinque Ports, and master of the ordnance in Ireland, temp. Queen Anne, and chancellor of the university of Oxford in the reign of King George I. His lordship m. Elizabeth, fourth daughter and coheiress of Thomas, Lord Crew, of Stene; but dying *s. p.* in 1759, all his HONOURS EXPIRED. His lordship was also lord high steward of Westminster, and a lieut.-general in the army.

Arms—Or. a chief indented as.

BUTLER — BARONS BUTLER, OF BRAMFIELD, IN THE COUNTY OF HERTFORD.

By Letters Patent, 20th September, 1628.

Lineage.

From the BOTELERS or BUTLERS, Barons of Wemrore and Oversley, descended

SIR JOHN BUTLER, BART., of Hatfield Woodhall, in the county of Herts, (so created in 17th James I.,) who was advanced to the peerage on the 20th September, 1628, as BARON BUTLER of BRAMFIELD, in the same shire. His lordship m. Elizabeth, sister of George Villiers, Duke of Buckingham, by whom he had six sons, whereof five predeceased him unmarried, and six daughters, of which,

Aubrey, m. first, Sir Francis Anderson, and secondly, Francis, Earl of Chichester.

Helen, m. Sir John Drake, Knt.

Jane, m. James Ley, Earl of Marlborough.

Olivera, m. Endymion Porter, Esq.

Mary, m. Edward, Lord Howard of Escrick.

Anne, m. first, Mounjoy Blount, Earl of Newport, and secondly, Thomas Weston, Earl of Portland.

His lordship d. in 1637, and was s. by his only surviving son,

WILLIAM, second baron, at whose decease without issue, in 1647, the BARONY OF BUTLER, of Bramfield, EXPIRED, while his lordship's estates devolved upon his sisters, or their representatives, and were purchased afterwards by George, Viscount

Grandeson, in Ireland, who thereby obtained possession of the manor of BRAMFIELD.

ARMS.—Gu. A fesse Chequée, ar. and sa. betw. six cross crosslets, or.

BUTLER — BARONS BUTLER, OF LANTHONY, IN THE COUNTY OF MONMOUTH, AND EARLS OF BRECKNOCK, IN THE PEERAGE OF ENGLAND.

By Letters Patent, dated 20th July, 1660,
12 Charles II.
Marquesses and Dukes of Ormonde, and Earls of Ossory, in Ireland.

Lineage.

The Right Hon.

JAMES BUTLER, Marquess of Ormonde, and Earl of Ossory, in Ireland, for his faithful adherence to King Charles I., was created a peer of England at the restoration of the monarchy, (20th July, 1660,) in the dignities of *Baron Butler, of Lanthony,* in the county of Monmouth, and EARL OF BRECKNOCK,[*] and the next year advanced to the Irish

---

[*] James Butler, Earl of Ormonde, his lordship's ancestor, m. Alianore, daughter of Humphrey De Bohun, Earl of Hereford and Essex, LORD OF BRECKNOCK, and constable of England, by Elizabeth Plantagenet, daughter of Edward I.—(See Bohun, Earl of Hereford.)

Note.—The illustrious house of ORMONDE, originally sprang from the great feudal family of Walter: thus,

In the 3rd Henry II., in the sheriff's account for Norfolk and Suffolk, mention is made in those shires, of

HUBERT WALTER, to whom succeeded,

HENRY WALTER, who had five sons, Hubert, Theobald, Walter, Roger, and Hamon, of whom,

Hubert, the eldest, a churchman, became Archbishop of Canterbury.

And, the second,

THEOBALD WALTER, obtained from King Richard I., a grant in fee, of the lordship of PRESTON, in Lancashire, with the whole Wapentake and forest of Amundernesse, to hold by three knights' fees: which grant bears date 22nd April, in the first year of that king's reign, being the Friday immediately after his coronation. In five years after, he was appointed sheriff of the county of Lancaster, and continued to fulfil the duties of that high office, from the 6th of Richard, to the 1st of John, inclusive. This feudal lord was a great benefactor to the church, and a founder of several religious houses, amongst which were the Augustinian Abbey of Cockersand, in Lancashire; and, (being BUTLER of Ireland,) the monastery of Arklow, and the abbeys of Mothany, county of Limerick, and Nenagh, county of Tipperary, in Ireland. In the 5th of King John, he gave two palfreys for license to go into that kingdom, and having espoused Maud, daughter of Robert Vava-

103

DUKEDOM OF ORMONDE. This nobleman distinguished himself first in public life, by a disposition to oppose the government of the Earl of Strafford in Ireland, and his political career commenced in the following singular manner. Lord Strafford, upon calling a parliament to meet at Dublin Castle, issued a proclamation that none of the members, lords or commons, should enter with their swords; an injunction obeyed by all but the young Marquess of Ormonde, who told the black rod at the door *"that he should have no swords of his except in his guts."* This so irritated the lord deputy, that the refractory lord was called upon in the evening to account for his conduct; when he produced his majesty's writ, summoning him to parliament, *"cinctus cum gladio."* So resolute a reply, at once fixed his lordship's fortune, and it being deemed more prudent to conciliate than to provoke so ardent a spirit, he was immediately called to the privy council; from that period he attached himself zealously to the cause of the king, and used all his efforts to defeat the accusations against the Earl of Strafford, who thenceforward felt so much gratitude towards him, that he made it his last request to his royal master to bestow the garter upon Ormonde; a request cheerfully complied with. The marquess was afterwards lord lieutenant of Ireland, and his valour, conduct, and loyalty, were in the highest degree conspicuous throughout the whole of the civil wars. He was a second time chief governor of Ireland after the restoration. Burnet says of this eminent person, "that he was every way well fitted for a court: of a graceful appearance, a lively wit, and a cheerful temper; a man of great expense, but decent even in his vices, for he always kept up the forms of religion: too faithful not to give always good advice; but when bad ones were followed, too complaisant to be any great complainer. He had got through many transactions with more fidelity than success; and in the siege of Dublin, miscarried so far, as to lessen the opinion of his military conduct: but his constant attendance on his master and his great sufferings, raised him (after the restoration), to be lord steward of the household, and lord lieutenant of Ireland."

His grace m. Elisabeth, only daughter of Richard Preston, Earl of Desmond, by whom he had issue—

Thomas, who d. young.

---

sour, with whom he acquired the manors of Edlington and Newborough, and the lands of Boulton, departed this life in the 9th of the same monarch. When Robert Vavasour above mentioned, gave to the king a fine of twelve hundred marks, and two palfreys for the benefit of the widow's marriage and dowrie. The lady married subsequently Fulke Fitz-warine. Theobald Walter left issue,

THEOBALD, who assumed from his office in Ireland, the surname of BOTELER or BUTLER, and from this great feudal lord, who m. Maude, sister of the celebrated Thomas-a-Becket, Archbishop of Canterbury, immediately descended the BUTLERS OF ORMONDE. Maud, whose tuition King John committed to Gilbert Fitz-Reinfrid, Baron of Kendall.

THOMAS, EARL OF OSSORY, who was summoned to parliament 24th September, 1666, as LORD BUTLER, *of Moor Park, in the county of Herts.* This nobleman was b. at Kilkenny on the 8th July, 1634, and by the time he had reached majority gave such proofs of discretion, talent, and noble bearing, that Sir Robert Southwell thus depicts him at that period. " He was a young man with a very handsome face; a good head of hair; well set; very good natured; rides the great horse very well; is a very good tennis player, fencer, and dancer; understands music, and plays on the guitar and lute; speaks French elegantly; reads Italian fluently; is a good historian; and so well versed in romances, that if a gallery be full of pictures and hangings, he will tell the stories of all that are there described. He shuts up his door at eight in the evening and studies till midnight; he is temperate, courteous, and excellent in all his behaviour." In 1661 his lordship was general of the horse in Ireland, and a member of the privy council. He was deputy to his father while lord lieutenant, and attained the highest reputation in the cabinet and the field. His lordship pre-eminently distinguished himself in the great naval engagement with the Dutch in 1673, *" wherein," (saith Anthony Wood,) " he gallantly acted beyond the fiction of romance."* He m. in 1659, Amelia, eldest daughter of Louis de Nassau, Lord of Beveweast, Odyke, and Auverquerque, natural son of Maurice, Prince of Orange, by whom he had two surviving sons and three daughters, viz.

JAMES, who s. his grandfather.

Charles, created Earl of Arran.

Elizabeth, m. to William Richard George, ninth Earl of Derby.

Emilia, ——.

Henrietta, m. to Henry D'Auverquerque, Earl of Grantham.

His lordship d. of a fever at Whitehall, in the life-time of his father, deeply lamented by the kingdom at large, on the 30th July, 1680.

Richard, created Earl of Arran in Ireland, and LORD BUTLER, OF WESTON, in England.

John, created EARL OF GOWRAN, d. in 1677, s. p.

The duke d. the year of the revolution, 1688, and was s. by his grandson,

JAMES BUTLER, second Duke of Ormonde in Ireland, and second EARL OF BRECKNOCK IN ENGLAND. This nobleman being one of the first to espouse the cause of the Prince of Orange, was made a KNIGHT of the GARTER, upon the elevation of his highness to the throne: and *constituted* LORD HIGH CONSTABLE OF ENGLAND for the day, at the coronation of his Majesty and Queen Mary. In 1690, his grace attended King William at the battle of the Boyne, and in three years afterwards was at Landen, where he received several wounds, had his horse killed under him, and was taken prisoner by the French, and carried to Namur. In 1702, he was appointed by Queen Anne, Commander-in-chief of the land forces sent against France and Spain, when he destroyed the French fleet, and the Spanish galleons, in the harbour of Viga; for which he received the thanks of parliament. In 1712, he succeeded the Duke of Marlborough, as Captain-general, and Commander-in-chief of all his majesty's land forces in Great Britain, or employed abroad in conjunction with her allies; and on the Queen's death was one of the privy council who signed the proclamation, declaiming George I. King of England; on whose arrival he was at first graciously received by his majesty, but in a few days after was removed from his great offices; and within a short time (1715), impeached in parliament of high crimes and misdemeanors. Whereupon retiring into France, he was attainted, his estates confiscated, and all his honours EXTINGUISHED, on the 20th August, 1715. But in 1721, an act of parliament passed, enabling his brother the Earl of Arran, to purchase the escheated property, which he accordingly did. The Duke m. twice, first Lady Anne Hyde, daughter of Laurence, Earl of Rochester, who died with her only infant child, and secondly, Lady Mary Somerset, daughter of Henry, Duke of Beaufort, by whom he had an only surviving daughter, Mary, m. to John, Lord Ashburnham. He died at Madrid, at the advanced age of ninety-four, on the 16th November, 1745.

ARMS.—Or. a chief indented az. *[handwritten annotation]*

BUTLER — BARON BUTLER, OF MOOR PARK, IN THE COUNTY OF HERTS.

See Butler, EARLS OF BRECKNOCK.
(Thomas, Earl of Ossory, son of the first lord.)

CAILLI—BARON CAILLI.

By Writ of Summons, dated 4th March 1309, 2nd Edward II.

Lineage.

In the 7th year of King John,
ADAM DE CAILLI accounted five pounds for license to plead before the king, in a cause depending between himself and Michael de Puninges, regarding the dowry of Margaret, the latter's wife. From this Adam descended,
THOMAS DE CAILLI, who in the 35th Edward I., obtained livery of the lands which he inherited from his cousin, Robert de Tatsthall, (nephew of his mother Emme,) and was summoned to parliament as a BARON, from the 4th March, 1309, to the 16th June, 1311, inclusive. In the 10th Edward II., this nobleman, with Margaret his wife, procured a charter of free-warren in all their demesne lands at Wymundham, Babingle, and Wulferton, in the county of Norfolk. In which year his lordship died, leaving Adam, the son of Roger de Clifton, by Margerie, his sister, then but nine years of age, his sole heir. Upon the decease of Lord Cailli, the BARONY became EXTINCT.

ARMS.—Ar. four bendlets gu.

From a collateral branch of this baronial house, descend the BARONETS CAYLEY, of Brompton, in the county of York.

CADOGAN—BARON CADOGAN, OF READING, IN THE COUNTY OF BERKS, VISCOUNT CAVERSHAM, EARL CADOGAN.

| Barony, | } by Letters | { 30th June, 1716, |
| Earldom, &c. | } Patent | { 8th May, 1718. |

Lineage.

WILLIAM CADOGAN, (eldest son of Henry Cadogan, barrister at law, by Bridget, his wife, daughter of Sir Hardress Waller, Knt.,) a general officer of great celebrity, the companion in arms of the Duke of Marlborough, and his grace's successor in the command of the army, was elevated to the peerage on 30th June, 1716, as BARON CADOGAN, *of Reading, in the county of Berks,* and created, on the 8th May, 1718, Baron Cadogan, of Oakley, in the county of Bucks, with remainder, in default of male issue, to his brother, Charles Cadogan, VISCOUNT CAVERSHAM, in the county of Oxford, and EARL CADOGAN. His lordship m. Margaretta-Cecilia, daughter of William Munster, counsellor of Holland, by whom he had issue,

Sarah, m. to Charles, second Duke of Richmond, K.G.

Margaret, died unmarried.

The earl d. on the 17th July, 1726, when the BARONY OF CADOGAN OF READING, the VISCOUNTY OF CAVERSHAM, and the EARLDOM OF CADOGAN, became EXTINCT, while the barony of Cadogan of Oakley devolved, according to the limitation, upon his lordship's brother, Charles Cadogan, and is now enjoyed by the present Earl Cadogan, the said Charles's grandson.

CAMOIS—BARONS CAMOIS.

By Writ of Summons, dated 14th Dec., 1264, 49 Henry III.

Lineage.

The first notice of this family occurs in the beginning of Henry the Third's time, when we find
RALPH DE CAMOIS restored to certain lands in Huntingdonshire, which had been seized upon by the crown, in the preceding reign, owing to his participation in the rebellion of the barons. After this, in the 26th Henry III., he executed the office of sheriff for the counties of Surrey and Sussex, and from that time until the thirteenth year of the same reign. He d. in thirteen years afterwards, and was s. by his son,
SIR RALPH DE CAMOIS, who, joining Montford, Earl of Leicester, and the rebellious barons, stood so high in their confidence, that, after the battle of Lewes, he was constituted one of their council of state for the government of the realm, having been summoned to parliament, as a BARON, on the 14th December, 1264. His lordship d. in 1276, and was s. by his son,
SIR JOHN DE CAMOIS, second baron, but never summoned to parliament. Of this nobleman the only remarkable circumstance recorded is, the granting, by a formal deed, his wife, Margaret, daughter and heiress of Sir John de Gatesden, and all her goods and chattels, to Sir William Painell,

Knt., with whom she had previously departed from her husband, and was then living in adultery. After the decease of Sir John Camois, the lady married Painell, and then demanded a portion of her deceased lord's lands as her dowry. But to that claim the king's attorney replied, that she had no right whatever, in as much as she had voluntarily forsaken her husband long before his death, to whom she had never subsequently been reconciled, and had been living in adultery with Painell. Unto which the claimant and her husband responded, that though she abode with him, it was not in an adulterous manner, but by virtue of the grant made by her deceased husband. The case was eventually referred to parliament, (29th and 30th Edward I.,) and the king's counsel urging the statute of ————, whereby it was enacted, " That if a wife do, of her own accord, forsake her husband, and live adulterously with another man, she shall for ever be debarred of her dowry, unless her husband, without ecclesiastical coercion, be reconciled to her, and cohabit with her," judgment was given against the claim, that the said Margaret should have no dowry out of her husband Camois' lands. This suit was very famous in its time. Sir John de Camois was *s.* by his son by the said Margaret,

SIR RALPH DE CAMOIS, third baron, summoned to parliament from 26th November, 1313, to 1st April, 1335. This nobleman distinguished himself in the Scottish wars of Kings Edward I. and Edward II., and was in the retinue of Hugh de Spencer the elder. But no mention is made of him, or of any descendant of his, after the year 1335.

ARMS.—Ar. on a chief gu. three plates (besants).

Copy of the very singular deed made by Sir John Camois to Sir William Painell—

Omnibus Christi fidelibus, ad quos præsens scriptum pervenerit, JOHANNES DE CAMEYS, filius et hæres Domini Radulphi de Cameys, salutem in Domino. Noveritis me tradisse et dimisisse, spontaneâ voluntate meâ, Domino WILLELMO PAYNEL militi, Margaretam de Cameys, filiam et hæredem Domini JOHANNIS DE GATESDEN, uxorem meam: et etiam dedisse et concessisse eidem Willielmo, relaxasse et quietum clamasse, omnia bona et catalla, quæ ipsa Margareta habet, vel de cætero habere posset: et etiam quicquid mei est de prædicta Margaretâ, bonis ve catallis, cum pertinentiis: ita quod nec ego, nec aliquis alius, nomine meo, in prædictâ Margaretâ, bonis et catallis ipsius Margaretæ, cum suis pertinentiis, de cætero exigere, vel vendicare poterimus, nec debemus imperpetuum. Ac volo et concedo, et per præsens scriptum confirmo; quod prædicta Margareta, cum prædicto Domino Willielmo, sit et maneat, pro voluntate ipsius Willielmi. In cujus rei testimonium huic præsenti scripto sigillum meum opposui: His testibus,

     Thomâ de Depeston.
     Johanne de Ferrings.
     Willielmo de Icombe.
     Henrico le Biroun.
     Stephano Camerario.
     Waltero le Blound.
     Gilberto de Batecumbe.
     Roberto de Bosco.
           et aliis.

CAMOIS—BARONS CAMOIS.

By Writ of Summons, dated 20th August, 1383,
7 Richard II.

Lineage.

In the 47th Edward III.,

THOMAS DE CAMOIS obtained the king's charter for a weekly market on the Saturday, at his manor at Broadwater, in Sussex: and in the 1st of Richard II. we find him serving the king in his fleet at sea, being then in the retinue of William, Lord Latimer. In three years afterwards he was in the expedition made into France, and in the 7th of the same monarch, being elected one of the knights for the shire of Surrey, he was, as a banneret, discharged from that service, it being amongst the privileges of that high order of knighthood not to be subject to serve in parliament. In the remainder of this reign he was in the wars of France and Spain; and he enjoyed the confidence of the succeeding monarchs, Henry IV. and Henry V. He had been summoned to parliament, as BARON CAMOIS, from the 7th of Richard II. to the 8th of Henry V., inclusive, and was a knight of the Garter. His lordship married Elizabeth, daughter and heiress of William de Louches, with whom he acquired the manor of Whateley, in Oxfordshire, and had issue,

    RICHARD, who d. before his father, leaving

        HUGH, successor to the barony.

        Margaret, m. to Ralph Rademilde.

        Alianor, m. to Roger Lewknor.

Lord Camois d. in 1421, and was s. by his grandson,

HUGH DE CAMOIS, second baron, at whose decease, without issue, in the 5th of Henry VI., the estates devolved upon his sisters, above mentioned, as co-heiresses, while the BARONY fell into ABEYANCE between them, as it so continues amongst their descendants.

A descendant from the younger sister, Alianor, by her husband, Roger Lewknor,

    Sir Roger Lewknor of Camois Court, in the county of Sussex, left issue, a daughter and heiress,

        Catherine, who m., temp. Henry VIII., John Mill, Esq., of Grantham, in Sussex, and had issue,

            Lewknor Mill, of Camois Court, whose eldest son and heir,

                JOHN MILL, Esq., was created a baronet in 1619, an honour enjoyed by his descendant, the present SIR CHARLES MILL.

ARMS.—Az. on a chief gules, three plates (besants).

CAMVILLE — BARONS CAMVILLE, OF CLIFTON.

By Writ of Summons, dated 23d June, 1295,
23 Edward I.

Lineage.

In the fifth year of King Stephen,

GERALD DE CAMVILLE, of Lilburne Castle, in the county of Northampton, granted two parts of the tithes of Charleton-Camville, in Somersetshire, to the monks of Bermondsey, in Surrey. To this Gerald s. his son,

RICHARD DE CAMVILLE, who was founder in the time of KING STEPHEN, of Combe-Abbey, in the county of Warwick, and was one of the witnesses in the 12th of the same reign, to the convention between that monarch and Henry, Duke of Normandy, regarding the succession of the latter to the crown of England. This feudal lord appears to be a person of great power during the whole of King Henry's reign, and after the accession of Richard I. we find him one of the admirals in the expedition made by that monarch into the Holy Land. He was subsequently governor of Cyprus: whence he went without the king's permission to the siege of ACON and there died. His lordship left four sons and a daughter, viz.

1. GERALD, his heir, who purchased from King Richard the custody of Lincoln Castle, and the province adjacent. This Gerald was a very powerful feudal lord in the reign of John, to which monarch he staunchly adhered. He m. Nichola, eldest daughter and co-heiress of Richard de Haya, and left an only son and heir,

> RICHARD, who m. Eustachia, daughter and heiress of Gilbert Basset, and widow of Thomas de Vernon, and left an only daughter and heiress,
>
>> IDONEA, who m. William, son of William de Longspee, Earl of Salisbury.

2. Walter, left issue—

> Roger, who had an only daughter,
>> Matilda, m. to Nigel de Moubray, and died s. p.
>
> Petronilla, m. to Richard Curson.
> Matilda, m. to Thomas de Astley.
> Alicia, m. to Robert de Esseby.

3. Richard left issue—

> Richard, died s. p.
> Isabella, heiress of her brother, m. in the 4th Richard I., Richard Harcourt, of Bosworth, in the county of Leicester.

4. William, with whom we shall proceed.

5. Matilda, m. to William de Ros.

WILLIAM DE CAMVILLE, the youngest son, m. Albreda, daughter and heiress of Geoffrey Marmion, and had issue—

GEOFFREY, his successor.

William, of Sekerton, in the county of Warwick, father of

> Thomas, whose grandson, Sir Gerard de Camville, left a daughter and heiress,
>> Elizabeth, m. to Robert Burdett, ancestor of the present Sir Francis Burdett, Bart.

Thomas, ——

William de Camville was s. by his eldest son,

GEOFFREY DE CAMVILLE, who, in the 22d Edward I. had summons to attend the king at Portsmouth, with horse and arms, to embark in the expedition then proceeding to Gascony; and was subsequently summoned to parliament as BARON CAMVILLE, *of Clifton, in the county of Stafford*, from 23d June, 1295, to 22d February, 1307. His lordship m. Maud, daughter and heiress of Sir Guy

de Bryan, by Eve, daughter and heiress of Henry de Traci, and had an only child,

WILLIAM, his successor.

He d. in 1308, seised of the lordships of Freymington, Bovey-Traci, Nymet-Traci, Barnstable, the fourth part of the manor of Toriton, and of the hamlet of Nimet St. George, as also of the lordship of Clifton Camville, in the county of Stafford, which he held by the service of three knights' fees; and which lordship and manors were holden by him (as tenant by the courtesy of England), in right of Maud, his wife. His lordship was s. by his son,

WILLIAM DE CAMVILLE, second baron, summoned to parliament 4th March, 1309, and 16th June, 1311, but never afterwards. Of the issue of this nobleman there are different statements. He d. however, without a son, when the BARONY OF CAMVILLE fell into ABEYANCE, as it probably so continues.

One authority, BURTON, in his Leicestershire, gives his lordship two daughters, his co-heiresses, viz.

Maud, m. to Sir Richard Stafford, of Pipe, in the county of Stafford, whose son,
> Richard, was summoned to parliament as Lord Stafford, of Clifton.
Margery, m. to Sir Richard Vernon, of Haddon, in the county of Derby.

Another, ERDEWIC, the historian of Staffordshire, says, he had but one daughter,

MAUD, who m. first, Richard Vernon, and secondly, Sir Richard Stafford.

While a third authority, Dr. Vernon, rector of Bloomsbury, in an interleaved copy of Erdewic, states,

That William de Camville, of Clifton-Camville, had issue five daughters and heirs, viz.

Maud, m. to Sir William Vernon, Knt., of Haddon, in the county of Derby.
Isabella, m. first, to Sir Richard Stafford, and secondly, to Gilbert de Bermingham.
Eleanor, ——
Nichola, m. to John St. Clere.
Catherine, m. to Robert Grisely.

ARMS.—Vert three lions passant ar. armed and langued gu.

CANTILUPE—BARONS CANTILUPE.

By Writ of Summons, dated 29th December, 1299, 28 Edward I.

Lineage.

WILLIAM DE CANTILUPE, the first of this family upon record, served the office of Sheriff for the counties of Warwick and Leicester in the 3rd, 4th, and 5th years of King John. In the next year he was made governor of the castles of Hereford and Wilton, and he was subsequently sheriff of Herefordshire. In the 11th of the same reign, being then the king's steward, he gave forty marks for the wardship of Egidia, Lady of Kilpeck, widow of William Fitz-Warine, and in three years afterwards, when the king was excommunicated by Pope Innocent III. he remained so faithful as to become one of the monarch's chief counsellors. We find him, however, arrayed afterwards under the baronial banner, and joining in the invitation to Lewis of

France. But within the same year he returned to the king, when he obtained grants of all the forfeited estates of Richard de Engaine and Vitalis de Engaine, two leading barons in the insurrection; and was appointed governor of Kenilworth Castle, in the county of Warwick. In the reign of Henry III. he continued attached to the cause of royalty and acquired immense possessions, in the shape of grants from the crown of forfeited lands. He d. in 1238, leaving five sons, viz.

1. WILLIAM, his heir, also steward to the king, and a person of great power, m. Millicent, daughter of Hugh de Gournal, and widow of Almeric, Earl of Eureux, and had issue,

WILLIAM, who m. Eve, daughter and coheiress of William Broase, Lord of Brecknock and Abergavenny, and in her right became possessed of that honour. He d. in the flower of his youth, leaving issue,

George, who died s. p.

Millicent, m. first, to John de Montalt, and secondly, to Eudo le Zouche, from which latter union descended the Lords Zouche, of Haryngworth.

Joan, m. to Henry de Hastings.

Thomas, Bishop of Hereford, and in the 34th Edward I., canonised.

Julian, m. to Robert de Tregos.

2. Walter, a priest, employed by King Henry as his agent to the court of Rome, afterwards Bishop of Worcester.

3. John, Lord of Snithfield, in the county of Warwick, m. Margaret, daughter and heiress of William Cummin, of that place, and was s. by his son,

JOHN, who d. in the 17th Edward II., and was s. by his grand-daughter,

Eleanor Cantilupe, who m. Sir Thomas _West_, from which union lineally descend the *extant* Earls of DELAWARR, and VISCOUNTS CANTILUPE.

4. Nicholas, of whom presently.

5. Thomas, elected lord chancellor of England, by the barons in the 49th Henry III.

NICHOLAS DE CANTILUPE, the fourth son, m. Eustachia, sister and eventual heiress of Hugh Fitz-Ralph, Lord of Greseley, in the county of Nottingham, and was s. by his son,

WILLIAM DE CANTILUPE, who having distinguished himself in the French and Scottish wars of King Edward I., was summoned to parliament, as BARON CANTILUPE, from 29th December, 1299, to 5th August, 1308. His lordship d. in the following year, and was s. by his elder son,

WILLIAM DE CANTILUPE, second Baron, but never summoned to parliament. This nobleman dying without issue, was s. by his brother,

SIR NICHOLAS DE CANTILUPE, third Baron. This nobleman served in the Flemish and Scottish wars of Edward III. and had summons to parliament, from 23rd April, 1337, to 15th March, 1354. His lordship d. in 1355, seised of the manor of Eselburgh, in the county of Buckingham; Ilkeston, in the county of Derby; Greseley, in Nottinghamshire; and Livington and others, in the county of Lincoln, and leaving a son, WILLIAM, but

108

neither that personage nor his sons, Nicholas and William, both of whom died s. p., were ever summoned to parliament, or deemed barons of the realm.

ARMS.—Gu. three leopards' heads inverted, jessant three fleurs de lis or.

CAPEL—BARON CAPEL OF TEWKSBURY, IN THE COUNTY OF GLOUCESTER.

By Letters Patent, dated 11th April, 1692.

Lineage.

SIR HENRY CAPEL, K.B., second son of Arthur, first Baron Capel, of Hadham, in the county of Hertford, and brother of Arthur, first Earl of Essex, having distinguished himself as a leading and eloquent member of the House of Commons, was elevated to the peerage on the 11th April, 1692, as BARON CAPEL, *of Tewksbury*. His lordship m. Dorothy, daughter of Richard Bennet, Esq., of Kew, in the county of Surrey, and niece of Sir Richard Bennet, Bart., of Babraham, in Cambridgeshire, but had no issue. Lord Capel was one of the Lords Justices of Ireland, upon the recal of Lord Sydney, in 1693, and died LORD LIEUTENANT of that kingdom, at the castle of Dublin, 30th May, 1696. His lordship was buried at Hadham, where an inscription states, that he was of the privy council to King Charles II., one of the lords of the treasury, and of the privy council to King William. At his lordship's decease the BARONY OF CAPEL, of Tewksbury, became EXTINCT.

ARMS.—Gu. a lion rampant, betw. three cross crosslets fitchy, or. with due difference.

CAREW — BARON CAREW, OF CLOPTON, IN THE COUNTY OF WARWICK. EARL OF TOTNESS.

Barony,	by Letters Patent,	4th June, 1605.
Earldom,		5th Feb. 1625.

Lineage.

Of this family, one of great antiquity in the Western parts of England, and which derived its surname originally from Carew Castle, in the county of Pembroke, was,

SIR GEORGE CAREW, Knt. who was made Captain of the Tower of Ruysbanke, at Calais, in the 31st of Henry VIII., which command Sir John Pecche and Sir Nicholas Carew formerly held. From this Sir George Carew descended another

GEORGE CAREW, who, being a churchman, was, first, archdeacon of Totness, in the county of Devon; next, dean of Bristol, and chief chanter in the cathedral of Salisbury; afterwards dean of the king's chapel, and dean of Christ Church, Oxford; lastly dean of Exeter and Windsor. This very reverend personage married Anne, daughter of Sir Nicholas Harvey, Knt., and had with other issue,

GEORGE CAREW, who adopting the profession of arms, was in the expedition to Cadis, in the 39th of Elizabeth, and afterwards served with great reputation in Ireland. In which kingdom he was made President of Munster, when uniting his forces with those of the Earl of Thomond, he reduced several castles, and other strong places, obtained many

He was 2d son of Sir Edmd Carew (who died 1513) and not descended from any George.

triumphs over the rebels, and brought the Earl of Desmond to trial. He was likewise a privy councillor in Ireland, and master of the ordnance. Upon the accession of King James I., he was constituted governor of the Isle of Guernsey, and having married Joyce, only daughter and heiress of William Clopton, Esq., of Clopton, in the county of Warwick, he was elevated to the peerage, on the 4th June, 1605, as *Baron Carew, of Clopton*. After which, he was made master of the ordnance for life, and sworn of the privy council; and, in the 1st year of King Charles I., created EARL OF TOTNESS. "Besides," says Dugdale, "these, his noble employments, 'tis not a little observable, that being a great lover of antiquities, he wrote an historical account of all those memorable passages, which hapned in Ireland, during the term of those three years, he continued there, intituled *Hibernia Pacata*, printed at London, in 1633, and that he made an ample collection of many chronological and choice observations, as also of divers exact maps, relating to sundry parts of that realm. Some whereof are now in the public library at Oxford, but most of them in the hands of Sir Robert Shirley, Bart., of Stanton Harold, in the county of Leicester, bought of his executors." His lordship *d.* 27th March, 1629, at the Savoy in the Strand, "in the suburbs of London," leaving an only daughter and heiress,

LADY ANNE CAREW, who married first, —— Wilford, Esq., of Kent, and secondly, Sir Allen Apsley.

The earl dying thus, without legitimate male issue, all his honours became EXTINCT.

ARMS.—Or. three lions passant, sa.

CAREY — BARONS HUNSDON, VISCOUNTS ROCHFORT, EARLS OF DOVER.

Barony,   ⎱ by Letters ⎰ 13th January, 1559.
Viscounty, ⎰ Patent, ⎱ 6th January, 1621.
Earldom,   8th March, 1628.

Lineage.

This family had their residence, anciently, at *Cockington*, in the county of Devon, and of that place, was

SIR JOHN CAREY, Knt, one of the barons of the exchequer, temp. Richard II. Sir John *m.* first, ——, and secondly, Margaret, daughter of William Holwell, of Holwell, in the county of Devon, and widow of Sir Guy de Brian, by whom he had issue, John, BISHOP OF EXETER, anno 1419, and an elder son, his heir,

SIR ROBERT CAREY, Knt., a person so valorous and so skilful in arms, that few presumed to enter the lists with him. Amongst his other exploits, is recorded his triumph over an ARRAGONIAN knight, in Smithfield; upon which occasion he was knighted, and allowed to adopt the arms of his vanquished rival—namely, " *Three roses on a bend.*" Sir Robert *m.* Margaret, daughter of Sir Philip Courtenay, of Powderham, in the county of Devon, and was *s.* by his son,

PHILIP CAREY, Esq., *of Cockington*, who *m.* Christian, daughter of Richard Orchard, Esq., and was father of

SIR WILLIAM CAREY, Knt., an eminent Lancastrian, who, upon the issue of the battle of Tewkesbury, 10th Edward IV., fled to a church for sanctuary, but was brought forth, under a promise of pardon, and beheaded. Sir William *m.* first, Anne, daughter of Sir William Paulet, Knt., and from that marriage, descended the Careys, who continued at Cockington. He *m.* secondly, Alice, daughter of Sir Baldwin Fulford, Knt., and had a son,

THOMAS CAREY, Esq., who *m.* Margaret, second daughter and co-heiress of Sir Robert Spencer, by Eleanor his wife, daughter of Edmund Beaufort, Duke of Somerset, by whom he had two sons, viz.—

     JOHN, (Sir) who *m.* ——, sister of Anthony Denny, Knt., and left issue.

        EDWARD, (Sir) *m.* Catherine, daughter of Sir Henry Knevet, and widow of Henry, Lord Paget, by whom he had

          HENRY, created VISCOUNT FALKLAND, in the peerage of Scotland, a dignity still EXTANT.

William, ——.
The younger son,

WILLIAM CAREY, an esquire of the body to King Henry VIII., and a favourite of that monarch, *m.* Lady Mary Boleyne, daughter of *Thomas*, EARL OF WILTSHIRE, and sister of the unfortunate *Queen*, ANNE BOLEYNE, and had issue,

HENRY.

Catherine, *m.* to Sir Francis Knolles, K.G.

He *d.* in 1528, being then of the bedchamber to the king, and was *s.* by his son,

HENRY CAREY, who, soon after the accession of his first cousin, QUEEN ELIZABETH, to the throne, received the honour of knighthood, and upon the 13th January following, (anno 1559,) was elevated to the peerage, by letters patent, as BARON HUNSDON, with a grant of the mansion of Hunsdon, in the county of Hertford, and a pension of £4000 a year. In the 5th of Elizabeth, his lordship was sent with the order of the garter to the King of France, then at Lyons; and in five years afterwards, being governor of Berwick, he drove the insurrectionary Earls of Northumberland and Westmoreland, into Scotland; the former of whom he subsequently got into his hands, and had beheaded at York. In the 29th of Elizabeth, Lord Hunsdon was appointed general warden of the Marches, towards Scotland, and lord chamberlain of the household. In 1588, the memorable year of the menaced Spanish invasion, his lordship had the protection of the queen's person, in the camp at Tilbury, and the command of the army for that purpose. He was likewise captain of the pensioners, and a KNIGHT of the GARTER. He *m.* Anne, daughter of Sir Thomas Morgan, Knt., and had issue,

GEORGE, his successor.

John.

Edmund, who was knighted for his valour, by the Earl of Leicester, in 1587. Sir Edmund *m.* Mary, daughter and heiress of Christopher Crocker, Esq., of Croft, in the county of Lincoln, by whom he had three sons, and two daughters, and was *s.* by the eldest son,

ROBERT, (Sir) a captain of horse, under

1. gon Cotham th. in bx Rec. Soc.

109

Horatio, Lord Vere of Tilbury, in the Netherlands, *m.* Alletta, daughter of Mynheer Hogenhove, secretary to the States General, by whom he had three sons, Horatio, Ernestus, and Ferdinand, and was *s.* by the eldest,

HORATIO, captain of horse in the service of King Charles I., *m.* Petronilla, daughter of Robert Conyers, Esq., and was father of

ROBERT, of whom hereafter, as sixth LORD HUNSDON.

ROBERT, created EARL OF MONMOUTH, (see that dignity).

Catherine, *m.* to Charles Howard, EARL OF NOTTINGHAM.

Philadelphia, *m.* to Thomas, Lord Scrope.

Margaret, *m.* to Sir Edward Hoby, Knt.

His lordship *d.* at Somerset House, 23rd July, 1596, and the illness which occasioned his death, is said to have arisen from disappointed ambition, in never having been able to attain the dignity of EARL OF WILTSHIRE. Fuller, in his Worthies of England, relates that, " when he lay on his death-bed, the queen gave him a gracious visit, causing a patent for the said earldom to be drawn, his robes to be made, and both to be laid on his bed; but this lord, (who could not dissemble, neither well nor sick,) replied, ' *Madam, seeing you counted me not worthy of this honour, while I was living, I count myself unworthy of it, now I am dying!* "

Sir Robert Naunton, in "Fragmenta Regalia," thus characterizes the first Lord Hunsdon : " My Lord of Hunsdon was one of the queen's nearest kindred, and on the decease of Sussex, both he and his son took the place of lord chamberlain; he was a fast man to his prince, and firm to his friends and servants; and though he might speak big, and therefore would be borne out, yet was he not the more dreadful, but less harmful; and far from the practice of my Lord of Leicester's instruction : for he was downright. And I have heard those that both knew him well, and had interest in him, say merrily of him, that his Latin and his dissimulation were both alike: and that his custom of swearing and obscenity in speaking, made him seem a worse christian than he was, and a better knight of the carpet than he should be. As he lived in a ruffling time, so he loved sword and buckler men, and such as our forefathers were wont to call men of their hands: of which sort, he had many brave men that followed him, yet not taken for a popular or dangerous person. And this is one that stood among the Togati of an honest stout heart, and such a one as (upon occasion,) would have fought for his prince and his country."

His lordship was *s.* by his eldest son,

GEORGE CAREY, second *Baron Hunsdon,* who had been educated for the public service, from his earliest youth, and obtained in the lifetime of his father, the honour of knighthood, for his distinguished conduct in the expedition made into Scotland, in the 13th of Elizabeth, under the Earl of Sussex. Sir George succeeded his father as captain of the band of pensioners, and was soon afterwards made lord chamberlain, and a KNIGHT of the

GARTER. His lordship *m.* Elizabeth, daughter of Sir John Spencer, of Althorp, Knt., by whom he had an only daughter and heiress,

Elizabeth, who *m.* Sir Thomas Berkeley, Knt., son and heir of Henry, Lord Berkeley.

He *d.* 9th September, 1603, and leaving no male issue, the peerage devolved upon his brother,

SIR JOHN CAREY, KNT., warden of the East Marches, towards Scotland, as third BARON HUNSDON. His lordship *m.* Mary, daughter of Leonard Hyde, Esq., of Throgkyn, in the county of Hertford, by whom he had issue,

HENRY, his successor.

Charles.

Anne, *m.* to Sir Francis Lovell, Knt., of East Harlyng, in the county of Norfolk.

Blanch, *m.* to Sir Thomas Woodhouse, Knt., of Kymberley, in the same shire.

He died in April, 1617, and was *s.* by his eldest son,

HENRY CAREY, fourth Baron Hunsdon, who was advanced, on the 6th June, 1621, to the *Viscounty of Rochford,* and created, 8th May, 1627, EARL OF DOVER. His lordship *m.* Judith, daughter of Sir Thomas Pelham, Bart., of Loughton, in the county of Sussex, by whom he had issue,

JOHN, *Viscount Rochford,* who was made a knight of the Bath at the coronation of King Charles I.

Pelham, } both died *s. p.*
George, }

Mary, *m.* to Sir Thomas Wharton, K.B., brother of Lord Wharton.

Judith, *d.* unmarried.

Philadelphia.

His lordship *d.* in 1668, and was *s.* by his eldest son,

JOHN CAREY, second EARL OF DOVER, and fifth *Baron Hunsdon.* This nobleman *m.* first, Lady Dorothy St. John, daughter of Oliver, EARL OF BOLINGBROKE, by whom he had no issue. His lordship *m.* secondly, Abigail, daughter of alderman Sir William Cokayne, Knt., of the city of London, by whom he had an only daughter,

Mary, *m.* to William Heveningham, Esq., of Heveningham, in the county of Sussex, by whom she had,

Sir William Heveningham, Knt.

Abigail, *m.* to John, son and heir of Sir John Newton, Bart.

He *d.* in 1677, and leaving thus no male issue, the *Viscounty of Rochford* and EARLDOM OF DOVER EXPIRED, while the BARONY OF HUNSDON reverted to his lordship's kinsman,

SIR ROBERT CAREY, KNT., (revert to descendants of the Hon. Sir Edmund Carey, third son of the first lord,) as sixth BARON HUNSDON. His lordship *m.* Margaret, daughter of Sir Gervase Clifton, Bart., and widow of Sir John South, Knt., but dying in 1692, without issue, the title devolved upon (the son of his uncle Ernestus,) his cousin,

ROBERT CAREY, as *seventh Baron Hunsdon,* who, at the time of his succession, was said to pursue the humble avocation of a *weaver.* His lordship *d.* unmarried in September, 1702, when the title devolved upon (the grandson of Colonel Ferdinand Carey, uncle of the last lord,) his cousin,

WILLIAM FERDINAND CAREY, as *eighth*

Baron Hunsdon. This nobleman was b. in Holland, the son of William Carey and Gertrude Van Oustoorn, but being naturalised in 1690, he inherited the honours of his family, and took his seat in the House of Peers on the 1st March, 1708. His lordship m. Grace, daughter of Sir Edward Waldo, Knt., and relict of Sir Nicholas Wolstenholme, Bart., but dying without issue, in 1765, the BARONY OF HUNSDON became EXTINCT.

ARMS.—Arg. on a bend sa. three roses of the field barbed and seeded ppr., a crescent for difference.

CAREY—BARONS CAREY, OF LEPPINGTON, IN THE COUNTY OF YORK. EARLS OF MONMOUTH.

By Letters Patent, dated 5th February, 1626.

Lineage.

The Honourable
ROBERT CAREY, fourth son of Henry, first LORD HUNSDON, was elevated to the peerage by King James I., by letters patent, dated 5th Feb., 1626, as *Baron Carey,* of Leppington, in the county of York, and EARL OF MONMOUTH. This eminent person, whose memoirs, written by himself, were published by *John,* EARL OF CORK AND ORRERY, in 1759, was b. about 1560. At the age of seventeen he accompanied Sir Thomas Leighton in his embassies to the States general, and to Don John of Austria: and he soon afterwards went with Secretary Walsingham into Scotland, where he appears to have insinuated himself into the good graces of James, the future king of England. He was on board the fleet in 1588, at the destruction of the Armada, and he states, " that he won a wager of two thousand pounds the next year by going on foot in twelve days to Berwick." " After this," goes on the memoir, " I married a gentlewoman, Elizabeth, daughter of Sir Hugh Trevanion, more for her *worth* than her *wealth,* for her estate was but £500. a year jointure. She had between £500. and £600. in her purse. Neither did she marry me for any great wealth; for I had in all the world but £100. a year out of the Exchequer, as a pension, and that was but during pleasure; and I was near £1,000. in debt. Besides, the queen was mightily displeased with me for marrying, and most of my best friends, only my father was no ways offended at it, which gave me great content." The tide of fortune, which he took in the spring, was the opportunity afforded him by the familiar intercourse with which his kinswoman, Queen Elizabeth, condescended to treat him, of being the first to announce her majesty's decease to her successor. Visiting her (he says,) in her last illness, and praying that her health might amend, she took him by the hand, and wringing it hard, replied, " No, Robin, I am not well," and fetching at the same time no fewer than forty or fifty sighs, which he declares, except for the death of Mary of Scotland, he never in her whole life knew her to do before. By those sighs the wily politician judged her majesty was near her dissolution, and with great candour he proceeds, " I could not but think in what a wretched state I should be left, most of my

livelihood depending on her life. And hereupon I bethought myself with what grace and favour I was ever received of the King of Scots whensoever I was sent to him." Upon the decease of the queen, Carey immediately proceeded to Scotland, and was the first person to announce to King James his accession to the crown of England, producing and presenting to his majesty, in proof of his veracity, a certain blue ring.[*] The king received him, of course, most graciously, and observed, " I know you have lost a near kinswoman, and a mistress, but take here my hand, I will be a good master to you, and will requite this service with honour and reward." Notwithstanding this royal pledge, however, full nineteen years elapsed before he attained the peerage, and in his Memoirs he observes, " I only relied on God and the king. The one never left me, the other, shortly after his coming to London, deceived my expectations, and adhered to those who sought my ruin." His lordship had issue by the lady already mentioned,

> HENRY, his successor, made a Knight of the Bath at the creation of Charles, Prince of of Wales, anno 1616.
>
> Thomas, one of the grooms of the bedchamber to King Charles I., and amongst that unfortunate monarch's most faithful servants; so faithful and attached, indeed, that, upon the execution of his royal master, he fell sick of grief, and died about the year 1648, in the 33d year of his age. The Hon. Thomas Carey obtained celebrity as a poet, and his remains repose in Westminster Abbey. He left an only daughter,
>
>> Elizabeth, who m. John Mordaunt, who was created *Viscount Mordaunt,* of Aveion, and left a son,
>>
>>> CHARLES, created EARL OF MONMOUTH.
>
> Philadelphia, m. to Sir Thomas Wharton, Knt.,

His lordship d. in 1639, and was s. by his elder son,
HENRY CAREY, second *Earl of Monmouth.* This nobleman, according to Anthony Wood, was noted, upon succeeding to his father's honours, " as a person well skilled in the modern languages, and a generous scholar; the fruit whereof he found in the trou-

---

[*] BLUE RING.—The account of the *blue ring* which Lady Elizabeth Spelman (daughter of Martha Countess of Middleton, who was daughter of the second earl of Monmouth, and grand-daughter of the nobleman to whom the anecdote refers), gave to Lord Cork, was this:—King James kept a constant correspondence with several persons of the English court for many years prior to Queen Elizabeth's decease; among others, with Lady Scroope, (sister of this Robert Carey,)to whom his majesty sent, by Sir James Fullerton, a sapphire ring, with positive orders to return it to him, by a special messenger, as soon as the queen actually expired. Lady Scroope had no opportunity of delivering it to her brother Robert whilst he was in the palace of Richmond; but waiting at the window till she saw him at the outside of the gate, she threw it out to him, and he well knew to what purpose he received it.

BANKS.

blesome times of the rebellion, when, by a forced retiredness, he was capacitated to exercise himself in studies, while others of the nobility were fain to truckle to their inferiors for company's sake." He wrote much; but, as Walpole observes, "we have scarce any thing of his own composition, and are as little acquainted with his character as with his genius." His lordship m. Lady Martha Cranfield, daughter of the lord treasurer, Lionel, Earl of Middlesex, by whom he had issue—

LIONEL, who fell in the ranks of the royalists at Marston-Moor, in 1644, and d. unmarried.

Henry, died in the small-pox, in 1641, also unmarried.

Anne, m. to James Hamilton, Earl of Clanbrasil, in the peerage of Ireland.

Philadelphia, d. unmarried.

Elizabeth-Mary, m. William, Earl of Desmond.

Trevaniana, d. unmarried.

Martha, m. to John, Earl of Middleton, in Scotland.

Theophila, } d. unmarried.
Magdalen, }

His lordship d. 13th June, 1661, and leaving no male issue, the *barony of Carey of Leppington* and the EARLDOM OF MONMOUTH became EXTINCT.

ARMS.—As. on a bend sa. three roses of the field, a crescent for difference.

CARLTON—BARON CARLTON OF IMBERCOURT, IN THE COUNTY OF SURREY, VISCOUNT DORCHESTER.

Barony, } by Letters { 22nd May, 1626.
Viscounty, } Patent, { 25th July, 1628.

Lineage.

SIR DUDLEY CARLTON, KNT., son of Anthony Carlton, of Baldwin Brightwell, in the county of Oxford, b. 10th March, 1573, having been employed, for a series of years, as ambassador to Venice, Savoy, and the Low Countries, was elevated to the peerage on the 22nd May, 1626, as BARON CARLTON, *of Imbercourt, in the county of Surrey*, and in two years afterwards created VISCOUNT DORCHESTER; in which year he was constituted one of his majesty's principal Secretaries of State. His lordship m., first, Anne, daughter and co-heiress of George Gerard, Esq., second son of Sir William Gerard, Knt., of Dogney, in the county of Bucks, by whom he had a son, HENRY, who d. young. He espoused secondly, Anne, daughter of Sir Henry Glemham, Knt., and widow of Paul, Viscount Bayning, which lady survived him, and gave birth to a posthumous child, Frances, who d. young. Lord Dorchester, whose negotiations have been published, had the reputation of being an able diplomatist, and a polished statesman. He was master of different languages, and a good ancient and modern historian. He composed some pieces, which are noticed by Walpole, and was esteemed a graceful and eloquent speaker. He d. in 1631, and his honours, in default of male issue, became EXTINCT.

ARMS.—Ar. on a bend, sa. three mascles of the first.

CARR—VISCOUNT ROCHESTER, EARL OF SOMERSET.

Viscounty, } by Letters { 25th March, 1611.
Earldom, &c. } Patent, { 3rd Nov., 1613.

Lineage.

SIR ROBERT CARR, K.B., of the ancient House of Fernihurst, in Scotland, and half brother of Andrew, first Lord Jedburgh, having ingratiated himself into the favour of King James I., was appointed, upon the decease of George, Lord Dunbar, treasurer of Scotland, and elevated to the peerage, as VISCOUNT ROCHESTER, on the 25th March, 1611. In the May following his lordship was installed a knight of the Garter, and created, on the 3rd November, 1613, *Baron Carr*, of Branspeth, in the bishopric of Durham, and EARL OF SOMERSET, being also nominated lord chamberlain of the household, and sworn of the privy council. At this time the earl was esteemed the first favorite of the court. "But having," says Dugdale, "thus seen his rise, let us now behold his fall, which I shall briefly here relate, with the occasion and chief circumstances thereof, from the report of the most Rev. Dr. Spotswood, late Archbishop of St. Andrew's in Scotland."

"This earl falling in love with the Lady Frances Howard, daughter of Thomas, Earl of Suffolk, (wife to Robert, Earl of Essex, from whom she had procured a divorce,) having formerly received into his intimate familiarity a knight of excellent parts, called Sir Thomas Overburie, was frequently by him dissuaded from her company, which being discerned by Overburie, and that, notwithstanding what had been said, he had a purpose to marry her; he so far presumed upon the friendly freedom which he had otherwise given him, to press him more earnestly to forbear her. And one night, dealing more plainly with him, said to this effect, ' My lord, I perceive you are proceeding in this match, from which I have often dissuaded you, as your true servant and friend: I now again advise you not to marry that woman, for if you do, you shall ruine your honour and yourself,' adding, 'that, if he went on in that business, he should do well to look to his standing.' Which free speech, this Earl taking impatiently, because he had touched the lady in her honour; replied in passion, ' That his legs were strong enough to bear him up, and that he should make him repent those speeches.' But Overburie, interpreting this to be only a sudden passion, thought not that their long continued friendship would break off by this occasion, and therefore continued his wonted attendance; neither did this earl wholly abandon him. Howbeit, having discovered his words to the lady, she never ceased, but by all means sought his overthrow. It happening therefore, about this time, that Overburie being designed for ambassador into Russia, this earl (whose counsel he asked,) advised him to refuse the service, but to make some fair excuse. Which advice he followed, supposing that it did proceed of kindness; but for his refusal he was committed to the Tower. The lady thus having him where she wished, and resolving to dispatch him by poison, wrought so with Sir Gervase Elways, then lieutenant of the Tower, as that he admitted one Richard Weston, upon her recommendation, to be his keeper, by whom (the very evening after he was so committed,) a yellow poison was ministered to him in a broth, at supper. But neither this nor the other poisons, which were continually put into his meats, serving to despatch him, Mistress Turner (the preparer of all,) procured an apothecary's boy, to give him a poisoned clyster, which soon brought him to his end. Being thus dead, he was presently buried; a general rumour, however, prevailed, that he had died by poison, but the greatness of the procurers kept all hidden for a time, till at length it pleased God to bring every thing to light, after a miraculous manner. It happened that the Earl of Shrewsbury, in conference with a counsellor of state, recommended the lieutenant of the Tower to his favour, as a man of good parts, and one who desired to be known to him. The counsellor answered, that he took it as a favour from the lieutenant that he should desire his friendship, but added, that there lay upon him an heavy imputation for Overburie's death, whereof he wisht that the gentleman should clear himself. Which being related to the lieutenant, he was stricken with it, and said, to his knowledge some attempts were made against Overburie, but that the same took no effect. Which being told to the king, he willed the counsellor to move the lieutenant to set down in writing what he knew of that matter, as he accordingly did. Whereupon certain of the council were appointed to examine and find out the truth. From Weston somewhat being found, he was made prisoner, Turner and Franklyn, the preparers of the poison, being examined, confessed every thing; whereupon, all breaking forth, this earl and his lady, as also the lieutenant, were committed. But Weston at his first arraignment stood mute, yet afterwards was induced to put himself on the trial of his country, and being found guilty, suffered death at Tyburne. Mistress Turner and James Franklyn were in like sort executed. The lieutenant, who had winked at their doings, being judged accessary to the crime, and condemned, suffered death also, expressing great penitency. And in May following, this earl and his lady were both brought to their trial, though, by their friends, laboured earnestly to eschew it. But King James would not be intreated, for the love he had to maintain justice. Thomas, Lord Ellesmere, at that time Lord Chancellor of England, was, by commission, constituted High Steward for that occasion, having for his assistants, Sir Edward Coke, Knt., Lord Chief Justice of the court of King's Bench, Sir Henry Hobart, Knt, Lord Chief Justice of the Common Pleas, Sir Laurence Tanfield, Knt., Lord Chief Baron of the Exchequer, Justice Alured, one of the barons of the Exchequer, Crook, Dodderidge, and Haughton, justices of the King's Bench, and Nichols, of the court of Common Pleas. The peers by whom they were tried being the EARL OF WORCESTER, lord privy seal, the EARL OF PEMBROKE, lord chamberlain, the Earls of RUTLAND, SUSSEX, HERTFORD, and MONTGOMERIE, the Viscount L'Isle, the Lord Zouch, warden of the cinque ports, the Lord Willoughby of Eresby, the Lord Dacres, the Lord Monteagle, the Lord Wentworth, the Lord Rich, the

Lord Willoughby of Parham, the Lord Hunsdon, the Lord Russel, the Lord Compton, the Lords Norris, Gerard, Cavendish, and Dormer. With the lady there was much ado; she, with many tears, confessing the fact, and desiring mercy. But this earl, being the next day presented, made some defence, which served no purpose; for the confessions of those who had suffered death already for the fact, and a letter which he himself had sent to the king, did so clearly convict him of being at least an accessary, that both himself and his lady had sentence of death passed upon them. Nevertheless, through his majesty's great clemency, their lives were spared." The event proved, however, miserable to both these guilty persons, ending in a total separation, and hatred of each other. The abandoned countess died 23rd August, 1632. The earl, who was released from the Tower in 1621, but afterwards confined to the house of Viscount Wallingford, died in July, 1645, leaving an only daughter,

ANNE, who m. William, fifth Earl of Bedford, and was mother of the illustrious patriot, William, LORD RUSSELL. The Countess of Bedford was as distinguished for purity as her unhappy mother had been for the reverse.

Upon his lordship's decease the *Viscounty of Rochdale* and EARLDOM OF SOMERSET became EXTINCT.

ARMS.—Gu. on a chevron, ar. three mullets, sa. in the dexter part of the escutcheon, a lion passant guardant or.

CARTERET—BARONS CARTERET, OF HAWNES, IN THE COUNTY OF BEDFORD, VISCOUNTS CARTERET, EARLS GRANVILLE.

| Barony, Earldom, &c. | } | By Letters Patent, | { | 19th October, 1681. 1st January, 1714. |

Lineage.

This family derived their surname from the seigniory of Carteret, in Normandy, of which they were formerly lords.

REGINALD DE CARTERET, Lord of Carteret, &c., in the last years of King Henry II., anno 1180, forfeited his lands in Normandy by his adhesion to the crown of England, when the duchy was delivered up to the French in 1904, and dying in three years afterwards, was *s.* by his son,

PHILIP DE CARTERET, who being with King Henry III. in his expedition into Britanny, in the 15th year of that monarch's reign, was the next year constituted, with Arnauld de St. Amand, governor of Jersey, Guernsey, Alderney, and Sark. This Philip was *s.* by his son,

PHILIP DE CARTERET, who was styled Lord St. Oven, in Jersey, in the year 1290, and was *s.* by his son,

REGINALD DE CARTERET, who obtained from King Edward I., in consideration of his military services, a grant of the manor of Melesches, in the Isle of Jersey, which he left to his second son, Sir John de Carteret. He was *s.* at his decease by his eldest son,

SIR PHILIP DE CARTERET, Lord of St. Oven, temp. Edward II., who was *s.* by his son,

REGINALD DE CARTERET. This feudal lord, by his prudence and valour, preserved the Island of Jersey from falling into the hands of the French in the year 1374, when Bertrand du Guesclin, constable of France, famous for his many victories over the English, past suddenly from Bretagne into Jersey, with an army of ten thousand men, wherein were the Duke of Bourbon, and the flower of the French chivalry. At that time this Reginald de Carteret secured Mount Orgueil Castle, and defended it so bravely, that after many violent assaults the constable withdrew his forces, leaving many of his best soldiers dead under the walls. For this great achievement, Reginald and his seven sons were all knighted by King Edward III. in one day. From this gallant personage we pass to his descendant,

SIR PHILIP CARTERET, who undertook, in the reign of Elizabeth, to plant such a colony in the Island of Sark, as should keep out the French, and he accordingly enlarged the settlement, and thereby improved his own estate. He m. Rachael, daughter and heir of Sir George Paulet, son and heir of Lord Thomas Paulet, of Cossington in the county of Somerset, second son of William, Marquess of Winchester, and had, with other issue,

> PHILIP, (Sir,) his successor, who m. Anne, daughter of Sir Francis Dowse, Knt., of Wallop, in the county of Southampton, and was s. by his eldest son,
>> PHILIP, in the seigniory of St. Oven, m. Anne, daughter of —— Dumasque, Esq., and dying in 1662, was s. by his son,
>>> PHILIP, created a BARONET 4th June, 1670, and dying in 1693, was s. by his son,
>>>> CHARLES, (Sir,) second baronet, who was one of the gentlemen of the privy chamber to Queen Anne, and high bailiff of the Island of Jersey. Sir Charles d. in 1715, when the baronetcy expired, but his estates passed to Lord Carteret.

> HELIER, of whom presently.
> Rachael, m. first, to —— Beaver, Esq., of the Island of Jersey, and secondly, to —— de Vic, Esq.
> Judith, m. to Sir Brian Johnson, of Buckinghamshire.

The second son,
HELIER CARTERET, Esq., deputy governor of Jersey, m. Elizabeth, daughter of —— Dumasque, Esq., and had, with other children,

SIR GEORGE CARTERET, a naval officer of high reputation, who, through the influence of the Duke of Buckingham, was appointed in the 2d of King Charles I. joint governor of Jersey, and at the breaking out of the civil war, held the office of comptroller of the navy. Sir George was, however, so much esteemed by all parties, that when the parliament passed the ordinance for the Earl of Warwick to command the fleet, then fully and entirely at their disposal, they likewise resolved that Captain Carteret should be vice-admiral: but he declined the appointment at the express command of the king. Upon which Lord Clarendon observes, "his interest and reputation in the navy was so great, and his diligence and dexterity in command

114

so eminent, that it was generally believed he would, against whatsoever the Earl of Warwick could have done, have preserved the major part of the fleet in their duty to the king."

Having thus retired from the navy, he withdrew with his family to Jersey; but subsequently returned to aid the projects of the royalists, when he was created by King Charles a baronet, 9th May, 1645. He again, however, went back to his government in Jersey, and there, in the ruin of the royal cause, afforded an asylum to.. the Prince of Wales, (who appointed him his vice-chamberlain,) Mr. Hyde, afterwards Lord Clarendon, and other refugees of distinction. After this he defended the Island of Jersey in the most gallant manner against the parliamentarians, and ultimately only surrendered upon receiving the command of King Charles II. so to do. Elizabeth Castle, in the Island of Jersey, under Sir George Carteret, was the last fortress that lowered the royal banner. At the restoration, Sir George formed one of the immediate train of the restored monarch in his triumphant entry into London: and the next day he was sworn of the privy council and declared VICE CHAMBERLAIN. He was afterwards returned to parliament by the corporation of Portsmouth. Sir George m. Elizabeth, daughter of Sir Philip Carteret, Knt., of St. Oven, and had issue,

> PHILIP (Sir), who had eminently distinguished himself during the civil wars, and was governor of Mount Orgueil Castle, when it was invested by the parliamentary forces in 1651. Sir Philip m. Jemima, daughter of Edward Montagu, first Earl of Sandwich, vice-admiral of England, and had issue,
>> GEORGE, who s. his grandfather.
>> Philip, captain of marines. Lost at sea in 1693.
>> Edward, M.P., joint post-master-general, m. Bridget, daughter of Sir Thomas Exton, judge of the high court of admiralty, and d. in 1739, leaving issue.
> Sir Philip Carteret being with his father-in-law, Lord Sandwich, in the great naval engagement off Solebay, 28th May, 1672, was blown up with that gallant officer in the Royal James.
> James, captain R.N., in the reign of King Charles II.
> George, d. unm. in 1656.
> Anne, m. to Sir Nicholas Slaning, of the county of Devon, K.B.
> Caroline, m. to Sir Thomas Scot, of Scot's Hall, Kent.
> Louisa-Margaretta, m. to Sir Robert Atkins, of Saperton, in the county of Gloucester.

Sir George d. 13th January, 1679, and was s. by his grandson,

SIR GEORGE CARTERET, second baronet, who was elevated to the peerage on the 19th October, 1681, as BARON CARTERET, of Hawnes, with remainder, default of male issue, to his brothers, and their heirs male. This nobleman, when only eight years of age, was m. to Lady Grace Granville, youngest daughter of John, Earl of Bath, and co-heiress of her nephew, William-Henry, last Earl of Bath of that family; a marriage agreed upon by his grandfather, Sir George Carteret, and the Earl of

Bath, to cement the friendship which had long subsisted between them. By this lady his lordship had issue, JOHN, his successor, with another son, Philip, and a daughter, Jemima, who both d. unmarried. His lordship, who was a zealous supporter of the revolution, d. at the early age of twenty-six, in 1695. His widow, Lady Carteret, having succeeded as co-heiress to the great Bath estates, upon the decease of her nephew, William-Henry Granville, Earl of Bath, in 1711 (when that dignity became extinct), was created on the 1st January, 1714, *Viscountess Carteret*, and COUNTESS GRANVILLE, with remainder of the viscounty, default of male issue in her son, John, Lord Carteret, to the uncle of that nobleman, Edward Carteret, Esq., and his male heirs. Her ladyship d. in 1744, and was s. by her only surviving son,

JOHN CARTERET, second Lord Carteret, as Earl Granville. His lordship was appointed one of the lords of the bedchamber at the accession of King George I., and constituted in 1716 lord lieutenant and custos rotulorum of the county of Devon. In 1719 he was accredited ambassador extraordinary to the court of Sweden. In 1721 he was declared principal secretary of State, and in 1724 constituted LORD LIEUTENANT OF IRELAND, which high office he retained for the six following years. He was thrice one of the lords justices during the occasional absence of the king, and a knight of the most noble order of the garter. His lordship m. first, 17th October, 1710, Frances, only daughter of Sir Robert Worsley, Bart., and grand-daughter maternally of Thomas Thynne, Viscount Weymouth, by whom he had surviving issue,

ROBERT, his successor.

Grace, m. to Lionel, Earl of Dorset.

Louisa, m. to Thomas Thynne, Viscount Weymouth, and had issue,

 THOMAS, Viscount Weymouth, created Marquess of Bath, d. in 1784, and left

  THOMAS, present Marquess of Bath, and other issue.

 HENRY-FREDERICK, having inherited the Carteret estates under the will of his grandfather, Earl of Granville, after the decease of his uncle, assumed the surname and arms of CARTERET, and was created in 1784 BARON CARTERET, of Hawnes, with remainder to the younger sons of his brother, the Marquess of Bath. His lordship d. in 1826, and the barony passed according to the limitation to his nephew, LORD GEORGE THYNNE, present LORD CARTERET.

Georgiana-Carolina, m. first, to the Hon. John Spencer, and secondly, to William, Earl Cowper.

Frances, m. to John, Marquess of Tweedale.

The earl espoused secondly, Lady Sophia Fermor, daughter of Thomas, Earl of Pomfret, and had an only daughter,

 Sophia, who m. in 1765, William Petty, second Earl of Shelburne, afterwards Marquess of Lansdown, by whom she had an only son,

  JOHN, second Marquess of Lansdown, half brother of Henry, present marquess.

His lordship d. 2d January, 1763, and was s. by his son,

ROBERT CARTERET, third Lord Carteret,

and second Earl Granville. His lordship d. without issue in 1776, when the BARONY OF CARTERET, and EARLDOM OF GRANVILLE, with the VISCOUNTY OF CARTERET, became EXTINCT, but the Barony of Carteret was recreated in 1784 (revert to issue of Lady Louisa Carteret, second daughter of John, first earl).

ARMS.—Quarterly, first and fourth gules, four fusils in fesse ar. for CARTERET, second and third three clarions, or claricords or. for GRANVILLE.

CAVENDISH — BARON OGLE AND VISCOUNTS MANSFIELD, EARLS OF NEWCASTLE-UPON-TYNE, &c., MARQUESSES OF NEWCASTLE, DUKES OF NEWCASTLE, &c.

Barony and Viscounty,		3d Nov. 1620.
Earldom, &c.	by Letters Patent.	7th Mar. 1628.
Marquisate,		27th Oct. 1643.
Dukedom, &c.		16th Mar. 1664.

Lineage.

This noble family, and the existing ducal house of Devonshire, have had a common progenitor in The Right Honorable

SIR WILLIAM CAVENDISH, who, by his distinguished lady, (his third wife,) Elizabeth, daughter of John Hardwick, Esq., of Hardwick, in the county of Derby, and eventually co-heiress of her brother, James Hardwick, had issue,

 Henry, of Tutbury Priory, in the county of Stafford, M.P. for Derbyshire, who died s. p. 12th October, 1616.

 WILLIAM, created EARL OF DEVONSHIRE, ancestor of the extant DUKES,

and

SIR CHARLES CAVENDISH, Knt., of Welbeck-Abbey, in the county of Notts, who m. first, Margaret, eldest daughter and co-heir of Sir Thomas Kitson, of Hengrave, Suffolk, by whom he had no issue; and secondly, Catherine, daughter of Cuthbert, seventh Baron Ogle, who, becoming eventually his lordship's sole heiress, succeeded to the barony of Ogle, which was confirmed to her ladyship by letters patent, dated 4th Dec. 1628: by this lady he left an only surviving son,

SIR WILLIAM CAVENDISH, K.B., who was elevated to the peerage on the 3d Nov. 1620, as *Baron Ogle, of Bothal*, and VISCOUNT MANSFIELD, *in the county of Nottingham*. This nobleman, afterwards so celebrated as a royalist general, filled originally the post of governor to the prince of Wales, eldest son of King Charles I., and was advanced in the peerage by that monarch on the 7th March, 1628, in the dignities of *Baron Cavendish, of Bolsover, in the county of Notts*., and EARL OF NEWCASTLE. When the proceeding of the Long Parliament ceased to be equivocal, his lordship hastened to rear the royal standard in the north, and planting it on the battlements of the Castle of Tynemouth, manned and fortified the town of Newcastle. He then levied forces, and, though in the midst of winter, placing himself at their head, routed the rebels in all directions in the county of York, and became master of their principal strong places there. In 1642 he received the queen, upon her majesty's arrival with arms and ammunition, and conducting her in safety to the king, at Oxford, was rewarded, by letters patent dated 27th Oct. 1643, with the MARQUISATE OF NEWCASTLE. Subsequently, his lordship sustained, upon every occasion, his high reputation, but particularly in his gallant defence of the city of York against three powerful armies of English and Scotch. He retired to the continent, however, after the fatal battle of Marston-Moor, owing to some misunderstanding between himself and PRINCE RUPERT, a misunderstanding which the royalists had eventually most deeply to deplore. Upon the restoration of the monarchy, the marquess was created, 16th March, 1664, *Earl of Ogle* and DUKE OF NEWCASTLE, as some compensation for the immense losses he had sustained, amounting in the aggregate, to nearly three parts of a MILLION sterling! His grace m. first, Elizabeth, daughter and heiress of William Basset, Esq., of Blore, in the county of Stafford, and widow of the Hon. Henry Howard, youngest son of Thomas, Earl of Suffolk, by whom he had surviving issue,

> CHARLES, who m. Elizabeth, daughter of Richard Rogers, Esq., of Brianston, in the county of Dorset, but d. in the life-time of his father, s. p.
>
> HENRY, his successor.
>
> Jane, m. to Charles Cheney, Esq., of Chesham-Boys, in the county of Bucks.
>
> Elizabeth, m. to John, second Earl of Bridgewater.
>
> Frances, m. to Oliver St. John, Earl of Bolingbroke.

The duke m. secondly, Margaret, sister of the Lord Lucas, but had no issue. Of his grace, Walpole, in his Noble Authors, says, that " he was a man extremely known from the course of life into which he was forced, and who would soon have been forgotten in the walk of fame which he chose for himself: yet as an author he is familiar to those who scarce know any other, from his Book of Horsemanship. Though amorous in poetry and music, as Lord Clarendon says, he was fitter to break Pegasus for a menage, than to mount him on the steeps of Parnassus. Of all the riders of that steed, perhaps there have not been a more fantastic couple than his grace and his faithful duchess, who was never off her pillion."

His grace, who, amongst his other honours, was a KNIGHT of the GARTER, d. in 1676, and a costly monument in Westminster Abbey records his virtues, dignities, and high public employments. He was s. by his only surviving son,

HENRY CAVENDISH, second duke, who m. Frances, daughter of William, second son of Robert Pierpoint, Earl of Kingston, by whom he had surviving issue,

1. HENRY, Earl of Ogle, who m. Lady Elizabeth Percy, only surviving child and heiress of Joceline, eleventh and last earl of Northumberland of the old Percys, upon which occasion his lordship assumed the surname of PERCY. He died s. p. 1st Nov. 1680, and his illustrious widow espoused, in two years afterwards, *Charles Seymour*, DUKE OF SOMERSET, from which union the present duke of Northumberland maternally descends.

2. Elizabeth, m. first, to Christopher Monk, Duke of Albemarle, and secondly, to Ralph Montagu, Duke of Montagu, but died issueless.

3. Frances, m. to John, second Earl of Breadalbane, but died s. p.

4. Margaret, m. to John Holles, fourth Earl of Clare, who was created, 14th May, 1694, *Marquess of Clare* and DUKE OF NEWCASTLE, by whom she had an only daughter,

> Lady Henrietta-Cavendish Holles, who m. Edward, Lord Harley, son and heir of Robert, Earl of Oxford, to whom she carried a very great real and personal estate.

His grace (John Holles, Duke of Newcastle,) dying thus without male issue, the honours ceased in the Holles family, but were revived in the descendants of his sister, GRACE HOLLES, who m. Thos. Pelham, Lord Loughton, and had issue,

> THOMAS, created *Earl* and *Marquess of Clare*, and DUKE OF NEWCASTLE, d. in 1768, s. p., when the husband of his niece inherited the dukedom.
>
> Henry Pelham, m. to Catherine, daughter of John, Duke of Rutland, and left issue,
>
>> Catherine, m. to *Henry Clinton*, EARL OF LINCOLN, who succeeded his wife's uncle in the DUKEDOM OF NEWCASTLE, and from him descend the extant DUKES OF NEWCASTLE.
>
> Grace, m. to George Nailor, Esq.
>
> Frances, m. to Viscount Castlecomer.
>
> Gertrude, m. to David Polhill, Esq.
>
> Lucy, m. to Henry, seventh Earl of Lincoln.
>
> Margaret, m. to Sir John Shelly.

5. Catherine, m. to Thomas, sixth Earl of Thanet.

6. Arabella, m. to Charles, Earl of Sunderland, and left an only daughter,

> FRANCES, who m., in 1717, Henry, fourth Earl of Carlisle, and had surviving issue,
>
>> Arabella, m. to Jonathan Cope, Esq.
>>
>> Diana, m. to Thomas Duncombe, Esq.

His grace d. in 1691, when, leaving no male issue, the dignities created in 1690, in 1698, in 1643, and in 1664,, (see commencement of this article,) became EXTINCT, while the old barony of OGLE, which came into the family with Catherine, Lady Ogle, wife of Sir Charles Cavendish, of Wilbeck Abbey, fell into ABEYANCE between his grace's five daughters and co-heiresses, and so continues amongst their descendants.

ARMS.—Sa. three bucks' heads caboshed, ar. attired or., a crescent for difference.

CECIL — BARON CECIL, OF PUTNEY, IN THE COUNTY OF SURREY, VISCOUNT WIMBLEDON.

Barony,	by Letters	9th November, 1625.
Viscounty,	Patent,	20th July, 1626.

Lineage.

The Hon.

SIR EDWARD CECIL, third son of Thomas,

first Earl of Exeter, and grandson of the celebrated Lord Treasurer Burghley, having adopted a military life, attained celebrity in the wars in the Netherlands, where he was engaged for a space of thirty-five years. He was marshal, lieutenant, and general of the forces, sent by King James and King Charles I. against the Spaniards and Imperialists, and was elevated to the peerage by King Charles II. on the 9th November, 1625, as *Baron Cecil, of Putney*, and created 25th July, 1626, Viscount Wimbledon. Walpole, in his noble authors, mentions that in the king's library are two manuscript tracts drawn up by this nobleman, on the several subjects of war, and the military defence of the nation; and he likewise states, that a manuscript was found by the Earl of Huntingdon in an old chest, purporting to be a warrant of King Charles I., directing, at the instance of Lord Wimbledon, the revival of the old English march, so famous in all the honorable achievements and glorious wars of this kingdom in ancient times; but which, by neglect, had been nearly lost and forgotten.

His lordship *m.* thrice, first, Theodosia, daughter of Sir Andrew Noel, of Dalby, in the county of Leicester, Knt., by whom he had four daughters, viz.

> Dorothy, ——.
> Albinia, *m.* to Sir Christopher Wray, Knt., of Barlings, in the county of Lincoln.
> Elizabeth, *m.* to Francis, Lord Willoughby, of Parham.
> Frances, *m.* to James, son and heir of William, Viscount Say and Sele.

The viscount *m.* secondly, Diana, daughter of Sir William Drury, of Halstede, in the county of Suffolk, Knt., and thirdly, Sophia, daughter of Sir Edward Zouche, of Woking, in Surrey, by whom he had a son,

> Algernon, who *d.* in infancy.

His lordship *d.* at Wimbledon on the 16th November, 1638, where he was interred, and leaving no male issue his honors became extinct.

Arms.—Barry of ten, ar. and sa. on six escutcheons, sa. three, two, one, as many lions rampant of the first.

CHANDOS—BARON CHANDOS.

By Writ of Summons, dated 20th December, 1337, 11 Edward III.

Lineage.

The first of this family upon record,

ROBERT DE CHANDOS, came from Normandy with the Conqueror, and obtained by arms large possessions in Wales. He was subsequently a munificent benefactor to the church. To this Robert *s.* another

ROBERT DE CHANDOS, who, upon the assessment in aid of marrying the king's daughter, in the 19th Henry II., certified his knights' fees to be thirteen and a sixth part, for which he paid £8 15s. 6d. He *d.* in 1173, and was *s.* by his eldest son,

ROBERT DE CHANDOS. This feudal lord paid forty marks for livery of the lands of his inheritance, in the 8th Richard I. He was *s.* by

ROBERT DE CHANDOS, who was *s.* by his son and heir,

ROGER DE CHANDOS, whose wardship was granted by the crown to William de Cantilupe. This Roger along with other barons-marchers had frequent summonses in the reign of Henry III. to march against the Welch. He was *s.* by his son,

ROBERT DE CHANDOS, who, in the 50th Henry III., doing his homage had livery of the lands of his inheritance, and in the 10th Edward I., was in the expedition then made into Wales. Upon his death, which happened in the 30th Edward I., it was found that he held the manor of Snodhull, with its appurtenances by barony, and the service of two knights' fees. He was *s.* by his son,

SIR ROGER DE CHANDOS. This feudal lord was in the Scottish wars temp. Edward II., and received the honor of knighthood with Prince Edward, and many others, by bathing, prior to going upon one of those expeditions. In the 15th Edward II. he was made sheriff of Herefordshire, and again in the 1st Edward III., when he was made governor of the castle of Hereford. "But of his successors," says Dugdale, "I am not able to continue a direct series." We come therefore to

ROGER DE CHANDOS, brother and heir of Thomas de Chandos, deceased. This Roger performing his fealty in the 7th Edward III. had livery of his lands, and the next year was constituted sheriff of Herefordshire, and governor of the castle of Hereford. In the 19th of the same reign, being then a banneret, he received a military summons to attend the king into France, and was summoned to parliament as a BARON from 20th December, 1337, to 23d October, 1355. In which latter year he *d.* leaving a son,

SIR THOMAS DE CHANDOS, Knt., but never summoned to parliament. He was *s.* by his son,

SIR JOHN CHANDOS, Knt., who *d.* in 1430, leaving his sister, Margaret, his heir; which

> MARGARET CHANDOS, *m.* Sir Thomas Berkeley, Knt., of Coberley, and left two daughters, her co-heirs, namely,
> > Margaret, *m.* to Nicholas Matteeden.
> > Alice, *m.* to Thomas Bruges, whence the DUKES OF CHANDOS.

Arms.—Or., a pile gules.

CHAVENT—BARON CHAVENT.

By Writ of Summons, dated 29th December, 1299, 28 Edward I.

Lineage.

PETER DE CHAUMPVENT, OR CHAVENT, having been engaged in the wars of Gascony in the 26th-28th Edward I., was summoned to parliament as a BARON in two years afterwards; but of his lordship, his family or descendants, nothing further is known.

Arms.—Payly of six, ar. and az. a fesse gules.

CHAWORTH—BARON CHAWORTH.

By Writ of Summons, dated 6th February, 1299. 27 Edward I.

Lineage.

About the latter end of King William the Conqueror's reign,

PATRICK DE CADURCIS, vulgarly called CHAWORTH, a native of Little Britanny, made a grant of certain mills in Gloucestershire to the monks of St. Peter's Abbey, in Gloucester. To this Patrick s. his son,

PATRICK DE CHAWORTH, who in the 33rd Henry II., upon the collection of the scutage of Galway, accounted six pounds for the knight's fees belonging to the honor of Striguil. This feudal lord was s. by

PAIN DE CHAWORTH, who, in the 2nd Henry III. being at that time one of the barons marchers, became surety for Isabel de Mortimer that she should come to the king's exchequer on the octaves of St. Michael to satisfy for such debts as she owed to the late King John. Pain de Chaworth m. Gundred, daughter and heir of William de la Ferte, (heir to Margaret de la Ferte, second daughter and co-heir of William de Briwere, a great feudal lord, who d. in 1296,) and was s. at his decease by his son,

PATRICK DE CHAWORTH, who, in the 23rd Henry III., being then under age, compounded with the king for his own wardship and marriage; paying £500 for the same. In the 29th of the same reign he received a precept from the crown, whereby he was commanded to use all his power and diligence to annoy the Welch then in hostility. He m. Hawyse, daughter and heir of Sir Thomas de Londres, Lord of Kidwilly, in Wales, and had issue,

    PAIN,⎫ all of whom, in 54th Henry III., being
    Hervey,⎬ signed with the cross, attended Prince
    Patric,⎭ Edward to the Holy Land,

with two daughters, Eve, and Anne. This feudal lord d. in 1257. and was s. by his eldest son,

PAIN DE CHAWORTH, who, in the 5th Edward I., was constituted general of the king's army in West Wales: whereupon Roger de Mortimer had command to aid him with all his power, and to admit him into all his castles and garrisons; at which time he was so successful that the Welch sued for peace, and did homage to the king. This gallant soldier died s. p. in 1278, and was s. by his only surviving brother,

PATRIC DE CHAWORTH, who m. the Lady Isabel de Beauchamp, daughter of William, Earl of Warwick, and d. in 1382, leaving an only daughter and heiress,

    MAUD DE CHAWORTH, who m. first, Henry Plantagenet, Earl of Lancaster, and secondly, Hugh le Despenser.

Thus terminated this great feudal branch of the family, but another branch had diverged from

WILLIAM DE CHAWORTH, son of Robert, brother of Patric, the first feudal lord. This William, in the 2nd year of King John, paid £5 fine that he might not go beyond sea. He was s. by his son and heir,

ROBERT DE CHAWORTH, who, in the 6th of John, paid a fine of one hundred marks, and one palfrey for his relief, and that he might have the king's charter for those lands he then held by military service, whereof he had no grant. He d. without issue, and was s. by his brother,

WILLIAM DE CHAWORTH, who m. Alice, daughter of Robert, and sister and co-heir (with her sister Joane, wife of Robert de Latham, of Lancashire), of Thomas de Alfreton, and was s. at his decease by his son,

118

THOMAS DE CHAWORTH, who was summoned to parliament as a BARON on the 6th February, 1299. But his lordship had no other summons, nor had any of his descendants, who long flourished in the counties of Derby and Nottingham.

ARMS.—Of the feudal Barons Chaworth—Barry of ten pieces, ar. and gu. an orle of martlets sa.

ARMS.—Borne by Lord Chaworth, being the arms of Alfreton, viz., Az. two chevrons or.

CHENEY—BARON CHENEY.

By Writ of Summons, dated 1st September, 1487, 3 Henry VII.

Lineage.

Although this family, founded by RALPH DE CAINETO, (that is CHENEY,) who came into England with the Conqueror, was from that period of considerable note, it did not attain the honour of the peerage, until the time of Henry VII.

JOHN CHENEY, Esq., of Sherland, in the Isle of Shepey, had with other issue, by his wife Alianore, daughter and heiress of Sir Robert de Shotestroke, Knt., a son and heir,

SIR JOHN CHENEY, Knt., an eminent soldier, under the banner of Henry of Richmond, at Bosworth field, whom, it is said, King Richard, personally encountering, felled to the ground, although he was a person of great bodily strength. Upon the accession of his chief to the crown, as Henry VII., Sir John Cheney was called to the privy council, and soon after, again stoutly fought for the king, against the Earl of Lincoln and his adherents, at Stoke. In the 3rd year of the new monarch, he was summoned to parliament as a BARON, and from that period to the 14th October, 1495. His lordship was also a knight banneret, and a KNIGHT of the most noble order of the GARTER. He d. without issue, in 1496, when the BARONY of CHENEY expired, while his lands devolved upon his nephew, Sir Thomas Cheney (see Cheney of Taddington).

ARMS.—Az. six lions rampant ar. a Canton ermine.

CHENEY — BARON CHENEY, OF TADDINGTON, IN THE COUNTY OF BEDFORD.

By Writ of Summons, dated 6th May, 1572.

Lineage.

SIR THOMAS CHENEY, Knt., nephew and heir of John, Lord Cheney, a dignity that expired in 1496, m. first, Frideswide, daughter and co-heiress of Sir Thomas Frowyke, Knt., Chief Justice of the Court of Common Pleas, and had issue,

    Catherine, m. to Thomas Kemp, Esq., of Glendich, in the county of Kent.

    Margaret, m. to George Nevil, Lord Abergavenny.

    Frances, m. to Nicholas Crips, Esq., son and heir of Sir Henry Crips, Knt.

    Anne, m. to Sir John Perrot, Knt.

Sir Thomas m. secondly, Anne, daughter and co-heiress of Sir John Broughton, of Taddington, in the county of Bedford, by whom he acquired that estate, and had an only son, HENRY, of whom hereafter. Sir Thomas Cheney appears to have been a person of great gallantry and note, in the reign of Henry VIII. At the celebrated interview between that monarch and Francis I., at Ardres, he was one of the challengers, against all gentlemen, who were to exercise feats of arms, on horseback, or on foot, for thirty days. He was a KNIGHT of the GARTER, warden of the Cinque Ports, and treasurer of the king's household. Upon the death of King Edward VI., he espoused the interests of Queen Mary, and he was called to the privy council in the first year of Elizabeth: about which period he deceased, and was s. by his son,

SIR HENRY CHENEY, Knt, who was summoned to parliament as BARON CHENEY, OF TADDINGTON, in the county of Bedford, from 8th May, 1572, to 15th October, 1586. His lordship, who was one of the peers, on the trial of Mary, Queen of Scots, m. Jane, daughter of Thomas Wentworth, Lord Wentworth, but died without issue, in 1587, when his estates devolved upon his widow, and the Barony of CHENEY, OF TADDINGTON, became EXTINCT. His lordship erected a noble mansion at Taddington, wherein he resided.

ARMS.—Erm: on a bend sa. three martlets, or.

CHERLTON—BARONS CHERLTON, OF POWYS.

By Writ of Summons, dated 26th July, 1313, 7 Edward II.

Lineage. CP III '60

In the first year of Edward II.

JOHN DE CHERLTON, (elder son of Sir Alan Cherlton, of Appleby Castle, in the county of Salop, from whose younger son, Alan, descended the Cherltons of Ludford,) obtained a charter of free warren, in all his demesne lands at CHERLTON, and PONTESBURY, in the county of Salop, and the next year had a confirmation of the manor of Pontesbury, (some time belonging to Rhese ap Howell,) to hold in general tail, by the services anciently imposed for the same. This John, by the gift of King Edward II., espoused Hawyse, sister and heiress of Gryffin ap Owen, otherwise known as Gryffin de la Pole, by reason of his residence at Pole, commonly called Welch-pole, in the county of Montgomery, and in her right acquired the feudal Barony of POLE, held in capite from the crown; but in the next year, Gryffin de la Pole, uncle to the said Hawyse, pretending a right to the castle of Pole, (afterwards denominated RED CASTLE,) raised a body of the Welch, and regularly besieged it, his niece and her husband being at the time residing therein; whereupon the king directed his precept to Roger de Mortimer, then Justice of Wales, to march thither for their relief and protection. Again, however, they were disturbed by the said Gryffin, who had summons to appear before the king, to answer for his proceedings, and to render John Cherlton and his wife more secure in their title, they had a royal charter in the 7th of Edward II., confirmatory of all their lands and castles, in NORTH WALES, SOUTH WALES, and

Powys. In which year, (26th July, 1313,) John Cherlton was summoned to parliament as BARON CHERLTON, and from that period, to the 25th July, 1353. His lordship was chamberlain to King Edward II., and took an active part in the wars of Scotland. In the reign of that monarch, he had license to make a castle of his manor house, at Cherlton, Shropshire; but notwithstanding the many important immunities he received from the crown, he was implicated in the rebellion of Thomas, Earl of Lancaster, and was taken prisoner at the battle of Boroughbridge, in Yorkshire, but was fortunate enough to obtain the king's pardon. In the next reign, he was constituted JUSTICE OF IRELAND, and landed there upon Thursday, the festival of St. Calixt, the pope, with his brother Thomas, Bishop of Hereford, chancellor, and about two hundred archers. His lordship was subsequently engaged in the wars of France, and dying in 1353, was s. by his son,

JOHN DE CHERLTON, second Baron, summoned to parliament, from the 15th March, 1354, to the 20th November, 1360, as BARON CHERLTON, and from 14th August, 1362 to 4th October, 1373, as Lord Cherlton, of Powys. This nobleman being LORD CHAMBERLAIN to the king, was in the wars of Gascony, in attendance upon the Black Prince. His lordship m. Joane, daughter of Ralph de Stafford, Earl of Stafford, and d. in 1374, was s. by his son,

JOHN DE CHERLTON, third Baron, summoned to parliament, as "Johanni de Cherlton, de Powys," from 9th August, 1399, to 3rd October, 1400. His lordship m. Maud, daughter of Roger de Mortimer, Earl of March; but d. without issue, anno 1400, was s. by his brother,

EDWARD DE CHERLTON, fourth Baron, summoned to parliament, from 2nd December, 1401, to 26th Feb., 1421. In the 9th of Henry IV. This nobleman sustained great loss by the insurrection of the Welch, under Owen Glendower. In the next reign, he had the thanks of parliament for his activity in apprehending the unfortunate Sir John Oldcastle, Lord Cobham, within the territory of Powys. His lordship m. Alianore, daughter of Thomas Holland, and sister and co-heir of Edmund Holland, both Earls of Kent, and widow of Roger Mortimer, Earl of March, by whom (who m. after his decease, John Sutton, Lord Dudley,) he had issue,

Joane, m. to Sir John Grey, K.G., Earl of Tankerville, in Normandy, whose grandson, John Grey, was summoned to parliament, as "Johanni Grey de Powys," on the 15th November, 1482, (see that dignity).

Joyce, m. to Sir John de Tiptoft, who was summoned to parliament, from 7th January, 1426, to 3rd December, 1441. (Dugdale says, he bore the title of Lord Tiptoft and Powys, but he was never summoned by any other designation than "Johanni Tiptoft, Chl'r;") and had issue,

JOHN, created EARL OF WORCESTER, in 1449, but beheaded and attainted, in 1470, when his honours expired, but his son, EDWARD DE TIPTOFT, was restored in blood, as EARL OF WORCESTER;

dying, however, *s. p.*, in 1485, his aunts became his coheiresses to the BARONY OB TIPTOFT, and to his estates, while the EARLDOM EX-PIRED.

Philippa, *m.* to Thomas, Lord Roos.

Johanna, *m.* to Sir Edmund Inglethorpe.

Joyce, *m.* to Edmund Sutton, son and heir of John, Lord Dudley.

His lordship *d.* in 1422, when the BARONY OF CHERLTON, OF POWYS, fell into ABEYANCE, between his daughters, and his estates devolved upon them, as co-heirs. The Lordship of Powys coming to the eldest daughter, Joane, that lady's grandson, John Grey, had summons to parliament, in 1482, as LORD GREY, OF POWYS, but Mr. Nicholas, in his "Synopsis," considers *that* summons a new creation, and not a revival of the original dignity, and he is borne out in the opinion, he says, by a careful examination of the parliamentary rolls, wherein he finds the old lords, denominated in almost all instances, LORDS CHERLTON, and he then very justly reasons, that if it were meant to revive the suspended barony in the great grandson of Edward, fourth and last Lord Cherlton, that personage would have been summoned as BARON CHERLTON, OF POWYS, and not as Lord Grey—a course which appears indisputable. The BARONY OF CHERLTON, must therefore be deemed still in ABEYANCE.

ARMS.—Or. a lion rampant, gu.

NOTE.—A younger branch of this family, was,

ALAN DE CHERLTON, brother of the first baron, who in the 11th of Edward II., had a charter for free warren, in all his demesne lands, at APPLEBY, and other places, in the county of Salop, and was constituted in three years afterwards, governor of Montgomery Castle; he *m.* Elen, widow of Nicholas de St. Maur, and one of the daughters and co-heirs of Lord Zouch—from which union descended the family of Charlton, of Ludford, in the county of Hereford, now represented by Edmund Lechmere Charlton, Esq., of Ludford.

CHOLMONDELEY — VISCOUNT CHOLMONDELEY, EARL OF LEINSTER, IN THE PEERAGE OF IRELAND, BARON CHOLMONDELEY, IN THE PEERAGE OF ENGLAND.

Viscounty,	by Letters	1628.
Earldom,	Patent,	5th March, 1646.
Barony,		1st Sept., 1645.

Lineage.

SIR HUGH CHOLMONDELEY, KNT., of Cholmondeley, (eldest son of Sir Hugh Cholmondeley, and his wife, Anne, daughter and co-heiress of George Dorman, Esq., of Malpas,) married Mary, only daughter and heiress of Christopher Holford, Esq. of Holford, and had issue,

ROBERT, of whom presently.

Hugh, *m.* Mary, daughter of Sir John Bodville, of Bodville Castle, in the county of Carnarvon, and dying in 1655, left

130

ROBERT, who inherited the estates of his uncle, and was the founder of the present noble House of Cholmondeley.

Thomas, of Vale Royal, from whom the present Lord Delamere descends.

Mary, *m.* to Thomas Middleton, Esq., eldest son of Sir Thomas Middleton, of Chirk Castle.

Catharine, *m.* to Charles Mainwaring, Esq., of Ightfield, in the county of Salop.

Sir Hugh died in the 43rd of Elizabeth, and his lady (designated by King James I. " the bold lady of Cheshire," in consequence of the spirit she displayed in carrying on a law suit with George Holford, Esq., of Newborough, for more than forty years, which finally terminated by compromise,) died on 15th August; 1626. Sir Hugh was *s.* by his eldest son,

ROBERT CHOLMONDELEY, ESQ., who was created a baronet on the 29th June, 1611, and advanced to the peerage of Ireland in 1628, as *Viscount Cholmondeley, of Kells.* His lordship afterwards, " in consideration of his special service, in raising several companies of foot in Cheshire, in order to the quenching those rebellious flames which began to appear anno 1642, and sending many other to the king, (Charles I.,) then at Shrewsbury, (which stood him in high stead in that memorable battle of Kineton, happening soon after,) as also raising other forces for defending the city of Chester, at the first siege thereof by his majesty's adversaries in that county, and courageous adventure in the fight of Tilton Heath, together with his great sufferings, by the plunder of his goods, and firing his houses," was created a peer of England, by letters patent, dated 1st September, 1645, in the dignity of BARON CHOLMONDELEY, *of Wichs Malbank,* otherwise Namptwich, in the county of Chester, and advanced the next year to the Irish EARLDOM OF LEINSTER. Subsequently, under the rule of the parliament, his lordship was obliged to compound for his estates, and paid the large fine of £7,742. He *m.* Catherine, daughter of John, Lord Stanhope of Harrington, but died without issue on 2nd October, 1659, when his large possessions devolved upon his nephew, Robert Cholmondeley, (son of his brother Hugh,) immediate ancestor of the existing noble house of Cholmondeley—and his lordship's honours, namely, the Irish BARONY OF CHOLMONDELEY, *of Kells,* and the EARLDOM OF LEINSTER, with the English BARONY OF CHOLMONDELEY, *of Namptwich,* became EXTINCT.

ARMS.—Gu. two helmets in chief ppr. garnished or. in base a garb of the last.

CLARE—LORDS OF CLARE, EARLS OF HERTFORD, EARLS OF GLOUCESTER.

The feudal lordship of Clare, from the conquest.

The earldom of Hertford, temp. King Stephen.

The earldom of Gloucester, by marriage with the heiress of Gloucester,

Lineage.

GEOFFREY, natural son of RICHARD I., Duke of Normandy, had a son,

GISLEBERT, surnamed Crispin, *Earl of Brion*, in Normandy, whose eldest son,

RICHARD FITZGILBERT, having accompanied the Conqueror into England, participated in the spoils of conquest, and obtained extensive possessions in the new and old dominions, of his royal leader and kinsman. In 1073, (6th William Conqueror,) we find him joined under the designation of *Ricardus de Benefacto*, with William de Warren, in the great office of Justiciary of England; with whom, in three years afterwards, he was in arms, against the rebellious Lords, Robert de Britolio, Earl of Hereford, and Ralph Waher, or Guader, Earl of Norfolk and Suffolk, and behaved with great gallantry. But afterwards, at the time of the *general survey*, which was towards the close of William's reign, he is called *Ricardus de Tonebruge*, from his seat at Tonebruge, (now Tunbridge,) in Kent, which town and castle he obtained from the Archbishop of Canterbury, in lieu of the Castle of Brion; at which time he enjoyed thirty-eight lordships in Surrey, thirty-five in Essex, three in Cambridgeshire, with some others in Wilts and Devon, and ninety-five in Suffolk, amongst those was Clare, whence he was occasionally styled Richard de Clare; and that place in a few years afterwards becoming the chief seat of the family, his descendants are said to have assumed thereupon the title of Earls of Clare. This great feudal lord m. Robese, daughter of Walter Gifford, Earl of Buckingham, and had issue,

Gilbert, his successor.

Roger, an eminent soldier in the reign of Henry I., died s. p. when his estates devolved upon his elder brother's son, Gilbert.

Walter, who having licence from the king to enjoy all he could conquer in Wales, possessed all Nether-Went; he d. also s. p.

Richard, a monk of Bec, in Normandy, and last Abbot of Ely.

Robert, steward to King Henry I., m. Maud, daughter of *Simon St. Liz*, Earl of Huntingdon, and had *Walter Fitz-Robert*, whose son, *Robert Fitz-Walter*, was one of the most distinguished of the barons, who rebelled against John, and was styled, Marshal of the Army of God, and Holy Church.

—— m. to Ralph de Teigers.

—— m. to Eudo Dapifer.

Richard de Tonebruge, or de Clare, who is said to have fallen in a skirmish with the Welsh, was s. by his eldest son,

GILBERT DE TONEBRUGE, who resided at Tonebruge, and inherited all his father's lands in England. This nobleman joined in the rebellion of Robert de Moubray, Earl of Northumberland, but observing the King (William Rufus) upon the point of falling into an ambuscade, he relented, besought pardon, and saved his royal master. We find him subsequently, however, again in rebellion, in the same reign, and fortifying and losing his castle at Tunbridge. He m. Adeliza, daughter of the Earl of Claremont, and had issue,

Richard, his successor.

Gilbert, created Earl of Pembroke, anno 1138; see that dignity. This nobleman was

father of Richard, surnamed Strongbow, so celebrated for his conquest of Ireland.

Walter, founder of the abbey of Tintern, in Wales, died s. p.

Hervey, famous in the conquest of Ireland, by the name of *Hervey, of Montmauricc*, but died a monk at Canterbury.

Baldwin, who left three sons, William, Robert, and Richard, and a daughter Margaret, m. to —— Montfichet.

Gilbert de Tonebruge, who was a munificent benefactor to the church, was s. by his eldest son,

RICHARD DE CLARE, who first bore the title of Earl of Hertford; and being one of those, who by power of the sword entered Wales, there planted himself, and became lord of vast territories, as also of divers castles, in those parts, but requiring other matters of moment from the king, in which he was unsuccessful, he reared the standard of revolt, and soon after fell in an engagement with the Welsh. His lordship in 1124 removed the monks out of his castle at Clare, into the church of St. Augustine, at Stoke, and bestowed upon them a little wood, called Stoke-Ho, with a doe every year out of his park at Hundenes. He m. Alice, sister of Ranulph, second Earl of Chester, and had issue, Gilbert, his successor, with two other sons, and a daughter, Alice, who m. Cadwalader-ap-Griffith, Prince of North Wales.

His lordship was s. by his eldest son,

GILBERT DE CLARE, second Earl of Hertford, who is said by Dugdale, to have also borne the title of Earl of Clare, but Hornby observes, that *that* meant only *Earl at Clare*; for his earldom was certainly at *Hertford*. This nobleman, in the 8th of King Stephen, anno 1140, was a hostage for his uncle, Ranulph, Earl of Chester, and subsequently, being in rebellion against the power of Stephen, was taken prisoner, and held in captivity, until he surrendered all his strong places. He d. in 1151, and having no issue, was s. by his brother,

ROGER DE CLARE, third Earl of Hertford, who is likewise said to have borne the title of Earl of Clare. In the 3rd Henry II., this nobleman obtaining from the king all the lands in Wales which he could win, marched into Cardigan with a great army, and fortified divers castles thereabouts. In the 9th of the same reign, we find him summoned by the celebrated Thomas-à-Becket, Archbishop of Canterbury, to Westminster, in order to do homage to the prelate for his castle of Tonebruge; which at the command of the king he refused, alleging that holding it by military service it belonged rather to the crown than to the church. His lordship m. Maude, daughter of James de St. Hillary, by whom (who married after his decease William de Albini, Earl of Arundel,) he had a son,

Richard, his successor.

This earl, who, from his munificence to the church, and his numerous acts of piety, was called the *Good*, d. in 1173, and was s. by his son,

RICHARD DE CLARE, fourth Earl of Hertford, who, in the 7th Richard I., gave a thousand pounds to the king for livery of the lands of his mother's inheritance, with his proportion of those some time belonging to Giffard, Earl of Buckingham. His lordship m. Amicia, second daughter and co-heiress (with her sisters Mabell, wife of the Earl of Evereux, in Normandy, and Isabel, the divorced wife of King John,) of *William*, EARL OF GLOUCESTER, by whom he had issue,

GILBERT, his successor.

Joane, m. to Rhys-Grig, Prince of South Wales. This earl, who was one of the twenty-five barons appointed to enforce the observance of MAGNA CHARTA, d. in 1218, and was s. by his son,

GILBERT DE CLARE, fifth earl of Hertford, who, after the decease of Geoffrey de Mandeville, Earl of Essex, the second husband of Isabel, the divorced wife of King John, (one of the co-heiresses mentioned above of William, Earl of Gloucester,) and in her right EARL OF GLOUCESTER, and her own decease, s. p. as also the decease of Almarick D'Evereux, son of the Earl of Evereux, by Mabell, the other co-heiress, who likewise succeeded to the Earldom of Gloucester, became EARL OF GLOUCESTER, in right of his mother Amicia, the other co-heiress. This nobleman was amongst the principal barons who took up arms against King John, and was appointed one of the twenty-five chosen to enforce the observance of MAGNA CHARTA. In the ensuing reign, still opposing the arbitrary proceedings of the crown, he fought at Lincoln, under the baronial banner, and was taken prisoner there by William Marshall, Earl of Pembroke; but he soon afterwards made his peace. His lordship m. Isabel, one of the daughters, and eventually, co-heiresses of the above mentioned earl, by whom, (who m. after his decease, Richard, Earl of Cornwall, brother of King Henry III.,) he had issue,

RICHARD, his successor.

William.

Gilbert.

Amicia, m. to Baldwin de Redvers, fourth Earl of Devon.

Agnes.

Isabel, m. to Robert de Brus.

The earl d. in 1229, and was s. by his eldest son,

RICHARD DE CLARE, sixth Earl Hertford, and second Earl of Gloucester, then in minority. The wardship of this young nobleman was granted to the famous Hubert de Burgh, Earl of Kent, Justiciary of England, whose daughter Margaret, to the great displeasure of the king, (Henry III.,) he afterwards clandestinely married, but from whom, he was probably divorced, for we find the king marrying him the next year to Maude, daughter of John de Lacy, Earl of Lincoln, in consideration whereof the said John paid to the crown five thousand marks, and remitted a debt of two thousand more. His lordship, who appears to have been a very distinguished personage in the reign of Henry III., was one of the chief nobles present in Westminster Hall, (40th Henry III.,) when *Boniface*, ARCHBISHOP OF CANTERBURY, with divers other prelates, pronounced that solemn curse, with candles lighted against all those who should thenceforth violate MAGNA CHARTA. In two years afterwards, an attempt was made by Walter de Scotenay, his chief counsellor, to poison the earl and his brother William, which proved effective as to the

122

latter, while his lordship narrowly escaped, with the loss of his hair and nails. In the next year, the earl was commissioned with others of the nobility, by the appointment of the king, and the whole baronage of England, to the parliament of France, to convey King Henry III.'s resignation of Normandy, and to adjust all differences between the two crowns; and upon the return of the mission, his lordship reported proceedings to the king, in parliament. About this period, he had licence to fortify the Isle of Portland, and to embattle it as a fortress. It is reported of this nobleman, that being at Tewkesbury, in the 45th Henry III., a Jew, who had fallen into a jakes, upon the Saturday, refusing to be pulled out in reverence to the Jewish sabbath, his lordship prohibited any help to be afforded him on the next day, Sunday, the Christian sabbath, and thus suffered the unfortunate Israelite to perish. He d. himself, in the July of the next year, (1262,) having been poisoned at the table of Peter de Savoy, the queen's uncle, along with Baldwin, Earl of Devon, and other persons of note. His lordship left issue,

GILBERT, his successor.

Thomas, who was governor of the city of London, in the 1st Edward I., and d. in the 15th of the same reign, leaving by ~~Amy~~, his wife, daughter of Sir Morris Fitz-Morris.

Gilbert, who died s. p.

Richard, d. in the lifetime of his father, leaving a son, *Thomas*, who died s. p.

Thomas, whose daughters,

Margaret, wife of Bartholomew Badlesmere.

Maud, wife of Robert, Lord Clifford, of Appleby, became eventually his co-heiresses.

Rose, m. to Roger de Mowbray.

Margaret, m. to Edmund, Earl of Cornwall, and died s. p.

The earl was s. by his elder son,

GILBERT DE CLARE, surnamed the Red, seventh Earl of Hertford, and third Earl of Gloucester, who, by the king's procurement, espoused, in the lifetime of his father, Alice, daughter of Guy, Earl of Angoulesme, and niece of the King of France, which monarch bestowed upon the lady a marriage portion of five thousand marks. This nobleman, who, like his predecessors, was zealous in the cause of the barons, proceeded to London, immediately after the defeat sustained by the insurrectionary lords at Northampton, (48th Henry III.,) in order to rouse the citizens, which having effected, he received the honour of knighthood, from *Montford*, EARL OF LEICESTER, at the head of the army at Lewes; of which army, his lordship, with John Fitz-John, and William de Montchensi, commanded the second brigade, and having mainly contributed to the victory, in which the king and prince became prisoners, while the whole power of the realm fell into the hands of the victors, the earl procured a grant under the great seal of all the lands and possessions lying in England, of John de Warren, Earl of Surrey, one of the most faithful adherents of the king, excepting the castles of Riegate and Lewes, to hold during the pleasure of the crown, and he soon after, with some of the principal barons, extorted from the captive monarch a commission authorizing Stephen, then BISHOP OF CHICHESTER, Simon Montford, EARL OF LEICESTER, and himself, to nominate nine persons of " the most faithful, prudent, and most studious of the public weal," as well prelates as others, to manage all things according to the laws and customs of the realm, until the consultations at Lewes should terminate. Becoming jealous, however, of the power of LEICESTER, the earl soon after abandoned the baronial standard, and having assisted in procuring the liberty of the king and prince, commanded the second brigade of the royal army, at the triumphant battle of EVESHAM, which restored the kingly power to its former lustre. In reward of these eminent services he received a full pardon for himself and his brother Thomas, of all prior treasons, and the custody of the castle of Bergavenny, during the minority of Maud, wife of Humphrey de Bohun. His lordship veered again though in his allegiance, and he does not appear to have been sincerely reconciled to the royal cause, until 1270, in which year demanding from Prince Edward repayment of the expenses he had incurred at the battle of Evesham, with livery of all the castles and lands which his ancestors had possessed, and those demands having been complied with, he thenceforward became a good and loyal subject of the crown. Upon the death of King Henry, the Earl of Hertford and Gloucester was one of the lords who met at the NEW TEMPLE IN LONDON, to proclaim PRINCE EDWARD, then in the Holy Land, successor to the crown, and so soon as the new monarch returned to England, his lordship was the first to entertain him and his whole retinue, with great magnificence, for several days at his castle of Tonebruge. In the 13th Edward I., his lordship divorced his wife, Alice, the French princess, and in consideration of her illustrious birth, granted for her support during her life, six extensive manors and parks, and he married in a few years afterwards JOANE OF ACRE, daughter of King Edward I., upon which occasion he gave up the inheritance of all his castles and manors, as well in England as in Wales, to his royal father-in-law, to dispose of as he might think proper; which manors, &c., were entailed by the king upon the earl's issue, by the said Joane, and in default, upon her heirs and assigns, should she survive his lordship. By this lady, he had issue,

GILBERT, his successor.

Alianore, m. first, to Hugh le Despencer, and secondly, to William, Lord Zouche, of Mortimer.

Margaret, m. first, to Piers Gaveston, and secondly, to Hugh de Audley, who was eventually created Earl of Gloucester.

Elizabeth, m. first, to John de Burgh, son of Richard, Earl of Ulster, by whom she had issue,

William, EARL OF ULSTER, who m. Maud, sister of Henry Plantagenet, Duke of Lancaster, and left a daughter and heiress,

ELISABETH DE BURGH, who m. Lionel Plantagenet, DUKE OF CLARENCE,

K.G., and had an only daughter and heiress,

PHILIPPA PLANTAGENET, who m. Edward Mortimer, EARL OF MARCH, and through her the house of York derived its claim to the throne.

His lordship d. in 1295, and the Countess Joane, surviving, married a " plain esquire," called Ralph de Monthermer, clandestinely, without the king her father's knowledge; but to which alliance he was reconciled through the intercession of Anthony Beke, the celebrated Bishop of Durham, and became eventually much attached to his new son-in-law,

RALPH DE MONTHERMER, who, during the lifetime of the Princess Joane, his wife, enjoyed the earldoms of HERTFORD AND GLOUCESTER, and was summoned to parliament in those dignities, from 6th February, 1299, to 3rd November, 1306, jure uxoris; but Joane dying in 1307, he never afterwards was so summoned but as a baron, under the designation of " Radulpho de Monthermer," (see Monthermer). We now return to

GILBERT DE CLARE, who succeeded his father, and at the decease of his mother, Joane, became EARL OF HERTFORD and EARL OF GLOUCESTER. His lordship m. Maud, daughter of Richard de Burgh, EARL OF ULSTER, but falling at the battle of BANNOCKBURN in 1313, and leaving no issue, his large possessions devolved upon his three sisters as co-heiresses, and the EARLDOMS OF GLOUCESTER AND HERTFORD became EXTINCT.

ARMS.—Or. three chevrons gu.

CLARE—EARLS OF PEMBROKE.

By Creation, anno 1138, 3rd of King Stephen.

Lineage.

GILBERT DE CLARE, second son of Gilbert de Tonebruge, feudal Lord of Clare, and brother of Richard de Clare, first Earl of Hertford, having obtained from King Henry I. a licence to enjoy all the lands he should win in Wales, marched a large force into Cardiganshire, and brought the whole country under subjection: here he soon afterwards built two strong castles; and his power increasing, he was created by King Stephen, in 1138, EARL OF PEMBROKE. His lordship m. Elizabeth, sister of Waleran, Earl of Mellent, and had issue,

RICHARD, surnamed STRONGBOW, his successor.

Baldwin, who fell at the battle of Lincoln, fighting under the banner of King Stephen.

Basilia, m. to Reymond, son of William Fitz-Gerald of Ireland.

The earl d. in 1149, and was s. by his elder son,

RICHARD DE CLARE, (the celebrated Strongbow,) second Earl of Pembroke. This nobleman was one of the witnesses to the solemn agreement, made in 1153, between King Stephen and Henry, Duke of Normandy, whereby the latter was to succeed to the English throne upon the decease of the former. But the leading part he subsequently had in the subjugation, Ireland procuring him a conspicuous place in history, we shall relate the particulars of that event in the words of the Monk of Jorevaulx —" The realm of Ireland," saith he, " being miserably opprest with warr by the many kings there, who banded against each other ; one of them sent his son into England to procure souldiers thence for his aid. Which souldiers for the hope of gain, giving him assistance, were so well recompenced, as that they rather chose to stay there than return into England. But after a short time the stoutest people of Ireland, being much offended with that king for getting aid from England, the English already fixed in Ireland, sent for more from hence, to strengthen their party ; and because they had no chief, they made choice of this EARL RICHARD, (a stout and valiant man,) to be their captain, who, yielding to their request, rigging a good fleet, prepared for the journey. Whereupon there were some who, in the king's behalf, endeavoured to restrain him. Howbeit, getting on shipboard, and landing safe, he assaulted Dublin, and took it ; the tidings whereof so terrified those that lived afar off, that they were content to be at peace with him ;' and, to confirm what he had got, gave him in marriage, Eva, daughter of Dermot McMurrough, one of their kings, with whom he had in dower a great part of the realm. Whereat the king of England growing much displeased, as well, for that he had not only, without his consent, but forbidden, made so great an attempt, seized upon all his patrimony here, prohibiting that he should have further aid ; and threatening him otherwise very sore, compelled him so to such a compliance, as that he got DUBLIN from him, and all the principal places he had won, requiring him to be content with the rest, and his patrimony in England ; soon after raising a great army the king sayled thither himself." In the end the earl was constituted Justice of Ireland by KING HENRY II., and having founded the priory of KILMAINHAM, in the province of Leinster, for knights' hospitalars, " This eminent person," Dugdale concludes, " died untimely upon the nones of April, anno 1176, and was buried in the Chapter-House at Gloucester, as may be seen by this inscription on the wall there ; Hicjacet RICARDUS STRONGBOW, filius GILBERTI Comitis de PEMBROKE." Leaving issue, as some say, one son, scarce three years old, to be his heir. But by others it is reported that, being by treachery abused and wounded, he departed this life the fifth year after his acquisition of the province of Leinster, and that he was buried at Dublin, leaving issue one only daughter and heiress,

ISABEL, who became in ward to King Henry II. and remained under the royal guardianship for the space of fourteen years, when she was given in marriage to WILLIAM MARSHAL, who thereupon became EARL OF PEMBROKE (see Marshal, Earl of Pembroke).

ARMS.—Or. three chevrons, gu. a label of five points, az.

Note.—HACKET, in his collection of epitaphs, gives the following from the tomb of STRONGBOW, at Christ's Church, Dublin :—

" Nate ingrate, mihi pugnauti terga dedisti,
" Non mihi, sed genti, regno quoque terga dedisti."

This alludes, says Banks, to a story that Strongbow's only son, a youth about seventeen, frighted with the numbers and ululations of the Irish in a great battle, ran away ; but being afterwards informed of his father's victory, he joyfully returned to congratulate him. But the severe general having first upbraided him with his cowardice, caused him to be immediately executed by cutting off in the middle with a sword. Such, in former times, was the detestation of dastardliness ! ! !

CLARE—BARON CLARE.

By Writ of Summons, dated 26th October, 1309, 3 Edward II.

Lineage.

RICHARD DE CLARE was summoned to parliament as a BARON on the 26th October, 1309, but never afterwards. Of this nobleman nothing further is known, and Dugdale makes no mention of him at all.

CLAVERING — BARONS CLAVERING.

By Writ of Summons, dated 2nd November, 1295, 23 Edward I.

Lineage.

EUSTACE FITZ-JOHN, (nephew and heir of Serlo de Burgh, the founder of Knaresborough Castle,) one of the most powerful of the northern barons, and a great favorite with King Henry I., married Beatrice, only daughter and heiress of Yvo de Vesci, Lord of ALNWICK in Northumberland, and of HALTON in Yorkshire, by whom he had issue,

WILLIAM, from whom the great baronial family of De Vesci sprang.

Geffery.

He m. secondly, Agnes, daughter and heiress of William Fits-Nigel, BARON OF HALTON, and constable of Chester, and with her acquired those dignities. By this lady he had a son, his successor,

RICHARD FITZ-EUSTACE, Baron of Halton, and constable of Chester. This Richard m. Albreda Lizures, half sister of Robert de Lacy, and had issue,

JOHN, who assumed the surname of Lacy, and succeeded his father as constable of Chester. He d. 25th Henry II., leaving one son,

Henry de Lacy, whose only daughter m. the Earl of Lancaster.

Robert, the hospitaller, that is of the hospital of St. John of Jerusalem, in England.

Roger.

The youngest son,

ROGER FITZ-RICHARD, who was feudal Baron of Warkworth, in the county of Northumberland, a lordship granted to him by King Henry II., m. Alianor, daughter and co-heir of Henry of Essex, Baron of Raleigh, and was s. by his only son,

ROBERT FITZ-ROGER, who m. Margaret,

only child and heiress of William de Cheney, by whom he acquired the barony of HORSFORD, in the county of Norfolk, and had an only son, JOHN. This Robert obtained a confirmation upon the accession of King John, of the castle and manor of WARKWORTH, of the manor of CLAVERING in Essex, and of the manor of EURE, in Buckinghamshire, to hold by the service of one knight's fee each. And in that monarch's reign he served the office of sheriff for Northumberland, Norfolk, and Suffolk; for each county thrice. In the conflict between John and the barons this powerful person, although indebted to the crown for immense territorial possessions, took part in the first instance with the latter, but under the apprehension of confiscation, and the other visitations of royal vengeance, he was very soon induced to return to his allegiance. He d. in 1240, and was s. by his son,

JOHN FITZ-ROBERT, to whom King John, in the 14th year of his reign, ratified the grant of the castle and manor of WARKWORTH, made by King Henry II., to his grandfather, Roger Fitz-Richard, as also of the manor of CLAVERING. In three years afterwards he was appointed joint governor with John Marshall, of the castles of Norwich and Oxford; but joining in the insurrection of the barons, and being chosen one of the twenty-five appointed to exercise the regal authority, his lands were seized by the king, and a part confiscated. Returning, however, to his allegiance in the next reign, his castles and estates were restored to him. In the 9th of Henry III. he was constituted sheriff of Northumberland, and governor of the town of Newcastle-upon-Tyne; and in the 13th of the same monarch he was one of the great northern barons appointed by special command of the king to wait upon Alexander, king of Scotland, at Berwick-upon-Tweed, and to conduct that prince to York, there to meet the king of England, "to treat upon certain affairs of great importance." His lordship m. Ada de Baliol, and had issue,

    ROGER, his successor.

    Hugh, surnamed " De Eure," from whom the Lords Eure descended.

    Robert, ancestor of the Eures of Axholm, in Lincolnshire.

He d. in 1240, and was s. by his eldest son,

ROGER FITZ-JOHN, feudal Baron of Warkworth and Clavering, who d. in 1249, and was s. by his son,

ROBERT FITZ-ROGER, then in infancy, whose tuition was committed to William de Valence, the king's brother, although Ada de Baliol, the grandmother of the child, offered two thousand two hundred marks for the wardship. This feudal lord became eventually so eminent in the Scottish wars of King Edward I., particularly in the battle of Faukirk, and other memorable conflicts, that he was summoned to parliament as a BARON on the 2nd November, 1295, and subsequently assisted with his son JOHN, who assumed, by the king's appointment, the surname of CLAVERING, at the celebrated siege of KARRLAVEROK. His lordship m. Margaret de la Zouche, and had issue, seven sons, viz.,—

    JOHN, his successor.

Edmund,
Alexander,
Robert, } all died s. p.
Henry,
Roger,

    Alan (Sir) m. Isabella, eldest daughter and co-heir of William Riddell; and from this union descended the Baronets CLAVERING of Axwell, in the county of Durham, the Claverings of Callaly, in Northumberland, the Claverings of Learchild, the Claverings of Tilmouth, in the county of Durham, and other eminent families.

He d. about the year 1311, and was s. by his eldest son,

JOHN DE CLAVERING, second baron, who had summons to parliament from the 10th April, 1299, to the 20th November, 1331. This nobleman had distinguished himself, in his father's lifetime, in the French and Scotch wars, and was taken prisoner at the battle of Strivelyn. His lordship m. Hawyse, daughter of Robert de Tibetot, and had an only daughter,

    Eve, who m. first, Ralph de Ufford, and secondly, Thomas de Audley, by both of whom she had issue.

Lord Clavering, long before his death, being doubtful of having male issue, made a feoffment to Stephen de Trafford, whereby he vested the inheritance of his castle and manor of WARKWORTH in the said Stephen, with other manors, for the intent that he should reconvey them to his lordship for life, with remainder to the king and his heirs. In consideration whereof the king granted unto the baron and his heirs divers lands and hereditaments, then valued at £400. per annum. His lordship d. at his manor of Aynho, in Northamptonshire, in 1332, when those great estates, falling to the crown, were divided thus—

    WARKWORTH, and the manors in Northumberland, granted to Henry de Perci, are still part of the possessions of the ducal family of Northumberland.

    AYNHO AND HORSFORD, in Northamptonshire and Norfolk, to Ralph de Neville, and his heirs.

    CLAVERING, in Essex, to the deceased lord's brother Edmund, for life, and in remainder to the above Ralph Neville and his heirs.

In this very unjustifiable manner were the descendants of his lordship's youngest brother deprived of their fair inheritance. At the decease of Lord Clavering the BARONY should have devolved upon his daughter, EVE, and it is now probably in ABEYANCE amongst that lady's descendants.

ARMS.—Quarterly or. and gu. over all a bend sa.

CLIFFORD — EARLS OF CUMBERLAND.

Created by Letters Patent, dated 18th June, 1525, 17 Henry VIII.

Lineage.

The first of this ancient family of whom DUGDALE takes notice, was called PONCE, who is represented as leaving three sons, Walter and Dru, considerable landed proprietors in the Conqueror's survey, and

RICHARD FITZPONCE, a personage of rank in the time of Henry I., and a liberal benefactor to the church; this Richard left also three sons, of whom the second, *Walter*, having obtained CLIFFORD Castle, in Herefordshire, with his wife, Margaret, daughter of Ralph de Toney, a descendant from William Fitzosborn, Earl of Hereford, by whom the castle was erected, assumed thence his surname, and became

WALTER DE CLIFFORD. This feudal lord, who was in influence in the reign of Henry II., left at his decease, two sons and two daughters, viz.—

WALTER, his heir.

Richard, from whom the *Cliffords* of Frampton, in Gloucestershire, descended.

ROSAMOND, so well known as "FAIR ROSAMOND," the celebrated *mistress* of Henry II., by whom she was 'mother of William Longespee, Earl of Salisbury. For this lady, the monarch caused to be constructed the famous labyrinth at Woodstock; and he is said to have presented her with a cabinet of such exquisite workmanship, that the devices upon it, representing champions in combat, moving cattle, flying birds, and swimming fishes, seemed as though they were, in reality, animated. At her decease, FAIR ROSAMOND was interred in the Chapter House of the nunnery, at Godstow, and the following epitaph placed upon her tomb:—

"Hic jacet in Tumbâ ROSA MUNDI, non ROSA MUNDA,

Non redolet, sed olet, quæ redolere solet."

Another account, however, states, that her memory and remains were treated with obloquy, after the death of her royal protector. In 1191, it is said that Hugh, Bishop of Lincoln, being at Godstow, upon his visitation, observing in the church, near the high altar, a herse covered with silk, and surrounded by numerous burning lights, demanded an explanation, and being informed by the nuns, that it contained the remains of "Fair Rosamond," whom King Henry so dearly loved, and for whose sake he had been a munificent benefactor to the house, having conferred large revenues for the maintenance of those lights, the indignant prelate exclaimed— "Hence with her! the king's affections were unlawful, and adulterous—remove her from this sacred edifice, and bury her with other common people—that religion be not vilified, and that other women be deterred from such abandoned courses!"

Lucia, m. first, to Hugh de Say, of Richard's Castle, and secondly, to Bartholomew de Mortimer.

Walter de Clifford was s. by his elder son,

WALTER DE CLIFFORD, who m. Agnes, only daughter and heiress of Roger de Cundi, Lord of the manors of Covenby and Glentham, in the county of Lincoln, by Alice his wife, Lady of Horncastle, daughter and heiress of William de Cheney,

126

lord of those manors in the Conqueror's time, by whom he had issue, WALTER, Roger, Giles, and Richard. He was sheriff of Herefordshire, in the 1st, 6th, 9th, and 17th John, and dying in the 7th of Henry III., was s. by his eldest son,

WALTER DE CLIFFORD. This feudal lord held a very high place in the estimation of King Henry III., until the rebellion of Richard Mareschal, Earl of Pembroke, when, taking part with that nobleman, his lands were confiscated and himself outlawed. The royal displeasure did not, however, endure any length of time, for we find him soon afterwards restored to his castle of Clifford, and during the many subsequent years of this same reign, enjoying the full confidence of the crown. At the coronation of Queen Eleanor, consort of King Henry, he claimed with the other barons-marchers, as *Jus Marchæ*, to carry the canopy, which belonged to the barons of the Cinque Ports. This Walter de Clifford m. Margaret, daughter of Lewelyn, Prince of Wales, and widow of John de Braose, by whom he had an only daughter and heiress,

Maud, who m. first, William de Longespee, Earl of Salisbury, and secondly, Sir John Gifford of Brimsfield.

Walter de Clifford d. in the 48th Henry III., when the continuation of the male line of the family devolved upon his nephew,

ROGER DE CLIFFORD, (son of Roger de Clifford, by Sibill, daughter and co-heiress of Robert de Ewyas, a great Baron of Herefordshire, and widow of Robert, Lord Tregoz,) who, for his staunch adherence to Henry III., was appointed, after the victory of Evesham, justice of all the king's forests south of Trent, and obtained a grant at the same time, of the lordship of Kingsbury, in the county of Warwick, forfeited by Sir Ralph de Bracebrigge, Knt. He was afterwards frequently employed against the Welsh, and lost his eldest son, Roger, who had married Isabel, daughter and co-heiress of Robert de Vipount, Lord and hereditary Sheriff of Westmoreland, in one of those conflicts. Roger de Clifford d. in 14th of Edward I., and was s. by (the son of his deceased son above mentioned) his grandson,

ROBERT DE CLIFFORD, who was summoned to parliament as a baron, from the 29th December, 1299, (28th Edward I.,) to 26th November, 1313, (7th Edward II.). This nobleman participated in the Scottish wars of King Edward I., and had a principal command in the English army. He fell in the following reign, at the battle of Bannockburn. His lordship m. Maud, daughter and co-heiress of Richard de Clare, Earl of Gloucester, and was s. by his son,

ROGER DE CLIFFORD, second baron, from whom we pass to

HENRY DE CLIFFORD, the eleventh baron who was created by letters patent, dated 18th June, 1525, EARL OF CUMBERLAND, and dignified with the Garter, in 1532. This nobleman obtained large grants out of the monastic spoliations, and was entrusted with a principal command in the army which invaded Scotland in the 34th of Henry VIII. His lordship m. first, Margaret, daughter of George Talbot, Earl of Shrewsbury, by whom he had no issue; and secondly, Margaret, daughter of Henry Percy, Earl of Northumberland, by whom he had,

HENRY, Lord Clifford, his successor.

Ingram (Sir), who m. Anne, daughter and sole heiress of Sir Henry Ratcliff, but dying s. p. left his property to his nephew, George, Earl of Cumberland.

Catherine, m. first, to John, Lord Scroope, of Bolton, and secondly, to Sir Richard Cholmeley, by the latter of whom she had

SIR HENRY CHOLMONELEY, of Grandmount and Raxby, who had

RICHARD (Sir), Sheriff of Yorkshire, in the last year of King James I., whose son,

HUGH, was created a baronet, 10th August, 1641, and was s. by his son,

SIR WILLIAM, second baronet, who left daughters only, his co-heirs, the eldest of whom, Elizabeth, m. Sir Edward Dering, of Surenden.

Maud, m. to John, Lord Coniers of Hornby, in the county of York.

Elizabeth, m. to Sir Christopher Metcalf, of Napper, Yorkshire.

Jane, m. to Sir John Huddlestone, of Millum Castle, in the county of Cumberland.

By the last will and testament of this nobleman, he devised, amongst other bequests, three hundred marks to be expended upon his funeral; to his daughter, Elizabeth, £1000, if she should marry an earl, or an earl's son; if a baron, a thousand marks; if a knight, eight hundred marks. His lordship d. in the 34th of Henry VIII., and was s. by his elder son,

HENRY CLIFFORD, second earl, who had been made a Knight of the Bath at the coronation of Queen Anne Boleyne. This nobleman m. first, Eleanor, daughter and co-heiress of Charles Brandon, Duke of Suffolk, and niece of King Henry VIII., by whom he had an only surviving child,

Margaret, m. to Henry Stanley, then Lord Strange, and afterwards Earl of Derby.

His lordship m. secondly, Anne, daughter of William Lord Dacres, of Gillesland, by whom he had surviving issue,

GEORGE, Lord Clifford.

Francis.

Frances, m. to Philip Lord Wharton.

The earl d. 8th January, 1569, and was s. by his elder son,

GEORGE CLIFFORD, third earl, then in his eleventh year, who was placed by Queen Elizabeth under the guardianship of Francis Russell, second Earl of Bedford, whose third daughter, Lady Margaret Russell, he eventually espoused, and had an only surviving daughter,

ANNE, born 30th January, 1758, who m. first, Richard Sackville, second Earl of Dorset, by whom she had three sons, who died young, and two daughters, viz.

MARGARET, m. to John Tufton, second Earl of Thanet.

ISABEL, m. to James, Earl of Northampton.

The Countess of Dorset m. secondly, Philip Herbert, Earl of Pembroke and Montgomery, K.G., and lord-chamberlain of the household; but had no issue. This lady claimed the barony of Clifford in 1698, and the hearing of her petition was appointed for the next session; but no further proceedings ensued. Her ladyship d. in 1675. Her descendant, however, Thomas, sixth Earl of Thanet, preferred his claim to the barony, and had it acknowledged by the house of lords in 1691; but the dignity fell into abeyance at his decease, in 1729, between his daughters and co-heirs, and so remained until terminated by the crown, in 1734, in favour of the third daughter, Margaret, Countess of Leicester, at whose decease, in 1775, it again became suspended, until again revived in favour of EDWARD SOUTHWELL, Esq., who became Lord de Clifford, and whose son is the present lord.

Earl George was educated at the university of Cambridge, and attaching himself to the study of mathematics, imbibed so decided a passion for navigation, that he became soon afterwards eminent as a naval commander, having undertaken at his own expense several voyages for the public service; but that, and a passion for tournaments, horse-racing, and similar pursuits, made such inroads upon his fortune, that he was said to have wasted more of his estate than any one of his ancestors. His lordship was elected a Knight of the Garter in 1592. His character is thus depicted in the MS. memoirs of his celebrated daughter, Anne, Countess of Dorset and Pembroke:—" He was endowed with many perfections of nature befitting so noble a personage, as an excellent quickness of wit and apprehension, an active and strong body, and an affable disposition and behaviour. But as good natures, through human frailty, are oftentimes misled, so he fell to love a lady of quality, which did, by degrees, draw and allene his love and affections from his so virtuous and well-deserving wife; it being the cause of many discontents between them for many years together, so that at length, for two or three years before his death, they parted houses, to her extreme grief and sorrow, and also to his extreme sorrow at the time of his death; for he died a very penitent man. He died in the duchy-house, called the Savoy, 30th October, 1605, aged forty-seven years, two months, and twenty-two days, being born at Brougham Castle, 8th August, 1558."

His lordship leaving no male issue, the barony remained for some years in abeyance, but eventually devolved upon the descendants his daughters, by one of whom it is at present inherited, while the earldom passed to his only brother,

FRANCIS CLIFFORD, fourth earl, who m. Grissel, daughter of Mr. Thomas Hughes, of Uxbridge, and widow of Edward Nevill, Lord Bergavenny, by whom he had surviving issue,

Henry, Lord Clifford.

Margaret, m. to Sir Thomas Wentworth, of Wentworth-Woodhouse, in the county of York, afterwards Earl of Strafford.

Frances, m. to Sir Gervase Clifton, Bart., of

Clifton, in the county of Nottingham, (his second wife).

Of this nobleman, the Countess of Dorset says, " He was an honourable gentleman, and of a good, noble, sweet, and courteous nature; and some twenty years before the Earl Francis died, his son, Henry Lord Clifford, did absolutely govern both him and his estate, he being then forty-nine years of age, wanting forty days, at the time of his father's decease." His lordship d. in 1641, and was s. by his son,

HENRY CLIFFORD, fifth earl, who m. Frances, only daughter of Robert Cecil, Earl of Salisbury, and had an only surviving daughter and heiress,

     Elizabeth, m. to Richard, second Earl of Cork, and first Earl of Burlington, who was created *Baron Clifford, of Lanesborough, in the county of York,* in 1644.

The earl died in the year previously, when the EARLDOM OF CUMBERLAND became EXTINCT. Upon his lordship's decease, all the castles and lands which he had inherited through his uncle, George, the fourth earl, reverted, by a deed of entail, to that nobleman's daughter, Anne, COUNTESS OF DORSET AND PEMBROKE.

Arms.—Chequée or. and az. a fesse gules.

NOTE.—" Beneath the altar, in Skepton church," says Whittaker, in his History of the Deanery of Craven, in the county of York, " is the vault of the Cliffords, the place of their interment from the dissolution of Bolton priory to the death of the last Earl of Cumberland, which, after having been closed many years, I obtained permission to examine, 29th March, 1803. The original vault, intended only for the first earl and his second lady, had undergone two enlargements; and the bodies having been deposited in chronological order, first, and immediately under his tomb, lay Henry, the first earl, whose lead coffin was much corroded, and exhibited the skeleton of a short and very stout man, with a long head of flaxen hair, gathered in a knot behind the skull. The coffin had been closely fitted to the body, and proved him to have been very corpulent as well as muscular. Next lay the remains of Margaret Percy, his second wife, whose coffin was still entire. She must have been a slender and diminutive woman. The third was ' the lady Ellenor's grave,' whose coffin was much decayed, and exhibited the skeleton (as might be expected in a daughter of Charles Brandon, and the sister of Henry VIII.), of a tall and large-limbed female. At her right hand was Henry, the second earl, a very tall and rather slender man, whose then envelope of lead really resembled a winding-sheet, and folded like a coarse drapery round the limbs. The head was beaten to the left side: something of the shape of the face might have been distinguished, and a long prominent nose was very conspicuous. Next lay Francis, Lord Clifford, a boy. At his right hand was his father, George, the third earl, whose lead coffin precisely resembled the outer case of an Egyptian mummy, with a rude face, and something like a female mammæ cast upon it, as were also the figures and letters, ' G. C. 1605.' The body was closely wrapped in ten folds of coarse cere cloth, which, being removed, exhibited the face so entire,

128

(only turned to a copper colour,) as plainly to resemble his portraits. All his painters, however, had the complaisance to omit three large warts upon the left cheek. The coffin of Earl Francis, who lay next to his brother, was of the modern shape, and alone had an outer shell of wood, which was covered with leather. The soldering had decayed, and nothing appeared but the ordinary skeleton of a tall man. This earl had never been embalmed. Over him lay another coffin, much decayed, which I suspect had contained the Lady Anne Dacre, his mother. Last lay Henry, the fifth earl, in a coffin of the same form with that of his father. Lead not allowing of absorption, nor a narrow vault of much evaporation, a good deal of moisture remained in the coffin, and some hair about the skull. Both these coffins had been cut open. Room might have been found for another slender body; but the Countess of Pembroke chose to be buried at Appleby, partly, perhaps, because her beloved mother was interred there, and partly that she might not mingle her ashes with rivals and enemies."

CLIFTON—BARONS CLIFTON.

By Writ of Summons, dated 1st December, 1376, 50 Edward III.

Lineage.

ROGER DE CLIFTON, Esquire to Thomas, LORD CAILLI, m. Margerie, the sister of that nobleman, and left issue,

ADAM DE CLIFTON, who, in his ninth year, inherited the great estates of his uncle, Lord Cailli, which included those of the family of Tatshall, derived by that nobleman from his mother, Emme, one of the co-heirs of Robert de Tatshall. This Adam had a son, CONSTANTINE, who predeceased him, leaving a son, the said Adam's successor,

JOHN DE CLIFTON, who was summoned to parliament as a BARON from 1st December, 1376, to 26th July, 1382. His lordship d. in the latter year at Rhodes possessed, amongst other lands, of the castle of Bokenham, and manor of Babingie, in the county of Norfolk; which castle he held by performing the office of butler at the king's coronation. He was s. by his son,

CONSTANTINE DE CLIFTON, second baron, summoned to parliament from 13th November, 1393, to the 20th of the same month in the next year. This nobleman d. in 1395, leaving issue,

     JOHN (Sir).

     Elizabeth, m. to Sir John Knevit, Knt., and had issue,

         JOHN KNEVIT.

His lordship's son and heir,

SIR JOHN DE CLIFTON, third baron, but never summoned to parliament, m. Joane, daughter and co-heir of Sir Edward Thorpe, by whom he had a daughter and heiress,

     Margaret, who m. Sir Andrew Ogard, but d. without issue.

His lordship d. ——, and the BARONY OF CLIFTON became vested at the decease of Lady Ogard, in

JOHN KNEVIT, amongst whose descendants and representatives it is now in ABEYANCE.

ARMS.—Cheque or. and gu. a bend erm.

CLINTON — BARON CLINTON, EARL OF HUNTINGDON.

Barony, by Writ of Summons, 6th Sept., 1330.
Earldom, by Letters Patent, dated 16th March, 1337.

Lineage.

SIR WILLIAM DE CLINTON, Knt., younger son of John de Clinton, Baron Clinton, espoused Julian, daughter and heiress of Sir Thomas de Leyburne, Knt., and widow of John, Lord Hastings, of Bergavenny, by which alliance it is presumed, that his subsequent advancement in life was considerably promoted; he was, however, himself a very eminent person, and fully entitled by his own deeds to the high honours he attained. In the year ensuing his marriage, Sir William was made justice of Chester, and within less than two months afterwards constable of Dover Castle, and warden of the cinque ports. Shortly after this, being one of those who surprised the great MORTIMER, at Nottingham Castle, he had summons to parliament as BARON CLINTON, on the 6th September, 1330, and from that period to the 14th January, 1337. In three years, subsequently, 7th Edward III., his lordship was constituted LORD ADMIRAL of the seas, from the Thames westwards, and in that year he was engaged in the Scottish wars, as he was in the 9th and 10th of the same reign. In the 11th Edward III., then enjoying the highest favour of the king, his lordship was created, by letters patent, dated 16th March, 1337, EARL OF HUNTINGDON, having, at the same time, not only £20. per annum given him out of the issues of the county to be paid by the sheriff, but one thousand marks per annum in land, to hold to himself and his male heirs for ever. He subsequently participated in his gallant sovereign's wars, both in Scotland and France, and was frequently employed in foreign embassies of the first importance. He was a second time constituted lord admiral, and a second time appointed constable of Dover Castle, and lord warden of the cinque ports. His lordship d. in 1354, leaving, according to Banks, an only daughter,

ELIZABETH, who m. Sir John Fitzwilliam, of Sprotborough, ancestor of the present EARL FITZWILLIAM.

The earl having no male issue, the dignity of EARL OF HUNTINGDON became EXTINCT, but the BARONY OF CLINTON, created by writ, should have devolved upon his daughter if legitimate, and if so, it is still extant in her descendants, the Earls Fitzwilliam. Of this, however, there must be strong doubt. Dugdale mentions no daughter, but says that the earl left all his extensive possessions to his nephew, Sir John de Clinton, Knt. Nicolas, in his synopsis, confirms Dugdale, by stating that the Earl of Huntingdon died s. p., " when his honours became extinct;" while Banks gives the particulars of the daughter as above. Collins and Jacob call

the lady " Elizabeth, daughter of William, Lord Clinton." Had she been legitimate, she would, doubtless, have been his lordship's heiress, and BARONESS CLINTON.

ARMS,—Arg. six cross crosslets fitchée sa. on a chief sa. two mullets or. pierced gu.

COBHAM — BARONS COBHAM, OF KENT.

By Writ of Summons, dated 8th January, 1313, 6 Edward II.

Lineage.

In the 12th King John, HENRY DE COBBHAM gave to that monarch a thousand marks for his royal favour. This Henry had three sons, namely,

Reginald, (the second son,) justice itinerant in Essex, in the 32nd Henry III., and the ensuing year in Middlesex and Wilts, when he was constituted sheriff of Kent, and he continued to execute the duties of that office for the nine following years. In the 39th of the same monarch he was made constable of Dover Castle, and warden of the cinque ports, when he had command to attend the ambassadors from the King of Castile, who then landed at Dover, to afford them hospitable entertainment, and to conduct them to the new temple at London, where they were to be lodged. He d. in three years afterwards.

William, (the youngest son,) one of the justices itinerant in the counties of Sussex, Southampton and Wilts, in the 39th Henry III., and for Norfolk and Suffolk in the 41st of the same reign.

JOHN DE COBBEHAM, (the eldest son,) executed in the 26th Henry III., the office of sheriff of Kent, on behalf of Peter de Savoy, brother of Queen Eleanor, for one-half of the year, and on behalf of Bertram de Criol for the other half. He was also one of the justices of the court of Common Pleas from the 26th to the 35th of the same reign. This eminent person married first, ———, daughter of Warine Fitz-Benedict, by whom he had issue—

John, his successor.

Henry (Sir), of Rundell, governor of the Islands of Guernsey and Jersey, and constable of the castle of Dover, and warden of the cinque ports, temp. Edward I. Sir Henry m. Joane, elder daughter and co-heiress of Stephen de Pencestre, and had issue—

STEPHEN.

He, John, m. secondly, Joane, daughter of Hugh de Nevill, and had a son,

REGINALD, from whom the Cobhams of Sterborough sprang.

JOHN DE COBBEHAM, the eldest son, succeeded his father, and was one of the justices of the courts of King's Bench and Common Pleas, and a baron of the exchequer, in the reigns of Henry III. and Edward I. This learned person m. Joane de Septvaus, one of the co-heirs of Rosse, the widow of Stephen de Pencestre, and had issue,

Henry, his successor.

Reginald, m. Joane, daughter of William de Evere, and obtained a charter in 32nd Edward I. for free warren in all his demesne lands at Pipard's Clive, in the county of Wilts.

The elder son,

HENRY DE COBBEHAM, s. his father, and doing homage in the 26th Edward I. had livery of his lands. In the 4th Edward II., being then styled Henry de Cobbeham, Jun. (his uncle Henry, of Rundell, still living), he was in an expedition into Scotland; and, in four years afterwards, he was constituted constable of Dover Castle, and warden of the cinque ports. In the 10th of the same reign he was again in the wars of Scotland, and in the 15th he was made governor of the castle of Tonebrugge. He had been summoned to parliament as a BARON on the 8th January, 1313, and in continuation for the remainder of his life. His lordship d. in 1339, and was s. by his eldest son,

JOHN DE COBHAM, second Baron Cobham, summoned to parliament from the 19th September, 1342, to 26th August, 1407. This nobleman, who had been made admiral of the king's fleet from the mouth of the Thames westward in the 9th Edward III., had the next year in remuneration of his services, whilst he was a justice of Oyer and Terminer, in Kent, a grant of one hundred marks out of the two hundred which the commons of that county gave to the king in furtherance of the Scottish war. In the 26th of the same monarch he was made a banneret, and in some years afterwards he was engaged in the French wars. In the beginning of Richard II.'s reign his lordship was appointed ambassador upon two occasions to negotiate a peace with the French, and joined in commission by the same monarch with John, Duke of Lancaster, and others, to treat with the Earl of Flanders, and others of that country, for the appeasing of certain discords between them and the English. In the 10th Richard he was one of the thirteen lords then appointed to govern the kingdom, but being impeached in the 21st of the same king he had judgment pronounced against him; his lordship received, however, a pardon, but was sent prisoner to the Isle of Jersey. Lord Cobham m. Margaret, daughter of Hugh Courtenay, Earl of Devon, and had issue,

Joane, who m. Sir John de la Pole, Knt., and dying before her father, left an only daughter,

JOANE, who m. first, Sir Robert Hemengdale, but had no surviving issue.

Her ladyship m. secondly, Sir Reginald Braybroke, by whom she had one surviving daughter,

JOANE, m. to Sir Thomas Brooke, Knt. (see Brooke, Lord Cobham).

She m. thirdly, Sir Nicholas Hawberke, but had no surviving issue; fourthly, SIR JOHN OLDCASTLE, KNT., and fifthly, Sir John Harpenden.

His lordship d. in 1407, leaving his above-mentioned grand-daughter, Joane, then Lady Hawberke, his sole heiress, who marrying subsequently,

SIR JOHN OLDCASTLE, KNT., that gentleman was summoned to parliament, jure uxoris, as BARON COBHAM, from the 26th October, (11th Henry IV.) 1409, to 22nd March, (1st Henry V.) 1413. Sir John Oldcastle is celebrated in history as leader of the LOLLARDS, the first sect of reformers that arose in England, and eventually by laying down his life in maintenance of his principles. Of this celebrated person Dugdale gives the following account—"In the 1st of Henry V., being tainted in his religion by those pretended holy zealots, then called LOLLARDS, he became one of the chief of that sect, which at that time gave no little disturbance to the peace of the church; for which he was cited to appear before the Archbishop of Canterbury. Whereupon, betaking himself to his castle of Couling, he was shortly after apprehended, and brought before the archbishop and others, in the cathedral of St. Paul, and there, by reason of his obstinacy in those dangerous tenets, received the sentence of an heretick. Under the cloak of this sanctity it was, that he and his party designed to murther the king upon Twelfth Night, then keeping his Christmas at Eltham, and to destroy the monasteries of Westminster and St. Albans, as also the cathedral of St. Paul in London, with all the houses of friers in that city; to which end about four score of his party were found, in arms, in the night time, expecting no less than twenty-five thousand the next day to appear with them in St. Giles Fields. Which pernicious purpose being seasonably prevented, divers of them suffered death at that time. But this Oldcastle escaping, lurked privily for a time in sundry places, and endeavoured to raise new commotions. Wherein failing of that success he expected, in anno 1417, 5th Henry V., (the king being then in his wars of France,) he incited the Scots to an invasion of this realm, which, through the vigilancy of John, Duke of Bedford, (the king's brother, and his lieutenant here in his absence,) was happily prevented, and at length being taken in Wales within the territory of the Lord Powys, was brought to his trial, where having judgment of death pronounced against him, viz. to be drawn, hanged, and burnt on the gallows; and accordingly brought to the place of execution, he desired Sir Thomas Erpingham, that in case he saw him rise again the third day after, that then he would be a means to procure favour for the rest of his sect." Walpole, in his Catalogue of Royal and Noble Authors, gives, however, a more flattering and just character of this unfortunate, though highly gifted nobleman—"The first author, as well as the first martyr, among our nobility, was Sir John Oldcastle, called ' the good Lord Cobham;' a man whose virtues made him a reformer, whose valour made him a martyr, whose martyrdom made him an enthusiast. His ready wit and brave spirit appeared to great advantage on his trial." He wrote "Twelve Conclusions, addressed to the parliament of England," and several other tracts. His lordship had an only daughter, Joane, by the heiress of Cobham, who d. young, and the BARONY OF COBHAM appears to have remained dormant from the period of his execution, until revived in the person of JOHN BROOKE, great grandson of the above mentioned Joane de la Pole, in 1445.

ARMS.—Gu. on a chevron or. three lions rampant sa.

COKE — BARON LOVEL OF MINSTER LOVEL, IN THE COUNTY OF OXFORD, VISCOUNT COKE OF HOLKHAM, IN THE COUNTY OF NORFOLK, EARL OF LEICESTER.

Barony,   } by Letters { dated — May, 1728.
Earldom, &c. } Patent, { dated 9th May, 1744.

Lineage.

The learned CAMDEN, who set forth the pedigree of this ancient family, deduced its origin from

WILLIAM COKE, *of Dodington,* in the county of Norfolk, mentioned in a deed anno 1206, who by his wife Felice had issue,

GEFFREY COKE, of the same place, from whom descended,

SIR EDWARD COKE, the celebrated lawyer. This eminent person, the son of Robert Coke, Esq., of Mileham, in the county of Norfolk, and Winifred, his wife, daughter, and one of the heirs of William Knightley, of Morgrave-Knightley, in the same shire, was born at the seat of his father, and at ten years of age sent to the grammar-school at Norwich, whence he removed to Trinity College, Cambridge, where he studied for four years, and was in some years afterwards chosen high-steward of that university. From Cambridge he removed to Clifford's-Inn, and, the year after, he was entered a student in the Inner Temple, whence he was called to the bar, and being chosen reader in Lyon's-Inn acquired so much celebrity, that he very soon attained considerable practice. About this period he married Bridget, daughter and co-heir of John Paston, Esq., of Huntingfield Hall, in the county of Suffolk, third son of Sir William Paston, of Paston, with whom he acquired a fortune of thirty thousand pounds. An alliance, too, that brought him honours and preferments as well as wealth. The cities of Coventry and Norwich soon after elected him their recorder. The county of Norfolk returned him to parliament, and the House of Commons placed him in the speaker's chair. In the 35th of Elizabeth, (1592,) Mr. Coke was appointed *Solicitor,* and the next year *Attorney-general.* In 1603 he received the honour of knighthood from King James I., at Greenwich, and in three years afterwards was elevated to the bench as chief of the court of Common Pleas, from which he was advanced, in 1613, to the dignity of CHIEF JUSTICE OF ENGLAND, (being the last person who bore that title,) and sworn of the privy council. His lordship incurred subsequently, however, the displeasure of the court; and while in disgrace, hearing that a noble lord had solicited from the crown a portion of the lands belonging to the church at Norwich, which he had recovered, and settled thereon, he cautioned the peer to desist, or that he would resume his gown and cap, and come into Westminster Hall once again, to plead the cause of the church. Between his paternal property, the great marriage portion he had with his wife, and his valuable offices and lucrative practice at the bar, Sir Edward Coke realised an estate so ample, that each of his sons

possessed a fortune equal to that of an elder brother. Camden, in his *Britannia,* says, "that he was a person of admirable parts, than whom, as none ever applied himself closer to the study of the law, so never did any one understand it better. Of which he fully convinced England, by his excellent administration for many years together, whilst Attorney-general, and by executing the office of Lord Chief Justice of the Common Pleas with the greatest wisdom and prudence; nor did he give less proof of his abilities in his excellent *Reports,* and Commentaries upon our Laws, whereby he was highly obliged both his own age and posterity." His lordship *d.* on the 3rd September, 1633, at the advanced age of 83. A noble monument was erected to his memory at Tittleshall-church, Norfolk, with his effigies habited in judge's robes, lying at full length, under a canopy supported by two marble pillars, on the top of which are four large figures, and between the pillars two marble tables, with these inscriptions:—

FIRST TABLE.

DEO OPTIMO MAXIMO
Hæ Exuviæ Humanæ Expectant
Resurrectionem Piorum
Hic Situs est non Perituri
Nominis EDVARDUS COKE
EQUES AURAT Legum anima
Interpres Oraculum non Dubium
Arcanorum Promicondus Mysteriorum
Cujus Fere unius Beneficio
Jurisperiti nostri sunt Jurisperiti Eloquentiæ Fulmen
Torrens Fulmen
Suadæ Sacerdos unicus
Divinus Heros
Pro Rostris ita Dixit
ut Literis Insudasse non nisi
Humanis
Ita Vixit ut non nisi Divinis
Sacerrimus intimæ Pietatis
Indagator
Integritas Ipsa Veræ Semper
Causæ Constantissimus Assertor
Nec favore nec Muneribus Violandus
Eximiæ Misericors Charior erat
Huic reus Quam sibi
(Miraculi instar est)
Siccoculus Sæpe ille audiit Sententiam
In se Prolatim Nunquam Hic Nisi
Madidoculus Protulit Scientiæ Oceanus
Quique Dum Vixit Bibliothecæ Parens
Duodecim Liberorum Tredecim
Librorum Pater
Facessant Hinc Monumenta
Facessant Marmora
(Nisi quod Pios Fuisse Denotarint Posteros)
Ipse sibi suum est monumentum
Marmore Perennius
Ipse sibi sua
Est Æternitas.

SECOND TABLE.

DEDICATED TO THE MEMORY OF
SIR EDWARD COKE, KNT.,
A late Reverend Judge. Born
at Mileham, in this County of Norfolk.

Excellent in all Learning, Divine
and Humane. That for his own, this
for his Country's Good, especially
in the Knowledge and Practice of the
Municipall Laws of this Kingdome,
a famous Reader, a sound
Counsellor; in his younger Years
Recorder of the Cities of Norwich and
London. Next, Solicitor-General
to Queen Elizabeth, and Speaker
of the Parliament in the XXXV Years
of hir Reigne. Afterwards Attorney-
General to the same Queen, as also to
her Successor, King James, to both a
faithfull Servant for their Majties.
for their Safties. By King James
constituted Chief Justice of both
Benches successively, in both a just,
in both an exemplary Judge, one of his
Majtys most Hon. Privie Councill, as also
of Council to Queen Anne, and Chief Justice
in Eire of all her Forrests, Parks, and Chases,
Recorder of the Citie of Coventrie, and
High Steward of the University of Cambridge, whereof he was sometime
a Member of Trinitie Colledge.
He had two Wives. By Bridget
his first Wife (one of the Daughters
and co-heirs of John Paston, Esq.,) he had
Issue seven Sons, and three Daughters; and by the Lady Elizabeth, his
second Wife, (one of the Daughters
of the Right Hon. Thomas, late Earl of
Exeter,) he had issue
two Daughters.
A CHAST HUSBAND,
A PROVIDENT FATHER.

And beneath the Effigies the following inscription:—

" He Crown'd his Pious Life with as Pious and
Christian Departure at STOKE POGES in the
County of BUCKINGHAM on Wednesdaye
the third Day of Sept. in the year of our
Lord MDCXXXIII
And of his Age LXXXIII
His Last Words
THY KINGDOME COME THY WILL BE DONE
Learn Reader to Live so
That thou mayst so die."

Sir Edward Coke's daughters, by his last wife, were,
Elizabeth, who d. unmarried.
Frances, m. to John Villiers, Viscount Purbeck, son and heir of Sir George Villiers,
by Mary, Duchess of Buckingham, and
eldest brother, of George, Duke of Buckingham, died s. p.
His surviving children, by his first wife were,
Robert, (Sir) m. Theophila, only daughter of
Thomas, Lord Berkeley, and d. 19th July,
1653, issueless.
Arthur, m. Elizabeth, daughter and heiress of,
Sir George Walgrave, Knt., of Hitcham,
in the county of Norfolk, and left at his
decease, 6th December, 1629, four daughters,
his co-heirs.

132

John, of Holkham, in the county of Norfolk,
m. Meriel, daughter and heiress of Anthony
Wheatley, Esq., (son of William Wheatley,
Prothonotary of the Court of Common
Pleas,) by whom he had seven sons and
seven daughters, whereof EDWARD, his heir
apparent, died before him, leaving no issue
by Elizabeth his wife, daughter of George,
Lord Berkeley, whereby the inheritance
devolved, eventually, upon his youngest
son,
JOHN, who dying unmarried, the estate
of HOLKHAM, came to the heirs of
HENRY COKE, of Thurrington, fifth
son of Sir Edward Coke, (next mentioned).
Henry, of Thurrington, in the county of Suffolk,
m. Margaret, daughter and heiress of Richard
Lovelace, Esq., of Kingsdown, in the
county of Kent, and was s. by his eldest
son,
RICHARD, who m. Mary, daughter of Sir
John Rous, Bart,, of Henham Hall,
in the county of Suffolk, and left an
only son,
ROBERT, of whom hereafter, as inheritor of the principal part of
Sir Edward Coke's fortune, and
grandfather of the first peer.
Clement, m. Sarah, daughter and co-heiress of
Alexander Redich, Esq., of Redich, in the
county of Lancaster, (by a daughter and
co-heiress of Sir Robert Langley, of Age-
croft, in the same shire,) by whom he ac-
quired the estate of Longford, in Derbyshire,
and was s., in May, 1619, by his elder son,
EDWARD COKE, who was created a
baronet, on the 30th December, 1641.
He m. Catherine, daughter and co-
heiress of Sir Lodowick Dyer, Knt., of
Great Stoughton, in the county of
Huntingdon, and had issue,
Robert, } successive Baronets.
Edward, }
Catharine, m. to Cornelius Clarke,
Esq., of Norton.
Sir Edward was s. by his elder son,
SIR ROBERT COKE, of Longford, second
Baronet, M.P. for the county of Derby,
in the 1st of James II., who m. Sarah,
daughter and co-heiress of —— Barker,
Esq., of Abrightlee, in the county of
Salop, but dying s. p., in 1617, the title
and estates devolved upon his brother,
SIR EDWARD COKE, of Longford, third
baronet, at whose decease, unmarried,
25th August, 1727, the baronetcy ex-
pired, while the estates passed by the
baronet's will, to Edward Coke, Esq.,
brother of Thomas, first Lord Lovel.
Anne, m. to Ralph Sadler, Esq., son and heir
of Sir Ralph Sadler, Knt.
Bridget, m. to William Skinner Esq., son and
heir of Sir Vincent Skinner.
So much for the lord chief justice's children, we
now return to the grandson of his son, HENRY,

ROBERT COKE, Esq., of Thurrington, who upon the decease of his cousin, (the son of his great uncle John,) John Coke, Esq., of Holkham, in the county of Norfolk, unmarried, inherited that estate, and thus became possessed of the chief part of (Sir Edward Coke) his great grandfather's property. Mr. Coke m. Lady Anne Osborne, daughter of Thomas, first Duke of Leeds, Lord Treasurer of England, by whom he had an only surviving son, his successor at his decease, 16th January, 1679.

EDWARD COKE, Esq., who m. Carey, daughter of Sir John Newton, Bart., of Barrows Court, in the county of Gloucester, and had issue,

    Thomas, his successor.

      Edward, of Longford, in the county of Derby, who bequeathed at his decease, unmarried, in 1733, that estate to his younger brother,

      Robert, Vice-Chamberlain to Queen Anne, who m. in June, 1733, Lady Jane Holt, widow of John Holt, Esq., of Redgrave, in the county of Suffolk, and sister and coheiress of Philip, Duke of Wharton, but died s. p.

      Carey, m. to Sir Marmaduke Wyvil, Bart., of Constable Burton, in the county of York.

      Anne, m. to Philip Roberts, a Major in the second troop of Horse Guards, and left a son,

        Wenman Roberts, of whom hereafter, as heir to the entire of the estates of his uncle, the Earl of Leicester.

Mr. Coke d. 13th April, 1707, and was s. by his eldest son,

THOMAS COKE, Esq., who was elected a knight of the Bath, on the 27th May, 1725, and elevated to the peerage, on the 28th May, 1728, as Baron Lovel, of Minster Lovel, in the county of Oxford. In 1733, his lordship was constituted joint post-master-general, and created on the 9th May, 1744, Viscount Coke, of Holkham, and Earl of Leicester; his lordship m., 2nd July, 1718, Lady Mary Tufton, fourth daughter and co-heiress of Thomas, sixth Earl of Thanet, (in which lady's favour, the abeyance of the Barony de Clifford, was terminated by the crown, in 1734,) by whom he had an only son,

      Edward, Viscount Coke, who m. in 1747, Lady Mary Campbell, daughter and coheiress of John, Duke of Argyll and Greenwich, but died s. p. in the lifetime of his father, anno 1753.

The earl d. 20th April, 1759, and thus leaving no issue, the Barony of Lovel, and Earldom of Leicester, with the viscounty, became extinct.

His lordship commenced the stately pile of building, called Holkham Hall, in Norfolk, which was completed by the countess, who survived him many years; her ladyship died in 1775. The whole of the extensive estates of the Earl of Leicester devolved upon his nephew, (refer to Anne, youngest daughter of Edward Coke, Esq., and Carey, daughter of Sir John Newton, Bart.,) Wenman Roberts, Esq., who thereupon assumed the surname of Coke, only, and marrying Miss Elisabeth Chamberlayne, left with two daughters, and a younger son, Edward, the present Thomas William

Coke, of Holkham, M.P. for the county of Norfolk.

Arms.—Parly per pale gu. and ar. three eagles displayed ar.

COLEPEPER — BARONS COLEPEPER, OF THORESWAY, IN THE COUNTY OF LINCOLN.

By Letters Patent, dated 21st October, 1644.

Lineage.

The family of Colepeper flourished in the counties of Kent and Sussex from the time of Edw. I., and produced many eminent characters, amongst whom were Sir Jeoffrey Colepeper, of Pepenbury, high-sheriff of Kent in the reign of that monarch, and Sir Thomas Colepeper, of Bedgbury, governor of Winchelsea, temp. Edward II. These eminent persons sealed with a bend engrailed, gules on a field argent; and Drayton, in his Barons' Wars, enumerating the arms of the distinguished families on each side, says,

    " And Colepeper, with silver arms inrail'd,
    Bare thereupon a bloody bend engrail'd."

JOHN COLEPEPER was a judge in the reign of Henry VI., and left an only daughter and heiress, who conveyed a considerable fortune to the family of Harrington, into which she married. Richard Colepeper, of Oxheath, was sheriff of Kent in the reign of Edward IV.; and King Henry VIII. set up the arms of two of the name in his gallery at Whitehall, for their military achievements at Tournay and the Battle of Spurs.

SIR JOHN COLEPEPER, of Bedgbury, knight of the shire for Kent in the parliament which met in 1641, chancellor of the exchequer, and afterwards master of the rolls, and one of the privy-council of King Charles I., was elevated to the peerage by that monarch on the 21st October, 1644, as Lord Colepeper, Baron of Thoresway, in the county of Lincoln. His lordship adhered zealously to the royal cause during the whole of the civil wars, and withdrew with King Charles II., in whose exile he shared for twelve years, but had the high gratification of witnessing the restoration of his royal master. Lord Colepeper m. first, Philippa, daughter of Sir ——— Snelling, Knt., and had issue,

    Alexander, who m. Catherine, daughter and heiress of Sir Edward Ford, Knt., of Harting, Sussex, but predeceased his father, issueless.

    Philippa, m. to Thomas Harlakenden, Esq., of Wood Church, in the county of Kent.

His lordship m. secondly, Judith, daughter of Sir Thomas Colepeper, of Hollingburn, Knt., by whom he had four sons,

    Thomas, his successor.

    John.

    Cheney.

    Francis

And three daughters, viz.,

    Elisabeth, m. to James Hamilton, Esq., and had by him,

JAMES, EARL OF ABERCORN.

Judith, *m.* to —— Colepeper, Esq.

Philippa.

Lord Colepeper *d.* master of the rolls, in July, 1680, and was *s.* by his eldest son,

THOMAS COLEPEPER, second baron, who *m.* Margaret, daughter and co-heir of Seigneur Jean de Hesse, of the noble family of HESSE, in Germany, by whom he had an only daughter and heiress,

Catherine, *m.* to Thomas, Lord Fairfax, and conveyed to her husband Ledes Castle, in Kent.

His lordship *d.* in 1688, and, leaving no male issue, the title devolved upon his brother,

JOHN COLEPEPER, third baron. This nobleman *m.* Frances, daughter of Sir Thomas Colepeper, of Hollingburn, in the county of Kent, but dying *s. p.* in 1719, was *s.* by his brother,

CHENEY COLEPEPER, fourth baron, at whose decease, issueless, (his younger brother, Francis, having previously died unmarried,) in 1725, the BARONY OF COLEPEPER became EXTINCT.

ARMS—Ar. a bend engrailed gu.

COLLINGWOOD — BARON COLLINGWOOD, OF COLDBURNE AND HETHPOOL, IN THE COUNTY OF NORTHUMBERLAND.

By Letters Patent, dated 20th Nov. 1905.

Lineage.

CUTHBERT COLLINGWOOD, *b.* 1750, son of Cuthbert Collingwood, Esq., of Ditchburne, in the county of Northumberland, having adopted the naval profession, obtained the rank of lieutenant in 1775 —was made post-captain in 1780—advanced to the rank of rear-admiral of the white in 1795—rear-admiral of the red in 1801—vice-admiral of the blue in 1804, in which commission he had the glory of being second in command at the memorable battle off Cape Trafalgar, on the 21st October, 1805, under the immortal Nelson; and for the services rendered upon that triumphant occasion, the vice-admiral obtained the professional promotion of vice-admiral of the blue, and was advanced to the peerage on the 20th November, 1805, as BARON COLLINGWOOD, of *Coldburne and Hethpool*, in the county of Northumberland. His lordship *m.* Patience, daughter and co-heiress of Erasmus Blackett, Esq., alderman of Newcastle-upon-Tyne, by whom he had issue,

Sarah.

Mary-Patience.

His lordship died in 1810, when, leaving no male issue, the barony of COLLINGWOOD became EXTINCT.

COLUMBERS — BARON COLUMBERS.

By Writ of Summons, dated 29th July, 1314, 8 Edward II.

Lineage.

In the second year of Henry II.,

PHILIP DE COLUMBERS paid *four pounds*

upon the collection of the impost, then denominated *danegelt*; and in twelve years afterwards, upon the assessment of aid for marrying the king's daughter, he certified, among the other barons, his knights' fees, *de vetori feoffamento*, to be ten, and *de novo*, one, for all which he paid the sum of six pounds thirteen shillings and four-pence. He *d.* soon afterwards, about the year 1186, leaving three sons,

PHILIP, his heir.

WILLIAM.

HENRY, whose daughter, Georgia, *m.* Hugh de Longchamp.

PHILIP DE COLUMBERS succeeded his father, and was *s.* himself, at his decease, anno 1216, by his son,

PHILIP DE COLUMBERS. This feudal lord, who distinguished himself in the French wars of Henry III., obtained license to impark his manor of Stavey, in the county of Somerset, which was the head of his barony. His lordship *m.* Egeline, daughter of Robert de Courtenay, and was *s.*, at his decease in 1256, by his elder son,

SIR PHILIP DE COLUMBERS, who, having been in the expedition made into Gascony in the 38th Henry III., received the honour of knighthood for his services upon that occasion. His lordship *d.* in 1276, and, having no issue, was succeeded by his brother,

JOHN DE COLUMBERS. This feudal lord was in the expedition made into Wales in the 10th Edward I; and in the 22d of the same monarch, he had summons to attend the king, to give his advice upon the urgent affairs of the realm; shortly after which he received command to be at Portsmouth, in order to proceed in the expedition to Gascony: but upon his arrival on the French soil, he abandoned his standard, and joined the enemy, for which treason his lands were all immediately seised. We find him, however, subsequently, (having made his peace,) in the Scotch wars, 32d Edward I., and again in two years afterwards. His lordship *m.* Alice, one of the daughters and co-heirs of Stephen de Pencester, and was *s.*, at his decease about the year 1305, by his elder son,

PHILIP DE COLUMBERS, who was summoned to parliament as BARON COLUMBERS, from the 29th July, 1314, to 3d March, 1341. In the 13th of Edward III., his lordship was associated with Hugh de Courtenay, Earl of Devonshire, in guarding the coast of Hampshire. He *m.* Alianore, one of the sisters and heirs of William, son of William Martin, but died without issue in 1342, leaving STEPHEN DE COLUMBERS, priest of the church of Shirewell, his brother and heir. At the decease of his lordship, the barony of COLUMBERS became EXTINCT.

ARMS—Gu., a bend or.

COLVILE—BARONS COLVILE.

By Writ of Summons, dated 14th December, 1264, 49 Henry III.

Lineage.

In the time of King Stephen,

PHILIP DE COLVILE, being opposed to that

monarch, built a castle in Yorkshire, and fortified it against him, but which Stephen invested, reduced, and demolished. In the ensuing reign we find this feudal lord one of the witnesses to the agreement between the King of England, and the King of Scots, by which the latter obliging himself to be faithful to King Henry, did homage to him at York. To this Philip succeeded,

WILLIAM DE COLVILE, one of the barons who took up arms against John, and was excommunicated by the Pope. This William, being taken prisoner at the battle of Lincoln, in the 1st Henry III, his wife Maude had safe conduct to the king, to treat for his liberation, and having accomplished her object, obtained a royal precept to William, Earl of Albemarle, for the restoration of her husband's castle, at Birham, in the county of Lincoln. William de Colvile was s. by his son,

ROBERT DE COLVILE, who had also taken up arms against John, and in the 17th of that monarch's reign, had letters of safe conduct, with Roger de Jarpevill, to the royal presence, to treat of peace on behalf of the barons. Continuing, however, in rebellion, he was taken prisoner by Falcase de Breant, in the 1st Henry III. To this Robert succeeded,

WALTER DE COLVILE, a person of no less turbulent disposition than his predecessors. Joining with Montfort, Earl of Leicester, he was taken prisoner by Prince Edward, at Kenilworth, in the 49th Henry III, but under the decree, called the "Dictum of Kenilworth," was admitted to a compensation for his lands which had been seized, and he appears to have been summoned to parliament as a BARON in the same year, 14th December, 1264. His lordship d. in 1276, and was s. by his son,

ROGER DE COLVILE, second baron, who was sheriff of Norfolk and Suffolk, in the 51st Henry III., and paid £100. fine in the 14th Edward I., for permission to marry Ermentrude, widow of Stephen de Cressy, by whom he had issue,

    EDMUND, his successor.

    Elizabeth, m. to —— Basset, of Sapcote, in the county of Lincoln, and had,

      SIMON, whose son and heir,

        RALPH BASSET, of Sapcote, became eventually co-heir to the Colviles.

    Alice, m. —— Gernun, and had,

    John Gernun, who became eventually co-heir to the Colviles.

His lordship d. in 1287, and was s. by his son,

EDMUND DE COLVILE, third baron, but never summoned to parliament. This nobleman m. Margaret, daughter of Robert de Ufford, and dying in 1315, was s. by his son,

ROBERT DE COLVILE, fourth baron, summoned to parliament, from 25th February, 1342, to 20th January, 1368. His lordship d. in 1368, and was s. by his son,

WALTER DE COLVILE, fifth baron, but never summoned to parliament. His lordship m. Margaret, daughter and heiress of Giles de Bassingburne, and had issue a son,

ROBERT DE COLVILE, who died without issue, leaving Ralph Basset, of Sapcote, and John

Gernun, (above mentioned,) his heirs, between whose descendants and representatives, it is presumed, the BARONY OF COLVILE is now in ABEYANCE.

ARMS.—Or. a fesse gules.

COMPTON — BARON WILMINGTON, OF WIMINGTON, IN THE COUNTY OF SUSSEX. VISCOUNT PEVENSEY, AND EARL OF WILMINGTON.

Barony, Earldom, &c. }	by Letters Patent, {	11th January, 1728. 14th May, 1730.

Lineage.

The Right Honourable

SIR SPENCER COMPTON, K.B., third son of James, third earl of Northampton, having filled the speaker's chair of the House of Commons, in the parliaments of 1714, and 1722, and subsequently, the offices of paymaster general of his majesty's land forces, and treasurer of Chelsea Hospital, was elevated to the peerage on the 11th January, 1728, as *Baron Wilmington*. In 1730, his lordship was constituted lord privy seal, and advanced on the 14th May, in that year, to the dignities of *Viscount Pevensey*, and EARL OF WILMINGTON. In the December following, he was declared lord president of the council, and installed on the 22nd August, 1726, a KNIGHT of the GARTER. He was also one of the lord's justices during the king's absence in Hanover, and one of the governors of the Charter House. This nobleman, who was esteemed a personage of great worth, abilities, and integrity, died unmarried in July, 1743, when ALL his honours became EXTINCT; while his estates, passed by his lordship's bequest to his brother, George, fourth Earl of Northampton, and have since been carried by that nobleman's great grand-daughter, Lady Elizabeth Compton, only daughter and heiress of Charles, seventh Earl of Northampton, into the Cavendish family, upon her ladyship's marriage in 1782, with Lord George Cavendish, uncle and heir presumptive of His Grace the Duke of Devonshire. The Barony of Wilmington was revived on 7th September, 1812, in the advancement of Charles, ninth and late earl, to the Marquisate of Northampton.

ARMS.—Sa. a lion, passant, guardant, or. betw. three helmets ar.

COMYN — EARL OF NORTHUMBERLAND.

Conferred by William, the Conqueror, anno 1068.

Lineage.

In the third year of King William, the Conqueror, that monarch conferred the Earldom of Northumberland, vacant by the death of Earl Copsi, upon

ROBERT COMYN; but the nomination accorded so little with the wishes of the inhabitants of the county, that they at first resolved to abandon entirely their dwellings; being prevented doing so, however, by the inclemency of the season, it was then determined, at all hazards, to put the new earl to death. Of this evil design, his lordship had intimation, through Egelivine, Bishop of Durham, but disregarding the intelligence, he repaired to Durham, with seven hundred soldiers, and commenced a course of plunder and bloodshed, which rousing the inhabitants of the neighbourhood, the town was assaulted and carried, by a multitude of country people, and the earl and all his troops, to a man, put to death. This occurrence took place in 1069, in a few months after his lordship's appointment to the earldom.

ARMS.—Gu. three garbs or.

CONINGSBY—BARON CONINGSBY, OF CONINGSBY, IN THE COUNTY OF LINCOLN, EARL OF CONINGSBY. BARONESS AND VISCOUNTESS CONINGSBY, OF HAMPTON COURT, IN THE COUNTY OF HEREFORD.

English Barony,	by Letters Patent,	18th June, 1715.
—— Earldom,		30th April, 1719.
Baroness and Viscountess,		26th Jan., 1716.

Lineage.

The surname of this family was originally assumed from the town of Coningsby, in the county of Salop, and the Coningsbys are said to have been of ancient descent, but they do not appear to have attained much importance until the period of the revolution. A THOMAS DE CONINGSBIE certainly distinguished himself in the martial reign of Edward III., and participated in the glory of POICTIERS, and the family of which we are about to treat may have sprung from him, but of that there is no evidence.

THOMAS CONINGSBY, Esq., having zealously promoted the revolution, attended King William into Ireland, and was present at the battle of the Boyne; where, being close to his majesty when the king received a slight wound in the shoulder, he was the first to apply a handkerchief to the hurt. He was, subsequently, upon William's departure from Ireland, constituted lord justice with Lord Sidney, and elevated to the peerage of that kingdom as BARON CONINGSBY, of Clanbrassil, in the county of Armagh, on the 17th April, 1693. In which year his lordship was sworn of the privy council in England, and again in the reign of Queen Anne, when he was made vice-treasurer and paymaster of the forces in Ireland. Upon the accession of King George I. he was made a peer of Great Britain, (18th June, 1715,) in the dignity of BARON CONINGSBY, of Coningsby, in the county of Lincoln, and created EARL OF CONINGSBY, also in the peerage of Great Britain,

136

on the 30th April, 1719, both honours being in remainder to MARGARET, Viscountess Coningsby, his eldest daughter by his second wife, and her heirs male. His lordship m. first, Miss Gorges, daughter of Ferdinando Gorges, Esq., of Eye, in the county of Hereford, by whom he had issue,

THOMAS, who m. ——, daughter of John Carr, Esq., of Northumberland, and dying in the lifetime of his father, left issue,

Thomas, who d. unmarried.

RICHARD, who s. his grandfather in the Irish BARONY of CONINGSBY, of Clanbrassil. His lordship m. Judith, daughter of Sir Thomas Lawley, Bart., but died s. p. on the 18th December, 1729, when the dignity EXPIRED.

Melior, m. to Thomas, first Lord Southwell.

Barbara, m. to George Eyre, Esq., of Eyre-Court, in the county of Galway.

Lettice, m. to Edward Denny, Esq., of Tralee, in the county of Kerry.

Lord Coningsby m. secondly, Frances, daughter and co-heir of Richard, Earl of Ranelagh, by whom he had two surviving daughters, viz.

Margaret, who, in the lifetime of her father (26th January, 1716), was created BARONESS AND VISCOUNTESS CONINGSBY, of Hampton-Court, in the county of Hereford, with remainder to her heirs male.

Frances, m. to Charles Hanbury Williams, Esq.

The earl d. on the 1st May, 1729, when the BARONY OF CONINGSBY, of Clanbrassil, devolved upon his grandson, RICHARD, as stated above, and EXPIRED with that nobleman in the same year, while his dignities of Great Britain passed according to the limitation to his eldest daughter (by his second wife),

MARGARET, Viscountess Coningsby, of Hampton-Court, who then became COUNTESS OF CONINGSBY. Her ladyship m. Sir Michael Newton, K.B., by whom she had an only son,

John, who d. in infancy.

Lady Coningsby d. in 1761, when leaving no issue, all her own honours and those inherited from her father became EXTINCT.

ARMS.—Gu. three conies sejeant ar.

CONWAY—BARONS CONWAY, OF RAGLEY, IN THE COUNTY OF WARWICK, VISCOUNTS CONWAY, OF CONWAY CASTLE, IN THE COUNTY OF CAERNARVON, AND EARL OF CONWAY.

The English Barony,	by Letters Patent,	22nd March, 1624.
—— Viscounty		6th June, 1696.
—— Earldom,		3rd Dec., 1679.

Lineage.

From

SIR HENRY CONWAY, who was retained in the 5th Richard II. to do that monarch service as a knight all his life, and in time of peace, to have diet for himself, one esquire, one chamberlain, and four grooms ; as also hay, oats, horse-shoes and nails for six horses, descended

JOHN CONWAY, Esq., of Potrithan, in the county of Flint, whose son,

SIR HUGH CONWAY, received the honour of knighthood at the coronation of Queen Elizabeth, consort of King Henry VII., having been previously a zealous supporter of the interests of that monarch, and master of his wardrobe. From this Sir Hugh lineally sprang,

EDWARD CONWAY, Esq., one of the gentlemen ushers of the chamber to King Henry VIII., who m. Anne, daughter and heiress of Richard Burdett, Esq., of Arrow, in the county of Warwick, and was s. by his son,

SIR JOHN CONWAY, Knt., who being in the great expedition made into Scotland in the 1st year of Edward VI., distinguished himself so highly as to be made a BANNERET. Sir John m. Catherine, daughter of Sir Ralph Verney, Knt., and was s. at his decease, some time in the reign of Edward VI. by his son,

SIR JOHN CONWAY, who was made governor of Ostend, by Robert, Earl of Leicester, in the year 1586. He m. Elene, daughter of Sir Fulke Greville, of Beauchamps Court, in the county of Warwick, and dying in the 1st year of King James I., was s. by his son,

SIR EDWARD CONWAY. This gallant person received the honour of knighthood from Robert, Earl of Essex, at the sacking of Cadix, where he commanded a regiment in 1596. After which he served in the Netherlands, and was governor of the Brill. In the 20th James I. he was constituted one of the principal secretaries of state, and elevated to the peerage on the 22nd March, 1624, as BARON CONWAY, of Ragley, in the county of Warwick, a manor acquired by purchase towards the close of Queen Elizabeth's reign. His lordship was appointed captain of the Isle of Wight in the December following, and being again secretary of state in the 1st King Charles I., was advanced to the IRISH VISCOUNTY OF KILLULTAGH, in the county of Antrim, in 1626, in which year, on the 6th June, he was created VISCOUNT CONWAY, OF CONWAY CASTLE, in the county of Caernarvon. His lordship filled afterwards the high office of PRESIDENT OF THE COUNCIL, and was accredited upon some occasion ambassador extraordinary to the court of Vienna. His lordship m. Dorothy, daughter of Sir John Tracy, Knt., of Lodington, in the county of Gloucester, and widow of Edward Bray, Esq., by whom he had issue, EDWARD, his successor; Thomas (Sir), a lieutenant-colonel in the army in the wars in Germany, and Ralph; with four daughters, viz.

Frances, m. to Sir William Pelham, Knt., of Brocklesby, in the county of Lincoln.

Brilliana, m. to Sir Robert Harley, Knt., of Brampton Bryan, in the county of Hereford.

Heligawrth, m. to Sir William Smith, Knt., of the county of Essex.

Mary.

The viscount d. in 1630, and was s. by his eldest son,

EDWARD CONWAY, second Viscount, who had been summoned to parliament in the 4th of Charles I., in his father's BARONY of CONWAY. His lordship m. first, Frances, daughter of Sir Francis Popham, Knt., of Littlecot, in the county of Somerset, by whom he had two surviving sons, Edward and Francis, and two daughters, Dorothy, m. to Sir George Rawdon, Bart., of Moira, in the county of Down, (ancestor of the Lords Moira, of Ireland ;) and Anne. His lordship m. secondly, Katherine, daughter of Giles Heicriblock, of Ghent, but had no issue. He d. in 1655, and was s. by his eldest surviving son,

EDWARD CONWAY, 4th Viscount, who was created EARL OF CONWAY, on the 3rd December, 1679, and was for some time secretary of state. His lordship m. first, Elizabeth, daughter of Sir Heneage Finch, Serjeant at Law, and Recorder of London, and sister of the Lord Chancellor, Heneage, (Finch,) first Earl of Nottingham, by whom he had an only son, Heneage, who died in infancy. He m. secondly, Elizabeth, daughter of Henry Booth, Earl of Warrington, and thirdly, Ursula, daughter of Colonel Stawel, but had no surviving issue. He died in 1683, when all his HONOURS became EXTINCT ; but the principal part of his extensive estates passed, by his lordship's will, to the sons of Sir Edward Seymour, Bart., of Bury Pomeroy, by his second wife, Lettice, daughter of —— Popham, Esq., of Littlecote, with the injunction, that the inheritor should assume the surname and arms of CONWAY. This fortune was first inherited by POPHAM SEYMOUR, Esq., who assumed, of course, the name of Conway, but that gentleman falling in a duel with Colonel Kirk, 4th June, 1699, and dying unmarried, it passed to his brother, FRANCIS SEYMOUR, Esq., who assumed likewise the surname of Conway, and was afterwards created BARON CONWAY, of Ragley, which BARONY now merges in the MARQUISATE OF HERTFORD.

ARMS.—S. on a bend cotised ar. a rose betw. two annulets gules.

COPSI — EARL OF NORTHUMBERLAND.

Conferred by William the Conqueror, anno 1068.

Lineage.

The EARLDOM of the county of NORTHUMBERLAND, was held at the time of the conquest, by

MORKAR, younger son of Algar, Earl of the county of Chester, and he was left undisturbed in the dignity, until he rose in rebellion against the new monarch, when he forfeited the earldom, which was then conferred upon

COPSI, (uncle of Tofti, a very distinguished Earl of Northumberland under the Saxon rule,) in consideration of the high character he had attained in council. The new earl immediately expelled from his territory, Osulph, whom Morkar had placed there as his deputy, but that chief collecting a force, compelled Earl Copsi to seek shelter in the church of Newburne, which being fired, the Earl of Northumberland was seized by his opponent in an attempt to escape, and was decapitated at the door of the church, on the fourth Ides of March, in the fifth week after he had the administration of those parts committed to him; but in the very next autumn, Osulph himself was slain by a robber, with whom he came casually into conflict.

CORBET—BARONS CORBET.

By Writ of Summons, dated 23rd June, 1295, 23 Edward I.

Lineage.

In the time of William the Conqueror,

The brothers, { ROGER } sons of CORBET, and { ROBERT, } held of Roger de Montgomery, divers lordships in the county of Salop, and were munificent benefactors to the church. From the younger descended

ROBERT CORBET, Lord of Caus, &c., in the county of Salop, who in the time of Henry II., paid twenty marks for trespassing in the king's forests. And in the 6th of Richard I., upon the collection of the scutage for that monarch's redemption, answered four pounds, as also twenty shillings more, for one knight's fee. This Robert, was s. by his son,

THOMAS CORBET, who, siding with the barons in the latter end of the reign of John, had his castle of Caus seised, but making his peace and doing homage, it was restored in the 2nd Henry III. This feudal lord d. in three years afterwards, and was s. by his son,

THOMAS CORBET, who in the 17th of Henry III., was compelled with other barons marchers to give a pledge to the crown for his good conduct. This Thomas was cast, in the 20th of the same reign, in a law-suit, which he had with Avice and Lucie, the daughters and heiresses of Roger de Say, for a wood at Ambaldeston. In the 22nd of Henry III., he had summons as a baron marcher, to attend the king at Oxford, to consult touching certain proceedings of Lewelin, Prince of Wales. In the 32nd of this same monarch, he was constituted sheriff of the counties of Salop and Stafford, and he held that office for two years and a half. In a few years afterwards, he attended the king in his expedition into Wales, and had command to aid Hamon le Strange, in driving the Welch from Montgomery. He was subsequently engaged several times in the Welch wars. This feudal lord m. Isabell, daughter of Reginald, and sister of Roger Valletort, Baron of Huberton, and had issue,

PETER, his successor.

Alice, m. to Robert de Stafford, and had issue, Nicholas de Stafford, whose son, Edmund de Stafford, was father of RALPH, LORD STAFFORD.

Emme, m. to Sir Bryan de Brampton, and had, Walter de Brampton, father of Sir Bryan de Brampton, who left two daughters, co-heiresses, Margaret, m. to Robert Harley, Esq., ancestor of the Earls of Oxford.

Elizabeth, m. to Edmund de Cornwall.

His lordship d. in 1273, and was s. by his son,

PETER CORBET, who having distinguished himself in the wars of King Edward I., was summoned to parliament as a BARON by that monarch, from the 23rd June, 1295, to 26th September, 1300. In the 27th of the same reign, his lordship was found by inquisition, to be one of the next heirs to Roger de Valletort. He d. in 1300, and was s. by his second, but eldest surviving son,

PETER CORBET, second Baron Corbet, summoned to parliament from 13th September, 1302, to 14th March, 1322. His lordship m. Beatrix, daughter of John, Lord Beauchamp, of Hacche, but died without issue, in 1322, when he was s. by his brother,

JOHN CORBET, third Baron, at whose decease, s. p., the BARONY OF CORBET, became EXTINCT, while (the descendants of the deceased lord's aunts,) Ralph, Lord Stafford, and Sir Robert Harley, became his heirs.

ARMS.—Or. a raven ppr.

CORBET—VISCOUNTESS CORBET, OF LINCHDALE, IN THE COUNTY OF SALOP.

By Letters Patent, dated anno 1679. The dignity for life only.

Lineage.

DAME SARAH CORBET, widow of Sir Vincent Corbet, Bart., of Moreton Corbet, in the county of Salop, (a descendant of the old Lords Corbet, of Caus Castle,) and daughter of Sir Robert Monson, of Carlton, in the county of Lincoln, was elevated to the peerage, by letters patent, dated in 1679, for life only, as VISCOUNTESS CORBET, OF LINCHDALE. Her ladyship's son, Sir Vincent Corbet, second Baronet, left a son, Sir Vincent Corbet, third Baronet, at whose decease, s. p., in 1688, the baronetcy became extinct. The peerage EXPIRED of course, with the viscountess.

NOTE.—Upon the demise of Sir Vincent Corbet, in 1688, the estates of the family reverted to that gentleman's great uncle, Richard Corbet, Esq., of Shrewsbury, whose lineal descendant, Andrew Corbet, Esq., was created a BARONET, in 1808, and is the present SIR ANDREW CORBET, of Moreton Corbet.

CORNWALL — BARON FANHOPE, IN THE COUNTY OF HEREFORD. BARON MILBROKE, IN THE COUNTY OF BEDFORD.

Barony of Fanhope, 17th July, 1433.
Barony of Milbroke, 30th January, 1442.

Lineage.

The first notice of
SIR JOHN CORNWALL, K.G., occurs in the

20th of Richard II., when, being retained to serve the king during his life, he obtained a grant of 100 marks per annum. In the 2d of Henry IV., Sir John, having deported himself with great gallantry in justing against a Frenchman at York, in the presence of the king, won the heart of that monarch's sister, Elizabeth, widow of John Holland, Earl of Huntingdon, whose hand he soon afterwards obtained, and with her considerable grants from the crown to enjoy during the lady's life, with a rent charge of 400 marks per annum for his own. In five years afterwards he was again distinguished at a tournament held in London, where he triumphed over a Scottish knight; and he was subsequently one of the companions in arms of the gallant Hen. V. at the glorious battle of AGINCOURT. In the 5th of the same reign, he was constituted one of the commissioners to treat with the captain of the castle of Caen for the surrender of that fortress; and upon the departure of his royal master from France, he was left behind for the defence of those parts; for all which important services, and in consideration of his connection with the house of Plantagenet, Sir John Cornwall was advanced by King Henry VI., in open parliament, to the dignity of a BARON of the realm, under the title of BARON FANHOPE, of Fanhope, in the county of Hereford, on the 17th July, 1433, and created, on the 30th January, 1442, BARON MILBROKE, to bear that title as a free denizen of this realm, &c.; but he was always summoned to parliament as "Johanni Cornewayll Chevalier." In the 12th of Henry VI., his lordship was made governor of the town of St. Selerine, then won by assault; shortly after which he had a grant of the custody of Charles, Duke of Orleans, during the time of the restraint of that prince in England.

This gallant nobleman outlived his wife, the Princess Elizabeth, by whom he had no issue,* and died in 1443, when the BARONIES OF FANHOPE AND MILBROKE became EXTINCT. His lordship left two illegitimate sons, JOHN and THOMAS, for whom he provided in his will.

ARMS.—Erm. a lion rampant, gu. crowned or. within a bordure sa. besantée.

CORNWALLIS — MARQUESSES CORNWALLIS.

By Letters Patent, dated 15th August, 1792.

Lineage.

CHARLES CORNWALLIS, second earl Cornwallis, born 31st December, 1738, having distinguished himself as a military commander in India, was created MARQUESS CORNWALLIS on the 15th August, 1792. In 1799 his lordship was appointed LORD LIEUTENANT OF IRELAND, and commander of the forces there; in which high situation he acquired the reputation of having restored public

* No issue, so says Dugdale; but Heylin, in his Lists of the Earls of Arundel, states that John Fitz-Alan, Lord Maltravers, espoused for his second wife, Maud, daughter of Sir John Cornwall, Lord Fanhope; and Lysson asserts that his lordship had one legitimate son slain in France in his own life-time.

tranquillity at that unhappy period by the firmness, moderation, and humanity which governed his councils. In 1804, the marquess had the honour of being placed a second time at the head of the government of India, as governor-general, and died there on the 5th October, in the following year. His lordship m., in July, 1768, Jemima, daughter of James Jones, Esq., and had issue,

  CHARLES, his successor.

  Mary, m. in 1785, to Mark Singleton, Esq., M.P., principal store-keeper to the ordnance.

The marquess, who was a KNIGHT of the GARTER, was s. by his eldest son,

CHARLES CORNWALLIS, third earl and second marquess, born 19th October, 1774, m. 17th April, 1797, Louisa, fourth daughter of Alexander, fourth Duke of Gordon, and had issue,

  Jane, m. to Richard, third and present Lord Braybroke.

  Louisa.

  Jemima, m. to Lord Eliot, eldest son of the Earl of St. Germans.

  Mary, m. to Charles Ross, Esq.

  Elizabeth.

His lordship d. in 1823, when the MARQUISATE OF CORNWALLIS EXPIRED; but the EARLDOM and other honours reverted to his uncle, John, Lord Bishop of Litchfield and Coventry, and are extant in his lordship's son, James, present EARL CORNWALLIS.

ARMS.—Sa. guttee d'eau, on a fesse ar., three Cornish choughs ppr.

COSPATRICK — EARL OF NORTHUMBERLAND.

Conferred by William the Conqueror, anno 1069.

Lineage.

Upon the death of Robert Comyn, Earl of Northumberland,

COSPATRICK, son of Maldred, son of Crinan, (which Maldred was progenitor to the second dynasty of the great family of Neville, still represented by the earls of Abergavenny,) obtained the earldom of the county of Northumberland from the Conqueror for a large sum of money; but soon afterwards becoming dissatisfied with the sway of the new ruler, his lordship, with other northern chiefs, fled into Scotland, taking with them young EDGAR ATHELING, Agitha, his mother, and Margaret and Christian, his sisters, and were well received by King Malcolm.

From Scotland the earl made several hostile incursions into England, and was deprived of the earldom for those repeated treasons. He subsequently obtained Dunbar, with the adjacent lands in Loudon, from the Scottish monarch for his subsistence, but died soon afterwards, leaving three sons and a daughter,

  Julian, whom King Henry II. gave in marriage to Ranulph de Merley, of Morpeth, a great Northumberland baron.

ARMS.—Gules, a saltier ar.

COTTINGTON—BARON COTTINGTON, OF HAMWORTH, IN THE COUNTY OF MIDDLESEX.

By Letters Patent, dated 19th July, 1631.

Lineage.

FRANCIS COTTINGTON, Esq., fourth son of Philip Cottington, Esq., of Godmanston, in the county of Somerset, having held the office of clerk of the council in the reign of King James I., and being secretary to Charles, Prince of Wales, was created a BARONET by that monarch on the 16th February, 1623. After the accession of King Charles I., Sir Francis Cottington was constituted chancellor and under treasurer of the exchequer; and being accredited ambassador to the court of Madrid, for the purpose of negociating a peace, he was elevated to the peerage on the 10th July, 1631, as LORD COTTINGTON, *Baron of Hanworth*, in the county of Middlesex. His lordship was next commissioned to exercise the important office of lord treasurer during the king's absence in Scotland, in the 9th Charles I., and was constituted master of the wards upon his majesty's return. During the civil wars, Lord Cottington remained faithfully attached to his royal master, and eventually went into exile with King Charles II., from which he never returned. His lordship married Anne, daughter of Sir William Meredith, Knt., and widow of Sir Robert Brett, by whom he had a son and four daughters, all of whom predeceased him unmarried. He d. at Valladolid, in 1653, when the the BARONY OF COTTINGTON became EXTINCT, and his estates passed to his nephew, CHARLES COTTINGTON, Esq., who had his lordship's remains brought over to England, and interred in Westminster Abbey, where he erected a stately monument.

ARMS.—Az. a fesse between three roses, or.

COVENTRY—BARONS COVENTRY, OF AYLESBOROUGH, IN THE COUNTY OF WORCESTER.

By Letters Patent, dated 10th April, 1628.

Lineage.

This family rose first into importance through

JOHN COVENTRY, an opulent mercer of the city of London, who filled the civic chair in 1425, and was one of the executors of the celebrated Sir Richard Whittington. From this worthy citizen descended

THOMAS COVENTRY, Esq., an eminent lawyer, temp. Elizabeth and King James I. In the 38th of the former reign, he was chosen autumnal reader by the society of the inner Temple, but was obliged to postpone the fulfilment of his task to the ensuing Lent, owing to the plague then raging in London. He was soon afterwards advanced to the dignity of the coif, and, in the 3d year of King James, was appointed king's serjeant; before the close of which year, being constituted one of the judges of the court of common pleas, he took his seat upon the bench, but survived his promotion a few months only. He m. Margaret, daughter and heiress of —— Jeffreys, Esq., of Croome-d'Abitot, and had issue,

THOMAS, his successor.

William, of Ridmarley, in the county of Worcester.

Walter, from whom the present Earls of Coventry derive.

Joan, m. to —— Rogers Esq., of Surrey.

Catherine, m. to William Child, Esq.

Anne, m. to George Frampton, Esq.

He was s. by his eldest son,

THOMAS COVENTRY, Esq., who, having adopted the learned profession of his father, attained the very highest honours of the bar. His advancement commenced with the recordership of London; he was then appointed solicitor-general, and honoured with knighthood, and, in the 18th of James I., succeeded to the attorney-generalship. In the first of King Charles I., Sir Thomas was constituted LORD KEEPER OF THE GREAT SEAL, and elevated to the peerage on the 10th April, 1628, as BARON COVENTRY, *of Aylesborough, in the county of Worcester*. His lordship m. first, Sarah, daughter of Edward Sebright, Esq., of Besford, in the county of Worcester, and had issue,

THOMAS, his successor.

Elizabeth, m. to Sir John Hare, of Stow-Bardolph, in the county of Norfolk.

He m. secondly, Elizabeth, daughter of John Aldersey, Esq., of Spurstow, and widow of William Pitchford, Esq., by whom he had

John, m. to Elizabeth, daughter and co-heir of John Coles, Esq., of Barton, in the county of Somerset, and widow of Herbert Doddington, Esq., and had

John, (Sir, K.B.) member of the Long Parliament for Weymouth. The outrage upon this gentleman, and its provocation, which gave rise to the well-known COVENTRY ACT, arose thus:— Upon the occasion of a money grant being carried in the House of Commons, it was proposed by opposition that the supplies for it should be raised by a tax upon playhouses, which being resisted by the court party, upon the plea " that players were the king's servants, and a part of his pleasure," Sir John Coventry asked whether did the king's pleasure lie among the men or the women that acted?—an observation that excited so much indignation in the royal circle, that it was determined to inflict summary punishment upon the utterer. The Duke of York told Burnet " that he had said every thing to divert the king from the resolution he had taken, which was to send some guards to watch in the street where Sir John Coventry lodged, and to set a mark upon him." The outrage, by bills of indictment, was found to have been committed by Sir Thomas Sandys, Knt., Charles O'Brien, Esq., Simon Parry, and Miles Reeves, who fled from justice, not daring to abide a legal trial. " As Coventry was going home," says Burnet, " they drew about him: he stood up to the wall, and snatched the flambeau out of his servant's hands; and with that in one hand, and his sword in the other, he defended himself so well, that he got great credit by it. He wounded some of them; but was soon disarmed, and then they cut his nose to the bone, to teach him to remember what respect he owed to the king; and so they left him, and went to the Duke of Monmouth's, where O'Brien's arm was dressed. The matter was executed by orders from the duke, for which he was severely censured, because he lived then upon terms of friendship with Coventry. Coventry had his nose so well needled up, that the scar was scarcely to be discerned. This put the house of commons in a furious uproar: they passed a bill of banishment against the actors of it, and put a clause in it, that it should not be in the king's power to pardon them, and that it should be death to maim any person." This Sir John Coventry died unmarried, and endowed an hospital at Wiveliscomb, in the county of Somerset.

Francis, married thrice, but had issue only by his third wife, Elizabeth, daughter and coheiress of John Manning, Esq., of London, and widow of Robert Cæsar, Esq., namely,

Francis, who d. unmarried in 1686.

Elizabeth, m. to Sir William Keyt, Bart., of Ebington, Gloucestershire.

Utrucia, m. to Sir Lacon-William Child, Knt.

Henry, one of the privy council of King Charles II., a diplomatist in the beginning of that monarch's reign, and subsequently one of his majesty's principal secretaries of state. He d. a bachelor on the 7th December, 1686.

William (Sir), a privy-councillor, secretary of the admiralty, temp. Charles II. " A man," says Burnet, " of great notions and eminent virtues; the best speaker in the House of Commons, and capable of bearing the chief ministry, as it was once thought he was very near it, and deserved it more than all the rest did." Sir William was, however, forbid the court for sending a challenge to the Duke of Buckingham; after which he resided in private until his decease in 1686, at Minster Lovel, near Whitney, in Oxfordshire. Sir William Coventry d. unmarried.

Anne, m. to Sir William Savile, Bart., of Thornhill, in the county of York.

Mary, m. to Henry Frederick Thynne, Esq., of Longlete, in the county of Wilts.

Margaret, m. to Anthony, Earl of Shaftesbury.

Dorothy, m. to Sir John Packington, Bart., of Westwood, in the county of Worcester. This lady, who was distinguished by her intelligence and piety, was esteemed the author of THE WHOLE DUTY OF MAN.

Thomas, Lord Coventry, died at Durham House, in the Strand, London, 14th January, 1640, and Lord Clarendon says that " he discharged all the offices he went through with great abilities and singular reputation of integrity; that he enjoyed his place of lord keeper with universal reputation (and, sure, justice was never better administered,) for the space of about sixteen years, even to his death, some months before he was sixty years of age." His lordship was s. by his eldest son,

THOMAS COVENTRY, second baron, who m. Mary, daughter of Sir William Craven, Knt., and sister of William, Earl Craven, by whom he had two sons, George and Thomas. His lordship d. 27th October, 1661, and was s. by the elder,

GEORGE COVENTRY, third baron, this nobleman m. 18th July, 1653, Margaret, daughter of John, Earl of Thanet, by whom he had surviving issue,

JOHN, his successor.

Margaret, m. to Charles, Earl of Wiltshire, afterwards Duke of Bolton, and died s. p. in 1683.

His lordship, d. 15th December, 1680, and was s. by his son,

JOHN COVENTRY, fourth baron, at whose decease, unmarried, 25th July, 1685, the title and estates reverted to his uncle,

The Honourable

THOMAS COVENTRY, of Snitfield, in the county of Warwick, as fifth Baron Coventry. His lordship was advanced by letters patent, dated 26th April, 1697, to the dignities of Viscount Deerhurst, and EARL OF COVENTRY, the limitation extending to William, Thomas, and Henry Coventry, grandsons of Walter Coventry, brother of the Lord Keeper Coventry. He m. first, Winifrede, daughter of Pierce Edgcombe, Esq., of Mount Edgcombe, in the county of Devon, and had two surviving sons, Thomas and Gilbert. His lordship m. secondly, Elizabeth, daughter of Richard Graham, Esq., (who espoused, after the earl's decease, Thomas Savage, Esq., of Elmley Castle, in the county of Worcester,) by whom he had no issue. He d. on the 15th July, 1699, and was s. by his elder son,

THOMAS COVENTRY, second earl, who m. Anne, daughter of Henry, Duke of Beaufort, and dying in 1710, was s. by his only surviving son,

THOMAS COVENTRY, third earl, at whose decease at Eton College, 28th January, 1711-12, the honours and estates reverted to his uncle,

GILBERT COVENTRY, fourth earl, who m. first, Dorothy, daughter of Sir William Keyt, Bart., of Ebrington, in the county of Gloucester, and had an only daughter,

Anne, m. to Sir William Carew, Bart., of Anthony, in Cornwall.

His lordship m. secondly, Anne, daughter of Sir Streynsham Masters, but had no issue. He d. on the 27th October, 1719, when the EARLDOM AND VISCOUNTY, with the bulk of his estates, passed to his relative, William Coventry, Esq., of the City of London, one of the clerks of the green cloth, according to the limitation of the patent of 1697, (from whom the extant Earls of Coventry inherit,) while the BARONY OF COVENTRY OF AYLESBOROUGH, became EXTINCT.

ARMS.—Sa. a fesse erm. between three crescents, or.

COURCY—EARL OF BEDFORD.

By charter, dated in 1366.

Lineage.

IGELRAM DE COURCY m. Catherine, daughter of the Duke of Austria, and had a son,

INGELRAM DE COURCY, who was so highly esteemed by King Edward III., that that monarch bestowed upon him his daughter Isabel, in marriage, and created him EARL OF BEDFORD, conferring upon him also the ribbon of the garter. His lordship d. in 1397, leaving issue by the princess,

  Mary, m. to Robert de Barr.

  Philippa, m. to Robert de Vere, Earl of Oxford, and Duke of Ireland, one of the unhappy favourites of Richard II.

Upon the decease of his lordship, the EARLDOM OF BEDFORD, became EXTINCT.

ARMS.—Barry of six, Vairée and gules.

COURTENAY — BARONS COURTE-NAY. EARLS OF DEVON.

Barony, by Writ of Summons, dated 6th February, 1299, 27 Edward I.
Earldom, by Letters Patent, dated 22nd February, 1335.

Lineage.

The Courtenays, one of the most illustrious races amongst the British nobility, and of which a branch still exists, deduced their pedigree paternally from ATHON, who himself descended from PHARAMOND, founder in 420 of the French monarchy, and common patriarch of all the kings of France. This ATHON, having fortified, during the reign of Robert the Wise, the town of COURTENAY, in the Isle of France, thence adopted his surname. But as the power of the Courtenays in England, principally arose from the great alliances formed by the first members of the family who settled here, we shall pass at once to their maternal pedigree.

GODFRY, Earl of Ewe and Brion, natural son of Richard I., Duke of Normandy, was father of

GILBERT, Earl of Brion, who had two sons, Richard, ancestor of the house of Clare, and

BALDWYN DE BRIONIS, who, for the distinguished part he had in the conquest, obtained from King William, the Barony of Okehampton, the custody of the county of Devon, and the government of the Castle of Exeter in fee. He m. Albreda, daughter of Richard, surnamed Goz, Count of Avranche, and had, with other issue,

  RICHARD, surnamed DE REDVERS.

  Robert, Governor of Brione.

  Emma, m. first, to William Avenal, and se-

149

condly, to William de Abrancis, by the latter of whom she had issue,

  ROBERT DE ABRANCIS, who, upon the resignation of his uncle, Richard de Redvers, obtained a grant of the Barony of Okehampton, the office of hereditary sheriff of Devon, and the government of Exeter Castle. He m. a daughter of Godwyn Dole, and left an only daughter and heiress,

    MAUD DE ABRANCIS, who m. first, —— Deincourt, by whom she had a daughter,

      HAWISE, m. to SIR REGINALD DE COURTENAY, of whom hereafter.

    Maud, espoused secondly, Robert Fitz-Edith, natural son of King Henry I., and had another daughter,

      MATILDA, m. to William de Courtenay, brother of Sir Reginald.

RICHARD DE ABRANCIS, surnamed DE REDVERS, having succeeded to the honours and possessions of his father, resigned the Barony of Okehampton, the sheriffalty of Devon, and the custody of the Castle of Exeter, in favour of his nephew Robert de Abrancis, mentioned above, and was created by King Henry I., EARL OF DEVON, with a grant of the Isle of Wight in fee. This nobleman, (who from residing chiefly at Exeter, was generally called Earl of Exeter,) m. Adeliza, daughter and coheiress of William Fitz-Osborne, Earl of Hereford, and had issue,

  BALDWYN DE REDVERS, his successor.

  William de Redvers, surnamed DE VERNON.

  Robert de Redvers.

  Hadewise, m. to William de Romare, Earl of Lincoln.

Richard de Redvers, first Earl of Devon, d. in 1137, and was s. by his eldest son,

BALDWYN DE REDVERS, as second Earl of Devon. This nobleman, upon the demise of King Henry I., espousing the cause of the Empress Maud, took up arms, and immediately fortified his Castle of Exeter, and the Isle of Wight; but being besieged by King Stephen, he was obliged to surrender the castle, and all his other possessions, and to withdraw with his family from the kingdom. We find him however soon again returning, and in the enjoyment of the Earldom of Devon; but, like his father, generally styled Earl of Exeter, from residing in that city. His lordship m. Lucia, daughter of Dru de Balm, and had issue,

  RICHARD, his successor.

  William, surnamed de Vernon, of whom hereafter, as sixth Earl of Devon.

  Maud, m. to Ralph Avenill.

He d. in June, 1155, and was s. by his son,

RICHARD DE REDVERS, third Earl of Devon, who wedded Dionysia, daughter of Reginald de Dunstanvill, (natural son of King Henry I.,) Earl of Cornwall, and had two sons, successive Earls. His lordship d. in 1162, and was s. by the elder,

BALDWIN DE REDVERS, fourth Earl of

Devon, at whose decease, without issue, the honours devolved upon his brother,

RICHARD DE REDVERS, fifth Earl of Devon, who died also *sine prole*, when the honours reverted to his uncle,

WILLIAM DE REDVERS, surnamed *Vernon*, as sixth Earl of Devon. This nobleman, upon the second coronation of King Richard I., was one of the four earls that carried the silken canopy, being then styled, "Earl of the Isle of Wight." His lordship appears to have adhered steadily to King John, for we find that monarch, in the eighteenth of his reign, providing for the security of the earl's property, against Louis of France, which from his advanced age, he was unable to defend himself. He *m.* Mabel, daughter of Robert, Earl of Mellent, by whom he acquired a considerable accession to his landed possessions, and had issue,

> Baldwin, who *m.* Margaret, daughter and heiress of Warine Fitzgerald, and left at his decease, 1st September, 1216, (in the lifetime of his father,) an only son,
>
>> BALDWIN, of whom presently, as 7th EARL OF DEVON.

Margaret, the widow, was forced, according to Matthew Paris, by King John, to marry "that impious, ignoble, and base conditioned man, *Falk de Breant*," of which marriage, he says, one wrote these lines at the time.

Lex connectit eos, amor et concordia lecti :
Sed Lex qualis ? Amor qualis ? Concordia qualis ?
Lex exlex ; amor exosus, concordia discors.

Paris continues—" On a time being in bed with him, he dreamed that a stone of an extraordinary bigness, like a thunderbolt, burst out of the tower of the church of St. Albans, and falling upon him, crusht him to pieces. Whereupon starting out of his sleep, and, with great amazement, trembling, she asked him what the matter was, and how he did? To whom he answered, ' I have in my time undergone many perils, but never was so much terrified, as in this dream,' And, having told her all particulars, she replied, that he had grievously offended St. Alban, by poluting that church with blood, and plundering the abbey; and therefore advised him, for preventing a more grievous revenge, to reconcile himself to that holy martyr. Wherefore, lodging then at Lupton, he forthwith arose and went to St. Albans; and having sent for the abbot, fell upon his knees with tears, and holding up his hands, said, ' Lord have mercy upon me, for I have grievously offended God, and his blessed martyr, St. Alban; but to a sinner there is mercy: let me therefore, by your leave, speak to your convent in chapter, to ask pardon of them in your presence for what I have done.' Whereunto, the abbot consented, admiring to see such lamb-like humility in a wolf. Therefore, putting off his apparel, he entered the chapter house, bearing a rod in his hand; and, confessing his fault, (which he said he did in time of war,) received a lash by every one of the monks upon his naked body; and when he had put on his clothes again, he went and sate by the abbot, and said, ' This my wife hath caused me to do for a dream; but if you require restitution for what I then took, I will not hearken to you.' And so he departed, the abbot and monks being glad, that they were so rid of him, without doing them any more mischief."

Joane, *m.* first, to William Brewere, and secondly, to Hubert de Burgh, chamberlain to the king, but had no issue.

Mary, *m.* ROBERT DE COURTENAY, feudal Baron of Okehampton, son and successor of Sir Reginald de Courtenay and Maud de Abrancis, (refer to Emma, daughter of Baldwin de Abrancis, first Baron of Okehampton,) and conveyed to her husband the head of the Barony of Devonshire, with the castle of Plimton. Of this marriage, were issue,

> SIR HUGH DE COURTENAY, successor to his father,
>
> Sir William de Courtenay, surnamed de Musberrie, who *m.* Joane, daughter of Thomas Basset, but died *s. p.*
>
> Hauise, *m.* to John de Nevil.

Robert de Courtenay, Baron of Okehampton, was *s.* by his elder son,

> SIR HUGH DE COURTENAY, as third Baron of Okehampton. His lordship *m.* Alianore, daughter of Hugh le Despencer, (father of Hugh, Earl of Winchester,) by whom, (who *d.* 11th October, 1328,) he had issue,
>
>> HUGH (Sir), his successor, of whom hereafter, as successor to the estates of the Redverses, and the person in whom the EARLDOM OF DEVON was revived.
>>
>> Philip (Sir), who fell at the battle of Shivelin, 24th June, 1314, and *d.* unmarried.
>>
>> Isabel, *m.* to John St. John, Baron St. John, of Basing.
>>
>> Aveline, *m.* to Sir John Gifford, Knt.
>>
>> Egeline, *m.* to Robert Scales.
>>
>> Margaret, *m.* to John de Moels.

His lordship *d.* 28th February, 1291. William, sixth Earl of Devon, *d.* 14th September, 1216, and was *s.* by his grandson,

BALDWIN DE REDVERS, seventh Earl of Devon. In the 11th Henry III. *Gilbert de Clare*, EARL OF GLOUCESTER AND HERTFORD, paid a fine of two thousand marks to the king for permission to marry his eldest daughter to this young nobleman: whereupon all his demesne lands, which were then valued at £900 per annum, were placed under the guardianship of the Earl of Gloucester, until he should attain maturity. In the 24th of the same reign, the king, keeping his Christmas at Winchester, at the instance of Richard, Earl of Cornwall, under whose tuition Baldwin then was, girded his lordship with the sword of knighthood; and investing him with the EARLDOM of the ISLE OF WIGHT, bestowed upon him Amicia, the daughter of the said Earl of Gloucester, in marriage. The Earl of Devon d. in five years afterwards, in the flower of his youth, anno 1245, leaving issue,

BALDWIN, his successor.

Margaret, a nun at Lacock.

ISABEL, successor to her brother.

His lordship was s. by his son,

BALDWIN DE REDVERS, eighth Earl of Devon, who was committed to the tuition of Peter de Savoy, uncle of Queen Eleanor, and a person of great note at that period. His lordship did homage, and had livery of his lands in the 41st Henry III., in which year he espoused Avis, daughter of the Earl of Surrey, by whom he had an only son, John, who d. in infancy. The earl d. in 1262, having been poisoned, with the Earl of Gloucester, and others, at the table of Peter de Savoy. With his lordship the male line of the ancient and eminent house of REDVERS expired, but its honours devolved upon his sister,

ISABEL DE FORTIBUS, widow of William de Fortibus, Earl of Albemarle and Holderness, as COUNTESS OF DEVON. Her ladyship had three sons, all of whom d. in infancy, and two daughters, viz.

Anne, d. unmarried.

Aveline, m. first, to Ingram de Percy, and secondly, to Edmund Plantagenet, Earl of Lancaster, but d. without issue in the lifetime of her mother,

The countess d. in 1293, and thus leaving no issue, the EARLDOM OF DEVON, and the other honours of the house of REDVERS expired, but so much of its extensive possessions as passed not to the crown, devolved upon the heir at law,

SIR HUGH COURTENAY, feudal baron of Okehampton, (the descendant of Lady Mary Redvers, daughter of William, sixth Earl of Devon, refer to that nobleman,) who was summoned to parliament as BARON COURTENAY from the 6th February, 1299 to the 94th July, 1334, and created on the 22nd February, 1335, EARL OF DEVON. The latter dignity was conferred upon his lordship in consequence of a representation made by him to the King (Edward III.), with whom he was in high estimation, to the purpose " that he was seised of a certain annuity of £18. 6s. 7d. for the tertium denarium of the county of Devon, with divers lands by right of inheritance, from Isabell de Fortibus, Countess of Albemarle and Devon, which she in her life-time did possess; and having accordingly received the same annuity at the hands of the sheriffs of that county, for which they had allowance upon their accounts in the exchequer, until Walter, Bishop of Exeter, lord treasurer to King Edward II., upon the investigation of some persons who were inclined to disturb the business, did refuse to admit thereof, alledging, that this annuity was granted to the ancestors of the said Isabell, by the king's progenitors, under the name and title of EARLS; and therefore, that he, the said Hugh, being NO EARL, ought not to receive the same: and, that upon the like pretence, the then sheriffs of

144

Devon did decline to pay it any longer to him." The king immediately instituted an inquiry into the affair, and finding it as stated, removed the difficulty by creating his lordship an earl, as stated above, and dispatching his royal precept to the then sheriff of Devon, commanding him to proclaim that all persons should forthwith style his lordship EARL OF DEVON. The earl m. when but seventeen years of age, Agnes, daughter of Sir John St. John, Knt., and sister of Lord St. John, of Basing, by whom he had issue,

JOHN, abbot of Tavistock.

HUGH, his heir.

Robert, of Moreton, who d. in youth.

Thomas, of Southpole, m. Muriel, daughter and heiress of Sir John de Moels, Knt., by whom he had,

Hugh, who died s. p.

Margaret, m. to Thomas Peverall.

Muriel, m. to John Dynham.

Eleanor, m. to John, Lord Grey, of Codnor.

Elizabeth; m. to Lord Lisle.

His lordship d. in 1340 and was s. by his son,

HUGH COURTENAY, second Earl of Devon. This nobleman distinguished himself in arms during the martial reign of Edward III., and was one of the first dignified with the GARTER upon the institution of that noble order. His lordship m. Margaret, daughter of Humphrey de Bohun, Earl of Hereford and Essex, and grand-daughter of King Edward I., by whom he had, with other issue,

HUGH (SIR), who was summoned to parliament as BARON COURTENAY on the 8th January, 1371, and was one of the orignal KNIGHTS of the GARTER. His lordship being in the expedition made into France twenty-four years before, (Edward III.,) participated in the glory of Cressy, and being the next year in the tournament at Eltham, he had a hood of white cloth, embroidered with dancing men, and buttoned with large pearls, presented to him by the king. He m. Elizabeth, daughter of Guy Brian, Lord of Tor-Brian, in Devonshire, and sister of the famous Guy, Lord Brian, standard-bearer to the King at Cressy, and a knight of the Garter, by whom he left at his decease, in the life-time of his father, an only son,

Hugh, who m. Matilda, daughter of Thomas Holland, Earl of Kent, and of Joane, his wife, commonly called the Fair Maid of Kent, daughter of Edmund, of Woodstock, son of King Edward I., which Joane, was subsequently m. to EDWARD, the Black Prince, and by him was mother of KING RICHARD II. Hugh Courtenay d. in 1377, a few years after his father, and before his grandfather, leaving no issue. His widow m. secondly, Waleran, Earl of St. Paul.

Edward, of Godlington, (who d. also before his father,) m. Emeline, daughter and heiress of Sir John D'Auney, Knt, and had issue,

EDWARD, of whom presently, as inheritor of the honours of the family.

Hugh (Sir), of Haccomb, m. first, Elizabeth, daughter of Sir William Cogan, and widow of Sir Fulk Fitzwarine, who d. without issue. He m. secondly, Philippa, daughter and co-heiress of Sir Warren Arcedekene, (by Elizabeth, daughter and heiress of John Talbot, of Ricard's Castle,) by whom he had an only daughter,

    Joane, m. first, to Nicholas, Lord Carew, of Mohuns Autrey, and secondly, to Sir Robert Vere.

Sir Hugh Courtenay m. thirdly, Maud, daughter of Sir John Beaumont, of Sherwell, in the county of Dorset, by whom he had a daughter,

    Margaret, who m. Sir Theobald Grenvill, Knt.

and a son and heir,

    Hugh (Sir), of Boconnock, in Cornwall, who fell at the battle of Tewkesbury, leaving issue by his wife, Margaret, daughter and co-heir of Thomas Carmino, Esq., of Devonshire,

        Edward, who was created Baron Okehampton, and Earl of Devon, in 1485, see those dignities.

        Elizabeth, m. to John Trethrif, Esq.

        Maud, m. to John Arundel, Esq., of Talvern.

        Isabel, m. to William Mohem, Esq.

        Florence, m. to John Trelawney, Esq.

William, Chancellor of the University of Oxford, anno 1367; Bishop of Hereford, 1369; Bishop of London 1375, and Archbishop of Canterbury 1381. His grace d. in 1396.

Philip (Sir), of Powderham Castle, lieutenant of Ireland in the reign of Richard II., ancestor of the existing noble house of Courtenay.

Piers (Sir), standard-bearer to King Edward III., constable of Windsor Castle, governor of Calais, chamberlain to King Richard II., and Knight of the Garter. This eminent and gallant person, who was celebrated for deeds of arms, d. unmarried in 1409.

Margaret, m. to John, Lord Cobham.

Elizabeth, m. first, to Sir John Vere, and secondly, to Sir Andrew Luttrel.

Catherine, m. first, to William, Lord Harington, and secondly, to Sir Thomas Engaine.

Joane, m. to Sir John Cheverston.

Hugh, second Earl of Devon, d. in 1377, and was s. by (the elder son of his son Edward), his grandson,

EDWARD COURTENAY, third earl. This nobleman served in the beginning of the reign of Richard II. as a naval officer, under John of Gaunt and Thomas of Woodstock respectively, and was appointed in the 7th of the same monarch, admiral of all the king's fleet from the mouth of the Thames westward. In the next year, being then Earl Marshal, his lordship was retained to serve the king in his Scottish wars; in two years afterwards he had the command of the fleet at sea to prevent invasion, and in the 13th of Richard was engaged in the French wars. His lordship espoused Maud, daughter of Thomas, Baron Camois, and had issue,

    Edward (Sir), K.B., and admiral of the king's fleet, who m. Eleanor, daughter of Roger Mortimer, Earl of March, but died s. p. in the life-time of his father.

    Hugh, his successor.

    James.

The earl d. on the 5th December, 1419, and was s. by his second, but eldest surviving son,

HUGH COURTENAY, fourth earl, K.B., who, in the 6th Henry V., (his father then living,) was appointed commander-in-chief of the king's fleet. His lordship m. Anne, daughter of Richard, Lord Talbot, and sister of the renowned John, Earl of Shrewsbury, by whom he had issue,

    Thomas, his successor.

    John, d. unmarried.

His lordship d. 16th June, 1422, and was s. by his elder son,

THOMAS COURTENAY, fifth earl. This nobleman commenced his military career at the age of sixteen, and was engaged for several years in the French wars of King Henry VI., with which monarch he sided upon the breaking out of the unhappy conflict between the houses of York and Lancaster; and the Courtenays continued to adhere to the red rose with unshaken fidelity from that period until the termination of the contest. In 1445 a dispute regarding precedency arose between the Earls of Devon and Arundel, but it was decided by parliament in favour of the latter, in consequence of the feudal possession of Arundel Castle. The earl m. Margaret Beaufort, second daughter of John, Marquess of Somerset, (one of the legitimised children of John of Gaunt,) and had issue,

    Thomas, his successor.

    Henry.

    John.

    Joane, m. to Sir Roger Clifford, Knt., who was beheaded in 1485.

    Elizabeth, m. to Sir Hugh Conway, Knt.

    Matilda.

    Eleanor.

His lordship d. 3rd February, 1458, in the abbey of Abingdon, upon his journey to London, with other lords, to mediate between the king and the Duke of York, and was s. by his eldest son,

THOMAS COURTENAY, sixth earl, then twenty-six years of age. This nobleman inheriting the political principles, as well as honours of his deceased father, was a strenuous upholder of the cause of Lancaster, and falling into the hands of the enemy at Towton-field, he was beheaded at York, by order of King Edward IV. in April, 1462. Under the attainder of this earl, the honours and possessions of the house of Courtenay fell; but his next brother,

HENRY COURTENEY, Esq., (as he was styled, but who should have been seventh earl,) finding favour with the new king, had restoration of some part of the lands. Engaging, however, in the Lancastrian quarrel with the zeal of his predecessors, he was attainted of treason, 4th March, 1466, before the king and justices at Sarum, and beheaded with the Lord Hungerford on the same day. The greater part of the Courtenay estates having been conferred upon Humphrey Stafford, Baron Stafford, of South-wicks, his lordship was created EARL OF DEVON, 7th May, 1469, but being beheaded and attainted in the August following, that earldom became forfeited. Upon the demise of Henry Courtenay, his only surviving brother,

JOHN COURTENAY, assumed to be eighth EARL OF DEVON, and the Lancastrian interest prevailing in 1470, when King EDWARD was driven into Holland by the Earl of Warwick, his lordship was restored, by parliament, with King Henry VI., to the *honours* and *estates* of his family. The defeat of the Earl of Warwick, however, after the return of King Edward by that prince, at the decisive battle of Barnet, 14th April, 1471, again placed the Earl of Devon in jeopardy: and attaching himself to Margaret, of Anjou, his lordship fell, gallantly fighting at the head of the rear guard of Margaret's army, at Tewkesbury, on the 4th May following. Thus the three brothers sealed with their blood their bond of fidelity to the house of Lancaster, and with these brave soldiers expired the senior branch of the ancient and illustrious house of Courtenay. The last earl was buried at Tewkesbury, and being attainted, the HONOURS and ESTATES of DEVON, became again FORFEITED.

ARMS.—Or, three torteauxes, with a label of three points, az. in chief.

COURTENAY—EARLS OF DEVON, MARQUESSES OF EXETER.

Earldom, by Letters Patent, dated 26th Oct., 1485.
Marquezate, by Letters Patent, dated 18th June, 1525.

Lineage.

SIR HUGH COURTENAY, Knt., of Bacon-nock, in the county of Cornwall, only son of Sir Hugh Courtenay, of Haccomb, brother of *Edward*, THIRD EARL OF DEVON, of the Courtenay family, (see descendants of Hugh, second Earl of Devon—article Courtenay, Earls of Devon,) m. Margaret, daughter and co-heiress of Thomas Carmino, Esq., (the last male heir of that ancient family,) by whom he had issue,

 EDWARD (Sir), his successor.
 Walter (Sir), d. unmarried.
 Elizabeth, m. to John Trethrif, Esq., and had a son,
  THOMAS TRETHRIF, who m. ——, daughter of —— Travisa, and left two daughters, viz.—
   Elizabeth, m. to John Vivian, Esq.
   Margaret, m. to Edward Courtenay, Esq. of Larrock.
 Maud, m. to John Arundel, Esq., of Talkern.
 Isabel, m. to William Mohun, Esq.
 Florence, m. to John Trelawney, Esq.

{ Heiresses, eventually, of their grand-nephew, Edward, second Marquess of Exeter. }

146

Sir Hugh, faithful to the Lancastrian interest, fell with his noble kinsman, the Earl of Devon, at the battle of Tewkesbury, and his elder son,

SIR EDWARD COURTENAY, being implicated with his brother, in Henry Stafford, Duke of Buckingham's conspiracy, in favour of Henry, Earl of Richmond, was forced to fly into Britanny, upon the failure of that plot, and the decapitation of the duke: and was attainted with the Earl of Richmond and others, by parliament, in the beginning of 1484, but returning with the earl, and assisting at the battle of Bosworth, he was elevated to the peerage, by King Henry VII., on the 26th October, 1485, in the ancient dignity of the family, *that* of EARL OF DEVON, the new monarch making him grants at the same time, of the greater part of the castles, manors, &c., which belonged to the late Thomas Courtenay, Earl of Devon. In the March following, the king made his lordship governor of Kesterwell, in Cornwall, and a Knight of the Garter. The earl was in all the parliaments of Henry VII. He was in the expedition to France, in 1491, and in six years afterwards, he defended the city of Exeter, against Perkin Warbeck and his adherents. He m. Elizabeth, daughter of Sir Philip Courtenay, of Molland, by whom he had only son,

 WILLIAM, K.B., who m. Katherine, seventh and youngest daughter of KING EDWARD IV. In the year 1502, this gentleman, with Lord William de la Pole, Sir James Tyrrel, and Sir John Windham, were arrested on the charge of holding a traiterous correspondence with Edmund de la Pole, Earl of Suffolk, (son of John, Duke of Suffolk and Lady Elizabeth, elder sister of Edward IV.,) who had fled to his aunt, Margaret, Duchess of Burgundy, and he (Sir William Courtenay) was attainted in consequence, in 1504: Tyrrel and Wyndham were beheaded on Tower Hill, while Sir William Courtenay was doomed to incarceration during the king's reign.

The earl d. in 1509, and King Henry VIII. ascending the throne in the same year, his highness immediately liberated

SIR WILLIAM COURTENAY, and took him into his gracious favour: but Sir William died in the third year of that monarch's reign, before he had either letters patent or a formal restoration of the earldom: he was, however, buried "*with the honours of an earl*," at the *especial* command of the king. By the Lady Katherine Plantagenet, he left an only son,

EDWARD COURTENAY, who being restored in blood and honours, became second EARL OF DEVON. In 1522, his lordship obtained a grant of Calliand, in Cornwall, and of "a fair mansion," situate in the parish of St. Lawrence Poultry, in the city of London, forfeited by the attainder of Edward Stafford, Duke of Buckingham, on whose trial he was one of the twenty-six peers that sat in judgment; and he was advanced, by letters patent, dated 18th June, 1525, to the dignity of MARQUESS OF EXETER. In the year 1530, at the interview between King Henry VIII. and the King of France, in the vale of Arden, when the two monarchs challenged all men at justs, the Marquess of Exeter ran a course with the French prince, when both their spears broke, and they maintained their seats. His lordship evinced his skill and valour in many other tournaments, and in the year 1532, on Henry's going to Calais, he was nominated by the king, prior to his highness's departure, heir apparent to the throne. His lordship subscribed the articles against Cardinal Wolsey, and the letter sent to Pope Clement VII., entreating his holiness to ratify the divorce between the king and Queen Catherine. In 1536, he sate in judgment upon Anne Boleyne, and in the same year, he suppressed, in conjunction with the Duke of Norfolk, and the Earls of Shrewsbury, Huntingdon, and Rutland, a rebellion in Yorkshire; but that very year he was committed to the Tower, with *Henry Pole*, LORD MONTACUTE, and Sir Edward Nevill, brother of Lord Abergavenny, accused by Sir Geoffrey Pole, brother of Lord Montacute, of high treason, and indicted for devising to maintain, promote, and advance, one Reginald Pole, late Dean of Exeter, enemy to the king, beyond sea, and to deprive the king, &c. The Marquess of Exeter and Lord Montacute, were tried on the 1st and 2nd of December, 1539, at Westminster, and being found guilty, were beheaded, with Sir Edward Nevill, on the 9th of January ensuing, on Tower Hill. Upon the attainder of the marquess, all his honours of COURSE EXPIRED, and *King* HENRY annexed to the Duchy of Cornwall, all his lands in that county, which came to the crown. The marquess had *m.* first, Elizabeth Grey, daughter and heiress of John, Viscount Lisle, by whom he had no issue, and secondly, Gertrude, daughter of William Blount, Lord Mountjoy, by whom he left an only son, (the Marchioness of Exeter was attainted with the Countess of Salisbury, the year after her husband, but the latter only suffered,)

EDWARD COURTENAY, who, although but twelve years of age when his father was beheaded, was committed prisoner to the Tower, and detained there during the remainder of King Henry's reign, and that of King Edward VI., but upon the accession of Queen Mary, he was released, and restored to his father's honours, as MARQUESS OF EXETER, &c., and to the estates which remained in the possession of the crown, by a private bill, passed in the 1st year of her majesty's reign, while another private bill reversed the attainder of his mother. His lordship had some command in suppressing Wyatt's rebellion, and yet with the Princess Elizabeth was afterwards accused of being accessory thereto, and sent with her highness to the Tower. He was subsequently confined in Fotheringhay Castle, but released through the interposition of Philip of Spain, upon his marriage with the queen, as was also the *Lady* ELIZABETH. His lordship after this, obtained the queen's permission to go abroad, and died at Padua, not without suspicion of poison, on the 4th October, 1566. This unfortunate nobleman seemed to be born to be a prisoner, for, from twelve years of age to the time of his death, he had scarcely enjoyed two entire years liberty. He *d.* unmarried, and was the last of the family who bore the titles of MARQUESS OF EXETER, EARL OF DEVON, and BARON OF OAK-

HAMPTON, those dignities expiring with his lordship, while his estates were divided amongst the four sisters of EDWARD, the first earl, his lordship's grand-aunts (refer to children of Sir Hugh Courtenay). The marquess's remains were interred in St. Anthony's church, in Padua, where a noble monument was erected to his memory.

ARMS.—Or. three Torteauxes, with a label of three points, az. in chief.

CRANFIELD—BARONS CRANFIELD; EARLS OF MIDDLESEX.

Barony, { by Letters } 9th June, 1621.
Earldom, { Patent, } 16th Sept., 1622.

Lineage.

LIONEL CRANFIELD, a merchant of London, and married to a kinswoman of Villiers, Duke of Buckingham, was introduced to the court of King James I., by that celebrated favourite, when he received the honour of knighthood, and soon after attracting the attention of the king, by his habits of business, he was appointed master of the requests —next, master of the king's great wardrobe, then master of the wards, after which he was sworn of the privy council, and elevated to the peerage, as BARON CRANFIELD, *of Cranfield*, in the county of Bedford, on the 9th July, 1621. In the October following, his lordship was constituted LORD TREASURER OF ENGLAND, and created, 16th September, 1622, EARL OF MIDDLESEX (the first person, says Dugdale, to whom that county gave the title of earl). But this tide of prosperity flowed too rapidly to be permanent, and a short time only elapsed, before its reflux became as remarkable. Within two short years, the lord treasurer found himself impeached by parliament, through the influence of the very nobleman who was the founder of his fortune, the favourite Buckingham, for bribery, extortion, oppression, and other heinous misdemeanours, for which he received judgment, viz.—

"That Lionel, Earl of Middlesex, now Lord Treasurer of England, shall lose all his offices which he holds in this kingdom, and shall be made for ever incapable of any office, place, or employment, in the state and commonwealth.

"That he shall be imprisoned in the Tower of London, during the king's pleasure.

"That he shall pay to our sovereign lord the king, the sum of £50,000.

"That he shall never more sit in parliament.

"That he shall never come within the verge of the court."

And a bill passed at the same time, to make his estate liable to the king's fine, and other accounts, and to make restitution to all whom he had wronged, as should be allowed by the discretion of the house. His lordship *m.* first, Elizabeth, daughter of Richard Shepherd, a merchant in London, by whom he had three daughters, viz.—

Martha, *m.* to Henry Carey, Earl of Monmouth.
Elizabeth, *m.* to Edmund, Lord Sheffield, grandson and heir of Edmund, Earl of Mulgrave.

The earl *m.* secondly, Anne, daughter of James Brett, Esq., of Houby, in the county of Leicester, (sister of Mary, Countess of Buckingham,) and had issue,

JAMES, } successive Earls.
LIONEL, }

Edward, d. unmarried.

William, d. young.

Frances, m. first, to Richard, Earl of Dorset, and secondly, to Henry Poole, Esq.

His lordship d. in 1645, and notwithstanding his disgrace, was buried in Westminster Abbey, where a monument was erected to his memory. He was s. by his eldest son,

JAMES CRANFIELD, second Earl, who m. Anne, third daughter and co-heiress, of Edward, Earl of Bath, by whom he had an only daughter,

Elizabeth, m. to John, Lord Brackley, eldest son of the Earl of Bridgewater.

His lordship d. in 1651, when his honours devolved upon his brother,

LIONEL CRANFIELD, third Earl, who m. Rachel, widow of Henry, Earl of Bath, and daughter of Francis, Earl of Westmoreland, but dying without issue, in 1674, the BARONY OF CRANFIELD, and EARLDOM OF MIDDLESEX, became EXTINCT, while his lordship's estates devolved upon his sister, the Countess of Dorset, whose eldest son, Charles, was created BARON CRANFIELD, and EARL OF MIDDLESEX, in 1675, honours which have descended with the Dukedom of Dorset.

ARMS.—Or. on a pale, as. three Fleur de lis of the first.

CRAVEN — BARON CRAVEN, OF HAMPSTED - MARSHALL, IN THE COUNTY OF BERKS, EARL CRAVEN, &c., BARON CRAVEN.

First Barony,		12th Mar., 1696.
Earldom & Viscounty,	by Let- ters Pa- tent.	15th Mar., 1663.
Second Barony,		15th Mar., 1663.

Lineage.

SIR WILLIAM CRAVEN, Knt., merchant-taylor, served the office of lord mayor of the city of London in 1611. He m. Elizabeth, daughter of William Whitmore, and had issue,

WILLIAM, his heir.

John, created Lord Craven, of Ryton.

Thomas, d. unmarried.

The eldest son,

WILLIAM CRAVEN, Esq., having distinguished himself in arms under GUSTAVUS ADOLPHUS, of Sweden, and HENRY, PRINCE OF ORANGE, was elevated to the peerage by King Charles I. on the 12th March, 1696, as BARON CRAVEN, of Hampsted-Marshall, with remainder, in default of male issue, to his brothers, John and Thomas; and having afterwards, during the civil wars, zealously and ably upheld the royal cause, his lordship was created, upon the restoration of the monarchy, 15th March, 1663, VISCOUNT CRAVEN, of Uffington, in the county of Berks, and EARL CRAVEN, in the county of York; and his brothers being both at this period defunct without issue, he was re-created BARON CRAVEN, of

148

Hampsted-Marshall, with remainder to his brothers, Sir William Craven, of Lendwike, and Sir Anthony Craven, his cousins; but the said Sir William dying without male issue, the earl had a new patent, dated 11th December, 1665, renewing the original barony, with an extended limitation to Sir Thomas Craven (a younger brother of the above-mentioned Sir William and Sir Anthony), and his male issue. His lordship, who lived to the advanced age of eighty-eight, was particularly famous for assisting in extinguishing fires in the city of London, of which he had such early intimation, and was so prompt to mount his horse upon such calamitous occasions, that it was commonly said, " Lord Craven's horse smelt a fire so soon as it happened." He d. a bachelor, 9th April, 1697, when the barony of 1696, and that of 1663, with the VISCOUNTY and EARLDOM OF CRAVEN, became EXTINCT; while the BARONY of 1665 devolved upon WILLIAM CRAVEN, Esq., of Combe Abbey, grandson of the Sir Thomas Craven limited in the patent, from whom the present EARL OF CRAVEN descends, and derives the said dignity.

ARMS.—Ar. a fesse between six crosslets fitchée or.

CRAVEN — BARON CRAVEN, OF RYTON, IN THE COUNTY OF SALOP.

By Letters Patent, dated 21st March, 1642.

Lineage.

JOHN CRAVEN, Esq., second son of Sir William Craven, Knt., merchant-taylor, and lord mayor of the city of London, anno 1611, was elevated to the peerage on the 21st March, 1642, as BARON CRAVEN, of Ryton. His lordship m. Elizabeth, daughter of William, Lord Spencer; but dying issueless in 1650, the barony became EXTINCT.

ARMS.—Ar. a fesse between six crosslets fitchée gules.

CRETING—BARON CRETING.

By Writ of Summons, dated 27th January, 1332, 6 Edward III.

Lineage.

SIR ADAM DE CRETING, Knt., having summons to attend King Edward I. at Portsmouth, and passing with the monarch into Gascony, was there slain by the treachery of one Walter Gifford. He was succeeded in his manor of GREAT STOCKTON, in the county of Huntingdon, and other lands, by his son and companion in arms,

JOHN DE CRETING, who, in the 4th of Edward III., obtained a charter for free-warren in all his demesne lands at Great Stokton, and, being a military man of reputation, was summoned to parliament, as a BARON, on the 27th January, 1332, but never afterwards; and nothing further is known of the family.

ARMS.—Ar. a chevron betw. three mullets gules, pierced of the field.

CREW—BARONS CREW, OF STENE, IN THE COUNTY OF NORTHAMPTON.

By Letters Patent, dated 20th April, 1661.

Lineage.

JOHN CREW, Esq., of Stene, in the county of Northampton, son of Sir Thomas Crew, Knt., serjeant-at-law to King Charles I., (of the ancient Cheshire family, of Crew Hall, represented by the present Lord Crewe, of Crewe,) by his wife Temperance, daughter and heiress of Reginald Bray, Esq., of Stene, was elevated to the Peerage on the 20th April, 1661, as BARON CREW, of Stene, in consideration for his zealous services in the restoration of the monarchy. His lordship m. Jemima, daughter and co-heiress of Edward Walgrave, Esq., of Lawford, in the county of Essex, by whom he had issue,

Thomas (Sir), his successor.
John.
Nathaniel, Bishop of Durham.
Walgrave.
Jemima, m. to Edward, first Earl of Sandwich.
Anne, m. to Sir Henry Wright, Bart., of Dagenham, in the county of Essex.

Lord Crew d. in 1679, and was s. by his eldest son,

THOMAS CREW, second baron, who m. first, Mary, daughter of Sir George Townshend, Bart., of Rainham, in the county of Norfolk, by whom he had surviving issue,

Anne, m. to —— Jolliff, Esq., of London.
Temperance, m. first, to Rowland, son and heir of Sir Thomas Alston, Bart., of Odell, in the county of Bedford, and secondly, to Sir John Wolstenholme, Knt.

His lordship m. secondly, Anne, daughter and co-heiress of Sir William Airmine, Bart., of Osgodly, in the county of Lincoln, and had four daughters, viz.,

Jemima, m. to Henry de Grey, Duke of Kent.
Airmine, m. to Thomas Cartwright, Esq., of Aynho, in the county of Northampton.
Catherine, m. to Sir John Harper, fourth baronet of Caulk, in the county of Derby, the great-grandson of which marriage, Sir Henry Harper, seventh baronet, assumed, by royal permission, the surname of CREWE only, and was succeeded, at his decease, by his son, the present SIR GEORGE CREWE, eighth Baronet of Caulk Abbey.
Elizabeth, m. Charles Butler, Earl of Arran, and Lord Butler, of Weston.

His lordship d. ————, and thus leaving no male issue, his fortune devolved upon his daughters, as co-heiresses, while the title passed to his brother,

The Right Reverend
NATHANIEL CREW, Lord Bishop of Durham, as third Baron Crew, of Stene. His lordship m. first, Penelope, daughter of Sir Philip Frowde, Knt., and secondly, Dorothy, daughter of Sir William Forster, of Balmborough Castle, in the county of Northumberland; but not having had any issue,

the BARONY OF CREW, of Stene, became, at his lordship's decease in 1721, EXTINCT.

ARMS.—Az. a lion rampant ar., a crescent for difference.

CROFTS—BARON CROFTS, OF SAXHAM, IN THE COUNTY OF SUFFOLK.

By Letters Patent, dated 18th May, 1658.

Lineage.

WILLIAM CROFTS, Esq., lineal male heir of the family of Crofts, which had flourished for several ages at Saxham, in the county of Suffolk, and descended by females from the first Lord Wentworth, of Nettlested, as also from the Montacutes, earls of Salisbury, and Nevills, earls of Westmorland, was elevated to the peerage on the 18th May, 1658, as BARON CROFTS, of Saxham, in the county of Suffolk. His lordship having been brought up at court from his youth, became, first, master of the horse to James Duke of York; next, captain of the guards to the queen-mother, and afterwards one of the gentlemen of the bed-chamber to King Charles II. He was subsequently employed as ambassador to Poland, and for his services on that occasion obtained the peerage. His lordship m. first, Dorothy, widow of Sir John Hele, Knt., daughter of Sir John Hobart, of Intwood, in the county of Norfolk, Bart., (son and heir of Lord Chief Justice Hobart, of the Common Pleas,) and secondly Elizabeth, daughter of William Lord Spencer, of Wormleighton; but having no issue, the barony of CROFTS became, at his lordship's decease in 1677, EXTINCT.

ARMS.—Or. three bulls' heads couped sa.

CROMWELL. — BARONS CROMWELL, OF TATSHALL, IN THE COUNTY OF LINCOLN.

By Writ of Summons, dated 10th March, 1308.
1 Edward II.

Lineage.

The family of Cromwell was of importance so far back as the time of King John, for we find in the 17th of that reign,

RALPH DE CROMWELL, paying a fine of sixty marks and a palfrey to make his peace for participating in the rebellion of the barons; and upon delivering up his eldest daughter in hostage, obtaining restitution of his lands. After which, in the 3rd Henry III., he was constituted justice itinerant in the counties of Lincoln, Nottingham, and Derby. To this Ralph s. another

RALPH DE CROMWELL, who m. Margaret, one of the sisters and co-heirs of Roger de Someri, Baron of Dudley, and was afterwards engaged in the French, Welch, and Scottish wars of King Edward I. He was s. by

SIR JOHN DE CROMWELL, who m. Idonea de Leyburne, younger daughter and co-heir of Robert de Vipount, hereditary sheriff of Westmoreland, and widow of Sir Roger de Leyburne. In the

33rd Edward I. Sir John Cromwell accused Sir Nicholas de Segrave of treason, and was answered by a defiance to battle, but the combat was not permitted. In the 1st Edward II. he had a grant for life from the crown of the Castle of Hope, in Flintshire, and the same year was made governor of Stritguil Castle, and constable of the Tower of London. He was likewise summoned to parliament as a BARON. His lordship was subsequently engaged in the French and Scotch wars of King Edward II., and having had summons to parliament until the 9th Edward III., d. in the latter year, (anno 1335,) and was s. by his son,

SIR RALPH DE CROMWELL, second baron, summoned to parliament from 28th December, 1375, to 19th August, 1399 inclusive. This nobleman m. Maud, daughter of John Barnack, and heiress of her brother William, in whose right he became lord of the manor of Tatshall, in the county of Lincoln, by lineal succession from the heirs female of Robert de Tatshall, sometime owner thereof, whereupon he fixed his chief residence there. In the 10th Richard II. Lord Cromwell being then a banneret, was retained to serve the king in defence of the realm against an invasion apprehended at that period. His lordship d. in 1399, and was s. by his son,

RALPH DE CROMWELL, third baron, summoned to parliament from 9th September, 1400, to 3rd September, 1417. His lordship d. in 1419, and was s. by his son,

SIR RALPH DE CROMWELL, fourth baron, who m. Margaret, daughter of John, Lord Deincourt, and Joane, his wife, daughter and heiress of Robert, Lord Grey, of Rotherfield, and co-heiress of her brother, William, Lord Deincourt. In the 11th Henry VI. this nobleman was constituted treasurer of the king's exchequer, and in three years afterwards had a grant of the office of master of the king's mues and falcons. In the 23rd of the same reign his lordship was appointed hereditary constable of Nottingham Castle, and warden of the forest of Sherwood. He d. in 1455, and leaving no issue, his sister became his heir, namely,

Maud Cromwell, who m. Sir Richard Stanhope, (ancestor of the existing noble houses of Chesterfield, Harrington, and Stanhope,) and had issue, two daughters, co-heiresses, viz.

Maud Stanhope, m. first, Robert, Lord Willoughby de Eresby, and had a daughter,

Joane, wife of Sir Robert Wells, Knt., afterwards Lord Wells, by whom the said Joane had issue,

Robert, Lord Willoughby and Wells, who died s. p.

Jane, heir to her brother, m. Sir Richard Hastings, Lord Wells and Willoughby, (in right of his wife,) and had issue,

Anthony Hastings, who died s. p., thus terminating the line.

Maude, Lady Willoughby, m. secondly, Sir Thomas Nevil, Knt., a younger son of Richard, Earl of Salisbury, and thirdly, Sir Gervase Clifton, Knt., but had issue by neither.

JANE STANHOPE, m. SIR HUMPHERY BOURCHIER, third son of Henry, Earl of Essex, which

SIR HUMPHREY BOURCHIER was summoned to parliament in right of his said wife, as BARON CROMWELL, from 25th July, 1461, to 15th October, 1470. This nobleman fell, gallantly fighting at the battle of Barnet-field, on the part of Edward IV. in 1471, and d. without issue. The BARONY OF CROMWELL, upon the decease of his lordship's widow, fell into ABEYANCE, amongst the descendants of Ralph, the fourth baron's three aunts,

Hawise, wife of Thomas, Lord Bardolph.

Maud, wife of Sir William Fitz-Williams, Knt.

Elizabeth, wife first of Sir John Clifton, Knt., and afterwards of Sir Edward Bensted, Knt.

and it still so continues, save as to the line of Bardolph, which was attainted.

ARMS.—Or. a chief gu. over all a bend, as.

CROMWELL—BARON CROMWELL, OF OKEHAM, IN THE COUNTY OF RUTLAND, EARL OF ESSEX.

| Barony, | by Letters Patent, | 9th July, 1536. |
| Earldom, | dated | 10th April, 1539. |

Lineage.

THOMAS CROMWELL, son of Walter Cromwell, a blacksmith at Putney, upon his return from foreign service under the Duke of Bourbon, obtained a situation in the suite of Cardinal Wolsey, and, after the fall of that celebrated prelate, was taken into the service of the king, (at Henry's especial command, from his fidelity to his old master,) in which he evinced so much zeal and ability, that the road to the highest honours of the state presented very soon an unimpeded course for his ambition. In a short time he filled successively the important situations of master of the jewel-office, clerk of the Hamper, principal secretary, justice of the forests, master of the rolls, and lord privy-seal, and was elevated to the peerage, in the dignity of BARON CROMWELL, of Okeham, on the 9th July, 1536. He was afterwards constituted the king's vice-regent in spirituals, honoured with the GARTER, and finally (17th April 1539) created EARL OF ESSEX, when he was invested with the LORD HIGH CHAMBERLAINSHIP OF ENGLAND. In the dissolution of the monastic institutions, and the establishment of the spiritual supremacy of his royal master, Cromwell, considering the powerful interests with which he had to contend, exhibited a boldness of character paralleled only by the profound political dexterity that accomplished those great and daring innovations. As a recompense, he shared largely in the spoil of the fallen church, and, amongst other grants, the sacerdotal revenues of St. Osythus, in Essex, and of the Gray Friars, at Yarmouth, flowed into his coffers. But his elevation was not more rapid than his decline, and his fall was hailed by all parties with satisfaction. So long as Essex ministered to the pleasures of Henry, the royal shield protected him from the indignation of the people; but the moment that was removed, his fate was sealed. His instrumentality in allying the king with Anne of Cleves, was the rock upon which his fortunes foundered, not very dissimilar to that upon which the papal power had previously perished. Unprepared for such a proceeding, the earl was arrested, under the king's especial order, by the Duke of Norfolk, at the controul-board, 10th June, 1540, hurried off to the Tower, attainted unheard, and beheaded on the 94th of the ensuing month, notwithstanding Archbishop Cranmer's powerful exertions in his behalf; and all the honours of the ex-minister were of course FORFEITED under the attainder; but his son, Gregory, who, in his life-time, had been summoned to parliament as Lord Cromwell, had that dignity confirmed to him, by letters patent, in the December following the earl's execution. (See Baron Cromwell.)

The annexed Letter was written, it appears, at the king's desire, by Cromwell himself.

" Most Gracious Kinge, and most mercifull Sovereying:

" Your most humble, most obeysant, and most bounden subject, and most lamentable servant and prisoner, prostrate at the feete of your most excellent Majesty, have herd your pleasure, by the mouth of your comptroller; which was, that I should wrytte to your most excellent Highness, such thynges as I thought mete to be wryttyn consernyng my most miserable state, and condition; for the which your most habundant goodness, benignyte and licens, the immortalle God, three and one, reward your magestye. And now most gracious Prince to the matyer,

" FYRST. Wher I have bene accusyd to your Magestye of Treason. To that I say, I never in alle my lyfe thought wyllingly to do that thyng that myght or sholde displease your Majesty; and much less to do or say that thyng, which of itself is so high and abbominable offence; as God knowyth, who I doubt not shall reveale the trewth to your Highness. Myne accusers your Grace knowyth, God forgive them: For as I ever have had love to your honor, - person, lyfe, prosperitye, helthe, welthe, joy and comfort; and also your most dere and most entyerly belovyd sone, the Prynce, his Grace, and your proceedyngs, God so helpe me in this myne adversitie and conffound me yf ever I thought the contrary. What labours, payns and travailes I have taken, according to my most bounden deutye, God also knowyth. For, yf it were in my power (as it is Godds) to make your Majestye to lyve ever young and prosperous, God knowyth I woolde. If it hadde bene, or were in my power to make yow so ryche, as ye myght enrych alle men, God helpe me as woolde do hit. If it had bene or were in my power to make your majesty so puyssant, as alle the worlde sholde be compellyd to obey yow, Christ he knowyth I wolde; for so am I of alle othyr most bounde: for your Magestye hath bene the most bountiful Prynce to me, that ever was a Kyng to his subject: ye, and more like a dere father (your Magestye not offendyd) than a master. Such hath bene your most grave and Godly counsayle towards me, at sundry tymes. In that I have offendid I ax your mercy. Should I now, for such exceeding goodness, benyngnyte, liberalitie and bounty be your traytor, nay then the greatest paynes were too little for me. Should any faccyon, or any affeccyon to any point make me a traytor to your magestie, then alle the Devylls in Hell confound me, and the vengeance of God light upon me, yf I sholde once have thought yt, most gracious Soverayn Lord. To my remembrance I never spake with the CHANCELOUR OF THE AUGMENTACYONS and THROGMORTON togethyr at one tyme; but yf I dyde, I am sure, I sake never of any such matyer; and your Grace knowyth, what manner of man Throgmorton hath evyr bene towards your Grace and your procedyngs, and what Mr. Chancelour hath bene towards me, God and he best knowyth, I will ne can accuse hym. What I have bene towards hym, your magestye right welle knowyth. I wolde in Christ I had obeyed your often most gracious, grave counsayles, and advertysements, that it had not bene with me as now hit is. Yet our Lord, yf hit be his wylle, can do with me as he dyd with Susan who was falsely accused: unto the whyche God I have only committyd my sowle; my body, and goods at your Mgestyes pleasure, in whose mercye and pyetie I do holly repose me: for othyr hope then in God and your Magestye I have not.

" Sir, as to your Common Welthe, I have aftyr my wytte, power, and knowledge, travayled therein; havyng had no respect to persons (your Magestie only except) and my dewtye tu the same: but, that I have done any injustice, or wrong, wyllfully, I trust God shall here my wytnes, and the world not able justly to accuse me. And yet I have not done my dewtye in alle thynges, as I was bounden, wherefore I ask mercy. If I have herde of any combynacyons, convencyons, or such as were offenders of your laws; I have, though not as I sholde have done, for the most part revealed them, and also causyd them to be punyshed; not of males, as God shall judge me. Nevertheless, Sir, I have medelyd in so many matyers, under your Highnes, that I am not able to answer them all. But one thyng I am well assured of; that willingly and wyttyngly I have not had wille to offend your Hyghness: but hard it is for me, or any other, medelyng, as I have done, to live under your Grace and your laws, but we must daylie offend; and where I have offendyd I most humbly aske mercy and pardon at your Grace's wyll and pleasure.

" Amongst othyr thynges, most Gracyous Soverayn, Mr. Comptroller shewed me, that your Grace shewed hym, that within this fourteen dayes, ye commytted a matyer of grete secresye, which I did revele, contrary to your expectation. Sir! I do remember well the matyer, which I nevyr revelyd to any creture: but this I dyd, Sir; after your Grace had openyd the matyer; fyrst to me in your chamber, and declared your lamentable fate; declarying the thynges, which your Highnes mysliked in the Quene; at whych time I shewyd your Grace, that she often desyred to speke wyth me, but I durst not; and ye sayd, why sholde I not? Allegyng, that I might do much good in goying to her; and to be playn wyth her, in declaring my mynde: I thereupon, takyng oportunitye, not being a lyttil grievyd, spake privylie with her Lord Chamberlayn, for the whych I aske your Grace mercy; desyring him, (not naming your Grace to hym,) to fynd some means that the Quene might be induced to order your Grace plesantly, in her behavyour towards you; thinking thereby, for to have had some faultes amendyd, to your Magesties content. And after that, by generalle wordes, the sayd Lord Chamberlane, and other of the Queene's counsayle, being with me, in my chamber at Westminster, for Lycens for the departure of the strange Maydens; I then required them to counsayl their Maystres, to use all plesantnees to your Highnes; the whych things undoubtedly weren both spoken before your Magestye told the secrete matyer unto me, only of purpose, that she might have by love inducyd to such plesant and honorable facyons, as myght have bene to your Grace's comforte; whych, above all things, as God knoweth, I dyd most covyt and desire. But that I openyd my mouth to any creature, aftyr your Magestye committyd the secresye thereof to me, othyr than only to my Lord Admyral; which I dyde by your Grace's commandement, which was upon Sunday last in the mornyng, whom I then fownd as wylling, and glad to seke remedye, for your comfort and consolacyon; and saw by hym that he did as much lament Your Highnes fate, as ever dyd man; and was wonderfully grevyed to see Your Highnes so troubelyd, wyshing gretely your comfort: for the attayning whereof he sayd, (your Honour salvyd) he would spend the best bloud in hys belye: and yf I wolde not do the lyke, ye and wyllingly dye for your comfort, I wolde I were in Hell; and I woolde I sholde receive a Thousand Dethis.

" Sir, This is all that I have done in that matyer; and yf I have offendyd your Magestie therein, prostrate at your Highnes fete, I most lowly aske mercy and pardon of your Highnes. Sir, this was also layd unto my chardge, at myne examination, that I had retayned contrary to your Laws. Sir, what exposycioun may be made upon retaynors, I know not: but thys wyll I say; that yf ever I retayned any man, but such only as were my household servants, but agaynst my will God confound me. But most Gracyous Soverayn, I have been so called on, and sewyd to by them, that sayd they were my Frendes; that constraynyd thereto, I retained their children and frendys, not as Retayners: for their fathers and parents did promyse me to fynde them, and so I took them, not as Ratayners, to my grete chardge, and for none evyll, as God best knowyth, interpret to the contrary who wylle; most humbly beseechyng your Magestye off pardon, yf I have offendyd therein.

" Sir, I acknowledge myself to have been a most miserable and wrechyd sinner; and that I have not towards God and your Highnes, behavyd myself as I ought and sholde have done: for the whych myne offence to God, whyle I lyve, I shall continually kall for his mercy. And for myne offencys to your Grace which God knowyth were never malycious and wylfull and that I never thought treason to Your Highnes, your realme, or Posteritie, so God helpe me, either in word or dede. Neverthelees, prostrate at your Magesties feet, in what thyng soever I have offendyd, I appel to your Highnes for mercy, grace, and pardon, in such wyse as shall be

152

your pleasure; beseechyng the Almighty Maker and redeemer of the World to send your Magestie continual and long helthe, welthe and prosperitie with Nestor's Yeares to reigne: and your dere son the Prince's Grace to prosper, reigne and continue long after you. And they that wolde contrary, short liffe, shame, and confusion. Wrytten with the quaking hand and most sorrowful heart of your most sorrowfull subject and most humble servant and prysoner, this Saturday at your Tower of London.

" THOMAS CROMWELL."

ARMS.—Ar. on a fesse between three lions rampant or., a rose gules between two Cornish choughs proper.   V. Ciwel

NOTE.—SIR ROBERT WILLIAMS, nephew of Thomas Cromwell, Earl of Essex, assumed the surname of Cromwell, and being in favour with King Henry VIII., was appointed a gentleman of the privy-chamber to that monarch, and constable of Berkeley Castle. Upon the dissolution of the monasteries, he obtained all the lands, in Huntingdonshire, belonging to any religious house in that county, and was s. by his son,

SIR HENRY CROMWELL, Knt., of Hinchinbroke, who left issue,

Sir Oliver Cromwell, K.B., and

ROBERT CROMWELL, who was father of

OLIVER CROMWELL, the Protector.

CROMWELL — BARONS CROMWELL.

By Writ of Summons, dated 28th April, 1539.
By Letters Patent, dated 18th December, 1540.

Lineage.

The Hon.

GREGORY CROMWELL, summoned to parliament 28th April, 1539, as LORD CROMWELL, (son of Thomas Cromwell, Earl of Essex, attainted and beheaded in July, 1540,) a servant of King Henry VIII., was created BARON CROMWELL, by letters patent, dated 18th December, 1540. His lordship m. Elisabeth, daughter of Sir John Seymour, sister of Edward, Duke of Somerset, and widow of Sir Anthony Oughtred, by whom he had three sons, HENRY, Edward, and Thomas, and two daughters, Frances, m. to Edward Stroude, Esq., of Devonshire; Catherine, m. to John Stroude, Esq., of the county of Dorset. Lord Cromwell, who had summons to parliament to the year 1548, d. in 1551, and was s. by his eldest son,

HENRY CROMWELL, second baron, summoned to parliament from the 5th to the 31st Elisabeth. His lordship m. Mary, daughter of John, Marquess of Winchester, and had issue, EDWARD, his successor, Sir Gregory Cromwell, Knt., and Catherine m. to Sir Lionel Talmache, Knt. He d. in 1592, and was s. by his elder son,

EDWARD CROMWELL, third baron, summoned to parliament in the 36th Elizabeth. This nobleman was with the Earl of Essex in his expedition at sea against the Spaniards in the 40th Elisabeth, and joined in the insurrection three years afterwards, which cost the earl his head. Lord Cromwell received, however, an especial pardon on the 9th July, 1691. His lordship m. first, ——, daughter of —— Umpton, Esq., and had an only daughter, Elizabeth, m. first, to Sir John Shelton, of Shelton, in Norfolk, and afterwards to Thomas Fitzhughes, Esq., of Oxfordshire. The baron m. secondly, Frances, daughter of William Rugge, Esq., of Norfolk, by whom he had THOMAS, his successor, with two daughters, viz. Frances, m. to Sir John Wingfield, of Tickencote, in the county of Rutland, and Anne, m. to Sir William Wingfield, of Poores Court, in Ireland. Lord Cromwell having alienated his estates in England by sale, purchased the barony of Lecale, in Ireland, from Mountjoy Blount, Earl of Devon, or, according to Noble, in his History of Cornwall, made an exchange thereof. His lordship d. in Ireland in 1607, and was s. by his son,

THOMAS CROMWELL, fourth baron, who was created by King Charles I. in 1625, *Viscount Lecale*, and EARL OF ARDGLASS, in the peerage of Ireland. His lordship remained firmly attached to the interests of the king during the civil wars, notwithstanding his friendship with the Earl of Essex. He m. Elizabeth, daughter and heiress of Robert Meverell, Esq., of Throwleigh, in the county of Stafford, by whom he had surviving issue, WINGFIELD, his successor, VERE-ESSEX, who inherited after his nephew, and Oliver, with a daughter Mary, who m. William Fitz-Herbert, Esq., of Tissington, in the county of Derby. He d. in 1653, and was s. by his eldest son,

WINGFIELD CROMWELL, FIFTH BARON CROMWELL, and SECOND EARL OF ARDGLASS. This nobleman m. Mary, daughter of Sir William Russell, of Strentham, in the county of Worcester, and was s. in 1668, by his only son,

THOMAS CROMWELL, SIXTH BARON and THIRD EARL, who m. ——, daughter of His Grace Michael Boyle, Archbishop of Dublin, and lord chancellor of Ireland, but dying issueless 11th April, 1682, his honours reverted to his uncle,

VERE-ESSEX CROMWELL, seventh baron and fourth earl. This nobleman m. Miss Hamilton, by whom (who subsequently espoused Richard Price, Esq.), he had an only daughter, ELIZABETH. His lordship d. in 1687, when the Irish VISCOUNTY OF LE-CALE and EARLDOM OF ARDGLASS, and the English Barony of Cromwell, created by patent, EXPIRED: but the BARONY OF CROMWELL, originating in the writ of 28th April, 1539, devolved upon his daughter,

ELIZABETH CROMWELL, as Baroness Cromwell, in which rank her ladyship assisted at the funeral of Queen Mary II., and coronation of Queen Anne. She m. Edward Southwell, Esq., principal secretary of state for Ireland, and had issue, two sons and a daughter, who d. all *sine prole*; and another, a son, Edward Southwell, who marrying Catherine, daughter of Edward Watson, Viscount Sondes, and sole heiress of her brothers, Lewis and Thomas, Earls of Rockingham, left a son,

EDWARD SOUTHWELL, who, in right of his mother, succeeded to the Barony of DE CLIFFORD.

Her ladyship d. in 1709, and the BARONY OF CROMWELL is now supposed to be vested in LORD DE CLIFFORD, son and successor of Edward, Lord de Clifford, mentioned above.

DACRE—BARONS DACRE, OF GIL-LESLAND OR THE NORTH.

By Writ of Summons, dated 15th November, 1482, 22nd Edward IV.

Lineage.

In the 20th year of King Henry III.

WILLIAM DACRE, *of Dacre*, in the county of Cumberland, served the office of sheriff for that shire, with John de Moore, and in the thirty-second of the same reign, he was constituted sheriff of Yorkshire, and governor of the castles of Scarborough and Pickering. He died in ten years afterwards, when again sheriff of Cumberland, and governor of the castle of Carlisle, and was s. by his son,

RANULPH DE DACRE, who had been in the life-time of his father a staunch adherent of King Henry III., in the conflicts between that monarch and the barons, and upon succeeding to his inheritance, was appointed sheriff of Cumberland. In the 7th Edward I., he was constituted sheriff of Yorkshire, and continued in that trust, until the end of the third quarter of the eighth succeeding year. This Ranulph, m. Joane de Luci, and dying in the 14th Edward I., was s. by his son,

WILLIAM DE DACRE, who, in the 32nd Edward I., was in the expedition made that year into Scotland, and about the same period obtained a charter for free Warren in all his demesne lands at Dacre, in the county of Cumberland, and at Halton, in Lancashire. In the first year of the next reign he had licence to encastellate his mansion at Dunwalloght, in Cumberland, on the marches of Scotland, and in three years afterwards was again engaged in the Scottish wars. His lordship m. Joane, daughter and heiress of Benedict Gernet, of Bluet, and having been summoned to parliament as a BARON, from the 26th Edward I., to the 19th Edward II., departed this life in the latter year, and was s. by his son,

RANULPH DE DACRE, who had summons to parliament as BARON DACRE, from 15th May, 1321, to 15th November, 1338. His lordship was made sheriff of Cumberland, and governor of Carlisle, in the 4th Edward III., and in the eighth of the same monarch, he obtained livery of all those castles and manors in Anandale, within the realm of Scotland, part of the possessions of Roger de Kirkpatric, and Humphrey de Bois, which had been given to him by Edward King of Scotland. He was also, in the same year, joined in commission with Robert de Clifford, for the defence of the town and marches of Carlisle, and for arraying so many "men at arms, hoblers, and foot soldiers," as should be needful for the service. In the next year he had license to make a castle of his house at Naworth, in the county of Cumberland. His lordship m. Margaret, only daughter and heiress of Thomas de Multon, BARON MULTON, *of Gillesland*, (by writ of Edward II., dated 26th August, 1307,) by whom he acquired considerable estates, and left at his decease, in 1339, three sons, viz.

WILLIAM, who succeeded to the Barony of

Dacre through his father, and to the Barony of MULTON, through his mother, but died *s. p.* in 1361.

RALPH, successor to his brother in the baronies, died also *s. p.* in 1375.

And

HUGH DE DACRE, who *s.* his brother Ralph as Lord Dacre and Lord Multon, and had summons to parliament from 1st December, 1376, to 20th August, 1383. His lordship *m.* Ela, daughter of Alexander, Lord Maxwell, and dying in 1383, was *s.* by his son,

WILLIAM DE DACRE, summoned to parliament from 3rd March, 1384, to 23rd November, 1403. His lordship *m.* Joane, daughter of James, Earl of Douglas, and dying about the year 1408, was *s.* by his son,

THOMAS DE DACRE, summoned to parliament from 1st December, 1412, to 26th May, 1455. This nobleman was constituted chief forester of Inglewood Forest, in the county of Cumberland, in the 8th Henry V., and was appointed in the 2nd Henry VI. one of the commissioners to treat for peace with James I. of Scotland. His lordship *m.* Philippa, daughter of Ralph Nevil, Earl of Westmorland, and had issue,

    THOMAS, who *m.* Elizabeth, daughter of Richard Bowes, Esq., and dying in the life-time of his father, left an only daughter and heiress,

        Joane, *m.* Sir Richard Fienes, Knt., who was declared *Baron* DACRE by King Edward IV., and from whom the BARONY has descended in regular succession to the present LORD DACRE.

    Ranulph, a stout adherent of the house of Lancaster, had summons to parliament as a BARON in the 38th Henry VI., but fell at Towtonfield, and was subsequently attainted, when his title and estates became forfeited.

    HUMPHREY, of whom presently.

    Joan, *m.* to Thomas, eighth Lord de Clifford.

SIR HUMPHREY DACRE, (the third son,) having deported himself obsequiously to the then triumphant house of York, attended King Edward IV. at the sieges and surrender of the different Lancastrian Castles in the north : for which good services, as well as his fidelity to the king's sister, Margaret, whom he escorted as chamberlain upon her journey into Flanders, on the occasion of her marriage with Charles, Duke of Burgundy, he was constituted master forester of Inglewood Forest for life, and continuing to enjoy the confidence of the king, he was summoned to parliament as a BARON on the 15th November, 1482, under the designation *of* " HUMFRIDIO DACRES OF GILLESLAND, *Chevalier.*" Sir Humphrey Dacre, who enjoyed Gillesland and other capital manors, by virtue of a fine levied by his father, had previously disputed the original BARONY OF DACRE, with his niece Joane, Lady Fienes, when the affair was referred to the arbitration of King Edward IV., who confirmed Sir Richard Fienes and his lady in the barony, with the precedency enjoyed by Lady Fienes's grandfather, and decreed to them divers castles and manors, but GILLESLAND, the ancient seat of the Vaux's, with several considerable estates was adjudged to Sir

Humphrey; who, at the same time, was created a BARON, with place next below Sir Richard Fienes, and for distinction was styled Lord Dacre, of Gillesland, or of the north; Sir Richard being entitled Lord Dacre, of the South. His lordship *m.* Maud, daughter of Sir Thomas Parr, Knt., and dying in 1509, was *s.* by his son,

SIR THOMAS DACRE, second Lord Dacre, of Gillesland, summoned to parliament from 17th October, 1509, to 12th November, 1515. This nobleman, in the 9th Henry VII., served under Thomas, Earl of Surrey, at the siege of Norham Castle, and his lordship obtained great celebrity in the command of a body of horse reserve, at the famous fight of FLODDEN, in the 4th Henry VIII. under the same gallant leader. He was, subsequently, at different times, engaged in Scotland, and he filled the important office of warden of the West Marches from the 1st year of King Henry VIII. He *m.* Elizabeth, grand-daughter and sole heiress of Ralph de Greystock, Baron Greystock, K.G., and had issue—

    WILLIAM, his successor.

    Humphrey.

    Mary, *m.* to Francis, Earl of Shrewsbury.

    Margaret, *m.* to Henry, Lord Scrope, of Bolton.

    Jane.

His lordship *d.* in 1525, and was *s.* by his elder son,

SIR WILLIAM DACRE, as third Lord Dacre, of Gillesland, summoned to parliament from 3rd November, 1529, to 21st October, 1555, in the first writ as " Willielmo Dacre de Dacre and Greystok, Chl'r," afterwards as " de Gillesland," or of Greystok, or " de North." In the 26th Henry VIII. this nobleman being accused of high treason by Sir Ralph Fenwike, was brought to trial before his peers at Westminster, in the July of that year, and acquitted, owing to the description of evidence by which the charge was sustained, namely, persons of mean degree from the Scottish border, who were either suborned, or brought forward by a vindictive feeling towards Lord Dacre, arising from the severity with which he had executed the duty of warden of the marches. In the reigns of Edward VI., Mary and Elizabeth, his lordship was captain of the Castle, and governor of Carlisle, and in the 2nd year of the last Queen he was joined in commission with the Earl of Northumberland to negotiate a peace with Scotland. His lordship *m.* Elizabeth, fifth daughter of George, Earl of Shrewsbury, and had issue,

    THOMAS, his successor.

    Leonard, who being dissatisfied with the distribution of the family estates amongst his nieces, at the decease of his nephew, George, Lord Dacre, joined in the conspiracy of the Earls of Northumberland and Westmorland, temp. Elizabeth for the rescue of Mary, Queen of Scots, and took possession of the Dacre Castles, of GREYSTOCK and NAWORTH, in the north, but was eventually obliged to fly into Scotland, when he was attainted, with the lords above-mentioned; died *s. p.*

    Edward, attainted with his brother Leonard for the same treason, died *s. p.*

Francis, attainted with his brothers, and for the same treason. He lived, however, several years after, dying about the 8th Charles I. He m. Dorothy, daughter of John, Earl of Derwentwater, and left,

Randal, (the last male heir of Humphrey, Lord Dacre, of Gillesland,) who d. two years after his father, without issue. The parish register of Greystock for 1634, contains the following entry (Buried), "Randal Dacre, Esq., sonne and hyre to Francis Dacre, Esquire, deceased, being the youngest son of the last Lord William Dacre, deceased, being the last hyre male of that lyne; which said Randal dyed at London, and was brought downe at the charges of the Right Hon. Thomas, Earle of Arundell and Surreye, and earle marshall of England."

Margaret, m. to Anthony Browne, Viscount Montacute.

Anne, m. to Henry Clifford, Earl of Cumberland.

Eleanor, m. to Henry Jerningham, Esq., of Costtessey Hall, in the county of Norfolk, by whom she had, with other issue,

HENRY JERNINGHAM, who was created a baronet 16th October, 1621; a dignity is inherited by Sir Henry's descendant, George-William (Stafford-Jerningham), present Lord Stafford.

Mary, m. to Alexander Culpepper, Esq.

Dorothy, m. to Sir Thomas Windsore, Knt., son and heir of William, Lord Windsore.

Lord Dacre d. in 1563, and was s. by his eldest son,

THOMAS DACRE, fourth Baron Dacre, of Gillesland, but never summoned to parliament. This nobleman m. Elizabeth, daughter of Sir James Leiburne, Knt., of Cunswick, in Westmorland, and had issue,

GEORGE, his successor.

Anne, m. to Philip Howard, Earl of Arundel.

Mary, m. to Thomas, Lord Howard, of Walden, and died s. p.

Elizabeth, m. to Lord William Howard, and her great-grandson, Charles Howard, Esq., was elevated to the peerage on the 20th April, 1661, by the titles of Baron Dacre, of Gillesland, Viscount Howard, of Morpeth, AND EARL OF CARLISLE. To which nobleman the present EARL OF CARLISLE, is great-great-great-grandson.

His lordship d. in 1566, and was s. by his only son,

GEORGE DACRE, fifth Lord Dacre, of Gillesland, who d. in minority, anno 1569, of a fall from a wooden horse, upon which he practised to leap. At the decease of his lordship the "BARONY OF DACRE, OF GILLESLAND," fell into abeyance between his sisters as co-heirs, and it so continues with their descendants. Of his estates, Greystock fell to the Earl of Arundel, and is now in the possession of the Duke of Norfolk. While Naworth Castle devolved upon Lord William Howard, where he settled, and it now belongs to the Earl of Carlisle.

Note:—The sisters of the last Lord Dacre are now represented, thus :—

Anne, Lady Arundel, by the Lords Petre and Stourton.

Elizabeth, Lady William Howard, by the Earl of Carlisle.

ARMS.—Gu. three escallops ar.

DAGWORTH — BARONS DAGWORTH.

By Writ of Summons, dated 13th November, 1347, 21 Edward III.

Lineage.

In the 19th of King Edward II., upon the death of Lora, widow of William Peyforer, which Lora died, seised of the third part of the office of *Huisher*, (Usher) in the exchequer court, and crier in the King's Bench, her grandson,

JOHN DE DAGWORTH, being found her next heir, upon doing his homage, had livery of the lands of his inheritance. To this John, succeeded his son,

THOMAS DE DAGWORTH, a very eminent soldier in the reigns of Edward II., and Edward III. In the 20th of the latter, being then a knight and commander of the king's forces in Britanny, he is recorded, as having defeated twice in one day, Charles de Blois, who had usurped in right of his wife, the title of Duke of Britanny, notwithstanding the great inequality of forces, the duke having fifteen hundred horse, eight thousand balistars, and thirty thousand foot, being treble the army of the English commander. In the next year following up his fortune, he marched to the relief of Rochedirian, invested by the same foe, and giving battle to the duke, obtained a decisive victory, making prisoners of thirty-six knights, slaying more than five hundred men-at-arms, and conveying Charles himself a captive to the Tower of London; for which good services he was appointed lieutenant and captain-general to the king, in the dukedom of Britanny; and the next year reaping fresh laurels on the French soil, he was summoned to parliament, as BARON DAGWORTH, on the 13th November, 1347, as an additional reward for his gallantry. His lordship resided from that period in Britanny until 1359, when he is said to have been slain by the treachery of the French. He was s. by his son,

SIR NICHOLAS DAGWORTH, second Baron Dagworth, but never summoned to parliament. Like his father, this gallant person acquired the highest military renown. In the year 1366, Sir Nicholas obtained a great victory over the French in Anjou, when amongst his prisoners, were the Dukes of Orleans and Anjou. It is further reported of him, that with thirteen English horse, he encountered sixty French near Flaveny, and by the means of chariots, which he employed for his defence, utterly vanquished them. In the reign of Richard II., he was imprisoned by the great lords then opposed to the court, but having obtained his freedom, he was employed with Walter Skirlaw, Bishop of Durham, to negociate a peace with France—"from which period," says Dugdale, "I have not seen any more of him."

ARMS.—Ermine, on a bend gules, three Besants.

DAMER—BARONS MILTON, VISCOUNTS MILTON, EARLS OF DORCHESTER.

Barony,	{ by Letters }	10th May, 1762.
Earldom, &c.	{ Patent, }	18th May, 1792.

Lineage.

This family had been long seated in the counties of Somerset and Dorset, and its founder, William D'Amory, came into England with the Conqueror.

JOSEPH DAMER, eldest son of John Damer, of Godmanston, embarked early in the service of the parliament, and was advanced by Cromwell to the command of a troop of horse: being in high confidence with the usurper, he was twice deputed by him upon secret negotiations to Cardinal Mazarine. After the restoration, Mr. Damer not deeming it safe to continue in England, disposed of his lands in Somerset, and Dorsetshire, and purchased other estates in Ireland, whither he removed. He d. on the 6th July, 1720, at the advanced age of ninty-one, never having experienced indisposition until these days before his decease. He died a bachelor, and bequeathed his estates to his nephew,

JOHN DAMER, Esq., of Shronehill, in the county of Tipperary, who m. in 1724, Margaret, eldest daughter of Andrew Roe, Esq., of Rossborough, in the same shire, but dying without issue in 1768, the estates devolved upon his brother,

JOSEPH DAMER, Esq., of Came, in the county of Dorset, b. in 1676, m. 9th December, 1714, Mary, daughter of John Churchill, Esq., of Henbury, in the same shire, and had issue,

    JOSEPH.

    John, of Came, in the county of Dorset, m. Martha, daughter of Samuel Rush, Esq., of Benhall, in the county of Suffolk.

    George, M. P. for Dorsetshire, in 1750-1, died in 1752, unmarried.

    Mary, m. to William Henry Dawson, Esq., of Dawson's Grove, in the Queen's county. This gentleman was advanced to the peerage of Ireland, as Viscount Carlow, and his son was created Earl of Portarlington. His grand-children, the present Earl of Portarlington, and his brothers, succeeded to the Damer estates, at the decease of Lady Caroline Damer.

    Martha, m. first, in 1741, to Sir Edward Crofton, Bart., of the Moat, in the county of Roscommon, and secondly, to Ezekiel Nesbitt, M.D.

Mr. Damer, who represented the county of Dorset in parliament, in 1722, died 1st March, 1736-7, and was s. by his eldest son,

JOSEPH DAMER, Esq., who having successively represented the borough of Weymouth, (1741,) Bramber, (1747) and Dorchester, (1754,) in

156

parliament, was elevated to the peerage of Ireland, on the 3rd July, 1753, as BARON MILTON, of Shronehill, in the county of Tipperary, and created a peer of Great Britain, on the 10th May, 1762, in the dignity of BARON MILTON, of Milton Abbey, in the county of Dorset. His lordship m., 27th July, 1742, Lady Caroline Sackville, only surviving daughter of Lionel, first Duke of Dorset, by whom (who d. 24th March, 1775) he had issue,

    John, b. 25th June, 1744, m. 14th June, 1767, Anne, only child of the Right Honourable Henry Seymour Conway, brother of Francis, first Marquess of Hertford, and died s. p., 15th August, 1776.

    GEORGE, who succeeded his father.

    Lionel, b. 16th September, 1748, m. 16th April, 1778, Williamsa, daughter of William Janssen, and niece of Sir Stephen Theodore Janssen, Bart.

    Caroline, b. 4th May, 1752, and d. unmarried, in 1829.

His lordship was advanced to the dignities of Viscount Milton, and EARL OF DORCHESTER, in the peerage of Great Britain, on the 15th May, 1792. He d. 12th February, 1798, and was s. by his eldest surviving son,

GEORGE DAMER, second earl of Dorchester, at whose decease in 1808, without issue, (his brother Lionel having died previously,) the Irish Barony of MILTON, with the British EARLDOM OF DORCHESTER, and inferior dignities, became EXTINCT.

ARMS.—Barry nebule of six, ar. and gu. a band ingrailed, az.

DANVERS—BARON DANVERS, OF DANTSEY, IN THE COUNTY OF WILTS. EARL OF DANBY, IN THE COUNTY OF YORK.

Barony,	{ by Letters }	27th July, 1603.
Earldom,	{ Patent, }	5th February, 1626.

Lineage.

JOHN NEVIL, last Lord Latimer, of that surname, m. Lucy, daughter of Henry, Earl of Worcester, and left at his decease, in 1577, four daughters, his co-heiresses, viz.—

    Catherine, m. to Henry Percy, Earl of Northumberland, by whom she had eight sons and three daughters. This earl was committed to the tower, for a supposed plot in favour of Mary, Queen of Scots, and there found dead in his bed, wounded by three pistol bullets, anno 1585.

    Dorothy, m. Thomas Cecil, first Earl of Exeter, by whom she was mother of

        WILLIAM, second Earl, who left at his decease, in 1640, three daughters, viz.—

            Elizabeth, m. to Thomas, Earl of Berkshire.

            Diana, m. first, to Thomas, Earl of Elgin, and secondly, to the Earl of Aylesbury.

Anne, m. to Henry Grey, Earl of Stamford.

Lucy, m. to Sir William Cornwallis, Knt., and left four daughters, viz.—

Frances, m. to Sir Edward Withipoole.
Elizabeth, m. to Thomas Sandys, Esq.
Catherine, m. to Richard Farmer, Esq.
Dorothy, m. to Archibald, Earl of Argyll.

Elizabeth, m. first, to Sir John Danvers, Knt., and secondly, to Sir Edmund Carey, Knt.

SIR JOHN DANVERS, acquired with the Honourable Elizabeth Nevil, the ancient Castle of Danby, in the North Riding of Yorkshire, and had issue,

CHARLES, (Sir) who lost his life, and was attainted for participating in the insurrection of Robert, Earl of Essex, 43rd Elizabeth.

HENRY, of whom presently.

John, (Sir) one of the Judges of King Charles I., d. in 1659.

Elizabeth, m. to Thomas Walmsley, Esq., of Dunkelhagh, in the county of Lancaster, and left an only daughter,

Anne Walmsley, who m. first, William Middleton, Esq., of Stockeld, in the county of York, and secondly, Sir Edward Osborn, Bart.; by the latter she had issue,

Sir Thomas Osborn, Bart., who was created *Viscount Latimer, Earl of Danby, Marquess of Carmarthen, and* DUKE OF LEEDS. His lordship was great-great, great-grandfather, of the present DUKE OF LEEDS.

Dorothy, m. to Sir Peter Osborn, Knt., from which union the *Baronets* OSBORN, of Chicksand Priory, in the county of Bedford, derive.

The second son,

SIR HENRY DANVERS, Knt., was elevated to the peerage, by letters patent, on the 27th July, 1603, as *Baron Danvers*, of Dantsey, in the county of Wilts, and in two years afterwards, his lordship was restored in blood, by special act of parliament, as heir to his father, notwithstanding the attainder of Sir Charles Danvers, his elder brother. Upon the accession of King Charles I., Lord Danvers was created by letters patent, dated 5th February, 1626, EARL OF DANBY, and his lordship was soon afterwards chosen a KNIGHT of the GARTER. This nobleman, who had adopted from his youth the profession of arms, distinguished himself both by sea and land, and was esteemed an able and gallant soldier.

His lordship was the founder of the famous Physic Garden, at Oxford, which cost him little short of £5,000. He d. 20th January, 1643, when never having married, the *Barony of Danvers* and EARLDOM OF DANBY, became extinct. His remains were interred in the chancel of the parish church at Dantsey, under a noble monument of white marble, with the following inscription:—

" HENRY, EARL OF DANBY, second son to Sir John Danvers, Knt., and Dame ELIZABETH, daughter and co-heir of John Nevil, Lord Latimer; born at Dauntesey, in the county of Wilts, 28th June, ann. Dom., 1573, and baptised in this church, the 1st of July following, being Sunday. He departed this life on the 20th of January, ann. Dom., 1643, and lyeth here interred.

" He was partly bred up in the low country wars, under MAURICE, Earl of Nassau, (afterwards Prince of Orange,) and in many other military actions of those times, both by sea and land. He was made a CAPTAIN in the wars of France, and there knighted for his good service, under Henry IV., then French King. He was employed as lieutenant-general of the horse, and serjeant-major of the whole army, in Ireland, under ROBERT, Earl of Essex, and Charles, Baron of Mountjoy, in the reign of Queen Elizabeth.

" He was made Baron of DAUNTSEY, and peer of the realm, by King James I.; and by him made Lord President of MUNSTER, and Governor of GARNSEY.

" By King Charles I., he was created Earl of Danby; made of his privy council, and knight of the most noble order of the Garter; but declining more active employments in his later time, (by reason of his imperfect health,) full of honour, wounds, and days, he died at his house at CORNBURY PARK, in the county of Oxford, in the 71st year of his age."

Laus Deo.

Sacred marble, safely keep
His dust, who under thee must sleep,
Untill the years again restore
Their dead, and time shall be no more.
Meanwhile, if He (who all things wears)
Does ruine thee; or if thy tears
Are shed for him: dissolve thy frame,
Thou art requited: for his fame,
His vertue, and his worth shall be
Another monument to thee.

ARMS.—Gu. a chevron between three mullets of six points, or.

D'ARCY—BARONS D'ARCY.

By Writ of Summons, dated 29th December, 1299,
28 Edward I.

Lineage.

At the time of the general survey,

NORMAN DE ARECI enjoyed no less than thirty-three lordships in the county of Lincoln, by the immediate gift of the CONQUEROR, of which NOCTON was one, where he and his posterity had their chief seat, for divers after ages. This Norman, in the 6th year of William Rufus, being with the king in his great council held at Gloucester, (together with several bishops, abbots, and others,) was a witness to that confirmation there made to the monks of St. Mary's Abbey, in York, of numerous possessions which had formerly been bestowed upon them. To Norman de Areci s. his son and heir,

ROBERT D'ARCY, who founded a priory of Augustines at his lordship at Nocton, and otherwise contributed liberally to the church. This Robert was s. by his son and heir,

THOMAS D'ARCY, who, upon the assessment

of the aid for marrying the king's daughter in the 19th Henry II., certified that he then held twenty knights' fees *de veteri feoffumento*, with half a knight's fee, and a fourth part *de novo*, for which he paid £13. 6s. 8d. This feudal lord *m.* Alice, daughter of Ralph D'Eincurt, by whom he had three sons and four daughters. He *d.* on St. Swithin's day, anno 1180, leaving Thomas his son and heir, then eighteen years of age. Upon the decease of his lordship, William Basset, sheriff of Lincolnshire, seised on his whole barony for the king, and committed it to the custody of Michael D'Arcy, but the baron's widow subsequently obtained the possession with the guardianship of her children, for which she paid £300. To Thomas D'Arcy *s.* his aforesaid son and heir,

THOMAS D'ARCY, who was with King Richard I. in the expedition which that monarch made into Normandy in the 6th year of his reign, and in the 5th John was retained to serve that king, with three knights for one whole year, in consideration of which King John remitted to him a debt of two hundred and twenty-five marks, which he then owed the Jews: but besides this retainer he was to perform the like service for his barony, that other barons did. His lordship was *s.* at his decease by his son,

NORMAN D'ARCY, who in the 7th of King John giving five hundred marks, six palfreys, with one horse for the great saddle, and doing his homage, had livery of all the lands of his inheritance: but taking part with the barons, those lands were seized upon by the crown a few years afterwards, and held until the pacification in the beginning of Henry III.'s reign, when they were restored. The baron *d.* soon after, and was *s.* by his son,

PHILIP D'ARCY, who had previously, for his adhesion to the king, in the turbulent times of John, a grant of all the lands of Robert de Camberling. In the 34th Henry III. this feudal lord is said to have been the accuser of *Sir Henry de Bathe*, an eminent judge of the period, for corruption in his judicial capacity. His lordship was afterwards engaged in the French wars, and involved himself so deeply in debt in the king's service that he was obliged to obtain in the 39th Henry III. certain letters hortatory, to all his tenants by military service, and other; earnestly moving them to yield unto him such reasonable aid as might extricate him from his pecuniary difficulties, and for which they should receive the especial thanks of the crown. He *m.* Isabel, sister and co-heir of Roger Bertram, of Mitford, and dying in 1263, was *s.* by his son,

NORMAN D'ARCY, then twenty-eight years of age, who doing his homage, and giving security for the payment of his relief as a baron, had livery of his lands, but the very next year, being one of the barons defeated at Evesham, those lands were all seised by the crown. His brother Roger, and his uncle Thomas, were likewise involved in the defeat, but all made their peace, under the memorable decree, denominated " *Dictum de Kenilworth*," John de Burgh, of Kent, Adam de Newmarch, of York, and Robert de Ufford, all barons, undertaking for their future loyalty and quiet demeanour. He was subsequently engaged in the Welsh wars, and in the

156

22nd Edward I. had summons to attend the king forthwith, and to give him his advice in those great and difficult affairs which then concerned his crown and kingdom. This feudal lord had issue,

    PHILIP, his successor.

    John, summoned to parliament as a baron 28th Edward I. (see another Lord D'Arcy).

    Robert, of Stallingburgh, in the county of Lincoln, *m.* Joan, ――――, and left an only daughter and heiress,

        Margaret, who *m.* John Argentine.

Norman D'Arcy *d.* 1296, and was *s.* by his eldest son,

PHILIP D'ARCY, who was summoned to parliament as BARON D'ARCY from 29th December, 1299, to 20th October, 1332. This nobleman was involved in the insurrection of Thomas, Earl of Lancaster, in the 15th Edward II., but made his peace, and had restitution of his lands. His lordship had issue,

    NORMAN, his successor.

    Robert, } died *s. p.*
    John,   }

    Julian, *m.* to Sir Peter de Limberry.

    Agnes, *m.* to Sir Roger de Pedwardine.

Lord Darcy was *s.* at his decease by his only surviving son,

NORMAN D'ARCY, second Baron D'Arcy, but never summoned to parliament; his lordship was likewise implicated in Lancaster's rebellion, but had pardon for his treason, and restitution of his lands. He *d.* in 1340, and was *s.* by his only child,

PHILIP D'ARCY, third Baron D'Arcy, at whose decease without issue,

    SIR PHILIP DE LIMBURY, KNT., son of Julian, the elder sister of Philip, first Lord D'Arcy,

And

    AGNES, wife of SIR ROGER DE PEDWARDINE, younger sister of Philip, first Lord D'Arcy,

were found to be his next heirs, and between those the BARONY OF D'ARCY fell into ABEYANCE, as it is still supposed to continue amongst their representatives.

ARMS.—Az. semée of cross crosslets, and three cinquefoils ar.

D'ARCY—BARONS D'ARCY.

By Writ of Summons, dated 27th January, 1332, 6 Edward III.

JOHN D'ARCY, (next brother of Philip D'Arcy, who was summoned to parliament, as Baron D'Arcy, 29th December, 1299,) being an active and distinguished person in the reigns of the first, second, and third Edwards, obtained some of the highest offices in the state, and attained eventually the peerage. In the latter years of Edward I., and the beginning of Edward II.'s reign, he was engaged in the wars in Scotland; and during the time of the last-mentioned monarch, he was governor of Norham Castle, sheriff of the counties of Nottingham, Derby, and Lancaster, and JUSTICE OF IRELAND. Upon the accession of Edward III., he was appointed sheriff of Yorkshire, and governor of the castle at York, and re-constituted JUSTICE OF IRELAND; to which latter post, with the government of the country, he was re-appointed the next year; and in the following year he had a grant from the king, for his good services, of the manor of Werk, in Tindale. In the 6th of Edward III., he was summoned to parliament, as BARON D'ARCY; and the next year, being then in his government of Ireland, his lordship marched with a great army into the province of Ulster, to avenge the death of William de Burgh, EARL OF ULSTER; but before he got thither, the people of the country having vindicated the murder, he transported himself and his army into Scotland, leaving Thomas Burke, his lieutenant, in Ireland, and joined the king, who was then pursuing the victorious course which placed Edward Baliol upon the Scottish throne. In two years afterwards, Lord D'Arcy, at the head of the Irish nobles, made a second inroad upon Scotland with fifty-six ships, and wasted the Isles of Arran and Bute, for which good service the king granted to him and his heirs the manors of Rathwere and Kildalk, in Ireland. His lordship was subsequently constable of the Tower of London, and steward of the king's household; and he was accredited ambassador to the courts of France and Scotland in the 11th Edw. III.; after which we find him acquiring fresh laurels on the French soil, until he finally shared in the glory of CRESSY. His lordship obtained further great immunities from Edward III., and was appointed JUSTICE OF IRELAND and CONSTABLE OF THE TOWER for life. This eminent nobleman espoused first, Emeline, daughter and co-heir of Walter Heron, of Hedleston, in the county of Northumberland, by whom he had issue,

JOHN, his successor.
Roger, from whom the D'Arcys of Essex derive.
Adomar.

His lordship married secondly, 3d July 1329, Joane, daughter of Richard de Burgh, Earl of Ulster, and widow of Thomas Earl of Kildare, and had issue of this marriage,

William, of Platin, from whom the Darcys of Ireland derive.
Elizabeth, m. to James, Earl of Osmonde.

Lord D'Arcy, who had summons to parliament from 1332 to 1342, d. 30th May, 1347, and was s. by his eldest son,

SIR JOHN D'ARCY, second Baron D'Arcy, b. in 1317, summoned to parliament from 20th November, 1348, to 15th March, 1354. This nobleman had acquired high military fame in the life-time of his father, and was also amongst the heroes of CRESSY. His lordship had custody of the king's liberty of HOLDERNESS, in the county of York, and was constable of the Tower of London. He m. Elizabeth, daughter and heiress of Nicholas Meinell, Lord Meinell, of Wherlton, and had issue,

JOHN, his successor.
PHILIP, successor to his brother.
Isabel.

His lordship d. in 1356, and was s. by his elder son,

JOHN D'ARCY, third Baron D'Arcy, at whose decease in minority (s. p.), 26th August, 1362, the barony devolved upon his brother,

PHILIP D'ARCY, fourth Baron D'Arcy, summoned to parliament from 4th August, 1377, to 5th November, 1397. This nobleman, in the 4th of Richard II., was in the expedition made into France with Thomas of Woodstock, Earl of Buckingham; and arriving at Calais three days before Maudlin-tide, in July, rode with his banner displayed. He became subsequently so eminent in the French wars, that, in the 6th of Richard II., he was especially excused, in consequence, from repairing into Ireland, as all persons having lands there were compelled to by act of parliament passed three years before, for the defence of the realm against the insurgents then in arms; and in the next year he was again excused, by reason of the great charge he was at in supporting himself in those wars, and likewise "that he was then marching towards Scotland against the king's enemies there." In the 9th of Richard II., his lordship was constituted ADMIRAL of the king's fleet from the river Thames northward. Lord Darcy m. Elizabeth, daughter of Sir Thomas Grey, of Heton, and had issue,

JOHN, his successor.
Thomas, of Seamer.
Philip.
Elizabeth.

His lordship d. 25th April, 1398, and was s. by his eldest son,

JOHN D'ARCY, fifth Baron D'Arcy, b. in 1377, summoned to parliament from 19th August, 1399, to 21st September, 1411. This nobleman m. Margaret, daughter of Henry, Lord Grey de Wilton, and had issue,

Philip, his successor.
John, m. Joan, daughter of John Lord Greystock; and his great-grandson, Thomas D'Arcy, was summoned to parliament, as Lord D'Arcy, of D'Arcy. (See that dignity.)
Elizabeth.
Maud.

His lordship d. in 1399, (leaving his widow, who m. secondly, Sir Thomas Swinford,) and was s. by his elder son,

PHILIP D'ARCY, sixth Baron D'Arcy. This nobleman m. Eleanor, daughter of Henry Lord Fitz-Hugh, and d. in 1418, before he had attained majority, leaving two daughters, viz.,

Elizabeth, m. to Sir James Strangeways, and had issue,
  1. Richard Strangeways, who m. Lady Elizabeth Nevil, one of the daughters and co-heirs of William Nevil, Lord Fauconberg, and Earl of Kent. The BARONY OF FAUCONBERG continues still in abeyance amongst the descendants of this marriage, and of the other coheirs, Joane, wife of Sir Edward Bedhowing, and Alice, wife of Sir John Conyers.
  2. James, ancestor of the Strangeways of Ormsby, in the county of York.
Margery, m. to Sir John Conyers, Knt.

Upon the decease of his lordship, the BARONY OF D'ARCY fell into ABEYANCE between those ladies, and it so continues with their representatives.

ARMS.—Az. semée of cross crosslets, and three cinquefoils ar.

DARCY — BARONS DARCY, OF CHICHE, IN THE COUNTY OF ESSEX.

By Letters Patent, dated 5th April, 1551.
5 Edward VI.

Lineage.

This is presumed to have been a branch of the great baronial house of D'Arcy, which flourished in the counties of Lincoln and York, but the exact line could never be traced. The first of the family, of note,

ROBERT DARCIE, was originally a lawyer's clerk, who laid the foundation of his fortune, by marrying the widow of a rich merchant of Malden, in Essex, which widow, called Alice, daughter and co-heiress of Henry Fitz-Langley, died in the 26th Henry VI., and was buried in the chapel of the Holy Trinity, within the church of All Hallows, in Malden, with this Robert Darcie, her husband, leaving issue by him,

    Sir Robert Darcy, of Danbury.
    John Darcy, of Tolshunt.

The elder son,

SIR ROBERT DARCY, died in the 9th Edward IV., and left a son,

THOMAS DARCY, Esquire of the body to King Henry VI., and King Edward IV., who d. in the first year of King Henry VIIth, and was s. by his son,

ROGER DARCY, Esquire of the body to King Henry VII., who m. Elizabeth, daughter of Sir Henry Wentworth, Knt., and was s. by his son,

SIR THOMAS DARCY, Knt., who in the 36th Henry VIII., was constituted master of the king's artillery, within the Tower of London, and in the next year made a gentleman of the privy chamber. In the 5th Edward VI., Sir Thomas, being then vice chamberlain of the king's household, captain of the guard, and one of the principal knights of the privy chamber, was advanced to the peerage, as BARON DARCY, *of Chiche, in the county of Essex*, by letters patent, dated 5th April, 1551, and thereupon had summons to the parliament then sitting. He was also made a KNIGHT of the GARTER. His lordship m. Lady Elizabeth de Vere, daughter of John, Earl of Oxford, and had surviving issue,

    JOHN, his successor.
    Thomasine, m. to Richard Southwell, Esq., of Wood-Rising, in the county of Norfolk.
    Constance, m. to Edmund Pyrton, Esq., of Bentley, in the county of Essex.

Lord Darcy, d. in 1558, and was s. by his son,

JOHN DARCY, second Lord Darcy, of Chiche. This nobleman accompanied William, Earl of Essex, into Ireland, in the 16th of Elizabeth. His lordship m. Frances, daughter of Richard, Lord Rich, LORD CHANCELLOR OF ENGLAND, and had issue,

    THOMAS, his successor.
    John, d. unmarried.
    Mary, m. to Robert, Lord Lumley.

He d. in 1580, and was s. by his elder son,

THOMAS DARCY, third Lord Darcy, of Chiche, who was advanced on the 5th July, 1621, to the

160

dignity of VISCOUNT COLCHESTER, with remainder to his son-in-law, Sir Thomas Savage, of Rocksavage, in the county of Chester, Bart., and created on the 4th November, 1626, EARL OF RIVERS, with a similar reversionary clause in the patent. His lordship m. Mary, daughter and heiress of Sir Thomas Kitson, Knt., and had issue,

    THOMAS, who d. in the life-time of his father, issueless.
    Elizabeth, m. to Sir Thomas Savage, to whom, and his male issue, by the said Elizabeth, the viscounty and earldom of her father, were granted in reversion; but previously to inheriting those honours, Sir Thomas was himself created VISCOUNT SAVAGE, of Rocksavage, in the county of Chester, by letters patent, dated 6th November, 1626.
    Mary, m. to Roger Manwood, Esq. son of Sir Peter Manwood, K.B.
    Penelope, m. first, to Sir George Trenchard, Knt., and secondly, to Sir John Gage, Bart., of Firle, in the county of Suffolk, from which union the family of Gage, Viscounts Gage, and that of Gage, Baronets of Hengrave, derive.
    Susan, d. unmarried.

His lordship d. in 1639, and his only son having died s. p., previously, the BARONY OF DARCY, of Chiche, became EXTINCT, while the viscounty and earldom devolved, according to the limitation, and his estates passed to his four daughters as co-heiresses.

ARMS.—Ar. three cinquefoils gu.

D'ARCY — BARONS D'ARCY, OF D'ARCY. BARONS D'ARCY, OF ASTON.

By Writ of Summons, dated 17th October, 1509, 1 Henry VIII.

Restored, as Baron D'Arcy, of Aston, to *heirs male only*, by act of parliament, 1548, 2 Edward II.

Lineage.

The Honourable

JOHN D'ARCY, second son of John, Lord D'Arcy, and Margery, daughter of Henry, Lord Grey de Wilton, became male representative of the family upon the decease of his brother Philip, Lord D'Arcy, 1418 (the barony fell, however, into ABEYANCE between the said Philip's two daughters as co-heirs, as it still continues with their descendants). Mr. D'Arcy, while a minor, living in ward to the king, m. without license, Joane, daughter of John, Lord Greystock, for which offence he paid a fine of two hundred marks. Of this marriage were issue,

    Richard, who d. in the life-time of his father, leaving by his wife, Eleanor, daughter of John, Lord Scroop, of Upsal, an only son,
        WILLIAM, who s. his grandfather.
    John.
    George.
    Thomas.
    Philip.
    Jane, m. first, to John Beaumont, and secondly, to Giles Daubeney.

John D'Arcy d. in the 32nd Henry VI., and was s. by his grandson,

SIR WILLIAM D'ARCY, then but four years of age. This gentleman m. Euphemia, daughter of Sir Thomas Langton, of Farnly, in the county of York, and dying in the 3rd Henry VII., was s. by his son,

SIR THOMAS D'ARCY, a person who obtained high honours and distinction in the reign of Henry VII., and was called to the peerage by the succeeding monarch. In 19th Henry VII. Thomas D'Arcy was one of the northern lords that marched with Thomas, Earl of Surrey, to the relief of Norham Castle, then besieged by the King of Scotland, and the next year being a knight of the king's body, he was made constable of Bamburgh Castle, in Northumberland; in two years, subsequently, he was constituted captain of the Town and Castle of Berwick, as also warden of the east and middle marches towards Scotland, and he had a special commission soon afterwards to exercise the office of constable and marshal of England against certain rebels, being appointed about the same time constable of Sheriff Hoton, in the county of York, and steward of that lordship. In the 17th of the same reign he was one of the commissioners appointed to receive the oath of James, the fourth King of Scotland, upon a treaty of peace, and in four years afterwards being then of the privy council, he was made general warden of the marches towards Scotland. An office confirmed to him jointly with Sir Thomas D'Arcy, Knt., upon the accession of King Henry VIII., when he was summoned to parliament as BARON D'ARCY, OF D'ARCY, installed a KNIGHT of the GARTER, and sworn of the privy council. From this period he enjoyed the confidence for several years of his sovereign, being amongst those who exhibited articles against Wolsey, and subscribed the celebrated letter to Clement VII., until, at length, absenting himself from parliament sooner than sanction the dissolution of the religious houses, and finally joining in Ask's rebellion, called "the Pilgrimage of Grace," he was convicted of high treason, on a charge of delivering up PONTIFRACT CASTLE to the rebels, and beheaded on Tower Hill, 20th June, 1538, when the BARONY OF D'ARCY fell under the attainder. His lordship had m. first, Dowsabel, daughter and heiress of Sir Richard Tempest, Knt., of Ridlesdale, in the county of Northumberland, by whom he had issue,

    George, of whom presently, as the restored Lord D'Arcy.

    Arthur, who m. Mary, daughter and co-heir of Sir Nicholas Carew, of Bedington, in the county of Surrey, K.G., and dying in 1561, left issue,

        Henry, m. Catherine, daughter of Sir John Fermor, and widow of M. Pulteney, Esq., and left an only daughter and heiress,

            Catherine, who m. Gervase, Lord Clifton, and had a daughter,

                Catherine, who laid claim to the Barony of Clifton in 1674, and had the same allowed in parliament; from this lady,

the present Lord Clifton derives.

Thomas, m. Elizabeth, co-heir of John, Lord Coniers, and had issue,

    Sir Coniers D'Arcy (see D'Arcy, Lords Holderness).

Edward, from whom the D'Arcys of Kent derive.

Arthur, ancestor of the D'Arcys of Aldington, in the county of Northampton.

Francis, m. to Catherine, daughter of Ed. Leigh, Esq., of Rushall, in the county of Stafford.

Elizabeth, m. to Lewis, Lord Mordaunt.

Lord D'Arcy espoused secondly, Elizabeth, sister of William Sandys, first Lord Sandys, by whom he had an only daughter,

    Elizabeth, m. to Sir Marmaduke Constable, of Spaldingmoor, in the county of York.

GEORGE D'ARCY, the eldest son, received the honour of knighthood from King Henry VIII. at the siege of Tournay, and was restored in blood, with the dignity of BARON D'ARCY to himself, and his heirs male, by an act of parliament passed in the 2nd Edward VI., anno 1548. This nobleman m. Dorothy, daughter and heiress of Sir John Melton, of Aston, in the county of York, by whom he had issue,

    JOHN, his successor.

    Agnes, m. to Sir Thomas Fairfax.

    Mary, m. first, to Henry Babington, Esq., and secondly, to Henry Foljamb, Esq.

    Edith, m. to Sir Thomas Dauney, Knt.

    Dorothy, m. to Sir Thomas Metham, Knt.

    Elizabeth, m. to Bryan Stapleton, Esq., of Carleton.

His lordship, who from the restoration of his honours bore the title of LORD D'ARCY, of Aston, d. 28th August, 1587, and was s. by his son,

JOHN D'ARCY, as second BARON D'ARCY, of Aston. This nobleman was with the Earl of Essex in the expedition made into Ireland in the 16th Elizabeth. His lordship m. Agnes, daughter of Thomas Babington, Esq., of Dethick, in the county of Derby, by whom he had an only son,

    MICHAEL, who m. Margaret, daughter of Thomas Wentworth, Esq., and dying in the lifetime of his father, left issue,

        JOHN, who s. to the title at the decease of his grandfather.

        Margaret, d. unmarried.

        Anna, m. to Thomas Savill, Esq.

Lord D'Arcy d. in 1587, and was s. by his grandson,

JOHN D'ARCY, third Lord D'Arcy, of Aston, who was summoned to parliament as "Johanni D'Arcie and Meinill." His lordship m. Rosamond, daughter of Sir Peter Freschevile, of Stavely, in the county of Derby, and had issue,

    JOHN, who predeceased his father unmarried.

    Rosamond, } both d. unmarried.
    Elizabeth, }

Lord D'Arcy d. 1635, when the BARONY OF D'ARCY, of Aston, for want of a male heir, became EXTINCT.

ARMS.—As. semée of cross crosslets, and three cinquefoils, ar.

D'ARCY—BARONS CONYERS, BARONS D'ARCY, EARLS OF HOLDERNESS.

Barony of Conyers, by inheritance, created originally by Writ, 17th October, 1509.
Barony of D'Arcy, by Letters Patent, dated 10th August, 1641.
Earldom, by Letters Patent, dated 5th December, 1682.

Lineage.

The Hon. Sir

ARTHUR D'ARCY, second son of the beheaded and attainted Lord D'Arcy, temp. Henry VIII., m. Mary, daughter and co-heir of Sir Nicholas Carew, of Bedington, in the county of Surrey, and dying in 1561, left, with several other children,

THOMAS D'ARCY, who, upon the decease of his elder brother Sir Henry D'Arcy, without male issue, became chief of the family. This gentleman m. Elizabeth, daughter and co-heir of John, Baron Conyers (see that dignity), and dying in 1605, was s. by his only child,

SIR CONYERS D'ARCY, who being the principal male branch then remaining of this ancient and noble family set forth in a petition to King Charles I. in that parliament, begun at Westminster 3rd November, 1640, that after the attainder of Thomas, Lord D'Arcy, his great-grandfather, in the 29th Henry VIII. Sir George D'Arcy, Knt., eldest son of the said Thomas, being restored in blood by King Edward VI., obtained a grant of the title and dignity of LORD D'ARCY to himself and the heirs male of his body; and that by the death of John, Lord D'Arcy, late of Aston, in Yorkshire, without issue male, in the 11th of his majesty's reign, the title and dignity of Lord D'Arcy was utterly extinct, did humbly desire, that being grandchild and heir-male of Sir Arthur D'Arcy, Knt., and likewise son and heir of Elizabeth, daughter and co-heir of John, Lord Conyers, lineal heir to Margery, daughter and co-heir to Philip, Lord D'Arcy, son of John, Lord D'Arcy, one of the barons of this realm in the time of King Henry IV., his majesty would be pleased to declare, restore and confirm to him, the said Sir Conyers D'Arcy, and to the heirs male of his body, the dignity of LORD D'ARCY, with such precedency as the said John, Lord D'Arcy had, and by right from his ancestors then enjoyed. Whereupon his majesty graciously condescending, he did by letters patent, dated at Westminster 10th August, 1641, restore and confirm to the said Sir Conyers D'Arcy, and the heirs male of his body, the dignity of BARON D'ARCY, as enjoyed by his aforesaid ancestor John, Lord D'Arcy, and he had summons to parliament accordingly.

His lordship was seated at Hornby Castle, and having m. Dorothy, daughter of Sir Henry Bellasise, Baronet, had issue,

CONYERS, his successor.
William (Sir), m. Dorothy, daughter of Sir George Selby, Knt.
Henry, of Newpark, in the county of York, m. Mary, daughter of William Scrope, Esq., of Highly, in the county of Durham.

Thomas, of Winkborne.
Marmaduke, gentleman usher of the privy council to King Charles II., d. unmarried.
James, of Sedbury Park, in the county of York, M.P. for Richmond, anno 1680, m. Isabel, daughter of Sir Marmaduke Wyvill, Bart., and had issue,
James, who s. to Sedbury Park.
Barbara, m. to Matthew Hutton, Esq., of Mask, in the county of York.
Ursula, m. to John Stillington, Esq., of Kelfield, in the county of York.
Dorothy, m. to John Dalton, Esq., of Hawkeswell, in the county of York.
Anne, m. to Thomas Metcalfe, Esq., of Routh Park, in the county of Lincoln.
Grace, m. first, to Geo. Bert, Esq., of Middleton, and secondly, (after his decease,) to Sir Francis Molineux, of Mansfield, in the county of Nottingham.
Margaret, m. to Acton Burnell, Esq., of Winckbourne Hall, in the county of Notts., whose descendant, Peter Pegge Burnell, Esq., continues to reside at the same seat.

Lord D'Arcy d. 3rd March, 1653, and was s. by his eldest son,

CONYERS D'ARCY, second Baron D'Arcy, summoned to parliament from 6th May, 1661, to 1st March, 1680, as "Conyers D'Arcie de D'Arcie," and in the two last writs with the addition of "Meynill." This nobleman was advanced to the dignity of EARL OF HOLDERNESS by letters patent, dated 5th December, 1682. His lordship m. Grace, daughter and heiress of Thomas Rokeby, Esq., of Skyers, in the county of York, and had issue,

CONYERS, his successor, who had been summoned to the House of Lords in November, 1680, as Baron Conyers.
Ursula, m. to Sir Christopher Wyvill, Bart., of Burton Constable.
Elizabeth, m. to Sir Henry Stapleton, Bart., of Myton, in the county of York.
Grace, m. to Sir John Legard, Bart., of Ganton, in the county of York.
Margaret, m. to Henry Marwood, Esq., of Little Bugby, in the county of York.

The earl d. 14th June, 1689, and was s. by his son,

CONYERS D'ARCY, Lord Conyers, as second Earl of Holderness. This nobleman m. no less than four times; first, Lady Catherine Fane, daughter of Francis, Earl of Westmorland, by whom he had no issue; secondly, Lady Frances Howard, daughter of Thomas, Earl of Berkshire, by whom he had,

JOHN, M.P., for the county of York, m. Bridget, daughter of Robert Sutton, Lord Lexington, and predeceasing his father and grandfather on the 7th June, 1688, left issue,
ROBERT, successor to his grandfather.
Conyers (Sir), M.P., for the county of York in 1707, and in several succeeding parliaments; Master of the Horse to Queen Anne and King George I., and subsequently comptroller of the household, and a member of the privy council; m. twice, but had no issue.

Elizabeth, *m.* to Sir Ralph Milbanke, Bart., of Halnaby, in the county of York.

Charlotte, *m.* to Wardel George Westley, Esq., a commissioner of the customs.

Philip,
Charles, } both *d.* unmarried.

The earl *m.* thirdly, Lady Frances Seymour, daughter of William, second Duke of Somerset, and widow of Richard, first Viscount Molineux, and of Thomas Wriothesly, Earl of Southampton. His lordship espoused fourthly, Elizabeth, daughter and co-heir of John, Lord Freschevile, and widow of Philip Warwick, Esq., but had no issue by those ladies. He *d.* in 1692, and was *s.* by his grandson,

ROBERT D'ARCY, third Earl of Holderness, first commissioner of trade in 1718, and sworn of the privy council. His lordship *m.* Frederica, eldest surviving daughter and co-heir of Meinhardt Schomberg, Duke of Schomberg, and had issue,

Meinhardt-Frederic, who *d.* young.
ROBERT, successor to the honours.
Carolina, *m.* to William-Henry, Earl of Ancram, afterwards (fourth) Marquess of Lothian.

The earl *d.* 20th January, 1721-2, and was *s.* by his only surviving son,

ROBERT D'ARCY, fourth Earl of Holderness. His lordship was appointed, in 1740, lord-lieutenant of the North Riding of Yorkshire, and in the following year, was admitted gentleman of his majesty's bed-chamber. In June, 1744, he was accredited ambassador to the republic of Venice; in 1749, minister plenipotentiary to the states-general of the United provinces—and in 1751, his lordship was constituted one of the principal secretaries of state, and sworn of the privy council. In 1752, he was appointed one of the lords justices during the king's absence at Hanover. He resigned the secretaryship of state, but was reappointed in 1754. He was subsequently admiral and warden of the Cinque ports. His lordship *m.* at the Hague, in November, 1742, Mary, daughter of Francis Doublet, member of the States of Holland, by whom he had issue,

George,
Thomas, } both died young before the earl.

Amelia, *b.* 12th October, 1754—*m.* first, in 1773, Francis-Godolphin, then Marquess of Carmarthen, afterwards fifth Duke of Leeds, by whom she had issue,

GEORGE - WILLIAM - FREDERIC, present Duke of Leeds.
Francis-Godolphin Osborne (Lord).
Mary-Henrietta-Juliana, *m.* to Thomas, second Earl of Chichester.

Her ladyship being divorced from the Marquess, by act of Parliament in May, 1779—*m.* secondly, John Byron, Esq., and had an only surviving daughter,

Augusta-Mary Byron, *b.* 26th January, 1783, *m.* in 1807 to John Leigh, Esq.

Lady Conyers (to which dignity she succeeded at the decease of her father,) *d.* in 1784, and Captain Byron *m.* subsequently Miss Gordon, by whom he was father of (an only son,)

George-Gordon Byron, the celebrated Lord Byron.

The Earl of Holderness *d.* in 1778, when the EARLDOM, for want of male issue, became extinct, as did the Barony of D'Arcy, created by the patent of 1641, but the Barony of "CONYERS" devolved upon his only surviving daughter, Amelia, then Marchioness of Carmarthen, and at her ladyship's decease passed to her eldest son,

George-William-Frederick, present Duke of Leeds.

ARMS.—Az. semée of cross crosslets, and three cinquefoils, ar.

DAUBENEY—BARONS DAUBENEY, EARL OF BRIDGEWATER.

Barony, {
by Writ of Summons,
by Letters Patent,
} {
dated 2nd November, 1296, 23 Edward I.
dated 13th March, 1486.
}

Earldom, by Letters Patent, dated 19th July, 1538.

Lineage.

Amongst the most distinguished companions in arms of the Conqueror, was

ROBERT DE TODENI, a nobleman of Normandy, upon whom the victorious monarch conferred, with numerous other grants, an estate in the county of Lincoln, upon the borders of Leicestershire. Here De Todeni erected a stately castle, and from the *fair view* it commanded, gave it the designation of BELVOIR CASTLE, and here he established his chief abode. At the time of the general survey this powerful personage possessed no less than eighty extensive lordships, viz., two in Yorkshire, one in Essex, four in Suffolk, one in Cambridge, two in Hertfordshire, three in Bucks, four in Gloucestershire, three in Bedfordshire, nine in Northamptonshire, two in Rutland, thirty-two in Lincolnshire, and seventeen in Leicestershire. "Of this Robert," saith Dugdale, "I have not seen any other memorial, than that the Coucher-Book of Belvoir recordeth: which is, that bearing a venerable esteem to our sometime much celebrated protomartyr, St. Alban, he founded, near to his castle, a priory for monks, and annexed it as a cell to that great abbey in Hertfordshire, formerly erected by the devout King Offa, in honour of that most holy man." Robert de Todeni, Lord of Belvoir, *d.* in 1088, leaving issue by his wife Adela, viz.

WILLIAM, who assumed, from what reason is unascertained, the surname of ALBINI, and was known as " William de Albini, Brito," in contradistinction to another great baron, " William de Albini, Pincerna," from whom the Earls of Arundel descended.

Beringar, who had divers lordships in the county of York, as well as others in Lincoln, Oxford, and Nottinghamshires.

Geoffery.

Robert.

Agnes, *m.* to Hubert de Rye, a person of note in Lincolnshire.

He was *s.* by his eldest son,

WILLIAM DE ALBINI, *Brito*, Lord of Belvoir, who, in the Chapter House of St. Albans, confirmed all the grants of his father and mother to the church of our lady at Belvoir, desiring that he might be admitted in the fraternity as those his parents had been. This feudal lord acquired great renown at the celebrated battle of Tenercheby, in Normandy, where, commanding the horse, he charged the enemy with so much spirit, that he determined at once the fate of the day. Of the exploit, Matthew Paris says, " In this encounter chiefly deserveth honour the most heroic William de Albini, the Briton, who, with his sword, broke through the enemy, and terminated the battle." He subsequently adhered to the Empress Maud, and had his castle of Belvoir, with all his other lands, seized by King Stephen, and transferred to Ranulph, Earl of Chester. He m. Maud, daughter of Simon de St. Liz, first Earl of Huntingdon, widow of Robert, son of Richard de Tunbridge, and dying about the year 1155, left two sons, viz.

1. WILLIAM, surnamed MESCHINES, and likewise BRITO, who had BELVOIR CASTLE, and a considerable portion of his lands, restored by King Henry II. In the 14th of which monarch's reign he died, and was *s.* by his son,

WILLIAM DE ALBINI, feudal Lord of Belvoir, who, in the 6th of Richard I., was with that monarch in the army in Normandy. And the next year was sheriff of the counties of Warwick and Leicester, as he was subsequently of Rutlandshire. In the 2nd of King John he had special license to make a park at Stoke in Northampton, and liberty to hunt the fox and hare, (it lying within the royal forest of Rockingham.) Afterwards, however, he took up arms with the other barons, and leaving Belvoir well fortified, he assumed the governorship of Rochester Castle, which he held out for three months against the Royalists, and ultimately only surrendered when reduced to the last state of famine. Upon the surrender of Rochester William Albini was sent prisoner to Corfe Castle, and there detained until his freedom became one of the conditions upon which Belvoir capitulated, and until he paid a ransom of six thousand marks. In the reign of Henry III. we find him upon the other side, and a principal commander at the battle of Lincoln, anno 1217, where his former associates sustained so signal a defeat. This stout baron, who had been one of the celebrated TWENTY-FIVE, appointed to enforce the observance of MAGNA CHARTA—m. first, Margery, daughter of Odonel de Umframville, by whom he had issue,

WILLIAM.
Robert.
Nicholas.

He espoused, secondly, Agatha, daughter and co-heir of William Trusbut, and dying in 1236, was *s.* by his eldest son,

WILLIAM DE ALBINI, feudal Lord of Belvoir, who, like his father, adhered firmly to King Henry III. He m. first, Albreda Bireth, and secondly, Isabel ——, and left issue, an only daughter and heiress,

ISABEL DE ALBINI, who m. Robert de Ros, Lord Ros of Hamlake, (see that dignity,) and conveyed to him the feudal barony and castle of BELVOIR, which eventually passed from the family of Ros to that of Manners, by which they are now enjoyed in the person of the DUKE OF RUTLAND.

2. Ralph.

The second son of William de Albini, Brito,

RALPH DE ALBINI, obtained fifteen knights' fees from his brother William, in the 12th of Henry II., and in the 28th of the same reign, he gave two hundred marks for license to marry the mother of Ebrard de Ross, (whose name was Sibilla de Valoines.) This feudal baron, who founded some religious houses, died at Acre, in the Holy Land, in 1190, and was *s.* by

PHILIP DE ALBINI, who, in the 8th of King John, was governor of Ludlow Castle, in Shropshire, and in six years afterwards of the Isle of Jersey. He was subsequently governor of the castle of Bridgenorth, and he obtained some territorial grants from the crown; but notwithstanding those favours, he enrolled himself under the baronial banner, and participated in the triumph of RUNNIMEDE. Again, however, he changed his colours, and adhered to King John during the remainder of his reign. Upon the accession of Henry III. he assisted at that monarch's coronation, and was one of his principal generals at the battle of Lincoln. Independently, however, of his military renown, he appears to have acquired the reputation of a man of learning, and Matthew Paris designates him " a most faithful teacher and instructor of the king." In this reign he was governor of Guernsey and Jersey, and governor of the castle of Devizes. Ultimately being signed with the cross, he repaired to the Holy Land, and dying there was *s.* by his nephew,

PHILIP DE ALBINI, who had acted as lieutenant to his uncle in the government of Guernsey and Jersey, and in the 8th of Henry III. had the hundred of Wichton granted to him for his better support in the king's service. He was *s.* at his decease by his brother,

ELIAS DAUBENEY, who was summoned to parliament as a BARON, from 2nd November, 1296, to 22nd January, 1305. His lordship was *s.* at his decease by his son,

SIR RALPH DAUBENEY, second baron, summoned to parliament 25th February, 1342. This nobleman was one of the Knights of the Bath, solemnly created in the 20th Edward II., and had his robes as a banneret. In the 8th of Edward III. he was in the expedition then made into Scotland, and again in a similar expedition made in four years afterwards. His lordship m. first, Katherine, daughter of William de Thweng, Lord Thweng, and sister and co-heir of Thomas de Thweng, Lord Thweng, a priest, by whom he had an only daughter,

ELIZABETH, m. to Sir William Botreaux, Knt.

The baron espoused secondly, Alice Montacute, daughter of Lord Montacute, and had a son,

SIR GILES DAUBENEY, Knt., third baron, but never summoned to parliament. This nobleman m. Alianor, daughter of Henry de Wylington, and was s. by his son,

GILES DAUBENEY, fourth baron, but never summoned to parliament. This Giles was sheriff of Bedfordshire and Bucks, in the 10th Henry VI. He d. about the year 1444, and was s. by his son,

WILLIAM DAUBENEY, fifth baron, but never summoned to parliament, who, doing homage in the 24th Henry VI., had livery of his lands: and in the following year obtained a royal charter for a fair at his lordship of SOUTH PEDERTON. To this William s. his son,

GILES DAUBENEY, sixth baron, who in the 17th Edward IV. being one of the esquires of the body to the king, had, in consideration of his many services, a grant for life of the custody of the King's Park at Petherton, near Bridgewater. Upon the accession of Richard III. he appears to have been one of the first consulted by the friends of the Earl of Richmond, and to have cordially joined in the conspiracy to place that nobleman upon the throne. Which, being accomplished by the victory of Bosworth, he was made one of the new monarch, Henry the Seventh's, chief counsellors—appointed constable of the castle of Bristol, master of the Mint, and created by letters patent, dated 12th March, 1486,* LORD DAUBENEY. In the 2nd of Henry VII. his lordship was retained by indenture to serve the king in his fleet at sea; and in the next year he was constituted one of the chamberlains of the exchequer. He was afterwards joined with Richard Fox, Bishop of Exeter, in an embassy to France, and subsequently made Justice Itinerant with Sir Reginald Bray, of all the king's forests on the south of Trent. Upon the fall of Sir William Stanley, in the 10th of Henry VII., Lord Daubeney succeeded to the lord chamberlainship of the king's household. In the 12th of the same reign his lordship was about to march at the head of a large army into Scotland, but his course was diverted by the insurrection of Lord Audley and the Cornishmen: and he participated in the victory obtained over those rebels at Blackheath—as he did in that of Taunton, the next year, achieved over Perkin Warbeck and his partisans. In the 19th of Henry VII. he was made con-

---

* The original barony does not appear to have been assumed from the period of the demise of Sir Ralph Daubeney, who had summons in 1342. This patent was probably but a confirmation of the dignity already in the family.

stable of the castle of Bridgewater, and he had previously been honoured with the Garter. His lordship m. Elizabeth, daughter of Sir John Arundel, of Lanhern, in Cornwall, by whom he had issue,

HENRY, his successor.

Cecily, m. to John Bourchier, Lord Fitz-Warine, afterwards Earl of Bath.

He d. 28th May, 1507, and was s. by his son,

HENRY DAUBENEY, second baron under the new creation, but seventh of the old, who was created EARL OF BRIDGEWATER on the 19th July, 1538. His lordship m. Lady Catherine Howard, daughter of Thomas, Duke of Norfolk, but had no issue. He d. in 1548, when the BARONY OF DAUBENEY, created in 1486, and the EARLDOM OF BRIDGEWATER, became EXTINCT—but the BARONY created by the writ of Edward I., anno 1295, should have passed to his sister Cecily, Countess of Bath, and it is probably now vested in the descendants of that lady, if such exist; if not, it is in the heirs general of Elias, the first BARON DAUBENEY.

ARMS.—Gules, four lozenges in fesse ar.

D'AUNEY—BARON D'AUNEY.

By Writ of Summons, 1 Edward III.

Lineage.

NICHOLAS D'AUNEY, lord of the manor of Shunock, in Cornwall, was summoned to parliament, as a BARON, in the 1st of Edward III., but never afterwards, nor any of his posterity. His lordship made a journey to the Holy Land, whence he brought home a rich and curious medal, said to be yet in the possession of the family of Burton-Dawnay, Viscounts Downe; in Ireland, which claims descent from this nobleman.

ARMS.—Ar. a bend sa. betw. two cottises sa.

DE DREUX — EARLS OF RICHMOND.

Creation of William the Conqueror.
By Letters Patent, dated 6th July, 32 Henry III.

Lineage.

The first EARL OF RICHMOND was

ALAN, surnamed RUFUS OF FERGAUNT, (by reason of his red hair,) son of Eudo, Earl of Britanny, in France; which Alan coming over into England with the Conqueror, commanded the rear of his army in the memorable battle of Hastings, and for his services upon that occasion, and at the siege of York, obtained the EARLDOM OF RICHMOND, with all the northern part of the county of York, vulgarly denominated Richmondshire, previously the honour and county of Edwyne, the Saxon, Earl of Mercia. This nobleman was esteemed a personage of great courage and ability—and his benefactions to the church were munificent. He m. Constance, daughter of King William the Conqueror, but had no issue. The earl who was likewise Earl of Britanny, died in 1089, and was s. by his brother,

ALAN NIGER, second Earl of Richmond, and

165

Earl of Britanny. This nobleman was also a very liberal benefactor to the church. He d. in 1093, and leaving no issue, was s. by his brother,

STEPHEN, third Earl of Richmond, and Earl of Britanny. This nobleman m. ——, daughter of the Earl of Guingampe, and had issue,

ALAN, his successor.

Henry, who had by charter of King Henry II., Waltham in Essex, the Stoke in the county of Lincoln, to hold in fee, as Stephen his father had it given to him, temp. Henry I.

Geoffrey, surnamed Botterell.

Maud, m. to Walter, son of Gilbert de Gant.

The earl d. in 1104, and was s. by his son,

ALAN, surnamed the Savage, fourth Earl of Richmond, and Earl of Britanny. This nobleman was an active partisan of King Stephen's in his contest with the Empress Maud. In 1149, he took the castle of Lincoln, with considerable treasure, from Ranulph, Earl of Chester, by scaling the walls at night. He also garrisoned the Castle of HOTUN, in Yorkshire, then part of the Bishop of Durham's possessions, and made great spoil at Ripon, upon the demesnes and tenants of the Archbishop of York. This Alan, who is described as a most deceitful, wicked person, wrote himself Earl of Britanny, Cornwall, and Richmond: but notwithstanding that character, he appears, like his progenitors, to have been a munificent benefactor to the church. His lordship m. Bertha, eldest daughter and coheir of Conan le Grosse, and had issue,

CONAN LE PETIT, his successor.

Brian, father of Alan, Lord of Bedale.

Guy, ancestor of the Barons Strange.

Reginald.

He d. in 1165, and was s. by his eldest son,

CONAN LE PETIT, fifth Earl of Richmond, who bore also the title of Duke of Britanny. Little more is recorded of this nobleman, than his numerous grants to the church. He m. Margaret, daughter of Henry, Earl of Huntingdon, and sister of William, King of Scotland, by whom he had an only daughter,

CONSTANCE, who m. first, Geoffrey Plantagenet, fourth son of King Henry II., and had issue,

ARTHUR, said to be put to death by his uncle JOHN, afterwards King John.

Eleanor, called Le Brit, died s. p.

——, daughter, name unknown.

Geoffrey Plantagenet was accidentally slain in a tournament, at Paris, in the twenty-eighth year of his age. His widow, Constance, of Britanny, espoused, secondly, RALPH DE BLONDVILLE, Earl of Chester, but from him she was soon afterwards divorced, and she married, thirdly, GUY, VISCOUNT OF THOUARS, by whom she had two daughters, viz.—

ALICE, m. to PETER DE DREUX.

Katherine, m. to Andrew de Vitre, in Britanny.

The three husbands of Constance are said to have been EARLS OF RICHMOND jure uxoris, but it is very questionable how far they were entitled to the dignity.

Conan, fifth Earl of Richmond, d. in 1171, and his grandson,

PETER DE DREUX, (called Mauclerc,) obtained on 6th July, 1268, a grant of the dignities of EARL OF RICHMOND, and Duke of Britanny: but he does not appear to have enjoyed the whole honour of Richmond, for in 1941, we find a grant from King Henry III., to Peter de Savoy,* of divers towns, castles, manors, lands, &c., belonging to the Honour of Richmond. This nobleman had issue by Alice, coheir of Constance of Britanny,

JOHN, his successor.

Joland, m. to Hugh le Brun, Earl of Picardy. His lordship d. about the year 1250, but previously, his son,

JOHN DE DREUX, seems to have become Earl of Richmond, and in the 50th of Henry III., had livery of the Honour of Richmond, from Guischard

---

* Peter de Savoy. This distinguished foreigner was uncle of Eleanor, Queen consort of King Henry III. Matthew Paris, taking notice of his coming into England, in 1941, saith, " That the king gave him Comitatum Richmundiæ, the Earldom of Richmond," which it seems he enjoyed for some time, " though it doth not appear," says Dugdale, " by any record I have seen, that he either used, or had the title attributed to him, until 50th Henry III.. Upon his arrival here," continues Dugdale, "certain it is, that the king entertained him with much joy, and made him chief of his council; after which, ere long, he held a tournament at Northampton, against Roger Bigod, Earl of Norfolk, to the end, that those aliens who came into England with him and others, might try masteries with the English. And the next ensuing year, fearing that his power and trust here might be displeasing to the English, prudently resigned the custody of those castles which had been committed to his charge, craving leave to return into his own country. But I do not discern that he went out of England accordingly; for before the end of that year, the king's subjects, in Poictou, being in no little fear of invasion from the French, and earnestly soliciting King Henry for some aid, he sent over this Peter de Savoy, with Peter de Egueblanch, Bishop of Hereford, to let them know that he was preparing to come speedily to them in person, with a very great power. In the 30th Henry III., the king granted to Peter de Savoy, the inheritance of those houses in the street, called the Strand, in the suburbs of London, and adjoining the river of Thames, formerly belonging to Brian de Lisle: paying yearly to the king's exchequer, three barbed arrows for all services; which houses, Queen Eleanor, in her widowhood, having obtained by purchase from the Provost and Chapter of the House of Mountjoy, granted to Edmund, her son, afterwards Earl of Lancaster." Here was erected the palace, called the SAVOY.

Peter de Savoy, uncle of Queen Eleanor, is often included (says the General Report of the Lords Committee, on the dignity of a Peer of the Realm,) in the lists of Earls of Richmond, but it is evident that he only obtained a grant of the Honour of Richmond, and never used the title.

de Charrun, a servant to Peter of Savoy, who had authority for granting the same. Having thus acquired Peter de Savoy's title, the king, by letters patent, dated 6th July, 1268, conferred upon him and his heirs, under the designation of *John, Duke of Britanny*, the EARLDOM OF RICHMOND, with the Castle and Honour of Richmond, &c., in fee. Soon after this, he obtained a grant from the king of the Honour and Rape of Hastings; and the next year, he attended Prince Edward to the Holy Land. His lordship *m.* Blanch, daughter of Theobald, King of Navarre, and dying in 1305, was *s.* by his son,

JOHN DE DREUX, Earl of Richmond, and Duke of Britanny. This nobleman was an eminent military leader, in the reigns of Edward I., and Edward II. In 1298, he had the command of the forces then sent into Gascony, and the ensuing year, being the king's lieutenant in Britanny, he was joined in commission with the seneschal of Aquitane, and others, to conclude a league of amity with the King of Castile. In 1300, he was with King Edward in the wars of Scotland; and in 1305, he was constituted the king's lieutenant in that kingdom: as he was again upon the accession of King Edward II. In the 18th of which latter monarch's reign, the Earl of Richmond was one of the ambassadors deputed to the King of France, for securing the Duchy of Aquitane from further spoil from the French. His lordship espoused the Lady Beatrix Plantagenet, daughter of King Henry III., and had surviving issue,

> ARTHUR, who inherited the Dukedom of Britanny, and whose son,
>> JOHN, *s.* his uncle in the Earldom of Richmond.
> JOHN, of whom presently, as inheritor of the Earldom of Richmond.
> Blanch *m.* to Philip, son of Robert, Earl of Artois.
> Gray, *m.* to Guy Castilion, Earl of St. Paul.
> Alice, Abbess of Fount Euerces.

He *d.* in 1305, and was *s.* by his younger son,

JOHN DE DREUX, as Earl of Richmond, who was summoned to parliament as "Johanni Britannia Juniori," in the 33d Edward I., and the next year as EARL OF RICHMOND. He died, however, in 1334, without issue, and was *s.* by his nephew,

JOHN DE DREUX, Duke of Britanny, who did his homage for the EARLDOM OF RICHMOND, and was summoned to parliament as Johanni Duci Britanniæ, and Comiti Richmund," on 1st April, 1335, and 22nd January, 1336. This nobleman *m.* first, Isabel, daughter of Charles, Earl of Valois; secondly, Blanch, daughter of the King of Castille; and thirdly, Margaret, daughter of Edward, Earl of Savoy, but had no issue. He *d.* in 1341, when his niece, Joane,* daughter of his

---

* This lady *m.* Charles, second son of Guy, Earl of Blois, who laid claim in her right, to the Duchy of Britanny, which caused a procrastinated war, wherein England and France became involved—one espousing the claim of John de Brenon, half-brother of the deceased, Duke John; the other that of Charles, of Blois, which latter was certainly

---

brother Guy, was constituted his heir, but the EARLDOM OF RICHMOND reverted to the crown—when King Edward III. created, on the 20th September, 1342,

JOHN PLANTAGENET, surnamed of "Gaunt," his younger son, EARL OF RICHMOND, but this prince resigned the dignity in 1372, when it was conferred upon

JOHN DE DREUX, surnamed *De Brenon*, Earl of Montford, half-brother of the last John, Duke of Britanny and Richmond. This nobleman being deprived by the King of France of his Earldom of Montfort, for siding with King Edward III., had the EARLDOM OF RICHMOND from the English monarch in its stead, with the castle, town, and honour of Richmond. His lordship was constantly engaged with King Edward, in the wars of France, but ultimately falling into the hands of his great foe, Charles of Blois, he was sent to Paris, and there died in prison, about the year 1375, leaving issue by Joane, his wife, daughter of Charles, King of Navarre—a daughter, Joane, who *m.* Ralph, Lord Basset, of Drayton, and a son, his successor,

JOHN DE DREUX, (surnamed the *Valient*,) in the EARLDOM OF RICHMOND. This nobleman in the 1st Richard II., was retained by indenture to serve the king, in his French wars, for one quarter of a year, with two hundred men at arms, (himself accounted,) twelve knights, and one hundred and eighty-seven archers. And the next year, in consideration of the Castle of Brest in Britanny, which he delivered up to King Richard, obtained a grant to himself, and Joane, his wife, sister of the king, of the castle and manor of RISING, in the county of Norfolk. In the 3rd of the same reign, bearing the titles of Duke of Britanny, Earl of Montfort, and EARL OF RICHMOND, he was in the wars of France, but shortly after this, deserting the banner of England for that of France, all his lands in the former kingdom were seized, and he was deprived of the EARLDOM OF RICHMOND, by special act of parliament, 7th Richard II., November 1363. He is said to have been afterwards restored to the dignity, but with the proviso, that if he died without issue, the earldom and honour should revert to the king; in the 14th Richard II, it was however again adjudged to be FORFEITED, and thus terminated the family of DE DREUX, EARLS OF RICHMOND. The last Earl *m.* the lady Mary Plantagenet, daughter of King Edward III., and had issue,

> JOHN, Duke of Britanny, who had issue,
>> PETER, } both Dukes of Britanny, and
>> FRANCES, } both died without issue.
> Richard, Earl of Estampes, married Margaret of Orleans, and was father of
>> FRANCIS, Duke of Britanny, who espoused Margaret, of Foix, and had a daughter,
>>> ANNE, heiress of Britanny, who espoused LEWIS XII., KING OF FRANCE, and thus annexed the DUCHY OF BRITANNY to the crown of France.

---

the more legitimate, the Lady Joan being daughter of Guy, brother of the whole blood to the duke.

ARMS.—*Of* Alan Fergaunt, and his immediate descendants. } Chequy or and as a Canton erm.—
Of De Dreux. } The same.

DEINCOURT — BARONS DEIN-COURT.

By Writ of Summons, dated 6th February, 1299,
27 Edward I.
By Writ of Summons, dated 27th January, 1332,
6 Edward III.

Lineage.

WALTER DEINCOURT, one of the distinguished companions in arms of the Conqueror, obtained as his portion of the spoil from the first William, no less than sixty-seven lordships, in different counties, of which Blankney, in the county of Lincoln, was his principal seat, and head of his feudal barony. "This Walter," says Dugdale, "had a son called William, probably the eldest, who, having his education in the court of King William Rufus, there died upon the 3rd of the calends of November, as appeareth by this inscription made on a plate of lead, in Saxon capital letters, with abbreviations; and lately found in his grave in the church-yard, near to the west door of the cathedral church at Lincoln."

"Hic jacet WILHELMUS filius WALTERI AIEN-CURIENSIS,
Consanguinei Remigii Episcopi LICOLIENSIS,
qui hanc
Ecclesiam fecit. Præfatus WILHELMUS. Regiâ
stirpe progenitus, dum in curia Regis WIL-
HELMI (filii
magni Regis WILHELMI, qui Angliam conqui-
sivit) aleretur,
3° Kalendas Novembris obiit."

To Walter Deincourt, succeeded his son,

RALPH DEINCOURT, who founded the Augustine priory of Thurgarton, in the county of Nottingham. This feudal lord had issue,

WALTER.
Hugh.
Ralph
Aelinda, *m.* to Thomas D'Arcy, and was *s.* by
his eldest son,

WALTER DEINCOURT. This nobleman was a great benefactor to St. Mary's Abbey, at York. He *d.* about the year 1167, and was *s.* by his eldest surviving son,

JOHN DEINCOURT, who, in the 22nd Henry II., paid twenty marks in Nottinghamshire, for trespassing in the king's forests, and ten marks in Northamptonshire, for a similar transgression. This John *m.* Alice, daughter of Ralph Murdach, and had three sons, viz., OLIVER, William, and Nicholas. By the eldest of whom, he was *s.* at his decease,

OLIVER DEINCOURT, who was employed in Normandy, in the king's service, in the reign of Richard I., and died in the beginning of the ensuing reign, when he was *s.* by his son,

OLIVER DEINCOURT, then a minor, for whose wardship John, Bishop of Norwich, paid a

184

fine of four hundred marks to the king. This feudal lord joined the baronial standard against King John, but little further is known regarding him. He *m.* Nichola, niece of Nichola de Haya, a lady of importance in the county of Lincoln, and was *s.* at his decease by his son,

JOHN DEINCOURT, who upon the death of his father, in the 30th Henry III., paid a hundred pounds for his relief, and had livery of the lands of his inheritance. This John died within ten or twelve years afterwards, leaving three sons, viz.

EDMUND.
William.
John.

And was *s.* by the eldest,

EDMUND DEINCOURT, who was summoned to parliament as a BARON, on the 6th February, 1299, having participated previously in the French and Scottish wars of King Edward I. His lordship had an only son, EDMUND, who died in his life-time, leaving one daughter, ISABEL. Upon the death of his son, Lord Deincourt, to perpetuate his own NAME and ARMS, which with his grand-daughter should of course cease, he obtained special license from the crown, in the 7th year of King Edward II., to entail his lands, &c., upon whomsoever he thought proper, and he accordingly settled the whole of his territorial possessions, upon his brothers primogeniturely, and their male heirs for ever. He *d.* in 1327, when the BARONY devolved upon his grand-daughter, the aforesaid Isabel, and is probably still in ABEYANCE, amongst her descendants and representatives, while the estates passed according to the entail upon his next brother,

WILLIAM DEINCOURT, who was summoned to parliament as BARON DEINCOURT, from 27th January, 1332, to 1st of June 1363. This nobleman was one of the eminent warriors of the martial reign of King Edward III., and participated for a series of years in the glorious achievements on the French soil. His lordship *m.* Milicent, daughter of William, Lord Roos, of Hamlake, and had issue,

WILLIAM, who *d.* in the life-time of his father, leaving an only son,
WILLIAM.
Margaret, *m.* to Robert de Tibetot.

Lord Deincourt, *d.* in 1379, and was *s.* by his grandson,

WILLIAM DEINCOURT, second Baron Deincourt, summoned to parliament from the 20th August, 1360, to 22nd August, 1381. This nobleman *m.* first, Margaret, daughter of Adam de Welle, by whom he had no issue, and secondly, Alice, daughter of John, Lord Nevil, by whom he had,

RALPH, his successor.
John, successor to his brother.
Robert, of Deincourt Hall, in the county of Lincoln, died *s. p.* in the 21st Henry VI.

His lordship *d.* 18th October, 1381, and was *s.* by his eldest son,

RALPH DEINCOURT, third Baron Deincourt, but never summoned to parliament. This nobleman *d.* a minor, and unmarried in 1400, when the title and fortune devolved upon his brother,

JOHN DEINCOURT, fourth Baron Deincourt,

but never summoned to parliament. His lordship
m. Joane, only daughter and heiress of Sir Robert
de Grey, Knt., Lord Grey, of Rotherfield, by whom
he had issue,

WILLIAM, his successor.

Alice, m. first, to Ralph, Lord Boteler, of
Sudley, by whom she had no issue, and
secondly, to William, Lord Lovell, of Tichmersh.

Margaret, m. to Ralph, Lord Cromwell, but
died s. p.

He d. 11th May, 1406, and was s. by his son,

WILLIAM DEINCOURT, fifth Baron Deincourt. His lordship m. Elizabeth, sister of John,
Viscount Beaumont, but died in minority, without
issue, anno 1422, leaving his two sisters, his co-
heirs: viz.

Alice, Lady Lovell, and Margaret, Lady Cromwell, but the latter dying without issue, the
BARONY OF DEINCOURT became then
vested (the abeyance terminating,) in Lord
and Lady Lovell's grandson, Francis, Viscount LOVELL, K.G., under whose attainder
it eventually EXPIRED in 1487. See Lovell,
Barons Lovell, of Tichmersh.

ARMS.—Az. a Fess indented between ten Billets
or. four in chief, six in base.

D'EIVILL—BARON D'EIVILL.

By Writ of Summons, dated 14th December, 1264,
49 Henry III.

Lineage.

In the reign of the First Henry, NIGEL DE ALBINI,
being enfeoffed of the manor of Egmanton, in the
county of Nottingham, by the crown, conferred it
upon

ROBERT D'EIVILL, from whom descended
another

ROBERT D'EIVILL, who, in the 15th King
John, attended that monarch in his expedition into
Poictou, and in the 26th Henry III. had summons
to fit himself with horse and arms, and to accompany the king into Gascony. To this Robert s.

JOHN D'EIVILL, who, in the 38th Henry III.,
was forced to fly the country under an excommunication, but soon afterwards having made his peace,
had permission to return, for in the third year following we find him constituted justice of all the
forests beyond Trent, and the next year the King
of Scots, King Henry's son-in-law, being in restraint
by his own subjects, he, with other of the northern
barons, received summons to fit himself with horse
and arms, and to be ready on command, to march
into Scotland for the captive monarch's rescue. In
the 44th Henry III. he was again constituted warden
of all the forests north of Trent. So, likewise, in
three years afterwards, when he was appointed governor of the Castle at York, and the next year he
obtained license to erect a castle at a place called
HODE, in Yorkshire, in which year he was constituted governor of Scarborough Castle. After this
we find him arrayed with the other discontented
barons against the crown, and so actively engaged in
the north, that the sheriff of Yorkshire could not

exercise his office for the king's service from Michaelmas in the 48th till the battle of Evesham in the
49th of that reign, during which period Henry was
in the hands of the barons a prisoner, and this feudal
lord was summoned to parliament, by the companions then ruling, as BARON D'EIVILL. The
subsequent triumph of the royal cause at Evesham
terminated for that time, however, the baronial
sway, but it did not bring back Lord D'Eivill to his
allegiance, for joining Robert, Lord Ferrers, his
lordship made head again at Chesterfield, in the
county of Derby, where, after the capture of Ferrers,
he was unhorsed by Sir Gilbert Haunsard, but
effected his escape to the Isle of Arholme, in the
county of Lincoln. Under the decree, called the
"Dictum of Kenilworth," he eventually, however,
made his peace, and redeemed his lands by a pecuniary fine. His lordship m. Maude, widow of Sir
James de Aldithley, without licence, for which
transgression he paid a fine of £200 to the king. Of
this nobleman nothing further is known, and his
posterity were never afterwards summoned to parliament.

ARMS.—Az. a chevron sa. a fleur de lis, or.

DELAVAL—BARON DELAVAL, OF SEATON DELAVAL, IN THE COUNTY OF NOR-THUMBERLAND.

By Letters Patent, dated 21st August, 1786.

Lineage.

FRANCIS BLAKE DELAVAL, Esq., (descended
from the old feudal Barons De la Val, who flourished
in the eleventh and twelfth centuries,) m. Rhoda,
daughter of Robert Apreece, Esq., of Washingly, in
the county of Huntingdon, by Sarah, daughter, and
eventually sole heiress of Sir Thomas Hussey, Bart.,
and had issue,

FRANCIS BLAKE, who was installed a knight
of the Bath in March 1761. Sir Francis Blake
Delaval m. Isabella, daughter of Thomas,
sixth Earl of Thanet, and widow of Lord
Nassau Paulett, but died s. p. in 1771.

John-Hussey, of whom presently.

Edward-Thomas, d. unmarried in 1787.

Rhoda, m. to Sir Edward Astley, Bart., of
Melton Constable, in the county of Norfolk.

Anne m. to the Hon. Sir William Stanhope,
K.B., second son of Philip, third Earl of
Chesterfield, and after his decease to Cap-
tain Morris.

Sarah, m. to John Saville, first Earl of Mex-
borough, by whom she was mother of the
present earl.

Mr. Blake-Delaval d. in 1752, and was s. by his eldest
son, Sir Francis Blake-Delaval, K.B., but we pass
to the second,

JOHN HUSSEY DELAVAL, who was created
a BARONET in 1761, and upon the decease of his
brother, Sir Francis, became the representative of
the family. In 1783 he was created a peer of Ireland, as Baron Delaval, of Redford, in the county
of Wicklow, and enrolled amongst the peers of
Great Britain on the 21st August, 1786, in the dig-

nity of BARON DELAVAL, of Seaton Delavél, in the county of Northumberland. His lordship m. first, Susannah, daughter of R. Robinson, Esq., and widow of John Potter, Esq., by whom (who d. 1st October, 1783), he had issue,

> John, b. in 1755, d. in 1775, unmarried.
> Sophia-Anne, m. to —— Jadis, Esq., and d. 24th July,.1793.
> Elizabeth, m. 19th May, 1781, to George, sixteenth Earl, Lord Audley, and d. in 1785, leaving issue.
> Frances, m. to John Fenton Cawthorn, Esq.
> Sarah, m. to George, Earl of Tyrconnel, by whom she left an only daughter, (heiress of the earl),
>> Lady Susanna Carpenter, who m. Henry, second Marquess of Waterford, and had with other Children,
>>> HENRY, PRESENT MARQUESS.

Lord Delaval, m. secondly, Miss Knight, but had no issue. He died in May, 1808, when his honours became EXTINCT; and his estates devolved upon his daughters as co-heiresses, or their representatives.

ARMS.—Quarterly—first and fourth, erm: two bars vert; second and third, a chevron betw. three garbs.

DENMARK, PRINCE OF—DUKE OF CUMBERLAND.

By Act of Parliament, dated 9th April, 1689.

Lineage.

GEORGE, PRINCE OF DENMARK, having espoused her Royal Highness, the Princess Anne, youngest daughter of His Majesty, King JAMES II., was created Baron Workingham, Earl of Kendal, and DUKE OF CUMBERLAND, with precedency of all other dukes, by act of parliament, dated 9th April, 1689. He was also constituted Lord High Admiral of Great Britain and Ireland, and installed a Knight of the Garter. By the princess, who subsequently to her marriage, ascended the throne as QUEEN ANNE, the duke had two sons and four daughters, all of whom died before the age of maturity, and in his lifetime. His own death occurred in 1708, when his British honours became EXTINCT.

ARMS.—Or. three lions passant guardant az. crowned ppr., and semée of hearts gules.

DENNY—BARONS DENNY, EARL OF NORWICH.

Barony, by Writ of Summons, dated 27th October, 1604, 2 James I.
Earldom, by Letters Patent, 24th October, 1696.

Lineage.

EDWARD DENNY, a Clerk in the Exchequer, was constituted King's Remembrancer, in the 20th Henry VII. To this Edward s. his son,

SIR ANTHONY DENNY, who in the reign of Henry VIII., was Gentleman of the Privy Council, and Groom of the Stole. This was the only individual, amongst the courtiers, who dared to apprise his royal master of his approaching dissolution;

Henry had, however, so high an esteem for Sir Anthony, that he could perform the sad office with impunity, and the monarch presented him with a magnificent pair of gloves worked in pearls. Sir Anthony Denny was also constituted one of the executors of his deceased sovereign, and appointed to be council to Prince Edward. Sir Anthony was s. by his son,

SIR HENRY DENNY, who m. Honora, daughter of William, Lord Grey, of Wilton, and had issue,

> EDWARD, (Sir) of whom presently.
> Anne, m. to George Goring, Esq., of Hurst Pierpont, in the county of Suffolk, and had issue,
>> George Goring, who was created Baron Goring, and Earl of ` Norwich, (see Goring, Earl of Norwich,)—from Edward Goring, Esq., uncle of this nobleman, the Gorings, Baronets, of Highden, in Sussex, derive.
> Dorothy, m. to —— Parney, Esq., of the county of Hertford.
> Catherine, m. to George Fleetwood, Esq., of Buckinghamshire.
> Elizabeth, d. unmarried.

Sir Henry was s. at his decease by his son,

SIR EDWARD DENNY, Knt., so created in 31st Elizabeth, anno 1589; who was summoned to parliament, in the 3rd James I., as BARON DENNY; of Waltham, in the county of Essex, and created by letters patent, dated 24th October, 1696, EARL OF NORWICH. His lordship m. Lady Mary Cecil, daughter of Thomas, Earl of Exeter, by Dorothy, daughter and co-heir of John Nevil, Lord Latimer, and had an only daughter and heir,

> Honora, who m. Sir James Hay, (of Pitcorthie, in the county of Fife, the celebrated favourite of King James I.,) Viscount Doncaster, and Earl of Carlisle, by whom she had an only son,
>> JAMES, second Earl of Carlisle, at whose decease, s. p., in 1660, the Viscountcy of Doncaster, and Earldom of Carlisle, with the BARONY OF DENNY, expired.

When King James I. passed from Scotland to London, upon succeeding to the throne of England, Sir Edward Denny was high sheriff of Hertfordshire; and met his majesty with a splendid retinue of one hundred and forty men, dressed in blue livery coats, with white doublets, hats, and feathers: being all well mounted, with red saddles on their horses. Sir Edward presented the king, at the same time, with a noble charger richly accoutred. His lordship d., 20th December, 1630, when the EARLDOM OF NORWICH became EXTINCT, but the BARONY of DENNY devolved upon his daughter, .

HONORA, as Baroness Denny, at her decease it passed to her son, the Right Honourable

JAMES HAY, second Earl of Carlisle, at whose decease, in 1660, it EXPIRED, with his lordship's other honours.

ARMS.—Gu. a saltier, ar. betw. twelve crosses patée or.

Note.—From Sir Edward Denny, Knt., youngest son of Sir Anthony Denny, Henry VIII.'s executor, descended the family Denny, Baronets of Tralee

Castle, in the county of Kerry, in Ireland, represented by the present Sir Edward Denny, Bart.

DESPENCER—EARL OF WINCHESTER.

Creation of Edward II. 10th May, 1322.

Lineage.

In the 18th year of William the Conqueror,

ROBERT LE DESPENCER, so called from being steward to the king, was a witness to the royal charter for removing the secular canons out of the cathedral of Durham, and placing monks in their stead. This Robert was brother of Urso de Abitot, then sheriff of Worcestershire, and he appears, as well by his high official situation, as by the numerous lordships he possessed, to have been a person of great eminence; but it has not been ascertained whether he first came into England with his royal master, or whether he was of Saxon or Norman extraction; nor is it clearly known, whether he had ever been married or had issue. In the reign of Henry I. there was a

WILLIAM LE DESPENCER, but whether he had the name from being son of Robert, or from succeeding to the post of steward, cannot be determined.

The next person we find holding this office, and in the same reign, was

THURSTAN DISPENCER. Of this steward, Camden, in his remains, relates the following story. "In the time of Henry I. it was the custom of the court, that books, bills, and letters, should be drawn and signed by servitors in court, concerning their own matters without fee. But at this time Thurstan, the king's steward, or Le Despencer, as they then called him, (from whom the family of the Lords Spencer came,) exhibited to the king a complaint against Adam of Yarmouth, clerk of the signet; for, that he refused to sign, without a fee, a bill passed for him. The king first heard Thurstan commending the old custom at large, and charging the clerk for exacting somewhat contrary thereunto, for passing his book. Then the clerk was heard, who briefly said, ' I received the book, and sent unto your steward, desiring only of him to bestow upon me two spice cakes made for your own mouth; who returned for answer, he would not, and thereupon I desired to seal his book.'"

The king greatly disliked the steward for returning this negative, and forthwith made Adam sit down upon the bench, with the seals and Thurstan's book before him, but compelled the steward to put off his cloak, to fetch two of his best spiced cakes for the king's own mouth, to bring them in a fair white napkin, and with low curtsie to present them to Adam, the clerk. Which being accordingly done, the king commanded Adam to seal and deliver him his book, and made them friends, adding this speech—" Officers of the court must gratifie and shew cast of their office, not only one to another, but also to strangers, whensoever need shall require.'

This Thurstan was s. by his son,

ALMARIC DE SPENCER, who served the office of sheriff of Rutland in the 34th Henry II., and again in the 1st of Richard I. From the latter monarch, to whom he was also steward, he obtained a confirmation in fee of the lordships of Wurdie and Stanley, in the vale of Gloucester. The former of which King Henry II. had given to Walter, the usher of his chamber, son of Thurstan, and uncle of this Almaric, for his homage and service, reserving a pair of gilt spurs, or twelve pence, to be yearly paid for the same into the exchequer. In the 6th of King John this Almaric paid a fine of a hundred and twenty marks and one palfry, to be exempted from attending upon the king in an expedition then proposed to be made beyond the sea. Almaric de Spencer m. Amabil, daughter of Walter de Chesnei, by whom he had two sons, Thurstan and Almaric, and was s. by the elder,

THURSTAN DE SPENCER, who appears, with his brother, to have taken arms with the other barons against King John, for, in the 18th of that reign, the king committed the custody of Thurstan de Spencer to Rowland Bloet, and gave away the lands of Almaric de Spencer to Osbert Giffard, his own natural son. Thurstan seems however to have regained his rank in the next reign, and to have twice served the office of sheriff for Gloucestershire. He died in 1248.

Contemporary with this Thurstan, and doubtless [*not*] of the same family, was [*to Lucy*]

HUGH DE SPENCER, whom King Henry III., in the 8th year of his reign, constituted sheriff of the counties of Salop and Stafford, and governor of the castles of Salop and Bruges (Bridgenorth). He was subsequently sheriff of Berkshire, and governor of Wallingford Castle. To this Hugh Henry III. gave the manor of Rithal, in the county of Rutland, and in the 21st of that monarch's reign, upon the death of John Scot, Earl of Chester, he was deputed with Stephen de Segrave and Henry de Aldithley to take charge of the castles of Chester and Beeston. After this Hugh came his grandson, another

HUGH DESPENCER, who, taking part with the barons, was nominated under the baronial power in the 44th of Henry III., Justiciary of England. After the battle of Lewes he was one of those to whom the custody of the captive monarch was committed, and he was then entrusted with the castles of Orford, in Suffolk, of Devizes, in Wilts, and Barnard Castle, in the bishopric of Durham. He was summoned to parliament on the 14th December, 1264, as " Hugh le Despencer, Justic' Anglie," and lost his life under the baronial banner at the battle of EVESHAM. His lordship m. Aliva, daughter of Philip Basset of Wycombe, in the county of Bucks, and widow of Roger Bigod, Earl of Norfolk, by whom he had issue, HUGH, of whom presently, and Alianore, m. to Hugh de Courtenay, father of Hugh, first Earl of Devonshire. After the forfeiture and decease of Lord Despencer his widow Aliva, for her father's sake, found such favour from the king, that she was enabled to retain a considerable proportion of the property, and at her death, in the 9th of Edward I., it devolved, on the payment of a fine of five hundred marks, upon her son,

HUGH DESPENCER, senior, so called to distinguish him from his son, who bore the designation of HUGH DESPENCER, junior, both so well known in history as the favourites of the unfortunate Edward II. Of HUGH, senior, we shall first treat, although as father and son ran almost the same course, at the same time, and shared a similar fate, it is not easy to sever their deeds.

HUGH DISPENSER paid a fine of two thousand marks to the king, in the 15th of Edward I., for marrying, without license, Isabel, daughter of William de Beauchamp, Earl of Warwick, and widow of Patrick Cheworth; by this lady he had an only son, the too celebrated

HUGH DISPENSER, jun.

In the 22d of the same reign, he was made governor of Oldham Castle, in the county of Southampton, and the same year had summons to attend the king at Portsmouth, prepared with horse and arms for an expedition into Gascony. In two years afterwards he was at the battle of Dunbar, in Scotland, where the English arms triumphed; and the next year he was one of the commissioners accredited to treat of peace between the English monarch and the kings of the Romans and of France. In the 26th and 28th years of Edward, he was again engaged in the wars of Scotland, and was sent by his sovereign, with the Earl of Lincoln, to the papal court, to complain of the Scots, and to entreat that his holiness would no longer favour them, as they had abused his confidence by falsehoods. To the very close of King Edward I.'s reign, his lordship seems to have enjoyed the favour of that great prince, and had summons to parliament from him from the the 23d June, 1295, to 14th March, 1322: but it was after the accession of Edward's unhappy son, the SECOND of that name, that the Spencers attained that extraordinary eminence, from which, with their feeble-minded master, they were eventually hurled into the gulph of irretrievable ruin. In the first years of Edward II.'s reign, we find the father and son still engaged in the Scottish wars. In the 14th year, the king, hearing of great animosities between the younger Spencer and Humphrey de Bohun, Earl of Hereford and Essex, and learning that they were collecting their followers in order to come to open combat, interfered, and strictly commanded Lord Hereford to forbear. About the same time, a dispute arising between the Earl of Hereford and John de Moubray regarding some lands in Wales, young Spencer seized possession of the estate, and kept it from both the litigants. This conduct, and similar proceedings on the part of the elder Spencer, exciting the indignation of the barons, they formed a league against the favourites, and placing the king's cousin, Thomas Plantagenet, Earl of Lancaster, at their head, marched, with banners flying, from Sherburne to St. Alban's, whence they dispatched the bishops of Salisbury, Hereford, and Chichester, to the king with a demand that the Spencers should be banished; to which mission the king, however, giving an imperious reply in the negative, the irritated nobles continued their route to London; when Edward, at the instance of the queen, acquiesced; whereupon the barons summoned a parliament, in which the Spencers were banished from England;

172

and the sentence was proclaimed in Westminster Hall. To this decision, HUGH the elder submitted and retired; but Hugh the younger lurked in divers places; sometimes on land, and sometimes at sea, and was fortunate enough to capture, during his exile, two vessels, near Sandwich, laden with merchandise to the value of forty thousand pounds; after which, being recalled by the king, an army was raised, which encountered and defeated the baronial forces at Boroughbridge, in Yorkshire. In this action, wherein numbers were slain, the Earl of Lancaster being taken prisoner, was carried to his own castle at Pontefract, and there, after a summary trial, (the elder Spencer being one of his judges,) beheaded. The Spencers now became more powerful than ever, and the elder was immediately created EARL OF WINCHESTER, the king loading him with grants of the forfeited estates. He was, about the same time, constituted warden of the king's forests on the south of Trent. Young SPENCER obtained, like his father, immense grants from the lands forfeited after the battle of Boroughbridge; but not satisfied with those, and they were incredibly numerous, he extorted by force whatsoever else he pleased. Amongst other acts of lawless oppression, it is related that he seized upon the person of Elizabeth Comyn, a great heiress, the wife of Richard Talbot, in her house at Kennington, in Surrey, and detained her for twelve months in prison, until he compelled her to assign to him the manor of Painswike, in Gloucestershire, and the castle and manor of Goderich, in the marches of Wales: but this ill-obtained and ill-exercised power was not formed for permanent endurance, and a brief space only was necessary to bring it to a termination. The queen and the young prince, who had fled to France, and had been proclaimed traitors through the influence of the Spencers, ascertaining the feelings of the people, ventured to return; and landing at Harwich, with the noblemen and persons of eminence who had been exiled after the defeat at Boroughbridge, raised the ROYAL standard, and soon found themselves at the head of a considerable force; when, marching upon Bristol, where the king and his favourites then were, they were received in that city with acclamation, and the elder Spencer being seized, (although in his ninetieth year,) was brought in chains before the prince and the barons, and received judgment of death, which was accordingly executed, by hanging the culprit upon a gallows in the sight of the king and of his son, upon St. Dennis's day, in October, 1326. It is said by some writers that he body was hung up with two strong cords for four days, and then cut to pieces, and given to the dogs. Young SPENCER, with the king, effected his escape; but they were both, soon afterwards, taken and delivered to the queen, when the unfortunate monarch was consigned to Berkeley Castle, where he was basely murdered in 1327. Hugh Spencer the younger, it appears, was impeached before parliament, and received sentence " to be drawn upon a hurdle, with trumps and trumpets, throughout all the city of Hereford," and there to be hanged and quartered, which sentence was executed, on a gallows fifty feet high, upon St. Andrew's eve, anno 1326 (20 Edw. II.)

Thus terminated the career of two of the most celebrated royal favourites in the annals of England. The younger Hugh was a peer of the realm, as well as his father, having been summoned to parliament, as a baron, from 29th July, 1314, to 10th October, 1325; but the two BARONIES of SPENCER, and the EARLDOM OF WINCHESTER, expired under the attainders of the father and son. For the family of the younger Spencer, see Despencer, Earl of Gloucester.

ARMS.—Quarterly ar. and gu.; in the second and third a fret, or. Over all a bend sa.

DESPENCER — BARONS DESPENCER, EARL OF GLOUCESTER.

Barony, by Writ of Summons, dated 15th June, 1338.
12 Edward III.
Earldom, anno 1337.

Lineage.

HUGH DESPENCER, Jun., (one of the hapless favourites of King Edward I.,) espoused Eleanor, daughter and co-heir of Gilbert de Clare, Earl of Gloucester, and had issue, *Eliz. & Maurice*

HUGH, of whom presently. *S? Birkeles*

Edward, m. Anne, daughter of Henry, Lord Ferrers, of Groby, and dying in 1342, left an only son,

198 Sept EDWARD, who succeeded his uncle, HUGH.

198 Pitchford —m. to Richard, Earl of Arundel.

After the execution of Hugh Despencer, in November, 1326, Eleanor, his widow, with her children and family, was confined in the Tower of London until the ensuing February, when she obtained her liberty, and married, subsequently, William la Zouch, of Mortimer. She died in July, 1337, possessed of several estates, in which she was s. by her elder son,

HUGH DESPENCER, who had already distinguished himself as a soldier in France and Scotland; and continuing actively and gallantly engaged in the same fields, he was summoned to parliament as a BARON, by King Edward III., from 15th June, 1338, to the 1st of January, 1349. His lordship m. Elizabeth, widow of Giles de Baddlesmere, but died without issue in 1349, when the barony EXPIRED, but his lands devolved upon his nephew,

EDWARD DESPENCER, who, in the 30th Edward III, being then a knight, attended Edward the Black Prince into France, and shared in the glory of POICTIERS. For several years afterwards Sir Edward continued in the French wars, and for his gallant conduct was summoned to parliament as BARON DE SPENCER, from 15th December, 1357, to 6th October, 1372, being also honoured with the Garter. His lordship m. Elizabeth, daughter and heiress of Bartholomew de Burghersh, Baron Burghersh, and had issue,

THOMAS, his successor.

Cicely, who d. young.

Elizabeth, m. first, to John Arundel, and secondly, to the Lord Zouch.

Anne, m. to Hugh Hastings, and afterwards to Thomas Morley.

Margaret, m. to Robert Ferrers.

Lord Despencer d. in 1375, and was s. by his son,

THOMAS DESPENCER, 2d Baron De Spencer, summoned to parliament 30th November, 1396, and 18th July, 1397. This nobleman, who was known as Lord Despencer of Glamorgan, was in the expedition to Ireland, made in the 18th Richard II.; and in the 21st of the same reign, having the sentence of banishment reversed, which had been passed by parliament in 15th Edward II. against his great grandfather, HUGH DESPENCER THE YOUNGER, was created EARL OF GLOUCESTER, anno 1337, by reason of his descent through Eleanor, wife of the said Hugh, from the De Clares, Earls of Gloucester. In the petition which his lordship presented for the reversal of Hugh his ancestor's banishment, it was set forth, that the said Hugh, at the time, possessed no less than fifty-nine lordships in different counties, twenty-eight thousand sheep, one thousand oxen and steers, one thousand two hundred kine, with their calves; forty mares, with their colts of two years; one hundred and sixty draught horses; two thousand hogs; three thousand bullocks; forty tuns of wine; six hundred bacons; four score carcases of martinmas beef; six hundred muttons in his larder; ten tuns of cider; armour, plate, jewels and ready money, better than ten thousand pounds; thirty-six sacks of wool, and a library of books. His lordship m. Constance, daughter of Edmund Plantagenet, surnamed De Langley, Duke of York, fifth son of King Edward III., and had issue,

RICHARD, who m. Elizabeth, daughter of Ralph, Earl of Westmorland, and d. issueless in 1414.

Isabel, m. to Richard Beauchamp, Lord Abergavenny and Earl of Worcester, by whom she had an only daughter and heiress,

ELIZABETH BEAUCHAMP, who m. Edward Nevel, a younger son of Ralph, Earl of Westmoreland, and brought into that family the Baronies of Burghersh and Despencer and Abergavenny.

Upon the marriage of the Earl of Gloucester, he obtained from King Richard II. a grant of divers manors; but adhering to that unfortunate monarch, he was degraded from his earldom, and dispossessed of most of his lands by the first parliament of Henry IV.; and before the same year elapsed, being taken prisoner, in an attempt to fly the kingdom, at Bristol, and being condemned by a vote of the House of Commons to die, he was carried into the market-place and there beheaded by the rabble, on the third day after St. Hillary, in the year 1400; when the EARLDOM OF GLOUCESTER and BARONY OF DE SPENCER fell under the attainder. Richard, his eldest son, dying in fourteen years afterwards, still a minor, without issue, Isabel, his only daughter, then became his heir. This lady, as stated above, married Richard Beauchamp, Earl of Worcester, by whom she had an only daughter and heiress, Lady Elizabeth Beauchamp. The attainder of Thomas, Lord Despencer and Earl of Gloucester, her grandfather, being reversed in the first year of Edward IV., the said Lady Elizabeth carried the Barony of Despencer (the Earldom of Gloucester could not of course be revived, having failed for want of a male heir), with the Baronies of Abergavenny and Burghersh, to her husband, the Hon. Edward Nevil, who was summoned to parliament, as Lord Abergavenny, in 1450; and the dignity of Despencer continued in his descendants, the Lords Abergavenny, until the decease of Henry, fourth baron, in 1597, when his lordship's only daughter and heiress, Elizabeth, then the wife of Sir Thomas Fane, Knt., claimed the baronies; but, after a long investigation, the House of Lords decided, that the Barony of Abergavenny belonged to the heir male at law; when the crown, by letters patent, confirmed the Barony of Le Despencer to her ladyship and her heirs. From that period it was enjoyed by Lady Fane's immediate descendants, the first seven Earls of Westmoreland; at the decease of John, the seventh earl, in 1762, the Barony of Despencer fell into abeyance between the heirs of his lordship's sisters, and was terminated the next year in favour of his nephew, Sir Francis Dashwood; at whose decease, s. p. in 1781, it again fell into abeyance; and so continued, until again terminated in 1788 in favour of Sir Thomas Stapleton, Baronet, present Lord Le Despencer, the descendant of Lady Catherine Paul, John, seventh Earl of Westmoreland's younger sister.

ARMS.—Same as those of Despencer, Earl of Winchester.

D'EVEREUX — EARLS OF SALISBURY.

Creation of the Empress Maud.

Lineage.

Amongst the principal Normans who accompanied the Conqueror in his expedition against England, and participated in the triumph and spoil of Hastings, was

WALTER DE EVEREUX, of Rosmar, in Normandy, who obtained, with other considerable grants, the lordships of Salisbury and Ambresbury, which, having devised his Norman possessions and earldom to Walter, his eldest son, he bequeathed to his younger son,

EDWARD DE EVEREUX, who was thenceforward designated "of Salisbury." This Edward was subsequently sheriff of Wiltshire, and, at the time of the general survey, possessed lordships in the counties of Dorset, Somerset, Surrey, Hants, Middlesex, Hereford, Buckingham, and Wilts. When Sheriff of the latter county, we are told that he received in rent, as belonging to his office, an hundred and thirty hogs—thirty-two bacons—two bushels and sixteen gallons of wheat—the same of barley—several bushels of oats—thirty-two gallons of honey, or sixteen shillings—four hundred and forty eight hens—a thousand and sixty eggs—an hundred cheeses—fifty-two lambs—two hundred fleeces of wool; having likewise one hundred and sixty-two acres of arable land, and, amongst the reves-land, to the value of forty pounds per annum. This Edward was standard-bearer at the battle of Brennevill, in Normandy, fought 20th Henry I., King Henry being present, and distinguished himself by his singular skill and valour. He left at his decease, a daughter,

Maude, wife of Humphrey de Bohun, and a son and heir,

174

WALTER DE EVEREUX, who m. Sibilla de Chaworth. This feudal lord founded the monastery of Bradenstoke, wherein, in his old age, he became a canon. He was s. by his son,

PATRIC DE EVEREUX, who, being steward of the household to the Empress Maud, was advanced by that princess to the dignity of EARL OF SALISBURY, and was one of the subscribing witnesses, as such, to the agreement made between King Stephen and Henry, Duke of Normandy, in the 18th year of that monarch's reign. In the 10th Henry II. his lordship was a witness to the recognition of the ancient laws and liberties of England; and in two years afterwards, upon the aid then assessed for marrying the king's daughter, he certified his knights' fees at seventy-eight and two-fifths. The earl being the king's lieutenant in Aquitaine, and captain-general of his forces there, was slain, in 1167, by Guy de Lezinnian, upon his return from a pilgrimage to St. James of Compostella, and was s. by his son,

WILLIAM DE EVEREUX, second Earl of Salisbury, who, at the coronation of King Richard I., bore the golden sceptre with the dove on the head of it; but the next year, when the king became a prisoner in Almaine, his lordship was one of those who adhered to John, Earl of Morton. In the 6th Richard I., the earl was with the king in the expedition then made into Normandy, and, upon his return to England, was one of his great council, assembled at Nottingham. At the second coronation of Richard, in the same year, the Earl of Salisbury was one of the four earls who supported the canopy of state. His lordship m. Alianore de Vitrei, daughter of Tirrel de Mainere, and left, at his decease, an only daughter and heiress,

ELA, " of whom (writes Dugdale) it is thus reported: that, being so great an inheiretrix, one William Talbot, an Englishman, and an eminent soldier, took upon him the habit of a pilgrim, and went into Normandy, where, wandering up and down for the space of two months, at length he found her out. Likewise, that he then changed his habit, and having entered the court where she resided in the garb of a harper, (being practised in mirth and jesting,) he became well accepted. Moreover, that, growing acquainted with her, after some time he conducted her into England, and presented her to King Richard, who, receiving her very courteously, gave her in marriage to WILLIAM, surnamed Longespee, (from the long sword which he usually wore,) his brother, that is, a natural son of King Henry II. by Fair Rosamond; and that thereupon King Richard rendered unto him the earldom of Rosmar, as her inheritance." Be this story true or false, it is certain, however, that the great heiress of the D'Evereux, Ela, espoused the above-named

WILLIAM LONGESPEE, who thereupon became, in her right, EARL OF SALISBURY. In the beginning of King John's reign this nobleman was sheriff of Wiltshire, he was afterwards warden of the marches of Wales, and then sheriff of the coun-tien of Cambridge and Huntingdon. About this period (14th John,) the baronial contest commencing, William Longespee at once espoused the royal cause, and maintained it so stoutly, that he was included, by the barons, amongst the evil councillors of the crown. The next year he was again constituted sheriff of Wilts, and he held the office from that time during the remainder of his life. He had also a grant of the honour of Eye, in Suffolk, and was the same year a witness to the agreement made between King John and the barons, as guarantee for the former. He was likewise a witness to the charter whereby John resigned his kingdom to the pope. After this we find him a principal leader in the royal army, until the very close of John's reign, when he swerved in his loyalty, and joined for a short period the ranks of Lewis of France. Upon the accession, however, of Henry III., he did homage to that monarch, particularly for the county of Somerset, which the king then gave him; and joining with William Marshall, (governor of the king and kingdom,) raised the siege of Lincoln: when he was constituted sheriff of Lincolnshire, and governor of Lincoln Castle, being invested at the same time with sheriffalty of the county of Somerset, and governorship of the castle of Shirburne. His lordship soon afterwards accompanied the Earl of Chester to the Holy Land, and was at the battle of DAMIETA, in which the crescent triumphed. He served subsequently in the Gascon wars, whence returning to England, Dugdale relates, " there arose so great a tempest at sea, that, despairing of life, he threw his money and rich apparel over board. But when all hopes were passed, they discerned a mighty taper of wax, burning bright at the prow of the ship, and a beautiful woman standing by it, who preserved it from wind and rain, so that it gave a clear and bright lustre. Upon sight of which heavenly vision both himself and the mariners concluded of their future security: but every one there being ignorant what this vision might portend except the earl; he however attributed it to the benignity of the blessed virgin, by reason, that upon the day when he was honoured with the girdle of knighthood, he brought a taper to her altar, to be lighted every day at mass, when the canonical hours used to be sung, and to the intent, that for this terrestrial light, he might enjoy that which is eternal.' A rumour, however, reached England of the earl's having been lost, and Hubert de Burgh, with the concurrence of the king, provided a suitor for his supposed widow, but the lady, in the interim, having received letters from her husband, rejected the suit with indignation. The earl soon after came to the king at Marlborough, and being received with great joy, he preferred a strong complaint against Hubert de Burgh, adding, that unless the king would do him right therein, he should vindicate himself otherwise, to the disturbance of the public peace. Hubert, however, appeased his wrath with rich presents, and invited him to his table, where it is asserted that he was poisoned, for he retired to his castle of Salisbury in extreme illness, and died almost immediately after, anno 1226. His lordship left issue, four sons and five daughters, viz.

WILLIAM, his successor.

Richard, a canon of Salisbury.

Stephen, chief justice of Ireland, m. Emmeline, Countess of Ulster, daughter and heir of Walter de Ridelsford, Baron of Bray, and left an only daughter and heiress, Ela, who m. Hugh Lacy, who was created Earl of Ulster by King John.

Nicholas, Bishop of Salisbury, d. in 1297.

Isabel, m. to William de Vesci, Lord Vesey.

Ela, m. first, to Thomas, Earl of Warwick; and secondly, to Philip Basset, of Hedendon.

Idonea, m. to William de Beauchamp, Baron of Bedford.

Lora, a nun at Lacock.

Ela, jun., m. to William de Odingselle.

His lordship's eldest son,

WILLIAM DE LONGESPEE, " commonly called," says Sir William Dugdale, " by Matthew Paris, and most of our other historians, EARL OF SALISBURY, but erroneously; for all records wherein mention is made of him, do not give him that title, but call him barely William Longespee. Nay, there is an old chronicle who saith expressly, that, in anno 1233, (17th Henry III.,) he was girt with the sword of knighthood, but not made Earl of Salisbury." This William made a pilgrimage to the Holy Land in 1240 — and again in 1247, having assumed the cross for a second pilgrimage, proceeded to Rome, and thus preferred a suit to the sovereign pontiff. " Sir, you see that I am signed with the cross, and am on my journey with the king of France, to fight in this pilgrimage. My name is great, and of note, viz., WILLIAM LONGESPEE; but my estate is slender: for the king of England, my kinsman, and liege-lord, hath bereft me of the title of earl, and of that estate; but this he did judiciously, and not in displeasure, and by the impulse of his will; therefore I do not blame him for it. Howbeit, I am necessitated to have recourse to your holiness for favour, desiring your assistance in this distress. We see here (quoth he,) that Earl Richard (of Cornwall,) who, though he is not signed with the cross, yet, through the especial grace of your holiness, he hath got very much money from those who are signed, and therefore I, who am signed, and in want, do intreat the like favour." The pope taking into consideration the elegance of his manner, the efficacy of his reasoning, and the comeliness of his person, conceded in part what he desired: whereupon he received above a thousand marks from those who had been so signed. In about two years after this, anno 1249, having received the blessing of his noble mother, Ela, then Abbess of Lacock, he commenced his journey at the head of a company of two hundred English horse, and being received with great respect by the king of France, joined that monarch's army. In Palestine he became subsequently pre-eminently distinguished, and fell, in 1250, in a great conflict with the Saracens, near Damieta, having previously killed above one hundred of the enemy with his own hand. It was reported that, the night before the battle, his mother Ela, the abbess, saw in a vision the heavens open, and her son armed at all parts, (whose shield she well knew,) received with joy by the angels. Remembering the occurrence, when news of his death reached her in six months after, she held up her hands, and with a cheerful countenance said, "I, thy handmaid, give thanks to thee, O Lord, that out of my sinful flesh thou hast caused such a champion against thine enemies to be born." It was also said, that in 1252, when messengers were sent to the Soldan of Babylon, for redemption of those who had been taken prisoners, he thus addressed them—"I marvel at you, christians, who reverence the bones of the dead, why you inquire not for those of the renowned and right noble William Longespee, because there be many things reported of them, (whether fabulous or not I cannot say,) viz., that, in the dark of the night, there have been appearances at his tomb, and that to some, who called upon his God, many things were bestowed from Heaven. For which cause, and in regard of his great worth and nobility of birth, we have caused his body to be here intombed." Whereupon the messenger desiring it, the remains were delivered to them by the Soldan, and thence conveyed to Acres, where they were buried in the church of St. Cross. This eminent and heroic personage m. Idonea, daughter and heir of Richard de Camville, and had issue,

WILLIAM DE LONGESPEE, his son and heir, who m. Maud, daughter of Walter Clifford, and died in the 41st Henry III., in the flower of his age, leaving an only daughter and heiress,

 MARGARET, commonly called Countess of Salisbury, who m. Henry de Lacy, Earl of Lincoln, and had issue, an only daughter and heiress,

  ALICE, m. to Thomas, Earl of Lancaster, who being outlawed, King Edward II. seized upon the lands which she had made over to her husband; some of which, viz.—Tenbrigge, Winterbourn, and Ambresbury, with other manors, King Edward III. gave to William de Montacute, to hold in as full and ample a manner, as ever the same had been holden by Margaret, Countess of Salisbury, or her predecessors.

Thus terminated the very eminent families of D'Evereux, and De Longespee, EARLS OF SALISBURY.

ARMS.—D'Evereux.—Three Pallets varry, on a chief, or. a lion passant, sa.

 De Longespee.—Az. six lions, (or lionels,) rampant, or. third, second, first.

DEVEREUX—BARONS DEVEREUX.

By Writ of Summons, dated 28th September, 1384, 8 Richard II.

Lineage.

Of this family, which derived its surname from the town of Eureux, in Normandy, and which came into England with the Conqueror, there were several generations, prior to that which attained the peerage. In the 7th King Henry III.,

STEPHEN DEVEREUX, being in the king's

army against the Welsh, had scutage of all his tenants in the counties of Gloucester and Hereford, who held of him by military service. To this Stephen succeeded his son,

WILLIAM DEVEREUX, who in the 42nd of Henry III., had summons to attend the king at Chester, with horse and arms to restrain the incursions of the Welch, and in two years afterwards, being then one of the barons marchers, received command, with the others, to repair to the marches without delay, for a similar purpose. He subsequently attended the king at the battle of Lewes, but there he forsook the royal standard, and afterwards fell fighting on the side of the Barons at Evesham, in the 49th Henry III., whereupon Maud, his widow, sister of Walter Giffard, Bishop of Bath and Wells, applied to the king, for "certain jewels and harness," which had been deposited in the church of Hereford, by the deceased baron, and obtained a precept to the treasurer of the cathedral, for their deliverance to her. But his lands being seized, continued with the crown, until the 51st Henry III., when his son and heir,

WILLIAM DEVEREUX, making his composition at three years value, according to the decree called "Dictum de Kenilworth," had livery of those estates. In the 22nd Edward I., we find this William Devereux employed in the great expedition made by the king himself into Gascony. To this feudal lord succeeded,

SIR JOHN DEVEREUX, Knt., who in the 42nd Edward III., attended Edward, the Black Prince, into Gascony, and the next year was seneschal and governor of Lymosin. Upon the accession of King Richard II., Sir John served in the fleet at sea, and was constituted governor of Ledes Castle, in Kent. In the 3rd of Richard, he was made captain of Calais, and in the eighth of the same monarch, being then a banneret, was summoned to parliament as a BARON. The following year, his lordship was installed a Knight of the Garter, and in the second year afterwards constituted constable of Dover Castle, and warden of the cinque ports, but the latter appointment was through the influence of the great lords then predominant. Upon the attainder of Sir Simon Burley, Knt., the Castle and Manor of Leonhales, in the county of Hereford, devolving to the crown, Lord Devereux obtained a special grant thereof, and being possessed of the lordship of Penshurst, he had a license in the 16th of Richard, to make a castle of his mansion house there. His lordship m. Margaret, daughter of Sir John Barre, Knt., and had issue,

JOHN, his successor.

Joane, m. to Walter Fitz-Walter, Lord Fitz-Walter.

He d. in 1394, and was s. by his son, *His bro Wm dead*

SIR JOHN DEVEREUX, Knt., second Baron Devereux, who m. Philippa, one of the daughters of Guy de Brien, then deceased, and grand-daughter and co-heiress of Sir Guy de Brien, but d. in 1397, still in minority, and without issue. When his lordship's barony and estates devolved upon his sister Joane, Lady Fitz-Walter, and thenceforward became united with the Barony of Fitz-Walter.

ARMS.—Ar. a fesse gu. in chief three Torteauxes.

176

DIGBY—BARONS DIGBY OF SHER-BORNE, IN THE COUNTY OF DORSET. EARLS OF BRISTOL.

Barony, } by Letters { 25th November, 1618.
Earldom, } Patent, { 15th September, 1622.

Lineage.

The surname of this ancient family is said to have originally been TILTON, assumed from their residence at Tilton, in the county of Leicester, where they possessed a fair estate in the reign of Henry II., in whose time lived SIR JOHN TILTON, who gave certain parcels of land in Billeraden and Kirby-Bellers, in that county, to the Lepers of St. Lazarus, of Jerusalem, which the king confirmed to the infirm brethren of Burton-Lazars. In 1266, 40th Henry III., the family removed from Tilton, to Digby, in the county of Lincoln, and assumed a new designation from that place, which they continued ever afterwards to retain. Of this line, was

JOHN DIGBY, who, in the reign of Edward I., was a commissioner for the gaol-delivery at Warwick, and served that prince, in his wars. He lies buried at Tilton, under a tomb, adorned with his effigies at full length, and cross-legged, holding a shield of his arms of the Fleur-de-lis, with the sun and moon thereon, and this line,

" Jehan de Digby, gist icy, praies pour luy."

To this John, succeeded

ROBERT DE DIGGEBY, to whom, temp. Richard II., William Francels conveyed certain lands in Billesdon, in Leicestershire; and by Catherine, daughter and co-heir of Simon Pakeman, he was father of

EVERARD DIGBY, who m. Agnes, daughter of John Clarke, and widow of Richard Seddale, and had, with three other sons, all of whom fell at Towton-field, in 1461, fighting under the Lancastrian banner, his successor.

EDWARD DIGBY, Esq., of Tilton, in the county of Leicester, and of Digby, in the county of Rutland, M.P., for the latter shire, temp. Henry VIth., who lost his life in the same cause and battle as his brothers, leaving by his wife, Jaqueta, daughter and co-heir of Sir John Ellys, of Devonshire, one daughter, Baringold, m. to Robert Hunt, Esq., of Lydnen, and seven sons, viz.

  I. EVERARD (Sir), progenitor of the Digbys, of Drystoke, in the county of Rutland, and of Sandon, in the county of Stafford. Sir Everard, was Sheriff of Rutland, in 1449, 1486, and 1499; and its representative in parliament, from the 25th to the 38th year of Henry VI., inclusive. He d. in 1509, and was s. by his son,

    SIR EVERARD, whose grandson,

      SIR EVERARD DIGBY, one of the most accomplished persons of the period in which he lived, being unfortunately involved in the gunpowder plot, was convicted on the 27th, and executed on the 30th January, 1605.

2. Simon, of Coles Hill, in the county of Warwick, of whom presently.

3. John (Sir), of Eye-Kettleby, in the county of Leicester, received the honour of knighthood from King Henry VII., for his services at Bosworth Field. In 1513, Sir John Digby, attended King Henry VIII. to Calais, and fought valiantly at Therouenne, but d. in 25th of the same king, leaving issue, by his wife, Catherine, daughter of Sir Nicholas Griffin, of Braybrook, in the county of Northampton.

4. Libeaus, of Luffenham, whose grand-daughter, Anne, (his only son, Thomas Digby's heiress,) m. John Burton, Esq., of Stockerston, in the county of Leicester.

5. Rowland, of Welby, in the county of Leicester, which estate he acquired, temp. Henry VII., with his wife, Agnes, daughter and heiress of John Sheiden, Esq., and which continued with his descendants until the reign of James I.

6. Thomas (Sir), of Oulney, in the county of Bucks, received the honour of knighthood from King Henry VII., after the battle of Bosworth Field. Sir Thomas's daughter, Catherine, m. first, Simon Wheeler, Esq., of Kenilworth, and secondly, John Fisher, Esq., of Packington Magna.

7. Benjamin, of Bathley, in the county of Norfolk.

SIR SIMON DIGBY, the second son, having taken a distinguished part with his brothers at Bosworth Field, was rewarded by the successful monarch, in the first year of his reign, (1485,) by a grant for life of all the lands which had belonged to George, Duke of Clarence, in the county of Rutland, being at the same time appointed steward and receiver of divers other manors in that shire, and in the county of York. In the next year having achieved a victory for the king, at Stoke, over the impostor Lambert Simnel, he obtained a grant from the crown of Ravysbury, in the county of Surrey, and in 1495, by letters patent, dated 23rd December, in that year, the lordship of Coles Hill, in the county of Warwick, forfeited by Sir Simon Montfort, the previous year. In 1496, Sir Simon Digby, was commissioned to exercise martial law in the counties of Devon and Cornwall, against several malefactors; and he filled the office of sheriff for Leicester and Warwickshires, in 1509, and 1517. He m. Alicia, daughter of John Walleys, Esq., of East Raddon, in the county of Devon, and had issue,

REGINALD, his successor.

Thomas, whose descendant,

  Thomas Digby, Esq., of Mansfield Wood-house, M.P., left a son, John, who died s. p., and two daughters, (co-heirs to their brother,) viz.

    Frances, m. in 1726, to Sir Thomas Legard, Bart.

    Philadelphia, m. in 1730, to Sir George Cayley, Bart.

Catherine, m. to Anthony Worth, Esq., of Worth.

Agnes, *m.* to William Tracy, Esq., of Todington.

Alice, *m.* to Robert Clifton, Esq.

Sir Simon Digby, *d.* 27th February, 1519, and was *s.* by his elder son,

REGINALD DIGBY, Esq., of Coles Hill, sheriff of Leicestershire, for the 26th and 36th years of Henry VIII., *m.* Anne, daughter and co-heir of John Danvers, Esq., of Calthorpe, in the county of Oxford, and dying 25th April, 1549, was *s.* by his son,

JOHN DIGBY, Esq., of Coles Hill, who *m.* Anne, eldest daughter of Sir George Throgmorton, and dying 26th November, 1558, was *s.* by his son,

SIR GEORGE DIGBY, who received the honour of knighthood for his services at the siege of Zutphen, in Flanders, from Robert, Earl of Leicester, in the 28th of Elizabeth. This gentleman *m.* Abigail, daughter of Sir Arthur Henningham, Knt., of Ketteringham, in the county of Norfolk, and had issue,

> ROBERT (Sir), whose son, Robert Digby, was elevated to the peerage of Ireland, in 1620, as BARON DIGBY, which barony now merges in the EARLDOM OF DIGBY, enjoyed by his lordship's descendants.
>
> Philip.
>
> JOHN, of whom presently.

Sir George Digby, *d.* 4th February, 1586, and was *s.* by his elder son, Sir Robert Digby, but we pass to the younger son,

SIR JOHN DIGBY, Knt., who having filled some high situations in the court of James I., and being twice accredited ambassador to the court of Spain, was elevated to the peerage, on the 25th November, 1618, as BARON DIGBY, *of Sherborne, in the county of Dorset.* His lordship was subsequently employed upon different embassies, but particularly to the court of Spain, in 1622, touching a marriage between Prince Charles, and the Lady Maria, when he was created EARL OF BRISTOL. In 1624, his lordship had a difference with the Duke of Buckingham, and they mutually impeached each other. From that period he lived in retirement, until the breaking out of the civil war, in which he first sided with the parliament, but afterwards went over to the king, and eventually withdrew into France. The earl *m.* Beatrix, daughter of Charles Walcot, Esq., of Walcot, in the county of Salop, and had issue,

> GEORGE, his successor.
>
> John, who was a general of horse, in Lord Hopton's army, and afterwards a secular *priest*, at Pontoise, in France, *d.* after the restoration.
>
> Abigail, *m.* George Freke, Esq., of Shroton, in the county of Dorset, and died *s. p.*
>
> Mary, *m.* to Arthur, Earl of Donegal, had no surviving issue.

His lordship *d.* in 1652, and was *s.* by his elder son,

GEORGE DIGBY, second Earl of Bristol, K.G. This nobleman suffered considerably during the civil wars, having had his estates confiscated, and himself banished. He lived, however, to be restored with the monarchy, to his country and fortune; but

having become a Roman catholic while abroad, he was thereby incapacitated from holding any place in the government. His lordship is noticed by Walpole, as an author, and a person of singularity, whose life was one contradiction. " He wrote against popery, and embraced it. He was a zealous opposer of the court, and a sacrifice for it; was conscientiously converted in the midst of his prosecution of Lord Strafford, and was most unconscientiously a prosecutor of Lord Clarendon. With great parts, he always hurt himself and his friends. With romantic bravery, he was always an unsuccessful commander. He spoke for the Test Act, though a Roman Catholic; and addicted himself to astrology, on the birth-day of true philosophy." His lordship *m.* Anne, daughter of Francis, fourth Earl of Bedford, by whom he had issue,

> JOHN, his successor.
>
> Francis, slain in the sea-fight with the Dutch, 28th May, 1672, and *d.* without issue.
>
> Diana, *m.* to the Baron Moll, in Flanders.
>
> Anne, *m.* to Robert, Earl of Sunderland, from whom descend the Dukes of Marlborough, and the Earls of Spencer.

His lordship *d.* in 1676, and was *s.* by his only surviving son,

JOHN DIGBY, third Earl of Bristol, who *m.* first, Alice, daughter and heiress of Robert Bourne, Esq., of Blackhall, in the county of Essex; and secondly, Rachael, daughter of Sir Hugh Windham, Knt., but having no issue, the BARONY OF DIGBY, and the EARLDOM OF BRISTOL, became, at his lordship's decease, in 1698, EXTINCT, while his large estates devolved upon his only surviving sister, Anne, Countess of Sunderland, whose son, George, third Earl of Sunderland, married, for his second wife, Anne, second daughter of John, first, and celebrated DUKE OF MARLBOROUGH.

ARMS.—Az. a Fleur de lis ar. with a mullet for difference.

DINAN—BARON DINAN.

By Writ of Summons, dated 23d January 1295, 23d Edward I.

Lineage.

The surname of DINAN appears to have been first adopted by *Fouke,* one of the knights of Roger de Montgomery, Earl of Shrewsbury, upon whom that nobleman conferred the castle which he had erected at *Dinan,* (now called Ludlow), and he was thence designated Sir Fouke de Dinan.

GEFFERY DINAN had summons, with other persons of note, in 41 Henry III., to repair to the king at Bristol, well fitted with horse and arms, in order to march against the Welch. He died in two years afterwards, seised of the manor of Hertland, in the county of Devon, which he held by service of two knights' fees, and was *s.* by his son,

OLIVER DINAN, who, upon doing homage in 48 Henry III., had livery of his lands. This Oliver, having married Isabel, widow of John de Courtenay, without license, had to pay a fine of £100. to the crown in consequence. In 14 Edward I. he procured the royal charter for free warren in all his demesne lands in the counties of Devon, Somerset and Cornwall; and was summoned to parliament as a BARON, from 23d June, 1295, to 29th December, 1299, and dying in the following year, was *s.* by his son,

JOSCE DINAN, second Baron Dinan, but never summoned to parliament; he died soon after his father (29 Edward I.), leaving two sons, viz.

John, his successor.

Oliver, who *d.* in 20 Edward III. and left a son,

    Oliver, who left, by his first wife, a son, Oliver, who died *s. p.*; and by his second, Margaret, daughter of Richard de Hydon, three daughters, viz.

        Margaret, *m.* to William de Asthorpe.

        Elene, } nuns.
        Isabel, }

The elder son,

JOHN DINAN, succeeded his father, and was succeeded himself by his son,

JOHN DINAN, (Dynant, or Dynham, as the name was differently written,) of Hertland, fourth baron, but never summoned to parliament. He *m.* Joane, daughter of Sir Thomas Courtenay and Muriell, his wife, daughter and co-heir of John, Lord Moels; which Joane was heiress of her brother, Sir Hugh Courtenay, Knt. To this nobleman succeeded his son,

JOHN DYNHAM, fifth baron, but not summoned to parliament. He *m.* a daughter of Lord Lovell, and was *s.* by his son,

SIR JOHN DYNHAM, sixth baron, who served in the wars of King Henry VI., and died in the 36th of that monarch, leaving by his wife, Joane, daughter and heiress of Richard de Arches, the following issue,

John, his successor.

Elizabeth, *m.* first, Fouke, Lord Fitz-Warren, and secondly, to Sir John Sapcoate, Knt.

Joane, *m.* to John, Lord Zouche, of Harringworth.

Margaret, *m.* to Sir John Carewe, Knt.

Catherine, *m.* to Sir Thomas Arundel, Knt.

Sir John Dynham was *s.* by his son,

SIR JOHN DYNHAM, Knt., who being in high favour with King Edward IV., was summoned to parliament as a BARON,* by that monarch, on the 28th February 1466, and continuing one of the most zealous and gallant supporters of the House of York, his lordship obtained, in two years afterwards, the custody of the Forest of Dartmore, with extensive territorial grants, amongst which were several manors, part of the possessions of Humphrey Stafford, Earl of Devon, then in the crown, by reason of the death of that earl, without issue, and the forfeiture of Thomas Courtenay, Earl of Devon. In 15 Edward IV. Lord Dynham was sworn of the privy council, and had a grant of an annuity of one

---

* No writ of summons having issued for several generations, (from the reign of Edward I.,) Sir John Dynham, although unquestionably a BARON by descent, is presumed to have been only raised to the dignity by this writ: and this has been deemed erroneously a new creation,

hundred marks for his attendance on that service, to be received out of the petty customs in the Port of London; in which office of Privy Counsellor he was continued by King Henry VII., and constituted by that monarch Treasurer of the Exchequer. His lordship was also a Knight of the Garter. He *m.* Elizabeth, daughter and heiress of Walter, Lord Fitz Walter, and widow of Sir John Ratcliffe; but dying without issue, about the year 1509, his barony, supposing it a new creation, EXPIRED; but *that* created by the writ of Edward I. fell into ABEYANCE between his heirs at law, and so continues amongst their representatives. Those heirs were,

Elizabeth, his lordship's sister, widow of Sir Fulke Fitz Warine.

Joane, his lordship's sister, widow of John, Lord Zouche, of Haryngworth.

Sir Edmund Carewe, his lordship's nephew, son of his sister Margaret, Lady Carewe.

Sir John Arundel, K.B., of Lanherne, in the county of Cornwall, his lordship's nephew, son of his sister Catherine, Lady Arundel. This Sir John Arundel *m.* first, Eleanor, daughter of Thomas Grey, Marquess of Dorset, from which union the noble family of ARUNDEL OF WARDOUR derives.

ARMS.—Gu. a fesse Dancettée Ermine.

DODDINGTON — BARON MELCOMBE, OF MELCOMBE REGIS, IN THE COUNTY OF DORSET.

By Letters Patent, dated in April, 1761.

Lineage.

GEORGE BUBB, Esq., assumed by Act of Parliament, in pursuance of the testamentary injunction of his maternal uncle, George Doddington, Esq., of Eastbury, in the county of Dorset, the surname of DODDINGTON; and under that designation was a very eminent personage in the reigns of George I. and George II.; during which period, he was member of parliament for Bridgewater, Weymouth and Melcombe Regis, and held many political posts of importance, being at one time Envoy Extraordinary at the Court of Spain; but his own curious and well-known Diary, published after his decease, best shews the high place he held in public life. He was elevated to the peerage in April, 1761, by the title of LORD MELCOMBE, of Melcombe Regis, in the county of Dorset; but dying in the following year, unmarried, the dignity became EXTINCT. This nobleman is so generally known, that it would be a work of supererogation to enter more into detail regarding him upon the present occasion. His mansion at Eastbury, when finished by his lordship, was esteemed a most superb and costly structure; it passed, at his decease, to the present Duke of Buckingham, and was pulled down and sold piece-meal; but the bulk of his fortune he left to Thomas Wyndam, Esq., of Wyndham.

ARMS.—Ar. a chevron between three bugle horns, sa.

DORMER—EARLS OF CARNARVON.

By Letters Patent, dated 2nd August, 1628.

Lineage.

ROBERT DORMER, (son of the Hon. William Dormer, and Alice, daughter of Sir Richard Molineaux, of Sefton,) succeeded as second BARON DORMER, *of Wenge,* on the decease of his grandfather, Robert, first lord, in 1616, and was advanced on 2nd August, 1628, to the *Viscounty of Ascot,* and EARLDOM OF CARNARVON. His lordship, who took up arms in the royal cause during the civil wars, was eminently distinguished as a military leader in those unhappy times. In the year 1643 he had the command of a regiment of horse, and went with Prince Rupert, the Marquess of Hertford, Prince Maurice, and Colonel Howard, into Dorsetshire, and charged as a volunteer in Sir John Byron's regiment, at the battle of Roundway-down, in the county of Wilts; after which he joined the king before Gloucester, being then a general of horse, but was slain at Newbury on the 20th September following. Of this gallant person Lord Clarendon gives the following account:—" Before the war, though his education was adorned by travel, and an exact observation of the manners of more nations than our common travellers use to visit, (for he had, after the view of Spain, France, and most parts of Italy, spent some time in Turkey, and those eastern countries,) he seemed to be wholly delighted with those looser exercises of pleasure, hunting, hawking, and the like, in which the nobility of that time too much delighted to excel. After the troubles however began, having the command of the first or second regiment of horse, that was raised for the king's service, he wholly gave himself up to the office and duty of a soldier, no man more diligently obeying, or more dexterously commanding; for he was not only of a very keen courage in the exposing of his person, but an excellent discerner and pursuer of advantage upon his enemy. He had a mind and understanding very present in the article of danger, which is a rare benefit in that profession. Those infirmities, and that licence which he had formerly indulged to himself, he put off with severity, when others thought them excusable under the notion of a soldier. He was a great lover of justice, and practised it then most deliberately, when he had power to do wrong; and so strict in the observation of his word and promise as a commander, that he could not be persuaded to stay in the west, when he found it not in his power to perform the agreement which he had made with Dorchester and Weymouth. If he had lived he would have proved a great ornament to that profession, and an excellent soldier; and by his death the king found a sensible weakness in his army." His lordship m. Anna-Sophia, daughter of Philip Herbert, Earl of Pembroke and Montgomery, and was s. by his only son,

CHARLES DORMER. third Baron Dormer, and second Earl of Carnarvon. This nobleman m. Elizabeth, daughter of Arthur, Lord Capel, by whom he had surviving issue,

Elizabeth, m. to Philip Stanhope, Earl of Chesterfield.

Isabella, m. to Charles Coote, Earl of Mountrath.

Anna-Sophia, d. of the small-pox, unmarried, in the twenty-second year of her age, anno 1695.

His lordship m. secondly, Mary, daughter of Montagu Bertie, Earl of Lindsey, but had no issue. He d. on the 29th November, 1709, when the EARLDOM OF CARNARVON became EXTINCT, while the BARONY OF DORMER devolved upon his kinsman, Rowland Dormer, Esq., of Grove Park, in the county of Warwick, great grandson of Robert, first lord, through his second son, the Hon. Anthony Dormer; and is still extant.

ARMS.—Az. ten billets, fourth, third, second, and first, or. in a chief of the second, a demi lion issuant, sa. armed and langued, gu.

DOUGLAS—DUKES OF DOVER.

By Letters Patent, dated 26th May, 1708.

Lineage.

JAMES DOUGLAS, who succeeded his father in 1695, as second DUKE OF QUEENSBURY, in the Scottish peerage, having taken a prominent part in the revolution, was appointed in 1693 one of the lords of the treasury in Scotland, and the following year had a patent to sit and vote in the parliament of that kingdom as LORD HIGH TREASURER.[*] After his accession to the Dukedom of Queensbury, his grace was made by King William lord privy seal of Scotland, and one of the extraordinary lords of Session; and in 1700 appointed lord high commissioner to represent the king in the parliament of Scotland, where he held two sessions under two distinct patents. Upon his return to court his grace was elected a Knight of the most noble order of the Garter: and at Queen Anne's accession to the crown, he was made secretary of State for Scotland. In 1703 he, for the fourth time, filled the office of lord high commissioner, and again in 1706, being the last session of the parliament of Scotland, in which, with the utmost efforts, his grace carried the measure of Union between the two kingdoms. For all these eminent services the duke was rewarded with a pension of £3,000 a year out of the post-office, and the first peerage of Great Britain, under the titles of *Baron Rippon, Marquess of Beverley,* and DUKE OF DOVER, with remainder to his second son, Charles, Earl of Solway. His grace m. Mary, second daughter of Charles, Lord Clifford, and grand-daughter of Richard Boyle, Earl of Burlington and Cork, and had, with other issue,

James, an imbecile.

CHARLES, b. 24th November, 1698, created 17th June, 1706, Viscount Tibbers, and Earl of Solway.

George, b. 20th February, 1701.

---

[*] The officers of state in Scotland, prior to the union, had seats in parliament ex-officio, and when an office was placed in commission the crown had the privilege to appoint any one person to represent the said office in parliament.

Jane, m. 5th April, 1720, to the Earl of Dalkeith.

Anne, m. 25th January, 1732, to the Hon. Wm. Finch.

The duke d. in 1711, and was s. by his eldest surviving son,

CHARLES DOUGLAS, Earl of Solway, as second Duke of Dover. His grace m. 10th March, 1720, Lady Catherine Hyde, second daughter of Henry, Earl of Clarendon and Rochester, and had two sons,

> HENRY, Earl of Drumlanrig, m. 1754, Lady Elizabeth Hope, and was killed a few months after by the accidental discharge of his own pistol.
>
> Charles, d. in 1756.

The duke d. at the age of eighty, on the 22nd October, 1778, and leaving no issue, the DUKEDOM OF DOVER, and his other British honours, became EXTINCT. The Scottish dignities devolved upon the heir at law, and are now enjoyed in part by the Duke of Buccleugh, and in part by the Marquess of Queensbury.

ARMS.—Quarterly, first and fourth, ar. a heart, gu. crowned with an imperial crown, or. on a chief, as. three mullets of the field, for Douglas; second and third, a bend between six cross-crosslets, fitché, or, (for the Earldom of Marr,) the whole within a bordure, or, charged with a double tressure fleury and counter fleury of the second, being an augmentation; as was also the heart in the first quarter, used in memory of the pilgrimage made by Sir James Douglas, ancestor of his grace, to the Holy Land, in the year 1330, with the heart of King Robert Bruce, which was there interred according to that monarch's own desire. The double tressure was added by King Charles II., when he honoured the family with the Marquisate of Queensbury, the bordure previously being plain.

DOUGLAS—BARON DOUGLAS, OF AMBRESBURY.

By Letters Patent, dated 21st August, 1786.

Lineage.

WILLIAM DOUGLAS, third Earl of March, who succeeded in 1778, as fourth Duke of Queensberry, in Scotland, was created a peer of Great Britain, on the 21st August, 1786, as BARON DOUGLAS, of Ambresbury, in the county of Wilts, but dying unmarried in 1810, the barony became EXTINCT.

ARMS.—Four grand quarterings, viz. first and fourth, quarterly: first and fourth, ar. a human heart gules, imperially crowned ppr. on a chief as. three mullets of the field, for DOUGLAS; second and third, as. a bend betw.: six cross-crosslets, fitchée, or. for MARR, all within a bordure of the last, charged with the double tressure of Scotland, which tressure was added by King Charles II., when he honoured the family with the Marquisate of Queensberry; second and third grand quarters, gu. a lion rampant, ar. within a bordure of the last, charged with eight roses of the first, for MARCH.

DUDLEY — VISCOUNTS L'ISLE, EARLS OF WARWICK, DUKE OF NORTHUMBERLAND.

Viscounty,	by Letters	12th March, 1542.
Earldom,	Patent,	17th Feb., 1547.
Dukedom,		11th Oct., 1551.

Lineage.

SIR JOHN SUTTON, K.G., fourth Baron Dudley, of that family, m. Elizabeth, daughter and co-heir of Sir John Berkeley, Knt., of Beveston, and widow of Sir Edward Charlton, Lord Powis, and had with other issue, John, his second son, who assuming the name of Dudley, became

JOHN DUDLEY; this gentleman m. Elizabeth, one of the daughters and co-heirs of John Bramshot, Esq., of Bramshot, and was father of

EDMUND DUDLEY, so well known, with his colleague, Richard Empson, as the rapacious minister of King Henry VII. Dudley was brought up to the bar, having studied at Gray's Inn, and before he entered the service of the king, he had attained considerable eminence in his profession. Upon the accession of Henry, he was sworn of the privy council, and he subsequently filled the speaker's chair of the House of Commons; whilst in the latter office, they were about making him a serjeant-at-law, when he petitioned the king, for what reason does not appear, that he might be discharged from assuming that dignity. This occurred in the 19th of Henry VII., and in three years afterwards, he obtained the stewardship of the rape of Hastings, in the county of Suffolk. "Whether, (writes Dugdale,) Dudley, with Richard Empson, another lawyer, son to a sieve-maker, discerning King Henry to be of a frugal disposition, did first project the taking advantage against such as had transgressed the penal laws, by exacting from them the forfeitures according to those statutes; or whether the king perceiving so fair a gap open, to rake vast sums of money from his subjects, finding those persons to be fit instruments for his purpose, did put them upon such courses for filling his coffers, 'tis hard to say. But certain it is, that these were they, whom he constituted his *judices fiscales*, (Dudley being an eminent man, and one that could put hateful business into good language, as Lord Verulam saith.)" The extortions of those men exciting universal clamour, Henry VIII. commenced his reign, by the popular acts of submitting their oppressive conduct to judicial investigation before a criminal court; Dudley was tried at Guildhall, in the city of London, and Empson at Northampton, and both being found guilty, were beheaded together, on Tower Hill, on the 28th August, in the 2nd year of Henry VIII. Dudley, in the day of his power, having obtained the wardship of Elizabeth Grey, daughter of Edward, first Viscount L'Isle, by Elizabeth Talbot, daughter of John Talbot, Viscount L'Isle, and sister and co-heir of Thomas Talbot, second and last Viscount L'Isle, of the Shrewsbury family, married the said Elizabeth Grey, and left issue by her,

> JOHN, of whom presently.

Andrew, (Sir) involved in the conspiracy to elevate Lady Jane Grey to the throne, and received sentence of death, in the 1st year of Mary.

Jerome.

Elizabeth, m. to William, sixth Lord Stourton. Of these, John, the eldest son, had scarcely attained his eighth year at the period of his father's execution, and being in ward to Edward Guifford, Esq., of the body of the king, that gentleman petitioned that the attainder of Edmund Dudley might be repealed, and obtained a special act of parliament, (3rd Henry VIII.,) which restored the said

JOHN DUDLEY, in name, blood and degree, so that he might inherit all his deceased father's lands. From this period twelve years elapsed before John Dudley appeared in public, and the first we afterwards hear of him is his receiving the honour of knighthood from Charles Brandon, Duke of Suffolk, general of the army sent into France against the Duke of Bourbon. In the 19th of Henry VIII., Sir John Dudley was in the train of Cardinal Wolsey upon an embassy into France; and in eight years afterwards, "being the king's servant," he was made master of the armory in the Tower of London for life, with the wages of twelve-pence per day for himself, and three-pence per day for his groom in the office. In the 31st of the same reign he was appointed master of the horse to Anne of Cleves; and the next year, in the justs held at Westminster, Sir John was one of the principal challengers, his horse being accoutred with white velvet. In about two years after this he was elevated to the peerage, in the ancient dignity enjoyed by his mother's family, that of VISCOUNT L'ISLE, and made, the same year, lord admiral of England for life. In this capacity his lordship displayed great gallantry, and did good service against France and Scotland. "To say truth," remarks Sir John Howard, "he was the minion of that time: so as few things he attempted, but he achieved with honour, which made him the more proud and ambitious. Generally he always increased both in estimation with the king and authority amongst the nobility; but doubtful, whether by fatal destiny to the state, or whether by his virtues or appearance of virtues." His lordship was one of the executors to the will of his royal master; and upon the accession of Edward VI., he was created EARL OF WARWICK, with a grant of Warwick Castle. At this period he was made lieutenant-general of the army, and acquired an accession of military fame under the Earl of Hertford, in Picardy and Scotland, as well as by his successful defence of Boulogne, of which he was governor. In the 3d of Edward VI. he was again made admiral of England, Ireland, and Wales, and the next year constituted lord steward of the household. Henceforward his lordship's ambition appears to have known no bounds, and to have hurried him into acts of great baseness and atrocity. Through his intrigues the quarrel arose between the Protector Somerset and his brother, Lord Thomas Seymour, which terminated in the public execution of the latter; and he is at this period accused of acquiring considerable wealth by plunder of the church. In the

6th of the same reign he was advanced to the dignity of DUKE OF NORTHUMBERLAND, a peerage which, by the death of the last earl of Northumberland without issue, and the attainder and execution of his brother, Sir Thomas Percy, with the Percy estate, became vested in the crown. His grace had previously been constituted earl-marshal of England. Having now attained the highest honour in the peerage, and power the most unlimited, the duke proceeded, with scarcely the semblance of restraint, in his ambitious projects; and the Protector Somerset, one of his earliest and steadiest patrons, soon fell a victim to their advancement. That distinguished personage was arraigned, through the intrigue of Northumberland, before his peers, and though acquitted of high treason, was condemned for felony, and sentenced to be hanged. The eventual fate of this unhappy nobleman is well known, and, considering his own conduct to his brother, not deplored. He was executed by decapitation on Tower Hill. From the death of Somerset, the Duke of Northumberland became so unremitting in his attentions upon the king, and had so much influence over him, that he prevailed upon his majesty to sign and seal a patent conferring the succession upon Lady Jane Grey, the wife of his son, Lord Guilford Dudley. His subsequent efforts, after the decease of Edward VI., to establish this patent by force of arms, proving abortive, he was arrested, upon a charge of high treason, at Cambridge, and being condemned thereof, he was beheaded, on Tower Hill, upon the 22d of August, 1553, when all his honours became forfeited under the attainder. His grace m. Jane, daughter of Sir Edward Guilford, Knt., and had issue,

Henry, died at the siege of Bologne.

John, Earl of Warwick, d. in the life-time of his father, s. p.

Ambrose, created EARL OF WARWICK. (See Dudley, Earl of Warwick.)

GUILFORD, who m. Lady JANE GREY, eldest daughter of Henry, Duke of Suffolk, by Mary, Queen Dowager of France, and sister of King Henry VIII. Lady Jane Grey was therefore grand-niece to King Henry VIII. Lord Guilford Dudley was attainted and beheaded with his father.

Robert, K.G., created baron of Denbigh and Earl of Leicester. (See those dignities.)

Henry, slain at St. Quintin.

Charles, d. young.

Mary, m. Sir Henry Sidney, K.G. *Churchill*

Catherine, m. Henry Hastings, Earl of Huntingdon.

ARMS.—Or. a lion rampant, az. double queves. vert.

NOTE.—John Sutton, the seventh Lord Dudley of that family, disposed of Dudley Castle to the Duke of Northumberland, and having alienated other property, was ever afterwards known as *Lord Quondam.*

DUDLEY—DUCHESS OF DUDLEY.

By Letters Patent, dated 23rd May, 1644.

Lineage.

ROBERT DUDLEY, Earl of Leicester, the notorious favourite of Queen Elizabeth, married for his second wife, Douglas Howard, daughter of William, Lord Effingham, and widow of John, Lord Sheffield, by whom he had an only son,

ROBERT.

The earl apprehending a diminution of his influence with his royal mistress, made an attempt to get rid of this wife, as he did of his first, the unhappy Amy Robsart, by poison, but ineffectually. He repudiated her, however, and denied his marriage—but he bequeathed, at his decease, the greater part of his property to their issue, calling him, nevertheless, his base son,

SIR ROBERT DUDLEY, who having in vain endeavoured to establish his legitimacy, retired in umbrage to Italy: whence, through the influence of his enemies, being summoned to return, and disobeying the mandate, his lands were seized under the statute of fugitives. Sir Robert m. Alice Leigh, daughter of Sir Thomas Leigh, Bart., and his wife, Catherine, daughter of Sir John Spencer, of Wormleighton, in the county of Warwick, and aunt of Thomas, first Lord Leigh, of Stoneleigh, by whom he had issue,

Alice, } died unmarried.
Douglas, }

Catherine, m. to Sir Richard Leveson, K.B.

Frances, m. to Sir Gilbert Kniveton, of Bradley, in the county of Derby.

Anne, m. to Sir Richard Holbourne, solicitor-general to King Charles I.

Sir Robert Dudley took up his abode in the territories of the Grand Duke of Tuscany, with which prince he became a favourite, owing to his extraordinary accomplishments, being not only well skilled in all kinds of mathematical learning, in navigation, and architecture, but being a great chymist and skilful physician; and his fame reaching the imperial courts, the emperor, Ferdinand II., by letters patent, dated 9th March, 1690, conferred upon him the dignity of DUKE, when he assumed the title of Duke of Northumberland. Sir Robert, like his father, deserted his lady, and took with him to the Continent Miss Southwell, daughter of Sir Robert Southwell, of Wood Rising, in the county of Norfolk, and there married her, under the pretence that his marriage with Alice Leigh was, by the canon law, illegal, in as much as he had carnal knowledge of her during the life-time of his first wife, Miss Cavendish, sister of Thomas Cavendish, the navigator. By Miss Southwell, Sir Robert Dudley had several children, of which Charles, the eldest son, bore, after his decease, the title of Duke of Northumberland. Notwithstanding the conduct of Sir Robert, his lady, who remained in England,

ALICE DUDLEY, was elevated to the peerage for life, by King Charles I., by letters patent, dated 23rd May, 1644, as DUCHESS OF DUDLEY, and her surviving daughters were allowed the precedency of a duke's children.

The following is a copy of the grant, viz.—

" CHARLES, by the grace of God, &c.

" Whereas, in the reign of King James, a suit was commenced in the Star Chamber Court against Sir Robert Dudley, for pretending himself lawful heir to the honours and lands of the earldoms of Warwick and Leicester, as son and heir of Robert, Earl of Leicester, by Douglas, wife to the said earl, and all proceedings stayed in the ecclesiastical courts, in which the said suit depended for proof of his legitimation; yet, nevertheless, did the said court vouchsafe liberty to the said Sir Robert to examine witnesses in the Star Chamber Court, to make good his legitimacy. Whereupon, by full testimony of the Lady Douglas herself, and other witnesses, it was made appear. But a special order being made, that the depositions should be sealed up, and no copies taken, did cause the said Sir Robert to leave the kingdom; whereof his adversaries taking advantage, occasioned his lands to be seised on, to the king, our father's use. And not long after, Prince Henry made overture to the said Sir Robert, to obtain his title by purchase of Kenilworth Castle, &c., valued at £50,000., but bought by the prince in consideration of £14,500., and promise of his princely favour to restore Sir Robert in honours and fortunes; but before payment thereof was made (if any at all,) to the said Sir Robert's hands, the prince was dead. And it appearing that Alice, Lady Dudley, wife of Sir Robert, had an estate of inheritance in the same, descendible unto her posterity, in the 19th of James I., an act was passed to enable her to alien her estate from her children as a feme sole; which she accordingly did, in consideration of £4,000., and further payments yearly to be made out of the exchequer, &c.; which having not been accordingly paid for many years, are to the damage of the said Lady Alice and her children, to a very great value. And the said Sir Robert settling himself in Tuscany, within the territories of the great duke, (from whom he had extraordinary esteem,) had from the emperor, Ferdinand II., the title of a duke given him, to be used by himself and his heirs throughout the sacred empire.

" And whereas, our father not knowing the truth of the lawful birth of the said Sir Robert, (as we piously believe,) granted away the titles of the said earldom to others, which we now hold not fit to call in question. And yet having a very deep sense of the injuries done to Sir Robert Dudley, and the Lady Alice, and their children, &c., and holding ourselves in honour and conscience obliged to make reparation; and also taking into consideration the said great estate which the Lady Alice had in Kenilworth, and sold at our desire to us at a very great undervalue, and yet not performed or satisfied to many thousand pounds damage. And we also, casting our princely eye upon the faithful services done by Sir Richard Leveson, who married the Lady Catherine, one of the daughters of the said duke, and also the great services which Robert Holbourne, Esq., hath done us by his learned pen, and otherwise, who married Anne, another of the daughters; we have conceived ourselves bound in honour and conscience to give the said Lady Alice and her children such honours and precedencies as is, or are due to them in marriage or blood. And therefore we do not only give and grant unto the said Lady Alice Dudley the title of Duchess of Dudley for life, in England, and other our realms, &c., with such precedencies as she might have had, i f she had lived in the dominions of the sacred empire, &c.; but we do also further grant unto the said Lady Catherine and Lady Anne, her daughters, the places, titles, and precedencies, of the said duke's daughters, as from the time of their father's creation during their respective lives, &c. Conceiving ourselves obliged to do much more for them, if it were in our power, in these unhappy times of distraction, &c., witness ourself, at Oxford, 23rd May, in the 20th year of our reign."

This honour was also confirmed to her grace by King Charles II.

The Duchess of Dudley died on the 22nd January, 1669-70, and was buried at Stoneleigh, in the county of Warwick, under a noble monument erected by herself, when her peerage, being for life only, EXPIRED.

DUDLEY—EARL OF WARWICK.

By Letters Patent, dated 26th September 1561.

Lineage.

Through the especial favour of the Queen, in the 3d and 4th of Philip and Mary.

LORD AMBROSE DUDLEY, then eldest surviving son of the attainted John Dudley, Duke of Northumberland, was restored in blood; and in the first year of Elizabeth, he obtained a grant of the manor of Ribworth Beauchamp, in the county of Leicester, to be held by the service of pantler to the kings and queens of England at their coronations, which manor and office his father and other of his ancestors, Earls of Warwick, formerly enjoyed. In the next year he was made master of the ordnance for life, and two years afterwards, 25th December 1561, advanced to the peerage as BARON L'ISLE, preparatory to his being created next day Earl of WARWICK, when he obtained a grant of Warwick Castle, and divers other lordships in the same county, which had come to the crown upon the attainder of his father. His lordship was afterwards elected a Knight of the Garter. In the 12th Elizabeth, upon the insurrection in the North of the Earls of Northumberland and Westmoreland, the Earl of Sussex being first dispatched against the rebels with seven hundred men, the Earl of Warwick, with the Lord Admiral Clinton, followed with thirteen thousand more, the earl being nominated lieutenant-general of the army. The next year his lordship was constituted Chief Butler of England, and soon afterwards sworn of her majesty's privy council; in which latter year, 15th Elizabeth, he was one of the peers who sate in Westminster Hall upon the trial and judgment of Thomas, Duke of Norfolk, as he did, in fourteen years after at Fotheringay, upon the trial of Mary of Scotland.

His lordship m. first, Anne, daughter and co-heir of William Whorwood, Esq., Attorney-General to King Henry VIII.; secondly, Elizabeth, daughter and heir of Gilbert Talboys, and sister and heir of George, Lord Talboys; and thirdly, Anne, daughter of Francis, Earl of Bedford; but died without issue in 1589, when all his HONOURS became EXTINCT, and the lordships and lands, which he had obtained by grant, (part of the inheritance of the old Earls of Warwick,) reverted to the crown. Of

184

these the ancient park of Wedgenock was granted in 1601 by Queen Elizabeth to Sir Fulke Greville, to whom, in four years afterwards, King James likewise granted the Castle of Warwick, with the gardens and dependencies. This Sir Fulke Greville was descended through his grandmother, Elizabeth, one of the daughters and co-heirs of Lord Beauchamp, of Powyk, from the old Beauchamps, Earls of Warwick; and from him have sprung the existing Earls of Brooke and Warwick.

ARMS.—Or. a lion rampant az. double queuee. vert.

DUFF—BARON FIFE.

By Letters Patent, dated 19th February 1790.

Lineage.

JAMES DUFF, second Earl of Fife, in the peerage of Ireland, was created a peer of Great Britain, in the dignity of BARON FIFE, on the 19th February 1790. His lordship m., in 1766, Lady Dorothea Sinclair, sole heir of Alexander, ninth Earl of Caithness; but dying without male issue in 1809, the British BARONY OF FIFE became EXTINCT, while his lordship's Irish honours devolved upon his brother, the Hon. Alexander Duff, as third Earl of Fife.

ARMS.—Quarterly; first and fourth, or. a lion rampant gu. for Mac Duff, second and third, vert, afemee, dancettée, erm. between a hart's head, cabossed, in chief, and two escallops in base or. for Duff.

DUNCOMBE — LORD FEVERSHAM, BARON OF DOWTON, IN THE COUNTY OF WILTS.

By Letters Patent, dated 23d June, 1747.

Lineage.

The Duncombes, originally of Barley-End, in the county of Buckingham, spread in different branches into other counties during the reigns of King Henry VIII. and his son Edward VI.

WILLIAM DUNCOMBE, of Ivingho, (at the time of the visitation in 1634,) married Mary, daughter of John Theed, gentleman, and had four sons, of whom the second,

ANTHONY DUNCOMBE, Esq., of Drayton, in the county of Bucks, m. —— daughter of Paulys, Lord of the Manor of Whitchurch, and had issue,

    Charles (Sir), a banker in London, who served the office of sheriff for that city, anno 1700, and filled, in nine years afterwards, the civic chair. Sir Charles died unmarried, possessed of immense wealth, acquired by himself, which he devised to his nephews, Anthony Duncombe, the son of his brother, and Thomas Brown, the son of his sister.

    Anthony, of whom presently.

    Mary, m. to Thomas Brown, Esq, of the city of London; by whom she had an only son,

        Thomas, whose grandson, Charles Duncombe, Esq. of Duncombe Park, in the county of York, was created Baron

Feversham in 1826, and is the present Lord Feversham.

ANTHONY DUNCOMBE, Esq. (the second son) m. Jane, eldest daughter and co-heiress of the Hon. Frederick Cornwallis, second son of Frederick, first Lord Cornwallis, and had an only son,

ANTHONY DUNCOMBE, Esq. who inherited, as stated above, a moiety of his uncle Sir Charles Duncombe's large fortune, and was elevated to the peerage by letters patent, dated 23d June, 1747, as LORD FEVERSHAM, *Baron of Downton*, in the county of Wilts. His lordship m. first, the Hon. Margery Verney, daughter of George, Lord Willoughby de Broke; by whom he had three sons, Charles and Anthony, who both died young, and George, who attained his nineteenth year, but died in 1741; he had likewise a daughter, that died in infancy. Lord Feversham m. secondly, Frances, daughter of — Bathurst, Esq.; this lady died in childbed, 21st November, 1757, and he m. thirdly, Anne, daughter of Sir Thomas Hales, by whom he had a daughter,

Anne, who m. Jacob, second Earl of Radnor, by whom she was mother of the present Earl of Radnor and his brothers.

His lordship d. in 1763, and leaving no male issue, the BARONY OF FEVERSHAM, OF DOWNTON, became EXTINCT. His widow m., 22d July, 1765, William, first Earl of Radnor.

ARMS.—Per chevron ingrailed, gu. and ar. three talbots heads erased, counterchanged.

Note.—Sir Saunders Duncombe, (probably a member of this family,) a gentleman pensioner to King James I. and his son King Charles, was the introducer of *sedans* or close chairs into this country in 1634, when he obtained a patent, vesting in himself and his heirs the sole right of carrying persons "up and down in them" for a certain sum. It is somewhat singular that the *same year* introduced hackney coaches into London: they were first brought into use by Captain Bayley.

DUNNING—BARON ASHBURTON, OF ASHBURTON, IN THE COUNTY OF DEVON.

By Letters Patent, dated 8th April, 1782.

Lineage.

JOHN DUNNING, second son of John Dunning, of Gnatham, in the county of Devon, m. Agnes, daughter of Henry Judsham, of Old Port, in the same shire, and left at his decease an only surviving son,

, JOHN DUNNING, b. at Ashburton, 18th October, 1731, who having applied himself to the study of the law, was called to the bar, and soon attained the first rank in his learned profession. In 1767 Mr. Dunning was appointed solicitor-general, an office which he resigned in 1770. He was elected to parliament by the borough of Calne, in 1768, and continued a member of the lower house until elevated to the peerage upon the accession of Lord Shelburne, his great patron to power, by patent, dated 8th

April, 1782, as BARON ASHBURTON, of Ashburton, in the county of Devon. On the 13th of the same month his lordship was appointed CHANCELLOR OF THE DUCHY OF LANCASTER. He was also recorder of Bristol, and a member of the privy council. He m. in 1780, Elisabeth, daughter of John Baring, Esq., of Larkbear, in the county of Devon, and sister of Sir Francis Baring, Bart., by whom he had two sons, John, who d. at about seventeen months old in April, 1783, and RICHARD-BARRE, his successor. Of this eminent lawyer, Sir Egerton Brydges says, " He was a man whose talents were so peculiar, and had such a singular kind of brilliance, that they are not yet forgotten at the bar. They were more remarkable for acuteness and for wit, than for elegance and chasteness. The combination of his words were so singular, and the tones of his discordant voice so served in him to rivet the attention, that, as they always conveyed powers of thinking eminently sharp and forcible, he was constantly listened to with eagerness and admiration. His temper was generous, his spirits lively, and his passions violent. The popular side' which he took in politics increased his fame; and he died generally lamented, just as he had attained the fond object of his ambition, aged fifty-two."

His lordship d. 18th August, 1783, and was s. by his son,

RICHARD-BARRE DUNNING, second baron, b. 16th September, 1782. His lordship m. 17th September, 1805, Anne, daughter of the late William Cunningham, Esq., of Lainshaw, but had no issue. He d. in 1823, when the BARONY OF ASHBURTON became EXTINCT.

ARMS.—Bendy sinister of eight, or. and vert. a lion rampant, sa.

DUNSTANVILL—EARL OF CORNWALL.

By Creation, anno 1140,
5 Stephen.

Lineage.

REGINALD DE DUNSTANVILL, one of the illegitimate sons of King Henry I., by the daughter of Robert Corbet, was made EARL OF CORNWALL, by King Stephen, anno 1140. Notwithstanding which, he subsequently espoused the cause of the Empress Maud, and was in rebellion, until the fall of Stephen's power at the battle of Lincoln. From which period we find nothing remarkable of him until the 10th Henry II., when he appears to have been an unsuccessful mediator between that monarch and the haughty prelate, Thomas à Becket. His lordship was afterwards in arms on the side of the king, against Robert, Earl of Leicester, (who had reared the standard of revolt in favour of Prince Henry, the king's son;) and joined Richard de Luci, justice of England, in the siege of Leicester; the town of which they carried, but not the castle. His lordship m. Beatrice, daughter of William Fitz-Richard, a potent man of Cornwall, and d. in 1175, when leaving no legitimate male issue, the EARLDOM OF CORNWALL reverted to the crown, and was retained by King Henry II. for the use of JOHN, his younger son, excepting a small proportion which devolved upon the deceased lord's daughters, viz.

Hawyse, m. to Richard de Redvers.

Maud, m. to Robert, Earl of Mellent.

Ursula, m. to Walter de Dunstanvill.

Sarah, m. to the Viscount of Limoges.

ARMS.—Gu. two lions passant guardant, or. a batune sinister, az.

Note.—Besides his legitimate daughters above-mentioned, the earl left by Beatrice de Vaus, lady of Torre and Karswell, two bastard sons, HENRY and WILLIAM, whereof the elder,

HENRY, surnamed FITZ-COUNT, became a person of great celebrity. In the 4th King John he had an assignation of £20 current money of Anjou, for his support in the king's service in ROAN; and about that time gave twelve hundred marks for the lands of William de Traci; which lands Hugh de Courtenay and Henry de Tracy afterwards enjoyed. In the 17th John he had a grant from the king of the whole COUNTY OF CORNWALL, with the demesnes, and all other appurtenances, to farm, until the realm should be in peace, and the king clearly satisfied, whether he ought to hold it in right of inheritance, or as a part of the demesne of the crown: and being then made constable of the CASTLE OF LANCESTON, rendered up the government of the Castle of PORCHESTER, which he had previously held. In the 4th of King Henry III. it appears that he stood indebted to the king in £597 and one mark, which sum was due by him to King John, and that the same year disobeying the king's commands, and departing the court without permission, the king discharged all his subjects, and in particular those of Cornwall, from having anything to do with him. He made his peace, however, soon after, through the mediation of the Bishops of Norwich, Winchester, and Exeter, and the friendship of Hubert de Burgh, then justice of England, upon surrendering to the crown the castle of Launceston, and the county of Cornwall, with all the homage and services thereto belonging as fully as King John enjoyed them at the beginning of the war with the barons: saving the right which he, Henry Fitz-Count, preferred to the county, and in which the king promised to do him justice when he attained maturity. The claimant died, however, before the arrival of that period, and the matter was consequently never determined. By some it has been thought that this HENRY FITZ-COUNT succeeded his father in the Earldom of Cornwall, because he obtained a grant of the county from the crown. "But considering," says Dugdale, "that the title of earl was never attributed to him, I cannot conceive any thing more passed by that grant, than the barony or revenue of the county."

DURAS—BARON DURAS, OF HOLDENBY, IN THE COUNTY OF NORTHAMPTON, EARL OF FEVERSHAM.

Barony, } by Letters Pa- { 19th January, 1673.
Earldom, } tent, dated { 8th April, 1676.

Lineage.

LEWIS DE DURAS, Marquess of Blanquefort,

186

and brother of the Duke de Duras, in France, was naturalized by act of parliament, 17th King Charles II., being at that period captain of the guard to the Duke of York, whom he afterwards attended in the celebrated sea-fight with the Dutch, in June, 1665, and behaved so gallantly therein, that he was elevated to the peerage by letters patent, dated 19th January, 1673, (in consideration of this and other services,) in the dignity of Baron Duras, of Holdenby. His lordship m. Mary, elder daughter and co-heiress of Sir George Sondes, of Lees Court, in the county of Kent, K.B., which Sir George was elevated to the peerage (see Sondes), as Baron Throwley, Viscount Sondes, and EARL OF FEVERSHAM, with remainder, in default of male issue, to his son-in-law, Lord Duras, by letters patent, dated 8th April, 1676, and dying in the following year, Lord Duras inherited accordingly, and became Earl of Feversham. His lordship had a command at the battle of Sedgemoor, and was commander of the army of King James, (by whom he was made a knight of the Garter,) when the Prince of Orange came to Whitehall. He survived the revolution, and died without issue in 1709, when all his honours became EXTINCT.

ARMS.—Gu. a lion rampant, ar. (a label of three points).

ECHINGHAM — BARON ECHINGHAM.

By Writ of Summons, dated 19th December, 1311, 5 Edward II.

Lineage.

SIMON DE ECHINGHAM, of Echingham, in the county of Sussex, served the office of sheriff for that shire and the county of Surrey in the 18th, 19th, and 20th of Henry III. To this Simon succeeded his son and heir,

WILLIAM DE ECHINGHAM, who held seven knights' fees of the honour of Hastings; and in the 31st of Henry III., having m. Margaret, eldest daughter and co-heir of William de Montacute, had livery of the moiety of the manor of Gysseberg, in the county of Somerset. After this WILLIAM, the next person of note of the family,

ROBERT DE ECHINGHAM, was engaged in the Scottish wars of Edward I.; and after him came

WILLIAM DE ECHINGHAM, who was summoned to parliament, as a BARON, from 19th December, 1311, to 14th March, 1322. His successor,

ROBERT DE ECHINGHAM, was summoned[*] to parliament in the 1st of Edward III. He died the next year, possessed of the manor of Echingham, in Sussex, and its members; but nothing authentic is further known of the family.

ARMS.—Az., a frett ar.

---

[*] Nicolas says this was a military summons, and not a summons to parliament.

EGERTON — BARONS OF EL-LESMERE, VISCOUNTS BRACKLEY, EARLS OF BRIDGEWATER, DUKES OF BRIDGEWATER.

Barony,		17th July, 1603.
Viscounty,	by Letters	7th Nov., 1616.
Earldom,	Patent,	27th May, 1617.
Marquisate &		
Dukedom,		18th June, 1720.

Lineage.

The DUKEDOM OF BRIDGEWATER and *Marquisate of Brackley* were conferred 18th June, 1720, upon

SCROOP EGERTON, fourth Earl of Bridgewater, and those honours EXPIRED with Francis Egerton, the third duke, in 1803. The earldom and minor titles then devolved upon the next male heir,

JO'IN WILLIAM EGERTON, Esq., as seventh earl, who transmitted them, at his decease in 1823, to his brother,

The Reverend

FRANCIS HENRY EGERTON, as eighth earl. At the decease of this nobleman, in 1829, the honours of the house of Bridgewater became suspended; but as we understand that they are likely *only to be suspended*, we have hesitated to consider them EXTINCT, and the particulars of the family may yet, therefore, he found in *Burke's Dictionary of the Peerage and Baronetage.*

EGERTON — BARON GREY DE WILTON.

By Letters Patent, dated 15th May, 1784.

Lineage.

This, and the noble house of BRIDGEWATER, originated with a common ancestor; but the branch of Grey de Wilton was the senior.

ROBERT FITZHUGH, BARON OF MALPAS, in Cheshire, left an only daughter and heiress,

————, who espoused

WILLIAM LE BELWARD, and conferred upon him the BARONY OF MALPAS. From this alliance sprang the two great Cheshire families of EGERTON and CHOLMONDELEY. Of the former,

SIR ROWLAND EGERTON, Knt., of Egerton and Oulton, in the county of Chester, (the latter estate inherited through an heiress of the *Donce*, from the family of *Kingsley*,) was created a baronet on the 15th of April, 1617. This gentleman resided at his manor of Farmingboe, in the county of Northampton, and m. Bridget, daughter of Sir Arthur Grey, fourteenth LORD GREY DE WILTON, lord-lieutenant of Ireland in 1560, and heir of her brother, Thomas Grey, fifteenth and last baron of that family, (see Grey, Barons Grey de Wilton,) by whom he had, with other issue,

> Thomas, who m. Barbara, daughter of Sir John St. John, Bart., and died *s. p.* in the life-time of his father.

JOHN, his successor.

Phillip, of Oulton, whose descendant is the present Baronet of Egerton and Oulton.

Sir Rowland d. in 1646, and was s. by his eldest surviving son,

SIR JOHN EGERTON, second baronet, who m. Anne, daughter of George Wintour, Esq., of Derham, in the county of Gloucester, and dying in 1674, was s. by his only surviving son,

SIR JOHN EGERTON, third baronet. This gentleman m. first, Elizabeth, daughter of William, and sister and sole heir of Edward Holland, Esq., of Heaton and Denton, in Lancashire, by whom he had six sons and two daughters. He espoused, secondly, Anne, sole daughter and heir of Francis Wolferstan, Esq., of Statfold, in Staffordshire. Sir John d. 4th November, 1729, and was s. by his eldest son,

SIR HOLLAND EGERTON, fourth baronet, who m., in 1712, Eleanor, youngest daughter of Sir Roger Cave, of Stanford, in Northamptonshire, Bart., and dying 25th April, 1730, was s. by his eldest surviving son,

SIR EDWARD EGERTON, fifth baronet, at whose decease, unmarried, in 1744, the title devolved upon his brother,

SIR THOMAS-GREY EGERTON, sixth baronet, who represented the county of Lancaster in three parliaments, and was elevated to the peerage, by letters patent dated 15th May, 1784, in the dignity of BARON GREY DE WILTON, in the county of Hertford. His lordship m., 12th December, 1769, Eleanor, daughter and co-heir of Sir Ralph Asheton, Bart., of Middleton, in the county of Lancaster, by whom he had two sons and three daughters, of which one daughter alone lived to maturity, namely,

> ELEANOR, who m., 26th April, 1794, Robert, Viscount Belgrave (present Earl Grosvenor).

The baron was advanced, on the 26th June, 1801, to the dignities of *Viscount Grey de Wilton* and EARL OF WILTON, with special remainder to Thomas Grosvenor, the second, and to the younger sons, successively, of his daughter Eleanor, by her then husband, Robert, Viscount Belgrave, or to her male issue by any future husband. His lordship d. 23d September, 1814, when the baronetcy reverted to John Grey Egerton, Esq., of Oulton Park. The viscounty and earldom devolved, according to the limitation, upon his grandson, the Hon. Thomas Grosvenor, now EARL OF WILTON, and the BARONY of GREY DE WILTON became EXTINCT.

ARMS.—Ar., a lion rampant, gules, betw. three pheons' heads sa.

ENGAINE—BARONS ENGAINE.

By Writ of Summons, dated 6th February, 1299, which became extinct; but revived by Writ, dated 25th February, 1342, 16 Edward III.

Lineage.

The first of this family taken notice of by our public records, is,

RICHARD INGAINE, chief engineer to King William the Conqueror, from which office he derived his surname; to whom succeeded,

· VITALIS ENGAINE; and after him came,

RICHARD ENGAINE, Lord of Blatherwick, in the county of Northampton, temp. Henry II., who m. Sara, daughter of the Earl of Oxford, and had two sons,

       Richard,
       Vitalis.

He was s. by the elder,

RICHARD ENGAINE, one of the insurrectionary barons, in the reign of King John, whose lands were in consequence seised by the crown. He d. in 1216, and was s. by his brother,

VITALIS ENGAINE, who had likewise espoused the baronial cause, and had not, therefore, possession of the estates of the family until the accession of King Henry III. In the 26th of this reign, this feudal lord made partition with William de Cantelupe, of Bergavenny, of the manor of Badmundsfields, in Suffolk, as heirs to William de Courtenai. He m. Roese, one of the three sisters and co-heirs of the honour of Montgomery, in Wales, and was s., at his decease in 1248, by his son,

HENRY ENGAINE, who in the 42nd Henry III. had a military summons to march against the Welch: but afterwards taking part with the barons, he was involved in the defeat at Evesham, and had his lands sequestered. They were soon restored, however, under the *Dictum of Kenilworth*. This feudal lord never married, and dying in 1271, was s. by his brother,

JOHN ENGAINE, who m. Joane, daughter and heir of Henry Gray, and dying in 1296, was s. by his son,

JOHN DE ENGAINE. This feudal lord having distinguished himself in the wars of Scotland, temp. Edward I., was summoned to parliament as a BARON by that monarch, from 6th February, 1299, to 15th May, 1321. His lordship died, however, the next year, when the BARONY became EXTINCT, but his landed property devolved upon his nephew as heir at law, namely—

JOHN DE ENGAINE, (son of Nicholas de Engaine, by Amicia, daughter of Walter Fauconberg,) who making proof of his age had livery of his estates. This John, in the 19th Edward III., then residing in Huntingdonshire, had a military summons to attend the king into France, and was summoned to parliament as a BARON, from 25th February, 1342, to 20th November, 1360. His lordship had previously the high military rank of knight banneret. He m. Joane, daughter of Sir Robert Peverell, and had issue,

       THOMAS, his successor.
       Joyce, m. to John de Goldington.
       Elizabeth, m. to Sir Lawrence Pakenham.
       Mary, m. to Sir William Bernak.

His lordship d. at his seat at Dillington, in the county of Huntingdon, seised of the manors of Haighton, in the county of Leicester; Noteley, in Essex; Handsdon, in Herts: Saundey, in Bedfordshire; Gideling and Dillington, in Huntingdonshire, and Laxton, in the county of Northampton. In which he was s. by his son,

THOMAS DE ENGAINE, second baron, but never summoned to parliament. His lordship m. the Lady Katherine Courtenay, daughter of Hugh,

Earl of Devonshire, but dying without issue in 1367, his great landed possessions devolved upon his sisters as co-heirs, while the BARONY OF ENGAINE fell into ABEYANCE amongst them, as it still continues with their representatives.

ARMS.—Gules, a fesse indented between seven cross croslets, four in chief, three in base, or.

EDRINGTON — BARON EDRINGTON.

By Writ of Summons, dated 22nd January, 1336.
9 Edward III.

The surname of this family was assumed from the lordship of Edrington, in the county of Warwick, bestowed by Gervase Paganell, Baron of Dudley, upon

HENRY DE EDRINGTON, whose grandson,

THOMAS DE EDRINGTON, was appointed, with Richard de Altacvipa, in the 6th King John, bailiff or substitute to Geoffrey Fitzpiers, then sheriff of the counties of Salop and Stafford. He was afterwards chamberlain to the king, and obtained some territorial grants from the crown. In the 15th of John, when the baronial influence predominated, this Thomas de Edrington, and Ralph Fitz-Nicholas, are said to have been despatched secretly by the king to Admiralius Murmelius, king of Africa and Spain, to offer to the infidel the whole realm of England, as a tributary state; and that he, John, would renounce the cross, and assume the crescent, if the Mahomedan monarch would afford him assistance against his powerful and rebellious subjects. Thomas de Edrington m. Roese de Cockfield, and dying in the latter end of John's reign, was s. by his son,

GILES DE EDRINGTON, who, in the 35th Henry III., was one of the justices itinerant for the City of London, and the next was constituted one of the justices of the court of common pleas: he was likewise one of the justices of assise for the county of Warwick, from the 34th to the 53rd of the same reign inclusive. This learned person was a munificent benefactor to the church. He was s. at his decease by his son,

HENRY DE EDRINGTON, who m. Maud, one of the daughters, and eventually co-heiresses of Roger de Someri, Baron of Dudley; and also one of the co-heirs of Nichola, daughter and co-heir of Hugh Albini, Earl of Arundel, and dying in the 10th Edward I., was s. by his son,

HENRY DE EDRINGTON, who, in the 30th Edward I., upon the decease of his mother, had livery of her lands. In four years afterwards he was made a knight of the Bath, and he then attended Prince Edward in the expedition made into Scotland: wherein he attained so much celebrity that he was summoned to parliament as a BARON on the 22nd January, 1336. His lordship m. Joane, daughter and co-heir of Sir Thomas de Wolvey, of Wolvey, in the county of Warwick, by whom he had an only son,

       GILES, who, not appearing in the 19th Edward III. to receive the honour of knighthood, obtained pardon for that omission.

Lord Edrington had but one summons, and his descendants none. He was *s.* by his son,

GILES DE EDRINGTON, whose great grandson,

THOMAS EDRINGTON, who lived in the reign of Henry VI., was the last of the family that enjoyed the lordship of Edrington, in the county of Warwick.

ARMS.—Or, two lions passant in pale az.

ELIOTT — BARONS HEATHFIELD, OF GIBRALTAR.

By Letters Patent, dated 6th July, 1787.

Lineage.

SIR GILBERT ELIOTT, of Stobbs, in the county of Roxburgh, a Baronet of Nova Scotia, *m.* Eleanor, daughter of William Eliot, of Weld, or Wells, in the same shire, and had, with other issue,

JOHN, his successor in the baronetcy.

And

GEORGE AUGUSTUS ELIOTT, (eighth son,) who was born at the paternal seat, 25th December, 1717, and received the rudiments of his education under a private tutor. At an early age he was sent to the university of Leyden, where he made rapid progress in classical learning, and spoke with elegance and fluency, the German and French languages. Being designed for a military life he was sent from thence to La Fere, in Picardy. This school was rendered the most celebrated in Europe, by means of the great Vauban, under whom it was conducted. It was afterwards placed under the management and care of the Count de Houroville; here it was, that the foundation was laid of that knowledge of military science in all its branches, and particularly in the arts of engineering and fortification, which afterwards so greatly distinguished this renowned officer. He completed his course, by a tour upon the continent, for the purpose of witnessing the practical effect of what he had been studying theoretically. Mr. Eliott returned, in his seventeenth year, to his native country of Scotland, and was introduced by his father, Sir Gilbert, in 1735, (the same year,) to Lieutenant-Colonel Peers, of the twenty-third regiment, then lying in Edinburgh. Sir Gilbert presented him as a youth, anxious to bear arms for his king and country; he was accordingly entered as a volunteer in that regiment, and continued as such for more than a year. From the twenty-third, he went into the engineer corps at Woolwich, and made great progress in that study, until his uncle, Colonel Eliott, brought him in as adjutant of the second troop of horse guards. With these troops he went upon service to Germany, and was wounded at the battle of Dettingen. Of this regiment, he eventually became lieutenant-colonel, and was soon afterwards appointed aid-de-camp to King George II. In the year 1759, he quitted the second troop of horse grenadier guards, being selected to raise, form, and discipline the fifteenth regiment of light horse, called after him *Eliott's light horse.* As soon as this corps was fit for service, he was appointed to the command of the cavalry in the expedition on the coasts of France,

with the rank of brigadier-general, thence he passed into Germany, and from that was appointed second in command in the memorable expedition against the Havannah. In 1775, General Eliott succeeded General A'Court, as commander-in-chief of the forces in Ireland. But he did not continue long on that station; not even long enough to unpack his trunks. He solicited his recal, which being complied with, he was appointed to the *command of Gibraltar.* The system of his life, as well as his education, peculiarly qualified him for this trust. He was perhaps the most abstemious man of the age. His food was vegetables, his drink, water. He never slept more than four hours at a time, so that he was up later and earlier than most other men. He had so inured himself to habits of severity, that the things which to others are painful, were to him of daily practice, and rendered agreeable by use. It could not be easy to starve such a man into a surrender. It would be quite as difficult to surprise him. The example of the commander-in-chief in a besieged garrison, has a most persuasive efficacy in forming the manners of the soldiery. Like him, his gallant followers came to regulate their lives by the most strict rules of discipline, before there arose a necessity for so doing; and severe exercise, with short diet, became habitual to them by their own choice. Thus General Eliott maintained his station upon the rock for three years of uninterrupted investment, in which the whole resources of Spain were employed. All the eyes of Europe were on his garrison, and his conduct justly raised him to a most elevated place in the military annals of his country.

Upon his return to England, the gratitude of the British senate was as prompt as the voice of the British public, in voting him that distinguished mark his merit deserved, to which his majesty was pleased to add that of Knight of the Bath, and an elevation to the peerage by the title of LORD HEATHFIELD, BARON GIBRALTAR, by letters patent, dated 14th June, 1787, permitting his lordship at the same time to take the arms of the fortress he had so bravely defended, to perpetuate to posterity his heroic conduct. His lordship *m.* 10th June, 1748, Anne Pollexfen Drake, daughter of Sir Francis Drake, Bart., of Buckland, in the county of Devon, and had surviving issue,

FRANCIS-AUGUSTUS, his successor.

Anne, *m.* in 1777, to John Trayton Fuller, Esq., of Brightling, in the county of Sussex, by whom she had THOMAS, and other issue.

Lord Heathfield died in the seventy-third year of his age, at his chateau, at Aix la Chapelle, 6th July, 1790, and was *s.* by his son,

FRANCIS-AUGUSTUS ELIOTT, second baron, *b.* 31st December, 1750. This nobleman was also a military man, and attained the rank of lieutenant-general. He died *s. p.* in 1813, when the BARONY OF HEATHFIELD EXPIRED, while his estates devolved upon his nephew, the present

SIR THOMAS-TRAYTON FULLER-ELIOTT-DRAKE, Bart.

ARMS.—G. on a bend ar. a baton az.: on a a chief azure, the fortress of Gibraltar, under it, PLUS ULTRA, as an augmentation.

EURE, OR EVRE—BARONS EURE, OR EVRE, OF WILTON, IN THE COUNTY OF DUR-HAM.

By Letters Patent, dated 24th February, 1544.

Lineage.

The surname of this family was derived from the lordship of EVRE, in the county of Buckingham, where HUGH, a younger son of the Bacons of Werkworth, in Northumberland, (which Bacons were afterwards known under the name of Clavering,) took up their abode, in the reign of Henry III., and thus became,

HUGH DE EVRE. He was succeeded by his son and heir,

SIR JOHN EVRE, who in the 35th Edward I., obtained a charter for Free-Warren, in all his demesne lands, at Esby, in Cleveland, in the county of York; and in the 8th Edward II., was in the expedition then made into Scotland. In two years afterwards, Sir John Evre, was constituted one of the commissioners to negotiate a truce with the Scots; and in the 19th of the same reign, we find him again in the Scottish wars. From Sir John Evre descended,

SIR RALPH EURE, who married Katharine, one of the daughters and co-heirs of Sir William Aton, second Lord Aton, and in the 13th Richard II., made partition with the other co-heirs,* of those lands which were of their inheritance; Sir Ralph being at that time sheriff of Northumberland, and governor of Newcastle-upon-Tyne. He was afterwards sheriff of Yorkshire, and constable of the Castle of York, and again sheriff of Northumberland. Sir Ralph Eure was s. by his son,

RALPH EURE, whose son and successor,

SIR WILLIAM EURE, m. Maud, daughter of Henry, Lord Fitz-Hugh, and had issue,

SIR RALPH EURE, who fell at Towton-field, in the 1st Edward IV., and from him descended,

SIR WILLIAM EURE, who, in the 30th Henry VIII., was made captain of the Town and Castle of Berwick upon Tweed, and afterwards, being warden of the west marches towards Scotland, was elevated to the peerage, by letters patent, dated 24th Feb., 1544, as BARON EURE, of Wilton, in the county of Durham; his lordship m. Elizabeth, sister of William, Lord Willoughby de Eresby, and had issue,

    RALPH (Sir), who being constable of Scarborough Castle, in the 28th Henry VIII., held that fortress so gallantly against the insurgents, calling themselves the " Pilgrimage of Grace," that he was made Commander-in-chief of all the king's forces appointed for guarding the marches towards Scotland. A post which he defended for

---

* The other co-heirs,
    Anastatia, m. Edward de St. John.
    Elizabeth, m. first, William Playtz, and secondly, John Coniers.
Between these ladies, and lady Eure, the barony of ATON fell into ABEYANCE, and so continues amongst their representatives.

190

several years with great reputation. Sir Ralph Eure after distinguishing himself by many valiant inroads upon Scotland, fell at last, in 1544, at the battle of Halydon Hill. He m. Margaret, daughter of Ralph Bowes, Esq., of Streatlam Castle, in the county of Durham, and left issue,

    WILLIAM, who s. his grandfather.
    Ralph.
    Thomas.
    Frances, m. to Robert Lambton, Esq., of Lambton, in the county of Durham, from which marriage the present Lord Durham descends.
    Anne, m. to Lancelot Merfeild, Esq.
    Henry.
    Anne, m. to Anthony Thorp, Esq., of Conyl Thorp, in the county of York.
    Muriel m. first, to George Bowes, Esq., and secondly, to William Wicliff, Esq., of Wicliff.
    Margaret, m. to William Buckton, Esq.

Lord Eure, who was one of the commissioners appointed in 5th Edward VI., to convey the Garter to the King of France, d. ——— and was s. by his grandson,

WILLIAM EURE, second baron. This nobleman was constituted one of the commissioners in the 29th of Elizabeth, to negotiate a league with Scotland. His lordship m. Margaret, daughter of Sir Edward Dymoke, of Scrivelsby, in the county of Lincoln, and had issue,

    RALPH, his successor.
    Francis (Sir), m. first, Elizabeth, daughter of John Leonard, Esq., and had issue,
        HORACE, who m. Debora, daughter and co-heir of John Bret, Esq., and had, with other issue,
            GEORGE,} who inherited as 7th and
            RALPH, } 8th lords.
            Elizabeth, m. to William Kay, Esq.
            Debora, m. to John Pickering, Esq.
    Sir Francis Eure m. secondly, Ellen, widow of Sir John Owen, and had an only son,
        Compton Eure.
    William.
    Charles.
    Anne, m. to John Malory, Esq.
    Meriol, m. to Richard Goodricke, Esq., of Ribstone, and her grandson,
        SIR JOHN GOODRICKE, Knt., of Ribstone Hall, in the county of York, was created a BARONET on 14th August, 1641, an honour enjoyed by his descendant, the present SIR JAMES GOODRICKE, of Ribstone.
    Martha, m. to William Ayrmin, Esq.

William, Lord Eure, d. in 1594, and was s. by his eldest son,

RALPH EURE, third baron, who was constituted, in the 5th of James I., the king's lieutenant within the principality of Wales. His lordship m. first, Mary, only daughter of Sir John Dauney of Cessay, in the county of York, and had an only son,

    WILLIAM, his successor.

He m. secondly, Lady Hunsdon, widow of George, second Lord Hunsdon, but had no issue. He was s. at his decease by his son,

WILLIAM EURE, fourth baron. This nobleman m. Lucia, daughter of Sir Andrew Noel, Knt., of Dalby, in the county of Leicester, and had issue,

RALPH, who d. in the lifetime of his father, leaving by his wife, Catherine, daughter of Thomas, Lord Arundel, of Wardour, an only child,

WILLIAM, who inherited as fifth lord.

WILLIAM, who succeeded as SIXTH lord.

Mary, m. to Sir William Howard, Knt., of Naworth Castle, in the county of Cumberland, and had, with other issue,

CHARLES HOWARD, who was elevated to the peerage on the 20th April, 1661, as *Baron Dacre, of Gillesland, Viscount Howard, of Morpeth*, and EARL OF CARLISLE—dignities enjoyed by his lordship's great-great-great grandson,

GEORGE, present EARL OF CARLISLE.

His lordship was s. by his grandson,

WILLIAM EURE, fifth baron. This nobleman dying unmarried, the BARONY reverted to his uncle,

WILLIAM EURE, sixth baron. This nobleman, who was a colonel in the army of King Charles I., fell at Marston Moor in 1645. His lordship m. ——, daughter of Sir Thomas Denton, Knt., of Helsden, in the county of Bucks, and left two daughters, viz.

Margaret, m. to Thomas Danby, Esq., of Thorpe, in the county of York—first mayor of Leeds.

Mary, m. to William Palmer, Esq., of Linley, in the county of York.

Lord Eure dying thus without male issue, the barony of Eure passed to his kinsman (revert to issue of Sir Francis Eure, second son of William, second lord),

GEORGE EURE, as seventh baron. This nobleman dying unmarried in 1672, was s. by his brother,

RALPH EURE, eighth baron, at whose decease, in 1698, without issue, the BARONY OF EURE is presumed to have become EXTINCT.

ARMS.—Quarterly or. and gu. on a bend sa. three eschallops ar.

EVERINGHAM — BARONS EVERINGHAM.

By Writ of Summons, dated 4th March, 1309, 2 Edward II.

Lineage.

In the 14th Henry III.,

ROBERT DE EVERINGHAM married Isabel, daughter of John de Birkin, and sister and sole heiress of Thomas de Birkin, (feudal lords who flourished to nearly the middle of the thirteenth century,) and paid a fine of two hundred marks to the crown for livery of her lands, and likewise for livery of the Bailiwick of the forest of Sherwood, that being also part of her inheritance. This

Robert held then five knights' fees and a half in the county of Nottingham, and one in Lexinton. He had issue,

ADAM, his successor.

John, to whom his mother gave the manor of Birkin.

Robert, a clergyman, rector of the church of Birkin.

He died in the 30th Henry III., and was s. by his eldest son,

ADAM DE EVERINGHAM, who in six years after, at the decease of his mother, had livery of her lands, upon doing homage, and giving security for the payment of fifty pounds for his relief. In the 42nd Henry III. this feudal lord was in the expedition made then into Wales, but he afterwards took up arms with Montfort, Earl of Leicester, and the other discontented barons of that period, and was at the battle of Evesham. He d. in the 9th of Edward I., being at the time seised of a moiety of the barony of Shelford, in Nottinghamshire, into which moiety twelve knights' fees and a half in several counties appertained, whereof ten were for the Bailiwick of Sherwood. He likewise possessed the manors of Everingham and Farburne, in the county of York, and Westbury, in the county of Lincoln. He was s. by his son,

ROBERT DE EVERINGHAM, who m. Lucia, daughter and heiress of Robert de Thwenge, a great feudal lord, temp. Edward I., (the lady had been previously the wife of Sir William Latimer, and divorced,) and dying in the 15th Edward I., was s. by his son,

ADAM DE EVERINGHAM, who, in the 31st of Edward I., was in the wars of Scotland, and in three years afterwards was created a Knight of the Bath with Prince Edward, and other persons of rank, when he attended the prince upon the expedition then made into Scotland. After which, in the 2nd of Edward II., he was summoned to parliament as a BARON, and from that period to the 9th inclusive; during those years he was constantly engaged in the wars of Scotland : but afterwards taking up arms with Thomas, Earl of Lancaster, he was made prisoner at the battle of Boroughbridge, and forced to pay a fine of four hundred marks to the king to save his life. In the 11th Edward III. his lordship entailed his manor of LEXINTON, in the county of Notts, where he principally resided, upon ADAM, his eldest son, and so successively in default of male issue upon Robert, Edmund, Alexander, and Nicholas, his younger sons. This manor was holden of the Archbishop of York, by the service of performing the office of butler in the prelate's house, upon the day of his inthronisation. Lord Everingham d. in 1341, and was s. by his eldest son,

ADAM DE EVERINGHAM, second baron, summoned to parliament, as "Adam de Everingham de Laxton," on the 8th January, 1371. This nobleman, who was several years actively engaged in the French wars, shared in the glory of CRESSY. His lordship had issue,

WILLIAM, who m. Alice, daughter of John, Lord Grey, of Codnor, and dying in the life-time of his father, left issue,

ROBERT, who succeeded his grandfather.

    Joan, *m.* to Sir William Elys, Knt.

    Catherine, *m.* to John Elton, Esq.

  Reginald, who inherited the manor of West-burgh, in Yorkshire, *m.* first, Agnes, daughter of John Lungvillers, and secondly, Joan, daughter of ——, and *d.* 1st Henry VI., leaving a son,

    EDMUND, who died *s. p.*

The baron *d.* in 1371, and was *s.* by his grandson,

ROBERT DE EVERINGHAM, third baron. This nobleman *d.* in minority a few months after he inherited the title, leaving his two sisters his heirs, and the BARONY OF EVERINGHAM fell into ABEY-ANCE, between those ladies, as it has continued since with their representatives.

ARMS.—Gules, a lion rampant, vairèe, ar. and az.

FALVESLEY—BARON FALVESLEY.

By Writ of Summons, dated 20th August, 1383,
7 Richard II.

Lineage.

SIR JOHN FALVESLEY, Lord of Falvesley, in the county of Northampton, one of the great military characters of the reign of Edward III., having *m.* Elizabeth Say, daughter of William, Lord Say, and sister and heiress of John, Lord Say, had livery of all her lands lying in the counties of Kent, Sussex, and Hertford, and the same year attended John, Duke of Lancaster, in the expedition then made into Spain. Sir John was summoned to parliament, as "Johanni de Falvesley, Chevalier," from 20th August, 1383, to 8th September, 1392. His lordship's last martial occupation was in the fleet, under the command of the Lord Admiral, Richard, Earl of Arundel, in the 11th Richard II. He *d.* about the year 1392, when, leaving no issue, the BARONY OF FALVESLEY became EXTINCT.

ARMS.—Gu. two chevrons or.   ✓. *Clark*

FELTON—BARONS FELTON.

By Writ of Summons, dated 8th January, 1313,
6 Edward II.

Lineage.

In the 25 Edward I.,

ROBERT DE FELTON obtained a charter from the crown for a weekly market at his manor of Luchin, in the county of Norfolk, and likewise for free-warren there. In the 34th of the same reign he was in the expedition then made into Scotland, and in 4 Edward II., he had a military summons for a similar service. The next year he was constituted Governor of Scarborough Castle, and was summoned to parliament as a BARON, on the 8th January, 22d May, 26th July, and 26th November, 1313. His lordship *d.* soon afterwards, and was *s.* by his son,

JOHN DE FELTON, second baron, who (according to Dugdale) had summons* to parliament

---

* His name does not appear in the list of summonses for that year—NICOLAS.

208

in the 16th Edward III., but not afterwards. This nobleman was Governor of Alnwick Castle in the 8th Edward II., and for some years afterwards, he was engaged in the Scottish wars. In the 18th of the same reign he was in the expedition then made into Gascony, being at that time one of the admirals of the fleet, sent out to annoy the French and their commercial adventurers. Of his lordship nothing further appears known, except that he was an ancestor of the Feltons of Playford, in the county of Stafford, and created BARONET in 1690, an honour now extinct.

ARMS.—Gu. two lions passant erm. crowned or.

Contemporary with this John, Baron Felton, was

WILLIAM DE FELTON, who was governor of Bamburgh Castle, in the county of Northumberland, in the reign of Edward II., and governor of Roxburgh Castle in Scotland, in the 11th Edward III. This personage, who appears to have taken a distinguished part in the wars of Scotland and France, was summoned to parliament as a BARON, on the 25th February 1342, but not afterwards. In the 39th Edward III. he attended Prince Edward into Gascony, and being then Seneschall of Limosin, he vanquished a considerable party of the *Britaine* there; but in two years subsequently, being in Spain with the Duke of Lancaster, and wishing to prove his charger, he made a descent upon a body of the enemy, with his spear in his rest, and piercing it through a knight, he was immediately surrounded and slain, 19th March, 1367, leaving a son and heir,

SIR JOHN DE FELTON, Knt., who was never summoned to parliament, nor were any of his descendants.

FERRERS—EARLS OF DERBY.

Creation of King Stephen, anno 1137.

Lineage.

The first of this eminent family that settled in England, was

HENRY DE FERIERS, (son of Gualcheline de Feriers, a Norman,) who obtained from William the Conqueror, a grant of Tutbury Castle, in the county of Stafford, with extensive possessions in other shires, of which one hundred and fourteen manors were in the single county of Derby. This person must have been of considerable rank, not only from these enormous grants, but from the circumstance of his being one of the commissioners appointed by the conqueror to make the great survey of the kingdom. He was the founder of the priory of Tutbury, which he liberally endowed, and dying ——, was *s.* at his decease by his only surviving son,

ROBERT DE FERRERS, who having contributed, at the head of the Derbyshire men, to King Stephen's victory over King David, of Scotland, at Northallerton, (commonly called the battle of the Standard,) was created by that monarch EARL OF DERBY. His lordship *m.* Hawyse ——, and had issue,

  ROBERT, his successor.

  Isolda, *m.* to Stephen de Beauchamp.

Maud, m. to Bertram de Verdon.

———, m. to Walcheline de Maminot.

The earl d. in 1139, and was s. by his son,

ROBERT DE FERRERS, as second Earl of Derby. This nobleman was distinguished by his munificence to the church. His lordship d. ———, and was buried at the Abbey of Meervale, in the county of Warwick, one of the religious houses which he had founded, wrapped in an ox's hide, according to his own desire. He was s. by his son,

WILLIAM DE FERRERS, third Earl of Derby, who, in the 12th Henry II., upon levying the aid for marrying the king's daughter, certified the knights' fees then in his possession to be in number seventy-nine, for which he paid the sum of sixty-eight marks. This nobleman was also a liberal benefactor to the church. His lordship m. Margaret, daughter and heiress of William Peverel, of Nottingham, by whom he had issue,

ROBERT, his successor.

Walcheline.

The earl was s. by his elder son,

ROBERT DE FERRERS, fourth Earl of Derby. This nobleman rebelled against Henry II., and marching at the head of the Leicestershire men (19th Henry II.), upon Nottingham, then kept for the king by Reginald de Luci, got possession of the town, which he sacked, putting the greater part of the inhabitants to the sword, and taking the rest prisoners. He was soon afterwards, however, reduced to submission, and obliged to surrender to the crown his castles of Tutbury and Duffield, which were demolished by order of the king. His lordship m. Sibilla, daughter of William de Braose, Lord of Abergavenny and Brecknock, by whom he had issue,

WILLIAM, his successor.

Millicent, m. to Roger, Lord Mortimer, of Wigmore.

Agatha. This lady being a concubine to King John, had by that prince a daughter,

Joane, who m. Lewelline, Prince of Wales.

This earl, who was also a benefactor to the church, having founded the priory of Woodham, commonly called Woodham-Ferrers, in Essex, was s. at his decease by his son,

WILLIAM DE FERRERS, fifth Earl of Derby. This nobleman was ousted of his dignities of Derby and Nottingham by King Richard I., but they were soon afterwards restored to him, and we find him accompanying the lion-hearted monarch to the Holy Land, where he lost his life at the siege of Acon, anno 1191. His lordship, amongst other gifts to the church, gave, in the 1st Richard I., for the health of his soul, and the soul of Sibel, his wife, to the monks of St. Denis, in France, one wax taper yearly, price thirteen pence; as also a stag and boar in their proper seasons, to be sent annually thither at the feast of St. Denis, by himself and his heirs. He was s. by his son,

WILLIAM DE FERRERS, sixth Earl of Derby. This nobleman, upon the return of King Richard from captivity, took arms in his behalf, and joining the Earl of Chester, besieged Nottingham Castle, which, after a brief resistance, surrendered. For this and other acts of fidelity, he was chosen by the king to sit with the rest of the peers in the great

council held at the said castle of Nottingham in the ensuing March. Moreover, at Richard's second coronation he was one of the four that carried the canopy over the king's head. Upon the accession of King John, his lordship, with the Earls of Clare and Chester, and other great men, swore fealty to the new monarch, but upon the condition that each person should have his right. His lordship was present at the coronation of King John, and on the 7th June following, being solemnly created EARL OF DERBY by special charter, dated at Northampton, he was girt with a sword by the king's own hands (being the first of whom in any charter that expression was used). He had also a grant of the third penny of all the pleas before the sheriff throughout the whole county, whereof he was earl, to hold to him and his heirs as amply as any of his ancestors had enjoyed the same. Moreover, in consideration of four thousand marks, he obtained another charter from the king of the manor of Higham-Ferrers, in the county of Northampton, with the hundred and park; as also of the manors of Bliseworth and Newbottle, in the same shire; which were part of the lands of his great grandfather, William Peverel, of Nottingham. King John also conferred upon him a mansion house, situated in the parish of St. Margaret, within the City of London, which had belonged to Isaac, a Jew, at Norwich, to hold by the service of waiting upon the king (the earl and his heirs), at all festivals yearly, without any cap, but with a garland of the breadth of his little finger upon his head. These liberal marks of royal favour were felt so gratefully by the earl, that in all the subsequent struggles between the king and the refractory barons, his lordship never once swerved from his allegiance, but remained true to the monarch; and after King John's decease, he adhered with the same unshaken loyalty to the interests of his son, King Henry III. His lordship assisted at the coronation of the new monarch; and immediately after the ensuing Easter he took part with the famous William Marshall, (governor of the king and kingdom,) the Earls of Chester and Albemarle, and many other great men in the siege of Mountsorell Castle, in Leicestershire, then held by Henry de Braybroke, and ten other stout knights. And the same year, was likewise with those noble persons at raising the siege of Lincoln, which place the rebellious barons with Lewis, King of France, had invested. His lordship m. Agnes, sister, and one of the co-heirs of Ranulph, Earl of Chester, by whom he had two sons, William and Thomas. He d. of the gout in 1246, and his countess d. in the same year, after a union, according to some authorities, of seventy-five, and by others, of fifty-five years. His lordship was s. by his elder son,

WILLIAM DE FERRERS, seventh Earl of Derby, who, upon doing homage in the 32nd Henry III. had livery of CHARTLEY CASTLE, and the other lands of his mother's inheritance; and the same year he sate in the parliament held in London, wherein the king made so stout an answer to the demands of his impetuous barons. His lordship m. first, Sibel, one of the daughters and co-heirs of William Mareschal, Earl of Pembroke, by whom he had seven daughters, viz.—

Agnes, *m.* to William de Vesci.

Isabel, *m.* first, to Gilbert Basset, and secondly, to Reginald de Mohun.

Maud, *m.* first, to William de Kyme, secondly, to William de Vyvon, and thirdly, to Emmerick de Rupel Canardi.

Sibil, *m.* to Franco de Mohun.

Joane, *m.* to William Aguillon, and secondly, to John de Bohun.

Agatha, *m.* to Hugh Mortimer, of Checimarsh.

Eleanor, *m.* first, to William de Vallibus, secondly, to Roger de Quinry, Earl of Winton, and thirdly, to Roger de Leybourne.

The earl *m.* secondly, Margaret, one of the daughters and co-heirs of Roger de Quinci, Earl of Winchester, and had issue,

ROBERT, his successor.

William, upon whom his mother conferred the Lordship of GROBY, in the county of Leicester. (See Ferrers, Barons Ferrers, of Groby.)

His lordship, who from his youth had been a martyr to the gout, and in consequence, obliged to be drawn from place to place in a chariot, lost his life by being thrown, through the heedlessness of his driver, over the bridge of St. Neotts, in the county of Huntingdon, in the year 1254. (38th Henry III.) He was *s.* by his elder son,

ROBERT DE FERRERS, eighth earl of Derby. This nobleman being a minor at the time of his father's decease, the queen and Peter de Savoy gave six thousand marks for the custody of his lands, during his minority. His lordship, when arrived at manhood, became one of the most active of the discontented nobles, arrayed against Henry III., and commencing his career by the plunder and destruction of Worcester, the king, to retaliate, sent a force under Prince Edward, into the counties of Stafford and Derby, which wasted the earl's lands with fire and sword, and demolished his castle at Tutworth. His lordship joining, afterwards, with Montford, Earl of Leicester, and Clare, Earl of Gloucester, participated in the victory achieved at Lewes, in Sussex, wherein the king and the prince were made prisoners; but continuing to adhere to Leicester, was defeated, with that nobleman, by his former companion in arms, the Earl of Gloucester, at Evesham, and obliged to throw himself upon the mercy of the king, which, in consideration of a cup of gold, adorned with precious stones, (obtained from Michal de Tony, upon a mortgage on one of his manors in Northamptonshire,) and fifteen hundred marks, was extended to him, and he received a full pardon for all his prior misdemeanours, the king undertaking to protect him against Prince Edward, and all others, towards whom, at any time during the troubles, he had done wrong; upon condition, that if he should transgress again, he was without hope of favour, to be wholly disinherited. For the strict observance of which provision, the earl not only obliged himself by special charter, then freely sealed to the king, but by his oath of allegiance at the time renewed. The charter and oath, however, were but feeble restraints upon his lordship, for in the very next spring, we find him again at the head

194

of a powerful army in the northern part of Derbyshire, and soon after defeated in a pitched battle, at Chesterfield, by Prince Henry, eldest son of the King of Almaine. Here, his lordship was amongst those who made their escape from the field, but hiding himself under some sacks of wool in a church, he was there discovered, through the treachery of a woman, and thence conveyed a prisoner to London; whereupon he was totally disinherited, by the parliament then sitting at Westminster, as well of the EARLDOM OF DERBY, as of his territorial possessions, the greater part of which were conferred by the king upon his second son, Edmund, (surnamed Crouchback,) Earl of Leicester and Lancaster; to whom many writers of authority attribute also the dignity of Earl of Derby; but Dugdale expressly says, "although he, (the prince,) had possession of the greater part of this Robert's land, and exercised (perhaps,) the power of earl in that county, I am not satisfied that he really was Earl of Derby; in regard, I cannot find that the same Edmund had any patent of creation to that honour, as he had to those of Leicester and Lancaster." It seems that this unfortunate nobleman continued in confinement about three years, but in the 53rd Henry III., there was so much interest made for him, that the king accepted of security, whereby he might receive satisfaction for his lordship's misdemeanours, and issued his precept to Prince Edmund, to make restitution of his lands; when an agreement was entered into, between the disinherited earl and the prince, by which the latter, for the sum of £50,000, to be paid at once upon a certain day, was to relinquish all interest in the lands; but that payment not being made good, the securities to the covenant passed over the lands to Prince Edmund and his heirs for ever. Subsequently, however, the ousted lord instituted a suit in the Court of King's Bench, against the prince, for the restitution of his property, upon the allegation that the agreement he had sealed was extorted from him when a prisoner, and under apprehension of his life; but after divers pleadings, a decision of the court in the beginning of Edward I.'s reign, confirmed the lands to Prince Edmund.

This Robert de Ferrers, last Earl of Derby, of the family, *m.* first, Mary, daughter of Hugh le Brun, Earl of Angoulesme, and niece of King Henry III., by whom he had no issue; and secondly, Eleanore, daughter of Ralph, Lord Basset, by whom he had an only son,

JOHN, who inherited CHARTLEY CASTLE.

(See Ferrers, Barons Ferrers, of Chartley).

The earl died in the 7th Edward I., the last EARL OF DERBY, of the house of FERRERS.

ARMS.—Ar. six horse-shoes sa. pierced or. three, two, and one.

FERRERS—BARONS FERRERS, OF WEMME, IN THE COUNTY OF SÁLOP.

By Writ of Summons, dated 28th December 1375, 49 Edward III.

Lineage.

SIR ROBERT FERRERS, Knt., younger son

of Robert, second Lord Ferrers, of Chartley, having m. Elizabeth, only daughter and heiress of Robert, Lord Boteler, of Wemme, was summoned to parliament, as BARON FERRERS, of *Wemme*, from 28th December, 1375, to 16th February, 1379. His lordship acquired, by this alliance, the Lordship of WEMME, in Shropshire, and that of OVERSLEY, in the county of Warwick, with other extensive estates, and had an only son,

ROBERT, his successor.

This nobleman, prior to his marriage, was engaged in the Flemish wars of Edward III. His lordship *d.* in 1380, and his widow married two husbands afterwards, viz. Sir John Say and Sir Thomas Molinton, but had issue by neither. Lord Ferrers was *s.* by his son,

SIR ROBERT FERRERS, second Baron Ferrers, of Wemme, but never summoned to parliament. His lordship m. Joane, daughter of John of Gaunt, by Catharine Swinford, and had issue,

  Elizabeth, m. to John, son of Ralph, Lord Greystock, (who succeeded to the barony in 1417,) and had issue,

    Ralph, Lord Greystock, who m. Elizabeth, daughter of William, Lord Fitzhugh, and was *s.* in 1487 by his granddaughter,

      Elizabeth, who m. Thomas, Lord Dacre, of Gillesland.

  Elizabeth, m. to Roger Thornton, Esq., whose only daughter and heiress,

    Elizabeth, m. Sir George Lumley, whose descendant, and eventual representative,

      Barbara Lumley, m. Humphrey Lloyd, Esq., of Denbigh, the great-great-grandson of this marriage. Rev. Dr. Robert Lloyd claimed, unsuccessfully, the Barony of Lumley in 1723.

  Mary, m. to Ralph, a younger son of Ralph Nevil, Earl of Westmoreland, and had issue,

    JOHN NEVIL, who m. Elizabeth, daughter and heiress of Robert Newmarch, and left an only daughter and heiress,

      JOANE NEVIL, m. to Sir William Gascoign, whose daughter and heiress,

        MARGARET GASCOIGN, m. Thomas Wentworth, ancestor of the Wentworths, Earls of Strafford.

Robert, Lord Ferrers, died in 1410, when the BARONY OF FERRERS, of *Wemme*, fell into ABEYANCE between his daughters, Elizabeth Greystock and Mary Nevil. His widow Joane, m. secondly, the above-mentioned Ralph Nevil, Earl of Westmoreland (his second wife). Elizabeth, Lord Ferrers's mother, outlived his lordship, and at her decease, the BARONY OF BOTELER, of WEMME, fell also into ABEYANCE between her ladyship's granddaughters, the said Elizabeth and Mary, and both baronies continue in the same state with their representatives.

ARMS.—Vaire or. and gu. a lion passant guardant of the first in a canton.

FERRERS—BARONS FERRERS, OF GROBY, IN THE COUNTY OF LEICESTER.

By Writ of Summons, dated 26th January, 1297, 25 Edward I.

Lineage.

The Honourable

WILLIAM FERRERS, second son of William, seventh Earl of Derby, obtained, by gift of Margaret, his mother, one of the daughters and co-heirs of Roger de Quinci, Earl of Winchester, the manor of Groby, in the county of Leicester, whereupon he assumed the arms of the family of De Quinci. He m. Joane, daughter of Hugh le Despencer, and had issue,

  WILLIAM, his successor.

  Anne, m. to John, Lord Grey, of Wilton.

He *d.* in 1287, and was *s.* by his son.

WILLIAM FERRERS, who doing homage had livery of his lands in England, in the 21st Edward I., and in the 24th, of the lands which he inherited in Scotland. In the following year he was summoned to parliament as BARON FERRERS, of *Groby*. His lordship was engaged in the wars of Scotland in the reigns of Edward I. and Edward II.; he m. Margaret, daughter of John, Lord Segreve, and dying in 1325, was *s.* by his son,

HENRY FERRERS, second Baron Ferrers, of Groby, summoned to parliament, from 5th June 1331, to 20th November 1342. This nobleman, being actively engaged in the wars of King Edward III., both in Scotland and France, acquired very large territorial possessions, by grants from the crown, for his services. His lordship m. Isabel, fourth sister, and one of the co-heirs of Theobald de Verdon, and in the 5th Edward III., upon doing homage, had livery of the lands of her inheritance lying in Ireland. Of this marriage there were issue,

  WILLIAM, his successor.

  Philippa, m. to Guy de Beauchamp.

  Elizabeth, m. to —— de Asselis.

His lordship *d.* in 1343, and was *s.* by his son,

WILLIAM FERRERS, third Baron Ferrers, of Groby, summoned to parliament, from 15th March 1354, to 6th April 1369. In the 29th Edward III. his lordship was in the expedition then made into France in the retinue of his father-in-law, Robert de Ufford, Earl of Suffolk; and again, in the 33d and 35th, in the latter of which years, his lands in Ireland being seised for the defence of that realm, the king directed his precept to the justice, chancellor and treasurer there, to discharge them, in consequence of his lordship's being then in the wars in France, with divers men at arms and archers, at a very considerable expense. His lordship m. first, Margaret, daughter and co-heir of Robert de Ufford, Earl of Suffolk, by whom he had issue,

  HENRY, his successor.

  Elizabeth, a nun, in the convent of *Minoresses* without Algate, in the suburbs of London.

195

Margaret, m. to Thomas Beauchamp, Earl of Warwick.

He m. secondly, Margaret, daughter of Henry de Percy, and widow of Robert, son of Gilbert de Umfravil, Earl of Angus, and dying in 1371, was s. by his son,

HENRY FERRERS, fourth Baron Ferrers, of Groby, summoned to parliament from 4th August, 1377, to 17th December, 1387. This nobleman was uninterruptedly engaged in the French wars from the 1st to the 7th Richard II. inclusive; and the next year, being then a banneret, he was retained to serve the king in the wars of Scotland. Upon the death of William de Ufford, Earl of Suffolk, his mother's brother, without issue, Lord Ferrers was found to be one of the deceased earl's next heirs. His lordship m. Joane, daughter of Thomas, Lord Poynings, and dying in 1387, was s. by his son,

WILLIAM FERRERS, fifth Baron Ferrers, of Groby, summoned to parliament from 30th November, 1396, to 3rd December, 1441. This nobleman was also in the French wars. His lordship m. ———, and had issue,

HENRY, who d. in his father's life-time, leaving an only daughter and heiress,

ELIZABETH, heiress to the Barony of Ferrers, of Groby, at the decease of her grandfather, m. Sir Edward Grey, Knt.

Thomas, who m. Elizabeth, sister and co-heir of Sir Baldwin Frevile, Knt., of Tamworth Castle, in the county of Warwick, from which union lineally descended,

Sir John Ferrers, Knt., of Tamworth Castle, who d. in 1680, leaving (the only child of his deceased son, Sir Humphrey Ferrers), his grand-daughter,

ANNE FERRERS, his heiress, who m. the Hon. Robert Shirley, eldest son of Robert, first Earl Ferrers (which Robert d. before his father had been advanced to the earldom). The only daughter and heiress of this marriage,

ELIZABETH SHIRLEY, married James Compton, Earl of Northampton, and their only daughter and heiress,

LADY CHARLOTTE COMPTON, Baroness Ferrers and Compton, marrying George, first Marquess Townshend, conveyed those baronies to the Townshend family, with Tamworth Castle, in the county of Warwick, which they have since enjoyed.

William, fifth Baron Ferrers, of Groby, d. in 1444, when his estates passed by an entail to his brother, the Hon. Thomas Ferrers, as heir at law, and the BARONY OF FERRERS, of Groby, devolved upon his daughter, Elizabeth, in which dignity, her husband, Sir Edward Grey, was summoned to parliament (see Grey, Baron Ferrers, of Groby).

ARMS.—Gu. seven mascles voided, or. (the arms of Quinci).

FERRERS—BARONS FERRERS, OF CHARTLEY.

By Writ of Summons, dated 6th February, 1299, 27 Edward I.

Lineage.

JOHN DE FERRERS, (only son of Robert de Ferrers, eighth, and last Earl of Derby of that family,) after the forfeiture of his father, was summoned to parliament as BARON FERRERS, of Chartley, in the county of Stafford, on the 6th February, 1299. (A seat which came into the family of Ferrers, by the marriage of William, fifth Earl of Derby, with Agnes, sister and co-heir of Ranulph, Earl of Chester.) This John, inheriting the turbulent spirit of his father, joined the Earl of Hertford and others, in the 25th Edward I., in opposing the collection of the subsidies granted by the parliament then held at St. Edmundsbury, to the crown, but the ferment was allayed by the king's confirming Magna Charta, and the charter of the Forests; and by declaring that in future, NO TAX SHOULD BE IMPOSED UPON THE SUBJECT WITHOUT THE CONSENT OF PARLIAMENT, at the same time granting a pardon to the discontented lords and their adherents, in which pardon John de Ferrers is especially named. Soon after this he petitioned Pope Nicholas III., that his holiness should interfere to procure him the lands of his late father which had been conferred upon Edmund, Earl of Lancaster, but his suit was ineffectual. He was subsequently in the Scottish wars, and was then raised to the peerage as stated above. His lordship m. Hawyse, niece and heiress of *Cecilia de Muscegros, by whom he acquired a great increase to his fortune. In the 34th Edward I. he was again in the wars of Scotland, and, subsequently, in the 4th Edward II., the year following which he was constituted Seneschal of Aquitaine. He d. in 1394, and was s. by his son,

ROBERT DE FERRERS, second Baron Ferrers, of Chartley, summoned to parliament 25th February, 1342. This nobleman, who was of a martial character, served frequently in the Scotch and French wars of Henry III., and, finally, the year before his decease, participated in the GLORIOUS VICTORY OF CRESSY, (23rd Edward III.) His lordship m. Agnes, daughter of Humphrey de Bohun, Earl of Hereford, by whom he had issue,

JOHN, his successor.

Robert, summoned to parliament as Baron Ferrers, of Wemme (see that dignity).

He d. in 1350, and was s. by his elder son,

JOHN DE FERRERS, third Baron Ferrers, of Chartley, but never summoned to parliament. This nobleman was in the wars of Gascony in the 33rd Edward III. His lordship m. Elizabeth, widow of Fulke le Strange, and dying beyond the seas, in 1367, was s. by his son,

ROBERT DE FERRERS, fourth Baron Ferrers,

* According to Dugdale; but by Edmonson, daughter and heiress of Robert de Muscegros, Lord of Charlton, in the county of Somerset.

of Chartley, but never summoned to parliament. His lordship m. Margaret, daughter of Edward, Lord Spencer, and dying in 1413, was s. by his son,

EDMUND DE FERRERS, fifth Baron Ferrers, of Chartley, but never summoned to parliament. This nobleman participated in most of the great victories of King Henry V. His lordship m. Helen, daughter and co-heir of Thomas de la Roche, by whom he acquired large landed possessions, amongst which was that of Castle Bromwich, in the county of Derby, and he had issue,

WILLIAM, his successor.

Edmund, upon whom the estates were entailed.

He d. in the 14th Henry VI., and was s. by his elder son,

WILLIAM DE FERRERS, sixth Baron Ferrers, of Chartley, who m. Elizabeth, daughter of Sir Hamon Belknap, Knt., and dying in the 28th Henry VI., left an only daughter,

ANNE, then wife of Walter Devereux, Esq., upon whom the Barony of FERRERS, OF CHARTLEY, devolved, a dignity, at present, enjoyed by the Marquess Townshend.

His lordship's great landed possessions passed in conformity with the entail upon his only brother, the Hon. Edmund Ferrers.

ARMS.—Vaire or. and gu.

FIENES — VISCOUNTS SAY AND SELE.

By Letters Patent, dated 7th July, 1694.

See Say, Lords Say and Sele.

FINCH—BARON FINCH, OF FORD-WICH, IN THE COUNTY OF KENT.

By Letters Patent, dated 7th April, 1640.

Lineage.

SIR THOMAS FINCH, Knt., a gallant soldier in the reigns of Mary and Elizabeth, m. Catherine, elder daughter and co-heiress of Sir Thomas Moyle, of Eastwell, in the county of Kent, and had issue,

MOYLE, from whom the EXTANT Earls of Winchelsea and Nottingham descend.

Henry, of whom presently.

Thomas, m. ——, daughter of —— Wilkins, Esq., of Tonge, and died s. p.

The second son,

SIR HENRY FINCH, serjeant at law, m. Ursula, daughter and heiress of John Thwaits, Esq., and had an only son,

SIR JOHN FINCH, an eminent lawyer, who filled the chair of the House of Commons in 1627, became attorney-general to the queen in 1635, justice of the common pleas the following year, and chief justice afterwards. In 1639, Sir John was appointed lord keeper of the great seal, and in the beginning of the next year, (7th April 1640,) he was advanced to the peerage, in the dignity of BARON FINCH, of Fordwich, in the county of Kent. His lordship m. first, Eleanor, daughter of Sir George Wyat, of Bexley, and secondly, Mabel, daughter of

the Very Rev. Charles Fortherby, Dean of Canterbury; but having no issue, save one daughter, who m. the Right Hon. Sir George Radcliffe, of Ireland, the BARONY OF FINCH, at his lordship's decease in 1660, became EXTINCT.

FITZ-ALAN—EARLS OF ARUNDEL, BARONS MALTRAVERS.

Earldom, by feudal possession of Arundel Castle.
Barony, by Writ of Summons, dated 5th June, 1330,
4 Edward III.

Lineage.

In the time of William the Conqueror,

ALAN, the son of Flathald (or Flaald) obtained, by the gift of that king, the Castle of Oswaldestre, with the territory adjoining, which belonged to Meredith ap Blethon, a Briton. This Alan, having married the daughter and heir of Warine, sheriff of Shropshire, had, in her right, the Barony of Warine, and was s. by his son,

WILLIAM FITZ ALAN, who, in the contest between King Stephen and the Empress Maud, being then governor of Shrewsbury and sheriff of the county of Salop, held the castle of Shrewsbury for the latter, until it was taken by assault. He was also with the empress at the siege of Winchester Castle, in the 6th Stephen, when she and her whole army were put to flight; and afterwards, continuing to adhere stoutly to the same cause, he was re-constituted sheriff of Salop, so soon as King Henry attained the crown. This William m. Isabel, daughter and heir of Helias de Say, Lady of Clun, niece of Robert, Earl of Gloucester, and dying some time before 1165, was s. by his son,

WILLIAM FITZ-ALAN, who, in the 12th Henry II., upon the assessment, in aid of marrying the king's daughter, certified his knights' fees to be in number thirty-five and a half. He was s. by his son,

WILLIAM FITZ-ALAN. This feudal lord served the office of sheriff for Shropshire, from 2d Richard I., until the 3d of John, inclusive. He was s. by his brother,

JOHN FITZ-ALAN, who took up arms with the other barons temp. John; but, upon the accession of King Henry, having had letters of safe conduct to come in and make his peace, he had livery of the lands of his inheritance, upon paying, however, a fine of ten thousand marks. This feudal lord m. first, Isabel, second daughter of William de Albini, Earl of Arundel, and sister and co-heir of Hugh, last earl of that family, by whom he had a son,

JOHN, his successor.

He espoused, secondly, Hawis de Blancminster, and dying in 1239, was s. by his son,

JOHN FITZ-ALAN, who, in the 26th Henry III., upon the division made of the property of Hugh Albini, Earl of Arundel, then made, had the castle of Arundel assigned to him for his principal seat, thus becoming fifth Earl of Arundel; and soon after that, in consideration of a thousand pounds' fine, had livery of his own castles of Clun, Blancminster and Schrawurthen. In the 42d Henry III., his lordship was made captain-general of all the forces designed for guarding the Welsh marches, and in the baronial war, he appears first to have

197

aided with the barons, and afterwards with the king. He died in the 52d Henry III., leaving issue by his wife, Maud, daughter of Rose de Verdun, his successor,

JOHN FITZ-ALAN, sixth Earl of Arundel, who m. Isabel de Mortimer, and dying in two years after his accession to the honours of the family, was s. by his son,

RICHARD FITZ-ALAN, seventh Earl of Arundel, who espoused Alice, daughter of the Marquess of Saluce in Italy, and had issue,

EDMUND, his successor.

Maud, m. to Philip, Lord Burnel.

Margaret, m. to William Boteler, of Wemme. His lordship d. in 1301, and was s. by his son,

EDMUND FITZ-ALAN, eighth Earl of Arundel. We find this nobleman, from the 34th Edward I., when he was made a Knight of the Bath with Prince Edward, to the fourth of the ensuing reign, constantly engaged in the wars of Scotland; but he was afterwards involved in the treason of Thomas, Earl of Lancaster, yet not greatly to his prejudice; for, in the 10th Edward II., his lordship was constituted lieutenant and captain-general to the king, from the Trent northwards, as far as Roxborough in Scotland, and for several years, subsequently, he continued one of the commanders of the English army in Scotland; in which service he so distinguished himself, that he obtained a grant from the crown of the confiscated property of Lord Baddlesmere, in the city of London and county of Salop; as well as the escheated lands of John, Lord Moubray, in the Isle of Axholme, and several manors and castles, part of the possessions (also forfeited) of Roger, Lord Mortimer, of Wigmore. But those royal grants led, eventually, to the earl's ruin; for, after the fall of the unhappy Edward into the hands of his enemies, Lord Arundel, who was implacably hated by the queen and Mortimer, suffered death, by decapitation, at Hereford in 1326. His lordship m. the Lady Alice Plantagenet, sister and sole heir of John, last Earl of Warren and Surrey of that family, by whom he had issue,

RICHARD, his successor.

Edmund.

Alice, m. to John de Bohun, Earl of Hereford.

Jane, m. to Warine Gerard, Lord L'Isle.

His lordship was s. by his eldest son,

RICHARD FITZ-ALAN, who being restored by parliament, 4th Edward III., had the Castle of Arundel, (which had been given to Edmund, Earl of Kent, the king's uncle,) rendered to him, and thus became ninth earl. In the 7th Edward III., this nobleman was constituted governor of Chirke Castle, in the county of Denbigh, and the ensuing year, had a grant of the inheritance of that castle, with all the territories thereunto belonging, being part of the possessions of Roger Mortimer, the attainted Earl of March; he was soon afterwards made governor of Porchester Castle, and the same year had a command in the wars of Scotland, where he continued engaged for some years. After this he was constituted admiral of the western seas, and governor of Caernarvon castle. In the 14th Edward III., his lordship embarked in the French wars, and participated in the glories of the

196

subsequent campaigns. He was at the siege of Vannes, the relief of Thouars, and the immortal battle of CRESSY. Besides his great military services, the earl was frequently employed in diplomatic missions of the first importance, and was esteemed one of the most eminent generals and statesmen of the era in which he lived. His lordship, who with his other honours had the GARTER, contracted in minority, and under constraint, marriage with Isabel, daughter of Hugh le Despenser, and had issue by her, an only daughter,

Philippa, m. to Sir Richard Sergeaux, Knt., of Cornwall. — A . -

He subsequently repudiated this lady, with the sanction of the Pope, and espoused the Lady Eleanor Plantagenet, daughter of Henry, Earl of Lancaster, by whom he had issue,

RICHARD, his successor.

John, m. Eleanor, grand-daughter and heir of John, Lord Maltravers, in whose right he bore that title, and had issue,

JOHN, who d. in his father's life-time, leaving a son,

JOHN, Lord Maltravers, who s. as eleventh Earl of Arundel.

Thomas, called Arundel, successively Bishop of Ely, Archbishop of York, and Archbishop of Canterbury, LORD CHANCELLOR OF ENGLAND. This prelate was impeached and banished the kingdom, in the reign of Richard II.; but returned with Henry IV. and was restored to the see of Canterbury. He was a person of great eminence in his time, but is accused of being a religious persecutor, particularly of the Wickliffites, and of Sir John Oldcastle, Lord Cobham. He d. 20th October, 1413, and was buried in the cathedral church of Canterbury.

Alice, m. to Thomas Holland, Earl of Kent.

Eleanor, died young.

Joane, m. to Humphrey de Bohun, Earl of Hereford.

Mary, m. to John, Lord Strange, of Blackmere.

His lordship d. in 1375, and was s. by his eldest son,

RICHARD FITZ-ALAN, tenth Earl of Arundel, K.G. In the 1st Richard II., this nobleman being constituted admiral of the king's fleet in the westwards, and soon after that to the southwards, was retained by indenture, to serve the king at sea, for one quarter of a year, in the company of John, Duke of Lancaster, King of Castile. He was afterwards engaged for some years in Scotland; and was in the commission, (9th Edward II.,) for the trial of Michael de la Pole, and some other of the king's favourites, whom the Commons had then impeached. His lordship was appointed the next year admiral of the whole fleet, and putting to sea, encountered and vanquished the united fleets of France and Spain, taking no less than one hundred ships, great and small, all laden with wines, comprising nineteen thousand tuns. This gallant exploit he followed up by entering the port of Brest, and reducing one of its castles and burning the other. He now returned to England in great triumph, but had to encounter the jealousy and hatred of the king's favourites, particularly of the Duke of Ireland, whose influence over the king he strenuously resisted. His lordship afterwards entered into the confederation of the Earls of Derby and Warwick, which assembled in arms at Haringhay Park, (now Hornsey,) in Middlesex, and compelled the king to acquiesce in their views. He was then, by the general consent of parliament, (11th Richard II.,) made governor of the castle and town of Brest, and shortly after, captain-general of the king's fleet at sea, with commission to treat of peace, with John de Montfort, then Duke of Britanny; whereupon hoisting his flag, soon after met with the enemy, of whose ships he sunk and took fourscore; entered the isle of Reas, which he burnt and spoiled, and several other ports which he likewise plundered, putting to flight all the French and Britons, that made any resistance. From this memorable period in the life of Lord Arundel, little is known of him, until the 15th Richard, when the king regaining his power, summoned a parliament at Westminster, and dismissed several of the great officers of state, amongst whom his lordship was removed from his command as admiral; and in two years afterwards, the parliament then sitting, he was accused of treason by the Duke of Lancaster, but escaped for the moment, and sought to retire from public life. The king entertaining, however, the strongest feeling of personal enmity to all those who had previously opposed his minions, contrived to get the Earl of Arundel into his hands by stratagem, and having sent him prisoner to the isle of Wight, brought him to immediate trial, when he was condemned to be hanged, drawn, and quartered, as a traitor. The sentence was however somewhat mitigated, and the gallant nobleman was simply beheaded at Cheapside, in the city of London, 21st of Richard II.; the king himself being a spectator, and Thomas de Mowbray, Earl Marshal, (who had married his daughter,) the executioner, who bound up his eyes, and according to some, the person who actually struck off his head. It is stated, that when the earl saw his son-in-law, Mowbray, and the Earl of Kent, his nephew, guarding him to the place of execution, he told them, it had been much more fit, that they should have absented themselves: "For the time will come," (said he,) "when as many shall wonder at your misfortune, as they now do at mine." His lordship m. first, Lady Elizabeth de Bohun, daughter of William, Earl of Northampton, and had surviving issue,

　　THOMAS, his successor.

　　Elizabeth, m. first, to William de Montacute, eldest son of William, Earl of Salisbury, which William was unhappily slain by his father in a tilting at Windsor, 6th Richard II. Her ladyship m. secondly, Thomas, Lord Mowbray, Earl Marshal, and through the daughter of this marriage, the

　　　　LADY MARGARET MOWBRAY, eventual heiress of the Mowbrays, who espoused Sir Robert Howard, Knt., the DUKEDOM of NORFOLK, the EARL MARSHALSHIP, and other honours, came

into the family of HOWARD, which they have since enjoyed.

　　Lady Elizabeth m. thirdly, Sir Gerard Ufflete, Knt., and fourthly, Sir Robert Gouphill, Knt.

　　Margaret, m. to Sir Rowland Lenthall, Knt.

　　Alice, m. to John Charlton, Lord Powis.

The earl was s. by his son,

　　THOMAS FITZ-ALAN, who, being restored in blood in the parliament 1st of Henry IV., when the judgment against his father was reversed, became *eleventh* EARL OF ARUNDEL. This nobleman was made a Knight of the Bath at the coronation of King Henry IV. He was afterwards made a Knight of the Garter—and upon the accession of King Henry V. he was constituted constable of Dover Castle, and lord warden of the Cinque Ports, as also LORD TREASURER of England. His lordship m. Beatrix, an illegitimate daughter of John, king of Portugal, and the nuptials were celebrated with great pomp in London, the king and queen assisting. He died, however, without issue, in 1415, leaving his four sisters his heirs, as to certain parts of his great possessions; but the CASTLE OF ARUNDEL, and with it the earldom, devolved upon his cousin,

　　JOHN FITZ-ALAN, Lord Maltravers, as twelfth Earl of Arundel[*] (refer to issue of Richard, ninth earl). This nobleman was in the king's fleet at sea under his kinsman, Richard, Earl of Arundel, and he was subsequently in the wars of Scotland and France. His lordship m. Alianore, daughter of Sir John Berkeley, Knt., of Beverston, in the county of Gloucester, by whom he had issue,

　　JOHN, his successor.

　　William, who s. as fifteenth earl.

────────

[*] Nicolas has the following note in his Synopsis— Until the 11th Henry VI., when it was decided that the tenure of the castle of Arundel alone, without any creation, patent, or investiture, constituted its possessor Earl of Arundel, neither this John, nor John his son and heir, were regularly considered to have possessed that dignity, although they were both seised of the said castle; in proof of which John Fitz-Alan, twelfth earl, was never summoned to parliament, and John, his son and heir, was summoned in the 7th Henry VI., as a BARON only; nor was it until the 3rd December, 1441, that the inheritor of the castle of Arundel sat in parliament by that title, which probably arose from this circumstance, that at the time of the decision alluded to, in the 11th Henry VI., 1432, John, Earl of Arundel, was engaged in the wars of France, and continued to be so until his death, which happened within two years afterwards; and Humphrey, his son and heir, died in 1437, then only ten years of age, and was succeeded by William, his uncle and heir, who was accordingly summoned to parliament as Earl of Arundel. Notwithstanding what has been observed, that John Fitz-Alan, who succeeded in 1415, was not admitted to this earldom, it is manifest he was generally styled Earl of Arundel, for Alice, his widow, in her will, describes herself as Countess of Arundel, and speaks of her late husband as John, Earl of Arundel.

Lord Arundel d. in 1421, and was s. by his elder son,

JOHN FITZ-ALAN, thirteenth Earl of Arundel, who, in the 7th of Henry VI., was summoned to parliament as Lord Maltravers, and the next year, according to Dugdale, as Earl of Arundel. In the 11th of Henry VI. this nobleman petitioned parliament for the confirmation of his title, as annexed to the castle, honour, and seigniory of Arundel, which was adjudged to him by virtue of the tenure only, after much opposition from John Mowbray, Duke of Norfolk, who was heir to Elizabeth, one of the sisters and co-heirs of Thomas, eleventh earl. His lordship was in the wars of France, under the celebrated general, John Talbot, first Earl of Shrewsbury, and for his achievements was created, by Henry VI., DUKE OF TOURAINE, in France, and invested with the Garter. But eventually having his leg shattered by a cannon ball, in an engagement with the enemy, he was taken prisoner, and conveyed to Beauvois, where he departed this life in 1434. The earl m. Maud, daughter of Robert Lovel, by Elizabeth, daughter of Sir Guy Bryen, the younger, Knt., and had issue,

HUMPHREY, his successor.

Amicia, m. to James Butler, Earl of Ormonde and Wiltshire, and died, temp. Edward IV., s. p.

His lordship was s. by his son,

HUMPHREY FITZ-ALAN, as Duke of Touraine, and fourteenth Earl of Arundel, then but six years old. This nobleman d. in three years afterwards, (1437,) when the dukedom of Touraine EXPIRED, but the castle of Arundel reverted to his uncle,

WILLIAM FITZ-ALAN, who thus became fifteenth Earl of Arundel. Between this nobleman and Thomas Courtenay, Earl of Devon, there arose, in the 23rd Henry VI., a great dispute in parliament regarding precedency, which being renewed in the parliament held four years afterwards, was then referred to the judges, who refused, however, to give any opinion upon the subject, declaring, "that it was a matter of parliament, belonging to the king's highness, and to his lords spiritual and temporal in parliament, by them to be decided." The question at issue was, whether this earl should have precedency of the Earl of Devon, or not? The Act of 11th Henry VI., expressing only that John, then Earl of Arundel, should have the place, precedency, &c., as Earl of Arundel, without mentioning his heirs. Upon which the lords ultimately resolved, "that he should have his place in parliament, and the king's council, as earl, by reason of the castle, lordship, and honour of Arundel, for himself, and his heirs for evermore, above the said Earl of Devon, and his heirs, as worshipfully as any of his ancestors Earls of Arundel before that time ever had." The Earl of Arundel, in the 10th Edward IV., was made constable of Dover Castle, and warden of the Cinque Ports, being then also justice of all the king's forests south of Trent. a post renewed to him upon the accession of Henry V. He was also a Knight of the Garter. His lordship m. the Lady Joane Nevil, daughter of Richard, Earl of Salisbury, by whom he had issue, THOMAS, Lord Maltravers, his successor, William, George, and John, with a daughter Mary. He d. in 1487, and was s. by his eldest son,

THOMAS FITZ-ALAN, sixteenth Earl of Arundel, who had been summoned to parliament, in 22nd Edward IV., and 1st Henry, as "Thomas Arundel, of Maltravers, Knight," his father being then alive. His lordship, who was a Knight of the Garter, was one of the English nobles sent over to Flanders, 5th Henry VII., to assist the Emperor Maximilian against the French. He m. Margaret, daughter of Richard Widvile, Earl Rivers, and had issue,

WILLIAM, Lord Maltravers, his successor.

Edward.

Margaret, m. to John de la Pole, Earl of Lincoln.

Joane, m. to George Nevill, Lord Bergavenny. The earl d. in 1524, and was s. by his elder son,

WILLIAM FITZ-ALAN, seventeenth Earl of Arundel, K.G. This nobleman's signature appears to the letter of remonstrance transmitted to Pope Clement II., in the 22nd Henry VIII., regarding the king's divorce from Queen Katherine. His lordship m. first, Anne, sister of Henry, Earl of Northumberland, upon which occasion he had grants from the crown of three manors, in the county of Somerset, and that of Hunton, in Southamptonshire, to hold by the service of a red rose yearly. By this lady he had issue, HENRY, Lord Maltravers, his successor, and two daughters, who both died unmarried. He espoused secondly, Elizabeth, daughter of Robert Willoughby, Lord Broke, by whom he had two daughters, Margaret and Elizabeth, who likewise died unmarried. In conformity with the policy recommended by Cromwell to the king upon the confiscation of the church lands, the Earl of Arundel was obliged to exchange several of his manors, for those which had belonged to the religious houses. His lordship d. in 1543, and was s. by his son,

HENRY FITZ-ALAN, eighteenth Earl of Arundel, K.G. This nobleman, in the 36th Henry VIII., was field marshal of the king's army at the siege of Boulogne, and in two years afterwards was constituted one of the assistants to that monarch's executors. After the fall of the Protector Somerset, temp. Edward VI., the Earl of Arundel having declined to enter into the views of Dudley, Earl of Warwick, was removed from the council by the intrigues of that nobleman, and fined £12,000. upon the frivolous charge of having removed bolts and locks from Westminster, and given away the king's stuff, in his capacity of lord chamberlain: and the ensuing year he was committed prisoner to the Tower. Upon the death of King Edward, his lordship zealously espoused the cause of Queen Mary, and was mainly instrumental in her ascending the throne without any effusion of blood; for which and other eminent services, he was made constable of the day at her majesty's coronation, as he was also the day immediately preceding the coronation of Queen Elizabeth, at which he officiated as LORD HIGH STEWARD. His lordship at this period aspired to the hand of the Virgin Queen, but being disappointed in his hopes, he obtained permission to travel; and while abroad served in the wars against the Turks. After his return to England he was upon the commission instituted to inquire into the murder of Henry, Lord Darnley, husband of Mary, Queen of Scots, and subsequently favouring the pretensions of the Duke of Norfolk, to the hand of that beautiful, but unfortunate princess, he suffered imprisonment (14th Elizabeth). His lordship m. first, Lady Catherine Grey, daughter of Thomas, Marquess of Dorset, by whom he had,

  HENRY, Lord Maltravers, who d. in the lifetime of his father, s. p.

  Joanna, m. to John, Lord Lumley, by whom she had no surviving issue.

  Mary, m. to Thomas Howard, Duke of Norfolk, and had issue,

    Philip Howard, who having inherited Arundel Castle, was summoned to parliament 16th January, 1580, as EARL OF ARUNDEL, and the castle and dignity have since remained in the FAMILY OF HOWARD.

The earl espoused secondly, Mary, daughter of Sir John Arundel, of Lanherne, in the county of Cornwal, but had no issue. His lordship, who, with the other high offices already enumerated, was president of the council to Queens Mary and Elizabeth, d. in 1579, when the EARLDOM OF ARUNDEL, and castle, passed with his daughter and eventually sole heiress, Lady Mary Fitz-Alan, to her husband, Thomas Howard, Duke of Norfolk, with the BARONY OF MALTRAVERS, which descended to her son, Philip Howard, who was attainted in the 32nd Elizabeth, when the barony became FORFEITED; it was, however, restored to his son, Thomas Howard, twentieth Earl of Arundel, and by act of parliament, 3rd Charles I., the Barony of Maltravers, with the Baronies of Fitz-Alan, Clun, and Oswaldestre, was annexed to the title, dignity, and honour of Earl of Arundel, and settled upon Thomas Howard, then Earl of Arundel and Surrey, and his heirs male, &c. &c. Until the passing of this act FITZ-ALAN was not a parliamentary barony, it was merely feudal. Thus terminated the noble and ancient family of *Fitz-Alan*, EARLS OF ARUNDEL.

ARMS.—Ar. a lion rampant within a bordure, or.

FITZ-CHARLES — EARL OF PLYMOUTH.

  Alice 4

By Letters Patent, dated 29th July, 1675, 27 Charles II.

Lineage.

CHARLES FITZ-CHARLES, illegitimate son of King Charles II. by Catherine, daughter of Thomas Pegg, Esq., of Yeldersley, in the county of Derby, was elevated to the peerage on 29th July, 1675, as *Baron Dartmouth, Viscount Totness,* and EARL OF PLYMOUTH. His lordship m. Lady Bridget Osborne, daughter of Thomas, first Duke of Leeds, but died without issue, at Tangier, during the siege of that city by the Moors, in 1680, when all his HONOURS became EXTINCT.

ARMS.—England, with a batune sinister, varry ar. and az.

FITZ-HERBERT — BARON FITZ-HERBERT, OR FITZ-REGINALD.

By Writ of Summons, dated 8th June, 1294, 22 Edward I.

Lineage.

In the fifth year of King Stephen,

HERBERT FITZ-HERBERT, then lord chamberlain to that monarch, gave £333, in silver, for livery of his father's lands. This Herbert m. first, ———, daughter and co-heiress of Robert Corbet, Lord of Alcester, in the county of Warwick, who had been some time concubine to King Henry I. He espoused secondly, Lucy, daughter of Milo, Earl of Hereford, and was s., at his decease, by his son by that lady,

PETER FITZ-HERBERT, who, being very obsequious to King John, was reputed one of that prince's evil counsellors. In 1214, he was constituted governor of Pykering Castle, in the county of York, and sheriff of the shire: but afterwards falling off in his allegiance, his lands at Alcester were seized by the crown, and given to William de Camvill. Returning, however, to his duty upon the accession of Henry III., those lands were restored to him. He d. in 1234, and was s. by his son,

HERBERT FITZ-PETER, who, in the 26th Henry III., had a military summons to attend the king into France. He d. soon after, however, (anno 1247,) and, leaving no issue, was s. by his brother,

REGINALD FITZ-HERBERT. This feudal lord had summons to march against the Welch in the 42d Henry III., and in two years afterwards received orders, as one of the barons marchers, to reside in those parts. In the 45th of the same reign, he was made sheriff of Hampshire, and governor of the Castle of Winchester; and in the 48th, he was one of those barons who undertook for the king's performance of what the king of France should determine regarding the ordinances of Oxford. He m. Joane, daughter of William de Fortibus, Lord of Chewton, in the county of Somerset, and dying in 1285, was s. by his son, *by Alice*

  Le Fort de Vivonne

JOHN FITZ-REGINALD, who had summons to parliament, as a BARON, on the 8th June, 1294, and from that period to 26th January, 1297. He was afterwards summoned from 29th December, 1299, to 26th August, 1307; but his descendants, who all bore the surname of FITZ-HERBERT, were never esteemed barons, nor had any of them summons to parliament as such. From PETER, a brother of this John, Lord Fitz-Reginald, the *Fitz-Herberts,* EARLS OF PEMBROKE, are said to descend.

ARMS.—Ar., a chief vairée or. and gu. Over all a bend az.

  3 lions

FITZ-HUGH—BARONS FITZ-HUGH.

By Writ of Summons, dated 15th May, 1321,
14 Edward II.

Lineage.

Although the surname of FITZ-HUGH was not
appropriated to this family before the time of Edward III., it had enjoyed consideration from the
period of the Conquest: when its ancestor,

BARDOLPH, was Lord of Ravenswath, with
divers other manors, in Richmondshire. This Bardolph assumed in his old age the habit of a monk,
in the Abbey of St. Mary, at York, to which he gave
the churches of Patrick Brompton and Ravenswath,
in pure alms. He was s. by his son and heir,

AKARIS FITZ-BARDOLPH, who, in the 5th
Stephen, founded the Abbey of Fors, in the county
of York, then called the Abbey of Charity, and
dying in 1161, was s. by his elder son,

HERVEY FITZ-AKARIS, who being a noble
and good knight, and much esteemed in his
country, gave consent, that Conan, then Earl of
Richmond and Britanny, should translate the Abbey
of Charity into the fields at East Wilton, and there
place it on the verge of the river Jore, from which
it was thenceforward called JOREVAULX. This
Hervey d. in 1182, and was s. by his son,

HENRY FITZ-HERVEY, who m. Alice, daughter of Randolph Fitz-Walter, (ancestor of the Barons
of Greystoke,) by whom he acquired considerable
estates in the north. He d. in 1201, and was s. by
his son,

RANDOLPH FITZ-HENRY. This feudal lord
m. Alice, daughter and heiress of Adam de Staveley,
Lord of Staveley, Dent, and Sadbergh, and dying
in 1263, was s. by his elder son,

HENRY FITZ-RANDOLPH, who was s. by
his son,

RANDOLPH FITZ-HENRY. This feudal baron dying without issue, was s. by his brother,

HUGH FITZ-HENRY, who d. in 1304, and was
s. by his son,

HENRY FITZ-HUGH, from whom his descendants ever afterwards adopted the surname of Fitz-Hugh. This Henry was engaged in the Scottish
wars from the 3rd to the 8th Edward II., the next
year he was constituted, owing to the minority of
the Earl of Warwick, (whose inheritance it was,)
governor of Barnard Castle, in the Bishoprick of
Durham; and being again employed in Scotland,
he was summoned to parliament as a BARON from
15th May, 1321, to 15th November, 1351. In 1327
his lordship acquitted Sir Henry Vavasor, Knt., of
a debt of five hundred marks, by special instrument
under his seal, upon condition that Henry Vavasor,
Sir Henry's son, should take to wife Annabil Fitz-Hugh, his daughter. In the 7th, 8th and 9th Edward III. Lord Fitz-Hugh was again in arms upon
the Scottish soil. His lordship m. Eve, daughter of
Sir John Bulmer, Knt., and had, beside the daughter already mentioned, a son,

> HENRY, who d. in the life-time of his father,
> leaving issue by his wife, Joane, daughter
> of Sir Richard Fourneys, and sister and
> heiress of William Fourneys,

Hugh, m. Isabel, daughter of Ralph, Lord
Nevill, and died s. p.

HENRY, who s. his grandfather.

Lord Fitz-Hugh d. in 1356, and was s. by his grandson,

HENRY FITZ-HUGH, second baron, summoned to parliament from 4th August, 1377, to 8th
August, 1385. His lordship was engaged in the
French wars of King Edward III., almost uninterruptedly from the 33rd to the 43rd of that gallant
monarch's reign. He m. Joane, daughter of Henry,
Lord Scrope, of Masham, and had issue,

> John, slain in the battle of OTTERBOURNE,
> better known as CHEVY CHASE, fought between the English, under Sir Henry Percy,
> son and heir of the Earl of Northumberland, and his brother, Sir Robert Percy,
> and the Scots, commanded by the Earl
> Douglas.
>
> HENRY, successor to his father.

His lordship d. in 1386, and was s. by his only surviving son,

HENRY FITZ-HUGH, third baron, summoned
to parliament from 17th December, 1387, to 1st September, 1423. This nobleman attained great eminence in the reigns of Henry IV. and Henry V. In
the beginning of the former we find his lordship included in a commission to negotiate a truce with
Scotland, and afterwards to accomplish a league of
amity between the two crowns (of England and
Scotland). In the 8th Henry IV. he was accredited
upon an important mission to Denmark, and in five
years afterwards he was again a commissioner upon
the affairs of Scotland. On the coronation of King
Henry V. Lord Fitz-Hugh was appointed constable
of England for that solemnity, and the next year he
obtained a grant from the crown of £100. per annum.
He was afterwards lord chamberlain of the king's
household, and assisted at the COUNCIL OF CONSTANCE. For which, and his other eminent services, he had a grant of all the lands which had
belonged to the attainted Henry, Lord Scrope, of
Masham, lying in Richmondshire, to hold during
the term that those lands should continue in the
king's hands; and upon the surrender of that grant
in the same year, he had another grant for life of
the manors of Masham, Clifton, Burton-Constable,
and ten others, likewise part of the possessions of
the aforesaid Lord Scrope. From the 5th to the 9th
Henry V. his lordship was uninterruptedly engaged
in the French wars, during which period he was at
the siege of Roan with the Duke of Exeter.

It is further reported of Lord Fitz-Hugh, that he
travelled more than once to JERUSALEM, and beyond that celebrated city, to GRAND CAIRO, where
the souldan had his residence, and that in his return
he fought with the Saracens and Turks. It is also
stated that by the help of the knights of Rhodes, he
built a castle there, called St. Peter's Castle. His
lordship m. Elizabeth, daughter and heir of Sir
Robert Grey, Knt., son of John, Lord Grey, of
Rotherfield, by Avica, sister and co-heir of Robert,
Lord Marmion, by whom he had, with other issue,

> WILLIAM, his successor.
>
> John, (Sir).
>
> Robert, in holy orders, Bishop of London.

Joane, m. to Sir Robert Willoughhy, Knt.

Eleanor, m. first, to William, Lord D'Arcy, and secondly, to Thomas Tunstal.

Maud, m. to Sir William Eure, ancestor of the Lords Eure.

Elizabeth, m. to Sir Ralph Grey, Knt.

Laura, m. to Sir Maurice Berkeley, Knt.

Henry, Lord Fitz-Hugh, K.G., d. in 1494, and was s. by his eldest son,

SIR WILLIAM FITZ-HUGH, fourth baron, summoned to parliament from 12th July, 1429, to 5th September, 1450. This nobleman attained distinction in the life-time of his father in the French wars, and after his accession to the title, he was in commission (11th Henry VI.), to treat with the commissioners of King James I., of Scotland, regarding compensation for injuries inflicted by the Scots upon the English. In two years afterwards his lordship was joined with the Earls of Northumberland and Westmoreland, and the great northern Lords, Dacre, Clifford, Greystoke, and Latimer, to repel an irruption of the Scots. Lord Fitz-Hugh m. Margery, daughter of William, Lord Willoughby de Eresby, and had issue,

    HENRY, his successor.

    Margery, m. to Sir John Milton, Knt.

    Joane, m. to John, Lord Scrope, of Bolton.

    Eleanor, m. to Thomas, Lord Dacre.

    Maud, m. to William Bowes.

    Lora, m. first, to John Musgrave, and secondly, to Thomas Constable, of Halsham.

    Lucy, a nun at Dartford.

His lordship d. in 1452, and was s. by his son,

HENRY FITZ-HUGH, fifth baron, summoned to parliament from 26th May, 1455, to 15th October, 1470. His lordship obtained, in 38th Henry VI., a grant of the stewardship of the honour of Richmond, and also of the office of chief forester of the new forest of Arkilgarth-Dale, and Le Hoppe, then escheated to the king by the forfeiture of Richard, Earl of Salisbury, to hold for life. During the reign of King Henry VI. Lord Fitz-Hugh remained firmly attached to the Lancastrian interest, but he seems nevertheless to have successfully cultivated the good opinion of King Edward IV., the champion of York, for we find his lordship, soon after the accession of that monarch, employed in his military capacity, and as a diplomatist. In 1468 he made a pilgrimage to the Holy Sepulchre, and upon his return founded a chantry for two priests in his castle at Ravenswath, there to celebrate divine service for himself and Alice during their lives, and for the health of their souls after their decease. His lordship m. the Lady Alice Nevill, daughter of Richard, Earl of Salisbury, and had, (with other issue,)

    RICHARD, his successor.

    Alice, m. to Sir John Fienes, Knt., and was mother of THOMAS, LORD DACRE.

    Elizabeth, m. first, to Sir William Parr, Knt., and had (with William, created Lord Parr, of Horton,)

        SIR THOMAS PARR, who had one son and two daughters, viz.,

            1. William Parr, Marquess of Northampton, died s. p.

2. Anne Parr, m. to William Herbert, Earl of Pembroke, and her male descendant continues to the present time to inherit that dignity, but Philip, eighth Earl of Pembroke, leaving at his decease an only daughter,

    LADY CHARLOTTE HERBERT, who m. first, John, LORD JEFFRIES, and secondly, Thomas, VISCOUNT WINDSOR, the coheirship to the Barony of Fitz-Hugh was thus severed from the Earldom of Pembroke. The representatives of her ladyship's two marriages are the present Earl Pomfret and Marquess of Bute.

2. CATHERINE PARR, m. first, to Edward Borough; secondly, to John Neville, Lord Latimer; thirdly, to KING HENRY VIII., and fourthly, to Thomas, Lord Seymour, of Sudley, but died s. p.

Elizabeth Fitz Hugh, m. secondly, Nicholas, Lord Vaux.

Anne, m. to Francis Lovell, but had no issue.

Margaret, m. to Robert Constable, died s. p.

Joane, a nun at Dartford.

Henry, fifth Baron Fitz-Hugh, d. in 1472, and was s. by his only son,

RICHARD FITZ-HUGH, sixth baron, summoned to parliament from 15th November, 1482, to 1st September, 1487. This nobleman was constituted, in the 1st Henry VII., governor of the castles of Richmond and Middleham, and of Barnard Castle. His lordship m. Elizabeth, daughter of Sir Thomas Borough, Knt., and was s. at his decease, about the year 1508, by his only child,

GEORGE FITZ-HUGH, seventh baron, summoned to parliament from 17th October, 1509, to 28th November, 1511, but dying without issue in 1512, his aunt Alice, Lady Fienes, and his cousin, Sir Thomas Parr, Knt., (refer to issue of Henry, fifth baron,) were found to be his next heirs, and between those the BARONY OF FITZ-HUGH fell into ABEYANCE, as it still continues amongst their representatives. Which representatives are at present, we believe,

    Thomas Brand, Lord Dacre, descended from Alice, Lady Fienes, whose husband was son of Richard, Lord Dacre, and father, by her ladyship, of Thomas, Lord Dacre. His lordship, if we are correct, is co-heir therefore to a moiety of the barony of Fitz-Hugh.

    Thomas-William, Earl of Pomfret, the great grandson of Lady Charlotte Herbert, (see issue of Henry, fifth Lord Fitz-Hugh,) by her first husband, John, Lord Jefferies.

    John, Marquess of Bute, the great grandson of Lady Charlotte Herbert, by her second husband, Thomas, Viscount Windsor.

                Co-heirs to the other moiety of the barony of Fitz-Hugh.

ARMS.—Az. three chevronels in base or. and a chief of the second.

FITZ-JAMES—DUKE OF BERWICK.

By Letters Patent, dated 19th March, 1687.

Lineage.

JAMES FITZ-JAMES, illegitimate son of King James II., by Arabella Churchill, sister of the celebrated John Churchill, Duke of Marlborough, was b. in 1671, and elevated to the peerage, on the 19th March, 1687, in the dignities of *Baron Boeworth, in the county of Leicester, Earl of Tinmouth, in the county of Northumberland*, and DUKE OF BERWICK UPON TWEED. His grace withdrew into France with his father, and entering into the French service, became one of the most distinguished commanders of the martial reign of Louis XIV. In 1690, he was at the siege of Londonderry, and the battle of the Boyne, and returning soon after the last engagement to France, he acquired high reputation at the sieges of Mons, Charleroi, and Ath, and at the battles of Leuse, Steinkirk, and Nerwinde. In the latter he was taken prisoner, and detained until exchanged for the Duke of Ormonde. In 1693, the French King made him lieutenant-general of his armies, and in ten years afterwards he commanded the expedition sent to aid the King of Spain. By which latter monarch he was created in 1704, a Spanish grandee of the first class. After a most successful campaign, the Duke returning into France, was nominated (anno 1715,) to the command of the troops destined to act against the fanatics in Languedoc, and upon the favourable issue of that campaign, he was presented by his royal master with a marshal's baton. Subsequently sent a second time into Spain, he achieved over the combined forces of England and Portugal, the glorious, though bloody victory of Almanza, for which eminent service Philip V., granted to the gallant marshal, with the dignity of Duke, the towns of Liria, and Xerica, in Valentia. Upon his return, the duke was placed at the head of the army on the Rhine, destined to oppose Prince Eugene, of Savoy, in which service, after a long series of brilliant achievements, he fell at the siege of Philipsburg, anno 1734. His grace espoused first in 1695, Honora de Burgh, widow of Patrick Sarsfield, Earl of Lucan, and daughter of the Earl of Clanricarde, by whom (who d. in 1698), he had issue,

JAMES-FRANCIS, an officer of eminence, chief of the branch, known in Spain as that of Liria; he m. Katherine, daughter of Pierre, Duke of Veragues; and had several children.

The Duke of Berwick, m. secondly, in 1700, Anne, daughter of Henry Bulkeley Esq., by Sophia Stuart, maid of honour to the queen, and had issue,

JAMES, b. in 1709, m. Victoire Felicité, daughter of John de Durfort, Duke of Duras, but died issueless in the life-time of his father, anno 1721.

Francis, who having entered into holy orders, never assumed the French title.

Henry, who likewise entered into holy orders, and for the same reason never assumed the French honours.

CHARLES, b. in 1714, heir eventually to the
204

French Dukedom of Fitz-James, and the estates in that kingdom. He m. in 1741, Victoria, daughter of the Marquess de Matignon, and had several children. His grace was s. by his eldest son,

JOHN-CHARLES, third Duke FitzJames, b. in 1743, m. ——, daughter of Charles, Count de Thiard.

Edward.

Henrietta, m. to the Marquess de Reuel.

Laura, m. to the Marquess de Bouzels.

Emelia, m. to the Marquess d'Escars.

Sophia, a nun.

Marshal Berwick was attainted in 1695, when the DUKEDOM OF BERWICK, and the minor English honours became EXTINCT. His grace was besides Duke of Liria and Xerica, in Valentia, a dignity which he transferred in his life-time to his eldest son, JAMES, who then became Duke of Liria, and having married, as already stated, Katherine, daughter of Pierre, Duke of Veragues, was succeeded in 1738, by his eldest son, JAMES, born in 1718, surnamed STUART, who was himself succeeded by his brother, PETER, b. in 1730, created MARQUESS OF ST. LEONARD, in 1764.

His grace of Berwick was created DUKE FITZ-JAMES in France, with remainder to the issue of his second marriage, and that dignity is enjoyed by his descendant, the present DUKE FITZ-JAMES.

ARMS.—Quarterly of four. First, England and France; second, Scotland; third, Ireland; fourth, as the first, within a border compone, gu. and az. the gu. charged with lions of Eng. the az. with fleur-de-lis of France.

FITZ-JOHN — BARONS FITZ-JOHN.

By Writ of Summons, dated 14th December, 1264,
49 Henry III.
By Writ of Summons, dated 23d June, 1295,
23 Edward I.

Lineage.

JOHN FITZ-GEOFFREY, son of Geoffrey Fitz-Piers, Earl of Essex, by Aveline, his second wife, being next male heir of that family on the death of William Fitz-Piers, Earl of Essex, in 1227, paid a fine to the king of three hundred marks for those lands which were his father's, and did by hereditary right belong to him, whereof this last Earl William died seised. In the 18th of Henry III., this John was constituted sheriff of Yorkshire; and in the 21st of the same reign, upon the treaty then made between the king and the barons, whereby, in consideration of the great charter and charters of the forest being confirmed, a thirtieth part of all men's moveables was given to the king, this feudal lord was admitted one of the privy council; and the same year, there being a grand council held at London, he was one of those at the time sent to the pope's legate, to prohibit his attempting any thing therein prejudicial to the interests of the king and kingdom. In eight years afterwards, John Fitz-Geoffrey was one of the commissioners sent from King Henry (with Roger Bigod, Earl of Norfolk, and others) to the council at Lyons, in order to complain of the great exactions made upon the realm by the holy see; and the next year he was constituted justice of Ireland, where, for his services, he received a grant from the crown of the Isles of Thomond. He m. Isabel, sister of John Bigod, and widow of Gilbert de Laci, and was s. by his son,

JOHN FITZ-JOHN, who had a military summons to march against the Welch in the 42d Hen. III. To this feudal lord succeeded his son,

JOHN FITZ-JOHN, who m. Margery, daughter of Philip Basset, justice of England. Joining Montford, Earl of Leicester, and the other turbulent barons, this John Fitz-John had a chief command at the battle of Lewes; after which, marching towards Wales, he reduced RICARD'S CASTLE (the chief seat of Hugh de Mortimer), and the CASTLE OF LUDLOW. He was subsequently constituted, by a grant from the barons, sheriff of Westmoreland, and keeper of the castles in those parts; as likewise governor of Windsor Castle; but sharing the fate of his party at the battle of Evesham, he became a prisoner in the hands of the royalists, when the inheritance of his lands appears to have been given, by the king, to Clare, Earl of Gloucester; but he had permission afterwards to compound for them under the "dictum of Kenilworth." He was summoned to parliament, as a BARON, on the 14th December, 1264, but died without issue the next year, when that dignity expired. His lordship was succeeded in his estates by his brother,

RICHARD FITZ-JOHN, who, upon doing homage, and paying his relief, had livery of all his lands in the counties of Norfolk, Bucks, Devon, Surrey, Wilts, Southampton, Essex, and Northampton. In the 10th Edward I., this feudal lord was in the Welch wars, and he was summoned to parliament, as a BARON, 23d June, 1295, but died the following year in the wars of France, without issue, when the BARONY OF FITZ-JOHN became EXTINCT, while his lands devolved upon his heirs, viz.,

> MAUD, *Countess of Warwick*, his eldest sister.
>
> ROBERT CLIFFORD, son of Isabel } Isabell de de Clifford, daughter of . . } Vipount,
> IDONEA DE LEYBURNE, another } his second daughter of . . . . } sister.
>
> RICHARD DE BUROH, *Earl of Ulster*, son of Aveline, his third sister.
>
> JOANE, wife of Theobald le Buteler, his fourth sister.

FITZ-PATRICK—BARON OF UPPER OSSORY, OF AMPHILL, IN THE COUNTY OF BEDFORD.

By Letters Patent, dated 12th August, 1794.

Lineage.

JOHN FITZ-PATRICK, Esq., of Castletown, (descended from the ancient monarchs of Ireland,) m. Elizabeth, fourth daughter of Thomas, Viscount Thurles, sister of James, first Duke of

Ormonde, and widow of James Purcell, Baron of Loughmoe, by whom he had issue,

> Edward.
> Richard.
> Arabella, m. to Sir Thomas Wiseman, Bart., of East Grinsted, in Sussex.

Mr. Fitz-Patrick, who suffered during the usurpation of Cromwell for his fidelity to the House of Stewart, was involved on King James's general Act of Attainder in 1689, and died in 1693. His elder son,

EDWARD FITZ-PATRICK, Esq., had the command at the revolution of a regiment given him, 31st December, 1688; was made colonel of the Royal Fusiliers, 1st August, 1692, and promoted to the rank of brigadier-general in 1694. General Fitz-Patrick was drowned in his passage from England to Ireland, 10th November, 1696, and died unmarried. His brother,

RICHARD FITZ-PATRICK, Esq., being bred to the sea-service, had the command of a ship of war, in which station he signalized himself by his valour and conduct; and to him and his brother, in consideration of their faithful services, King William granted, in 1696, the estate of Edmond Morris, (one of the adherents of King James, killed at the battle of Aghrim,) situated in the Queen's County. Mr. Fitz-Patrick was elevated to the peerage of Ireland on 27th April, 1715, as *Baron Gowran, of Gowran*, and took his seat in parliament the November following. His lordship m. Anne, younger daughter and co-heir of Sir John Robinson, Bart., of Farming-Wood, in the county of Northampton, and had two sons, JOHN and Richard. He d. 9th June, 1727, and was s. by his elder son,

JOHN FITZ-PATRICK, second baron, who was advanced to the *earldom of Upper-Ossory*, in the peerage of Ireland, 5th October, 1751. His lordship m. in 1744, Lady Evelyn Leveson Gower, eldest daughter of John, Earl Gower, and had issue,

> JOHN, *Lord Gowran*.
>
> Richard, b. 24th January, 1748, a general officer in the army, a privy counsellor, and M.P. for the county of Bedford. In 1783 General Fitz-Patrick was appointed secretary at war, which office he resigned in the course of the year. Under the whig administration of 1806 he again filled the same department, and for hardly a longer period. He d. ————.
>
> Mary, m. to Stephen Fox, second Lord Holland, by whom she was mother of
>> Henry-Richard, present LORD HOLLAND.
>
> Louisa, m. to William, second Earl of Shelburne, and first Marquess of Lansdowne, (his lordship's second wife,) and was mother of
>> Henry, present MARQUESS OF LANSDOWNE.

The earl d. 23rd September, 1758, and was s. by his elder son,

JOHN FITZ-PATRICK, second earl, who was created a peer of Great Britain on the 12th August, 1794, as BARON OF UPPER-OSSORY, of Amphill, in the county of Bedford. His lordship *m.* in 1769, Anne, daughter of Henry Liddell, Lord Ravensworth, by whom (who had been divorced from the Duke of Grafton,) he had two daughters, Lady Anne and Lady Gertrude. The earl died in 1818, when, with his Irish honours, the British barony of UPPER-OSSORY became EXTINCT.

ARMS.—Sa., a saltire, arg., and chief, azure, the latter charged with three fleur de lis.

FITZ-PAYNE — BARONS FITZ-PAYNE.

By Writ of Summons, dated 6th February, 1299, 27 Edward I.

Lineage.

The first that assumed this surname was ROBERT, son of Pain Fits-John, whose nephew, taking the name of VESCI, was founder of that eminent family. This

ROBERT FITZ-PAIN served the office of sheriff for the counties of Dorset and Somerset, from the 31st to the 34th Henry II. inclusive; and in the 13th of John, upon the collection of the scutage of Wales, he paid thirty marks for fifteen knights' fees. He was *s.* by

ROGER FITZ-PAIN, who *m.* Margery, eldest of the three sisters and co-heirs of Alured de Lincolne,[*] and thereby acquired considerable property in the counties of Somerset, Dorset, Wilts, and Devon, whereof Ockford Fitz-pain, in Dorsetshire, constituted a part. He *d.* about the year 1237, and was *s.* by his son,

ROBERT FITZ-PAIN, who, during his homage in the 30th Henry III., had livery of his lands in the counties of Wilts, Somerset and Dorset, and Netherwent, in Wales. In the 41st of the same reign, he had two military summonses to march against the Welch; but after this he appears to have joined the barons, and to have taken a prominent part in the battle of Lewes, where the baronial banner waved in triumph. He *d.* in the 9th Edward I. (1280), and was *s.* by his son,

ROBERT FITZ-PAYNE. This feudal lord was in the expedition made against the Welch, in the 10th Edward I., and the same year, during his homage, had livery of the lands of his inheritance. He was summoned to parliament as a BARON on the 6th February, 1299, and from that time, to the 23d October, 1314. In 1303 he was in the Scottish wars,

---

[*] ALURED DE LINCOLNE. The Lincolnes were great feudal barons, from the period of the conquest, until the death of Alured Lincolne, in the 48th Henry III., when their great possessions devolved upon the deceased baron's sisters, as co-heirs, viz.

Margery, *m.* to Roger Fits-pain.

Beatrix, *m.* to Sir William de Gouis, and her portion of the property passed eventually, by an heiress, to the family of Latimer, Lords Latimer, of Corby.

Albreda, *d.* without issue.

and again in 1306, in the immediate train of Prince Edward, having been created a knight of the bath in the same year. In the 1st Edward II. his lordship was constituted governor of the castle of Winchester, and the next year, being then steward of the king's household, he was deputed, with Otto de Grandison, upon an important mission to the Sovereign Pontiff. In the eighth of the same reign he had a military summons to march against the Scots, but died the ensuing year, 1315, seised of manors in the counties of Devon, Wilts, Dorset, Gloucester, and Somerset; and, jointly with his wife Isabel, of the manor of Stourton, in Wiltshire. His lordship was *s.* by his son,

ROBERT FITZ-PAYNE, second baron, summoned to parliament, from 7th August, 1327, to 15th November, 1351. This nobleman was in the wars of Scotland in the 10th and 12th Edward II., and in the 16th Edward III. (residing then at his seat of Mershwode, in the county of Dorset) he had command to provide ten men at arms, and ten archers, for the king's service in France, and in three years afterwards, being then a BANNERET, he had a military summons to attend the king into that realm. His lordship *m.* Ela, daughter and co-heir of Guy de Bryan, and dying in 1354, left an only daughter and heir,

ISABEL FITZ-PAYNE, then thirty-six years of age, and the wife of John Chideocke; by whom she had a son and heir,

 SIR JOHN CHIDEOCKE, Knt., whose son and heir,

  SIR JOHN CHIDEOCKE, Knt., left two daughters, his co-heirs, viz.

   1. KATHERINE CHIDEOCKE, *m.* first, to Sir William Stafford, and had an only child, HUMPHREY STAFFORD, EARL OF DEVON, who died *s. p.*

   She espoused, secondly, Sir John Arundel, Knt., and from this union descend the LORDS ARUNDEL, of WARDOUR.

   2. Margaret Chideocke, *m.* to William, second Lord Stourton, and from this marriage the Lords Stourton descend.

The BARONY OF FITZ-PAYNE, upon the decease of ROBERT, the second baron, appears to have been suspended, and it is now in ABEYANCE between the representatives of Sir John Chideocke's co-heirs, namely, the above-mentioned Katherine and Margaret Chideocke; which representatives are,

JAMES EVERARD, LORD ARUNDEL, OF WARDOUR, elder son of Mary Christiana, elder daughter and co-heir of Henry, eighth Lord Arundel, of Wardour.

ELEANOR MARY, wife of Charles, late Lord Clifford, of Chudleigh, younger daughter of Henry, eighth Lord Arundel, of Wardour.

 Co-heirs to a moiety of the Barony of Fitz-payne.

WILLIAM, LORD STOURTON, heir to a moiety of the BARONY OF FITZ-PAYNE.

ARMS.—Gu. three lions passant guardant in pale, over all a bend, az.

Certain manors in the county of Dorset, part of the property of Robert, last Lord Fitz-payne, and Ela, his wife, being so entailed, devolved, at the decease of the said Ela, (then his lordship's widow,) upon her presumed brother-in-law,
The Honourable
ROBERT GREY, of Charlton Grey, in the county of Somerset, younger son of Richard, Lord Grey, of Codnor, who thereupon assumed the surname of FITZ-PAYNE, and Dugdale says, was summoned to parliament as BARON FITZ-PAYNE; but the name of such a baron does not appear upon the roll. He m. Elizabeth, daughter and co-heir of Guy de Bryan, (sister of Ela, Lady Fitz-payne,) and left an only daughter and heiress,

    ISABEL FITZ-PAYNE, who m. Richard, Lord Poynings, and was mother of

      ROBERT, *Lord Poynings*, whose granddaughter and heiress,

        ALIANORE POYNINGS, m. Sir Henry Percy, son and heir of the Earl of Northumberland,* and conveyed her great inheritance to the noble HOUSE of PERCY.

FITZ-PIERS—EARL OF ESSEX.

See Mandeville, Earl of Essex.

FITZ-ROY — DUKES OF CLEVELAND, DUKES OF SOUTHAMPTON.

| Dukedom of Cleveland, | by Letters | 3rd Aug., 1670. |
| Dukedom of Southampton, | Patent, | 10th Sep., 1674. |

Lineage.

BARBARA VILLIERS, daughter and heiress of William Villiers, Viscount Grandison, in Ireland, grand-niece of George, Duke of Buckingham, the celebrated favourite of King James I., and wife of Roger Palmer, Earl of Castlemaine, in Ireland, becoming the mistress of King Charles II., was elevated to the peerage by letters patent, dated 3rd August, 1670, as *Baroness Nonsuch, in the county of Surrey, Countess of Southampton,* and DUCHESS of CLEVELAND, with remainder to Charles and George Fitzroy, two of her sons by the king. Her grace had issue by his majesty,

CHARLES, of whom presently.
Henry, created Duke of Grafton, from whom the present Dukes of Grafton descend.
George, created Duke of Northumberland, died s. p., in 1716, when that dignity expired.

----

* Through this alliance the Percys claimed the ancient BARONY of FITZ-PAYNE, but they had no pretensions whatever to it.

Charlotte, m. to Edward Lee, Earl of Litchfield.
The Duchess married, secondly, Robert Fielding, Esq.; she d. 9th October, 1709, and was succeeded by her eldest son,
CHARLES FITZROY, b. in June, 1662, who had been elevated to the peerage himself, by letters patent, dated 10th September, 1674, as *Baron Newbury, in the county of Berks, Earl of Chichester, in the county of Sussex,* and DUKE OF SOUTHAMPTON, with remainder, in default of male issue, to his brother George. He was installed a KNIGHT of the GARTER, the year preceding. His grace m. first, Mary, daughter and sole heiress of Sir Henry Wood, one of the Clerks of the Green Cloth, temp. Charles II., by whom he had no issue. This lady died in 1680; but in Michaelmas term, 1685, the duke had a decree in Chancery for £30,000, against her uncle, Doctor Thomas Wood, Bishop of Litchfield and Coventry, as a portion of her fortune. His grace espoused, secondly, Anne, daughter of Sir William Pulteney, of Misterton, in the county of Leicester, Knt., by whom he had,

WILLIAM, his successor.
Charles, b. in 1699, d. in 1723.
Henry, b. in 1701, d. in 1708.
Barbara.
Grace, m. to Henry Vane, third Baron Barnard, of Barnard Castle, (who was created Viscount Barnard, and Earl of Darlington, and was mother of,

    HENRY, second Earl of Darlington, whose son and successor,

      WILLIAM HENRY, third Earl of Darlington, was created MARQUESS OF CLEVELAND, in 1827, and is the PRESENT MARQUESS.

Anne, m. to Francis Paddy, Esq.
The duke died 9th September, 1730, and was s. by his eldest son,
WILLIAM FITZROY, second Duke of Cleveland and Southampton. His grace m. Lady Henrietta Finch, daughter of Daniel, Earl of Winchelsea, but died without issue, in 1774, when all his HONOURS became EXTINCT.

ARMS. — Quarterly — first and fourth, grand quarters, *France and England;* second, *Scotland,* and third, Ireland, (being the arms of King Charles II.,) over all a Baton Sinister, Counter-Componé, Erm: and az.

FITZ-ROY — DUKE OF RICHMOND AND SOMERSET.

By Letters Patent, dated 18th June, 1525,
17 Henry VIII.

Lineage.

HENRY FITZROY, natural son of King Henry VIII., by Elizabeth, daughter of Sir John Blount, Knt., and widow of Gilbert, Lord Talboys; was first made a KNIGHT of the GARTER, and then created by letters patent, dated 18th June, 1525, *Earl of Nottingham,* and DUKE OF RICHMOND AND SOMERSET; the ceremony being performed at the royal palace, called Bridewell, in the city of London, at which time he was little more than six years of age. Upon the same day he was appointed lieutenant-general of all the king's forces north of Trent, and warden of the Marches of Scotland. In five years afterwards, his grace was constituted lieutenant of Ireland, and Sir William Skeffington appointed his deputy there. The Duke was educated with Henry, Earl of Surrey, at Windsor Castle, and went with that nobleman to Paris, in 1532, where he formed an attachment to the earl's sister, Lady Mary Howard, and married her, but the marriage was never consummated. His grace was a youth of great promise, and much beloved by his royal father. He died, aged about seventeen, in 1536, when all his honours became EXTINCT.

FITZ-WALTER — BARONS FITZ-WALTER.

By Writ of Summons, dated 23rd June, 1295, 23 Edward I.

Lineage.

ROBERT, fifth son of Richard de Tonbridge, Earl of Clare, being steward to King Henry I., obtained from that monarch the Barony of Dunmow, in Essex, as also the Honour of Baynard's Castle, in the city of London, both which came into the possession of the crown, by the forfeiture of William Baynard. This Robert m. Maud de St. Liz, Lady of Bradham, daughter of Simon de St. Liz, first Earl of Huntingdon, and had two sons,

WALTER, his successor.
Simon, to whom he gave Daventre, in Northamptonshire.

He d. in 1134, and was s. by his elder son,

WALTER FITZ-ROBERT, who in the 12th of Henry II., upon the assessment in aid of marrying the king's daughter, certified his knight's fees to be in number, sixty-three and a half, de Veteri Feoffamento; and three and a fourth part, de Novo, for all of which he paid £44. 10s. In the great controversy between John, Earl of Moreton, (brother of King Richard,) and William de Longcamp, Bishop of Ely, whom the king left governor of the realm during his absence in the Holy Land; this Walter adhered to the bishop, and had at that time the custody of the Castle of Eye, in Suffolk. He m. first, Maud de Lucy, with whom he had the Lordship of Dis, in Norfolk; and secondly, Margaret de Bohun. He d. in 1198, and was s. by his son,

ROBERT FITZ-WALTER. This feudal lord, upon the assessment of the scutage of Scotland, in the 13th of John, had the king's especial writ of acquittal for sixty-three knights' fees and a half, which were of his own proper inheritance; and for thirty knights' fees, and a third part which he had acquired by marriage. But the next year he was forced to fly with his family into France, in order to avoid being arrested, upon the first disposition of the barons to revolt; and was soon afterwards charged with treason and rebellion, when his house, called Baynard's Castle, in the city of London, was demolished by order of the king.

" The primary occasion of these discontents," (says Dugdale,) " is by some thus reported: viz.—that this Robert Fitz-Walter having a very beautiful daughter, called Maude, residing at Dunmow, the king frequently solicited her chastity, but never prevailing, grew so enraged, that he caused her to be privately poisoned, and that she was buried at the south side of the quire at Dunmow, between two pillars there."

Fitz-Walter, however, is said, subsequently, to have made his peace with King John, by the great prowess and valour he displayed at a tournament, held in Normandy before the kings of France and England; where, running a tilt with his great lance, he overthrew his rival at the first course; which act of gallantry caused the English monarch to exclaim, " By God's Tooth, he deserves to be a king who hath such a soldier of his train;" and afterwards, ascertaining the name of the victorious knight, he immediately sent for him, and having restored his barony, gave him liberty to repair his castle of Baynard. In the 17th of King John, Fitz-Walter had so far regained the confidence of the crown, that he was appointed governor of the castle at Hertford; but soon after, arraying himself under the baronial banner, his lands were all seized, and those in Cornwall committed to Prince Henry, the king's son: a course of proceeding that had the immediate effect of riveting the haughty baron to the cause which he had espoused, while his high rank, tried courage and acknowledged abilities, soon gave him a lead amongst his compeers. We find him, therefore, amongst the first commissioners nominated to treat with the king; when it was agreed, that the city of London should be delivered up to the barons, and twenty-five of those powerful feudal chiefs chosen to govern the realm. The insurrectionary lords subsequently assembled at St. Edmundsbury, and there pledged themselves, by solemn oath at the high altar, that if the king refused to confirm the laws and liberties granted by Edward the Confessor, they would withdraw their allegiance from him and seize upon his fortresses. After which, forming themselves into a regular army, they appointed this Robert Fitz-Walter their GENERAL, with the title of MARSHAL OF THE ARMY OF GOD AND THE CHURCH, and under his command, they eventually extorted the GREAT CHARTERS OF FREEDOM from John on the plains of RUNNYMEDE, when Fitz-Walter was elected one of the celebrated TWENTY-FIVE, appointed to see the faithful observance of those laws. He continued, during the remainder of John's reign, equally firm to his purpose; and after the accession of Henry III., until the battle of LINCOLN, where the baronial army sustained a signal defeat under his command, and he became a prisoner himself, after displaying a more than ordinary degree of valour. He does not appear, however, to have remained long under restraint, for we find him, the very next year, in the Holy Land, and assisting at the great siege of Damietta. This eminent feudal baron m. first, Gunnora, daughter and heiress of Robert de Valonies, and had issue,

WALTER, his successor.
Matilda.

- Christian, *m.* to William Mandevil, Earl of Essex.

He espoused, secondly, Roese ———, and dying in 1234, was *s.* by his son,

WALTER FITZ-WALTER, who, in the 24th Henry III., paid into the exchequer a fine of three hundred marks for livery of his lands, and in the 42d of the same king had a military summons to march against the Welsh, in which year (1257) he died, and was succeeded by his son,

SIR ROBERT FITZ-WALTER, who had a licence, in 1275, to pass away the inheritance of Baynard's Castle to Robert Kilwardby, then Archbishop of Canterbury, which prelate translated thereto the Dominican or Black Friars, from Holborn, near Lincoln's-inn. In alienating this part of his property, Sir Robert took especial care, however, to preserve the immunities of his barony, which, as appertaining to Baynard's Castle, are thus specified: "That the said Robert, as constable of the Castle of London, (so Baynard's Castle was designated,) and his heirs, ought to be banner-bearers of that city, by inheritance, as belonging to that castle; and in time of war, to serve the city in the manner following, viz. to ride upon a light horse, with twenty men-at-arms on horseback, their horses covered with cloth or harness, unto the great door of St. Paul's church, with the banner of his arms carried before him; and being come in that manner thither, the mayor of London, together with the sheriffs and aldermen, to issue armed out of the church, unto the same door, on foot, with his banner in his hand, having the figure of St. Paul depicted with gold thereon, but the feet, hands and head of silver, holding a silver sword in his hand; and as soon as he shall see the mayor, sheriffs, and aldermen come on foot out of the church, carrying such a banner, he is to alight from his horse, and salute him as his companion, saying, *Sir mayor, I am obliged to come hither to do my service, which I owe to this city.* To whom the mayor, sheriffs and aldermen are to answer: *We give to you, as our banner-bearer by inheritance for this city, this banner of the city, to bear and carry to the honour and profit thereof to your power.* Whereupon the said Robert and his heirs shall receive it into their hands, and the mayor and sheriffs shall follow him to the door, and present him with a horse worth twenty pounds; which horse shall be saddled, with a saddle of his arms, and covered with silk, depicted, likewise, with the same arms; and they shall take twenty pounds sterling, and deliver it to the chamberlain of the said Robert, for his expenses that day.

"This being done, he shall mount upon that horse, with his banner in his hand, and being so mounted, shall bid the mayor to choose a marshal for the city army; who, being so chosen, shall command the mayor and burgers of the city to assemble the commons, who shall go under this banner of St. Paul, which he shall bear to Aldgate; and being come thither, they shall give it to whom they shall think fit.

"And if it shall so happen, that they must march out of the city, then shall the said Robert make choice of two of the gravest men out of every ward, to guard the city in their absence, and their consul-

tation shall be in the priory of the Holy Trinity near Aldgate; and before what town or castle this city army shall come, and shall continue the siege, for one whole year, this Robert shall receive, from the commonalty of the city, one hundred shillings for his pains and no more. Those were his rights and privileges in time of war; in time of peace they were these:—

"That the said Robert should have a *soke* (that is, a jurisdiction) in the same city; extending, from the canonry of St. Paul's, along the street before Paul's brewhouse, unto the Thames, and thence to the side of the mill, which is in the water, that comes down from Fleet-bridge, and thence up to London-wall, all about the Black-friars unto Ludgate, and so back to the house of the said friars, to the corner of the wall of the same canonry of St. Paul's; that is, all St. Andrew's parish, which was the gift of his ancestors for that royalty.

"In this soke, the said Robert should have the nomination of a *sokeman*, who should possess certain privileges in the trial and execution of criminals.

"Moreover, the said Robert was to enjoy as extensive privileges in the city as the mayor and citizens; and when the mayor held a great council, he was to be summoned thereto; and at all times that he came to the hustings in Guildhall, the mayor was to rise and to place him next to himself." So much for the immunities attached to the ancient office of standard-bearer of the city of London, originally held by the Baynards, and afterwards by the Fitz-Walters.

This Robert Fitz-Walter was in the wars of Gascony, in the 22d Edward I., in the retinue of Edmund, Earl of Lancaster, and continued there the next year; at which period he was summoned to parliament, as a BARON, and from that time to the 19th Edward II. His lordship was afterwards continually engaged in the Scottish wars. He *m.* first, Alianore, daughter of William, Earl of Ferrers, by whom he had an only son,

    ROBERT, his successor.

His lordship espoused secondly, Devorgil, one of the daughters and co-heirs of John de Burgh, and grand-daughter of Hubert de Burgh, Earl of Kent, and had an only daughter,

    Christian, *m.* to John le Marshal, and left a son,

        William Marshal, who left two children, viz.

           JOHN MARSHAL, who died *s. p.*

           Hawyse, who *m.* to Robert Morley.

The baron *d.* in 1325, and was *s.* by his son,

ROBERT FITZ-WALTER, second baron, but never summoned to parliament. This nobleman *m.* Joane, daughter and co-heir of John de Multon, of Egremond; and dying in 1328, was *s.* by his son,

JOHN FITZ-WALTER, third baron, summoned to parliament from 3d March, 1341, to 20th November, 1360. In the latter year, being then in the wars of France with the king, his lordship was one of those appointed to assist Sir Walter Manny in an attack upon the barriers of Paris, the Duke of Normandy being at the time within the city; and he was knighted for his good services therein.

Lord Fitz-Walter *m.* Eleanor, daughter of Henry, Lord Percy, and was *s.*, at his decease in 1361, by his son,

WALTER FITZ-WALTER, fourth baron, summoned to parliament from 6th April, 1369, to 3d September, 1385. This nobleman, in the 44th Edward III., was in the expedition made into Gascony, being esteemed at that time one of the most expert soldiers in the realm; but being taken prisoner, he was constrained to mortgage his castle and lordship of Egremond for the sum of a thousand pounds to accomplish his release by ransom. In three years afterwards, he was again in France under John, Duke of Lancaster; and in the 1st of Richard II., he served with Thomas of Woodstock against the Spaniards. In the 5th of the same reign, he did great service in Essex against Jack Straw, and the next year he was constituted one of the wardens of the west marches towards Scotland. In the 9th, being with John, Duke of Lancaster, in his expedition into Spain, when he went to receive possession of the kingdom of Castile, his lordship displayed great valour in storming the forts raised against the castle of Brest, in Britanny, and relieving that fortress, then closely besieged. He *m.* first, Eleanor ——, but had no issue; and secondly, Philippa, daughter and co-heir of John de Mohun, Lord of Dunster, and widow of Edward, Duke of York, and dying in 1386, was *s.* by his son,

WALTER FITZ-WALTER, fifth baron, summoned to parliament from 12th September, 1390, to 25th August, 1404. This nobleman *m.* Joane, daughter of Sir John Devereux, and sister and heiress of John, second Baron Devereux, (by which alliance the baronies of Fitz-Walter and Devereux became united,) and had issue,

   HUMPHREY, } successive barons.
   WALTER, }
   Eleanor.

His lordship *d.* in 1407, and was *s.* by his elder son,

HUMPHREY FITZ-WALTER, sixth baron, who died a minor, without issue, in 1422, and was *s.* by his brother,

WALTER FITZ-WALTER, seventh baron, summoned to parliament from 12th July, 1429, to 27th November, 1430. This nobleman became so distinguished in the French wars of King Henry V., that he obtained from that monarch, in consideration of his services, a grant to himself and his heirs male of all the lands and lordships which Sir John Cheney held within the duchy of Normandy, and which had reverted to the crown upon the decease *s. p.* of the said Sir John. At this time Lord Fitz-Walter had not attained his full age: he was, however, equally eminent in majority upon the same field. His lordship *m.* ———, and had an only daughter and heiress,

   ELIZABETH, who *m.* Sir John Ratcliffe, K.G., and conveyed the baronies of Fitz-Walter and Devereux into that family.

He *d.* in 1432, when the male line of the FITZ-WALTERS became *extinct;* but the honours of the family passed, as stated above, to the Ratcliffes. (See Ratcliffe, Barons Fitz-Walter.)

ARMS.—Or., a fesse between two chevronels gu.

210

FITZ-WARINE — BARONS FITZ-WARINE.

By Writ of Summons, dated 23rd June, 1295,
23 Edward I.

Lineage.

Amongst the first persons of note, to whom William the Conqueror committed the defence of the Marches towards Wales, was

GUARINE DE MEEZ, (a member of the house of Lorraine,) to whose custody he confided Adderbury, in the county of Salop, and Alestoun, in Gloucestershire, of which former county Guarine was sheriff, in the year 1083; and he was at the same time one of the chief councillors to Roger de Montgomerie, Earl of Shrewsbury. Of this Guarine, it is stated, that having heard that William, a valiant knight, sister's son to Pain Peverell, Lord of Whittington, in Shropshire, had two daughters, one of whom, Mallet, had resolved to marry none but a knight of great prowess; and that her father had appointed a meeting of noble young men, at Peverel's Place, on the PEKE, from which she was to select the most gallant, he came thither; when entering the lists with a son of the King of Scotland, and with a Baron of Burgundy, he vanquished them both, and won the fair prize, with the Lordship and Castle of Whittington. At this place he subsequently took up his abode, and founded the Abbey of Adderbury. He was *s.* at his decease, by his son,

SIR FULKE FITZ-WARINE, who being under the tutelage of Sir Josce de Dinant, fell in love with his daughter, Hawise, and marrying her, proceeded with her father to Ireland, and assisted him in his wars against Walter de Lacie. This Fulke was constituted by King Henry I., about the year 1122, lieutenant of the Marches of Wales, and afterwards steward of the household, and lord and governor of those Marches. Of Sir Fulke it is stated, that at one time falling out with Prince John, King Henry's son, at a game of chess, and having had his head broken by a blow of the chess-board, from the prince, he returned the assault so violently, as nearly to deprive his opponent of life. He *d.* some time before the year 1195, and was *s.* by his eldest son,

FULKE FITZ-WARINE, who had a castle at Adderbury, the ruins of which were remaining at the time Dugdale wrote. This Fulke was left by King Richard I., to defend the Marches of Wales, when that monarch set out himself for the Holy Land; and in the 7th of the same reign, he paid forty marks to the crown for livery of Whittington Castle, in conformity with the judgment then given in his favour, by the Court of King's Bench. After the accession of John, however, this castle was forcibly seized by the crown, and conferred upon another person, which act of injustice drove Fitz-warine and his brothers into rebellion, and they were in consequence outlawed; but through the mediation of the Earl of Salisbury, (the king's brother,) and the Bishop of Norwich, the outlawry was reversed, and Fitz-Warine, upon paying two hundred marks, and two coursers, had livery of the castle as his hereditary right; command being given to the sheriff of Shropshire to yield him possession thereof accordingly. About this time he paid to the crown, twelve hundred marks and two palfreys, for permission to marry Maud, daughter of Robert Vavasour, and widow of Theobald Walter. In the 12th John, he attended that prince into Ireland, and in the 17th he had livery of his wife's inheritance, lying in Amunderneuse, in Lancashire. After this we find him active in the baronial cause, and amongst those excommunicated by the Pope; nor did he make his peace until the 4th of Henry III., when he compromised by paying £262, and two great coursers, for the re-possession of Whittington Castle, which, in the baronial conflict, had again been alienated. Whereupon undertaking that it should not be prejudicial to the king, he had licence the next year, to fortify the same; and he thenceforward evinced his loyalty, by the good services he rendered against the Welch, under William Marshal, Earl of Pembroke, and by his personal attendance upon the king himself, in his army at Montgomery. He had subsequently military summonses upon several occasions, and fought at the battle of Lewes, anno 1263, under the royal banner; in which action he lost his life, by being drowned in the adjacent river. This celebrated feudal lord, m. first, as already stated, Maud, daughter of Robert Vavasour; and secondly, Clarice ——. He left at his decease, a daughter, Eve, who became second wife of Lewelline, Prince of Wales, and a son, his successor,

FULKE FITZ-WARINE, who having distinguished himself in the Welch wars, was summoned to parliament as a BARON, by King Edward I., on 23rd June, 1295, and he had summons from that period, to the 24th October, 1314. His lordship was afterwards equally eminent in the wars of Scotland and Flanders, and was made a knight of the Bath, prior to attending Prince Edward into the former kingdom, in the expedition made against Robert Bruce. Lord Fitz-Warine m. the daughter of Gryffin, son of Wenovewyn, by whom he acquired the territory of Ballesley; and dying about the year 1314, was s. by his son,

FULKE FITZ-WARINE, second Baron, summoned to parliament from 6th October, 1315, to 22nd January, 1336. This nobleman being at the time of his father's death, in the wars of France, Alianore, his wife, by the king's especial favour, had livery of the manor of Whittington until his return. During the remainder of King Edward II.'s reign, he was engaged either in Scotland or Gascony, and he was constable of the royal army which advanced against the barons in insurrection under the Earl of Lancaster. In the 7th of Edward III., he was again in Scotland; and in the 20th, he was in the expedition then made into France. His lordship d. in 1349, and was s. by his son,

FULKE FITZ-WARINE, third Baron, but never summoned to parliament. This nobleman, in the 41st Edward III., attended Edward, the Black Prince, into Gascony, and was subsequently engaged in the wars in Flanders. His lordship m. Margaret, daughter of James, Lord Audley, and third sister and co-heir of Nicholas, Lord Audley,

of Heleigh, in the county of Stafford, and dying in 1373, was s. by his son,

FULKE FITZ-WARINE, fourth Baron, but never summoned to parliament. This nobleman d. in 1377, and was s. by his son,

FULKE FITZ-WARINE, fifth Baron, but, like his two immediate predecessors, never summoned to parliament. His lordship making proof of his age, in 7th Richard II., had livery of his lands. He m. Elizabeth, sister and heir of Sir William Cogan, Knt., by Elizabeth, widow of Sir Hugh Courtenay, Knt., and was s. at his decease, in 1391, by his son,

FULKE FITZ-WARINE, sixth Baron, but never summoned to parliament. His lordship d. in minority, anno 1407, and was s. by his son,

FULKE FITZ-WARINE, seventh Baron, never summoned to parliament. This nobleman died also in minority, anno 1429, and left his only sister,

ELIZABETH FITZ-WARINE, his heir. This lady m. afterwards, Richard Hankford, Esq., and left an only daughter and heiress,

THOMASINE HANKFORD, who espoused SIR WILLIAM BOURCHIER, Knt., who was summoned to parliament, in her right, as

LORD FITZ-WARINE. (See Bourchier, Barons Fitz-Warine.)

ARMS—Quarterly arg. and gu. per fesse indented.

FITZ-WARINE — BARONS FITZ-WARINE.

By Writ of Summons, dated 25th February, 1342, 16 Edward III.

Lineage.

Besides the BARONY OF FITZ-WARINE, conferred by the writ of Edward I., upon Fulke Fitz-Warine, in 1295, and which barony was eventually conveyed by an heiress to a branch of the great house of Bourchier, another member of the same family,

WILLIAM FITZ-WARINE, called Le Frere, was elevated to the peerage, as a BARON, by writ of summons, dated 25th February, 1342. This William had been constituted governor of the castle of Montgomery, in the beginning of King Edward the Third's reign, and was afterwards engaged in the French and Scottish wars. The year he attained the peerage he was in France, being then of the rank of banneret, with one knight, eight esquires, and ten archers, on horseback, in his immediate train—and again in four years afterwards. His lordship m. Amicia, daughter and heir of Henry Haddon, of Candel Haddon, in the county of Dorset, and dying in 1361, possessed of estates in the counties of Berks, Somerset, and Dorset, was s. by his son,

IVO or JOHN FITZ-WARINE, second baron, but never summoned to parliament. This nobleman was at the siege of Nantes in the beginning of the reign of Richard II., under THOMAS OF WOODSTOCK. He d. in 1414, leaving an only daughter and heiress,

ELEANOR FITZ-WARINE, who m. Sir John Chediock, and left a son,

SIR JOHN CHEDIOCK, Knt., who *m.* Katherine, daughter of Ralph Lumley, and left, at his decease, two daughters, his co-heirs, viz.

> Margaret, *m.* to William, second Lord Stourton, ancestor of the present lord.
>
> Katherine, *m.* first, to Sir William Stafford, and secondly, to Sir John Arundel, from whom the Lords Arundel, of Wardour, descend.

ARMS.—Quarterly gu. and erm. per fesse indented. In the first quarter a fret gules.

FITZ-WILLIAM — BARON FITZ-WILLIAM.

By Writ of Summons, dated 5th April, 1324, 1 Edward III.

Lineage.

In the reign of Henry II., William, the son of William Fitz-Godrick, was the first, according to Dugdale, who assumed this surname, and called himself

WILLIAM FITZ-WILLIAM, in which opinion Seager, Garter-king-of-arms, temp. Charles I., coincides. William Fitz-Godrick is stated to have been cousin in blood to King Edward the Confessor, and to have been deputed upon an embassy by that monarch to William, Duke of Normandy, at whose court he remained until he returned with the expedition in 1066, as marshal of the invading army, and it is added, that the CONQUEROR bestowed upon him a scarf from his own arm, for the gallantry he had displayed at Hastings. Sir William Fitz-William (Fitz-Godrick's son,) *m.* Eleanor, daughter and heir of Sir John de Elmley, Lord of Elmley and Sprotborough, in Yorkshire, and was *s.* by his son,

SIR WILLIAM FITZ-WILLIAM, who was living in 1117, Lord of Elmley and Sprotborough. This feudal lord *m.* Ella, daughter and co-heir of William, Earl of Warren and Surrey, and had Roger, to whom the Earl of Warren gave the lordship of Gretewell; and an elder son, his successor,

SIR WILLIAM FITZ-WILLIAM, Lord of Elmley and Sprotborough, who *m.* Albreda, daughter and heir of Robert de Lizures, widow of Richard Fitz-Eustace, constable of Chester, and sister of the half blood to Robert de Laci, Baron of Pontefract, and had issue, a daughter, Donatia, to whom her mother gave lands in Crowle—with a son, his successor,

SIR WILLIAM FITZ-WILLIAM. This feudal lord took up arms in the baronial cause, temp. King John, but returned to his allegiance in the 5th Henry III. He *m.* Ella, daughter of Hamlyn, Earl Warren and Surrey, and was *s.* by his son,

SIR THOMAS FITZ-WILLIAM, who *m.* Agnes, one of the daughters and co-heirs of Roger Bertram, feudal Lord of Mitford, by whom he had three sons,

WILLIAM, his successor.

212

Roger (Sir), who had the lands of Woodhall from his father.

Peter, who was settled at Denby.

He had besides five daughters, of whom Albreda *m.* Sir Richard Walleis, Knt., of Burgh Walleis. Sir Thomas Fitz-William was *s.* by his eldest son,

SIR WILLIAM FITZ-WILLIAM, of Sprotborough, who, in the 29th Edward I., was in the Scottish wars; but the next reign, joining in the great insurrection of Thomas, Earl of Lancaster, he was made prisoner with that nobleman at Boroughbridge, and hanged immediately after at York. He *m.* Agnes, daughter of Richard, Lord Grey, of Codnor, and left an only son,

SIR WILLIAM FITZ-WILLIAM, who was summoned[*] to parliament, in the 1st Edward III., as a BARON, but never afterwards. This nobleman *m.* Maud, daughter of Edmond, Lord Deincourt, and had several children, but as none were subsequently esteemed barons, we presume, with Nicolas, that the summons was not a parliamentary, but a military one. From this Sir William the present noble house of Fitz-William, Earls Fitz-William, lineally derive.

ARMS.—Losengy, ar. and gules.

FITZ-WILLIAM—EARL OF SOUTHAMPTON.

By Letters Patent, dated 18th October, 1537.

Lineage.

From Sir William Fitz-William, son of William Fitz-Godrick, marshal of the victorious army at Hastings, descended,

SIR JOHN FITZ-WILLIAM, who *m.* Elizabeth, daughter and heiress of William Clinton, Earl of Huntingdon, and had several children, of whom,

EDMOND FITZ-WILLIAM, was grandfather of

SIR THOMAS FITZ-WILLIAM, Knt., of Aldwarke, in the county of York, who *m.* Lucy, daughter and co-heir of John Nevill, Marquess of Montacute, and had issue, THOMAS, slain at Flodden-Field, in the 4th Henry VIII., and another son,

WILLIAM FITZ-WILLIAM, who was made by King Henry VIII. one of the esquires of his body, and knighted soon after for his good services at the siege of Tournay. Upon the attainder of Edward Stafford, Duke of Buckingham, Sir William Fitz-William, being then vice-admiral of England, obtained a grant of the manor of Navesby, in the county of Northampton, part of that nobleman's possessions. In the 15th Henry VIII. Sir William, as admiral of the English fleet, went to sea for the purpose of intercepting the Duke of Albany, who

---

[*] So says Dugdale, "but it appears from his list of summonses in that year, that Sir William Fitz-William was not included in either of the summonses *to parliament,* but only in the summons, dated at Ramsay, 5th April, 1324, to attend at Newcastle-upon-Tyne with horse and arms.

."NICOLAS."

was about returning to Scotland with a large body of French. The next year he was captain of Guisnes, in Picardy, and he was soon after, being at the time treasurer of the household, deputed with John Taylor, doctor of law, to take the oath of the Lady Regent, then at Lyons, (King Francis I. being a prisoner in Spain,) for ratifying the articles of a treaty just concluded between the crowns of England and France. In the 24th of the same reign he was joined in another embassy to France with the Duke of Norfolk and Dr. Cox, regarding the marriage of the French king's third son, with the English monarch's daughter, the Lady ELIZABETH; after which (28th Henry VIII.), being a Knight of the Garter, treasurer of the household, and chancellor of the Duchy of Lancaster, he was constituted ADMIRAL OF ENGLAND, WALES, IRELAND, NORMANDY, GASCONY, AND AQUITAINE, and elevated to the peerage, by letters patent, dated 18th October, 1537, as EARL OF SOUTHAMPTON. He was subsequently appointed lord privy seal. His lordship d. at Newcastle in 1543, upon his march into Scotland, leading the van of the English army, but so highly was he esteemed, that to do honour to his memory, his standard was borne in the forward, throughout the whole of the ensuing campaign. The earl m. Mabel, daughter of Henry, Lord Clifford, and sister of Henry, first Earl of Cumberland, but had no issue, in consequence of which the EARLDOM OF SOUTHAMPTON at his decease became EXTINCT, while his estates devolved upon (his brother's daughters) his nieces,

> Margaret Fitz-William, wife of Godfrey Fuljambe, Esq.
>
> Alice Fitz-William, wife of Sir James Fuljambe, Knt.

ARMS.—Lozengy, ar. and gu. a mullet for difference.

FOLIOT—BARON FOLIOT.

By Writ of Summons, dated 23rd June, 1295, 23 Edward I.

Lineage.

In the 12th year of King Henry II.

ROBERT FOLIOT, upon the assessment of the aid for marrying the king's daughter, certified that he had fifteen knights' fees, which his ancestors had held from the Conquest. This feudal lord m. Margery, daughter and heiress of Richard de Reincurt, Lord of Sutton, in the county of Bedford, whereupon King Henry II. confirmed to him the manor of Burton, in the county of Northampton, and all other, the lands and honour of Guy de Reincurt, ancestor of the said Richard. He was s. by his son,

RICHARD FOLIOT, who left an only daughter and heiress, wavy gu 4 ermin

> Margery, who m. Whyschard Ledet, son of Christian Ledet, Lady of Langtone, in the county of Leicester. The inheritance of this lady (Margery Foliot) was litigated in the 8th Richard I., by Thomas Foliot,

Richard de Hidon, Emme de Boterel, and Geffrey de Barinton, grand-children of Robert Foliot, and the suit was pending in the reign of King John.

With this heiress this branch of the family appears to have terminated, but many of the same race were distinguished for several years afterwards, until the reign of Edward I., when

JORDAN FOLIOT was summoned to parliament as a BARON from 23rd June, 1295, to 26th January, 1297, but of his lordship and descendants nothing further is known.

ARMS.—Gu. a bend ar..

Note.—Gilbert Foliot, Bishop of Hereford, anno 1149, and of London, in 1161, is another eminent person of this name. Of his lordship, distinguished by his fidelity to King Henry II., in the struggles between that monarch and Thomas à Becket, Matthew Paris states the following circumstance:— As he lay in bed one night after a conference with the king, a terrible and unknown voice sounded these words in his ears: "O Gilbert Foliot, dum revolvis tot, et tot Deus tuus est Astaroth." Which he taking to come from the devil, answered as boldly: "Mentiris, dæmon, Deus meus est Deus Sabbaoth." He was the author of an apology for Henry, against Becket; and he also wrote an invective against the proud prelate, with several other works.

FORTESCUE—EARL OF CLINTON.

By Letters Patent, dated 5th July, 1746.

Lineage.

LADY MARGARET-CLINTON, one of the daughters and co-heirs of Theophilus, fourth Earl of Lincoln, and tenth Baron Clinton, m. Hugh Boscawen, Esq., of Tregotham, in the county of Cornwall, and left an only daughter and heiress,

BRIDGET BOSCAWEN, who espoused Hugh Fortescue, Esq., of Filley, in the county of Devon, and had (with two other sons and two daughters, all of whom died s. p.) a son and heir,

HUGH FORTESCUE, Esq., in whose favour the ABEYANCE of the ancient BARONY OF CLINTON was terminated by the crown, and he was summoned to parliament, as LORD CLINTON, on the 16th March, 1721. His lordship was made a Knight of the Bath in 1725, and created, by letters patent, dated 5th July, 1746, Baron Fortescue, of Castle Hill, and EARL OF CLINTON, with special remainder of the barony to his half brother, Matthew Fortescue, Esq. The earl d. in 1751, without issue, when the BARONY OF CLINTON fell again into ABEYANCE between his sister and heir, Margaret Fortescue, Countess of Orford, and Margaret, daughter of Lady Arabella Clinton, by her husband, Robert Rolle, Esq., of Haynton, in the county of Devon. The BARONY OF FORTESCUE passed according to the limitation, and is enjoyed by the present EARL FORTESCUE, while the EARLDOM OF CLINTON became EXTINCT.

ARMS.—Az. a bend engrailed ar. cottised, or.

FRESCHEVILLE — BARON FRESCHEVILLE, OF STAVELEY, IN THE COUNTY OF DERBY.

By Letters Patent, dated 6th March, 1664.

Lineage.

In the 9th of Henry III., upon the death of Robert Fitz-Ralph, Lord of Cryche, in Derbyshire,

RALPH DE FRESCHEVILLE, being his heir, and paying one hundred marks for his relief, had livery of his lands. This Ralph, in the 26th of the same reign, paid a fine of thirty marks to be excused from attending the king into Gascony. He d. in nineteen years afterwards, and was s. by his son,

ANKERE DE FRESCHEVILLE, who, having joined the baronial standard, was made prisoner at the battle of Northampton, when his lands were seized by the crown, and conferred upon Brian de Brompton, according to the tenor of the *Dictum de Kenilworth*, until the heir of the said Ankere should accomplish his full age. Ankere d. in the 54th Henry III., when it was found that he held the manor of BONEY, in the county of Nottingham, by barony, of the king in Capite, so likewise the manor of Cryche, in Derbyshire. He had married Amice, eldest daughter and co-heir of Sir Nicholas Musard, Lord of Staveley, in the county of Derby, and sister and co-heir of Nicholas Musard, and was s. by his son,

RALPH DE FRESCHEVILLE, who, in the 15th Edward I., doing his homage, had livery of all his father's lands, save the manor of Boney, which Richard de Grey still retained until the fine imposed by the Dictum of Kenilworth should be liquidated. In ten years afterwards this Ralph distinguished himself in the wars of Scotland, and was summoned to parliament, as a BARON, in the 25th Edward I., but never afterwards. His lordship was s. by his son,

RALPH DE FRESCHEVILLE, who was never summoned to parliament, nor esteemed a BARON; nor were any of his descendants. Of whom his direct male heir,

SIR PETER DE FRESCHEVILLE, had the honour of knighthood conferred upon him by KING EDWARD VI., for his valour at the battle of Musselborough, in Scotland. Sir Peter was great grandfather of

JOHN FRESCHEVILLE, Esq., of Staveley, in the county of Derby, who, having adhered firmly to the royal cause during the civil wars, was elevated to the peerage by King Charles II., on 16th March, 1664, as BARON FRESCHEVILLE, of *Staveley*. In 1677 his lordship claimed to be allowed to sit in the House of Peers under the writ of summons to his ancestor, RALPH, in the reign of Edward I., but it being contended, that to give the party summoned to parliament an estate of inheritance, a sitting under the writ was necessary, as the onus of proving such sitting rested with the party claiming the dignity, and no such proof being extant in the case of Ralph Frescheville, the claim was not admitted. Lord Frescheville m. first, Sarah, daughter

214

of Sir John Harington, Knt., and had three daughters, viz.

    Christian, m. to Charles Paulet, then Lord St. John, afterwards Duke of Bolton.

    Elizabeth, m. first, to Philip, son and heir of Sir Philip Warwick, Knt., and secondly, (his lordship's fourth wife,) to Conyers Darcy, second Earl of Holdernesse.

    Frances, m. to Colonel Thomas Colepeper. This lady became eventually sole heiress of her father.

His lordship espoused, secondly, Anna-Charlotta, daughter and heir of Sir Henry Vick, Knt., but had no issue. He d. in 1682, when the BARONY OF FRESCHEVILLE of *Staveley* became EXTINCT.

ARMS.—Az. a bend betw. six eschallop shells ar.

FREVILLE—BARON FREVILLE.

By Writ of Summons, dated 5th April, 1327, 1 Edward III.

Lineage.

This family was anciently seated in the county of Cambridge, and of considerable note. In the 15th of Henry III.,

BALDWIN DE FREVILLE, having obtained the wardship of Lucia, daughter and heir of Richard de Scalers, for which he gave two hundred marks, made her, very soon after, his wife; and in the 30th of the same reign, paid towards the marriage-portion of the king's daughter, fifteen pounds, for fifteen knights' fees which he had of her inheritance. To this Baldwin succeeded his son and heir,

RICHARD DE FREVILLE, who was engaged in the Welsh wars. He was s., at his decease, by his son,

BALDWIN DE FREVILLE, who died without issue, and was s. by his brother,

ALEXANDER DE FREVILLE, who m. Joane, daughter of Mazere, second daughter and co-heir of Sir Philip Marmion, and wife of Ralph de Cromwell. This Alexander was in the Scottish wars of Edward I., and had a military summons for that service in the 8th of Edward II.; in the 3d of which latter monarch's reign, upon partition of the lands of Isabel, wife of William Walraund, he had, in right of his wife, heir to the said Isabel, the manors of Winterborne and Asserton, in the county of Wilts. He was afterwards summoned[*] to parliament as a BARON, in the 1st of Edward III., but never again, nor any of his descendants. He d. in 1328, leaving a son,

BALDWIN DE FREVILLE, who d. in the 17th Edward III., and was s. by his son,

BALDWIN DE FREVILLE, then twenty-six years of age, who, doing homage, the next ensuing

---

[*] On referring to Dugdale's List of Summonses, it appears that this ALEXANDER is not included in either summons to parliament issued in that year, but only in a summons dated at Ramsey, 5th April, 1st Edward III., 1327, to be at Newcastle-upon-Tyne, with horse and arms, to serve against Robert Bruce.—NICOLAS.

year had livery of the lands of his inheritance lying in the counties of Warwick, Hereford, Salop, Stafford, Wilts, Norfolk, and Suffolk. In the 38th Edward III., this Baldwin was made seneschal of Fantoigne for life, by Edward, the renowned Black Prince, and he was afterwards in the wars of Gascony with that illustrious personage. He *m.* first, Elizabeth, sister and co-heir of Sir John Montfort, of Beldesert, in the county of Warwick; secondly, Ida, daughter of ——— Clinton, a lady of honour to Queen Philippa; and thirdly, Joane, daughter of Lord Strange, and dying in the 49th Edward III., was *s.* by his son,

SIR BALDWIN DE FREVILLE, who, in the 1st of Richard II., claimed, as feudal lord of Tamworth Castle, in the county of Warwick, to be the king's champion on the day of his coronation; but the same was determined against him, in favour of Sir John Dymoke, Knt., (see Marmion,) in right of the tenure of the manor of Scrivelsby, in the county of Lincoln, and the Dymokes have ever since enjoyed that honour. Sir Baldwin *m.* two wives, both of them daughters of Sir John Botetourt, of Weoly Castle, namely, Elizabeth, who died very young, and Joice, by whom, at his decease, 11th Richard II., he left issue,

SIR BALDWIN DE FREVILLE, who *m.* Joane, daughter of Sir John Green, Knt., and had issue,

BALDWIN, his successor.

Elizabeth, *m.* to Sir Thomas Ferrers, second son of William, Lord Ferrers, of Groby, from whom lineally descended

ANNE FERRERS, grand-daughter and heiress of Sir John Ferrers, of Tamworth Castle, who *d.* in 1680. This great heiress *m.* the Hon. Robert Shirley, first Earl of Ferrers of that family, and had issue,

Robert, who died *s. p.* in 1714.

Elizabeth, heir to her brother, *m.* to James, fifth Earl of Northampton, and carried the baronies of Ferrers, of Chartley, &c. &c. into that family.

Margaret, *m.* to Sir Hugh Willoughby, Knt., and afterwards to Sir Richard Bingham, Knt., one of the justices of the King's Bench.

Joice, *m.* to Roger Aston, Esq., ancestor of the Lord Astons, of Forfar, in Scotland.

Sir Baldwin *d.* in the 2d of Henry IV., and was *s.* by his son,

BALDWIN DE FREVILLE, at whose decease in minority, and issueless, 6th Henry V., his sisters became his heirs, and the great possessions of the Frevilles were thus divided:—

Sir Thomas Ferrers had the castle and manor of Tamworth, with other estates in the county of Warwick, and lands in Hereford and Stafford shires.

Roger Aston had the manor of Newdigate, in Surrey, with other lands in Wiltshire and Warwickshire.

Sir Richard Bingham obtained the manors of Middleton and Whitnash, in Warwickshire,

and other lordships in the counties of Nottingham and Hereford.

ARMS.—Or., a cross patonce gu.

FURNIVAL — BARONS FURNIVAL.

By Writ of Summons, dated 23rd June, 1295,
23 Edward I.

Lineage.

In the time of Richard I.

GIRARD DE FURNIVAL came into England from Normandy, and, accompanying the lion-hearted monarch to the Holy Land, assisted at the celebrated siege of Acon. To this gallant soldier succeeded his son, another

GIRARD DE FURNIVAL, who *m.* Maud, daughter and heiress of William de Luvetot, a powerful Nottinghamshire Baron, and had livery of her lands in the fifth year of King John. This feudal lord, being one of the barons who adhered to John, was included in the commission to treat, on part of the monarch, with Robert de Ros and the other insurrectionary lords, and was appointed by the king to reside at Bolsover Castle, in the county of Derby, for the better preservation of the peace in those parts. He *d.* at Jerusalem, in the 3d Henry III., leaving three sons, viz.

THOMAS, of whom presently.

Girard, who *m.* Christian Ledet, daughter and heiress of Wischard Ledet, and widow of Henry de Braybroc, in whose right he held the barony of Wardon. He left, at his decease, two daughters, his co-heiresses, viz.

Christian, *m.* to William Latimer.

Agness, *m.* to John Latimer.

William, *m.* Ada ———, and left an only daughter and heiress,

Helewyse, *m.* to Eustace de Baliol.

The eldest son,

THOMAS DE FURNIVAL, succeeded to the feudal barony, and Henry III. committed to his wardship, William de Moubray, son of Roger de Moubray, a great Yorkshire baron. Of this Thomas nothing more is known, than his being slain by the Saracens in the Holy Land, whither he had journeyed upon a pilgrimage, and that his body was brought from thence by his brother Girard, and buried at Worksop. He was succeeded by his son,

THOMAS DE FURNIVAL, who had licence, in the 54th Henry III., to make a castle of his manor-house, of Sheffield, in the county of York. To this Thomas *s.* his son and heir,

GERARD DE FURNIVAL, who *d.* some time before 1280, and was *s.* by his son,

THOMAS DE FURNIVAL, who, in the 22d Edward I., had summons, amongst other great men, to attend the king, in order to advise of the affairs of the realm; and having so done, received command to repair to Portsmouth, upon the first day of the ensuing September, well fitted with horse and arms, for the expedition then intended against France. In the next year, 23d June, 1295, he was first summoned to parliament as a BARON, and from that period his lordship appears, for several years, to have taken a distinguished part in the Scottish wars. In the 27th Edward I., he was constituted captain-general and lieutenant to the king for the counties of Nottingham and Derby, and had summons to parliament, uninterruptedly, until 27th January, 1332, (6th Edward III.,) but he did not hold his lands by barony. Lord Furnival *m.* Elizabeth, daughter of Peter de Montfort, of Beldesert Castle, in the county of Warwick, and was *s.* at his decease, in 1332, by his eldest son, *viz. [?]*

THOMAS DE FURNIVAL, who was himself a BARON, having been summoned to parliament as "Thomæ de Furnival, Junior," from 25th August, 1318, to 27th January, 1332, and without "junior," until 15th November, 1338 (12th Edward III.). This nobleman, who, like his father, was engaged in the Scottish wars, *m.* Joan, eldest daughter and coheiress of Theobald de Verdon, (a great baron,) and widow of William, son of William de Montacute, but without the king's licence, for which he had to pay a fine of £200. By this lady he acquired extensive estates in the county of Stafford, and had two sons, Thomas and William. His lordship *d.* in 1339, and was *s.* by the elder,

THOMAS DE FURNIVAL, third baron, then seventeen years of age. In the 19th Edward III. this nobleman embarked in the expedition made into France, and the next year participated in the glories of CRESSY. His lordship continued in the French wars some years subsequently, and he was afterwards in Scotland under Henry, Lord Percy. He *d.* about the year 1364, having been summoned to parliament, from the 20th November, 1348, to the 4th October in that year; and leaving no issue, was *s.* by his brother,

WILLIAM DE FURNIVAL, fourth baron, summoned to parliament, from 20th January, 1366, to 7th January, 1383. This nobleman permitted the pale of his park at Worksop to be so defective, that divers of the king's deer, out of the forest of Sherwood, came freely into it, and were destroyed. In consequence of which, William de Latimer, warden of the forests beyond Trent, seized the said park for the king; but it was soon afterwards released, and Lord Furnival pardoned, upon the payment of a fine of £20. His lordship *m.* Thomasin, daughter and heiress of —— Dagworth, (in whose right he acquired the manor of Dagworth, in Suffolk,) by whom he had an only daughter,

     Joane, who *m.* Thomas Nevill, brother of Ralph, first Earl of Westmoreland.

With this nobleman, in the year 1383, expired the male line of the Furnivals, and the barony was conveyed by his heiress, Joane Nevill, to her husband,

THOMAS NEVILL, who was summoned to parliament on the 20th August, 1383, (7th Richard II.) as "Thomæ Nevyll de Halumshire," and thenceforward styled, "Lord Furnival." In which year, making proof of his wife's age, he had livery of her great inheritance. By this lady he had two daughters, viz.

     Maud, *m.* to Sir John Talbot, Knt.
     Joane, who *d.* unmarried.

His lordship *m.* secondly, Ankaret, widow of Sir

216

Richard Talbot, and sister of John, son to John, Lord Strange, of Blackmere, but had no issue. This nobleman, who was a personage of distinction, in the reigns of Richard II. and Henry IV., died in 1406, leaving his two daughters, his co-heiresses. The elder of whom, Maud, as stated above, married the celebrated

GENERAL SIR JOHN TALBOT, who was summoned to parliament as "Lord Furnival," from 26th October, 1409, to 26th February, 1421; and subsequently, for his many heroic achievements, created EARL OF SHREWSBURY, in the peerage of England, and EARL OF WATERFORD AND WEXFORD, in that of Ireland. In which higher honours the BARONY OF FURNIVAL merged for two centuries, until the demise of Gilbert, seventh Earl of Shrewsbury, in 1616, without male issue, when the earldom passed to that nobleman's brother; but the baronies of TALBOT, FURNIVAL, STRANGE, OF BLACKMERE, &c. fell into abeyance between his three daughters, viz.

   Mary, *m.* to William, Earl of Pembroke.
   Elisabeth, *m.* to Henry, Earl of Kent.
   Alethea, *m.* to Thomas, (Howard,) Earl of Arundel; by which marriage the manor of Worksop came into the Howard family; and by virtue of possessing which, the Dukes of Norfolk claim to support the king's left arm on the day of coronation, so long as his majesty holds the royal sceptre; George, fourth Earl of Shrewsbury, having exchanged with the crown, his manor of Farnham Royal, (holden by that tenure,) for the inheritance of the site of the priory of Worksop, with divers other lands.

The baronies finally, however, devolved upon Alethea, COUNTESS OF ARUNDEL, and thenceforward became merged in the Earldom of Arundel and the Dukedom of Norfolk, until the decease of Edward Howard, ninth Duke, 20th September, 1777, without issue, when the higher honours passed to the male heir; and the baronies in fee, amongst which was that of FURNIVAL, fell into ABEYANCE between the daughters of his grace's deceased brother, Philip Howard, of Buckinham, in the county of Norfolk, viz., the said

PHILIP HOWARD, *m.* first, Winefrede, daughter of Thomas Stoner, Esq., and had issue,
   Thomas, who *d.* in 1763, *s. p.*
   Winefrede, *m.* to WILLIAM, fifteenth Lord Stourton, and had issue,
     CHARLES PHILIP, sixteenth Lord Stourton, father of the present LORD STOURTON.

Mr. Howard *m.* secondly, Harriet, daughter and co-heir of Edward Blount, Esq., by whom he had,
   Edward, who *d.* unmarried in 1767.
   Anne, *m.* to Robert Edward, ninth Lord Petre, by whom she had,
     ROBERT EDWARD, tenth Lord Petre, father of the present LORD PETRE.

The baronies thus continue still in ABEYANCE between the LORDS STOURTON AND PETRE.

ARMS.—Ar. a bend between six mascles, Gu.

GAGE—BARON GAGE OF FIRLE, IN THE COUNTY OF SO-MERSET.

By Letters Patent, dated 27th October, 1780.

Lineage.

WILLIAM HALL GAGE, second Viscount Gage, in the peerage of Ireland, (see the extant Viscounts Gage, *Burke's Peerage and Baronetage,*) was created a peer of Great Britain on 27th October, 1780, as BARON GAGE, of Firle, in the county of Somerset. His lordship m. in 1757, Elizabeth, sister of Sampson, Lord Eardley, by whom he had an only son, who died in infancy. His lordship obtained, subsequently, another British peerage as Lord Gage, of High Meadow, in the county of Glouceater, with remainder to his nephew and presumptive heir, Major-General Henry Gage, who inherited that dignity and the Irish viscounty at his decease, 11th October, 1791, when the BARONY OF GAGE, *of Firle,* became EXTINCT.

ARMS.—Per saltier, as. and ar. a saltier gules.

GANT—EARLS OF LINCOLN.

Inherited by marriage from the family of ROMARE, (see Romare, Earl of Lincoln).

Lineage.

GILBERT DE GANT, son of Baldwin, Earl of Flanders, by Maud, sister of William the Conqueror, accompanied his uncle into England, and participating in the triumph of HASTINGS, obtained a grant of the lands of a Danish proprietor, named *Tour,* with numerous other lordships; for we find him at the general survey, possessed of manors in Berks, Oxford, Yorkshire, Cambridgeshire, Buckinghamshire, Huntingdonshire, Northamptonshire, Rutland, Leicestershire, Warwickshire, Nottinghamshire, and Lincolnshire, in all a hundred and seventy-three lordships; of which Folkingham was one, and his seat, as the head of his barony. This Gilbert happened to be at York, anno 1069, and had a narrow escape, when the Danes, in great force on behalf of Edgar Etheling, entered the mouth of the Humber, and marching upon that city, committed lamentable destruction by fire and sword, there being more than three thousand Normans slain. Like most of the great lords of his time Gilbert de Gant disgorged a part of the spoil which he had seized to the church, and amongst other acts of piety restored Bardney Abbey, in the county of Lincoln, which had been utterly destroyed many years before by the Pagan Danes, Inquar and Hubba. He m. Alice, daughter of Hugh de Montford, and had issue,

> WALTER, his successor.
> Robert, lord chancellor of England, anno 1153.
> Emma, m. to Alan, Lord Percy.

This great feudal chief died in the reign of William Rufus, and was s. by his elder son,

WALTER DE GANT, a person of great valour and piety: who, at an advanced age, commanded a brave regiment of Flemings and Normans, in the celebrated conflict with the Scots, at Northallerton, in Yorkshire, known in history as the *Battle of the Standard,* "where," says Dugdale, "by his eloquent speech and prudent conduct the whole army received such encouragement, as that the Scots were utterly vanquished." He m. Maud, daughter of Stephen, Earl of Britanny, and had issue, Gilbert, Robert, and Geffrey. He d. in the 4th King Stephen, and was s. by his eldest son,

GILBERT DE GANT, who, in his youth, being taken-prisoner with King Stephen at the battle of Lincoln, (1142,) was compelled by Ranulph, Earl of Chester, to marry his niece, the Lady Hawyse Romare, daughter of William, Earl of Lincoln, whereby he became eventually in her right* EARL OF LINCOLN. This nobleman founded, in 1148, the Abbey of Rutford, in Nottinghamshire, and otherwise contributed munificently to the church. He d. in 1156, leaving two daughters, his co-heirs, viz.

> Alice, m. to Simon de St. Liz, (the last of that name,) Earl of Huntingdon and Northampton.
> Gunnora.

At the decease of these ladies, without issue, the great inheritance reverted to their uncle,

ROBERT DE GANT, who does not, however, appear to have succeeded to the Earldom of Lincoln. This Robert m. first, Alice, daughter and heir of William Paganel, and of Avice de Romelli, (daughter and co-heir of William Meschines, Lord of Copeland,) by whom he had an only daughter,

> ALICE, m. to Robert Fitzhardinge, of the family of Fitzhardinge, from which the Earls of Berkeley derive. This Robert assumed the name of Gant, and had issue,
>> Maurice de Gant, who died s. p., anno 1230.
>> Eve, m. to Thomas de Harpetre, and had issue,
>>> Robert de Harpetre, surnamed Gournay.
>> This Eve was heir to her brother Maurice.

Robert de Gant m. secondly, Gunnora, niece of Hugh de Gournay, and had issue,

> GILBERT, surnamed the Good.
> Stephen, who adhered to the rebellious barons about the latter end of King John's reign, and d. in 1162.

He d. about the 4th Richard I., and was s. by his elder son,

GILBERT DE GANT, then under age, and in ward to William de Stutevill. In the last year of King John's reign, this Gilbert adhering to the barons, was constituted EARL OF LINCOLN, by Lewis, of France, at that time in London, and at the head of the baronial party, and was despatched into Nottinghamshire to oppose the royalists. Shortly after which, assisted by Robert de Ropesie,

---

* In the succession of this earldom there is something very singular. William Romare, Earl of Lincoln, left at his decease a grandson, William Romare, son of his only son, who had predeceased him, and this grandson ought surely to have been earl before the husband of his aunt, but he never appears to have borne the title (see Romare, Earl of Lincoln).

he reduced the city of Lincoln, but at the subsequent battle, the baronial force being totally broken, he was taken prisoner, and never after assumed the title of Earl of Lincoln; which dignity was then conferred upon Randall de Meschines, surnamed Blundeville, Earl of Chester. This ex-earl d. in 1242, leaving issue,

GILBERT, who inherited a considerable property, for in the 29th Henry III. he paid £68 for as many knights' fees, upon collection of the aid for marrying the king's daughter. In the 42nd of the same reign he was made governor of Scarborough Castle, but afterwards adhering to the barons, he was taken prisoner at Kenilworth, and was obliged to pay no less than three thousand marks for the redemption of his lands. Whereupon the king received him again into favour; but he d. soon afterwards, anno 1274, leaving issue,

GILBERT, summoned to parliament as a baron (see Barons Gant).
Margaret, m. to William de Kerdeston.
Nichola, m. to Peter de Mauley.
Julian, d. unmarried.

Julian, m. to Geffrey, son of Henry de Armentiers.

ARMS.—Barry of six, or. and az. a bend gules.

GANT—BARON GANT.

By Writ of Summons, dated 23rd June, 1295, 23 Edward I.

Lineage.

GILBERT DE GANT, grandson of Gilbert, last Earl of Lincoln of that family, (see Gant, Earls of Lincoln,) succeeded to his father's possession in 1274, and having served in the Welch wars of King Edward I., was summoned to parliament as a BARON from 23rd June, 1295, to 26th August, 1296, His lordship m. Lora, sister of Alexander de Baliol, but having no issue, he constituted King Edward I. his heir in the lands of his barony; viz. Falkingham, Barton, Heckyngton, and Edenham, retaining only Swaledale, and his portion of Skendelley. He d. in 1297, when the BARONY OF GANT became EXTINCT, and his property passed to Roger, son of William de Kerdeston, by Margaret, his elder sister; Peter, son of Peter de Mauley, by Nicola, his second sister; and Julian de Gant, his third sister.

ARMS.—Barry of six, or. and az. a bend, gules,

GAVESTON—EARL OF CORNWALL.

Creation about the year 1308.

Lineage.

PIERS DE GAVESTON, the notorious favourite of King Edward II., was elevated to the peerage by that monarch, as Baron Wallingford and EARL OF CORNWALL.

Gaveston, the son of a private gentleman in Gascony, who had been distinguished in the wars, was brought to court by King Edward I., as a companion for his son, Prince Edward, but that monarch before his death was so sensible of the danger incurred by the prince, in having so evil an adviser, compelled Gaveston to abjure the realm, and forbad his son recalling him, under the penalty of his curse. Upon the accession of the young monarch, however, he not only invited Gaveston back, but elevated him to the peerage, and loaded him so profusely with favours, that the rest of the nobility found it imperatively necessary to interfere, and to beseech the king to remove him. Edward for the moment acquiesced—but only for the moment—Gaveston was recalled, and new honours awaited him. This at length so exasperated the haughty nobles, that they flew to arms, under Thomas Plantagenet, Earl of Lancaster, and determined to compel the king to comply with their wishes. Edward being apprised of these proceedings, conducted the favourite to Scarborough Castle, and there left him with sufficient forces for its defence, whilst he himself marched into Warwickshire. The lords thereupon invested Scarborough, and the unhappy Gaveston soon after surrendered upon conditions of personal safety. He was, however, conveyed by the Earl of Warwick to Warwick Castle, and beheaded by his orders at Blacklow Hill, about a mile from the town of Warwick, without any form of trial whatsoever.

Gaveston m. Margaret, daughter of Gilbert de Clare, Earl of Gloucester, by Joane of Acres, the king's sister, and co-heir of her brother, Gilbert de Clare, Earl of Gloucester, by whom (who m. after his decease, Hugh de Audley,) he had an only daughter, JOANE, who died young. The execution of his lordship took place in 1314, when the EARLDOM OF CORNWALL became EXTINCT.

ARMS.—Vert. six eagles displayed or. membered and beaked gules.

GENEVILL—BARON GENEVILL.

By Writ of Summons, dated 6th February, 1299, 27 Edward I.

Lineage.

In the 28th Henry III.,

PETER DE GENEVA having married Maud, niece, and one of the co-heirs of Walter de Laci, obtained with her the CASTLE OF LUDLOW, and its members. To this Peter, who was governor of Windsor Castle, succeeded his son and heir,

GEOFFREY DE GENEVILL, who, in the 36th Henry III., had livery of the castle of Trim, in Ireland, as the right by inheritance of Maud de Laci, daughter of Gilbert de Laci, who died in his father's life-time. In four years afterwards this Geoffrey received a military summons to march against the Welch, and in the 44th of the same king, being then one of the barons marchers, he had command to repair to the castle of Wales, and to reside there. In the 10th of Edward I. he was in the expedition made against the Welch, and in fifteen years subsequently he was in the wars of Gascony. For all which services he was summoned to parliament, as a BARON, on the 6th February, 1299, and from that period to 3rd November, 1306. He m. ——, and had issue,

GEOFFREY, who died *s. p.* in the life-time of his father.

PETER, his successor.

SIMON, m. Joan Fitz-Lues, Lady of Tull-Malyn, and had issue, one son and six daughters, viz.,

    Nicholas, who left an only daughter and heiress,

        Joane, wife of John Cusak, of Beaurepaire.

    1. ——, m. to John Huse, Lord of Saltrim.

    2. ——, m. to William de Loundres, of Ashboy.

    3. ——, m. to the Baron of Slane.

    4. ——, m. to Walter de Hyde.

    5. ——, m. to John Cruce.

    6. ——, m. to John Fitz-Thomas, nephew of Gerard Fitz-Maurice.

His lordship d. about the year 1307, and was s. by his eldest surviving son,

PETER DE GENEVILL, second baron, but never summoned to parliament, who m. Joane, daughter of Hugh le Brune, Earl of Angolesme, and had three daughters, viz.

    JOANE, who m. Roger Mortimer, Earl of March, and conveyed eventually the whole inheritance of the Grenevilles, and half the lands of the Lacies, into that family.

    Isabel,   } nuns at Aconbury.
    Beatrice, }

Upon the decease of this Peter, the BARONY OF GENEVILL, if he were ever esteemed a baron, fell into ABEYANCE between those ladies.

ARMS.—Az. three horses' bits, or. on a chief, ermine, a demy lion issuant gules.

GEORBODUS—EARL OF CHESTER.

Creation of the Conqueror.

Lineage.

The EARLDOM OF CHESTER, after the Norman conquest, was first conferred upon

GEORBODUS, a Fleming, who, having encountered many difficulties, as well from the English as his troublesome neighbours the Welch, and being at length sent for into Flanders by some of his friends, to whom he had entrusted his affairs there, obtained licence from King William to attend the summons, but he had no sooner reached his native soil, than, falling into the power of his enemies, he was cast into prison, where he remained a considerable time. He does not appear to have ever returned to England, and the earldom of Chester was subsequently bestowed upon HUGH DE ABRINCES, (see Abrinces, Earl of Chester.)

GERARD — BARONS GERARD, OF GERARD'S BROMLEY, IN THE COUNTY OF STAFFORD.

By Letters Patent, dated 21st July, 1603.

Lineage.

In the first year of Queen Mary,

GILBERT GERARD, a branch of the ancient Gerards, of Bryn, in Lancashire, derived from the great Geraldine stock, in Ireland, having attained eminence in the profession of the law, was chosen autumn-reader by the benchers of Grey's Inn, and the next year appointed, with Nicholas Bacon, (afterwards lord-keeper,) joint-treasurer of the society. In some time after, when the princess Elizabeth was brought before the council, Mr. Gerard advocated her cause so ably, that he was committed to the Tower, where he remained during the rest of Queen Mary's reign. Upon the accession of Elizabeth, he was released, and constituted attorney-general. He afterwards received the honour of knighthood, and was appointed master of the rolls, when he had held the attorney-generalship no less than three-and-twenty years. This Sir Gilbert erected a stately mansion in the county of Stafford, where he resided, called Gerard's Bromley. He m. Anne, daughter of William Ratcliffe, Esq., of Wimersley, in the county of Lancaster, and had issue,

    THOMAS, his successor.

    Ratcliffe, from whom the Gerards, Barons Gerard, of Brandon, and Earls of Macclesfield, derived. (See Gerard, Barons Gerard, of Brandon.)

    Frances, m. to Sir Richard Molineux, Bart., ancestor of the extant Earls of Sefton.

    Margaret, m. to Peter Leigh, Esq.

    Catherine, m. to Sir Richard Hoghton, Bart., of Hoghton Tower, in the county of Lancaster, ancestor of the present Sir Henry Philip Hoghton, Bart.

    Ratcliffe, m. to —— Wingfield, Esq.

Sir Gilbert Gerard d. in 1593, and was s. by his elder son,

SIR THOMAS GERARD, who was advanced to the peerage on the 21st July, 1603, as BARON GERARD, of *Gerard's Bromley*, in the county of Stafford; and in the 14th of King James I., was constituted lord president of Wales. His lordship m. first, Alice, daughter and heiress of Sir Thomas Rivet, Knt., and had three sons,

    GILBERT,

    William,

    John.

He espoused secondly, Elisabeth, daughter of —— Woodford, Esq.; but had no issue. He d. in 1618, and was s. by his eldest son,

GILBERT GERARD, second Baron Gerard, of Gerard's Bromley, who m. Eleanor, daughter and heiress of Thomas Dutton, Esq., of Dutton, in the county of Chester, by whom he had surviving issue,

    DUTTON, his successor.

    Alice, m. to Roger Owen, Esq., son and heir of Sir William Owen, of Cundover, in the county of Salop, Knt.

    Frances, m. to the Hon. Robert Needham, son and heir of Robert, Viscount Kilmorey.

    Elisabeth, m. to Sir Peter Leicester, Bart., of Nether Tabley, the celebrated antiquary and historian of Cheshire, maternal ancestor of the present Lords de Tabley.

His lordship d. in 1622, (his widow re-married the above-mentioned Robert, Lord Kilmorey.) He was s. by his son,

219

[handwritten notes at bottom of page, partially legible]

DUTTON GERARD, third Baron Gerard. This nobleman m. first, Lady Mary Fane, daughter of Francis, Earl of Westmorland, by whom he had issue, .

CHARLES, his successor.

Mary, m. to Sir Anthony Cope, Bart., of Hanwell, in the county of Oxford.

His lordship espoused secondly, Lady Elizabeth O'Bryen, daughter and co-heir of Henry, Earl of Thomond, in Ireland, and had an only daughter,

Elizabeth, m. to William Spencer, of Ashton, in the county of Lancaster, third son of William, Lord Spencer, and had a daughter,

Elizabeth Spencer, who m. Robert Hesketh, Esq., of Rufford, in the county of Lancaster, and left a daughter and heiress,

ELIZABETH HESKETH, who m. Sir Edward Stanley, Bart., afterwards eleventh Earl of Derby, and had, with other issue,

JAMES, Lord Stanley, father of EDWARD, present EARL OF DERBY.

Lord Gerard d. in 1640, and was s. by his son,

CHARLES GERARD, fourth Baron Gerard, who m. Jane, only surviving daughter and heiress of George Digby, Esq., of Sandon, in the county of Stafford; and dying in 1667, was s. by his only child,

DIGBY GERARD, fifth Baron Gerard. This nobleman espoused his distant relation, Elizabeth, daughter of Charles Gerard, first Earl of Macclesfield, and had an only daughter and heiress,

ELIZABETH, who m. James, Duke of Hamilton, in Scotland, and first Duke of Brandon, in England.

Lord Gerard died in 1711, when the BARONY OF GERARD, of Gerard's Bromley, became EXTINCT, in default of a male heir, while his lordship's estates devolved upon his daughter, the Duchess of Hamilton and Brandon.

ARMS.—Quarterly, first and fourth ar., a saltier gules. Second and third az., a lion rampant crowned or.

GERARD — BARONS GERARD, OF BRANDON, IN THE COUNTY OF SUFFOLK, EARLS OF MACCLESFIELD.

| Barony, | by Letters | 3rd November, 1645. |
| Earldom, | Patent, | 23rd July, 1679. |

Lineage.

RATCLIFFE GERARD, Esq., of Hatsall, in the county of Lancaster, second son of Sir Gilbert Gerard, attorney-general and master of the rolls, in the reign of Elizabeth, m. Elizabeth, daughter and heiress of Sir Charles Somerset, K.B., and granddaughter of Edward, Earl of Worcester, and was s. by his son,

SIR CHARLES GERARD, Knt., who m. Penelope, sister and co-heir of Sir Edward Fitton, of

Gosworth, in the county of Chester, Knt., and was s. by his son,

CHARLES GERARD, who, being brought up from his youth to the profession of arms, upon the usual theatre of European warfare, the NETHERLANDS, joined his majesty, King Charles I., at Shrewsbury, soon after he had reared the royal standard, and became eminently distinguished amongst the cavaliers. First, at KINETON, where he received some dangerous wounds. And soon afterwards at the taking of Lichfield, the first battle of Newberry, and the relief of Newark. General Gerard then accompanied Prince Rupert into South Wales, and acquired high reputation by his victories at Cardiffe, Kidwelly and Caermarthen—and his success in taking the castle of Cardigan, and other fortresses, and reducing the strong garrison of Haverford-West, with the castles of Picton and Carew. In consideration of which gallant services he was made, by the king, lieutenant-general of his horse, and elevated to the peerage, as BARON GERARD,[*] of Brandon, on the 8th November, 1645. His lordship, after the restoration, was created, 23rd July, 1679, Viscount Brandon, and EARL OF MACCLESFIELD—but in the time of James II. he was committed, with the Earl of Stamford and the Lord Delamere, to the Tower, and condemned to death, but pardoned. He lived to see the revolution, and, "in fact, to witness," says Banks, "three singular occurrences in the annals of British history;" (he might have characterised them as the three most singular,) "first, the deposition and decapitation of King Charles I.; secondly, the restoration of his son; and thirdly, the REVOLUTION and total expulsion of the royal family so recently restored." His lordship married a French lady, and had issue,

CHARLES, } successively earls.
FITTON, }

Charlotte, m. first, —— Mainwaring, Esq., of Cheshire, and had a daughter,

CHARLOTTE, who m. Charles, Lord Mohun. To this nobleman, Charles, second Earl of Macclesfield, left the chief of his estates, which causing a law-suit between him and James, Duke of Hamilton, an unhappy personal quarrel

[*] Besides his lordship, there were of his family the following persons actively engaged upon the royal side, in those unhappy conflicts—

| His brothers, | Edward Gerard, a colonel of foot, wounded in the first battle of Newberry. Sir Gilbert Gerard, slain near Ludlow. |
| His uncles, | Sir Gilbert Gerard, governor of Worcester. Ratcliffe Gerard, lieut.-col. to his brother. This gentleman had three sons, Radcliffe. John, put to death by Cromwell. Gilbert, created a baronet. } All in the battle of Kineton. |

arose, which terminated in a duel, wherein both lost their lives, 15th November, 1712.

Lady Charlotte Mainwaring espoused, secondly, Sir Thomas Orby, of Lincolnshire.

Anne, m. to Captain Ebrington.

Elizabeth, m. to Digby, Lord Gerard, of Bromley.

The earl d. in 1693, and was s. by his elder son,

CHARLES GERARD, second Earl of Macclesfield, a colonel in the army. This nobleman was ambassador to Hanover, upon the subject of the succession to the throne of England. His lordship m. first ——, daughter of Sir Richard Mason, Knt., of Shropshire, from whom he separated; and secondly, Miss Harbourd, but had no issue. His lordship d. in 1697, leaving the greater part of his estates to Charles, Lord Mohun, (who had married his niece, Miss Mainwaring,) owing to some dispute with his brother and successor,

FITTON GERARD, third Earl of Macclesfield, who d. unmarried in 1702, when the BARONY OF GERARD, of Brandon, with the *Viscounty of Brandon*, and EARLDOM OF MACCLESFIELD, became EXTINCT.

ARMS.—AL. sa. saltier gules, a crescent for difference.

GHISNES—BARON GHISNES.

By Writ of Summons, dated 23rd June, 1295, 23 Edward I.

Lineage.

INGELRAM DE GHISNES, otherwise DE CURSI, a noble baron of France, related to the Counts De Ghisnes, of that kingdom, who were feudal lords in England, temp. John and Henry III., had a daughter, Mary, married to Alexander II., king of Scotland, and was s. by another

INGELRAM DE GHISNES, who, having married Christian, daughter and heir of William de Lindesey, descended from Alice, one of the sisters and co-heirs of William de Lancaster, and doing his fealty in the 11th Edward I., had livery of the lands of her inheritance, amongst which was the manor of Wyresdale, in Lancashire. This feudal lord having distinguished himself in the wars of Scotland, was summoned to parliament, as a BARON, from 23rd June, 1295, to 14th March, 1322. His lordship d. in the 17th of Edward II., seised of the manor of Middleton, near Richmond, and was s. by his son,

WILLIAM DE GHISNES, alias DE CURSI, second baron, but never summoned to parliament. This nobleman died s. p., seised of the moiety of the manor of Kirby, in Kendale, and was s. by his brother and heir,

INGELRAM DE GHISNES, or DE COURCY, who m. Katherine, daughter and heir of the Archduke of Austria, and was s. by his son,

INGELRAM DE GHISNES, or DE COURCY, who espoused the Lady Isabella Plantagenet, one of the daughters of King Edward III., and was

---

* His lordship was first created Earl of Newberry, but the title was changed to MACCLESFIELD.

---

created Earl of Bedford, (see De Courcy, Earl of Bedford). The BARONY OF GHISNES is now vested in the descendant and representative of INGELRAM, who was summoned to parliament in the reign of Edward I.

ARMS.—Barry of six vairée and gu.

GIFFORD — EARLS OF BUCKINGHAM.

Creation of William the Conqueror, anno 1066.

Lineage.

The *first* EARL of this county, after the conquest, was

WALTER GIFFARD, son of Osborne de Bolebec, and Aveline, his wife, sister of Gunnora, Duchess of Normandy, great-grandmother of the Conqueror, who was so dignified for his gallant services at the battle of Hastings. At the time of the general survey, this nobleman was sent with Remigius, Bishop of Lincoln, and others, into Worcestershire, and some other counties, to value the lands belonging to the crown, as well as to private individuals in those parts. He himself possessed at that time two lordships in Berkshire; one in Wilts; one in Somersetshire; one in Huntingdon; five in Cambridgeshire; nine in Oxfordshire; nine in the county of Bedford; three in Suffolk; twenty-eight in Norfolk; and forty-eight in Buckinghamshire; in all ONE HUNDRED AND SEVEN. In 1069, his lordship adhering to William Rufus, fortified his mansions in Normandy, for that king, and became chief general of his army there: yet in some years afterwards, (1102,) he sided with Robert Curthose, against King Henry I. The earl m. Agnes, daughter of Gerard Flaitell, and sister of William, Bishop of Eureux, and had, with other issue,

WALTER, his successor.

Rohais, m. to Richard Fitz-Gilbert, feudal lord of Clare, in the county of Suffolk, (see Clare,) and had, besides other children,

  GILBERT, who m. Adeliza, daughter of the Earl of Cleremont, and was father of

    Richard de Clare, Earl of Hertford.

    GILBERT DE CLARE, created *Earl of Pembroke*, whose son,

      RICHARD, surnamed STRONGBOW, became so distinguished in the conquest of Ireland.

Isabel, m. to Richard Granville, or Grenville, progenitor of the noble house of Grenville, now Dukes of Buckingham.

His lordship d. in 1102, and was s. by his son,

WALTER GIFFARD, second Earl of Buckingham. This nobleman adhered faithfully to King Henry I., and distinguished himself in that monarch's cause at the battle of BRENNEVILLE, in 1119, against the French, commanded by their king in person, where Henry obtained a victory. His lordship, during this reign, founded the Abbey of Nutley, in the county of Bucks. He died in 1164, without issue, when the lands of his Barony came, according to Dugdale, to be shared amongst his relatives; "for it beems," (says that writer,) "in the 1st of Richard I., that Richard de Clare, Earl of Hertford, (in respect of his descent from Rohaise, sister of the Earl, and wife of Richard Fitz-Gilbert, his lineal ancestor,) and William Mareschall, Earl of Pembroke, (in right of Isabel de Clare, his wife,) obtained a confirmation from that king, of all the lands of this Walter, Earl of Buckingham, both in England and Normandy; of which lands, Richard, Earl of Hertfort, was to have the chief seat in England, and William, Earl of Pembroke, the chief seat in Normandy; the residue in both countries to be equally divided between them." Thus terminated the house of Giffard, EARLS OF BUCKINGHAM. The title is said by Camden to have been subsequently borne by Richard de Clare, surnamed Strongbow, Earl of Pembroke.

ARMS.—Gu. three lions passant ar.

GIFFARD — BARONS GIFFARD, OF BRIMSFIELD, IN THE COUNTY OF GLOUCESTER.

By Writ of Summons, dated 24th June, 1295, 23 Edward I.

Lineage.

In the Conqueror's time,

OSBERT GIFFARD, held one lordship in Berkshire; one in Oxfordshire; three in Cornwall, one in Dorsetshire, and four in Gloucestershire, whereof Brimsfield was one, and his chief seat. To this feudal lord, who died before the year 1086, succeeded his son,

HELIAS GIFFARD, who, in conjunction with Ala, his wife, granted in 1086, part of his woods, with three borderers, to the Abbey of St. Peter, at Gloucester. He was s. at his decease, by another

HELIAS GIFFARD, who, like his father, was a liberal benefactor to the church, having made grants to divers religious houses, amongst which was the above mentioned Abbey of St. Peter, upon which he conferred his lordship of Cronham. He was s. by a third

HELIAS GIFFARD. This feudal lord, upon the assessment for the marriage portion of King Henry II.'s daughter, Maud, certified that he possessed nine knights' fees, and the same year, (12th Henry II.,) gave one hundred marks' fine, for livery of his inheritance. He d. in 1190, and was s. by

THOMAS GIFFARD, who in the 6th of Richard I., paid £9. upon levying the scutage for the king's redemption. He was s. by his son,

HELIAS GIFFARD, who took up arms with the other barons against King John, and in the 18th of that monarch's reign, all his lands in the counties of Wilts, Northampton, Gloucester, Somerset, Dorset, Oxford, and Berks, were given by order of the king, to Bartholomew Peche, but restored by Henry III., at the general pacification. By the inquisition taken after the death of this feudal baron, 33rd Henry III., he appears to have been possessed of the manor of Winterborne, in the county of Wilts, and that that lordship was then

the head of his barony. He d. in 1248, and was s. by his son,

JOHN GIFFARD, then in his seventeenth year, during whose minority the queen had a grant of his lands, towards the maintenance of Prince Edward. In the 41st Henry III., this John Giffard was commanded to be at Bristol with horse and arms, thence to march into South Wales, against Lewelin ap Griffin. In six years subsequently, he was constituted governor of St. Briavel's Castle, and of the Forest of Dean, in Gloucestershire; but soon after, taking part with the rebellious barons, was amongst those whom the Archbishop of Canterbury ordered to be excommunicated. He was at the battle of Lewes, under the baronial banner, but adopting a different course at the battle of Evesham, he obtained pardon for his former treasons, in consideration of the services which he then rendered to the royal cause.

In the 55th of Henry III., Maud Longspe, widow of William Longspe, son of William, Earl of Salisbury, and daughter and heiress of Walter de Clifford, having by letter complained to the king, that this John Giffard, had taken her by force from her manor house, and carried her to his Castle of Brimsfield, where he kept her in restraint; he was summoned before the king, when denying the charge, but confessing his marriage with the lady without the royal licence, he made his peace by paying a fine of three hundred marks.

In the 10th Edward I. John Giffard was in the expedition then made by Gilbert de Clare, Earl of Gloucester, against Lewelin, Prince of Wales; and observing that Lewelin had separated, with a small party, from the body of his army, he joined with Edward Mortimer, and slaying the prince, despatched his head to the king, who caused it to be set upon the tower of London, crowned with ivy. In the eighteenth of the same reign he was constituted governor of Dynevor Castle, in Wales, and having had summons to parliament as a BARON, from 24th June, 1295, to 10th April, 1299, died in the latter year, and was buried at Malmesbury. His lordship m. first, (as already stated,) Maud, widow of William Longspe, by whom he had issue,

　　Katherine, m. to Nicholas Aldithley, first Baron Aldithley, or Audley, of Helegh.

　　Alianore, m. to Fulk le Strange, Baron Strange, of Blackmere.

He m. secondly, Alicia Maltravers, by whom he had no child; and thirdly, Margaret de Nevile, by whom he had an only son, his successor,

SIR JOHN GIFFARD, K.B., second baron, summoned to parliament, from 8th October, 1311, to 15th May, 1321, as "Johanni Giffard de Brymesfield." This nobleman was constituted, in the 9th Edward II., constable of the castles of Glamorgan and Morgannoc. Adhering subsequently, however, to Thomas, Earl of Lancaster, in his opposition to the Spencers, he sate in the parliament by which those favourites were condemned to banishment, and afterwards, when the king marched into Wales, plundered the royal carriages, which so incensed Edward, that, in passing from Cirencester towards Worcester, he sent a party of soldiers to demolish Lord Giffard's castle at Brimsfield. His lordship eventually, sharing the fortune of his leader, the Earl of Lancaster, was taken prisoner, with that nobleman, after the defeat at Boroughbridge, and being condemned for high treason, was hanged at Gloucester in 1322, when the BARONY OF GIFFARD fell under the attainder; but the proceedings against Thomas, Earl of Lancaster, and his adherents, being reversed in the 1st Edward III., anno 1327, the dignity was revived, and may now probably be considered to be vested in the descendants and representatives of his half sisters, the above-mentioned

　　Katherine, Lady Aldithley,
　　　　　　　and
　　Alianore, Lady Strange, of Blackmere.

ARMS.—Gules, three lions passant in pale ar. and langued as.

GODOLPHIN — BARONS GODOLPHIN, OF RAILTON, IN THE COUNTY OF CORNWALL. EARLS OF GODOLPHIN. BARONS GODOLPHIN, OF HELSTON, IN THE COUNTY OF CORNWALL.

Barony,	by Letters Patent,	8th September, 1684.
Earldom,		29th December, 1706.
Barony,		23rd January, 1735.

Lineage.

This family derived its surname from Godolphin,* (anciently written Godolghan,) in the county of Cornwall,

JOHN DE GOLDOLPHIN was living about the time of the Norman Conquest, and amongst his other feudal possessions, was lord of the manor of Godolphin, and resided there. From this John descended, through several generations,

DAVID GODOLPHIN, Esq., who m. Meliora, daughter of John Cowling, Esq., of Trewerveneth, and left an only daughter and heiress,

ELEANOR GODOLPHIN, who m. John Rinsey, Esq., and being a great heiress, covenanted, that her issue should bear her own family name. The heir of this marriage was,

THOMAS GODOLPHIN, Esq., of Godolphin, whose great-grandson,

JOHN GODOLPHIN, Esq., of Godolphin, was sheriff of Cornwall in the 19th and 23d Henry VII.; he was also joint steward with Sir Robert Willoughby, Lord Brooke, of the mines in Cornwall and Devonshire. He m. Margaret, daughter of John Trenouth, Esq., and had issue,

　　WILLIAM, his successor.
　　John, whose descendants were seated at Morewall and Trewerveneth, in the county of Cornwall.
　　Elizabeth, m. to William Canell, Esq.

He was s. by his son,

WILLIAM GODOLPHIN, Esq., who m. Mar-

* Godolphin, in Cornish, signifies a WHITE EAGLE, which was always borne in arms of this family.

garet, daughter and co-heir of John Glinne, Esq., of Moreval and Lowewater, by whom he had two sons, viz.

　　WILLIAM (Sir), his successor.
　　Thomas, who m. ――――, daughter of Edmund Bonithon, Esq., and left issue,
　　　　FRANCIS, who succeeded his uncle, Sir William Godolphin, and carried on the line of the family.
　　　　William, M.P. for Helston, in the 28th of Elizabeth.

Mr. Godolphin was s. by his elder son,

SIR WILLIAM GODOLPHIN, a very distinguished person in the reign of Henry VIII., who, for his services, had the honour of knighthood, and was constituted warden and chief steward of the Stanneries. Sir William lived to an advanced age, and was chosen several times one of the knights of the shire for Cornwall, in the parliament of King Henry VIII. and King Edward VI. He was thrice sheriff of Cornwall, in the reign of Henry VIII., and once in the reign of Edward VI., and again in that of Elizabeth. He, likewise, attained a high military reputation, particularly for his gallant conduct at the siege of Boulogne. Mr. Carew, in his survey of Cornwall, ranks Sir William Godolphin amongst the principal worthies of that shire; thus speaking of him: " He demeaned himself very valiantly beyond the seas, as appeared by the scars he brought home, no less to the beautifying of his fame, than the disfiguring of his face." Sir William m. Blanch, daughter of Robert Langden, Esq., and had issue,

　　Margaret, m. to Sir Robert Verney.
　　Grace, m. to Sir John Sydenham, of Brimpton, in the county of Somerset.
　　Anne, m. to Sir John Arundel, of Talvern, in the county of Cornwall.

Having thus no male issue, the estates passed at Sir William's decease to his nephew,

SIR FRANCIS GODOLPHIN, M.P. for the county of Cornwall, in the 31st Elizabeth, and colonel of a regiment of twelve companies armed with four hundred and seventy pikes, four hundred and ninety muskets, and two hundred and forty calivers. He was also governor of Scilly, " which," Carew says, " by her majesty's order, was reduced to a more defensible plight by him, who with his invention and purse, bettered his plot and allowance, and therein so tempered strength and delight, and both with use, as it serveth for a sure hold, and a commodious dwelling." Of Sir Francis, the same author gives the following character:—" Sir Francis Godolphin, Knt., whose zeal in religion, uprightness in justice, providence in government, and plentiful housekeeping, have won him a very great and reverent reputation in his country; and these virtues, together with his services to her majesty, are so sufficiently known to those of highest place, as my testimony can add but little light thereunto. But by his labours and inventions in tin matters, not only the whole county hath felt a general benefit, so as the several owners have thereby gotten very great profit out of such refuse works, as they before had given over for unprofitable; but her majesty hath also received increase of her customs by the same, at least to the value of £10.000. Moreover, in those works, which are of his own particular inheritance, he continually keepeth at work three hundred persons or thereabouts; and the yearly benefit, that out of those his works accrueth to her majesty, amounteth *communibus annis* to £1,000 at the least, and sometimes so much more. A matter very remarkable, and, per chance, not to be matched again, by any of his sort and condition in the whole realm." Sir Francis undertook the coinage of silver out of the mines in Wales and Cornwall; and King Charles I. (for he was living at the accession of that monarch), granted him the power of coining at Aberrusky, in Cornwall. The pence, groats, shillings, half-crowns, &c., there afterwards coined, were distinguished by a plume of ostrich feathers, the arms of Wales.

Sir Francis Godolphin m. Margaret, daughter of John Killigrew, Esq., of Arnwick, in Cornwall, and had three sons and six daughters, of whom,

> WILLIAM, was his successor.
>
> Blanch, m. George Keckwith, Esq., of Catch-French.
>
> Ursula, m. ——— Creyde, Esq.
>
> Thomasin, m. Sir George Carew, afterwards Earl of Totness.

Sir Francis was s. by his eldest son,

SIR WILLIAM GODOLPHIN, who accompanied Robert, Earl of Essex, in his expedition to Ireland against the rebels in 1599, and received the honour of knighthood for his gallantry at Arklow. In the following year he was so highly esteemed by the lord deputy Mountjoy, that he entrusted him with the command of his own brigade of horse, in the decisive battle between the queen's forces, and the Spaniards and Irish, fought on the 24th December, in the immediate vicinity of Kinsale: which victory was chiefly owing to his courageous conduct, having broken through the Spanish line, and made prisoner of their commander, when the whole was put to the rout. In this action Sir William was slightly wounded in the thigh with a halbert; but in six days afterwards was so far recovered, that when Don John D'Aquila, commander of the Spaniards in the town of Kinsale, offered a parley, desiring the lord deputy, that some gentleman of special trust and sufficiency might be sent into the town to confer with him, he was employed in the negotiation. Sir William Godolphin represented the county of Cornwall in the first parliament of King James, and dying in 1613, left issue by Thomasin, daughter and heir of Thomas Sidney, Esq., of Wrighton, in the county of Norfolk,

> FRANCIS, his successor.
>
> Sidney, a very accomplished personage, and a poet of some celebrity, of whom Lord Clarendon thus speaks.—" A young gentleman of incomparable parts, who being of a constitution and education more delicate and unacquainted with contentions, upon his observation of the wickedness of those men in the House of Commons, of which he was a member, out of pure indignation of his soul against them, and conscience to his country, had, with the first, engaged himself with that party in the west; and though he

224

thought not fit to take command in a profession he had not willingly chosen, yet as his advice was of great authority with all the commanders, being always one in the council of war, and whose notable abilities they had still use of in their civil transactions, so he exposed his person to all action, travel, and hazard; and by too forward engaging himself, (in this action at Chagford,) received a mortal shot by a musket, a little above the knee, of which he died in the instant." He was buried at Okehampton, 10th February, 1642.

William, was colonel of a regiment, and performed many signal services for King Charles I., in several remarkable actions in the west: Penelope, m. to Sir Charles Berkeley, Viscount Fitzhardinge.

Sir William was s. by his eldest son,

FRANCIS GODOLPHIN, Esq., M.P. for St. Ives, prior to the breaking out of the rebellion. After which unhappy proceeding he retired to his seat in Cornwall, secured the Island of Scilly for the king, and raised a regiment of foot, the command of which was given to his brother, Colonel William Godolphin. He subsequently waited upon his majesty at Oxford, and was amongst those members, who met there by royal appointment in January, 1643. The Island of Scilly was under Mr. Godolphin's command, until the incarceration of the king, when finding it hopeless any longer to resist, he capitulated upon honourable terms: the commons having voted, 4th January, 1646-7, " that Mr. Godolphin, governor of Scilly, upon his surrender of that island, with all forts, &c., should enjoy his estate, and be free from arrest for any acts of war." For these services, and his known loyalty, he was created a Knight of the Bath at the coronation of King Charles II. He m. Dorothy, second daughter of Sir Henry Berkeley, Knt., of Yarlington, in the county of Somerset, and had no less than sixteen children, of whom,

> WILLIAM, (the eldest son,) was created a BARONET the 29th April, 1661. Sir William lived in retirement, and dying unmarried, 17th August, 1710, bequeathed his estates to his nephew, the Earl of Godolphin.
>
> Francis, d. unmarried in the reign of Charles II.
>
> Sidney, we shall treat of presently.
>
> Henry, D.D., Provost of Eton College, and Dean of St. Paul's. Dr. Godolphin, who was greatly esteemed for his learning, piety, and benevolence, d. at the advanced age of eighty-four, 29th January, 1732-3, leaving a son and daughter, viz.
>
>> William, who succeeded to the Barony of Godolphin, of Helston, upon the decease of Francis, second Earl of Godolphin
>>
>> ———, m. to ——— Owen, Esq., of Porkington, in Shropshire.

The third son,

SIDNEY GODOLPHIN, was, from his youth, in the service of King Charles II., who, when Prince of Wales, coming into Cornwall, there took particular notice of him, and after the restoration made him one of the grooms of the bed-chamber. In 1678 he was accredited to the states general upon a special mission, and the next year, upon the dismission of the Earl of Danby from the office of LORD HIGH TREASURER OF ENGLAND, he was constituted one of the commissioners of the treasury, and sworn of the privy council. Soon after which he acquired, by his prudent management, a great ascendant in the council, and Sir William Temple informs us, "that the Earl of Sunderland, Mr. Hyde, and Mr. Godolphin were esteemed to be alone in the secret and management of the king's affairs, and looked upon as the ministry." On the resignation in 1684 of Sir Leoline Jenkins, one of his majesty's principal secretaries of state, Mr. Godolphin was sworn into that office, but he returned to the treasury in a few months after as first commissioner, and was elevated to the peerage on the 8th September in that year, as BARON GODOLPHIN, of Rialton, in the county of Cornwall. Upon the accession of King James II. his lordship was appointed lord chamberlain to the Queen, and upon the removal of the Earl of Rochester from the lord treasurership in January, 1686-7, he was again constituted one of the commissioners of the treasury. After the landing of the Prince of Orange, his lordship was one of those deputed by the reigning sovereign to wait upon the prince, and to demand the object he had in view; and when King James retired, in the debates regarding the vacancy of the throne that followed, his lordship voted for a regency: nevertheless, when their majesties, King William and Queen Mary were proclaimed king and queen of England, knowing his great abilities and integrity, they constituted him one of the lords commissioners of the treasury, and he was sworn of the privy council. In the year 1695 his lordship was declared one of the seven lords justices, for the administration of the government during the king's absence beyond the seas, as he was again the following year, as also in the year 1701.

Upon the accession of Queen Anne, Lord Godolphin was constituted LORD HIGH TREASURER OF ENGLAND. Under his lordship's administration in this high office, public credit, which had previously been declining, revived. The war was carried on with success, and the nation was entirely satisfied with his prudent management. He neglected nothing that could engage the subject to bear the burthen of war with cheerfulness; and it was owing to his lordship's advice that her majesty contributed £100,000 out of the civil list towards that object. In 1704, he was installed a KNIGHT of the GARTER; the next year he was constituted lord-lieutenant of the county of Cornwall; and his lordship so managed affairs before the end of that year, that her majesty was empowered by the parliaments, both of Scotland and England, to appoint commissioners to treat about a union. This important affair was set on foot by King James I.; but no prince before Queen Anne, nor any council but her's, could effect it: for by the assiduity and dexterity of Lord Godolphin, all obstacles were removed, and the long-desired union of the two kingdoms accomplished. For those eminent services her majesty created his

lordship, on the 29th December, 1706, *Viscount Railton* and EARL OF GODOLPHIN, and constituted him LORD HIGH TREASURER OF GREAT BRITAIN; from which office he was removed by the spirit of political animosity in 1710, the celebrated trial of Dr. Sacheverel having previously taken place. His lordship, who had laboured for some years under an indisposition of the stone and gravel, died on 15th September, 1712, and was buried, on the 8th of the next month, in the south aisle of Westminster Abbey, where a monument was erected to his memory by his daughter-in-law, the Duchess of Marlborough.

His lordship m. Margaret, fourth daughter and one of the co-heirs of Thomas Blague, Esq., groom of the bed-chamber to Kings Charles I. and II., by whom he left an only child,

FRANCIS GODOLPHIN, second earl, born 3d September, 1678. This nobleman represented the county of Oxford, in the life-time of his father, in parliament; and in the reign of Queen Anne, was lord warden of the stanaries, and cofferer to her majesty. In 1723, his lordship was appointed groom of the stole, and first gentleman of the bed-chamber, and the same year was constituted one of the lords justices during the temporary absence of the king. In 1733, the earl was appointed governor of the Islands of Scilly, and he was created, on the 23d January, 1735, BARON GODOLPHIN, of HELSTON, with special remainder, (in default of his own male issue,) to the heirs male of his deceased uncle, the very reverend Henry Godolphin, D.D., dean of St. Paul's (revert to issue of Henry Godolphin, Esq., father of the first earl). He was subsequently sworn lord privy-seal. His lordship espoused Lady Henrietta Churchill, eldest daughter and co-heir of John Churchill, the great Duke of Marlborough, which lady, upon her illustrious father's decease, became Duchess of Marlborough, by virtue of the act of parliament which entailed his grace's honours upon his daughters. By this lady the earl had issue,

WILLIAM, Marquess of Blandford, M.P. for Woodstock. His lordship m., in 1729, Maria-Catherine, daughter of Peter D'Jong, of the province of Utrecht, but died without issue, 24th August, 1731.

Henry, died young.

Henrietta, m. to Thomas Pelham Holles, Duke of Newcastle, and died s. p.

Margaret, died young.

Mary, m. to Thomas Osborne, fourth Duke of Leeds, K.G., of which marriage, George-William, present Duke of Leeds, is grandson.

Her grace died 24th October, 1733, and his lordship, on the 17th January, 1766, when the EARLDOM OF GODOLPHIN, VISCOUNTY OF RAILTON, and BARONY OF GODOLPHIN, of Railton, became EXTINCT; but the barony of GODOLPHIN, OF HELSTON, devolved, according to the limitation, upon his first cousin,

FRANCIS GODOLPHIN, Esq., of Baylis, in the county of Bucks, as second baron, who had previously represented Helston in parliament. His lordship m. first, in 1734, Lady Barbara Bentinck, daughter of William, Earl of Portland. He espoused secondly, Lady Anne Fitz-William, daughter of John, Earl Fitz-William : but dying without issue, in 1785, the BARONY OF GODOLPHIN, of HELSTON, also EXPIRED.

ARMS.—Gules, an eagle with two heads displayed between three fleur-de-lis ar.

GORGES—BARON GORGES.

By Writ of Summons, dated 4th March, 1309, 2 Edward II.

Lineage.

In the 41st of Henry III.,

RALPH DE GORGES had a military summons to march against the Welch, and in a few years afterwards was made governor of Sherburne and Exeter Castles. He was likewise sheriff of the county of Devon. In the 54th of the same reign, he attended Prince Edward to the Holy Land, and dying within the two next years, was s. by his son,

RALPH DE GORGES, who, in the 21st Edward I., was marshal of the king's army in Gascony, and the next year, continuing in those parts, was made prisoner and carried to Paris. He was not detained long, however, in captivity, for we find him soon after again in active service upon the same field, and subsequently engaged in the wars of Scotland; in consideration of which services he was summoned to parliament, as a BARON, by King Edward II., on the 4th of March, 1309, and from that period to the 18th September, 1322; but his descendants enjoyed no similar honours. His lordship was s. by his son,

RALPH DE GORGES, who, dying without issue, was s. by his sister,

ELEANOR DE GORGES, who m. Theobald Russel, son of Sir William Russel, of Kingston-Russel, in the county of Dorset, and had issue,

THEOBALD, of whom presently.

Ralph (Sir), of Kingston-Russel and Derham, m. ———, and left issue,

Theobald, } died issueless.
John, }

Maurice (Sir), of Kingston-Russel, who had issue,

Thomas-Fitzmaurice, whose daughter,

Mary, died s. p.

Isabel, m. to Sir Stephen Heytfield.

Margaret, m. first to Gilbert Denys, Esq., and secondly to John Kemys, Esq.

The elder son,

SIR THEOBALD RUSSEL, assuming his maternal surname, became Sir THEOBALD GORGES. He also adopted the armorial bearings of the family, which occasioned a dispute, in the 21st Edward III., between him and Warburton of Cheshire, for bearing also those arms; but the latter established his right thereto in the court of the Earl Marshal, Henry, Earl of Lancaster, and Gorges had then assigned him, a chevron gules on the lozenge or. and ez., for difference; which his posterity bore for some time, until they again resumed 296

their ancient and hereditary coat, namely, " Ar. a gurges or., whirlpool az."

Sir Theobald died in the 4th of Richard II., leaving four sons,

Ralph,
Bartholomew, } all of whom d. issueless.
William,

And

THOMAS GORGES, who succeeded his brothers, and carried on the line of the family; and dying in the 5th of Henry IV., was s. by his son,

JOHN GORGES, who died in minority, and was s. by his brother,

THEOBALD GORGES, who had, by his first wife,

WALTER GORGES, who continued the Wraxal line;

And, by his second,

RICHARD GORGES, who, and his descendants, held lands for some time in Sturminster Marshall, in the county of Dorset.

NOTE.—There were other branches of this family in the counties of Hereford, Somerset, and Wilts, particularly at Langford, in the latter shire; one of which was created a baronet in the reign of James I., and an Irish peer, by the title of Lord Dundalk.

GORING — BARONS GORING, OF HURST PIERPONT, IN THE COUNTY OF SUSSEX. EARLS OF NORWICH.

Barony, } by Letters { 14th April, 1632.
Earldom, } Patent, { 8th November, 1644.

Lineage.

GEORGE GORING, Esq., of Hurspierpont and Ovingdene, both in the county of Suffolk, m. Anne Denny, eldest sister of Sir Edward Denny, Baron Denny, and Earl of Norwich, (an earldom that expired in 1630,) and was s. by his son,

SIR GEORGE GORING, Knt., who was elevated to the peerage on the 14th April, 1632, as BARON GORING, of Hurst Pierpont, in the county of Sussex, and in two years afterwards obtained a grant of the offices of secretary, clerk of the signet, and clerk of the council within the principality of Wales. His lordship subsequently rendering the highest services to King Charles I., after the breaking out of the civil wars, was advanced to the dignity of EARL OF NORWICH, by letters patent, dated 8th November, 1644. He m. Mary, daughter of Edward, Lord Bergavenny, by whom he had issue,

GEORGE, so gallantly distinguished in the civil wars as General Goring. This heroic personage fought to the last in the cause of his royal and unfortunate master—and after the surrender of Oxford, retiring to the Netherlands, he acquired fresh laurels as lieutenant-general of the king of Spain's army—he m. Lettice, daughter of Richard, Earl of Cork, and died s. p. in 1662, prior to his father.

CHARLES, second earl.

Elizabeth, m. to Lord Brereton, of Ireland.

Lucy, m. to Sir Dru Dene, of Maptested, in the county of Essex, Knt.

Diana, m. first, to Thomas Covert, Esq., of Slaugham, Sussex; and secondly, to George, eldest son of Endymion Porter, Esq.

Catherine, m. to William Scott, Esq., of Scott's Hall, Kent.

His lordship d. in 1662, and was s. by his only surviving son,

CHARLES GORING, second Earl of Norwich. His lordship m. ——, daughter of —— Leman, Esq., and widow of Sir Richard Baker, Knt., but dying without issue in 1672, the *Barony of Goring* and EARLDOM OF NORWICH, became EXTINCT.

ARMS.—Ar. a chevron between three annulets, gules.

NOTE.—From Edward Goring, Esq., uncle of George, first Earl of Norwich, the extant baronets Goring, of Highden, in Sussex, derive, which are now represented by Sir Charles Forster Goring. Bart.

GRANDISON—BARON GRANDISON.

By Writ of Summons, dated 21st September, 1299, 27 Edward I.

Lineage.

In the 55th of Henry III.,

OTHO DE GRANDISON attended Prince Edward into the Holy Land; and after that prince ascended the throne as Edward I., he was constituted governor of the islands of Guernsey and Jersey. In this reign he appears to have been a person of great note, and to have held some high political employment. Amongst others that of secretary to the king. He was knighted, and deputed ambassador to Rome, (17th Edward I.,) when he had the king's letters to the merchants of LUCA, to supply him with money there, by bills of exchange. He had previously obtained grants from the crown of the town of Tipperary, and other extensive possessions in Ireland, all which he transferred, with the sanction of the king, to his brother, William de Grandison. In the 24th of the same reign Sir Otho was joined in commission with the Bishop of Ely and others, to treat of peace with the French; and he was summoned to parliament, as a BARON, on the 21st September, 1299. The period of his lordship's death is not ascertained, but in the 12th Edward II. all those castles, manors, and lands, which he held in Ireland for life, were given, by the king, to Prince Edward, his eldest son, and to his heirs, KINGS OF ENGLAND. He died without issue, when the BARONY OF GRANDISON became EXTINCT.

ARMS.—Paly of six ar. and vert. on a bend gules three eagles displayed or.

GRANDISON — BARONS GRANDISON.

By Writ of Summons, dated 6th February, 1299, 27 Edward I.

Lineage.

WILLIAM DE GRANDISON, (brother of Sir Otho de Grandison, secretary to King Edward I.,

and afterwards Lord Grandison,) being originally a menial servant to Edmund, Earl of Lancaster, obtained from that prince, in consideration of his own faithful services, and the services of his ancestors, a grant of the manors of Radley and Menstreworth, in the county of Gloucester. In the 20th Edward I. he procured licence to make a castle of his house at Asperton, in the county of Hereford, and in two years afterwards he was in the expedition made into Gascony, where he continued for some time, and while so engaged was summoned to parliament as a BARON. He was afterwards engaged in the Scottish wars. His lordship m. Sibilia, youngest daughter and co-heiress of Sir John de Tregos, and upon partition of the lands of that inheritance, acquired the manors of Burnham, in the county of Somerset, and Eton, in Herefordshire. He had issue by this lady, three sons and a daughter, viz.

PETER, his successor.

John, Bishop of Exeter.

Otto, a distinguished soldier in the reigns of Edward II. and Edward III., m. Beatrix, daughter and co-heir of Nicholas Malmains, and had issue,

THOMAS, who succeeded his uncle, the Bishop of Exeter, in the barony of Grandison.

Elizabeth.

Agnes, m. to John de Northwode.

His lordship d. ——, and was s. by his eldest son,

PETER DE GRANDISON, second baron, summoned to parliament from 23rd April, 1337, to 22th March, 1349. This nobleman being implicated in the insurrection of Thomas, Earl of Lancaster, 15th Edward II., was obliged to pay three hundred marks fine for his pardon. He was afterwards in the wars of France, and attained the rank of banneret. His lordship m. Blanch, one of the daughters of Roger de Mortimer, Earl of March, but had no issue. He d. in 1358, and was s. by his brother,

JOHN DE GRANDISON, Bishop of Exeter, third baron, but never summoned to parliament as Lord Grandison, having already a seat in his episcopal dignity. Of this prelate it is related, that he got the wealth of all the clergy in his diocese into his own hands, by inducing them to leave him every thing they possessed at their death, for the purpose of laying the same out in charitable uses, in endowing churches, and building hospitals and colleges; trusts which he is said, however, very piously to have performed. He d. in 1370, and was s. by his nephew,

SIR THOMAS GRANDISON, as fourth Baron Grandison, but never summoned to parliament. He died s. p. in the 49th Edward III., and the BARONY is now vested in the representatives of Agnes, daughter of William, the first lord, if any such exist.

ARMS.—Paly of six ar. and vert. on a bend gules, three eagles displayed or.

GRANVILLE—EARLS OF BATH.

By Letters Patent, dated 20th April, 1661.

Lineage.

This noble family claimed descent from Rollo,

227

first Duke of Normandy, and its founder in England, ROBERT FITZ-HAMON, was nephew of King William the Conqueror, and one of his companions in arms.

SIR BEVILL GRANVILLE, Knt., one of the most eminent generals, upon the part of King Charles I., during the civil wars, after attaining the highest reputation in several engagements, lost his life at the battle of Lansdowne, near Bath, and left, by his wife Anne, eldest daughter and co-heir of Sir John St. Leger, a son and heir,

JOHN GRANVILLE, Esq., who, pursuing the same loyal course as his father, although then but fifteen years of age, first headed that celebrated officer's own regiment, and soon after, became commander-in-chief of five others, in all the considerable fights and skirmishes in the west; and in the second battle of NEWBERRY, wherein he received several severe wounds. Mr. Granville, subsequently, withdrew with Prince Charles, to whom he was gentleman of the bedchamber, and attended him in France, Flanders, Holland and the Isle of Jersey. He was afterwards mainly instrumental in the restoration of the monarchy, by successfully negociating with his near kinsman, General Monk; and as a reward for his services and sufferings, was elevated to the peerage on 20th April, 1661, as *Baron Granville, of Kilkhampton, in Cornwall, and Biddeford, in Devonshire, Viscount Granville, of Lansdowne, and EARL OF BATH;* and it being suggested, at this time, that he had, by inheritance, a real right to the titles of Earl of Carboile, Thorigny and Granville, in Normandy, in as full and ample a manner as his ancestors formerly enjoyed those dignities, before that dukedom was lost to the crown of England; he was, three days after, allowed, by his majesty's warrant, under his royal signet, to use the same; the preamble to which warrant runs thus : " Whereas, it appears to us, that our right trusty, &c., John, Earl of Bath, &c. is descended, in a direct line, as heir male to Robert Fitz-Haman, Lord of Gloucester and Glamorgan, in the reigns of William the Conqueror, William Rufus, and King Henry I., and who was the son and heir of Hamon Dentatus, Earl of Corboile, and Lord of Thorigny and Granville, in Normandy, which titles they held before Normandy was lost to the crown of England, whereby he justly claims his descent from the youngest son of the Duke of ·Normandy, as we ourselves do from the eldest." His lordship m. Jane, daughter of Sir Peter Wiche, comptroller of the household to King Charles I., and ambassador at Constantinople, by whom he had issue,

    CHARLES, his successor.

    JOHN, created, by Queen Anne, 9th March 1702, BARON GRANVILLE, of Potheridge, in the county of Devon, m. Rebecca, daughter of Sir John Child, of Wanstead, in Essex, and widow of Charles, Marquess of Worcester, but had no issue. His lordship was lord warden of the stanneries. He d. in 1707, when the BARONY became EXTINCT.

    Bevil, d. a bachelor.

    Jane, m. to Sir William Gower, and thus became great-great-grandmother to George

228

Granville Leveson Gower, present Marquess of Stafford.

    Catherine, m. to Craven Payton, Esq., of Lancashire.

    Grace, m. to Sir George Carteret, Bart., afterwards created BARON CARTERET, of Hawnes, in the county of Bedford, with remainder, in default of male issue, to his brothers, Philip and Edward. Her ladyship, after the decease of her husband, was herself elevated to the peerage, as Viscountess Carteret and Countess Granville (see Carteret, Lord Carteret).

    (These ladies became, eventually, co-heirs to their nephew, William Henry, Earl of Bath.) His lordship d. in August 1701, and was s. by his eldest son,

CHARLES GRANVILLE, second Earl of Bath, who had been summoned to parliament in the lifetime of his father, anno 1689, and had been created a count of the Roman empire by Emperor Leopold, for his eminent services, in the war of Hungary, where he was a volunteer in the army that defeated the Turks before Vienna, in 1683, and was the same year at the taking of Gran. His lordship m. first, Lady Martha Osborne, daughter of Thomas, first Duke of Leeds, by whom he had no surviving issue. He espoused, secondly, Isabella, daughter of Henry de Nassau, Velt Marshal Auverque, commander of the Dutch forces under the Duke of Marlborough, and had an only child,

    WILLIAM HENRY, his successor.

The earl died in twelve days after his father, being killed by the accidental discharge of his own pistol, at the time he was preparing for the interment of that nobleman. He was s. by his son,

WILLIAM HENRY GRANVILLE, third Earl of Bath, born 30th January 1691-2, but d., unmarried, of the small pox, in May 1711; when the EARLDOM OF BATH and inferior dignities became EXTINCT, while his estates passed to his lordship's aunts (revert to issue of John, first earl) as co-heiresses.

ARMS.—Gules, three suffiues or organ rests or.

GRANVILLE — BARON LANSDOWNE, OF BIDDEFORD, IN THE COUNTY OF DEVON.

By Letters Patent, dated 31st December, 1711.

Lineage.

GEORGE GRANVILLE, Esq., grandson of Sir Bevill Grandville, (being second son of his son, Bernard Granville,) and nephew of John Granville, first Earl of Bath, was elevated to the peerage, on the 31st December, 1711, as BARON LANSDOWNE, of *Biddeford, in the county of Devon.* His lordship m. Lady Mary Villiers, daughter of Edward, Earl of Jersey, and had issue,

    Mary, m. to William Graham, Esq., of Ireland.

    Grace, m. to Thomas Foley, Esq., of Stoke, in the county of Hereford, who was created

BARON FOLEY, of Kidderminster, in the county of Worcester, in 1776, of which marriage,

THOMAS, *present Lord Foley*, is grandson.

Elizabeth.

Anne.

Lord Lansdowne was secretary at war, and comptroller and treasurer of the household, in the reign of Queen Anne. He died in 1734, when the BARONY OF LANSDOWNE, in default of a male heir, became EXTINCT, and his estates devolved upon his daughters as co-heirs.

ARMS.—Same as those of Granville, Earls of Bath, with the necessary distinctive junior mark.

GRANVILLE—BARON GRANVILLE, OF POTHERIDGE, IN THE COUNTY OF DEVON.

Refer to Granville, Earl of Bath,
(John, second son of John, first Earl.)

GRENDON—BARON GRENDON.

By Writ of Summons, dated 29th December, 1299,
28 Edward I.

Lineage.

Of this family, deriving its appellation from a fair lordship of that name in the county of Warwick, where they had originally their chief residence, (and whereof there were several knights before,) was

SIR RALPH DE GRENDON, Knt., who in the 26th of Edward I., received command to be at Carlisle, (amongst other great men of that time,) well fitted with horse and arms, to march against the Scots, and was summoned to parliament as a BARON, in the 28th, 39d, and 33d, of the same monarch, but not afterwards. His lordship m. ——, and had issue,

ROBERT, his successor.

Joane, m. to John de Rochfort, and had issue,

Sir Ralph de Rochfort, Knt., who m. Joane, daughter of Sir Hugh Meynil.

Lord Grendon d. in 1331, and was s. by his son,

ROBERT GRENDON, second Baron. This being a person of weak intellect, Sir Roger de Chetwind, and Sir Philip de Chetwind, knights, with John de Freford, who had married his aunts, Joane, Alice, and Margaret Grendon, alleging that A. de Clinton, second wife of old Sir Ralph de Grendon, father of the late baron, had a joint estate with her husband in all their lands, challenged the whole inheritance, and accordingly entered upon the lands; whereupon ROBERT sought the protection of Henry, duke of Lancaster, yielding unto his grace the entire manor of Shenston, near Lichfield, in the county of Stafford, conditionally, that he would protect him in the possession of Grendon, and certain other lands in other places. In consequence of which arrangements, his uncles and aunts relinquished their pretended claim. He died

about the 22nd of Edward III., when those lands descended to his nephew, Sir Ralph Rochfort, Knt., whereupon Sir Ralph entailed them upon the issue of his own body, by Joane, his wife, daughter of Sir Hugh Meynil, with remainder to his three sisters successively, and then to Sir Richard Stafford, Knt., and his heirs. According to which settlement, the possession continued for divers years, until Sir Ralph Rochfort's death, when Joane, his widow, marrying, secondly, Hugh de Ashby, made an agreement with Sir William Chetwynd, Knt. (son and heir of Sir Philip,) by which Grendon at length came into the possession of the Chetwynds, and is now held by Sir George Chetwynd, Bart. The BARONY OF GRENDON, which fell into abeyance amongst the Rochforts, so continues with their representatives, if such exist.

ARMS.—Ar. two chevrons gules.

GRESLEY—BARON GRESLEY.

By Writ of Summons, dated 10th March, 1308,
1 Edward II.

Lineage.

In the year 1134,

ROBERT DE GRESLEI, of Manchester, in the county of Lancaster, having a large proportion of marsh land, at Swineshed in Lincolnshire, founded an abbey of Cistertian monks there. To this Robert s. his son,

ALBERT DE GRESLEI, who m. first, Agnes, daughter of Nigel, Baron of Halton; and secondly, a daughter of Thomas Basset. He d. about the year 1185, and was s. by his son,

ROBERT DE GRESLEI, who in the 6th of Richard I., being then of full age, attended that monarch in the expedition made into Normandy; but taking part with the barons towards the close of King John's reign, his lands were all seised by the crown. Making his peace, however, in the 2nd of Henry III., he had restitution of those lands, which lay in the counties of Oxford, Rutland, Lincolnshire, Lancashire, Norfolk, and Suffolk. He m. ——, daughter of Henry de Longchamp, (brother of William de Longchamp, Chancellor to King Richard I.,) and dying in 1230, was s. by his son,

THOMAS DE GRESLEI, who, in the 26th Henry III., had a military summons to march into France, but paid one hundred marks, beside his ordinary scutage, to be freed from the journey. In the 42nd of the same reign, he had another military summons to march against the Welch, and the next year he was constituted warden of the king's forests, south of Trent. He d. about the year 1261, and was s. by his son,

ROBERT DE GRESLEI, who in the 8th of Edward I., having married Hawyse, one of the daughters and co-heirs of John de Burgh, son of Hubert, Earl of Kent, had livery of her share of her father's lands: namely, Waukerley, Ringeston, and Porteslade. He d. in 1283, and was s. by his son,

THOMAS DE GRESLEY, who in the 34th of

Edward I., was made a knight of the Bath, and was summoned to parliament as a BARON, from the 1st to the 4th of Edward II., inclusive. His lordship died without issue, in 1347, when the BARONY OF GREBLEY became EXTINCT, but his great estates devolved upon his only sister and heiress,

> JOANE DE GREBLEY, who married John, son of Roger de la Warre, and brought her noble inheritance into that family.

ARMS.—Vairée, ermines and gules.

GREY—BARONS GREY, OF WILTON, IN THE COUNTY OF HEREFORD.

By Writ of Summons, dated 23rd June, 1295, 23 Edward I.

Lineage.

SIR JOHN DE GREY, second son of Henry de Grey, of Thurrock, in the county of Essex, (see Grey, of Codnor,) served the office of sheriff for the counties of Buckingham and Bedford, in the 23d of Henry III., and had summons to attend the king, in the 26th of the same reign, with horse and arms, upon the expedition then made into Flanders. In four years afterwards, Sir John was made constable of the Castle of Gannoc, in North Wales, and in the 33d of Henry, being then justice of Chester, had a grant of all the king's lands in Cheshire, and North Wales, to hold from the feast of the Purification of our Lady, for one whole year, rendering to the king five hundred marks at the feast of St. John Baptist, and the Nativity of Our Lord, by equal portions. The next year he had a similar grant: but Wales being then subjugated, Alan la Zouche supplanted him, and gave a higher rent: viz., eleven hundred marks per annum, for those lands. "In the 35th Henry III.," says Dugdale, "the Lady Joane Peyvre, widow of Pauline Pevere, (a great man in that age,) being possessed of all her husband's estate, sold to this John, the marriage of her son, for five hundred marks; he undertaking to discharge her of any fine to the king: whereupon he married him to his own daughter; and when this Joane heard that the king had given her in marriage, (as she was a widow,) to one Stephen de Salines, an alien, she by the advice of her friends, (being then in London,) matched herself to this John de Grey, which being told to the king, he grew much offended, but at length accepted of a fine of five hundred marks from him, for that transgression." In the 37th Henry III., Sir John de Grey was made governor of Northampton Castle, and the next year constituted steward of all Gascony; but in three years afterwards, "being an aged knight, much esteemed for his civility and valour, as also chief of the king's council," yet weary of the vanities of the court, he withdrew from public life. In the very next year, however, we find him nominated to the governorship of Shrewsbury Castle, and soon after appointed constable of that of Dover. In the 47th Henry III., he was sheriff of Herefordshire, and governor of Hereford Castle. The next year he had the custody of all the lands of Anker de Frescheville, in the counties of Nottingham and Derby. And was one of those barons who undertook that the king should abide the arbitration of Lewis, King of France, touching the misunderstanding with the barons. Remaining subsequently loyal to the king, he was appointed, after the victory of Evesham, sheriff for the counties of Nottingham and Derby. Sir John de Grey had issue,

> REGINALD, his successor.
> ———, m. to Robert de Tatshall.

He d. in 1265, and was s. by his son,

REGINALD DE GREY, who, in consideration of his faithful services to the king, obtained special livery of all his father's lands, although he had not then done his homage. In the 9th of Edward I., he was made justice of Chester, and merited so well, that for his manifold services, he had part of the honour of Monmouth conferred upon him by the king; and in further recompence of his services, obtained the Castle of Ruthyn and other lands. In 22d of Edward I., he received command to be at Portsmouth, to attend the king in Gascony, then menaced by the French, and the next year was summoned to parliament as a BARON. In two years afterwards, King Edward going into Flanders, committed the government of England in his absence, to Prince Edward, and appointed Lord Grey the prince's assistant; and the same year his lordship was one of the sureties on the part of the king, for the observance of the charters; after this we find him in the wars of Scotland. His lordship m. Maud, daughter and heiress of William, Lord Fitz-Hugh, by Hawys, daughter and heiress of Hugh de Longchamp, of Wilton Castle, in the county of Hereford, which came into the family of Grey by this marriage—by whom he had issue,

> JOHN, his successor.
> Joane, m. to Ralph, Lord Basset.

The baron, who had been summoned to parliament from 23d June, 1295, to 26th August, 1307, died in 1308, and was s. by his son,

JOHN DE GREY, second Baron, summoned to parliament, from 9th June, 1309, to 18th September, 1322. This nobleman, who at the decease of his father was forty years of age, had been previously distinguished in the service of the king; and we find him afterwards, constantly employed in the Scottish wars. In the 10th Edward II., he was constituted justice of North Wales, and Governor of the Castle of Caernarvon. His lordship m. first, Anne, daughter of William, Lord Ferrers of Groby, and had issue,

> HENRY, his successor.

He m. secondly, Maud, daughter of Ralph, Lord Basset, and had,

> Roger, who was summoned to parliament, as Lord Grey, de Ruthyn, in the 18th Edward II., a dignity enjoyed by his descendant.
>> Barbara Yelverton, present Baroness Grey de Ruthyn.

His lordship d. in 1323, seised, amongst other possessions, of the manor of Eston Grey, in Wilts, and the Castle of Ruthyn, in North Wales, and was s. by his elder son,

HENRY DE GREY, third Baron, summoned to

parliament from 30th December, 1334, to 12th September, 1342. This nobleman being abroad in the French wars, at the time of his father's death, and therefore not able to come to claim his inheritance so soon as he should, according to custom, have done, King Edward III., in the first year of his reign, in consideration of his eminent services, remitted him a debt he owed to the exchequer. His lordship m. Anne, daughter and heiress of Ralph Rockley, by Elizabeth, his wife, daughter of William Clare, (a younger son of Robert, Earl of Clare,) and dying in 1342, was s. by his only son,

REGINALD DE GREY, fourth Baron, summoned to parliament from 24th February, 1343, to 20th November, 1360. His lordship m. Maud, daughter and co-heir of John Botetourt, of Weoly, and dying in 1370, was succeeded by his son,

SIR HENRY DE GREY, fifth Baron, summoned to parliament as "Henry Grey, of Shirland, 1st December, 1376, and as "Henry Grey, of Wilton," from 4th August, 1377, to 20th November, 1394. This nobleman, during the life-time of his father, was in the immediate retinue of John of Gaunt, in the expedition made by that prince into Gascony, in 40th Edward III. His lordship m. Elizabeth, daughter of Thomas, Lord Talbot, and had issue,

    RICHARD, his successor.

    Margaret, m. to John, Lord Darcy.

Lord Grey d. in 1395, and was s. by his son,

RICHARD DE GREY, sixth Baron, but never summoned to parliament. This nobleman, at the decease of his father, was but three years of age, so that nothing occurs regarding him, until the 3rd of Henry V., when he appears to have been in the retinue of Thomas, Earl of Dorset, uncle of the king, and governor of Normandy, in an expedition made thither. His lordship m. first, Blanche, daughter and co-heiress of Sir Philip de la Vacche, K.G., by whom he had a son,

    REGINALD, his successor.

He m. secondly, Margaret ——, and had another son, William.

His lordship d. in 1442, and was s. by his elder son,

SIR REGINALD DE GREY, seventh baron, summoned to parliament from 13th January, 1445, to 14th October, 1495, as "Reginaldo Grey de Wilton, chevalier." His lordship m. Tacina, daughter of Sir Owen Tudor, by the Queen Dowager, Katherine, widow of King Henry V., and youngest daughter of Charles VI. of France, and dying in 1495, was s. by his son,

JOHN DE GREY, eighth baron, summoned to parliament as "Johanni Grey de Wilton," 16th January, 1497. In the 1st of Richard III., this nobleman obtained a grant from the crown of the manor of Wilsamstede, in the county of Bedford; and in the 11th of Henry VII., he fought stoutly at Blackheath against the Cornishmen, then in rebellion, under James, Lord Audley. In the next year he was in the wars of Scotland, under Giles, Lord D'Aubeny. His lordship m. Lady Anne Grey, daughter of Edmund, Earl of Kent, lord-treasurer, and dying before 1508, was s. by his son,

SIR EDMUND DE GREY, ninth baron, summoned to parliament, as "Edmundo Grey de Wil-

ton, Chl'r," 17th October, 1509. His lordship m. Florence, daughter and co-heir of Sir Ralph Hastings, third brother of William, first Lord Hastings, by whom he had issue,

    George,
    Thomas,   all successively Lords Grey, of
    Richard,   Wilton.
    William,

    Elizabeth, m. to John Brydges, first Lord Chandos.

His lordship d. in 1511, and was s by his eldest son,

GEORGE DE GREY, tenth baron, who d. in minority, and was s. by his brother,

THOMAS DE GREY, eleventh baron, at whose decease, also in minority, the title devolved upon his brother,

RICHARD GREY, twelfth baron, likewise a minor at his decease, when the title devolved upon his brother,

SIR WILLIAM GREY, thirteenth baron, summoned to parliament from 3d November, 1529, to 5th November, 1558, as "Willielmo Grey de Wilton, Chl'r." This nobleman was one of the commanders in the expedition made into France in the 36th of Henry VIII., under John, Lord Russell; and in the first year of Edward VI., being then a field-marshal and captain-general of horse in the army sent into Scotland, he placed himself at its head, and in that position made the first charge against the enemy. In the next year his lordship fortified Haddington, fired Dalkeith, and won the castle, spoiling much of the country around Edinburgh; after which, upon the commotions raised in England against the Reformation, he marched, at the head of fifteen hundred horse and foot, into Oxfordshire, and immediately restored tranquillity. His lordship was afterwards committed to the Tower as one of the partizans of the Protector Somerset, but was restored to his liberty after the decapitation of that unfortunate nobleman, and the next year made deputy of Calais, and governor of the castle of Guisnes, in Picardy. Lord Grey joined the Duke of Northumberland in his abortive effort to place Lady Jane Grey upon the throne; and it was to him the duke observed, in reference to the multitude of people that stood gazing at them when about to march from London, "Do you see, my Lord, what a conflux of people here is drawn together to see us march?—and yet, of all this multitude, you hear not so much as one that wisheth us success."

As governor of the castle of Guisnes, his lordship, after a gallant defence of that fortress against the French, was obliged to surrender it, and became, with all his officers, prisoner to the Duke of Guise, then commander-in-chief of the French army, by whom he was transferred to Marshal Stoszy, and finally passing to Count Rouchefoucalt, he continued in captivity until ransomed for twenty thousand crowns, which considerably impaired his fortune. "How he came to be attainted," says Dugdale, "I have not seen; but in the 1st of Elizabeth he was restored in blood;" and the next year, being then a KNIGHT of the GARTER, he was constituted governor of Berwick-upon-Tweed, and warden of the east and middle marches towards

Scotland. His lordship m. Lady Mary Somerset, daughter of Charles, Earl of Worcester, and had issue,

ARTHUR, his successor.

William.

Honora, m. to Henry Denny, Esq.

Lord Grey d. in 1562, at Cheston, in Hertfordshire, the house of his son-in-law, Denny ; and it was remarked, " that, on the same day died the greatest scholar and the greatest soldier of the nobility," namely Henry Manners, Earl of Rutland, and William Grey, Lord Grey, of Wilton. His lordship was s. by his elder son,

SIR ARTHUR GREY, fourteenth baron, summoned to parliament, as " Arthuro Grey de Wilton, Chl'r.," from 30th September, 1566, to 19th February, 1593. This nobleman was lord-lieutenant of Ireland in 1580, and acquired great fame by suppressing the rebellion of Desmond. He was subsequently one of the commissioners who sate in judgment on the unfortunate Mary, Queen of Scots, at Fotheringay, and he afterwards defended secretary Davison from the accusation of delivering the warrant of execution without the knowledge of Elizabeth, and, in a long speech, justified the foul murder of the Scottish princess. In the 31st of Elizabeth, he was one of the council of war, for the defence of the ports and havens against the celebrated Armada. His lordship m. first, Dorothy, natural daughter of Richard, Lord Zouch, of Harringworth, by whom he had an only daughter,

Elizabeth, m. to Sir Francis Goodwin, by whom she had a son,

Arthur Goodwin, whose daughter and heiress,

Jane, m. Philip, Lord Wharton.

Lord Grey espoused, secondly, Jane-Sibylla, daughter of Sir Richard Morison, Knt., and Countess Dowager of Bedford, and had issue,

THOMAS, his successor.

William, died s. p. in 1605.

Bridget, m. to Sir Rowland Egerton, Bart.

His lordship, who was a KNIGHT of the GARTER, d. in 1593, and was s. by his elder son,

SIR THOMAS GREY, fifteenth baron, summoned to parliament from 24th October, 1597, to 27th October, 1601. This nobleman being involved in what has been termed "Raleigh's Conspiracy," was arrested on the 19th July, 1603, and tried with Lord Cobham, at Winchester, on the 25th and 26th November following. Sir Dudley Carleton says, that after the abject defence of Cobham, " Grey, quite in another key, began with great assurance and alacrity, telling the lords, the judges, and the king's council, their duties in a long speech, and kept them the whole day to subtle traverses and subterfuges; but the evidence that he was acquainted with the surprise of the king, was too conspicuous, by Broke's and Markham's confessions. The lords," (continues Sir Dudley,) " were long ere they could agree, and loth to come out with so hard a censure against him ; most of them strove with themselves, and would fain, as it seems, have dispensed with their consciences, to have shewn him favour. After sentence, when he was

asked what he would say against its being denounced ? he replied, ' I have nothing to say, yet a word of Tacitus comes in my mouth :

' Non eadem omnibus decora.'

The house of Wilton have spent many lives in their prince's service, and Grey cannot ask his.'" His lordship was removed to the Tower, where he died 6th July, 1614, having received a pardon so far as the remission of the capital part of the sentence: but the barony of GREY OF WILTON expired under his lordship's attainder, and his estates became forfeited. Those at Whaddon, in Buckinghamshire, were, after his attainder, leased out to his widow, and after his death granted in fee to the favourite George Villiers, Duke of Buckingham. Wilton Castle, on the banks of the Wye, in Herefordshire, had been sold in the reign of Elizabeth, to the Hon. Charles Brydges, ancestor to the Dukes of Chandos—and upon the decease of the first duke it was, together with other large estates in the neighbourhood, sold to Guy's Hospital. Lord Grey having died without issue, and his only brother, William, previously also issueless, his sister of the whole blood, Bridget, wife of Sir Rowland Egerton, of Egerton, in Cheshire, became his heir. Her ladyship's interest in the estates, according to Carte, was purchased by Villiers for £11,000., and the procuring a baronetcy for Sir Rowland. Villiers was subsequently himself created Baron Whaddon, the mansion of the Greys.

From Sir Rowland Egerton, and Bridget Grey, his lady, descended lineally,

Sir Thomas Egerton, the seventh baronet, who was elevated to the peerage on 15th May, 1784, as Baron Grey, of Wilton Castle, in the county of Hereford, and advanced, on the 26th June, 1801, to the dignities of Viscount Grey de Wilton and EARL OF WILTON, with remainder to the second and younger sons of his daughter Eleanor, who had married Robert, Viscount Belgrave—now Earl Grosvenor—and the said honours, at his lordship's decease in 1814, were inherited by his grandson (according to the limitation),

The Honourable Thomas Grosvenor, who assumed the name of Egerton, and is the present EARL OF WILTON.

ARMS.—Barry of six ar. and az. in chief three fortesauxes, a tile of three points ar.

GREY — BARONS GREY, OF ROTHERFIELD, IN THE COUNTY OF OXFORD.

By Writ of Summons, dated 26th January, 1297, 25 Edward I.

Lineage.

ROBERT DE GREY, fourth son of Henry de Grey, of Thurroc, (see Barons Grey, of Codnor,) obtained from his brother, Walter de Grey, Archbishop of York, a gift of the major part of the lordship of Rotherfield, in the county of Oxford, and was s. by his son,

WALTER DE GREY, to whom the same prelate extended his bounty by a grant of all his lands in Gilesford, in Kent, Brighthelmstone, in Sussex, with Herdewyke and Coges, in the county of Oxford, which he had by assignment from Joan and Alice, the daughters and co-heirs of Robert de Araie, Baron of Coges, and likewise the residue of the manor of Rotherfield, together with divers other lordships. This Walter d. in 52nd Henry III., and was s. by his son,

ROBERT DE GREY, who m. Avice, daughter of William de St. Lis, and dying in 1294, was s. by his son,

JOHN DE GREY, then twenty-four years of age, who, soon after doing his homage, had livery of his inheritance; and in the 25th Edward I. had summons to the parliament, then held at Westminster, as a BARON. This nobleman appears to have taken part in the Scottish wars of Edward I. His lordship m. Margaret, daughter and co-heiress of William de Odingsells, of Maxtock, in the county of Warwick, and dying in 5th Edward II., was s. by his son,

JOHN DE GREY, second baron, who, in the 15th Edward II., making proof of his age, had livery of his lands; and in the 1st of Edward III. was in the wars of Scotland. In the 6th of the same reign, upon some difference between his lordship and William le Zouch, of Haryngworth, another great baron, which was heard before the king, Lord Grey, under the irritation of the moment, drew his knife upon Lord Zouch in the royal presence, whereupon both lords were committed to prison; but the Lord Zouch was soon afterwards released, while Lord Grey was remanded, and his lands seized upon by the crown. He was, however, within a short time, upon making submission, restored to favour; and in three years afterwards we find his lordship in Scotland upon the king's service, being of the retinue with Henry, Earl of Lancaster. From this period, for several years, he was engaged in the French wars, and in the 20th of Edward's reign he obtained licence to fortify his houses at Rotherfield Grey, in the county of Oxford, and Sculcotes, in the county of York, with embattled walls of lime and stone. The next year there being a tournament held at Eltham, in Kent, amongst other accoutrements prepared for that military exercise, his lordship had a hood of white cloth, embroidered with dancing men, in blue habits, buttoned before with large pearls, presented to him by the king. In the 26th Edward III. he was one of the commissioners in the counties of Oxford and Berks, for arraying and arming all men of ability within those shires, and leading them against the king's enemies, invasion being at that time threatened by the French. In the next year he was steward of the king's household, and had summons to parliament from the 1st to the 29th of Edward III. inclusive. His lordship m. first, Katherine, daughter and co-heir of Bryan Fitz-Alan, of Bedall, in the county of York, and had issue,

　　JOHN, his successor.
　　Maud, m. first, to John de Botetourt, of Weoley, and secondly, to Thomas de Harcourt.

He m. secondly, Avice, daughter and co-heir of

John, Lord Marmion, and had two sons, John and Robert, who both assumed their mother's name of Marmion (see Barons Marmion).

Lord Grey d. in 1359, and was s. by his eldest son, JOHN DE GREY, third baron, summoned to parliament as "Johanni de Grey de Rotherfeld," from 20th November, 1360, to 4th October, 1373. His lordship m. ———, and had issue,

　　JOHN, who m. Elizabeth, daughter of Sir Richard de Poynings, Knt., and dying before his father, left issue,
　　　　BARTHOLOMEW, who succeeded his grandfather.
　　　　Robert, who succeeded his brother.
　　　　Richard, died s. p.
　　Robert, who died without male issue, in the 41st Edward III.

Lord Grey d. in 1375, and was s. by his grandson, BARTHOLOMEW DE GREY, fourth baron, but never summoned to parliament. This nobleman, dying in 1376, unmarried, the title and estates devolved upon his brother,

ROBERT DE GREY, fifth baron, summoned to parliament in the 1st Richard II., but not afterwards. His lordship m. Elizabeth, daughter and co-heir of William de la Plaunche, of Haversham, in the county of Bucks, and dying in 1387, left an only daughter and heiress,

　　JOANE, who m. Sir John Deincourt, Knt., and by him left, at her decease, two daughters, viz.,
　　　　Alice, who m. first, William, Lord Lovel, and secondly, Sir Ralph Boteter.
　　　　Margaret, m. to Ralph, Lord Cromwell, of Tattersall, and died s. p.

The barony of GREY, OF ROTHERFIELD, vested, eventually, in John, Lord Lovel, son and heir of the above-mentioned Alice Deincourt, by William, Lord Lovel, and passed, at his decease, to his son Francis, Viscount Lovel, K.G., under whose attainder, in 1487, it EXPIRED.

ARMS.—Same as Grey, of Codnor.

GREY — BARON GREY, OF CODNOR, IN THE COUNTY OF DERBY.

By Writ of Summons, dated 6th February, 1299, 27 Edward I.

Lineage.

In the sixth year of King Richard I., that monarch conferred the manor of Thurrock, in the county of Essex (afterwards called Thurrock Grey), upon

HENRY DE GREY, which grant was confirmed by King John, who vouchsafed, by special charter, to permit the said Henry de Grey to hunt the hare and fox in any land belonging to the crown, save the king's own demesne-parks. In the 1st Henry III. he had also a grant of the manor of Grimston, in the county of Nottingham, and having afterwards married Isolda, niece and heiress of Robert Bardolf, shared in the inheritance of his lands. By this lady Henry de Grey had issue,

　　RICHARD, of whom presently.

2 H　　　　　　　　　　233

John, some time justice of Chester, progenitor of the Greys of Wilton, and Greys of Ruthyn.

William, of Landford, in the county of Notts, and Sandiacre, in the county of Derby.

Robert, of Rotherfield.

Walter, Archbishop of York.

This prelate lies buried in the cathedral church of York, under a tomb of curious gothic workmanship, having the bishop's effigy at full length, with his crosier lying at the bottom part.

Henry.

RICHARD DE GREY, of Codnor, in the county of Derby, the eldest son, having adhered to King John, had the lands of John de Humes, in Leicestershire, and Simon de Canci, in Lincolnshire, two of the rebellious barons, conferred upon him; and in the 10th Henry III. he was made governor of the Isles of Guernsey, Jersey, Alderney and Sarke: of which, in the 36th of the same king, he had a grant, in fee farm, for 400 marks, to be paid yearly into the king's exchequer. In which year the king, intending a pilgrimage to the Holy Land, and causing the bishops of Worcester and Chichester to preach a similar course to the people, this Richard and John, his brother, came forward, although, generally speaking, the discourses of the prelates had but little effect, which so pleased the king, that he embraced them in his arms, kissed them, and called them brothers. In a few years afterwards (42d Henry III.) we find Richard de Grey constable of Dover Castle and warden of the cinque ports, and being both diligent and trusty in those offices, discovered much treasure, which the Poictovins (then in high favour with the king) had ready to convey into France. "But about this time," says Dugdale, "there being no little contest, touching Athelmure, the king's brother, by the mother, then elect Bishop of Winchester; divers of the great barons opposing him, in regard he was of that party, against whom they took high exception, for misleading the king, and consuming the wealth of the land. Whereupon he fled to Rome, and by false suggestions, procured the pope's letters for his institution, which were sent by Walescho, a grey friar, who landed at Dover. The barons grew so incensed, that they forthwith sent Hugh Bigot, then Justice of England, thither, to inquire by what authority he was suffered to come on shore; who went to this Richard (then constable of the castle) and said, 'Have you been trusted by the people of England, as a faithful warden of the ports, and suffered this person to land, without our knowledge, to the manifest violation of your oath? We think you, not only unworthy of this place any longer, but to be farther questioned, for so great a transgression, tending to the public damage of the whole realm.' And thereupon took the custody of the castle, and of all the ports into his own hands." Subsequently to this period Richard de Grey arrayed himself under the baronial standard, and being, with his son John, in the army of young Simon de Montfort, at Kenilworth, was surprised in the night-time by a party from Prince Edward's army, and taken prisoner, with several other barons. For this treason

234

his lands were seised upon by the crown; but were afterwards restored, upon the payment of a fine under the decree, denominated "*Dictum de Kenilworth*." Richard de Grey m. Lucia, daughter and heiress of the John de Humes mentioned above, and was s. at his decease by his son,

JOHN DE GREY, who died in 1271, and was s. by his son,

HENRY DE GREY, who being in the king's army in Wales, in the 10th Edward I., had scutage from all his tenants, in the counties of Norfolk, Suffolk, Kent, Nottingham and Derby, that held of him by military service, and had summons, in the 22d of the same monarch, amongst other great men, to repair forthwith to the king, to consult about the urgent affairs of the realm, as also to be at Portsmouth, upon the first of the ensuing September, with horse and arms, to attend the king in his expedition into Gascony. After which he had summons to parliament as a BARON, from 6th February, 1299, to 6th August, 1308. His lordship was, for several years, actively engaged in the French and Scottish wars; in the latter of which he formed one of the immediate retinue of Prince Edward. He d. in 1308, and was s. by his elder son,

RICHARD DE GREY, second baron, summoned to parliament from 4th March, 1309, to 3d February, 1335. This nobleman was seneschal of Gascony in the 6th Edward II. In the 12th of the same reign he was in the wars of Scotland, and again the next year, when he was in the retinue of Thomas of Brotherton, Earl of Norfolk. In four years after, he was constituted steward of the duchy of Aquitaine, and within two years appointed constable of Nottingham Castle. In the 7th of Edward III., he had summons to attend the king at Newcastle, with horse and arms, to march against the Scots, but had a special dispensation from the service in consequence of his bodily infirmities. His lordship m. ———, and had issue,

JOHN, his successor.

Robert, of Cheriton-Grey, in the county of Somerset, which, with other lands, he inherited from Robert Fitz-Payn, and in consequence assumed the surname of Fitz-Paine. He m. Elizabeth, daughter and co-heir of Sir Guy de Bryan, and left an only daughter and heiress,

ISABEL, who m. Richard, Lord Poynings.

Richard, Lord Grey, d. in 1335, and was s. by his elder son,

JOHN DE GREY, third baron, summoned to parliament from 1st April, 1335, to 8th September, 1392, as "Johanni Grey de Codenore." This nobleman, during the life-time of his father, attained distinction in the Scottish wars, and, after his accession to the title, was engaged in those of Flanders; and so eminent were his services esteemed by the king, that his lordship received, about the 20th year of Edward's reign, from the hands of the monarch himself, a hood of white cloth, embroidered with blue men, buttoned before with great pearls; and being to perform divers military exercises in a tournament at Canterbury, had certain accoutrements of Indian silk, whereon the arms of Sir Stephen Cosyngton, Knt., were painted, bestowed upon him by the king. In two years afterwards, he again went into France, continuing in the retinue of Henry, Earl of Lancaster; and in four years subsequently, we find him joined in commission with Lord D'Eincourt, to array all the knights, esquires, and other able persons residing in the counties of Nottingham and Derby, and to conduct them to such places as should be needful for the defence of the realm, there being an invasion threatened at that time by the French. In the 29th of Edward III., his lordship was once more in France, as he was again in the 33d. But after all these military services, he obtained licence, in the 39th Edward III., to go on a pilgrimage; and in the 45th of the same reign, being then very aged, and not able to endure the fatigues of travelling, he had a special dispensation from the king (wherein his great and manifold services were gratefully acknowledged), to exempt him from coming to parliament and councils, and likewise from being charged with setting forth any soldiers whatsoever in the wars of that king, his heirs, or successors. His lordship m. ————, and had issue,

    HENRY, m. ————, and dying in the life-time of his father, left a son,
        RICHARD, who inherited the title.
    JOHN.
    Alice, m. to William de Everingham.
John, Lord Grey, of Codnor, KNIGHT of the GARTER, d. about the year 1392, and was s. by his grandson,

RICHARD DE GREY, fourth baron. This nobleman, who was in the French wars in the 17th and 21st of Richard II., was made admiral of the king's fleet from the mouth of the Thames to the northward, in the 2d of Henry IV., and soon afterwards constituted joint-governor of the castle of Roxborough, in Scotland, with Sir Stephen le Scrope. In the next year he was again in France upon the king's service; and in the 8th of the same monarch, his lordship was constituted constable of the castle of Nottingham, and chief ranger of Shirewood Forest, for life. After this we find him constantly employed upon confidential missions to the courts of France and Scotland, and he had summons to parliament, as "Richardo Grey de Codenore," from 13th November, 1393, to 3d September, 1417, being also a KNIGHT of the GARTER. His lordship m. Elizabeth, one of the daughters and co-heirs of Ralph, Lord Basset, of Sapcoate, and had issue,

    JOHN, his successor.
    Henry, successor to his brother.
    Elizabeth, m. to Sir John Zouche.
    Eleanor, m. to Thomas Newport.
    Lucie, m. to Rowland Lenthall.
His lordship d. in 1418, and was s. by his elder son,

JOHN DE GREY, fifth baron, summoned to parliament from 26th February, 1490, to 3d August, 1428, as John Grey, of Codnor. This nobleman d. in 1430, s. p. and was s. by his brother,

HENRY DE GREY, sixth baron, summoned to parliament, as Henry Grey, of Codnor, from 27th November, 1430, to 3d December, 1441. His lord-

ship m. Margaret, one of the daughters and co-heirs of Sir Henry Percy, of Athol, by whom (who m., after his decease, Sir Richard Vere, Knt.) he had an only son, his successor, at his decease in 1443.

HENRY DE GREY, seventh baron, summoned to parliament, as "Henrico Grey, Militi," but never with the addition of Codnor. This nobleman much affecting the study of chemistry, obtained, in the 3d of Edward IV., a licence from the crown to practise the transmutation of metals. His lordship d. in 1496, and, leaving no legitimate issue, his estates reverted to his aunts,

Elizabeth, wife of Sir John Zouche;	amongst whom, the BARONY OF GREY, OF CODNOR, fell into
Eleanor, wife of Thomas Newport;	ABEYANCE, as it continues with their de-
Lucie, wife of Sir Rowland Lenthall;	scendants.

Lord Grey left two illegitimate sons,
    Richard Grey, to whom he devised the manor of Radcliffe-upon-Trent, in the county of Notts.
    Henry Grey, from whom the Greys of Langley, in the county of Leicester, descended.
ARMS.—Barry of six, ar. and az., in chief three torteauxes.

NOTE.—"The last Lord Grey, of Codnor," says Leland, "left three daughters, whereof one was married to Sir Rowland Lentalle, of Nottyngham-shire; another to Newport, in Shropshire; and the third to one Souche, a younger brother of the house of the Lord Souches. These three had the Lord Greyes landes in copartion, whereof the lordship of Ailesford, in Kent, and How Hundred, was parte. There were some of the Lord Greyes, of Codnor, buryed at Ailesford Freres."

"Lentalle, dying without issue male, left two daughters, whereof one, called Catherine, was married to one of the Lord Zouches; the other to Cornwale, Baron of Burford; and so cam they to be copartiners in the Lord Grey of Codnor's lands."

GREY—BARONS GREY, OF GROBY, MARQUESSES OF DORSET, DUKE OF SUFFOLK.

Barony, by Writ of Summons, dated 26th Sept., 1300, 28 Edward I.

Marquisate, Dukedom,	} created, {	18th April, 1475. 11th October, 1551.

Lineage.

SIR EDWARD GREY, Knt., (eldest son of Reginald, Lord Grey, of Ruthyn, by Joan, his second wife, daughter and heir of Sir William de Astley, son and heir of Thomas, seventh Lord Astley,) espoused Elizabeth Ferrers, grand-daughter and heir of William Ferrers, Lord Ferrers, of Groby, and was summoned to parliament in her right, as Baron Ferrers, of Groby, from 14th December, 1446, to 2nd January, 1449, and as LORD GREY, OF GROBY, from 23rd September, 1449, to 26th May, 1455. That his lordship bore, in 1446, the former title is evident, from a special dispensation, which he obtained on 8th November in that year, from John Stafford, then Archbishop of Canterbury, whereby, in consequence of the distance of the manor house of Groby from the parish church, and "foulness of the ways thereto," he had licence to hristen the child, of which his lady was then pregnant, by the vicar of his chapel. The dispensation being addressed thus—"Nobili viro Edmundo Domino de Ferrers de Groby." His lordship had issue,

    JOHN (Sir), his successor.

    Edward, who m. Elizabeth Talbot, eldest daughter of Thomas, Lord L'Isle, and was created VISCOUNT L'ISLE.

    Reginald, slain at the battle of Wakefield.

    Anne, m. to Sir Edward Hungerford.

He d. in 1457, and was s. by his eldest son,

SIR JOHN GREY, second baron, but never summoned to parliament, who m. ELIZABETH WIDVILLE, daughter of Richard Widville, Earl Rivers, and had issue,

    THOMAS (Sir), his successor.

    Richard (Sir), beheaded in the 1st of Richard III.

Sir John Grey fell in the 39th Henry VI., at the battle of St. Albans, fighting under the colours of Lancaster. His widow becoming subsequently a suitor to King Edward IV., for some lands which had been given to her in jointure; the king was so enamoured of her beauty and gracefulness, that he, upon his part, became a suitor to the lady. But she, it is said, wisely answered him when he became importunate, "that as she did account herself too base to be his wife, so she did think herself too good to be his harlot." The result is well known. The king married her, and thereby incurred the wrath of the Earl of Warwick, which had nearly lost him his crown. In consequence of this great alliance her eldest son,

SIR THOMAS GREY, was created, on the 4th August, 1471, Earl of Huntingdon,* and advanced, on the 18th April, 1475, to the MARQUISATE OF DORSET, only "per Cincturam Gladii et Capæ Honoris impositionem." On which day he sate in his habit at the upper end of the table, among the knights, in St. Edward's chamber; and in the 22nd Edward IV., had livery of his lands without making proof of his age. But on the death of King Edward he was attainted of high treason, 1st Richard III., owing to his near relationship to the young King Edward V.; he was, however, fortunate enough to make his escape into Britanny, and joined the Earl of Richmond, who, after the battle of Bosworth-field, having ascended the throne, as HENRY VII., sent for the Marquess of Dorset, and restored him to all his honours. His lordship subsequently enjoyed the favour of the king, although at one time he was committed to the Tower. In the 7th of Henry VII. he was with the army sent to assist the Emperor Maximilian against the French; and in four years afterwards we find him one of the commanders who vanquished Lord Audley and the rebels at Blackheath. His lordship m. Cecilie,

daughter and heir of William, Lord Bonvile, of Harrington, and had, with other issue,

    THOMAS, his successor.

    Leonard, created Viscount Graney of the kingdom of Ireland, executed 31st Henry VIII.

    George, in holy orders.

    Dorothy, m. first, to Robert, Lord Willoughby de Broke, and secondly, to William Blount, Lord Mountjoy.

    Cecily, m. to John Sutton, Lord Dudley.

    Eleanor, m. to John Arundel, of Lanhern, in the county of Cornwall.

    Elizabeth, m. to Gerald Fitz-Gerald, Earl of Kildare.

    Mary, m. to Walter, Lord Ferrers, of Chartley.

    Margery, m. to Richard Wake, of Blisworth.

    Anne, m. to Richard Clement.

The Marquess, who was a Knight of the Garter, d. in 1501, and was s. by his eldest son,

THOMAS GREY, who was summoned to parliament on the 17th October, 1509, as Lord Ferrers, of Groby, but in the second parliament, in 1511, as MARQUESS OF DORSET. This nobleman, in the 3rd Henry VIII., was commander-in-chief of the army sent about the beginning of May into Spain, consisting of ten thousand men, whereof a moiety were archers, who, along with their bows and arrows, carried halberts, which they pitched in the ground until their arrows were shot, and then resumed them to charge the enemy. In this expedition were also his lordship's brothers, Lord Thomas Howard, son and heir of the Earl of Surrey, and the Lords Brooke, Willoughby, and Ferrers. This armament returned, however, to England without performing any service. It was designed as an augmentation of the forces of the Emperor Ferdinand in the invasion of Guyenne, but that monarch proposing another designation, not warranted by the commission which the general had received, he thought it his duty to re-embark, not, however, before he had lost some of his soldiers by sickness, and suffered indisposition himself. In two years afterwards the marquess and his brothers were with the Duke of Suffolk in France, at a just at St. Denis, where he acquired singular honour, as also in those celebrated tournaments, the 12th Henry VIII., at the interview, in Picardy, between the English and French monarchs. In the 14th of the same reign his lordship was sent to Calais, to attend the Emperor, Charles V., into England, who was at that period so sumptuously entertained by King Henry, being himself lodged in Black Friers, and his train in the king's (then newly beautified,) palace at Bridewell. "This Thomas, Marquess of Dorset, was esteemed the best general of those times for embattling an army, always observing the number, strength, and experience of his camp, and the nature and extent of the place, as well as the time, ground, persons, and quality of his enemies. And he was ever careful of good pay, lest his soldiers mutinied; of good diet and quarters, lest they failed; and of order, discipline, and temperance, lest they should be confused by sudden attacks, or enfeebled by sickness and distemper. His speech was soldier-like, plain, short, smart, and material;

---

* This dignity he relinquished upon being created Marquess of Dorset.

and notwithstanding the times could not endure his virtues, nor he their vices; he died full of honour at court, and applause in the country, with this monument from the king, (Henry VIII.,) ' That honest and good man.' The Collegiate Church of Astley, in the county of Warwick, (founded by Thomas, Lord Astley, whose heiress general married the ancestor of this marquess,) a most rare and beautiful piece of workmanship, having fallen down, a new chancel was erected by the parishioners. When, on opening the vault where the body of the marquess was laid, a large and long coffin of wood was found, which, at the curious desire of some, being burst open, the body, which had lain there seventy-eight years, appeared perfect in every respect, neither perished nor hardened, but the flesh, in colour, proportion, and softness, alike to any ordinary corpse newly interred. The body was about five feet eight inches in length, the face broad, and the hair yellow. All which seemed so well preserved from the strong embalming thereof." The marquess was one of those lords who, in the 22nd Henry VIII., signed the celebrated letter to Pope Clement, touching the king's divorce: and was also one who subscribed the forty-four articles of impeachment against Cardinal Wolsey. His lordship m. first, Eleanor, daughter of Oliver, Lord St. John, but had no issue. He espoused, secondly, Margaret, daughter of Sir Robert Wotton, Knt., of Bacton, in Kent, by whom he had (with other issue,)

> Henry, his successor.
> John, of Pergo, from whom the present Earl of Stamford derives.
> Elizabeth, m. to Thomas, Lord Audley.
> Catherine, m. to Henry, Earl of Arundel.
> Anne, m. to Henry Willoughby, of Wollaton, Notts.

This eminent personage died in 1530, and was s. by his eldest son,

HENRY GREY, third Marquess of Dorset, who in the 1st Edward VI., was constituted lord high constable of England, for three days only, by reason of the solemnity of the king's coronation. In the fourth of the same reign, he was made justice in eyre, of all the king's forests; and the next year warden of the east, west, and middle Marches, towards Scotland. His lordship was created Duke of Suffolk, on the 11th October, 1551, and installed a Knight of the most noble order of the Garter. He m. first, Katherine, daughter of William, Earl of Arundel, but by her had no issue. His grace espoused secondly, the Lady Frances Brandon, eldest daughter and co-heir of Charles, Duke of Suffolk, by Mary, dowager Queen of France, and sister of King Henry VIII., by whom he had,

> Jane, who m. Lord Guildford Dudley, and having aspired to the crown, at the decease of Edward VI., suffered decapitation for high treason, with her husband, Lord Guildford Dudley. In Walpole's Catalogue of Noble Authors, he terms the Lady Jane Grey, "this admiral young heroine," and the fairest ornament of her sex. "The works of this lovely scholar's writing," he says,

"are four Latin epistles; three to Bullinger, and one to her sister, the Lady Katharine, which was written the night before her death, in a Greek Testament, in which she had been reading, and sent to her sister. Her conference with Feckenham, Abbot of Westminster, who was deputed to convert her to the Catholic religion. A letter to Dr. Harding, her father's chaplain, who had apostatised a prayer for her own use, under imprisonment. Four Latin verses written in prison, with a pin." Her speech on the scaffold; and various others, of which mention is made by Baker and Hollingshed.

> Katherine, m. first, Henry, Lord Herbert, eldest son of William, Earl of Pembroke, from whom she was divorced. Her ladyship espoused secondly, Edward Seymour, Earl of Hertford, but not having the permission of Queen Elizabeth, she was committed, as well as her husband, to the Tower, where she died, 26th January, 1567; having had, by her second husband, three sons: Edward, the eldest, who died young; Thomas, the youngest, who m. Isabel, daughter of Edward Onley, Esq., of Catesby, in the county of Northampton, and died issueless—and
>
>> Edward, Lord Beauchamp, whose male line failed with William, third Duke of Somerset; but the youngest sister of that nobleman, Elizabeth, having espoused Thomas Bruce, first Earl of Aylesbury, had issue,
>>
>>> Charles, Earl of Aylesbury, whose eldest daughter and co-heir, Mary, espoused Henry Chandos, Marquess of Caernarvon; and her grand-daughter, Anne Elizabeth, present Duchess of Buckingham and Chandos, is now sole representative of this branch of the Grey family; and of Frances, eldest daughter of Charles Brandon, Duke of Suffolk, and his wife, Mary, Queen Dowager of France, sister of King Henry VIII.
>
> Mary, m. to Martin Keys, Groom Porter to Queen Elizabeth, and died, s. p.

Upon the demise of King Edward VI., the Duke of Suffolk, at the instigation of Dudley, Duke of Northumberland, (father of Lord Guildford Dudley,) proclaimed his daughter, the Lady Jane Grey, Queen of England, upon the allegation that the deceased monarch had so designated her ladyship in his will. This attempt proving abortive, the unhappy lady and her youthful husband, with her father-in-law, the ambitious Northumberland, were brought to the block, while Suffolk himself was reserved for a subsequent fate, for joining in Wyat's rebellion; he made an effort to raise the people in the counties of Warwick and Leicester, but being pursued by the Earl of Huntingdon, at the head of some forces, he was obliged to conceal himself within a hollow tree, in his park, at Astley, when being betrayed by Underwood, one of the keepers in whom he had confided, he was delivered up to his enemies, and beheaded on Tower Hill, 23rd February, 1554; being also attainted, his honours, viz., the DUKEDOM OF SUFFOLK, the BARONY OF GREY, OF GROBY, the MARQUISATE OF DORSET, and the Baronies of ASTLEY, BONVILE and HARRINGTON, became EXTINCT.

ARMS.—Barry of six ar. and az. three torteauxes in chief, and a label of three points ermine.

GREY—BARONS GREY, OF POWIS.

By Writ of Summons, dated 26th July, 1313, 7 Edward II.

Lineage.

EDWARD CHERLETON, *Lord Powis*, whose ancestor had been summoned to parliament in that dignity, in the 7th year of Edward II., died in 1422, leaving two daughters, his co-heirs, (between whom the barony fell into abeyance,) namely,

    JOAN, *m.* to Sir John de Grey, of whom we are about to treat.

    JOYCE, *m.* to John, Lord Tiptoft, and had issue,

        JOHN, created EARL OF WORCESTER, who was attainted of treason, 10th Edward IV., 1478.

The husband of the elder daughter,

SIR JOHN DE GREY, Knt., who was son of Sir Thomas Grey, of Berwyke, in the county of Northumberland, by Jane, daughter of John, Lord Moubray, was a very eminent military character in the time of Henry V. In the 2nd of that monarch's reign, he was with the king at the siege of Caen, and behaved himself so valiantly, that he had a grant of the castle and lordship of Tilye, in Normandy, then forfeited by Sir William Harcourt, an adherent of the king's enemies. He was subsequently sent with a guard into Powisland, where Sir John Oldcastle, the chief of the Lollards, had been taken, to bring that unfortunate personage before parliament. The next year, (6th Henry V.,) being again in the French wars, we find him Captain of Maunt, and obtaining, in further consideration of his services, a grant of the EARLDOM OF TANKERVILLE, in Normandy, to hold by homage, and delivery of a bassinet, or helmet, at the Castle of Roen, on the feast of St. George, yearly. Continuing in those wars, his lordship had several further grants, and was made governor of the castle of Tournay. But he was soon after slain, (at the battle of Baugy Bridge,) in fording a river, near the Castle of Beaufort, with the Duke of Clarence, and divers others of the English nobility. His lordship was *s.* by his son,

SIR HENRY GREY, Knt., as Earl of Tankerville. This nobleman being young at the time of his father's decease, (9th Henry V.) had not livery of his lands, until the 20th Henry VI., yet the fourth year of that reign, he was knighted, by John, Duke of Bedford: at which time, the king himself received the same honour, at Leicester. He *m.* Antigone, natural daughter of Humphrey Plan-

tagenet, Duke of Gloucester, and dying in the 28th Henry VI., (1449,) left issue,

    RICHARD, his successor.

    Humphrey, who *d.* issueless.

    Elizabeth, *m.* to Sir Roger Kynaston, Knt., from whom lineally descended,

        JOHN KYNASTON, Esq., who claimed the Barony of GREY DE POWIS, in 1732. He *d.* in 1733, and was *s.* by his elder surviving son,

            EDWARD KYNASTON, Esq., who died *s. p.*, in 1772, and was *s.* by his brother,

            ROGER KYNASTON, Esq., who *m.* Mary, only child of Henry Powell, Esq., of Worthin, in the county of Salop, and dying in 1786, was *s.* by his eldest son,

                JOHN KYNASTON, who assumed, by sign manual, the additional surname of POWELL. This gentleman claimed, unsuccessfully, in 1800, the BARONY OF POWIS. He was subsequently created a BARONET.

The elder son,

RICHARD GREY, Earl of Tankerville, adhering to the house of York, was attainted, with divers others, in the 38th of Henry VI. He was with the Earl of Warwick at the siege of Alnwick Castle, in the 2nd of Edward IV. "It does not appear," says Nicolas, "that this nobleman was ever summoned to parliament, but strong evidence exists that he sat in that assembly as a baron of the realm, in 1455." His lordship *m.* Margaret, daughter of James, Lord Audley, and dying 6th Edward VI., left issue,

    JOHN, of whom hereafter.

And a (presumed) daughter,

    Elizabeth, who *m.* Sir John Ludlow, of Hodnet, in the county of Salop, and had issue,

        ANNE, *m.* to THOMAS VERNON, Esq., of Stokesley, from whom descended through his daughter,

            ELEANOR VERNON, who *m.* Frances Curson, Esq., of Kidleston,

                SIR NATHANIEL CURZON, Bart., who opposed the claim of Mr. Kynaston, to the BARONY OF POWIS, and from whom the LORDS SCARSDALE derive.

        Alice, *m.* to Humphrey Vernon, Esq., (brother of the above Thomas,) from whom descended,

            SIR HENRY VERNON, Bart., (so created in 1660,) who was *s.* by his son,

                SIR THOMAS VERNON, second Baronet, who *d.* in 1684, leaving two daughters, Diana and Harriot, who both died unmarried, and a son, his successor,

                    SIR RICHARD VERNON, third Baronet, at

whose decease unmarried, his title and line became EXTINCT.

The Earldom of Tankerville, fell not only by the attainder of the earl, but France being lost to the English crown, it shared a similar fate. His lordship's son,

JOHN GREY, who obtained livery of his lands, in the 20th Edward IV., without making proof of his age, was summoned to parliament as a BARON, under the designation of "Johanni Grey de Powes," from 15th November, 1482, 22d Edward IV., to 16th January, 1497, 12th Henry VII. His lordship m. Lady Anne Herbert, daughter of William, Earl of Pembroke, and dying in 1494, was s. by his son,

JOHN GREY, second Baron Grey, of Powis, but never summoned to parliament. This nobleman m. Margaret, daughter of Edward, Lord Dudley, and dying in 1504, was s. by his son,

SIR EDWARD GREY, third Baron Grey, of Powis, summoned to parliament, from 3d November, 1529, to 23d January, 1552. This nobleman accompanied the Duke of Suffolk, 15th Henry VIII., in the expedition then made into France, and was at the taking of Bray and other places, won, at that time, from the French. His lordship m. Lady Anne Brandon, daughter and co-heir of Charles, Duke of Suffolk, by whom (who m., after his decease, Randle Hauworth, Esq.) he had no issue. He had illegitimate children by one Jane Orwell, namely, Edward, Anne, Jane and —— Grey, upon whom he entailed the greater part of his estates, composing the Barony of Powis. His lordship d. in 1552, when the BARONY OF GREY DE POWIS fell, it is supposed, into ABEYANCE, but between whom, has not been determined. Mr. Harris Nicolas, in his able Synopsis of the Peerage, to which the author of this work has been much indebted, deems the BARONY OF GREY DE POWIS created by the summons of Edward IV., not a continuation of that of CHERLETON OF POWIS, but a new and distinct peerage, and if he be right, the FORMER is EXTINCT.

Banks says, "Since this time (the death of Edward, the last lord) much uncertainty has prevailed respecting the right to the inheritance to the title; it being contended, on the one hand, that Richard, Earl of Tankerville, who d. 6th Edward ÷V., besides his son and successor JOHN, left a daughter Elizabeth, who m. Sir John Ludlow; who by her had issue, two daughters and co-heirs, Anne and Alice Ludlow, who m. the brothers, Thomas and Humphry Vernon; but on the other hand it is objected, that the said Richard, Earl of Tankerville, had not a daughter Elizabeth, m. to Ludlow, but had a sister ELIZABETH, m. to Sir Roger Kynaston, Knt. It appears, however, that anno 1584 (which is the first notice of Elizabeth in the herald's books) Henry Vernon (descended from the aforesaid Vernons) petitioned Queen Elizabeth, setting forth his claim to the barony of Powis; the matter was referred to the Lord Treasurer Burghley and the Earl of Leicester. Those two lords join in a letter, dated 22d September, 1584, to Cooke, Clarencieux, (garter being then vacant,) and Glover, Somerset Herald,

requiring them to examine into the proof of Mr. Vernon's claim, and to certify their opinion. And by a report, dated 22d October, 1584, they certified that they had examined into the descent of the Powis family, and after searching all the records and books of office, they find that none of the Lords Grey, of Powis, had a daughter, except Henry, who had a daughter, named Elizabeth, m. to Sir Roger Kynaston, from whom the Kynastons, of Hordley, are descended.

"After this, viz. in March 1731-2, John Kynaston, Esq. laid claim to this barony, as lineal heir of Edward Kynaston, of Hordley, next cousin in blood and heir of Edward, the last Lord Grey, of Powys; but he was opposed by Sir Nathaniel Curzon, Bart., (descended from the Vernons,) and resting his pretensions on the ground of being nearer in blood to the said Edward, Lord Powys; that is, from Elizabeth, daughter and at length heir of Richard, Lord Powis; whereas Mr. Kynaston claimed from Elizabeth, sister of the said Richard; and in support of the position, Sir Nathaniel adduced,

1. Three inquisitions, post mortem.
2. Three verdicts in actions at law.
3. Enjoyment of part of the Powys estate.
4. Printed books, herald's books and pedigrees.

"To the first it was answered, by Mr. Kynaston, that in hilary term, 27th Elizabeth 1585, in a cause in the court of wards, (inter Vernon and Grey, the bastard,) that court, by a solemn decree, reciting, that the said three inquisitions had been traversed, and in due form avoided, declared all these inquisitions insufficient.

"To the second head it was observed, that it was apprehended these verdicts would not affect Mr. Kynaston, as the then Mr. Kynaston, nor any person under whom he claims, are not made parties to the suits, and as such, the verdicts were to be considered as 'res inter alios acta.'

"On the third head it was asserted, it did not appear that the Vernons, (from whom Sir Nathaniel derived himself,) by any of their disputes, enjoyed any part of the Lord Powys' estate, excepting a small portion, part of which being in the neighbourhood of Curzon, might probably be purchased, as was the other part.

"And in relation to the last head, it was alleged, that none of the old heralds' books made any mention of this daughter Elizabeth, and the first visitation book, wherein mention is made of her, is above 118 years after the death of Richard, her supposed father. Whereas, Mr. Kynaston's family hath his marriage regularly entered in the herald's books according to the time; and though the name of John Ludlow be entered in the books of the time, yet a blank is left for his marriage; which, if it had been with Elizabeth Grey, is the more remarkable, as the Greys were one of the most considerable families of those days; and further, the last book, (G 15 Salop,) a visitation book, Salop 1584, page 61, has a pedigree of the Ludlows, and in one circle is entered, John Ludlow, of Stokesay, county of Salop, Esq., and in the circle adjoining is entered, Elizabeth, daughter of Richard Grey, Lord Powys; but these last words are of a different hand and ink from the rest of the pedigree, and were not the original entry in that circle, but the first words were 'D. of Robert Corbet, Knt.,' which were crossed out."

In 1800, JOHN KYNASTON POWELL, grandson of the aforesaid John Kynaston, became a new petitioner for the barony; but his case never came to a decision.

ARMS.—Gu. a lion rampant, within a border ingrailed, ar.

GREY — BARONS L'ISLE, VISCOUNTS L'ISLE.

Barony, } by Letters { ————, 1475.
Viscounty, } Patent, { 28th June, 1483.

Lineage.

SIR EDWARD GREY, Knt., second son of Edward Grey, Lord Ferrers, of Groby, having married Elizabeth Talbot, elder daughter of John Talbot, Viscount L'Isle, and sister and co-heir of Thomas Talbot, last Viscount L'Isle of that family, was created in the 15th Edward IV., BARON L'ISLE, the patent reciting to the effect of the preamble in that granted to John Talbot, (see Talbot, Viscount L'Isle,) and further stating, "that the said John Talbot had issue, Thomas, late Viscount L'Isle, and Elizabeth, then the wife of Edward Grey, Lord L'Isle, and Margaret, late the wife of George Vere; that the manor of Kingston L'Isle, descended to Thomas, late Viscount L'Isle, and that he dying s. p. the manor descended to Elizabeth and Margaret, as his heirs, and Margaret, dying without issue, Edward Grey, Lord L'Isle, and Elizabeth, his wife, were seised in fee of the manor, in right of Elizabeth, and had issue, John and others; the king, therefore, considering the premises, and that Warine L'Isle before mentioned, by reason of the lordship and manor of Kingston L'Isle, aforesaid, had the dignity of Baron and Lord de L'Isle, &c., recognised the right to the dignity of Edward Grey, and the heirs of his body, by the aforesaid Elizabeth, and granted the said BARONY to him, and the heirs of his body by the said Elizabeth." His lordship was subsequently created VISCOUNT L'ISLE, also by patent, dated 28th June, 1483. This nobleman in the 14th Edward IV., was retained by indenture to serve the king, in his "Duchy of Normandy and realm of France," for one whole year, with seven spears and fifty archers. In the 4th Henry VII., he was one of the commissioners for choosing archers in the county of Warwick, for the relief of the Duchy of Britanny. By the heiress of Talbot, his lordship had issue,

JOHN, his successor.

Anne, m. to John Willoughby.

Elizabeth, m. first, to Edmund Dudley, so notorious in the reign of Henry VII., and had, with other issue,

JOHN DUDLEY, created VISCOUNT L'ISLE, (see Dudley, Viscount L'Isle).

Muriel, m. to Henry Stafford, Earl of Wiltshire, and died s. p.

The Viscount had a second wife, Jane, who survived him, but he had no issue by her. He d. in 1491, and was s. by his son,

240

JOHN GREY, second Viscount L'Isle, who m. the lady Muriel Howard, daughter of Thomas, Duke of Norfolk, and dying in 1512, left an only daughter and heiress,

ELIZABETH GREY,

Upon the decease of Lord L'Isle, the VISCOUNTY OF L'ISLE expired, but the barony must have devolved upon his daughter, as his sole heiress, and likewise tenant of the manor of Kingston L'Isle. This lady was contracted to Charles Brandon, (afterwards Duke of Suffolk,) who was therefore created Viscount L'Isle, but refusing when at majority to fulfil the contract, the patent was cancelled. She afterwards m. Henry Courtenay, second Earl of Devon, but died s. p. before 1596, leaving her aunt Elizabeth, her father's only surviving sister, her heir, and who being seised of the manor of Kingston L'Isle, and heir general of John Talbot, Viscount L'Isle, is presumed to be legally entitled to the Barony of L'Isle, both under that patent, of 26th June, 1443, and under that to Edward Grey, her father; at her decease both these qualifications devolved upon her son, (by her first husband,) John Dudley,* but who never enjoyed the dignity; he was however created Viscount L'Isle, (see Dudley, Lord L'Isle).

ARMS.—Barrule of six, ar. and az. in chief three tortesuxes, a label ar.

GREY — EARLS OF KENT, VISCOUNT GOODERICH, OF GOODERICH CASTLE, IN THE COUNTY OF HEREFORD, EARL OF HAROLD, IN THE COUNTY OF BEDFORD, MARQUESS OF KENT, DUKE OF KENT, MARQUESS DE GREY.

Earldom of Kent, 3rd May, 1465.
Marquisate of Kent, and } 14th Dec., 1706.
  inferior honours, }
Dukedom, 28th April, 1710.
Marquisate, 9th May, 1740.

Lineage.

EDMUND GREY, fourth Lord Grey, of Ruthyn, having espoused the cause of the Yorkists, after the battle of Northampton, obtained from King Edward IV., the estate of Ampthill, in the county of Bedford, and other lands, which had belonged to the Lord Fanhope, and was subsequently made LORD TREASURER OF ENGLAND. Leland gives

---

* Sir John Dudley, sold the manor of Kingston L'Isle, to Mr. Hyde, from whom it passed in lineal succession to John Hyde, Esq., who died seised thereof, in May, 1745, and his widow sold the same in the following year to Abraham Atkins, Esq., of Clapham, in Surrey, whose case, as claimant to the Barony of L'Isle, as possessor of the manor of Kingston L'Isle, and consequently assignee of John Talbot, first Viscount L'Isle, was drawn up by the Hon. Hume Campbell, in 1790, under the title of "Case of the Barony of L'Isle."

the following account of this nobleman's conduct upon that occasion. "In the time of the civil war betwixt King Henry VI., and King Edward IV., there was a battel fought without the south suburbs of Northampton. The Lord Fanhope took totally King Henry's part. The Lord Grey, of Ruthyn, did the same in countenance; but a little afore the field, he practised with King Edward. Others saying that he had a title to the Lord Fanhope's lands at Antehille, and thereabout, or depraving him with false accusations, so wrought with King Edward, that he, with all his strong band of Walschemen, fell to King Edward's part, upon promise, that if Edward wan the field, he should have Antehille, and such lands as Fanhope had there. Edward wan the field, and Grey obtained Antehille, *cum pertinentiis*," &c.* His lordship appears to have attained in a very great degree the favour of King Edward, who besides conferring the treasureship upon him, created him, (he then bearing the titles of Lord Hastings, Wexford, and Ruthyn,) EARL OF KENT, with limitation to his heirs male. Which dignity was confirmed by King Richard III., and afterwards by Henry VII., so that his lordship seems to have played the part of the Vicar of Bray, long before that celebrated divine is supposed to have existed; and to have reposed in equal security upon a bed of *white* or *red* roses. The earl married the Lady Katherine Percy, daughter of Henry, Earl of Northumberland, and had surviving issue,

GEORGE, his successor.

John.

Elizabeth, *m.* to Sir Robert Greystock, Knt., son and heir of Ralph, Lord Greystock.

Anne, *m.* to John, Lord Grey, of Wilton.

His lordship *d.* in 1488, and was *s.* by his eldest surviving son,

GEORGE GREY, fifth Baron Grey de Ruthyn, and second Earl of Kent, who, being a military commander of high reputation, was one of the principal persons in the army, sent the 7th Henry VII. into France, under Jasper Tudor, Duke of Bedford, to the assistance of the Emperor Maximilian, but which army returned in a short time, without achieving any memorable action, by reason that Maximilian, for want of money, was unable to make his appearance. The earl was afterwards the chief commander against the Cornish men, who had risen under Lord Audley, and defeated those insurgents at Blackheath. His lordship *m.* first, Anne, daughter of Richard Widville, Earl Rivers, and widow of William, Viscount Bouchier, by whom he had an only son, RICHARD, his successor. He espoused secondly, Lady Katherine Herbert, daughter of William, Earl of Pembroke, and had issue,

HENRY (Sir), of Wrest, who inherited as fourth earl.

George, *d.* unmarried.

Anthony, of Branspeth, whose grandson, the

Rev. Anthony Grey, Rector of Burbache, inherited as NINTH EARL.

Anne, *m.* to John, Lord Hussey.

The earl *d.* in 1504, and was *s.* by his eldest son,

RICHARD GREY, sixth Baron Grey de Ruthyn, and third earl of Kent, K.G. This nobleman attended King Henry VIII., at the siege of Therouenne; but becoming an inveterate gamester, he wasted the whole of his estate, and died in poverty at the sign of the George, in Lombard-street, within the city of London, anno 1523. He *m.* Elizabeth, daughter of Sir William Hussee, Knt., Chief Justice of the King's Bench, and sister of John, Lord Hussey, but having no issue, the honours devolved upon his half brother,

SIR HENRY GREY, of Wrest, in the county of Bedford, who should have been, seventh Baron Grey de Ruthyn, and fourth Earl of Kent, but from the narrowness of his estate he declined assuming the peerage: He *m.* Anne, daughter of John Blanerhasset, Esq., by whom he had an only son,

　　HENRY, who *d.* in the life-time of his father, anno 1545. This gentleman *m.* Margaret, daughter of John St. John, Esq., of Bletsho, by whom he had issue,

　　　　Reginald,
　　　　Henry,　　} successively Earls of Kent.
　　　　Charles,

　　　　Katherine, *m.* first, —— Spencer, Esq., and secondly, —— Slayton, Esq., but died *s. p.*

Sir Henry Grey, *d.* in 1562, and was *s.* by his grandson,

REGINALD GREY, eighth Baron Grey de Ruthyn, and fifth Earl of Kent, which honours, having by frugality much improved his fortune, he assumed in 1571, and sate as one of the peers on the trial of the Duke of Norfolk in two years afterwards. His lordship *m.* Susan, daughter of Richard Bertie, Esq., and Katherine, Duchess of Suffolk, but dying *s. p.* in 1579-3, was *s.* by his brother,

SIR HENRY GREY, as ninth Baron Grey de Ruthyn, and sixth Earl of Kent. This nobleman was one of the peers on the trial of the unhappy Mary, of Scotland, (29th Eliz.,) and " evinced," says Dugdale, "much more zeal for her destruction, than befitted a person of honour." His lordship *m.* Mary, daughter of Sir John Cotton, and widow of Edward, Earl of Derby, by whom he had no issue, and dying in 1615, was *s.* by his brother,

CHARLES GREY, tenth Baron Grey de Ruthyn, and seventh Earl of Kent. His lordship *m.* Susan, daughter of Sir Richard Cotton, of Bedhampton, in the county of Hants, and had issue,

　　HENRY, his successor.

　　Susan, heir to her brother, *m.* Sir Michael Longueville, and her son,

　　　　CHARLES LONGUEVILLE, was confirmed in the BARONY OF GREY DE RUTHYN, in 1640. His lordship *d.* in 1643, leaving an only daughter and heiress,

　　　　　　SUSAN LONGUEVILLE, Baroness Grey de Ruthyn, who *m.* Sir Henry Yelverton, Bart., and from this marriage descends

　　　　　　BARBARA YELVERTON, pre-

---

* This account seems however quite erroneous, for Lysons, in his " Magna Britannia," relates, that the Lord Fanhope died in peace at Ampthill, seventeen years before the battle.

sent Baroness GREY DE RUTHYN.

The earl d. in 1695, and was s. by his son,

HENRY GREY, eleventh Baron Grey de Ruthyn, and eighth Earl of Kent, who m. Elizabeth, one of the daughters and co-heirs of Gilbert Talbot, Earl of Shrewsbury, but died in 1639, without issue. When the BARONY OF GREY DE RUTHYN, devolved upon his sister, Susan, Lady Longueville, and has since been enjoyed by her descendants; while the EARLDOM OF KENT passed according to the limitation to his distant relation, (revert to children of George, second earl,)

The Reverend

ANTHONY GREY, Rector of Burbace, in the county of Leicester, as ninth EARL OF KENT. This nobleman resisted strenuously the claim of Charles Longueville, to the Barony of GREY DE RUTHYN, upon the plea, "that when a barony by writ was once involved in an earldom, it should wait upon such earldom, and might not be subsequently transferred to another family, by a daughter and heiress, so long as the earldom continued in the male." But the decision was against his lordship, and it established the point, that an earldom, or other superior dignity, does not attract a barony in fee. The earl m. Magdalene, daughter of William Purefoy, Esq., of Caldecote, in the county of Warwick, by whom he had, with other issue,

HENRY, his successor.

Grace, m. to James Ward, Esq.

Magdalen, m. to John Brown, Esq.

Christian, m. to —— Burdet, Esq.

Patience, m. to —— Wood, Esq.

His lordship d. in 1643, and was s. by his eldest son, (there were four other sons, John, Job, Theophilus, and Nathaniel,)

HENRY GREY, tenth Earl of Kent, who m. first, Mary, daughter of Sir William Courteen, Knt., by whom he had a son,

Henry, who died young, in the earl's lifetime.

His lordship espoused, secondly, Amabel, daughter of Sir Anthony Benn, recorder of London, and widow of the Hon. Anthony Fane, a younger son of Francis, Earl of Westmorland, by whom he had issue,

ANTHONY, his successor.

Elizabeth, m. to Banastre Maynard, third Lord Maynard.

The earl d. in 1651, and his lady, who, from her numerous acts of benevolence, was called the "Good Countess," lived to the advanced age of ninety-two, surviving her husband forty-seven years. The Earl was succeeded by his only son,

ANTHONY GREY, eleventh Earl of Kent. His lordship m. Mary, daughter and heiress of John, first Baron Lucas, of Shenfield, in the county of Essex, which lady was created, on the 7th May, 1663, BARONESS LUCAS, of Crudwell in the county of Wilts, with remainder to her heirs male by the said earl; failing which, "the title not to be suspended, but to be enjoyed by such of the daughters and co-heirs, if any shall be, as other indivisible inheritances, by the common law of this realm, are usually possessed." The earl had issue by her ladyship,

HENRY, his successor.

Amabel, who d. unmarried.

His lordship d. in 1702, and was s. by his only son,

HENRY GREY, Lord Lucas, (a dignity which he had inherited at the decease of his mother, in 1700,) as twelfth Earl of Kent. His lordship was created, on the 14th December, 1706, Viscount Goodrich, of Goodrich Castle, in the county of Hereford; Earl of Harold, in the county of Bedford, and MARQUESS OF KENT. On the 23d April, 1710, his lordship obtained a dukedom, as DUKE OF KENT, and in three years afterwards was installed a KNIGHT of the GARTER. At the demise of Queen Anne, he was one of the lords entrusted with the administration of the kingdom, until the arrival of his majesty, King George I., by whom he was received with so much favour as to have several of the most honourable and important places and offices at court conferred upon him. Nor was he less esteemed by King George II., at whose coronation he carried St. Edward's staff, and was afterwards constituted lord-lieutenant and custos-rotulorum of the county of Bedford. His grace m. first, Jemima, eldest daughter of Thomas, Lord Crewe, of Steane, by whom he had, with two other sons who both died young,

ANTHONY, Earl of Harold, who was summoned to parliament as Lord Lucas, of Crudwell, in 1719, and the next year appointed one of the lords of the bed-chamber. His lordship m. Lady Mary Tufton, daughter of Thomas, Earl of Thanet; but d. without issue in 1723. His death is mentioned as having arisen from an ear of barley which his lordship had inadvertently put into his mouth, by which he was choked.

Henry, d. in the twenty-first year of his age, in 1717.

Amabel, m. John, Viscount Glenorchy, son and heir of John Campbell, Earl of Breadalbane; and dying in 1727, left an only daughter,

Lady Jemima Campbell, who m. Philip, second Earl of Hardwicke, and had two daughters,

Amabel, who s. as Baroness Lucas, and was created COUNTESS DE GREY.

Mary-Jemima, m. to Thomas Robinson, Lord Grantham, and had issue,

Thomas-Philip, present LORD GRANTHAM.

Frederick-John, created VISCOUNT GODERICH.

Jemima, m. to John, third Lord Ashburnham, and became grandmother of

George, present Earl of Ashburnham.

Anne, m. to Lord Charles Cavendish, brother of William, Duke of Devonshire.

Mary, m. to Dr. Gregory, Dean of Christ Church.

His grace espoused, secondly, Sophia, daughter of William, Duke of Devonshire, by whom he had a son, who died in infancy, and a daughter,

Anne-Sophia, m. to the Right Rev. John Egerton, Lord Bishop of Durham.

The duke having arranged the marriage of his granddaughter, Lady Jemima Campbell, with the Hon. Philip York, son and heir of Philip, Lord Hardwicke, was created MARQUESS DE GREY on the 9th May, 1740, with limitation to himself and his issue male; and in default thereof, to the said Lady Jemima Campbell, and her issue male. His grace died at Wrest House,* in Bedfordshire, on the 5th June, in the following year, when ALL HIS HONOURS became EXTINCT, save the MARQUISATE DE GREY and the BARONY OF LUCAS, which devolved upon his aforesaid grand-daughter, then Lady Jemima York, at whose decease, in 1770, without male issue, the MARQUISATE also became EXTINCT; but her ladyship's eldest daughter, Lady Amabel York, who m., in 1772, Alexander, Lord Polwarth, (created a British peer, as Lord Hume, of Berwick,) succeeded to the BARONY OF LUCAS, and was created, 5th October, 1816, COUNTESS DE GREY, with remainder, in default of male issue, to her sister, Jemima, Dowager-Baroness of Grantham, and her male issue.

ARMS.—Barry of six, ar. and az.; in chief three torteauxes.

GREY—BARONS GREY, OF WERKE, EARL OF TANKERVILLE.

Barony,	{ by Letters	11th February, 1694.
Earldom, &c.,	{ Patent,	11th June, 1695.

Lineage.

SIR THOMAS GREY, of Berwyke, in the county of Northumberland, m. Jane, (or Anne,) daughter of John, Lord Moubray, and had issue,

JOHN, from whom descended the BARONS GREY DE POWIS; see that dignity.

Thomas, (Sir) of whom presently.

Henry, (Sir) of Kettringham, in Suffolk.

William, Bishop of London.

Maud, m. to Sir Henry Ogle, Knt.

From the second son,

SIR THOMAS GREY, of Heton, descended

RALPH GREY, who m. Isabel, daughter and heir of Sir Thomas Grey, of Horton, and had issue,

* WREST HOUSE, *Bedfordshire.*—At this ancient seat of the Grey family, now in possession of Amabel, Countess de Grey, Lysons relates, that there is a great number of portraits, forming nearly a series of the Grey family from Henry, Earl of Kent, who assisted at the trial of Mary, Queen of Scots, down to the present time; amongst which is one of Elizabeth, Countess of Kent, who, in her widowhood, residing at Wrest, there patronised Butler the poet, and frequently entertained the learned Selden as her guest. The Duke of Kent, who was very partial to this seat, adorned the gardens with obelisks and various other buildings, particularly a magnificent banqueting-house, and a large room where he spent many convivial hours with some great statesmen who were his contemporaries, after enjoying his favourite amusement in the adjoining bowling-green.—BANKS.

WILLIAM GREY, Esq., of Chillingham, who was created a baronet, on 15th June, 1619, and elevated to the peerage, on 11th February, 1694, as BARON GREY OF WERKE, in the county of Northumberland. His lordship m. Anne, daughter and co-heir of Sir John Wentworth, of Gosfield, in the county of Essex, and had surviving issue,

RALPH, his successor.

Elizabeth, d. in 1692.

Katherine, m. first, to Sir Edward Moseley, Bart., of Hough, in the county of Lancaster; and secondly, to Charles, eldest son of Dudley, Lord North.

Lord Grey* died in 1674, and was s. by his son,

RALPH GREY, second Lord Grey, of Werke, who m. Catherine, daughter of Sir Edward Forde, Knt., of Hartling, in the county of Sussex, and widow of Alexander, eldest son of John, Lord Colepeper, by whom he had issue,

FORDE, his successor.

RALPH, who succeeded his brother.

Charles.

Catherine, m. to Richard Neville, Esq., and had issue,

GREY, m. Elizabeth, daughter of Sir John Boteler, and died s. p., in 1723.

HENRY, who assumed the surname of Grey, and died s. p., in 1740, leaving a widow, Elizabeth, who re-married John Wallop, Earl of Portsmouth.

Catherine, m. Richard Aldworth, Esq., of Stanlake, in the county of Oxford, and dying in 1740, left a son,

RICHARD, who assumed the surname and arms of NEVILLE, and was father of

RICHARD ALDWORTH NEVILLE, who succeeded, as second LORD BRAYBROOKE.

His lordship d. in 1675, and was s. by his eldest son,

FORDE GREY, third Lord Grey, of Werke. This nobleman joining in the rebellion of the Duke of Monmouth, commanded the horse at Sedgemoor, where he is accused of having treacherously deserted his post, and of flying at the first charge: certain it is, that he subsequently made terms for himself, and preserved his life by giving evidence against his associates. After the revolution, his lordship obtained the favour of King William, and was created by letters patent, dated 11th June, 1695, *Viscount Grey, of Glendale,* and EARL OF TANKERVILLE. He was afterwards a lord of the treasury, sworn of the privy council, and in 1700, Lord Privy-seal. He m. Mary, daughter of George, Lord Berkeley, and had an only daughter,

Mary, m. to Charles Bennet, second Lord Ossulston, who was created, after the extinction of the male line of the Greys, EARL OF TANKERVILLE. His lordship was great-

* When the Lord Keeper Lyttleton, deserted the House of Lords, in 1643, and carried the great seal to King Charles, at Oxford, this William, Lord Grey, of Werke, was elected Speaker for the House, at Westminster.

great grandfather, of the present Earl of Tankerville.

His lordship d. in 1701, when the Earldom of Tankerville and Viscounty of Glendale, became EXTINCT, while the Barony of Grey, of Werke, devolved upon his brother,

RALPH GREY, as fourth Baron. This nobleman attended King William in most of his campaigns, and was made governor of Barbadoes, in 1698. He died in 1706, when the Barony of GREY, OF WERKE, EXPIRED. His lordship devised a considerable estate to his cousin, William, Lord North and Grey, son of Charles, Lord Grey, of Rolleston.

ARMS.—Gules, a lion rampant within a border ingrailed ar.

GREYSTOCK — BARONS GREY-STOCK.

By Writ of Summons, dated 23rd June, 1295, 23d Edward I.

Lineage.

This family derived its surname from the Manor of GREYSTOKE in Cumberland, at which place,

THOMAS DE GREYSTOKE obtained a royal charter, 29th Henry III., to hold a weekly market and yearly fair. This Thomas m. Christian, daughter of Roger de Vipount, and was s. by his son,

ROBERT DE GREYSTOCK, who dying in the 38th Henry III., was s. by his brother,

WILLIAM DE GREYSTOCK, who paying £100. for his relief, and doing his fealty, had livery of the lands of his inheritance. This William had a military summons to attend the king, at Chester, 42nd Henry III., in order to restrain the hostilities of the Welch. He m. Mary, the eldest of the three daughters and co-heirs of Roger de Merlay, an eminent baron of the north, by whom he acquired the Manor of MORPETH, in Northumberland, and had issue, two sons, JOHN, and William, and a daughter, Margaret, m. to Sir Robert de la Val, Knt. This feudal lord died in 1288, and was s. by his elder son,

JOHN DE GREYSTOCK, who in the 22d Edward I., had summons with other great men, to attend the crown to advise upon certain important affairs of the nation, and in pursuance of that advice, went with the king into Gascony, the French monarch having then invaded those territories; where distinguishing himself in arms, he was the next year summoned to parliament as a BARON, and subsequently to all the parliaments of his time. In two years afterwards, we find his lordship again in the wars of Gascony, and then in the retinue of Anthony Bec, Bishop of Durham, and Patriarch of Jerusalem. In the 28th and 29th of Edward I., he was in the wars of Scotland. His lordship d. issueless, in 1305, when he settled his Manor and Barony of GREYSTOCK, upon his cousin RALPH, son of William Fitz-Ralph, Lord of Grimthorpe, in Yorkshire, son of the baron's aunt, Joane; his brothers and uncles being then all dead, without issue male, which

RALPH FITZ-WILLIAM, in the 10th Edward I.,

244

paid a fine to the king of one hundred marks, for licence to marry Margery, Widow of Nicholas Corbet, and daughter and heir of Hugh de Bolebec; and in the 24th of the same reign, as brother and heir of Geffery Fitz-William, of Yorkshire, had livery of the said Geffery's lands, upon doing his homage. This nobleman was much engaged in the wars of Scotland; and in the 7th of Edward II., we find him governor of Berwick, and joined in commission with John, Lord Moubray, and others, in the wardenship of the Marches. He was the next year governor of Carlisle, and founded a chantry at Tinemouth, for the soul of John, Lord Greystock, his kinsman, and all his ancestors. His lordship died in 1316, having had summons to parliament as a BARON, under the designation of "RALF FITZ-WILLIAM," from 23rd June, 1295, to 6th October, 1315. He was s. by his second, but eldest surviving son,

ROBERT FITZ-RALPH, second Baron, but never summoned to parliament, who m. Elizabeth, daughter of —— Nevill, of Stainton, in the county of Lincoln, and dying the year after his father, was s. by his son,

RALPH DE GREYSTOCK, which surname he assumed, and was summoned to parliament by that designation, from 15th May, 1321, to 17th September, 1322. His lordship by virtue of a special dispensation from the Pope, espoused Alice,[*] daughter of Hugh, Lord Audley, they being within the third and fourth degrees of consanguinity: and had an only son, WILLIAM. Lord Greystock having been a principal in seizing Sir Gilbert de Middleton, in the Castle of Mitford, for treason, was soon afterwards poisoned, while at breakfast, through the contrivance of that person. His death occurred in 1323, when he was s. by his son,

WILLIAM DE GREYSTOCK, fourth Baron, summoned to parliament from 20th November, 1348, to 15th December, 1357. This nobleman shared in the martial glories of Edward III.'s reign, and served in France under the Black Prince. He obtained permission to make a castle of his manor house, at Greystock, and was constituted governor of Berwick; but during his governorship, being commanded to attend, personally, King Edward into France, Berwick fell into the possession of the Scots, whereupon the king was much offended; it being clearly proved, however, that Lord Greystock was absent upon no other occasion, he obtained his pardon at the request of Queen Philippa. His lordship m. first, Lucy de Lucie, daughter of Lord Lucie, from whom he was divorced, without issue. He espoused, secondly, Joane, daughter of Lord Fitz-Hugh, by whom, (who married after his decease, Anthony de Lucie, and Sir Matthew Redman, Knt.) he had issue, RALPH, his successor, Robert and William, and a daughter, Alice, m. to Sir Robert de Harrington. He died in 1388, and was s. by his eldest son,

---

* Dugdale in one place, calls this lady, "Alice de Audeley," daughter of Hugh, Lord Audeley, and in another, "Alice," daughter of Ralph, Lord Nevill.

RALPH DE GREYSTOCK, fifth baron, summoned to parliament from 29th November, 1375, to 5th October, 1417, as "Radulfo Baroni de Greystok." This nobleman was constituted in the 39th Edward III., governor of Loughmaban castle, in Scotland, and one of the commissioners for guarding the west marches. Moreover, in the 1st Richard II., he was joined in commission with Henry, Duke of Northumberland, and others, for guarding the east and west marches, and the next year he assisted the earl in taking the castle of Warwick, of which the Scots had possessed themselves, by surprise. In the 4th Richard II. his lordship had the direction of the military expedition against the Scots; but was made prisoner by George, Earl of Dunbar, at Horseridge, in Glendail. His ransom cost 3,000 marks. His brother William went as a hostage for him to Dunbar, and died there of the pestilence. After his enlargement he was again constituted one of the commissioners for guarding the west marches. His lordship m. Catherine, daughter of Roger, Lord Clifford, and dying in 1417, was s. by his son,

SIR JOHN DE GREYSTOCK, sixth baron, summoned to parliament from 24th August, 1419, to 5th July, 1435. This nobleman was constituted, 9th Henry V., governor of Roxborough Castle, in Scotland, for four years, with an allowance of a thousand pounds per annum in time of peace, and two thousand in war. In the 1st of Henry VI. he was joined in commission, with the Bishop of London, and others, to treat of peace with James, king of Scotland; and was twice subsequently in a similar commission. In the 13th of the same reign his lordship was one of the chief commanders sent with the forces to the relief of Berwick, then besieged by the Scots. He m. Elizabeth, daughter and co-heir of Robert Ferrers, of Wemme, and had issue, RALPH, his successor, with three other sons, William, Richard, and Thomas, and a daughter, Elizabeth, married to Roger Thornton, whose only child and heiress, Elizabeth Thornton, espoused Sir George Lumley, Lord Lumley, from whom the present Earl of Scarborough collaterally descends. Lord Greystock d. in 1435, and was s. by his eldest son,

SIR RALPH DE GREYSTOCK, seventh baron, summoned to parliament from 29th October, 1439, to 15th September, 1485. This nobleman, who was frequently in commissions to treat with the Scots, m. Elizabeth, daughter of William, Lord Fitz-Hugh, and had an only son,

    ROBERT, who m. Elizabeth, daughter of Edmund Grey, Earl of Kent, and dying in the life-time of his father, 1st Richard III., left an infant daughter and heiress,

        ELIZABETH, who m. Thomas, LORD DACRE, of Gillesland, K.G., and conveyed the BARONY OF GREYSTOCK to her husband, when it became united with that of GILLESLAND.

Lord Greystock died in 1487, and was succeeded by his grand-daughter Elizabeth, who married, as stated above, Lord Dacre, of Gillesland—by this marriage, as also stated above, the baronies of Dacre and Greystock became united, and so continued until the decease of George, fifth Baron Dacre, of Gillesland, and Baron Greystock, in 1569, when it fell into ABEYANCE between his lordship's three sisters and co-heirs, viz.

    Anne, m. to Philip Howard, Earl of Arundel, ancestor of the Dukes of Norfolk.

    Mary, m. to Thomas, Lord Howard, of Walden, and died s. p.

    Elisabeth, m. to Lord William Howard, ancestor of the Earls of Carlisle.

And between the representatives of these co-heirs the BARONY OF GREYSTOCK is presumed still to be in ABEYANCE. Those representatives are,

William-Frances, LORD PETER, William, LORD STOURTON,	Representatives of Anne Dacre, through Winifred Howard, who married William, fifteenth Lord Stourton, and Anne Howard, who m. Robert - Edward, ninth Lord Petre, sisters and co-heirs of Philip Howard, brother of Edward, ninth Duke of Norfolk.

George, EARL OF CARLISLE, representative of Elisabeth Dacre.

ARMS.—Barry of six ar. and az. over all three chaplets gules.

GRIFFIN — BARONS GRIFFIN, OF BRAYBROKE CASTLE, IN THE COUNTY OF NORTHAMPTON.

By Letters Patent, dated 3rd December, 1688.

Lineage.

By a pedigree attested by *Sir Richard St. George*, and the learned *Camden*, it appears, that in the reign of Edward II.,

SIR JOHN GRIFFIN married the heiress of the family of the Favells, of Weston-Favel, in the county of Northampton, and obtained that seat, which became the place of his abode, and of his posterity, until the time of Henry IV., when

SIR THOMAS GRIFFIN married Elisabeth Latimer, only daughter of Warine, Lord Latimer, of Braybroke, by Katherine, sister and heir of John, Lord La Warr, and was s. by his son,

RICHARD GRIFFIN, who m. Anne, daughter of Richard Chamberlain, and was s. by his son,

JOHN GRIFFIN, Esq., who, in the 12th of Henry IV., upon the death of his great uncle, Edward, last Lord Latimer of Braybroke, was found to be his next heir, and had livery thereupon of the manor of Warden, and the castle of Braybroke, in the county of Northampton, with divers other lands in other shires. In the 4th of Henry VI. he was also found to be next heir to Thomas, the last Lord La Warr, but by virtue of an entail, made by the said Lord La Warr, Sir Reginald West was heir to his lands, being son of Sir Thomas West,

Knt., by Joan, his wife, daughter of Roger, Lord La Warre. To John Griffin, who died without issue, succeeded his brother,

SIR NICHOLAS GRIFFIN, of Braybroke, who was sheriff of Northamptonshire, in the 35th Henry VI. This gentleman m. Catherine, daughter of John Curson, Esq., and was s. by his son,

JOHN GRIFFIN, Esq., of Braybroke, who m. Emmot, daughter of Richard Wheathill, Esq., of Callis, and had issue,

　NICHOLAS (Sir), his successor.
　Mary, m. to John Touchet, Lord Audley.

He was s. at his decease by his son,

SIR NICHOLAS GRIFFIN, who was made one of the Knights of the Bath at the marriage of Prince Arthur, eldest son of King Henry VII., 17th November, 1501, and was sheriff of Northamptonshire in 1504. Sir Nicholas m. Alice, daughter of John Thornborough, Esq., and had two sons,

　1. THOMAS (Sir), who succeeded his father, and was sheriff of the county of Northampton in the 26th and 36th of Henry VIII. Sir Thomas m. Jane, eldest daughter and co-heir of Richard Newton, Esq., and was s. by his son,

　　RICE (Sir), who m. Elizabeth, daughter of Sir Thomas Brudenel, Knt., of Dean, in the county of Northampton, and left an only daughter and heiress,

　　　MARY GRIFFIN, who m. Thomas Markham, Esq., of Allerton. Thus terminated this branch of the family.

　2. Edward.

The younger son,

SIR EDWARD GRIFFIN having pursued the study of the law, was constituted solicitor-general in the 37th Henry VIII., and retained in that office till 6th Edward VI., when he was advanced to the attorney generalship; which he continued to hold during the reign of Mary. Sir Edward m. first, Elizabeth, daughter of —— Palmer, Esq., of Bowden, in the county of Northampton, by whom he had (with four daughters),

　EDWARD, his successor.

He m. secondly, Anne, daughter of Mr. Baron (John) Smith, of the exchequer, but had no issue; and he espoused thirdly, Elizabeth, daughter and heiress of Geffrey Chambers, Esq., of Stanmore, in the county of Middlesex, and widow of —— Coniers, Esq., of Wakerley, in the county of Northampton; of Lord St. John, and of Sir Walter Stoner, Knt., by whom he had a son,

　Rice (Sir), of Bickmarsh, who left a son,
　　EDWARD, who d. in 1659, leaving,
　　　Nicholas.
　　　Lucy.

The attorney-general was s. by his elder son,

SIR EDWARD GRIFFIN, of Dingley, K.B., who m. Lucy, daughter of —— Coniers, Esq., of Wakerley, by his step-mother, (the Attorney-General Griffin's last wife,) and had issue,

　THOMAS, his successor.
　Edward (Sir).
　Frances, m. to Sir Gregory Cromwel, Knt.
　Elizabeth, m. to Cecil Hall, Esq.

246

Anne, m. to Sir William Villiers, Bart.

Sir Edward was s. by his eldest son,

SIR THOMAS GRIFFIN b. in 1580, m. Elizabeth, daughter of George Touchet, Lord Audley, and widow of Sir John Stawel, K.B., and was s. by his son,

SIR EDWARD GRIFFIN, Knt., of Braybroke and Dingley, treasurer of the chamber to King Charles II. This gentleman m. ——, daughter of —— Uvedale, Esq., and dying in 1681, was s. by his son,

SIR EDWARD GRIFFIN, Lieut.-Colonel of the Duke of York's regiment of foot guards, (now called the Coldstream,) in the reign of King Charles II., who was advanced to the peerage, by letters patent, dated at Salisbury 3rd December, 1688, in the dignity of BARON GRIFFIN, of Braybroke. His lordship m. the Lady Essex Howard, only daughter and heiress of James, third Earl of Suffolk, and Baron Howard, of Walden. Lord Griffin adhering to the fortunes of King James II., attended that monarch upon his abdication into France, and was outlawed. He remained abroad until 1708, when, upon an intended invasion of Scotland, he embarked on the Salisbury man of war at Dunkirk; and was taken prisoner, with several others, by Sir John Byng, Knt., off the coast of North Britain. His lordship was then committed to the Tower of London, where he died in November, 1710, and was s. by his son,

JAMES GRIFFIN, second Baron Griffin, of Braybroke, who m. Anne, daughter and sole heiress of Richard Rainsford, Esq., eldest son of Sir Richard Rainsford, of Dallington, in the county of Northampton, lord chief justice of England, by whom he had issue,

　EDWARD, his successor.
　James, } both died s. p.
　Richard, }
　Elizabeth, m. first, to Henry Grey, Esq., of Billingbear, in the county of Berks, and secondly, to John Wallop, Earl of Portsmouth, but d. issueless.
　Anne, m. to William Whitwell, Esq., of Oundle, in the county of Northampton. This lady succeeded eventually as sole heiress of her brother, Edward, Lord Griffin.

Her eldest son,

　　JOHN GRIFFIN-WHITWELL, having obtained from his aunt the Countess of Portsmouth, her share of the estate of Saffron Walden, in Essex, assumed the surname and arms of GRIFFIN, and having his claim to the ancient Barony of Howard, of Walden, admitted, (as great-grandson of Lady Essex Howard, only child of James, Earl of Suffolk and Lord Howard, of Walden,) was summoned to parliament in that dignity. He was afterwards created BARON BRAYBROKE, with a special remainder, and that BARONY is now extant under the limitation.

His lordship d. in October, 1715, and was s. by his son,

EDWARD GRIFFIN, third Baron Griffin, who,

on the 1st February, 1796-7, took the oaths and his seat in parliament, having conformed to the established church. His lordship m. Mary, daughter of Anthony Welden, Esq., of Well, in the county of Lincoln, some time Governor of Bengal, by whom he had an only daughter, ESSEX, who d. unmarried in 1738. He d. himself in 1742, when the BARONY OF GRIFFIN, of Braybroke, became EXTINCT, and his lordship's estates devolved upon his sisters, as co-heirs (refer to the daughters of James, second baron).

ARMS.—Sa. a griffin segreant, az. his beak and fore legs, or.

GUELPH — DUKE OF CAMBRIDGE.

By Letters Patent, dated 9th November, 1706.

Lineage.

GEORGE AUGUSTUS GUELPH, Prince Electoral of Hanover, only son of *His Majesty* KING GEORGE I., was created a peer of Great Britain, 9th November, 1706, in the dignities of *Baron Tewkesbury, of Tewkesbury, in the county of Gloucester, Viscount Northallerton, in the county of York, Earl of Milford Haven*, and MARQUESS AND DUKE OF CAMBRIDGE. (His Royal Highness was created Prince of Wales, 22nd September, 1714). The prince succeeded to the throne as KING GEORGE II., on the demise of his father, 11th June, 1727, when all these honours merged in the CROWN.

GUELPH — DUKE OF CUMBERLAND.

By Letters Patent, dated 27th July, 1762.

Lineage.

WILLIAM AUGUSTUS GUELPH, second son of *His Majesty* KING GEORGE II., was created a peer of Great Britain by his grandfather, GEORGE I., 27th July, 1762, as *Baron of the Isle of Alderney, Viscount Trematon, in Cornwall, Earl of Kennington, Marquess of Berkhampsted*, and DUKE OF CUMBERLAND. His royal highness, who adopted early in life the profession of arms, attained a very high military reputation, for courage, conduct, and ability. He was with his father at the battle of Dettingen, and there displaying great gallantry, received a wound in the brunt of the engagement. In this conflict the British arms were victorious; but, subsequently, sustained a defeat under his royal highness at FONTENOY, owing, in a great measure, to the irresistible valour of the celebrated IRISH BRIGADE, which formed the rear guard of Marechal Saxe's army. It was upon that memorable occasion that the English monarch is said to have exclaimed in the bitterness of his fortune, "curst be those laws that array my own subjects against me." The duke, in 1746, commanded the English troops against the CHEVALIER, and terminated that very formidable rebellion by his decisive victory of CULLODEN.

The duke,[*] who was a KNIGHT of the most noble order of the GARTER, died unmarried in 1765, when all his honours became extinct.

GUELPH — DUKE OF CUMBERLAND AND STRATHERN.

By Letters Patent, dated 18th October, 1766.

Lineage.

HENRY-FREDERICK GUELPH, third son of His Royal Highness, Frederick, Prince of Wales, and brother of *His Majesty* KING GEORGE III., was created a peer of Great Britain, as DUKE OF CUMBERLAND AND STRATHERN, and of Ireland, as Earl of Dublin, on the 18th October, 1766. His Royal Highness was likewise installed a KNIGHT of the most noble order of the GARTER. This prince, after figuring in the annals of gallantry, espoused, in 1771, the Lady Anne Horton, widow of Christopher Horton, Esq., of Cotton Hall, in the county of Derby, and daughter of Simon Luttrell, first Earl of Carhampton. This marriage was received very unfavourably at court, and gave rise to the law soon after passed, known as the ROYAL MARRIAGE ACT, by which the subsequent marriages of the royal family were confined within specific limitations. His royal highness died in 1790, without issue, when all his honours became EXTINCT.

GUELPH — DUKE OF YORK AND ALBANY.

By Letters Patent, dated 29th June, 1716.

Lineage.

His Majesty KING GEORGE I., soon after his accession to the throne, created his brother,
EARNEST AUGUSTUS GUELPH, Bishop of Osnaburgh, DUKE OF YORK AND ALBANY, in the peerage of Great Britain, and Earl of Ulster, in that of Ireland. His royal highness was likewise invested with the GARTER. He died, unmarried, in 1728, when his honours became EXTINCT.

GUELPH — DUKE OF YORK AND ALBANY.

By Letters Patent, dated 1st April, 1760.

Lineage.

EDWARD AUGUSTUS GUELPH, second son of His Royal Highness, Frederick, Prince of Wales, and brother of *His Majesty* KING GEORGE III., was created DUKE OF YORK AND ALBANY, in the peerage of Great Britain, and Earl of Ulster in Ireland, on 1st April, 1760, but at the decease of this promising youth in 1767, those honours became again EXTINCT.

---

[*] There is a pedestrian statue of this prince upon a pillar of considerable altitude in the town of Birr, King's County, Ireland.

GUELPH — DUKE OF YORK AND ALBANY.

By Letters Patent, dated 27th November, 1784.

Lineage.

FREDERICK GUELPH, second son of His Majesty King George III., born 16th August, 1763, was elected the following year BISHOP OF OSNABURG, and chosen a Knight of the Bath in 1767. In June, 1771, he was elected a KNIGHT of the most noble order of the GARTER, and installed at Windsor, 25th of the same month. His royal highness was created a peer of Great Britain, as DUKE OF YORK AND ALBANY, and of Ireland, as Earl of Ulster, 27th November, 1784. The prince adopting the profession of arms, attained the rank of FIELD-MARSHAL and held for several years the high and important office of COMMANDER-IN-CHIEF of all the king's land forces in the united kingdom; during which period, and greatly owing to the efficiency of his royal highness's government, the British army acquired an unprecedented degree of glory, and the military banner of Great Britain waved as triumphantly as her naval pennant. The Duke of York espoused, 29th September, 1791, Princess Frederica Charlotte, eldest daughter of Frederick, King of Prussia, by whom, (who died 6th August, 1820,) he had no issue. His royal highness died, deeply lamented, 5th January, 1827, when all his honours became EXTINCT.

GUELPH — DUKE OF KENT AND STRATHERN.

By Letters Patent, dated 23rd April, 1799.

Lineage.

EDWARD GUELPH, fourth son of His Majesty KING GEORGE III., born 2nd November, 1767, was created a peer of Great Britain, as DUKE OF KENT AND STRATHERN, and of Ireland, as Earl of Dublin, on 23d April, 1799. His royal highness was a KNIGHT of the GARTER, and of St. Patrick, a Knight Grand Cross of the Bath, a field-marshal in the army, and colonel of the first regiment of foot. The duke espoused, in 1818, Her Serene Highness Victoria-Mary-Louisa, daughter of Francis, Duke of Saxe-Coburg-Saalfield, by whom he had an only daughter,

ALEXANDRINA-VICTORIA, born 24th May, 1819.

His royal highness died, deeply lamented, 23d January, 1820, when all his honours became EXTINCT; but his daughter is now HEIR PRESUMPTIVE to the crown.

HACCHE—BARON HACCHE.

By Writ of Summons, dated 6th February, 1299, 27 Edward I.

Lineage.

EUSTACE DE HACCHE, originally a menial servant to King Edward I., obtained from that monarch a charter of free-warren in all his demesne lands at Hacche, in the county of Wilts, as also at Norton-Merhull and Cestreton, in Warwickshire. He was afterwards, 22nd Edward I., made governor of Portsmouth, in which year he accompanied Edmund, Earl of Lancaster, in the expedition then made into Gascony. In two years afterwards he received command to attend the king at Carlisle, thence to march into Scotland against Robert Bruce, who had at that time assumed the sovereignty of that kingdom. In the 26th of Edward I., he was at the memorable battle of Fawkirk, and he continued for several years subsequently in the Scottish wars. He was summoned to parliament, as a BARON, from 6th February, 1299, to 22nd January, 1305. His lordship d. in the following year, leaving an only daughter and heiress,

JULIAN, m. to John Hansard, in whose representatives, if such are in being, the BARONY OF HACCHE is vested.

ARMS.—Or., a cross engrailed, gules.

HARCLA—BARON HARCLA. EARL OF CARLISLE.

Barony, by Writ of Summons, dated 15th May, 1321. 14 Edward II.
Earldom, by Charter, dated 25th March, 1322.

Lineage.

ANDREW DE HARCLA, (son of Michael de Harcla, Sheriff of Cumberland, from 13th to the 16th of Edward I., inclusive,) having distinguished himself in the Scottish wars, was constituted by King Edward II., governor of the castle of Carlisle, warden of the marches, and elevated to the peerage, by writ of summons, dated 15th May, 1321, as BARON HARCLA; in which year his lordship had the good fortune to completely rout the insurgents under Thomas Plantagenet, Earl of Lancaster, at Boroughbridge, and to seize the earl himself, whom he conveyed a prisoner to the king at York, and had soon afterwards executed at Pontefract. In consideration of this eminent service, his lordship was created an earl, under the title of EARL OF CARLISLE, by the girding of a sword, accompanied by a charter, in which it was covenanted, that for the better support of the dignity, he should have to himself, and the heirs male of his body, lands and rents in the counties of Cumberland and Westmoreland, of a thousand marks per annum value, and five hundred marks per annum more, in the marches of Wales, and until such provision should be made, that he should receive a thousand marks, per annum, out of the exchequer. Besides these substantial records of royal favour, this charter, for the first time, in such a grant, set forth in the preamble, a detail of the merits of the dignified person: it was dated at Pontefract, 25th March, 15th Edward II., anno 1332. "Thus elevated," says Dugdale, "from a mean condition, for he was merely a knight of small fortune, he grew so lofty, that he began to manifest the hatred publicly, which he had long privately borne, towards Hugh le Despencer, (the greatest and most powerful favourite of his time,) whom the king had recently advanced to the Earldom of Winchester."

This feeling towards Despencer, led the earl to make private overtures to the Scots, which being communicated to the king, he was seized (by Anthony de Luci,) at Carlisle, and brought to trial there, by virtue of a commission, dated at Knaresborough, 27th February, 16th Edward II., and directed to Edmund, Earl of Kent, John, Lord Hastings, Sir Ralph Basset, Sir John Peche, Sir John Wisham, and Geffrey le Scrope, Esq. Before this court, his lordship was accused of having conspired with James Douglas, a Scot, whereby the king, for lack of his assistance, was defeated in a battle, near the Abbey of Biland, in Yorkshire: so that he was necessitated for the security of his person, to fly to York: and the earl being found guilty, sentence was then and there pronounced against him: viz.—"That his sword should be taken from him, and his gilt spurs hacked from his heels. That he should then be drawn and hanged by the neck; his heart and bowels taken out of his body, burnt to ashes and winnowed; his body cut into quarters; one to be set on the principal tower of Carlisle Castle; another upon the tower at Newcastle-upon-Tyne; a third upon the bridge at York; and the fourth at Shrewsbury; while his head was to be placed upon London Bridge;" which judgment was executed upon the unhappy nobleman accordingly, on the morrow, after St. Chad's day, (3rd March,) 1322, and all his honours became, of course, FORFEITED.

His lordship had a brother, John de Harcla, who died the same year, seised of the Manor of Whitehall, in the county of Cumberland, leaving a son and heir, ANDREW, then three years of age.

ARMS.—Ar. a cross gules, in the first quarter, a martlet sa.

HAMILTON — EARLS OF CAMBRIDGE.

By Letters Patent, dated 16th June, 1619.

Lineage.

THE EARLDOM OF CAMBRIDGE merged in the crown, in 1461, upon the accession of *King Edward IV.*, who had previously borne that dignity, and it remained dormant from that period, until conferred, 16th June, 1619, by King James I., upon

JAMES HAMILTON, second Marquess of Hamilton, in Scotland, who was then created by letters patent, *Baron of Ennerdale, in Cumberland*, and EARL OF CAMBRIDGE, and was installed a knight of the Garter, at Windsor, 7th July, 1623. His lordship was lord steward of the household. He m. Anne, daughter of James, seventh Earl of Glencairne, by whom he had issue,

 JAMES, his successor.
 William, Earl of Lanark.
 Anne, m. to the Earl of Crawford.
 Margaret.
 Mary.

His lordship d. in 1625, and was s. by his elder son,

JAMES HAMILTON, second Earl of Cambridge. This nobleman carried the sword of state, at the coronation of King Charles I., and was advanced by that monarch, to the Scottish Dukedom of Hamilton. His grace espousing, actively, the cause of his royal master, was defeated and taken prisoner, by Cromwell, at the battle of Preston, and suffered decapitation, in old Palace Yard, 9th March, 1648. He m. Mary, daughter of William Fielding, Earl of Denbigh, by Susan, his wife, sister of George Villiers, Duke of Buckingham, and had surviving issue,

 ANNE, who, upon the decease of her uncle, became Duchess of Hamilton, in Scotland.

 Susanna, m. to John, Earl of Cassilis.

The duke dying thus, without male issue, was s. in all his honours, by his brother,

WILLIAM HAMILTON, Earl of Lanark, thus third Earl of Cambridge. This nobleman m. Elizabeth, daughter and co-heir of James Maxwell, Earl of Dirleton, by whom he had four daughters, viz.: Anne, Elizabeth, Mary, and Margaret. His grace fell like his brother, in the royal cause, having received a mortal wound, at the unfortunate battle of Worcester, in 1651, when the EARLDOM OF CAMBRIDGE, AND BARONY OF ENNERDALE, became EXTINCT; his own Scottish honour shared a similar fate, while the Dukedom of Hamilton, in Scotland, devolved, according to special limitation in the patent, upon his niece, the LADY ANNE HAMILTON, who married William Douglas, Earl of Selkirk, and from this union the present Duke of Hamilton lineally descends.

ARMS.—Gules, three cinque-foils ermine pierced.

HAMPDEN — VISCOUNTS HAMPDEN.

See TREVOR, Viscounts Hampden.

HANDLO—BARON HANDLO.

By Writ of Summons, dated 25th February, 1342, 16 Edward III.

JOHN DE HANDLO was summoned to parliament, as a BARON, on 25th February, 1342, but never afterwards. His lordship m. Maud, widow of John Lovel, and sister and heir of Edward Burnell. He d. in 1346, leaving his grandson,

EDMUND DE HANDLO, his heir. This Edmund died before he attained majority, anno 1355, leaving two daughters, his co-heirs, viz.,

 Elizabeth, m. to Sir Edmund de la Pole.
 Margaret, m. to Gilbert Chastlein.

 Both these ladies having died without issue, were succeeded in the estates by their kinsman, Hugh, Lord Burnell, son and heir of Nicholas de Handlo, second son of John, Lord Handlo; which Nicholas assumed his mother's name of Burnell.

As only one writ of summons was issued to John, Lord Handlo, the BARONY OF HANDLO is presumed to have, at his lordship's decease in 1346, become EXTINCT.

HARCOURT—BARONS HARCOURT, OF STANTON HARCOURT, IN THE COUNTY OF OXFORD, VISCOUNTS HARCOURT, EARLS HARCOURT.

Barony,	by Letters Patent,	3rd September, 1711.
Viscounty,		24th July, 1721.
Earldom,		1st December, 1749.

Lineage.

This ancient and eminent family traced its pedigree to BARNARD, a nobleman of the royal blood of Saxony, who acquired, in 876, when ROLLO, the Dane, made himself master of Normandy, the lordships of *Harcourt*, Calleville, and Beauficel, in that principality. From this nobleman descended

ERRAND DE HARCOURT, commander of the archers of Val-de-Ruel, in the army which successfully invaded England in 1066, under the Duke of Normandy. The second son of this warrior, Robert de Harcourt, is said to be the ancestor of the present Earl of Harcourt; but the immediate founder of the honours of the family was

SIMON HARCOURT, Esq., (grandson of Sir Simon Harcourt, Knt., a military officer of high renown, who was appointed governor of Dublin in 1642, and immediately raised the blockade of that city, then invested by the rebels, but fell soon after, before the castle of Carrick-Main, in the county of Wicklow,) a lawyer of eminence, who filled the offices of solicitor and attorney-general, with little interruption, from 1702 until 1710, when he was nominated lord-keeper of the great seal, and sworn a member of the privy-council. In the following year, 3rd September, 1711, he was elevated to the peerage, by the title of BARON HARCOURT, *of Stanton-Harcourt, in the county of Oxford;* and on the 7th April, 1712, declared LORD HIGH-CHANCELLOR OF GREAT BRITAIN, which great office he continued to fill until the accession of George I., in 1714. On the 24th July, 1721, his lordship was created *Viscount Harcourt,* and, in the following month, again called to the council-board. The viscount was appointed one of the lords-justices in 1723, 1725, and 1727. His lordship m. thrice, but had issue only by his first wife, Rebecca, daughter of the Rev. Thomas Clark, M.A., viz., one surviving son and two daughters. He d. on the 29th of July, 1727, and was s. by his grandson, (the son of the Honourable Simon Harcourt, M.P., by Elizabeth, daughter of John Evelyn, Esq., of Wotton,)

SIMON HARCOURT, second viscount, who was created, on the 21st December, 1749, *Viscount Nuneham, of Nuneham-Courtney,* and EARL OF HARCOURT, *of Stanton-Harcourt.* His lordship was the twenty-seventh in paternal descent from Bernard, Lord of Harcourt, in Normandy. He m., in 1735, Rebecca, only daughter and heiress of Charles Le Bas, Esq., of Pipwell Abbey, in the county of Northampton, by whom he had issue,

GEORGE-SIMON, his successor.

WILLIAM, successor to his brother.

Elizabeth, who was one of the ten young ladies,

250

daughters of dukes and earls, who supported the train of Queen Charlotte, at her majesty's nuptials, 8th of September, 1761. Her ladyship m., in 1763, Sir W. Lee, Bart., and d. in 1811, leaving issue.

The earl, who had filled some high diplomatic stations during the reign of King George II., was constituted, in 1751, governor to his late majesty, King George III., then Prince of Wales; and in 1761, his lordship was nominated ambassador-extraordinary to demand the Princess Charlotte, of Mecklenburgh Strelits, in marriage for that monarch. In 1772 he was appointed viceroy of Ireland. His lordship lost his life, on the 16th September, 1777, by unfortunately falling into a well in his own park, at Nuneham, and was s. by his eldest son,

GEORGE SIMON HARCOURT, second earl, who died without issue, in April, 1809, when the honours devolved upon his brother,

WILLIAM HARCOURT, third earl. This nobleman was born 20th March, 1743, and, adopting the profession of arms, attained the high rank of FIELD-MARSHAL. He was colonel of the 16th regiment of dragoons, and a Knight Grand Cross of the Bath. His lordship m., in 1778, Mary, relict of Thomas Lockhart, Esq., and daughter of the Rev. William Danby, D.D., of Marhamshire, in the county of York; but dying s. p. 18th June, 1830, ALL HIS HONOURS became EXTINCT.

ARMS.—Gu., two bars, or.

HARINGTON — BARONS HARINGTON.

By Writ of Summons, dated 30th December, 1324, 18 Edward II.

Lineage.

The family of HARINGTON derived their surname from HAVERINGTON, in the county of Cumberland, a lordship which they very anciently possessed; but from the time of Edward I., their chief seat and residence was at ALDINGHAM, in Lancashire, which manor was acquired by

ROBERT DE HARINGTON, with his wife, Agnes, sister and heir of William de Cancefield, son and heir of Richard de Cancefield, by Alice his wife, sister and heir of Michael Flameng, LORD OF ALDINGHAM. To this Robert succeeded his eldest son,

JOHN DE HARINGTON, who, in the 34th Edward I., amongst the rest of those stout young soldiers which were then to attend the king into Scotland, received the honour of knighthood, with Prince Edward, by bathing and other sacred ceremonies. Sir John had a military summons, in the 4th of Edward II., for the Scottish wars. In the the 12th of the same reign he had a charter of free-warren in all his demesne-lands in the counties of York and Lancaster, and in the 14th of Edward III., a licence to impark six hundred acres of wood, moor, and marsh, within the precincts of his lordship of Aldingham. He was summoned to parliament, as a BARON, from 30th December, 1324, to 13th November, 1348. His lordship m. Margaret, daughter of Sir Richard Bartingham, Knt., and had an only son,

    ROBERT, who died in the life-time of his father, leaving issue, by his wife, Elizabeth, one of the daughters and co-heirs of John de Multon, of Egremond,

      JOHN, successor to his grandfather.

      Robert, from whom descended the Lords Harington, of Exton.

      Simon, ancestor of the Harringtons, of Rishton.

Lord Harington died in 1347, and was s. by his grandson,

JOHN DE HARINGTON, second baron, summoned to parliament from 14th February, 1348, to 10th March, 1349. This nobleman d. in 1363, seised of the third part of the manor of Multon, in the county of Lincoln—of the manors of Aldingham, Thirnum, and a moiety of the manor of Ulveston, in Lancashire—of the manor of Austwyke, in the county of York, and of those of Millum, Mosearghe, Haverington, with its members, and a third part of the manor of Egremond, in Cumberland. He was s. by his son, then in minority,

ROBERT DE HARINGTON, third baron, summoned to parliament from 4th August, 1377, during the remainder of his life. This nobleman received the honour of knighthood at the coronation of Richard II., and was the same year employed in that monarch's service at Calais. His lordship m. Isabel, daughter and co-heir of Sir Nigel Loryng, K.G., and had issue,

    JOHN (Sir), his successor.

    William, successor to his brother.

He died in 1406, and was s. by his elder son,

SIR JOHN DE HARINGTON, fourth baron, summoned to parliament under the misnomer of ROBERT,[*] from his accession to the peerage until 3rd September, 1417. This nobleman was in the expedition made into France in the 3rd Henry V.; and the next year, being retained by indenture to serve the king in those wars, he received £295. in hand, towards his wages, upon that account. But soon after, purposing to travel into foreign parts, he declared his testament, 8th June, 1417, bequeathing his body to be buried wheresoever he should happen to die, and leaving to Elizabeth, his wife, one-half of all his silver vessels; after which he survived not a year, for the probate of that will bears date 27th April, next ensuing year. Leaving no issue, his lordship was s. by his brother,

SIR WILLIAM DE HARINGTON, fifth baron, summoned to parliament from 26th February, 1421, to 6th September, 1439. This nobleman served the

_____

* The name of *Robert* de Harington occurs regularly in the summonses to parliament, from 1st Richard II. to 4th Henry V.; but as Robert, the last baron, died in 1406, (twelve years before the latter period,) and as *John*, Baron Harington, is stated in the Rolls of Parliament to have been present on the 22nd December, 8th Henry IV., 1406, it may be inferred that all the writs after the 7th Henry IV. were directed to this baron, and that the christian name of *Robert* on the rolls, after that year, was an error.—NICOLAS.

office of sheriff for Yorkshire, and was governor of the castle at York, in the 10th Henry V., he was afterwards several years engaged in the wars of France in the reigns of Henry V. and Henry VI. His lordship m. Margaret, the sister of Thomas, son of Sir Robert Nevill, of Thornby, Knt., and had an only child,

    ELIZABETH, (who died in her father's life-time,) m. to William, Lord Bonville, and had a son,

      WILLIAM BONVILLE, who, in her right, became Lord Harington, died in the life-time of his father, leaving a daughter,

        CECILY BONVILLE, who m. first, Thomas Grey, Marquess of Dorset, and secondly, Henry Stafford, Earl of Wiltshire.

Lord Harington d. in 1457, leaving his grandson, WILLIAM BONVILLE, above-mentioned, his heir. CECILY BONVILLE, the daughter and heiress of the said William, having espoused Thomas Grey, first Marquess of Dorset, for her first husband, she conveyed the BARONIES OF BONVILLE AND HARINGTON to the noble house of Grey, where they continued until the attainder in 1554 of Henry Grey, Duke of Suffolk, grandson of the said Cecily Bonville, and the said Thomas, Marquess of Dorset, when those dignities, along with his grace's other high honours, became EXTINCT. By her second husband, Henry Stafford, Earl of Wiltshire, Cecily Bonville had no issue.

ARMS.—Sa. a fret, ar.

HARINGTON — BARONS HARINGTON, OF EXTON, IN THE COUNTY OF RUTLAND.

By Letters Patent, dated 21st July, 1603.

Lineage.

This is a branch of the ancient family of Harington, barons by writ, springing from

SIR ROBERT DE HARINGTON, grandson of Sir John de Harington, who had been summoned to parliament in the reign of Edward II., and second son of Robert de Harington, and his wife, Elizabeth, daughter and co-heir of John de Multon, of Egremond. This Sir Robert left a son,

JOHN DE HARINGTON, who m. Agnes, daughter of Lawrence Flete, Esq., of Flete, in the county of Lincoln, and dying in 1421, was s. by his son,

ROBERT DE HARINGTON, who wedded one of the daughters and co-heirs of John de la Laund, and was s. by his son,

JOHN DE HARINGTON, who having married Catherine, daughter and heir of Sir Thomas Colepeper, acquired thereby the manor of EXTON, in Rutlandshire, and fixed his residence there. He was s. by his son,

ROBERT HARINGTON, Esq., of Exton, who served the office of sheriff for the county of Rutland in 1492 and 1498. He m. Maud, daughter of Sir John Prisett, Knt., chief justice of the court of

Common Pleas, and dying in 1591, was *s.* by his son,

SIR JOHN HARINGTON, Knt., of Exton, whose son,

SIR JOHN HARINGTON, Knt., *m.* Elizabeth, daughter and heir of Robert Moton, of Peckleton, in the county of Leicester. This Sir John was treasurer of the army at Boulogne, temp. Henry VIII., he was *s.* at his decease by his son,

SIR JAMES HARINGTON, Knt., of Exton, who *m.* Lucy, daughter of Sir William Sidney, of Penshurst, and sister of Sir Philip Sidney, K.G., by whom he had three sons, viz.

> JOHN, his successor.
> Henry, (Sir).
> James, of Ridlington, in the county of Rutland, who was created a BARONET, 29th June, 1611; a dignity now enjoyed by his descendants, SIR JOHN EDWARD HARINGTON, BART., of Ridlington.

Sir James *d.* in 1592, and was *s.* by his eldest son,

SIR JOHN HARINGTON, Knt., who was elevated to the peerage by letters patent, dated 21st July, 1603, as BARON HARINGTON, *of Exton.* His lordship was tutor to the Princess Elizabeth, daughter of King James I., until her marriage with the Electoral-Palatine, when he attended her royal highness into Germany. He *m.* Anne, only daughter and heiress of Robert Kelway, Esq., surveyor of the court of wards and liveries, and had issue,

> JOHN, his successor.
> Lucie, *m.* to Edward Russell, third Earl of Bedford, and died *s. p.*
> Frances, *m.* to Sir Robert Chichester, K.B., and had an only daughter,
>> Anne, *m.* to Robert, Lord Kinlosse, by whom she was mother of
>>> Robert, Earl of Aylesbury.

His lordship *d.* in 1613, and was *s.* by his son,

JOHN HARINGTON, second baron, at whose decease in the following year, (1614,) the BARONY OF HARINGTON, OF EXTON, became EXTINCT, and his lordship's estates devolved upon his sisters. The Countess of Bedford, Dugdale says, notwithstanding her large fortune, wasted by her profuseness, not only her own estate, but some portion of her husband's. Pennant, in describing the pictures at Woburne Abbey, notices "a full length of that fantastic lady, Lucy, Countess of Bedford, dressed in as fantastic a habit, with an immense veil distended behind her. Her ladyship was a patroness of literature, and there are several Epistles of Daniel, the poet, and the celebrated Doctor John Donne, dedicated to her."

Nicholas Stone, statuary to King James I., made a tomb for her father, mother, brother, and sister, and for which the countess paid him £1080, and had it erected at Exton.

ARMS.—Sa. a frett, ar.

HASTANG—BARON HASTANG.

By Writ of Summons, dated 19th December, 1311.
5 Edward II.

Lineage.

Of this family (whose chief seat was at Leming-
252

ton, in the county of Warwick, and thence called Lemington Hastang), was

ATROP HASTANG, who gave to the canons of Nostell, in the county of York, the churches of Lemington and Newbold; and bestowed on the canons of Kenilworth the church of Whitnash. To this Atrop succeeded his son,

ATROP HASTANG, who was succeeded by his son,

HUMPHREY HASTANG, who joining the rebellious barons against King John, had his lands seized, but returning to his allegiance, they were restored in the 1st Henry III. This Humphrey was *s.* by his son,

ROBERT HASTANG, who *m.* Joane, daughter and co-heir of William de Curli. This Robert gave a mark in gold, in 41st Henry III., for respiting his knighthood. But afterwards taking part with Montford, Earl of Leicester, he was one of those who held out the castle of Kenilworth, for which his lands were seized, and given to Sir James de Aldithley, and Sir Hugh de Turbervill. He had restitution of them, however, upon paying a fine under the "Dictum de Kenilworth." Robert de Hastang was *s.* by his son,

ROBERT DE HASTANG, who, in the 10th Edward II., was constituted one of the commissioners to treat with Robert de Brus, and his party in Scotland, upon a truce betwixt both realms; and was summoned to parliament as a BARON in 5th Edward II., but not afterwards, nor was his son,

JOHN DE HASTANG, second baron, but his son,

THOMAS DE HASTANG, third baron, had summons 25th February, and 20th November, 1342, but not afterwards. His lordship had a son,

> SIR JOHN DE HASTANG, who *m.* first, Blanch ———, but had no issue, and secondly, Maud, daughter of Sir William Trussel, Knt., by whom he had two daughters, his co-heirs,
>> Maud, *m.* to Ralph Stafford, of Grafton.
>> Joane, *m.* to Sir John Salisbury, Knt.

In the representatives of those ladies, the BARONY OF HASTANG is now vested.

ARMS.—Az. and a chief gules, over all a lion rampant, or.

HASTINGS — BARONS HASTINGS, EARLS OF PEMBROKE.

Barony, by Writ of Summons, dated 14th Oct., 1264,
49 Henry III.
Earldom, by Letters Patent, dated 13th Oct., 1339.

Lineage.

This noble family derived its surname from HASTINGS, (one of the Cinque Ports,) in Sussex, the lastage of which they farmed for a considerable period from the crown.

ROBERT, Portreve of Hastings, was *s.* by

WALTER DE HASTINGS, who held the office of steward to King Henry I., by Sergeantie, in respect of his tenure of the manor of Ashele, in the county of Norfolk, viz., by the service of taking charge of the naperie, (table linen,) at the solemn coronation of the kings of this realm. This Walter was *s.* by his son,

HUGH DE HASTINGS, Lord of Fillongley, in the county of Warwick, who *m.* Erneburga, daughter of Hugh de Flamville, and niece and heir of Robert de Flamville, of Aston-Flamville, in the county of Leicester, by whom he acquired that manor, as well as Grissing, in Norfolk, and the stewardship of the abbey of St. Edmundsbury, and had two sons and a daughter, viz.

WILLIAM, his successor.

Richard, a priest, rector of Barewell, in Leicestershire.

Mahant, to whom he gave the manor of Arke, in Devonshire, on her marriage with Robert de Wyford: from this lady descended,

Sir Geffery de Anke, or Hanke, who, temp. Henry III., conveyed that estate, in marriage with his daughter, to Michael Davyll.

Hugh de Hastings was *s.* by his elder son,

WILLIAM DE HASTINGS, steward to King Henry II., from whom he obtained a confirmation of all the lands which William, his grandfather, and Hugh, his father, had enjoyed in the reign of Henry I., as also Aston-Flamville and the other lands, which Robert de Limesi, Bishop of Coventry, with the consent of the chapter, and approbation of King Henry I., gave to the above mentioned Robert de Flamville. This feudal lord *m.* first, Margery, daughter of Roger Bigot, Earl of Norfolk, and had issue, Henry, who died issueless, and WILLIAM, who became heir to his brother. He espoused, secondly, Ida, daughter of Henry, Earl of Eu, by whom he had two other sons, of which Thomas, the elder, was father of Hugh de Hastings, progenitor of the Hastings, Earls of Huntingdon. The younger son of the first marriage, and the heir upon the decease of his elder brother, in 1194,

WILLIAM DE HASTINGS, in the 6th of Richard I., paid one hundred marks for his relief of those lands held in serjeanty, which had descended to him, and a hundred marks more to obtain the king's favour, in regard that he did not at that time attend him into Normandy. This William de Hastings was one of the peers in the parliament, held at Lincoln, 1st of King John, wherein William, king of Scotland, did homage to the English monarch. In the 15th of the same reign he was with the king in Poitou; but in three years afterwards we find him in the ranks of the insurrectionary barons, and his lands at that time granted by the crown to William de Roeley, and Eleas, his uncle, for their support in the service of the king. He seems, however, to have made his peace in the beginning of Henry III.'s reign, and was with the royal army at the siege of Bitham Castle, in Lincolnshire. He died in 1226, and was *s.* by his son,

HENRY DE HASTINGS, who, upon paying a fine of fifty marks, and doing his homage, had livery of his lands in the counties of Warwick, Leicester, Salop, Bedford, Norfolk, and Suffolk. This Henry espoused Ada, fourth daughter of David, Earl of Huntingdon, and of Maud, his wife, daughter of Hugh, and one of the sisters and co-heirs of Ranulph, Earl of Chester: and through

her he eventually shared in the great estates of the Earls of Chester. By this lady he had issue, HENRY, his successor, and two daughters, Margery and Hillaria, who, at the time of his decease, were in the nunnery of Alneston, and their tuition was then committed to William de Cantelupe. This Henry de Hastings attending King Henry into France, in the 26th of that monarch's reign, was taken prisoner at the great defeat which the English army then sustained at Zante, but was soon afterwards released. In a few years subsequently he accompanied Richard, Earl of Cornwall, with divers other of the principal nobility, into France, whither the said earl proceeded at that period with a splendid retinue, but for what purpose does not appear. About the close of the same year (1250) Henry de Hastings died, and was *s.* by his son,

HENRY DE HASTINGS, then in minority, whose wardship was granted to Guy de Lusignan, King Henry III.'s half brother. This Henry, in the 44th Henry III., had a military summons to be at Shrewsbury, with horse and arms, to march against the Welsh; and the next year had a similar summons to be at London. But very soon afterwards we find him in arms with Simon de Montfort, Earl of Leicester, and other turbulent spirits, against the king, and with those excommunicated by the Archbishop of Canterbury. After which he became one of the most zealous of the baronial leaders, and distinguishing himself at the battle of Lewes, wherein the king was made prisoner, received the honour of knighthood at the hands of Montfort; and was constituted governor of Scarborough and Winchester Castles. Moreover, after the defeat of the barons at Evesham, being then appointed governor of the strong castle of Kenilworth, by the younger Simon Montfort, he held it out stoutly against the victorious army for the full space of six months; and when the king sent his messenger to him with gracious offers, in case he should surrender, he caused the envoy to be maimed, and made much havoc amongst the besiegers, by casting forth huge stones from the engines, and by occasional bold and daring sallies, not at all daunted by the anathema, which Ottobon, the pope's legate, then there, thundered out against him: he was eventually, however, from want of supplies, compelled to submit, but upon honourable terms, viz., " to march out of the fortress with bag and baggage," which he accordingly did upon the eve of St. Thomas the apostle. In consequence of this stubborn resistance he was excluded from the benefits of the *Dictum de Kenilworth*, and condemned to seven years' imprisonment, or submission to the king's mercy. But within two years he was admitted, through the mediation of Prince Edward, to the full advantages of the said decree of Kenilworth. The period of the decease of this stout baron has not been ascertained, but he was *s.* by his son,

HENRY DE HASTINGS, who *m.* Joane, sister, and at length co-heir, of George de Cantilupe, Baron of Bergavenny, and had issue,

JOHN, his successor.

Edmund, who had summons to parliament, as a BARON, from 29th December, 1299, 28th Edward I., to 26th July, 1313, 7th Edward II., but nothing is known of his descendants.

And three daughters, Audra, Lora, and Joane. This feudal lord was summoned to parliament, as BARON HASTINGS, on 14th December, 1264. He d. in 1268, and was s. by his son,

JOHN HASTINGS, second baron, summoned to parliament as LORD HASTINGS, from 23rd June, 1295, to 22nd May, 1313, although in right of his mother, and the tenure of the castle of Bergavenny, he was unquestionably BARON OF BERGAVENNY. This nobleman was in the expedition to Scotland in the 12th Edward I., and in three years afterwards attended Edmund, Earl of Cornwall, regent of the kingdom during the king's sojourn in Gascony, into Wales. He was subsequently in an expedition to Ireland, and again in Scotland, 28th Edward I., where he performed military service for five knights' fees. The next year he continued in the Scottish wars, under Edward, Prince of Wales, and in the 31st Edward I. he assisted at the celebrated siege of KARRLAVEROCK. His lordship had afterwards, 34th Edward I., a grant from the king of the whole county of Menteth, with the isles, as also of all the manors and lands of Alan, late Earl of Menteth, then declared an enemy and rebel to the king. He was likewise seneschal of Aquitaine, and one of the competitors, in 1290, for the crown of Scotland, in right of his descent from Ada, daughter of David, Earl of Huntingdon, brother of Malcolm and William, kings of Scotland. His lordship m. first, Isabel, daughter of William, and sister and co-heir of *Aymer de Valence*, EARL OF PEMBROKE, by whom he had, with other issue,

John, his successor.

Elizabeth, m. to Roger, Lord Grey, of Ruthyn.

Lord Hastings espoused, secondly, Isabel, daughter of Hugh Despencer, Earl of Winchester, and had two other sons, viz., HUGH, of Gressing Hall, in the county of Norfolk, and Thomas. From the elder son lineally descended EDWARD HASTINGS, of whom in the sequel, as competitor with Lord Grey de Ruthyn, for the arms of Hastings. His lordship d. in 1313, and was s. by his eldest son,

JOHN HASTINGS, third baron, summoned to parliament as LORD HASTINGS, from 26th November, 1313, to 20th February, 1325. This nobleman was actively engaged in the wars of Scotland from the 4th to the 12th Edward II., and the next year, upon the insurrection of the lords, when they banished the two Spencers, his lordship being one of their adherents, deserted the barons, and joined the king at Cirencester. Moreover, he was the same year again in the Scottish wars; and in the 16th Edward II. he was made governor of Kenilworth Castle. Lord Hastings espoused Julian, granddaughter and heir of Thomas de Leybourne, Baron Leybourne, and dying in 1325, was s. by his son,

LAURENCE HASTINGS, fourth baron, then but five years of age, who, upon attaining majority, was, by royal favour, by letters patent dated 13th October, 1339, declared EARL OF PEMBROKE: and about the same time, was in the expedition made into Flanders. The next year, he attended King Edward III., in the notable adventure at sea against

the French, where he participated in the glory of the victory achieved near Sluys. He was afterwards constantly in the French wars, wherein he displayed great valour. The earl m. Agnes, daughter of Roger Mortimer, Earl of March, and dying in 1375, was s. by his only son,

JOHN HASTINGS, second Earl of Pembroke, K.G., who, in the 46th Edward III., being selected for his experience and valour, was sent lieutenant into Aquitaine, and arrived at the port of Rochel, then besieged by the French, on the eve of St. John the Baptist. But no sooner had he got his ships within the harbour, than being suddenly attacked by the Spanish fleet, before he had been able to form his line of battle, he suffered so signal a defeat that few of his men escaped. His squadron was entirely consumed, himself and his principal officers made prisoners, and treasure to the amount of twenty thousand marks, which King Edward had sent over to maintain the war, became a prize to the enemy. He subsequently endured four years' harsh captivity in Spain, from which he was eventually released through the interference of Bertrand Clekyn, Constable of France, but died on his journey from Paris (whither he had removed from Spain) to Calais, being considered to have been poisoned by the Spaniards, anno 1375. His lordship m. first, the Lady Margaret Plantagenet, fourth daughter of King Edward III., by whom he had no issue. He espoused secondly, Anne, daughter, and at length sole heir of Sir William Manny, K.G., by whom he had an only son,

John, his successor.

This John, Earl of Pembroke, according to Dugdale, in the 43d Edward III., having obtained the king's licence for so doing, made a feoffment of all his castles, lordships, manors, &c. in England and Wales, to certain uses. Which feoffment upon his decease, was, by the feoffees, delivered to the king's council at Westminster to be opened; when it was found, that in case he died without issue of his body, the town and castle of Pembroke should come to the king, his heirs and successors; and the castle and lordship of Bergavenny, with other lands in England and Wales, to his cousin, William de Beauchamp (his mother's sister's son), in fee, provided he should bear the arms of Hastings, and endeavour to obtain the title of Earl of Pembroke—in default thereof, then to his kinsman, William de Clinton, upon similar conditions. This Earl of Pembroke was the first English subject who followed the example of King Edward III., in quartering of arms; as may be seen in his escutcheon on the north-side of that monarch's tomb, in Westminster abbey, whereon he beareth quarterly, *Or a Maunch gules*, for HASTINGS, and *Barry ar. and az. an Orle of Martlets gules*, for VALENCE. His lordship d. in 1389, and was s. by his son,

JOHN HASTINGS, third Earl of Pembroke, then but two years and a half old. At the coronation of Richard II., this nobleman (not having attained his fifth year) claimed to carry the great golden spurs; and proving his right to that honourable service, it was adjudged, that by reason of his minority, another should be appointed in his behalf; viz. Edmund Mortimer, Earl of March, whose daughter, Philippa, he married, although very young. The 13th Richard II. that monarch keeping his Christmas at Woodstock, his lordship, only then seventeen years of age, adventuring to tilt with Sir John St. John, was so severely wounded, by an unlucky slip of Sir John's lance, in the abdomen, that he died almost immediately, 30th December, 1399, when leaving no issue, the EARLDOM OF PEMBROKE became EXTINCT. At his lordship's thus premature decease, *Reginald*, LORD GREY DE RUTHYN, (grandson of Roger, Lord Grey, and his wife, Elizabeth Hastings, daughter of John, second Baron Hastings,) was found to be *his heir* of the WHOLE BLOOD. And Hugh, Baron Hastings, eldest son of Hugh Hastings, of Gressing Hall, in the county of Norfolk, (eldest son of the said John, second Baron Hastings, by his second wife, Isabel, daughter of Hugh de Spenser, Earl of Winchester,) *his heir* of the HALF BLOOD; between the son of this Lord Hastings of Gressing Hall, Edward Hastings, and Reginald Lord Grey, there was a memorable competition in the court military, before the constable and marshals of England, for the right of bearing the arms of Hastings, which lasted the full period of twenty years, and was eventually decided against Hastings, who, besides being condemned in the heavy costs of £970. 17s. 1d. was imprisoned sixteen years for disobeying the judgment.

"Unless the BARONY OF HASTINGS," says Nicolas, "be considered the same as Bergavenny," (and he proves that it was totally unconnected with the feudal tenure of the castle of Bergavenny,) "it must be vested in the descendants and representatives of the said Edward Hastings."

Note.—The superstition of the period attributed the untimely fate of the last and youthful Earl of Pembroke to a divine judgment upon the family, in regard that *Aymer de Valence*, EARL OF PEMBROKE, his ancestor, was one of those who passed sentence of death upon Thomas Plantagenet, Earl of Lancaster at Pontefract: for it was observed, that subsequently to that judgment, none of the Earls of Pembroke saw his father, nor any father of them took delight in seeing his children.

ARMS.—Or, a Maunch gules.

HASTINGS—BARON HASTINGS, OF GRESSING HALL, IN THE COUNTY OF NORFOLK.

By Writ of Summons, dated 25th February, 1342, 16 Edward III.

Lineage.

JOHN HASTINGS, second Lord Hastings, (grandfather by his first wife of Laurence Hastings, Earl of Pembroke,) *m.* for his second wife, Isabel, daughter of Hugh Despencer, Earl of Winchester, and had, with a younger son,

HUGH HASTINGS, of Gressing Hall, in the county of Norfolk, whose grandson,

HUGH HASTINGS, of Gressing Hall, having distinguished himself in arms, in Flanders, was summoned to parliament as a BARON, by King Edward III., on the 25th February, 1342. In the

20th of the same reign, being designated *the king's cousin*, his lordship was constituted lieutenant of Flanders, and commander of all the king's forces there, against the French. At this period, he took three hundred prisoners, and brought them all to England. In 1359, Lord Hastings was in the wars of Gascony, and in some years afterwards, he attended John, Duke of Lancaster, into Spain; but further nothing is mentioned of this nobleman, because neither himself nor any descendants were subsequently summoned to parliament. His son, and eventual heir,

EDWARD HASTINGS, who assumed the title of LORD HASTINGS AND STOTVILLE, but by what authority remains to be established, is the person mentioned in the account of the Hastings, Earls of Pembroke, as having twenty years' litigation with the Lord Grey de Ruthyn, regarding the right to bear the arms of Hastings, (viz.: or, a maunch gu). This celebrated cause was heard and decided, in the court military, by the constable and marshal of England, and it went finally against Hastings, who was also condemned in heavy costs, and imprisoned sixteen years for disobeying the judgment of the court. Edward Hastings, having likewise questioned the entail of John Hastings, second Earl of Pembroke, by which the Bergavenny and other estates, passed to William de Beauchamp. "Beauchamp invited," says Dugdale, "his learned counsel, to his house in Pater-Noster-Row, in the city of London; amongst whom were Robert Charlton, (then a judge,) William Pinchebek, William Brenchesley, and John Catesby, (all learned lawyers;) and after dinner, coming out of his chappel, in an angry mood, threw to each of them a piece of gold, and said, ' *Sirs, I desire you, forthwith to tell me, whether I have any right* and title to HASTINGS' lordships and lands?' whereupon Pinchebek stood up, (the rest being silent, fearing that he suspected them,) and said, ' *No man here, nor in England, dare say that you have any right in them, except* HASTINGS *do quit his claim therein; and should he do it, being now under age, it would be of no validitie.* ' " Perhaps," (continues the same authority,) "there had been some former entail, to settle them upon the heir, male, of the family; but whatever it was, HASTINGS apprehended the injury thereby done to him, to be so great, that with extreme anguish of mind, at his latter end, he left God's curse and his own, upon his descendants, if they did not attempt the vindication thereof."

Nicolas considers the BARONY OF HASTINGS, which had belonged to the Earls of Pembroke, to be vested in the representatives of this Edward Hastings.

HASTINGS—BARON HASTINGS, OF LOUGHBOROUGH, IN THE COUNTY OF LEICESTER.

By Letters Patent, dated 19th January, 1558.

Lineage.

GEORGE HASTINGS, first Earl of Huntingdon, espoused Lady Anne Herbert, widow of Sir

Walter Herbert, Knt., and daughter of Henry Stafford Duke of Buckingham, by whom he had, with several other children, FRANCIS, his successor in the Earldom of Huntingdon, and

SIR EDWARD HASTINGS, a very eminent person in the time of Queen Mary. In the 4th Edward VI., he served the office of sheriff for the counties of Warwick and Leicester; and the same year, he was sent with his brother, the Earl of Huntingdon, to dislodge the French from a position which they had taken up between Bologne and Calais. Upon the accession of Mary, he was constituted receiver of the honour of Leicester, parcel of the Duchy of Lancaster, in the counties of Leicester, Warwick, Northampton, and Nottinghamshire; and being the same year made a privy counsellor to the queen, and master of her horse, was appointed collector general to all her revenues within the city of London, and the counties of Middlesex, Essex, and Hertfordshire. He obtained a grant at this time, of the Manor of Bosworth, in the county of Leicester; and was subsequently made a Knight of the Garter. In the 4th and 5th of Philip and Mary, Sir Edward was constituted lord chamberlain of the household, and was elevated to the peerage, by letters patent, dated 19th January, 1558, as BARON HASTINGS, of Loughborough, in the county of Leicester. His lordship died at Stoke Pogis, in the county of Bucks, (where he had built a chapel, and founded and endowed an hospital,) in 1558, when leaving no male issue, the BARONY became EXTINCT.

ARMS.—Ar. a maunch sa.

HASTINGS—BARON HASTINGS, OF LOUGHBOROUGH.

By Letters Patent, dated 22nd October, 1643.

Lineage.

HENRY HASTINGS, fifth Earl of Huntingdon, married Elizabeth, third daughter and co-heir of Ferdinand Stanley, fifth Earl of Derby, and had, besides two daughters, Ferdinando, who succeeded as sixth Earl of Huntingdon, and

HENRY HASTINGS, who, having espoused, zealously, the cause of King Charles I., at the breaking out of the rebellion, and become one of the most distinguished in arms, amongst the gallant cavaliers, was elevated to the peerage by the ill-fated monarch, on the 22d October, 1643, as BARON HASTINGS, of Loughborough, in the county of Leicester, a dignity which had been borne by, and expired with his gallant ancestor, Sir Edward Hastings, K.G., in the reign of Queen Mary. His lordship had the gratification of living to witness the restoration of the monarchy, but dying unmarried, in January, 1665-6, the BARONY OF HASTINGS, of Loughborough, for the second time, EXPIRED.

ARMS.—Ar. a maunch, sa.

HASTINGS—BARON HASTINGS, OF WELLES.

See Welles.

256

HATTON — BARONS HATTON, OF KIRBY, IN THE COUNTY OF NORTHAMPTON, VISCOUNTS HATTON, OF GRETTON.

Barony, } by Letters { 29th July, 1643.
Viscounty, } Patent, { 17th January, 1682.

Lineage.

This family which derived its surname from the Lordship of HALTON, in Cheshire, deduced its pedigree from Nigel, BARON OF HALTON in that county, and constable to the old Earls of Chester.

The principal branch of the Hattons, in the days of Queen Elizabeth, was,

CHRISTOPHER HATTON, Esq., then of Holdenby, in the county of Northampton, "who," says Dugdale, "being a private gentleman of the Inns of Court, was for his activity and comeliness, taken into favour. "Besides those accomplishments," continues the same author, "and the grace of dancing, he had likewise the addition of a strong and subtle capacity, so that, soon learning the discipline and garb of the times and court, he first became one of the queen's gentlemen pensioners; afterwards gentleman of the privy chamber, captain of the guard, vice chamberlain, and one of the privy council, lastly, LORD CHANCELLOR OF ENGLAND, and a Knight of the most noble Order of the Garter."

Of this eminent person, the following character is given. "He had a large portion of gifts and endowments; his features, his gait, his carriage, and his prudence, strove to set him off. Every thing he did, was so exactly just and discreet, and what he spoke so weighty, that he was chosen to keep the queen's conscience, as her chancellor, and to express her sense as her speaker. The courtiers that envied him, were forced by his superior power, to own themselves in error; and the serjeants, who at first refused to plead before him, could not at length but confess his abilities. His place was above his law, but not above his parts, which were infinitely pregnant and comprehensive. His station was great, but his humility was greater; giving an easy access to all addresses. He was so just, that his sentence was a law to the subject, and so wise, that his opinion was an oracle with the queen." Sir Christopher Hatton died a bachelor, 20th November, 1591, of a broken heart, it is stated, in consequence of his royal mistress having demanded rigorously, an old debt, which he owed her. He adopted (his sister Dorothy's son, by her husband, John Newport, Esq.,) his nephew,

SIR JOHN NEWPORT, Knt., who thereupon assumed the name of HATTON. This gentleman m. Elizabeth, daughter and heiress of Sir Francis Gawdy, chief justice of the court of Common Pleas, and left an only daughter, FRANCES, who married Robert Rich, Earl of Warwick. Upon his decease, the greater part of the estates of the Lord Chancellor Hatton, devolved by virtue of an entail upon the great-great nephew of that eminent individual,

SIR CHRISTOPHER HATTON, K.B., who m. Alice, daughter of Thomas Fanshaw, Esq., of Ware Park, and dying in 1619, was s. by his son,

SIR CHRISTOPHER HATTON, who was made a Knight of the Bath at the coronation of King Charles I., and afterwards distinguishing himself by his ardent zeal in the royal cause, he was elevated to the peerage on the 29th July, 1643, as BARON HATTON, of Kirby, in the county of Northampton. Upon the restoration of King Charles II., his lordship was sworn of the privy council, and constituted governor of Guernsey. Lord Hatton m. Elizabeth, eldest daughter and co-heir of Sir Charles Montagu, and niece of Henry, Earl of Manchester, by whom he had issue,

    CHRISTOPHER, his successor.
    Charles.
    Mary.
    Jane.
    Alice.

He d. in 1670, and was s. by his eldest son,

CHRISTOPHER HATTON, second baron. This nobleman, like his father, was governor of Guernsey, and while in that government had one of the most singular escapes from death, probably upon record. During his residence at Cornet Castle, the magazine of powder caught fire at midnight by lightning; and his lordship, while sleeping in his bed, was blown out of the window, and remained for some time struggling on the ramparts, without sustaining any injury. His lady, and several of her female attendants perished: but one of his children, an infant, was found the next day alive, sleeping in its cradle, under a beam. His lordship was advanced in 1682, to the dignity of VISCOUNT HATTON, of Gretton, in the county of Northampton. He m. first, Lady Cecilia Tufton, daughter of John, Earl of Thanet, and had one surviving daughter,

    ANNE, who m. Daniel Finch, second Earl of Nottingham, and sixth Earl of Winchelsea, and had, with three elder sons,

        The Hon. EDWARD FINCH, who assumed the additional surname of HATTON, and his grandson,

            GEORGE FINCH-HATTON, Esq., inheriting, in 1826, the Earldoms of Winchelsea and Nottingham, is the present earl.

The viscount espoused, secondly, Frances, only daughter of Sir Henry Yelverton, of Gaston Mauduit, in the county of Northampton, Bart., by whom he had no surviving issue. He m. thirdly, Elizabeth, daughter and co-heir of Sir William Haslewood, of Maidwell, in the county of Northampton, and had three sons, William, Charles, and John, and three daughters, Elizabeth, Penelope, and Anne. His lordship d. in 1706, and was s. by his eldest son,

WILLIAM HATTON, second viscount. This nobleman dying unmarried in 1762, and his brothers having deceased previously without male issue, the

BARONY AND VISCOUNTY OF HATTON became EXTINCT. The estates eventually devolved upon the Honourable Edward Finch Hatton, mentioned above.

ARMS.—As. a chevron betw. three garbs gu.

HAUSTED—BARON HAUSTED.

By Writ of Summons, dated 20th July, 1332,
6 Edward III.

Lineage.

JOHN DE HAUSTED, in the first year of Edward II., obtained a grant to himself and the heirs of his body, of the manor of Deusangre, and divers other lands in the county of Northumberland: he was subsequently engaged in the wars of Scotland; and was invested with the power of receiving into protection all those who in the county of Northumberland, and parts adjacent, submitted to the authority of the king. In the 15th of the same monarch he had the castle and honour of Clare, in the county of Suffolk, committed to his charge; and after the accession of Edward III. he was made seneschal of Gascony. For all these services he obtained a grant of two hundred marks sterling, to be received yearly during his life out of the customs of Bourdeaux, until such time as provision should be made for the payment thereof within this realm: and he was summoned to parliament as a BARON from the 20th July, 1332, to the 22nd January, 1336, but never afterwards, and nothing further is known of his lordship or his descendants.

ARMS.—Gules, a chief componée, or. and az.

HAY—BARONS HAY, OF SAWLEY, VISCOUNTS DONCASTER, EARLS OF CARLISLE.

Barony,	by Letters Patent,	29th June, 1615.
Viscounty,		5th July, 1618.
Earldom,		13th Sept., 1622.

Lineage.

Amongst the natives of Scotland who accompanied King JAMES I. into England was a gentleman of the name of HAY, whom Sir Anthony Weldon thus describes: "The king no sooner came to London, but notice was taken of a rising favourite, the first meteor of that nature appearing in our climate; as the king cast his eye upon him for affection, so did all the courtiers, to adore him, his name was

MR. JAMES HAY, a gentleman that long lived in France, and some say of the Scottish guard to the French king; this gentleman coming over to meet King James, and share with him in his new conquest, (according to the Scottish phrase,) it should seem had some further acquaintance with the then leiger embassadour in Scotland for the French monarch, who coming with his majesty into England, presented this gentleman as a well accomplished person to the king, in such high commendation as engendered such a liking as produced a favourite;

in thankful acknowledgement whereof, he did him many fair offices for the present, and coming afterwards an extraordinary embassador to our king, made him the most sumptuous feast at Essex House, that ever was seen before, never equalled since, in which was such plenty, and fish of that immensity, brought out of Muscovia, that dishes were made to contain them, (no dishes in all England before could ne're hold them,) and after that a costly voydee, and after that a mask, of choyse noble-men and gentlemen, and after that a most costly banquet, the king, lords, and all the prime gentlemen then about London being invited thither. Truly, he was a most compleat, and well accomplished gentleman, modest and court-like, and of so fair a demeanour, as made him be generally beloved; and for his wisdom, I shall give you but one character for all: he was ever great with all the favourites of his time, and although the king did often change, yet he was (semper idem), with the king, and favourites, and got by both; for although favourites had that exorbitant power over the king, to make him grace and disgrace whom they pleased, he was out of that power, and the only exception to that general rule; and for his gettings, it was more than almost the favourites of his time, which appeared in those vast expenses of all sorts, and had not the bounty of his mind exceeded his gettings, he might have left the greatest estate that ever our age or climate had heard of; he was, indeed, made for a courtier, who wholly studied his master, and understood him better than any other."

"He was employed in very many of the most weighty affairs, and sent with the most stately embassies of our times, which he performed with that wisdom and magnificency, that he seemed an honour to his king and country, for his carriage in state affairs." This celebrated favourite having, by the influence of his royal master, obtained Honora, sole daughter and heir of Edward, Lord Denny, in marriage, had a grant of the name and title of LORD HAY, with precedence next to the barons of England, but no place or voice in parliament. On 29th June, 1615, he was, however, advanced to the dignity of a baron of the realm, under the title of LORD HAY, of Sauley, in the county of York, without any solemn investiture, his lordship being the first ever so created, the lawyers then declaring that the delivery of the letters patent was sufficient without any ceremony. He was the next year sent ambassador to the court of France. In March, 1617, his lordship was sworn of the privy council, and created Viscount Doncaster on the 5th July, 1618, preparatory to his proceeding upon an embassy into Germany. In 1622 he was again employed as ambassador in France, and was advanced on the 13th September in that year to the EARLDOM OF CARLISLE. Besides all these high honours and trusts he was master of the great wardrobe, gentleman of the robes to King James I., and Knight of the most noble order of the Garter. He was also first gentleman of the bed-chamber to King Charles I. His lordship m. as already stated, Honora, only daughter and heiress of Edward, Lord Denny, and after her decease he espoused the Lady Lucy Percy, youngest daughter of Henry, Earl of Northumberland. He d. 25th April, 1636, and was s. by his only surviving son,

JAMES HAY, second Earl of Carlisle, who m. Lady Margaret Russell, daughter of Francis, Earl of Bedford, but dying s. p. in 1660, ALL his HONOURS became EXTINCT.

ARMS.—Ar. three escutcheons gules.

HENLEY — BARONS HENLEY, OF GRAINGE, EARLS OF NORTHINGTON.

Barony,	} by Letters {	27th March, 1760.
Earldom, &c.	} Patent, {	19th May, 1764.

Lineage.

ANTHONY HENLEY, Esq., m. Mary, daughter and co-heir of the Hon. Peregrine Bertie, a younger son of Montagu, Earl of Lindsey, and was father of

SIR ROBERT HENLEY, Knt., a lawyer of great eminence, who was appointed, in 1756, attorney-general, when he received the customary honour of knighthood, and the next year he was constituted keeper of the great seal. In 1760 Sir Robert was elevated to the peerage as BARON HENLEY, of Grainge, in the county of Southampton, and appointed LORD CHANCELLOR OF ENGLAND in 1761. In three years afterwards he was advanced to the dignities of Viscount Henley, and EARL OF NORTHINGTON. His lordship officiated as lord high steward at the trial of Earl Ferrers. He m. Jane, daughter of Sir John Huband, of the county of Warwick, and had surviving issue,

  ROBERT, his successor.

  Bridget, m. first, to Robert, only son of Lord Bingley; and secondly, to the Hon. John Talmash, but had no issue.

  Jane, m. to Sir Willoughby Aston, Bart.

  Mary, m. to the Earl of Legonier, and died s. p.

  Catherine, m. to George, Viscount Deerhurst.

  Elizabeth, m. to Frederick Morton Eden, Esq., a diplomatist of the first grade, who was created a peer of Ireland, as BARON HENLEY, of Chardstock, and had, with other issue,

    ROBERT, present BARON HENLEY, of Chardstock.

The earl d. in 1772, and was s. by his son,

ROBERT HENLEY, second Earl of Northington, who was constituted LORD-LIEUTENANT OF IRELAND in 1783, but filled the vice-regal office until the next year only. His lordship, who was a Knight of the Thistle, died unmarried in 1786, when the BARONY and VISCOUNTY OF HENLEY, with EARLDOM OF NORTHINGTON, became EXTINCT, while his estates devolved upon his sisters as co-heirs.

ARMS.—Quarterly first and fourth az. a lion rampant ar. ducally crowned or. within a border ar. charged with eight forteauxes, for HENLEY—second and third, ar. three battering rams bar-ways ppr. (Brown) armed and garnished az. for BERTIE.

HERBERT—BARONS HERBERT, OF HERBERT, AND OF CHEPSTOW, EARLS OF PEMBROKE, EARL OF HUNTINGDON.

Barony, by Writ of Summons, dated 20th July, 1461, 1 Edward IV.

Earldom of Pembroke, by Letters Patent, 27th May, 1468.

Earldom of Huntingdon, by Charter, 4th July, 1472.

Lineage.

The first of this family raised to the rank of an earl was,

SIR WILLIAM DE HERBERT, Knt., Lord of Ragland, in the county of Monmouth, an estate which he derived from Maud, his grandmother, daughter and heiress of Sir John Morley, Knt. Sir William Herbert is said by some to have deduced his line from Henry, the son of Herbert, chamberlain to King Henry I., but by others, from Henry Fitz-Roy, one of the natural sons of that king. He was a staunch supporter of the house of York, and for his fidelity and services, King Edward IV., soon after his accession, constituted him chief justice and chamberlain of South Wales, and made him likewise steward of the castle and lordship of Brecknock, and of all other the castles of Humphrey, Duke of Buckingham, in the same part of the principality. Sir William was summoned to parliament, as BARON HERBERT, *of Herbert*, on the 26th July, 1461, and by letters patent, bearing date the 3d of February following, wherein his manifold services and eminent deserts are recorded, (such as hazarding his life in numerous conflicts against King Henry VI. and the Lancastrians, particularly against Henry Holland, Duke of Exeter, Jasper Tudor, Earl of Pembroke, James Butler, Earl of Wiltshire, &c., reducing castles, fortresses, &c.,) obtained a grant in general tail of the castle, town, and lordship of Pembroke, with all its appurtenances. His lordship had subsequently other extensive grants; was constituted chief justice of North Wales for life, and created EARL OF PEMBROKE on the 27th May, 1468. He was afterwards appointed chief forester of Snowdon, and constable of Conway castle. In the August ensuing the earl won the castle of Harlow, one of the strongest forts in Wales, by assault, and he was shortly after elected a KNIGHT OF THE GARTER. " Whereunto I shall add," says Dugdale, " what I find further memorable of him, from a certain manuscript book in the custody of Edward, now Lord Herbert, of Chirbury, viz.— Upon the advancing of WILLIAM HERBERT to be Earl of Pembroke, and his instalment at Windsor, King Edward IV. commanded the said earl, and Sir Richard, his brother, to take their surnames after their first progenitor, HERBERT FITZ-ROY, and to forego the British manner, whose usage is to call every man by father's, grandfather's, and great-grandfather's name. And in regard the English heralds were ignorant of the Welch descents, the king was pleased, under his great seal, unto YVAN

AP KYTHECK AP EVAN LLHOYD, of Cardiganshire, Esq., to summon before him, at the castle of Pembroke, the eldest heralds and bards in South Wales, to certifie the linage and stock of the said earl and his brother, which was accordingly done the 17th day of August, 1462, by HOWEL AP DAVID, AP EVAN AP RICE, EVAN BRECVA, EVAN DULIUN, and HOWELL SWERDWALL, the chief men of skill in pedigrees in all South Wales; who, being led by warrant of old doctors' books, records of court barons, histories and wars of princes, books of remembrances found in the ancient abbies of Strata Florida, books of pedigrees of Howell Morthey, of Castle Dolwyn, Esq., the roll of Morgan, the abbot, and several other books and warrants of authority, as also by the evidence of this earl, they presented to his majesty their certificate in three several languages, Brittish, Latine, and French; viz.

" The said Hon. EARL is named WILLIAM HERBERT, a noble knight, son of Sir William, son of Thomas, son of Guillim, son of Jenkyn, son of Adam, son of Reginald, son of Peter, son of Herbert, the son of HERBERT, a noble lord, descended of the royal blood of the crown of ENGLAND, for he was son natural to KING HENRY I., son of WILLIAM, commonly called the CONQUEROR."

Upon the breaking out of the insurrection anno 1469, 9th Edward IV., in the north, on behalf of the Lancastrians, headed by SIR JOHN CONIERS, *Knight*, and ROBERT HILLYARD, who called himself Robin of Riddesdale, the Earl of Pembroke was despatched by the king, with his brother, Sir Richard Herbert, of Colebrook, in command of eighteen thousand Welchmen, to meet the rebels, but being deserted by Humphrey Stafford, Earl of Devonshire, who had joined him with six thousand archers at Banbury, he was compelled to give the insurgents battle with an inferior force, and experienced a signal defeat at Danesmore, Northamptonshire, when himself and his brother fell into the hands of their enemies, and were immediately executed at Northampton, with *Richard Widevile*, LORD RIVERS, and his son, by order of the Duke of Clarence, and the Earl of Warwick, who had recently revolted from the banner of York. His lordship m. first, Anne, daughter of Sir Walter Devereux, and sister of Walter, Lord Ferrers, of Chartley, by whom he had issue,

WILLIAM, his successor.

Walter (Sir).

George (Sir), of St. Gillians, who succeeded eventually to a portion of the estates of the Earl of Pembroke; and his descendant and inheritor of those estates, Mary Herbert, married the celebrated Edward, LORD HERBERT, of Chirbury.

Philip, of Lanyhangel.

Cecilie, m. to Lord Greystock.

Maud, m. to Henry Percy, Earl of Northumberland.

Katherine, m. to George Grey, Earl of Kent.

Anne, m. to John Grey, Lord Powis.

Isabel, m. to Sir Thomas Cokesey, Knt.

Margaret, m. first to Thomas Talbot, Viscount L'Isle, and secondly to Sir Henry Bodringham, Knt.

The earl espoused,* secondly, Maud, daughter and heiress of Adam ap Howell Graunt, and had issue,

> RICHARD (Sir), of Ewyas, from whom the *extant Earls* of Pembroke, derive.
>
> George (Sir), of Swansey.

His lordship was *s.* by his eldest son,

WILLIAM HERBERT, second Earl of Pembroke. King Edward IV. wishing to confer the Earldom of Pembroke upon his son, *Prince Edward*, this nobleman made a resignation† thereof to the crown, and was created in stead EARL OF HUNTINGDON, by charter, bearing date, at York, 4th July, 1479. In the 1st Richard III., his lordship was constituted justice of South Wales, and in the February ensuing, he entered into covenants with that king, to take Dame Katherine Plantagenet, his daughter, to wife, before the feast of St. Michael following; as also to make her a certain jointure, and the king to settle lands and lordships of a large annual value upon them, and the heirs male of their bodies. The king further undertaking to be at the expense of the wedding. But this lady dying in her early years, the marriage did not take effect. His lordship afterwards espoused lady Mary Widvile, daughter of Richard, and sister and co-heir of Richard, Earl Rivers, by whom he had an only daughter and heiress,

> ELIZABETH HERBERT, who *m.* Sir Charles Somerset, Knt., illegitimate son of Henry Beaufort, third Duke of Somerset, of that family (the descendants of John of Gaunt, by Catherine Swinford), which Charles was created in 1513-14, EARL OF WORCESTER, and from this union the present ducal family of Beaufort derives.

In the 3d year of Henry VII., his lordship obtained from the crown a confirmation of the Earldom of Huntingdon. He *d.* —— when the BARONY OF HERBERT, created by the writ of Edward IV., devolved upon his daughter, and the EARLDOM OF HUNTINGDON became EXTINCT.

ARMS.—Per pale az. and gu. three lions rampant, ar. on a border componée, or. and of the second besanty.

HERBERT—BARONS HERBERT, OF CHIRBURY.

By Letters Patent, dated 7th May, 1629.

Lineage.

Of the family of the celebrated,

EDWARD HERBERT, first Lord Herbert, of Chirbury, we shall speak in the words of that chivalrous and eminent person himself. " My father was Richard Herbert, Esq., son of Edward Herbert, Esq., and grandchild of Sir Richard Herbert, Knt., of Colebrook, in Monmouthshire, of all whom I shall say a little. And first, of my father, whom I

---

* This marriage is doubtful, and the branch springing from it is generally deemed illegitimate.

† Resolutions of the House of Lords in 1640 and 1678, declare that no surrender of a patent can be a bar to a claim of the dignity so surrendered; but previously such surrenders were not uncommon.

remember to have been black-haired, and bearded, as all my ancestors of his side are said to have been, of a manly or somewhat stern look, but withal very handsome, and well compact in his limbs, and of a great courage, whereof he gave proof, when he was so barbarously assaulted by many men, in the church-yard at Lanervil, at what time he would have apprehended a man who denied to appear to justice; for, defending himself against them all, by the help only of one John ap Howell Corbet, he chaced his adversaries, until a villain coming behind him, did over the shoulders of others, wound him on the head behind, with a forest-bill, until he fell down, though recovering himself again, notwithstanding his skull was cut through to the *pia mater* of the brain, he saw his adversaries fly away, and after, walked home to his house 'at Llyssyn, where, after he was cured, he offered a single combat to the chief of the family, by whose procurement it was thought the mischief was committed; but he disclaiming wholly the action as not done by his consent, my father desisted from prosecuting the business further. My grandfather was of a various life; beginning first at court, when, after he had spent most part of his means, he became a soldier, and made his fortune with his sword, at the siege of St. Quintens in France, and other wars, both in the north, and in the rebellions happening in the times of King Edward VI., and Queen Mary, with so good success, that he not only came off still with the better, but got so much money and wealth, as enabled him to buy the greatest part of that livelihood which is descended to me. My grandfather was noted to be a great enemy to the outlawys and thieves of his time, who robbed in great numbers in the mountains of Montgomeryshire, for the suppressing of whom he went often, both day and night, to the places where they were; concerning which, though many particulars have been told, I shall mention one only. Some outlaws being lodged in an alehouse, upon the hills of Llandinam, my grandfather and a few servants coming to apprehend them, the principal outlaw shot an arrow against my grandfather, which stuck in the pummel of his saddle; whereupon my grandfather coming up to him with his sword in his hand, and taking him prisoner, he shewed him the said arrow, bidding him look what he had done; whereof the outlaw was no farther sensible, than to say, he was sorry that he left his better bow at home, which he conceived would have carried his shot to his body; but the outlaw being brought to justice, suffered for it. My grandfather's power was so great in the country, that divers ancestors of the better families now in Montgomeryshire were his servants, and raised by him. He delighted also much in hospitality; as having a very long table twice covered every meal, with the best meats that could be gotten, and a very great family. It was an ordinary saying in the country at that time, when they saw any fowl rise, *fly where thou wilt, thou wilt light at Blackhall;* which was a low building, but of great capacity, my grandfather erected in his age; his father and himself, in former times, having lived in Montgomery Castle. Notwithstanding, yet these expenses at home, he brought up his children well, marrying his daughters to the better sort of persons near him, and bringing up his younger sons at the university; from whence his son Matthew went to the low country wars; and, after some time spent there, came home, and lived in the country, at Dolegsog, upon a house and fair living, which my grandfather bestowed upon him. His son also, Charles Herbert, after he had passed some time in the low countries, likewise returned home, and was after married to an inheretrix, whose eldest son, called Sir Edward Herbert, Knt., is the king's attorney-general. His son, George, who was of New College, in Oxford, was very learned, and of a pious life, died in a middle age of a dropsy. My grandfather died at the age of fourscore, or thereabouts, and was buried in Montgomery church, without having any monument made for him, which yet for my father is there set up in a fair manner. My great grandfather, Sir Richard Herbert, was steward, in the time of King Henry VIII., of the lordships and marches of North Wales, East Wales, and Cardiganshire, and had power, in a marshal law, to execute offenders; in the using thereof he was so just, that he acquired to himself a singular reputation; as may appear upon the records of that time, kept in the paper chamber at Whitehall, some touch whereof I have made in my history of Henry VIII.; of him I can say little more, than that he likewise was a great suppressor of rebels, thieves, and outlaws, and that he was just and conscionable. He lieth buried likewise in Montgomery; the upper monument of the two placed in the chancel being erected for him. My great grandfather, Sir Richard Herbert, of Colebrook, was that incomparable hero, who (in the History of Hall and Grafton, as it appears), twice passed through a great army of northern men alone, with his poleax in his hand, and returned without any mortal hurt. This Sir Richard Herbert lieth buried in Abergaveny, in a sumptuous monument for those times; whereas his brother, the Earl of Pembroke,* being buried in Tintirne Abbey, his monument, together with the church, lie now wholly defaced and ruined. This Earl of Pembroke had a younger son, who had a daughter, which married the eldest son of the Earl of Worcester, who carried away the fair castle of Ragland, with many thousand pounds yearly, from the heirmale of that house, which was the second son of the said Earl of Pembroke, and ancestor of the family of St. Gilliams, whose daughter and heir I after married, as shall be told in its place. My mother was Magdalen Newport, daughter of Sir Richard

---

* In the 9th Edward IV. an insurrection, headed by Sir John Coniers and Robert Riddesdale, in favour of Henry VI., having broken out, this earl and his brother, Sir Richard Herbert, being sent to suppress it, were joined by the Earl of Devonshire, but a dispute arising between the two earls, the Earl of Devon separated from Pembroke, who, engaging the enemy at Danesmoore, near Edgcote, in Northamptonshire, was defeated and taken prisoner, with his brother, and both were put to death, with Richard Widville, Earl Rivers, father of the queen, by command of the Duke of Clarence and the Earl of Warwick, who had revolted from Edward.

Newport, and Margaret, his wife, daughter and heir of Sir Thomas Bromley, one of the privy council, and executors of King Henry VIII. By these ancestors I am descended of Talbot, Devoreux, Gray, Corbet, and many other noble families, as may be seen in their matches, extant in the many fair coats the Newports bear. The names of my brothers and sisters were, Richard, William, Charles, George, Henry, Thomas, Elizabeth, Margaret, and Frances (I was myself the eldest). My brother Richard, after he had been brought up in learning, went to the low countries, where he continued many years with much reputation, both in the wars, and for fighting single duels, which were many; insomuch, that between both, he carried, as I have been told, the scars of four-and-twenty wounds upon him to his grave, and lieth buried in Bergenopsoom. My brother William, also a person of great bravery, died a military man in the low countries. My brother Charles was fellow of New College, Oxford, where he died young. My brother George,* was so excellent a scholar, that he was made the public orator of the University of Cambridge. Henry came to court, and was made gentleman of the king's privy chamber, and master of the revels; by which means, as also by a good marriage, he attained to great fortunes for himself and posterity to enjoy. Thomas was a naval officer, who won a very high reputation, but finding himself, after many eminent services, as he thought undervalued, he retired to a private and melancholy life, being much discontented to find others preferred to him; in which sullen humour having lived many years, he died, and was buried in London, in St. Martin's, near Charing Cross. Elizabeth, my eldest sister, was married to Sir HENRY Jones, of Albemarle. Margaret was married to John Vaughan, son and heir of Owen Vaughan, of Llwydiart. Frances, my youngest sister, was married to Sir John Brown, Knt., of the county of Lincoln, who had by her divers children; the eldest son of whom, although young, fought divers duels, in one of which it was his fortune to kill one Lee, of a great family in Lancashire. I shall now come to myself. I was born at Eyton, in Shropshire, in 1581;" but as our limits prevent our proceeding farther, so much in detail— we shall state at once that Mr. Herbert married about the time that he had attained his fifteenth year, his kinswoman, Mary, daughter and heir of Sir William Herbert, of St. Gilliams, in the county of Monmouth, (the lady had been enjoined by the will of her father to marry a Herbert,) then twenty-one years of age, and had issue, RICHARD, Edward, Beatrix, and Florence. About the year 1608 he resolved to travel, and for that purpose came to court and obtained licence to go beyond sea. In his sojourn upon the Continent he became a proficient in military exercises, and a most accomplished

---

* George took orders, and was rector of Bamerton, near Salisbury. He died between 1630 and 1640. His poems were printed at London in 1635, under the title of " The Temple;" and his " Priest to the Temple," in 1652. Lord Bacon dedicated to him a translation of some Psalms into English Verse.

cavalier. He was made a Knight of the Bath at the coronation of King James I., and was afterwards of that monarch's council for military affairs, and his majesty's ambassador to Lewis XIII. of France, to mediate for the relief of the protestants of that kingdom, in which service he continued more than five years; managing the high trust with so much fidelity and discretion, that he was advanced to the dignity of a baron of Ireland, (where he had a fair estate,) by the title of Lord Herbert, of Castle Island; and afterwards proving himself a faithful servant of King Charles I. in the council and the field, his lordship was created a peer of England by letters patent, dated 7th May, 1629, as BARON HERBERT, of Chirbury, in the county of Salop. " This noble lord" (says Dugdale,) " was author of that learned Philosophical Tract (in Latin), de Veritate, printed in 1658, and since, as I have heard, translated into sundry languages." As also of these others—

De Causis Errorum, et de Religione Laici, Edit. Lon. 1656.

De Expeditione in Ream Insulam, Edit. Lon. 1649.

The Life and Reign of King Henry VIII., Edit. Lon. 1649.

De Religione Gentilitium, &c., Ed. Amstelodami, 1663.

The history of Henry VIII.'s reign was undertaken by command of King James I., and is much esteemed. His lordship's historical collections are preserved in the library of Jesus College, Oxford. This so celebrated Lord Herbert, of Chirbury, died in 1648, and was s. by his eldest son,

RICHARD HERBERT, second Lord Herbert, of Chirbury, who, during his father's life-time, being a person of great courage and valour, served King Charles I. as captain of a troop of horse, in the first engagement against the Scotch : and afterwards in England against the parliamentarians. His lordship m. Mary, daughter of John, Earl of Bridgewater, and had issue,

EDWARD, his successor.

John, who d. young.

Henry, captain in the service of King Charles I.

Thomas, d. unmarried.

Frances, m. to William Brown, Esq.

Florence, m. to Richard Herbert, and her grandson,

HENRY ARTHUR HERBERT, had the dignity of HERBERT, OF CHIRBURY, revived in his favour in 1743; see Herbert, Earl Powis.

Arabell, d. unmarried.

Alice, m. Paul Berrard, Esq.

His lordship d. in 1655, and was s. by his eldest son,

EDWARD HERBERT, third Lord Herbert, of Chirbury. This nobleman, like his predecessors, was zealously attached to the fortunes of King Charles I., and had the gratification to witness the restoration of the monarchy. His lordship espoused first, Anne, daughter of Sir Thomas Middleton, Knt., of Chirk Castle, in the county of Derby, and secondly, Elizabeth, daughter and co-heir of George, Lord Chandos, but having no issue, the honours, at his lordship's decease, in 1678, devolved upon his brother,

202

HENRY HERBERT, fourth Lord Herbert, of Chirbury, who m. Lady Catherine Newport, daughter of Francis, Earl of Bradford, but having no issue, the Irish barony, and that of HERBERT, OF CHIRBURY, at his lordship's decease, in 1691, became EXTINCT.

ARMS.—Party per pale, az. and gu. three lions rampant, ar. armed and langued, or.

HERBERT — BARONS POWIS, OF POWIS CASTLE, IN THE COUNTY OF MONTGOMERY, EARLS OF POWIS, MARQUESSES OF POWIS.

Barony, Earldom, Marquisate,	by Letters Patent,	2nd April, 1629. 4th April, 1674. 24th March, 1687.

Lineage.

The Honourable

SIR EDWARD HERBERT, Knt., of Red Castle, anciently called Poole Castle, but now POWIS CASTLE,* second son of William Herbert, first Earl of Pembroke, of the existing peerage, espoused Mary, only daughter and heiress of Thomas Stanley, Esq., of Standen, in the county of Hertford, Master of the Mint, in 1570, by whom he had issue,

WILLIAM, his successor.

George, d. unmarried.

John (Sir), died s. p.

Edward, d. unmarried.

Anne, m. to William, son and heir of Sir William Stanley, of Horton, in the county of Chester.

Catherine, m. to Sir William Massey, of Puddington, in Cheshire.

The eldest son,

WILLIAM HERBERT, was made a Knight of the Bath, at the coronation of King James I., and elevated to the peerage, as BARON POWIS, of Powis Castle, on 2nd April, 1629. His lordship m. Eleanor, daughter of Henry Percy, Earl of Northumberland, and had issue,

PERCY, who was created a baronet, in the lifetime of his father.

Katherine, m. first, to Sir Robert Vaughan, Knt., of Lydiard, in the county of Montgomery : and secondly, to Sir James Palmer, Knt., of Dorney Court, Bucks, father of Roger, Earl of Castlemain.

Lucy, m. to William Abington, Esq., of Hinlop, in the county of Worcester.

His lordship d. at the advanced age of eighty-three, on the 7th March, 1655, and was s. by his son,

SIR PERCY HERBERT, Bart., second Lord Powis. This nobleman, m. Elizabeth, daughter of Sir William Craven, an alderman of London,

---

* This castle, anciently the seat of inheritance of the Charletons and Greys, Barons Powis, was purchased by the Herberts, in the reign of Elizabeth.

and sister of William, Earl Craven, by whom he had,

WILLIAM, his successor.

Mary, m. to George, Lord Talbot, eldest son of John, Earl of Shrewsbury.

His lordship d. in 1666, and was s. by his son,

WILLIAM HERBERT, third Lord Powis, who was created, 4th April, 1674, EARL OF POWIS; and upon the accession of King James II., 24th March, 1686, Viscount Montgomery, and MARQUESS OF POWIS. This nobleman attaching himself to the fortunes of his royal master, withdrew with his majesty into France, at the revolution, and was subsequently created by the fallen monarch, Marquess of Montgomery, and Duke of Powis, but those dignities were never recognised in England. His lordship was outlawed for not returning within a certain period, and submitting to the new government. He m. Lady Elizabeth Somerset, daughter of Edward, Marquess of Worcester, and had issue,

WILLIAM, his successor.

Mary, m. first, to Richard, son of Carril, Viscount Molineaux, in Ireland; and secondly, to Francis, Viscount Montague.

Frances, m. to Kenneth Mackenzie, Earl of Seaforth.

Anne, m. to Francis Smith, Lord Carrington.

Winifred, m. to William Maxwell, Earl of Nithisdale.

The marquess died at St. Germans, on 2nd June, 1696, and his son,

WILLIAM HERBERT, was restored to the dignities of Viscount Montgomery, and Earl and Marquess of Powis, and took his seat in the House of Lords, in 1722. His lordship m. Mary, daughter and co-heir of Sir Thomas Preston, Bart., of Furness, in the county of Lancaster, by whom she had issue,

WILLIAM, his successor.

Edward, who m. Henrietta, daughter of the Earl of Waldegrave, and dying in 1734, left his lady enceinte, who was delivered of a daughter, BARBARA HERBERT, who m. HENRY-ARTHUR HERBERT, Esq., created LORD HERBERT, OF CHIRBURY, in 1743; see that dignity.

Mrs. Herbert married secondly, Mr. Beard, the comedian.

The marquess died in 1745, and was s. by his elder son,

WILLIAM HERBERT, third Marquess of Powis. This nobleman dying unmarried, the MARQUISATE AND EARLDOM OF POWIS, with his other honours, became EXTINCT; but he devised the whole of his estates to the husband of his niece, HENRY-ARTHUR, LORD HERBERT, of Chirbury.

ARMS.—Party per pale, az. and gu. three lions rampant, ar. a crescent for difference,

HERBERT — EARL OF TORRINGTON.

By Letters Patent, dated 29th May, 1689.

Lineage.

ARTHUR HERBERT, Esq., grandson of Charles,

uncle of Sir Edward Herbert, the celebrated LORD HERBERT, of Chirbury, was elevated to the peerage by King William III., on the 29th May, 1689, as Baron Torbay, and EARL OF TORRINGTON, in the county of Devon. His lordship, who was brought up to the naval service, had the command of a fleet, temp. Charles II., before Tangier, and afterwards against Algiers; but being removed from his commissions by King James II., he retired into Holland, and was graciously received by the Prince of Orange. "He was a man of good understanding, but profusely luxurious, and on every occasion so sullen and peevish, that it was plain he valued himself much, and expected the same from others; and it was thought, his private quarrel with Lord Dartmouth, for having more of the king's confidence than himself, was the root of his resentment against his majesty. The reputation he had gained with the people in England, and his skill in sea affairs, made it necessary to endeavour to keep him in good temper, so far as homage and observance could do it."

His lordship was admiral of the Dutch fleet, on the coming over of the Prince of Orange, and was subsequently first commissioner of the admiralty, and commander-in-chief of the British fleet. In 1690, he engaged the French fleet, near Beechy Head, but although he fought most gallantly against a superior force, yet not achieving a victory, subjected him to considerable reprehension, deprivation of his command, and committal to the Tower He was eventually tried by court-martial, and acquitted, but never again employed.

His lordship m. first, Miss Anne Hadley; and secondly, Anne, daughter of Sir William Airmine, and widow of Sir Thomas Woodhouse, but having no issue, the EARLDOM OF TORRINGTON and minor dignity, at his lordship's decease, 14th April, 1716, became EXTINCT.

ARMS.—Party per pale, az. and gu. three lions rampant, ar. a mullet for difference.

HERBERT—BARONS HERBERT, OF CHIRBURY.

By Letters Patent, dated 28th April, 1694.

Lineage.

HENRY HERBERT, only son and heir of Henry Herbert, gentleman of the king's chamber, and master of the revels, and nephew of the celebrated Edward, Lord Herbert, of Chirbury, was elevated to the peerage by King William III. on 28th April, 1694, as BARON HERBERT, of Chirbury. His lordship m. Anne, daughter and co-heir of Mr. Alderman Ranney, of the city of London; and dying in 1709, was s. by his only son,

HENRY HERBERT, second baron. This nobleman m. Mary, daughter of John Wallop, Esq., of Farley, in the county of Southampton; but dying in 1738, without issue, this BARONY OF HERBERT, OF CHIRBURY, became EXTINCT.

ARMS.—Party per pale az. and gu., three lions rampant, ar., armed and langued, or.

HERBERT—BARON SHERBERT, OF CHERBURY, EARLS OF POWIS, &c., BARONS HERBERT, OF CHERBURY AND LUDLOW.

Barony, Earldom, &c., Barony, with special remainder,	by Letters Patent,	21st Dec., 1743. 27th May, 1748. 7th Oct., 1749.

Lineage.

HENRY ARTHUR HERBERT, Esq., grandson of Richard Herbert, and son of the Hon. Florence Herbert, (one of the daughters and co-heirs of Richard, second Lord Herbert, of Cherbury, and grand-daughter of EDWARD, the *celebrated* LORD HERBERT, OF CHERBURY,) was created Baron Herbert, of Cherbury, 21st December, 1743, and was advanced, in three years afterwards, to the barony of *Powis, of Powis Castle*, the *viscounty of Ludlow*, and the EARLDOM OF POWIS, having espoused BARBARA, niece of William Herbert, third and last Marquess of Powis, and succeeded, under the will of that nobleman, to his large estates. The earl obtained another peerage, 7th October, 1749, as BARON HERBERT, OF CHERBURY AND LUDLOW, with limitation, in default of issue male of his own body, to his next brother, FRANCIS, and his issue male. His lordship d. in 1749, and was s. by his son,

GEORGE - EDWARD - HENRY - ARTHUR HERBERT, second Earl of Powis, Who d., without issue, in 1801, when the BARONY OF HERBERT, *of Cherbury*, the EARLDOM OF POWIS and its minor dignities, with the BARONY OF HERBERT, *of Cherbury and Ludlow*, (his lordship's uncle having predeceased him, unmarried, to whom the last barony was in reversion,) became EXTINCT, while the earl's estates passed to his sister, *Lady HENRIETTA-ANTONIA HERBERT*, who m. in 1784, Edward, Lord Clive, of the kingdom of Ireland, which nobleman was advanced subsequently to the EARLDOM OF POWIS, &c., and is the present earl.

ARMS.—Party per pale az. and gu., three lions rampant, ar., armed and langued, or.

HERVEY — BARON HERVEY, OF KIDBROKE, IN THE COUNTY OF KENT.

By Letters Patent, dated 7th February, 1628.

Lineage.

WILLIAM HERVEY, Esq., of Ickworth, in the county of Suffolk, (said to have descended from Robert Fitz-Hervey, a younger son of Hervey, Duke of Orleans, who came over with the Conqueror,) died in 1538, leaving, with other issue,

John Hervey, ancestor of the present Marquess of Bath, and

SIR NICHOLAS HERVEY, of the privy-chamber to King Henry VIII., and ambassador from that monarch to the emperor's court at Ghent.

This eminent person m. first, Elizabeth, daughter of Sir Thomas Fitz-Williams, and widow of Sir Thomas Maleverer, by whom he had an only son,

Thomas (Sir), knight-marshal to Queen Mary. Sir Nicholas espoused, secondly, Bridget, daughter and heiress of Sir John Wiltshire, of Stone Castle, in the county of Kent, and relict of Sir Richard Wingfield, of Kimbolton Castle, in the county of Huntingdon, by whom he had two sons, viz.,

HENRY, his successor.

George, ancestor of the Herveys, of Marshal, in Essex.

Sir Nicholas was s. by his elder son,

HENRY HERVEY, whose son and heir,

WILLIAM HERVEY, Esq., of Kidbroke, in the county of Kent, obtained great eminence as a military character in the reigns of Queen Elizabeth, King James I., and King Charles I. Mr. Hervey first signalised himself in the memorable conflict with the ARMADA, having boarded one of the galleons, and killed the captain, Hugh Mongade, with his own hand. He was subsequently knighted; and being employed successfully in Ireland, was created a baronet, 31st May, 1619, and in the following year elevated to the peerage of that kingdom, in the dignity of Baron Hervey, of Ross, in the county of Wexford. His lordship continuing his eminent public services, was created a peer of England, on the 7th February, 1628, as BARON HERVEY, *of Kidbroke, in the county of Kent*. He m. first, Mary, relict of Henry, Earl of Southampton, and daughter of Anthony, Viscount Montacute, by whom he had no issue. His lordship espoused, secondly, Cordelia, daughter and co-heir of Brian Anslow, Esq., of Lewisham, in Kent, and had issue,

William, killed in Germany.

John, who died in Ireland.

Henry, died young.

ELIZABETH, m. to John Hervey, Esq., of Ickworth, who died in 1679, s. p., when his estate devolved upon his brother, SIR THOMAS HERVEY, whose eldest surviving son, JOHN HERVEY, was created Baron Hervey, of Ickworth, and Earl of Bristol, dignities enjoyed by the present MARQUESS OF BRISTOL.

Lord Hervey died in 1642, and his sons having predeceased him, the Irish barony of Hervey, of Ross, with the baronetcy and English barony of HERVEY, OF KIDBROKE, became EXTINCT, while his estates devolved upon his only surviving child, ELIZABETH HERVEY.

ARMS.—Gu. on a bend ar., three trefoils slipped vert.

HERON — BARON HERON.

By Writ of Summons, dated 8th January, 1371, 44 Edward III.

Lineage.

About the beginning of King John's reign,

JORDAN HAIRUN possessed a barony in Northumberland, which he held by the service of one knight's fee, as his ancestors had done from the time of King Henry I., who enfeoffed them thereof. He was s. by his son,

WILLIAM HERON, who, in the 32nd Henry III., was made governor of Bamburgh Castle, in the county of Northumberland, and in the 39th of the same reign was governor of the castle of Pickering, in Yorkshire, and warden of the forests north of Trent. The next year he filled the office of sheriff of Northumberland, and was constituted governor of Scarborough Castle. He m. ———, daughter and heir of Odonel de Ford, and was s. by his son,

WILLIAM HERON. This feudal lord was one of the barons on the part of the king at the battle of Lewes; and was summoned by Edward I., with the other northern barons, to meet him at Norham, with horse and arms, when he went to give judgment between the competitors for the crown of Scotland. William Heron m. Christian, daughter and heir of Roger de Notton, and had issue,

> WALTER, who m. Alicia de Hastings, and dying before his father, left an only daughter and heir, EMMELINE, m. to John, Lord Darcy, steward of the household to Edward III., and who, on the decease of her grandfather, was his heir, whereby the Darcy family became possessed of the ancient barony of HERON, and of the manors of SILKSTON and NOTTON, in the county of York.
>
> Roger, of whom presently.
> Odonel.

At the decease of his father, his elder brother having died previously, as stated above, the representation of the family devolved upon

ROGER HERON, who inherited the manors of Ford and Bokenfield, in the county of Northumberland; and with his brother Odonel, attended King Edward I., as one of his knights, to the siege of Stirling Castle. In the 10th of Edward II. he was governor of Bamburgh Castle, and was s. at his decease by his son,

WILLIAM HERON. This feudal lord obtained licence, in the 12th Edward III., to make a castle of his house at Ford—and was summoned to parliament, as a BARON, on the 8th January, 1371, but never afterwards. The BARONY OF HERON became therefore, at his decease, EXTINCT.

ARMS.—Gules a chevron between three herons ar.

HERON — BARON HERON.

By Writ of Summons, dated 13th November, 1393, 17 Richard II.

Lineage.

SIR WILLIAM HERON, of Applynden, grandson of Odonel Heron, and grand nephew of the Lord Heron, of Ford, having m. Elizabeth, widow of John de Falvesley, daughter and heiress of William, Baron Say, and cousin and heiress of Thomas de Brewose, had summons to parliament, from 13th November, 1393, to 25th August, 1404, as "Willielmo Heron, Chl'r," although it is certain that he was generally considered as Lord Say, jure uxoris ; for in a charter of 1st Henry IV., to which he was a witness, he is styled "Willielmo Heron, Dominus

de Say, Seneschallus Hospitii Regis." This nobleman was a gallant soldier, and eminent diplomatist. He died 30th October, 1404, without issue, when, if his barony be deemed a distinct dignity from that of SAY, it became EXTINCT.

ARMS.—Gules a chevron between three herons ar.

HILTON — BARON HILTON, OF HILTON, IN THE COUNTY OF DURHAM.

By Writ of Summons, dated 23rd June, 1295, 23 Edward I.

Lineage.

ROBERT DE HILTON, of Hilton Castle, in the county palatine of Durham, was summoned to parliament, as a BARON, in the 23rd, 24th, and 25th of Edward I. His lordship m. Margaret, one of the three co-heirs of Marmaduke de Thwenge, by whom he acquired large estates, and left two daughters,

> Isabel, m. to Walter de Pedwardyn.
> Maud, m. to Sir John Hothum, Knt.

At his lordship's decease the BARONY OF HILTON fell into ABEYANCE between those ladies, as it continues amongst their representatives, should any exist.

ARMS.—Ar. two bars az. and fleur de lis or.

HILTON—BARON HILTON.

By Writ of Summons, dated 27th January, 1332, 6 Edward III.

Lineage.

ALEXANDER DE HILTON, who served in the Scottish wars under Ralph, Lord Nevill, had summons to parliament, as a BARON, from 27th January, 1332, to 22nd January, 1336. But of this nobleman, or his descendants, nothing further is known.

ARMS.—Ar. two bars az. and fleur de lis or.

HOESE—BARON HOESE.

By Writ of Summons, dated 23rd June, 1295, 23 Edward I.

Lineage.

In the 4th year of King Henry III.

HENRY HOESE, of Herting, in the county of Sussex, gave ninety marks for livery of his father's lands, and dying in fifteen years after, was s. by his son,

MATTHEW HOESE, who thereupon gave seven hundred marks for livery of his inheritance. This Matthew, in the 37th Henry III., entered into covenants with John Maunsell, provost of Beverley, that Henry, his son and heir, should espouse Joane Fleming, niece of the said John. Matthew died in two years afterwards, and was s. by his aforesaid son,

HENRY HOESE, for whose wardship, and custody of his lands, the above named John Maunsell paid six hundred marks. This feudal lord took up arms with the other barons, in the 49th Henry III.,

2 M

against the king; but when he died does not appear. He was *s.*, however, by his son, another

HENRY HOESE, who *d.* in 1289, and was *s.* by his son,

HENRY HOESE. This feudal lord had summons in the 22nd Edward I., upon the 8th June in that year, to attend the king, with divers other persons of note, to advise concerning the important affairs of the realm; and the next year he was summoned to parliament, as a BARON, under the designation of " Henrico Husee," and from that period to the 10th October, 1325 (19th Edward II.). His lordship, who was engaged in the wars of Scotland, *d.* in 1332, and was *s.* by his son,

HENRY HOESE, second baron, summoned to parliament, from 19th August, 1337, to 10th March, 1349. This nobleman, in the 21st Edward III., on the marriage of Henry, his son and heir, with Elizabeth, the daughter of John de Bohun, settled certain estates upon him and her, and their issue, default to Richard, another son, with remainder to the issue of himself, by Catherine, his then wife, and in default of such issue, on Elizabeth, his daughter. His lordship appears to have survived this settlement but two years, when he was *s.* by his son,

HENRY HOESE, but neither this person, nor any of his descendants, were afterwards summoned to parliament.

ARMS.—Barry of six, ermine and gules.

HOESE OR HUSEE—BARON HOESE, OF BEECHWORTH, IN THE COUNTY OF SURREY.

By Writ of Summons, dated 20th November, 1348, 22 Edward III.

Lineage.

ROGER HOESE, or HUSE, presumed to be of the same family as the Lords Hoese of Herting, in Sussex, having distinguished himself in the wars of Scotland, was summoned to parliament as a BARON, from 20th November, 1348, to 10th March, 1349. His lordship *d.* in 1361, seised, amongst other lands, of the manor of West Beechesworth, and Heggercourt, in the county of Surrey; Ringstede, in Dorsetshire; a moiety of Burton Sacy, in the county of Southampton; and Northinkton, and Kingston Deverell, in Wilts. He was *s.* by his son,

SIR JOHN HUSEE, of Beechworth Castle, who had livery of his inheritance, but was never summoned to parliament. The only daughter of this baron, Alice, is said, by Collins, to have married Richard de Wallop, ancestor of the Earls of Portsmouth, and the lady is called heir of Robert Husee, her brother; but Vincent mentions her as sister of Sir John, and daughter of course, of Roger, Lord Huse. It would appear by both authorities, however, that the Earls of Portsmouth represent this branch of the old baronial house of HOESE, or HUSEE.

ARMS.—Barry of six, ermine and gules.

HOLAND—BARONS HOLAND.

By Writ of Summons, dated 29th July, 1314, 8 Edward II.

Lineage.

That this family was of great antiquity in the county of Lancaster, is evident from the register of the county of COKERSAND ABBEY, to which religious house some of its members were benefactors, in King John's time. The first person of any note, however,

ROBERT DE HOLAND, who was in the wars of Scotland, in the 31st Edward I., owed his advancement to his becoming secretary to Thomas, Earl of Lancaster, for previously he had been but a " *poor knight.*" In the 1st Edward II., he obtained large territorial grants from the crown, viz. the manors of Melburne, Newton, Osmundeston, Swarkeston, Chelardeston, Normanton, and Wybeleston, in the county of Derby, and the same year had a military summons to march against the Scots. In the 8th Edward II., he was first summoned to parliament as a BARON; and in the 10th and 12th, he was again in the wars of Scotland, in which latter year he had licence to make a castle of his manor house of Bagworth, in the county of Leicester. Upon the insurrection of his old master, Thomas, Earl of Lancaster, (15th Edward II.) his lordship promised that nobleman, to whom he owed his first rise in the world, all the aid in his power; but failing to fulfil his engagement, Lancaster was forced to fly northwards, and was finally taken prisoner at Boroughbridge, when Lord Holand rendered himself to the king at Derby, and was sent prisoner to Dover Castle. For which duplicity he became so odious to the people, that being afterwards made prisoner a second time, anno 1328, in a wood, near Henley park, towards Windsor, he was beheaded on the nones of October, and his head sent to Henry, Earl of Lancaster, then at Waltham Cross, in the county of Essex, by Sir Thomas Wyther, and some other private friends. His lordship *m.* Maud, one of the daughters and co-heirs of Alan le Zouch, of Ashby, and had issue,

 ROBERT, his successor.

 Thomas, who became EARL OF KENT, see Holand, Earl of Kent.

 Alan, who had the manors of Dalbury, and Weeksworth, in the county of Derby.

 Otho, a person of great valour in the reign of Edward III., and one of the original KNIGHTS OF THE GARTER. He fell into disgrace, however, by suffering the Earl of Ewe, (a prisoner at war,) who had been committed to his custody, to go at large armed; and was committed to the Marshalsey, after being examined in the presence of the Lord Chancellor, and other noblemen. He died soon after in Britanny, (33d Edward III.) where he was engaged in his military capacity: and having no issue, his elder brother, Sir Robert Holand, by his last will, became his heir.

Robert, Lord Holand, was *s.* by his eldest son,

SIR ROBERT HOLAND, second baron, summoned to parliament from 25th February, 1342, to

6th October, 1372. This nobleman was engaged for several years in the French wars of King Edward III., part of the time under Thomas de Beauchamp, Earl of Warwick, and the remainder in the retinue of his brother, Thomas Holland. His lordship d. in 1373, leaving his grand-daughter,

> MAUD HOLLAND, then seventeen years of age, his sole heir; who m. John Lovel, fifth LORD LOVEL, OF TICHMERSH; and carried the BARONY OF HOLLAND into that family, (see Lovel, Barons Lovel, of Tichmersh).

ARMS.—Az. a lion rampant guardant, between six fleur-de-lis, ar.

HOLLAND — BARONS HOLLAND, EARLS OF KENT, AND BARONS WOODSTOCK AND WAKE, DUKE OF SURREY.

Barony, by Writ of Summons, dated 15th July, 1353, 27 Edward III.
Earldom, &c., by marriage, with Joane Plantagenet, the Fair Maid of Kent.
Dukedom, 29th September, 1397.

Lineage.

SIR THOMAS DE HOLLAND, second son of Robert de Holand, Lord Holland, having been engaged from the 14th to the 20th Edward III., in the wars of France, and in the last year commanded the van of Prince Edward's army, at the famous battle of CRESSY, was made a KNIGHT OF THE GARTER, and summoned to parliament as a BARON. At the siege of Caen, Sir Thomas had the good fortune to make prisoner of the EARL OF EWE, then Constable of France, whom he delivered up to King Edward, for the sum of four thousand florens: and he (Sir Thomas) subsequently assisted at the siege of Calais. His lordship m.* Joane Plantagenet, celebrated for her beauty, under the name of "the Fair Maid of Kent," only daughter of Edmund Plantagenet, surnamed "of Woodstock," Earl of Kent, second son of King Edward I.* This distinguished woman inherited, upon the decease of her brother, JOHN, third Earl of Kent, that dignity, with the Barony of WOODSTOCK, honours of her father, and the BARONY OF WAKE, a dignity of her mother's;

---

* It is said by some that this Thomas, being steward of the household to William de Montacute, Earl of Salisbury, married his mistress, viz., Joane, daughter of Edmund, and sister and heir of John, Earl of Kent. But herein there is a mistake: for, by his petition to Pope Clement VI., representing that the said Earl of Salisbury had a purpose to have wedded her, had not a precontract with her by him been formerly made, and carnal knowledge ensued: also that nevertheless the same earl, taking advantage of his absence in foreign parts, made a second contract with her, and unjustly withheld her. His holiness, upon a full hearing of the cause, gave sentence for him; in which the Earl of Salisbury acquiesced.   DUGDALE.

from which latter peerage, she styled herself "LADY OF WAKE."

In the 28th Edward III., his lordship was made lieutenant, and captain general of the Dukedom of Britanny, and he was constituted, in two years afterwards, governor of the islands of Jersey and Guernsey. He had summons to parliament as LORD HOLLAND, from the 27th to the 31st Edward III.: but in the 34th, (anno 1360,) he assumed the title of EARL OF KENT, and was so summoned on the 20th November, in that year, in right of his wife, for it does not appear that he had any other sort of creation. In this year his lordship was appointed the KING'S LIEUTENANT AND CAPTAIN GENERAL IN FRANCE AND NORMANDY. He did not long, however, enjoy that high office, for he died on the 28th December, in the same year, leaving issue by the great heiress of Kent, (who espoused, after his lordship's decease, Edward the Black Prince, and was mother of King Richard II.,) three sons, and a daughter, viz.,

> THOMAS, his successor.
> Edmund.
> John, created EARL OF HUNTINGDON, AND DUKE OF EXETER (see Holland, Duke of Exeter).
> Maud, m. Hugh, son of Hugh de Courtney, Earl of Devon.

Thomas Holland, EARL OF KENT, was s. by his eldest son,

THOMAS HOLLAND, second Earl of Kent, Baron Woodstock, Baron Wake, and Baron Holland. This nobleman was engaged in the French wars in the immediate retinue of his gallant stepfather, EDWARD, the Black Prince, and attained distinction at the battle of Castile. Upon the accession of his half-brother, King RICHARD II., his lordship obtained a grant of £200 per annum out of the exchequer, and was constituted general warden of all the forests south of Trent. In the 9th of the same reign, at the decease of his mother, JOANE, Princess of Wales, he had special livery of all the lands of her inheritance; having had previously his grant out of the exchequer extended to £1000 a year. He was also constituted MARSHAL OF ENGLAND, but he was afterwards discharged of that office, which was conferred upon Thomas Mowbray, Earl of Nottingham: and appointed governor of CARISBROKE CASTLE for life. His lordship m. the Lady Alice Fits-Alan, daughter of Richard, Earl of Arundel, by whom he had, with other issue,

> THOMAS, } successively EARLS OF KENT.
> EDMUND, }
> Alianore, m. first, to Roger Mortimer, Earl of March, and secondly, to Edward Charlton, Lord Powis.
> Margaret, m. first, to John Beaufort, Marquess of Dorset, and secondly, to Thomas Plantagenet, Duke of Clarence, son of King Henry IV.
> Joane, m. first, to Edward, Duke of York, secondly, to William, Lord Willoughby, and thirdly, to Sir Henry de Bromfiete.
> Eleanor, m. to Thomas Montacute, Earl of Salisbury.

Elisabeth, *m.* to Sir John Nevill, Knt.

Bridget, a nun at Barking.

The earl *d.* in 1397, and was *s.* by his eldest son,

THOMAS HOLLAND, third Earl of Kent. This nobleman, upon the attainder of Thomas de Beauchamp, Earl of Warwick, 22nd Richard II., had a grant in special tail of the castle, manor, and lordship of WARWICK, with sundry other manors: having been created DUKE OF SURREY, the preceding year, by his uncle, King Richard, sitting in parliament, with the crown upon his head. He was also constituted MARSHAL OF ENGLAND, and about the same time appointed LIEUTENANT OF IRELAND. The earl was likewise a KNIGHT of the GARTER. But all his honours terminated with the power of his unhappy and royal kinsman; for being engaged in a conspiracy to subvert the government, after the accession of the Duke of Lancaster, as Henry IV., he was taken prisoner and beheaded, with the Earl of Salisbury, by the populace, at Cirencester, in 1400, when his head was sent to London, and placed upon the bridge there, and parliament passed an act of attainder, by which his HONOURS and LANDS became FORFEITED. His lordship *m.* the Lady Joane Stafford, daughter of Hugh, Earl of Stafford, but had no issue. Notwithstanding the attainder, (although no reversal is upon record,) the earl's brother and heir,

EDMUND HOLLAND, appears to have succeeded to the Earldom of Kent, and, of course, to the Baronies of Woodstock, Wake, and Holland. He had, subsequently, a special livery of certain castles, manors and lands, which had devolved upon him by virtue of an old entail made of them by his ancestors. In the 9th Henry IV. his lordship was appointed one of the commissioners to treat of peace, between the king and the Duke of Britanny, and was constituted LORD ADMIRAL OF ENGLAND. But soon after that besieging the castle and isle of Briak, in Britanny, he received a mortal wound in his head by an arrow from a cross bow, on the 15th September, 1407. His lordship *m.* Lucy, daughter of the Duke of Milan, but having no legitimate issue, his sisters, or their representatives, became his heirs, (revert to the children of Thomas, second earl,) and amongst those, the BARONIES OF WOODSTOCK, WAKE, and HOLLAND, are in ABEYANCE, supposing them unaffected by the attainder of THOMAS, Duke of Surrey.

With Edmund, Earl of Kent, who was a Knight of the Garter, that EARLDOM EXPIRED in the Holland family.

ARMS.—Al. semy de lis, a lion rampant guardant, or.

HOLLAND — EARL OF HUNTINGDON, DUKE OF EXETER.

Earldom, 2nd June, 1337.

Dukedom, 29th September, 1397.

Lineage.

JOHN DE HOLLAND, third son of Thomas de Holland, Earl of Kent, by the celebrated heiress, JOANE PLANTAGENET, " the Fair Maid of Kent," (see Holland, Earls of Kent,) was in the expedition made into Scotland in the 29th Edward III., and

after the accession of his half-brother, King Richard II., was constituted JUSTICE OF CHESTER. From which period we seldom find him out of some great public employment. In the 7th Richard he attended the king in the expedition then made into Scotland, when having some dispute with Ralph de Stafford, elder son of the Earl of Stafford, he slew the said Ralph with his dagger, and fled to sanctuary at Beverley. But the king becoming highly incensed at this foul murder, caused the assassin to be indicted and outlawed for the crime, and seised upon all his lands and offices.

It is said that the Princess Joane, his mother, bearing that the king had vowed that Holland should suffer according to law, sent earnestly to him, imploring his favour, (she being their common parent,) and that upon return of the messenger to Wallingford, where she then was, finding that her request availed not, she became so absorbed in grief, that she died within five days. De Holland, however, eventually made his peace through the mediation of the Duke of Lancaster, and other noblemen, and was pardoned by the Earl of Stafford. The year after this unfortunate affair he was retained to serve the king in his Scottish wars for forty days, and the next year being in Castile with the Duke of Lancaster, he tilted at Besances with Sir Reginald de Roy, in the presence of the King of Portugal, being then constable of the duke's host. About this time, being also in the wars of France, he obtained a grant of five hundred marks per annum during his life. And, at length, in expiation of the murder he had the misfortune to commit, he came to an agreement with the Earl of Stafford to find three priests to celebrate divine service every day, to the world's end, for the soul of Ralph Stafford, in such place as the king should appoint. In the 11th of the same reign he was again in the wars of France, as also in Spain, with John of Gaunt, Duke of Lancaster, and, upon his return was created EARL OF HUNTINGDON, at the especial desire of the Commons in parliament assembled, having therewith a grant of £20 per annum out of the profits of the county: as also lands of two thousand marks per annum, to himself and Elizabeth, his wife, and to the heirs male of their bodies. Shortly after which he was made admiral of the king's fleet westwards, and constituted governor of the castle, town, and Bastile of Brest, in Britanny, for three years, where he accordingly went to reside. He subsequently obtained large grants from the crown, and was constituted GREAT CHAMBERLAIN OF ENGLAND for life. His lordship was one of those nobles who impeached the Duke of Gloucester, in the parliament held at Nottingham, and he is accused of having assisted at the execution of his grandfather, Richard, Earl of Arundel. He was advanced in 1397 to the DUKEDOM OF EXETER, by King Richard, in open parliament, being at the time captain of Calais: and he accompanied that monarch soon afterwards into Ireland. Upon the accession, however, of the Duke of Lancaster, as Henry IV., his grace was doomed to a reverse of fortune, and parliament adjudged that he should lose his honours and lands. He retained, however, the Earldom of Huntingdon, which, with his whole estate, he might probably have continued to enjoy, had he not joined with his brother, the Earl of Kent, in a conspiracy to overturn the new government. The plot having, however, failed, he endeavoured to escape beyond sea, but was driven back by contrary winds to the coast of Essex, where he landed, and was made prisoner by the populace while at supper at the house of a friend. He was immediately conveyed to Chelmsford, and thence to Plessy, where he was beheaded by the common people on the very spot where the Duke of Gloucester had suffered in the reign of his brother, King Richard. His grace died in 1400, and was subsequently attainted. He had married the Lady Elizabeth Plantagenet, daughter of John of Gaunt, and had issue,

- *Richard*, d. unmarried.
- JOHN, his heir, created DUKE OF EXETER (see Holland, Duke of Exeter).
- Edward (Sir).
- Constance, m. first, to Thomas Mowbray, Duke of Norfolk; and afterwards to John, Lord Grey, of Ruthven.

By this alliance, John, Earl of Huntingdon, and Duke of Exeter, was brother-in-law to King Henry IV., the monarch, for conspiring against whom he lost his life. The EARLDOM and DUKEDOM fell under the attainder of his grace.

ARMS.—Of England, and a bordure of France.

HOLLAND—DUKES OF EXETER.

By Letters Patent, dated 6th January, 1443.

Lineage.

JOHN HOLLAND, second but eldest surviving son of John Holland, Earl of Huntingdon and Duke of Exeter, (attainted and beheaded in 1400,) was restored in blood, as heir to his father and brother, in the 4th Henry V., and the next year made general of all the men at arms and archers at that time employed in the king's fleet at sea, in which capacity he assisted at the siege of Caen. He did not, however, make proof of his age until the ensuing year, when it was stated by the witnesses then examined, that the abbot of Tavestoke, in the county of Devon, being one of his godfathers, gave him, immediately after the baptism, a cup of gold, with a circle about it, framed after the fashion of a lilley, and with ten pounds in gold therein, and to the nurse twenty shillings. That the prior of Plimpton, being the other godfather, gave him twenty pounds in gold; and that Joane, the wife of Sir John Pomeraie, Knt., carried him to the church to be christened: her husband, and Sir John Dynham, Knt., conducting her by the arms. Likewise, that twenty-four men did precede them, bearing twenty-four torches, which torches, as soon as the name was given, were kindled.

This John Holland was engaged, during the whole reign of Henry V., in active warfare upon the French soil, and displayed extraordinary skill and valour. He was at the siege of Roan; and the next year, upon the taking of Pontoise by the Captain de la Bouche, he intercepted those of the garrison who endeavoured to get to Paris; and he was in that great fight against the French who came to raise

the siege of Fresney, wherein five thousand were slain and six hundred made prisoners. He was subsequently commissioned to reduce all the castles and strong places in Normandy that continued to hold out against the king; and he was soon after, in consideration of his eminent services, constituted constable of the Tower of London. In the reign of Henry VI., he continued his gallant career in France, and assisted, in 1431, at the coronation of that monarch, then solemnised at Paris. In the 11th of the same reign, he had a grant of the office of MARSHAL OF ENGLAND, to hold during the minority of John, son and heir of John, late Duke of Norfolk; and two years afterwards, being sent ambassador to the city of Arras, to treat of peace with the French, he had licence to carry with him gold, silver, plate, jewels, robes, twenty-four pieces of woollen cloth, and other things, to the value of six thousand pounds sterling. In the 14th, he was joined in commission with the Earl of Northumberland for guarding the east and west marches towards Scotland, and at the same time constituted admiral of England and Aquitaine. He was afterwards in a commission to try all manner of treasons and sorceries which might be hurtful to the king's person; and was created, by letters patent, dated at Windsor, 6th January, 1443, DUKE OF EXETER, with this special privilege, "that he and his heirs male should have place and seat in all parliaments and councils, next to the Duke of York and his heirs male."

His grace was constituted lord high-admiral of England, Ireland, and Aquitaine, for life, in the 24th Henry VI., his son, Henry, being joined in the grant, and, the next year, made constable of the Tower of London, his son, Henry, being, in like manner, joined with him. His lordship m. first, Anne, widow of Edward Mortimer, Earl of March, and daughter of Edmund, Earl of Stafford, by whom he had an only son,

HENRY, his successor.

He espoused, secondly, Lady Anne Montacute, daughter of John, Earl of Salisbury, and had a daughter,

Anne, m. to John, Lord Nevil, son and heir of Ralph, Earl of Westmoreland, which Lord Nevil fell at Towton-Feld, and died s. p. Her ladyship espoused, secondly, Sir John Nevil, Knt., uncle of her first husband, and by him was mother of Ralph Nevil, third Earl of Westmoreland.

His grace, who was a KNIGHT of the GARTER, died in 1446, and was s. by his only son,

HENRY HOLLAND, second Duke of Exeter, who, in the 28th Henry VI., in consideration of his father's services, had livery of all his castles, manors, and lands, both in England and Wales, although at that time he had not accomplished his full age: after which (33rd Henry VI.) the Yorkists then prevailing, his grace having fled to sanctuary at Westminster, he was forced thence, and sent prisoner to Pontefract Castle. We find him, however, at the battle of Wakefield, sharing the triumph of the Lancastrians; when King Henry VI., being re-established in power, his grace's fidelity was rewarded by a grant of the office of constable of Fotheringay Castle. But the tide again turning, the duke fled from Towton-Field, with the Duke of Somerset and some others, to York, where the king and queen then were, and thence proceeded with the royal fugitives into Scotland. In the parliament assembled upon the accession of King Edward IV., his grace, with the other leading Lancastrians, was attainted; but nothing further is recorded of him until he appeared again in arms under the red banner of Lancaster at Barnet-Field, where his party sustained so signal a defeat. In this conflict the Duke of Exeter fought with extraordinary courage and resolution, and, being severely wounded, was left for dead, from seven o'clock in the morning until four in the afternoon, when, being conveyed to the house of one of his servants, called Ruthland, he had the assistance of a surgeon, and was then carried for sanctuary to Westminster: but in the 13th Edward IV. 1473, he was found dead in the sea between Calais and Dover: by what accident, however, was never ascertained. *Comines* reports that he saw this unhappy nobleman in such deep distress, (after the defeat at Barnet, it is presumed,) that he ran on foot, bare-legged, after the Duke of Burgundy's train, begging his bread for God's sake, but that he uttered not his name; and that when he was known, the duke conferred upon him a small pension. His grace m. Anne, daughter of Richard, Duke of York, and sister of King Edward IV., by whom, according to Sandford, he had an only daughter,

ANNE, m. to Thomas Grey, Marquess of Dorset. From his lady the Duke of Exeter was divorced, *at her suit*, and his DUKEDOM fell under the attainder, in 1461, twelve years before his melancholy death. Thus terminated one of the staunchest partisans of the house of Lancaster, although brother-in-law to King Edward, the successful monarch of the house of York. Such was the heart-rending dissension which that terrible quarrel had sown amongst the nearest and dearest connections, and such the misery and wretchedness it entailed upon a great majority of the most illustrious houses in England.

ARMS—Of England, and a bordure of France.

HOLLES — BARONS HOUGHTON, EARLS OF CLARE, DUKES OF NEWCASTLE.

Barony,	by Letters	9th July, 1616.
Earldom,	Patent,	2nd Nov., 1624.
Dukedom,		14th May, 1694.

Lineage.

The first of this family who became of note was

SIR WILLIAM HOLLES, an alderman of London, and lord mayor in 1540. This opulent citizen left three sons, viz.

Thomas (Sir), who succeeded to a considerable estate, but squandered the whole, and died in prison.

WILLIAM, of whom presently.

Francis, died s. p.

The second son,

WILLIAM HOLLES, inherited the manor of

270

Houghton, in the county of Nottingham, and took up his abode there. He m. Anne, daughter and co-heir of John Danzell, Esq., of Danzell, in Cornwall, and had, with other issue, DANZELL, who m. Anne, sister of John Sheffield, Lord Sheffield, and dying before his father, left a son (who eventually succeeded to the estates),

JOHN HOLLES, of Houghton, who was elevated to the peerage by King James I., on 9th July, 1616, (through the influence of the Duke of Buckingham, to whom he paid £10,000.,) in the dignity of BARON HOUGHTON, OF HOUGHTON, and was created, under the same powerful patronage, for the additional sum of £5,000., EARL OF CLARE,[*] on the 2nd November, 1624. His lordship m. Anne, daughter of Sir Thomas Stanhope, of Shelford, in the county of Nottingham, and had surviving issue,

JOHN, his successor.

DANZELL, created BARON HOLLES, *of Ifield* (see that dignity).

Eleanore, m. to Oliver Fitz-Williams, Earl of Tirconnel, in Ireland.

Arabella, m. to Thomas Wentworth, first Lord Strafford.

His lordship d. 4th October, 1637, and was s. by his eldest son,

JOHN HOLLES, second earl, who espoused Elizabeth, eldest daughter, and one of the co-heirs of the celebrated General Sir Horatio Vere, Lord Vere, of Tilbury, and had issue,

GILBERT, his successor.

Anne, m. to Edward Clinton, Lord Clinton, eldest son of Theophilus, fourth Earl of Lincoln, and was mother of *Edward*, fifth EARL OF LINCOLN.

Elizabeth, m. to Wentworth, Earl of Kildare.

Arabella, m. to Sir Edward Rosseter, Knt., of Somerley, in the county of Lincoln.

Susan, m. to Sir John Lort, Bart., of Stockpole Court, in the county of Pembroke.

Diana, m. to Henry Bridges, son and heir of Sir Thomas Bridges, of Keynsham, in the county of Somerset.

Penelope, m. to Sir James Langham, Bart., of Colesbroke, in the county of Northampton.

Of this nobleman, Lord Clarendon says, " he was a man of honour and of courage, and would have been an excellent person, if his heart had not been too much set upon keeping and improving his estate." His lordship appears to have lived in retirement at his country houses during the usurpation. He survived to witness the restoration of the monarchy, and dying 2nd January, 1665, was s. by his son,

GILBERT HOLLES, third Earl of Clare. This nobleman opposed strongly the measures of the Stewarts, and was a strenuous supporter of the revolution. He m. Grace, daughter of William

[*] This dignity had been just before refused to Robert Rich, Earl of Warwick, on a solemn declaration by the crown lawyers, that it was a title peculiar to the royal blood, and not to be conferred upon a subject.

Pierpont, of Thoresby, in the county of Nottingham, second son of Robert, Earl of Kingston, and had issue,

JOHN, who succeeded to the honours.

William, who fell at Luxemburgh, in the twenty-first year of his age.

Densell, died unmarried.

Elizabeth, m. to Sir Christopher Vane, Knt., who was created BARON BARNARD, of Barnard Castle, in the county of Durham. From this marriage *William-Henry*, present MARQUESS OF CLEVELAND, is fourth in lineal descent.

Mary, m. to Hugh Boscawen, Esq.

Ann.

Grace, m. to Sir Thomas Pelham, Bart., created afterwards BARON PELHAM, *of Laughton*, in the county of Sussex, and had, with other issue, a son THOMAS, who inherited the greatest part of the Holles estates, and had the honours of the family partly revived in his person, (see PELHAM-HOLLES, Earls of Clare).

His lordship d. 16th January, 1689, and was s. by his eldest son,

JOHN HOLLES, fourth Earl of Clare. This nobleman having married Lady Margaret Cavendish, third daughter and co-heir of Henry, second Duke of Newcastle, inherited the greater part of his grace's estates upon the decease in 1691, and was created, on the 14th May, 1694, *Marquess of Clare* and DUKE OF NEWCASTLE. He likewise succeeded to the fortune of his kinsman, Densell, Lord Holles, of Ifield, and thus became one of the richest subjects in the kingdom. His grace enjoyed several high offices at court, and was a KNIGHT OF THE GARTER. He died from the effects of a fall while stag-hunting, on 15th July, 1711, leaving an only daughter,

LADY HENRIETTA CAVENDISH HOLLES, who m. in 1713, *Edward*, LORD HARLEY, son and heir of Robert, Earl of Oxford, to whom she conveyed a very considerable estate, and by whom she had an only surviving daughter,

LADY MARGARET CAVENDISH HARLEY, who espoused *William Bentinck*, second DUKE OF PORTLAND, K.G.

At the decease of the Duke of Newcastle ALL HIS HONOURS became EXTINCT. He had adopted his nephew, THOMAS PELHAM, eldest son of Thomas, *Lord Pelham*, who succeeded to a portion of his great estates, and assumed the surname and arms of HOLLES (see Pelham-Holles, Earl of Clare).

ARMS.—Erm. two piles in point sa.

HOLLES-PELHAM — BARONS PELHAM, EARLS OF CLARE, DUKE OF NEWCASTLE.

Barony,		29th December, 1706.
Earldom,	by Letters Patent.	26th October, 1714.
Dukedom,		2nd August, 1715.

Lineage.

SIR THOMAS PELHAM, Bart., was elevated to the peerage, 29th December, 1706, as BARON PELHAM, *of Laughton, in the county of Sussex*. He had married, previously, Lady Grace Holles, youngest daughter of Gilbert, third Earl of Clare, and dying in 1712, was s. by his eldest son,

THOMAS PELHAM-HOLLES, as second Baron Pelham. This nobleman having been adopted, by his uncle, John Holles, fourth Earl of Clare, and first Duke of Newcastle, assumed the additional surname and arms of HOLLES, upon the decease of his grace; and was created, 26th October, 1714, *Viscount Pelham*, of Houghton, and EARL OF CLARE. His lordship was advanced the next year, to the dignities of *Marquess of Clare*, and DUKE OF NEWCASTLE, with remainder, default of male issue, to his brother, the Right Honourable HENRY PELHAM. His grace, under the three first sovereigns of the house of Brunswick, fulfilled the several posts of lord chamberlain of the household; secretary of state; first lord of the treasury, and one of the lords justices, during the temporary absences of Kings George I. and II. The duke was likewise chancellor of the University of Cambridge, a privy counsellor, and a KNIGHT of the GARTER.

His grace m. Lady Harriet Godolphin, daughter of Francis, Earl of Godolphin, by Henrietta, his wife, daughter of the celebrated John Churchill, Duke of Marlborough, but had no issue.

The duke was created, in 1756, DUKE OF NEWCASTLE UNDER LYNN, with special remainder to his nephew, Henry Fiennes-Clinton, ninth Earl of Lincoln, K.G., son of his grace's sister, the Honourable Lucy Pelham, by Henry, seventh Earl of Lincoln; and he was also created BARON PELHAM, *of Stanmore, in Sussex*, with remainder to his kinsman, Thomas Pelham, Esq., of Stanmore, (grandson of Henry Pelham, younger brother of the first Lord Pelham,) which honours devolved, at his grace's decease, in 1768, according to the said limitations, and are now enjoyed by the DUKE OF NEWCASTLE and the EARL OF CHICHESTER, (see those dignities, in *Burke's Dictionary of the Peerage and Baronetage*;) while ALL HIS OWN HONOURS, including the DUKEDOM OF NEWCASTLE, in remainder to his brother, the Right Honourable Henry Pelham, (that gentleman having predeceased his grace, leaving daughters only,) became EXTINCT.

ARMS.—Quarterly, first and fourth, as. three pelicans ar. vulning themselves in the breast, gu. second and third, erm. two piles in point sa.

HOLLES — BARONS HOLLES OF IFIELD, IN THE COUNTY OF SUSSEX.

By Letters Patent, dated 20th April, 1661.

Lineage.

The Honourable DANZILL HOLLES, second son of John, first Earl of Clare, by Anne, eldest daughter and co-heir of John Danzill, of Danzill, in Cornwall, Serjeant at Law, was elevated to the peerage, at the restoration, by letters patent, dated 20th April, 1661, as BARON HOLLES, of *Ifield, in the county of Sussex*. This nobleman, in the beginning, opposed the assumed prerogative of Charles I. and his ministers; carrying up the impeachment against Laud; suffering a severe imprisonment, and being marked by the king in that wild attempt of accusing the five members. When brought before the privy council, with Sir Henry Hammond and others, in those times of arbitrary power, Mr. Holles deported himself with a more than ordinary degree of firmness, and, as characteristic of the epoch, we give the following passage from his examination. "Why did you sit above some of the privy council, so near the speaker's chair?" "I seated myself there, some other times before, and took it as my due, there and in any place whatsoever, on account of my noble birth, as son of the Earl of Clare!" continuing to state, "that he came into the house, with as much zeal as any other person, to serve his majesty; yet, finding his majesty was offended, he humbly desired·to be the subject, rather of his mercy than of his power." To which the treasurer Weston, answered; "You mean rather of his majesty's mercy than of his justice." Mr. Holles replied, emphatically, "I say of his majesty's power." Subsequently discovering the designs of the republican party, and disgusted with them, he exerted himself zealously, at the decease of Cromwell, in furtherance of the restoration; and for some time after the accomplishment of that great event, accepted employments and embassies from the court. In 1663, his lordship was ambassador extraordinary to France, and afterwards, plenipotentiary to the treaty of Breda; but he again joined the ranks of opposition, and maintained the consistency of his patriotic character.

Burnet thus describes this patriotic personage:— "He was a man of courage,* and as great pride. The head of the presbyterian party, for many years; and who, during the whole course of his life, never once changed side. He had indeed, the soul of an old stubborn Roman in him; was a faithful, but a rough friend; and a severe, but open enemy. His sense of religion was just; his course of life regular; and his judgment, where passion did not bias him, sound enough. He was well versed in the records of parliament; and argued well but too vehemently; for he could not bear any contradiction."

His lordship m. first, Dorothy, only daughter and heiress of Sir Francis Ashley, of Dorchester, by whom he had one surviving son, FRANCIS, who was created a baronet. He espoused, secondly, Jane, eldest daughter and co-heir of Sir John Shirley, of Isville, in Sussex; and thirdly, Esther, second daughter and co-heir of Gideon de Lou, Lord of the manor of Columbiers, in Normandy, but had no other issue. He d. 17th February, 1679-80, and was s. by his son,

SIR FRANCIS HOLLES, Bart., of Winterbourn St. Martin, in the county of Dorset, as second

Lord Holles. His lordship m. first, Lucy, youngest daughter of Sir Robert Carr, of Sleford, in the county of Lincoln, Bart., by whom he had two daughters, who both died young. He espoused secondly, Anne, eldest daughter and co-heir, of Sir Francis Pile, Bart., of Compton Beauchamp, in the county of Berks, and had a son, DANZIL, his successor, and daughter, Jane, who died in infancy. His lordship d. 1st March, 1689-90, and was s. by his son,

DANZILL HOLLES, third baron. This nobleman died in his nineteenth year, (anno 1694,) unmarried, when the BARONY OF HOLLES, OF IFIELD, with the baronetcy, became EXTINCT, while his lordship's estates devolved upon his heir at law, John Holles, Duke of Newcastle.

ARMS.—Erm. two piles sa. a crescent for difference.

HOO — BARON OF HOO, IN THE COUNTY OF BEDFORD, AND OF HASTINGS, IN THE COUNTY OF SUSSEX.

By Letters Patent, dated 2nd June, 1447.

Lineage.

Of this family, whose chief seat was at Hoo, in Bedfordshire, were divers persons of note, prior to its elevation to the peerage.

ROBERT DE HOO, obtained the king's charter, 20th Edward I., for a weekly market, and an annual fair, at his manor of Knebbeworth, in the county of Hertford. As also free-warren in all his demesne lands, within his respective lordships of the above-mentioned Knebbeworth, and Harpeden, in the same shire; of Hoo and other estates in the county of Bedford; of Clopton, in Cambridgeshire, and Sivethorpe, in the county of Oxford. The next of the family we meet with,

SIR THOMAS HOO, Knt., had similar grants for fairs and markets, upon his different estates, in the 11th Edward III. He was s. by his son,

SIR WILLIAM HOO, Knt., who, in the 10th Richard II., assisted Michael de la Pole, Earl of Suffolk, in effecting his escape to Calais, in which garrison Sir William afterwards served (8th Henry IV.) under John, Earl of Somerset, then captain thereof. Sir William Hoo m. Alice, daughter and heir of Sir Thomas St. Maur (by Jane, his wife, daughter and heir of Nicholas Malmains), and was s. by his son,

SIR THOMAS HOO, who, having been employed in the suppression of a rebellion in Normandy, obtained a grant, 20th Henry VI., in consideration of his special services, and great expenses in the wars, of eleven pounds a year during his life, out of the revenues in the county of York. In the 24th of the same reign, having again distinguished himself in the French wars, he was elevated to the peerage, by letters patent, dated 2nd June, 1447, by the titles of LORD HOO, of Hoo, *in the county of Bedford*, and of HASTINGS, in the county of Sussex, with remainder to the heirs male of his body. Moreover, he was made a knight of the most noble order of the Garter. His lordship, married first, Elizabeth,

---

. * A remarkable instance of his spirit was his challenging General Ireton, who pleading, "That his conscience would not permit him to fight a duel;" Holles pulled him by the nose; telling him, "That if his conscience would not let him give redress, it ought to prevent his offering injuries."

daughter and heir of Sir Thomas Felton, Knt., by whom he had an only son, Thomas, who died in his father's life-time issueless. He espoused, secondly, Elizabeth, daughter and heir of Sir Nicholas Wichingham, Knt., by whom he had an only daughter, Anne, who m. Sir Geffery Bullen, Knt., some time, Lord Mayor of London. His lordship m. thirdly, Alianore, daughter of Leo, Lord Welles, and sister and co-heir of Richard, Lord Welles, by whom he had issue,

> Alianore, m. to Sir James Carew, Knt., of Bedington, in the county of Surrey.
>
> Jane, m. to Sir Roger Copley, Knt., from which marriage the present Sir Joseph Copley maternally descends.
>
> Elizabeth, m. to Sir John Davenish, Knt.

Lord Hoo died about the year 1453, and thus leaving no male issue, the Barony of Hoo became extinct.

Arms.—Quarterly, sa. and ar.

HOOD — BARON BRIDPORT, VISCOUNT BRIDPORT.

Barony, } by Letters { 13th June, 1796.
Viscounty, } Patent, { 10th June, 1801.

Lineage.

ALEXANDER HOOD, a very eminent naval officer, having served as rear admiral, under Lord Howe, at the relief of Gibraltar, in 1782, was invested with the military order of the Bath; and having, as second in command, contributed to the ever-memorable victory of the 1st June, 1794, was rewarded with a peerage of Ireland, in the dignity of Baron Bridport, of Cricket St. Thomas. In 1795, his lordship achieved a splendid victory over the French fleet, and was made, in consequence, a peer of Great Britain, 13th June, 1796, as Baron Bridport, of Cricket St. Thomas, in the county of Somerset. In 1801, he was advanced to the dignity of Viscount Bridport, being then vice-admiral of Great Britain, and general of marines. His lordship m. first, Maria, daughter of the Rev. Dr. West, prebendary of Durham; and secondly, Maria-Sophia, daughter and heiress of Thomas Bray, Esq., of Edmonton, but dying without issue, 3d May, 1814, his English honours, namely, the Barony and Viscounty of Bridport, became extinct, while the barony in the Irish peerage devolved according to a special limitation in the patent.

Arms.—Az. a fret, ar. on a chief or. three crescents, sa.

HOPTON — BARON HOPTON OF STRATTON, IN THE COUNTY OF CORNWALL.

By Letters Patent, dated 4th September, 1643.

Lineage.

ROBERT HOPTON, Esq., of Wytham, in the county of Somerset. m. Jane, daughter and heir of Rowland Keymiah, Esq., of Wardry, in the county of Monmouth, and left a son,

SIR RALPH HOPTON, who was made a Knight of the Bath, at the coronation of King Charles I., and became afterwards one of the most zealous supporters of that unfortunate monarch. Sir Ralph represented Welles, in parliament in 1642, when, perceiving the course of public affairs, he took up arms in the royal cause, and obtained distinction at Sherbourne Castle, Lanceston, Saltash, and Bradock, but particularly at Stratton, in Cornwall, when, in consideration of the gallant part he had in that victory, he was elevated to the peerage, on the 4th September, 1643, as Baron Hopton, of Stratton; with limitation, in default of male issue, to his uncle, Sir Arthur Hopton, Knt., and the heirs male of his body. His lordship was subsequently constituted general of the ordnance, in his majesty's armies, throughout the whole realm of England, and dominion of Wales. Lord Hopton m. Elizabeth, daughter of Arthur Capel, of Hadham, in the county of Hertford, Esq., and widow of Sir Justinian Leven, Knt., but had no issue. During the usurpation, his lordship retired to Bruges, where he died, in 1652, when (his uncle having predeceased him also issueless) the Barony of Hopton, of Stratton, became extinct.

Arms.—Erm. on two bars sa. six mullets or.

Sir Arthur Hopton, upon whom the title was entailed, died about the year 1650, without issue, when his four sisters, or their representatives, became his heirs. Those sisters were,

> Rachel, m. to ——— Morgan, Esq.
>
> Mary, m. first to ——— Hartop, Esq., and secondly, to Sir Henry Mackworth, Bart.
>
> Catherine, m. to John Windham, Esq.
>
> Margaret, m. to Sir Baynam Throgmorton, Bart.

HOWARD—BARONS HOWARD.

By Writ of Summons, dated 15th October, 1470, 49 Henry VI.

The first of this very eminent family, mentioned by Dugdale, after a fruitless inquiry to discover a more ancient founder,

SIR WILLIAM HOWARD, was chief justice of the court of Common Pleas from 1297 to 1308. This learned person had large possessions in Wigenhale, in the north-west parts of the county of Norfolk; and he had summons in the 23rd Edward I. amongst the rest of the judges, and the king's learned council, to the parliament then held at Westminster, as also to those parliaments of 25th, 26th, and 32nd of Edward I., and 1st Edward II. Sir William m. first, Alice, daughter, and eventually heir of Sir Edward Fitton, Knt., by whom he had two sons, John and William. He espoused secondly, Alice, daughter of Sir Robert Ufford, but had no issue. He was s. by his elder son,

SIR JOHN HOWARD, of Wiggenhall, who, in the 34th Edward I., being one of the gentlemen of the king's bed-chamber, obtained the wardship of the lands and heir of John de Crokedale, a person of note in Norfolk; and on the accession of King Edward II. had orders to attend his coronation at

Westminster, the Sunday next after the feast of St. Valentine. He subsequently distinguished himself in the wars of Gascony and Scotland; and was sheriff of the counties of Norfolk and Suffolk, from the 11th to the 16th Edward II. inclusive. Sir John m. Joan, sister of Richard de Cornwall, and dying in 1331, was s. by his son,

SIR JOHN HOWARD, who, in the 9th Edward III., was constituted admiral and captain of the king's navy from the mouth of the Thames northward, and the next year had an assignation of £183. 7s. 6d. for the wages of himself, with his men at arms and archers in that service. This gallant person m. Alice, daughter of Sir Robert de Boys, and sister and heir of Sir Robert de Boys, of Fersfield, in Norfolk, by which marriage the whole inheritance of the Boys's came into the Howard family. He had issue,

> ROBERT (Sir), of Fersfield. This gentleman was committed, in the 2nd Richard II., to the Tower, for detaining Margery de Narford, from Alice, Lady Nevil, her grandmother, with whom, on her petition to the king and council, she had been appointed to remain till the cause of divorce between her and John de Brewer should be determined in the court of Rome. This Sir Robert Howard m. Margery, daughter of Robert, Lord Scales, of Newcells, and, at length, one of the heirs of that family, by whom he left at his decease, (1388,) prior to the death of his father,
>
> > JOHN, successor to his grandfather.
> > Margaret, m. to William de Lisle.

Sir John Howard was s. by his grandson,

SIR JOHN HOWARD, who was sheriff of the counties of Essex and Hertford, 2nd Henry IV., and again in the 3rd and 7th Henry V., and in the 9th of the latter reign he was one of the knights of the shire for the county of Cambridge. He m. first, Margaret, daughter and heir of Sir John Plaiz, of Tofts, in Norfolk, and of Slansted Mountfitchet, in Essex, by whom he had issue,

> JOHN (Sir), who m. Joan, daughter of Sir Richard Walton, and sister and heir of John Walton, Esq., of Wyvenhoe, in Essex, by whom, dying in the life-time of his father, he left an only daughter and heir,
>
> > ELIZABETH, who m. John Vere, Earl of Oxford, whereby the Barony of Scales centered in the Veres.
>
> Margaret, m. first, to Sir Constantine Clifton, of Buckinham Castle, Norfolk, and secondly, to Sir Gilbert Talbot.

Sir John Howard espoused, secondly, Alice, daughter and heir of Sir William Tendring, of Tendring, and had two sons, viz.

> 1. ROBERT (Sir), who m. Margaret, eldest daughter of Thomas de Mowbray, Duke of Norfolk, by Elizabeth, his wife, daughter and co-heir of Richard Fitz-Alan, Earl of Arundel, and cousin and co-heir of John Mowbray, Duke of Norfolk. By this marriage the inheritance of those great families became eventually vested in this of the Howards, and by Isabel, the other co-heir in

274

that of Berkeley. Sir Robert dying before his father, left issue by this great heiress,

> JOHN, successor to his grandfather.
> Margaret, m. to Sir William Daniel, Baron of Rathwire, in Ireland.
> Cathárine, the second wife of Edward Nevil, Lord Abergavenny.

> 2. Henry, who, by the gift of his father, had Wigenhall, and other manors, in the county of Norfolk, m. Mary, daughter of Sir Henry Hussey, and left an only daughter and heiress,
>
> > ELIZABETH HOWARD, who m. Henry Wentworth, Esq., of Codham, in Essex.

Sir John Howard was s. by his grandson,

SIR JOHN HOWARD, an eminent Yorkist, distinguished not only by his birth and possessions, but by the various places of high trust which he filled during the reigns of Edward IV. and Richard III. He was first summoned to parliament as a BARON on the 15th October, 1470, and had summons from that period as LORD HOWARD, until the 15th November, 1582. In the next year he was created Duke of Norfolk, and made earl marshal of England. The ultimate fall of this nobleman, at Bosworth-field, under the banner of Richard III., is so well known that it is hardly necessary to mention it here. From the creation of the Dukedom of Norfolk, in the Howard family, the BARONY OF HOWARD continued merged therein, and was included in the numerous forfeitures and restorations which attended that dignity, until the demise of EDWARD HOWARD, eleventh Duke of Norfolk, in 1777, when, with several other baronies, it fell into ABEYANCE between the two daughters and co-heirs of his grace's brother, PHILIP HOWARD, Esq., of Buckenham, in the county of Norfolk, namely, Winifrede, LADY STOURTON, and Anne, LADY PETRE, thus:—

HENRY HOWARD, created Baron of Castle Rising, and Earl of Norwich, m. Anne, daughter of Edward, Marquess of Worcester, and left issue,

> HENRY, who succeeded his uncle, as Duke of Norfolk.
> Thomas, who m. Elizabeth-Maria, only daughter and heir of Sir Henry Savile, Bart., of Copley, in the county of York, and had issue,
>
> > THOMAS, who succeeded his uncle as Duke of Norfolk.
> > EDWARD, who s. his brother as Duke of Norfolk, and died s. p. in 1777.
> > Philip, m. first, Winifrede, daughter of Thomas Stoner, Esq., and had an only surviving daughter,
> >
> > > WINIFREDE, m. to William, LORD STOURTON, by whom she was mother of
> > >
> > > > CHARLES-PHILIP, Lord Stourton, father of
> > > >
> > > > > WILLIAM, present LORD STOURTON.
> >
> > Mr. Philip Howard espoused, secondly, Harriet, daughter and co-heir of Edward Blount, Esq., and had an only surviving daughter,
> >
> > > ANNE, who m. Robert-Edward,

LORD PETRE, and was mother of

> Robert-Edward, Lord Petre, father of
>> *William - Francis*, present LORD PETRE.

Upon the decease of *Edward Howard*, eleventh DUKE OF NORFOLK, in 1777, issueless, as stated above, the BARONY OF HOWARD, separated from the dukedom, and fell into ABEYANCE between his grace's nieces, as it still continues between their grandsons, the LORDS PETRE AND STOURTON.

ARMS.—Gules, on a bend between six cross croslets, fitchy, ar.

HOWARD—DUKES OF NORFOLK.

The DUKEDOM OF NORFOLK came into the Howard family, by the creation of JOHN HOWARD, Earl Marshal, and Duke of Norfolk, on the 28th June, 1483. The said John Howard was son and heir of Sir Robert Howard, by Margaret, daughter of Thomas Mowbray, first Duke of Norfolk of that family, and cousin, and ultimately co-heir of John Mowbray, fourth and last Duke of Norfolk, of the Mowbrays. The DUKEDOM OF NORFOLK has since been frequently forfeited by the Howards; but as it has now continued uninterruptedly for the greater part of two centuries in the family, it is deemed more correct to place it amongst *extant* than *extinct* honours; the reader is therefore referred to Burke's Dictionary of the Peerage and Baronetage for a full and accurate detail of the family of Howard, Dukes of Norfolk.

ARMS.—Quarterly, first gu. on a bend betw. six cross-croslets, fitchée, ar. an escucheon or. charged with a demi-lion, rampant, pierced through the mouth with an arrow, within a double tressure, flory, counterflory, gu. for HOWARD; second, gu. three lions, passant, gardant, in pale, or. in chief a label of three points, ar. for BROTHERTON; third, chequy, or. and az. for WARREN; fourth, gu. a lion rampant, ar. armed and langued, az. for MOW-BRAY; behind the shield two truncheons, or marshals staves, in saltier, or. enamelled at the ends, sa. (the insignia of earl marshal).

HOWARD—VISCOUNTS HOWARD, OF BINDON, IN THE COUNTY OF DORSET.

By Letters Patent, dated 13th January, 1559.

Lineage.

THOMAS HOWARD, third Duke of Norfolk, married, first, the Lady Anne Plantagenet, one of the daughters of King Edward IV., by whom he had an only son, Thomas, who died young. His grace espoused, secondly, Lady Elizabeth Stafford, daughter of Edward, Duke of Buckingham, by whom he had issue,

> HENRY, the celebrated EARL OF SURREY, who suffered decapitation in 1547, leaving a son, THOMAS, who inherited the honours of the house of Norfolk.
> Thomas, of whom presently.

Mary, m. to Henry Fitz-Roy, Duke of Richmond, natural son of King Henry VIII.

The second son,

LORD THOMAS HOWARD, was restored in blood, (his father having been attainted, and only saved from execution by the death of King Henry VIII.,) in the first year of Queen Mary, and was elevated to the peerage on the 13th January, 1559, as VISCOUNT HOWARD, OF BINDON,* in the county of Dorset. His lordship m. first, Elizabeth, younger daughter and co-heir of John, Lord Marney, by Christian, daughter, and eventually sole heiress of Sir Roger Newburgh, of East Lullworth, in the county of Dorset. By this lady Lord Bindon acquired very considerable estates in Dorsetshire, amongst which was the manor of Bindon, and had issue,

> Henry.
> Thomas.
> Francis, } died young.
> Giles,
> Elizabeth, died unmarried.
> Grace, m. John, son and heir of Sir John Horsey, of Clifton, in the county of Dorset, but died *s. p.*

His lordship espoused, secondly, Gertrude, daughter of Sir William Lyte, of Billesdon, in Somersetshire, and had a son,

> Charles Lyte Howard, who left two daughters, viz.
>> Catherine, m. to Thomas Thynne, Esq., and had issue,
>>> Sir Henry Thynne, Bart., ancestor of the Marquess of Bath.
>> Anne, m. to Sir William Thornyhurst, Knt., of Agencourt, in Kent.

Lord Bindon m. thirdly, Mabell, daughter of Nicholas Burton, Esq., of Carshalton, in Surrey, by whom he had a daughter, Frances, m. first, to Henry Pranel, Esq., of Barkway, in the county of Hertford; secondly, to Edward Seymour, Earl of Hertford; and thirdly, to Lodowick Stuart, Duke of Richmond, but had no issue. His lordship wedded, fourthly, Margaret, daughter of Henry Manning, Esq., of Greenwich. He died 5th April, 1582, and was s. by his eldest son,

HENRY HOWARD, second Viscount, who espoused Frances, daughter of Sir Peter Mewtas, Knt., of Essex, by whom he had an only daughter, Douglass, who m. Sir Arthur Gorges, Knt. His lordship d. in 1590, and was s. by his brother,

THOMAS HOWARD, third Viscount, who was installed a Knight of the Garter in May, 1606. His lordship m. Grace, daughter of Bernard Duffield, Esq., but died without issue in 1619, when the VIS-COUNTY OF BINDON became EXTINCT. His lordship devised his estate to his kinsman, Thomas, Earl of Suffolk, and entailed it on Henry, Viscount Howard, Giles Howard, Henry, Earl of Northampton, William, Lord Howard, and their heirs.

ARMS.—Same as the other noble house of Howard.

---

* DUGDALE states, "Howard of Bindon" to have been his lordship's title. BRATSON, makes it "Viscount Bindon, of Bindon."

HOWARD — EARLS OF NOTTING-HAM, EARLS OF EF-FINGHAM, IN THE COUNTY OF SURREY.

| Earldom of Not-tingham, | by Letters | 22nd October, 1597. |
| Earldom of Ef-fingham, | Patent, | 8th December, 1731. |

Lineage.

LORD WILLIAM HOWARD, eldest son of Thomas, Duke of Norfolk, by Agnes, his second duchess, sister and heiress of Sir Philip Tilney, of Boston, in the county of Lincoln, having been accredited by King Henry VIII. and Edward VI., upon numerous confidential missions to foreign courts, amongst others, in 1553, to the Czar of Muscovy, (being the first ambassador from England to Russia,) was elevated to the peerage in the first year of Queen Mary, on the 11th March, 1554, as BARON HOWARD, OF EFFINGHAM, and consti-tuted in the same month LORD HIGH ADMIRAL of her majesty's dominions. His lordship was soon afterwards installed a Knight of the Garter, and in the ensuing reign he was made lord chamberlain of the household, and then lord privy seal. His lord-ship m. first, Katharine, one of the sisters and heirs of John Broughton, Esq., by whom he had an only daughter, AGNES, who m. William Paulet, third Marquess of Winchester, and died in 1601. Lord Howard espoused, secondly, Margaret, second daughter of Sir Thomas Gamage, Knt., of Coity, in the county of Glamorgan, and had issue,

CHARLES, his successor.

> William (Sir), of Lingfield, in the county of Surrey, who m. Frances, daughter of Wil-liam Gouldwell, Esq., of Gouldwell Hall, Kent, and had issue,
>
>> Edward,
>> Francis, } all knights.
>> Charles,
>
> Sir William d. in 1600, and was s. by his eldest son,
>
>> SIR EDWARD HOWARD, who died s. p. in 1620, and was s. by his brother,
>>
>> SIR FRANCIS HOWARD, of Great Book-ham, who m. Jane, daughter of Sir William Monson, of Kinnersley, in Surrey, and was s. by his eldest son,
>>
>>> SIR CHARLES HOWARD. This gen-tleman m. Frances, daughter of Sir George Courthorpe, of Whi-ligh, in the county of Sussex, and dying in 1672, left issue,
>>>
>>>> FRANCIS, who succeeded as fifth LORD HOWARD, OF EF-FINGHAM.
>>>>
>>>> George, whose great grand-son,
>>>>
>>>>> KENNETH - ALEXANDER HOWARD, Esq., suc-ceeded to the BARONY upon the decease of the last EARL OF EFFING-HAM, in 1816, and is the

present Lord Howard, of Effingham.

Douglas, m. first, to John, Lord Sheffield; secondly, to Robert, Earl of Leicester; and thirdly, to Sir Edward Stafford, of Grafton, Knt.

Mary, m. first, to Edward, Lord Dudley, and secondly, to Richard Mompesson, Esq.

Frances, m. to Edward, Earl of Hertford, and died s. p. in 1598.

Martha, m. to Sir George Bourchier, Knt., third son of John, Earl of Bath.

His lordship d. in 1573, and was s. by his eldest son,

SIR CHARLES HOWARD, second Baron Howard, of Effingham, so celebrated for his glo-rious defeat of the formidable armada. This emi-nent person was initiated, in the life-time of his father, in the affairs of state, having been de-puted by Queen Elizabeth on a special embassy to Charles IX. of France. Upon his return he was elected to parliament by the county of Surrey, and was made general of horse, in which capacity he distinguished himself in suppressing the rebellion raised by the Earls of Northumberland and West-morland. The following year he was sent with a fleet of men of war, to convey the Lady Anne of Austria, daughter of the Emperor Maximilian, going into Spain, over the British seas. In 1574 he was installed a Knight of the Garter, and appointed lord chamberlain of the household. In 1586 his lordship was one of the commissioners for the trial of the unhappy Queen of Scotland; he had been previously, on the death of the Earl of Lincoln in 1585, constituted LORD HIGH ADMIRAL OF ENG-LAND, in which capacity he had the high honour of preserving his native shores from the hostile foot of the foreigner, and the dispersion of the SPANISH ARMADA, has stamped with immortality the illus-trious name of HOWARD OF EFFINGHAM. For this great service his royal mistress not only rewarded him with a pension, but ever after considered him as a person born for the especial preservation of her realm. His next achievement was the conquest of Cadiz, for which he was created, 22nd October, 1597, EARL OF NOTTINGHAM. Upon the accession of King James I. his lordship was continued in the post of lord admiral, and constituted for the occa-sion of that monarch's coronation LORD HIGH STEWARD OF ENGLAND. We afterwards find the earl taking a prominent part at the nuptials of the Princess Elizabeth with the elector Palatine, which is thus recorded by Arthur Wilson. "In February (1613) following the death of Prince Henry, the prince palatine, and that lovely princess, the Lady Elizabeth, were married on Bishop Valentine's day, in all the pomp and glory that so much grandeur could express. Her vestments were white, the em-blem of innocency; her hair dishevelled, hanging down her back at length, an ornament of virginity; a crown of pure gold upon her head, the cognizance of majesty, being all over beset with precious gems, shining like a constellation; her train supported by twelve young ladies in white garments, so adorned with jewels, that her path looked like a milky way. She was led to church by her brother, Prince Charles, and the Earl of Northampton. And while the Archbishop of Canterbury was solemnizing the marriage some coruscations and lightnings of joy appeared in her countenance, that expressed more than an ordinary smile, being almost elated to a laughter, which could not clear the air of her fate, but was rather a forerunner of more sad and dire events; which shews how slippery nature is to toll us along to those things that bring danger, yea sometimes destruction with them.

"She returned from the chapel between the Duke of Lenox, and the Earl of Nottingham, lord high admiral, two married men. The city of London (that with high magnificence feasted the prince palatine and his noble retinue,) presented to the fair bride a chain of oriental pearl, by the hand of the lord mayor and aldermen, (in their scarlet and gold chain accoutrements,) of such a value as was fit for them to give, and her to receive. And the people of the kingdom in general being summoned to a contribution for the marriage of the king's daughter, did shew their affections by their bounty. And though it be the custom of our kings to pay their daughters' portions with their subjects' purses, yet an hundred years being almost past since such a precedent, it might have made them unwilling (if their obedience had not been full ripe,) to recal such obsolete things, as are only in practice now by the meanest of the people."

In 1619, the earl resigned the office of LORD ADMIRAL. He was now eighty-three years of age, and desirous of repose; but not caring to lose the precedence which that dignity gave him, the king, according to Collins, conferred upon him, by a special patent, the privilege of taking place, as his ancestor (John, Lord Mowbray, Earl of Nottingham) had done in the time of Richard II. His lordship m. first, Katherine Carey, daughter of Henry, Lord Hunsdon, and had issue,

> WILLIAM, who was summoned to parliament in his father's life-time. He m. Anne, daughter and sole heir of John, Lord St. John, of Bletso, but died before his father, leaving an only daughter and heiress,
>> Elizabeth, who m. John, Lord Mordaunt, afterwards Earl of Peterborough.
> CHARLES, who succeeded his father as second earl.
> Elisabeth, m. first, to Sir Robert Southwell, of Woodrising, in Norfolk, and secondly, to John Stewart, Earl of Carrick, in Scotland.
> Frances, m. first, to Henry, Earl of Kildare, and secondly, to Henry Broke, Lord Cobham.
> Margaret, m. to Sir Richard Leveson, of Trentham, in Staffordshire.

The earl espoused, secondly, Lady Margaret Stewart, daughter of James, Earl of Moray, and had an only surviving son,

> SIR CHARLES HOWARD, who succeeded his half-brother in the dignities.

This great person died at Haling House, in Surrey, on the 14th December, 1624, and was s. by his eldest surviving son,

CHARLES HOWARD, second Earl of Nottingham, who m. first, in 1597, Charity, daughter of Robert White, of Christ Church, Hants, and widow of William Leche, of Sheffield, in Fletching, in Sussex. He espoused, secondly, Mary, eldest daughter of Sir William Cockayne, Knt., alderman, and some time lord mayor of London; but had issue by neither. He d. 3rd October, 1642, and was s. by his half-brother,

SIR CHARLES HOWARD, third Earl of Nottingham. This nobleman m. Arabella, daughter of Edward Smith, Esq., of the Middle Temple, and sister of Sir Edward Smith, lord chief-justice of the court of Common Pleas in Ireland; but died, s. p., 26th April, 1681, when the EARLDOM OF NOTTINGHAM became EXTINCT, and the BARONY OF HOWARD, OF EFFINGHAM, devolved upon his kinsman, (refer to descendants of Sir William Howard, of Langfield, second son of first baron,)

FRANCIS HOWARD, Esq., of Great Bookham, in Surrey, as fifth BARON HOWARD, OF EFFINGHAM. This nobleman was governor of Virginia in the reign of Charles II. His lordship m. first, Philadelphia, daughter of Sir Thomas Pelham, Bart., great-grandfather of Thomas, Duke of Newcastle, and had surviving issue,

> THOMAS, } successive peers.
> FRANCIS, }
> Elizabeth, m. first, to William Roberts, Esq., of Wellesden, in the county of Middlesex; and secondly, to William Hutcheson, Esq.

Lord Howard m. secondly, Susan, daughter of Sir Henry Felton, of Playford, in the county of Suffolk, and widow of Thomas Herbert, Esq.; but had no issue. He d. 30th March, 1694, and was s. by his elder son,

THOMAS HOWARD, sixth baron Howard, of Effingham. This nobleman, who was one of the gentlemen of the bed-chamber to George, Prince of Denmark, m. first, Mary, daughter and heir of Ruishe Wentworth, Esq., son and heir of Sir George Wentworth, a younger brother of Thomas, Earl of Strafford, by whom he had two daughters,

> Anne, m. to Sir William Yonge, K.B., and Baronet of Escote, Devon.
> Mary, m. to George-Venables Vernon, Esq., of Sudbury in Derbyshire, afterwards created LORD VERNON.

His lordship espoused, secondly, Elizabeth, daughter of John Rotheram, Esq., of Much-Waltham, in the county of Essex, and widow of Sir Theophilus Napier, Bart., of Luton-Hoo, in the county of Bedford; but had no issue. He d. 10th July, 1725, and was s. by his brother,

FRANCIS HOWARD, as seventh Lord Howard, of Effingham. This nobleman, who was a military officer of high rank, was advanced to the EARLDOM OF EFFINGHAM, 8th December, 1731, in consideration of his gallant professional services. In the same year he was constituted deputy earl-marshal of England. His lordship married first, Diana, daughter of Major-general O'Farrel, by whom he an only son,

> THOMAS, his successor.

He espoused, secondly, Anne, sister of Robert Bristow, Esq., one of the commissioners of his majesty's board of green cloth, by whom he had a son,

> George, who died young.

277

The earl d. 12th February, 1742-3, and was s. by his only surviving son,

THOMAS HOWARD, second Earl of Effingham, who, on the decease of his father, was appointed DEPUTY EARL-MARSHAL OF ENGLAND. This nobleman was also a military character, and attained the rank of lieutenant-general in the army. His lordship m., in 1745, Elizabeth, daughter of Peter Beckford, Esq., of the Island of Jamaica, by whom (who espoused, after the earl's decease, Sir George Howard, K.B.) he had issue,

THOMAS, } successive earls.
RICHARD, }

Elizabeth, m. to the Right Rev. Henry Reginald Courtenay, LL.D., Bishop of Exeter, by whom she had issue,

    William Courtenay, clerk assistant of the parliament.

    Thomas Peregrine Courtenay, a privy-councillor.

Anne, m. to lieutenant-colonel Thomas Carleton, of the 29th regiment of foot, who died in Canada, 1787.

Maria, m. to Guy Carleton, Lord Dorchester, who d. in 1808.

Frances-Herring, d. unmarried, in 1796.

His lordship d. 19th November, 1763, and was s. by his elder son,

THOMAS HOWARD, third Earl of Effingham, who m., in 1765, Catherine, daughter of Metcalfe Proctor, Esq., of Thorpe, near Leeds, in Yorkshire, by whom he had no issue. His lordship was deputy-marshal of England. In 1782 he was appointed treasurer of the household, and, in 1784, master of the mint. He was afterwards constituted governor of Jamaica, in which government he died, 15th November, 1791, when his honours devolved upon his brother,

RICHARD HOWARD, fourth Earl of Effingham. This nobleman espoused, in 1785, Miss March, daughter of John March, Esq., of Waresly Park, in the county of Huntingdon; but had no issue. His lordship d. 11th December, 1816, when the BARONY OF HOWARD, OF EFFINGHAM, devolved upon his kinsman, Kenneth-Alexander Howard, Esq., (refer to descendants of Sir William Howard, second son of the first lord,) while the EARLDOM OF EFFINGHAM became EXTINCT.

ARMS.—Gu., a bend between six cross crosslets, fitché, ar. on a bend; an escocheon or., charged with a demi-lion rampant, pierced through the mouth with an arrow, within a double tressure, flory, counterflory gu.

HOWARD—EARL OF NORTHAMPTON.

By Letters Patent, dated 13th March, 1604.

Lineage.

HENRY HOWARD, the celebrated EARL OF SURREY, beheaded on Tower Hill, 19th January, 1547, left by Frances, his wife, daughter of John de Vere, Earl of Oxford,

    THOMAS, who was restored to the Dukedom of Norfolk.

    Henry, of whom presently.

Jane, m. to Charles Neville, Earl of Westmorland.

Margaret, m. to Henry, Lord Scrope of Bolton.

Catherine, m. to Henry, Lord Berkeley.

The second son,

HENRY HOWARD, who, with his three sisters, was restored in blood, in the first parliament of Queen Elizabeth, during the remainder of that reign, having but a limited fortune, lived in retirement, and made little figure; but upon the accession of King James, he rose rapidly into honour, wealth, and power. He was first sworn of the privy council, soon afterwards constituted warden of the Cinque Ports, and constable of Dover Castle, and elevated to the peerage on the 13th March, 1604, in the dignities of Baron Howard, of Marnhill, and EARL OF NORTHAMPTON. The next year he was made one of the commissioners for exercising the office of Earl Marshal, and installed a Knight of the Garter, and in 1608, he was appointed Lord Privy Seal.

" The character of this nobleman," says Banks, " is unnoticed by the Baronagians in general, though other authors represent him as the most contemptible and despicable of mankind; a wretch, that it causes astonishment to reflect, that he was the son of the generous, the noble, and accomplished Earl of Surrey! He was a learned man, but a pedant, dark and mysterious, and consequently far from possessing masterly abilities. He was the grossest of flatterers; as his letters to his friend and patron, the Earl of Essex, demonstrate. But while he professed the most unbounded regard for Essex, he yet paid his suit to the treasurer Burghley; and on the fall of Essex, insinuated himself so far into the confidence of his mortal enemy, Cecil, as to become the instrument of the secretary's correspondence with the King of Scots, which passed through his hands. Wherefore, this circumstance, his intriguing spirit, and the sufferings of his family, for Mary, Queen of Scots, may, in some measure, account for the very great favour he experienced on the accession of King James I."

His lordship died unmarried, 15th June, 1614, at the palace he had erected at Charing Cross, (the present Northumberland House,) when the BARONY OF HOWARD, OF MARNHILL, and the EARLDOM OF NORTHAMPTON, became EXTINCT.

ARMS.—Gu. on a bend between six cross. fitchée, ar. an escucheon or. charged with a demi-lion, vulnerated in the mouth with an arrow, all within a double tressure counterflory, gu. a crescent, for difference.

HOWARD—BARONS HOWARD, OF ESCRICK, IN THE COUNTY OF YORK.

By Letters Patent, dated 29th April, 1628.

Lineage.

SIR EDWARD HOWARD, K.B. (seventh son of Lord Thomas Howard, who had been created EARL OF SUFFOLK, in 1603), having derived the Lordship of Escrick, from his mother Catherine, eldest daughter, and co-heiress of Sir Henry Knevit, and heir of her uncle, Thomas, Lord Knevit, of Escrick, was elevated to the peerage on the 29th April, 1628, as BARON HOWARD, of *Escrick*. This nobleman acquired an infamous immortality by his betrayal of the celebrated patriots, LORD RUSSEL, and ALGERNON SIDNEY. His lordship, who was involved in the conspiracy for which these illustrious persons suffered in the reign of Charles II., was the chief evidence against Russel, and the only one against Sidney, and thus made his own peace with the court. Lord Howard *m.* Mary, daughter and co-heir of John, Lord Butler, of Bramfield, and had issue,

> THOMAS, } successors to the barony.
> WILLIAM, }
>
> Cecil (Sir), had an only daughter, who died in infancy.
> Edward, killed before Dunkirk, *d. s. p.*
> Anne, *m.* to Sir Charles Howard, Earl of Carlisle.

His lordship *d.* in 1675, and was *s.* by his eldest son,

THOMAS HOWARD, second baron. This nobleman *m.* first, Elizabeth, daughter of John, Earl of Peterborough, by whom he had no surviving issue. He espoused, secondly, Joane, daughter of —— Drake, Esq., but had no issue. His lordship *d.* in 1683, and was *s.* by his brother,

WILLIAM HOWARD, third baron, who *m.* Frances, daughter of Sir James Bridgman, of Castle Bromwich, in the county of Warwick, and niece of the Lord Keeper, Sir Orlando Bridgman, by whom he had Charles, with three other sons, and two daughters, who all deceased issueless. His lordship *d.* in 1694, and was *s.* by his eldest son,

CHARLES HOWARD, fourth baron. This nobleman *m.* Elizabeth, daughter and co-heir of George Brydges, Lord Chandos, widow of the Earl of Inchiquin, and of Lord Herbert, of Cherbury, but dying without issue in 1714, the BARONY OF HOWARD, OF ESCRICK, became EXTINCT.

ARMS.—Gu. on a bend between six cross crosslets fitchée ar. an escocheon or. thereon a demi-lion rampant, pierced through the mouth with an arrow, within a double tressure counterflory gu. with a fleur-de-lis for difference.

HOWARD—VISCOUNT STAFFORD, EARLS OF STAFFORD.

By Letters Patent, dated 12th September, 1640.

Lineage.

The BARONY OF STAFFORD having been surrendered by Roger Stafford, the last male heir of that illustrious family, to King Charles I., (see Stafford, Barons Stafford, Earls Stafford, &c.,) that monarch created by letters patent, dated 12th September, 1640,

SIR WILLIAM HOWARD, K.B., (younger son of Thomas, Earl of Arundel,) and his wife, Mary Stafford, only sister and heiress of Henry Stafford, Lord Stafford, who *d.* in 1637, BARON and BARONESS STAFFORD, with remainder to the heirs *male*, of their bodies, failing of which, to the *heirs female;* and in two months after, 11th November, his lordship was advanced to the VIS-

COUNTY OF STAFFORD. The unjust fate of this nobleman is so well known, that it were a waste of time and space to particularise it here, further than his having been tried at Westminster Hall, for high treason, as a participator in the mock popish plot, and his becoming the last victim of Titus Oates and his perjured associates. His lordship suffered death by decapitation, on Tower Hill, in December, 1670—and having been attainted, his honours became FORFEITED, while the BARONY of his lady was placed pretty much in a similar situation, owing to the bar raised by that penal act, to the inheritance of her children. The viscount left issue,

> HENRY, of whom presently.
>
> John, *m.* first, Mary, daughter of Sir John Southcote, Knt., of Merstham, in the county of Surrey, and had issue,
> > WILLIAM, who *s.* his uncle.
> > JOHN-PAUL, who succeeded his nephew.
> > Mary, *m.* to Francis Plowden, Esq., and had issue, an only daughter and heiress,
> > > MARY PLOWDEN, who *m.* Sir George Jerningham, and was mother of Sir William Jerningham, whose son and heir, Sir George William Jerningham, was restored to the BARONY OF STAFFORD, created in 1640, by the reversal of the iniquitous attainder of VISCOUNT STAFFORD, in 1636, and is the present Lord Stafford.
> >
> > John Howard, *m.* secondly, Theresa, daughter of Robert Strickland, Esq., and had a son and daughter, Edward, and Harriott.
> >
> Francis, *m.* Eleanor, daughter of Henry Stanford Esq., and had a son,
> > Henry, who died *s. p.*
> Isabella, *m.* to John Paulet, Marquess of Winchester.
> Anastasia, *m.* to George Holman, Esq., of Warkworth, in the county of Northampton.

After the decease of the viscount, the viscountess was created, on 5th October, 1688, countess of Stafford, for life, (a dignity that *expired*, in 1693). Upon the same day that her ladyship had this new honour, her eldest son,

HENRY STAFFORD HOWARD, was created Earl of Stafford, with remainder, default of male issue, to his brothers. Upon the abdication of King James II., his lordship, following the fortunes of the fallen monarch, retired into France, and there married, 3rd April, 1694, Claude-Charlotte, eldest daughter of Philibert, Count de Gramont, and Elizabeth, daughter of Sir George Hamilton, Knt., but dying in 1619, without issue, was *s.* by his nephew,

WILLIAM STAFFORD HOWARD, second Earl of Stafford, who *m.* his first cousin, Anne, daughter of George Holman, Esq., and had issue,

> WILLIAM MATHIAS, his successor.
> Mary, *m.* to Count Chabot, of the house of Rohan, in France.
> Anastasia, } Nuns.
> Anne, }

His lordship d. in France, in January, 1733-4, and was s. by his son,

WILLIAM-MATHIAS STAFFORD HOWARD, third Earl of Stafford. This nobleman m. in 1743, Henrietta, daughter of Richard Cantillon, Esq., and dying issueless, in February, 1750-1, was s. by his uncle,

JOHN-PAUL STAFFORD-HOWARD, fourth Earl of Stafford, who m. Elizabeth, daughter of —— Ewen, Esq., of the county of Somerset, but having no issue, the EARLDOM OF STAFFORD, at his lordship's decease, in 1762, became EXTINCT.

The BARONY OF STAFFORD, created in 1640, has since been restored, in the person of Sir George William Jerningham, Bart., (see issue of the first Visct.) by the reversal of the unjust attainder of Sir William Howard, first Baron Stafford.

ARMS.—Gules, a bend betw. six crosslets, fitchée ar. a crescent for difference.

HOWARD—BARONS HOWARD, OF CASTLE RISING, IN THE COUNTY OF NORFOLK, EARLS OF NORWICH.

Barony, } by Letters { 27th March, 1669.
Earldom, } Patent, { 19th October, 1672.

Lineage.

HENRY HOWARD, second son of Henry-Frederick Howard, Earl of Arundel, Surrey, and Norfolk, who d. in 1652, was created on the 27th March, 1669, Baron Howard, of Castle Rising, and advanced, 19th October, 1672, to the EARLDOM OF NORWICH. His lordship succeeded his brother, THOMAS, (who had been restored to the dukedom,) as DUKE OF NORFOLK, in 1677. His grace was likewise created EARL MARSHAL of England. He m. first, Anne, eldest daughter of Edward, Marquess of Worcester, and had issue,

HENRY, his successor.

Thomas, of Worksop, in the county of Nottingham, who m. Mary-Elizabeth, daughter and sole heiress of Sir John Saville, Bart., of Copley, in the county of York, and had, with other issue,

THOMAS, } who succeeded in turn to
EDWARD, } the honours.

Philip, of Buckenham, in the county of Norfolk, who left two daughters and co-heirs, namely:—

WINIFRED, m. to WILLIAM, LORD STOURTON.

ANNE, m. to Robert Edward, LORD PETRE.

His grace espoused secondly, Jane, daughter of Robert Bickerton, Esq., and had four sons, all of whom died issueless, and three daughters. He d. in 1684, and was s. by his elder son,

HENRY HOWARD, seventh Duke of Norfolk, and SECOND EARL OF NORWICH. His grace, m. Mary, daughter and heiress of Henry Mordaunt, Earl of Peterborough, from whom he was divorced, in 1700. He died in the following year, and leaving no issue, the honours devolved upon his nephew,

THOMAS HOWARD, eighth Duke of Norfolk,

and THIRD EARL OF NORWICH. His grace m. Mary, daughter and sole heiress of Sir Nicholas Shireburne, of Stoneyhurst, in the county of Lancaster, but dying s. p., in 1732, was s. by his brother,

EDWARD HOWARD, ninth Duke of Norfolk, and FOURTH EARL OF NORWICH, and BARON HOWARD, OF CASTLE RISING. This nobleman, m. Mary, second daughter and co-heiress, of Edward Blount, Esq., of Blagdon, in the county of Devon, but dying without issue, 20th September, 1777, the Baronies of Mowbray, Howard, &c., fell into abeyance, between his two nieces, the daughters and co-heirs of Philip Howard, of Buckenham, as they still continue with their representatives. The DUKEDOM OF NORFOLK, &c., passed to the heir at law, while the Barony of HOWARD, OF CASTLE RISING, and EARLDOM OF NORWICH, became EXTINCT.

ARMS.—Quarterly ;—first, gu. on a bend, betw. six cross-crosslets, fitchée, ar. an escocheon or. charged with a demi-lion, rampant, pierced through the mouth with an arrow, within a double treasure, flory, counterflory, gu., for HOWARD ; second gu. three lions passant, gardant, in pale, or in chief a label of three points ar. for BROTHERTON ; third, chequy, or. and az. for WARREN ; fourth gu. a lion rampant, or. armed a langued az. for MOWBRAY ; behind the shield two truncheons, or marshal's staves in saltier or. enamelled at the ends sa. (the insignia of Earl Marshal).

HOWARD — EARLS OF BINDON.

By Letters Patent, dated 30th December, 1706.

Lineage.

THOMAS HOWARD, VISCOUNT BINDON, at whose decease, s. p. in 1619, that dignity expired, devised his estate to his kinsman, Thomas Howard, Earl of Suffolk ; from whom lineally descended,

HENRY HOWARD, fifth Earl of Suffolk, who married the Hon. Mary Stewart, only daughter and heiress of Andrew, Lord Castle Stewart, of Ireland, and had, with other issue,

HENRY HOWARD, (the eldest son,) who was elevated to the peerage in the life-time of his father, by letters patent, dated 30th December, 1706, as Baron Chesterfield, in the county of Essex, and EARL OF BINDON. His lordship was likewise constituted deputy Earl Marshal, and in that capacity he held a Court of Chivalry, 26th September, 1707. The Earl Suffolk dying in 1709, Lord Bindon succeeded as sixth Earl of Suffolk. His lordship m. first, Penelope, daughter of Henry, Earl of Thomond, and had issue,

CHARLES-WILLIAM, his successor.

James,   }
Thomas, } all died unmarried.
Arthur, }

Sarah, m. in 1721, to Thomas Chester, Esq., of Knoole Park, in the county of Gloucester, and died in the following year.

The earl espoused, secondly, Henrietta, daughter of Henry, Duke of Beaufort, but had no issue. He d. 2nd October, 1718, and was s. by his eldest son,

CHARLES-WILLIAM HOWARD, seventh Earl

of Suffolk, as second EARL OF BINDON. This nobleman espoused Arabella, daughter and co-heir of Sir Samuel Astry, Knt., but had no issue. His lordship, who was Lord Lieutenant, and Custos Rotulorum of the county of Essex, died in February, 1722, when the Earldom of Suffolk devolved upon his uncle, and the BARONY OF CHESTERFIELD and EARLDOM OF BINDON, became EXTINCT.

ARMS.—Same as those of the other members of the Howard family.

HOWARD—BARONS FURNIVAL.

See FURNIVAL.

HOWE—BARONS CHEDWORTH.

By Letters Patent, dated 12th May, 1741.

Lineage.

This is a branch of the family of HOWE, Earls Howe, in the *existing* peerage.

JOHN HOWE, Esq. of Stowell, succeeded to the estates of Sir Richard Howe, Bart., of Compton, in the county of Gloucester, and Weshford, Wilts, at the decease, without issue, of that gentleman, in 1730, and was elevated to the peerage on 12th May, 1741, as BARON CHEDWORTH, *of Chedworth, in the county of Gloucester*. His lordship m. Dorothy, daughter of Henry Frederick Thynne, Esq., grandfather of Thomas, Viscount Weymouth, by whom he had surviving issue,

JOHN-THYNNE, his successor.

Henry-Frederick, successor to his brother.

Thomas, m. Frances, daughter of Thomas White, Esq., and left JOHN, who inherited as fourth baron.

Charles, who d. a bachelor, in 1640.

James, m. Susan, daughter of Sir Humphrey Howarth, but died s. p.

William, died in 1762.

Mary, m. to Alexander Wright, Esq.

Anne, m. to Roderick Gwynne, Esq.

His lordship d. in 1742, and was s. by his eldest son,

JOHN THYNNE HOWE, second Baron Chedworth. This nobleman m. Martha, daughter and co-heir of Sir Philip Parker-a-Morley Long, Bart., of Arwarton, Suffolk, but dying s. p. in 1762, the title devolved upon his brother,

HENRY FREDERICK HOWE, third Baron Chedworth, who d. unmarried, in 1781, and was s. by his nephew,

JOHN HOWE, fourth Baron Chedworth, at whose decease, unmarried, in 1804, the barony became EXTINCT.

ARMS.—Or, a fesse between three wolves' heads, couped sa, a crescent for difference.

HOWE — VISCOUNT HOWE, EARL HOWE.

Viscounty, } by Letters { 30th January, 1782.
Earldom, } Patent, { 19th August, 1788.

Lineage.

RICHARD HOWE, so celebrated as Admiral Howe, succeeded his brother *General* GEORGE AUGUSTUS HOWE, Viscount Howe, of Ireland, in

that dignity in 1758, and was created for his own gallant achievements a peer of Great Britain, on 30th January, 1782, as VISCOUNT HOWE, *of Langar*, in the county of Nottingham, and on the 19th August, 1788, he was advanced to the EARLDOM OF HOWE, being at the same time created *Baron Howe, of Langar*, with remainder of the latter dignity in failure of male issue, to his daughters and their male descendants respectively. His lordship was elected a KNIGHT OF THE GARTER in 1797. He m. in 1758, Mary, daughter of Chiverton Hartopp, Esq., of Welby, in Nottinghamshire, by whom he had three daughters, viz.

SOPHIA-CHARLOTTE, who inherited the barony at his lordship's decease (see *Burke's Peerage and Baronetage*).

Maria-Juliana, d. unmarried.

Louisa-Catherine, m. first, to John-Dennis, Marquess of Sligo; and secondly, to Sir William Scott, Knt., Lord Stowell.

His lordship d. 5th August, 1799, when the VISCOUNTY and EARLDOM OF HOWE EXPIRED. The BARONY OF HOWE passed, according to the limitation, to his eldest daughter—and his Irish honours devolved upon the General, Sir William Howe, with whom they also expired.

ARMS.—Or, on a fesse between three wolves' heads erased sa,

HUME — BARON HUME, OF BERWICK.

By Letters Patent, dated 7th July, 1604.

Lineage.

SIR GEORGE HUME, Knt., sprung from one of the most ancient families in Scotland, having accompanied King James I. into England, was elevated to the English peerage on the 7th July, 1604, as BARON HUME, *of Berwick*. He had previously succeeded Lord Elphinston in the treasurership of Scotland, and was created a peer of that kingdom subsequently in the dignity of EARL OF DUNBAR. His lordship, who was in great favour with his royal master, was a KNIGHT OF THE GARTER, chancellor of the exchequer, and master of the wardrobe. He is characterised by the Archbishop of St. Andrews "as a person of deep wit, few words; and in his majesty's service, no less faithful than fortunate. The most difficile affairs he compassed without any noise, never returning when he was employed, without the work performed that he was sent to do." He d. in 1611, leaving a daughter and heiress,

Lady ELIZABETH HUME, who m. Theophilus Howard, second Earl of Suffolk.

Upon his lordship's decease the BARONY OF HUME, of BERWICK became EXTINCT.

ARMS.—Or, a lion rampant reguardant vert.

HUME-CAMPBELL—BARON HUME, OF BERWICK.

By Letters Patent, dated 20th May, 1776.

Lineage.

HUGH HUME, third Earl of Marchmont in the

peerage of Scotland, LORD KEEPER OF THE GREAT SEAL in that kingdom, from January, 1764, to May, 1766—espoused, first, in 1731, Anne, daughter of —— Western, Esq., by whom he had three daughters, viz.

> Anne, m. to John Paterson, Esq., eldest son and successor of Sir John Paterson, Bart., of Eccles.
>
> Margaret, m. to Colonel James Stuart.
>
> Diana, m. to Walter Scot, Esq., of Arden.

His lordship m. secondly, Elizabeth, daughter of Mr. Windmill Crompton, of London, by whom he had an only son,

ALEXANDER HUME, (by courtesy Viscount Polwarth,) who m. in 1772, Amabel, elder daughter and co-heir of Lady Jemima Campbell, Marchioness Grey, by her husband, Philip, Earl of Hardwicke, and was created a peer of England on the 20th May, 1776, as BARON HUME, of Berwick. His lordship assumed the additional surname of CAMPBELL. He died without issue in 1781, when the BARONY OF HUME became EXTINCT. (See Countess de Grey, Burke's Dictionary of the Peerage and Baronetage.)

ARMS.—Quarterly, first grand quarter, counter quartered; 1st and 4th vert, a lion rampant ar. for HUME; 2nd and 3rd., ag. three popinjays of the first for PEPDIE; 2nd., ar. three piles ingrailed, gu. for POLWARTH; 3rd., ar. a cross ingrailed, sa. for SINCLAIR; the 4th grand quarter as the first; and over all, as a surtout, an escutcheon, ar. charged with an orange, ensigned with an imperial crown, all ppr. as a coat of augmentation, given by King William III., when he created his lordship's ancestor, Sir Patrick Hume, Lord Polwarth.

HUNGERFORD—BARONS HUNGERFORD.

By Writ of Summons, dated 7th January, 1426, 4 Henry VI.

Lineage.

The antiquity of this family in the county of Wilts is proved by the sheriff's accounts, rendered the 11th of Henry II., wherein

EVERARD DE HUNGERFORD is mentioned, by reason of a fine of twenty pounds having been then levied upon him. From this Everard we shall pass to

SIR ROBERT DE HUNGERFORD, who, in the 1st year of Edward III., was constituted one of the commissioners to inquire and certify to the barons of the exchequer what lands and tenements, &c., Hugh le Despenser, Earl of Winchester, and Hugh, his son, (with others, who suffered death in the last year of King Edward II.'s reign,) were possessed of. This Sir Robert, who was distinguished by his piety, gave to the warden of the hospital of St. John, at Calne, lands of considerable value, to maintain a priest to pray for the soul of Joane, his wife, for the health of his own soul, and those of his parents, benefactors, and all the faithful deceased. But in the event of the said warden falling

to fulfil the trust thus reposed in him, the said lands were to devolve upon his brother WALTER. Sir Robert died in the 36th Edward III., and was s. by his said brother,

SIR WALTER DE HUNGERFORD, who m. Elizabeth, daughter of Sir Adam Fitz-John, and was s. by his son,

SIR THOMAS DE HUNGERFORD, who, in the 30th Edward III., was escheator for the county of Wilts; and in the 51st of the same reign, filled the chair of the House of Commons as SPEAKER, being the first person elected to that high office; the Commons not having had previously such an officer. In the 3rd Richard II. Sir Thomas obtained a confirmation of the office of forester of Selwood, which he had formerly acquired from Roger de Sturton. In the 6th of the same monarch he purchased from Elizabeth, the widow of Edward, Lord Spenser, the manor of Haytesbury, called the West Court, together with the hundred of Haytesbury. The next year having fortified his house at FARLE-MONTFORD, in the county of Somerset, without licence, he obtained a pardon for the same, and soon after procured a charter for free warren in all his demesne lands. Sir Thomas m. Joane, daughter and co-heir of Sir Edmund Hussie, Knt., and dying 3rd December, 1398, was s. by his son,

SIR WALTER HUNGERFORD, Knt., who, in consideration of his eminent services obtained, upon the accession of King Henry IV., a grant of £100. per annum, to be received out of the lands of Margaret, Duchess of Norfolk. In three years afterwards Sir Walter was engaged in the wars of France, and, subsequently, for his expenses in those wars, and especially at Calais, where he acquired great honour by encountering a knight of France, he had a further grant of one hundred marks per annum, payable out of the town and castle of Marlborough, in Wilts, and the same year was constituted sheriff of that county. In the 13th Henry IV., upon the death of Joane, his mother, he had livery of the manors of Haytesbury and Tesfount-Ewyas, in the county of Wilts, and of Farle-Mountfort, and others in Somersetshire, his homage being respited. In the 4th Henry V. Sir Walter was constituted admiral of the whole fleet under John, Duke of Bedford, and during that and the next two years he appears to have been been entirely engaged in the wars of France. In the latter year, being at the time steward of the king's household, and in his service at the siege of Roan, he obtained a grant in special tail, of the Barony of Homet, in Normandy, which had formerly been enjoyed by Sir William de Montney, Knt.; rendering to the king and his heirs one lance, with a fox-tail hanging thereat yearly, upon the feast day of the exaltation of the Holy Cross; and finding ten men at arms and twenty archers, to serve him, or his lieutenant during his wars with France. About this time Sir Walter was chosen a KNIGHT of the GARTER. Continuing to acquire fresh laurels on the French soil, this gallant soldier obtained a further grant for his services in the 9th of the same reign, of the castle of Neville, and territory of Breant, in Normandy, with divers other lands, which had been the possessions of Sir Robert de Breant, Knt. Sir Walter was one of the executors to the will of Henry V., and in the 2nd of the ensuing reign he was constituted, by advice of the lords then sitting in parliament, steward of the household to the young king; and in two years afterwards he was appointed treasurer of the exchequer. In the 6th Henry VI., bearing then the title of "Sir Walter Hungerford, Knt., Lord of Heightresbury and Homet, and treasurer of England;" he gave to the dean and canons of the Free-Royal-Chapel of St. Stephen, within the king's palace of Westminster, divers houses and shops in the parish of St. Anthony, within the city of London, in consideration whereof, they covenanted to make him partaker of all their masses and suffrages, during his life, and after his death to celebrate his obit annually, with *Placebo* and *Dirige*, and mass of *Requiem*, and to make distribution thereof, of twenty pence to the dean, to every canon twelve pence, to every vicar sixpence, to every clerk fourpence, and to the virger sixpence. In three years afterwards, being still lord treasurer of England, his lordship had licence to transport three thousand marks for the ransom of Sir Walter Hungerford, his son, then a prisoner in France. His lordship m. first, Catherine, one of the daughters and co-heirs of Thomas Peverell, by his wife, Margaret, daughter of Sir Thomas Courtenay, Knt., by whom he had issue,

Walter (Sir), who d. in Provence, before his father.
ROBERT (Sir), of whom presently.
Edmund (Sir), m. Margery, daughter and co-heir of Edward Burnell, and grand-daughter and co-heir of Hugh, Lord Burnell, between whom and her sisters, the BARONY OF BURNELL fell into abeyance in 1420, and so remains with their representatives.
Elizabeth, m. to Sir Walter Courtenay, Knt.
Margaret, m. to Sir Walter Rodeney, Knt.

Lord Hungerford espoused, secondly, Alianore, Countess of Arundel, daughter of Sir John Berkeley, Knight, but had no issue. He was summoned to parliament as a BARON, from the 4th to the 26th of King Henry VI.'s reign inclusive. By his testament bearing date 1st July, 1449, wherein he styleth himself Lord Hungerford, Haytesbury, and Homet, he directs his body to be buried in a certain chapel in the cathedral church at Salisbury, in which he had founded a perpetual chantry for two chaplains, and wherein Catherine, his first wife lay buried; and after some pious bequests, he leaves to Alianore, Countess of Arundel, his then wife, all his plate, both of silver and gold, and likewise all those other goods and chattels, which were hers while she was unmarried. To Sir Robert Hungerford, his son, his best Dorser of Arras. To the Lady Margaret, wife of his said son, his best legend of the lives of saints, written in French, and covered with red cloth. To Robert Hungerford, Lord Molines, his grandson, his best pair of curasses, with all belonging thereto; to be made choice of by him, out of the armory at Farley-Hungerford. To his son, Sir Edmund Hungerford, Knt., a cup of gold, with a cover, and a saphire on the head thereof. To Elizabeth, his daughter, a cup of gold. To Margaret, his other daughter, a bed of silk, of black and green

colour. And because his much honoured lord, the Viscount Beaumont, was lineally descended from the Dukes of Lancaster, he bequeathed unto him a cup of silver, with a cover bordered with gold, with which cup the most noble Prince John, Duke of Lancaster, was often served; and in which he did use to drink so long as he lived. And lastly, for the better advancement of Arnulph and William Hungerford (sons of the said Sir Robert Hungerford, Knt., his son), in their marriages, and Mary, daughter of the said Sir Robert, he bequeaths to them seven hundred marks sterling. His lordship d. in 1449, and was s. by his eldest surviving son,

SIR ROBERT HUNGERFORD, Knt., as second Baron Hungerford, summoned to parliament from 5th September, 1450, to 26th May, 1455. Of this nobleman very honourable mention is made regarding his services in France, during the life-time of his father, under the Regent Bedford. In the 17th Henry VI. he inherited the estates of his aunt, Alianore Talbot, the only sister of his mother, and the co-heir of Thomas Peverell. His lordship m. Margaret Botreaux,[*] only daughter and heir of

---

[*] "Of this Margaret," says Dugdale, "besides her being so great an heir, and that she lived to be very aged, I find much that is memorable." After recounting these numerous charitable and pious bequests upon a most liberal scale in her ladyship's will, which bore date 12th January, 1470, Sir William Dugdale proceeds with the following particulars of the enormous sums her ladyship expended in procuring the redemption of her son Robert, Lord Hungerford and Molines, who had been taken prisoner at Chastillon, and some other disbursements, viz.:—

	£.	s.	d.
In sending Chester-Herald into France, sundry times, by the space of seven years and sixteen weeks, to procure his enlargement - - - - - -	140	0	0
In gifts and rewards to those, who had part in him - - - - - - - - -	733	6	8
In apparel sent to him, with an ambling horse to please his friends; and for healing his wounds - - - - - -	176	0	0
For meat and drink by the space of seven years, and sixteen weeks, for himself and his servants, before he was put to his finance - - - - - - - - -	760	0	0
For the like board for himself and his servants after he was put to his finance - - - - - - - - -	126	13	4
For his finance, over and above all other expences and costs - - - - - -	6909	0	0
For exchange of money viii. by the noble (for payment of his ransom, being £7690.) paid - - - - - -	769	0	0
In gifts to divers noblemen, which were sureties for her, upon borrowing of money to pay this ransom; and to quit those lords harmless - - - - -	945	6	0
Lost in the sale of plate, which she sold towards that payment - - - - -	160	0	0
Item—Paid for her son's expences, from			

William, Lord Botreaux, who *d.* in 1462, and had issue,

 Robert, his successor, who inherited the Barony of Botreaux, in right of his mother.
 Arnulph.
 William.
 Mary.

Lord Hungerford *d.* in 1459, and was *s.* by his eldest son,

ROBERT HUNGERFORD, third Baron Hungerford, who had been summoned to parliament, (having married the heiress of Molines) in the lifetime of his father, as Lord Molines. This nobleman served in the French wars, under the great captain, Sir John Talbot, the gallant and renowned Earl of Shrewsbury, and was with him at the unfor-

tunate battle of Chastillon, where that illustrious soldier lost his life, and Lord Molines became a prisoner. Whereupon Alianore, Countess of Arundel, some time wife of his grandfather, Walter, Lord Hungerford, bestowed upon him all the wool then in her manor of Haytesbury, valued at an hundred marks, towards the payment of his ransom, provided that he came alive out of prison. By which, and considerable supplies from Margaret, Lady Hungerford and Botreaux, his mother, he obtained his freedom, after an incarceration of seven years and four months. In the 36th Henry VI., his lordship, in consideration of his services and his sufferings, obtained licence to transport fifteen hundred sacks of wool into any foreign parts, without payment of custom for the same: as also to travel beyond sea, and to take as many

	£.	*s.*	*d.*
the time he landed in England, until the time he went into Florence, with gifts and rewards to great lords and other after he escaped out of the Tower of London; and for his licence to go to Florence - - - - - - - - -	768	13	4
Paid for shipping and expences - - -	255	0	0
Paid in expences of his wife, children, and servants, by the space of seven years and sixteen weeks; with the expenses of Sir Thomas Hungerford, Knt., son and heir of her said son, waiting upon the Earl of Warwick, in the king's service, (after the departing of King Henry,) arrayed and accompanied for the war - - - - - - - -	800	0	0
Paid to her said son's creditors to whom he was indebted before he went out of England - - - - - - - - - -	400	0	0
Paid and spent for the composition of the lands of her late husband, Robert, Lord Hungerford, which had been divers times seised, and given to several great lords - - - - - - - - - -	2160	0	0
In the charge of being under the arrest of the Earl of Wiltshire, by the king's command; and to be restored to her lands and goods - - - - - - - -	400	0	0
In the loss which she sustained, when she was put into the abbey of Ambresbury by the lord chancellor of England, at the king's command; her moveable goods of great value being there burnt, (viz. :—Beds of cloth of gold, arras and silk hangings for halls and chambers; plate, money, and other stuff,) to the value of £1000 more; besides repairing the lodgings so burnt - - - - -	200	0	0
Item—When the Duke of Clarence and the Earl of Warwick went out of England against the king's will: she being then put in ward to the young Duchess of Norfolk: In making means to the king to be at Syon; cost her - -	200	0	0
Item—Whereas Robert, Lord Hungerford, her husband, ordained by his last -			

264

	£.	*s.*	*d.*
will to have a chappel for his sepulture builded, adjoining to our lady chappel, in the cathedral church of Salisbury, and two priests there to be founded; and livelyhood amortised thereof; and his and her *obit* to be kept solemnly in the said church. Which chappel she did make accordingly; and removed his body thither into a vault of marble, and made another tomb for herself: all this cost - - - - - - - - -	497	0	0
Item—In ornaments for said chappel; viz. three pair of candlesticks of silver; whereof one pair gilt; three pair of cruets, whereof one pair gilt; three pax-bredes; one bell of silver; nine pair of altar cloths; nine pair of vestments; mass books, leigers, and other necessaries to the chappel - - - -	200	0	0
Item—For license to amortise the manors of Immer and Homyngton, in the county of Wilts, and the manor of Folke, in the county of Dorset, to the dean and chapter of Salisbury; for maintenance of those two priests, and keeping the said *obit* for ever - - -	176	13	4
Item—Whereas Walter, Lord Hungerford, built an alms-house for twelve poor men and one woman; and a house for a school-master, being a priest, as well to teach grammar, as to have the rule and oversight of those poor men and women, at Haytesbury, in the county of Wilts, and ordained that the manors of Chyverell-Burnell, and Chyverell-Halys, alias Chyverell-Magna, should be amortised to the said school-master, poor men, &c., and their successors. This being not performed in his days, she paid for the effecting thereof - - - - - - - - - -	200	0	0
Item—In other sums, upon other occasions which she paid, all which computed, amounted to 26,180 marks, 6*s.* and 8*d.*			

         £8726 0 0

with him in his company, with gold, silver, and other necessaries, as should be suitable to his degree. Upon this occasion, his lordship travelled into Italy. But returning before long, he espoused the Lancastrian interests, and fought under the red banner at TOWTON-FIELD, from which conflict, after the defeat of his party, he fled to York, where he joined King Henry, and thence accompanied the monarch into Scotland. His lordship was, in consequence, attainted by the parliament assembled in the 1st Edward IV. Notwithstanding which, King Edward regarded his wife, Alianore, and his younger children, with such feelings of compassion, that he committed them to the care of Lord Wenlok, to whom he had granted the attainted lord's estates, for a fitting support. In three years afterwards, the Lancastrians again making head, Lord Hungerford was in their ranks at the battle of HEXHAM, and being made prisoner, he was conveyed to Newcastle, and there beheaded, anno 1463, He was buried in the cathedral church of Salisbury. His lordship m. Alianore, daughter and heir of William, Lord Molines, and had issue,

THOMAS (Sir), of whom presently.

Walter, ancestor of the Lords Hungerford, of Haytesbury, *see that dignity.*

Leonard.

Fridiswide, who became a nun at Sion.

Upon the attainder of Robert, Lord Hungerford and Molines, these honours became EXTINCT. His lordship's widow espoused Sir Oliver Manningham. His eldest son,

SIR THOMAS HUNGERFORD, sided for a while with Richard Nevil, Earl of Warwick, who then espoused the cause of Edward IV., but afterwards falling off, and exerting his influence for the restoration of King Henry VI., he was seized, and tried for his life at Salisbury, in the 8th Edward IV., and having had judgment of death as a traitor, was executed the next day. Sir Thomas m. Anne, daughter of Henry, Earl of Northumberland, by whom (who m. secondly, Sir Laurence Raynesford, Knt., and thirdly, Sir Hugh Vaughan, Knt.,) he had an only daughter and heiress,

MARY HUNGERFORD, who espoused EDWARD HASTINGS, son and heir apparent of William, first Lord Hastings, of Ashby-de-la-Zouche. This Mary, the attainders of her father and grandfather having been reversed in the first parliament of King Henry VII., had restitution of the honours and estates of her family, and in consequence bore the title of Lady Hungerford, Botreaux, and Molines. Her ladyship's son and successor, George Hastings, was created EARL OF HUNTINGDON, in which Earldom, those baronies became merged until the death of Francis, tenth earl, in 1780, without issue, when they became vested in Elizabeth, his sister and heir, wife of John, Earl of Moira, of the kingdom of Ireland, and they are now enjoyed by her ladyship's grandson, GEORGE, present MARQUESS OF HASTINGS.

ARMS.—Barry of four ar. and gu. in chief three plates.

HUNGERFORD—BARON HUNGERFORD, OF HEYTESBURY, IN THE COUNTY OF WILTS.

By Writ of Summons, dated 8th June, 1536, 28th Henry VIII.

Lineage.

The Honourable

WALTER HUNGERFORD, second son of Robert, third Baron Hungerford, who was attainted and beheaded in 1463, having joined the banner of the Earl of Richmond, shared in the triumph of Bosworth, and participated in the spoils of conquest. We find him subsequently again in arms for his royal master, against Perkyn Warbeck, and the Cornish men, who had risen in his behalf, and he was eventually of the privy council, to King Henry VIII. He m. Jane, daughter of William Buistrode, and had issue,

EDWARD (Sir), his successor.

Elizabeth m. to Sir John Bourchier.

He was s. at his decease by his son,

SIR EDWARD HUNGERFORD, Knt., of Heytesbury, in the county of Wilts, who m. Jane, daughter of John Lord Zouche of Haryngworth, and was s. by his only son,

SIR WALTER HUNGERFORD, who was summoned to parliament as BARON HUNGERFORD, *of Heytesbury,* on the 8th June, 1536, but never afterwards. His lordship m. first, Susan, daughter of Sir John Danvers, Knt., and had issue,

WILLIAM (Sir), of Farley Castle, in the county of Wilts.

Lord Hungerford espoused, secondly, Alice, daughter of William, Lord Sandys, by whom he had,

Edward (Sir), gentleman-pensioner to Queen Elizabeth, died s. p.

Anthony (Sir), of Burton Inges, in the county of Oxford.

Mary, m. to —— Baker, Esq., of the county of Essex.

This nobleman in the 31st Henry VIII., being attainted in parliament, was beheaded on Tower Hill, with Cromwell, Earl of Essex, on the 28th July, 1541, when the BARONY OF HUNGERFORD OF HEYTESBURY, EXPIRED. The crimes laid to his lordship's charge, were "retaining a chaplain, called William Bird, who had called the king a heretic.—Procuring certain persons to ascertain, by conjuration, how long the king should live;—and having been guilty of unnatural offences." The attainder of Lord Hungerford was reversed by Queen Mary in favour of his children, to all intents and purposes, save the enjoyment of the peerage. The eldest son,

SIR WILLIAM HUNGERFORD, Knt., of Farley Castle, m. Anne, daughter of Sir William Dormer, Knt., and had issue,

EDWARD, who died young.

Susan, m. to Michael Ernley, Esq., of Cannings, in the county of Wilts.

Lucy, m. to Sir John St. John, of Lydiard.

Jane, m. to Sir John Kerne, Knt., of the
county of Glamorgan.

ARMS.—Barry of four ar. and gu. in chief three
plates.

HUNTERCOMBE — BARON HUN-
TERCOMBE.

By Writ of Summons, dated 23rd June, 1295,
23 Edward I.

Lineage.

In the 35th Henry III.

WILLIAM DE HUNTERCOMBE having mar-
ried Isabel, one of the daughters and co-heirs of
Robert de Muscamp, had livery of the lands of her
inheritance. In some years after which he had summons to be at Chester, well fitted with horse and
arms, to oppose the hostilities of the Welch. And
in the 54th of the same reign he was signed with the
cross, in order to accompany Prince Edward in a
voyage to the Holy Land. He died the next year,
seised of the manor of Huntercombe, in the county
of Oxford, and other estates, and was s. by his
son,

SIR WALTER DE HUNTERCOMBE, Knt.,
who, in the 5th of Edward I., answered fifty pounds
for his relief of the moiety of the barony of Mus-
champ, which he then possessed. In the 10th year
of the same reign we find him in an expedition made
into Wales. In the 22nd he had summons to attend
the king at Portsmouth, with horse and arms,
thence to sail into Gascony, and the next year he
was summoned to parliament as a BARON. In the
25th his lordship was in the expedition made into
Scotland, and the 26th he was made governor of
Edinburgh Castle. In the 27th he was constituted
lieutenant of Northumberland, and for several
years subsequently he continued with the army in
Scotland. In the 35th he petitioned parliament,
setting forth his being in all the Scottish wars, first
at Berwick, with twenty light horse; afterwards at
Strivelin, with thirty-two in the retinue of the Earl
Warren; next at La Vaire Chapelle, with thirty in
the retinue of the Bishop of Durham; lastly, at
Galloway, with sixteen. And since that, in the last
battle, that he sent eighteen, though absent himself, being then warden of the marches towards
Northumberland. And his lordship prayed that
his scutage for all these expeditions might be remitted, which request was accordingly conceded.
Lord Huntercombe m. Alice, one of the daughters
and co-heirs of Hugh de Bolebec, of Bolebec, in the
county of Northumberland, and also co-heir of
Richard de Montfichet, by reason that Margery, the
mother of the said Hugh, was one of the sisters and
co-heirs of the said Richard. His lordship d. in
1312 without issue, when his nephew, Nicholas, son
of Richard de Newband, and Gunmore, his sister,
succeeded to his lands, and the BARONY OF HUN-
TERCOMBE became EXTINCT.

ARMS.—Ermine two bars gemells gules.

302

HUNTINGFEILD — BARONS HUNT-
INGFEILD.

By Writ of Summons, dated 26th January, 1297,
25 Edward I.

Lineage.

In the time of King Stephen,

WILLIAM DE HUNTINGFEILD, with the
consent of Roger, his son and heir, gave the whole
Isle of Mendham, in the county of Suffolk, and
divers other lands, to the monks of Castle Acre, in
the county of Norfolk. He d. in 1155, and was s.
by his said son and heir,

ROGER DE HUNTINGFEILD, who was s. by
his son,

WILLIAM DE HUNTINGFEILD, who being
made constable of Dover Castle in the 5th of King
John, obliged himself, by oath in the king's presence, faithfully to preserve the safe custody of that
fortress, so that it should not be surrendered to any
person, save the king himself, or the lord chamberlain, Hubert de Burgh, and as hostages for his
loyalty, delivered up his son and daughter, the
former to remain in the hands of the Earl of Arundel, the latter in those of the Earl Ferrers. In the
8th of John this William de Huntingfeild paid a
fine of two marks and two palfreys, for the wardship of the heir and lands of Osbert Fits-Hervie,
and the next year obtained a grant of all the possessions of Roger de Huntingfeild, his brother,
which had been seised by the crown by reason of
the interdict. In the following year we find him
justice-itinerant for Lincoln, and afterwards sheriff
for the counties of Norfolk and Suffolk; for four
successive years subsequently, however, he became
eminent amongst the barons who extorted the
GREAT CHARTERS from John, and was one of the
twenty-five chosen to enforce their observance, for
which conduct he came under the excommunication
of the pope, and had his lands in Lincolnshire
seised by the crown, and transferred to Nichola de
Haya during the king's pleasure. In the reign of
Henry III., he seems to have made his peace,
for he then journeyed to the Holy Land with a
licence from the crown. This feudal lord m. Alice
de St. Liz, and had issue,

ROGER, his successor.

Alice, m. to Richard de Solers, whom she survived, and her father, in the 15th of John,
she being then a widow, gave to the king
six fair Norway goshawkers for licence to
have the disposal of her in marriage, and
for an assignation of her dowry out of the
lands of her deceased husband.

His lordship was s. at his decease by his son,

ROGER DE HUNTINGFEILD, who, in the
26th Henry III., paid a fine of two hundred marks,
to be exempted from the expedition then making
into Gascony. He m. Joane, one of the daughters
and co-heirs of William de Hobrugg, and dying in
1256, was s. by his son,

WILLIAM DE HUNTINGFEILD, who, at
the battle of Evesham, 49th Henry III., was one

of the principal barons in hostility to the crown. He d. in 1222, and was s. by his son,

ROGER DE HUNTINGFEILD, who, in the 22nd Edward I., had summons, with other eminent persons, to attend the king with all despatch to advise about the important affairs of the realm; and soon after received command to be at Portsmouth well fitted with horse and arms, to sail into Gascony. In the 25th Edward I. (30th January, 1297,) he was summoned to parliament as a BARON, but never afterwards. His lordship m. Joyce, daughter of John de Engaine, and dying in 1301, was s. by his son,

WILLIAM DE HUNTINGFEILD, second baron, but never summoned to parliament. This nobleman was engaged in the Scottish wars, temp. Edward I. and Edward II., and died in 1313, being then possessed of the manor of Bekesworth, in the county of Cambridge, and the manors of Mendham and Huntingfield, in the county of Suffolk, as also divers lordships and lands in other shires. His wife Sibell survived him, and married William le Latimer. His lordship was s. by his son,

ROGER DE HUNTINGFEILD, third baron, but never summoned to parliament. This nobleman m. Cecilia, daughter of Sir Walter de Norwich, Knt., and dying in 1337, was s. by his son,

SIR WILLIAM DE HUNTINGFEILD, fourth baron, summoned to parliament from 15th November, 1351, to 20th January, 1376. His lordship served in the French wars in the 33rd and 34th of Edward III., being latterly of the retinue of Henry, Duke of Lancaster. He d. in 1377, sine prole, leaving his aunt Alicia, daughter of William, his grandfather, and widow of Sir John Norwich, Knt., his heir; but, according to another inquisition, the said Alice, and Sir John Copledick, grandson of Johanna, daughter of the said William, his grandfather, by Sybilla, his second wife, were his heirs. Amongst whose descendants, if the writ of Edward I. be that which created the dignity, the BARONY OF HUNTINGFEILD is now in ABEYANCE.

ARMS.—Or. on a fess gules, three plates.

HUNTINGFEILD — BARON HUNTFEILD.

By Writ of Summons, dated 14th August, 1362, 36 Edward III.

Lineage.

JOHN DE HUNTINGFEILD, was summoned to parliament as a BARON, from 14th August, 1362, to 6th April, 1369, but nothing further is known of his lordship or his descendants.

ARMS.—Or. on a fess gules, three plates.

HUSSEY—BARON HUSSEY, OF SLEFORD, IN THE COUNTY OF LINCOLN.

By Writ of Summons, dated 5th January, 1534, 25 Henry VIII.

Lineage.

SIR WILLIAM HUSSEY, Knt., an eminent lawyer in the time of Edward IV., after filling the office of attorney-general, and having been called by writ, to the degree of serjeant at law, was constituted LORD CHIEF JUSTICE of the Court of King's Bench, in the 17th of that monarch's reign, when he received an allowance of one hundred and forty marks, for greater state. He was living temp. Henry VII., as is evident by this inscription over his arms, in the semicircular or bow window, of Grey's Inn Hall, viz:—

"W. Hussee miles capitalis justiciarius de banco regis, temp. R. Henry VII."

In one of the windows of the chapel, belonging to the same inn, are his arms impaling those of his wife, with the following inscription:—

"Will. Hussee miles capitalis justic. ad placita coram rege, et Elizabetha uxor ejus filia Thomæ Berkeley arm."

The lady mentioned above, was of the Berkeleys of Wymondham, and Sir William had issue by her,

> JOHN, his successor.
>
> Robert (Sir), whose grandson, Sir Edward Hussey, Bart., of Honington, in the county of Lincoln, (so created by King James I.,) was grandfather of Sir Thomas Hussey, with whom the baronetcy expired. Sir Thomas left two surviving daughters, his co-heirs, viz.
>
>> Elizabeth, m. to Richard Ellis, Esq., and died s. p.
>>
>> Sarah, m. to Robert Apreece, Esq., of Washingley, in the county of Huntingdon, and had issue,
>>
>>> THOMAS APREECE, whose son and heir,
>>>
>>>> THOMAS-HUSSEY APREECE, Esq., of Washingley, was created a baronet, 4th June, 1782, and is now (1831) living.
>
> William, from whom descended the Husseys of Yorkshire.
>
> Elizabeth, m. to Richard Grey, Earl of Kent.
>
> Mary, m. to William, Lord Willoughby.

The eldest son,

SIR JOHN HUSSEY, Knt., in the 2nd Henry VII., was in arms for the king, at the battle of Stoke, against John, Earl of Lincoln, and his adherents; and in the 13th of Henry VIII., was made chief butler of England. In the 21st of the same reign, he was one of the knights of the king's body; and being summoned as BARON HUSSEY, of SLEFORD, in the county of Lincoln, (where he had erected a noble mansion,) to the parliament begun at Westminster, 3rd November, in that year, was admitted into the house upon the 1st December following; but his lordship's name does not occur in the list of summonses for that year, nor before the 5th January, 1534, yet it is clear that he was summoned; for the year after, (22d of Henry,) he had, under the title of Lord Hussey, a grant of the custody of the Manor of Harewoole, in the county of York; and he was one of the lords, who at that time signed the declaration to the pope, regarding the king's divorce. In 1533, being then a lord of the council, he had a grant of the wardship and marriage of Thomas, the son and heir of Christopher Wymbushe, deceased; but in a few years afterwards, engaging in the common insurrection, (anno 1537,) when the feuds and differences about religion broke out, he was attainted of high treason; his Manor of Sleford, with lands adjacent, worth £5000. a year, confiscated, and he himself beheaded at Lincoln, when the BARONY OF HUSSEY, OF SLEFORD, EXPIRED. His lordship m. first, Lady Anne Grey, daughter of George, Earl of Kent, and had issue,

> Giles, } who both died s. p.
> Thomas, }
>
> Bridget, m. first, to Sir Richard Morison, Knt., by whom she had issue,
>
>> Charles, whose son, Sir Charles Morison, Bart., of Cashiobury, in the county of Herts, left an only daughter and heiress, ELIZABETH, who espoused Arthur, LORD CAPEL, OF HADHAM, from whom the present EARL OF ESSEX, descends, and inherits Cashiobury Park.
>> Elizabeth, m. first, to Henry Norris, Esq.; and secondly, Henry Clinton, Earl of Lincoln.
>> Mary, m. to Barth Hales, Esq.
>> Jane-Sibilla, m. first, to Edward, Lord Russel; and secondly, to Arthur, Lord Grey, of Wilton.
>> Bridget, Lady Morison, espoused secondly, Henry, Earl of Rutland; and thirdly, Francis, Earl of Bedford, but had issue by neither.
>
> Elizabeth, m. to —— Hungerford, Esq.
> Anne, m. first, to Sir Humphrey Browne, Knt., one of the Justices of the Court of Common Pleas; and secondly, to —— Dimock, Esq.
> Dorothy, m. to —— Dockwray, Esq.

Lord Hussey, m. secondly, Margaret, daughter and heir of Sir Simon Blount, of Mangerfield, in the county of Gloucester, and had issue,

> William (Sir), of whom presently.
> Giles (Sir), of Caythorpe, in the county of Lincoln.
> Gilbert (Sir).
> Reginald.
> Elisabeth.

The attainder of his lordship was reversed in parliament, the 5th of Elizabeth, and his children restored in blood, but neither the estate or honour granted to the heir, which heir,

SIR WILLIAM HUSSEY, was sheriff of the county of Lincoln, in the 22d Henry VIII.. He m. ——, daughter, and eventually sole heir, of Sir Thomas Lovell, Knt., and left two daughters, viz.—

> Nella, m. to Richard Disney Esq., of Norton Disney.
> Anne, m. to William Gell, Esq., of Darley, in the county of Derby.

Sir William d. in the 3rd and 4th of Philip and Mary.

ARMS.—Or. a cross vert.

HYDE — BARONS HYDE, OF HINDON, EARLS OF CLARENDON, BARONS HYDE OF WOTTON BASSETT, VISCOUNTS HYDE, OF KENELWORTH, EARLS OF ROCHESTER.

Barony of Hyde, of Hindon,		3rd November, 1660.
Earldom of Clarendon,	by Letters Patent,	20th April, 1661.
Barony of Hyde, of Wotton Basset, and		23rd April. 1681.
Viscounty of Hyde, of Kenilworth, Earldom of Rochester,		29th November, 1682.

Lineage.

SIR EDWARD HYDE, Knt., a person eminently learned in the law, and as eminent for his attachment to the CHARLESES, was made chancellor of the exchequer and a privy councillor, by the first monarch of that name; and having shared the fortunes of the second, was declared by his majesty, while in exile, at Bruges, in Flanders, LORD HIGH CHANCELLOR OF ENGLAND, in the year, 1657, which office he held, until 1667, when he was succeeded by Sir Orlando Bridgman. Sir Edward was elevated to the peerage, by letters patent, dated 3d November, 1660, as *Baron Hyde, of Hindon*, in the county of Wilts; and created, 20th April, 1661, *Viscount Cornbury*, and EARL OF CLARENDON.* His lordship obtained celebrity, not only as a lawyer and statesman, but as a man of letters. By command of King Charles II., he wrote his popular "History of the Rebellion," and he produced several other works, which are enumerated in Walpole's Catalogue of Royal and Noble Authors. "One may pronounce," says Walpole, "on my Lord Clarendon, in his double capacity of statesman and historian, that he acted for liberty, but wrote for prerogative;" and Burnet characterizes him, "as a good minister, indefatigable in business, but little too magisterial, and not well enough acquainted with foreign affairs." "He was a good chancellor," continues the same authority, "and impartial in the administration of justice; but a little too rough. He had a levity in his wit, and a loftiness in his carriage, that did not well become the station he was

---

* CLARENDON. This title, first enjoyed by Sir Edward Hyde, was derived from a spacious park, near Salisbury, formerly the site of a royal palace, but more remarkable, as the place where King Henry II. summoned the great council of peers and prelates, in 1164, from which emanated the celebrated regulations, so well known, as "the CONSTITUTIONS OF CLARENDON," by which the clergy were made amenable to the jurisdiction of the civil power. From those regulations, arose the subsequent hostility between Henry II., and Thomas à Becket.

in: for those that addressed him, and those that thought themselves neglected, he was apt to reject with contumely, and some disparagement of their services, which created him many enemies, and at last procured his fall." Upon his disgrace, the earl retired into France, and died at Roan, in Normandy, 19th December, 1674. His lordship m. Frances, daughter, and eventually sole heir, of Sir Thomas Aylesbury, Bart., and had four sons and two daughters, viz.

1. HENRY, *Viscount Cornbury*, his successor.
2. Laurence, Master of the Robes to King Charles II., who was advanced to the peerage, on the 23d April, 1681, as *Baron Hyde, of Wotton Basset*, in the county of Wilts, and *Viscount Hyde*, of Kenilworth, in the county of Warwick, and was created EARL OF ROCHESTER, on 29th November, 1682. This nobleman concurred in the revolution of 1688, and was constituted LORD LIEUTENANT OF IRELAND, in 1700. He was a person of great natural parts, and esteemed as a statesman, incorruptible: indeed his disposition was deemed too warm, to be insincere. He married Lady Henrietta Boyle, daughter of Richard, Earl of Burlington, and had issue,

    HENRY, his successor.
    Anne, m. to James, Duke of Ormonde.
    Henrietta, m. to James, Earl of Dalkeith, eldest son of the unfortunate James, Duke of Monmouth, and from this marriage, the Dukes of Buccleugh descend.
    Mary, m. to Francis Seymour, Lord Conway, ancestor of the extant Marquesses of Hertford.
    Catherine, died unmarried,
    His lordship d. in 1711, and was buried in Westminster Abbey. He was s. by his son,
    HENRY, second Earl of Rochester, of whom hereafter, as fourth EARL OF CLARENDON.
3. Edward, student at law, died unmarried.
4. James, drowned on board the Gloucester frigate, in his passage to Scotland, with several other persons of distinction, in the train of the Duke of York.
1. ANNE, married to JAMES, *Duke of York*, afterwards KING JAMES II. This lady was maid of honour to the princess royal, and her marriage with the duke was concealed, until her pregnancy compelled an avowal. The prince is accused of using both promises and menaces, to deter her from claiming him as a husband, but her ladyship had the spirit to declare, that it should be known she was his wife, be the consequences what they might.
2. Frances, m. to Sir Thomas Knightley, K.B., of Harlingfordbury, in the county of Herts.
Edward, Earl of Clarendon, was s. by his eldest son,
HENRY HYDE, second Earl of Clarendon, who in the first year of King James II., was lord privy seal, but retired from office the next year. At the

revolution, he refused to act with the new government, and lived subsequently, in retirement. His lordship espoused first, the Honourable Theodosia Capel, daughter of Arthur, first Lord Capel, by whom he had an only son, EDWARD, *Viscount Cornbury*, his successor. He espoused secondly, Flower, daughter and sole heir of William Backhouse, Esq., of Sallowfield, but had no issue. His lordship d. 31st October, 1709, and was s. by his son,
EDWARD HYDE, third Earl of Clarendon. This nobleman, in the lifetime of his father, was master of the horse to Prince George, of Denmark, and in the reign of Queen Anne, his lordship was governor of New York. He m. Catherine, daughter of Henry, Lord O'Brien, eldest son of Henry, Earl of Thomond, which Catherine, at the decease of her mother, became BARONESS CLIFTON. By this lady he had issue,

    EDWARD, Viscount Cornbury, who died unmarried, at the age of twenty-two, 12th February, 1712-13.
    Catherine, d. unmarried.
    Theodosia, m. to John Bligh, Esq., and from this marriage the extant EARLS OF DARNLEY derive: who enjoy the Barony of Clifton, through this lady.
His lordship d. 31st March, 1723, and his only son having died previously, the honours devolved upon his kinsman (revert to Laurence, second son of Edward, first earl).
HENRY HYDE, second Earl of Rochester, as fourth EARL OF CLARENDON. This nobleman was joint treasurer of Ireland with Arthur, Earl of Anglesey. His lordship m. Jane, youngest daughter of Sir William Leveson-Gower, and sister of John, Lord Gower, by whom he had surviving issue,

    HENRY, Viscount Cornbury, who d. in 1753, before his father.
    Jane, m. to William Capel, third Earl of Essex, and had four daughters; of whom two lived to maturity, viz.
        CHARLOTTE, who became heir to her grandfather, Henry, Earl of Clarendon and Rochester. Her ladyship espoused the Hon. Thomas Villiers, second son of William, second Earl of Jersey, which Thomas, was elevated to the peerage on 31st May, 1756, as *Baron Hyde, of Hindon*, and created EARL OF CLARENDON 8th June, 1776. His lordship left at his decease, with other issue,
            John-Charles, present Earl of Clarendon.
        Mary, m. in 1756, to Admiral, the Hon. John Forbes, second son of George, third Earl of Granard.
    Catherine, m. to Charles, Duke of Queensberry and Dover. This lady was the celebrated Duchess of Queensberry, the patroness of Gray, the poet.
The earl d. 1753, and his only son deceasing in the same year before him, the BARONY OF HYDE, OF HINDON, the VISCOUNTY OF CORNBURY, the EARLDOM OF CLARENDON, the BARONY OF HYDE,

of Wotton Basset, the VISCOUNTY OF HYDE, of Kenilworth, and the EARLDOM OF ROCHESTER, became ALL EXTINCT.

ARMS.—As. a chevron betw. three losanges, or.

HYDE—EARLS OF ROCHESTER.

See Hyde, Earls of Clarendon.

INGHAM—BARON INGHAM.

By Writ of Summons, dated 15th June, 1328, 2 Edward III.

Lineage.

In the 2d year of King John,

JOHN DE INGHAM, of Ingham, in the county of Norfolk, having m. Albreda, one of the daughters and co-heirs of Walter Waleran, paid a fine of sixty marks, and one palfrey to the king, for livery of the third part of his barony, and for the relief due thereupon, excepting the serjeanty of the forest, which William de Nevill then had. He d. in the 5th of the same reign, and was s. by his son,

OLIVER DE INGHAM, who d. in the 10th Edward I., possessed of estates in the counties of Norfolk, Southampton, Dorset, and Wilts, and was s. by his son,

JOHN DE INGHAM, of Ingham, who was s. by his son,

OLIVER DE INGHAM, of Ingham, who was summoned to parliament as a BARON, in the 2d year of Edward III., and from that period to the 16th of the same reign. This nobleman was a very eminent person during the martial times in which he lived. In the beginning of Edward II.'s reign he was in the wars of Scotland, and we find him for several years afterwards actively engaged in that kingdom. In the 14th Edward II., he was constituted governor of the castle of Ellesmere, in Shropshire, and upon the breaking out of the insurrection under Thomas, Earl of Lancaster, he marched with the king to Cirencester, Gloucester, Shrewsbury, and other places. The next year he was made governor of the castle at Devizes, in Wilts, and sheriff of Cheshire; and in two years afterwards seneschal of Aquitaine, when he proceeded thither at the head of seven thousand men. Upon the deposition of Edward II., his lordship was appointed one of the twelve guardians of the young King Edward III., and soon after constituted justice of Chester for life. In this reign, (Edward III.,) his patent for the seneschalcy was renewed, and he obtained a grant of five hundred marks sterling for his support in that service. His lordship had issue,

Elizabeth, m. to John Curson, and d. before her father, leaving a daughter,
MARY CURSON.

Joane, m. to Roger le Strange, Lord Strange, of Knokyn.

Lord Ingham d. in 1344, when the BARONY OF INGHAM fell into ABEYANCE, between his grand-daughter, Mary Curson, and his daughter Joane, Lady Strange, his co-heirs, as it still continues with their representatives.

ARMS.—Per pale, or. and vert. a cross recercele, or moline, gu.

290

JEFFERYS — BARONS JEFFERYS, OF WEM, IN THE COUNTY OF SALOP.

By Letters Patent, dated 15th May, 1685.

Lineage.

SIR GEORGE JEFFERYS, Baronet, was elevated to the peerage, in the 1st year of King James II., (15th May, 1685,) as BARON JEFFERYS, OF WEM, in the county of Salop.

This infamous person was a younger son of John Jefferys, Esq., of Acton, in the county of Denbigh, by Margaret, daughter of Sir Thomas Ireland, Knt., of Bewsey, in Lancashire. The rudiments of education he acquired at a school in the country, whence he removed to Westminster, and thence, became a student of the Middle Temple. He was subsequently a practising barrister, in good business, although it is asserted that he was never regularly called to the bar. His first official employment was that of a Welch judge, from which he was promoted in 1680 to the chief justiceship of Chester, In 1681 he was created a baronet, and in two years afterwards sworn of the privy council, and constituted LORD CHIEF JUSTICE OF THE COURT OF KING's BENCH. The conduct of this monster in ermine has rendered his memory justly odious, and made his name the most opprobrious epithet by which the bench can be assailed. He was partial, morose, and cruel, violent, savage, and bloodthirsty. It would be, however, a work too horrid and disgusting to pursue his sanguinary course, did not its notoriety render the task one of supererogation; his deeds in the west, after the suppression of the unfortunate Monmouth's rebellion, have been so indelibly imprinted in blood, that the tide of time washes over them without removing a single stain; and so long as the English language finds a tongue, JEFFERYS will be a synonyme for everything unjust, cruel, and tyrannical. In 1685 he was constituted LORD HIGH CHANCELLOR, and in the same year he presided as lord steward of England at the trial of Lord Delamere, who was acquitted. Upon the landing of the Prince of Orange, Jefferys attempted to withdraw in disguise from the kingdom, and for that purpose had got on board a Newcastle collier, which was to convey him to Hamburgh, but he was discovered, seized, brought before the lords of the council, and by them committed to the Tower, where he remained until his decease in 1689. He m. first, ————, by whom he had one surviving son, JOHN, his successor, and two daughters, viz.

Margaret, m. to Sir Thomas Stringer, of Durance, in the county of Middlesex.

Sarah, m. to Captain Harmage, of the marines.

His lordship wedded, secondly, Lady Jones, widow of Sir John Jones, of Funman, in Glamorganshire, and daughter of Sir Thomas Bloodworth. Lord Jefferys was s. by his son,

JOHN JEFFERYS, second baron, who espoused Lady Charlotte Herbert, daughter and heir of Philip, Earl of Pembroke, by whom he had an only surviving daughter,

Henrietta-Louisa, who m. Thomas, first Earl of Pomfret, and was mother of

GEORGE, second Earl of Pomfret, father of

THOMAS, present EARL POMFRET.

His lordship d. in 1703, when the BARONY OF JEFFERYS, OF WEM, became EXTINCT.

ARMS.—Arm. a lion rampant and canton, sa. with a mullet for difference on a canton.

JERMYN — BARONS JERMYN, OF ST. EDMUNDSBURY, IN THE COUNTY OF SUFFOLK, EARL OF ST. ALBANS.

| Barony, | by Letters | 8th September, 1643. |
| Earldom, | Patent, | 27th April, 1660. |

Lineage.

SIR THOMAS DE JERMYN m. Agnes, sister and co-heir of Thomas de Rushbroke, with whom he acquired the manor of Rushbroke, in the county of Suffolk. From this Sir Thomas descended

SIR THOMAS JERMYN, of Rushbroke, treasurer of the household to King Charles I., whose second son,

HENRY JERMYN, master of the horse to the queen, having devoted himself with a more than ordinary degree of zeal to the fortunes of his royal master during the civil wars, was elevated to the peerage on the 8th September, 1643, as BARON JERMYN, of St. Edmundsbury, in the county of Suffolk, with remainder, default of male issue, to his elder brother, Thomas Jermyn. His lordship subsequently attended the queen into France, and presided over her majesty's small establishment for a great many years. While abroad he was employed in several embassies by King Charles II., and in consideration of all his faithful services, his lordship, immediately upon the restoration, was created by letters patent, dated at Breda, 27th April, 1660, EARL OF ST. ALBANS. He was soon after made a Knight of the Garter, and constituted lord chamberlain of the household. His lordship died unmarried in 1683, when the EARLDOM OF ST. ALBANS became EXTINCT, and the Barony of Jermyn devolved upon (his deceased brother Thomas's son,) his nephew,

THOMAS JERMYN, second Baron Jermyn. This nobleman was governor of Jersey. His lordship m. Mary ———, and had issue,

———, m. to Thomas Bond, Esq., and d. in the life-time of her father.

Mary, m. to Sir Robert Davers, Bart.

Merelina, m. first, to Sir William Spring, and secondly, to Sir William Gage, Bart., of Hengrave.

Penelope, m. to Gray James Grove, Esq.

Delariviere, m. to Symonds D'Ewes, Bart.

He d. in 1703, when the BARONY OF JERMYN, OF ST. EDMUNDSBURY, became EXTINCT.

ARMS.—Sa. a chevron between two mullets in pale ar.

JERMYN — BARON JERMYN, OF DOVER.

By Letters Patent, dated 13th May, 1685.

Lineage.

HENRY JERMYN, next brother of Thomas, second Lord Jermyn, of St. Edmundsbury, was himself elevated to the peerage, on the 13th May, 1685, as BARON JERMYN, OF DOVER. His lordship d. without issue in 1708, when the barony became EXTINCT—and his estates devolved upon his nieces, the daughters of his above mentioned brother.

ARMS.—Same as Jermyn, Earl of St. Albans, with the requisite difference.

JERVIS — EARL OF ST. VINCENT.

By Letters Patent, dated 27th May, 1797.

Lineage.

JOHN JERVIS, Esq., second son of Swynfen Jervis, Esq., a lawyer of eminence, (descended from James Jervis, of Chatkyll, in the county of Stafford, living temp. Henry VIII.,) by Elizabeth, daughter of George Parker, Esq., of Park Hall, was b. at Meaford, on the 19th of January, 1734, and having entered the royal navy at a very early period of life, (in his tenth year,) attained the highest honours of that gallant profession, and was elevated to the peerage the 27th May, 1797, by the titles of Baron Jervis, of Meaford, in the county of Stafford, and EARL of ST. VINCENT, as a reward for the splendid victory he had achieved, in that year, over the Spanish fleet, off Cape St. Vincent. His lordship was nominated first lord of the admiralty in 1801; and created, on the 27th April, in the same year, VISCOUNT ST. VINCENT, with remainder, in default of male issue, to his nephews, William-Henry Ricketts, and Edward-Jervis Ricketts, successively, and afterwards, to these gentlemen's sister, Mary, Countess of Northesk, and her male descendants. The earl m. in 1783, Martha, daughter of Lord-chief-baron Parker, who d. without issue in 1816. His lordship d. in March, 1823, when the EARLDOM AND BARONY EXPIRED, but the viscounty devolved upon his younger nephew, (the elder, Captain William-Henry Ricketts, of the royal navy, having been unfortunately drowned in 1805, leaving only daughters,) EDWARD-JERVIS, the present viscount, who is second son of William-Henry Ricketts, Esq., of Canaan, in the island of Jamaica, by the deceased earl's sister, Mary, who d. in 1828.

ARMS.—Sa. a chev. erm. between three martlets ar.

KEPPEL — VISCOUNT KEPPEL, OF ELVEDEN, IN THE COUNTY OF SUFFOLK.

By Letters Patent, dated 22nd April, 1782.

Lineage.

The Honourable

AUGUSTUS KEPPEL, (second son of William-

Anne, second Earl of Albemarle,) a naval officer of eminence, was constituted first lord of the admiralty; and created a peer of the realm, as VISCOUNT KEPPEL, *of Elveden, in the county of Suffolk*, by letters patent, dated 22nd April, 1782.

This celebrated officer was with Commodore Anson in the South Seas; where, at the taking of Paita, he had a narrow escape from a cannon ball, which shaved off the peak of a jockey-cap, then on his head, close to his temple. In 1751, he was commodore of a squadron in the Mediterranean, and he took the island of Goree from the French in 1758. The same year he was with Admiral Hawke, in that memorable battle with Conflans, when at a second broad-side he sunk a seventy-four gun-ship, with all her crew; and he accompanied his brother, the Earl of Albemarle, in 1762, at the siege of Havannah, where, under Admiral Pococke, he was greatly instrumental in taking that important place and its dependencies. In 1778, he attained the rank of Admiral of the Blue; but having then the command of the British fleet, his conduct in the engagement with the French, under Compte D'Orvilliers, was so unsatisfactory, that he was brought before a court marshal, by which, however, he was honourably acquitted.

His lordship d. unmarried in 1786, when the BARONY OF KEPPEL, OF ELVEDEN, became EXTINCT.

ARMS.—Gules three escallop shells ar. a crescent for difference.

KER — EARLS KER, OF WAKEFIELD.

By Letters Patent, dated 24th May, 1722.

Lineage.

ROBERT KER, who succeeded his father in the Dukedom of Roxburghe, in the peerage of Scotland, anno 1741, had been previously created a peer of Great Britain, by letters patent, dated 24th May, 1722, as *Baron Ker* and EARL KER, *of Wakefield*, in the county of York. His grace m. in 1739, Essex, daughter of Sir Roger Mostyn, Bart., and had issue,

JOHN, his successor.
Robert, lieutenant-colonel, who d. unmarried in 1781.
Essex (daughter).
Mary.

The duke d. in 1755, and was s. by his elder son,

JOHN KER, third Duke of Roxburghe, and second EARL KER. This nobleman, who was a KNIGHT OF THE GARTER, and a Knight of the Thistle, and groom of the stole to King George III., died unmarried 19th March, 1804, when his Scottish honours passed to his kinsman, William, Lord Bellenden, and the British EARLDOM OF KER, with the inferior dignity, EXPIRED.

ARMS.—Quarterly first and fourth vert, on a chevron between three unicorn's heads erased ar. as many mullets sa. second and third gules three mascles, or.

292

KERDESTON — BARONS KERDESTON.

By Writ of Summons, dated 27th January, 1332, 6 Edward III.

Lineage.

In the 1st year of King John's reign,

ROGER DE KERDESTON paid a fine to the crown of thirty marks to have a confirmation of those lands which formerly belonged to Hubert de Rie. To this Roger s.

WILLIAM DE KERDESTON, who was sheriff of Norfolk and Suffolk, in the 25th and 26th of Edward I. He m. Margaret, daughter of Gilbert de Gant, Baron of Folkingham, in Lincolnshire, and was s. by his son,

ROGER DE KERDESTON, who, in right of his mother, was one of the co-heirs of his uncle, Gilbert de Gant, Lord Gant, who died s. p. in 1297: and doing homage, had livery of the lands which so descended to him. In the 34th Edward I. this Roger received the honour of knighthood with Prince Edward, by bathing, &c., having his livery of robes, and all accoutrements relating to that solemnity out of the king's wardrobe. In the 5th Edward III. he was made sheriff of Norfolk and Suffolk, and governor of the castle at Norwich. In the next year, (1332,) he was summoned to parliament as a BARON, and from that period to the 21st June, 1337. His lordship d. in the latter year, and was s. by his son,

WILLIAM DE KERDESTON, second baron, summoned to parliament from 20th December, 1337, to 3rd April, 1360. This nobleman distinguished himself in the French wars, and had the honour of participating in the glories of CRESSY. He d. in 1361, leaving, according to one inquisition, WILLIAM, his son and heir, then thirty-six years of age; but by another inquisition, John, the son of John de Burghersh, then nineteen years of age, was found to be his cousin and heir. The former, however,

SIR WILLIAM DE KERDESTON, Knight, claimed part of his father's lands as his heir, and not being opposed, was admitted to them. He was, however, never summoned to parliament, and probably some doubt hung over his legitimacy. In Morant's History of Essex, which is partly corroborated by a pedigree in the college of arms, it appears that William de Kerdeston, the last baron, left issue by Alice de Norwich, his second wife, a son WILLIAM; but by his first wife, two daughters, who are called in the MS. pedigree above cited, his co-heirs, viz.

Margaret, who m. Sir William de Tendring, and her son and heir,
SIR WILLIAM TENDRING, left issue,
Alice, m. to Sir John Howard, ancestor of the Dukes of Norfolk.
Maud, m. to John de Burghersh, and left two daughters, his co-heirs,
Margaret, m. first, to Sir John Granville, and secondly, to John Arundel.
Maud, m. to Thomas Chaucer, son of the poet, Geoffrey Chaucer, and left a daughter,

Alice Chaucer, who was thrice married.

Upon the failure of issue of Sir William de Kerdeston, the reputed son of the last baron, the BARONY OF KERDESTON fell into ABEYANCE between his half-sisters, or their representatives, as it still continues with their descendants.

ARMS.—Gu. a saltier engrailed, ar.

KIRKETON—BARON KIRKETON.

By Writ of Summons, dated 25th February, 1342, 16 Edward III.

Lineage.

THOMAS DE KIRKETON, was summoned to parliament as a BARON on the 25th February, 1342, but never afterwards, and Dugdale makes no further mention of himself or his descendants.

ARMS.—Barry of six, gu. and ar.

KIRKETON—BARON KIRKETON.

By Writ of Summons, dated 14th August, 1362, 37 Edward III.

Lineage.

JOHN DE KIRKETON, of Kirketon, in that part of the county of Lincoln, called Holland, received the honour of Knighthood, in the 19th Edward II., by bathing, &c., having had allowance of his robes for that solemnity out of the king's wardrobe: and being possessed of the castle and manor of Tatshall, and manor of Tumby in the same shire, with the knight's fees, and advowsons of churches thereunto belonging, made a feoffment in the 16th Edward III., of that castle and lordship, to Adam de Welles, and others, to stand feoffed thereof, to the use of himself, and Isabel, his wife; and to the heirs of their two bodies lawfully begotten, with divers remainders; his lands at Kirketon being at the time valued at £10. per annum.

In the 26th Edward III., upon the danger of an invasion by the French, Sir John de Kirketon was constituted one of the commissioners of Array, in the county of Lincoln, for arming all knights, esquires, and others, for defending the sea coasts in that shire. And in the 33rd of the same reign, KING JOHN, OF FRANCE, being then prisoner in England, he was one of the persons appointed to remove that prince from the castle of Hertford, to Somerton Castle, in the county of Somerset, and there to secure him. Sir John de Kirketon was summoned to parliament as a BARON on 14th August, 1362, and 1st June, 1363. He d. in 1367, without issue, when the BARONY became EXTINCT. His lordship died, seised of the manor of Tatshall, by the grant of Sir Ralph de Cromwell, Knt., and Maud, his wife, as also of the manors of Tumby, Kirkeby, &c., leaving Sir John de Tudenham, Knt., Richard de Lina, John de Tilney, and William de Sutton, rector of the church of Whitwell, his next heirs.

ARMS.—Barry of six, gu. and ar.

KIRKHOVEN — BARON WOTTON, OF WOTTON, IN THE COUNTY OF KENT.

By Letters Patent, dated 31st August, 1650.

Lineage.

THOMAS WOTTON, second Baron Wotton, of Marley, in Kent, died in 1630, without male issue, when that title became EXTINCT; his lordship left, however, by his wife, Mary, daughter and co-heir of Sir Arthur Throckmorton, of Paulers-Perry, in Northamptonshire, four daughters, his co-heirs, viz.

KATHERINE, who m. first, to Henry, Lord Stanhope, son and heir of Philip, Earl of Chesterfield, by whom, who predeceased his father, she had,

Philip, who succeeded to the Earldom of Chesterfield.

Mary, who d. unmarried.

Katherine, m. to William, Lord Alington.

Her ladyship espoused, secondly, John POLLIANDER KIRKHOVEN, Lord of Hemfleet, in Holland, and had a son,

CHARLES HENRY KIRKHOVEN, of whom presently.

She married, thirdly, Colonel Daniel O'Neile, one of the grooms of the bedchamber to Charles II., but had no issue by him. This lady was governess to the Princess of Orange, daughter of Charles I., and attending her highness into Holland, sent over money, arms, and ammunition, to his majesty's aid, for which service she was created, at the restoration, COUNTESS OF CHESTERFIELD for life (see Wotton, Countess of Chesterfield).

Heather, m. to Baptist, Viscount Campden.

Margaret, m. to Sir John Tufton, Knt.

Anne, m. to Sir Edward Hales, Knt., of Tunstal, Kent.

The eldest of these co-heiresses, Katherine, had, by her second husband, as stated above, an only son,

CHARLES HENRY KIRKHOVEN, who, by reason of his descent, was created BARON WOTTON, of Wotton, in Kent, by letters patent, dated 31st August, 1650: and was naturalized by act of parliament, in September, 1660. His lordship was advanced to the Earldom of Bellomont, in Ireland, in 1677, but died s. p. in 1672, when ALL HIS HONOURS became EXTINCT, and his estates devolved, by his lordship's bequest, upon his nephew by the half-blood, CHARLES STANHOPE, a younger son of his half-brother, Philip, Earl of Chesterfield, who, upon inheriting, assumed the surname of WOTTON.

ARMS.—Ar. a saltier, sa.

KNIVET—BARON KNIVET, OF ESCRICK, IN THE COUNTY OF YORK.

By Writ of Summons, dated 4th July, 1607, 5 James I.

Lineage.

The family of KNIVET, anciently seated in Norfolk,

came at length to possess BUCKINGHAM CASTLE, in that shire, by the marriage of

SIR JAMES KNIVET, with Margaret Clifton, an heiress, to whom it descended (through females) from the founder in the time of the conquest, William de Albini. From this Sir James we pass to

SIR THOMAS KNIVET, Knt., one of the gentlemen of the privy chamber to King James I., who, in 1605, upon the mysterious intimation conveyed by letter to the Lord Monteagle, was sent, being a Justice of the Peace in Westminster, to make search, with others, in the vaults and cellers under the House of Lords, where Guydo Faux was discovered, and the gunpowder plot detected and prevented. After which, he was summoned to the parliament, then sitting, 4th July, 1607, as BARON KNIVET, OF ESCRICK, in the county of York. His lordship m. Elizabeth, widow of Richard Warren, Esq., and daughter of Sir Rowland Hayward, an alderman of London, but had no issue. He d. 27th April, 1622, when the BARONY OF ESCRICK became EXTINCT. His lordship's estates devolved upon his niece, Elizabeth, daughter and co-heir of Sir Henry Knivet, of Charlton, in the county of Wilts; which Elizabeth, married Thomas Howard, Earl of Suffolk, and her seventh son, Sir Edward Howard, K.B., was created BARON HOWARD OF ESCRICK, on the 29th April, 1628 (see that dignity).

ARMS.—Ar. a plain bend and a border ingrailed, sa.

NOTE.—Of this family was JOHN KNIVET, CHANCELLOR OF ENGLAND, in the 46th Edward III.

KNOLLYS—BARON KNOLLYS, VISCOUNT WALLINGFORD, EARL OF BANBURY.

Barony,	} by Letters {	13th May, 1603.
Viscounty,	Patent,	14th November, 1616.
Earldom,		18th August, 1626.

Lineage.

In the 41st Edward III.,

SIR ROBERT KNOLLYS, K.G., having from humble fortune attained great wealth, and high reputation, in the Norman wars, was chosen by the BLACK PRINCE, to accompany him into Spain, in aid of Don Pedro, then King of Castile and Leon, against Henry, the bastard son of (his father) King Alfonsus. And in three years afterwards was made general of all the forces then sent by King Edward into France. In the 1st Richard II. Sir Robert was governor of the castle of BREST, and in the 3rd he went with Thomas Plantagenet, (of Woodstock,) Earl of Buckingham, and other gallant persons, to assist the Duke of Britanny against the French, when, landing at Calais, they marched quite through France, without resistance. The next year, upon the breaking out of Jack Straw's insurrection, Sir Robert led the citizens of London against the rebels. Besides his military achievements which rendered him famous in those days, Sir Robert Knollys left other memorials behind him. He erected a stately bridge over the river Medway, near Rochester, in Kent, called Rochester Bridge, and he enlarged the house of Friers-Carmelites, commonly called White

x 4

Friers, in the city of London. He likewise founded a collegiate church of secular priests, at Pontefract, in Yorkshire. He died at his seat of Scene Thorpe, in the county of Norfolk, anno 1407, and was buried with the Lady Constance, his wife, in the body of the church at the White Friers. From this gallant personage descended,

ROBERT KNOLLYS, who, in the 9th of Henry VIII., being then one of the gentlemen ushers of the privy chamber, had a lease for a certain number of years, from the king, of the manor of Rotherfield Grey, commonly called GREYS, in the county of Oxford. He was s. by his son,

SIR FRANCIS KNOLLYS, who obtained from King Henry VIII., a grant of the lordship in fee of Rotherfield Grey, or Greys, and was one of that monarch's gentlemen pensioners. In the reign of Edward VI., he was so staunch an upholder of the reformation, that he deemed it prudent upon the accession of Mary, to retire into Germany. But when Elizabeth ascended the throne, he returned and enjoyed in a high degree, the favour and confidence of the crown. He was immediately sworn of the privy council, made vice-chamberlain of the household; next, captain of the guard; afterwards treasurer; and lastly, installed a Knight of the Most Noble Order of the Garter. In the 11th of Elizabeth, Sir Francis Knollys had the custody of Mary, Queen of Scots, then confined at Bolton Castle, in Yorkshire, and in eighteen years afterwards, he was one of those who sat in judgment upon her life. Sir Francis m. Catherine, daughter of William Carey, Esq., (by Mary, his wife, daughter of Thomas Boleyn, Earl of Wiltshire, and sister of Queen Anne Boleyn) and was s. at his decease, by his eldest surviving son,

WILLIAM KNOLLYS, treasurer of the household, in the reign of Elizabeth, who was advanced to the peerage by King James I., by letters patent, dated 13th May, 1603, in the dignity of LORD KNOLLYS, of Greys, in the county of Oxford (his chief seat). In 1614, his lordship was appointed master of the wards, and within a short time installed a Knight of the Garter. In 1616, he was created VISCOUNT WALLINGFORD, and advanced by King Charles I., on 18th August, 1626, to the EARLDOM OF BANBURY, with precedency of all earls who were created before him. His lordship m. first, Dorothy, daughter of Edward, Lord Bray, sister and co-heir of John, Lord Bray, and widow of Edmund, Lord Chandos, by whom he had no issue. He espoused, secondly, Lady Elizabeth Howard, daughter of Thomas, Earl of Suffolk, and dying 25th May, 1632, at the advanced age of eighty-eight,· was buried in the church of Greys. The subsequent history of this peerage is one of the most curious in the whole record of peerage claims. Upon the decease of the EARL OF BANBURY, the inquisition found that he died without issue, but leaving a widow, Elizabeth, his last wife. His honours were then deemed EXTINCT, and his estates passed to his collateral heirs, excepting such as he had devised to his widow, who remarried Lord Vaux. In a few years this lady produced two sons, born during her marriage with Lord Banbury, her first husband. They had at first been called

VAUX, but now she set them up as the sons of the Earl of Banbury, and gave to the eldest the title of that Earldom. They were not of age before the civil wars had broken up the House of Lords. The elder died. Nicholas, the survivor, availing of the convention parliament in 1660, took his seat therein, and during the continuation of its sittings, voted upon several occasions. It seems, however, that on the 13th July, 1660, it was moved, "That there being a person that now sits in this house as a peer of the realm, viz. the Earl of Banbury, it is ordered that this business shall be heard at the bar by counsel, on Monday come sennight." Whether, in fact, any such hearing did take place or not, the journals are silent, yet they furnish abundant proof, that the doubt had been removed by some means: for they shew, that the said Earl was present in the house every day preceding the day appointed for the hearing. That he was also present on that very day; and that the day following, he was named of the committee on the excise bill. That he was present on the 13th September, when the king was in the house; and, in short, was only absent seven days, from the 13th July, when the said motion was made, to the 21st November, when it was ordered, "That the Earl of Banbury hath leave to be absent for some time." Shortly after this, however, the parliament was dissolved, viz., 29th December, 1660; and in the new parliament, which met the 8th May, 1661, the name of the Earl of Banbury was omitted; his lordship presented therefore, a petition to the king for his writ of summons, which petition was referred to the lords for their opinion, and by them transferred to a committee of privileges. Here a regular examination of witnesses took place, and the attorney-general, who attended on behalf of the crown, confessed the law to be clear; when the committee reported to the house, 1st July, 1661, "That Nicholas, Earl of Banbury, was a legitimate person." Upon receiving the report, the house ordered that the cause should be heard at the bar; where having been accordingly heard, it was again referred to the committee of privileges, with an additional direction, to consider the matter of the right of precedency between the said earl and several other peers; which committee once more having taken the matter into consideration, on the 19th July, 1661, reported, "That the Earl of Banbury, in the eye of the law, was son of the late William, Earl of Banbury; and the House of Peers should therefore advise the king, to send him a writ to come to parliament, and that he ought to have a place in the House of Peers, according to the date of his patent, and not according to that part thereof, which ranked him before the other earls created before William, Earl of Banbury." This report was made on Friday, and the house resolved to take it into consideration on the Monday following; but nothing appears to have been done on that day: from which period it was postponed day after day, to the 9th December; when it appears from the journals, that a bill was brought in, and read a first time, entitled, "An act for declaring Nicholas, called Earl of Banbury, to be illegitimate." But such a measure was found too unjust to become a law, and the bill

therefore dropped. Nicholas, the petitioner, died 14th March, 1673-4, without bringing the matter to a conclusion, leaving a son, CHALME, then twelve years of age. Which Charles, in the first parliament after he came of age, anno 1695, presented a petition to the House of Peers, who referred it to a committee of privileges, and he was treated with the same procrastination as his father had experienced. He had, however, the misfortune to kill his brother-in-law, Philip Lawson, Esq., in a duel, in 1692, and that event placed his right to the peerage in a different point of view, and raised a new question upon it. He was indicted at the quarter sessions of Middlesex, and the indictment being removed by certiorari, into the Court of King's Bench, the assumed Earl of Banbury petitioned the lords to be tried by his peers. The house having again entered into the investigation of his father's legitimacy, resolved, *that he had no right to the Earldom of Banbury*, and the petition was ordered to be dismissed. Meantime, the proceedings went on in the King's Bench, and he being indicted in the name of Charles Knollys, pleaded in abatement that he was Earl of Banbury. To this the attorney-general rejoined, that he *was not* Earl of Banbury, because the lords adjudged that he had no right to that honour. To this he demurred as a bad replication, contending that the lords had no jurisdiction over that question. And the point which the Court of King's Bench had now to determine, was "whether the plea or replication was good?"

Lord Holt, and his brother judges, entered upon the investigation, with the most profound labour, learning, courage, and integrity; and they finally adjudged "*the replication bad, the resolution of the lords invalid*:" upon the following grounds.

First. That the decision of the lords was no judgment, but only an opinion.

Secondly. That it was not the decision of the court of parliament, which consisted of king, lords, and commons; and that the lords had no original jurisdiction, but in case of appeal.

Thirdly. That the case was not before the lords, the petitioner having only prayed for his privilege, and not having submitted his right of peerage to the house at all.

Fourthly. That there was no reference from the crown.

Fifthly. That the right to the inheritance to the peerage was as much under the protection of the common law as any other question of legal inheritance. The defendant, therefore, having exhibited in court the patent of creation, and having stated his descent under it, the attorney-general could only oppose him, by referring the question of fact as to descent to a jury, but declining to adopt that course, the plea was adjudged good, and the defendant acquitted accordingly. The lords, enraged at this decision, moved that the Chief Justice Holt be called to their bar to explain the grounds of his judgment, and his lordship was consequently summoned. But he calmly and firmly set them at open defiance, telling their lordships that he owed it to the dignity of his place, and the laws which he had to administer, not to account to them in that extrajudicial manner: but if the prosecutors were dissatisfied, they might bring a writ of error, and then he should be prepared in the regular form to give the reasons of his judgment. But so conclusive were the arguments and authorities of the court deemed, that no writ of error was resorted to.

The claimant now again petitioned for his writ of summons, and the crown again referred it to the lords, anno 1698, who got rid of the affair, by sending a message to his majesty "that they had already determined the question, of which they supposed the king was not aware." In the reign of Queen Anne the claimant once more petitioned, and it was referred to the privy council, but what became eventually of the petition is not known.

On the accession of George II., 1727, he again petitioned. Sir Philip Yorke, afterwards Lord Hardwicke, was then attorney-general, and · this petition being referred to him, he reported, that whether the crown would refer it to the lords, was a matter of discretion, not of law: the crown therefore declined to interfere. Thus the claim continued to be hung up from reign to reign, Lord Hardwicke was undoubtedly right: it was a matter of pure option on the part of the crown, whether it would take the opinion of the lords; and prudence counselled the negative, after the flame which had been kindled between the house of peers and the courts of law. At length, in 1776, the heirship devolved upon William Knollys, an officer in the army, who has attained the rank of general, now living, who from that time enjoyed, as his ancestors had, since the Restoration, the *titular* honour, and been so named in all the king's commissions. The awkwardness of his situation, however, impelled him to make an effort in his own person to have the question of his right to a writ of summons finally decided. He accordingly petitioned the crown; and the case was referred to the attorney-general, Sir Vicary Gibbs, in 1806. That able lawyer reported that he was bound by the high authority of the judgment of Lord Chief Justice Holt, in 1693, to give it as his opinion, that the resolution of the lords on that occasion was not conclusive, because, if that judgment had been erroneous it might have been reversed by a writ of error.

The case thus again came before a lords' committee; Sir Samuel Romilly was counsel for the claimant, and his speech on the occasion is said to have been his happiest effort; but unluckily no note of it has been found among his papers: so that the memoranda of it were very scanty. There is enough, however, to pronounce it unanswerable. Two subjects were raised, that of LEGITIMACY, and that of JURISDICTION. The law of the former Sir Samuel takes up, as it had always been held in England, and other countries, from the Roman law: that the issue of the wife must be acknowledged in law to be the issue of the husband, where there is access, and no natural impossibility: and among other authorities he cites the celebrated speech of Lord Chancellor Nottingham, in the case of the Viscounty of Purbeck. The noble lords who took an active part in this discussion were, Redesdale, Ellenborough, Erskine, and the Lord Chancellor Eldon. Lord Redesdale violently opposed the claim upon both questions. On that of legiti-

macy his whole reasoning turned upon the circumstances, which raised the presumption that Nicholas Knollys or Vaux, was, in fact, the son of Lord Vaux, born in adultery, principally on account of the mother's concealment of his birth, and his non-succession to Lord Banbury's inheritance; which, according to Romilly's law, had no concern with the matter, it not being allowable to enter upon such questions, where husband and wife cohabit, and where no natural impossibility exists on the part of the husband; the concealment of the birth having been the act of the wife, and no act of the wife, not even her direct declaration being allowed to bastardise the issue. Lord Redesdale could not produce a single authority in answer to this; but chose to rely upon his own dictum and opinion as paramount to it. On the point of jurisdiction his arguments were still more contradictory. He takes no notice of Lord Holt's reasonings, except to say, in general terms, he was wrong, and that the lords were right: and he insists on the lapse of time, and the claimants' abandonment, to crush the claim. Now where is the law, that lapse of time applies to honours? and where was the abandonment in this case? Did not every successive generation do all in its power to insist on its claim? And was the house to take advantage of its own wrong in having suspended and adjourned and delayed the case. No close reasoner would be a convert to Lord Redesdale, even in one of his propositions or arguments. Next came Lord Ellenborough, who having much less leisure than Lord Redesdale, seems to have mainly borrowed his line of argument. He begins with rather an ill-timed protestation of his enchainment to the law: and then, throughout his discourse, tries every effort to discover reasons for overturning the law. He declares Lord Chief Justice Holt wrong, and that he had peculiar notions on the jurisdiction of the lords. Now if they were peculiar, why were they not reversed by a writ of error? He finally gives his decision in direct opposition to the solemn unreversed judgment of Lord Holt, by which the Attorney-General Gibbs had reported himself bound. This was rather a strange mode of shewing himself chained to the law! He closes, with using the harsh terms of calling upon the house to prevent the claimant from *intruding* himself upon them.

Lord Erskine then rose; his great genius, his beautiful eloquence, his profound knowledge of the law of evidence, rendered his speech a treasure of constitutional principles of enlightened axioms, of acute logic, of felicitous expression, and generous pleading for oppressed rights. His exposition of the law in the claimant's favour was as full of wisdom, as it was of legal justice. He afterwards entered a long and eloquent PROTEST to the same effect on the lords' journal.

The Lord Chancellor Eldon came last, but he was equally unable to stem the tide of authority in support of the law, as laid down by Sir Samuel Romilly. He gave it as his opinion that circumstances might rebut the inference of legitimacy even where there was access, and no natural impossibility. As to jurisdiction he did not deny that of the regular courts of law, but pronounced that the lords might also have it incidentally when questions of privilege arose; and, therefore, that the court of King's Bench ought to have paid deference to the lords' resolution of 1685. In those speeches the application of the word "judgment," to the resolution of a lords' committee, is not becoming the precision of legal lips.

The result was a resolution on the part of the majority of the committee in 1813, that the claimant was not entitled to the Earldom of Banbury. It cannot be denied to have been a very hard case. The opinion of the judges was taken on the abstract question of law; and it must be confessed that that opinion does not exactly coincide with the law as laid down by Sir Samuel Romilly and Lord Erskine: but it surely does not bear out the resolution of the lords in the Banbury case. The judges say, that evidence may be admitted to prove that the reputed father *could not* have been the father of the child, not confining it to natural impossibility; but in the Banbury case no evidence was even attempted to prove that Lord Banbury *could not* have been the father of Nicholas. That the old law was as Romilly laid it down, seems to admit of no question.

There never can be wanting instances to prove how dangerous it is to remove the land-marks of the law. If once the question of expedience or particular inconvenience is admitted, there are no further guides, or pole-stars: all is afloat in the sea of uncertainty: and men's rights are at the mercy and caprice of individual opinion. The claimant's ancestor was born under those unquestionable facts which by the law entitled him to the inheritance of the husband of his mother. Is not this to be legitimate? Let us admit private conviction as to the fact of filiation, and whither will it lead? do we not continually in society meet persons in possession of honours and riches in right of blood, which we privately feel assured does not belong to them, viz. the children of the wife; and not of the husband. The claimant's ancestor may have been the son of Lord Vaux, and probably was so; but even that fact is not conclusive.

They who can look upon this case without interest must have strange hearts. Upon what are we justified in relying, but on the settled law of the land? Perhaps it will be answered—"but here was the pursuit of a shadow." A peerage is not a shadow; not a mean pursuit of wealth, and vulgar power, but the desire of a high legislative and legal function. Was there, or was there not, cause for the assumption of this peerage, in the outset? It has been shewn, that the law was with the claimant. Why then should he decline it? when once embarked, how could he draw back? Is it nothing, after having enjoyed the titular honour of an earldom, for nearly two hundred years, under the sanction of the highest court of law, to be cast amongst the undistinguished crowd; to be trampled on, sneered at, and triumphed over? Is it nothing to have been driven to support the right, at the bar of the lords, at an enormous expense, as well as great anxiety, and then to be sent away, beaten and degraded, in defiance of the law? Is it any apology, to have it answered, when the law is pleaded, "Oh, but it was an inconvenient and foolish law! we are wiser than our ancestors; and will make a new law?" It will perhaps be deemed very arrogant, to run contrary, in this way, to great names ! but have we not great names on our side? Are not Lord Holt, and Romilly, and Lord Erskine, and Sir Vicary Gibbs, and Lord Coke, and Lord Nottingham, and Sir Geoffery Palmer, great names ? There is but one on the other side, which will be put in competition with any of these names, and that is Lord Eldon ! but Lord Eldon's speech on this occasion, was somewhat wavering and indecisive.

Lawyers will hereafter, sit and study this case, with greater care than they have hitherto done. We are obliged to Mr. Le Marchant, in his appendix to the Gardiner claim, for a fuller report of this case, in 1808-1813, than had hitherto been published. It is strange, that even Hargrave had not thoroughly investigated it, and the manner in which the lords argue the jurisdiction—sliding without notice over the main doctrines and arguments of Lord Holt, seems to call for comments in which delicacy forbears to indulge. To treat about extinct and dormant peerages, and not thoroughly to discuss this case, would be to pass over the chief feature which belongs to the work. He who is not completely master of Lord Holt's decision in the Banbury case, knows nothing of peerage-law ! It is a study worth the labour; a familiarity with Lord Holt's doctrines shews the whole extent of this branch, in a luminous point of view; all connected, forming one clear whole; while the modern usage of a reference to committees, is continually drawing the investigation into perplexities, which leads to all sorts of defeats of justice. If the question of legitimacy had arisen in a regular court of law, it would have been argued in a very different way; and probably Lord Ellenborough himself would not have come to the same conclusion in his own Court of King's Bench. In the courts of law, the presence of an intelligent bar is always a check upon new and speculative law; while a committee of privileges, though it sometimes affects to be governed by the same rules—(at other times it puts them at defiance) altogether, feels itself free and unfettered, and the law lords are surrounded, be it remembered, by those, whose lack of legal habits deprives them of all weight upon purely legal questions. Mr. Le Marchant has forborne to comment on the Banbury case, and taken on himself the mere province of a reporter. The present observations may appear bold, they have not been ventured without long and deep pondering on the subject. Nothing of the kind will be found in "*Cruise on Dignities*," a work of utility, truly, but superficial. It is a branch of the law, which has been hitherto little attended to; but yet it is very important. Of late years, a disposition has been evinced, in particular quarters, to apply more minute care to it; but unluckily, in directions where there is a tendency to erect a new tribunal, with new rules drawn up; in a spirit that trenches on those constitutional customs and enactments, to which a Briton has looked to shield his rights, from the time of Magna Charta. Whatever removes questions of right from the courts of common law, is a mischievous innovation.

Our peerage is greatly enlarged; to an extent indeed, which many sage persons consider perilous to the poise of the constitution. The tendency of our manners and political institutions, has been by manufactures, commerce, and taxation, to extinguish the old families, more rapidly than in the ordinary course of events. This is not the time, therefore, by new rules of an injurious effect, to add still more to the number of those extinctions. An ancient name and house has still a hold upon the veneration of the people; a new aristocracy is what the nature of the human mind revolts at. The people will not patiently submit to those, to whose progenitors their progenitors have not bowed. They will not either succumb to a tyrant or fool, because his ancestors were great or liberal. Antiquity must unite with talent and virtue.

It is as little wise therefore, as it is generous, in the state, to do its utmost to dry up any of these few remaining fountains, whence their issue have passed down the stream of time, and collected tinctures and infusion, grateful to the people. The tribunals which were sufficient to guard the rights of the crown, in ages when the greater part of the titles were ancient, and families still continued to survive in their numerous branches, are surely sufficient to preserve those rights against the effects of new grants of honours, where it can rarely happen, that the stock is removed at any distance from the memory of living persons. Lord Redesdale seems to have been greatly mistaken, as to the duties imposed upon the lords, with regard to questions of peerage, referred to them by the crown. He appears to have assumed, that the lords had a sort of original jurisdiction of their own, over peerages, and that they had an interest and a right to interfere; and were therefore entitled, to make such new rules and regulations, as would, in their opinion, most effectually guard the door, and render the entry difficult. We may confidently assert, that this is an erroneous view of the subject. The lords have no right of interference whatsoever, except as to the order of precedence among their own body. If the crown allows a peerage with a date of precedence, which the lords can prove not to belong to it, they may then, upon due investigation, refuse that precedence—a case not likely to happen, but certainly possible. But if, when the crown demands the opinion of the lords, and the opinion which they give is arrived at by any other means or processes, than those which are conformable to the common law, and which in consequence of such variation of means, are different from those which the rules and customs of the common law would give, then they mislead the crown, for the crown is restrained to act according to the common law.

Note.—For these commentaries upon the celebrated BANBURY PEERAGE, we are indebted to a gentleman, whose literary works, particularly in genealogy and antiquities, have attained very high reputation; but we do not hold ourselves responsible for all the opinions he has advanced.

Descent

OF THE BANBURY PEERAGE THROUGH THE ASSUMED EARLS OF BANBURY.

NICHOLAS KNOLLYS, (or Vaux, the person whose birth was concealed by his mother, during the life-time of her first husband, William, Earl of Banbury,) assumed the dignity of Earl of Banbury, and as such voted in the convention parliament. He m. first, Isabella, daughter of Mountjoy Blount, Earl of Newport, and had a daughter,

   Anne, m. to Sir John Briscal, Knt.

His lordship espoused secondly, Anne, daughter of William Sherard, Lord Leitrim, in Ireland, and had, with other issue, his successor, in 1673-4,

CHARLES KNOLLYS, who also assumed the title of Earl of Banbury. He m. first, Margaret, daughter of Edward Lister, Esq., of Burwell, in the county of Leicester, and had issue,

   CHARLES, Viscount Wallingford, who died s. p., in the lifetime of his father.

His lordship m. secondly, Mary, daughter of Thomas Woods, Esq., and dying in 1740, was s. by the son of this marriage,

CHARLES KNOLLYS, assumed Earl of Banbury, m. Miss Martha Hughes, and had with other issue,

   WILLIAM, his successor.

   THOMAS-WOODS, successor to his brother.

He died 13th March, 1771, and was s. by his elder son,

WILLIAM KNOLLYS, assumed Earl of Banbury, who died unmarried, 29th August 1776, and was s. by his brother,

THOMAS-WOODS KNOLLYS, assumed Earl of Banbury, m. Mary, daughter of William Porter, Esq., of Winchester, and left, with other issue,

   WILLIAM KNOLLYS, a general officer in the army, who, unsuccessfully, preferred his claim to the EARLDOM OF BANBURY, in 1808-1813.

ARMS.—Az. a cross recercele voided. Semee of cross crosslets, or.

KNOVILL — BARON KNOVILL.

By Writ of Summons, dated 23rd June, 1295, 23 Edward I.

Lineage.

BOGO DE KNOVILL, in the 16th of King John, had livery of those lands at Horsed, in Cambridgeshire, which Stephen of Oxford some time held. But in the 18th of Henry III., being involved in the insurrection of Richard, Earl Marshall, all his possessions were seized by the crown. Upon making submission, however, he obtained precepts to the sheriffs of Northamptonshire, Buckinghamshire, Sussex, Herefordshire, and Cambridgeshire, to make restitution to him of what lay in their respective counties. To this Bogo succeeded (his son and heir it is presumed),

BOGO DE KNOVILL, who, in the 3rd of Edward I., was constituted sheriff of the counties of Salop and Stafford, and governor of the castle of

Blanomineter, (subsequently called Oswestre,) in the former shire. In which office he continued for three years, and was then made governor of Dolvoron Castle, in the marches of Wales. This feudal lord was summoned to parliament as a BARON, from 23rd June, 1295, to 26th August, 1307, in which latter year he died, leaving a son and heir, then thirty years of age,

BOGO DE KNOVILL, who doing homage, had livery of his lands, but, according to Dugdale, was never summoned to parliament. His name appears, however, in the rolls of the first year of King Edward II., amongst others therein mentioned, as having been summoned to the parliament held at that period. In the 4th of Edward II. this Bogo was in the wars of Scotland, and in four years after he had a military summons for the same field. He was subsequently involved in the rebellion of Thomas, Earl of Lancaster, and paid the very large fine of £1,000 to preserve his life. He then resided in Gloucestershire. Of this nobleman, or his descendants, Dugdale gives no further account.

Kimber, in his Baronetage, states, that Eleanor, daughter and co-heir of Sir John Knovill, married about the 13th of Edward III., Grey de St. Aubyn, ancestor of the present Sir John St. Aubyn, Baronet, of Clowrance, in the county of Cornwall.

ARMS.—Ar. three estoils, gules.

KYME—BARONS KYME.

By Writ of Summons, dated 23rd June, 1295,
23 Edward I.

Lineage.

Of this ancient family, which assumed the surname of *Kyme*, from a fair lordship, the principal place of their residence, in Kesteven, in the county of Lincoln, the first mentioned is

SIMON DE KYME, (the son of William,) who founded, temp. Stephen, the PRIORY OF BOLINTON, in Lincolnshire. This Simon m. Roese, daughter of Robert Dapifer, (that is Steward, to Gilbert de Gant, Earl of Lincoln,) which lady was commonly called Roese de Bulinton. He was s. by his son,

PHILIP DE KYME, who was constituted sheriff of Lincolnshire in the 14th of Henry II., and was one of the barons in the great council held at London in the year 1177, where he was a subscribing witness to the instrument of arbitration there made by King Henry II., for according the difference betwixt *Alfonso*, king of Castile, and *Sanctius*, king of Navarre. This feudal lord was the founder of the priory of Kyme, and he granted twenty acres of land to the canons and nuns at Bolinton, for supporting the charge of their garments. He was steward to Gilbert de Gant, Earl of Lincoln, and was s. at his decease by his son,

SIMON DE KYME, who, in the 21st of Henry II., was indebted to the crown in the sum of forty marks, as a fine for not disclaiming his right to certain lands after he had lost them upon a trial by battel. In the 6th of Edward I. he paid a hundred marks to be excused serving in Normandy, and in the 8th of the same reign he was sheriff of Lincolnshire. In the reign of John he took up arms with the barons,

and was excommunicated by the pope, when his lands were all seized, and transferred to Geoffry Nevill. He subsequently negotiated for their restoration, but died before any thing effectual in the matter could be accomplished. He died in 1309, and was s. by his son,

PHILIP DE KYME, who, upon paying one hundred pounds for his relief, had the lands of his father restored to him. He m. Agnes de Wales, and dying in 1242, was s. by his eldest son,

SIMON DE KYME, who died s. p. in 1247, and was s. by his brother,

WILLIAM DE KYME, who died (also) without issue in 1258, and was s. by

PHILIP DE KYME. This feudal lord had a military summons in the 22nd of Edward I., for the French wars, and in three years afterwards he was engaged in Gascony. In the 28th of the same reign he obtained a grant for a weekly market at his manor of Burwell, in the county of Lincoln, and we find his lordship for several years subsequently actively employed in the wars of Scotland. In the 10th of Edward II. he had an indemnity granted him, being then much decayed in strength, in consideration of his great service in the wars, in the time of King Edward I., and the then king, from any the like service in future. Furthermore, in the 19th of the same monarch, he obtained a special discharge for a debt of fifty pounds, owing to the king's exchequer, by a recognisance, which money had been borrowed in the time of King Edward I., as a supply for the charge of his passage into Gascony. This eminent person was summoned to parliament, as a BARON, from 23rd June, 1295, to 26th November, 1313. His lordship m.——, daughter of Hugh Bigot, (to which Hugh he had been a ward in his minority,) and dying in 1322, was s. by his son,

WILLIAM DE KYME, second baron, summoned to parliament, from 26th December, 1323, to 22nd January, 1336. His lordship died without issue in 1338, leaving Joane, his widow, who remarried Nicholas de Cantilupe. Whereupon Gilbert de Umfranvill, Earl of Angus, who had married LUCIA DE KYME, his lordship's sister, came by virtue of a fine, levied in the 8th Edward III., to possess the inheritance; and amongst the descendants of the said Gilbert and Lucie, the BARONY OF KYME must be considered now to be in ABEYANCE.

ARMS.—G. a chevron. * Ten crosslets are added.

LACY—EARLS OF LINCOLN.

By Charter of Creation, dated 23rd November, 1232.

Lineage.

Two distinguished members of this ancient family, namely, WALTER DE LACI, and ILBERT DE LACI, came into England with the CONQUEROR, but in what degree allied, if at all, has not been ascertained. From ILBERT the noble house, of which we are about to treat, derived, and to him and his descendants, after disposing of the line of Walter, we shall direct our attention.

WALTER DE LACI, when the power of his royal master was firmly established in England, was one of the commanders whom WILLIAM sent into Wales to subjugate the principality, and being victorious, acquired large possessions there, in addition to those already obtained as his portion of the spoil of Hastings. He was killed in April, 1084, by falling from a ladder, which he had ascended to inspect the completion of the church of St. Peter in Hereford, of which he was the founder. Walter de Laci left three sons, ROGER, Hugh, and Walter, a monk in the abbey of St. Peters, at Gloucester. The eldest son,

ROGER DE LACI, through the bounty of the Conqueror, as well as by inheritance from his father, had large possessions in the counties of Berks, Salop, Gloucester, Worcester, and Hereford, where the castle of Ewyas was the head of his barony. But joining in the rebellion against WILLIAM Rufus, in favour of ROBERT Curthose, he was banished England, and all his lands were conferred upon his brother,

HUGH DE LACI, who, with many other Norman soldiers of fortune, had been permitted by Rufus to invade the principality of Wales, and to acquire, by their good swords, lands there—which lands Sir John Dodderidge, Knt., one of the justices of the Court of King's Bench, a learned antiquary as well as lawyer, describes as becoming, when conquered, *Baronies Marchers*, held *in capite* of the crown—wherein the barons enjoyed a kind of palatine jurisdiction, with power to administer justice to the tenants in each of their territories, holding courts, invested with divers privileges, franchises, and immunities, so that the king's writs were not current, unless the whole barony had been in question. Such was the state of the government of the marches of Wales down to the reign of Henry VIII. This Hugh, who upon all occasions liberally supported the church, was the founder of the PRIORY of LANTHONY, in Wales. He died without issue, bequeathing his great inheritance to his two sisters, ERMELINE, who had no children, and Emme, whose son,

GILBERT, assumed the surname of LACI. This feudal lord, in the conflict between STEPHEN and the EMPRESS, espoused the cause of the latter. He eventually became a Knight Templar, and was succeeded by (whether son or brother, not known,)

HUGH DE LACI, who was employed in the conquest of Ireland, and for his services there obtained from King Henry II. the whole county of Meath. He was subsequently constituted governor of Dublin, and justice of Ireland. But incurring the displeasure of his royal master by marrying without licence the king of Connaught's daughter, he was divested, in 1181, of the custody of the metropolis. In four years afterwards he was murdered by one Malvo Miadaich, a mean person, in revenge for the severity with which he had treated the workmen employed by him in erecting the castle of Lurhedy. He left issue,

WALTER, his successor.

HUGH, constable of Ireland, who, according to Matthew Paris, a most famous soldier, obtained the Earldom of Ulster from King John, by betraying and delivering into that monarch's power the celebrated *John de*

Courcy, EARL OF ULSTER, ancestor of the Lords Kinsale. He subsequently, however, incurred the displeasure of the king, and was himself driven out of Ireland. His wife was Emeline, daughter and heir of Walter de Ridelesford, by whom, at his decease, 26th Henry III., he left issue, an only daughter and heir,

MAUD DE LACY, who espoused, first, Walter Bourke, Lord of Connaught, and secondly, Stephen de Longespe.

Elayne, m. to Richard de Beaufo.

The elder son,

WALTER DE LACI, paid, in the 10th Richard I., two thousand marks for the king's favour, and to have livery of his lands, but this being the last year of that monarch's reign, his brother and successor, JOHN, exacted no less than £1200 for similar favour of livery. In the 9th of the latter king's reign, Walter de Laci obtained a confirmation of his dominion of Meath, to be held by him and his heirs for the service of fifty knights' fees; as also of all his fees in FINGALL, in the valley of Dublin, to be held by the service of seven knights' fees. But in three years afterwards, *King John* passing into Ireland with his army, Laci was forced to deliver up himself and all his possessions in that kingdom, and to abjure the realm. He was subsequently banished from England, but in the 16th of the same reign, he seems to have made his peace, for he was then allowed to repossess LUDLOW, with the CASTLE: and the next year he recovered all his lands in Ireland, except the castle and lands of Drogheda, by paying a fine of four thousand marks to the crown. After this we find him sheriff of Herefordshire, in the 18th of John, and 2nd of Henry III., and in the 14th of the latter king, joined with Geffrey de Marisco, then Justice of Ireland, and Richard de Burgh, in subduing the King of Connaught, who had taken up arms to expel the English from his territories. So much for the secular acts of this powerful feudal baron. Of his works of piety, it is recorded that he confirmed to the canons of Lanthony, all those lands and churches in Ireland, granted to them by his father, Hugh de Laci; and of his own bounty, gave them the church of our lady at Drogheda, with other valuable gifts. To the monks of Creswil, in Herefordshire, he was a special benefactor, having conferred upon them two hundred and four acres of his wood, called Ham; as also six hundred acres, with the woods to them belonging; and common pasture for their cattle, in New Forest, and in divers other pasturages. Moreover the ninth sheaf of wheat and other corn, except oats, throughout all his lordships of England and Wales. Likewise the tithe of all the hides of those cattle which were yearly sold at the larder of his castle at Ewyas. In Ireland, he founded the abbey of BEAUBEC, which was first a cell to the great abbey of Bec, in Normandy, and afterwards to Furneise, in Lancashire. Walter Laci married Margaret, daughter of William de Braose, of Brecknock, and in the year 1241, being then infirm and blind, departed this life, " Vir, inter omnes nobiles Hiberniæ, eminentissimus," leaving his great inheritance to be divided amongst females, viz., the daughters of GILBERT DE LACY, his son, (who died in his life-time,) and Isabel, his wife, sister of John Bigod. Which daughters were,

> Maud, wife of Peter de Geneva, who had livery of Ludlow Castle in her right, and after this, in 38th Henry III., of Geffery de Genevill, who had livery of the castle of Trim, in Ireland, as part of her inheritance.
>
> Margery, m. to John de Verdon, and had for her share of the property, the castle of Webbeley. The honour of Ewyas-Lacy having been assigned for the dower of Isabel, her mother.

Having thus brought the line of WALTER DE LACY, the companion of the CONQUEROR, to a close, we return to his fellow-soldier, if not kinsman,

ILBERT DE LACI, to whom King William gave the castle and town of Brokenbridge, in the county of York, which he afterwards denominated, in the Norman dialect, PONTFRACT. He had besides other territorial grants of vast extent; and at the time of the general survey, possessed nearly an hundred and fifty lordships in Yorkshire, ten in Nottingham, and four in Lincolnshire. This Ilbert left two sons, Robert and Hugh. The elder,

ROBERT DE LACI, otherwise Robert de Pontfract, had a confirmation from King WILLIAM Rufus, of all those lands whereof Ilbert, his father, died possessed. Attaching himself, however, to the interest of Robert Curthose, after the death of Rufus, himself and his son, ILBERT, were expelled the realm by King Henry I., and the honour of Pontfract bestowed upon Henry Traverse; which Henry, having shortly after been mortally wounded by one Pain, a servant of his own, caused himself to be shorn a monk, and so died within three days. After which the king gave this honour to Guy de la Val, who held it until King Stephen's time, when, it is stated by an old historian, that,

ILBERT DE LACY, (the personage mentioned above as exiled with his father,) by the special favour of Stephen, re-obtained his BARONY OF PONTFRACT, and was ever afterwards one of the staunchest adherents of that monarch. In the 3d year of whose reign he was a principal commander at the celebrated battle of the STANDARD, fought at Northallerton, where the Scots sustained so signal a defeat from the northern barons. He subsequently obtained a pardon on behalf of his servants, for all forfeitures whatsoever; and especially for the death of William Maltravers. This feudal lord m. Alice, daughter of Gilbert de Gant, but dying s. p. he was s. by his brother,

HENRY DE LACY, who was received into favour by the empress, and her son, King Henry II., and obtained from them a remission of the displeasure which King Henry I. bore towards Robert, his father; as also of the forfeiture, which he himself had made before he did his homage; with full restitution of his whole honour of Pontfract, and all other his lands in England and Normandy. He was s. by his son,

ROBERT DE LACY, who attended as one of the barons at the coronation of King Richard I.

This feudal lord died without issue, in 1193, when (the daughter of his mother, Albrida, by her second husband, Eudo de Lisours), his half sister,

ALBREDA LISOURS, then the wife of Richard Fitz-Eustace, feudal baron of Halton, and constable of Chester, possessed herself of the Barony of Pontfract, and all the other lands of her deceased brother; under pretence of a grant from Henry de Lacy, her first husband. By Fitz-Eustace, she had a son, JOHN, who becoming heir to his half uncle, Robert de Lacy, assumed that surname, and inherited, as

JOHN DE LACY, the Baronies of Halton and Pontfract, with the constableship of Chester. This feudal lord espoused Alice de Vere, and dying in the Holy Land, anno 1179, was s. by his eldest son,

ROGER DE LACY, Constable of Chester. This nobleman assisted at the siege of ACON, in 1192, under the banner of the lion-hearted RICHARD, and shared in the subsequent triumphs of the chivalrous monarch. At the accession of John, he was a person of great eminence, for we find him shortly after the coronation of that prince, deputed with the Sheriff of Northumberland, and other great men, to conduct William, King of Scotland, to Lincoln, where the English king had fixed to give him an interview; and the next year he was one of the barons present at Lincoln, when David of Scotland did homage and fealty to King John. In the time of this Roger, Ranulph, EARL OF CHESTER, having entered Wales at the head of some forces, was compelled, by superior numbers, to shut himself up in the castle of Rothelan, where, being closely besieged by the Welch, he sent to the Constable of Chester, who forthwith marched to his relief, at the head of a concourse of people, then collected at the fair of Chester, consisting of minstrels, and loose characters * of all descriptions, forming altogether so numerous a body, that the besiegers, at their approach, mistaking them for soldiers, immediately raised the siege. For this timely service, the Earl of Chester conferred upon De Lacy and his heirs, the patronage of all the minstrels in those parts, which patronage the constable transferred to his steward, DUTTON and his heirs; and it is enjoyed to this day by the family of Dutton. It is doubtful, however, whether the privilege was transferred to the Duttons by this constable or his successor. The privilege was, "That at the midsummer fair held at Chester, all the minstrels of that country, resorting to Chester, do attend the heir of Dutton, from his lodging to St. John's church, (he being then accompanied by many gentlemen of the country, one of them walking before him in a surcoat of his arms, depicted on taffata; the rest of his fellows proceeding two and two, and playing on their seve-

---

* HUGH LUPUS, first Earl of Chester, in his charter of foundation of the abbey of St. Werburg, at Chester, gave a privilege to the frequenters of Chester fair, "That they should not be apprehended for theft, or any other offence during the time of the fair, unless the crime were committed therein." Which privilege made the fair of course the resort of thieves and vagabonds from all parts of the kingdom.

ral sorts of musical instruments. When divine service terminates, the like attendance upon Dutton to his lodging, where a court being kept by his steward, and all the minstrels formally called, certain orders and laws are made for the government of the society of minstrels.

JOHN DE LACY, Constable of Chester, who, in the 15th year of King John, undertook the payment of seven thousand marks to the crown, in the space of four years, for livery of the lands of his inheritance, and to be discharged of all his father's debts due to the exchequer: further obliging himself by oath, that in case he should ever swerve from his allegiance, and adhere to the king's enemies, all his possessions should devolve upon the crown; promising also, that he would not marry without the king's licence. By this agreement, it was arranged, that the king should retain the CASTLES OF PONTEFRACT and DUNNINGTON, still in his own hands; and that he, the said John, should allow £40 per annum, for the custody of those fortresses. But the next year, he had Dunnington restored to him, upon hostages. About this period, he joined the baronial standard, and was one of the celebrated TWENTY-FIVE barons, appointed to enforce the observance of MAGNA CHARTA. But the next year, he obtained letters of safe conduct to come to the king to make his peace, and he had similar letters, upon the accession of Henry III., in the 2d year of which monarch's reign, he went with divers other noblemen into the Holy Land. He married MARGARET, daughter and heir of Robert de Quincy, Earl of Winchester, by Hawyse, fourth sister and co-heir of Ranulph de Meschines, Earl of Chester and Lincoln, which Ranulph, by a formal charter under his seal, granted the EARLDOM OF LINCOLN, that is, so much as he could grant thereof, to the said Hawyse, "to the end that she might be a countess, and that her heirs might also enjoy the earldom;" which grant was confirmed by the king, and at the especial request of the countess, this John de Lacy, Constable of Chester, was created, by charter, dated at Northampton, 23d November, 1232, EARL OF LINCOLN, with remainder to the heirs of his body, by his wife, the above mentioned Margaret. In the contest which occurred during the same year, between the king and Richard Marshal, Earl of Pembroke, Earl Marshal, the Earl of Lincoln, Matthew Paris states, was brought over to the king's party, with John le Scot, Earl of Chester, by Peter de Rupibus, Bishop of Winchester, for a bribe of one thousand marks. In 1237, his lordship was one of those appointed to prohibit OTO, the pope's legate, from establishing any thing derogatory to the king's crown and dignity, in the council of prelates then assembled; and the same year he had a grant of the sheriffalty of Cheshire, being likewise constituted governor of the Castle of Chester. The earl died in 1240, leaving Margaret, his wife, surviving, who re-married William Marshal, Earl of Pembroke. His lordship left issue,

EDMUND, his successor,

and two daughters; which ladies, in the 27th Henry III., were removed to Windsor, there to be educated with the king's own daughters; of these,

Maud, m. Richard de Clare, Earl of Gloucester. The earl was s. by his son,

EDMUND DE LACI, (presumed second Earl of Lincoln). This young nobleman married, in 1247, "an outlandish lady," (says Dugdale,) "from the parts of Savoy, brought over purposely for him, by Peter de Savoy, uncle to the queen, which occasioned much discontent amongst the nobles of England." The lady thus designated, was ALICE, daughter of the Marquess of Saluces, in Italy, and cousin of the queen. By her, his lordship had issue,

HENRY, his successor.

John.

Margaret, m. to George de Cantilupe, Baron of Bergavenny.

As to the title of EARL OF LINCOLN, this nobleman never used it, nor was it ever attributed to him in any charter, by reason that he died before his mother, through whom the dignity came; but as he enjoyed the Tertium Denarium of that county, he must nevertheless be esteemed the second earl, and Nicolas so places him. His lordship d. in 1257, and was s. by his elder son,

HENRY DE LACY, third Earl of Lincoln, who, having espoused Margaret, daughter and co-heir of William de Longespee, son of William de Longespee, Earl of Salisbury, became jure uxoris, EARL OF SALISBURY. This nobleman was one of the most eminent of the period in which he lived, and enjoyed the highest favour of King Edward I., in whose Welch wars he had early a distinguished part, and obtained from the king the land of Denbigh, upon which he began the town of that name, walling it in and protecting it by a castle, upon the front whereof was his statue in long robes. In the 21st year of Edward I., his lordship was sent ambassador to the King of France, to treat concerning the restraint of pirates; and the next year he attended the king into Wales, where he experienced a great repulse, not far from the Castle of Denbigh. He was subsequently, for some years, engaged in the French wars: first under Edmund, Earl of Lancaster, but after the decease of that prince, he had the sole command of the army himself. In the 27th and 28th of the same reign, his lordship was in the wars of Scotland; in the 29th he was constituted governor of Corff Castle, and two years afterwards, joined in commission with the Bishop of Winchester and others, to treat of peace with the Court of France. In 1305, the earl was deputed with the Bishops of Lichfield and Worcester, to the solemn inauguration of the POPE at Lions, and presented his holiness with divers vessels of pure gold, from his royal master. After this, we again find him in the wars of Gascony and Scotland; and in the 3rd Edward II., upon that monarch's march into Scotland, the Earl of Lincoln was constituted governor of England, during the king's absence. His lordship died in 1312, "at his mansion house, called LINCOLN's INN, in the suburbs of London, which he himself had erected, in that place, where the BLACKFRIARS habitation anciently stood." Immediately before his decease, he called his son-in-law, the Earl of Lancaster, to his bedside, and addressed him in words to the following effect.—"Seest thou the church of England, heretofore honourable and free, enslaved by Romish oppressions, and the king's unjust exactions? Seest thou the common people impoverished by tributes and taxes, and from the condition of freemen, reduced to servitude? Seest thou the nobility, formerly venerable through Christendom, vilified by aliens, in their own native country? I therefore charge thee, in the name of Christ, to stand up like a man; for the honour of God, and his church, and redemption of thy country; associating thyself to that valiant, noble, and prudent person, *Guy*, EARL OF WARWICK, when it shall be most proper to discourse of the public affairs of the kingdom; who is so judicious in counsel, and mature in judgment. Fear not thy opposers, who shall contest against thee in the truth. And if thou pursuest this, my advice, thou shalt gain eternal Heaven!" This great earl left an only daughter, and heiress,

> ALICE DE LACY, who *m.* first, Thomas Plantagenet, Earl of Lancaster, who is said to have been Earl of Lincoln, in her right; she espoused secondly, Eubold le Strange; and thirdly, Hugh le Frenes. Her ladyship assumed the title of COUNTESS OF LINCOLN AND SALISBURY, but died without issue, in 1348, when those honours became EXTINCT, in the family of Lacy.

ARMS.—Or. a lion rampant, purpuré.

Note.—One important service of the last earl's, we had nearly omitted. In 1290, (18th Edward I.,) his lordship was appointed the chief commissioner for rectifying and discovering abuses and briberies amongst the judges, complained of in parliament: when THOMAS WEYLAND, Chief Justice of the Common Pleas, was banished, and all his estates forfeited; Sir JOHN LOVETOT, compounded for five hundred marks; ROGER LEICESTER, (clerk,) for one thousand; Sir William Brompton for six thousand, with several others, who were also fined; a proof that the judgment-seat is not always as immaculate, as it is *at all times* represented to be.

LANCASTER — BARON LANCASTER.

By Writ of Summons, dated 29th December, 1299, 28 Edward I.

Lineage.

The LANCASTERS, feudal Lords of Kendal, deduced their descent from IVO TAILBOYS, brother of Fulk, Earl of Anjou, through his great grandson, WILLIAM, who assumed, Dugdale presumes, from being governor of Lancaster Castle, the surname of Lancaster. This

WILLIAM DE LANCASTER, Baron of Kendal, *m.* Gundred, daughter of William, second Earl of Warren, and widow of Roger, Earl of Warwick; by whom he had issue; William, his successor, and a daughter, married to Richard de Morevill. He was *s.* at his decease by his son, called

WILLIAM DE LANCASTER, the second, who was steward to King Henry II. This William *m.* Helewise de Sluteville, and left an only daughter and heiress,

> HELEWISE DE LANCASTER, whom King Richard I., shortly after his coronation gave

in marriage to (the son and heir of Roger Fitz-Reinfride, one of the justices of the King's Bench)

GILBERT FITZ-REINFRIDE, and in consideration of a fine of sixty marks of silver, relieved him and his heirs from a certain tribute, called NUTGELD, which used to be paid by his lands in Westmoreland and Kendal. This Gilbert obtained a grant of the honour of Lancaster for life from King John, and filled the office of sheriff of Lancashire from the 7th to the 17th year of the same reign. But we find him, notwithstanding, taking up arms with the other barons, and only reduced to allegiance by the capture of his son and heir, William, by the royalists, upon the fall of Rochester Castle. This event compelled the haughty baron to sue for pardon, which the king granted with the freedom of the captive, in consideration of the sum of twelve thousand marks, the custody of some of his castles, and hostages for future good conduct. This Gilbert *d.* in 1219, leaving issue,

> WILLIAM, his heir, who assumed his maternal surname, of Lancaster.
>
> Helewise, *m.* to Peter de Brus, of Skelton, and left a son, Peter, who died *s. p.*, and four daughters,
>
>> 1. Margaret, *m.* to Robert de Ros, whose descendant, in the fifth degree, and representative of the family.
>>
>>> Elizabeth de Ros, *m.* Sir William Par, Knt., the great-great-great grand-children, of which marriage were,
>>>
>>>> WILLIAM PARR, Baron of Kendall, and Marquess of Northampton.
>>>>
>>>> CATHERINE PARR, last Queen of King Henry VIII.
>>>>
>>>> Anne Parr, wife of William Herbert, first Earl of Pembroke.
>>
>> 2. Agnes, *m.* to Walter de Fauconberg, (see Nevill, Lord Fauconberg.)
>> 3. Lucy, *m.* to Robert de Tweng.
>> 4. Laderine, *m.* to John de Bella-Aqua.
>
> Alice, *m.* to William de Lindesey, whose descendant,
>
>> Christian de Lindesey, *m.* Ingleram de Ghisnes, Lord of Courcy, in France.
>
> Serota, *m.* to Allan de Multon, and died *s. p.*

Gilbert Fitz-Reinfride, was *s.* by his son,

WILLIAM DE LANCASTER, called the third. This feudal lord was sheriff of Lancashire from the 18th to the 30th Henry III. inclusive, and had likewise the custody of the honour of Lancaster. He *d.* about the year 1246 *s. p.*, when his estates devolved upon the representatives of his two elder sisters, the youngest sister having died without issue, and were thus divided. The Brus's had what was called, the Marquis and Lumley fee; the Lindesays, the Richmond fee. Thus terminated the legitimate line of the Lancasters, Barons of Kendall; but the last baron had a bastard brother, called

ROGER DE LANCASTER, who held the manor of Barton, in the county of Westmorland, by gift of his brother, as also *that* of Patterdale, in the same shire, and was sheriff of Lancashire in 49th Henry III. He *m.* Philippa, eldest daughter, and one of the co-heirs of Hugh de Bolebec, of —————, in the county of Northumberland, and dying in 1290, was *s.* by his son,

JOHN DE LANCASTER. This feudal lord having distinguished himself in the wars of Scotland, temp. Edward I., was summoned to parliament as a BARON from 29th December, 1299, to 12th December, 1309. His lordship *d.* in 1334, without issue, when the BARONY OF LANCASTER became EXTINCT, while his estates, which included the feudal Barony of Rydale, in Westmoreland, with divers other lordships, in the counties of Northumberland and Essex, devolved upon his heir at law, Richard, the son of Richard de Plaiz, then twelve years old.

ARMS.—Ar. two bars gemels, on a canton of the second, a lion passant guardant, or.

LANGDALE—BARONS LANGDALE, OF HOLME.

By Letters Patent, dated 4th February, 1658.

Lineage.

The family derived its surname from the town of LANGDALE, in the hundred of Pickering, in Yorkshire, of which they were lords prior to the time of King John.

In the reign of Edward II.

PATRICK DE LANGDALE espoused Amanda, daughter and heiress of Lawrence de Elton, and was *s.* by his son,

PATRICK DE LANGDALE, who *m.* Helen, daughter and heir of Sir Thomas Houghton, of Houghton, county of York, and with her acquired that estate; from this Patrick descended,

ANTHONY LANGDALE, of Houghton, who *d.* in the 19th Elizabeth, leaving with other issue, RICHARD, his successor, at Houghton, and

PETER LANGDALE, who was seated at Pighill, near Beverley, and having *m.* Anne, daughter of Michael Wharton, Esq., of Beverley Park, was *s.* by his son,

SIR MARMADUKE LANGDALE, of Holme, in Spaldingmore, Yorkshire. This gentleman received the honour of knighthood from King Charles I., at Whitehall, in 1627, "and was esteemed," says Banks, "a serious and wise man, of most scholarlike accomplishments, and of good husbandry." During the civil wars Sir Marmaduke became one of the most distinguished amongst the cavalier generals. At the head of a corps raised by himself, consisting of three companies of foot, and a troop of seventy horse, he encountered and defeated the Scots at Corbridge, in Northumberland; and next, being commander-in-chief of the troops sent by the king into Lincolnshire, he there encountered the rebels under Colonel Rosseter. Thence marching against the Lord Fairfax, and putting that officer to the rout, he relieved Pontefract Castle, then beleaguered by a numerous body of the northern insurgents. He subsequently besieged and reduced Berwick-upon-Tweed, and the strong castle of Carlisle. But afterwards involved in the defeat of the Duke of Hamilton and the Scotch army at Preston,

Sir Marmaduke was made prisoner; he was fortunate, enough, however, to effect his escape, and retiring abroad, became one of the attendants of King Charles II. in his exile, by whom he was elevated to the peerage, on the 4th February, 1658, as BARON LANGDALE, *of Holme, in Spaldingmore, in the county of York.* His lordship *m.* Lenox, daughter of Sir John Rhodes, of Barborough, in Derbyshire, by whom he had surviving issue,

MARMADUKE, his successor.

Philip.

Lenox, *m.* to Cuthbert Harrison, Esq., of Alaster Selby, in the county of York.

Mary.

Anne.

Lord Langdale returned to England at the Restoration, and *d.* at his seat, Holme, on the 5th August, 1661. His lordship is thus mentioned by Lloyd: "He was a very lean and much mortified man, so that the enemy called him ghost (and deservedly, they were so haunted by him;) and carried that gravity in his converse, that integrity and generosity in his dealings, that strictness in his devotion, that experience, moderation, and wariness in his counsel, and that weight in his discourse, as very much endeared strangers to his royal master's cause, and to his own person, in all the countries he travelled, as he did in many; and to all the armies he engaged in, as he did in most then afoot in Europe, till he was restored with his majesty in 1660; when, after appearing in parliament as Baron Langdale, of Holme, he returned to his considerable estates in Yorkshire; having lost £160,000. in his majesty's service, without any other recompence, than the conscience of having suffered in a good cause, acquitted himself bravely, and played the man." He was *s.* by his elder son,

MARMADUKE LANGDALE, second baron, who wedded Elisabeth, daughter of Thomas Savage, Esq., of Beeston, in the county of Chester, and niece of John, Earl Rivers, by whom he had issue,

MARMADUKE, his successor.

Philip, } both died *s. p.*
Peter, }

Jane, *m.* to Michael Anne, Esq., of Frickley, Yorkshire.

Elisabeth, *m.* to Sir Hugh Smithson, Bart., and was grandmother of SIR HUGH SMITHSON, first EARL OF NORTHUMBERLAND, of that family.

Bridget, *d.* unmarried.

This nobleman was governor of Hull in the reign of James II., where, upon the landing of the Prince of Orange, he was surprised and made prisoner by Colonel Copeley. His lordship *d.* in 1703, and was *s.* by his eldest son,

MARMADUKE LANGDALE, third baron. This nobleman espoused Frances, daughter of Richard Draycott, Esq., of Painesley, in the county of York, and had issue,

MARMADUKE, his successor.

Elisabeth, *m.* to Peter Middleton, Esq., of Stockeld, in Yorkshire.

Frances, *m.* to Nicholas Blundell, Esq., of Crosby, in the county of Lancaster.

His lordship *d.* in 1718, and was *s.* by his son,

MARMADUKE LANGDALE, fourth baron, who m. Elizabeth, youngest daughter of William, Lord Widrington, and had issue,

MARMADUKE, who succeeded to the title.

Alathea, d. unmarried.

Dorothy, m. to Sir Walter Vavasor, Bart., of Haselwood, in the county of York, and had two sons,

Walter Vavasor, Thomas Vavasor,	successive baronets, with the latter of whom the baronetcy expired, and Sir Thomas bequeathed his estates to his cousin, *the Hon.* EDWARD MARMADUKE STOURTON, who, assuming the name of Vavasor, is the present SIR EDWARD VAVASOR, Bart.

Elizabeth.

His lordship d. in 1771, and was s. by his only son,

MARMADUKE LANGDALE, fifth baron. This nobleman m. Constantia, daughter of Sir John Smythe, Bart., of Acton-Burnel, in the county of Salop, by whom he had

MARMADUKE, who died young, and before his father.

Constantia, died young.

Elizabeth, m. to Robert Butler, Esq., of Bally-ragget, in Ireland.

Mary, m. to Charles-Philip, sixteenth Lord Stourton, and had, with other issue,

WILLIAM, present Lord Stourton.

Edward-Marmaduke Stourton, who assumed the surname of VAVASOUR, as stated above, and was created a baronet in 1828.

Charles Stourton, who assumed the surname of LANGDALE *only*, in compliance with the testamentary injunction of Philip Langdale, Esq., of Houghton, in the county of York.

Apolonia, m. to *Hugh-Edward-Henry*, sixth LORD CLIFFORD, *of Chudleigh*, and was grandmother of *Hugh-Charles*, present LORD CLIFFORD.

His lordship d. in 1777, when the BARONY OF LANGDALE, *of Holme*, became EXTINCT.

ARMS.—Sa. a chevron between three estoils ar.

LASCELS—BARON LASCELS.

By Writ of Summons, dated 23rd June, 1295, 23 Edward I.

Lineage.

"Of this ancient family, seated in the county of York, were divers persons," says Dugdale, "of great note many ages since." The chief of whom was

ROGER DE LASCELS, who, in the 22nd Edward I., had summons, with several of the peers of the realm, and other eminent persons, to attend the king, and to advise touching the most important affairs of the kingdom. Nicolas doubts whether this writ could be deemed a *baronial* summons to parliament, as he observes, that none of the higher temporal nobility, nor any of the spiritual peers, were included in it, and that no regular day was fixed for the meeting. The same learned authority further remarks, "that the writ in question is the earliest on record, excepting that of the 49th Henry III.; that the majority of the persons summoned by it were never again summoned save in the 23rd of Edward I.; that several of those persons were not considered as barons by tenure; and that of those who were barons by tenure, and summoned on those occasions, many were never included in any subsequent summons to parliament. The writ has, however, (continues Mr. Nicolas,) on one occasion (in the case of the Barony of Roos,) been admitted as a writ of summons to parliament at the bar of the House of Lords; but the last 'General Report of the Lords' Committee,' appointed to search for matters touching the dignity of a peer of the realm, appears to confirm the objections thus raised." Roger de Lascels was, however, summoned in the following year, on the 23rd June, 30th September, and 2nd November, and on the 26th August, 1296. His lordship d. about the year 1297, leaving four daughters, his co-heirs, amongst whom the BARONY OF LASCELS fell into ABEYANCE, and it still continues in that state with the representatives of those ladies.

*** The noble house of Lascelles, Earls of Harewood, claims descent from this ancient baronial family.

ARMS.—Ar. three chaplets gu.

LASCELLES—BARON HAREWOOD.

By Letters Patent, dated 9th July, 1790.

Lineage.

HENRY LASCELLES, Esq., of Harewood, in the county of York, M.P., and an East India Director, m. Janet, daughter of John Whetstone, Esq., of Barbadoes, and was s. at his decease, in 1754, by his son,

EDWIN LASCELLES, Esq., who was elevated to the peerage on the 9th July, 1790, as BARON HAREWOOD, of Harewood, in the county of York. His lordship married twice, but dying without issue, 25th January, 1795, the BARONY OF HAREWOOD became EXTINCT, while his lordship's estates passed to his heir at law, EDWARD LASCELLES, Esq., who was created Baron Harewood the next year, and was father of the present Earl of Harewood.

ARMS.—Sa. a cross flory, within a bordure or.

LATIMER—BARONS LATIMER, OF DANBY.

By Writ of Summons, dated 29th December, 1299, 28 Edward I.

Lineage.

The surname of LATIMER is remarked from an old inquisition to have been attributed to Wrenoc, the son of Meirric, who held certain lands by the service of being *latimer*, that is *interpreter* between the Welsh and English. Of this name, English history has since boasted of several distinguished personages. In the 2nd Richard I.,

WILLIAM LE LATIMER paid one hundred shillings to have a trial at law with Geffry de Valoins, who had possessed himself of part of his park at Billenges, in the county of York. To this William succeeded another,

WILLIAM LE LATIMER, who, in the 38th of Henry III., was made sheriff of Yorkshire, and governor of the castle at York, and the next year governor of Pickering Castle. In this sheriffalty he continued for nearly five years, during which period he had a military summons to march into Scotland in aid of (the minor) King Alexander, (Henry III.'s son-in-law,) against his rebellious subjects: and he was constituted escheator-general throughout all the counties of England. In the 47th Henry III., he obtained the king's precept to the conservators of the peace, in the counties of York, Cumberland, Northumberland, Lincoln, and Northampton, to make restitution to him of all his lands which had been seised in the baronial war. He appears, however, in those contests to have sided with the crown, for we find him upon the full re-establishment of the power of the king, again filling the office of the sheriff of Yorkshire, and again governor of the castles at York and Scarborough. He also received a compensation of one hundred marks for the expenses he had incurred. In the 54th of Henry III., he was, amongst others, signed with the cross, to accompany Prince Edward to the Holy Land. In the 10th of Edward I., he was in an expedition against the Welsh, and in several years after he accompanied the famous soldier, John St. John, in an expedition into Gascony. From this period he seems to have been almost uninterruptedly employed in the wars of Scotland and Gascony, and for his services was summoned to parliament as a BARON, from the 29th December, 1299, to 22nd January, 1305. He obtained, about the same time, a grant from the crown, of the manor of Danby, in the county of York. His lordship m. Alice, daughter and co-heir of Walter Ledet, by whom he acquired a moiety of the Barony of Warden, in the county of Northampton, and a moiety of the town and whole hundred of Corby, in the same shire. He had, with other issue,

    WILLIAM, his successor.

    John (Sir), who m. Joane, daughter, and at length heir of Sir William de Goule, Knt., by whom he acquired, amongst other estates, the manor of Duntish, in the county of Dorset; where he and his posterity continued to flourish, eminent for several generations, until the attainder of

        SIR NICHOLAS LATIMER, in the reign of Edward IV., but that attainder was subsequently reversed. Sir Nicholas died in 1505, leaving an only daughter and heiress,*

---

* By a MS. in the British Museum, in a collection of miscellaneous pedigrees, by William Penson, Lancaster herald, it is, however, stated that Sir Nicholas Latimer left, by another wife, another

306

EDITH LATIMER, who m. Sir John Mordaunt, Knt., ancestor of the Earls of Peterborough, by which alliance those (now extinct) noblemen acquired DUNTISH, and other considerable lordships, in the county of Dorset.

Lord Latimer d. in 1305, and was s. by his eldest son,

WILLIAM LE LATIMER, who had himself been summoned to parliament as a BARON, under the designation of "Willielmo de Latimer, juniori," from 6th February, 1299, to 22nd January, 1305, and enjoyed precedency of his father. After the decease of that nobleman, he was summoned without the addition of junior. His lordship was an experienced soldier, and highly distinguished in the Scottish wars of Edward I. and Edward II. In the latter reign he fought at BANNOCKBURN, and was made prisoner there. He was subsequently involved in the treason of Thomas, Earl of Lancaster, but obtained a pardon; and in three years afterwards, (15th Edward II.,) upon the breaking out of the grand insurrection of that prince, Lord Latimer was one of the principal commanders, by whom he was defeated at BOROUGHBRIDGE: for which service his lordship was the next year made governor of the city of York. He m. first, Lucia, daughter and heir of Robert de Thweng, and grand-daughter of Marmaduke, Baron Thweng. This lady seems to have proved unfaithful, for during one of his lordship's campaigns in Scotland, she was taken away from his manor house of BRUNNE, in Yorkshire, and the king's precept to the sheriff of the shire immediately issued, directing a strict search to be instituted after her. His lordship was, however, eventually divorced, and her ladyship married Robert de Everingham; and after him she espoused Bartholomew de Fancourt. Lord Latimer wedded, secondly, Sibill, widow of William de Huntingfield, and dying in 1397, was s. by his son (by his second wife),

WILLIAM LE LATIMER, third baron, summoned to parliament from 6th August, 1327, to 1st April, 1335. This nobleman having, without licence, purchased the office of coinage in the Tower of London, and city of Canterbury, from Maud, the widow of John de Botetourt, (who held it by inheritance of the king in capite,) obtained pardon for that offence in the 3rd of Edward III. His lordship m. Elizabeth, daughter of Lord Botetourt, and dying in 1335, was s. by his son,

WILLIAM LATIMER, fourth baron, summoned to parliament from 24th February, 1368, to 20th October, 1379. This nobleman was one of the eminent warriors of the martial times of Edward III. At the period he succeeded to the representation of his family, he was in minority, and did not make proof of his age until the year 1361, when his homage was respited in consequence of his being then engaged in the king's service at Calais. His lord-

---

daughter, ELIZABETH LATIMER, who married William Apreece, Esq., of Washingley, in the county of Huntingdon, lineal ancestor of the present Sir Thomas Hussey Apreece, Bart.

ship continued for several succeeding years in France, performing numerous gallant exploits;—amongst others, he is celebrated for a victory achieved over CHARLES DE BLOIS, at the siege of Doveroy; where, with only 1600 men, (English and Britons,) he encountered that prince, who had come to the relief of the place at the head of 3600 men, and defeated and slew him, with nearly a thousand knights and esquires; taking prisoners, two earls, twenty-seven lords, and fifteen hundred men at arms. In the 43d Edward III., his lordship was again in the wars of France, being at that time steward of the king's household; and the next year he was constituted lieutenant, captain, and governor of the castle, town, and viscounty of St. Saviour's, in Normandy. Nevertheless, in a few years afterwards, we find him, with the Duke of Lancaster, falling under the displeasure of the commons, and impeached by the parliament then (50th Edward III.) assembled at Westminster, of peculation, and of squandering, whilst belonging to the king's council, the royal treasure. Being convicted of these offences, he was deprived of all his public offices, and sentenced to pay a fine of twenty thousand marks, and to be imprisoned during the king's pleasure: but the fine and imprisonment were both remitted by the king. The parliament roll of that year states, that the loss of the town of St. Saviour's, in Normandy, and Becherell, in Britanny, were laid to his charge: but afterwards that the lords and commons, representing to the king, that he had been deprived of his offices, and erased from the privy council by untrue suggestion, he was reinstated in those offices again. Upon the death of King Edward III., Lord Latimer was one of those whom King Richard II. deputed to acquaint the citizens of London with the event: and for the remainder of his life, he enjoyed the full confidence of the new monarch; was of his privy council, a knight of the garter, &c. &c. In this reign his lordship's last service was at the siege of Nantes, with Thomas of Woodstock, being then constable of the Host. He m. the lady Elisabeth Fitz-Alan, daughter of Edmond, Earl of Arundel, and dying in 1380, left an only daughter and heiress,

> ELIZABETH LATIMER, who espoused John de Nevill, Lord Nevill of Raby, (his lordship's second wife,) and had issue,
>
>> JOHN NEVILL, of whom presently.
>> Elizabeth Nevill, m. to Sir Thomas Willoughby, Knt.
>> Margaret, died issueless.
>
> She married secondly, Robert, Lord Willoughby de Eresby, and died in the 7th of Richard II.

The son of the above Elisabeth Latimer,

JOHN NEVILL, was summoned to parliament in right of his mother, as BARON LATIMER, from 26th August, 1404, to 27th November, 1430. His lordship m. Maud, daughter of Thomas, Lord Clifford, and widow of Richard Plantagenet, Earl of Cambridge—but died s. p., in 1430, when the BARONY OF LATIMER devolved upon his only surviving sister of the whole blood, Elizabeth, Lady Willoughby, and was claimed in the reign of Henry VIII., by her ladyship's great grandson, *Robert,*

LORD WILLOUGHBY DE BROKE, against Richard Nevill, second Lord Latimer, (under a new writ, 10th Henry VI.,) and though his lordship did not prosecute his claim,[*] the original BARONY OF LATIMER must still be considered as vested in his descendant, HENRY, present LORD Willoughby de Broke.

ARMS.—Gu. a cross patonce, or.

LATIMER — BARON LATIMER, OF BRAYBROOKE.

By Writ of Summons, dated 29th December, 1299, 28 Edward I.

Lineage.

JOHN LE LATIMER, brother of William, first Lord Latimer, of Danby, espoused Christian, second daughter and co-heir of Walter Ledit, (Lord Latimer, of Danby, m. the other daughter,) and dying in the 11th Edward I., was s. by his son, (then 12 years of age,)

THOMAS LATIMER, who took up his abode at Braybroke, in the county of Northampton, (part of his mother's inheritance, that lady having been great-grandchild and co-heir of Henry de Braybroke,) and in the 32nd Edward I., obtained licence to make a castle of his manor house there. In the 18th of Edward II., being then called Thomas le Latimer Bochard, he was in the expedition made at that time, into Scotland; and he was summoned to parliament, as a BARON, from 29th December, 1299, to 16th June, 1311. He died in 1334, seised, amongst other manors, of those of Warden and Braybroke, in the county of Northampton, and was s. by his son,

WARINE LATIMER, who, being subsequently a banneret, was in the expedition made into France, in the 19th of Edward III., and died in four years afterwards; never having been summoned to parliament. He m. Catherine, sister of John, Lord de la Warre, and was s. by his eldest son,

JOHN LATIMER, who died s. p., and was s. by his brother,

SIR THOMAS LATIMER, who, in the 39th of Edward III., was of the retinue of Prince Edward in Gascony. This Sir Thomas is deemed the same person whom historians mention as a leader in the religious sect so well known, as *"Lollards,"* in the

---

[*] To end this contest, the Lord Broke was informed by a herald, that Sir George Nevill, grandfather to Richard, had been created Lord Latimer, by a new title, which therefore lineally descended to Richard, by Henry, son and heir of the said George; and that the Lord Broke had made a wrong claim, who should have claimed his style from William Latimer, first created Lord Latimer, of Danby, (the head of his barony,) temp. Edward I. On this, Lord Broke perceiving his error, and having a title of his own, was contented to conclude a match between their children; and Richard suffered a recovery on certain manors and lordships, demanded by the Lord Broke; with which adjustment both parties were well satisfied.—BANKS.

reign of Richard II. He d. without issue, and was s. by his brother,

EDWARD LATIMER, who died s. p., in 1411, then seised of the manor of Warden, and Castle of Braybroke, with divers other estates in Northampton and other shires, which devolved upon (his sister, Elizabeth's, son,) his nephew, JOHN GRIFFIN, whose descendant,

EDWARD GRIFFIN, was created in 1688, BARON GRIFFIN, of Braybroke Castle, a dignity that expired with his grandson,

EDWARD GRIFFIN, third baron, in 1742.

ANNE GRIFFIN, his lordship's younger sister, and eventually, sole heiress, married William Whitwell, Esq., of Oundle, and her son,

JOHN GRIFFIN WHITWELL, Esq., having assumed the name of GRIFFIN only, and established his claim to the Barony of HOWARD DE WALDEN, was summoned to parliament, in that dignity. He was afterwards created BARON BRAYBROKE, with special remainder, under which that barony has passed to the present LORD BRAYBROKE.

ARMS.—Gu. a cross patonce, or.

LEA—BARON DUDLEY.

See SUTTON, Barons Dudley.

LECHMERE — BARON LECHMERE, OF EVESHAM, IN THE COUNTY OF WORCESTER.

By Letters Patent, dated 25th August, 1721.

Lineage.

NICHOLAS LECHMERE, Esq., an eminent lawyer, having filled the office of solicitor and attorney-general, was elevated to the peerage by King George I. in the dignity of BARON LECHMERE, of Evesham, in the county of Worcester, by letters patent, dated 25th August, 1721. His lordship was likewise chancellor of the Duchy of Lancaster. He m. Lady Elizabeth Howard, daughter of Charles, Earl of Carlisle, but dying issueless in 1727, the BARONY OF LECHMERE became EXTINCT

ARMS.—Quarterly, first and fourth gules, a fesse and in chief two pelicans, or. vulning themselves sanguine; second vert frettèes, or.; third ar. a chevron ingrailed between three chess rooks, sa.

LEE—EARLS OF LITCHFIELD.

By Letters Patent, dated 5th June, 1674.

Lineage.

This family derived its surname from the lordship of LEE, in Cheshire, where resided in the time of Edward III.,

SIR WALTER LEE, Knt., who was father of

SIR JOHN LEE, of Lee Hall, whose great-grandson,

JOHN LEE, of Lee Hall, m. Margaret, daughter of Sir Ralph Hocknel, and had issue, JOHN, his successor, at Lee, with a younger son,

BENEDICT LEE, who, in the reign of Edward IV., became seated at Quarendon, in the county of Bucks. This gentleman m. Elizabeth, daughter and heir of John Wood, Esq., of Warwick, and was s. by his son,

RICHARD LEE, of Quarendon, who altered his arms to " Argent, a fesse between three crescents, as.," and marrying Elizabeth, daughter and co-heir of William Sanders, Esq., of the county of Oxford, had issue,

ROBERT (Sir), of Burston, in the county of Bucks, grandfather of Sir Henry Lee, K.G., temp. Elizabeth.

Benedict, of Hulcote.

Roger, of Pickthorn.

John, from whom the Lees, of Binfield, in the county of Berks, derived.

The second son,

BENEDICT LEE, Esq., of Hulcote, m. Elizabeth, daughter of Robert Cheney, Esq., of Chesham-Boyes, in the county of Bucks, and was father of

SIR ROBERT LEE, whose son, *[manuscript note]*

HENRY LEE, Esq., of Quarendon, was cousin and heir of Sir Henry Lee, K.G., and was knighted. In the 9th James I. this gentleman was created a baronet; and was s. by his son,

SIR FRANCIS-HENRY LEE, of Ditchley, in the county of Oxford, and of Quarendon, Berks, as second baronet. This gentleman m. Anne, daughter of Sir John St. John, of Lidiard-Tregos, in the county of Wilts, Bart., and was s. by his son,

SIR EDWARD LEE, third baronet, who was elevated to the peerage, by letters patent, dated 5th June, 1674, as Baron of Spellesbury, in the county of Oxford, Viscount Quarendon, Bucks, and EARL OF LITCHFIELD. His lordship m. Lady Charlotte Fitz-Roy, natural daughter of King Charles II., by Barbara Villiers, Duchess of Cleveland, and had surviving issue,

Edward, who d. unmarried.

James, m. Sarah, daughter of John Bagshaw, and d. in 1711.

Charles, d. unmarried.

GEORGE-HENRY, who s. his father.

Fitzroy-Henry, died s. p. in 1730.

ROBERT, who inherited as fourth earl.

Charlotte, m. to Benedict Calvert, Lord Baltimore.

Anne.

Elizabeth, m. first, to Colonel Lee, and secondly, to George, son of Sir George Broom, Bart.

His lordship, who refused to swear allegiance to the new government of the REVOLUTION, d. in 1716, and was s. by his eldest surviving son,

GEORGE-HENRY LEE, second Earl of Litchfield, who took his seat in the House of Lords soon after his accession to the peerage. His lordship m. Frances, daughter of Sir John Hales, of St. Staphens, Tunstall, and Woodchurch, in Kent, and had issue,

GEORGE-HENRY, his successor.
James, d. in 1742.
Charles-Henry, d. in 1740.
Charlotte, m. to Henry, eleventh Viscount Dillon. This lady became eventually heiress of her father, and the fortune is now enjoyed by her grandson, Henry-Augustus Dillon Lee, thirteenth VISCOUNT DILLON.
Mary, m. to Cosmas Neville, Esq.
Frances, d. unmarried.
Harriot, m. to John, Lord Bellew.
Anne, m. to Hugh, fifth Baron Clifford, of Chudleigh.

The earl d. in 1743, and was s. by his eldest son,

GEORGE-HENRY LEE, third earl. This nobleman was chancellor of the university of Oxford, captain of the band of gentlemen pensioners, and custos brevium in the Common Pleas. His lordship m. Diana, only daughter and heir of Sir Thomas Frankland, Bart., of Thirkelby, in the county of York, but dying s. p. in 1775, the honours reverted to his uncle,

ROBERT LEE, as fourth earl. This gentleman represented the city of Oxford for some time in parliament. He m. Katherine, daughter of Sir John Stonehouse, of Radley, Berks, but had no issue. His lordship d. in 1776, when the EARLDOM OF LITCHFIELD, and minor honours, became EXTINCT.

ARMS.—Ar. a fesse betw. three crescents, sa.

LEGGE—BARONY OF STAWEL.

By Letters Patent, dated 20th May, 1760.

Lineage.

For the line of the STAWELS, refer to STAWEL, BARONS STAWEL, of Somerton.

EDWARD STAWEL, fourth LORD STAWEL, of Somerton, left at his decease, in 1755, when his peerage became EXTINCT, an only daughter and heiress,

The Honourable

MARY LEGGE, then the wife of the *Honourable* HENRY BILSON LEGGE, (whom she had espoused, 3rd September, 1750,) fourth son of William, first Earl of Dartmouth. Mr. Legge, who was one of the most prominent statesmen of his time, sat in the eighth parliament of Great Britain for one of the Cornish boroughs, at which period he was a commissioner of the navy, and soon afterwards joint secretary to the treasury. He subsequently represented the county of Hants, was appointed a lord of the admiralty in 1745, and the next year a lord of the treasury. In 1748 he was accredited envoy extraordinary to the court of Berlin, and upon his return, in 1749, was constituted treasurer of the navy. In 1754 he was appointed chancellor of the exchequer, and sworn of the privy council, and he was, subsequently, twice removed from, and twice re-appointed to the same important office, from which, however, he was finally dismissed, or, to use his own expression, *turned out,* upon the change of administration in 1762. He had pre-

viously obtained the dignity of BARONESS STAWEL, of Somerton, in the county of Somerset, for his lady, with remainder to the heirs male of her body by himself: and dying 21st August, 1764, left an only son,

HENRY-STAWEL.

The baroness re-married in 1768, with the Right Hon. Wills Hill, Earl of Hillsborough, afterwards Marquess of Downshire, but had no issue. Her ladyship d. in 1780, when the Barony of Stawel devolved upon her only child,

HENRY STAWEL LEGGE, as Baron Stawel. This nobleman m. in 1779, the Hon. Mary Curzon, youngest daughter of Asheton, first Viscount Curzon, by whom (who d. in 1804) he left an only daughter and heiress,

MARY, who espoused John Dutton, present Earl of Sherborne.

His lordship d. in 1820, when the BARONY OF STAWEL became extinct.

ARMS.—Gu. a cross of losenges, ar. for STAWEL, a buck's head, cabossed, ar. for Legge.

LEIGH — BARONS LEIGH, OF STONELEIGH, IN THE COUNTY OF WARWICK.

By Letters Patent, dated 1st July, 1643.

Lineage.

The ancestors of this noble family assumed their surname from the town of HIGH-LEIGH, in Cheshire, where they were seated before the conquest.

HAMON, Lord of the mediety of High-Leigh, temp. Henry II., was father of

WILLIAM DE LEIGH, of West-Hall, in High-Leigh, whose grandson,

RICHARD DE LEIGH, left an only daughter and heiress,

AGNES-LEIGH, who espoused, first, Richard de Lymme, and had a son,
　THOMAS, who had half of the said mediety of High-Leigh, and taking the surname of LEIGH, left a son,
　　THOMAS LEIGH, who was patriarch of the LEIGHS, of West-Leigh, in High-Leigh.

AGNES LEIGH, married, secondly, William Venables, of Bradwell, second son of Sir William Venables,-Baron of Kinderton, and had a son,
　JOHN, who assumed the name of LEIGH, and of him presently.

She wedded, thirdly, William de Hawardyn, and had a son,
　RALPH DE HAWARDYN, who had the other half of the mediety of High-Leigh, and sold it to Sir Richard Massey, of Tatton, in 1286.

The son of Agnes Leigh, by her second husband,

JOHN LEIGH, m. Ellen, daughter of Richard Dent, of Cheshire, and had issue,
　JOHN (Sir), of Booths.
　Robert, of Adlington.
　Peter, of Beckington, whose only daughter

and heir —— m. Thomas Fitten, of Gawsworth, in Cheshire.

The second son,

ROBERT LEIGH, of Adlington, in Cheshire, m. Sibil, daughter of Henry Handford, of Handford, in the same county, and had issue,

> ROBERT (Sir), his successor, at Adlington, and progenitor of the LEIGHS, of that place.
>
> Peter (Sir), of whom presently.
>
> Alice.
>
> Joan.

The second son,

SIR PETER LEIGH, of Maxfield and Lyme, m. Margaret, widow of Sir John Savage, of Clifton, Kent, and daughter and heir of Sir Thomas Denyers, Jun., of Bradley and Clifton, and had a son and heir,

SIR PETER LEIGH, who serving under the victorious Henry V., in his French wars, was made a knight banneret, and was slain at the battle of Agincourt, 24th October, 1415. This gallant person m. first, Joan, daughter and heir of Sir Gilbert Haydock, Knt., by whom he had,

> PETER, who was knighted at the battle of Wakefield, by Richard, Duke of York, 31st December, 1460. From this Sir Peter Leigh, the Leighs of Lyme descend.

He m. secondly, Cecilie, daughter of John del Hagh, and heir to Thomas; and in her right was styled of Ridge. By this lady he had a son and two daughters, viz.

> JOHN, of whom presently.
>
> Agnes, m. to Richard Leversage.
>
> Alice, m. to William Clayton.

The son,

JOHN LEIGH, who inherited his mother's estate, of Ridge, was escheator of Cheshire for seven years, from the 19th Henry VI., and was living in 1459, being then also escheator. He m. Alice, daughter and heir of Thomas Alcock, and had issue,

> ROGER, who by Ellen, his wife, daughter of Robert Leigh, Esq., of Adlington, was ancestor of the Leighs of Ridge.
>
> Richard, of whose line we are about to treat.
>
> John, from whom descended Sir John Leigh, K.B., of Stockwell, in Surrey.

The second son,

RICHARD LEIGH, was seated at Rushall, in Staffordshire, in 1456, and was s. by his son,

ROGER LEIGH, of Wellington, in Shropshire and Rushall, in the county of Stafford. This gentleman had issue,

> WILLIAM, who succeeded to the estates, and marrying Elizabeth, daughter of Sir John Harpur, Knt., and co-heir of her brother, was progenitor of the Leighs, of Rushall. This William Leigh, was gentleman usher to KING HENRY VII.

And a younger son,

THOMAS LEIGH, who was brought up under Sir Rowland Hill, a rich merchant of London, and Lord Mayor of that city; by whom, for his knowledge and industry, he was made his factor beyond sea: and in that trust deporting himself with the highest integrity, Sir Rowland bestowed upon him

310

the hand of his favourite niece, Alice, daughter of John Barker, alias Coverall, of Wolverton, in the county of Salop, by Elizabeth, his wife, daughter of Thomas Hill, and upon the issue of the marriage he entailed the greater part of his estate. Thomas Leigh subsequently served the office of Sheriff of London, and was Lord Mayor at the death of Queen Mary. He was knighted during his mayoralty, and dying in 1571, was buried in Mercer's Chapel, London, with this epitaph upon his tomb:

> Sir Thomas Leigh bi civil life,
> All offices did beare,
>   Which in this city worshipfull
>   Or honourable were:
> Whom as God blessed with great wealth,
> So losses did he feele;
> Yet never changed he constant minde,
> Tho' fortune turn'd her wheele.
>   Learning he lov'd and helpt the poore
>   To them that knew him deere;
> For whom this lady and loving wife
> This tomb hath builded here.

His widow lived at Stoneleigh to a very advanced age, having seen her children's children to the fourth generation. She died in 1603, and was buried at Stoneleigh, where she had founded an hospital for five poor men, and five poor women, all of them to be unmarried persons, and nominated after her decease by Sir Thomas Leigh, her son, and his heirs for ever. Sir Thomas Leigh had issue by this lady,

> ROWLAND, who was largely provided for at Longborough, in Gloucestershire, by Sir Rowland Hill, his godfather. He m. first, Margery, daughter of Thomas Lawe, of London, vintner, and secondly, ——, daughter of Sir Richard Berkeley, Knt., of Stoke-Gifford, in Gloucestershire.
>
> Richard, died s. p.
>
> THOMAS, of whom presently.
>
> William (Sir), of Newnham-Regis, in Warwickshire, who m. Frances, daughter of Sir James Harrington, of Exton, in Rutlandshire, and left a son,
>
>> FRANCIS (Sir, K.B.), who m. Mary, daughter of Lord Ellesmere, Lord Chancellor of England, and left a son,
>>
>>> FRANCIS, who was elevated to the peerage as Earl of Chichester (see Leigh, Earl of Chichester).
>
> Mary, m. first, to Robert Andrews, of London, and secondly, to —— Cobb.
>
> Alice, m. to Thomas Connye, of Lincolnshire.
>
> Katherine, m. Edward Barber, of Somersetshire, Serjeant at Law.
>
> Winifred, m. to Sir George Bond, Lord Mayor of London.

The second surviving son,

THOMAS LEIGH, was knighted by Queen Elizabeth, and created a baronet, upon the institution of that order, 29th June, 1611. Sir Thomas m. Catherine, fourth daughter of Sir John Spencer, Knt., of Wormleighton, in the county of Warwick, and had issue,

> JOHN (Sir), who married, first, Ursula, daugh-

ter of Sir Christopher Hoddesdon, Knt.,
lord of the manor of Leighton, in Bedfordshire, by whom he had a son,

    THOMAS, successor to his grandfather.

Sir John espoused, secondly, Anne, eldest
daughter of Sir John Cope, Bart., of Hanwell, in Oxfordshire, but had no issue. He
died before his father.

    Thomas (Sir), } both d. issueless.
    Ferdinando,

    Alice, m. to Sir Robert Dudley, Knt., and was
    created Duchess of Dudley for life (see Dud-
    ley, Duchess of Dudley).

Sir Thomas d. in February, 1626, and was s. by his
grandfather,

SIR THOMAS LEIGH, second baronet, M.P.
for the county of Warwick, temp. Charles I., who,
for his zeal in the royal cause, was elevated to the
peerage by letters patent, dated at Oxford, 1st July,
1643, as BARON LEIGH, of Stoneleigh, in the county
of Warwick. Before the king set up his standard
at Nottingham his majesty marched to Coventry,
but finding the gates shut against him, and that no
summons could prevail with the mayor and magistrates to open them, he went the same night to
Stoneleigh, the house of Sir Thomas Leigh, where,
as Clarendon observes, he was well received. Sir
Thomas was afterwards an ardent supporter of the
royal cause, and at one time paid no less than
£4,895, as a compensation for his estate. He had
the gratification, however, of seeing the monarchy
restored.

His lordship m. Mary, one of the daughters and
co-heirs of Sir Thomas Egerton, eldest son of the
Lord Chancellor Ellesmere, by whom he had, with
other issue,

    THOMAS (Sir), who m. first, Anne, daughter
    and sole heir of Richard Bingham, Esq., of
    Lambeth, in Surrey, by whom he had an
    only daughter, ANNE, who d. young. Sir
    Thomas espoused, secondly, Jane, daughter
    of Patrick Fitz-Maurice, Lord Kerry, in
    Ireland, and dying before his father, left

        THOMAS, who succeeded his grandfather.

        Honora, m. first, to Sir W. Egerton, and
        secondly, to Hugh, Lord Willoughby,
        of Parham.

        Mary, m. to Arden Bagot, Esq., of Pipe
        Hall, in the county of Warwick.

        Jane, m. to William, Viscount Tracy.

    Charles, of Leighton, who m. twice, but sur-
    viving his children, left his estates to his
    grand-nephew, the Hon. Charles Leigh.

    Elizabeth, m. to John, Lord Tracy.

    Vere, m. to Sir Justinian Isham, of Lamport,
    Notts, Bart.

    Ursula, m. to Sir William Bromley, K.B., of
    Bagington, in the county of Warwick.

Lord Leigh d. 22nd February, 1671, and was s. by
his grandson,

THOMAS LEIGH, second baron. This nobleman m. first, Elizabeth, daughter and heir of
Richard Brown, Esq., of Shingleton, but had no
issue. He espoused, secondly, Eleanor, eldest
daughter of Edward, Lord Rockingham, by whom
he had surviving issue,

EDWARD, his successor.

    Charles, who succeeded to the estates of his
    uncle, the Hon. Charles Leigh, of Leighton,
    and m. Lady Barbara Lumley, but died s. p.
    in 1749.

    Anne, d. unmarried in 1734.

    Eleanor, m. to Thomas Verney, Esq., and d.
    in 1756.

His lordship d. in 1710, and was s. by his elder son,

EDWARD LEIGH, third baron, who espoused
Mary, only daughter and heiress of Thomas Hol-
becke, Esq., of Fillongley, in the county of Warwick, and heir also by Elizabeth, her mother, to
Bernard Paulet, Esq., by whom he had issue,

    Edward, who d. in the life-time of his father,
    anno 1737.

    THOMAS, his successor.

    Mary,

    Eleanor, } d. unmarried.
    Anne,

His lordship d. 9th March, 1737-8, and was s. by his
only surviving son,

THOMAS LEIGH, fourth baron. This noble-
man m. first, Maria-Rebecca, daughter of the Hon.
John Craven, and sister of William, fifth Lord
Craven, by whom he had surviving issue,

    EDWARD, his successor.

    Mary, d. unmarried.

His lordship espoused, secondly, Catherine, daughter of Rowland Berkeley, Esq., of Cotheridge, in
the county of Worcester, and had a daughter ANNE,
who m. Andrew Hesket, Esq. He d. 30th November, 1749, and was s. by his son,

EDWARD LEIGH, fifth baron. This nobleman
dying unmarried in 1786, the BARONY OF LEIGH,
OF STONELEIGH, is presumed to have EXPIRED.

ARMS.—Gu. a cross ingrailed ar. a lozenge in the
dexter, chief of the second.

LEIGH—BARON DUNSMORE, EARL
OF CHICHESTER.

Barony, } by Letters { 31st July, 1628.
Earldom, } Patent, { 3rd June, 1644.

Lineage.

SIR FRANCIS LEIGH, Baronet, of Newnham
Regis, in Warwickshire, was elevated to the peerage
on the 31st July, 1628, in the dignity of BARON
DUNSMORE, of Dunsmore, in the county of Warwick. His lordship espoused Audrey, daughter and
co-heir of John, Lord Butler, of Bramfield, (by
Elizabeth, sister of George Villiers, Duke of Buckingham,) and widow of Sir Francis Anderson, Knt.,
by whom he had issue,

    Elizabeth, m. to Thomas Wriothesley, Earl of
    Southampton (his lordship's second wife).

    Mary, m. to George Villiers, Viscount Grandi-
    son, in the peerage of Ireland.

Lord Dunsmore having distinguished himself by
his zeal in the royal cause during the civil wars, was
advanced, on the 3rd July, 1644, to the Earldom of
Chichester, with remainder to the Earl of Southampton, and his issue male by his lordship's above-
mentioned daughter Elizabeth. He d. 21st December, 1653, when the BARONY OF DUNSMORE

became EXTINCT, and the Earldom of Chichester devolved according to the limitation (see Wriothesley, Earl of Southampton).

ARMS.—G. a cross ingrailed, and in the first quarter a lozenge ar.

LEIGH—DUCHESS DUDLEY.

By Letters Patent, (for life only,) dated 23rd May, 1644.

(See DUDLEY, DUCHESS DUDLEY.)

LEKE — BARONS DEINCOURT, OF SUTTON, EARLS OF SCARSDALE.

Barony, } by Letters { 26th October, 1624.
Earldom, } Patent, { 11th November, 1645.

Lineage.

Upon the institution of the order of BARONET, SIR FRANCIS LEKE, Knt., of Sutton, in the county of Derby, being a person of very ancient family in those parts, and of ample fortune, was advanced to that dignity by patent, dated 22nd May, 1611, and elevated to the peerage on the 26th October, 1624, as BARON DEINCOURT, of Sutton.* His lordship taking an active part during the civil war in the royal cause, under whose banner two of his sons laid down their lives, was created by King Charles I., 11th November, 1645, EARL OF SCARSDALE. He m. Anne, daughter of Sir Edward Carey, Knt., of Berkhampstede, in the county of Hertford, and sister of Henry, Viscount Falkland, by whom he had issue, viz.

    Francis, slain in France.
    NICHOLAS, his successor.
    Edward, } fell fighting under the royal banner.
    Charles, } ner.
    Henry, d. unmarried.
    Anne, m. Henry Hillyard, Esq.
    Catherine, m. Cuthbert Morley, Esq.
    Elizabeth, } d. unmarried.
    Muriel, }
    Frances, m. the Viscount Gormanston, of Ireland.
    Penelope, m. Charles, Lord Lucas.

His lordship became so much mortified, it is said, by the murder of King Charles I., that he clothed himself in sackcloth, and causing his grave to be dug some years before his death, laid himself therein every Friday, exercising himself frequently in divine meditation and prayer. He d. in 1655, and was s. by his eldest surviving son,

NICHOLAS LEKE, second Earl of. Scarsdale, who espoused Lady Frances Rich, daughter of Robert, Earl of Warwick, and had issue,

    ROBERT, Lord Deincourt, his successor.
    Richard, who m. Mary, daughter of Sir John Molineaux, Bart., and had issue,
        NICHOLAS, who s. as fourth earl.
        Robert, d. young.
        Frances.
        Lucy.
    Mary.

His lordship d. in 1680, and was s. by his elder son,

ROBERT LEKE, third Earl of Scarsdale. This nobleman, in the reign of JAMES II., was lord-lieutenant of the county of Derby, colonel of horse, and groom of the stole to Prince George of Denmark. His lordship m. Mary, daughter and co-heir of Sir John Lewis, Bart., of Ledstone, in the county of York, by whom he had no surviving issue. He died in 1707, and was s. by his nephew,

NICHOLAS LEKE, fourth Earl of Scarsdale. This nobleman dying unmarried in 1736, the BARONY OF DEINCOURT and EARLDOM OF SCARSDALE became EXTINCT.

ARMS.—Ar. on a saltier ingrailed sa. nine annulets or.

LENNARD—EARL OF SUSSEX.

By Letters Patent, dated 5th October, 1674.

Lineage.

THOMAS LENNARD, fifteenth Baron Dacre, (see Baron Dacre, Burke's Dictionary of the Peerage and Baronetage,) was created EARL OF SUSSEX, on 5th December, 1674. His lordship m. Anne, daughter of Barbara, Duchess of Cleveland, prior to her formal separation from her husband, Roger Palmer, Earl of Castlemain, which Anne was acknowledged by King Charles II. as his natural daughter, and his majesty assigned her the royal arms, with the Batton sinister. By this lady the Earl of Sussex had two sons, who both died in infancy, and two daughters, viz.

    Barbara, who m. Lieutenant General Charles Skelton, of the French service, (eldest son of Bevil Skelton, son and heir of Sir John Skelton, Lieutenant-Governor of Plymouth, which Bevil was envoy extraordinary to the states general, temp. James II., and followed the fortunes of his fallen master into France.) Lady Barbara Skelton died without issue in 1741.
    Anne, who m. first, Richard Barrett Lennard, by whom she had an only son,
        THOMAS BARRETT LENNARD, who succeeded as seventeenth Lord Dacre.
    Lady Anne Lennard espoused, secondly, Henry, eighth Lord Teynham, by whom she had, with other children,
        CHARLES ROPER, whose son,
            TREVOR-CHARLES ROPER, succeeded as eighteenth Baron Dacre.
    Her ladyship wedded, thirdly, the Hon.

---

* This manor was acquired by the marriage of Richard de Grey, (son of William de Grey, of Landford Nolts, and Sandiacre, in Derbyshire, a younger son of Henry de Grey, of Thurrock,) with Lucy, daughter and heir of Robert de Hareston, Lord of Sutton, in the Dale; which, with divers other lordships, by issue male failing, came by a female branch to the Hilarys, who took the name of Grey; by a female heir of which line, married to Sir John Leke, in the reign of Henry IV., the same came to this family.—BANKS.

Robert Moore, son of Henry, third Earl of Drogheda, by whom she also had issue.

The Earl of Sussex, who was one of the lords of the bed-chamber, entering deeply into the dissipations of the court, considerably impaired his estate; a great part of which he was obliged at different times to dispose of, particularly the fine seat at Herstmonceaux, in Sussex. He d. in 1715, when, leaving no male issue, the EARLDOM OF SUSSEX became EXTINCT, and the Barony of Dacre fell into ABEYANCE between his daughters—but the elder, Lady Barbara Skelton, dying s. p. in 1741, the younger, Lady Anne Lennard, became then sole heiress, and BARONESS DACRE.

ARMS.—Or. on a fesse gules, three fleur de lys of the first.

LEY — BARONS LEY, OF LEY, IN THE COUNTY OF DEVON, EARLS OF MARLBOROUGH.

Barony, } by Letters { 31st December, 1625.
Earldom, } Patent, { 5th February, 1626.

Lineage.

JAMES LEY, sixth son of Henry Ley, Esq., of Teffont Evias, in the county of Wilts, having been bred to the bar, and having attained great eminence in his learned profession, was raised to the coif, in the 1st of James I., and the next year constituted chief justice of the Court of King's Bench, in Ireland. In the 17th of the same reign, his lordship then residing at Westbury, in Wilts, was created a BARONET, having previously had the honour of knighthood; and the next year was appointed chief justice of the Court of King's Bench, in England. In three years afterwards, he was constituted LORD TREASURER, and upon the last day of the same year, elevated to the peerage as BARON LEY, of Ley, in the county of Devon. In the 1st of Charles I., his lordship was created EARL OF MARLBOROUGH; and was soon after appointed president of the council. He m. first, Mary, daughter of John Pettey, Esq., of Stoke-Talmage, in the county of Oxford, and had issue,

> HENRY, his successor.
> James, who d. in 1618, unmarried.
> William, successor to his nephew.
> Elizabeth, m. to Morice Carant, Esq., of Toomer, in the county of Somerset.
> Anne, m. to Sir. William Long, of Draycot, Wilts.
> Mary, m. to Richard Erisey, Esq., of Erisey, in Cornwall.
> Dionysia, m. to John Harington, Esq., of Kelneyton, in Somersetshire.
> Margaret, m. to —— Hobson, Esq., of Hertfordshire.
> Esther, m. to Arthur Fuller, Esq., of Bradfield, Hertfordshire.
> Martha, d. unmarried.
> Phoebe, m. to —— Biggs, Esq., of Hurst, in the county of Berks.

His lordship wedded secondly, Mary, widow of Sir William Bower, Knt.; and thirdly, Jane, daughter

of John, Lord Butler, of Bramfield, but had no issue by either of these ladies.

This nobleman, who was esteemed a person of talents, and integrity, and who left behind him several learned works, both in law and history—died on the 14th March, 1628, and was s. by his eldest son,

HENRY LEY, second Earl of Marlborough, who, m. Mary, daughter of Sir Arthur Capel, of Hadham, in Hertfordshire, by whom he had a son, JAMES, his successor, and a daughter, Elizabeth, who died unmarried. His lordship was s. at his decease, by his son,

JAMES LEY, third Earl of Marlborough. This nobleman, who was an eminent mathematician and navigator, was appointed, being a naval officer, lord admiral of all his majesty's ships at Dartmouth, and parts adjacent. In 1662, he was employed in the American plantations. But in 1665, commanding "that huge ship, called the Old James, in that great fight at sea, with the Dutch, upon the 3rd June, was there slain by a cannon bullet." His lordship dying s. p., his honours reverted to his uncle,

WILLIAM LEY, fourth earl. This nobleman m. Miss Hewet, daughter of Sir William Hewet, Knt., but dying without issue, in 1679, the BARONY OF LEY, and EARLDOM OF MARLBOROUGH, became EXTINCT.

ARMS.—Ar. a chevron betw. three seal heads couped sa.

LEYBURN—BARON LEYBURN.

By Writ of Summons, dated 6th February, 1299, 27 Edward I.

Lineage.

In the 10th of Richard I., ROBERT DE LEEBURN being dead, Stephen de Turnham paid three hundred marks to the king, for the wardship and marriage of his son and heir,

ROGER DE LEIBURN. This feudal lord espousing the cause of the barons, at the commencement of the contest, in the reign of John, was made prisoner with several of his associates, at Rochester Castle, and committed to the custody of John Mareschall. In the time of Henry III., we find him first mentioned, in the 36th year of that king's reign, as slaying, presumed accidentally, but shrewdly suspected, designedly, through revenge, Sir Ernauld de Mountney, in a tournament, held at Walden, in Essex. The next year, after this unhappy affair, he attended the king in an expedition into Gascony. In the 44th of the same reign, he was constituted constable of the Castle at Bristol, but before two years elapsed, again siding with the barons, he was one of those prohibited by royal precept, to meet at any tournament, without especial licence; and soon after included in the excommunication of the Archbishop of Canterbury. Within a very short period, however, he forsook the baronial banner, (drawn off, it was said, by promised rewards,) and was made warden of the Cinque Ports. He was subsequently one of the most zealous commanders in the royal army—at the taking of the town and Castle of Northampton—in defending Rochester, when assaulted by the insurrectionary lords, where he was severely wounded, and at the battle of Lewes, for which services, after the king's restoration to power, by the victory of Evesham, he was made warden of all the forests beyond the Trent; sheriff of Cumberland and Kent, and warden of the Cinque Ports. He obtained likewise, a grant of the wardship of Idonea, younger of the two daughters and co-heirs of Robert de Vipount, a great baron in the north; and in the 50th of Henry III., joining with Robert de Clifford, the guardian of Isabel, the elder co-heir, he procured the king's pardon for those ladies, for the rebellious proceedings of their father, in the time of the grand insurrection of Montfort, Earl of Leicester, and his adherents. He was afterwards re-appointed sheriff of Cumberland and Kent, and governor of the Castle of Carlisle. This great feudal lord, m. first, Eleanore, daughter of his guardian, Stephen de Turnham; and secondly, Eleanore de Vaux, widow of Robert de Quinci, Earl of Winchester. He d. in the 56th Henry III., and was s. by his son,

WILLIAM DE LEYBURN, who, in the 10th Edward I., was in the expedition then made into Wales. In the 22d of the same reign, he was made constable of the Castle of Pevensey; and about this period, the king having concluded a league with Rodulph, King of the Romans, and sending in conformity with its provisions, an army into Gascony, this William de Leyburn was appointed admiral of the fleet, lying at Portsmouth, upon which one third of the expedition was to embark. In three years afterwards, he attended the king into Flanders; and he was summoned to parliament as a BARON, on the 6th February, 1299. His lordship was subsequently engaged in the Scottish wars. He died in 1309, leaving his grand-daughter JULIAN, (daughter of his son, Thomas de Leyburn, who had predeceased him,) his heir. This lady, afterwards, became the wife of John de Hastings, Lord Hastings, father of Laurence, first Earl of Pembroke of that family, and subsequently of William de Clinton, Earl of Huntingdon; her issue by her first husband failed, in 1389, and having none by her second marriage, the BARONY OF LEYBURN, in that year, became EXTINCT.

ARMS.—Az. six lioncels rampant ar.

LEYBURN—BARON LEYBURN.

By Writ of Summons, dated 21st June, 1337,
11 Edward III.

Lineage.

SIR JOHN DE LEYBURN, of the county of Salop, having been involved in the insurrection of Thomas, Earl of Lancaster, in the 15th Edward II., had all his lands in the county of Northumberland seized by the crown; but paying a fine in two years afterwards, he had full restitution of those estates. The next year he accompanied John de Felton in the expedition then made into Gascony: and in the 4th Edward III., upon the death of John le Strange, of Cheswardyne, in the county of Salop, he was found to be his next heir; that is, son of Lucia, sister

of the said John. In three years afterwards, he had summons to attend the king in his Scottish wars; but being prevented by some unforeseen circumstances, he obtained pardon for his absence, upon his humble petition setting forth the cause in the 9th of Edward III. The next year he was, however, in those wars. In the 19th of the same reign, being then a banneret, and residing in Shropshire, he had a military summons to attend the king into France, and the next year distinguished himself in the celebrated battle of Durham, wherein David, king of Scotland, was vanquished and made prisoner. Sir John was summoned to parliament as a BARON, from 21st June, 1337, to 14th February, 1348, in the latter of which years he died issueless, when the BARONY OF LEYBURN became EXTINCT.

LIDDELL — BARON RAVENSWORTH.

By Letters Patent, dated 29th June, 1747.

Lineage.

THOMAS DE LIDDEL, or LYDDALE, m. Margaret, daughter of John de Layburne, and was s. by his son,

THOMAS LIDDELL, Esq., an alderman of Newcastle-upon-Tyne, who m. Barbara, daughter and heiress of Richard Strangeways, Esq., and had four sons and two daughters. This gentleman acquired by purchase, in 1607, Ravensworth Castle, and other estates, in the county of Durham, in which he was s. by his eldest son,

THOMAS LIDDELL, Esq., of Ravensworth Castle, who d. in 1619, and was s. by his eldest son,

THOMAS LIDDELL, Esq., of Ravensworth Castle, who was created a baronet, on the 2nd November, 1642, in consideration of his gallant defence of Newcastle against the Scots, during the civil wars. Sir Thomas m. Isabel, daughter of Henry Anderson, Esq., and was s. at his decease, in 1650, by his grandson,

SIR THOMAS LIDDELL, second baronet. This gentleman m. Anne, daughter of Sir Henry Vane, the elder, of Raby Castle, in the county of Durham, and dying in 1697, was s. by his eldest son,

SIR HENRY LIDDELL, third baronet, who m. Catherine, daughter and heiress of Sir John Bright, of Badsworth, in the county of York, by whom he had several children. The eldest son, THOMAS, m. in 1707, Jane, eldest daughter of James Clavering, Esq., of Greencroft, in the county of Durham, and dying before his father, left a son, HENRY, who succeeded to the title; and another son, THOMAS, whose son, by Margaret, daughter of Sir William Bowes, of Gibside, HENRY-GEORGE inherited as fifth baronet. The second son of Sir Henry Lyddel having been adopted by his grandfather, Sir John Bright, assumed the surname of Bright, and was seated at Badsworth. This gentleman's son, Thomas Bright, left an only daughter and heiress, Margaret, who m. Charles-Watson Wentworth, Marquess of Rockingham.

Sir Henry Liddell d. in 1723, and was s. by his eldest son,

SIR HENRY LIDDELL, fourth baronet, who

.was elevated to the peerage, 29th June, 1747; as BARON RAVENSWORTH, *of Ravensworth Castle.* His lordship *m.* in 1735, Anne, only daughter of Sir Peter Delme, Knt., alderman and lord mayor of London, by whom he had an only daughter,

     Anne, who *m.* Augustus-Henry, Duke of Grafton, from whom she was divorced, and afterwards espoused the Earl of Upper Ossory.

His lordship *d.* in 1749, and leaving thus no male issue, the BARONY OF RAVENSWORTH became EXTINCT, while the baronetcy devolved upon his nephew, HENRY GEORGE LIDDELL, Esq., as fifth baronet.

ARMS.—Ar. a frette gu. on a chief of the second, three leopards faces or.

LIGONIER—BARON LIGONIER, OF RIPLEY, IN THE COUNTY OF SURREY, EARL LIGONIER.

Barony, } by Letters { 27th April, 1763.
Earldom, } Patent, { 10th September, 1766.

Lineage.

Of the ancient French family of *Ligonier,* the two brothers, FRANCIS and JOHN LIGONIER, members of the church of England, entered into the British military service, and attained very high distinction therein. The elder, FRANCIS, was colonel of dragoons, and in that rank fought at the battle of Falkirk, in 1745-6. To attend his duty, however, upon that occasion, he rose from a sick-bed, and died soon after the engagement, from the combined effects of disease and fatigue. A monument has been erected to his memory in Westminster Abbey. The younger brother,

· JOHN LIGONIER, having distinguished himself under the Duke of Marlborough, in Flanders, and afterwards attaining high reputation, temp. George II., in Germany, was made a KNIGHT BANNERET, under the royal standard, at the battle of Dettingen, in 1742. Sir John was created an Irish Peer, in 1757, as Viscount Ligonier, of Enniskillen, in the county of Fermanagh: and in 1762, he obtained a new patent in the same kingdom, conferring upon his lordship the Viscounty of Ligonier, of Clonmell, with remainder to his nephew, Edward Ligonier, Esq. In the next year he was made a peer of Great Britain, as BARON LIGONIER, *of Ripley, in the county of Surrey,* and created EARL OF LIGONIER, on the 10th September, 1766. His lordship, after filling the first military offices, and establishing the highest military reputation, died at the advanced age of ninety-one, 1770, and was buried in Westminster Abbey, when, leaving no issue, the BRITISH BARONY and EARLDOM OF LIGONIER, became EXTINCT. While the Irish Barony of Ligonier, of Clonmell, passed according to the patent, to (the son of his brother, Colonel Ligonier) his nephew, EDWARD LIGONIER, Esq., who married, first, Penelope, daughter of George Pitt, Lord Rivers, from whom he was divorced, and secondly, Mary, daughter of Robert, Earl of Northington,

but dying *s. p.* in 1782, the Barony of Ligonier, of Clonmell, also expired.

ARMS.—Gu. a lion rampant ar. on a chief of the second, a crescent between two mullets, az.

L'ISLE—BARONS L'ISLE.

By Writ of Summons, dated 15th December, 1347, 31 Edward III.

Lineage.

Of this surname were several families, springing originally from two; which had derived the designation, one from the Isle of Ely, the other from the Isle of Wight. This first person of rank, upon record, was,

BRYAN DE L'ISLE, who, in the beginning of King John's reign, paid one hundred and twenty marks, and a palfrey, for the wardship and marriage of the heir of William Briston; and in a few years afterwards, married Maud, daughter and heiress of Thomas, son of William de Saleby. This Bryan adhering to King John in his dispute with the barons, was reputed one of the evil advisers of the crown. He was governor of Bolsover Castle, in the county of Derby, and a principal commander of the royal army raised in Yorkshire. At that time King John conferred upon him the lands of the Barons, Robert de Percy, and Peter de Plumpton. In the reign of Henry III., remaining stedfast to the cause he had espoused, he had a command at the siege of Montsorel, and the subsequent battle of Lincoln. In the 5th of Henry, he was made warden of all the forests throughout England: and he was afterwards sheriff of Yorkshire. He *d.* about the 18th Henry III., possessed of the manor of Brianston, otherwise Blandford Brian, in the county of Dorset—"which," says Hutchins, in his history of that shire, "is called Brientius town, by Camden; and very properly derived its additional denomination of Brian, from Brian de Insula, of L'Isle, its ancient lord."

"I now come (says Dugdale) to WARINE DE L'ISLE, son of Robert, son of Alice, daughter of Henry, a younger son of Warine Fitzgerald, as the descent sheweth." Which Warine was in the Scottish wars, temp. Edward I., and in the beginning of Edward II.'s reign, was constituted governor of Windsor Castle, and warden of the forest. For years subsequently, he was engaged in Scotland, but joining Thomas, Earl of Lancaster, against the Spencers, 14th Edward II., and sharing in the discomfiture of his chief, he was taken prisoner, and hanged at York, with the Lord Mowbray, and several others. After which, it was found in the 1st Edward III., that he died seised of the manors of Bouden, Kingston, and Fanfiore, in Berks; Mundiford, in Norfolk; and Kistingbury, in Northamptonshire; leaving Gerard, his son, twenty-three years of age, and Alice, his wife, sister and heir of Henry, Baron Tayes, surviving, which

GERARD DE L'ISLE, having become eminent in the Scotch and French wars of Edward III., was summoned to parliament as a BARON, by the designation of "Gerardo de Insula," on the 15th Decembber, 1347, but never afterwards. His lordship d. in 1360, and was s. by his son,

WARINE DE L'ISLE, second baron, summoned to parliament from 6th April, 1369, to 24th May, 1368. This nobleman, like his father, participated in the great martial achievements of King Edward III. In the 1st of Richard II. he was also in the wars of France—and in two years afterwards he went to Ireland. From King Edward he obtained licence to make a castle of his house at Shirbourne, in the county of Oxford. His lordship m. Margaret, daughter of William Pipard, by whom he left, at his decease in 1381, an only daughter,

    Margaret de L'Isle, who m. Thomas, Lord Berkeley, and had an only daughter and heiress,

        Elizabeth Berkeley, who m. Richard Beauchamp, twelfth Earl of Warwick, by whom she had three daughters, her co-heirs, viz.

           Margaret, second wife of John Talbot, first Earl of Shrewsbury.

           Eleanor, m. first, to Thomas, Lord Ros, and secondly, to Edmund, Duke of Somerset.

           Elizabeth, m. to George Nevill, Lord Latimer.

Amongst the representatives of which descendants of Margaret de L'Isle, the BARONY OF L'ISLE, is presumed to be now in ABEYANCE.

ARMS.—Gu. a lion passant ar. crowned or.

L'ISLE — BARONS DE L'ISLE, OF ROUGEMONT.

By Writ of Summons, dated 19th December, 1311, 5 Edward II.

Lineage.

ROBERT DE L'ISLE, of Rougemont, in the county of Bedford, having married Rohese de Tatshall, widow of Robert de Tatshall, and daughter and co-heir* of John de Wahull, feudal Lord of Wahull, (now Wodhull,) in the county of Bedford, had livery of the lands of her inheritance upon paying his relief in the 1st Henry III., at which period he had restitution of his own estates, in the counties of Lincoln, Kent, York, Norfolk, and Suffolk, which had been seised by the crown in the preceding reign during the baronial contest. After this feudal lord came another,

ROBERT DE L'ISLE, who, in the 48th of Henry III., was constituted governor of the castles of Marlborough and Lutgareshull: and the next year taking part with the barons, was made by them governor of Newcastle-upon-Tyne. "From this Robert," says Dugdale, "I must make a large leap to another,"

ROBERT DE L'ISLE, who was summoned to parliament, as a BARON, from 19th December, 1311, to 25th February, 1342. This nobleman was in the expedition made, 13th Edward III., into Flanders, but he subsequently took holy orders, having,

---

* AGNES WAHUL, the other daughter and co-heir, married Robert de Bassingham.

316

before doing so, settled the manors of Rampton, Cotenham, West-Wike, with the advowson of the church of Winpole, in the county of Cambridge, upon Alice, daughter of Robert de L'Isle, Elizabeth Peverell, and Richard Bayeaux, for life, with remainder to John, son of Robert de L'Isle, and his heirs. He was also then seised of the manors of Hayford-Warin, in Oxfordshire, and Pishiobury, in Hertfordshire. His lordship d. in 1342, and was s. by his son,

JOHN DE L'ISLE, second baron, summoned to parliament as "Johanni de Insulâ de Rubeo Monte," from 25th November, 1350, to 15th December, 1357. This nobleman, in the 19th of Edward III., had obtained a grant from his father of the manor of HARWOOD, in the county of York, valued at four hundred marks per annum, to enable him the better to serve the king in his wars. In three years subsequently he was in the English army, then drawn up to encounter the French at Vironfosse—and we find him soon after engaged in an expedition made into Gascony. In the 16th of the same reign he was one of the commanders at the siege of Nantes. In the 18th he was again in Gascony, and in the 20th he had a pension from the king of £200 per annum, to be paid out of the exchequer, to enable him to sustain his rank of BANNERET. It is said by some, that in the 20th Edward III., Sir Thomas Dagworth, Knt., with eighty men at arms, and a hundred archers, worsting Charles de Bloys, and the great men of Britanny, who had a thousand horse, the king thereupon made two barons, viz., Alan Zouche, and John L'Isle, as also fifty knights; but others affirm, that this was at the battle of CRESSY, which happened the same year. John L'Isle was, however, so highly esteemed by King Edward III. for his courage and martial prowess, that he was made one of the Knights Companions of the GARTER, at the institution of that order. He subsequently obtained from the crown a grant for life of the sheriffalty of the counties of Cambridge and Huntingdon, with the governorship of the castle of Cambridge: and the year before he died (29th Edward III.,) he was again with Prince Edward in the wars of France. His lordship d. in 1356, and was s. by his son,

ROBERT L'ISLE, third baron, who was summoned to parliament as LORD L'ISLE, of Rougemont, on 20th November, 1360, but never afterward: and of his lordship or his descendants nothing further is known.

ARMS.—Gu. a lion passant guardant or, crowned ar.

LONGESPEE — EARL OF SALISBURY.

(See D'Evereux, Earl of Salisbury.)

LONGVILLIERS — BARON LONGVILLIERS.

By Writ of Summons, dated 25th February, 1342, 16 Edward III.

Lineage.

In the 25th Edward I.

JOHN DE LONGVILLIERS died, seised of

the manors of Cokesford, in the county of Notts, and Glossborne, in Yorkshire, and was *s.* by his brother,

THOMAS DE LONGVILLIERS, who had summons to parliament, as a baron, on 25th February, 1342, but never afterwards. His lordship died in 1374, when the BARONY OF LONGVILLIERS became EXTINCT. According to Dugdale, his lordship left an only sister, AGNES, wife of Robert, son of Ralph Cromwell, his next heir. Under the head of Everingham, however, the same authority states, that Agnes, daughter of John Longvilliers, married Reginald de Everingham. And Collins says, that Agnes, the wife of Everingham, was daughter and co-heir of Sir John Longvillers, whose sister, Elizabeth, was mother of Stephen Maulovel, whose daughter and heir, Elizabeth, espoused John de Stanhope, ancestor of the Earls of Chesterfield.

ARMS.—Sa. a bend between six cross crosslets ar.

L'ORTI—BARON L'ORTI.

By Writ of Summons, dated 6th February, 1299, 27 Edward I.

Lineage.

In the 6th of Henry III.,

HENRY DE ORTRAI, (which is the same with *L'Orti*, or *De Urtiao*,) having married Sabina, daughter and heir of Richard Revel, (a person of great note in the west, viz., sheriff of the counties of Devon and Cornwall, from the 7th to the end of King Richard I.'s reign,) and of Mabel, his wife, sister and heir of Walter de Esselegh, of Esselegh, in the county of Wilts, had livery of the lands of the inheritance of the said Sabina, and in some years afterwards obtained licence to impark his woods in the county of Somerset, so that he might be free of any regard of the king's forests. He *d.* in 1241, and was *s.* by his son,

HENRY L'ORTI, who, having been engaged in the Welch and French wars, was summoned to parliament, as a BARON, on the 6th February, 1299. His lordship was *s.* at his decease by his son,

JOHN L'ORTI, second baron, but never summoned to parliament. This nobleman left, at his decease, two daughters, viz.

Sybil, wife of Sir Lawrence de St. Martin.

Margaret, wife of Henry de Esturmie.

Amongst whose descendants and representatives the BARONY OF L'ORTI is now in ABEYANCE.

ARMS.—Vert a pale or.

LOVEL—BARON LOVEL, OF KARY.

By Writ of Summons, dated 20th November, 1348, 22 Edward III.

Lineage.

The first of this family that came into England was

ROBERT, Lord of Breherval, &c., in Normandy, (where he likewise held the castle of Yvery, by the service of three knights' fees,) a younger son, as it is said, of Eudes, sovereign Duke of Britanny. This nobleman accompanied the Conqueror in 1066, and was rewarded with the lordships of Kary and Harpetre, in the county of Somerset; but returning into Normandy, and being there attacked by a severe illness, he became a monk in the abbey of Bec, and died soon after, about the year 1083, leaving three sons, of whom the eldest,

ASCELIN GOUEL DE PERCEVAL, succeeded his father. This feudal lord, like his predecessor, held a distinguished place in the Norman army of the conquest, and for his services had a grant of divers manors, particularly of Weston and Stawel, in the county of Somerset. He was a man of violent temper, and hence acquired the surname of LUPUS, or the Wolf. *Odericus Vitalis* gives the particulars of a long and extraordinary dispute which this Ascelin had with the Earl of Bretevil, in Normandy, and which terminated by his obtaining his own terms, after sustaining a siege of two months in his castle of Breherval, against a powerful army, commanded by the ablest captains of the age—which terms included the retention of the fortress, and the hand of Isabella, the Earl of Bretevil's only daughter, in marriage. This lady, although illegitimate, upon the failure of the earl's legitimate issue, became, through the favour of Henry I., heir in part to her father, and her husband ASCELIN was established in the Earldom of Yvery in 1119. The issue of the marriage were seven sons, and a daughter, married to Radulfus Rufus, a noble Norman. Of the sons, three alone have been handed down to us, namely, ROBERT, William, and John, whereof the youngest, John, acquired from his father the manor of Harpetré, and assumed that as a surname, but it was afterwards changed by his descendants to GOURNAY. Ascelin died soon after his accession to the Earldom of Yvery, and was *s.* by his eldest son,

ROBERT, Earl of Yvery, who died *s. p.* in 1121, and was *s.* in his Norman and English estates by his brother,

WILLIAM, Earl of Yvery. This nobleman was nicknamed *Lupellus*, or the little wolf, which designation was softened into *Lupel*, and thence to LUVEL, and became the surname of most of his descendants. He defended his castle of Kary in 1153 against King Stephen, but died in two years afterwards. He *m.* Auberic, sister of Walleran de Bellemonte, Earl of Mellent, in Normandy, and had five sons, namely,

WALERAN, who succeeded to the Norman dominions, and was Baron of Yvery, but the title of earl never, subsequently, occurs. His line continued until the fifteenth century.

RALPH, of whom presently.

Henry, successor to his brother Ralph.

William, ancestor of the Lovels, of Tichmersh, &c.

Richard, who retained the original surname of PERCEVAL, and from him descend the Percevals, Earls of Egmont; the second son having adopted the surname of Lovel, and inherited the estate of Castle Kary, became

RALPH LOVEL, Lord of Castle, of Kary. He *m.* Maud, daughter of Henry de Newmarch, but dying without issue, was *s.* by his brother,

HENRY LOVEL. This feudal lord, upon the collection of the scutazoon, 5th Henry II., paid five marks; and in seven years after, upon the assessment in aid of marrying the king's daughter, certified his knight's fees, de veteri feoffamento, to be eighteen, and de novo, one. In the 22nd Henry II. he was amerced for trespassing in the king's forests at a hundred marks. He d. before the year 1199, and was s. by his son and heir,

RALPH LOVEL, who, in the 1st year of King John, paid sixty pounds for livery of his Barony of Kary, and afterwards bestowed the lands of Ethelberge on the monks of Montacute. He d. in 1207 without issue, and was s. by his brother,

HENRY LOVEL. This feudal lord, in the 13th King John, gave three hundred marks, and seven good palfries, for permission to go into Ireland. He d. in 1218, and was s. by his son,

RICHARD LOVEL, who, in the 2nd Henry III., giving £100 as a security for payment of his relief, had livery of his Barony of Kary, and all his other lands in Somersetshire. In the 26th of the same king he paid a fine of fifteen marks to be exempted from going into Gascony, and in twelve years afterwards, upon the collection of the aid for making the king's eldest son a knight, he answered for eleven knights' fees and a half for the honour of Moreton. He died in this latter year, (1253,) and was s. by his son,

HENRY LOVEL, who, the ensuing year, paid £100 for his relief, and had livery of his lands: but enjoyed the estates only a short period. He d. in 1262, then seised of the manor of Castle Kary, held in capite from the crown, by barony, and the service of finding two soldiers in the king's army at his own charge for forty days, and was s. by his elder son,

RICHARD LOVEL. This feudal lord died s. p. the year after his father, and was s. by his brother,

HENRY LOVEL, who died about the year 1280, leaving a daughter, Oliva, m. to John de Gournay, and his successor,

HUGH LOVEL, against whom his brother-in-law, John de Gournay, instituted a suit at law in the time of Edward I. for the fortune of his wife, Oliva: which fortune, in the 8th of that reign, the said Hugh entered into a stipulation to pay. He d. in 1291, and was s. by his son,

SIR RICHARD LOVEL, who, in the 9th Edward III., in conjunction with Muriel, his wife, had the custody of the castles of Corf and Purbeck, in the county of Dorset, and was summoned to parliament as a BARON from 20th November, 1348, to 25th November, 1350. His lordship m. Muriel, daughter of William, first Earl Douglas, in Scotland, and had issue,

> JAMES, who predeceased the baron, anno 1342, leaving issue,
>
>> Richard, who d. in the same year issueless.
>>
>> MURIEL, m. to Sir Nicholas de St. Maur, Lord St. Maur.
>
> Joan, m. to John de Moels.
> Elianore, m. to Sir Roger Ruhaut.

Lord Lovel d. in 1351, seised of the manor of Winfred Egle, in the county of Dorset, and of Castle
318

Kary and Mersh, in the county of Somerset. Upon the decease of his lordship the BARONY OF LOVEL, OF CASTLE KARY, and his estates, devolved upon his grand-daughter, MURIEL LOVEL, who conveyed them to the family of her husband, Nicholas, Lord St. Maur (see St. Maur.)

ARMS.—Or. seme of cross crosslets, a lion rampant, az.

LOVEL—BARONS LOVEL, OF TICHMERSH, IN THE COUNTY OF NORTHAMPTON, VISCOUNT LOVEL.

Barony, by Writ of Summons, dated 26th Jan., 1297, 25 Edward I.
Viscounty, by Letters Patent, dated 4th Jan., 1483.

Lineage.

This branch of the family of Lovel was founded by WILLIAM LOVEL, fourth son of William, Earl of Yvery, in Normandy, and brother of Ralph and Henry Lovel, feudal lords of Castle Kary. This William, who was lord of Minster Lovel, in the county of Oxford, died previously to the year 1196, and was s. by his son,

WILLIAM LOVEL, who, in the 13th John, held Dockinges by barony. He was s. by his son,

JOHN LOVEL, Lord of Dockinges, and of Minster Lovel. This feudal baron was a minor at the period of his father's decease, and under the guardianship of Alan Basset, of Mursdewall and Wycombe, in Surrey, whose daughter, Aliva, by Aliva, daughter of Stephen Gay, he eventually espoused, (as was frequently the case in those times,) and settled upon her the manor of Minster Lovel. On his marriage he quitted the ancient coat of arms of his own family, and assumed that of the Bassets, the colours only changed from as and sa. to or. and gules. He had issue,

> JOHN, his successor.
>
> Philip, who, in the 25th Henry III., being then guardian to the Jews, was charged with great bribery, in taking plate of much value to exempt some of them from the tallage then imposed, and he incurred thereby the high displeasure of the king. He made his peace, however, and through powerful interest at court got off with a fine of a thousand marks. He was, subsequently, so well established in royal favour that he was constituted treasurer of England. But in the 43d of the same reign, the barons caused him to be brought to trial for the offence abovementioned, and had him removed from the treasurership: he was likewise subjected to a heavy penalty, and his estates were seised by the crown, until that penalty should be discharged. This persecution so affected him that he is supposed to have died in the following year, 1258, of grief and vexation, at his rectory (having taken orders,) at Hamestable. He is stated to have married, before, of course, he became a priest, the widow of Alexander de Aric, and had two sons,

John (Sir), who left an only daughter and heiress.

    Margaret, who m. Thomas de Botetourt.

Henry, a priest.

Fulco, Archdeacon of Colchester.

Agnes, m. to Adam de Chetwynd, ancestor of the Viscounts Chetwynd, of Ireland.

William Lovel was s. at his decease by his eldest son,

JOHN LOVEL, who in the 41st Henry III., had a military summons to march against the Welsh, and in four years afterwards was constituted sheriff of the counties of Cambridge and Huntingdon. In the 48th of the same reign he was made governor of the castle of Northampton, and subsequently governor of Marlborough Castle. He espoused Maud Sydenham, a great heiress, by whom he acquired the lordship of Tichmersh, and had issue,

    JOHN (Sir), his successor.

    Thomas (Sir), of Tickwell.

He d. in 1286, and was s. by his elder son,

SIR JOHN LOVEL, who performing his fealty had livery of his lands in the year of his father's decease. In the 22d Edward I. Sir John attended the king in his wars in Gascony, and was summoned to parliament as BARON LOVEL on 26th January, 1297, and afterwards as Baron Lovel, OF TICHMERSH. His lordship was subsequently engaged in the Scottish wars, and deserved so well for his services there, that he was rewarded with a licence from the king, 31st Edward I., permitting him to make a castle of his house at Tichmersh, also for a market to be held there weekly, and a fair annually. He m. first, Isabel, daughter of Ernald de Bois, of Thorpe Ernald, and sister and heir of William de Bois, by whom he had an only daughter,

    Maud, m. to William, Lord Zouch, of Haryngworth, and, as heir to her mother, carried with her the manor of Dockinges, which had been settled on that lady.

His lordship espoused, secondly, Joan, daughter of Robert, Lord Roos, of Hamlake, and had two sons, viz.

    JOHN, his successor.

    James, who left a son,

        Sir Ralph Lovel, Knt.

Lord Lovel died 1311, and was s. by his elder son,

JOHN LOVEL, second Baron, summoned to parliament, as LORD LOVEL, OF TICHMERSH, from 8th January, 1313, to 29th July, 1314. His lordship m. Maud, daughter of Sir Philip Burnell, Knt., and sister and heir of Edward, Lord Burnell, by whom he had an only son, his successor at his decease, in 1314,

JOHN LOVEL, third Baron, but never summoned to parliament. This nobleman was engaged for several years in the wars of Scotland and France, temp. Edward III. His lordship is said to have married, Isabel, daughter of William, Lord Zouch, but the fact is doubtful; he had issue, however,

    JOHN, his successor.

    JOHN, successor to his brother.

    Isabella, m. to Thomas Greene.

His lordship d. in 1347, and was s. by his elder son,

JOHN LOVEL, fourth Baron, who dying in minority, issueless, anno 1361, was s. by his brother,

JOHN LOVEL, fifth Baron, summoned to parliament as LORD LOVEL, OF TICHMERSH, from 29th December, 1375, to 26th August, 1407. This nobleman, in the 42d Edward III., being then a knight, was in the wars of France, and of the retinue of Lionel, Duke of Clarence; he continued in this service for some years, and was constituted governor of the Castle of Banelyngbam, in France. In the reign of Richard III., when the influence exercised by Robert de Vere, Duke of Ireland, caused so much discontent amongst the nobility, he at first espoused the populace-side, but afterwards going over to the king, he was one of those expelled the court by the confederated lords. His lordship, who was a Knight of the Garter, m. Maud, daughter* and heir of Robert de Holand, Lord Holand, and dying in 1408, (in his testament, he styles himself, Lord Lovel and Holand,) was s. by his only son,

SIR JOHN LOVEL, BARON HOLAND, in right of his mother, and summoned to parliament as LORD LOVEL, of TICHMERSH, from 20th October, 1409, to 26th September, 1414. This nobleman espoused, Alianore, daughter of William, Lord Zouch, of Haryworth, and had issue,

    WILLIAM, his successor.

    William, m. Elizabeth, daughter and co-heir of Thomas St. Clere, of Barton St. John, in the county of Oxford.

His lordship died in 1414, and was s. by his elder son,

SIR WILLIAM LOVEL, BARON LOVEL AND HOLAND, summoned to parliament, from 24th February, 1425, to 20th January, 1453. This nobleman was engaged in the French wars of King Henry V. His lordship m. Alice, widow of Ralph Butler, of Sudley, and daughter and eventual heir of John, Lord Deincourt, by Johanna, daughter and sole heir of Robert, Lord Grey, of Rotherfield, by which alliance the Baronies of DEINCOURT and GREY, OF ROTHERFIELD, became united with those of LOVEL AND HOLAND. Of this marriage there were issue,

    JOHN, his successor.

    William, m. Alianore, daughter and heir of Robert, Lord Morley, and was summoned to parliament, as LORD MORLEY. (See Lovel, Baron Morley.)

    Robert died s. p.

    William.

His lordship d. in 1454, and was s by his elder son,

SIR JOHN LOVEL, Baron Lovel and Holand, summoned to parliament, from 9th October, 1459, to 28th February, 1463. This nobleman, in consideration of his good services, obtained a patent from the king, 38th Henry VI., appointing him chief forester of the forest of Whichwoode, in the county of Northampton; but before the end of that year, the face of public affairs suddenly changed: for upon the landing of the Duke of York, this

---

* This lady, in the printed pedigrees produced before the House of Lords, in a committee of privileges, on the claim of the late Sir Cetil Bishop, to the Barony of Zouch, is called the grand-daughter and heir of Robert, Lord Holand.

John, Lord Lovel, proceeding to London, with the Lords Scales and Hungerford, for the purpose of raising the good citizens in favour of King Henry, was forced to take refuge in the Tower, as a place of security. Soon after which, the Yorkists prevailed in all parts of the kingdom, to the total ruin of the unfortunate Henry, and his faithful adherents. Of this nobleman, nothing further is related, than his death, which happened in the 4th of Edward IV., being then seised among divers other considerable lordships, of the Manors of Minster Lovel, in the county of Oxford; Bainton, otherwise Deincourts Manor, in Yorkshire; Tichmersh, Northamptonshire; Holgate Burnell, and Acton Burnell, in Shropshire; and likewise of the moiety of the Manor of Askham-Bryan, in the county of the city of York. His lordship had married Joane, only sister and heir of William, Viscount Beaumont, by whom he had issue,

FRANCIS, his successor.

Joane, who m. Sir Brian Stapleton, of Carlton, Knt., and from her lineally descended,

GILBERT STAPLETON, who left issue,

Richard, died s. p.

Gregory, a monk, died s. p.

Miles, created a BARONET, and had two daughters, both of whom died in infancy; died himself, in 1707.

John, died s. p., in 1644.

Mary, a nun, died in 1668.

ANNE, m. to Mark Errington, Esq., of Conteland, and her son,

NICHOLAS took the name of STAPLETON, and left a son,

NICHOLAS STAPELTON, whose son,

THOMAS STAPLETON, Esq., of Carleton, claimed the BARONY OF BEAUMONT, in 1798, when the House of Lords came to a resolution, that the BARONY OF BEAUMONT remains in ABEYANCE, between the co-heirs of William, Viscount Beaumont, (in whom it was vested by descent, from his father, John, Lord Beaumont, who was summoned to and sat in parliament, 2nd Henry VI., as a barony in fee;) descended from his lordship's sister, Joane, and that the petitioner is one of these co-heirs."

Fridiswide, m. to Sir Edward Norris, Knt., and had issue,

John Norris, Esq., of the body to King Henry VIII., d. without legitimate issue.

HENRY NORRIS, who fell a sacrifice to the suspicious temper of Henry VIII., and under the charge of a criminal intercourse with the unhappy Queen, Anne Boleyn, was tried, condemned, and executed, 14th May, 28th Henry VIII. Mr. Norris being attainted, it is presumed, that the moiety of the Barony of Beaumont, to which he was heir, became vested in the crown. From this Henry Norris, descends the present EARL OF ABINGDON.

His lordship was s. by his son,

SIR FRANCIS LOVEL, ninth Baron, summoned to parliament as such, on the 15th November, 1482, and created on the 4th January, 1483, VISCOUNT LOVEL. This nobleman being in high favour with King Richard III., was made, by that monarch, chamberlain of the household, constable of the Castle of Wallingford, and chief butler of England. He subsequently fought under the banner of his royal master, at Bosworth, and was fortunate enough to escape with life, from the field; whence flying to St. John's, at Colchester, he there, for some time, took sanctuary, but deeming that no place of permanent security, he removed privately, to Sir John Broughton's house, in Lancashire, and thence effected his escape into Flanders, where he was graciously received by Margaret, Duchess of Burgundy, the late king's sister; by whom, with two thousand soldiers, under the conduct of the eminent German General, Martin Swarts, he was sent into Ireland, to uphold the pretensions of Lambert Simnell, and thence invading England, his lordship is said to have fallen at the battle of Stoke, in 1487. That circumstance, however, admits of doubt, for after the battle, he was certainly seen endeavouring, on horseback, to swim the river Trent; yet from this period, no further mention is made of him, by any of our historians. A rumour prevailed, that he had, for the time, preserved his life, by retiring into some secret place, and that he was eventually starved to death, by the treachery or negligence of those in whom he had confided. Which report, (says Banks,) in later days seems to be confirmed by a very particular circumstance, related in a letter from William Cowper, Esq., Clerk of the Parliament, concerning the supposed finding of the body of Francis, Lord Lovel, viz.

"Hertingfordbury Park, 9th August, 1737.

"Sir,

"I met t'other day with a memorandum I had made some years ago, perhaps not unworthy of notice. You may remember, that Lord Bacon, in his history of Henry VII., giving an account of the battle of Stoke, says of the Lord Lovell, who was among the rebels, that he fled and swame over the Trent on horseback, but could not recover the further side, by reason of the steepness of the bank, and so was drowned in the river. But another report leaves him not there, but that he lived long after, in a cave or vault.

"Apropos to this; on the 6th May, 1728, the present Duke of Rutland related in my hearing, that about twenty years then before, viz., in 1708, upon occasion of new laying a chimney at Minster Luvel, then was discovered a large vault underground, in which was the entire skeleton of a man, as having been sitting at a table, which was before him, with a book, paper, pen, &c.; in another part of the room lay a cap, all much mouldered and decayed. Which the family and others judged to be this Lord Lovel, whose exit has hitherto been so uncertain."

From hence, (continues Banks) it may be concluded, that it was the fate of this unhappy lord, to have retired to his own house after the battle, and there to have entrusted himself to some servant, by whom he was immured, and afterwards neglected, either through treachery, fear, or some accident which befel that person. A melancholy period to the life and fortunes of one of the greatest and most active nobleman of the era wherein he had lived.

To complete the tragedy, King Henry VII., aspiring after the vast inheritance of this family, confiscated, by an act of attainder, the whole estate, then inferior to few or none in the kingdom; and which, by grants at different times from Henry VIII. to James I., has passed to the families of Compton, Earls of Northampton; Cecil, Earls of Salisbury, and other great houses now existing. Under this attainder, the BARONIES OF LOVEL, OF HOLAND, OF DEINCOURT, and OF GREY OF ROTHERFIELD, fell, and could not be inherited by his lordship's sisters and co-heirs; but those ladies became heirs to their maternal uncle, William, Viscount Beaumont, which, as already stated, continues in ABEYANCE amongst their descendants.

ARMS.—Barry nebule of six or. and gu.

Note.—The title of Baron Lovell, of Minster Lovell, in the county of Oxford, was revived in the person of Sir Thomas Coke, (maternal ancestor of the present T. W. Coke, Esq., of Holkham), in 1728, but expired with that nobleman for want of a male heir.

The Barony of Lovell and Holland was conferred in 1762, upon John Perceval, second Earl of Egmont, in Ireland, the representative of RICHARD PERCEVAL, youngest son of William, Earl of Yvery, and brother of the founders of the houses of LOVEL OF CASTLE KARY, and LOVEL OF TICHMERSH (see Lovel of Castle Kary).

LOVEL—BARONS MORLEY.

By Writ of Summons, dated 29th December, 1299, 28 Edward I.

See MORLEY, BARONS MORLEY.

LOVELACE — BARONS LOVELACE, OF HURLEY, IN THE COUNTY OF BERKS.

By Letters Patent, dated 31st May, 1627.

Lineage.

SIR RICHARD LOVELACE, Knt., son of Richard Lovelace, Esq., of Hurley, (which place had been a religious house of Benedictine monks, and a cell to Westminster Abbey) was elevated to the peerage, 31st May, 1627, as BARON LOVELACE, of Hurley. His lordship m. first, Katherine, daughter of George Hill, Esq., and widow of William Hide, Esq., of Kingston L'Isle, Berks, but had no issue. He espoused, secondly, Margaret, only daughter and heir of William Dodsworth, citizen of London, and had two sons and two daughters, viz.,

JOHN, his successor.

Francis, whose son,

> William, m. Mary, daughter of William King, Esq., of Iver, Bucks, and left a son, JOHN, who inherited as fourth baron.

Elizabeth, m. to Henry, son and heir of Sir Henry Martin, Knt.

Martha, m. to Sir George Stonehouse, Bart.

His lordship d. in 1670, and was s. by his son,

JOHN LOVELACE, second baron, who m. Lady Anne Wentworth, daughter of Thomas, Earl of Cleveland, (which lady, upon the decease of her niece, Henrietta-Maria Wentworth, Baroness Wentworth, in 1686, succeeded to that BARONY,) and had issue,

JOHN, his successor.

Anne, d. unmarried.

Margaret, m. to Sir William Noel, Bart., of Kirby-Malory, in the county of Leicester, and her great grandson,

> SIR EDWARD NOEL, Bart., eventually succeeded in her right to the BARONY OF WENTWORTH.

Dorothy, m. to Henry, son of Sir Henry Drax, Knt.

His lordship d. in 1670, and was s. by his son,

JOHN LOVELACE, third baron. This nobleman, an early and zealous promoter of the Revolution, was in the habit of assembling the leading friends of that measure, in a vault beneath the hall of his splendid mansion at Lady Place, in Berkshire; a council chamber into which he had afterwards the pleasure of introducing King William, when that monarch honoured him with a visit. His lordship was captain of the band of pensioners. He lived in so much splendour and profuseness, however, that a great portion of his estates came to the hammer, under a decree of the Court of Chancery. He m. Margery, one of the daughters and co-heirs of Sir Edmund Pye, Bart., of Bradenham, in the county of Bucks, by whom he had several children, one of whom only survived himself, viz.,

> MARTHA, who, upon the decease of her grandmother, ANNE, Lady Wentworth, and Dowager Lady Lovelace, (who survived her son, Lord Lovelace,) succeeded to the Barony of Wentworth. Her ladyship m. Sir Henry Johnson, an opulent ship-builder, but died without issue, in 1745, when the BARONY OF WENTWORTH passed to her kinsman, Sir Edward Noel (refer to Margaret, daughter of the second lord).

His lordship d. before his mother, Lady Wentworth, in 1693, when the Barony of Lovelace passed to his cousin (refer to the second son of first lord),

JOHN LOVELACE, fourth baron, who m. Charlotte, daughter of Sir John Clayton, Knt., by whom he left two surviving sons, John and Nevil. His lordship was governor of New York, and died in his government, 6th May, 1709, when he was s. by his elder son,

JOHN LOVELACE, fifth baron, who survived his father but a fortnight, when the barony devolved upon his only brother,

NEVIL LOVELACE, sixth baron. This nobleman d. in 1736, without issue, when the BARONY OF LOVELACE OF HURLEY, became EXTINCT.

ARMS.—Gu. on a chief indented a. three martlets, ar.

LOWTHER.— VISCOUNTS LONSDALE.

By Letters Patent, dated 28th May, 1696.

Lineage.

The family of LOWTHER is of great antiquity in the counties of Westmorland and Cumberland, having been seated at Lowther-Hall in the former, from a period too remote to be specified.

SIR RICHARD LOWTHER, Knt., was sheriff of Cumberland in the 8th and the 30th years of Queen Elizabeth. He succeeded his uncle, Henry, Lord Scroop, as warden of the west marches, and was thrice commissioner in the great affairs between England and Scotland in the same reign; when Mary, of Scotland, seeking safety in England, arrived at Workington, in May, 1568, Sir Richard, being then sheriff, was directed to convey the Scottish Queen to Carlisle Castle; but while the princess remained in his custody the sheriff incurred the displeasure of Elizabeth, by permitting the Duke of Norfolk to visit his fair prisoner. Sir Richard d. in 1607, and was s. by his eldest son,

SIR CHRISTOPHER LOWTHER, Knt., who was father of

SIR JOHN LOWTHER, M.P. for the county of Westmorland, in the reigns of James I. and Charles I. He d. in 1637, and was s. by his eldest son,

SIR JOHN LOWTHER, who was created a baronet of Nova Scotia in 1640, and was s. at his decease in 1675 by his grandson,

SIR JOHN LOWTHER, second baronet. This gentleman was the thirty-first knight of the family, in almost regular succession. He was returned to parliament by the county of Westmorland in 1675, and he continued to represent that shire so long as he remained a commoner. At the accession of King William, Sir John was sworn of the privy council. In 1689 he was constituted lord lieutenant of Westmorland and Cumberland; in 1690 appointed first commissioner of the treasury, and elevated to the peerage 28th May, 1696, in the dignities of *Baron Lowther, of Lowther, in the county of Westmorland,* and VISCOUNT LONSDALE. In 1699 he was made lord privy seal; and was twice one of the lords justices for the government of the kingdom during his majesty's absence. His lordship m. Catherine, daughter of Sir Frederick Thynne, and sister of Thomas, Viscount Weymouth, by whom he had issue,

338

RICHARD, } successors in turn to the vis-
HENRY,   } county.

Anthony, a commissioner of the revenue in Ireland, d. unmarried in 1741.

Mary, m. to Sir John Wentworth, Bart., of North-Elmsal and Broadsworth, Yorkshire.

Jane, d. unmarried.

Margaret, m. to Sir Joseph Pennington, Bart., of Muncaster, in Cumberland.

Barbara, m. to Thomas, son and heir of William Howard, Esq., of Corby, in Cumberland.

The viscount d. 8th July, 1700, and was s. by his eldest son,

RICHARD LOWTHER, second viscount Lonsdale, who died of the small-pox, the same year that he had attained his majority, (1713,) and being unmarried, was s. by his brother,

HENRY LOWTHER, third Viscount Lonsdale. Of this nobleman, Banks thus speaks: " If considered in his attachment to the protestant succession, his love to the king, and his readiness to cooperate with his ministers whenever he thought them right, he was *a perfect courtier.* But if we regard his constant adherence to the interest of his country, his contempt of honours, and advantage to himself, and his steady opposition to every measure which he considered detrimental to the public, then *he was, indeed, a patriot.* Beloved by his friends, respected even by his enemies, he was in the senate honoured with attention from both: courted by all parties, he enlisted with none, but preserved through life a remarkable independency. These public virtues arose from the excellence of his private disposition, from the benevolence of his heart, from the uprightness of his intentions, from his great parts, and uncommon penetration." His lordship d. unmarried 12th May, 1750-1, when the *Barony of Lowther* and VISCOUNTY OF LONSDALE became EXTINCT: while the estates and baronetcy devolved upon his kinsman, and heir at law,

JAMES LOWTHER, Esq., as fifth baronet, (see Lowther, Earl of Lonsdale).

ARMS.—Or. six annulets three, two, and one, sa.

LOWTHER—EARL OF LONSDALE.

By Letters Patent, dated 24th May, 1784.

Lineage.

Upon the decease of Sir Henry Lowther, Bart., Viscount Lonsdale, 12th May, 1751, unmarried, the baronetcy and estates of the family passed to his heir at law,

JAMES LOWTHER, Esq., as fifth baronet. This gentleman was son and heir of Robert Lowther, Esq., Governor of Barbadoes, by Catherine, daughter of Sir Joseph Pennington, Bart. Sir James, who represented the counties of Cumberland and Westmorland for several years in parliament, was elevated to the peerage on the 24th May, 1784, as *Baron Lowther, of Lowther,* in the county of Cumberland, Baron of the Barony of Kendal, in the same county, Baron of the Barony of Bury, in the county of Westmorland, Viscount Lonsdale, in the county of Westmorland, and county Palatine of

Lanchester, *Viscount Lowther and Earl of Lons-dale*. His lordship m. in 1761, Lady Margaret Stuart, daughter of John, Earl of Bute, but had no issue. In 1797 he obtained a new patent, conferring upon him the dignities of *Baron and Viscount Low-ther, of Whitehaven*, with remainder to the heirs male of his cousin, the Rev. Sir William Lowther, Bart., of Swillington. His lordship d. in 1802, when the EARLDOM OF LONSDALE, and *minor honours*, created in 1784, became EXTINCT, while the peerage, created in 1797, devolved according to the limita-tion, and is enjoyed by the present EARL OF LONS-DALE.

ARMS.—Same as Lowther, Viscounts Lonsdale.

LUCAS—BARON LUCAS, OF SHEN-FIELD, IN THE COUNTY OF ESSEX.

By Letters Patent, dated 3rd January, 1644.

Lineage.

The family of LUCAS flourished for many ages in the counties of Suffolk and Essex, and was en-nobled in the person of

SIR JOHN LUCAS, Knt., one of the most faith-ful and zealous supporters of the royal cause, during the civil wars, who was elevated to the peerage by King Charles I. on the 3rd January, 1644, in the dignity of BARON LUCAS, *of Shenfield, in the county of Essex*, with remainder, default of male issue to his brothers, Sir Charles Lucas,[*] and Sir Thomas Lucas, his lordship's gallant companions in arms in those unhappy times.

Lord Lucas m. Anne, daughter of Sir Christopher Nevill, K.B., of Newton St. Lo, in the county of Somerset, by whom he had an only daughter,

MARY LUCAS, who m. Anthony Grey, eleventh Earl of Kent, and was created, 7th May, 1663, BARONESS LUCAS, *of Crudwell, Wilts*, with remainder of the dignity of Baron Lucas, of Crudwell, to her heirs male, by the Earl of Kent, falling which, " the title not to be suspended, but to be enjoyed by such of the daughters and co-heirs, if any shall be, as other indivisible inheritances by the common law of this realm are usually possessed." Her ladyship d. in 1700, and her son and heir,

HENRY GREY, twelfth Earl of Kent, in-herited the Barony of Lucas. This nobleman was afterwards created MAR-QUESS DE GREY, with remainder to his grand-daughter, and sole heir,

LADY JEMIMA CAMPBELL, and dying in 1740, the said Lady Jemima succeeded as

JEMIMA, Marchioness de Grey,

---

[*] SIR CHARLES LUCAS. This gallant person having become pre-eminently distinguished in the ranks of the cavaliers, was shot in cold blood, with Sir George Lisle, by order of Cromwell, upon the surrender of Colchester to the parliamentarians in 1648.

and BARONESS LUCAS. She espoused, Philip, second Earl of Hardwick, and dying in 1797, was s. in the Barony of Lucas, (the marquisate becoming extinct,) by her eldest daughter,

ARNABELL HUME-CAMP-BEL, relict of Lord Pal-warth, as BARONESS LUCAS. This lady was afterwards created COUNTESS DE GREY (see Burke's Dictionary of the Peerage and Ba-ronetage).

His lordship d. in 1670, and his celebrated brother, Sir Charles Lucas, having predeceased him, as well as his elder brother, Sir Thomas Lucas,[*] he was s. by the son of the latter, his nephew,

CHARLES LUCAS, second baron. This noble-man m. Penelope, daughter of Francis Leke, Earl of Scarsdale, but dying without male issue, the title devolved upon his brother,

THOMAS LUCAS, third baron, who d. unmar-ried in 1705, when the BARONY OF LUCAS, *of Shenfield*, became EXTINCT.

ARMS.—Ar. a fesse betw. six annulets, gu.

LUCY—BARONS LUCY.

By Writ of Summons, dated 15th May, 1320, 14 Edward II.

Lineage.

The first mention of this family is in a render made by King Henry I., of the lordship of Dics, in Norfolk, (whether in requital of services, or as an inheritance, the record saith not) to

RICHARD DE LUCIE, who was governor of Faleis, in Normandy, temp. King Stephen, and defended that place with great valour, when be-sieged by Geoffrey, Earl of Anjou: for which heroic conduct he had a grant of lands, in the county of Essex, with the services of divers persons, to hold by ten knights' fees. In the subsequent contest between Stephen and the Empress Maud, he re-mained steady in his allegiance to the former, and obtained a victory of some importance near Wal-lingford Castle. Upon the adjustment of the dis-pute, the tower of London, and the castle of Win-chester, were by the advice of the whole clergy, placed in the hands of this feudal lord, he binding himself by solemn oath, and the hostage of his son, to deliver them up on the death of King Stephen, to King Henry. Which being eventually fulfilled, Richard de Lucy was constituted sheriff of Essex and Hertfordshire, in the 2nd of Henry II., and in three years afterwards, being with the king in Normandy, he was despatched to England to pro-cure the election of Thomas à Becket, then Lord

---

[*] SIR THOMAS LUCAS. This gentleman was illegitimate, having been born prior to the marriage of his parents; the other brothers, Sir John and Sir Charles, were born subsequently.

Chancellor, to the archiepiscopal see of Canterbury, vacant by the death of Theobald, Abbot of Becco. Soon after this he was appointed to the high office of JUSTICE OF ENGLAND. In the 12th of this reign, upon the aid then assessed for marrying the king's daughter, he certified his knights' fees, (lying in the counties of Kent, Suffolk, and Norfolk) de veteri feoffamento, to be in number seven, and that his ancestors performed the service of CASTLE GUARD at Dover, for the same, as also that he held one knight's fee more, de novo feoffamento, in the county of Devon. About this time Becket having fled into Normandy from the power of King Henry, came to Wiceliac to celebrate the feast of the ascension, and observing several persons of distinction present, amongst whom was this Richard de Lucie, he ascended the pulpit, and there with lighted candles, pronounced the sentence of excommunication against them all, as public incendiaries betwixt the king and himself, but being neither convicted nor called to answer, they appealed and entered the church. Soon after this, (13th Henry II.) during a temporary absence of the king beyond sea, de Lucie was constituted LIEUTENANT OF ENGLAND, and again in 1173, when the Earl of Leicester and others having reared the standard of rebellion in behalf of Prince Henry, he besieged, in conjunction with Reginald, Earl of Cornwall, the town of Leicester, and having reduced it, demolished its walls, and laid it in ashes.

In 1178, he founded the priory of Westwode, in the diocese of Rochester, in honour of St. Thomas, of Canterbury, the martyr: and began, about the same time the foundation of the priory of Lesnes, in Kent, which he munificently endowed. In this priory he subsequently assumed the habit of a canon regular, and departing this life soon after, (about 22nd Henry II.) was buried in the chapter-house there. He m. Rohais ——, and had issue,

Geffrey, who died in his father's life-time, leaving,

RICHARD, his son and heir, who departing this life, s. p., the inheritance devolved upon his aunt, ROHAIS.

Hubert, who had the lordship of STANFORD, in Essex, and hundred of ANGRE, for his livelihood, but died issueless.

Maude, m. first, to Walter Fitz-Robert, to whom she brought the lordship of DISCE, and secondly, to Richard de Repariis, and d. 27th Henry III., leaving issue,

Rohais, m. to Fulbert de Dovor, Lord of Chilham, in Kent. This Rohais, upon the decease of her nephew, succeeded to the estates of her elder brother, and upon the death of her younger brother, Hubert, she had livery of the whole barony, on paying a fine to the crown, in the 9th of King John.

Having thus disposed of the celebrated RICHARD DE LUCIE, and his family, we come to

REGINALD DE LUCIE, whose parentage Dugdale declares his inability to discover, but who, upon the rebellion of the Earl of Leicester, in the reign of Henry II., was governor of Nottingham for the king; and attended at the coronation of

Richard I., with the rest of the barons. This feudal lord espoused Annabell, second of the three daughters, and co-heirs of William Fitz-Duncan, Earl of Murray, in Scotland, by Alice, daughter and heir of Robert de Rumeli, Lord of Skypton, with whom he acquired the HONOUR OF EGREMONT, in the county of Cumberland, and by whom he had issue, his successor,

RICHARD DE LUCIE, who, in the 1st of John, paid a fine to the crown of three hundred marks for livery of his lands, and licence to marry with whom he should think proper, In four years afterwards, he paid five marks and one palfrey to the king, that he might have jurors to inquire what customs and services his tenants had used to perform, and to do, him and his ancestors for their lands in Coupland. And the same year he obtained a grant from the king to himself and Ada, his wife, daughter and co-heir of Hugh de Morvill, of the forester-ship of Cumberland. The next year he paid nine hundred marks, and five palfreys, to have livery of the property of the said Ada, and to enjoy the foresterahip of Cumberland as amply as Hugh de Morvill had it, without any partition whatsoever. By an ample charter about this period, he granted to the burgesses of Egremont, divers immunities and privileges; namely, "that they should not go beyond the gates of the castle there, upon any summons, either with the lord, or his steward, to take distresses in Coupland. That in time of war they should not be obliged to find any more than twelve armed men for forty days, for the defence of the castle, at their own proper costs. That they should not give aid, unless for making his eldest son knight, marrying one of his daughters, or towards his own ransom, in case he were taken prisoner, and at such other times as his tenants, by military service, gave aid. Moreover, that they should be quit of pawnage for their hogs in certain of his woods." But by this charter he obliged them to grind at his mills, and to give the thirteenth part for toll of their own corn, and of that which they should buy, the sixteenth part. Upon the purchase of any burgage, the buyer to give him four-pence at the taking possession. He died on or before the 15th of King John, for then Ada, his widow, gave a fine of five hundred marks for livery of her inheritance; as also for her dowry of his lands, and that she might not be compelled to marry again. She espoused without compulsion, however, and without the king's licence, Thomas de Multon, in consequence of which the castle of Egremont, and her other lands, were seized by the crown. But upon paying a compensation they were restored, and she had livery of them again. Her first husband, Richard de Lucie, left two daughters, his co-heirs, who became wards to her second husband, and were married to his sons, thus,

ANNABELL DE LUCIS espoused the eldest son, Lambert de Multon, and conveyed to him the Lordship of Egremont (see Multon of Egremont).

ALICE DE LUCIE, married the younger son, ALAN DE MULTON, and had a son,

THOMAS DE MULTON.

The son of the younger co-heir, Alice, Thomas de

Multon, having assumed the surname of his maternal family, became,

THOMAS DE LUCIE, and in the 16th Edward I., had livery of all the lands which were of the inheritance of Alice, his mother.

He m. Isabell, one of the daughters and co-heirs of Adam de Bolteby, by whom he acquired the manor of Langley, in the county of Northumberland, and dying in 1304, was s. by his son,

THOMAS DE LUCY, who, in the 34th of Edward I., was in the wars of Scotland; and dying in 1308, without issue, was s. by his brother,

ANTHONY DE LUCY, who had been companion in arms of his deceased brother in the wars of Scotland. In the 10th Edward II., this Anthony was joined in commission with William, Lord Dacre, for defending the counties of Cumberland and Westmorland against the incursions of the Scots. The next year he was made sheriff of Cumberland, and constituted sole guardian of that county, and of Westmorland, and again sheriff of Cumberland the ensuing year, when he was appointed governor of the castles of Carlisle and Cockermouth. He was summoned to parliament soon after, as a BARON, and from that period to the 17th of Edward III. In the 16th Edward II. he obtained a grant from the crown of the honour of Cockermouth, with the manor of Hapcastre, pertaining thereto, to hold by the service of one knight's fee. Amongst the other actions of this nobleman was the surprisal and capture of Andrew de Harcla, Earl of Carlisle, who had gone over to the Scots; whom he sent up to London a prisoner, where he was degraded and sentenced to death. Lord Lucy was subsequently appointed JUSTICE OF IRELAND, and governor of the town and castle of Berwick-upon-Tweed. His lordship m. ———, and had issue,

    THOMAS, his successor.

    Joane, m. to —— Melton, and had issue,
      Sir William Melton, Knt.

He d. in 1343, and was s. by his son,

THOMAS DE LUCY, second baron, summoned to parliament 25th February, 1342, in the lifetime of his father, and afterwards from 2nd April, 1344, to 4th December, 1364. This nobleman, prior to the decease of his father, had attained high eminence in arms, particularly in Flanders, and at the siege of Loughmaban Castle, 17th Edward III. He was afterwards constantly employed to defend the northern marches towards Scotland, and had a part in the victory of Durham, wherein David, King of Scotland, was made prisoner. His lordship m. Mary, sister and co-heir of John de Multon, of Egremont, by whom he acquired considerable estates in the county of Cumberland, and had issue,

    ANTHONY, his successor.

    Maud, m. first, to Gilbert de Umfraville, Earl of Angus, who died s. p., and secondly, to Henry, first Earl of Northumberland. Upon the marriage of this lady, then sole heiress of the Barons Lucy, with the earl of Northumberland, it was stipulated that the castle and honour of Cockermouth, part of her inheritance, should be settled upon the earl and herself, and the heirs male of their two bodies; failing which, upon the heirs of

her body; and in case she should die without issue, then upon Henry, Lord Percy, the earl's son and heir by his first wife, and the heirs male of his body, upon condition that the said Henry and his heirs male should bear the arms of Percy quarterly with the arms of Lucy, viz. " gules, three lucies ar.," in all shields, banners, &c.; and notwithstanding the said Maud died without issue, the descendants of the said earl were often styled Barons Lucy, their pretensions to that dignity being manifestly without a shadow of foundation. In 1557, however, Thomas Percy, brother and heir of Henry, the sixth earl, was created Baron Percy, of Cockermouth and Petworth, Baron Poynings, LUCY, Bryan, and Fitzpayne—all which honours expired, in 1670, upon the decease of Joceline, Earl of Northumberland, without issue.

His lordship d. in 1365, and was s. by his son,

ANTHONY DE LUCY, third baron, but never summoned to parliament. This nobleman was joined with Roger de Clifford in the guardianship of the marches towards Cumberland and Westmorland. In the 41st Edward III., his lordship, with divers other noble persons, procured licence to travel beyond sea, and died the ensuing year, 1368, leaving an infant daughter, Joane, by his wife, Joane, widow of William, Lord Greystoke, which infant daughter died the next year, when her aunt, Maud, then Countess of Angus, succeeded to the BARONY OF LUCY and the honour of Cockermouth, with the other estates. (Refer to issue of Thomas, second baron.) This lady m. subsequently the Earl of Northumberland, and made the settlement already stated; but she died issueless, when the BARONY OF LUCY reverted certainly to the descendant of her aunt, Joane, (refer to issue of Anthony, first baron,) Sir William Melton, Knt., and it is now vested in his representatives, should any such exist.

ARMS.—Gules, three lucies hauriant, ar.

LUMLEY—BARON LUMLEY.

By Writ of Summons, dated 28th September, 1384, 8 Richard II.

Lineage.

The surname of LUMLEY was assumed from Lumley on the Wear, in the bishoprick of Durham, and the family deduced its lineage from

LIULPH, (son of Osbert de Lumley,) who m. Algitha, daughter of Aldred, Earl of Northumberland, by Edgina, daughter of King ETHELRED II. This Liulph, who was a nobleman of great popularity in the time of the CONFESSOR, was murdered by means of Leofarin, chaplain to Walcher, bishop of Durham; a crime that the populace of Durham soon after avenged by sacrificing both the chaplain and the prelate to their just resentment. The eldest son of Liulph and Edgina, assuming the surname of Lumley, succeeded as

UCHTRED DE LUMLEY, and from him lineally descended

ROGER DE LUMLEY, who m. Sybil, one of the

daughters and co-heirs of the great Northumberland feudal Baron, HUGH DE MORBWIC,[*] and was s. by his son,

SIR ROBERT DE LUMLEY, who m. Lucia, one of the three sisters and co-heirs of William, Robert, and Thomas de Thweng, Barons Thweng, of Kilton Castle, in the county of York, (Robert and Thomas were priests,) and was s. by his son,

SIR MARMADUKE DE LUMLEY, who assumed the arms of Thweng, and was s. by his elder son,

ROBERT DE LUMLEY. This feudal lord died in the 48th Edward III., and was s. by his brother,

SIR RALPH DE LUMLEY, who, in the 9th of Richard II., was in the expedition then made into Scotland, in the retinue of Hugh de Percy, Earl of Northumberland. In the 10th of Edward II. he was made governor of Berwick-upon-Tweed, and continued therein until the 19th, when he was taken prisoner by the Scots. In three years after he was deputy governor of the same place under the Earl of Northumberland, and the next year had licence to make a castle of his manor house at Lumley. Sir Ralph was summoned to parliament, as a BARON, from the 8th of Richard II. to the 1st of Henry IV., inclusive. In which latter year, joining in the insurrection of Thomas de Holand, Earl of Kent, for the restoration of the former monarch, he was slain in a skirmish at Cirencester, and being attainted in 1400, his lands were seized by the crown, and the BARONY OF LUMLEY fell under the attainder. His lordship left issue by his wife, Eleanor, daughter of John, Lord Nevill, of Raby, four sons and three daughters, of whom the youngest, Marmaduke de Lumley, was successively master of Trinity Hall, Cambridge, and chancellor of the University; Bishop of Carlisle (1430), treasurer of England (1446), and Bishop of Lincoln (1451). Lord Lumley was s. by his eldest son,

THOMAS DE LUMLEY, who had been attainted with his father, and dying without issue in 1404, was s. by his brother,

SIR JOHN DE LUMLEY, who, in the 6th of Henry IV., doing his homage, had livery of all the castles, manors, and lands, whereof his father, Ralph, Lord Lumley, was seised at the time of his attainder; and was restored in blood by act of parliament in the 13th of the same reign. He was subsequently, temp. Henry V., distinguished in the wars of France, and fell at the battle of Baugy, in Anjou, anno 1421. Sir John m. Felicia, daughter of Sir Matthew Redman, governor of Berwick, and was s. by his only son,

SIR THOMAS DE LUMLEY, who, in the 33rd of Henry VI., was governor of SCARBOROUGH CAS-

TLE, and upon the accession of King Edward IV. having petitioned the parliament for the reversal of the attainder of his grandfather, Ralph, Lord Lumley, and that prayer being granted by the repeal of the said attainder, was summoned to parliament, as BARON LUMLEY, on the 26th July, 1461, and from that period to 16th January, 1497. His lordship m. Margaret, daughter of Sir James Harrington, Kat., and was s. at his decease by his only son,

SIR GEORGE LUMLEY, third baron, but never summoned to parliament. This nobleman m. Elizabeth, daughter and co-heir of Roger Thornton, Esq., an opulent merchant of Newcastle-upon-Tyne, by his wife, Elizabeth, daughter of John, Lord Greystoke, and had issue,

    THOMAS, who m. Elisabeth Plantagenet, natufal daughter of KING EDWARD IV., by Lady Elizabeth Lucy, and dying in the lifetime of his father, (anno 1487,) left a son and heir, and three daughters, viz.

        RICHARD, who succeeded his grandfather.

        Anne, m. to Ralph, Lord Ogle.

        Sybil, m. to William, Baron Hilton.

        Elizabeth, m. to ——— Croswell.

    Roger.

    Ralph.

Lord Lumley acquired by his marriage the lordships of WILTON, in Northumberland, and LULWORTH, and Isle, in the bishoprick, but had a great contest regarding those lands with Giles Thornton, the bastard son of his father-in-law, which quarrel terminated by his lordship's killing his antagonist in the ditch of Windsor Castle. The baron, who, in the 7th of Henry VII., was in the expedition then made into Scotland under the command of Thomas, Earl of Surrey, when Norham Castle was besieged, died in 1508, and was s. by his grandson,

RICHARD DE LUMLEY, fourth baron, summoned to parliament from 17th October, 1509, to 28th November, 1511; to the last writ the following edition is made on the roll, "Mortuus est, ut dicitur." His lordship m. Anne, daughter of Sir John Coniers, K.G., of Hornby Castle, in the county of York, and sister of William, first Lord Coniers, by whom he had two sons,

    JOHN, his successor.

    Anthony, who m. a daughter of Richard Gray, Esq., of the county of Northumberland, and left a son,

        Richard Lumley, whose son,

        SIR RICHARD LUMLEY, was elevated to the peerage of Ireland, as VISCOUNT LUMLEY, OF WATERFORD, and from this nobleman lineally descend the artsnt EARLS OF SCARBOROUGH.

His lordship d. in 1511, and was s. by his elder son,

JOHN DE LUMLEY, fifth baron, summoned to parliament on the 23rd November, 1514. This nobleman was at the celebrated battle of FLODDEN FIELD, under the Earl of Surrey. His lordship m. Joane, daughter of Henry, Lord Scroop, of Bolton, and had issue,

    GEORGE, who, being concerned in an insur-

---

[*] The male line of this nobleman terminated in 1351, when his estates devolved upon his three daughters, as co-heirs. Those daughters were,

    Sybil, who m. first, as stated above, Roger de Lumley, and secondly, Roger de St. Martin.

    Theophania, m. to John de Bulmer.

    Beatrice, m. to John de Roseles.

396

rection with Lord Darcy and others, was apprehended, committed to the Tower, and being convicted of high treason, was executed and attainted in the 29th Henry VIII. (his father then living.) He m. Jane, second daughter and co-heir of Sir Richard Knightley, of Fausley, in the county of Northampton, and left issue,

> JOHN, who was restored in blood, and created BARON LUMLEY. (See that dignity.)
> Jane, m. to Geffrey Markham, Esq., and died s. p.
> Barbara, m. to Humphrey Lloyd, Esq., of Denbigh, and had issue,
>> Splandinian Lloyd, who died s. p.
>> HENRY LLOYD, of Cheam, who m. Mary, daughter of Robert Brome, of Bromefield, Essex, and was s. by his son,
>>> HENRY LLOYD, who m. Isabella, daughter of Sir Isham Parkyns, Bart., and was s. by his son,
>>>> HENRY LLOYD, who m. Elizabeth, daughter of Benjm. Goodwin, Esq., of Stretham, and had, (with three daughters,)
>>>>> REV. DR. ROBERT LLOYD, who claimed the Barony of Lumley in 1723.

Lord Lumley, in the 29th of Henry VIII., was implicated in the insurrection, called the "Pilgrimage of Grace;" when a pardon being offered by the Duke of Norfolk, who commanded the army sent against the rebels, his lordship was deputed to treat with the duke, and succeeded so well, that all concerned in the affair were allowed to return home without being further molested. Upon his decease his only son, GEORGE LUMLEY, having been, as stated above, previously attainted, the BARONY OF LUMLEY became extinct. It was claimed, however, in 1723, by the Rev. Robert Lloyd, as lineal descendant of BARBARA LUMLEY, sister of the attainted George, when the House of Lords came to the resolution, " That the petitioner had no right to a writ of summons in parliament, as prayed by his petition"—which resolution was founded upon the previous report—

" That by the act of parliament* of 1st Edward VI., a new Barony of Lumley was created, and limited by express words to John, Lord Lumley, in tail male; and that upon his death, without issue male, the said barony became extinct.

" That the attainder of George Lumley is not reversed by the said act, but remains yet in force; and that the restitution of John, Lord Lumley, in blood only, while the attainder remains unreversed, could not possibly revive the ancient barony, which was before merged in the crown, in consequence of that attainder."

---

* Which conferred the barony upon John Lumley, son and heir of the attainted George.

ARMS.—Originally. Gu. six martlets ar.
    After the alliance with de Thweng, ar. a fesse betw. gules, three parrots, ppr. collared as the second.

NOTE.—In consequence of the marriage of Sir Robert Lumley with Lucia de Thweng, one of the co-heirs of the Lords Thweng, a third of the BARONY OF THWENG devolved upon the Lumleys, which third, it is presumed, merged in the crown under the attainder of GEORGE LUMLEY in the reign of Henry VIII.

LUMLEY—BARON LUMLEY.

By Act of Parliament, anno 1547.

Lineage.

JOHN LUMLEY, only son of the Honourable George Lumley, who had been attainted and executed for high treason, in the 29th of Henry VIII., having petitioned parliament, in the 1st Edward VI., praying that the attainder might be reversed, " It was enacted, that the said John Lumley, and the *heirs male of his body*, should have, hold, enjoy, and bear the name, dignity, state, and pre-eminence of a baron of the realm." By this law, a new Barony of Lumley was created, the old one having merged in the crown under the attainder; nothing but a positive appeal of that statute could have restored it, and the new act did not effect that object. His lordship m. first, Jane, elder daughter and co-heir of Henry Fitz-Alan, Earl of Arundel, by whom he had a son and two daughters, who died all in infancy. He espoused secondly, Elizabeth, daughter of John, Lord Darcy, of Chiche, but had no issue. Of Lord Lumley, Camden says, " That he was of entire virtue, integrity, and innocence; and in his old age, a complete pattern of true nobility. Having so great a veneration for the memory of his ancestors, that he caused monuments to be erected for them, in the collegiate church of Chester le Street, (opposite Lumley Castle,) in the order as they succeeded one another, from Liulphus down to his own time: which he had either picked out of the demolished monasteries, or made new. He also took care that his estates should descend to one of his own name and blood, by his last will and testament; in which he bequeaths to his kinsman and heir male, Richard, eldest son and heir apparent of Roger, the son of Anthony Lumley, brother to John, Lord Lumley, his grandfather, his Castle of Lumley, together with divers manors, lands, tenements, &c."

His lordship d. 11th April, 1609, and was interred in the Church of Cheam, having a noble monument of white marble erected to his memory. With his lordship the new BARONY OF LUMLEY EXPIRED.

ARMS.—Ar. a fesse gu. betw. three parrots, ppr. collared as the second.

Note.—The Sir Richard Lumley, who inherited the estates under the will of John, Lord Lumley, (as stated above,) was created in 1628, Viscount Lumley, of Waterford. He was the great-great-great grandfather of the present Richard Lumley Saunderson, Earl of Scarborough.

LUTEREL—BARON LUTEREL.

By Letters Patent, dated 24th June, 1295.
23 Edward I.

Lineage.

In the time of Richard I., the lands of
GEOFFREY DE LUTEREL, in the counties of
Nottingham and Derby, were seized by the crown,
for his adherence to the Earl of Moreton, but he
was compensated, upon the accession of that personage to the throne, as King John, by extensive
territorial and other grants. He d. in the 2nd year
of Henry III., and was s. by his son,

ANDREW DE LUTEREL, who, in the 14th of
Henry III., upon the collection of the scutage, for
the first journey of that king into Britanny, accounted £30. for fifteen knights' fees. In this year,
he laid claim to lands in the county of Somerset,
as well as the Manor of Berham, in the county of
Lincoln, which formerly belonged to Maurice de
Gant, and had descended to him, by right of inheritance: and the next year he had livery of the
same, upon paying one hundred marks to the crown.
He subsequently served the office of Sheriff of Lincolnshire, and dying in 1264, was s. by his elder
son,

GEOFFREY DE LUTEREL, feudal Baron of
Irnham. This Geoffrey being insane, his brother,
Alexander Luterel, had the custody of his person,
and William de Gray, whose daughter he had married, the education of his children. To these succeeded,

ROBERT DE LUTEREL, who, in the 5th of
Edward I., was in the expedition then made into
Wales, and had summons amongst other great men,
in the 22nd of the same reign, to attend the king,
touching the important affairs of the realm. He
was summoned to parliament as a BARON, on the
24th June, and 2nd of November, 1295, and dying
in the following year, possessed of Irnham, in the
county of Lincoln, and Hoton Painell, in the
county of York, left a son and heir,

GEOFFREY DE LUTEREL, feudal Lord of
Irnham, but never summoned to parliament as a
baron, nor were any of his descendants.

ARMS.—Or. a bend betw. six martlets sa.

Note.—There were two other branches of the Lute-
rels, of distinction; ONE, seated at Dunster, in Somersetshire,—an honour and castle inherited from the
Mohuns, once Lords of Dunster, and reputed Earls
of Somerset: and which came by a sole heiress, to
Henry Fownes, Esq., who assumed the surname of
Luttrell. This gentleman m. in 1782, a Miss Drew,
and was s. at his decease, by John Fownes Luttrell, Esq., of Dunster Castle, M. P. for Minehead,
in the county of Somerset.

The other branch was of Luttrell's town, in the
county of Dublin, of which the late Earl of Carhampton, of the Irish peerage, who was also Baron
Irnham, was the chief. His lordship died 17th
March, 1799, when all his honours, in default of
male issue, became EXTINCT; he left an only
daughter,

Lady Mary Saunderson, wife of Major Saunderson, of the Grenadier Guards, son of

Francis Saunderson, Esq., of Castle Saunderson, in Ireland.

LYTTLETON — BARON LYTTLE-TON, OF MOWNSLOW, IN THE COUNTY OF SALOP.

By Letters Patent, dated 18th February, 1640.

Lineage.

The family of Luttelton, of LYTTLETON, is of
long standing in the county of Worcester, where
it possessed lands in the vale of Evesham, particularly at South LYTTLETON, (whence the surname,) in the beginning of the 13th century.

THOMAS DE LUTTELTON, m. about the
19th of Henry III., Emma, only daughter and heir
of Sir Simon de Frankley, Knt., by whom he had
an only daughter, Emma, who wedded Augerus de
Tatlynton; he espoused, secondly, Anselm, daughter and heiress of William Fitz-Warren, of Upton,
in the county of Worcester, one of the Justices-Iti-
nerant, and Judges of the Common Pleas, in the
12th of Henry III., by whom he had three sons,
and was s. by the eldest,

EDMUND DE LUTTELTON, who dying s. p.,
was s. by his brother,

THOMAS DE LUTTELTON, M. P. for the
county of Worcester, from 9th Edward II., to 34th
Edward III. This Thomas was s. by his eldest
son,

THOMAS DE LUTTELTON, who recovered
the Manor of Frankley, by writ of right, on failure
of the issue of his cousin, Thomas de Tatlynton;
this Thomas was Esquire of the Body, to Richard
II., Henry IV., and Henry V. He died in the 1st
of Henry VI., leaving an only daughter and heiress,

ELIZABETH DE LUTTELTON, who espoused
Thomas Westcote, Esq., providing, prior to her
marriage, that her issue should bear her own surname. By this gentleman she had four sons and
four daughters: of whom succeeded to the estates,
the eldest son,

THOMAS LUTTELTON, (or LYTTLETON,
as he began to write it). This gentleman being
bred to the bar, was called, in 1454, to the degree
of sergeant-at-law, and was constituted next year,
king's sergeant, when he rode justice of the assise
in the northern circuit. In 1464, he was raised to
the bench, in the Court of Common Pleas, and was
made a knight of the Bath. Sir Thomas Lyttleton
wrote his celebrated "Treatise on Tenures," after
he had become a judge; a book which lord Coke
has described, "as the ornament of the common
law, and the most perfect and absolute work that
ever was wrote in any human science." This celebrated person m. Joan, widow of Sir Philip Chetwynd, of Ingestrie, in the county of Stafford, and
daughter and co-heiress of Sir William Burley, of
Bromscroft Castle, in the county of Salop, by
whom he had issue,

WILLIAM, his successor, ancestor of the Lords
Lyttleton, of Frankley (see that dignity).

Richard, to whom the treatise was addressed,
and who followed his father's profession.

From this gentleman descended the LITTLE-TONS of Pillaton Hall, in Staffordshire; which family continued without interruption, always through Sir Edwards, at first knights, afterwards baronets, until the death of Sir Edward Littleton, Bart., in 1812, when the TITLE became extinct, and the estates passed to his grandnephew, the present

> EDWARD JOHN LITTLETON, Esq., M.P. for the county of Stafford; which gentleman is grandson of the deceased baronet's sister —— by Moreton Walhouse, Esq., of Hatherton, in Staffordshire.

Thomas, of whose descendants we are about to treat.

This great lawyer, "to whose tenures," says Dr. Holand, in his additions to Camden, "the students of the common law are no less beholden, than the civilians are to Justinian's Institutes," died at Frankley, 23d August, 1481, and was *s.* by his eldest son, Sir William Lyttleton, of Frankley (see Barons Lyttleton of Frankley). The youngest son,

THOMAS LYTTLETON, was seated at Spechley, near Worcester, and *m.* Anne, daughter and sole heir of John Botreaux, Esq., of Botreaux Castle, in Cornwall, from whom descended Sir Thomas Lyttleton, speaker of the house, temp. William III., and an elder branch,

SIR EDMUND LYTTLETON, of Mounslow, in the county of Salop. This gentleman, like his great ancestor, attained fame, honours, and fortune, by the profession of the law. In the 10th year of King Charles I., Mr. Lyttleton was appointed solicitor-general, when he received the honour of knighthood. In five years afterwards, he was made lord chief justice of the court of Common Pleas, and the next year constituted LORD KEEPER OF THE GREAT SEAL; when he was elevated to the peerage, 18th February, 1640, as BARON LYTTLETON, of *Mounslow*, in the county of Salop. At the commencement of the civil wars, when CHARLES retired to the city of York, the lord keeper immediately followed his majesty with the great seal, and continued afterwards in attendance upon him. His lordship *m.* Anne, daughter of John Lyttleton, Esq., of Frankley, M.P. for the county of Worcester, by whom he had an only daughter and heiress,

> ANNE, who *m.* her second cousin, Sir Thomas Lyttleton, Bart.

Of this eminent person, Banks says: " his learning was various and useful; his skill in the maxims of government, and of the fundamental statutes and customs of the kingdom, was particular; as was his experience, long and observing. His eloquence was powerful and majestic: in fact, such a man was worthy of that honour to which he was advanced; namely, of a peer of the realm." His lordship *d.* in 1645, when the BARONY OF LYTTLETON, OF MOUNS-LOW, became EXTINCT.

ARMS.—Ar. a chevron between three eschallop shells, sa.

LYTTLETON — BARONS LYTTLE-TON, OF FRANKLEY.

By Letters Patent, dated 19th November, 1757.

Lineage.

The celebrated

SIR THOMAS LYTTLETON, one of the Justices of the court of Common Pleas, and author of the " Treatise on Tenures," (see Baron Lyttleton, of Mownslow,) *d.* 23d August, 1481, and was *s.* by his eldest son,

SIR WILLIAM LYTTLETON, of Frankley, who was knighted by Henry VII., for his conduct at the battle of Stoke. He *m.* first, Ellyn, widow of Thomas Fielding Esq., and daughter and heir of William Walsh, Esq., of Wanslip, in the county of Leicester, by whom he had an only daughter, Joan, who *m.* Sir John Aston, of Haywood, in Staffordshire, and carried the manor of Tixhale, in that county, and Wanlip, into the Aston family. Sir William espoused, secondly, Mary, daughter of William Whittington, of Pauntley, in the county of Gloucester, and had issue,

> JOHN, his successor.
>
> Elizabeth, *m.* to Thomas Rouse, Esq., of Rouse-Lench, in Worcestershire, a family now represented by SIR WILLIAM-EDWARD ROUSE BOUGHTON, Bart.

He *d.* at Frankley, in 1507, and was *s.* by his son,

JOHN LYTTLETON, Esq., of Frankley, who endowed his family (saith Habington, in his MS. Antiquities of Worcestershire,) with abundance of noble blood, by having in marriage, Elizabeth, the daughter and co-heir of Sir Gilbert Talbot, of Grafton, by Anne, his wife, the daughter and co-heir of Sir William Paston, by Anne, third sister and co-heir of Edmund Beaufort, Duke of Somerset. By this lady he had a numerous family, and dying 17th May, 1532, was *s.* by his eldest son,

JOHN LYTTLETON, Esq., then a minor, whose wardship was granted by the king to Sir John Packington, Knt., of Hampton Lovell. Mr. Lyttleton *m.* Bridget, the daughter and heir of his guardian, and acquired a considerable increase of fortune by the alliance. He was thus enabled to rebuild, in a magnificent manner, his seat at Frankley, and to purchase other estates. In 1553 Queen Mary granted him for life the office of Constable of Dudley Castle, in the county of Stafford, together with the rangership of the old and new parks there. The same year he was chosen one of the knights for Worcestershire, and served the office of sheriff once in the reign of Mary, and twice in that of Elizabeth; in which latter reign, although a Roman Catholic, he enjoyed places of honour and trust. In 1556 he was knighted by the queen, with other gentlemen of great distinction, at Kenilworth Castle, when her majesty honoured the Earl of Leicester with a visit there.

Sir John Lyttleton had, with other issue,

> GILBERT, his successor.
>
> William, *m.* to Margaret, only daughter and heir of William Smyth, Esq., of Sherford, in the county of Warwick, but *d.* before the age of consummation, by a fall from his horse in hunting.
>
> George, settled at Holbeach, in the county of

Stafford, who m. Margaret, his brother's widow.

Elizabeth, m. to Francis Willoughby, Esq., of Wollaton, in the county of Nottingham.

Margaret, m. to Samuel Marrow, Esq., of Berkeswell, in the county of Warwick.

Amphilis, m. to William Barneby, Esq., of Bockleton, in Worcestershire.

He d. 15th February, 1589-90, and was s. by his eldest son,

GILBERT LYTTLETON, Esq., M.P. for the county of Worcester. This gentleman resided chiefly at Prestwood, in that shire, where his father had erected a large mansion. It was purchased by Sir John Lyttleton, from Sutton, Lord Dudley; but there was great contention between the two families, before the Lyttletons could obtain quiet possession of the estate. In the month of October, 1592, Lord Dudley armed one hundred and forty persons, and coming by night to Prestwood, forcibly carried off 341 sheep, 14 kine, 1 bull, and 8 fat oxen, which they drove to Dudley, and there kept. Replevins were immediately taken, but not delivered by the bailiffs, for fear of being cut to pieces. After Lord Dudley had killed and eaten part of those cattle, the remainder were sent towards Coventry, accompanied by sixty armed men, in order to be sold; but his lordship changing his mind, he raised the inhabitants of several villages to the number of six or seven hundred, who brought them back to Dudley Castle, when they roasted them all. Upon this violent proceeding, a bill was filed in the Star Chamber against Lord Dudley and his adherents; where, on full proof of these illegal outrages, a reference was proposed, and accepted, and articles were signed 24th May, 1595, whereby Lord Dudley agreed to pay one thousand marks to Mr. Lyttleton, and all further suit to cease. This Gilbert m. Elizabeth, daughter of Humphrey Coningsby, Esq., of Nyend-Solers, in Shropshire, and of Hampton Court, in the county of Hereford, and dying in 1599, was s. by his eldest son,

JOHN LYTTLETON, Esq., M.P. for the county of Worcester, temp. Elizabeth. This gentleman (to use the words of Sir Francis Bacon) being much respected for his wit and valour, and a Roman Catholic, was courted by Lord Essex and his friends, and in some measure drawn in by Sir Charles Danvers to that conspiracy which cost Essex his head, and Lyttleton his estate: for he was tried and convicted of high treason at the queen's bench bar on 20th February, 1601, and d. in prison the July following. He m. Muriel, daughter of Sir Thomas Bromley, which lady obtained, upon the accession of James I., a reversal of the attainder of her late husband, and a grant of the whole of his estate. She was a person of so much prudence, that she was enabled not only to discharge debts of her husband and his father to the amount of £9000, but to acquire a high reputation for benevolence and hospitality. She survived Mr. Lyttleton a great many years, and brought up her children in the reformed religion. The eldest son,

SIR THOMAS LYTTLETON, Knt., M.P. for the county of Worcester, was created a baronet in 1618, and from him we pass to the fifth baronet,

330

SIR GEORGE LYTTLETON, M.P., who, in 1737, was appointed secretary to the Prince of Wales; in 1744, one of the commissioner of the treasury; in 1754, cofferer of the household, when he was sworn of the privy council; and in 1755 he was constituted chancellor and under treasurer of the exchequer. Sir George was elevated to the peerage 19th November, 1757, as BARON LYTTLETON, of Frankley, in the county of Worcester. This nobleman acquired the reputation of an excellent scholar, and a great patron of literature. He was also justly esteemed as an author, and his works are still highly valued; his Persian Letters, Dialogues of the Dead, History of the Age and Reign of Henry II., &c. &c. His lordship m. first, Lucy, daughter of Hugh Fortescue, Esq., of Filleigh, in the county of Devon, by whom he had issue,

THOMAS, his successor.

Lucy, m. to Arthur Annesley, Viscount Valentia, in Ireland.

He espoused, secondly, Elizabeth, daughter of Sir Robert Rich, Bart., but had no child by that lady. His lordship d. in 1773, and was s. by his son,

THOMAS LYTTLETON, second baron. This nobleman was a person of great eccentricity, and the vision which is said immediately to have preceded his dissolution, has ever been a subject of interest and marvel, to those who place implicit reliance upon narratives of that description. His lordship m. in 1772, Apphia, second daughter of Broome Witts, Esq., and widow of Jos. Peach, Esq., Governor of Calcutta, but dying s. p. in 1779, the BARONY OF LYTTLETON, of Frankley, became EXTINCT, while the baronetcy reverted to his uncle, William Henry Lyttleton, Baron Westcote, in Ireland, in whom the expired dignity was revived.

ARMS.—Ar. a chevron betw. three escallops, sa.

MACARTNEY — BARON MACARTNEY, OF PARKHURST, IN THE COUNTY OF SURREY, AND OF AUCHINLECK, IN THE STEWARTRY OF KIRKCUDBRIGHT.

By Letters Patent, dated 8th June, 1796.

Lineage.

GEORGE MACARTNEY, K.B., Earl Macartney, in the peerage of Ireland, was created a baron of Great Britain, by letters patent, dated 8th June, 1796, as LORD MACARTNEY, of Parkhurst, in the county of Surrey, and of Auchinleck, in the stewartry of Kirkcudbright. This nobleman was employed upon several important diplomatic missions, and particularly in an embassy to the emperor of China, of which his secretary, the late Sir George Staunton, published a very full narrative. His lordship m. Lady Jane Bute, daughter of the Earl of Bute; but died without issue in 1806, when ALL HIS HONOURS became EXTINCT.

ARMS.—Or., a buck trippant within a bordure gules.

MACKENZIE — BARON SEAFORTH, OF KINTAIL, IN THE COUNTY OF ROSS.

By Letters Patent, dated 26th October, 1797.

Lineage.

COLONEL ALEXANDER MACKENZIE, third son of Kenneth, third Earl of Seaforth, in Scotland, (whose peerage was forfeited in 1715,) by Isabel, daughter of Sir J. Mackenzie, of Tarbat, was father of

MAJOR MACKENZIE, who m. Mary, daughter of Matthew Humberston, Esq., and had issue,

> Thomas-Frederick-Humberston, a colonel in the army, and actively engaged in the East Indies, where he died of wounds received in action.
>
> FRANCIS-HUMBERSTON, of whom presently.
>
> Frances-Cerjet, m. Sir Vicary Gibbs, chief baron of the exchequer.
>
> Maria-Rebecca, m. to Alexander Mackenzie, Esq.
>
> Elizabeth.
>
> Helen, m. to Colonel Alexander Mackenzie.

The second but eldest surviving son,

FRANCIS - HUMBERSTON MACKENZIE, Esq., having inherited the family estates, and distinguished himself as a military officer, was elevated to the peerage, 26th October, 1797, as BARON SEA-FORTH, of Kintail, in the county of Ross. His lordship m. Mary, daughter of the Rev. Baptist Proby, Dean of Lichfield, and had issue,

> William-Frederick, }
> Francis-John, Midsh., R.N. } who both predeceased his lordship.
>
> Mary.
>
> Frederica-Eliz. m. to Admiral Sir Samuel Hood.
>
> Frances-Catherine.
>
> Caroline.
>
> Charlotte-Eliz.
>
> Augusta-Anne.

Lord Seaforth was a lieutenant-general in the army, and governor, successively, of Barbadoes, (in 1800,) and Berbice. His lordship was lord-lieutenant of the county of Ross. He died in 1814, when the BARONY OF SEAFORTH, of Kintail, became EXTINCT.

ARMS.—Az. a deer's head carbossed, or.

MAITLAND — EARL OF GUILD-FORD.

By Letters Patent, dated 25th June, 1674.

Lineage.

JOHN MAITLAND, second Earl of Lauderdale, in the peerage of Scotland, having distinguished himself by his zealous support of the royal cause during the civil wars, was advanced to the Scottish dukedom of Lauderdale in 1672, and created a peer of England on the 25th June, 1674, as Baron Petersham, and EARL OF GUILDFORD. This nobleman was a conspicuous public character in the reign of Charles II., and, under the title of Lauderdale, supplied the letter L to the CABAL administration. His grace was a Knight of the Garter, and high commissioner of the church of Scotland. The duke espoused first, Anne, daughter and co-heir of Alexander, Earl of Hume, and had an only daughter and heiress,

> ANNE, who m. to John Hay, second Marquess of Tweeddale.

He m. secondly, Elizabeth, Countess of Dysart, daughter and heir of William Murray, Earl of Dysart, and widow of Sir Lionel Tollemache, Bart.; but had no issue.

His grace d. in 1682, when the English BARONY OF PETERSHAM and EARLDOM OF GUILDFORD, with the Scottish dukedom of Lauderdale, became EXTINCT, and his other honours devolved upon his brother, the Hon. Charles Maitland, as third Earl of Lauderdale.

Burnet, speaking of the Duke of Lauderdale, thus characterises him :—

"For many years he was a zealous covenanter, but, in 1647, turned to the king's interest, and, at the battle of Worcester, was taken prisoner, and detained in custody till the restoration. In his person he made a very ill appearance: he was very big; his tongue was too large for his mouth, which made him bedew all that he talked to; and his whole manner was rough and boisterous, and very unfit for a court.

"He was very learned, not only in Latin, in which he was a great master, but in Greek and Hebrew. He had read a great deal of divinity, and almost all the historians, ancient and modern, so that he had a great store of materials. He was a man (as the Duke of Buckingham called him) of a blundering understanding. He was haughty beyond expression, abject to those he saw he must stoop to, but imperious to all others. He had a violence of passion that carried him often to fits like madness, in which he had no temper. If he took a thing wrong, it was a vain thing to study to convince him: that would rather provoke him to swear he would never be of another mind. He was to be let alone; and, perhaps, he would have forgot what he said, and come about of his own accord. He was the coldest friend, and the violentest enemy I ever knew. He, at first, seemed to despise wealth; but he afterwards delivered himself up to luxury and sensuality, and by that means ran into a vast expense, and stuck at nothing that was necessary to support it. In his long imprisonment, he had great impressions of religion on his mind; but he wore these out so entirely, that scarce any trace of them was left. His great experience in affairs, his ready compliance with every thing that he thought would please the king, and his bold offering at the most desperate counsels, gained him such an interest in the king, that no attempt against him, nor complaint, could ever shake it, till a decay of strength and understanding forced him to let go his hold. He was in his principles much against popery and arbitrary government, and yet, by a fatal train of passions and interests, he made way for the former, and had almost established the latter; and whereas some, by smooth deportment, made the first beginnings of tyranny less discernible and unacceptable, he, by the fury of his behaviour, heightened the severity of his ministry, which was more like the cruelty of an inquisition, than the legality of justice. With all this, he was a Presbyterian, and retained his aversion to King Charles and his party to his death."

. ARMS—Or., a lion rampant dechaussée, within a double tressure, flory, counter-flory, gu.

MALTRAVERS—BARON MALTRAVERS.

By Writ of Summons, dated 5th June, 1330, 4 Edward III.

Although none of this family were barons by tenure, nor had summons to parliament before the time of the third Edward, yet were they anciently persons of note. In the reign of Henry I., Hugh Maltravers was a witness to the charter made by that monarch to the monks of Montacute, in the county of Somerset ; and in the 5th of Stephen, Maltravers gave a thousand marks of silver, and one hundred pounds, for the widow of Hugh de la Val, and lands of the same Hugh, during the term of fifteen years, and then to have the benefit of her dowry and marriage.

JOHN MALTRAVERS took up arms with the barons against king John ; but in the 1st Henry III., returning to his allegiance, was of the retinue of William, Earl-Mareschall, and had summons (26th Henry III.) to attend the king, with horse and arms, into France. He died in the 24th Edward I., at an advanced age, seised, amongst others, of the manors of Lychet and Wychampton, in the county of Dorset, leaving his son and heir,

JOHN MALTRAVERS, then thirty years of age, who, upon doing homage in the 25th Edward I., had livery of his lands ; and in the 34th of the same reign, was made a knight, with Prince Edward and others, by bathing, &c., whereupon he attended that prince into Scotland, being of the retinue with Maurice de Berkeley ; and the same year he obtained a charter for free warren in all his demesne lands at Lychet-Maltravers, in the county of Dorset. In the 7th Edward II. he was again in the wars of Scotland, and the next year had a military summons to attend the king with horse and arms at Newcastle-upon-Tyne, to restrain the incursions of the Scots : in which year he had a grant for a market weekly on the Tuesday in *Limerick*, in Ireland, but wherefore does not appear ; for although large possessions of his are enumerated in the counties of Dorset, Somerset, Wilts, Gloucester, and Berks, none are mentioned as lying out of England. After this we find him again in the wars of Scotland, and upon the deposal of the unhappy Edward II., being in high estimation with those who were then in power, he was summoned to the parliament held in the 4th Edward III., as "John Maltravers, sen." The infamous part which this nobleman subsequently took in the cruel murder of the unfortunate Edward, is too well known to need recitation here —enough that the wretched monarch was removed

from the custody of Lord Berkeley, who had treated him with some degree of humanity, and placed under Lord Maltravers and Sir Thomas Gournay, for the mere purpose of destruction, and that those ruffians ultimately fulfilled their diabolical commission, in the most horrible manner possible, in one of the chambers at Berkeley Castle. So conscious was Maltravers of guilt, that he fled immediately after the foul deed into Germany, where he remained for several years, having had judgment of death passed upon him in England—but in the 19th of the same reign, King Edward being in Flanders, Lord Maltravers came and made a voluntary surrender of himself to the king, who, in consideration of his services abroad, granted him a safe convoy into England to abide the decision of parliament ; in which he had afterwards a full and free pardon, (25th Edward III.,) and was summoned as a BARON to take his seat therein. That was not, however, sufficient—King Edward constituted the murderer of his father, soon after, governor of the Isles of Guernsey, Jersey, Alderney, and Sarke. His lordship m. first, Ela, daughter of Maurice Berkeley, and had issue,

JOHN, who was knighted, and in the reign of Edward III. had summons to parliament as a BARON, but d. in the life-time of his father, leaving

> HENRY, died s. p.
>
> Joan, m. first, to Robert Rous, and secondly, to Sir John Kynes, but died issueless.
>
> Eleanor, m. first, to John Fitz-Alan, second son of Richard, ninth Earl of Arundel, and had issue,
>
>> JOHN FITZ-ALAN, who succeeded to the Barony of Maltravers, and eventually as eleventh Earl of Arundel (see Fitz-Alan, Earls of Arundel).
>
> She married, secondly, Reginald, Lord Cobham.

Lord Maltravers espoused, secondly, Agnes, daughter of William Berneford, and relict of Sir John Argentine, Knt., by whom he had a son,

JOHN, who m. Elizabeth, daughter and heir of Robert Cefrewast, of Hooke, in the county of Dorset, and Crowel, in the county of Oxford, by whom he had,

> JOHN (Sir), of Hooke and Crowel, who m. Elizabeth, daughter and co-heir of Sir William Aumerle, and left two daughters, viz.
>
>> Matilda, m. first, to Peter de la Mare, and secondly, to Sir John Dynham, Knt., and died s. p. 11th Henry IV.
>>
>> Elizabeth, m. to Sir Humphrey Stafford, Knt., whose grandson and heir,
>>
>>> SIR HUMPHREY STAFFORD, of Hooke, was slain by Jack Cade's mob, leaving a son,
>>>
>>>> HUMPHREY STAFFORD, who died s. p., and was s. by

HUMPHREY STAF-
FORD, of Suthwike
(see Staffords, of
Suthwike).

After the decease of John, Lord Maltravers, the
BARONY passed to his grand-daughter, (the even-
tual sole heiress of his predeceased son, Sir John
Maltravers,) Eleanor, wife of the Hon. John Fitz-
Alan, whose son JOHN was summoned to parliament as Lord Maltravers, and succeeded as eleventh
Earl of Arundel—and the Barony of Maltravers has
since merged in that superior dignity. Lady Mary
Fitz-Alan, the daughter, and ultimately sole heiress
of Henry, eighteenth Earl of Arundel, married
Thomas Howard, Duke of Norfolk, and brought
the barony and earldom into the Howard family.
Those dignities descended to her son, Philip, who
was ATTAINTED in the 32nd Elizabeth, when the
barony fell under the attainder, but it was restored
to his son, Thomas Howard, twentieth Earl of
Arundel; and by act of parliament, 3rd Charles I.,
the BARONY OF MALTRAVERS, together with those
of Fitz-Alan, Clun, and Oswaldestre, was annexed
to the title, dignity, and honour, of ARUNDEL, and
settled upon Thomas Howard, then Earl of Arundel (see Fitz-Alan, Earls of Arundel).

ARMS.—Sa. a fret, or. with a file of three points,
erm.

MANDEVILLE—EARLS OF ESSEX.

By Special Charter of King Stephen.

Lineage.

Upon the first arrival in England of Duke William, the Norman, amongst his companions was a
famous soldier, called
GEFFREY DE MAGNAVIL, so designated
from the town of *Magnavil*, in the duchy, which he
then possessed, who obtained as his share in the
spoil of conquest, divers fair and widespreading
domains, in the counties of Berks, Suffolk, Middlesex, Surrey, Oxford, Cambridge, Herts, Northampton, Warwick, and Essex; whereof WALDENE was
one, which afterwards became the chief seat of his
descendants. He was subsequently made constable
of the Tower of London, and continued to execute
the duties of that important office for the remainder
of his life. This Geffrey, among other benefactions
to the church, founded a Benedictine Monastery at
Hurley, in Berkshire, conferring upon it the whole
lordship of that place, and the woods adjoining
thereto. He was *s.* at his decease by his son,
WILLIAM DE MAGNAVIL, corrupted into
MANDEVILLE, who *m.* Margaret, only daughter
and heiress of Eudo Dapifer,[*] and had issue,

Geoffrey, who inherited from his mother the
stewardship of Normandy.
Beatrix, *m.* first, Hugh Talbot, from whom
she was divorced, and secondly, William de
Say.

He was *s.* at his decease by his son,
GEOFFREY DE MANDEVILLE, who in the

[*] Dapifer, *id est*, steward to King William for
Normandy.

5th year of King Stephen, had livery of his inheritance, upon paying the sum of £866. 13s. 4d. to
the crown; and was advanced by that monarch,
from the degree of baron, (by special charter, dated
at Westminster,) to the dignity of EARL OF THE
COUNTY OF ESSEX, unto which charter were witnesses: "William de Ipre, Henry de Essex, John,
the son of Robert Fitz-Walter, Robert de Newburgh, William de St. Clair, William de Dammar-
tin, Richard Fitz-Urse, and William de Owe;" but
notwithstanding this high honour conferred upon
him by King Stephen, the Empress Maud, by a
more ample charter, made at Oxford, allured him
to her party; for she not only conferred whatsoever
Geoffrey, his grandfather, or William, his father,
ever enjoyed, either in lands, forts, or castles, particularly the Tower of London, with the castle
under it, to strengthen and fortify at his pleasure;
but bestowed upon him the HEREDITARY SHE-
RIFFALTY of LONDON and MIDDLESEX, as also that
of HERTFORDSHIRE, with the sole power of trying
causes in those counties: for which offices and privileges he paid the sum of £360. Moreover she
granted him all the lands of Eudo Dapifer, in
Normandy, with his office of steward, as his rightful inheritance, and numerous other valuable immunities, in a covenant witnessed by Robert,
Earl of Gloucester, and several other powerful
nobles — which covenant contained the singular
clause, "that neither the Earl of Anjou, her husband, nor herself, nor her children, would ever
make peace with the burgesses of London, but
with the consent of him, the said Geffrey, because
they were his mortal enemies." Besides this, he had
a second charter, dated at Westminster, re-creating
him EARL OF ESSEX, to hold to himself and his
heirs, and to have the third penny of the pleas of
the sheriffalty, as an earl ought to enjoy in his earldom. Of which proceedings King Stephen having
information, seised upon the earl in the court,
then at St. Alban's, some say after a bloody affray,
in which the Earl of Arundel, being thrown into
the water with his horse, very narrowly escaped
drowning; certain it is, that to regain his liberty,
the Earl of Essex was constrained, not only to give
up the Tower of London, but his own Castles of
Walden and Blessey. Wherefore, being transported
with wrath, he fell to spoil and rapine, invading
the king's demesne lands and others, plundering the
Abbeys of St. Alban's and Ramsay; which last
having surprised at an early hour in the morning,
he expelled the monks therefrom, made a fort of
the church, and sold their religious ornaments to
reward his soldiers; in which depredations he was
assisted by his brother-in-law, William de Say, a
stout and warlike man, and one Daniel, a counter-
feit monk. At last, being publicly excommunicated
for his many outrages, he besieged the Castle of
Burwell, in Kent, and going unhelmed, in consequence of the heat of the weather, he was shot in
the head with an arrow, of which wound he soon
afterwards died. This noble outlaw had *m.* Rohesia, daughter of Alberic de Vere, Earl of Oxford,
Chief Justice of England, and had issue, Ernulph,
Geoffrey, William, and Robert; and by a former
wife, whose name is not mentioned, a daughter,

Alice, who *m.* John de Lacy, Constable of Chester. Of his death, Dugdale thus speaks:—"Also that for these outrages, having incurred the penalty of excommunication, he happened to be mortally wounded, at a little town, called Burwell; whereupon, with great contrition for his sins, and making what satisfaction he could, there came at last some of the Knights Templars to him, and putting on him the habit of their order, with a red cross, carried his dead corpse into their orchard, at the old Temple, in London, and coffining it in lead, hanged it on a crooked tree. Likewise, that after some time, by the industry and expenses of William, whom he had constituted Prior of Walden, his absolution was obtained from Pope Alexander III., so that his body was received among christians, and divers offices celebrated for him; but that when the prior endeavoured to take down the coffin and carry it to Walden, the templars being aware of the design, buried it privately in the church-yard of the NEW TEMPLE, viz. in the porch before the west door."

After the decease of this Earl Geoffrey, his son, ERNULPH, within the same year, was taken prisoner in the Castle of Ramsey, which he had fortified, and banished, when

GEOFFREY, surnamed the younger, (the second son,) was restored by King Henry II., to all the lands of his ancestors, and confirmed in the EARLDOM OF ESSEX. This nobleman being an eloquent and accomplished person, was associated with Richard de Lacy, to march against the Welsh, then near Chester, at which city falling sick, it happened that his servants being all gone to dinner, and nobody left with him, he died. Whereupon divers ancient knights then assembled there, who had served his father, and enjoyed large possessions through his bounty, consulting together, resolved to carry his corpse to WALDEN, there to be interred as patron of that house: and for that purpose having taken out his brain and bowels, and committed them to holy sepulture, with honour and alms, they seasoned the rest of his body with salt, then wrapt it in a good hide, and coffined it: and thus proceeded, accompanied by the earl's servants, towards Walden; but upon the way, one of the deceased lord's chaplains, named Hasculf, took out his best saddle horse, in the night, and rode to CHICKSAND, where the *Countess Rohese* then resided with her nuns, and having acquainted her with the death of her son, advised her to send speedily, whatever force she could, to intercept the corpse, and to bring it thither, to the end that the kindred and friends of the deceased, might become benefactors to the Convent of Chicksand; of which design the conductors of the corpse having, however, been apprised, they immediately drew their swords, and thus brought the noble remains in safety to Walden, where they were most magnificently interred. His lordship *m.* Eustachia, a kinswoman of King Henry II., but did not live long with her, and the lady, thereupon, making a complaint to her royal relative, the king is said to have caused, in great wrath, a divorce betwixt them. The earl *d.* on the 12th November, 1167, and leaving no issue, was *s.* by his brother,

WILLIAM DE MANDEVILLE, as third EARL OF ESSEX. This nobleman attended King Henry II. into France, in the 19th of that monarch's reign, as one of the generals of his army. In two years afterwards, (1175,) his lordship was one of the witnesses to the agreement made at Windsor, between the English monarch and Roderic, King of Connaught. In 1177, the earl made a pilgrimage to the Holy Land, and upon his return, repairing to WALDEN, was received by the whole convent in solemn procession, "all of them singing with one heart and voice, *Benedictus qui venit in nomine Domini.*" After which, ascending to the high altar, and there receiving formal benediction from the prior, he offered divers precious relics, some of which he had acquired in the Holy Land, and others from the Emperor of Constantinople, and the Earl of Flanders. Then standing before the altar, the prior began the hymn of *Te Deum Laudamus*, which being ended, he went into the chapter house, and saluted all the monks, and thence into the abbey, where he was feasted honourably. His lordship *m.* first, Hawise, daughter and heiress of William le Gross, Earl of Albemarle, in whose right he bore that additional title; and secondly, Christian, daughter of Robert, Lord Fitz-Walter, (who wedded after the earl's decease, Reymond de Burgh,) but had issue by neither of those ladies. The earl being a person chiefly engaged in military affairs, spent the greater part of his life in Normandy, where he was entrusted with divers forts and castles, by King Henry. He *d.* in 1190, when the EARLDOM must have EXPIRED, but the feudal lordship and estates devolved upon his aunt, BEATRIX, wife of William de Say, whose eldest son, William de Say, dying in the life-time of his father, left two daughters, viz.

    Beatrix, *m.* to Geoffrey Fitz-Piers.

    Maud, *m.* to William de Boeland.

Upon the decease of William de Mandeville, Earl of Essex, as mentioned above, much dispute arose regarding the inheritance; Beatrix, his aunt and heir, in the first place, preferring her claim, sent Geoffrey de Say, her younger son, to transact the business for the livery thereof; but Geoffrey Fitz-Piers insisted upon the right of Beatrix, his wife; nevertheless, Geoffrey de Say, in consideration of seven thousand marks, promised to be paid on a certain day, obtained an instrument in right of his mother, under the king's seal, for the whole of the barony, but the said Geoffrey de Say, making default of payment, this

GEOFFREY FITZPIERS, being a man of great wealth and reputation, made representation that the barony was the right of his wife; and promising to pay the money, obtained livery thereof, and procured the king's confirmation of his title. One of the earliest acts of this feudal lord, was to dispossess the monks of Walden, of certain lands which they had derived from his predecessors, a proceeding followed by a long controversy, which, after being referred to the pope and the king, was finally compromised. Upon the removal of Hubert, archbishop of Canterbury, from the office of Justice of England, by Richard I., this Geoffrey was appointed to succeed him; and at the coronation of King

John, he was girt with the sword, as EARL OF ESSEX, and then served at the king's table. Being nominated patron of the monastery of Walden, he appears soon after to be received with great ceremony by the monks, and to be perfectly reconciled to those holy fathers. In the 7th of King John, he had a grant of the castle and honour of Berkhamstead, with the knights' fees thereunto belonging, to hold to him and the heirs of his body, by Aveline, his second wife. His lordship espoused first, as already stated, Beatrix de Say, by whom he had issue,

GEOFFREY, his successor.
. William, successor to his brother. } These all assumed the name of MANDEVILLE.
Henry, Dean of Wolverhampton.
Maud, m. to Robert de Bohun, Earl of Hereford, whose son and heir became eventually EARL OF ESSEX, as well as Earl of Hereford.

He m. secondly, Aveline —— and had an only son, John Fitspiers, Lord of Berkhamstead. His lordship, of whom Matthew Paris characterises as "ruling the reins of government so, that after his death, the realm was like a ship in a tempest without a pilot." He d. in 1212, and was s. by his eldest son,

GEOFFREY DE MANDEVILLE, who, in the 15th of King John, had livery of the lands of his inheritance, and the same year, bearing the title of EARL OF ESSEX, the king gave him to wife, Isabel, Countess of Gloucester, third daughter and co-heir of William, Earl of Gloucester, (which Isabel had first been married to King John himself, but repudiated on account of consanguinity). · This nobleman afterwards distinguished himself amongst the barons, who rebelled against the tyrannical power of John, and was one of the twenty-five lords chosen to enforce the observance of MAGNA CHARTA: about which period, attending a tournament at London, he received a wound from a lance, which proved mortal. His lordship d. in 1219, and leaving no children, was succeeded by his brother,

WILLIAM MANDEVILLE, as EARL OF ESSEX. This nobleman, like his deceased kinsman, espoused the cause of the barons, and stoutly maintained it even after the decease of King John; being one of those who then assisted Lewis of France, in the siege of Berkhamstead Castle, occupied by the king's forces. A sally having been made, however, from the garrison, much of the baggage of the besiegers was captured, and amongst other things the banner of this Earl William. His lordship seems to have made his peace soon after, for we find him engaged in the Welsh wars. He d. in the flower of his age, anno 1227, and leaving no issue, the EARLDOM OF ESSEX devolved upon his sister, Maud, Countess of Hereford, (see Bohun, Earl of Hereford,) while the lands which he inherited passed to his half brother,

JOHN FITZ-PIERS, who was sheriff of Yorkshire, in the 18th Henry III. He m. Isabel, sister of John Bigod, and was s. by his son,

John Fitz-John Fitz-Geoffrey, whose son and heir,

JOHN FITZ-JOHN, was summoned to parliament as a BARON, temp. Henry III. (see Fitz-John).

ARMS.—Quarterly or. and gules.

MANNY—BARON MANNY.

By Writ of Summons, dated 13th November, 1347, 21 Edward III.

Lineage.

WALTER DE MANNY, (an alien, born in the diocese of Cambray,) being a person of high military repute, was made a knight of the Bath, in the 5th Edward III.; after which we find him one of the most gallant and enterprising characters of the martial period, in which he had the fortune to flourish. In the 8th, 9th, and 10th, of the same reign, Sir Walter was engaged in the Scottish wars, and in the 11th, he was constituted admiral of the king's fleet, northwards, being the same year sworn of the privy council. "Shortly after this," says Dugdale, " he was in the battel of Cagant, against the French; and seeing Henry, Earl of Derby, son to Henry, Earl of Lancaster, felled to the ground, he brought him out of danger, and cryed, *Lancaster for the Earl of Derby.*" In the week also, that defiance was made to the French king, he rode through Brabant night and day, with forty spears, until he reached Hainault; having pledged himself to divers " ladies fair," previously to leaving England, that he should be the first to invade France, and to win some town or castle there: in redemption of which chivalrous promise, he entered Mortaigne, with his penon borne him, through the high-street; but coming to the great tower, found the gate closed against him. Upon which, causing the watch of the castle to sound his horn, and cry, *Treason, treason,* he retraced his steps, and fired the adjoining street. Thence he proceeded to Conde, and on to Valenciennes, from which place he marched to CHINE, and took by assault, the strong castle there; whereof, making it a garrison, he appointed his brother, Giles Manny, governor. He thence joined the king at MACHLINE. In about two years after this, Sir Walter Manny was in an expedition made into the north of France, and there his usual fortune attended him—he spoiled the country, slew more than a thousand soldiers, and burnt three hundred villages. In the same year (14th Edward III.) he was in the great sea fight, between the French and English, before Sluce, in Flanders; and for his disbursements in that and other services, had an assignation of two thousand pounds, payable by the receiver of the subsidy then levied in Essex. In the 16th Edward III., he attended the king to the siege of NANTES; and in consideration of four thousand pounds, which he remitted of the sum of eight thousand pounds, then due to him from the crown, he obtained a grant for life, of the sheriffalty of Merionethshire; and an assignation of sixty-eight sacks, and one quartern of the king's wools in Sussex, for the support of himself, and fifty men at arms, with fifty archers on horseback, in the expedition then made into France. His own wages as a banneret, being four shillings

335

per day; the knights, (twelve in number,) two shillings each, per day; the esquires, one shilling, and the archers, sixpence. In two years afterwards, being one of the marshals of the host to the Earl of Derby, when he went to assault Bergerath, he said to his lordship, as he sate at dinner, "Sir, if we were good men at arms, we should drink this evening with the French lords at BERGERATH." Whereupon all that heard him, cried, "to arms," and the town being immediately assaulted, surrendered to its gallant assailants.

"Amongst other towns," saith Dugdale, "then won by the Earl of Derby, RYOL being one; this Walter found the tombe of his father, who had been buried there. Of whose death, Froisard makes this relation; viz. "That at a certain tourneament before Cambray, (there being on both parts, five hundred knights,) he tourneyed with a knight of Gascoine, a kinsman to the bishop of Cambray; and wounded him so sore, as that he died soon after. Which so incensed the kindred of that knight, that upon a pacification made, he was, for expiation of the knight's death, to go on a pilgrimage to St. James: and that upon his return thence, finding RYOL besieged by COUNT CHARLES, OF VALOIS, brother to King PHILIP, (it being then in the hands of the English,) coming back at night towards his lodging from a visit, which he had made to that count, he was murthered by some of the knight's kindred, who lay purposely in wait for him. And that upon tidings brought to the count, he caused his body to be buried in a little chappel without the town; which when the town came to be enlarged, was encompassed by the walls."

Sir Walter Manny was subsequently one of the most conspicuous heroes of CRESSY, having a principal command in the VAN of the English army. From this celebrated field he repaired to the siege of Calais, where King Edward and his victorious son, the BLACK PRINCE, condescended to array themselves under Sir Walter's banner, and fighting beneath it reduced that strong and important place. About this period, in reward of all those heroic achievements, Sir Walter Manny was summoned to parliament as a BARON, and thenceforward during the remainder of his life. He had likewise large grants from the crown, and was made a KNIGHT of the GARTER. His lordship continued actively engaged in the French war, until the peace concluded with France in the 49d Edward III., when he was one of those who swore to observe the articles of the treaty. His lordship espoused the Lady Margaret Plantagenet, styled Countess of Norfolk, eldest daughter, and eventually co-heiress of Thomas of Brotherton, Duke of Norfolk, and widow of John, Lord Segrave, by whom he left an only daughter and heiress,

ANNE MANNY, who m. John de Hastings, Earl of Pembroke.

This great and gallant nobleman d. in 1372. His will bears date at LONDON, upon St. Andrew's Day, in the preceding year. By that testament he bequeathed his body to be buried in the midst of the quire of the Carthusians, (commonly called the Charter-house,) near West Smithfield, in the suburbs of London, of his own foundation, but

without any great pomp; appointing that his executors should cause twenty masses to be sung for his soul; and that every poor body coming to his funeral, should have a penny to pray for him, and for the remission of his sins. To Mary, his sister, (at that time a nun,) he bequeathed £10. To his two bastard daughters, nuns also, (namely, Malbosel and Malpiesant,) the one two hundred franks, the other one hundred. To Margaret, his wife, all his silver vessels; likewise his girdle of gold, with all his girdles and knives. Also his beds, and dressers in his wardrobe; excepting his folding bed, pale of blue and red, which he gave to his daughter of PEMBROKE. Moreover, he ordained, that a tomb of alabaster, with his image as a knight, and his arms thereon, should be made for him, like unto that of Sir John Beauchamp, in the cathedral of St. Paul, at London, as a remembrance of him, and that men might pray for his soul. And whereas the king did owe him an old debt of a £1000, by bills of his wardrobe; he appointed, that if it could be had, it should be given to the prior and monks of the CHARTER-HOUSE, whereof he was founder. And whereas, there was due to him from the prince, from the time he had been Prince of Wales, the sum of one hundred marks per annum for his salary, as governor of Hardelagh Castle, he bequeathed a moiety thereof to the said prior and monks of the Charter-house before-mentioned, and the other moiety to his executors, (of which he constituted Sir Guyde de Bryene one,) for the performance of his testament.

Upon the decease of Lord Manny, the BARONY OF MANNY devolved upon his daughter, Anne, COUNTESS OF PEMBROKE, and at the decease of her son, John Hastings, third Earl of Pembroke, without issue, it became EXTINCT.

ARMS.—Sa. a cross voided, ar.

MANSELL—BARONS MANSELL OF MARGAM IN THE COUNTY OF GLAMORGAN.

By Letters Patent, dated 31st December, 1711.

Lineage.

The family of MANSELL, according to genealogists, sprang from an ancient stock; whereof

PHILIP MANSEL is said to have come over with the Conqueror: and from his eldest son,

HENRY MANSEL descended

JOHN MANSELL, who, in the reign of Henry III., being chancellor of the church of St. Paul's, was appointed keeper of the king's seal, and was a very eminent person at that period. This John m. Joane, daughter of Simon Beauchamp, of Bedford, and was father of

SIR HENRY MANSELL, whose son,

HENRY MANSELL settled in Glamorganshire, temp. Edward I., and from him descended

THOMAS MANSELL, Esq., who was created a baronet, at the institution of the order, in 1611. From Sir Thomas we pass to his lineal descendant,

SIR THOMAS MANSELL, fourth baronet, who was elevated to the peerage on 31st December, 1711, as BARON MANSELL, of Margam, in the county of

Glamorgan. His lordship m. Martha, daughter and heiress of Francis Mellington, Esq., of the city of London, merchant, by whom he had, (with three daughters,)

    ROBERT, who m. Anne, daughter and co-heir of the celebrated Admiral Sir Cloudesley Shovel, Knt., and dying before his father, (29th April, 1723,) left, with one daughter,

        THOMAS, successor to his grandfather.

    Christopher, } who both succeeded eventually
    Bussey,   } to the title.

His lordship d. in 1723, and was s. by his grandson,

THOMAS MANSELL, second baron. This nobleman d. unmarried in 1743, when the honours reverted to his uncle,

CHRISTOPHER MANSELL, third baron, who d. in the ensuing year unmarried, and was s. by his brother,

BUSSEY MANSELL, fourth baron. This nobleman espoused, first, Lady Betty Hervey, daughter of John, Earl of Bristol, by whom he had no issue. He m. secondly, Barbara, widow of Sir Walter Blacket, Bart., and daughter of William, Earl of Jersey, and had an only daughter and heiress,

    LOUISA-BARBARA MANSELL, who m. George, second Baron Vernon, by whom she had two daughters, who both d. in infancy, and a third, LOUISA, who d. unmarried in 1786. Her ladyship d. in the same year.

His lordship d. in 1750, when the BARONY OF MANSELL became EXTINCT.

ARMS.—A chevron betw. three maunches, sa.

MARE—BARON LA MARE.

By Writ of Summons, dated 6th February, 1299, 27 Edward I.

Families of the surname of DE LA MARE flourished simultaneously in the counties of Wilts, Somerset, Hereford, and Oxford, whereof

HENRY DE LA MARE, (of the Oxfordshire House,) upon the demise of his father, in the 5th year of King Stephen, paid a fine of £26. 6s. 8d., that he might enjoy his office of *veltrare*, or huntsman to the king; for so he was, holding the post by petty serjeanty. To this Henry succeeded

ROBERT DE LA MARE, who was sheriff of Oxfordshire in the 34th Henry II., and of Oxford and Berks, in the 1st and 2d years of Richard I. He was s. by

GEFFERY DE LA MARE, who gave a fine of one hundred marks, and one palfrey for warranty of his lands at Dudercote, in the county of Berks. From this Geffery descended

JOHN DE LA MARE, of Gersyndon, afterwards called Garsyngton, in the county of Oxford, who, having been engaged in the French and Scottish wars of King Edward I., was summoned to parliament as a Baron from 6th February, 1299, to 26th July, 1313. But of his lordship nothing further is known, and Dugdale says, that his descendants had never afterwards summons to parliament.

ARMS.—Gules, two lions passant in pale, ar.

MARMYON, OR MARMION — BARONS MARMYON.

FEUDAL.

[Although it is not intended that this work shall embrace personages who were *merely* feudal lords, the present family, as that from which the CHAMPIONSHIP OF ENGLAND is inherited, demands to be noticed.]

Lineage.

At the period of the Norman conquest,

ROBERT DE MARMYON, Lord of Fontney, in Normandy, having by grant of King William the castle of Tamworth, in the county of Warwick, with the adjacent lands, expelled the nuns from the abbey of Polesworth, to a place called Oldbury, about four miles distant. "After which," (writes Sir William Dugdale,) "within the compass of a twelvemonth, as it is said, making a costly entertainment at Tamworth Castle, for some of his friends, amongst whom was Sir Walter de Somervile, Lord of Whichover, in the county of Stafford, his sworn brother: it happened, that as he lay in his bed, St. Edith appeared to him in the habit of a veiled nun, with a crosier in her hand, and advertised him, that if he did not restore the abbey of Polesworth, which lay within the territories belonging to his castle of Tamworth, unto her successors, he should have an evil death, and go to hell. And, that he might be the more sensible of this her admonition, she smote him on the side with the point of her crosier, and so vanished away. Moreover, that by this stroke being much wounded, he cryed out so loud, that his friends in the house arose; and finding him extremely tormented with the pain of his wound, advised him to confess himself to a priest, and vow to restore the nuns to their former possessions. Furthermore, that having so done, his pain ceased; and that in accomplishment of his vow, accompanied by Sir Walter de Somervile, and the rest, he forthwith rode to Oldbury; and craving pardon of the nuns for the injury done, brought them back to Polesworth, desiring that himself, and his friend Sir Walter de Somervile, might be reputed their patrons, and have burial for themselves and their heirs in the abbey—the Marmions in the chapter house—the Somerviles in the cloyster. However, (continues Dugdale,) some circumstances in this story may seem fabulous, the substance of it is certainly true; for it expressly appeareth by the very words of his charter, that he gave to Osanna the prioress, *for the establishing of the religion of those nuns there, the church of St. Edith, of Polesworth, with its appurtenances, so that the convent of Oldbury should remain in that place.* And likewise bestowed upon them the whole lordship of Polesworth: which grant King Stephen afterwards confirmed." The castle and manor of Tamworth, in Warwickshire, and the manor of Scrivelsby, in the county of Lincoln, were granted by the Conqueror to this Robert de Marmion, to be held by grand serjeanty, " to perform the office of champion at the king's coronation," (the Marmions, it is said, were hereditary champions to the Dukes of Normandy, prior to the conquest of England). Robert

Marmion was succeeded at his decease by his son and heir,

ROBERT DE MARMYON, Lord of Fontney, in Normandy, where he possessed a fortified castle, which was besieged by Geoffrey, of Anjou, in the 6th of King Stephen, and demolished. This Robert having a great enmity to the Earl of Chester, who had a noble seat at Coventry, entered the priory there in the 8th of Stephen, and expelling the monks, turned it into a fortification, digging at the same time divers deep ditches in the adjacent fields, which he caused to be covered over with earth, in order to secure the approaches thereto; but the Earl of Chester's forces drawing near, as he rode out to reconnoitre, he fell into one of those very ditches, and broke his thigh, so that a common soldier, presently seizing him, cut off his head. He was s. by his son,

ROBERT DE MARMION, who, in the 31st Henry II., being constituted sheriff of Worcestershire, continued in that office until the end of the four-and-thirtieth year. He was also justice itinerant in Warwickshire, and some other counties—and again sheriff of Worcestershire in the 1st of Richard I. In five years afterwards he attended that monarch into Normandy, and in the 15th of King John he was in the expedition then made into Poictou. This feudal lord died about the year 1217, leaving issue, by different mothers,

 ROBERT, his successor.
 Robert, jun., who had the estates of Witringham and Coningsby, in the county of Lincoln (see Marmion, Barons Marmion, of Witrington).
 William, of Torington (see Marmion, Barons Marmion).

He was s. by his eldest son,

ROBERT DE MARMION, who appears to have sided with the French, when they seized upon Normandy in the beginning of King John's reign, for the murder of Arthur, Duke of Britanny; but afterwards making his peace, for in the 5th of Henry III. he had livery of Tamworth Castle, and his father's other lands. He is supposed to have returned to Normandy in twelve years afterwards, and to have died there in 1241, when he was s. by his son,

PHILIP DE MARMION, who was sheriff for the counties of Warwick and Leicester, from the 33rd to the 36th of Henry III. In the latter of which years he was questioned for sitting with Richard de Mundevill, and the rest of the justices, for gaol-delivery at Warwick, having no commission so to do. The next year he attended the king into Gascony; upon his return whence he was taken prisoner by the French at Pontes, in Poictou, with John de Plessets, then Earl of Warwick, notwithstanding they had letters of safe conduct from the king of France. In the 45th of the same reign this feudal lord had summons to be at London with divers of the nobility, upon the morrow after *Simon and Jude's day*; in which year the defection of many of the barons began further to manifest itself, by their assuming the royal prerogative, in placing sheriffs throughout different shires. In this period of difficulty Philip de Marmion, being of

unimpeachable loyalty, had, by special patent from the king, the counties of Suffolk and Norfolk committed to his custody, with the castles of Norwich and Oxford: a well-judged confidence, for through all the subsequent fortunes of Henry III. he never once swerved from his allegiance. He was present at the battle of Lewes—and his fidelity was rewarded after the royal victory of Evesham, by some valuable grants for life, and the governorship of Kenilworth Castle. He m. Joane, youngest daughter, and eventually sole heiress of Hugh de Kilpec, by whom he had four daughters, his co-heirs, viz.

Joane, m. to William Mosteyn, and died s. p. in 1294.

Mazera, m. to Ralph Cromwell, and had an only daughter and heiress,

 Joane, m. to Alexander, Baron Freville, whose grandson,
  Sir Baldwin de Freville, Lord Freville, claimed the championship in the 1st Richard II., by the tenure of Tamworth Castle, but the matter was determined against him in favour of Sir John Dymoke.

Maud, m. to Ralph Botiller, and died s. p.

Joane, m. to Sir Thomas de Ludlow, Knt., and had issue,

 John de Ludlow, who died s. p.
 Margaret de Ludlow, sole heiress at the decease of her brother, m. Sir John Dymoke, Knt., and brought into the family of her husband the manor of SCRIVELABY, in Lincolnshire, by which the Dymokes have from the accession of Richard II. exercised the chivalrous office of CHAMPION at the CORONATIONS of the KINGS OF ENGLAND: and have intermarried with the most eminent families. Our space compels us to pass over the various champions to JOHN DYMOKE, champion to King George III., who d. in 1784, leaving issue, by his wife, Martha, daughter of Josiah Holmes, Esq.,

  Lewis.
  JOHN, Prebendary of Lincoln.
  Catherine, m. to John Bradshaw, Esq.
  Elizabeth, died s. p.
  Sophia, m. John Tyrwhit, Esq.
 Lewis Dymoke succeeded his father at Scrivesby, and served the office of sheriff of Lincolnshire. He was s. by his brother,
 THE REV. JOHN DYMOKE, who was called upon to act as champion at the coronation of King George IV., but owing to his clerical station, he deputed his son, HENRY DYMOKE, Esq., who executed the office accordingly. The reverend gentleman d., we believe, in 1828, and has been succeeded by his son above-mentioned, who is now in his own right CHAMPION OF ENGLAND.

Upon the decease of Philip de Marmion, his estates

passed to his co-heiresses, and eventually the barony and manor of Tamworth to Freville, and Scrivelsby to Dymoke.

At the coronation of King Richard II. Sir Baldwin Freville, then Lord of Tamworth, exhibited his claim to be king's champion that day, and to do the service appertaining to that office, by reason of his tenure of Tamworth Castle, viz.

"To ride completely armed upon a barbed horse into Westminster Hall, and there to challenge the combat with whomsoever should dare to oppose the king's title to the crown."

Which service the Barons de Marmion, his ancestors, lords of that castle, had theretofore performed. But Sir John Dymoke counterclaimed the same office as Lord of Scrivelsby. Whereupon the constable and marshal of England, appointed the said Sir John Dymoke to perform the office at that time.

The chief part of Scrivelsby Court, the ancient baronial seat, was destroyed by fire sixty or seventy years ago. In the part consumed was a very large hall, on the panels of the wainscoting of which was depicted the various arms and alliances of the family through all its numerous and far-traced descents. The loss has been, in some degree, compensated by the addition which the late proprietors made to those parts which escaped the ravages of the flames. Against the south wall of the chancel in the parish church of Scrivelsby, is a very handsome marble monument, ornamented with a bust of the Hon. Lewis Dymoke, champion at the coronation of the two first sovereigns of the House of Brunswick. On the north side of the chancel is a marble tablet to the memory of the Hon. John Dymoke, who performed the duties of champion at the coronation of King George III. On the floor of the south side of the communion table is a plate of copper, on which is an inscription to the memory of Sir Charles Dymoke, Knt., who was champion at the coronation of King James II. At the eastern end of the aisle are two tombs, on one of which is the figure of a knight in chain armour, cross-legged, on the other that of a lady with a lion at her feet. By the side of these is the tomb of Sir Robert Dymoke, who was champion at the coronations of Richard III., Henry VII., and Henry VIII. On the floor of the aisle is also a stone which once contained a brass figure, with corner shields, and an inscription, all of which are now gone.

In July, 1814, Lewis Dymoke, Esq., uncle of the present champion, presented a petition to the crown, praying to be declared entitled to the BARONY OF MARMION, of Scrivelsby, in virtue of the seisure of the manor of Scrivelsby; which petition was referred to the attorney-general, who having reported thereon, the same was referred to the House of Lords, where evidence was received at the bar, and the claimant's counsel summoned up, when the attorney-general was heard in reply, and tendered some documents on the part of the crown; but the claimant died before the judgment of the house was given.

"With respect to this claim," says Mr. Nicolas, "it is to be observed, that though the manor of Scrivelsby was held by the service of performing the office of king's champion by Robert de Mar-

myon, in the reign of William the Conqueror, he was not by seisure thereof a baron, but by seisure of the barony and castle of TAMWORTH, which he held of the king in capite by knights' service; so that, if at this period baronies by tenure were admitted, the possessor of the manor and lordship of Tamworth, (which in the division of his property fell to the share of Joane, his eldest daughter, wife of William Mosteyn, and on her death s. p. to Alexander Freville, husband of Joan, daughter and heir of Ralph Cromwell, by Mazera, the next sister of the said Joan de Mosteyn,) would possess the claim to the barony enjoyed by Robert de Marmion, he having derived his dignity from that barony instead of from the seisure of the manor of Scrivelsby. Moreover, if Philip Marmyon, the last baron, had died seised of a barony in fee, Lewis Dymoke was not even a co-heir of the said Philip, though he was the descendant of one of his daughters and co-heirs."

ARMS.—Vairée, a fesse gules.

MARMYON, OR MARMION — BARONS MARMION OF WETRINGTON, IN THE COUNTY OF LINCOLN.

By Writ of Summons, dated 26th January, 1297,
25 Edward I.

Lineage.

ROBERT DE MARMYON, eldest son by his second wife, of Robert de Marmyon, third feudal Lord of Tamworth, had the lordships of Witringham, and Coningsby, in the county of Lincoln; Dueinton, in the county of Gloucester; and Berwick, in the county of Suffolk; by especial grant of his father: and in the 16th of King John, he gave to the king, three hundred and fifty marks, and five palfreys, for licence to marry Amice, the daughter of Jerneygan Fitz-hugh. After which, being in arms with the rebellious barons, he obtained letters of safe conduct for coming in to the king, to make his peace. He again, however, took up arms in the baronial cause, in the ensuing reign, along with his brother William, and appears to have held out to the last. This Robert acquired a large accession of landed property with his wife, Alice Fitz-hugh, and was s. at his decease, by his son,

WILLIAM DE MARMION, who m. Lora, daughter of Roese de Dovor, by whom he acquired the town of Ludington, in Northamptonshire, and was s. by his son,

JOHN DE MARMION, who, in the 22nd of Edward I., had summons, with other great men, to attend the king to advise upon the affairs of the realm: and was summoned to parliament as a BARON, from 26th January, 1297, to the 14th March, 1322. In the 4th of Edward II., his lordship had, licence to make a castle of his house, called the Hermitage, in the county of York. He d. in 1322, and was s. by his son,

JOHN DE MARMION, second baron, summoned to parliament, from 3d December, 1326, to 1st April, 1335. This nobleman was engaged in the

Scottish wars. His lordship m. Maud, daughter of Lord Furnival, and had issue,

    Robert, his successor.

    Joane, m. to Sir John Bernack, Knt.

    Alice, second wife of Sir John de Grey, Lord Grey, of Rotherfield, and had issue,

        John de Grey, who assumed the surname of Marmion, d. s. p. in 1385.

        Robert de Grey assumed the name of Marmion—m. Lora, daughter and co-heir of Herbert de St. Quintin, and had an only daughter and heiress,

            Elizabeth Marmion, who m. Henry, Lord Fitz-hugh, K.G.

The baron d. in 1335, and was s. by his son,

ROBERT DE MARMION, third baron, but never summoned to parliament. This nobleman being of infirm constitution, and having no issue, married his younger sister, Alice, by the advice of his friends, to Sir John Grey, Lord Grey of Rotherfield, upon condition that the issue of the said Sir John Grey and Alice, should bear the surname of Marmion. At the decease of his lordship, the BARONY OF MARMION, of Witrington, fell into ABEYANCE between his sisters (refer to children of second baron). The elder of whom, Joane, Lady Bernack, died without issue. The younger Alice, as stated above, espoused Lord Grey, and her grand-daughter, Elizabeth, m. Henry, Lord Fitz-hugh, amongst whose representatives, this BARONY continues suspended.

ARMS.—Vairée ar. and as. a fesse gules.

MARMYON, OR MARMION—BARON MARMION.

By Writ of Summons, dated 24th December, 1264, 49 Henry III.

Lineage.

WILLIAM DE MARMYON, youngest son of Robert de Marmyon, third feudal Lord of Tamworth, having taken a leading part in the baronial war against King Henry III., was summoned as a BARON to the parliament called in the king's name, by those turbulent lords, after their triumph at Lewes, but never subsequently. His lordship appears to have d. without issue, when the BARONY became, of course, EXTINCT.

ARMS.—Vairée ar. and as. a fesse gules.

MARNEY — BARONS MARNEY, OF LEYR-MARNEY, IN THE COUNTY OF ESSEX.

By Letters Patent, dated 9th April, 1523.

Lineage.

In the 9th Edward III.,

WILLIAM DE MARNEY obtained a charter for free warren in all his demesne lands, at Leyr-Marney, in the county of Essex. To this William s. another

WILLIAM DE MARNEY, who, in the 3rd Henry IV., was constituted sheriff of the counties of Essex and Hertford. He d. in the 2nd Henry V., and was s. by

SIR THOMAS MARNEY, Knt., who left an only daughter and heir,

MARGARET MARNEY, at whose decease in minority, and unmarried, the estates reverted to her uncle,

JOHN MARNEY, who was s. by his son,

SIR HENRY MARNEY, Knt., who being " a person of great wisdom, gravity, and of singular fidelity to that prudent prince King Henry VII.," was made choice of for one of his privy council, in the first year of his reign, and the next year he commanded against the Earl Lincoln, at the battle of Stoke. He was subsequently engaged against Lord Audley and the Cornish rebels, at Blackheath. Upon the accession of Henry VIII., he was re-sworn of the privy council, and soon afterwards installed a Knight of the Garter. Sir Henry was subsequently appointed captain of the guard to the king, and upon the attainder of Edward Stafford, Duke of Buckingham, he had grants of a large proportion of that nobleman's estates. He was appointed keeper of the privy seal in February, 1523, and elevated to the peerage in the April following, as BARON MARNEY, of Leyr-Marney, in the county of Essex.

His lordship m. first, Thomasine, daughter of John Arundel, Esq., of Lanherne, in Cornwall, by whom he had two sons, John, his successor, and Thomas, who died young, and a daughter Elizabeth, who m. Thomas Bonham, Esq. He espoused, secondly, Elizabeth, daughter of Alderman Nicholas Wifield, Lord Mayor of London, and had a daughter, who m. Sir Henry Bedingfield. His lordship d. in 1524, and was s. by his son,

JOHN MARNEY, second baron. This nobleman in the time of his father, was one of the esquires of the body to King Henry VIII., and governor of Rochester Castle. His lordship m. first, Christian, daughter and heir of Sir Roger Newburgh, by whom he had two daughters, viz.

    Katherine, m. first, to George Ratcliffe, Esq., and secondly, to Thomas, Lord Poynings.

    Elisabeth, m. to Lord Thomas Howard, afterwards created Viscount Bindon.

Lord Marney, espoused, secondly, Margaret, daughter of Sir William Waldegrave, Knt., and widow of Thomas Finderne, Esq., but had no issue. He died in 1525, when the BARONY OF MARNEY became EXTINCT, and his estates devolved upon his daughters as co-heirs.

ARMS.—Gu. a lion rampant, guardant ar.

MARSHAL—BARONS MARSHAL.

By Writ of Summons, dated 9th January, 1309, 2 Edward II.

Lineage.

The earliest notice of this family occurs in the time of Henry I., when Gilbert Mareschall, and John, his son, were impleaded by Robert de Venois, and William de Hastings, for the office of Mareshall to the king, but without success. The son, (bearing the same surname, derived from his office,)

JOHN MARESCHALL, attaching himself to the

fortunes of MAUD, against King Stephen, was with ROBERT, the *Consul*, Earl of Gloucester, at the siege of Winchester Castle, when the party of the empress sustained so signal a defeat. Upon the accession of Henry II., however, his fidelity was amply rewarded by considerable 'grants in the county of Wilts; and in the 10th of that monarch's reign, being then marshal, he laid claim, for the crown, to one of the manors of the see of Canterbury, from the celebrated prelate, Thomas à Becket, who about that period had commenced his contest with the king. To this John succeeded his son and heir,

JOHN MARESCHALL, to whom King Henry II., confirmed the office of marshal, and the lands which he held of the crown in England, and elsewhere. At the coronation of RICHARD I., this John Mareschall bore the great gilt spurs, and the same year obtained a grant from the crown of the manor of BOSHAM, in Sussex, in fee farm, paying forty-two pounds yearly, to the exchequer; with other extensive lordships. He died soon after, and it appears issueless, for his brother, *William Mareschall*, EARL OF PEMBROKE, succeeded as his heir. We now come to the nephew of the said William, Earl of Pembroke,

SIR JOHN MARSHAL, who married Aliva, elder daughter and co-heir of HUBERT DE RIE, feudal Lord of HINGHAM, in the county of Norfolk, by whom he acquired that lordship. Espousing the cause of *King John* against the BARONS, Sir John Marshal acquired from the crown, all the forfeited lands of the Earl of Evreux, in England, as also the lands of Hugh de Gornai, lying in the counties of Norfolk and Suffolk, whereof the said Hugh was possessed, when he deserted the royal banner; and he likewise obtained a grant in fee, of the office of MARSHAL OF IRELAND. He was, subsequently, in the same reign, constituted guardian of the Marches of Wales, and Sheriff of Lincolnshire, and afterwards joined with John Fitz-Robert, in the Sheriffalty of the counties of Norfolk and Suffolk, and the custody of the Castles of Norwich and Orford. He was likewise made governor of Dorchester Castle; moreover, in the same year, livery of the office of marshal of Ireland, and whatsoever did appertain thereto; so that he should appoint a knight to execute its duties effectually. Continuing steadfast in his allegiance to King John, he was made sheriff of Worcestershire, and governor of the Castle of Worcester: and he was one of those who marched with the king into the north, to waste the lands of the insurrectionary barons there. Upon the accession of Henry III., Sir John Marshal was constituted sheriff of Hampshire, and governor of the Castle of Devizes, in Wilts, and retained, during the remainder of his life, the favour of that monarch. He d. in 1234, and was s. by his son,

WILLIAM MARSHAL, who, adopting a different line of politics, joined the baronial standard, in the 49th of Henry III., and died about the same period, leaving two sons, JOHN and WILLIAM, then under age, who, the next year, through the intercession of William de Say, obtained the king's pardon for their father's transgression, and had permission to enjoy his lands, with whatever pos-

sessions they had, by gift of Aliva, their grandmother. The elder of these sons,

JOHN MARSHAL, died in the 12th Edward I., and was s. by his son,

WILLIAM MARSHAL, who, in the 34th Edward I., was in the wars of Scotland, and was summoned to parliament as a BARON, from 9th January, 1309, to 26th November, 1313. His lordship d. in the next year, and was s. by his son,

JOHN MARSHAL, second Baron, but never summoned to parliament. In the 7th of Edward II., this John attended Queen Elizabeth into Scotland, and the ensuing year doing his homage, had livery of his lands, lying in the counties of Norfolk and Lincoln. He died soon after, about the year 1316, leaving his sister, HAWYSE, wife of *Robert*, LORD MORLEY, his heir, who carried the BARONY OF MARSHAL into the MORLEY family, from which it passed into that of LOVEL, and thence to the PARKERS, when it finally fell into ABEYANCE, upon the decease of THOMAS PARKER, LORD MORLEY, in 1696, between the issue of that nobleman's aunts,

　　Katherine, wife of John Savage, second Earl Rivers.

　　Elizabeth, wife of —— Cranfield, Esq., and amongst whose descendants it so continues.

ARMS.—Gu. a bend lozengée, or.

MARSHAL—EARLS OF PEMBROKE.

EARLDOM, conferred upon the family of CLARE, in 1138.

Conveyed to the MARSHALS by an heiress.

Lineage.

ISABEL DE CLARE, only child and heiress of RICHARD DE CLARE, (surnamed *Strongbow*,) EARL OF PEMBROKE, who had been under the guardianship of Henry II., was given in marriage by *King* RICHARD I., to

WILLIAM MARSHAL, of the great baronial family of Marischal, (see Marshal, Barons Marshal,) Marshal to the King. This William is first noticed as receiving from *Prince* HENRY, the rebellious son of Henry II., upon the prince's death-bed, his cross, as his most confidential friend, to convey to Jerusalem. He espoused the great heiress of the CLARES, in 1189, and with her acquired the EARLDOM OF PEMBROKE—in which rank he bore the royal sceptre of gold, surmounted by the cross, at the coronation of King Richard I.; and he was soon afterwards, on the king's purposing a journey to the Holy Land, appointed one of the assistants to Hugh, Bishop of Durham, and William, Earl of Albemarle, Chief Justice of England, in the government of the realm. Upon the decease of his brother,[*] John Mareschall, Marshal of the King's

---

[*] He was brother and heir male, of John Marshal, otherwise Mareschall (for whose descent, see Marshal, Barons Marshal). This family enjoyed the office of MARSHAL of the King's House, and from that post assumed its surname: which gave occasion, says Banks, to their being often styled Earls Marshal, as well as Earls of Striguil and

House, in 1199, he became lord marshal; and on the day of the coronation of King John, he was invested with the sword of the Earldom of Pembroke, being then confirmed in the possession of the said inheritance. In the first year of this monarch's reign, his lordship was appointed sheriff of Gloucestershire, and likewise of Sussex, wherein he was continued for several years. In the 5th he had a grant of GOEBRICH CASTLE, in the county of Hereford, to hold by the service of two knights' fees; and in four years afterwards, he obtained, by grant from the crown, the whole PROVINCE OF LEINSTER, in Ireland, to hold by the service of one hundred knights' fees. Upon the breaking out of the baronial insurrection, the Earl of Pembroke was deputed, with the Archbishop of Canterbury, by the king, to ascertain the grievances and demands of those turbulent lords; and at the demise of King John, he was so powerful, as to prevail upon the barons, to appoint a day for the coronation of Henry III., to whom he was constituted guardian, by the rest of the nobility, who had remained firm in their allegiance. He subsequently took up arms in the royal cause, and after achieving a victory over the barons, at Lincoln, proceeded directly to London, and investing that great city, both by land and water, reduced it to extremity, for want of provisions. Peace, however, being soon after concluded, it was relieved. His lordship, at this period, executed the office of sheriff for the counties of Essex and Hertford. This eminent nobleman was no less distinguished by his wisdom in the council, and valour in the field, than by his piety and his attachment to the church, of which his numerous munificent endowments bear ample testimony. His lordship had, by the HEIRESS OF CLARE, FIVE SONS, who succeeded each other in his lands and honours, and five daughters, viz.

Maud, m. first to Hugh Bigot, Earl of Norfolk; secondly, to William de Warren, Earl of Surrey: and thirdly, to Walter de Dunstanville. This lady, upon the decease of her youngest brother, Anselm, Earl of Pembroke, s. p., in 1245, and the division of the estates, obtained, as her share, the manor of Hempsted-Marshall, in Berks, with the office of MARSHAL of ENGLAND, which was inherited by her son, Roger Bigot, fourth EARL OF NORFOLK, and surrendered to the crown by her grandson, Roger Bigot, fifth Earl of Norfolk.

Maud, Countess of Norfolk, had likewise the manors of Chepstow and Carlogh.

Joane, m. to Warine de Montchensy.

Isabel, m. to Gilbert de Clare, Earl of Gloucester; and secondly, to Richard, Earl of Cornwall. This lady had, as her portion, Kilkenny.

Pembroke; but such denomination was matter of curiosity more than of reality. The Manor of Hempsted-Marshal, in Berkshire, belonging to the Marshals, was held of old by grand serjeanty of the Kings of England, to be the knights marshals, as the offices of steward, constable, &c., were in those times granted.

342

Sybil, m. to William de Ferrers, Earl of Derby, to whom she brought Kildare.

Eve, m. to William de Brosse, of Brecknock. The earl died in 1219, and was s. by his eldest son,

WILLIAM MARSHAL, Earl of Pembroke, who, in the time of his father, was as strenuous a supporter of the baronial cause as that nobleman was of the royal interests; and was constituted one of the celebrated TWENTY-FIVE BARONS appointed to enforce the observance of MAGNA CHARTA, being then styled " Comes Mareschal, Jun." After the decease of King John, however, he made his peace, and, becoming loyally attached to the new monarch, obtained grants of the forfeited lands of his former companions, Seier de Quincy, Earl of Winchester, and David, Earl of Huntingdon. His lordship was subsequently engaged against the Welch, and defeated their Prince, LEOLINE, with great slaughter; and in the 14th Henry III., he was captain-general of the king's forces in Britanny. He m. first, Alice, daughter of Baldwin de Betun, Earl of Albermarle; and secondly, the Lady Alianore Plantagenet, daughter of King John, and sister of Henry III., but had issue by neither. He d. in 1231, and was s. by his next brother,

RICHARD MARSHAL, Earl of Pembroke. This nobleman returned to England upon the decease of his brother, and repairing to the king, then in Wales, offered to do homage for his inheritance; but Henry, at the suggestion of HUBERT DE BURGH, justiciary of England, declined receiving it, under the plea that the late earl's widow had been left in a state of pregnancy; and the king, at the same time, commanded Marshal forthwith to depart the realm within fifteen days; upon which he repaired to Ireland, where his brothers then were, who, with the army, received him cordially, and, delivering up the castles to him, did their homage. He immediately afterwards took possession of the castle of Pembroke, and prepared to enforce his rights by arms; but the king, fearing to disturb the public tranquillity, accepted his fealty, and acknowledged him EARL OF PEMBROKE. This reconciliation was not, however, of long endurance, for we find him soon afterwards in open hostility to the king, defending his own castles, storming and taking others, fighting and winning pitched battles, until his gallant career was finally arrested by the treachery of his own followers in Ireland, where, being inveigled, under the pretext of entering into a league of amity, he was assailed by superior numbers, and mortally wounded. His lordship, who is termed by Matt. Paris " the flower of chivalry," died in 1234, and was buried in the oratory of the Friars Minors, at Kilkenny. Dying unmarried, his estates and honours devolved upon his brother,

GILBERT MARSHAL, fourth Earl of Pembroke, who was restored to the whole of the late earl's lands, by the king, although he had taken part in the proceedings of that nobleman. But notwithstanding this act of grace, his lordship never appears to have been cordially reconciled to the crown. His death occurred in 1241, and was occasioned by a fall from his horse at a tournament. He had m. first, Margaret, daughter of William,

King of Scotland, and secondly, Maud de Lanvaley; but having no issue, he was s. by his brother,

WALTER MARSHAL, fifth Earl of Pembroke. This nobleman had no little difficulty in obtaining livery of his inheritance, for when he came to do his homage, the king upbraided him with the injuries he had sustained from his predecessors. First, that Earl William, his father, had traitorously suffered Lewis of France to escape out of England. Next, that Earl Richard, his brother, was a public enemy, and slain in fight as his enemy. That Gilbert, his brother, to whom at the instance of Edmund, archbishop of Canterbury, he had more through grace than favour, vouchsafed livery of his lands, had against his express prohibition, met at the tournament, wherein he was killed. "And thou," continued the king, "in contempt of me, wast also there. With what face, therefore, canst thou lay claim to that inheritance?" Whereupon Walter replied: "Though I could give a reasonable answer to what you have said, nevertheless I refer myself solely to your highness. You have hitherto been gracious to me, and reputed me as one of your family, and not amongst the meanest of your servants. I never demerited your favour, but now, in being at this tournament with my brother, whom I could not deny: and if all who were there should be thus disinherited, you would raise no small disturbance in your realm. Far be it from a good king, that I should suffer for the faults of all, and that amongst so great a number be the first punished." The king soon after, through the intercession of the Bishop of Durham, vouchsafed him livery of the earldom and marshal's office. His lordship m. Margaret, daughter and heir of Robert de Quincy, but dying issueless in 1245, was s. by his only remaining brother,

ANSELME MARSHAL, fifth Earl of Pembroke, who enjoyed the honours but eighteen days. He d. 5th December, 1245, when leaving no issue by his wife, Maud, daughter of Humphrey de Bohun, Earl of Hereford, ALL HIS HONOURS became EXTINCT—and his great inheritance devolved upon his sisters, as co-heirs—(refer to issue of the first earl).

ARMS.—Party per pale or. and vert. a lion rampant gu. armed and langued, az.

These arms were not borne until the family came to be Marshals of England, prior to which period the coat was, "Or a bend losengée or."

MARTIN—BARONS MARTIN.

By Writ of Summons, dated 23rd June, 1295, 23 Edward I.

Lineage.

The first of this family upon record, is

MARTIN DE TOURS, a Norman, who, making a conquest of Kemyst, in Pembrokeshire, founded a monastery for benedictine monks, at St. Dogmaels, which his son and successor,

ROBERT MARTIN, endowed with lands in the time of Henry I. This Robert m. Maud Peverell, and was s. by his son,

WILLIAM MARTIN. This feudal lord m. the daughter of Rhese ap Griffin, Prince of South Wales, and dying in 1209, was s. by his son,

WILLIAM MARTIN, who, upon the decease of his father, paid 300 marks for livery of his lands, and dying in 1215, was s. by his son,

NICHOLAS MARTIN. This feudal lord espoused Maud, daughter of Guy de Brien, and Eve, his wife, daughter and heir of Henry de Tracy, Lord of Barnstaple, in the county of Devon, by which alliance he acquired that lordship. In the 29th Henry III. this Nicholas received command to assist the Earl of Glocester, and other barons marchers, against the Welch. He died in 1282, and was s. by his grandson,

WILLIAM MARTIN, who, being in the Scottish wars, was summoned to parliament, as a BARON, from 23rd June, 1295, to 10th October, 1395. His lordship m. Eleanor, daughter of William de Mohun, and had issue,

WILLIAM, his successor.

Eleanor, m. to William de Columbers.

Joan, m. first, to Henry de Lacy, Earl of Lincoln; and secondly, to Nicholas de Audley, by whom she had a son,

JAMES DE AUDLEY.

He d. in 1325, and was s. by his son,

WILLIAM MARTIN, second baron, but never summoned to parliament. His lordship d. the year after he inherited, seised of the whole territory of KEMEYS, which he held of the king, in capite, by the fourth part of one knight's fee. Upon the baron's decease the BARONY OF MARTIN fell into ABEYANCE between his heirs, Eleanor Columbers, his sister, and James de Audley, his nephew, as it still continues with their representatives.

ARMS.—Ar. two bars gules.

NOTE.—Of this family the MARTINS, of Long Melford, now represented by Sir Roger Martin, Baronet, is said to be a branch.

MASHAM — BARONS MASHAM, OF OTES, IN THE COUNTY OF ESSEX.

By Letters Patent, dated 31st December, 1711.

Lineage.

SIR WILLIAM MASHAM, of High-Laver, in the county of Essex, (created a baronet on the 20th December, 1621,) m. Winifred, daughter of Sir Francis Barrington, Bart., of Barrington Hall, son of Sir Thomas Barrington, by Winifred, his wife, widow of Sir Thomas Hastings, and second daughter and co-heir of Henry Pole, Lord Montagu, (attainted and beheaded in 1539,) son and heir of Sir Richard Pole, K.G., by his wife Margaret, Countess of Salisbury, daughter, and eventually co-heir of George Plantagenet, Duke of Clarence, younger brother of King Edward IV. By this marriage the family of Masham allied itself with the noblest blood in the realm. From Sir William we pass to his great grandson,

SIR SAMUEL MASHAM, fourth baronet, who m. Abigail, daughter of Francis Hill, Esq., a turkey merchant, and sister of General John Hill. This lady was nearly related to the celebrated Sarah,

Duchess of Marlborough, and was introduced by her grace, whom she eventually supplanted, to the notice of Queen Anne. Sir Samuel, who was an eighth son, was originally a page to the queen, whilst Princess of Denmark, and also one of the equerries, and gentlemen of the bed-chamber to Prince George. Upon the discomfiture of the Marlborough party, and the establishment of his wife as the reigning favourite, he was elevated to the peerage 31st December, 1711, as BARON MASHAM, *of Otes, in the county of Essex:* and having had a grant in reversion of the office of remembrancer of the exchequer, succeeded to that post on the death of Lord Fanshaw in 1716. His lordship had issue,

    George, who died *s. p.* in the life-time of his father.

    SAMUEL, successor to the title.

    Francis, died *s. p.* in the life-time of his father.

    Anne, *m.* to Henry Hoare, Esq., and had issue,

        Susannah, *m.* first, to Charles, Viscount Dungarvon, and secondly, to Thomas, first Earl of Aylesbury.

        Anne, *m.* to Sir Richard Hoare, Bart.

    Elizabeth, *d.* unmarried in 1794.

Lord Masham died in 1758, and was *s.* by his only surviving son,

SAMUEL MASHAM, second baron. This nobleman *m.* first, Harriet, daughter of Salway Winnington, Esq., of Stanford Court, in the county of Worcester, by whom (who *d.* in 1761,) he had no issue. He espoused, secondly, Miss Dives, one of the maids of honour to the dowager Princess of Wales, but had no issue. His lordship, who filled several public employments, died in 1776, when the BARONY OF MASHAM became EXTINCT.

ARMS.—Or. a fesse humette gu. between two lions passant sa.

MAUDUIT—EARL OF WARWICK.

See Newburgh, Earls of Warwick.

MAUDUIT—BARON MAUDUIT.

By Writ of Summons, dated 12th September, 1342, 16 Edward III.

Lineage.

Of the same family as William Mauduit, Earl of Warwick, was (according to Dugdale,)

JOHN MAUDUIT, who, in the 8th of Edward II., had a military summons, amongst other great men, to march against the Scots, and was engaged for some years afterwards in the wars of Scotland. In the 3rd Edward III. he was constituted sheriff of Wiltshire, and governor of the castle of Old Sarum; and was summoned to parliament as a BARON on the 12th September, 1342, but not afterwards. In the 19th of the same reign his lordship obtained a charter for free warren in all his demesne lands at Farnhull, Somerford, Maduit, Funtel, and Uptele, in the county of Wilts, as also

at Stanlake and Broughton, in Oxfordshire. His lordship *d.* in 1347, leaving a son and heir,

    JOHN MAUDUIT, but neither this John, nor any of his posterity, were ever summoned to parliament, nor deemed barons of the realm.

The BARONY OF MAUDUIT is therefore presumed to have become EXTINCT upon the demise of the said John, Lord Mauduit.

ARMS.—Ar. two bars gules.

MAULEY—BARONS MAULEY.

By Writ of Summons, dated 23rd June, 1295, 23rd Edward I.

Lineage.

The first mention of this name and family occurs shortly after the decease of King Richard I., when his brother JOHN, Earl of Moreton, to clear his own way to the throne, employed Peter de Mauley, a Poictovin, his esquire, to murder his nephew, Prince Arthur, of Britanny, and in reward of the foul deed, gave to the said

PETER DE MAULEY, in marriage, Isabel, daughter of Robert de Turnham, and heiress of the Barony of Mulgrave. This Peter, throughout the whole reign of King John, adhering to his royal master, obtained considerable grants from the crown, and was esteemed amongst the evil advisers of the king. In the height of the baronial war, most of the prisoners of rank were committed to his custody, and he was constituted, (18th John,) sheriff of the counties of Dorset and Somerset. In the 4th of Henry III., upon the coronation of that monarch, Peter de Mauley had summons to assist thereat, and to bring with him the *regalia*, then in his custody, at Corfe Castle, which had been entrusted to him by King John; and the next year, being again sheriff of the counties of Somerset and Dorset, he delivered up the Castle of Corfe to the king, with Alianore, the king's kinswoman, and Isabel, sister to the king of Scots, as well as all the jewels, military engines, and ammunition there, which the late monarch had formerly committed to his custody. Soon after this, he was made governor of Sherburne Castle, in the county of Dorset, and *d.* in 1221, was *s.* by his son,

PETER DE MAULEY, who giving one hundred marks for his relief, had livery of his lands. Amongst the causes of discontent avowed by Richard Mareschall in his contest with Henry III. was, that the king by the advice of foreigners, had dispossessed Gilbert Basset, a great baron of the time, of the manor of Nether-Haven, in the county of Wilts, and conferred it upon this Peter de Mauley. The king, nevertheless, continuing his favour to Peter, constituted him governor of the castle of Devizes, and the next year (20th Henry III.), made him sheriff of Northamptonshire. Moreover, in 1239, he was one of the godfathers, at the baptismal font to Prince Edward, (the king's eldest son,) and in 1241 he accompanied William de Fortibus, Earl of Albemarle, and divers other noble persons, to the Holy Land. This feudal lord *m.* Joane, daughter of Peter de Brus, of Skelton, and *d.* in 1242. Upon his decease Gerard le Grue, paid five hundred marks for the *firms* of his lands, and had the custody of the castle of Mulgrave; maintaining his widow with necessaries; keeping the buildings in repair; and not committing waste in the woods. Peter de Mauley was *s.* by his son,

PETER DE MAULEY, (commonly called the THIRD,) who doing his homage in the 31st Henry III., had livery of his lands. In the 42nd of the same reign, the Scots having made a prisoner of their King Alexander III., (son-in-law of the English monarch,) Peter de Mauley received summons with the other northern barons to fit himself with horse and arms, for the relief of the Scottish prince. He *m.* Nichola, daughter of Gilbert de Gant, son of Gilbert, Earl of Lincoln, and had issue,

    PETER, his successor.

    Edmund, a very eminent person in the reigns of Edward I. and II., and greatly distinguished in the Scottish wars. He had a grant of the manor of Seton, in the county of York. He was successively governor of the castle of Bridgenorth, of the town and castle of Bristol, and the castle of Cockermouth. He fell at the battle of Bannockburn, and dying *s. p.*, his estates passed to his nephew,

    Peter de Mauley.

He was *s.* at his decease by his elder son,

PETER DE MAULEY, (called the fourth,) who, in the 7th Edward I., doing his homage, and paying £100 for his relief, had livery of all his lands, which he held of the king in capite, by barony of the inheritance of William Fossard (whose grand-daughter and heir, Isabel de Turnham, was wife of the first Peter de Mauley). This feudal lord having been engaged in the Welsh and Scottish wars, was summoned to parliament as a BARON by King Edward I. on the 23rd June, 1295, and he had regular summons from that period to the 12th December, 1309. In the 25th Edward I. his lordship was in the expedition then made into Gascony, and in consideration of his good services there, obtained from the king, a grant of the marriage of Thomas, the son and heir of Thomas de Multon, of Gillesland, deceased. For several years after this he was actively employed in the warfare of Scotland. His lordship *m.* Eleanor, daughter of Thomas, Lord Furnival, and dying in 1310, was *s.* by his son,

SIR PETER DE MAULEY, K.B., second baron, summoned to parliament from 19th December, 1311, to 15th March, 1354. This nobleman was for several years actively engaged in the wars of Scotland, and was a commander at the battle of Durham, (20th Edward III.,) wherein the Scots, under their king, David Brus, sustained so signal a defeat, the monarch himself being made prisoner. His lordship *m.* Margaret, daughter of Robert, Lord Clifford, and dying in 1355, was *s.* by his son,

PETER DE MAULEY, third baron, summoned to parliament from 20th September, 1355, to 7th January, 1383. This nobleman, in the 30th Edward III., shared in the glorious victory of POICTIERS, and in three years afterwards he was in the expedition then made in Gascony. In the 41st of the same reign he was joined in commission with the Bishop of Durham, Henry, Lord Percy, and others, for guarding the marches of Scotland; and again, in the 3d Richard II., with the Earl of Northumberland. His lordship *m.* first, in the 31st Edward III., Elizabeth, widow of John, Lord Darcy, and daughter and heir of Nicholas, Lord Meinill, without licence, for which office he paid a fine of £100, and obtained pardon. He espoused, secondly, Constance, one of the daughters and co-heirs of Thomas de Sutton, of Sutton, in Holderness, and had issue, (by which wife not known,)

    Peter, who *m.* Margery, one of the daughters and co-heirs of Sir Thomas de Sutton, Knt., and dying in the life-time of his father, left issue,

        PETER, successor to his grandfather.

        Constance, *m.* first, to William Fairfax, by whom she had no issue, and secondly, to Sir John Bigot.

        Elizabeth, *m.* to George Salvin, Esq., from whom, we believe, the present William Thomas Salvin, Esq., of Croxdale, in the county of Durham, (one of the most ancient Catholic families,) derives.

His lordship *d.* in 1383, seised of the manor and castle of Mulgrave; the manor of Doncaster with its members; and a moiety of the manor of Helagh, all in the county of York. He was *s.* by his grandson,

PETER DE MAULEY, fourth baron, who, making proof of his age in the 22d Richard II., had livery of the lands of his inheritance, as well as those derived from his grandfather, as from Thomas, his uncle. This nobleman was made a Knight of the Bath at the coronation of King Henry IV., and was summoned to parliament from 18th August, 1399, to 19th August, 1415. His lordship *m.* the Lady Maud Nevil, daughter of Ralph, Earl of Westmorland, but *d.* in 1415, without issue, when his sisters (refer to issue of third baron) became his heirs, and between those the BARONY OF MAULEY fell into ABEYANCE, as it still continues amongst their representatives. In the distribution of the Mauley estates, Leland says, "Bigot had the castle of Maugreve, (Mulgrave,) with eight tounelettes therabout the se cost longging to it, whereof Seton thereby was one. Saulwayne had, for his part, the Barony of Eggeston on Eske, not far from Whitby; also Lokington-Barugh, not far from Watton-on-Hull ryver; Nesseark, and the lordship of Doncaster."

ARMS.—Or. a bend sa.

MEINILL—BARON MEINILL.

By Writ of Summons, dated 23rd June, 1295,
23 Edward I.

Lineage.

About the close of King Henry I.'s reign,

ROBERT DE MEINEL, bestowed certain lands upon the monks of St. Mary's Abbey, at York, which his son and successor,

STEPHEN DE MEINEL, ratified. In the 25th Henry II. this Stephen was fined £100 for trespassing in the forests of Yorkshire. He *d.* about the 9d Richard I., and was *s.* by his elder son,

, ROBERT DE MEINEL, who m. Emme, daughter of Richard de Malbisse, and had a son,* STEPHEN, who predeceased him, leaving a son,

NICHOLAS DE MEINEL, who s. his grandfather in the 8th King John. · This Nicholas was in the Welsh wars, and in consideration of his services had a debt of one hundred marks remitted by King Edward I., besides obtaining grants of free warren throughout all his lands and lordships in the county of York. In the year 1299 he brought a charge against Christian, his wife, of an intent to poison him, and although she clearly established her innocence, he refused ever afterwards to be reconciled to her. In the 22d Edward III. he had summons, amongst many other persons of note, to attend the king, to advise about the affairs of the realm; and he was summoned to parliament as a BARON from the 23d June, 1295, to 6th February, 1299, during which interval he took a prominent part in the wars of Scotland. His lordship d. in 1299, without legitimate issue, when JOHN MEINILL, his brother, was found to be his heir, and the BARONY OF MEINILL became EXTINCT.

ARMS.—AZ. three bars gemels, and a chief, or.

MEINILL—BARON MEINILL.

By Writ of Summons, dated 22nd May, 1313,
6 Edward II.

Lineage.

NICHOLAS DE MEINILL, Baron Meinill, who d. in 1299 without legitimate issue, when his BARONY expired, left by Lucie, his concubine, daughter and heir to Robert de Thweng, a natural son,

NICHOLAS DE MEINILL, who doing his homage, had livery of divers lordships and lands which had been settled upon him. This feudal lord was frequently in the Scottish wars in the reigns of Edward I. and Edward II., and was summoned to parliament as a BARON by the latter monarch from 22d May, 1313, to 14th March, 1322. His lordship d. in the latter year without issue, when the BARONY OF MEINILL became again EXTINCT. His estates devolved upon his brother,

JOHN MEINILL, whose grand-daughter,

ALICE MEINILL, eventually conveyed them to her husband, JOHN DE BOULTON.

ARMS.—AZ. three bars gemels, and a chief, or.

MEINILL—BARON MEINILL.

By Writ of Summons, dated 22nd January, 1336,
9 Edward III.

Lineage.

NICHOLAS DE MEINILL, called by Dugdale, the "chief of the family," but how related to the other Barons Meinill does not appear, was summoned to parliament as a BARON from 22d January, 1336, to 25th February, 1342. This nobleman possessed large estates in Yorkshire; one of which, the

---

* He had also a natural son,

ROBERT MEINILL, who m. Agnes, sister and heir of Adam de Hilton, of Hilton, in Cleveland, from whom the Meinills in those parts descended.

---

manor of WHERLTON, he held of the Archbishop of Canterbury, by the tenure of serving him with the cup, in which he should drink upon the day of his inthronization, and receiving the fees belonging to that office. His lordship m. Alice, daughter of William, Lord Ros, of Hamlake, and left an only daughter and heiress,

ELIZABETH, who espoused, first, John, second Baron Darcy, and conveyed the BARONY OF MEINILL to the Darcy family, in which it remained until the decease of Philip, eleventh Baron Darcy, in 1418, when, with the Barony of Darcy, it fell into ABEYANCE between his lordship's daughters and co-heirs.

Elizabeth Meinill espoused, secondly, Peter, sixth Baron Mauley.

Her ladyship d. in the 42d Edward III.

His lordship d. in 1342, when the BARONY OF MEINILL devolved as stated above upon his daughter, ELIZABETH, who espoused Lord Darcy.

"Although," says Nicolas, "the abeyance of the Baronies of Meinill and Darcy has never been terminated, yet Conyers Darcy, second Baron Darcy, under the patent of 10th August, 1641, and Baron Conyers, in right of his grandmother, probable, under the presumption that the said patent not only restored the ancient barony of Darcy, but also that of Meinill, was styled, in the writs of summons to parliament of 7th October, 31 Car. 2, 1679, and 1st March, 31st March, 1680, ' Conyers Darcie de Darcie and Meinill, Chi'r.' He was created Earl of Holderness in 1682, which title, as well as the Barony of Darcy, created by the patent of 1641, became EXTINCT in 1778; but it is manifest that the assumption of the title of the Barony of Meinill was without any legal foundation."

ARMS.—AZ. three bars gemels, and a chief, or.

MESCHINES, EARLS OF CHESTER.

By Inheritance, anno 1119.

Lineage.

HUGH (LUPUS,) DE ABRINCIS, the celebrated Earl of Chester, had four sisters, viz.

1. Judith, m. to Richard de Aquita.
2. ———, m. to William, Earl of Ewe.
3. Isabel, m. to Gilbert, a younger son of Richard, Earl of Corboil, in Normandy, and had issue.

ROBERT, who, for his attachment to Robert de Stafford, and the king's service in those parts, as also "ratione consanguinitas" held Peshall, in the county of Stafford, with its appurtenances, anno 1098, from whither he assumed that surname, and is said to have been ancestor to the family of PESHALL, created baronet in 1612.

4. MAUD, m. to Ralph de Meschines, and had a son,

RANULPH DE MESCHINES, surnamed de Briossard, Viscount Bayeux, in Normandy, upon whom King Henry I. conferred the EARLDOM OF CHESTER, at the decease of his first cousin, Richard de Abrincis, second Earl of Chester of that family, (see Abrincis,) without issue. By some of our historians this nobleman is styled Earl of Carlisle, from residing in that city; and they further state, that he came over in the train of the Conqueror, assisted in the subjugation of England, and shared, of course, in the spoil of conquest. He was Lord of Cumberland and Carlisle, by descent from his father, but having enfeoffed his two brothers, William, of Coupland, and Geffery, of Gillesland, in a large portion thereof, he exchanged the Earldom of Cumberland for that of Chester, on condition, that those whom he had settled there, should hold their lands of the king " *in capite*." His lordship m. Lucia, widow of Roger de Romera, Earl of Lincoln, and daughter of Algar, Earl of Mercia, and had issue,

   RANULPH, his successor.

   William, styled Earl of Cambridge, but of his issue nothing is known.

   Adeliza, m. to Richard Fitz-Gilbert, ancestor of the old Earls of Clare.

   Agnes, m. to Robert de Grentemaisnil.

The earl d. in 1128, and was s. by his elder son,

RANULPH DE MESCHINES, (surnamed de *Gernons*, from being born in Gernon Castle, in Normandy,) as EARL OF CHESTER. This nobleman, who was a leading military character, took an active part with the Empress Maud, and the young Prince HENRY against King Stephen, in the early part of the contest, and having defeated the king, and made him prisoner at the battle of Lincoln, committed him to the castle of Bristol. He subsequently, however, sided with the king, and finally, distrusted by all, died, under excommunication, in 1163, supposed to have been poisoned by William Peverell, Lord of Nottingham, who being suspected of the crime, is said to have turned monk, to avoid its punishment. The earl m. Maud, daughter of Robert, surnamed *the consul*, Earl of Gloucester, natural son of King Henry I., and had issue,

   HUGH, his successor, surnamed *Kevelick*, from the place of his birth, in Merionethshire.

   Richard.

   Beatrix, m. to Ralph de Malpas.

His lordship was s. by his elder son,

HUGH (Kevelick), third Earl of Chester. This nobleman joined in the rebellion of the Earl of Leicester and the king of Scots, against King Henry II., and in support of that monarch's son, Prince HENRY's pretensions to the crown. In which proceeding he was taken prisoner, with the Earl of Leicester, at Alnwick, but obtained his freedom soon afterwards, upon the king's reconciliation with the young prince. Again, however, hoisting the standard of revolt, both in England and in Normandy, with as little success, he was again seized, and then detained a prisoner for some years. He eventually, however, obtained his liberty and restoration of his lands, when public tranquillity became completely re-established some time about the twenty-third year of the king's reign. His lordship m. Bertred, daughter of Simon, Earl of Evereux, in Normandy, and had issue,

   RANULPH, his successor.

   Maud, m. to David, Earl of Huntingdon, brother of William, king of Scotland, and had one son and four daughters, viz.

   1. JOAN, surnamed *Le Scot*, who succeeded to the Earldom of Cheshire.

   1. Margaret, m. to Alan de Galloway, and had issue,

     Divorgal, m. to John de Baliol, and was mother of JOHN DE BALIOL, declared king of Scotland in the reign of Edward I.

     Christiana, m. to William de Fortibus, Earl of Albemarle, and died s. p.

   2. Isabel, m. to Robert de Brus, and was mother of ROBERT DE BRUS, who contended for the crown of Scotland temp. Edward I.

   3. Maud, d. unmarried.

   4. Ada, m. to Henry de Hastings, and had issue,

     HENRY DE HASTINGS, one of the competitors for the Scottish crown temp. Edward I.

   Mabill, m. to William de Albini, Earl of Arundel.

   Agnes, m. to William de Ferrers, Earl of Derby.

   Hawise, m. to Robert, son of Sayer de Quincy, Earl of Winchester.

The earl had another daughter, whose legitimacy is questionable, namely,

   Amicia, m. to Ralph de Mesnilwarin, justice of Chester, " a person," says Dugdale, " of very ancient family," from which union the Mainwarings, of Over Peover, in the county of Chester, derive. Dugdale considers Amicia to be a daughter of the earl by a former wife. But Sir Peter Leicester, in his Antiquities of Cheshire, totally denies her legitimacy. " I cannot but mislike," says he, " the boldness and ignorance of that herald, who gave to Mainwaring, (late of Peover,) the elder, the quartering of the Earl of Chester's arms; for if he ought of right to quarter that coat, then must he be descended from a co-heir to the Earl of Chester: but he was not; for the co-heirs of Earl Hugh married four of the greatest peers in the kingdom."[*]

The Earl d. at Leeke, in Staffordshire, in 1181, and was s. by his only son,

RANULPH, surnamed *Blundevil*, (or rather Blandevil, from the place of his birth, the town of *Album Monasterium*, modern Oswestry, in Powis,) as fourth EARL OF CHESTER. This nobleman was made a knight in 1186, by King Henry II., and the same monarch bestowed upon him in marriage, CONSTANCE, Countess of Britanny, daughter and

---

[*] Upon the question of this lady's legitimacy there was a long paper war between Sir Peter Leicester and Sir Thomas Mainwaring—and eventually the matter was referred to the judges, of whose decision Wood says, " At an assize held at Chester, 1675, the controversy was decided by the justices itinerant, who, as I have heard, adjudged the right of the matter to Mainwaring."

heiress of Conon, EARL OF BRITANNY, and widow of King Henry's son Geffrey, with the whole of Britanny, and the Earldom of Richmond, wherefore he is designated in most charters, " Duke of Britanny and Earl of Richmond." In the 4th of Richard I. we find his lordship aiding David, Earl of Huntingdon, and the Earl Ferrers, in the siege of Marlborough, then held for John, Earl of Moreton, the king's brother; and in two years afterwards with the same parties, besieging the castle of Nottingham. In which latter year he was also with the army of King Richard in Normandy, and so highly was he esteemed by the lion-hearted monarch, that he was selected to bear one of the three swords at his second coronation. In the commencement of King John's reign his lordship divorced his wife Constance, " by reason," saith Dugdale, " that the king haunted her company,". and espoused Clementia, daughter of Ralph de Fuegers, widow of Alan de Dinant, and niece of William de Humet, constable of Normandy, with whom he acquired not only a large accession of landed property in France, but some extensive manors in England. In the 6th of John his lordship had a grant from the crown of all the lands belonging to the honour of Richmond, in Richmondshire, excepting a small proportion, which the king retained in his own hands; and he gave in the same year to the king a palfrey for a lamprey, which shews the value of that description of fish in those days.

This was the earl, who, marching into Wales too slenderly attended, was compelled to take refuge in Rothelan Castle, in Flintshire; and being there closely invested by the Welsh, was delivered from his precarious situation by the rabble, which then happened to have been assembled at the fair of Chester. For sending to Roger de Lacy, Baron of Halton, his constable of Cheshire, to come with all speed to his succour, Roger, (surnamed Hell, from his fiery spirit,) gathered a tumultuous rout of fiddlers, players, cobblers, debauched persons, both men and women, and marched immediately towards the earl; when the Welsh, descrying so numerous a multitude advancing, at once raised the siege, and sought safety in flight. Wherefore the earl conferred upon the constable patronage over all the fiddlers and shoemakers in Chester, in reward and memory of this service. Of which patronage De Lacy retained to himself and his heirs that of the shoemakers, and granted the fiddlers and players to his steward, DUTTON, of Dutton, whose heirs still enjoy the privilege. For upon Midsummer-day, annually, the fair of Chester, a Dutton, or his deputy, rides attended through the city of Chester, by all the minstrelsy of the county, playing upon their several instruments, to the church of St. John's, where a court is held for the renewal of their licences.

In the conflicts between John and the barons the Earl of Chester remained stoutly attached to the former, and it was through his exertions chiefly that Henry III. ascended the throne. Of which an old MONK OF PETERBOROUGH gives the following narrative:—

" Upon the death of King John, the great men of England fearing that the son would follow his father's steps in tyranny over the people, resolved to extirpate him, and all of his blood, not considering that saying of the prophet, viz., ' THAT THE SON SHALL NOT SUFFER FOR THE INIQUITY OF THE FATHER.' And to that end determined to set up LEWES, son to the king of France, (a youth then but fourteen years old,) in his stead; whom, at the instance of the rebellious barons, that king, for the purpose alleged, sent over into England, in the last year of King John, under the tuition of the Earl of Perch, and other great men of that realm. Who having landed himself in England accordingly, and received homage of the Londoners, expecting the like from the southern nobility, advanced to Lincolne. Which being made known to the Earl of Chester, who did abominate any conjunction with them in that their conspiracy, he convened the rest of the northern peers; and being the chief and most potent of them, taking with him young Henry, son of King John, and right heir to the crown, raised a puissant army, and marched towards Lincolne. To which place, at the end of four days after Lewes got thither, expecting him, he came. To whom the Earl of Perch, observing his stature to be small, said, ' Have we staid all this while for such a little man, such a dwarf.' To which disdainful expression he answered, ' I vow to God and our lady, whose church this is, that before to-morrow evening I will seem to thee to be stronger, and greater, and taller than that steeple.' Thus parting with each other, he betook himself to the castle.

" And on the next morning, the Earl of Perch, armed at all parts, except his head, having entered the cathedral with his forces, and left Lewes there, challenged out our earl to battle: who no sooner heard thereof, but causing the castle gates to be opened, he came out with his soldiers, and made so fierce a charge upon the adverse party, that he slew the Earl of Perch, and many of his followers; and immediately seizing upon Lewes in the church, caused him to swear upon the gospel and relics of those saints then placed on the high altar, that he would never lay any claim to the kingdom of England, but speedily hasten out of the realm, with all his followers; and that when he should be king of France, he would restore NORMANDY to the crown of England. Which being done, he sent for young Henry, who during that time lay privately in a cow-house, belonging to BARDNEY ABBEY, (near Lincolne, towards the west,) and, setting him upon the altar, delivered him seisin of this kingdom; as his inheritance by a white wand, instead of a sceptre; doing his homage to him, as did all the rest of the nobility then present.

" For which signal service, the king gave him the body of Gilbert de Gant, his enemy, with all his possessions: which Gilbert was a great baron, and founder of Vaudey Abbey, in Kesteven." Thus far for the monk of Peterborough. Further, it appears that after the coronation of the king, the Earl of Cheshire brought all his resources to bear upon the rebellious barons; first in the siege of Mountsorell, in Leicestershire, and afterwards at Lincoln, " The castle whereof," says Dugdale, " was then beleagured by a great strength of barons; which in that notable battle there, were utterly vanquished."

In the course of the same year his lordship had the Earldom of Lincoln, forfeited by Gilbert de Grant, conferred upon him, to which dignity he had a claim, in right of his great grandmother, who bore the title of Countess of Lincoln. His lordship subsequently assumed the cross, for the second time, and embarked for the Holy Land, having previously granted to his Cheshire barons a very ample charter of liberties. As a soldier, the stout Earl of Chester was not less distinguished abroad than at home, and the laurels which he had so gallantly won upon his native soil, were not tarnished in the plains of Palestine. His lordship had a command at the celebrated siege of Damieta, "where," saith Henry, archdeacon of Huntingdon, "being general of the Christian army, he did glorious things." *Ubi Dux Christianæ Cohortis præsidit gloriosa.* Immediately upon his return to England, anno 1220, the earl begun the structure of CHARTLEY CASTLE, in Staffordshire, and of BEESTON CASTLE, in Cheshire, as also the abbey of DEULACRES, for white monks, near Leek, in the former shire; which monastery he had been incited, it was said, to found by the ghost of Earl Ranulph, his grandfather, which appeared to him one night while he was in bed, as the story went, and "bade him repair to a place called, CHOLPESDALE, within the territory of Leek, and there found and endow an abbey of white monks," adding, "there shall be joy to thee, and many others, who shall be saved thereby: for there, quoth he, shall be a ladder erected, by which the prayers of angels shall ascend and descend, and vows of men shall be offered to God, and they shall give thanks, and the name of our Lord shall be called upon in that place, by daily prayers; and the sign of this shall be, when the pope doth interdict England. But do thou in the mean time, go to the monks of Pulton, where Robert Butler hath in my name built an abbey, and thou shalt there be partaker of the sacrament of the Lord; for such privileges belong to the servants of the foundation. And in the seventh year of that interdict, thou shalt translate those monks to the place I have foretold." The earl having communicated this dream, or ghost-mandate, to his wife, the Lady Clementia, she exclaimed in French, *Dieu encres*, which exclamation his lordship deeming propitious, declared should give name to the projected monastery: hence the designation of DEULACRES.

After this period we find the earl coinciding with the barons rather than the king, in some misunderstanding regarding the charters, which was, however, peaceably settled in the 11th of Henry's reign. The most remarkable subsequent event of his lordship's life, was his resistance to one Stephen, a commissary from the pope, who was deputed to collect the tenths from the bishops, and all religious orders; and did so throughout England, Ireland, and Wales, except within the jurisdiction of the Earl of Chester, where his lordship's proclamation interposed. This potent nobleman d. at Wallingford, in the November of 1231, after governing the county palatine of Chester for more than half a century; and as a proof of the simplicity of the age, so far as faith in supernatural events may be so characterised, we give the following story, which, according to Henry Huntendon, met with general credence. "It is reported," saith our author, "of this earl, that when he died, a great company in the likeness of men, with a certain potent person, hastily passed by a hermite's cell, near Wallingford; and that the hermite asking one of them, what they were? and whither they went so fast? he answered, *We are devils, and are making speed to the death of Earl Randulph, to the end we may accuse him of his sins.* Likewise that the hermites thereupon adjuring the devil, that he should return the same way, within thirty days, and relate what was become of this earl. He came accordingly, and told him, *That he was, for his iniquities, condemned to the torments of hell; but that the great dogs of Deulacres, and with them many other, did bark so incessantly, and fill their habitations with such a noise, that their prince, being troubled with it, commanded he should be expelled his dominions; who is now, saith he, become a great enemy to us; because their suffrages, together with others, hath released many souls from purgatory.*" So much for the ingenuity of the good monks of Deulacres.

His lordship never having had issue, his great possessions devolved, at his decease, upon

His nephews,
- JOHN SCOTT, (son of Maud, Countess of Huntingdon, the earl's eldest sister, then dead,) who succeeded to the Earldom of Chester, (see Scot, Earl of Chester,) with the whole county palatine, and the advowson of the priory of COVENTRY.
- Hugh de Albany, EARL OF ARUNDEL, (son of Mabel, the earl's second sister, then dead,) who succeeded to COVENTRY, as his chief seat, with the manors of CAMPDEN, in Gloucestershire; DINEY, in Buckinghamshire; and LEDES, in Yorkshire.

His sisters,
- Agnes, COUNTESS OF DERBY, who, with her husband, William de Ferrers, Earl of Derby, had the castle and manor of CHARTLEY, in Staffordshire, with all the lands belonging to her late brother, which lay between the rivers Ribble and Merse, together with a manor in Northamptonshire, and another in Lincolnshire.
- Hawise, wife of Robert de Quincy, who had the castle and manor of BOLINGBROKE, in the county of Lincoln, and other large estates in that shire. It appears that her brother, in his lifetime, had granted to this lady, the Earldom of Lincoln, in order that she might become countess thereof, and that her heirs might also enjoy it. Which grant seems to have been confirmed by the crown so far, that at her ladyship's desire, the king conferred the dignity of Earl of Lincoln upon John Lacy, Constable of Chester, and the heirs of his body, by Margaret de Quincy, the Lady Hawise's daughter.

349

ARMS, borne by RANULPH, surnamed DE BAI-
CASAND.—Or. a lion rampant, his tail erected, gu.

ARMS, borne by HOAR, surnamed KEVELIOK.—
Az. six garbs or. three, two, and one.

ARMS, borne by RANULPH, surnamed BLUNDER-
VIL.—Az. three garbs or. two and one.

MILDMAY — BARONS FITZ-WAL-
TER, EARL FITZ-WALTER.

BARONY, { Originally by Writ of Summons, dated
23rd June, 1295, 23 Edward I.
To the Mildmays, by Writ of Summons, dated 10th February, 1669.
EARLDOM, by Letters Patent, dated 14th May, 1730.

Lineage.

LADY FRANCES RATCLIFFE, only daugh-
ter, by his second wife, of Henry, third Lord Fitz-
Walter, and second Earl of Sussex, (revert to
Ratcliffe, Barons Fitz-Walter,) married Sir Thomas
Mildmay, Knt., of Moulsham, in the county of
Essex, and had issue,

THOMAS (Sir), created a Baronet, and died
s. p. in 1690.

HENRY, of whom presently.

The second son,

SIR HENRY MILDMAY, Knt., becoming at
the decease of his brother representative of the
family, and his mother, at the death of her nephew,
by the half blood, Robert Ratcliffe, sixth Lord
Fitz-Walter, and fifth Earl of Sussex, having become sole heiress of that ancient barony, preferred
his claim in her right, by petition to the long parliament, in 1640; but the civil war breaking out
immediately after, he was unable to accomplish
anything in the affair. Sir Henry m. Elizabeth,
daughter of John Darcy, Esq., of Toleshurst Darcy,
in the county of Essex, and dying in 1654, left
issue,

ROBERT, who m. Mary, daughter and co-heir
of Sir Thomas Edmonds, Knt., and had two
sons and a daughter, viz.

1. HENRY, who petitioned for the barony,
but died s. p., before there was any
decision.

2. Benjamin, of whom presently, as
LORD FITZ-WALTER.

3. Mary, m. to Henry Mildmay, Esq.,
of Graces, and had five daughters,
namely—

Mary, m. to Charles Goodwin, Esq.

Lucy, m. to Thomas Gardener, Esq.

Elizabeth, m. to Edmund Waterson,
Esq.

Frances, m. to Christopher Fowler,
Esq.

Katherine, m. to Colonel Thomas
Townshend.

Henry, died s. p.

Charles, m. to Martha, daughter and heiress
of Sir Cranmer Harris, Knt., and left an
only daughter,

Mary, m. to Sir Charles Tyrrell, Bart., of
Thornton.

Sir Henry Mildmay's grandson,

BENJAMIN MILDMAY, Esq., having inhe-
rited the estates of the family, upon the decease of
his brother Henry, without issue, pursued the
claim to the BARONY OF FITZ-WALTER, already
preferred by his grandfather and brother; but he
met a strenuous opponent in Robert Cheeke, Esq.,
son of Henry Cheeke, Esq., by Frances Ratcliffe,
daughter of Sir Humphrey Ratcliffe, of Elneston,
and sister of Sir Edward Ratcliffe, who succeeded
as sixth Earl of Sussex, and died s. p., in 1641,
when that earldom expired. (See Ratcliffe, Barons Fitz-Walter, issue of Robert, second Lord,
and Earl of Sussex.) Mr. Cheeke's claim chiefly
rested on the question, whether there could be a
possessio fratris in dignity; and after several hearings at the bar of the House of Lords, the parliament was prorogued, and nothing further was done
in that session; but on the 29th December following, Mr. Mildmay again petitioned the king, and
his majesty was then pleased to order, that the
cause should be heard by the privy council, in 19th
January, 1669, on which day the two chief justices,
and the chief baron, were directed to attend.

"The counsel for the said Robert Cheeke affirmed, that the same was a barony by tenure, and
ought to go along with the land;[*] which the counsel of the petitioner denied, and offered to argue on
the same; upon which both parties being ordered
to withdraw, the nature of a barony by tenure being
discussed, it was found to have been discontinued
for many ages, and not in being, and so not fit to
be revived, or to admit any pretence of right of succession thereto; and the other points urged by
Mr. Cheeke[†] being over-ruled, it was ordered by
his majesty in council, that the petitioner is admitted, humbly to address himself to his majesty,
for his writ, to sit in the House of Peers, as Baron
Fitz-Walter, and he was so summoned accordingly."[‡] There being, after this, some doubts, as
to the place and precedency of the Lord Fitz-Walter, it was ultimately settled, that his lordship
should be placed the last baron of the reign of King
Edward I. This Benjamin, first Lord Fitz-Walter,
of the Mildmay family, m. Catherine, daughter
and co-heiress of John, Viscount Fairfax, of the kingdom of Ireland, and had surviving issue, two sons,

---

[*] It does not appear on what grounds Mr.
Cheeke's counsel claimed the Barony of Fitz-Walter
by tenure, for that barony was originally attached
to the possession of the Manor of Little Dunmow,
in Essex, granted to Robert Fitz-Walter, in the
reign of Henry I.; and at the period when this
claim was discussed, it was not the property of
either of the claimants.—Nicolas.

[†] First, half blood in Mildmay; and secondly,
that the Barony or Title of Lord Fitz-Walter, was
merged in the Earldom of Sussex, and became
extinct with that dignity. Upon which it was decided, that the half blood could not be any impediment in the case of a dignity; and that, although
a baron in fee simple be created an EARL, the
barony shall descend to the heir general, whether
or not, the earldom continue, or be extinct.

[‡] Collins's Precedents.

CHARLES and HENRY, who inherited, successively, the barony. His lordship d. in 1679, and was s. by the elder,

CHARLES MILDMAY, second Baron Fitz-Walter. His lordship m. Elizabeth, daughter of the Honourable Charles Bertie, of Uffington, youngest son of Montague, Earl of Lindsey, but died in 1728, without issue, and was s. by his brother,

HENRY MILDMAY, third Baron Fitz-Walter, who was created by letters patent, dated 14th May, 1730, Viscount Harwich, and EARL FITZ-WALTER. In 1735, his lordship was sworn of the privy council, appointed first lord commissioner of trade and plantations; and constituted, in 1737, treasurer of the household. He m. Frederica, eldest daughter and co-heir of Meinhardt, Duke of Scombergh, and widow of Robert, Earl of Holderness, by whom he had an only son, ROBERT-SCOMBERGH, who died in infancy. His lordship d. 29th February, 1755, when the VISCOUNTY OF HARWICH, and EARLDOM OF FITZ-WALTER, became EXTINCT, but the ancient BARONY OF FITZ-WALTER fell into ABEYANCE, between his aunts and their representatives, (revert to descendants of Sir Henry Mildmay,) as it still continues amongst their descendants.

ARMS.—Ar. three lions rampant az.

MOELS—BARONS MOELS.

By Writ of Summons, dated 6th February, 1299, 27 Edward I.

Lineage.

In the time of Henry III.,

NICHOLAS DE MOELS, in right of Hawyse, his wife, daughter and co-heir of James de Newmarch, possessed the lordships of CADBURY, and SAPERTON, in the county of Somerset, part of the feudal barony of the said James. In the same reign, this Nicholas was made sheriff of Hampshire, and governor of the castle of Winchester, and continued in office for four years. He had subsequently the islands of Guernsey, Jersey, Serke, and Aurency (Alderney,) committed to his care, and was again constituted sheriff of Hampshire, after which he was sheriff of Yorkshire, and held that office until the 25th Henry III. The next year he was deputed with Ralph Fitz-Nicholas, ambassador to France, for the purpose of denouncing war against the king of that realm; and he was soon after appointed seneschal of Gascony. Being at the time a person so highly regarded by the king, that JAMES, his son and heir, was by special command, admitted to have his education with Prince Edward: the prince's tutors, Hugh de Giffard and Berard de Savoy, having directions to receive him, with one servant, and to provide him with necessaries. In the 28th of the same reign, he obtained a signal victory over the king of Navarre, and returning to England the ensuing year, he was employed in the Welsh wars, and constituted governor of the castles of Caermarthen and Cardigan. He was subsequently appointed Constable of Dover Castle, and warden of the Cinque Ports; and the March following, made sheriff of Kent, and governor of the castles of Rochester and Canterbury. This celebrated and gallant person was s. by his son,

ROGER DE MOELS, who served in the Welsh wars, and in the beginning of Edward I.'s reign, had the honour and castle of Lampadervaur, in Cardiganshire, committed to his custody. He m. Alice, daughter and heir of William de Preux, and dying in 1294, was s. by his son,

JOHN DE MOELS, who, doing his homage in the same year, had livery of his lands. This feudal lord having distinguished himself in the Scottish wars of Edward I., was summoned to parliament as a BARON, from 6th February, 1299, to 16th June, 1311. His lordship m. ———— daughter of Lord Grey de Ruthyn, and dying in 1311, was s. by his son,

NICHOLAS DE MOELS, second baron, summoned to parliament from 19th October, 1311, to 8th October, 1315. This nobleman, like his predecessors, distinguished himself in arms, and was engaged in the Scotch wars. His lordship m. Margaret, daughter of Sir Hugh Courtenay, Knt., and sister of Hugh, Earl of Devon, by whom he had issue,

> ROGER, his successor.
> JOHN, who succeeded his brother.

His lordship d. in 1316, and was s. by his elder son,

ROGER DE MOELS, third baron, who paying an hundred marks fine, and doing homage, had livery of his lands the same year, through the king's especial favour, being at the time not of full age. His lordship d. in the 19th Edward II. s. p., and was s. by his brother,

JOHN DE MOELS, fourth baron, but never summoned to parliament. This nobleman was created a knight of the Bath, 20th Edward II., and in the 7th Edward III., he was in the expedition then made into Scotland. His lordship m. Joane, one of the daughters and co-heirs of Sir Richard Luvel, Knt., of Castle Cary, and had issue,

> MURIEL, m. to Sir Thomas Courtenay, Knt., a younger son of the Earl of Devon, and had issue,
>> HUGH COURTENAY, who died s. p.
>> Margaret Courtenay, m. to Sir Thomas Peverel, and had issue,
>>> Katherine Peverel, m. to Sir Walter Hungerford.
>>> Alianore Peverel, m. to ———— Talbot.
>> Muriel Courtenay, m. to John Denham.
> Isabel, m. to William de Botreaux, Lord Botreaux, and her great grand-daughter,
>> MARGARET BOTREAUX, m. to Sir Robert Hungerford, Knt., and carried the Barony of Botreaux, with the moiety of that of MOELS, to Robert, second Lord Hungerford, whose mother, Katherine, Lady Hungerford, daughter, and eventually sole heir of Sir Thomas Peverel, and Margaret, daughter and co-heir of Sir Thomas Courtenay, by MURIEL DE MOELS, his wife, above mentioned, was also the co-heir of the other moiety of the BARONY OF MOELS; which representation, viz.,

of one moiety, and half of the other moiety, is now vested in the present MARQUESS OF HASTINGS, Baron Hungerford, Molines, and Botreaux, the heir general of the body of the said Robert, Lord Hungerford, and of Margaret, daughter and heiress of Lord Botreaux, his wife. The other half moiety of the Barony of MOELS, is vested in the representatives of the Lords Dinham.

His lordship d. in 1337, when the BARONY OF MOELS fell into ABEYANCE, between his daughters, as it still continues, as stated above, with their representatives. His lordship's estates passed likewise to his daughters, and were divided thus:

    MURIEL, Lady Courtenay, had the manor of of King's Creswell, with the hundred of Haytore, in the county of Devon; the manor of Stoke-Moels, in the county of Oxford, with one hundred shillings rent, out of the manor of Langford, also in Devonshire.

    ISABEL, Lady Botreaux, had the manor of North-Cadbury, in the county of Somerset, and Duppleford, Langeford, and the hundred of Stanburgh, in the county of Devon.

ARMS.—Ar. two bars gu. in chief three torteauxes.

MOHUN—BARONS MOHUN.

By Writ of Summons, dated 6th February, 1299, 27 Edward I.

Lineage.

The first of this family upon record is,

SIR WILLIAM DE MOHUN, one of the companions in arms of the CONQUEROR, who had no less than forty-seven stout knights of name and note in his retinue, at the battle of Hastings; and for the good services rendered to his royal master, in that celebrated conflict, obtained the CASTLE DUNSTER, with fifty-five manors, in the county of Somerset, besides several other lordships in Wilts, Devonshire, and Warwickshire. Sir William was s. by his son,

WILLIAM DE MOHUN, Lord of Dunster, who, with Anne, his wife, granted the Church of Whichford, to the canons of Bridlington, King HENRY I. confirming the grant. This William was s. by his son,

WILLIAM DE MOHUN, who, espousing the fortunes of the Empress Maude, fortified his CASTLE OF DUNSTER on her behalf, and breaking out into open rebellion against King Stephen, laid the country waste around him. He subsequently, in conjunction with David, KING OF SCOTLAND, Robert, Earl of Gloucester, and the other partisans of Maude, besieged Henry de Bloys, (Stephen's brother,) Bishop of Winchester, in the castle at that place; and in consideration of these eminent services, is said to have been created EARL OF DORSET, by the Empress. He founded the Priory of Bruton, in the county of Somerset, and endowed

358

it largely with lands, in England and Normandy. He died before the year 1165, and was s. by his son,

WILLIAM DE MOHUN, surnamed Meschyn. In the 19th Henry II., this feudal lord, upon levying the aid for marrying the king's daughter, certified his knights' fees, de veteri feoffamento, to be in number, forty, and those de novo, four. He confirmed his father's grants to the Priory of Bruton, and like him was buried there. He d. about the year 1202, and was s. by his son,

REGINALD DE MOHUN, who, in the sixth of John, espoused Alice, (or Joane,) one of the sisters and co-heirs of William de Briwere, by whom he acquired considerable estates in the counties of Cornwall, Devon, and Somerset. He d. in 1213, and was s. by his son,

REGINALD DE MOHUN, then in minority, whose wardship was committed to Henry Fitz-Count, son of the Earl of Cornwall. In the 26th Henry III., this Reginald was constituted Chief Justice of all the forests south of Trent; and, in some years afterwards, governor of Saubeye Castle, in Leicestershire. In the 41st of the same reign, he had a military summons to march against the Welsh. He m. first, ——, sister of Humphrey de Bohun, Earl of Hereford, and had a son, JOHN, his successor. He espoused secondly, Isabel, daughter and co-heir of William de Ferrers, Earl of Derby, (and co-heir, likewise, to Sibilla, her mother, sister and co-heir of ANSELM MARSHAL, last Earl of Pembroke, of that family,) by whom he had a son,

    WILLIAM, who, by the gift of his father, had the Manors of Ottery, Stoke-Fleming, Monkton, and Galmeton, with the Manor of Mildenhall, in the county of Wilts, and Greylkell, in the county of Southampton. He m. Beatrix, daughter of Reginald Fitz-Piers, and left two daughters, his co-heirs, viz.

        Elinor, m. to John de Carru.

        Mary, m. to John de Meryet.

Reginald Mohun d. in 1256, and was s. by his elder son,

JOHN DE MOHUN, who wedded Joane, daughter of Sir Reginald Fitz-Piers, and dying 1278, was s. by his son,

JOHN DE MOHUN (called John de Mohun the second). This feudal lord, at the decease of his father, was but ten years of age. He was afterwards distinguished in the wars of Gascony and Scotland, and was summoned to parliament as a BARON, from 6th February, 1299, to 23rd October, 1330. In the 27th Edward I., he exchanged with the crown, all his lands in Ireland, for the Manor of Long Compton, in Warwickshire. His lordship m. Auda, daughter of Sir Robert de Tibetot, and dying in 1330, was s. by his grandson,

JOHN DE MOHUN, second baron, summoned to parliament from 25th February, 1342, to 4th October, 1373 (the latter part of the time, as BARON MOHUN, of Dunster). This nobleman was one of the martial heroes of the reign of Edward III., and was of the retinue of the BLACK PRINCE, and subsequently, of that of John of Gaunt. His lordship m. Joane, daughter of his guardian, Bartholomew de

Burgherah, and dying ——, left three daughters, his co-heirs, viz.

    Philippa, m. to Edward Plantagenet, Duke of York, and secondly, to Sir Walter Fitz-Walter, Knt.

    Elizabeth, m. to William de Montacute, Earl of Salisbury.

    Maud, m. to John, Lord Strange, of Knocking.

Upon the decease of his lordship, the BARONY OF MOHUN, fell into ABEYANCE, amongst those ladies, and so continues with their descendants and representatives.

ARMS.—Gu. a maunch ermine, the hand ppr. holding a Fleur de Lis, ar.

MOHUN — BARONS MOHUN, OF OKEHAMPTON, IN THE COUNTY OF DEVON.

By Letters Patent, dated 15th April, 1628.

Lineage.

REGINALD MOHUN, Esq., of Boconnoc, in Cornwall, lineally descended from Reginald de Mohun, younger son of John, first Baron Mohun, of Dunster, (a dignity that fell into abeyance, in the time of Edward III.,) was created a baronet by King James I. He m. Philippa, daughter of John Hele, Esq., and was s. by his son,

SIR JOHN MOHUN, second baronet, who was elevated to the peerage on the 15th April, 1628, in the dignity of BARON MOHUN, of Okehampton, in the county of Devon. His lordship, during the civil wars, was one of the chief cavalier commanders in Cornwall, and the west of England, and did essential service to the royal cause. He m. Cordelia, daughter of Sir John Stanhope, of Shelford, in the county of Notts, and widow of Sir Roger Aston, by whom he had issue,

    JOHN, his successor.

    Warwick, heir to his brother.

    Charles, slain at Dartmouth, fighting under the royal banner.

    Cordelia, m. to John Harris, Esq., of Heane, in the county of Devon.

    Theophila, m. to James Campbell, Esq., son of Mr. Alderman Campbell, of London.

    Philadelphia.

His lordship d. in 1644, and was s. by his eldest son,

JOHN MOHUN, second baron, who died unmarried, and was s. by his brother,

WARWICK MOHUN, third baron. This nobleman m. Catherine, daughter of —— Welles, Esq., of Brember, in the county of Southampton, and dying in 1665, was s. by his son,

CHARLES MOHUN, fourth baron, who espoused Lady Philippa Annesley, daughter of Arthur, first Earl of Anglesey, and had issue,

    CHARLES, his successor.

    Elizabeth, who d. unmarried, in 1709.

His lordship d. before the year 1682, and was s. by his son,

CHARLES MOHUN, fifth baron. This nobleman was of a vehement and passionate temper, which led him into many excesses in his youth,

and subjected him to be twice arraigned for murder, but he was, upon both occasions, honourably acquitted. Having had a dispute with James, Duke of Hamilton, regarding an estate left him by the Earl of Macclesfield, he challenged that nobleman, and a duel ensued in Hyde Park, on the 15th November, 1712, wherein both the combatants were slain. His lordship m. first, Charlotte, daughter of —— Mainwaring, Esq., by Lady Charlotte Gerard, sister of Charles, Earl of Macclesfield, and secondly, Elizabeth, daughter of Dr. Thomas Lawrence, and widow of Colonel Griffith, but had no issue, in consequence of which the BARONY OF MOHUN, of Okehampton, at his decease, became EXTINCT.

ARMS.—Or. a cross ingrailed sa.

MOLINES—BARONS MOLINES.

By Writ of Summons, dated 18th February, 1347, 21 Edward III.

Lineage.

This family, which was of French extraction, assumed its surname from a town so called, in the Bourbonnois: but no member of the house became of note in England, before the reign of Edward III., when

JOHN DE MOLINES attained high rank, and great importance, as well from enjoying the favour of the king, as by his large possessions in several counties, but particularly in Buckinghamshire: In the beginning of King Edward's reign, he was one of those who surprised the castle of Nottingham, and seized the person of Mortimer, Earl of March, for which act, he shortly afterwards received a pardon. In the 14th of the same reign, he had several grants from the crown, and was summoned to parliament as a BARON, on 18th February, 1347, but never afterwards. His lordship had been treasurer of the chamber to King Edward, and amassed a very large estate by the favour and grants of that monarch. He was engaged in the wars of France, and received the honour of knighthood for his services. He m. first, Egidia, heir of John Mauduit, of Somerford, in Wilts, and secondly, Margaret, daughter and co-heir of Roger Pogeys, of Stoke-Pogeys, in the county of Buckingham, and was s. by his son,

WILLIAM MOLINES, second baron, who m. Margery, daughter and heir of Edmund Bacoun, and dying in the reign of Richard II., was s. by his son,

RICHARD MOLINES, third baron, who was s. by his son,

WILLIAM MOLINES, fourth baron, who, dying in the 3d of Henry VI., was s. by his son,

WILLIAM MOLINES, fifth baron. This nobleman was slain at the siege of Orleans, in the reign of Henry VI., leaving an only daughter and heiress,

    ALIANORE MOLINES, who espoused ROBERT HUNGERFORD, second Lord Hungerford, who had summons to parliament, as Lord Molines, in 1445.

ARMS.—Paly of six wavey, or and gules.

Note.—Nicolas is of opinion, although the title of Lord Molines was attributed to each of the descendants of John, the first baron, that the dignity became EXTINCT, at the demise of that nobleman, because it has been decided that a *single* summons to parliament, without proof of sitting, does not constitute a barony in fee.

MONK — DUKES OF ALBEMARLE.

By Letters Patent, dated 7th July, 1670.

Lineage.

The family of LE MOYNE, or MONK, was of great antiquity in the county of Devon, and in that shire they had, from a remote period, possessed the MANOR OF POTHERIDGE, which lineally descended to

GEORGE MONK,* the celebrated general under the *usurper*, CROMWELL, who, for his exertions in restoring the monarchy, was created by King Charles II., on the 7th July, 1670, *Baron Monk, of Potheridge, Baron Beauchamp, of Beauchamp, Baron of Teys, Earl of Torrington, all in the county of Devon,* and DUKE OF ALBEMARLE: and shortly after was installed a knight of the garter. To explain his grace's titles, it is necessary to state, that Elizabeth Grey, the wife of his ancestor, Arthur Plantagenet, was sister and heir of John Grey, Viscount L'Isle, and daughter of Edward Grey, by Elizabeth, daughter and heir of John Talbot, eldest son of John, Earl of Shrewsbury, by his second wife, Margaret, eldest daughter and co-heir of Richard Beauchamp, EARL OF WARWICK, and ALBEMARLE, by Elizabeth, his wife, daughter and heiress of Thomas, Lord Berkeley, by Margaret, his wife, daughter and heiress of Gerard Warine, Lord L'Isle, by Alice, daughter and heiress of Henry Lord Teyes.

---

* This eminent person was lineally descended from ARTHUR PLANTAGENET, *Viscount L'Isle,* natural son of King Edward IV., thus:

> ARTHUR PLANTAGENET m. Elizabeth, sister and co-heir of John Grey, Viscount L'Isle, and widow of Edmund Dudley, and left, with other issue,
>
> FRANCES PLANTAGENET, who espoused, for her second husband, Thomas Monk, Esq., of Potheridge, and was mother of
>
> ANTHONY MONK, who m. Mary, daughter of Richard Arscot, Esq., and was *s.* by his son,
>
> SIR THOMAS MONK, Knt., who wedded Elizabeth, daughter of Sir George Smith, Knt., and had issue,
>
> > Thomas, who m. Mary, daughter of William Gold, and had a son, THOMAS, who *d.* in his twelfth year, and two daughters.
> > GEORGE, created DUKE OF ALBEMARLE.
> > Nicholas, who m. Susanna, daughter of Thomas Paine, Esq., and had issue,
> > > Mary, *m.* to Arthur Fairwell, and had several children.
> > > Elizabeth, *m.* to Curwen Rawlinson, and had issue,
> > > > Monk Rawlinson, *d.* unmarried, in 1695.
> > > > Christopher Rawlinson.

The military and naval achievements of Monk have shone so conspicuously in history, that any attempt to depict them in a work of this description could have no other effect than that of dimming their lustre. He crowned his reputation by the course he adopted after the death of Cromwell, in restoring the monarchy, and thus healing the wounds of his distracted country. To the gloomy and jealous mind of the usurper, general Monk was at times a cause of uneasiness and distrust; and to a letter addressed to the general himself, Cromwell once added the following singular postscript: " There be that tell me there is a certain cunning fellow in Scotland, called George Monk, who is said to lie in wait there to introduce Charles Stuart; I pray you use your diligence to apprehend him, and send him up to me." From the time of the restoration to that of his death, his Grace of Albemarle preserved the confidence and esteem of the restored monarch, and his brother, the Duke of York; the former always calling him his "political father." With the people, Monk always enjoyed the highest degree of popularity, and his death was lamented as a national misfortune. His obsequies were public, and his ashes were deposited in Henry VIII.'s chapel, at Westminster, with the remains of royalty. The Duke espoused Anne, daughter of John Clarges, and sister to Sir Thomas Clarges, Bart., by whom he had an only son,

CHRISTOPHER, his successor.

His grace *d.* in 1670, and was *s.* by his son,

CHRISTOPHER MONK, second Duke of Albemarle. This nobleman was made a KNIGHT of the GARTER, in 1671, and sworn of the privy council. His grace espoused Lady Elizabeth Cavendish, daughter and co-heir of Henry, Duke of Newcastle, by whom he had an only son, that died immediately after his birth. The duke went out GOVERNOR-GENERAL to Jamaica, in 1687, accompanied by Sir Hans Sloane, and died there in the next year, when ALL HIS HONOURS became EXTINCT.

ARMS.—Gu. a chevron betw. three lion's heads erased, ar.

Note.—The following singular circumstance occurred during the trial of an action of trespass, between William Sherwin, plaintiff, and Sir Walter Clarges, Baronet, and others, defendants, at the bar of the King's Bench, at Westminster, 15th November, 1700.

" The plaintiff, as heir and representative of Thomas Monk, Esq., elder brother of George, Duke of Albemarle, claimed the Manor of Sutton, in the county of York, and other lands, as heir at law to the said duke, against the defendant, devisee under the will of Duke Christopher, his only child, who *d.* in 1688, *s. p.* Upon this trial it appeared, that Anne, the wife of George, Duke of Albemarle, was daughter of John Clarges, a farrier in Savoy, and farrier to Colonel Monk. In 1632, she was married at the Church of St. Lawrence Pountney, to Thomas Ratford, son of Thomas Ratford, late a farrier's servant to Prince Charles, and resident in the Mews. She had a daughter, born in 1634, who *d.* in 1638; her husband and she lived at the three Spanish Gipsies, in the New Exchange, and sold wash-balls, powder, gloves, and such things, and she taught girls plain work. About 1647, she being sempstress to Monk, used to carry him linen. In 1648, her father and mother died; in 1649, she and her husband fell out, and parted; but no certificate from any parish register appears, reciting his burial. In 1652, she was married in the Church of St. George, Southwark, to General George Monk, and in the following year, was delivered of a son, CHRISTOPHER, *who was suckled by Honour Mills, who sold apples, herbs, oysters, &c.*," which son, CHRISTOPHER, succeeded his father, as stated in the text.

MONTALT — BARONS MONTALT.

By Writ of Summons, dated 23rd June, 1295,
23 Edward I.
By Writ of Summons, dated 6th February, 1299,
27 Edward I.

Lineage.

Upon the foundation of the Abbey of St. Werburg, in the city of Chester, temp. William Rufus, HUGH, the son of Norman, being at that time one of the barons to Hugh, Earl of Chester, granted certain lands to the monks of that house, Ralph and Roger, his brothers, being witnesses. To Ralph succeeded his son and heir,

ROBERT, who assumed the surname of Montalt, from the chief place of his residence, an elevation in the county of Flint, where he erected a castle. This Robert, being steward to the Earl of Chester, was also one of his barons. After the death of Ranulph de Gernons, Earl of Chester, the lands of that great earldom were, it appears, for sometime in the king's hands, for in the 6th of Henry II., this Robert de Montalt was one of those, who accounted in the king's exchequer for the farm of them: and likewise for what was then expended, in building the Castle of Chester. This Robert was s. by his son and heir,

ROBERT DE MONTALT, Lord of Montalt, in the county of Flint, who was s. by his son,

ROGER DE MONTALT, who was deemed one of the greatest feudal barons in the realm, temp. Henry III., and accompanied Prince Edward to the Holy Land. This feudal lord was constantly employed against the Welsh, and in the 44th Henry III., he had command to repair to the borders, with the other Barons-Marches and there to reside for the defence of the country. He m. Cecilia, second sister, and one of the co-heirs of Hugh de Albini, Earl of Arundel, and had issue,

JOHN.

Robert.

Leucha, m. to Philip de Orreby, the younger.

He d. in 1260, and was s. by his elder son,

JOHN DE MONTALT, who m. first, Elene, widow of Robert de Stockport; and secondly, Milisent, daughter of William de Cantilupe, but dying without issue, was s. by his brother,

ROBERT DE MONTALT, who had two sons, Roger, and Robert, and was s. by the elder,

ROGER DE MONTALT, who was one of the barons in rebellion against Henry III., but returning to his allegiance, he subsequently defended Cambridge for the king. In the reign of Edward I., he was in the wars of Gascony, and was summoned to parliament as a BARON, on the 23rd June, 1295, His lordship m. Julian, daughter of Roger de Clifford, but dying without issue, in 1297, the barony expired—his lands devolved, however, upon his brother,

ROBERT DE MONTALT. This gallant person having distinguished himself in the wars of Scotland and Gascony, temp. Edward I. and Edward II., was summoned to parliament by the former monarch, on 6th February, 1299, and he had summons from that period, to the 13th June, 1329, in which year he died without issue, when the BARONY OF MONTALT became EXTINCT, and his extensive estates, according to a settlement made by the deceased lord, passed to Isabel, Queen Consort of England, mother of Edward III., for life, and afterwards to John, of Eltham, brother to the king, and his heirs for ever.

ARMS.—Az. a lion rampant, ar.

MONTFORT — BARONS MONTFORT.

By Writ of Summons, dated 23rd June, 1295.

Lineage.

HUGH DE MONTFORT, commonly called Hugh with a Beard, son of Thurstan de Bastenburgh, accompanied William the Conqueror into England, and aided that prince's triumph at Hastings, for which eminent service he obtained divers fair lordships, and at the time of the general survey, was possessor of twenty-eight in Kent, with a large portion of Romney Marsh; sixteen in Essex; fifty-one in Suffolk, and nineteen in Norfolk. This gallant soldier eventually lost his life in a duel, with Walcheline de Ferrers, and was s. by his son,

HUGH DE MONTFORT, who had issue by his first wife, two sons, viz.

> Robert, general of the army to King William Rufus, but favouring the title of Robert Curthose, in opposition to Henry I., he was impeached for his disloyalty, whereupon, being conscious of guilt, he got permission to go to Jerusalem, and left all his possessions to the king; he died s. p.
> Hugh died in a pilgrimage also, s. p.

Hugh de Montfort, senior, had, besides these sons, a daughter by his second wife, who m. Gilbert de Gant, and had issue,

> HUGH, who, on account of his mother being so great an heiress, assumed the name of Montfort.
> ———, m. to Simon, Earl of Huntingdon.

Which

HUGH DE MONTFORT, (Olim Gant,) inherited all the possessions of his grandfather, and was called Hugh *the Fourth*. This Hugh, having married Adeline, daughter of Robert, Earl of Mellent, joined with Waleran, her brother, and all those who endeavoured to advance William, son of Robert Curthose, against King Henry I., in 1124, and entering Normandy for that purpose, he was made prisoner, with the said Waleran, and confined for the fourteen years ensuing. The time of his death is not ascertained, but he left issue,

> Robert.
> Thurstan.
> Adeline, m. to William de Britolio.
> ——, m. to Richard, son of the Earl of Gloucester.

He was s. by his elder son,

ROBERT DE MONTFORT. This feudal Lord having in 1163, charged, Henry de Essex, the King's Standard Bearer, with cowardice, in fleeing from his colours, vanquished him in a subsequent trial by battle. He does not not appear to have had any issue, for he was s. at his decease, by his brother,

THURSTAN DE MONTFORT, who, being enfeoffed of divers fair lordships, by Henry de Newburgh, the first Earl of Warwick, erected a stony castle, called Beldesert, at the chief seat of his family, in Warwickshire, which it continued for several subsequent ages. To this Thurstan succeeded his son,

HENRY DE MONTFORT, who, in the 2nd of Richard I., regained the manor of Wellesbourne, in the county of Warwick, commonly called Wellesbourne-Montfort, whereof he had been dispossessed by King Henry II. He was s. by

THURSTON DE MONTFORT, who had great law suits in King John's time, with Eustace de Stutevill and Nicholas de Stutevill, regarding a portion of the lordship of Cotingham, in the county of York. He d. in 1216, and was s. by his son,

PETER DE MONTFORT. This feudal lord for several years, in the reign of King Henry III., took an active part in the wars of that monarch, but at length, on the breaking out of the barons' insurrection, he became one of the most zealous amongst those turbulent lords, and after the battle of Lewes, was of the *nine* nominated to rule the kingdom—in which station he enjoyed and exercised more than regal power—but of short duration, for he fell at the subsequent conflict of Evesham, so disastrous to the baronial cause. Peter de Montfort m. Alice, daughter of Henry de Aldithley, a great Staffordshire baron, and had issue,

> Peter, his successor.
> William, who by gift of his father had the manor of Uppingham, in the county of Rutland.
> Robert, who had lands also in the county of Rutland.

The eldest son,

PETER DE MONTFORT, participated in his father's treasons, and was taken prisoner at the battle of Evesham, but being allowed the benefit of the dictum of Kenilworth, he was restored to his paternal inheritance—and afterwards enjoyed the favour of King Edward I., in whose Welsh wars he took a very active part. He d. in 1287, leaving a daughter Elizabeth, (who m. first, William, son and heir of Simon de Monticute, and secondly, Sir Thomas de Furnivall,) and a son and heir,

JOHN DE MONTFORT, who, in the 22nd Edward I., being in the wars of Gascony, was the next year summoned to parliament as a BARON.

His lordship m. Alice, daughter of William de Plaunch, and had issue,

> John, } successively barons.
> Peter, }
> Elizabeth, m. to Sir Baldwin de Freville, Knt.
> Maud, m. to —— Ludley.

He d. in 1296, and was s. by his elder son,

JOHN DE MONTFORT, second baron, summoned to parliament 26th July, 1313, in which year he received pardon for his participation in the murder of Piers de Gaveston—and afterwards marching with the English army into Scotland, was killed at the battle of Stryvelin, when, leaving no issue, he was s. by his brother,

PETER DE MONTFORT, third baron, summoned to parliament from 22nd January, 1336, to 10th March, 1349. This nobleman, prior to the decease of his brother, was in priest's orders, but upon inheriting the honours of his family the sacred function was dispensed with. In the 15th Edward II. he was joined in commission with William de Beauchamp, and Roger de Aylesbury, in the custody of the city of Worcester, and five years afterwards was constituted governor of Warwick Castle, then vested in the crown, by reason of the minority of the Earl of Warwick. His lordship m. Margaret, daughter of the Lord Furnival, and had a son,

> GUY, who m. Margaret, one of the daughters of Thomas de Beauchamp, Earl of Warwick, but died in the life-time of his father, without issue.

Peter, last Lord Montfort, d. in 1367, when the barony fell into ABEYANCE between his sisters, (refer to children of John, first lord,) as it still continues amongst their representatives.

ARMS.—Bendy of ten, or and as.

NOTE.—Peter, last Lord Montfort, had by a concubine, called Lora de Ullenhale, daughter of one Richard Astley, of Ullenhale, in the county of Warwick, a son,

> SIR JOHN MONTFORT, Knt., whose posterity flourished in the male line for several subsequent ages, at Coleshill, in the county of Warwick, until the attainder of Sir Simon Montfort, Knt., temp. Henry VII., whose descendants continued at Bescote, in the county of Stafford.

MONTFORT — EARLS OF LEICESTER.

Creation of King John, anno 1206.

Lineage.

The first of this family that settled in England was

SIMON DE MONTFORT, surnamed the Bald, great grandson of Almaric, an illegitimate son of Robert,[*] king of France. Which Simon having

---

[*] Thus,

> ROBERT, king of France.
> Almaric, who had the town of Montfort by

espoused Amicia, one of the two sisters and co-heirs of ROBERT BEAUMONT, surname Fitz-Parnel, fourth and last Earl of Leicester of that family, obtained a grant of the EARLDOM OF LEICESTER from King John, with a confirmation of the STEWARDSHIP of England, which he acquired by the possession of the honour of HINKLEY, a portion of the immense fortune of his wife. But notwithstanding these marks of royal favour, the earl, within a brief period, revolted from the king of England to the king of France, for which act of treason the Earldom of Leicester was transferred to Ranulph, Earl of Chester, the honours of Hinkley seised upon by the crown, and De Montfort himself banished the realm. Soon after this (1209) we find him, under the title of Earl of Montfort, a commander in the papal crusade against the primitive christians, called *Albigenses*, and in nine years subsequently a leader in the besieging army of Lewis, king of France, before the walls of Tholouse, where he was slain by a slinger from the battlements. His lordship had two sons by the co-heiress of Beaumont, namely, Almaric and Simon, the younger of whom,

SIMON DE MONTFORT, is said to have first sought an asylum in England from the hostility of Blanch, queen of France, and to have obtained a restitution of the EARLDOM OF LEICESTER, and stewardship of England, from King Henry III., through the petition of his brother Almaric, then Earl of Montfort, and constable of France. Certain it is, however, that in 1232, (16th Henry III.,) he bore the title of Earl of Leicester, and had obtained a grant of all his mother's inheritance in England from his brother. In 1236 his lordship officiated as steward at the nuptials of Henry III., and held the ewer in which the king washed. And in two years afterwards he obtained the hand of the king's sister, Eleanor, widow of William Marshal, Earl of Pembroke; the marriage ceremony being performed by Walter, one of the royal chaplains at Westminster, "within a little chappel at the corner of the king's chamber." This marriage was, however, opposed by the princess's other brother, Richard, Earl of Cornwall, (afterwards king of the Romans,) and the kingdom at large, because the lady had made in her widowhood a vow of chastity, in the presence of Edmund, Archbishop of Canterbury, and several of the nobility. And so strongly did public discontent manifest itself, that the earl was obliged to repair in person to Rome for the purpose of obtaining a dispensation, which with considerable difficulty he at length accomplished; and returning to England was most graciously received at court by the king, who appointed him his chief counsellor. Notwithstanding this, however, William de Abindon, a Dominican friar, and many other of the clergy, continued to exclaim against the marriage. The birth of Prince Edward, the king's eldest son, occurring soon after, the earl was chosen one of the spon-

sors of the royal infant, and as such officiated at the baptismal font. But before the close of the same year, he felt the influence of one of those clouds which so constantly hang over the brightest beams of royal sunshine: for the king observing him and his countess amongst the nobility who attended the queen at her purification, called him an excommunicated person, and prohibited his entering the church. "Which sudden unkindness," (says Dugdale,) "much dismaying him, he went away by water to Winchester House, which (the bishop being dead), the king had lent him. But there he could not be permitted to stay, the king in great wrath causing him to be put out of doors. Whereupon he returned sorrowing and weeping, yet could not appease his anger, the king plainly telling him, that he had abused his sister before marriage: and that, though he afterwards gave her to him for a wife, it was unwillingly, and to avoid scandal. Upbraiding him, that to ratify this his unlawful marriage, he went to Rome, and there corrupted that court with large bribes and promises: adding, that having failed in payment of the money, he ought justly to be excommunicated." This storm ultimately drove his lordship from the kingdom, but only for a short period, as we find him returning in 1940, and having then an honourable reception from the king and all his court. Soon after this he made a journey to Jerusalem, having previously disposed of one of his woods to the knights hospitallers and canons of Leicester for somewhat less than a £1000 to defray part of the necessary expences of the undertaking. Henceforward he appears for a series of years to have enjoyed the high favour of the king, and to have fully merited it by his eminent services. In the 39d Henry III. his lordship was appointed commander-in-chief of the forces in Gascony, and in the end of that year he sate in the great convention of parliament held at London; about which time he obtained from the king a grant of the custody of Kenilworth Castle, for Eleanor, his wife, to hold during her life; and, returning into Gascony, he forced Guaston de Bearne, who had raised the standard of rebellion, to an honourable truce. The earl came back to England the next year, and was received at court with great honour. Soon after which, in fulfilment of a vow he had made as penance for his marriage, he began a journey to the Holy Land, and in the 34th of the same reign returned safely, with his brother-in-law, Richard, Earl of Cornwall, and others. For the two following years he was actively and victoriously employed in Gascony, until the king hearkening to complaints against him for cruelty and oppression, which appear to have been unsustainable, removed him from the seneschalship of that country. Upon the subsequent insurrection of the barons against the king, the Earl of Leicester siding with the former, was appointed their general-in-chief, in which character he fought the great battle of Lewes, where the royal army sustained so signal a defeat, the king himself being made prisoner with Prince Edward, his son, his brother, Richard, king of the Romans, and many other personages of eminence, attached to his cause. This victory placing the

gift of his royal father, and thence assumed that surname.
    Simon de Montfort.
    Almaric, Earl of Montfort, father of Simon, above-mentioned.

government in the hands of the earl and his adherents; HIMSELF, the Bishop of Chichester, the Earl of Gloucester, and a few others of less note, were nominated to discharge the executive functions. One of the earliest acts of the usurpation was to summon a parliament in the king's name, by writs dated 24th December, 48th Henry III., directed to the bishops and abbots, and to such lay lords as could be relied upon; by which, signifying " the realm to be then in peace and quiet, and the desire of the king to establish the same to the honour of God, and benefit of his people;" they were summoned to meet at LONDON, on the octaves of St. Hilary, there to sit in parliament, " to treat and give their advice." At the same time precepts were issued to the sheriffs, ordering them to return two knights for each county; to the cities and boroughs the like number of citizens and burgesses; and to the barons of the cinque ports, a certain number of their discreetest men for the same purpose. This is deemed the first precedent of a parliament, such as ever since has been established, and Sir William Dugdale thus speculates upon the causes of the revolution. " If I may be so bold as to give my opinion, what reasons these potent rebels then had, thus to alter the former ancient usage, I shall take leave to conjecture, that it was, because they discerning what large retinues the nobility and other great men in those elder times had; as also the great number of the king's tenants in capite, then called *barones minores*, it might have proved dangerous to themselves to permit such a multitude to come together." The new government did not, however, endure long, for a breach taking place between the two chiefs, Leicester and Gloucester, the arms of those powerful persons were directed against each other, and Prince Edward effecting his escape about the same time, the Earl of Gloucester reared the royal standard, and formed a junction with the forces of the prince. With this army, marching towards Kenilworth, they surprised young Simon Montfort, the earl's son, and made prisoners of no less than thirteen of his chief adherents, driving himself within the walls of the castle for protection. Elated with this triumph they proceeded to EVESHAM, where the Earl of Leicester and his great force lay, expecting the arrival of his son; whose banners the royal army as a stratagem of war alone displayed, and thereby completely deceived this able commander. His lordship undismayed, however, drew out his army in order of battle, and fighting gallantly to the last, fell in the midst of his enemies, when victory declared for the royal cause. It is said, that when the earl discerned the form of his adversaries *bataglia*, he swore " by the arm of St. James, (his usual exclamation,) they have done discreetly; but this they learned from me; let us therefore commend our souls to God, because our bodies are theirs." Nevertheless, encouraging his men, he told them, " it was for the laws of the land, yea, the cause of God and justice, that they were to fight." The principal persons slain in the memorable engagement were, the earl himself, Henry de Montfort, his eldest son, Hugh Despenser, then justice of England, Ralph Basset, of Drayton. Amongst the prisoners, were Guy de

Montfort, a younger son of the earl; John Fitz-John; Humphrey de Bohun, the younger; John de Vesci, Peter de Montfort, junr., and Nicholas de Segrave. The body of the earl was removed from the field of battle by some of his friends upon an old ladder covered with a poor torn cloth, and thus conveyed to the abbey of Evesham, where, folded in a sheet, it was committed to the grave. But within a short time, some of the monks alleging, that the earl being an excommunicated person, and attainted of treason, his remains were unworthy christian burial, the body was taken up, and interred in a remote place, known but to few. Thus fell, in 1264, Simon de Montfort, Earl of Leicester; one of the most eminent soldiers and statesmen of the period in which he lived, and being attainted, the EARLDOM became EXTINCT. Of his widow, Eleanor, the king's sister, it is stated, that after the fatal battle of Evesham, she fled into France, and took up her abode in the nunnery of the order of preachers, at Montarges, which had been founded by her husband's sister. Of his issue,

HENRY fell at Evesham, leading the van of the baronial army.

Simon, who for some time gallantly defended the castle of Kenilworth, was eventually made prisoner in the Isle of Ely, by Prince Edward; afterwards effecting his escape he fled into France, and in 1270 being at Viterbuirm, in Italy, he joined with his brother, Guy, in the murder of their cousin, Henry, eldest son of Richard, king of the Romans, in the church of St. Silvester, as the prince assisted at mass.

Guy, fought in the van of the baronial army at Evesham, and being made prisoner, was confined in Dover Castle, from which escaping, he fled into Tuscany, and there acquiring high reputation as a soldier, he obtained the daughter and heiress of the Earl Rufus for his wife. Meeting with Prince Henry, son of the king of the Romans, himself, and his brother, Simon, slew him in revenge, in the church of St. Silvester, at Viterbuirm. For which barbarous act, being first excommunicated by Pope Gregory X., he was thrown into prison; but released in 1283 by Pope Martin II., and placed at the head of an army, in which situation he displayed his characteristic prowess. He subsequently, at the decease of his wife's father, returned to Tuscany, and inherited a very considerable fortune. He is said to have been Earl of Angleria, in Italy, and progenitor of the Montforts, of Tuscany, and of the Earl of Campobachi, in Naples.

Amaric, who, when conveying his sister from France to be married to Leoline, Prince of Wales, was taken prisoner, with her at sea, and suffered a long imprisonment. He was at last, however, restored to liberty, and his posterity are said to have flourished in England under the name of Wellsburne.

Eleanor, m. to Leoline, Prince of North Wales.

ARMS.—Gules, a lion rampant, quevé forchée, ar.

MONTACUTE — BARONS MONTA- CUTE, EARLS OF SALISBURY.

Barony, by Writ of Summons, dated 26th Sept., 1300, 28 Edward I.

Earldom, by Charter, dated 16th March, 1337.

Lineage.

The ancestor of this celebrated family,

DROGO, surnamed De MONTE-ACUTO, MONTA- CUTE, or MONTAGUE, came into England with Robert, Earl of Moreton, at the CONQUEST, and appears, by Domesday Book, to have held of him divers manors in Somersetshire, whereof Sceptone, or Shipton-Montacute, was one, and Sutone, other- wise Sutton-Montacute, was another. The grand- son of this Drogo,

RICHARD DE MONTACUTE, paid twenty marks for his knights' fees, upon the collection of the scutage, levied in the 7th of Henry II. He was s. by his son,

DRU DE MONTACUTE, (commonly called, young Dru,) who, in the 19th of Henry III., upon the assessment of the aid for marrying the king's daughter, certified his knights' fees to be in num- ber, nine, an half, and third part, de veteri feoffa- mento, and one de novo, besides one, whereof he was dispossessed by Henry Lovel. This feudal lord m. Aliva, daughter of Alan Basset, of Wycombe, and had issue,

DRU, whose line terminated in two grand- daughters and heirs, viz.

Margaret, m. to William de Echingham.

Isabel, m. to Thomas de Audham.

William.

The younger son,

WILLIAM DE MONTACUTE, was sheriff of Dorsetshire, in the time of King John, and was s. by his only son,

WILLIAM DE MONTACUTE. This feudal lord had military summonses in the 41st and 42nd of Henry III., to march against the Welch. He was s. at his decease, by his son,

SIMON DE MONTACUTE, one of the most eminent persons of the period in which he lived. In the 10th of Edward I., he was in the expedition made into Wales, and within a few years after, re- ceived considerable grants from the crown. In the 22d, he was in the wars of France, where he appears to have been engaged for the two or three following years, and then we find him fighting in Scotland. In the 27th he was constituted governor of Corfe Castle, and summoned to parliament, next year, as a BARON. In the 4th of Edward II., his lord- ship was appointed admiral of the king's fleet, then employed against the Scots: and he obtained, in three years afterwards, licence to make a castle of his mansion house, at Perlynton, in Somersetshire. He m. Aufrick, daughter of Fergus, and sister and heir of Orry, King of the Isle of Man, and had issue,

WILLIAM, his successor.

Simon, m. to Hawise, daughter of Aimeric, Lord St. Amand.

His lordship d. about the year 1316, and was s. by his elder son,

SIR WILLIAM DE MONTACUTE, K. B. se- cond baron, summoned to parliament, from 20th November, 1317, to 26th August, 1318. This noble- man had distinguished himself in the Scottish wars, in the life-time of his father, and was made a Knight of the Bath. In the 11th Edward II., being then steward of the king's household, his lordship was constituted seneschal of the Duchy of Aqui- taine, and had licence to make a castle of his house at Kersyngton, in Oxfordshire. He subse- quently obtained other extensive grants from the crown. He m. Elizabeth, daughter of Sir Peter de Montfort, of Beaudesert, by whom (who es- poused secondly, Thomas, Lord Furnival,) he had surviving issue,

WILLIAM, his successor.

Simon, in holy orders, Bishop of Worcester, translated to the see of Ely, in 1336, and knighted about two years after, by Edward the Black Prince.

Edward (Sir), summoned to parliament as a BARON, temp. Edward III., (see Montacute, Baron Montacute).

Katherine, m. to Sir William Carrington, Knt.

Alice, m. to —— Auberie.

Mary, m. to Sir —— Cogan.

Elizabeth, Prioress of Haliwell.

Hawise, m. to Sir —— Bavent.

Maud, Abbess of Berking.

Isabel, a nun at Berking.

His lordship d. in Gascony, but was buried at St. Frideswide, now Christ Church, Oxford, in 1320. He was s. by his eldest surviving son,

WILLIAM DE MONTACUTE, third baron, who, the next ensuing year, although in minority, obtained a grant from the king, of the wardship of all his own lands; and in the 16th Edward II., making proof of his age and doing his homage, had livery thereof. In three years afterwards, he was made a Knight of the Bath, and had an allowance of robes for that solemnity, as a banneret. In the 4th of Edward III., his lordship was deputed am- bassador to the pope, with Bartholomew de Burgh- ersh, to return thanks to HIS HOLINESS, for confirming a bull of Pope Honorius, IV., touching certain favours, by him granted, to the monks at Westminster; moreover, before the end of the year, a parliament being then held at NOTTINGHAM, he was the principal person who apprehended Roger de Mortimer, EARL OF MARCH,[*] in the night-time,

* A parliament being held at Nottingham, in 1330, Sir William Montacute, (Lord Montacute,) was the chief person who laid the conduct of Roger de Mortimer, Earl of March, before the king, who, immediately, thereupon, taking into consideration his own dishonour and damage, as also the impover- ishment of his people, and revealing his mind, pri- vately, to Sir William Montacute, gave him com- mand to take to his assistance, some trusty and resolute persons, which he accordingly did, by selecting, as his associates, Sir Humphrey Bohun, John, Lord Molines, Robert, Lord Ufford, Ralph, Lord Stafford, William, Lord Clinton, and Sir

within the queen's lodgings there, and sent him prisoner to London, where he was soon afterwards executed for high treason. For this service, Lord Montacute had a grant in tail, to himself, and Katherine his wife, of the Castle of Sherburne, in the county of Dorset, and of several other manors in Southampton, Berkshire, Buckinghamshire, and Cambridge: part of the possessions of the attainted Earl of March. In the 8th of Edward III. his lordship was constituted governor of the Isles of Guernsey, Jersey, &c., and the next year made constable of the Tower of London.

About this time Lord Montacute acquired great distinction in the Scottish wars, but at the expence of one of his eyes, which he lost in the campaign. In the 10th of Edward III., he was appointed admiral of the king's fleet, westward, and the next year, in consideration of his numerous gallant achievements, he was advanced in full parliament held at London, to the title and dignity of EARL OF SALISBURY, with a grant of twenty pounds out of the profits of that county. Shortly after this, he

was joined in command of the army in Scotland, with Richard, Earl of Arundel; and pursued his victorious career as well in Scotland as in France, for the two ensuing years, when in storming the town of L'Isle, he had the misfortune to be made prisoner with Robert de Ufford, Earl of Suffolk, and conveyed in fetters, amidst the acclamations of the places through which he passed, to Paris, where the French king would have put him to death, but for the interference of the King of Bohemia. His lordship and his fellow-captive, the Earl of Suffolk, were soon after, however, delivered up in exchange for the Count of Murref, (a Scotchman) and the sum of three thousand pounds sterling. With his liberty, he recommenced his martial career, and won fresh laurels on the French soil. In the 16th of Edward III., having conquered the Isle of Man, he was crowned king thereof, by his royal master. His lordship m. Katherine, daughter of William, Lord Grandison, and had issue,

WILLIAM, his successor.

JOHN (SIR), a distinguished warrior, and one

John Nevil, of Horneby. While these noble persons were consulting how to seize on Mortimer, he was at the same time holding a council in the Castle of Nottingham, with Isabel, the Queen Mother, Henry Burwash, Bishop of Lincoln, Sir Simon Beresford, Sir Hugh Turplington, Sir John Monmouth, and others, his creatures, how to bring to utter ruin all those that accused him of treason and felony. But the Lord Montacute, and those of the council concerned with him, not being admitted to take up their lodgings in the castle, had a suspicion that Mortimer designed their destruction: and thereupon his lordship told the king, "That since neither he nor any of his partakers, were admitted to lodge in the castle, they should never be able to seize Mortimer, without the consent and assistance of the Constable, Sir William Eland." "Now, surely," said the king, "I love you well, and therefore advise you to go to the constable in my name, and command him to be aiding and assistant to you, in taking Mortimer, all other things laid aside, on peril of life and limb." "Sir," said Montacute, "then God grant success;" thereupon he went to the said constable, and telling him the king's will before the rest of his accomplices, in general terms; the constable answered, that "The king's will should be obeyed;" and thereupon, he was sworn to be constant and secret to the Lord Montacute, and Montacute to him, in the hearing of all the assistants. "Now, surely, dear friend," said Lord Montacute to the constable, "it behoved us to gain your acquaintance, in order to seize on Mortimer, since you are keeper of the castle, and have the keys at your dispose." "Sirs," replied the constable, "you shall understand, that the gates of the castle are locked, with the locks that Queen Isabell sent hither, and at night, she hath all the keys thereof, and layeth them under the pillow of her bed, until the morning: and so I may not help you into the castle, at the gates, by any means; but I know an hole that stretcheth out of the ward, under earth, into the castle, beginning on the west side; which hole,

neither Isabel, the Queen, nor Mortimer himself, nor none of his company, know anything of; and through this passage I shall lead you, till you come into the castle, without the espial of any of your enemies." That same night, Sir William Montacute, (Lord Montacute,) and all the lords, his assistants, with the constable, took horse, pretending to go out of town, which when Mortimer heard of, he thought they fled away for fear of him, and devised how to entrap them. But about midnight, on Friday, 19th October, returning back again, they all came to the passage aforesaid, and following the direction of Sir William Eland, entered a dismal cave, which went under the castle, dug unequally, through stony, and other sort of ground, till it came to the rock on which the castle stood, through which it also passed with stairs, till it opened itself above, within the keep, or chief tower. This wonderful passage had been hewed and dug, during the Danish invasions, by some of the Saxon kings, for their better security in case of a siege; but since the action of this night, it hath the name of Mortimer's Hole; whom, without any great noise, and with little resistance, they at last took, not in the queen's chamber, but in another, not far from it, in the company of the said Bishop of Lincoln. Before he could be seized, Montacute finding some resistance from the earl's attendants, slew Sir Hugh Turplington, Steward of the King's Household, and Sir John Monmouth, and at last secured Mortimer's person, to be reserved for a more public death. The queen mother, then in bed, heard the noise of this rencontre, and supposing what the matter really was, and that the king himself must needs be there, she called out to him in these words, "Bel Fitz, Bel Fitz, ayez pitie du gentil Mortimer!" Mortimer was hurried thence, and brought before the king, who immediately commanded him into safe custody in the castle, the keys thereof being put into the king's hands, that none might issue out, to discover what hath been done, till the rest of Mortimer's abettors had been secured.—COLLINS.

of the heroes of CRESSY, who m. Margaret, daughter and heir of Thomas, Lord Montherner, and was summoned to parliament as a BARON, from 15th February, 1357, to 6th December, 1369. His lordship had issue,

JOHN, second baron, who succeeded his uncle, as third Earl of Salisbury.

Thomas, Dean of Salisbury, d. in 1404.

Robert, of Sutton-Montague, in Somersetshire. The issue of this gentleman, according to Banks, flourished there until William Montague, the last of the family, left three daughters and coheirs, of which, EMMA m. James Dupote, who, in her right, possessed one moiety of Sutton-Montague, whose son, THOMAS, was father of Henry Duport, Esq., of Leicestershire, and John Duport, D.D., Master of Jesus College, Cambridge.

Simon (Sir),* from whom the extinct Dukes of Montague, and the extant Dukes of Manchester, and the Earls of Sandwich, are said to have derived.

Eleanor.

Sibyl, a nun.

Katherine.

Margaret, a nun.

---

* SIR SIMON MONTACUTE. The fifth in direct lineal descent from this gentleman,

THOMAS MONTAGUE, m. Agnes, daughter of William Dudley, of Clopton, Northamptonshire, and issue,

JOHN, his successor,

And

SIR EDWARD MONTAGUE, Knt., one of the most celebrated lawyers of the period in which he lived. In the reign of Henry VIII., he was speaker of the House of Commons, and not a little obsequious to his royal master. Upon one occasion, a bill of subsidies not passing, Mr. Speaker was sent for by the king, and thus addressed, while upon his knees, in the royal presence, "Ho! will they not let my bill pass?" and laying his hand on the head of Montague, his Highness continued, "Get my bill to pass by such a time to-morrow, or else by such a time this head of yours shall be off." The speech was brief but conclusive; for we are told that Sir Edward "wrought so effectually, that before the time prescribed, the bill passed with the approbation of the house, and the sovereign's satisfaction." Sir Edward was afterwards CHIEF of the Court of King's Bench, and then of the Common Pleas. He was likewise of the privy council. He was s. by the eldest son of his third marriage,

SIR EDWARD MONTAGU, who was father of

SIR HENRY MONTAGU, M.P. for London, temp. James I., and subsequently created EARL OF MANCHESTER. His lordship was great-grandfather of the first Duke of Manchester, who was great-great-grandfather to the present Duke.

Robert.

Sibyl, m. to Edmund, son of Edmund, Earl of Arundel.

Philippa, m. to Roger Mortimer, Earl of March.

Elizabeth, m. to Giles, Lord Badlesmere.

Anne, contracted to John, son of Roger, Lord Grey.

This great earl d. in 1343, of bruises received in a tilting at Windsor, and was s. by his eldest son,

WILLIAM DE MONTACUTE, second Earl of Salisbury. This nobleman, in 1346, attended King Edward III., into France, and was at the siege of Caen, and the glorious battle of CRESSY. From this period he was seldom absent from the theatre of war, so that his whole life may be denominated one continued campaign. At the battle of POICTIERS, he commanded the rear-guard of the English army, and is said to have contended with the Earl of Warwick, in the heat of action, as to which should shed most French blood. His lordship was one of the original KNIGHTS OF THE GARTER, the foundation of which noble order, tradition attributes to the love which King Edward bore to his lordship's countess. The earl m. first, Joane, daughter of Edmund Plantagenet, Earl of Kent, from whom he was divorced, on account of the lady's precontract with Sir Thomas Holland (this was the celebrated FAIR MAID OF KENT, who eventually became the wife of Edward, the Black Prince). His lordship espoused, secondly, Elizabeth, daughter and coheir of John, Lord Mohun, of Dunster, and had an only son,

WILLIAM, who m. Elizabeth, daughter of Richard, Earl of Arundel, and died before his father, s. p. in 1383.

The earl d. in 1397, when leaving no issue, his honours devolved upon his nephew,

SIR JOHN DE MONTACUTE, Baron Montacute and Montherner, as third Earl of Salisbury. This nobleman was not less distinguished in the field than his martial predecessors. In the 21st of Richard II., he did his homage, and had livery of the lands which he inherited from his uncle, "and being," says Dugdale, "a great favourite of the king, he was one of those whom that monarch suborned to impeach Thomas, of Woodstock, Duke of Gloucester, as also the Earls of Warwick and Arundel, in the ensuing parliament." The next year his lordship was constituted marshal of England, in the absence of Thomas Holand, Duke of Surrey, then employed in Ireland: and he remained faithful to the fortunes of King Richard, when almost every body else deserted him, upon the invasion of Henry, Duke of Lancaster, who eventually drove that weak monarch from the throne. "It is reported of this earl," says Dugdale, "that though, upon the deposal of King Richard II., (to whom he had been most obsequious) he had such fair respect from King Henry IV., that his life was not brought in question; nevertheless, he confederated with the Earls of Huntingdon and Kent, in designing his destruction; and accordingly came with them to Windsor Castle, under the disguise of Christmas players, with purpose to murder him and his sons, and to restore King

Richard. But finding that their plot was discovered, they fled by night to Cirencester, in the county of Gloucester. Whereupon the townsmen, being much affrighted at their coming thither with such numbers, at that unseasonable time; stopping up all the avenues, to prevent their passage out, there grew a sharp fight betwixt them, which held from midnight, until three of the clock next morning; so that being tired out, they yielded themselves, desiring that they might not suffer death till they could speak with the king, which was granted: but that a priest of their party setting fire to the town, to give them an opportunity for escape, so irritated the inhabitants, that, (neglecting to quench the fire) they brought them out of the abbey in great fury, and beheaded them about break of the day." His lordship had m. Maud, daughter of Sir Adam Francis, Knt., of London (widow of John Aubrey, son of Andrew Aubrey, citizen of London, and of Sir Alan Buxhull, Knt.), by whom he had issue,

THOMAS, who was restored to the Earldom of Salisbury, and the other honours.

Richard, d. s. p.

Anne, m. first to Sir Richard Hankford, Knt., secondly, to John Fits-Lewis, and thirdly to John Holland, Duke of Exeter.

Elizabeth, m. to Robert, Lord Willoughby, of Eresby.

Margaret, m. to William, Lord Ferrers, of Groby.

This John, Earl of Salisbury, was one of the most zealous of the sect called Lollards. His death as stated above, occurred upon the 5th January, 1400, and ALL HIS HONOURS expired under the subsequent attainder. But King Henry taking compassion upon his widow and children, restored some of the late earl's manors in Devonshire for their support; and to the elder son,

THOMAS DE MONTACUTE, he also granted a large proportion of his father's estates: and within a few years restored him to the EARLDOM OF SALISBURY, and the other honours. "This nobleman," in the words of Banks, "was concerned in so many military exploits, that to give an account of them all, would be to write the history of the reign of Henry V. Suffice it then to say, that as he lived, so he died in the service of his country; being mortally wounded when commanding the English army at the siege of Orleans in 1428." His lordship m. first, the Lady Eleanor Plantagenet, daughter of Thomas, and sister and co-heir of Edmund, Earl of Kent, and had an only daughter,

ALICE, who m. Richard Nevill, second son of Ralph, first Earl of Westmorland (see Nevill, Earls of Salisbury).

The earl espoused, secondly, Alice, daughter of Thomas Chaucer, Esq., and widow of Sir John Philipps, Knt., but had no issue. Upon the decease of his lordship, who, with his other honours, was a KNIGHT OF THE GARTER, the EARLDOM OF SALISBURY became EXTINCT, but the Baronies of MONTACUTE, created by writ in 1300, of MONTACUTE, created by writ in 1357, and MONTHERMER, devolved upon his daughter and heiress,

362

LADY ALICE MONTACUTE, and was conveyed by her to the NEVILLS.

ARMS.—Ar. three fusils in fesse, gu.

NOTE.—The illustrious house of Montacute is now represented by the Dukes of Manchester and the Earls of Sandwich, who descend from Sir Simon Montacute, a younger son of Sir John Montacute, Lord Montacute, second son of William, first Earl of Salisbury, and father of John, third earl.

MONTACUTE — BARONS MONTACUTE.

By Writ of Summons, dated 15th February, 1357, 31 Edward III.

[See MONTACUTE, EARLS OF SALISBURY,' Sir John Montacute, second son of William, first Earl of Salisbury.]

MONTACUTE — BARON MONTACUTE.

By Writ of Summons, dated 25th February, 1342, 26 Edward III.

Lineage.

SIR EDWARD DE MONTACUTE, youngest brother of William, first Earl of Salisbury, in the 4th of Edward III. had a grant from the crown for his good services, and to support his rank as a knight, of £100 per annum: and was summoned to parliament as a BARON, from 25th February, 1342, to 20th November, 1360. His lordship was an eminent soldier, and served with high reputation in the wars of Scotland and France, having at one time in his train nine knights, fifteen esquires, and twenty archers on horseback, when his banner bore the following arms, viz., "Ar. three fusils in fesse, on each an eagle displayed with a label of three points." He m. the Lady Alice Plantagenet, daughter and co-heir of Thomas, of Brotherton, Duke of Norfolk, by whom he had an only child,

JOANE, who m. William Ufford, Earl of Suffolk, and died issueless,

His lordship d. in 1361, when the BARONY OF MONTACUTE devolved upon his daughter Joane, and at her decease it became EXTINCT.

ARMS.—Ar. three fusils in fesse, on each an eagle displayed, with a lable of three points.

MONTAGUE — BARONS HALIFAX, EARL OF HALIFAX, EARLS OF HALIFAX.

Barony,	by Letters Patent,	4th Dec., 1700.
First Earldom,		14th Oct., 1714.
Second Earldom,		14th June, 1715.

Lineage.

The Honourable

GEORGE MONTAGUE, eldest son of Henry, first Earl of Manchester, by his third wife, Margaret, daughter of John Crouch, Esq., m. Elizabeth, daughter of Sir Anthony Irby, Knt., and was father of

CHARLES MONTAGUE, (a younger son,) who became one of the most eminent statesmen of the important period of King William III. Mr. Montague was returned to parliament by the city of Durham, and afterwards by the city of Westminster. In 1692 he was appointed one of the commissioners of the treasury, and in two years afterwards chancellor of the exchequer, in which office he projected, and caused to be executed, the great recoinage of silver in 1695. In 1698 he adjusted the affairs of the East India Company to universal satisfaction: and was elevated to the peerage, in compliance with the recommendation of the House of Commons, on 4th December, 1700, in the dignity of BARON HALIFAX, *of Halifax, in the county of York,* with remainder, failing his issue male, to his nephew, GEORGE MONTAGU, son and heir of his elder brother, Edward Montagu. In the reign of Queen Anne his lordship was constituted a commissioner for the union between England and Scotland; and was created, 14th October, 1714, *Viscount Sunbury, in the county of Middlesex,* and EARL OF HALIFAX. His lordship was not more distinguished as a politician than as a wit and man of letters. " Addison," says Banks, " has celebrated this nobleman in his account of the greatest English poets. Sir Richard Steel has drawn his character in the dedication of the second volume of the Spectator, and of the fourth of the Tatler; but Pope in the portrait of Bufo, in the Epistle to Arbuthnot, has returned the ridicule which his lordship, in conjunction with Prior, had heaped on Dryden's Hind and Panther; besides which admirable travestie, Lord Halifax wrote divers other works, most of which have been published together in an octavo volume, with memoirs of his lordship's life (1716); and are noticed by Walpole in his catalogue of Noble Authors."

The earl m. Anne, countess dowager of Manchester, daughter of Sir Christopher Yelverton, Bart., of Easton Mauduit, Notts, but had no issue. His lordship, who was a KNIGHT OF THE GARTER, d. in 1715, when the EARLDOM EXPIRED, but the BARONY devolved, according to the limitation, upon his nephew,

GEORGE MONTAGUE, second Baron Halifax, who was created, on the 14th June, 1715, *Viscount Sudbury* and EARL OF HALIFAX. This nobleman was made a Knight of the Bath upon the revival of that order in 1725. His lordship m. first, Richarda-Posthuma, daughter of Richard Saltenstale, Esq., of Chippen-Warden, in the county of Northampton, by whom he had an only daughter,

LUCY, m. to Francis, Lord Guilford.

The earl espoused, secondly, Lady Mary Lumley, daughter of Richard, Earl of Scarborough, and had issue,

GEORGE, his successor.
Frances, m. to Sir Roger Burgoyne.
Anne, m. to Joseph Jekyll, Esq.
Mary, m. to Sir Danvers Osborn, Bart.
Elizabeth, m. to Henry Archer, brother of Lord Archer.
Barbara, d. unmarried.
Charlotte, m. to Col. Johnston.

His lordship d. in 1739, and was s. by his son,

GEORGE MONTAGU, second Earl of Halifax. This nobleman espoused Anne, daughter of William Richards, Esq., and that lady having succeeded to the estates of Sir Thomas Dunk, of Tonges, in Kent, his lordship assumed the surname of DUNK. He had issue,

Anne, d. unmarried in 1761.
Frances, d. unmarried in 1674.
Elizabeth, m. to John, fifth Earl of Sandwich.

His lordship filled the offices of first lord of the admiralty, and secretary of state. He died in 1771, when ALL HIS HONOURS became EXTINCT.

ARMS.—AZ. three losanges in fesse gules, within a border s. a mullet for difference.

MONTAGU — BARONS MONTAGU, OF BOUGHTON, EARLS OF MONTAGU, DUKES OF MONTAGU.

Barony,	by Letters Patent,	29th June, 1621.
Earldom,		9th April, 1689.
Dukedom,		19th April, 1705.

Lineage.

SIR JOHN MONTACUTE, brother of William, first Earl of Salisbury, m. Margaret, daughter and heiress of Thomas, Lord Monthermer, and had, with other issue, JOHN, who inherited as third Earl of Salisbury, (see Montacute, Earls of Salisbury,) and

SIR SIMON MONTACUTE, who m. Elizabeth, daughter and heir of William Boughton, Esq., of Boughton, in the county of Northampton, and from this marriage lineally descended

SIR EDWARD MONTAGU, Knt., chief justice of the King's Bench, and afterwards of the Common Pleas, (temp. Henry VIII.,) having previously filled the chair of the House of Commons. This celebrated person was in such favour with King Henry VIII., that he was appointed by that monarch one of the executors to his will. He m. Helen, daughter of John Roper, Esq., of Eltham, and had several sons. He was s. by the second, but eldest surviving,

SIR EDWARD MONTAGU, who espoused Elizabeth, daughter of Sir James Harington, of Exton, in the county of Rutland, and had issue,

EDWARD (Sir), his successor.
Walter (Sir).
Henry (Sir), progenitor of the DUCAL HOUSE OF MANCHESTER.
Charles (Sir).
James, Bishop of Winchester.
Sydney (Sir), ancestor of the EARLS OF SANDWICH.

Sir Edward, who served the office of sheriff for Northamptonshire in 1567, was s. by his eldest son,

SIR EDWARD MONTAGU, K.B., who was elevated to the peerage, 29th June, 1621, as BARON MONTAGU, of Boughton, in the county of Northampton. His lordship m. first, Elizabeth, daughter and heir of Sir John Jeffries, Knt., of Chitting-Leigh, in the county of Sussex, chief baron of the exchequer, by whom he had an only daughter,

ELIZABETH, who m. Robert, Lord Willoughby, of Eresby, afterwards EARL OF LINDSEY.

His lordship espoused, secondly, Frances, daughter of Thomas Cotton, Esq., of Conington, in Huntingdonshire, and sister of Sir Robert Cotton, Bart., by whom he had,

> Christopher, who predeceased his father, dying in the twenty-fourth year of his age, anno 1641.

EDWARD, successor to the title.

William, lord chief baron of the exchequer in 1687, from which he was removed by King James II. He lived, subsequently, in retirement. By Mary, his wife, daughter of Sir John Aubrey, Bart., he had a son and daughter,

>> William, who m. Anne, daughter and heir of Richard Evelyn, Esq., of Woodcot, in Surrey.

>> ———, m. first, to —— Drake, Esq., and second, to Samuel Totsman, Esq., of Syston, in Gloucestershire.

Frances, m. to John, Earl of Rutland.

This nobleman is characterised " as a person of a plain, downright English spirit; of a steady courage, a devout heart; and though no puritan, severe and regular in his life and manners. That he lived amongst his neighbours with great hospitality; was very knowing in country affairs, and exceedingly beloved in the town and county of Northampton. That he was no friend to changes either in church or state; that when the civil wars began, he was brought prisoner to town by the parliament party, and confined in the Savoy: where he d. in the eighty-second year of his age, anno 1644." His lordship was s. by his eldest surviving son,

EDWARD MONTAGU, second baron, who m. Anne, daughter, and eventually heir of Sir Ralph Winwood, of Ditton Park, principal secretary of state to King James I., by whom he had issue,

> Edward, who was appointed by King Charles II. master of the house to the queen. Afterwards going to sea with his gallant kinsman, the Earl of Sandwich, he was slain in an attack upon the Dutch East India fleet, in the port of Bergen, 3d August, 1665.

> RALPH, successor to the title.

> Elizabeth, m. to Sir Daniel Harvey, Knt., ambassador at Constantinople in 1668.

His lordship d. in 1683, and was s. by his only surviving son,

RALPH MONTAGU, third baron, who, in the life-time of his father, represented the county of Huntingdon in parliament, and was a very distinguished member of the house. He was an active and zealous promoter of the Revolution, and in consequence, upon the accession of King William and Queen Mary, he was created 9th April, 1689, Viscount Monthermer, and EARL OF MONTAGU. In 1669 his lordship was ambassador to the court of France, and then formed that taste in building and landscape gardening, which he afterwards acted upon, in erecting his mansion at Boughton, as much after the model of Versailles, as the extent would

permit. His town house was in Bloomsbury, and is now the BRITISH MUSEUM. In 1705 he was advanced by Queen Anne to the Marquisate of Monthermer, and Dukedom of MONTAGU. His grace m. first, Lady Elizabeth Wriothesley, daughter of Thomas, Earl of Southampton, and widow of Joceline, Earl of Northumberland, by whom he had issue,

> Ralph, } who both d. in the life-time of the
> Winwood, } duke.

> JOHN, his successor.

> Anne, m. first, to Alexander Popham, Esq., and secondly, according to Collins, to Lieut.-General Hervey, but by Edmondson, to Edward, Viscount Hinchinbroke.

The duke espoused, secondly, Lady Elizabeth Cavendish, daughter and co-heir of Henry, Duke of Newcastle, widow of Christopher Monk, Duke of Albemarle, but by her had no issue. His grace d. in 1709, and was s. by his son,

JOHN MONTAGU, second duke. This nobleman officiated as lord high constable of England at the coronation of King George I. His grace m. Mary, daughter and co-heir of the celebrated General, John, DUKE OF MARLBOROUGH, and had three sons, John, George, and Edward-Churchill, who all d. young, in his life-time, and three daughters, viz.

> Isabella, m. first, to William, Duke of Manchester, by whom she had no issue, and secondly, to Edward Hussey, Earl of Beaulieu.

> Eleanor, d. young.

> Mary, m. to George Brudenell, fourth Earl of Cardigan, who, after the decease of his father-in-law, was created Marquess of Monthermer, and DUKE OF MONTAGU.

In the reign of George I. the Duke of Montagu filled several public situations of the highest honour. He was a Knight of the Garter, and a Knight of the Bath. At the accession of King George II. he was continued in favour, and at the coronation of that monarch, he carried the sceptre with the cross. His grace d. in 1749, when ALL HIS HONOURS became EXTINCT.

ARMS.—Quarterly, first and fourth, ar, three losenges conjoined in fesse gules within a border, sa. for MONTAGU. Second and third, or, an eagle displayed vert, beaked and membered gules, for MONTHERMER.

MONTAGU — BARON MONTAGU, OF BOUGHTON.

By Letters Patent, dated 8th March, 1762.

Lineage.

The Honourable

JOHN MONTAGU, only son of John, fourth Earl of Cardigan, by Lady Mary Montagu, daughter and co-heir of John, second Duke of Montagu, (who d. in 1749,) was created by letters patent, dated 8th March, 1762, BARON MONTAGU, of Boughton, in the county of Northampton, but dying unmarried in the life-time of his father the DIGNITY became EXTINCT.

ARMS.—Same as the Dukes of Montagu.

MONTAGU—DUKE OF MONTAGU.

By Letters Patent, dated 5th November, 1766.

Lineage.

GEORGE BRUDENELL, fourth Earl of Cardigan, having espoused Lady Mary Montagu, one of the daughters and co-heirs of John, second Duke of Montagu, (who d. in 1749, when his honours expired,) assumed the surname and arms of MONTAGU, and was created 5th November, 1766, *Marquess of Monthermer*, and DUKE OF MONTAGU. His grace was governor of Windsor Castle, a member of the privy council, and a KNIGHT of the GARTER. He had issue,

JOHN, created BARON MONTAGU, *of Boughton*, but d. unmarried in 1770, in the life-time of his father.

Elizabeth, m. in 1767, to Henry, third Duke of Buccleuch, by whom she had, with four daughters, two sons, viz.

CHARLES - WILLIAM - HENRY, fourth Duke of Buccleuch.

HENRY-JAMES, who s. his grandfather as Baron Montagu, of Boughton.

Mary,
Henrietta, } both d. unmarried.

The duke was created in 1786, BARON MONTAGU, OF BOUGHTON, with remainder to Henry, second son of his daughter, Elizabeth, Duchess of Buccleuch. His grace, who was governor to the Prince of Wales, (George IV.,) and Prince Frederick, (Duke of York,) sons of King George III., d. 23rd May, 1790, when the Earldom of Cardigan devolved upon his brother, the Hon. James Brudenell. The Barony of Montagu, of Boughton, passed according to the limitation, and the MARQUISATE OF MONTHERMER and DUKEDOM OF MONTAGU became EXTINCT.

ARMS.—Same as the Duke of Montagu, who d. in 1749.

MONTHERMER — BARON MONTHERMER, EARL OF GLOUCESTER AND HERTFORD.

Earldom, *Jure Uxoris*, by Writ of Summons, 6th February, 1299, 27 Edward I.
Barony, by Writ of Summons, dated 4th March, 1309, 2 Edward II.

Lineage.

RALPH DE MONTHERMER, "a plain Esquire," having espoused the *Lady* JOANE PLANTAGENET, (commonly called Joane of Acres,) daughter of *King* EDWARD I., and widow of Gilbert, Earl of Clare, Gloucester and Hertford, had the title of EARL OF GLOUCESTER AND HERTFORD, in her right, and was summoned to parliament as "Comiti Gloucester' et Hertf." from 6th February, 1299, to 3d November, 1306. In the 26th year of Edward I. his lordship was in the expedition then made into Scotland, and behaved so valiantly, that the king rendered to him and his wife, the said Joane, the castle and honour of Tonebrugge, with other lands in Kent, Surrey, and Sussex; as also the Isle of Portland, and divers other estates belonging to the said Joane, which had been seised by the crown in consequence of her marriage without licence with the said Ralph; and the king became eventually much attached to his son-in-law, to whom he had been reconciled through the intercession of Anthony Beke, the celebrated Bishop of Durham. In the 31st, 39d, and 34th of his father-in-law, the earl was again in Scotland, and in the contest with Bruce, King Edward conferred upon him the whole of Anandale, with the title of Earl of Atholl, the Scottish nobleman who held that dignity, having espoused the fortunes of Bruce. But it was not long after this that Joane of Acres departed this life, (viz. 1 Edward II.,) and he never, subsequently, assumed the title of Earl of Gloucester and Hertford, although he lived for several years; in a grant of considerable landed property made to him and his sons in two years afterwards, he is styled Ralph de Monthermer only. Nor is he otherwise denominated, in the 5th Edward II., at which time, in recompence of his service in Scotland the king gave him three hundred marks, part of the six hundred marks which he was to have paid for the wardship of John ap Adam, a great man of that age. Nor in two years afterwards, when again in the wars of Scotland, he was made prisoner at Bannockburn, but he then found favour from his former familiarity with the king of Scotland, at the court of England, and obtained his freedom without paying ransom. He was, however, summoned to parliament as a BARON from 4th March, 1309, to 30th October, 1324. His lordship espoused, secondly, Isabel, widow of John de Hastings, and sister and co-heir of Aymer de Valence, Earl of Pembroke, by whom he had no issue. But by his first wife, the Princess Joane, he had two sons, viz.

THOMAS, who d. before his father, (being killed in a sea fight with the French in 1340,) leaving an only daughter and heiress,

MARGARET DE MONTHERMER, who m. Sir John de Montacute, and conveyed the BARONY OF MONTHERMER to the family of Montacute. Her eldest son,

JOHN, *Baron Montacute and Monthermer*, s. as third Earl of Salisbury (see Montacute, Earl of Salisbury).

EDWARD, who was summoned to parliament as a BARON on the 23rd April, 1337, 11th Edward III., but never afterwards, and nothing further is known of him or his descendents.

ARMS.—Or. an eagle displayed, vert. membered and beaked, gu.

MONTGOMERY — BARON MONTGOMERY.

By Writ of Summons, dated 25th February, 1342, 16 Edward III.

In the 20th Edward III.,

JOHN DE MONTGOMERY was in the great

expedition then made into France, and the next year was made captain of Calais, as also admiral of the king's whole fleet, from the mouth of the Thames, westwards. He had summons to parliament as a BARON, on 25th February, 1342, but never afterwards, and the dignity is presumed to have become EXTINCT, at his lordship's decease.

ARMS.—Or. an eagle displayed, &c.

MORDAUNT — EARLS OF PETER-BOROUGH, VISCOUNTS MORDAUNT OF AVALON, EARLS OF MONMOUTH.

Earldom of Peterborough, Viscounty, &c. Earldom of Monmouth,	by Letters Patent,	9th March, 1628. 10th July, 1659. 9th April, 1689.

Lineage.

It appears from the records of this family, collected in the reign of King Charles II., and printed at the charge of *Henry*, EARL OF PETERBOROUGH, that

SIR OSBERT LE MORDAUNT, a Norman knight, was possessed of Radwell, in Bedfordshire, by the gift of his brother, who derived it from the CONQUEROR, in recompense of his own and his father's good services. The grandson of this successful soldier,

EUSTACH LE MORDAUNT, m. Alice, eldest daughter and co-heir of Sir William de Alneto, modernly called Dauney, and acquired by her the lordship of Turvey, in Bedfordshire. He was s. by his son,

WILLIAM MORDAUNT, who became Lord of Turvey, Radwell, Asthull, and other manors. He was s. by his son,

WILLIAM MORDAUNT. This feudal lord had licence to inclose his pasture of Wolesey, his field called Turvey-Lees, his pasture of Maselgrove, and other lands in Turvey, to form a park. He m. Rose, daughter of Sir Ralph Wake, and was s. by his eldest son,

ROBERT MORDAUNT, who was knight of the shire for the county of Bedford, in the parliament held at Westminster in the 15th Edward III. From this gentleman we pass to his descendant,

SIR JOHN MORDAUNT, Knt., of Turvey, in the county of Bedford, who was one of the royal commanders at the battle of Stoke, 16th June, 1484. Being likewise learned in the laws, he was constituted king's serjeant in the 11th of Henry VII., justice of Chester in four years after, subsequently chancellor of the duchy of Lancaster, and made one of the knights of the sword at the creation of Henry, Prince of Wales, 18th February, 1509-3. This gallant and learned person d. in the 21st year of Henry VII., and was s. by his eldest son,

WILLIAM MORDAUNT, Esq., who died s. p., when the estates devolved upon his brother,

SIR JOHN MORDAUNT, who was sheriff of Bedford and Bucks in the 1st year of Henry VIII.,

366

and in the 5th of the same reign was one of the commissioners, appointed by act of parliament, for assessing and collecting the Poll-Tax. He was knighted before, 4th June, 1520, when he was one of those appointed to attend the queen at the interview with Francis I. of France; and in May, 1522, he waited upon the king at Canterbury, at his second meeting in England with the Emperor Charles V. In 1530 he was appointed, with others, to inquire into the landed possessions of Cardinal Wolsey, and he was summoned to parliament, as a BARON, from 4th May, 1532, to 5th November, 1558. In the year 1551, a great dearth of provisions being in the nation, his lordship was the first in commission, with other persons of rank in the county of Bedford, to prevent the enhancing the prices of corn, &c., and to punish offenders therein, as also to supply the said county. He m. Elizabeth, daughter and co-heir of Sir Henry Vere, Knt., of Drayton and Adington, in the county of Northampton, and had issue,

> JOHN, his successor.
> William, m. Agnes, daughter and heir of Charles Booth, Esq.
> George, of Oakley, in the county of Bedford, m. Cecilia, daughter and co-heir of John Harding, Esq., of Harding, in Bedfordshire, and was father of
> > Edmund Mordaunt, Esq., of Thundersley, in Essex.
> Anne, m. first, to James Rodney, Esq., and secondly, to John, son and heir of Sir Michael Fisher.
> Elizabeth, m. to Silvester Danvers, Esq., of Dauntsey, Wilts.
> Margaret, m. to Edward Fettiplace, Esq., of Blessils-Lee, Bucks.
> Winifrid, m. to John Cheyney, of Chesham-Boys.
> Editha, m. to John Elmes, Esq., of Huntingdonshire.
> Dorothy, m. to Thomas More, Esq., of Haddon, in Oxfordshire.

His lordship d. in 1562, and was s. by his eldest son,

JOHN MORDAUNT, second baron, summoned to parliament from 11th January, 1563, to 8th May, 1572. This nobleman, in the life-time of his father, was made one of the Knights of the Bath at the coronation of Queen Anne Boleyn, 1st June, 1553; and was sheriff for Essex and Hertfordshire in 1540. At the demise of Edward VI. he was one of the first in arms on behalf of Queen Mary; whereupon he was sworn of the privy council; and in her majesty's reign served in four parliaments for Bedfordshire. His lordship m. first, Ellen, cousin and heir of Sir Richard Fitz-Lewes, of West-Thorndon, in Essex, by whom he had issue,

> LEWIS, his successor.
> Elizabeth, m. to George Monneux, Esq., of Walthamstow.
> Anne, m. to Clement Tanfield, Esq., of Eberton.
> Margaret, m. to William Acklam, Esq., of Moreby, in Yorkshire.
> Ursula, m. to Edward, son of Sir Nicholas

Fairfax, of Gilling Castle, in the county of York.

Lord Mordaunt m. secondly, Joan, daughter of Robert Wilford, Esq., of Kent, but had no issue by that lady. He d. in 1572, and was s. by his son,

LEWIS MORDAUNT, third baron, summoned to parliament from 8th February, 1576, to 24th October, 1597. This nobleman received the honour of knighthood from Queen Elizabeth, in 1567, and was one of the peers who sate in judgment upon Thomas, Duke of Norfolk; and upon the unhappy MARY, OF SCOTLAND. His lordship espoused Elizabeth, daughter of Sir Arthur Darcy, Knt., second son of Thomas, Lord Darcy, and had issue,

HENRY, his successor.

Mary, m. to Thomas Mansel, Esq., eldest son of Sir Edward Mansel, Knt.

Katherine, m. to John Heveningham, Esq., eldest son of Sir Arthur Heveningham, Knt.

Elizabeth.

He d. 16th June, 1601, and was s. by his son,

HENRY MORDAUNT, fourth baron, summoned to parliament from 27th October, 1601, to 5th November, 1615. This nobleman, under suspicion of being concerned in the gunpowder-plot, was committed to the Tower, and fined by the starchamber before he obtained his liberty. He m. Margaret, daughter of Henry, Lord Compton, by whom he had issue,

JOHN, his successor.

Henry.

Francis, m. Frances, daughter of Sir Edward Gostwick, Bart.

Lewis.

Frances.

Elizabeth, m. to Sir Thomas Nevil, K.B.

His lordship d. in 1608, and was s. by his son,

JOHN MORDAUNT, fifth baron, summoned to parliament from 30th January, 1620, to 17th May, 1625. This nobleman, who was bred a Roman Catholic, is said to have been converted to the established church by a disputation which occurred in his own house, between Bishop, then Dr. Usher, and a Catholic churchman. His lordship was advanced to the dignity of EARL OF PETERBOROUGH, by letters patent, dated 9th March, 1628. He m. Elizabeth, only daughter and heir of William Howard, Lord Effingham, son and heir of Charles, Earl of Nottingham, by whom he had (with Elizabeth, who m. Thomas, son and heir of Edward, Lord Howard, of Escrick), two sons, viz.

HENRY, his successor.

JOHN; this gentleman obtained great fame by his zeal in the cause of King Charles II., and stood a trial during the usurpation for his exertions in behalf of the exiled monarch, but upon which he was acquitted, by the connivance chiefly, as stated by Lord Clarendon, of the celebrated JOHN LISLE, the presiding judge. The other judges were equally divided as to the guilt or innocence of Mr. Mordaunt, and the president gave the casting vote in his favour. He subsequently made several daring but fruit-less attempts to restore the king, and for all those faithful services was, eventually, elevated to the peerage 10th July, 1659, as BARON MORDAUNT, of Ryegate, in the county of Surrey, and VISCOUNT MORDAUNT, OF AVALON, in Somersetshire. His lordship and Sir John Greenvile were the bearers of the letters which the king, prior to his restoration, addressed to Monk, to parliament, and to the corporation of London. In the latter of which, his majesty says:—
"How desirous we are to contribute to the obtaining the peace and happiness of our subjects without effusion of blood, and how far we are from desiring to recover what belongs to us by war, if it can be otherwise done, will appear to you by the inclosed declaration; which, together with this our letter, we have intrusted to our right trusty and well-beloved cousin, the Lord Viscount Mordaunt, and our trusty and well-beloved servant, Sir John Greenvile, Knt., one of the gentlemen of our bed-chamber, to deliver to you, to the end, &c." His lordship, after the restoration, was constituted Constable of Windsor Castle, and appointed Lord Lieutenant, and Custos Rot. of the county of Surrey. He m. Elizabeth, daughter and sole heiress of Thomas Carey, second son of Robert, Earl of Monmouth, by whom he had five sons and three daughters.

1. CHARLES, his successor.

2. Harry, M.P. lieutenant-general in the army, and treasurer of the Ordnance, to which last office he was appointed in 1699. General Mordaunt m. first, Margaret, daughter of Sir Thomas Spencer, of Yarnton, in the county of Oxford, Bart., by whom he had, with other children,

John (Sir), K.B., a general officer in the army.

Eliza-Lucy, m. to Sir Wilfred Lawson, Bart., of Isell, in Cumberland.

General Mordaunt espoused, secondly, Penelope, daughter and heir of William Tipping, Esq., by whom he had,

Penelope, m. to Sir Monoux Cope, Bart.

3. Lewis, a brigadier-general in the army, who died in 1712-13, leaving issue by two wives.

4. Osmond, slain at the battle of the Boyne.

5. George, in holy orders. This gentleman m. thrice, and left by his second wife,

Anna-Maria, m. to Jonathan Shipley, D.D., Bishop of St. Asaph;

and by his third consort,

Mary, m. to Valentine Maurice, Esq., of Perafield, Monmouthshire.

Elizabeth, m. to Sir William Milner, Bart.

1. Charlotte, m. to Benjamin Albin, Esq.
2. Sophia, m. to James Hamilton, Esq., of Bangor, in Ireland.
3. Anne, m. to James Hamilton, Esq., of Tullamore, in Ireland.

His lordship d. 5th June, 1675, and was s. by his eldest son,

CHARLES MORDAUNT, second viscount, who was created EARL OF MONMOUTH, 9th April, 1689, and succeeded to the EARLDOM OF PETERBOROUGH, at the decease of his uncle, in 1697.

The Earl of Peterborough was General of Ordnance, and colonel of a regiment of foot, in the army raised in 1642, by order of parliament, under the command of Robert, Earl of Essex. His lordship d. in the same year, and was s. by his elder son,

HENRY MORDAUNT, second Earl of Peterborough. This nobleman was distinguished during the civil wars by his zeal in the royal cause. He raised a regiment at his own expense, was wounded at the battle of Newbury, and often imprisoned for his loyal exertions. In 1648, he was in the rising with the Earl of Holland to release the king from his confinement; and on their defeat, though Holland was taken and beheaded, Peterborough with his brother, escaped, but they were voted traitors to the commonwealth, and their estates sequestered. His lordship was, after the restoration, of the privy council to King Charles II., and entrusted with several honourable embassies. At the coronation of King James II., he carried the sceptre with the cross, and was elected, in the same year, a KNIGHT OF THE GARTER. After the accession of William and Mary, the commons resolved (26th October, 1689) that the Earl of Peterborough, and the Earl of Salisbury, should be impeached for high treason, for departing from their allegiance, and being reconciled to the church of Rome; but the impeachment was dropped. His lordship m. Penelope, daughter of Barnabas, Earl of Thomond, in Ireland, by whom he had issue,

Elizabeth, d. unmarried.

MARY, who became sole heiress, m. first, Henry, Duke of Norfolk, from whom she was divorced in 1700, and then married Sir John Germain, Bart., but had issue by neither. Her ladyship inherited the BARONY OF MORDAUNT, of Turvey, at the decease of her father, but the dignity again attached to the Earldom of Peterborough, at her own decease, in 1705. Her ladyship bequeathed her whole estate to her second husband.

The earl d. in 1697, when the BARONY OF MORDAUNT, of Turvey, devolved upon his only surviving daughter, as stated above, and the Earldom of Peterborough passed to his nephew (revert to issue of the first earl),

CHARLES MORDAUNT, first Earl of Monmouth, as third Earl of Peterborough. This nobleman, who had distinguished himself as a military character prior to the revolution, was, upon the accession of William and Mary, sworn of the privy council, and made one of the lords of the bedchamber, and in order to attend at their coronation as an earl, was raised to the Earldom of Monmouth, having, the day before, been constituted first lord commissioner of the treasury. In 1692, his lordship made the campaign of Flanders, under King William; and soon after the accession of Queen Anne, he was declared GENERAL, AND COMMANDER-IN-CHIEF, of the FORCES sent to SPAIN; in which command he acquired great military fame, by the capture of Montjovi—by driving the Duke of Anjou, and the French army, consisting of twenty-five thousand men, out of Spain, with a force not exceeding ten thousand, and by acquiring possession of Catalonia, of the kingdoms of Valencia, Arragon, Majorca, &c. His lordship was, however, recalled from the scene of those gallant achievements, and his conduct subsequently examined by parliament; when a vote passed the House of Lords, 12th January, 1710-11, that during the time he had the command in Spain, he performed many great and eminent services;" and his lordship received the thanks of the house, through the lord chancellor. In 1710, and 1711, he was employed in embassy to the Court of Turin, and other Italian states, on especial missions; and in 1713, he was installed Knight of the Garter. In the reign of King George I., his lordship was constituted general of all the marine forces in Great Britain. The earl espoused, first, Carey, daughter of Sir Alexander Fraser, of Dores, N.B., and had issue,

JOHN, Lord Mordaunt,—a military officer— Colonel of the Grenadier Guards, at the celebrated battle of BLENHEIM, 13th August, 1704, wherein he lost one of his arms. His lordship m. Lady Frances Powlett, daughter of Charles, Duke of Bolton, and dying of the small-pox, 6th April, 1710, left two sons,

CHARLES, who s. his grandfather in the honours of the family.

John, a Lieutenant-Colonel in the army, M.P., m. first, in 1735, Mary, sister of Scroop, Viscount How, and widow of Thomas, Earl of Pembroke. He espoused, secondly, Elizabeth, daughter of Samuel Hamilton, Esq., but died issueless, in 1767.

Henry, a naval officer of high character, and a member of parliament—d. unmarried, (of the small-pox,) 27th February, 1709-10.

Henrietta, m. to Alexander Gordon, second Duke of Gordon, from whom lineally descended,

ALEXANDER, fourth Duke of Gordon, who, upon the decease of lady Mary-Anastacia-Grace Mordaunt, daughter of Charles, fourth Earl of Peterborough, in 1819, inherited the BARONY of MORDAUNT, of Turvey.

His lordship m. secondly, in 1735, Anastasia Robinson, and going to Lisbon for the recovery of his health, died there, on the 25th October, in the same year. Upon the decease of his lordship's cousin, Mary, Baroness Mordaunt, of Turvey, (revert to issue of second Earl of Peterborough,) he inherited that ancient dignity of the family. He was s. in all his honours, by his grandson,

CHARLES MORDAUNT, fourth Earl of Peterborough, and second Earl of Monmouth. His lordship m. first, Mary, daughter of John Cox, Esq., of London, and had issue,

> Frances, who, m. the Rev. Samuel Bulkeley, of Hatfield, in Hertfordshire, and died s. p.
>
> MARY-ANASTASIA-GRACE, who succeeded, eventually, to the BARONY OF MORDAUNT, of Turvey.

The Earl espoused, secondly, Robiniana, daughter of Colonel Brown, and d. in 1779, was s. by his only surviving son, by that lady,

CHARLES HENRY MORDAUNT, fifth Earl of Peterborough, and third Earl of Monmouth, born in 1758, and d. unmarried, in 1814, when the EARLDOM OF PETERBOROUGH, and the EARLDOM OF MONMOUTH, with the Viscounty of Mordaunt, and Barony of Mordaunt, of Ryegate, became EXTINCT, while the BARONY OF MORDAUNT, OF TURVEY, devolved upon his lordship's half sister, Lady MARY-ANASTASIA-GRACE MORDAUNT, as BARONESS MORDAUNT, and at her ladyship's decease, in 1819, s. p., it passed to Alexander Gordon, fourth Duke of Gordon, as heir general, of Charles, third Earl of Peterborough, and is now enjoyed by his present Grace of Gordon.

ARMS.—Ar. a chevron betw. three estoils of six points, sa.

MORDAUNT — VISCOUNTS MORDAUNT, OF AVALON, EARLS OF MONMOUTH.

See Mordaunt, EARLS OF PETERBOROUGH.

MORETON, or (more correctly,) DE BURGO, EARLS OF CORNWALL.

Creation of William the Conqueror, in 1068.

Lineage.

HARLOWEN DE BURGO, founder of the abbey of Grasteim, in Normandy, m. Arlotta, the mother of the Conqueror, and dying before his father, John, Earl of Comyn, left two sons,

> ROBERT, Earl of Moreton, in Normandy,
>
> Odo, Bishop of Bayeux,

who both accompanied their illustrious brother in his expedition against England, and were aggrandised after his triumph. Odo being created Earl of Kent, and

ROBERT DE MORETON, Earl of Cornwall, with a grant of seven hundred and ninety-three manors. In the time of William Rufus, this nobleman joining his brother, the Earl of Kent, raised the standard of rebellion in favour of Robert Curthose, and held the castle of Pevensey for that prince. He delivered it up, however, upon its being invested by the king, and made his peace. His lordship m. Maud, daughter of Roger de Mont-

gomery, Earl of Shrewsbury, and had issue, WILLIAM, his successor, and three daughters, whose christian names are unknown: the eldest m. Andrew de Vitrei; the second m. Guy de Val, and the youngest m. the Earl of Tholouse. The time of the Earl of Cornwall's death has not been ascertained, "but if he lived," (says Dugdale,) "after King William Rufus so fatally lost his life by the glance of an arrow in New Forest, from the bow of Walter Tirell; then was it unto him, that this strange apparition happened, which I shall here speak of; otherwise, it must be to his son and successor, Earl William, the story whereof is as followeth. In the very hour that the king received the fatal stroke, the Earl of Cornwall being hunting in a wood, at a distance from the place, and left alone by his attendants, was accidentally met by a very great black goat, bearing the king all black, and naked, and wounded through the midst of his breast. And adjuring the goat by the Holy Trinity to tell what that was he so carried; he answered, I am carrying your king to judgment, yea, that tyrant, WILLIAM RUFUS, for I am an evil spirit, and the revenger of his malice which he bore to the church of God; and it was I that did cause this his slaughter; the protomartyr of England, St. Alban, commanding me so to do; who complained to God of him for his grievous oppressions in the Isle of Britain, which he first hallowed. All which the earl soon after related to his followers." His lordship was s. by his son,

WILLIAM DE MORETON, second Earl of Cornwall, in England, and Earl of Moreton, in Normandy. This nobleman being from childhood of an arrogant and malevolent disposition, envied the glory of King Henry I.; and not contented with the great honours he had derived from his father, demanded the Earldom of Kent, which had been borne by his uncle ODO; giving out secretly, that he would not put on his robe, unless the inheritance, which he challenged by descent from his uncle, might be restored to him. In this demand the king refusing to acquiesce, the earl fled to Normandy, and with Robert de Belesme reared the standard of revolt in the Duchy; which caused Henry to seize upon his possessions in England, to rase his castles to the ground, and to banish him the kingdom. He subsequently led the van at the battle of Tenerchebray, and, after displaying great personal valour, fell into the hands of his opponents, and was sent prisoner to England, where he was treated with great cruelty, the king causing his eyes to be put out, and detaining him in captivity for life. His honours became, of course, FORFEITED. The period of his decease has not been recorded; nor does Dugdale mention either his wife or issue— but in Archdale's edition of Lodge's Peerage of Ireland, (vol. i., in the article regarding the house of Clanricarde) it is stated that the unfortunate earl left two sons, viz.—

> ADELM, from whom the noble house of CLANRICARDE derives.
>
> JOHN, who was father of the celebrated Hubert de Burgo, Earl of Kent, Justiciary of England, temp. Henry III.

ARMS.—Erm. a chief indented gules.

MORLEY—BARONS MORLEY.

By Writ of Summons, dated 29th December, 1299, 28 Edward I.

Lineage.

In the 25th Edward I.,

WILLIAM DE MORLEY, was in the expeditions made in that and the next year, into Scotland, and had summons to parliament as a BARON, from 29th December, 1299, to 3rd November, 1306. His lordship was *s.* by his son,

ROBERT DE MORLEY, second baron, summoned to parliament, from 20th November, 1317, to 15th February, 1357. This nobleman was one of the eminent warriors, of the martial times of King Edward III. In the 13th of that monarch's reign, after previously distinguishing himself in the wars of Scotland, he was constituted ADMIRAL of the king's whole fleet, from the mouth of the Thames, northwards; and the next year, achieved the greatest naval victory, up to that period, ever won, over the French, near SLUCE, in Flanders; subsequently sailing to Normandy, he burnt fourscore ships of the Normans, with three of their sea-port towns, and two villages. The next year, (16th Edward III.), being still admiral, he was in the great expedition then made into France, and in four years afterwards, his banner waved amongst the victorious, upon the plains of CRESSY. His lordship continued admiral several years afterwards, and in each successive year, reaped fresh laurels. In the 29th Edward III., he was made constable of the Tower of London. In the 33rd., he was again in arms on the French soil, and died there the next year, while in immediate attendance upon the king. His lordship m. Hawyse, daughter and heir of Sir William Mareschall, Knt., and had issue,

    WILLIAM (Sir), his successor.

He espoused secondly, Joane ———, and had, with other issue,

    ROBERT (Sir), who, in the 41st Edward III., attended *Prince* EDWARD into Aquitaine; and in the reign of Richard II. was in the wars of France. Sir Robert had issue,

        SIR ROBERT MORLEY, father of

            SIR THOMAS MORLEY, whose daughter and heiress,

                MARGARET MORLEY, *m.* Sir Geffery Ratcliffe, Knt.

His lordship was *s.* by his eldest son,

·SIR WILLIAM MORLEY, third baron, summoned to parliament from 4th December, 1364, to 3d December, 1378. This nobleman, in the time of his father, was in the wars of France, with Robert de Ufford, Earl of Suffolk; and in the 38th Edward III., he had licence to travel beyond sea. As also to grant the office of marshal of Ireland (which he had inherited from his mother) to Henry de Ferrers, to hold during good conduct. His lordship m. Cicily, daughter of Thomas, Lord Bardolph, and had an only son, THOMAS, his successor. Lord Morley *d.* in 1380, and by his last testament, bequeathed his body to be buried in the church of the *Friers-Augustines,* at Norwich. Appointing that two of his best

370

horses should be disposed of for mortuaries, viz., his best black horse to those friers, on the day of his funeral: and, his palfrey, called DON, to the Rector of the church of Hallingbury. He likewise left large sums for masses for his soul, as all the great personages of that period were in the habit of bequeathing. He was *s.* by his son,

SIR THOMAS MORLEY, fourth baron, summoned to parliament from 16th July, 1381, to 3d September, 1417. This nobleman in the 4th of Richard II., arriving at CALAIS, with divers other English lords, rode with his banner displayed. And in the 15th of the same reign (being marshal of Ireland) was in the expedition then made into France, as he was again in the 3d of Henry V.; and the next year he was appointed lieutenant and captain-general of all the forces assembled at London from the different ports, in order to proceed to France. His lordship m. Anne, daughter of Edward, Lord Despenser, (by Elizabeth de Burghersh, his wife) and widow of Sir Hugh de Hastings, Knt., by whom he had a son,

    THOMAS, who died in the life-time of his father, leaving by Isabel, his wife, daughter of John, Lord Molines, a son,

        THOMAS, successor to his grandfather.

He *d.* in 1417, and was *s.* by his grandson,

THOMAS MORLEY, fifth baron, who, in the 6th Henry V., being then marshal of Ireland, was in the expedition made into France, and so likewise, in the 9th of the same reign. His lordship being in the service of *King* HENRY V., when that gallant prince died in France, bore one of the banners of saints, which were carried at the monarch's solemn obsequies. His lordship espoused Lady Isabel de la Pole, daughter of Michael, Earl of Suffolk, and dying in 1435, was *s.* by his son,

ROBERT MORLEY, sixth baron, summoned to parliament 3rd December, 1441. This nobleman m. Elizabeth, daughter of William, Lord Roos, and dying in 1442, left an only daughter and heir,

    ALIANORE MORLEY, who espoused WILLIAM LOVEL, second son of William, Baron Lovel, of Tichmersh, and he was summoned to parliament, *jure uxoris,* as LORD MORLEY. Of this marriage there were issue,

        HENRY LOVEL, *Lord Morley,* who died *s. p.*

        ALICE LOVEL, *m.* to Sir William Parker, Knt., standard bearer to Richard III. Upon the death of her brother this lady inherited the BARONY, and her son,

            HENRY PARKER, was summoned as LORD MORLEY (see Parker, Lords Morley).

Upon the decease of this Robert, last Lord Morley, the male line of that family expired: while his daughter, ALIANORE MORLEY, carried the BARONY OF MORLEY into the family of LOVEL, whence it passed, as stated above, to that of PARKER (see Parker, Lords Morley).

ARMS.—Ar. a lion rampant, sa. crowned or.

MORTIMER — BARONS MORTIMER, OF WIGMORE, EARLS OF MARCH.

Barony, by Writ of Summons, dated 8th June, 1294, 22 Edward I.
Earldom, by Charter, dated anno 1328.

Lineage.

The first of this name upon record,

ROGER DE MORTIMER, is deemed by some to have been son of William de Warren, and by others, of Walter de St. Martin, brother of that William. Which Roger was founder of the abbey of St. Victor, in Normandy. "It is reported," says Dugdale, "that in the year 1054, (which was twelve years before the Norman Conquest,) when Odo, brother of Henry, King of France, invaded the territory of Evreux, Duke William sent this Roger, then his general, (with Robert, Earl of Ewe, and other stout soldiers,) to resist his attempts; who meeting with Odo near to the castle of Mortimer, gave him battle, and obtained a glorious victory. It is further observable of this Roger, that he was by consanguinity allied to the Norman duke, (afterwards king, by the name of William the Conqueror,) his mother being niece to Gunnora, wife of Richard, Duke of Normandy, great-grandmother to the Conqueror." The presumed son of this Roger,

RALPH DE MORTIMER, accompanying the Duke of Normandy in his expedition against England, was one of his principal commanders at the decisive battle of Hastings; and shortly after, as the most puissant of the victor's captains, was sent into the marches of Wales to encounter Edric, Earl of Shrewsbury, who still resisted the Norman yoke. This nobleman, after much difficulty, and a long siege in his CASTLE OF WIGMORE, Mortimer subdued, and delivered into the king's hands. When, as a reward for his good service, he obtained a grant of all Edric's estates, and seated himself thenceforward at WIGMORE. Independently of these great Welsh territorial possessions, Ralph Mortimer enjoyed by the bounty of his royal master sundry lordships and manors in other parts of the realm, which he held at the time of the general survey. In the beginning of RUFUS's reign Mortimer took part with Curthose, but he subsequently changed sides, and being constituted general of the forces sent to oppose that prince in Normandy, by King Henry I., he totally routed the enemy, and brought CURTHOSE prisoner to the king. This gallant person m. Milicent, daughter of —————, by whom he had issue,

Hugh, his successor.
William, Lord of Chelmersh, and afterwards of Netherby.
Robert, ancestor of the Mortimers, of Richard's Castle (see Mortimer, Baron Mortimer, of Richard's Castle).
Hawise, m. to Stephen, Earl of Albemarle.

He was s. by his son,

HUGH DE MORTIMER, who being a person of a proud and turbulent spirit, opposed strenuously the accession of King Henry II. upon the demise of Stephen, and induced Roger, Earl of Hereford, to fortify his castles of GLOUCESTER and HEREFORD against the new monarch; himself doing the same with his castles of Cleobury, Wigmore, and Brugges (commonly called Bridgenorth). Whereupon Gilbert Foliot, at that time Bishop of Hereford, addressing himself to the Earl of Hereford, (his kinsman,) by fair persuasions soon brought him to peaceable submission. But Mortimer continuing obstinate, the king was forced to raise an army, and at the point of the sword to bring him to obedience. Between this rude baron, and Joceas de Dynant, at that time Lord of Ludlow, existed a feud, carried to so fierce a pitch, that Dynant could not pass safely out of his castle for fear of being taken by Mortimer's men. But it so happened, that setting his spies to take all advantages of Dynant, he was surprised himself, and carried prisoner to Ludlow, where he was detained until he paid a ransom of three thousand marks of silver. He was oftentimes engaged against the Welsh, and he erected some strong castles in Wales. He likewise finished the foundation of the ABBEY OF WIGMORE, begun by his father, and in his old age became a canon of that house. He m. Maud, daughter of William Longespe, Duke of Normandy, and had four sons,

Roger, his successor.
Hugh, who m. Felicia de Sancto Sydonio, and had, by gift of his father, the manors of Sudbury and Chelmers.
Ralph.
William.

He d. in 1185, and was s. by his eldest son,

ROGER DE MORTIMER, Lord of Wigmore. This feudal lord, like his predecessors, was in constant strife with the Welsh. At one time he sustained a great defeat in conjunction with Hugh de Say, but in the end he was victorious, and took twelve of their principal leaders in one battle. He also enlarged considerably his territories, and drove thieves and robbers from those parts. Being at one time present at the solemn anniversary of his father, he confirmed all his grants to the canons of Wigmore; adding, of his own gift, a spacious and fruitful pasture, lying adjacent to the abbey, called the *Treasure of Mortimer.* Upon which occasion his steward remonstrating with him for parting with so valuable a treasure, he replied; "I have laid up my treasure in that field, where thieves cannot steal or dig, or much corrupt." This Roger m. first, Millicent, daughter of ——— Ferrers, Earl of Derby, and had issue, Hugh, his successor, and two daughters; the ELDER, married to Stephen le Gross; the YOUNGER, to Walkeline de Beauchamp. He espoused, secondly, Isabel, sister and heir of Hugh de Ferrers, of OAKHAM, in Rutlandshire, and of LECHELADE and LAGNBIRY, in Gloucestershire. All which lands he inherited upon the death of the said Hugh Ferrers; and by the lady he had three sons, Ralph, Robert, and Philip. He d. in 1215, and was s. by his eldest son,

HUGH DE MORTIMER. This feudal lord in the baronial war adhered with unshaken fidelity to King John. In the 16th of that monarch's reign he had a military summons to attend the king at Cirencester, with the other Barons Marchers. He espoused Annora, daughter of William de Braose, and had one hundred shillings in land with her. But having been severely wounded in a tournament, departed this life in November, 1227, leaving no issue, when he was s. by his half-brother,

RALPH DE MORTIMER, who, in the 12th Henry III. paying £100 for his relief, had livery of all his lands, lying in the counties of Gloucester, Southampton, Berks, Salop, and Hereford. This nobleman being of a martial disposition, erected several strong castles, by which he was enabled to extend his possessions against the Welsh: so that Prince Lewelin, seeing that he could not successfully cope with him, gave him his daughter, Gladuse Duy, widow of Reginald de Braose, in marriage, and by this lady he had issue, ROGER, his successor; Peter John, a grey friar at Shrewsbury; and Hugh, of Chelmersh. He d. in 1246, and was s. by his eldest son,

ROGER DE MORTIMER, who, in the 31st of Henry III, paying two thousand marks to the king, had livery of all his lands, excepting those whereof Gladuse, his mother, then surviving, was endowed. In six years afterwards he attended the king in his expedition into Gascony, and in a few years subsequently, when Lewelin, Prince of Wales, began again to make incursions upon the marches, received command to assist Humphrey de Bohun, Earl of Hereford, in the defence of the country lying between Montgomery and the lands of the Earl of Gloucester. In the 42nd of the same reign he had another military summons to march with the king against the Welsh; and being in that service, had a special discharge of his scutage for those twenty-six knights' fees, and a sixth part which he held in right of Maud, his wife, one of the daughters and co-heirs of William de Braose, of Brecknock. In two years afterwards he was made captain-general of all the king's forces in Wales, all the barons marchers receiving command to be attendant on him with their whole strength; and he was the same year constituted governor of the castle of Hereford. But, notwithstanding this extensive power, and those great resources, he was eventually worsted by Lewelin, and constrained to sue for permission to depart, which the Welsh prince, owing to his consanguinity, conceded. After this he took an active part in the contest between Henry III. and the insurrectionary barons, in favour of the former. He was at the battle of Lewes, whence he fled into Wales, and afterwards successfully planned the escape of Prince Edward. The exploit is thus detailed by Dugdale: "Seeing therefore his sovereign in this great distress, and nothing but ruine and misery attending himself, and all other the king's loyal subjects, he took no rest till he had contrived some way for their deliverance; and to that end sent a swift horse to the prince, then prisoner with the king in the castle of Hereford, with intimation that he should obtain leave to ride out for recreation, into a place called Widmersh; and that upon sight of a person mounted on a white horse, at the foot of Tulington Hill, and waving his bonnet, (which was the Lord of CROFT, as it was said,) he should haste towards him with all possible

372

speed. Which being accordingly done, (though all the country thereabouts were thither called to prevent his escape,) setting spurs to that horse he overwent them all. Moreover, that being come to the park of Tulington, this Roger met him with five hundred armed men; and seeing many to pursue, chased them back to the gates of Hereford, making great slaughter amongst them." Having thus accomplished his prince's freedom, Mortimer, directing all his energies to the embodying a sufficient force to meet the enemy, soon placed Prince Edward in a situation to fight, and win the great battle of EVESHAM, (4th August, 1265,) by which the king was restored to his freedom and his crown. In this celebrated conflict Mortimer commanded the third division of the royal army, and for his faithful services obtained, in the October following, a grant of the whole earldom and honour of Oxford, and all other the lands of Robert de Vere, Earl of Oxford, at that time, and by that treason, forfeited. The DICTUM OF KENILWORTH followed soon after the victory of Evesham, by which the defeated barons were suffered to regain their lands upon the payment of a stipulated fine; but this arrangement is said to have caused great irritation amongst the barons marchers, (Mortimer with the rest,) who had acquired grants of those estates. He was, however, subsequently entrusted, by the crown, with the castle of Hereford, which he had orders to fortify, and was appointed sheriff of Herefordshire. After the accession of Edward I. he continued to enjoy the sunshine of royal favour, and had other valuable grants from the crown. He married, as already stated, Maud, daughter and co-heir of William de Braose, of Brecknock, and had, with other issue, three sons, EDMUND, William, and Geffrey: upon whom, having procured the honour of knighthood to be conferred by King Edward I., he caused a TOURNAMENT to be held, at his own cost, at KENILWORTH, where he sumptuously entertained an hundred knights and as many ladies, for three days, the like whereof was never before known in England; and there began the ROUND TABLE, so called from the place wherein they practised those feats, which was encompassed by a strong wall, in a circular form. Upon the fourth day the golden lion, in token of triumph, having been yielded to him, he carried it (with all that company,) to Warwick. The fame whereof being spread into foreign countries, occasioned the queen of Navarre to send him certain wooden bottles, bound with golden bars and wax, under the pretence of wine, but in truth filled with gold, which for many ages after were preserved in the abbey of Wigmore. Whereupon, for the love of that queen, he had added a carbuncle to his arms. By his wife he had several sons, whereof

Ralph (Sir), d. in his life-time.

EDMUND (Sir), was his successor.

Roger, was Lord of CHIRKE, which lordship his grandson sold to Richard Fitz-Alan, Earl of Arundel. It subsequently passed to the family of MIDDLETON (see Mortimer, of Chirke).

William (Sir), an eminent soldier, who m. Hawyse, heir of Robert de Musegross, but d. issueless.

Geffrey (Sir), died *s. p.* in his father's life-time.

This celebrated feudal lord *d.* in 1282, and was *s.* by his eldest surviving son,

SIR EDMUND MORTIMER, Lord of Wigmore, who *m.* Margaret, daughter of Sir William de Fandles, a Spaniard, kinswoman to Queen Eleanore, the wedding being kept at the court at Winchester, at the king and queen's charge. In the 10th of Edward I. he succeeded his father, and the next year doing his homage, had livery of his lands. He was afterwards constantly employed in the Welsh wars, and was summoned to parliament as a BARON, from 8th June, 1294, to 2nd June, 1302. His lordship was mortally wounded in 1303 at the battle of BUELT, against the Welsh, and dying almost immediately, at Wigmore Castle, was buried in the abbey there. He left issue,

ROGER, his successor.

John, accidentally slain in a tournament at Worcester 12th Edward II., by John de Leyburne, being not more than eighteen years of age, and unable to wield his lance.

Hugh, a priest, rector of the church at Old Radnor.

Walter, a priest, rector of KINGSTON.

Edmund, a priest, rector of Hodnet, and treasurer of the cathedral at York.

Maud, *m.* to Theobald de Verdon.

Joan, } nuns.
Elizabeth, }

His lordship was *s.* by his eldest son,

ROGER MORTIMER, second baron, summoned to parliament from 6th February, 1299, to 3rd December, 1326, (from the accession of Edward II., with the addition of "De Wigmore"). This nobleman, so notorious in our histories as the paramour of ISABEL, queen consort of the unfortunate Edward II., was in his sixteenth year at the time of his father's decease, and was placed by the king (Edward I.,) in ward with PIERS GAVESTON, so that to redeem himself, and for permission to marry whom he pleased, he was obliged to pay Gaveston two thousand five hundred marks, and thereupon espoused Joane, daughter of Peter de Genevill, son of Geffrey de Genevill, Lord of Trim, in Ireland. In the 34th of Edward I. he received the honour of Knighthood, and the same year attended the king into Scotland; where we find him again in the 3rd of Edward II., and the same year he was constituted governor of the castle of Buelt, in Brecknockshire. In the 7th, 8th, and 10th years he was likewise in Scotland, and was then appointed LORD-LIEUTENANT OF IRELAND. During the remainder of the unhappy Edward's reign he attached himself to the interests of the queen, and at length fled with her and Prince Edward into France. Returning, however, and his party triumphing, he was advanced to the dignity of EARL OF MARCH soon after the accession of King Edward III., and he held a *round table* the same year at Bedford. But hereupon becoming proud beyond measure, (so that his own son, Geffrey, called him the King of Folly,) he kept a round table of knights in Wales, in imitation of King Arthur. "Other particulars," says Dugdale, "of his haughtiness and

insolence were these, viz., that with queen Isabel he caused a parliament to be held at Northampton, where an unworthy agreement was made with the Scots, and Ragman's Roll of Homage of Scotland was traitorously delivered, as also the black cross, which King Edward I. brought into England, out of the abbey of Scone, and then accounted a precious relique. That (with the queen,) he caused the young king to ride twenty-four miles in one night, towards Bedford, to destroy the Earl of Lancaster and his adherents, saying that they imagined the king's death. That he followed Queen Isabel to Nottingham, and lodged in one house with her. That he commanded the treasure of the realm, and assumed the authority, which by common consent in parliament was conferred upon Henry, Earl of Lancaster, at the king's coronation." His career was not, however, of long continuance, for, the king becoming sensible of his folly and vices, had him suddenly seised in the castle of Nottingham, and conveyed prisoner to London, where, being impeached before parliament, he was convicted under various charges, the first of which was privity to the murder of King Edward II. in Berkeley Castle; and receiving sentence of death, was hanged at the common gallows, called Elmes, near Smithfield, where his body was permitted to hang two days and two nights naked, before it was interred in the Grey-Friers; whence in some years afterwards it was removed to Wigmore. This great but unfortunate man left issue, four sons and seven daughters, viz.

EDMUND (Sir), of whom presently.

Roger (Sir).

Geffrey (Sir), Lord of Towyth.

John, slain in a tournament at Shrewsbury.

Katherine, *m.* to Thomas de Beauchamp, Earl of Warwick.

Joane, *m.* to James, Lord Audley.

Agnes, *m.* to Laurence, Earl of Pembroke.

Margaret, *m.* to Thomas, son and heir of Maurice, Lord Berkeley.

Maud, *m.* to John de Cherlton, son and heir of John, Lord Powis.

Blanch, *m.* to Peter de Grandison.

Beatrix, *m.* first, to Edward, son and heir of Thomas, of Brotherton, Earl Marshal of England, and secondly, to Sir Thomas de Braose.

Upon the execution and attainder of the earl ALL HIS HONOURS became FORFEITED. But his eldest son,

SIR EDMUND MORTIMER, although he did not succeed to the earldom, was summoned to parliament, as LORD MORTIMER, on 20th November, 1331. His lordship espoused Elizabeth, one of the daughters, and at length co-heirs of Bartholomew, (commonly called the Rich,) Lord Badlesmere, of Ledes Castle, in Kent, by whom (who married, after his decease, William de Bohun, Earl of Northampton,) he had an only surviving son, his successor in 1331,

ROGER MORTIMER, summoned to parliament as BARON MORTIMER, and Baron Mortimer, OF WIGMORE, from 20th November, 1348, to 15th March, 1354. This nobleman, at the time of his father's decease, was only three years of age, and during his minority his castles in the marches of Wales were committed to the custody of William, Earl of Northampton, who had married his mother. In the 20th Edward III. he accompanied the king into France, and then received the honour of knighthood. In the 26th he was in a similar expedition, and in two years afterwards, obtaining a reversal of the attainder of his grandfather, he was restored to the EARLDOM OF MARCH, and to his forfeited lands. His lordship the next year was constable of Dover Castle, and warden of the cinque ports, and for some years afterwards he was in the wars of France. He m. Philippa, daughter of William de Montacute, Earl of Salisbury, and had issue,

     Roger, who d. in his life-time.

     EDMUND, his successor.

     Margaret, m. to Robert Vere, Earl of Oxford.

     Margery, m. to John, Lord Audley.

His lordship d. at Romera, in Burgundy, in 1360, being then commander of the English forces there, and a Knight of the Garter. He was s. by his son,

EDMUND MORTIMER, third Earl of March. This nobleman, at the time of his father's death, was in minority, yet by reason of his singular knowledge and parts, he was employed at eighteen years of age, to treat with the commissioners of the King of France, touching a peace betwixt both realms. In the 1st of Richard II., he was sworn to the privy council, and in two years afterwards constituted LORD LIEUTENANT OF IRELAND, in which government he died in 1381. His lordship m. the Lady PHILIPPA PLANTAGENET, daughter and heir of Lionel, Duke of Clarence, (by Elizabeth, his wife, daughter and heir of William, son and heir of John de Burgh, Earl of Ulster,) by whom he had issue,

     ROGER, his successor.

     Edmund (Sir), m. the daughter of Owen Glendour.

     John (Sir), who, being arraigned in parliament, temp. Henry VI., for treasonable speeches, was condemned and executed.

     Elizabeth, m. to Henry Percy, the celebrated HOTSPUR.

     Philippa, m. first to John, Earl of Pembroke; secondly, to Richard, Earl of Arundel, and thirdly, to John Poynings, Lord St. John.

His lordship was s. by his eldest son,

ROGER MORTIMER, fourth Earl of March, who being but seven years old, at the decease of his father, was committed in ward, by the king, to Richard, Earl of Arundel; and when he came of age, found, by the care of those who had the management of his estate, all his castles and houses in good repair, and amply stored with rich furniture, while his lands were completely stocked with cattle, and in his treasury, no less than forty thousand marks. This Roger being a hopeful youth, and every way accomplished, was, soon after his father's death, made lieutenant of Ireland; and in parliament, held 9th Richard II., was declared, by reason of his descent from Lionel, Duke of Clarence, heir apparent to the crown. His lordship m. Alianore, daughter of Thomas Holland, Earl of Kent, sister of Thomas, Duke of Surrey, and sister

374

and co-heir of Edmund, Earl of Kent, by whom he had issue,

     EDMUND, his successor.

     Roger, died s. p.

     Anne, m. to Richard Plantagenet, Duke of Cambridge, younger son of Edmund, Duke of York, (fifth son of King Edward III.,) and conveyed the right to the crown to the HOUSE OF YORK.

     Alianore, m. to Edward, son of Edward Courtenay, Earl of Devon, but died s. p.

His lordship was slain in battle, in Ireland, in 1398, and was s. by his son,

EDMUND MORTIMER, fifth Earl of March. This nobleman being but six years of age, at his father's death, was committed by King Henry IV., to Henry, Prince of Wales, his son; out of whose custody, he was shortly after stolen away, by the Lady de Spencer; but being discovered in Chittham Woods, they kept him afterwards, under stricter guard, for he was the rightful heir to the crown of England, by his descent from Lionel, Duke of Clarence. This nobleman was frequently engaged in the wars of France, temp. Henry V., and in the 1st of Henry VI., he was constituted lord lieutenant of Ireland. His lordship m. Anne, daughter of Edmund, Earl of Stafford, but died without issue, in 1424, when the EARLDOM OF MARCH became EXTINCT, but the BARONIES OF MORTIMER, created by the writs of Edward I. and Edward III., devolved upon his lordship's nephew,

     RICHARD PLANTAGENET, Duke of York, son of his sister Anne, Countess of Cambridge; and upon the accession of the son and heir of the said Duke of York to the throne, as EDWARD IV., these baronies, with his other dignities, became merged in the crown.

Thus terminated the male line of the illustrious family of Mortimer, EARLS OF MARCH; and their great estates, with the right to the throne, passed to Richard, DUKE OF YORK, son of the last earl's sister, the Lady ANNE MORTIMER, by her husband, Richard Plantagenet, Duke of Cambridge.

ARMS.—Barry of six, or and az. on a chief of the first, three pallets between two esquires, bust dexter, and sinister of the second, and in escutcheon. ar.

MORTIMER—BARON MORTIMER, OF RICHARD'S CASTLE.

By Writ of Summons, dated 26th January, 1297, 25 Edward I.

Lineage.

The founder of this branch of the MORTIMERS in England, was

ROBERT DE MORTIMER, (the presumed son or brother of the first Hugh de Mortimer, of Wigmore, ancestor of the Earls of March,) who m. Margery, only daughter and heiress of Hugh de Ferrers, and grand-daughter of Hugh de Say,[*] Lord

---

[*] HUGH DE SAY was feudal lord of RICHARD'S CASTLE, in the county of Hereford, one of the possessions of his ancestor, RICHARD, (surnamed

of RICHARD'S CASTLE, in the county of Hereford, by which alliance he acquired that, and other considerable manors, and in the 12th Henry II. he certified his knight's fees of this honour to be in number twenty-three. In the 17th of John he had a grant from the king of all those lands in Berwic, in Sussex, which had belonged to Mabel de Say, mother of Margery, his wife, and then in the possession of Robert Marmion, the younger. He d. about the year 1219, and was s. by his son,

HUGH DE MORTIMER, who, in the 43rd Henry III., upon the death of William de Stutevill, second husband of his mother, had livery of all those lands of her inheritance, upon the payment of £100 for his relief, which he the said William held as tenant by the courtesy of England during his life. In the next year Hugh Mortimer, being one of the Barons Marchers, had command to repair personally to his house, at Richard's Castle, and there to attend the directions of Roger, LORD MORTIMER, of Wigmore, whom the king had then constituted captain-general of all his forces in those parts, to oppose the hostilities of Lewelin, PRINCE OF WALES. In the contest between Henry III. and the barons, this feudal lord siding with the former, was obliged to surrender Richard's Castle, after the defeat of LEWES, but he regained possession of that and all his other lands, by the triumph of EVESHAM. In the 1st Edward I., he executed the office of sheriff for the counties of Salop and Stafford, and dying in two years afterwards, was s. by his son,

ROBERT DE MORTIMER, who m. Joice, daughter and heir of William La Zouch, second son of Roger, second Baron Zouch, of Ashby, and had issue,

Hugh, his successor.

William, who, inheriting from the Zouches the Lordship of Ashby de la Zouch, assumed the surname of ZOUCHE (see ZOUCHE, of Mortimer).

This feudal lord d. in 1287, and was s. by his elder son,

HUGH DE MORTIMER, who was summoned to parliament as a BARON, on 26th January, 1297, and from that time to 10th April, 1299, in which latter year he was in the wars of Scotland. His lordship d. in 1304, leaving two daughters, his co-heirs, viz.

1. JOANE MORTIMER, m. first, to Thomas de Bikenore, by whom she had no issue, and secondly, to Richard Talbot, (a younger son of Richard, Lord Talbot, of Eccleswal, in Herefordshire,) who thus founded the House of "TALBOT, of Richard's CASTLE."

Scrupe,) in Edward the Confessor's days, whence it derives its denomination. In the 22nd Henry II. this Hugh paid twenty marks to the king for trespassing in the royal forests, and in the 31st of the same reign two hundred marks for livery of his lands. He m. Lucia, daughter of Walter de Clifford, and left an only daughter and heir,

Mabel, who m. HUGH DE FERRERS, by whom she had an only daughter and heir,

MARGERY FERRERS, who m. Robert Mortimer, as in the text.

By this, her second husband, Joane Mortimer had three sons, JOHN, Thomas, and Richard, and was s. by the eldest,

SIR JOHN TALBOT, of Richard's Castle, who m. Joane, daughter of Roger, Lord Grey, of Ruthyn, and was s. by his elder son,

JOHN TALBOT, of Richard's Castle, who left two sons, Richard and John, who both d. unmarried, and three daughters, his eventual heirs, viz.

ELIZABETH TALBOT, m. to Sir Warine Archdeakene, of Lanherne, in Cornwall.

PHILIPPA TALBOT, m. to Sir Matthew Gournay.

ELEANOR TALBOT, d. unmarried.

2. MARGARET MORTIMER, m. to Geffery Cornwall.

Upon the decease of his lordship, the BARONY OF MORTIMER, of Richard's Castle, fell into ABEYANCE, in which state it is supposed still to remain, amongst the descendants and representatives of his above-mentioned daughters.

ARMS.—Similar to those of the Earls of March, with a bend gules.

MORTIMER—BARON MORTIMER, OF CHIRKE.

By Writ of Summons, dated 26th August, 1307, 1 Edward II.

Lineage.

ROGER MORTIMER, second son of Roger Mortimer, fifth feudal Lord of Wigmore, by Maud, daughter of William de Braose, of Brecknock, settled himself at CHIRKE, part of the territories of Griffith ap Madoc, and was summoned to parliament, as BARON MORTIMER, of Chirke, from 26th August, 1307, to 15th May, 1321. The manner in which his lordship acquired Chirke, is thus detailed by Powel, the Welch historian:—"Griffith ap Madoc," saith he, "took part with King Henry III., and King Edward I., against the Prince of North Wales, and died, leaving his children within age; shortly after which followed the destruction of two of them: for King Edward gave the wardship of Madoc, (the elder of them,) who had for his part the Lordship of BROMFIELD, &c., as also the Castle of DINAS-BRAN, to John, Earl of Warren; and of Lewelin, the younger, to whose part the Lordship of CHIRKE, &c., fell, to Roger Mortimer, a younger son of Roger Mortimer, Lord of Wigmore; which guardians forgetting the services done by Griffith ap Madoc, their father, so guarded these, their wards, that they never returned to their possessions, and shortly after obtained these lands to themselves by charter." Being thus seated here, he built the Castle of Chirke; and during the reign of Edward I., was constantly employed in the wars of France, Scotland, and Wales, of which latter he was constituted the king's lieutenant, having all the castles in the principality committed to his custody; and he was subsequently made justice of all Wales. In the time of Edward II., his martial spirit continued, and we find him ever in the field, either in Scotland or in Wales; he ended his career, however, in the Tower; for being one of the opponents of the Spencers, and amongst those lords who condemned them to exile, so soon as the king recovered his authority, his lordship and his nephew, Lord Mortimer, of Wigmore, submitting themselves, were committed to the Tower of London, in which confinement this nobleman is said to have died, anno 1336. His lordship *m.* Lucia, daughter of Sir Robert de Wafre, Knt., and was *s.* by his son,

ROGER MORTIMER, of Chirke, but never summoned to parliament; who *m.* Joane Turbaville, and was *s.* by his son,

JOHN MORTIMER, never summoned to parliament. This personage sold his lordship of CHIRKE, to Richard Fitz-Alan, EARL OF ARUNDEL.

ARMS.—Same as the Earls of March.

MOWBRAY—BARONS MOWBRAY, EARLS OF NOTTINGHAM, DUKES OF NORFOLK, EARLS-MARSHAL, EARL OF WARREN AND SURREY.

Barony, by Writ of Summons, dated 23rd June, 1295, 23 Edward I.
Earldom, by Charter, anno 1377, and recreated 1383.
Dukedom, by Charter, 29th September, 1396.
Earldom of Warren and Surrey, 29th March, 1451.

Lineage.

This family was founded by
NIGIL DE ALBINI, brother of William de Albini, from whom the ancient Earls of Arundel descended. The Albinis, who were maternally of the house of Mowbray, came into England with the Conqueror, and obtained large possessions after the victory of Hastings. Nigil's grants lay in the counties of Bucks, Bedford, Warwick, and Leicester, and comprised several extensive lordships. In the reign of Rufus, he was bow-bearer to the king; and being girt with the sword of knighthood by King Henry I., had the manor of Egmanton, with divers parks in the forest of Shirwood, of that monarch's gift; which lordship he transferred, however, to his particular friend, Robert Davil. But when King Henry had further experience of his great valour and military skill, he augmented his royal bounty, and conferred upon him the vavassories of Camvile and Wyvile; which gracious mark of favour so attached Albini to the interests of his sovereign, that he espoused with the most devoted zeal the cause of Henry, against his brother, Robert Curthose, and taking a conspicuous part at the battle of Tenerchebray, he there slew the horse of Curthose, and brought the prince himself prisoner to the king; for which eminent service Henry conferred upon him the lands of Robert, Baron of Frontebeof, namely, Stuteville, in

376

England, which Frontebeof had fortified in behalf of Curthose. After which, King Henry besieging a castle in Normandy, this gallant Sir Nigil first entered the breach, sword in hand, and delivered up the fortress to the king, which achievement was remunerated by a royal grant of the forfeited lands of his maternal uncle, Robert de Mowbray, Earl of Northumberland, both in Normandy and England: as also his castles, with the castle of Bayeux and its appurtenances; so that he had no less than one hundred and twenty knights' fees in Normandy, and as many in England; thus becoming one of the most powerful persons of the period in which he lived. Sir Nigil de Albini *m.* first, Maud, daughter of Richard de Aquila, by permission of Pope Paschall; her husband, Robert de Mowbray, Earl of Northumberland, before mentioned, being then alive, and in prison for rebellion against William Rufus: from this lady he was, however, divorced, on account of consanguinity, and by her he had no issue. He espoused, secondly, in 1118, Gundred, daughter of Girald de Gorney, by the especial advice of King Henry I., and had two sons,

ROGER, his successor, who, possessing the lands of Mowbray, assumed, by command of King Henry, the surname of MOWBRAY.

HENRY, who had the Lordship and Barony of Camho, and was ancestor of the Albinis, feudal lords of that place.

This great feudal baron *d.* at an advanced age, and was buried with his ancestors, in the abbey of Bec, in Normandy. He was *s.* by his elder son,

ROGER DE MOWBRAY, who, although not yet of age, was one of the chief commanders, at the memorable battle fought, anno 1138, with the Scots near Northalerton, known in history as the BATTLE OF THE STANDARD; and adhering to King Stephen, in his contest with the empress, he was taken prisoner with that monarch at the battle of Lincoln. In 1148, he accompanied Lewis, King of France, to the Holy Land, and there acquired great renown by vanquishing a stout and hardy Pagan in single combat. He was afterwards involved in the rebellion of Prince Henry, against King Henry II., and lost some of his castles. His grants to the church were munificent in the extreme; and his piety was so fervent, that he again assumed the cross, and made a second journey to the Holy Land, where he was made prisoner, but redeemed by the Knights Templars; he died, however, soon after in the east, and was buried at Surea. Some authorities say that he returned to England, and living fifteen years longer, was buried in the abbey of Byland. He *m.* Alice de Gant, and was *s.* by his elder son,

NIGEL DE MOWBRAY, who attended amongst the barons, in the 1st of Richard I., at the solemn coronation of that monarch; and in the 3d of the same reign, assuming the cross, set out for Palestine, but died upon his journey. He *m.* Mabel, daughter of the Earl of Clare, and had issue, WILLIAM, Robert, Philip, and Roger. Of which Robert, having married a countess in Scotland, acquired a fair inheritance there, and was founder of the family of Mowbray in that kingdom. Nigil de Mowbray was *s.* by his eldest son,

WILLIAM DE MOWBRAY, who, in the 6th of

Richard I., paying £100 for his relief, had livery of his lands. This feudal lord, upon the accession of King John, was tardy in pledging his allegiance, and at length only swore fealty upon condition that the king should render to every man his right. At the breaking out of the baronial war, it was no marvel then, that he should be found one of the most forward of the discontented lords, and so distinguished, that he was chosen with his brother, Roger, amongst the TWENTY-FIVE celebrated barons appointed to enforce the observance of MAGNA CHARTA. In the reign of Henry III., adhering to the same cause, he was at the battle of Lincoln, and taken prisoner there, when his lands were seized, and bestowed upon William Marschal the younger, but he was subsequently allowed to redeem them. After which he appears to have attached himself to the king, and was with the royal army at the siege of Bitham Castle, in Lincolnshire. He m. Agnes, daughter of the Earl of Arundel, and dying in 1222, was s. by his elder son,

NIGEL DE MOWBRAY, who, in the 8th of Henry III., paying five hundred pounds for his relief, had livery of his lands. He m. Maud, daughter and heiress of Roger de Camvil, but dying without issue in 1228, was s. by his brother,

ROGER DE MOWBRAY, then in minority. This feudal lord had several military summonses to attend King Henry III. into Scotland and Wales. He m. Maud, daughter of William de Beauchamp, of Bedford, and dying in 1266, was s. by his eldest son,

ROGER DE MOWBRAY, who, in the 6th of Edward II., upon making proof of his age, had livery of his lands. He was engaged in the wars of Wales and Gascony, and was summoned to parliament as a BARON, from 23rd June, 1295, to the 26th August, 1296. His lordship m. Rose, great grand-daughter of Richard de Clare, Earl of Hertford, and dying in 1296, was s. by his son,

JOHN DE MOWBRAY, second baron, summoned to parliament from 26th August, 1307, to 5th August, 1320. This nobleman during his minority was actively engaged in the Scottish wars of King Edward I., and had livery of all his lands before he attained minority, in consideration of those services. In the 6th of Edward II., being then sheriff of Yorkshire, and governor of the city of York, he had command from the king to seize upon Henry de Percy, then a great baron in the north, in consequence of that nobleman's suffering Piers de Gaveston, Earl of Cornwall, to escape from Scarborough Castle, in which he had undertaken to keep him in safety. The next year Lord Mowbray was in another expedition into Scotland, and he was then constituted one of the wardens of the marches towards that kingdom. In the 11th of the same reign he was made governor of Malton and Scarborough Castles, in Yorkshire, and the following year he was once more in Scotland, invested with authority to receive into protection all who should submit to King Edward. But afterwards taking part in the insurrection of Thomas, Earl of Lancaster, he was made prisoner with that nobleman and others at the battle of Boroughbridge, and immediately hanged at York, anno 1321, when his

lands were seized by the crown, and Aliva, his widow, with her son, imprisoned in the Tower of London. This lady, who was daughter and co-heir of William de Braose, Lord Braose, of Gower, was compelled, in order to obtain some alleviation of her unhappy situation, to confer several manors of her own inheritance upon Hugh le Despenser, Earl of Winchester. In the next reign, however, she obtained from the crown a confirmation of Gowerland, in Wales, to herself and the heirs of her body by her deceased husband, remainder to Humphrey de Bohun, Earl of Hereford and Essex, and his heirs. Lady Mowbray m. secondly, Sir Richard Peshale, Knt., and d. in the 8th of Edward III. Her ladyship's son,

JOHN DE MOWBRAY, third baron, was summoned to parliament from 10th December, 1327, to 20th November, 1360. This nobleman found much favour from King Edward III., who, in consideration of the eminent services of his progenitors, accepted of his homage, and gave him livery of his lands before he came of full age. He was subsequently the constant companion in arms of this martial sovereign, attending him in his glorious campaign in France, where he assisted at the siege of Nantes, and the raising that of Aguillon. He was likewise at the celebrated battle of Durham, (20th Edward III.,) and at one time was governor of Berwick-upon-Tweed. His lordship m. the Lady Joan Plantagenet, daughter of Henry, Earl of Lancaster, by whom he had issue, JOHN, his successor. Lord Mowbray, who was styled in the charters, lord of the Isle of Axholme, and of the honour of Gower and Brember, d. in 1361, and was s. by his son,

JOHN DE MOWBRAY, fourth baron, summoned to parliament from 14th August, 1362, to 20th March, 1366, as "John de Mowbray, of Axholm." This nobleman in the life-time of his father was in the wars of France; and he eventually fell anno 1368, in a conflict with the Turks, near Constantinople, having assumed the cross, and embarked in the holy war. His lordship m. Elizabeth, daughter and heiress of John, Lord Segrave, by Margaret, Duchess of Norfolk, (daughter, and eventually sole heiress, of Thomas Plantagenet, of Brotherton, Earl of Norfolk—see that dignity,) whereby he acquired a great inheritance in lands, and the most splendid alliance in the kingdom. By this lady he had two sons, JOHN and Thomas, and a daughter, Anne, who became Abbess of Barking, in Essex. His lordship was s. by his elder son,

JOHN DE MOWBRAY, fifth baron, who was created EARL OF NOTTINGHAM, upon the day of the coronation of King Richard II., anno 1377, with a special clause in the charter of creation, that all his lands and tenements whereof he was then possessed, should be held sub honore comitali, and as parcel of this earldom. His lordship d. two years afterwards, still under age, and unmarried, when the EARLDOM OF NOTTINGHAM expired, but the Barony of Mowbray and his great possessions devolved upon his brother,

THOMAS DE MOWBRAY, as sixth baron, then seventeen years of age, who was created EARL OF NOTTINGHAM, as his brother had been, by charter, dated in 1383, and three years afterwards was constituted EARL MARSHAL, by reason of his descent from Thomas, of Brotherton; his lordship being the first who had the title of earl attached to the office. In the 10th of Richard II. his lordship participated in the naval victory achieved by Richard, Earl of Arundel, over the French and Spaniards, and the subsequent conquest of the castle of Brest. In the 16th of the same reign he was made governor of Calais, and in four years afterwards obtained the king's charter of confirmation of the office of earl marshal of England to the heirs male of his body, and that they, by reason of the said office, should bear a golden truncheon, enamelled with black at each end, having at the upper end the king's arms, and at the lower their own arms engraven thereon. Moreover, he stood in such favour, that the king, acknowledging his just and hereditary title to bear for his crest a *golden leopard*, with a *white label*, which of right belonged to the king's eldest son, did, by letters patent, grant to him and his heirs, authority to bear the *golden leopard* for his crest, with a *coronet of silver* about his neck, instead of the *label*; and the same year appointed him justice of Chester and Flintshire for life. In the 18th of Richard he attended the king into Ireland, but afterwards siding with the parasites, who controlled that weak and unfortunate prince, he not only aided in the destruction of his father-in-law, Richard, Earl of Arundel—being one of the chief persons that guarded the unhappy nobleman to the place of execution—but he is also accused of being an accomplice in the murder of Thomas, of Woodstock, Duke of Gloucester, the king's uncle. Certain it is that he was at this period in high estimation with the prevailing party, and obtained a grant of all the lands of the unfortunate Lord Arundel, with those of Thomas Beauchamp, Earl of Warwick, which had also vested in the crown, by forfeiture. These grants bore date on the 29th September, 1396, and the next day he was created DUKE OF NORFOLK (his grandmother, Margaret, Duchess of Norfolk, being still alive). Prosperous, however, as this nobleman's career had hitherto been, it was doomed, eventually, to a disgraceful termination; and such be the fate of every man, who attains elevation through the shedding of blood. Henry, Duke of Hereford, (afterwards Henry IV.,) having accused his grace of Norfolk, of speaking disrespectfully of the king, a challenge ensued, and a day was named for the combat, when the lists were accordingly set up, at Gosford Green, Coventry, and the king and court were present; but just as the combatants were about to engage, and the charge had been sounded, Richard interfered, and by advice of his council, prohibited the conflict, banishing the Duke of Hereford for ten years, and the Duke of Norfolk for life—who, thereupon going abroad, died at Venice, of the pestilence, but according to Sandford, of grief, in 1400. The duke, who, along with his other great honours, was a KNIGHT of the GARTER, m. first, Elizabeth, daughter of John, Lord Strange, of Blackmere, but had no issue; he espoused, secondly, Lady Elizabeth Fitz-Alan, daughter of Richard, Earl of Arundel, sister and co-heir of Thomas, Earl of Arundel, and widow

of William de Montacute, by whom he had issue,

> THOMAS, who simply bore the title of Earl Marshal.
>
> JOHN, of whom hereafter, as restored Duke of Norfolk.
>
> Margaret, m. Sir Robert Howard, Knt. This lady became eventually co-heiress of the Mowbrays—and her son,
>
> > Sir John Howard, Knt., succeeded by creation to the Dukedom of Norfolk and the Earl Marshalship—from whom the existing Dukes of Norfolk derive.
>
> Isabel, m. to James, Lord Berkeley, ancestor of the extant Earls Berkeley.

The elder son,

THOMAS DE MOWBRAY, seventh Baron Mowbray, was but fourteen years of age, at the decease of his father, and never had the title of Duke of Norfolk, but was simply styled, EARL MARSHAL. He was beheaded at York, in 1405, for participating in the conspiracy of Richard Scrope, Archbishop of York, against Henry IV. His lordship m. Constance, daughter of John Holland, Duke of Exeter, but having no issue, was s. by his brother,

JOHN DE MOWBRAY, eighth Baron Mowbray, who was restored, 3rd Henry VI., in the parliament then held at Westminster, to the dignity of DUKE OF NORFOLK, having previously used only the titles of Earl of Nottingham, and Earl Marshal. This nobleman was engaged in the French wars of King Henry V., and was only prevented by indisposition, sharing the glories of Agincourt. His grace, who was a Knight of the Garter, m. the Lady Katharine Nevil, daughter of Ralph, Earl of Westmoreland, (who, subsequently, espoused Thomas Strangways, Esq., and after his decease, John, Viscount Beaumont, and lastly, Sir John Widvile, Knt.,) and dying in 1432, was s. by his son,

JOHN DE MOWBRAY, third Duke of Norfolk. This nobleman attained majority in the 14th Henry VI., and in three years afterwards, was sent ambassador into Picardy, to treat of peace, with the King of France. In the 23rd of the same reign, upon obtaining a confirmation of the Dukedom of Norfolk, he had a place assigned him in parliament, and elsewhere, next to the Duke of Exeter. His grace m. Eleanor, daughter of William, Lord Bourchier, and dying in 1461, was s. by his son,

JOHN DE MOWBRAY, Earl of Warren and Surrey, (so created, 29th March, 1451,) as fourth Duke of Norfolk, and Earl Marshal. This nobleman, in the 14th Edward IV., was retained to serve the king in his wars in France, for one year—and he was made a KNIGHT of the GARTER. His grace m. the Lady Elizabeth Talbot, daughter of John, Earl of Shrewsbury, by whom he had an only daughter,

> Lady Anne Mowbray, contracted to Richard, son of King Edward IV., but died before consummation of marriage.

The duke d. in 1475, when all his HONOURS, except the Baronies of Mowbray and Segrave, EXPIRED; but those, on the decease of Lady Anne Mowbray, above mentioned, fell into ABEYANCE, amongst the descendants of the Ladies Margaret Howard, and Isabel Berkeley, (refer to issue of Thomas, first Duke of Norfolk,) and so continued until the suspension of the Barony of Mowbray was terminated, by the summoning of Henry Howard, son, and heir apparent, of Thomas, Earl of Arundel, Norfolk, and Surrey, to parliament, 13th April, 1639, as BARON MOWBRAY. The eldest son of that nobleman was restored to the Dukedom of Norfolk, and the barony merged in that dignity, until the death of Edward, eleventh duke, in 1777, when, with several other baronies, it again fell into ABEYANCE, between the two daughters and co-heirs of Philip Howard, Esq., younger brother of the said duke, namely,

Winifred, m. to Charles-Philip, fifteenth Lord Stourton, grandfather of the present lord.

Anne, m. to Robert-Edward, ninth Lord Petre, grandfather of the present lord.

And it still so remains with their representatives. The BARONY OF SEGRAVE, never having been called out of ABEYANCE, continues yet in a state of suspension, between the descendants of the Ladies Margaret Howard, (the Lords Stourton and Petre, as heir general,) and the representative of the Lady Isabel Berkeley, (the present Earl Berkeley).

ARMS.—Gu. a lion rampant ar.

MULTON—BARONS MULTON, OF EGREMONT.

By Writ of Summons, dated 26th February, 1297, 25 Edward I.

Lineage.

In the time of King HENRY I.,

THOMAS DE MULTON, so called from his residence at Multon, in Lincolnshire, bestowed at the funeral of his father, in the Chapter House, at Spalding, (his mother, brothers, sisters, and friends, being present,) the Church of Weston, upon the monks of that abbey. After this Thomas, came

LAMBERT DE MULTON, who, in the 11th Henry II., residing then in Lincolnshire, was amerced one hundred marks. In the 9th and 10th of King John, flourished another

THOMAS DE MULTON, who at that period was sheriff of the county of Lincoln, and in the 15th of the same reign, attended the king in his expedition then made into POICTOU. This Thomas gave a thousand marks to the crown for the wardship of the daughters and heirs of Richard de Luci, of Egremont, in the county of Cumberland, and bestowed those ladies afterwards in marriage upon his two sons, Lambert and Alan. In the 17th John, being in arms with the rebellious barons, and taken at Rochester Castle, he was committed to the custody of Peter de Mauley, to be safely secured, who conveyed him prisoner to the castle of Corff, but in the 1st of Henry III., making his peace, he had restitution of his liberty and his lands. The next year having espoused Ada, daughter and co-heir of Hugh de Morvill, widow of Richard de Lacy, of Egremont, without the king's licence,

command was sent to the archbishop of York, to make seizure of all his lands in Cumberland, and to retain them in his hands until further orders. Multon giving security, however, to answer the same, whensoever the king should require him so to do, he had livery of all those lands which had been seized for that transgression, with the castle of EGREMONT. In three years afterwards he paid £100 fine to the king, and one palfry for the office of forester of Cumberland, it being the inheritance of Ada, his wife. In the 17th of Henry III., he was sheriff of Cumberland, and remained in office for several succeeding years. Moreover, he was one of the Justices of the king's Court of Common Pleas, from the 8th Henry III., and a justice itinerant for divers years, from the 9th of the same reign. He m. first ——, and had issue,

LAMBERT, m. Annabel, daughter and co-heir of Richard de Lucie.

Alan, m. Alice, daughter and co-heir of Richard de Lucie, and had a son,

THOMAS DE MULTON, who assumed the surname of LUCIE (see LUCY, OF EGREMONT).

Thomas de Multon espoused, secondly, Ada, daughter and co-heir of Hugh de Morville, and had, by that lady,

THOMAS (see MULTONS, of Gillesland).

Julian, m. to Robert le Vavasour.

This celebrated feudal lord, who was a liberal benefactor to the church, is thus characterized by Matthew Paris: "In his youth he was a stout soldier, afterwards very wealthy, and learned in the laws; but overmuch coveting to enlarge his possessions, which lay contiguous to those of the monks of Crowland, he did them great wrong in many respects." He d. in 1240, and was s. by his eldest son,

LAMBERT DE MULTON, who, as stated above, m. Annabel, the elder daughter and co-heir of Richard de Lucy, of Egremont, and in 1246, obtained by large gifts from the pope, an extraordinary privilege; namely, that no one should have the power to excommunicate him, but by a special mandate from his holiness. But he, who had this liberty, saith Matthew Paris, to sin without punishment, and to do injury to others, riding with rich trappings very proudly, from a trial at law, no sooner alighted from his horse, but (meriting God's judgment) was suddenly smitten with a grievous disease, of which falling to the ground, he died before his spurs could be taken off, being then at his house at Multon, in Lincolnshire. By his first wife he had a son, THOMAS, his successor. He espoused, secondly, Ida, widow of Geoffrey de Oilli, but had no issue. His death occurred in 1247, when he was s. by his son,

THOMAS DE MOULTON, designated of EGREMONT, who was in arms against the king, in 49th Henry III., with the rebellious barons of that period. In the 22d Edward I., he had a grant of free warren in all his demesnes lands, at Egremont, and dying in 1294, was s. by his son,

THOMAS DE MULTON, who was summoned to parliament as BARON MULTON, of Egremont, from 26th January, 1297, to 15th May, 1390. During which interval, he was almost constantly engaged in the Scottish wars. His lordship *d.* in 1322, and was *s.* by his son,

JOHN DE MULTON, second baron, summoned to parliament from 27th January, 1332, to 24th July, 1334. This nobleman *m.* Annabel, daughter and heiress of Laurence de Holbeche, but dying without issue in 1334, his estates, including the manors of THURSTANESTON, in Suffolk, and EGREMONT and COCKERMOUTH, in Cumberland, were divided amongst his three sisters, thus, viz.—

> JOANE, wife of Robert, Baron Fitz-Walter, had for her share the CASTLE OF EGRE- MONT, with the third part of that manor, and the third part of other manors.
>
> ELIZABETH, wife of Walter de Bermichan, had certain lands at Gosford, parcel of the manor of Egremont, and a proportion of other manors.
>
> MARGARET, wife of Thomas de Lucy, had certain lands in Cumberland, parcel of the manor of Egremont, besides a proportion of other estates,

while the BARONY OF MULTON, of *Egremont*, fell into ABEYANCE amongst those ladies, as it still continues with their descendants and representa- tives.

ARMS.—Ar. three bars, gules.

MULTON — BARON MULTON, OF GILLESLAND.

By Writ of Summons, dated 26th August, 1307, 1 Edward II.

Lineage.

THOMAS DE MULTON, Lord of Multon, in Lincolnshire, who *d.* in 1240, (see Multon of Egre- mont,) espoused, for his second wife, Ada, daughter and co-heir of Hugh de Moreville, and had, with a daughter, Julian, who married Robert de Vavasour, a son,

THOMAS DE MULTON, who inherited the office of forester of Cumberland from his mother, and in the 36th Henry III., paid a fine of four hundred marks to the crown, for trespassing in the forest there, and for the future enjoyment of all the privileges which his ancestors had possessed with the forestership. In the 42d of the same reign, he had a military summons to march with the other northern barons, into Scotland, for the purpose of rescuing the Scottish monarch, King Henry's son-in-law, from the restraints imposed upon him by his own subjects: and again in the 55th, to take up arms against the Welch. This feudal baron espoused MAUD, only daughter and heiress of HUBERT DE VAUX,* Lord of GILLES-

---

* RANULPH DE MESCHINES, in the time of the Conqueror, granted the Barony of GILLESLAND † to a Norman called,

HUBERT, who was ever afterwards denominated

† *Gill,* in the provincial dialect of Cumberland, signifies a *dale* or *valley,* which corresponds with the Latin word, *vallis,* whence the French derived their term, *l'aulx.*

LAND, and with her acquired that lordship. He *d.* in 1270, and was *s.* by his son,

THOMAS DE MULTON, who doing his ho- mage, had livery of his lands, and the ensuing year, upon the death of Helewise de Levinton, widow of Eustace de Balliol, was found to be her heir as to a moiety of the Barony of *Burgh upon the Sands,* (he already enjoyed the other moiety by inheritance,) and divers other considerable manors. He *d.* in 1293—his mother, the heiress of Gillesland, being still alive—and was *s.* by his son,

THOMAS DE MULTON, who doing his homage the same year, had livery of his lands, but died in two years afterwards, being then seised of the manor of Donham, in Norfolk; of Burgh-upon-Sands; of Kirk-Oswald; and of the Barony of GILLESLAND, with divers other estates, all in the county of Cum- berland. He was *s.* by his son,

THOMAS DE MULTON. This feudal lord having been engaged in the Scottish wars, in the 31st and 34th of Edward I., was summoned to parlia- ment as BARON MULTON, OF GILLESLAND, upon the accession of Edward II. (from 26th August, 1307, to 20th November, 1313). After which we find his lordship again upon the theatre of war, in Scotland, in the 3d and 4th years of the new mo- narch: and he subsequently obtained some immu- nities from the crown, in the shape of grants for fairs and markets upon his different manors. He *d.* in 1313, leaving an only daughter and heiress,

> MARGARET DE MULTON, who *m.* Ranulph de Dacre, LORD DACRE, *of the North,* and conveyed her great estates with the BARONY OF MULTON, to the DACRE family (see DACRE, of *Gillesland*).

ARMS.—Az. three bars gules.

MUNCHENSI — BARON MUN- CHENSI.

By Writ of Summons, dated 24th December, 1264, 49 Henry III.

It was not long after the Norman Conquest, that

HUBERT DE MUNCHENSI, made grants of lands to the monks of Eye and Thetford, in the county of Suffolk and Norfolk. " It is said that this Hubert," observes Dugdale, " had issue, *Wa- rine de Munchensi,* and he another Hubert, which is likely enough to be true: for in the 33d of Henry II., it appears that Hubert de Munchensi was in

either HUBERT VAULX," or HUBERT DE VALLI- BUS." He was *s.* by his son and heir,

ROBERT DE VAUX, who *m.* Ada, daughter and heir of William Engaine, and widow of Simon de Morville, and was *s.* by his elder son,

ROBERT DE VAUX. This baron outliving his only son, was *s.* at his decease, by his brother,

RANULPH DE VAUX, who was father of

ROBERT DE VAUX, one of the barons who took up arms against King John. He was *s.* by his son,

ROBERT DE VAUX, who left at his decease, an only daughter and heir,

> MAUD DE VAUX, who *m.,* as in the text, THO- MAS DE MULTON, and conveyed to him the BARONY OF GILLESLAND.

ward to the Bishop of Ely, with his land at Stratford, part of the honour of Henry de Essex. At the same time also *Agnes de Munchensi* (widow of Warine, as I guess) daughter of Payne Fitz-John, then sixty years of age, had three sons, viz., Ralph, and William, both knights, and Hubert, a clerk; as also two daughters, the one *m.* to Stephen de Glanvile, and the other to William Painell, her lands at HOLKHAM, in Norfolk, being then valued at eleven pounds per annum."

The next member of the family upon record is,

WILLIAM DE MUNCHENSI, who *d.* about the 5th of John, and was *s.* by his son,

WILLIAM DE MUNCHENSI, who was succeeded in about seven years afterwards, by his uncle,

WARINE MUCHENSI, a person of military reputation, temp. Henry III. He *m.* Joan, daughter and heir of William Marshall, Earl of Pembroke, and had issue,

WILLIAM, his successor.

Joane, *m.* to William Valence, the king's half brother.

Warine *d.* in 1255, and was *s.* by his son,

WILLIAM MUSCHENSI. This feudal lord was one of the leading persons who took up arms against Henry III., and one of the chief commanders at the battle of LEWES. After this victory he was summoned to parliament by the baronial government, acting in the name of the king. His lordship was subsequently made prisoner at Kenilworth, and his lands being seised, were transferred to his brother-in-law, William Valence. They were soon, however, restored upon his making the necessary submission. He was eventually slain, anno 1289, in battle, by the Welsh. He left a daughter and heiress,

DYONISIA MUSCHENSI, who *m.* Hugh de Vere, younger son of Robert, Earl of Oxford.

This dignity can hardly be deemed, however, an inheritable barony. A young brother of the barons, William de Munchensi, *m.* Beatrix, daughter and co-heir of William de Beauchamp, Baron of Bedford, and *d.* in 1286, leaving William, his son and heir, who *d.* in 1302, leaving male issue, but none of this branch were ever summoned to parliament.

ARMS.—Or. three escutcheons barry of six varée and gules.

MURRAY — VISCOUNTESS BAYNING, OF FOXLEY, IN THE COUNTY OF WILTS.

By Letters Patent, dated 17th March, 1674.

Lineage.

The Honourable

ANNE BAYNING, second daughter of Sir Paul Bayning, Bart., first VISCOUNT BAYNING, *of Sudbury*, in the county of Suffolk, and sister of Paul, second Viscount Bayning, was created for life, after the decease of the latter lord, without male issue, and the extinction of the honours of her family, VISCOUNTESS BAYNING, *of Foxley, in the county of Wilts*, on the 17th March, 1674. She had previ-

ously married Henry Murray, Esq., one of the Grooms of the Bedchamber to King Charles I. Her ladyship *d.* in 1696, when the dignity of course EXPIRED. Mr. Murray's eldest daughter and co-heiress, by Lady Bayning,

The Honourable Elizabeth Murray, *m.* Randolph Egerton, Esq., and had a daughter,

ANNE EGERTON, (sole heiress of her father,) who *m.* Lord William Paulet, second son of Charles, first Duke of Bolton, by whom she had an only daughter,

HENRIETTA PAULET, (heiress of her father,) who *m.* the Honourable William Townshend, third son of Charles, second Viscount Townshend, K. G., and left a son,

CHARLES TOWNSHEND, who was created BARON BAYNING, OF FOXLEY, on the 27th October, 1797, and was father of the present LORD BAYNING.

MUSGRAVE—BARON MUSGRAVE.

By Writ of Summons, dated 25th November, 1350, 24 Edward III.

Lineage.

The MUSGRAVES are said to have come originally from Germany, and to have been MUSGRAVES, or Lords Marchers, there. Banks tells the following story of their good fortune in obtaining an alliance with the imperial family. " The emperor had two great generals, who made court to his daughter at the same time; and as he had experienced singular services from both, did not care to prefer one before the other. But to decide the matter, ordered the two heroes to run at the ring for her (an exercise then in use): it so happened, that this Musgrave (one of the contending generals) had the fortune to pierce the ring with the point of his spear; by which action he gained her for a reward of his gallantry and dexterity, and had six annulets or. given him for his coat of arms; and for his crest, two arms in armour, holding an annulet. From this marriage issued that MUSGRAVE, who being a man of an enterprizing genius, accompanied William the Conqueror into England, and was the founder of the Musgraves in this country."

SIR THOMAS MUSGRAVE, one of the commanders in the van of the English army that gave battle to, and totally defeated David, King of Scotland, at Durham, 20th Edward III., was summoned to parliament as a BARON from 25th November, 1350, to 4th October, 1373. His lordship appears to have been generally employed upon the borders in resisting the incursion of the Scotch. He was made, 21st of Edward III., governor of Berwick-upon-Tweed; and sole justiciar through all the lands in Scotland, whereof the king had then possession. He was afterwards sheriff of Yorkshire and governor of the castle of York. His lordship *m.* Isabel, widow of Robert, son of Robert, Lord Clifford, and daughter of Thomas, Lord Berkeley; but the barony did not continue in his descendants, nor have any of those been deemed BARONS of the realm. Descended from his lordship are the three existing houses of Musgrave, Baronets, viz.

The MUSGRAVES of Eden Hall, in Cumberland, created BARONETS 29th June, 1611.

The MUSGRAVES of Hayton, created BARONETS in 1683.

The MUSGRAVES of Myrtle Grove, in the county of Cork, created BARONETS of Ireland, in 1782.

ARMS.—Gu. six annulets or.

NANSLADRON — BARON NANSLADRON.

By Writ of Summons, dated 29th December, 1299, 28 Edward I.

Lineage.

In the 29th Edward I.,

SERLO DE NANSLADRON was in the expedition then made into Scotland, and had summons to parliament as a BARON, from the 28th to the 34th of the same reign, but never afterwards, and of his lordship nothing further is known.

ARMS.—Sa. three chevronels ar.

NASSAU — EARLS OF ROCHFORD.

By Letters Patent, dated 10th May, 1695.

Lineage.

This noble family descended from

FREDERICK DE NASSAU, natural son of Henry-Frederick de Nassau, Prince of Orange, (grandfather of King William III.,) who was endowed by his father with the lordship of Zuleistein, and thereupon assumed that surname. He subsequently commanded the infantry in the service of the States-General, when his country was invaded by the French, in 1672. In that gloomy conjuncture, when the Prince of Orange was elected stadtholder, his highness's first action was an attack on Naerden; in furtherance of which he detached General Zuleistein, to take up a position between Utrecht and the object of the prince's operations; whereupon the Duke of Luxemburgh marched to relieve the besieged, and fell upon General Zuleistein with between eight and nine thousand men, who bravely met the assault, and repulsed his assailant. The town was afterwards bombarded, and reduced to such extremity, as to be compelled to offer terms of capitulation; in which interval the Duke of Luxemburgh, having been reinforced, marched through swamps, guided by peasants, and re-attacked General Zuleistein, who, after a gallant resistance, fell, sword in hand, on the 12th of October, 1672. The son of this brave soldier,

WILLIAM-HENRY DE ZULEISTEIN, confidential friend of William III., accompanied that prince to England, and was elevated to the peerage on the 10th May, 1695, as *Baron of Enfield, Viscount Tunbridge,* and EARL OF ROCHFORD. His lordship m. Jane, daughter and heiress of Sir Henry Wroth, of Durans, in the county of Middlesex, by whom 382

he had four sons and five daughters. He d. at Zuleistein, in 1708, and was s. by his eldest son,

WILLIAM-HENRY DE NASSAU, second earl. This nobleman was a military officer of considerable renown, and, participating in the triumphs of the Duke of Marlborough, was the bearer of the despatches announcing the glorious victory of Blenheim, on the 2nd August, 1704. His lordship fell at the battle of Almanza, in Spain, on the 27th of July, 1710; and, dying unmarried, the honours devolved upon his brother,

FREDERICK NASSAU, third earl, then one of the nobles of the province of Utrecht. His lordship m. Bessey, daughter and heiress of Richard Savage, Earl of Rivers, by whom he left two sons: .

WILLIAM-HENRY, his successor.

Richard-Savage, one of the clerks of the board of green-cloth,' and M.P.; b. in 1723; m. in December, 1751, Elizabeth, daughter and heiress of Edward Spencer, Esq., of Rendlesham, Sussex,. and Dowager of James, Duke of Hamilton and Brandon, by whom he had, (with a son and daughter, deceased,)

WILLIAM-HENRY.

His lordship d. on the 14th of June, 1738, and was s. by his elder son,

WILLIAM-HENRY NASSAU, fourth earl, who was installed a Knight of the Garter, in 1778, having previously resided as ambassador at the courts of Madrid and Versailles, and filled the offices of groom of the stole,. first lord of the bedchamber, and secretary of state. His lordship m. Lucy, daughter of Edward Young, Esq., of Durnford, in the county of Wilts, by whom he had no issue; and dying on the 20th of September, 1781, the honours devolved upon his nephew,

WILLIAM-HENRY NASSAU, fifth earl, at whose decease, unmarried, 3rd September, 1830, all his honours became EXTINCT.

ARMS.—Quarterly; first, az. semee of billets, or, a lion, rampant, of the second, for NASSAU; second, or, a lion, rampant, gu. ducally crowned az. for DIETZ; third, gu. a fesse ar. for VIANDEN; fourth, two lions, passant, gardant, in pale, or, for CATZNELLOGEN; over all, in an escocheon gu. three rulei ar. in chief a label of three points of the last, for ZULEISTEIN.

NASSAU, OR DE AUVERQUERQUE— EARL OF GRANTHAM.

By Letters Patent, dated 24th December, 1698.

Lineage.

HENRY DE NASSAU, Lord of Auverquerque, general of Dutch infantry, and governor of Hortogenbosh, d. 28th February, 1668, leaving by his wife, Elizabeth, daughter of Count de Horn, the following issue,

Maurice, Earl of Nassau, being so created by the Emperor Leopold, Lord of La Leek, in Holland, and governor of Sluce, d. in 1683.

William Adrian, Lord of Odyke, Zeist, &c., was created likewise an earl of the empire, and was premier nobleman of Zealand.

Henry, of whom presently.

Emilia, *m.* to the celebrated Thomas Butler, Earl of Ossory, son and heir of James, Duke of Ormond.

Isabella, *m.* to Henry Bennet, Earl of Arlington.

Mauritia, *m.* to Colin Lindsey, Earl of Belcarras.

Charlotte, lady of the bed-chamber, *d.* unmarried, in 1702.

Anne-Elizabeth, *m.* to Heer van Baron Rutenburgh, and was mother of,

George, Earl of Cholmondeley.

The youngest son,

HENRY DE NASSAU, Lord of Auverquerque, came into England with the Prince of Orange, in 1670, and being with his highness when he visited the university of Oxford, had the degree of Doctor of Civil Law conferred upon him. He was subsequently the companion in arms of the prince, and at the battle of St. Dennis, in 1678, had the good fortune to save his life, by striking to the ground an officer in the act of charging his highness: for which gallant achievement, the states-general presented him with a sword, whereof the hilt was of massy gold, a pair of pistols richly inlaid with gold, and a pair of horse-buckles of the same valuable metal. Being captain of the guard to the Prince of Orange, he attended him in that station into England, anno 1688. And upon the accession of William and Mary to the throne, he was naturalised by act of parliament, and appointed master of the horse. His lordship was at the battle of the Boyne, and subsequently attended his royal master in all his campaigns against the French. At the decease of King William, he returned to Holland, and was appointed by the states, velt-marshal of the army. In the campaign of 1708, his lordship lost his life in the field, as he had always desired. He *d.* in the camp at Rouselaer, in the 67th year of his age, after a procrastinated indisposition, on the 17th October, 1708, and was interred with great pomp at Auverquerque. His lordship *m.* Isabella van Arsens, daughter of Cornelius, Lord of Somerdyke and Placata, by whom he had issue,

Louis, *d.* in 1687.

Henry, of whom presently.

Cornelius, Count Nassau, of Woudenburgh, major-general in the service of the States-general, killed at the battle of Denain, anno 1712.

William-Maurice, lieutenant-general in the service of the States-general, and governor of Sluce.

Francis, colonel of dragoons, killed at the battle of Almenara, in Spain.

Isabella, *m.* in 1691, to Charles, Lord Lansdown, heir apparent to John Granville, Earl of Bath, by whom he had an only son,

William-Henry, Earl of Bath.

Frances, *m.* to Nanfant Cote, Earl of Bellamont, in the peerage of Ireland.

HENRY DE AUVERQUERQUE, the eldest surviving son, had been elevated to the peerage in the life-time of his father, on the 24th December, 1698, by the titles of *Baron Alford, Viscount Boston,*

and EARL OF GRANTHAM. His lordship *m.* Lady Henrietta Butler, sister of James, Duke of Ormonde, and daughter of the celebrated Thomas, Earl of Ossory, by whom he had issue,

Henry, Viscount Boston, *d.* 19th June, 1718, unmarried.

Thomas, Viscount Boston, *d.* 27th April, 1730, unmarried.

Frances, *m.* to Captain Elliot.

Emilia-Maria, *d.* at ten years of age.

Henrietta, *m.* 27th June, 1732, to William, Earl Cowper.

His lordship *d.* in 1754, and having previously buried both his sons, all his honours EXPIRED.

ARMS.—Quarterly, first, as. semee of billets, and a lion rampant or; second or. a lion rampant guardant, gu., crowned with a ducal coronet as.; third, gu. a fesse ar.; fourth, gu. two lions passant guardant in pale or., over all in an escutcheon, ar., a lion rampant as.

NEREFORD — BARON NEREFORD.

By Writ of Summons, dated 26th January, 1297, 25 Edward I.,

Lineage.

In the year 1206,

ROBERT DE NEREFORD; and his wife, Alice, daughter of John Pouchard, founded the abbey of Pree, in the county of Norfolk, as also an hospital there, for thirteen poor people. This Robert was governor of Dovor Castle, in the 1st of Henry III., under Hubert de Burgh, Justiciary of England. He was *s.* by

WILLIAM DE NEREFORD, who had been in arms with the barons against King John, and had his lands seized, but returning to his allegiance in the beginning of the next reign, they were restored to him. He *m.* Petronill, one of the daughters and co-heirs of John de Vaux, without licence, for which offence he paid a fine of two hundred and thirty pounds to the crown. In the division of the lands of de Vaux, with William de Ros, who had married the other co-heir, this William de Nereford had the manors of Sherston and Sholesham, in the county of Norfolk, with other lands in the same shire, and in the counties of Suffolk and Cambridge. In the 22d of Edward I., he received command, with divers other great men, to attend the king, with his best advice, upon the great affairs of the realm, and was summoned to parliament as a BARON, in the 25th of the same reign, but never afterwards. His lordship was *s.* by his son,

JOHN DE NEREFORD, who was never summoned to parliament as a baron, nor esteemed such. He *d.* without issue, and was *s.* by his brother,

THOMAS DE NEREFORD, who was father of SIR JOHN DE NEREFORD, Knt., who was slain in the wars in France, in 36th of Edward III., leaving an only daughter and heiress,

MARGERY DE NEREFORD, then but five years old, who afterwards vowed chastity.

ARMS.—Gules, a lion rampant, ermine.

383

NEVILL — BARONS NEVILL, OF RABY, EARLS OF WEST-MORLAND.

Barony, by Writ of Summons, 8th June, 1294, 22 Edward I.
Earldom, by Charter, dated 29th September, 1397.

Lineage.

This noble, ancient, and far-spreading family was founded in England, by

GILBERT DE NEVIL, a Norman, one of the companions in arms of the Conqueror, and called, by some of our genealogists, his admiral; although there is no mention of him, or of any person of the name, in the general survey. The grandson of this Gilbert,

GEOFFREY DE NEVILL, m. Emma, daughter and heir of Bertram de Bulmer, a great baron of the north, and had issue,

HENRY, who d. s. p. in 1227.
Isabel.

By the heiress of Bulmer, Geoffrey de Nevill acquired extensive estates, which, after the death of his son, as stated above, issueless, devolved upon his daughter,

ISABEL DE NEVILL. This great heiress espoused Robert Fitz-Maldred,* Lord of RABY, in the bishopric of Durham, and had a son, GEOF-FREY, who, adopting his maternal surname, and inheriting the estates, became

GEOFFREY DE NEVILL, of Raby, and left issue,

　ROBERT, his successor.
　Geoffrey, who, in the 54th of Henry III., was constituted governor of SCARBOROUGH CASTLE, and a justice itinerant. He m. Margaret, daughter and heir of Sir John Longvillers, of HORNBY-CASTLE, in Lancashire, and died in the 13th of Edward I., being then seised of the manor of APPLEBY, and other lands in Lincolnshire; the castle and manor of HORNBY, in the county of Lancaster; and HOTON-LONGVILLERS, and other manors in Yorkshire; the entire of which he acquired by his wife. He left a son and heir,
　　JOHN NEVILL, from whom descended the Nevills of Hornby, whose heir-female,
　　　MARGARET NEVILL, m. Thomas Beaufort, Duke of Exeter.

The elder son,

ROBERT NEVILL, in the 38th Henry III., upon doing his fealty, had livery of all the lands which he inherited from his grandfather, Robert Fitz-Maldred. In the 42d of the same reign, he had a military summons to march to the relief of the King of Scotland, and he was then constituted

* ROBERT FITZ-MALDRED was the lineal heir-male of UCHTRED, Earl of Northumberland, in the days of King EDMUND, Ironside; that is, son of Dolfin, son of Earl Gospatric, son of Maldred Fitz-Crinan, by ALGITHA, daughter of the said UCH-TRED.

governor of the CASTLES OF NORHAM AND WERKE. In the next year, he was entrusted with BAMBOROUGH CASTLE: and two years afterwards, made warden of all the king's forests beyond Trent; which was followed by the appointment of justice-itinerant, for the pleas of those forests. In the 47th, he was one of the barons who undertook for the king's observance of the ordinances of Oxford; and in the same turbulent period, was made captain-general of all the king's forces beyond Trent, as also sheriff of Yorkshire, and governor of the Castle of York; but notwithstanding these great trusts, he subsequently joined the baronial banner, yet was fortunate enough, after the discomfiture of his party, not only to obtain his pardon, but to be constituted governor of Pickering Castle, in Yorkshire. He m. Ida, relict of Robert Bertram, and had a son,

　ROBERT, who m. Mary, elder daughter and co-heir of Ralph Fitz-Randolph, Lord of Middleham, by which alliance he acquired that manor, with the manor of Carleton, and the forest of Coverdale. He d. in the life-time of his father, leaving a son,
　　RANULPH, who succeeded his grandfather.

Robert de Nevill died in 1282, and was s. by his grandson,

RANULPH DE NEVILL, who, being in minority, at the time of his grandfather's decease, obtained liberty of the king, that his friends might plough and manage his lands; and in the 13th Edward I., had livery of certain manors, part of his inheritance; soon after this, he had a warm contest with the PRIOR OF DURHAM, about the presentation of a stag, upon St. Cuthbert's day, in September; "which, in truth," (says Dugdale,) "was rather a rent than an obligation, in regard he held RABY, with the eight adjoining townships, by the yearly rent of £4 and a stag. For, contrary to the custom of his ancestors, he not only required that the PRIOR OF DURHAM, at the offering of that stag, ought to feast him, and all the company he should bring, but that the prior's own menial servants should, for that time, be set aside, and his peculiar servants and officers be put in their stead. Whereupon, amongst other of his guests, he invited John de Baillol, of Barnard Castle, who refused to go with him, alleging that he never knew the Nevills to have such a privilege there; Sir William de Brompton, the bishop's chief justice, likewise acknowledging that he himself was the first that began that extravagant practice; for being a young man, and delighting in hunting, he came with the Lord Nevill, at the offering of the stag, and said to his companions, 'Come, let us go into the abbey and wind our horns,' and so they did. The prior further adding, that before the time of this Ranulph, none of his predecessors ever made any such claim; but when they brought the stag into the hall, they had only a breakfast, nor did the lord himself ever stay dinner, except he were invited." This Ranulph was summoned to parliament as a BARON, on 8th June, 1294, and from that period, to 18th February, 1331. His lordship was in the wars of France, temp. Edward I., and in those of Scotland in the next reign. It is said, however, that he little minded secular business, but devoted the principal part of his time to conversation with the canons of Merton and Coverham, upon whom he bestowed some considerable grants. He m. first, Eufemia, daughter of Sir John de Clavering, and had two sons,

Robert, called the "*Peacock of the North,*" who died *s. p.*, in his father's life-time.

Ralph, his successor.

His lordship espoused, secondly, Margery, daughter of John, son of Marmaduke de Thweng, but had no issue. He *d.* in 1331, and was *s.* by his only surviving son,

RALPH DE NEVILL, second baron, summoned to parliament, from 20th November, 1331, to 20th January, 1336. This nobleman, in the time of his father, was retained by indenture, to serve the Lord Henry de Percy, for life, in peace and war, against all men except the king, with twenty men-at-arms, whereof five to be knights, receiving £100 sterling per annum. The dispute with the prior of Durham, regarding the presentation of the stag, was revived, and finally set at rest, in the abandonment of his claim, by this Lord Nevill. The matter is thus detailed by Dugdale: " In this year, likewise, doing his fealty to William, Prior of Durham, upon Lammas day, for the manor of Raby, he told him, ' that he would offer the stag as his ancestors had done; saving that, whereas his father required, that the prior's servants should be set aside at that time, and his own serve in their stead; he would be content, that his should attend together, with those of the prior's; and whereas, his father insisted, that his servants should only be admitted at dinner; he stood upon it, that his should be there entertained the whole day, and likewise the morrow at breakfast.' Whereupon the prior made answer, ' that none of his ancestors were ever so admitted, and that he would rather quit the stag, than suffer any new custom to the prejudice of their church.' But, to this Ralph replied, ' that he would perform the whole service, or none, and put the trial of his right upon the country.' The prior, therefore, knowing him to be so powerful, and that the country could not displease him, declined the offer; howbeit, at length, to gain his favour, in regard he had no small interest at court, and might do him a kindness or a displeasure, was content for that one time, he should perform it as he pleased, so that it might not be drawn into example afterwards: and to the purpose proposed, that, that indentures should be made betwixt them. Whereupon the Lord Nevill brought but few with him, and those more for the honour of the prior, than a burthen; and so, shortly after dinner, took his leave, but left one of his servants to lodge there all night, and to take his breakfast there on the next day; ' protesting, that being both a son and tenant to the church, he would not be burthensome to it, in respect it would be no advantage to himself, but might much damnifie him, if he should bring with him as great a train as he would,' saying, ' *what doth a breakfast signify to me ? nothing.* And likewise, that if the prior would shew that he had no right to what he so claimed, he would freely

recede therefrom; and if he had a right, he would accept of a composition for it, rather than be burthensome to the convent; but if they should put him to get his right by law, then he would not abate anything thereof.' Whereupon inquiry being made amongst the eldest monks of the house, they affirmed, that being of eight years standing when his father was before repulsed, they had often seen the stag offered, and that he never staid dinner, but when the prior invited him; and some ancient men of the country testified as much: as also, that so soon as the stag was brought, they carried him to the kitchen, and those who brought him were taken into the hall to breakfast, as they that bring their rents used to be.

" Moreover, when it happened any of the Lords Nevill to be desired to stay dinner with the prior, his cook was admitted into the kitchen to prepare a dish for him; so likewise, another servant in the cellar, to choose his drink, and in like manner, some other at the gate, who knew his servants and followers, merely to let them in, and keep out others, who, under pretence of being servants, might then intrude. But this was only done by the prior, as out of courtesy and respect, and not at all out of right."

In the 7th Edward III., Lord Nevill was one of the commissioners sent into Scotland, there to see that the covenants between Edward de Bailiol, King of Scots, and his royal master, were ratified by the parliament of that kingdom; and the next year he was joined with Henry de Percy, in the wardenship of the Marches of Northumberland, Cumberland, and Westmorland. He had, subsequently, other high and confidential employments, and was constantly engaged in the wars of Scotland and France. His lordship m. Alice, daughter of Hugh de Audley, and had issue,

John (Sir), his successor.

William (Sir), Gentleman of the Bedchamber to Richard II.

Thomas, m. Margaret, daughter of William Babington, and had a daughter and heir,

Jane, m. first, to Thomas Thurland; and secondly, to Sir Gervase Clifton, Knt.

Robert (Sir), of Eldon, eminent in arms.

Alexander, Archbishop of York, *d.* in 1391.

Ralph, of Candall.

Euphemia, m. to Reginald de Lucy,

Catherine.

Margaret, m. to Henry Percy, Earl of Northumberland.

He *d.* in 1367, and was buried in the church of Durham, on the south-side thereof, being the first secular person that had sepulture there, which favour he obtained from the prior and convent, for a vestment of red velvet, richly embroidered with gold, silk, great pearls, and images of saints standing in tabernacles; by him given to St. Cuthbert. His body being brought in a chariot drawn by seven horses, to the boundary of the churchyard, and thence conveyed upon the shoulders of knights, into the middle of the church, where the abbot of St. Mary's, in York, (by reason of the bishop's absence and impotency of the dean,) performed the office of the dead, and celebrated the morrow mass, at which were offered eight horses, viz., four for the war, with four men armed, and all their harness and habiliments; and four others for peace; as also three cloths of gold, of blue colour, interwoven with flowers. Four of those horses were redeemed, after the funeral, by Sir John, his son and heir, for one hundred marks. His lordship was s. by his eldest son,

SIR JOHN DE NEVILL, third baron, summoned to parliament as LORD NEVILL, OF RABY, from 24th February, 1368, to 28th July, 1388. This nobleman was with his father at the battle of Durham, in the 20th Edward III., and received the honour of knighthood some years afterwards, when in arms before the barriers of Paris. In the 44th of the same reign he was again in the wars of France, and then constituted admiral of the king's fleet from the mouth of the Thames northwards. During the remainder of King Edward's reign he was constantly in active service either in France or Scotland. In the 2nd Richard II. he was constituted lieutenant of Aquitaine, and he was likewise seneschall of Bordeaux. It is reported of this nobleman that he was some time employed against the Turks; and that being lieutenant of Aquitaine, he reduced that province to tranquillity, and that in his service in those parts, he won, and had rendered to him, eighty-three walled towns, castles, and forts. His lordship was a Knight of the Garter. He m. first, Maud, daughter of Lord Percy, by whom he had issue,

> RALPH, his successor.
> Thomas, who m. Joane, only daughter and heiress of William de Furnival, Lord Furnival, and was summoned to parliament in her right, as LORD FURNIVAL (see Furnival, Lords Furnival).
> Maud, m. to William, Lord Scroop.
> Alice, m. to William, Lord Deincourt.
> Eleanor, m. to Ralph, Lord Lumley.

His lordship espoused, secondly, Elizabeth, daughter and heir of William, Lord Latimer, K.G., and had

> JOHN, who, in right of his mother, was summoned to parliament as LORD LATIMER (see Latimer, Barons Latimer, of Danby).
> Elizabeth, m. to Sir Thomas Willoughby, Knt.
> Margaret.

He d. in 1388, and was s. by his eldest son,

RALPH DE NEVILL, fourth baron, summoned to parliament from 6th December, 1389, to 30th November, 1396. This nobleman took a leading part in the political drama of his day, and sustained it with more than ordinary ability. In the life-time of his father (9th Richard II.), he was joined with Thomas Clifford, son of Lord Clifford, in the governorship of the city and castle of Carlisle, and was appointed a commissionership for the guardianship of the West Marches. In three years after this he succeeded to the title, and in two years subsequently he was one of the commissioners appointed to treat with the kings of France and Scotland, touching a truce made by them with the king of England. In the 21st Richard II. he was made constable of the Tower of London, and

shortly afterwards advanced in full parliament to the dignity of EARL OF WESTMORLAND. His lordship was of the privy council to King Richard, and had much favour from that monarch, yet he was one of the most active in raising HENRY, of Lancaster, to the throne, as HENRY IV., and was rewarded by the new king in the first year of his reign, with a grant of the county and honour of Richmond for his life, and with the great office of EARL MARSHALL OF ENGLAND. Soon after this he stoutly resisted the Earl of Northumberland in his rebellion, and forced the PERCIES, who had advanced as far as Durham, to fall back upon PRUDHOE, when the battle of Shrewsbury ensued, in which the gallant HOTSPUR sustained so signal a defeat, and closed his impetuous career. The earl was afterwards governor of the town and castle of Carlisle, warden of the West Marches towards Scotland, and governor of Roxborough. He was also a KNIGHT OF THE GARTER. His lordship m. first, Lady Margaret Stafford, daughter of Hugh, Earl Stafford, K.G., for which marriage a dispensation was obtained from Pope URBAN V., the Earl and his bride being within the third and fourth degrees of consanguinity: by this lady he had issue,

> JOHN, Lord Nevill, who, in the 12th Henry IV., was made governor of the castle of Roxborough for ten years, and the next year constituted warden of the West Marches towards Scotland. His lordship m. Lady Elizabeth Holland, daughter of Thomas, Earl of Kent, and sister and co-heir of Edmund, Earl of Kent, by whom (dying in 1423, his father still living) he left issue,
>> RALPH, who succeeded as second Earl of Westmorland.
>> John, slain at Towton, in 1461, m. Lady Ann Holland, daughter of John, Duke of Exeter, and widow of his nephew, John, Lord Nevill, and left a son,
>>> RALPH, who succeeded as third Earl of Westmorland.
>> Thomas.
> Ralph, who m. Margery, daughter and co-heir of Sir Robert Ferrers, of Oversley, and left a son,
>> John, who m. Elizabeth, daughter and heir of Robert Newmarch, and left an only daughter and heir,
>>> MARGARET, m. to Thomas Wentworth, ancestor of the Earls of Strafford.
> Maud, m. to Peter, Lord Mauley.
> Philippa, m. to Thomas, Lord Dacre.
> Alice, m. first, to Sir Thomas Grey, Knt., and secondly, to Sir Gilbert Lancaster, Knt.
> Margaret, m. to Richard, Lord Scroop, of Bolton.
> Anne, m. to Sir Gilbert Umfravill.
> Margery, abbess of Barking.
> Elizabeth, a nun.

The earl espoused, secondly, Joane de Beaufort, daughter of John of Gaunt, by Katherine Swynford, and widow of Robert, Lord Ferrers, of Wem, by whom he had issue,

RICHARD, who m. Lady Alice Montacute, only daughter and heiress of Thomas, Earl of Salisbury, and was created EARL OF SALISBURY himself (see Nevill, Earl of Salisbury).

William (see Nevill, Lord Fauconberg and Earl of Kent).

George (see Nevill, Lord Latimer).

Edward (Sir), who m. Lady Elizabeth Beauchamp, only daughter and heiress of Richard Beauchamp, LORD BERGAVENNY, and Earl of Worcester, and was summoned to parliament, *jure uxoris*, as Baron Bergavenny: a dignity enjoyed by his lordship's lineal descendant, the present Earl of Abergavenny.

Robert, a churchman, Bishop of Durham.

Cuthbert,
Henry, } died s. p. *7h Strssrgn ry*
Thomas,

Catherine, m. first, to John Mowbray, Duke of Norfolk, and secondly, to Sir John Widvile, Knt., son of Richard, Earl Rivers.

Eleanor, (or Elizabeth,) m. first, to Richard, Lord Spencer, and secondly, to Henry Percy, Earl of Northumberland.

Anne, m. first, to Humphrey, Duke of Buckingham, and secondly, to Walter Blount, Lord Mountjoy.

Jane, a nun.

Cicily, m. to Richard Plantagenet, Duke of York.

This great earl d. in 1425, and was s. by his grandson,

RALPH NEVILL, fifth Baron Nevill, of Raby, and second Earl of Westmorland. This nobleman, after the death of Elizabeth, his mother, had £40 per annum, allowed him by the king for his maintenance, being then in minority. His lordship m. first, Elizabeth, daughter of Henry, Lord Percy, (*Hotspur,*) and widow of John, Lord Clifford, by whom he had issue,

JOHN, Lord Nevill, who m. Lady Anne Holland, daughter of John, Duke of Exeter, and d. in the life-time of his father s. p. His widow re-married her late husband's uncle, Sir John Nevill.

The earl espoused, secondly, Margaret, daughter of Sir Reginald Cobham, Knt., but had no issue. His lordship d. in 1485, and was s. by his nephew,

RALPH NEVILL, sixth Baron Nevill, of Raby, and third Earl of Westmorland. This nobleman m. Margaret, daughter of Sir Roger Booth, of Barton, in the county of Lancaster, and had an only son,

RALPH, Lord Nevill, who m. Elizabeth, daughter of Sir William Sandys, and dying in the life-time of his father, left a son and daughter, viz.

RALPH, who s. as fourth earl.

Anne, m. to Sir William Conyers, Knt.

The earl is said to have d. of grief for the loss of his son at Hornby Castle, in 1523, and was s. by his grandson,

RALPH NEVILL, seventh Baron Nevill, of Raby, and fourth Earl of Westmorland. This nobleman was made a Knight of the Garter by King Henry VIII., and was one of those who signed the celebrated letter to *Pope* CLEMENT regarding the divorce of Queen Katherine. His lordship m. Lady Catherine Stafford, daughter of Edward, Duke of Buckingham, and had, with other issue,

HENRY, Lord Neville, his successor.

Thomas (Sir).

Eleanor.

Dorothy, m. to John, Earl of Oxford.

Mary, m. to Sir Thomas Danby, Knt.

Joane.

Margaret, m. to Henry Manners, Earl of Rutland.

Elizabeth, m. to Thomas, Lord Dacre, of Gillesland.

Eleanor, m. to Sir Bryan Stapleton, Knt.

Anne, m. to Sir Fulke Greville, Knt., of Beauchamps Court, in the county of Warwick.

Ursula.

The earl d. in 1549, and was s. by his eldest son,

HENRY NEVILL, eighth Baron Nevill, of Raby, and fifth Earl of Westmorland; who m. first, Lady Jane Manners, daughter of Thomas, Earl of Rutland, and had issue,

CHARLES, Lord Nevill.

Eleanor, m. to Sir William Pelham, Knt.

Katherine, m. to Sir John Constable, Knt., of Kirby Knowle, in the county of York.

Adeline, d. unmarried.

His lordship espoused, secondly, Margaret, daughter of Sir Richard Cholmondeley, Knt., and widow of Sir John Gascoigne, Knt., by whom he had two daughters, Margaret and Elizabeth. The earl, who was a Knight of the Garter, d. in 1549, and was s. by his son,

CHARLES NEVILL, ninth Baron Nevill, of Raby, and sixth Earl of Westmorland. This nobleman, joining in the insurrection of Henry Percy, Earl of Northumberland, in the 13th of Elizabeth, was attainted, and preserved his life only by first flying into Scotland, and afterwards to the Netherlands, where he lived to an advanced age, Banks says, "meanly and miserably." His lordship m. Anne, daughter of Henry Howard, Earl of Surry, and sister of Thomas, Duke of Norfolk, by whom he had issue,

Catherine, m. to Sir Thomas Grey, of Chillingham.

Eleanor, d. unmarried.

Margaret, m. to Nicholas Pudsey, Esq.

Anne, m. to David, brother of Sir William Ingleby, Knt.

Under the attainder of this nobleman the old BARONY OF NEVILL, OF RABY, and the EARLDOM OF WESTMORLAND became both FORFEITED.

ARMS.—Gules, a saltier, ar.

Note.—In the reign of James I. the Earldom of Westmorland was claimed by Edward Nevill, and the case appears thus :—

In the time of Richard II., Ralph, Lord Nevill, of Raby, was created Earl of Westmorland, to him and the heirs male of his body; and had issue by his first wife a son, Ralph, whose issue male, during several successions, enjoyed the title, and to him Charles, last Earl of Westmorland, was heir male. That Ralph, the first earl, by his second wife, had issue, George Neville, Lord Latimer, of whom the then claimant, Edward Neville, was the lineal descendant, and heir male. And that Charles, then late Earl of Westmorland, was attainted for high treason. It was, however, adjudged that Edward Neville should not succeed to the earldom, though heir male of the first donee. The authority for which decision was grounded on the statute of 26 Henry VIII., cap. 13, whereby, in cases of high treason, it is enacted, that the offender shall forfeit all such lands, tenements, and *hereditaments*, *wherein he shall have any estate of inheritance.—* BANKS.

NEVILL — EARLS OF SALISBURY, EARL OF WARWICK, BARON MONTACUTE, BARON MONTHERMER.

Earldom of Salisbury,	by Letters	4th May, 1442.
Earldom of Warwick,	Patent,	
Barony of Montacute,	by Writ of	8th June, 1294, 22 Edward I.
Barony of Monthermer,	Summons,	4th March, 1309, 2 Edward II.

Lineage.

RICHARD NEVILL, eldest son of *Ralph Nevill*, first EARL OF WESTMORLAND, by his second wife, Joane de Beaufort, daughter of JOHN OF GAUNT, and widow of Robert, Lord Ferrers, of Wem, espoused the Lady Alice Montacute, daughter and heir of Thomas, Earl of Salisbury, (see Montacute, Earl of Salisbury,) and had that EARLDOM revived in his person, by letters patent, dated 4th May, 1442, with remainder to the said Alice, and with twenty pounds annual rent out of the issues of the county of Wilts. Her ladyship inherited the old Baronies of MONTACUTE and MONTHERMER, which had been so long in her family. This nobleman obtained from King HENRY VI. numerous substantial grants, and some of the highest and most important trusts, amongst others he was appointed warden of the marches towards Scotland, and governor of Carlisle, had had large territorial gifts from the crown, with a grant of £9,063. 6s. 8d. per annum, out of the customs, for thirty years, yet he was one of the earliest to espouse the cause of the house of York, and one of the most determined in maintaining it. His lordship fought and won, in conjunction with the Duke of York, the first pitched battle, that of ST. ALBANS, between the contending Roses; and he followed up his success by defeating the Lord Audley at BLORE HEATH in 1458, and again in 1460, at NORTHAMPTON, when he was constituted by the Yorkists LORD GREAT CHAMBERLAIN OF ENGLAND. The fortune of war changing, however, in the very next rencounter, the battle of WAKEFIELD, the Duke of York fell, the Yorkists were routed, Salisbury's son, Sir Thomas Nevill, slain, and the earl himself made prisoner, when his head was immediately cut off, and fixed upon a pole over one of the gates of the

388

city of York. His lordship had issue by the heiress of the Montacutes,

RICHARD, *Earl of Warwick*, his successor.

Thomas (Sir), m. Maud, widow of Lord Willoughby, and was slain at Wakefield—died s. p.

John (Sir), created MARQUESS OF MONTAGU (see that dignity).

George, in holy orders, became Archbishop of York, and CHANCELLOR OF ENGLAND.

Ralph, }
Robert, } d. young.

Joane, m. to William Fitz-Alan, Earl of Arundel.

Cicely, m. first, to Henry Beauchamp, Duke of Warwick, and secondly, to John Tiptoft, Earl of Worcester.

Alice, m. to Henry, Lord Fitz-Hugh.

Eleanor, m. to Thomas Stanley, first Earl of Warwick.

Katherine, m. to William, Lord Bonville.

Margaret, m. first, to John de Vere, Earl of Oxford, and secondly, to William, Lord Hastings.

The decapitation of the earl (who was a Knight of the Garter) occurred in December, 1460, when his eldest son,

RICHARD NEVILL, the *stout* EARL OF WARWICK, became second Earl of Salisbury, and he inherited from his mother the baronies of Montacute and Monthermer. His lordship married Lady Anne Beauchamp, daughter of Richard, fifth Earl of Warwick, and heiress of the Beauchamps, upon the decease, in 1449, of her young niece, Anne, COUNTESS OF WARWICK, daughter and heiress of Henry, Duke of Warwick, and had a confirmation of the EARLDOM OF WARWICK, with all its preeminences to himself and his wife, the said Lady Anne Beauchamp, by letters patent, dated 23rd July, in the same year. This nobleman, so well known in English history as the KING MAKER, espoused with his father the fortunes of the house of York at the very commencement of the lamentable contest between the Roses, and was made CAPTAIN-GENERAL OF CALAIS after the first battle of St. Albans. He subsequently commanded the van of the Yorkists at Northampton, where MARGARET OF ANJOU, sustained so signal a defeat. He shared, however, in the reverses of his party in the ensuing battles of Wakefield and St. Albans, but outgeneralled the heroic Margaret, in reaching London, with the young Earl of March, son of the Duke of York, before her victorious army. Here he caused his *protegee* to be proclaimed as EDWARD IV., and following the queen and Lancastrians into the north, *fixed* the sceptre in the hand of the new monarch by the great victory of Towton FIELD. After which he was constituted general warden of the east marches towards Scotland, constable of Dover Castle, LORD GREAT CHAMBERLAIN of England for life, and LORD HIGH STEWARD. He likewise obtained immense grants from the crown, so that his revenues are said to have amounted, independently of his own heritable estates, to the annual income of *four score thousand crowns!* It is not possible, however, in a work of this description; to enter into any thing like a detail of the deeds of this, probably most potent, noble in the whole range of English story. We must, therefore, be content in briefly stating, that his lordship, becoming in a few years discontented with the order of things which he had thus established, projected the restoration of the Lancastrian monarch, Henry VI., and having embodied an army under the sanction of his former foe, MARGARET, OF ANJOU, landed in the west of England from Normandy, proclaimed King Henry VI., forced King Edward to fly the kingdom, marched upon London, and releasing the restored monarch from his captivity in the Tower, re-established him upon the throne; when he was himself constituted LORD HIGH ADMIRAL OF ENGLAND. This revolution was, however, but of brief endurance, for within one short year King Edward reappeared upon the scene of action, and soon found himself at the head of a sufficient force to contend for, and to recover his diadem. The battle was fought on Easter-day 1471, at BARNET-FIELD, when, notwithstanding the personal valour, and great martial prowess of the Earl of Warwick, and his brother, the Marquess of Montagu, victory declared for the Yorkists, but his lordship survived not the defeat—he fell in the brunt of the conflict, with a numerous train of eminent associates. The earl's remains, with those of his brother, the Marquess of Montagu, were conveyed to London, and there exposed to public view in the cathedral of St. Paul, whence they were transferred to Bitham, in Berkshire, and interred in the tomb of the MONTACUTES. *Comines* reports, that the earl was so popular at Calais, of which he was governor, that every body wore his badge, no man esteeming himself gallant whose head was not adorned with his *ragged staff;* nor no door frequented that had not his *white cross* painted thereon. Moreover, he saith, that this earl never used to fight on foot; but his manner was, when he had led his men to the charge, then to take horse. And if the victory fell on his side, to fight among his soldiers, otherwise to depart in time. But in this last battle he was constrained by his brother, the Marquess of Montagu, to alight and to send away his horse. Of his extraordinary hospitality it is recorded, that, at his house in London, six oxen were usually eaten at breakfast, and every tavern full of his meat; "for, who that had any acquaintance in his family, should have as much sodden and roast as he might carry upon a long dagger." As admiral to King Henry VI. his lordship was styled GREAT CAPTAIN OF THE SEA, and through the favour of the same monarch, he had a grant of precedency above all the earls of England, and to augment his grandeur, had a peculiar office at arms, for his services in martial employments, called WARWICK HERALD. After his lordship's death, his countess, such the mutability of human affairs, the great heiress of the BEAUCHAMPS, endured the deepest distress, being constrained to take sanctuary in the Abbey of *Beaulieu,* in Hampshire, where she continued a long time in a very mean condition; thence removing privately into the north, she there too abode in most humble circumstances, all her vast inheritance being, by

authority of parliament, taken from her and settled upon ISABEL and ANNE, her two daughters and heirs, as if she herself had been naturally dead. But upon the death of these ladies, without surviving issue, her inheritance was restored, 3rd Henry VII., with power to alienate the same or any part thereof. This appears, however, to have been merely granted, in order that she might transfer it to the king; for soon after, by special deed, and a fine thereupon, she passed the Warwick estates, of no less than one hundred and fourteen lordships, together with the isles of Jersey, &c., to King Henry VII., and his issue male, with remainder to herself and her heirs for ever. When she died, is not exactly known, but she was living in the 5th of Henry VII. By this lady the Earl of Warwick left two daughters,

ISABEL, *m.* to George Plantagenet, Duke of Clarence, brother of King Edward IV., and died *a* 1477 *2 children - see Plantagenet.*

ANNE, *m.* first, to Edward Prince of Wales, son of King Henry VI., and secondly, to Richard Duke of Gloucester, afterwards RICHARD III., who killed the young prince, her first husband, in cool blood, after the battle of Tewksbury. By Richard she had a son,

EDWARD PLANTAGENET, who was created by his uncle, King Edward IV., EARL OF SALISBURY, in the first year of his reign, and afterwards Earl of Chester, and PRINCE OF WALES. He *d.* the next year, 1484, when all his honours became EXTINCT.

An attainder immediately followed the death of the *stout* EARL OF WARWICK, and under *that,* the EARLDOMS OF WARWICK AND SALISBURY, with the BARONIES OF MONTACUTE AND MONTHERMER, became FORFEITED.

ARMS.—Gules, a saltier, ar.

NEVILL — BARON NEVILL, OF MONTAGU, EARL OF NORTHUMBERLAND, MARQUESS OF MONTAGU.

Barony, by Writ of Summons, dated 30th July, 1460, 38 Henry VI.

Earldom,	by Letters	27th May, 1467.
Marquisate,	Patent,	25th May, 1470.

Lineage.

SIR JOHN NEVILL, third son of Richard Nevill, Earl of Salisbury, by the Lady Alice Montacute, daughter and heir of Thomas Montacute, Earl of Salisbury, was summoned to parliament as BARON NEVILL, *of Montague,* by King Henry VI., in 1460, and afterwards espousing, with his father and elder brother, Richard, the celebrated EARL OF WARWICK, the interests of the House of York, he had similar summons upon the accession of *King* EDWARD IV., which latter monarch constituted him general warden of the east Marches towards Scotland, and the ensuing year, (27th May, 1467,) advanced him to the dignity of EARL OF NORTHUM-

BERLAND (in consequence of the flight of Henry Percy, Earl of Northumberland, into Scotland, with Henry VI.). His lordship in this year defeated the Lancastrians under the Duke of Somerset, at HEXHAM; and he was subsequently rewarded with extensive grants from the forfeited lands in the counties of Norfolk, Leicester, Nottingham, Suffolk, and York. In the 10th of Edward IV., the earl was induced to resign the peerage of Northumberland, in order that *the Percy* might be restored; and in lieu thereof, he was created MARQUESS OF MONTAGU. Soon after this, however, his lordship joined his brother, the Earl of Warwick, in the restoration of *King* HENRY VI., and eventually shared the fate of that eminent nobleman, at the battle of Barnet, 14th April, 1471; in that conflict both brothers fell, and both were afterwards attainted. The marquess *m.* Isabel, daughter of Sir Edmund Ingoldesthorp, Knt., and had issue,

> GEORGE, who was created DUKE OF BEDFORD, on the 5th January, 1469, by *King* EDWARD IV., with the intention of bestowing upon him, in marriage, his eldest daughter, the Lady Elizabeth Plantagenet. After the attainder of his father, and the consequent confiscation of his heritable estates, having no means of sustaining the ducal dignity, his grace was degraded from all his dignities and honours; by parliament, in 1477. He died in 1483, *s. p.*, and was interred at Sheriff Hoton.
>
> John, *d.* and was buried at Salston, in Cambridgeshire.
>
> Anne, *m.* to Sir William Stoner, Knt., of Oxfordshire.
>
> Elizabeth, *m.* to Lord Scrope, of Upsall.
>
> Margaret, *m.* first, to Sir John Mortimer, and secondly, to Robert Horne.
>
> Lucy, *m.* first, to Sir Thomas Fitz-Williams, of Aldwarke, Knt., and secondly, to SIR ANTHONY BROWN, Knt., Standard-Bearer of England. Her ladyship's grandson,
>
>> SIR ANTHONY BROWN, Knt., was created Viscount Montagu.
>
> Isabel, *m.* to Sir William Huddleston, Knt., of Salston.

Under the attainder of this nobleman, the BARONY OF NEVILL, OF MONTAGU, and the MARQUESATE OF MONTAGU, became FORFEITED.

ARMS.—Gules. a saltier, ar. a label gobonny ar. and az. a crescent for difference.

NEVILL—DUKE OF BEDFORD.

See *Nevill*, MARQUESS OF MONTAGU.

NEVILL, AND FAUCONBERG— BARONS FAUCONBERG, EARL OF KENT.

Barony, by Writ of Summons, dated 23rd July, 1295, 23 Edward I.
Earldom, by Letters Patent, dated 1462.

Lineage.

Of this ancient family, the first upon record is
PETER DE FALKEBERGE, son of Agnes de
390

Arches, foundress of the house of nuns, Nunkeiling, in Holderness, in the county of York. This Peter had three sons,

> William.
>
> Walter, *m.* Agnes, one of the three daughters and co-heirs of Simon Fitz-Simon, by Isabel, his wife, daughter and heir of Thomas de Cukeney, founder of Welbeck Abbey, in Nottinghamshire.
>
> Stephen, *m.* Petronill, another of the daughters and co-heirs of Simon Fitz-Simon.

To Walter de Falkeberg, (the second son,) succeeded,
PETER DE FAUCONBERG, who was *s.* by his son,
WALTER DE FAUCONBERG, of Ryse, in Holderness, who, in the 8th of Henry III., was constituted governor of Plympton Castle, in the county of Devon. He *m.* Agnes, one of the sisters and co-heirs of Peter de Bruss of Skelton Castle, and by her he acquired that castle, with other extensive lands, in all of which he obtained charter for free warren, in the 8th Edward I. In the 23d of the same reign, he had summons* to attend the king, amongst divers other persons of note, to advise concerning the important affairs of the realm, and soon after had a military summons to be at Portsmouth, in order to sail with the king into France. He was summoned to parliament as a BARON, from 23rd June, 1295, to 24th July, 1301, and d. in 1303—was *s.* by his eldest son,
WALTER DE FAUCONBERG, second baron, but never summoned to parliament. His lordship *m.* Isabel, daughter of Lord Roos, of Hamlake, by whom he had a numerous family. He d. ——, and was *s.* by his eldest surviving son,
SIR WALTER DE FAUCONBERG, K.B., third baron, summoned to parliament from 13th November, 1303, to 25th August, 1318. This nobleman distinguished himself in the Scottish wars. His lordship *m.* Anastasia, daughter of Ralph de Nevil, and d. in 1313—was *s.* by his son,
JOHN DE FAUCONBERG, fourth baron, summoned to parliament from 23d January, 1336, to 10th March, 1349. This nobleman was in the wars of Scotland, 7th Edward III., and he was afterwards in the expedition made into Flanders. In the 15th of the same reign, he was constituted sheriff of Yorkshire, and governor of the Castle of York; and the next year he was made governor of Berwick-upon-Tweed. His lordship *d.* in 1349, and was *s.* by his son,
SIR WALTER DE FAUCONBERG, fifth baron, summoned to parliament, from 25th November, 1359, to 14th August, 1362. This nobleman being a banneret, had an assignation, in the 34th Edward III., of £239. 9*d.*, to be paid out of the exchequer, for wages due to him, for his services and expenses in the wars beyond sea. In two years afterwards, upon an apprehended inva-

---

* NICOLAS doubts whether this writ could be deemed a regular summons to parliament, as none of the higher temporal nobility, nor any of the spiritual peers were included in the summons, nor was there any day fixed for the meeting.

sion by the French, his lordship was appointed, with the Lord Mowbray and other eminent persons, to guard the sea coast of Yorkshire; and he was subsequently again in the wars of France. He m. first, Maud, daughter of John, Lord Pateshull, and sister and co-heir of William de Pateshull, and had a son THOMAS, his successor. His lordship espoused, 'secondly, Isabel, sister of John Bigot. He d. in 1362, and was s. by his son,

SIR THOMAS DE FAUCONBERG, sixth baron, but never summoned to parliament. This nobleman was with William de Windsore, in the expedition made into Ireland, in the 43rd of Edward III., and in the 50th of the same reign, he was in the wars of France. He d. about the year 1376, leaving an only daughter and heiress,

JOAN DE FAUCONBERG, who espoused

SIR WILLIAM NEVILL, Knt., (youngest son of Ralph, first Earl of Westmorland, by his second wife, Joane de Beaufort, daughter of John of Gaunt;) he was summoned to parliament, *jure uxoris*, as LORD FAUCONBERG, from 3rd August, 1429, to 23d May, 1461. His lordship, who was a military person of great valour, distinguished himself at the siege of Orleans, in the 9th of Henry VI.; and subsequently took a leading part in the wars of France. He was governor of the Castle of Roxborough, in the same reign; but being sent ambassador into Normandy to treat of peace, he was perfidiously seized upon by the French, and detained for some time a prisoner in France. In consideration of which captivity, he had an assignation, in the 30th of Henry VI., of £4180, then in arrear, due to him for his pay, whilst he was governor of Roxborough, to be received out of the customs of the ports of Bristol, Kingston-upon-Hull, and Ipswich. After this he was again constituted, in conjunction with Sir Ralph Grey, Governor of Roxborough Castle for twelve years, and they were to receive jointly, in times of truce, £1000 per annum, and in time of war, double that income. In the 35th of the same reign, he was again in the wars of France, in the retinue of his nephew, Richard, Earl of Warwick, then governor of Calais, and lieutenant of the Marches there. His lordship espousing the cause of Edward IV., and fighting valiantly for that prince, at the battle of TOWTON, was rewarded, after the accession of the new monarch, by being raised to the dignity of EARL OF KENT, constituted LORD ADMIRAL OF ENGLAND, and made a Knight of the Garter. But those honours his lordship enjoyed a few months only, as he died some time in the same year, 1462, leaving three daughters his co-heirs, viz.

Joane, m. to Sir Edward Bedhowing, Knt.

Elisabeth, m. to Sir Richard Strangeways, Knt.

Alice, m. to Sir John Coniers, Knt., K.G., and her eldest son,

SIR WILLIAM CONYERS was summoned to parliament by King HENRY VIII. as LORD CONYERS. His lordship m. Lady Anne Neville, daughter of Ralph, Earl of Westmorland, and dying in 1524, left issue,

CHRISTOPHER, his successor.

Katherine, m., to Sir Francis Bigod, of Settrington.

Margaret, m. to Richard, son of Sir Roger Cholmeley, of Rockley, Knt.

His lordship was s. by his son,

SIR CHRISTOPHER CONYERS, second baron, who m. Anne, daughter of William, Lord Dacre, of Gillesland, and had issue,

JOHN, his successor.

Leonard.

Elizabeth, m. to George Playce, Esq., of Halnaby.

Jane, m. to Sir Marmaduke Constable, Knt.

His lordship was s. by his elder son,

JOHN CONYERS, third baron. This nobleman m. Maud, daughter of Henry Clifford, first Earl of Cumberland, and d. in 1557, leaving three daughters, his heirs, viz.

Anne, m. to Anthony Kempe, Esq.

Elizabeth, m. to Thomas, son of Sir John D'Arcy, Knt. (see D'Arcy, Barons Conyers).

Catherine, m. to John, son and heir of John Atherton, Esq., of Atherton, in Lancashire.

Of these daughters, the descendants of Elizabeth, Lady D'Arcy alone remain, and in one of those, WILLIAM, present DUKE OF LEEDS, the BARONY OF CONYERS now centres.

Upon the decease of the EARL OF KENT that dignity became EXTINCT, while the BARONY OF FAUCONBERG fell into ABEYANCE between his three daughters, as it still continues with their REPRESENTATIVES.

ARMS.—Gu. a saltier, ar. a mullet, sa. for difference.

Note.—In an old inquisition, it was found that Henry de Fauconberge held the manor of Cukeney, in Nottinghamshire, by serjeanty, for shoeing the king's horses when he came to Mansfield, which was formerly a place where our kings were wont frequently to retire to for the purpose of enjoying the chase.

NEVILL—BARON LATIMER.

See Latimer, Barons Latimer, of Danby.

NEVILL—BARONS LATIMER.

By Writ of Summons, dated 25th February, 1432, 10 Henry VI.

Lineage.

Upon the decease, without issue, of *John Nevill*, LORD LATIMER, OF DANBY, several of his lordship's estates passed by entail to his elder brother of the half-blood,

RALPH NEVILL, first Earl of Westmorland, who settled those lands by feoffment on Sir George

Nevill, one of his sons by his second wife, Joane, daughter of John of Gaunt, which

SIR GEORGE NEVILL was, thereupon, the next ensuing year, on the 25th February, 1432, summoned to parliament as BARON LATIMER. In the 13th Henry VI. this nobleman was one of the chief commanders of the king's forces then raised in the north, for the defence of those parts against the Scots. And the same year his lordship came to an agreement with Maud, Countess of Cambridge, (widow of his half-uncle, John, Lord Latimer, of Danby,) to this effect, viz.:—That if they should, by advice of their counsel, grant unto Sir John Willoughby, Knt., (for the purpose of avoiding litigation,) any of those lands which formerly belonged to the said John, Lord Latimer, that she should give of the said grants, two parts, and he, Lord Latimer, one. And in case of any suit commenced by Sir John Willoughby against them (by reason of his being the next heir of blood of the said John, Lord Latimer,) for any of those lands, she to pay two-third parts, and he the other part of the costs incurred thereby.

Lord Latimer m. Lady Elizabeth Beauchamp, third daughter by his first wife, of Richard, Earl of Warwick, by whom he had, with a daughter, who d. issueless,

> HENRY (Sir), who m. Joanna, daughter of John Bourchier, Lord Berners, and falling at the battle of Edgcot, near Banbury, in the 9th Edward IV., his father still living, left two sons and a daughter, viz.
>
>> RICHARD (Sir), successor to his grandfather.
>> Thomas, of Mathon, m. Anne, daughter of Robert Grenville.
>> Joane, m. to Sir James Ratcliffe.
>
> Thomas, of Shenstone, in the county of Stafford.

Lord Latimer, it appears, in the latter years of his life became an idiot, and King Edward IV., in consequence, committed all his lands and lordships to the care of his nephew, Richard Nevill, Earl of Warwick. He d. on the 30th December, 1469, and was s. by his grandson,

SIR RICHARD NEVILL, second baron, summoned to parliament from 12th August, 1492, to 3rd November, 1529. This nobleman was one of the commanders (1st Henry VII.) of the king's army at the battle of Stoke, wherein John de la Pole, Earl of Lincoln, and his adherents, sustained so signal a defeat. In the 6th Henry VII. he had special livery of all the lands which descended to him, by the death of his grandfather; and the next year he was again a commander in the English army, under the Earl of Surrey, which marched to the relief of Noham Castle, then invested by the Scots; but the besiegers raised the siege and fled, at the approach of the English forces. In the 5th Henry VIII. Lord Latimer acquired high reputation at the battle of Flodden Field, where the Scottish army was totally routed, and King James IV., of Scotland, slain. In the 20th of the same reign he was one of the peers who subscribed the letter to Pope Clement VII., touching the king's divorce from Queen Katherine. His lordship m. Anne,

daughter of Sir Humphrey Stafford, of Grafton, and had issue.

> JOHN, his successor.
> William, of Penwyn, m. Elizabeth, daughter of Sir Giles Greville, Knt., and his issue became extinct in 1631.
> Thomas, m. Mary, daughter and co-heir of Thomas Teys, Esq., and had a son,
>> Thomas.
> Marmaduke, m. Elizabeth, daughter and co-heir of Thomas Teys, Esq., and had issue,
>> Christopher, who d. young.
>> Alianore, who m. Thomas Teys, Esq., of Layer-de-la-Hay.
> George.
> Christopher.
> Margaret,* m. to Edward, son and heir of Robert, Lord Broke.
> Dorothy, m. to Sir John Dawney, Knt.
> Elizabeth.
> Catherine.
> Susanna, m. to Richard Norton, Esq., high sheriff of Yorkshire, 13th Elizabeth. From a younger son of this marriage, Edmund Norton, the Lords Grantley are said to derive.
> Joane.

Lord Latimer d. in 1530, and was s. by his eldest son,

SIR JOHN NEVILL, third baron, summoned to parliament from 5th January, 1534, to 16th January, 1542. This nobleman, upon the insurrection in Yorkshire, temp. Henry VIII., called the Pilgrimage of Grace, was one of those deputed by the rebels (the others were the Lords Scrope, Lumley, and Darcy,) to treat with the Duke of Norfolk, then advancing at the head of an army against them. His lordship m. first, Lady Dorothy de Vere, daughter and co-heir of John, Earl of Oxford, and had issue,

> JOHN, his successor.
> Margaret.

He espoused, secondly, Catherine, daughter of Sir Thomas Parr, of Kendall, Knt., by whom (who

---

* Memorable, also, is this Richard, Lord Latimer, for the dispute he had with Robert, Lord Broke, touching the Barony of Latimer; to which, as next heir in blood to John, Lord Latimer, of Danby, who died s. p., the 9th Henry VI., he claimed a right. But to end the contention, the Lord Broke was informed by an herald, that Sir George Nevill, grandfather to Richard, was created Lord Latimer by a new title, which therefore lineally descended to Richard, by Henry, son and heir of the said George; and that the Lord Broke had made a wrong claim: who should have claimed his style from William Latimer, first created Lord Latimer, of Danby, (the head manor of his barony,) temp. Edward I., on this, the Lord Broke perceiving his error, and having a title of his own, was contented to conclude a match between their children; and Richard suffered a recovery on certain manors and lordships demanded by the Lord Broke; with which adjustment both parties were well satisfied.—BANKS.

became, after his decease, the last wife of KING HENRY VIII.) he had no issue. His lordship d. in 1542, and was s. by his son,

SIR JOHN NEVILL, fourth baron, summoned to parliament from 14th June, 1543, to 6th January, 1561. His lordship m. Lucy, daughter of Henry, Earl of Worcester, and had issue,

    Katherine, m. to Henry Percy, eighth Earl of Northumberland.

    Dorothy, m. to Thomas Cecil, first Earl of Exeter, and had issue,

        WILLIAM, second Earl of Exeter, who left three daughters, viz.

            Elizabeth, m. to Thomas, Earl of Berkshire.

            Diana, m. first, to Thomas, Earl of Elgin, and secondly, to the Earl of Aylesbury.

            Anne, m. to Henry Grey, Earl of Stamford.

    Lucy, m. to Sir William Cornwallis, Knt., and had two sons, who both died s. p., with four daughters, viz.

        Frances, m. to Sir Edward Withipoole.

        Elizabeth, m. to Thomas Sandys, Esq.

        Catherine, m. to Richard Farmer, Esq.

        Dorothy, m. to Archibald, Earl of Argyll.

    Elizabeth, m. to Sir John Danvers, Knt., and had issue,

        SIR CHARLES DANVERS, Knt., attainted in 43rd Elizabeth.

        Sir Henry Danvers, Knt., created EARL OF DANBY. His lordship, who was a Knight of the Garter, d. in 1644 unmarried, when his honours became extinct.

        Sir John Danvers, one of the judges of King Charles I., d. in 1659.

        Elizabeth Danvers m. Thomas Walmsley, Esq., of Dunkelhagh, in the county of Lancaster, and left a daughter,

            Anne, who m. first, William Middleton, Esq., of Stockeld, in the county of York, and secondly, Sir Edward Osborn, Bart., whose son, Sir Thomas Osborn, was created Viscount Latimer, Earl of Danby, and afterwards Marquess of Carmarthen, and DUKE OF LEEDS; all which honours are enjoyed by his descendant, the present Duke of Leeds.

Lord Latimer d. in 1577, when the BARONY OF LATIMER fell into ABEYANCE between his lordship's four daughters and co-heirs, as it still continues with their descendants and representatives.

ARMS.—Gu. a saltier, ar. an annulet for difference.

NEVILL—BARON FURNIVAL.

See FURNIVAL.

NEVILL — BARONS NEVILL OF ESSEX.

By Writ of Summons, dated 22nd January, 1336, 9 Edward III.

Lineage.

In the 8th Henry III.,

HUGH DE NEVILL was constituted principal warden of the king's forests throughout England, and chief justice of the same. This Hugh m. Joane, daughter and co-heir of Warine Fitz-Gerald, by Alice, his wife, daughter and heir of William de Courcy, and paid one hundred marks for livery of the moiety of the manor of Stoke Courcy, with the castle there, and moiety of the knight's fees thereunto belonging, which he had of her inheritance. He founded the priory of Stoke-Courcy, in the county of Devon, and was s. by his son,

JOHN DE NEVILL, who, like his father, was chief warden of the forests. In the 26th Henry III., this John had a military summons to attend the king into France; but in two years afterwards, being convicted of trespassing in the royal forests, he was fined two thousand marks and dismissed from the wardenship with disgrace; which so affected him, that he d. in the same year of a broken heart, at his manor house of Walperfield. He was s. by his son,

HUGH DE NEVILL, a minor at the time of his father's decease, and then removed to Windsor Castle, there to be educated with other of the king's wards. For the custody of this Hugh, and benefit of his marriage, John de Courtenay paid to the crown, 31st Henry III., two thousand five hundred marks. From this Hugh, Dugdale surmises, descended

HUGH DE NEVILL, who was father of

JOHN DE NEVILL, who, in the 9th Edward III., upon doing his homage, had livery of his lands, and was summoned to parliament as a BARON NEVILL, of Essex, from 22nd January, 1336, to 10th March, 1349. His lordship was in the wars of France and Flanders. He d. in 1358, seised of two parts of the manors of Great and Little Wakering, in Essex, for life only, the remainder to William de Bohun, Earl of Northampton; and also jointly with Alice, his wife, the manors of Wethers's-field, Parva, Halyngbury, Chigenhale-Zoin, Chigenhale-Tany, and Peltingdou; the reversion of all which belonged to the said William, Earl of Northampton.

Upon the decease of Lord Nevill without issue, the Barony of NEVILL, OF ESSEX, became EXTINCT.

Note.—The connection, if any, between this family of Nevills, and the NEVILLS, OF RABY, does not appear.

NEVILL—BARON NEVILL.

By Writ of Summons, dated 25th February, 1342, 16 Edward III.

Lineage.

ROBERT DE NEVILL was summoned to parliament, as a BARON, on the 25th February, 1342, but never afterwards—nor is there any thing further known of himself or his family. It is presumed that the barony became, at his decease, EXTINCT.

NEWBURGH — EARLS OF WARWICK.

Creation of William the Conqueror.

Lineage.

The first who bore the title of EARL OF WARWICK, after the Norman conquest, was

HENRY DE NEWBURGH, (so called from the castle of that name in Normandy,) a younger son of Roger de Bellomont, Earl of Mellent. When this eminent person obtained the earldom is not exactly ascertained, but Sir William Dugdale presumes the period to be towards the close of the Conqueror's reign, "for then," saith he, "King William having begirt Warwick with a mighty ditch, for the precinct of its walls, and erected the gates at his own charge, did promote this Henry to the earldom, and annexed thereto the royalty of the borough, which at that time belonged to the crown." But, though Henry de Newburgh was made Earl of Warwick by the first Norman sovereign, he was not invested with all the lands attached to the earldom until the ensuing reign, as we find WILLIAM Rufus, soon after his accession to the throne, conferring upon him the whole inheritance of Turchil de Warwick, a Saxon, who, at the coming of Duke William, had the reputation of earl; and thenceforth the "bear and ragged staff," the device of Turchil's family, derived from the chivalrous Guy, Earl of Warwick, was assumed by the first of the Newburgh dynasty; and it has been continued ever since as a badge of the successive Earls of Warwick. The name of this Henry, Earl of Warwick, appears as a witness to the charter of King Henry I., whereby that prince confirmed the laws of Edward the Confessor, and granted many other immunities to the clergy and laity. His lordship m. Margaret, daughter of Rotrode, Earl of Perch, and had issue, two daughters, whose names are not mentioned, and five sons, viz.

    ROGER, his successor,

    Henry.

    Geffrey.

    Rotrode, Bishop of Eureaux.

    Robert, seneschal and justice of Normandy.
        This Robert was a great benefactor to the abbey of Bec, in which he was afterwards shorn a monk, and d. in 1123.

This Earl Henry commenced imparking WEDGENOCK, near his castle of Warwick, following the example of his sovereign, King Henry, who made the first park that had ever been in England, at WOODSTOCK. His lordship, who was memorable for pious foundations as for military achievements, d. in 1123, and was s. by his eldest son,

ROGER DE NEWBURGH, second Earl of Warwick. This nobleman, in the contest between the Empress Maud and King Stephen, espoused the cause of the former—but his lordship is much more distinguished by his munificent grants to the church

than his martial deeds. He m. Gundred, daughter of William, Earl of Warren, and had issue,

    WILLIAM, } successive earls.
    WALERAN, }

    Henry, who had for his patrimony Gowerland, in Wales—he died s. p.

    Agnes, m. to Geffery de Clinton, the king's chamberlain, son of Geffery, founder of KENILWORTH CASTLE.

The earl d. on the 12th June, 1153, and was s. by his eldest son,

WILLIAM DE NEWBURGH, third Earl of Warwick, who, in the 12th Henry II., upon the assessment of aid for marrying the king's daughter, certified the number of his knights' fees to be one hundred and five, and one half, an enormous fortune at that period. His lordship m. first, Maud, elder daughter and co-heir of William, Lord Percy, and secondly, Margaret D'Eivill, but had no issue. This nobleman was distinguished by the splendour of his style of living, and, like his father, he was a liberal benefactor to the church. He d. in the Holy Land 15th November, 1184, and was s. by his brother,

WALERAN DE NEWBURGH, fourth Earl of Warwick. This nobleman, Dugdale says, "had much ado a great part of his time touching his inheritance; there starting up one who feigned himself to be his brother, Earl William, deceased in the Holy Land, which occasioned him no little trouble and vexation; so that it is thought by some, that the grant which he made to Hubert, Archbishop of Canterbury, then chancellor of England, of the advowson of all the prebendaries belonging to the Collegiate Church, in Warwick, to hold during his life, was to purchase his favour in that weighty business." His lordship m. first, Margery, daughter of Humphrey de Bohun, Earl of Hereford, by whom he had issue,

    HENRY, his successor.

    Waleran, who had the manors of Gretham and Cotismore, in the county of Rutland—died s. p.

    Gundred, who took the veil at Pinley.

He espoused, secondly, Alice, daughter of John de Harcourt, and widow of John de Limesi, by whom he had an only daughter,

    ALICE, m. to William Mauduit, feudal Baron of Hanslape, (great grandson of William Mauduit, chamberlain to King Henry I., by Maud, daughter and heiress of Michael de Hanslape,) and had issue,

        William Mauduit, Baron of Hanslape, who eventually succeeded to the Earldom of Warwick.

        Isabel, m. to William Beauchamp, Baron of Elmeley, from whom the Beauchamps, Earls of Warwick, descended.

The earl d. in 1205, and was s. by his elder son,

HENRY DE NEWBURGH, fifth Earl of Warwick, a minor at his father's decease, and committed to the guardianship of Thomas Basset, of Hedendon, who accordingly had livery of his lands, with the castle of Warwick. His lordship attained majority in the 15th of King John, and, although that monarch had, during his minority, taken away his inheritance of Gower, in Wales, and bestowed it upon William de Braose, his lordship, nevertheless, adhered to the royal cause in all the subsequent conflicts between the crown and the barons, in the reigns of King John and his son Henry III. His lordship *m.* first, Margery, elder daughter and co-heir of Henry D'Oyley, of Hoke Norton, in the county of Oxford, by whom he had issue,

 THOMAS, his successor.

  Margery, *m.* first, to John Mareschal, and secondly, to John de Plassets, both of whom, in her right, assumed the Earldom of Warwick.

The earl *m.* secondly, Philippa, one of the three daughters and heirs of his guardian, Thomas Basset, of Hedendon, but had no issue. This countess, outliving his lordship, paid one hundred marks to King Henry III. that she might not be *compelled* to marry again, but that she might select her own husband, provided he were a loyal subject. She afterwards espoused Richard Siward, a turbulent person, but of a martial disposition from his youth, who took an active part with the barons. From this boisterous soldier her ladyship was, however, eventually divorced. Henry, fifth Earl of Warwick, was *s.* by his son,

THOMAS DE NEWBURGH, sixth Earl of Warwick. This nobleman *m.* Ela, daughter of William Longespee, Earl of Salisbury, but dying without issue the earldom and great inheritance devolved upon his half sister,

 The Lady MARGERY DE NEWBURGH, then wife of

WILLIAM MARESCHALL, who assumed the title of Earl of Warwick, but dying the following year, 1243, without issue, the countess espoused, by especial appointment of the king,

JOHN DE PLESSETS, an eminent Norman, who came to England in the beginning of the reign of Henry III., and achieved a high reputation in the Welsh wars. In the 28th of the same reign this John was made constable of the Tower of London, but not by the title of Earl of Warwick, nor does it appear that he acquired that designation for some time after his union with the heiress of Warwick. He eventually assumed it, however, under a clause in a fine levied in the 31st Henry III., whereby William Mauduit, and Alice, his wife, did, as much as in them lay, confer the earldom upon him for life, so that, if he outlived the countess, his wife, he should not be forced to lay it aside. In the August ensuing the king granting to him licence to fell oaks in the forest of Dene, styles him EARL OF WARWICK, and thenceforward he bore the dignity. His lordship appears to have been one of the first favourites of King Henry III., and to have enjoyed every honour and privilege that monarch could confer. At the commencement of the troubles between Henry and the barons the earl was appointed sheriff of the counties of Warwick and Leicester, but he lived not to witness the issue of those conflicts, for, falling sick in the beginning of the month of February, 1263, he died before its expiration. His lordship left issue by his first wife, (see Plessets, Baron Plessets,) but none by the Countess of Warwick. Lady Warwick survived her husband but a short

time, when the Earldom of Warwick, and the great inheritance of the Newburghs, reverted to the son of her aunt, Lady Alice Mauduit, (refer to issue of Waleran, fourth Earl,) her cousin,

WILLIAM MAUDUIT, who inherited the feudal Barony of Hanslape at the decease of his father in the year 1256, and upon succeeding the Countess of Warwick, assumed the title of Earl of Warwick, in which dignity he had summons to attend the king at Worcester, to march against the Welsh (47th Henry III.). During the civil war between King Henry and the barons his lordship was surprised by a division of the baronial army, under John Giffard, governor of Kenilworth, at his castle of Warwick, and being taken prisoner with his countess, Alice, daughter of Gilbert de Segrave, was detained at Kenilworth until freed by paying a ransom of nineteen hundred marks. The earl *d.* in 1267, without issue, when his sister, Isabel, wife of William Beauchamp, of Elmeley, called the Blind Baron, became his lordship's heir, (see Beauchamp, Earls of Warwick,) and thus terminated the earls of the houses of Newburgh, Plessets, and Mauduit.

 ARMS.—Newburgh, Earls of Warwick.—Losengy or. and az. on a bordure, gu. eight plates.

  Mauduit, Earl of Warwick.—Ar. two bars gu.

NEWMARCH—BARON NEWMARCH.

By Writ of Summons, dated 24th December, 1264.

Lineage.

Amongst the companions of the CONQUEROR was

BERNARD DE NEWMARCH, who won the province of *Brecknock*, in Wales, and settled there. In this place he founded a priory of Benedictine Monks, and, endowing it with extensive lands and revenues, gave it to the abbey of Battel, which his victorious master had founded in commemoration of the CONQUEST. This Bernard *m.* Nesta, or Agnes, daughter of Griffyn, son of Lewelyn, Prince of Wales, and had a son, MABEL, who, by the infamous conduct of his mother, was deprived of his inheritance. She was a woman of licentious habits, and her son having enraged her by offending one of her paramours, she swore before the king that he was not the offspring of her husband, but begotten in adultery. Upon which, Mabel being excluded, the estates devolved to his sister, Sibyl, and in her right to her husband, Miles, Earl of Hereford, whose ~~only surviving child and~~ heiress, BERTHA, inherited eventually the county of Brecknock, and *m.* Philip de Braose.

The next person of this name mentioned, but unascertained how allied, if at all to the last, is

ADAM DE NEWMARCH. And after him comes

WILLIAM DE NEWMARCH, who, in the 10th Richard I., paid £100 for his relief, and £100 for livery of his father's lands. But of him nothing further is stated, than that he became a *leper*, and that Godfrey de St. Martin had custody of his lands in Hampshire. From this William, we pass to

HENRY DE NEWMARCH, who, upon the assessment of the aid for marrying the king's daughter, 12th Henry II., certified his knights' fees to be sixteen, an half, two thirds, and two fifth parts; for which he paid £11 14s. 9d. To this feudal lord succeeded his brother and heir,

JAMES DE NEWMARCH, who d. about the year 1232, leaving two daughters, his co-heirs, viz.

    ISABEL DE NEWMARCH, m. to Ralph Russel, who, in the 8th of Henry III., had livery of her lands, in the counties of Somerset, Wilts, and Gloucester.

    HAWYSE DE NEWMARCH, m. first to John de Botreaux, who, in the 2d of Henry III., had livery of her proportion of her father's property. She espoused, secondly, Nicholas de Moels.

Thus terminated this branch of the family: but there was another, of which was

ADAM DE NEWMARCH, who, joining the baronial standard, temp. Henry III., was summoned to parliament as a BARON, after the battle of Lewes, by the lords who then usurped the government: but he was subsequently made prisoner, and compounded for his estates under the DICTUM DE KENILWORTH. He m. ———, daughter of Roger de Mowbray, and had a son and successor,

ROGER DE NEWMARCH, who was never esteemed a BARON, nor summoned to parliament. In the 11th of Edward II., he had free warren granted him, in certain demesne lands, in the county of York; and left a son, ROGER, but nothing further is recorded of the family.

ARMS.—Gules, five lozenges conjoined in fesse or.

NEWPORT — BARONS NEWPORT, VISCOUNTS NEWPORT, EARLS OF BRADFORD.

Barony,	by Letters	14th October, 1642,
Viscounty,	Patent,	11th March, 1675.
Earldom,		11th May, 1694.

Lineage.

The NEWPORTS were of great antiquity in the county of Salop, and descended from

JOHN DE NEWPORT, a person of some note, in the time of Edward I., from whom, after several generations, sprang

THOMAS NEWPORT, Esq., who marrying Anne, daughter and co-heir of John Ercall, Esq., of High Ercall, in Shropshire, settled there, and made it the designation of his family. From this marriage lineally descended,

SIR RICHARD NEWPORT, Knt., of High Ercall, who, for his eminent services to King Charles I., was elevated to the peerage by that monarch, on the 14th October, 1642, as BARON NEWPORT, of High Ercall. His lordship m. Rachael, daughter of John Levison, Esq., of Haling, and sister and co-heir of Sir Richard Levison, of Trentham, in the county of Stafford, K.B., and had issue,

    FRANCIS, his successor.
296

Andrew, a commissioner of the Customs, d. unmarried.

Beatrix, m. to Sir Henry Bromley, Knt., of Shrawarden Castle, Salop.

Christian, d. unmarried.

Mary, m. first, to John Steventon, Esq., of Dothill, in Shropshire, and secondly, to Francis Forester, Esq., of Watlingstreet, in the same county.

Margaret, m. to Richard Fowler, Esq., of Harnage Green.

Anne, m. to Edward Corbet, Esq., of Longnor

Christian, d. unmarried.

Elizabeth, m. to Henry Powle, Esq., of Williamsthorpe, in the county of Gloucester.

Lord Newport having suffered much during the civil wars, and being aged and infirm, retired into France, and d. there, 8th February, 1650, when he was s. by his eldest son,

FRANCIS NEWPORT, second Baron Newport. This nobleman, in the time of his father, fought valiantly under the Royal banner until 1644, when he was taken prisoner by the parliamentarians. Upon the restoration, he was constituted by King Charles II., first, comptroller, and afterwards, treasurer of the household, and was advanced to the dignity of VISCOUNT NEWPORT, of Bradford, by letters patent, dated 11th March, 1675. His lordship m. Lady Diana Russell, daughter of Francis, Earl of Bedford, and had issue,

    RICHARD, his successor.

    THOMAS, elevated to the peerage, 25th June, 1716, as BARON TORRINGTON, in the county of Devon, died s. p. in 1718, when the BARONY became EXTINCT.

    Francis, d. unmarried.

    Elizabeth, m. first, to Sir Henry Littelton, of Frankley, Bart., and secondly, to Edward Harvey, Esq., of Combe, in the county of Surrey.

    Catherine, m. to Henry, Lord Herbert of Cherbury.

    Diana, m. first, to Thomas, son of Sir Robert Howard, Knt., of Ashstead, in the county of Surrey, and secondly, to William Fielding, brother of Basil, Earl of Denbigh.

    Anne, d. unmarried.

His lordship, after the revolution, was created EARL OF BRADFORD, by letters patent, dated 11th May, 1694. He d. in 1708, and was s. by his eldest son,

RICHARD NEWPORT, second earl. This nobleman m. Mary, daughter of Sir Thomas Wilbraham, Bart., of Woodhey, in the county of Chester, and had issue,

    HENRY,
    RICHARD, successively Earls of Bradford.
    THOMAS,

    William, died s. p.

    Mary, d. unmarried.

    Elizabeth, m. to James Cocks, Esq., in the county of Worcester, and died s. p.

    Anne, m. to Sir Orlando Bridgeman, Bart., and her eldest son,

        SIR HENRY BRIDGEMAN, was created in 1794, BARON BRADFORD. His lordship d. in 1800, and was s. by his son,

ORLANDO BRIDGEMAN, second baron, who was created EARL OF BRADFORD, in 1815. He d. in 1825, and was s. by his son,

George-Augustus, present EARL OF BRADFORD.

Diana, m. to Algernon Coote, Earl of Montrath, in Ireland, by whom she had an only son,

Charles-Henry, Earl of Montrath, who died s. p. in 1802.

His lordship, who was Lord Lieutenant, and Custos Rotulorum, of the county of Salop, d. in 1723, and was s. by his eldest son,

HENRY NEWPORT, third earl, who d. without legitimate issue, in 1734, and was s. by his next brother,

RICHARD NEWPORT, fourth earl, at whose decease, unmarried, the honours devolved upon his brother,

THOMAS NEWPORT, fifth earl. This nobleman d. a lunatic, in 1762, when, leaving no issue, the BARONY OF NEWPORT, of High Ercall, the VISCOUNTY OF NEWPORT, and the EARLDOM OF BRADFORD, became EXTINCT.

ARMS.—Ar. a chevron gu. between three leopards' faces, sa.

NEWPORT — BARON TORRINGTON.

Refer to Newport, EARLS OF BRADFORD (Thomas, second son of the first earl, was created Baron Torrington).

NOEL — BARONS WENTWORTH, VISCOUNTS WENTWORTH, OF WELLESBOROUGH, IN THE COUNTY OF LEICESTER.

Refer to WENTWORTH, Barons Wentworth.

NOEL — BARONS NOEL, OF RIDLINGTON, VISCOUNTS CAMPDEN, BARONS NOEL, OF TITCHFIELD, EARLS OF GAINSBOROUGH.

Barony,		23rd March, 1617.
Viscounty,	by Letters	5th May, 1628.
Barony,	Patent,	3rd February, 1681.
Earldom,		1st December, 1682.

Lineage.

It is evident, say modern genealogists, from the foundation of the PRIORY OF RAUNTON, in Staffordshire, that NOEL, the ancestor of this family, came into England with the CONQUEROR in 1066, and for his services obtained the manors of Ellenhall, Wiverstone, Podmore, Milnece, and other lands, by grants from the new monarch. His eldest son,

ROBERT, was Lord of Ellenhall, &c., and in the reign of Henry I. had a grant of the greatest part of Granborough, in the county of Warwick,

from Lawrence, the prior of Coventry, and the monks of that house. In the reign of Henry II. he founded the priory of Raunton, or Ronton, near Ellenhall, his chief seat, for Canons Regular of St. Augustine. This Robert had two sons,

Thomas, who was sheriff of Staffordshire for seven years, in the reign of Henry II., and for one year upon the accession of Richard I.—left, at his decease, two daughters,

Alice, m. to William Harcourt, of Stanton Harcourt, and had Ellenhall and other estates as her moiety of her father's property.

Joan, m. to William de Dunston, and had for her share Ronton, &c.

Philip.

The second son,

PHILIP NOEL, had Hilcote, in Staffordshire, from his father, and was s. by his son,

ROBERT NOEL, Lord of Hilcote, who m. Joan, daughter of Sir John Acton, Knt., and from this Robert we pass to his lineal descendant,

JAMES NOEL, Esq., of Hilcote, who, in the 5th Henry VIII., was nominated, by act of parliament, one of the justices of the peace for assessing and collecting the poll tax, &c. He m. a daughter of Richard Pole, of Langley, in the county of Derby, by whom he had seven sons, of which ROBERT, the eldest, continued the line at Hilcote, while another branch was founded by the third son,

ANDREW NOEL, Esq., who, at the dissolution of the monasteries, had a grant of the manor and scite of the late preceptory of Dalby-upon-Wold, in Leicestershire, which had belonged to the knights of St. John of Jerusalem, and of the manor of Purybarre, in Staffordshire. In the 26th Henry VIII. he was sheriff of the county of Rutland, as he was afterwards, both in the reign of Edward VI. and in that of Mary. In 1548 he purchased the seat and manor of Brook, in Rutlandshire, and was elected for that county in the first parliament of Queen Mary. He m. first, Elizabeth, daughter and heir of John Hopton, Esq., of Hopton, in Shropshire, and widow of Sir John Perient, by whom he had ANDREW, his heir, and several other children. He espoused, secondly, Dorothy, daughter of Richard Conyers, Esq., of Wakerley, in the county of Northampton, widow of Roger Flower, Esq., by whom he had one son,

JOHN, father of

WILLIAM NOEL, Esq., of Kirby Mallory, high sheriff of Leicester in the 2nd of James I., whose son and successor,

VERE NOEL, Esq., of Kirby Mallory, was created a baronet in 1660, and was ancestor of

SIR EDWARD NOEL, who s. to the Barony of Wentworth in 1762, and was created VISCOUNT WENTWORTH.

Mr. Noel was s. at his decease by the eldest son of his first marriage,

SIR ANDREW NOEL, Knt., of Dalby, in the county of Leicester, who was a person of great note in the time of·Elizabeth, living in such magnificence as to vie with noblemen of the largest fortunes. Fuller, in his Worthies of England, saith, that this Andrew, "for person, parentage, grace, gesture, valour, and many other excellent parts, (amongst which skill in music,) was of the first rank in the court." He was knighted by Queen Elizabeth, and became a favourite, but the expences in which he was involved obliged him to sell his seat and manor at Dalby. Her majesty is said to have made the following distich upon his name—

" The word of denial, and letter of fifty,
" Is that gentleman's name, who will never be
   thrifty."

He was thrice sheriff of the county of Rutland, and member for that shire in several parliaments during the reign of Queen Elizabeth. Sir Andrew m. Mabel, sixth daughter of Sir James Harrington, Knt., and sister and heir of John, Lord Harrington, of Exton, by whom he had issue,

   EDWARD (Sir), his heir.

   Charles, d. unmarried in 1619.

   Arthur.

   Alexander, of Whitwell.

   Lucy, m. to William, Lord Eure.

   Theodosia, m. to Sir Edward Cecil, afterwards
     Lord Wimbledon.

   Elizabeth, m. to George, Earl of Castlehaven,
     in Ireland.

He d. at his seat, BROOK, in Rutlandshire, 9th October, 1607, and was s. by his eldest son,

SIR EDWARD NOEL, Knt., who was created a BARONET 29th June, 1611, and elevated to the peerage, by letters patent, dated 23rd March, 1616-17, as BARON NOEL, of Ridlington, in the county of Rutland. His lordship m. Julian, eldest daughter and co-heir of Sir Baptist Hicks, Bart., which Sir Baptist was created Baron Hicks, of Ilmington, in the county of Warwick, and VISCOUNT CAMPDEN, in Gloucestershire, 5th May, 1628, with remainder to his son-in-law, Lord Noel; and upon his decease, on the 18th of October, in the following year, these dignities were inherited by his lordship. He had issue,

   BAPTIST, his successor.

   Henry, m. Mary, daughter of Hugh Perry,
     Esq., of London, but died s. p.

   Anne.

   Penelope, m. to John, Viscount Chaworth.

   Eleanor.

   Mary, m. to Sir Erasmus de la Fountain, of
     Kirby Bellers, in the county of Leicester.

On the breaking out of the civil war Lord Noel raised forces for the royal cause, and departed this life in his garrison at Oxford, 10th March, 1643, when he was s. by his elder son,

BAPTIST NOEL, second Baron Noel, and third Viscount Campden. This nobleman was as faithful a cavalier as his father, and raised a troop of horse and company of foot for the service of the king. For his estates he was obliged to pay to the sequestrators £9,000 composition, and an annuity of £150 settled on the Teachers of the period. While he sustained the loss of his princely seat at Campden, which had been burnt down by the royal army to prevent its becoming a garrison to the par-

liamentarians. His lordship lived to witness the restoration of the monarchy, and was made lord-lieutenant of the county of Rutland. He m. first, Lady Anne Fielding, daughter of William, Earl of Denbigh, by whom he had no surviving issue. He espoused, secondly, Anne, widow of Edward, Earl of Bath, and daughter of Sir Robert Lovet, Knt., but had only one still-born child. His lordship wedded, thirdly, Hester, daughter and co-heir of Thomas, Lord Wotton, by whom he had issue,

   EDWARD, his successor.

   Henry, of North Luffenham, in Rutlandshire,
     who m. Elizabeth, daughter and heir of Sir
     William Wale, and left an only daughter
     and heir,

     JULIANA, who m. Charles Boyle, Earl of
       Burlington.

   Mary, m. to James, Earl of Northampton.

   Juliana, m. to William, Lord Alington.

   Elizabeth, m. to Charles, Earl Berkeley.

The viscount m. fourthly, Lady Elisabeth Bertie, daughter of Montague, Earl of Lindsey, and had surviving issue,

   BAPTIST, of Luffenham, in the county of
     Rutland, M.P. for that shire, m. Susannah,
     daughter and heir of Sir Thomas Fanshaw,
     and left at his decease, one son,

     BAPTIST, who inherited, as third Earl of
       Gainsborough.

   John, m. Elizabeth, daughter of Bennet, Lord
     Sherrard, and had issue,

     John, M.P. for Northamptonshire, who
       d. unmarried.

     Thomas, m. Elizabeth, widow of Baptist,
       fourth Earl of Gainsborough.

     Bennet, m. to ——, daughter of Adam,
       Esq.

     Elizabeth, d. unmarried.

     Bridget, m. to David, Lord Milsington.

     Alice.

   Catherine, m. to John, Earl of Rutland.

   Martha-Penelope, m. to —— Dormer, Esq.

His lordship died at Exton, 29th October, 1682, and was s. by his eldest son,

EDWARD NOEL, third Baron Noel, and fourth Viscount Campden, who had been created by King Charles II., by letters patent, dated 3rd February, 1681, BARON NOEL, of Titchfield, with remainder, default of male issue, to the younger sons of his father, and was advanced to the dignity of EARL OF GAINSBOROUGH, 1st December, 1682, with similar limitation. His lordship was constituted lord lieutenant of the county of Southampton, warden of the New Forest, and governor of Portsmouth. He m. first, Lady Elizabeth Wriothesley, daughter and co-heir of Thomas, fourth Earl of Southampton, by whom he acquired the lordship of Titchfield, and had issue,

   WRIOTHESLEY-BAPTIST, his successor.

   Frances, m. to Simon, Lord Digby, and d. in
     1684.

   Jane, m. to William, Lord Digby, brother and
     successor of Simon, Lord Digby.

   Elizabeth, m. to Richard Norton, Esq., of the
     county of Southampton.

   Juliana, d. unmarried.

The earl m. secondly, Mary, widow of Sir Robert Worseley, of Appledercomb, in the Isle of Wight, and daughter of the Honourable James Herbert, of Kingsey, in Buckinghamshire. He d. in 1689, and was s. by his son,

WRIOTHESLEY-BAPTIST NOEL, fourth Baron Noel, fifth Viscount Campden, and second Earl of Gainsborough, who m. Catherine, eldest daughter of Fulke Greville, fifth Lord Brooke, and had two daughters, his co-heirs, viz.

> Elizabeth, m. in 1704, to Henry, first Duke of Portland.
> Rachel, m. in 1705-6, to Henry, second Duke of Beaufort.

His lordship d. 21st September, 1690, when all the honours devolved upon his kinsman, (refer to issue of Baptist, third Viscount Campden, by his fourth marriage).

BAPTIST NOEL, Esq., of Luffenham, in the county of Rutland, as third Earl of Gainsborough. His lordship m. Lady Dorothy Manners, daughter of John, Duke of Rutland, and had issue,

> BAPTIST, Viscount Campden, his successor.
> John, d. in 1718.
> James, M.P. for Rutlandshire, d. unmarried, in 1752.
> Susan, m. to Anthony, fourth Earl of Shaftesbury.
> Catherine.
> Mary, d. in 1718.

The earl d. in 1751, and was s. by his son,

BAPTIST NOEL, fourth Earl of Gainsborough. This nobleman espoused Elizabeth, daughter of William Chapman, Esq., by whom, (who m. secondly, Thomas Noel, Esq., grandson of the third Viscount Campden,) he had issue,

> BAPTIST, } fifth and sixth Earls.
> HENRY, }
> Charles, d. young.
> Elizabeth.
> Jane, m. to Gerard-Anne Edwards, Esq., of Welham Grove, in the county of Essex, and her only son, GERARD EDWARDS, having been created a baronet, and assuming the name and arms of NOEL, upon inheriting the estates of his uncle, Henry, sixth Earl of Gainsborough, is the present,
>> SIR GERARD-NOEL NOEL, BART.
> Juliana, m. to George Evans, Lord Carberry, and d. in 1760.
> Penelope, d. young.
> Anne.
> Lucy, m. to Sir Horatio Mann, K.B.
> Mary.
> Susanna.
> Sophia, m. to Christopher Neville, Esq.

His lordship d. 21st March, 1750-51, and was s. by his eldest son,

BAPTIST NOEL, fifth Earl, who died in minority, on his travels, at Geneva, in 1759, when the honours devolved upon his brother,

HENRY NOEL, sixth earl, at whose decease, unmarried, in 1798, the EARLDOM OF GAINSBOROUGH, and ALL the other HONOURS became EXTINCT; while the estates passed to his lordship's nephew, Gerard-Noel Edwards, Esq., who, there-

upon assuming the surname and arms of NOEL, and being created a BARONET, became Sir Gerard-Noel Noel (refer to children of fourth Earl).

ARMS.—Or. fretty gu. a canton erm.

NORTH — BARONS NORTH, OF KIRTLING.

By Writ of Summons, dated 17th February, 1554, 1 Phil. and Mary.

Lineage.

This family sprang from

ROBERT NORTH, Esq., who died in the reign of Edward IV., leaving issue by Alice, his wife, daughter of John Harcourt, Esq., of the county of Oxford,

THOMAS NORTH, Esq., of Walkringham, in the county of Nottingham, who was s. by his son,

ROGER NORTH, Esq., who d. in the reign of Henry VII., leaving two sons, viz.

> THOMAS, who continued the line of Walkringham.

And

ROGER NORTH, Esq. This gentleman m. Christian, daughter of Richard Warcup, of Sconington, near Appleby in Kent, and widow of Ralph Warren, by whom he had issue,

> EWDARD, his successor.
> Joan, m. to William Wilkinson, an Alderman of London.
> Alice, m. to Thomas Burnet, Auditor of the Exchequer.

Mr. North d. in 1509, and was s. by his son,

SIR EDWARD NORTH, a lawyer of eminence, who was appointed, in the 22nd Henry VIII., joint clerk of the parliament, with Sir Bryan Tuke, Knt., but that office they surrendered at the expiration of ten years, Sir Edward being then treasurer of the court of augmentations, of which he became afterwards chancellor. In the 37th Henry VIII., he was sworn of the privy council, having some years before been made one of the king's serjeants, and elected to parliament by the county of Cambridge; and having had large grants of lands from the crown. Thus, he stood high in the favour of King Henry, but as that monarch was remarkable for any thing rather than stability in his attachments, Sir Edward North felt the precariousness of his situation, and was more than ordinarily cautious in his deportment towards his royal master. One morning, however, being sent for at an unusually early hour by the king, (he was then residing at the Charter House,) he was observed by the servant who delivered the command to tremble exceedingly, but he hastened, nevertheless, to obey the summons, and brought the same servant with him who witnessed the subsequent interview between bluff King HAL, and the cautious politic lawyer. Upon their admission, they found the king walking up and down in an apparent state of disquietude, and Sir Edward was received with a scowl that boded no good; it was met, however, by a very still and sober carriage. At last Henry thundered out: " We are informed you have cheated us of certain lands in

Middlesex." To which a simple negative was the reply. " How is it then, did we give those lands to you?" " Yes, Sir," answered Sir Edward, " your majesty was pleased so to do." The king upon this immediately relaxed, and taking Sir Edward into a closet conferred with him confidentially for some time. From that period his influence with his royal master increased, and the king upon his death-bed nominated him one of his executors, with a legacy of £300, and appointed him a member of the council to his son and successor, King Edward VI. Upon King Edward's accession Sir Edward North was re-elected for Cambridgeshire, and continued during the reign one of his majesty's privy council, but upon that king's decease he was one of those who espoused the cause of Lady Jane Grey, yet he appears to have played his cards judiciously, for we find him afterwards not only of the privy council to Queen MARY, but summoned to parliament by that monarch in the 1st year of her reign, as BARON NORTH, *of Kirtling, in the county of Cambridge.* At the accession of Elizabeth, his lordship was constituted one of the commissioners to decide upon the claims of persons who were to perform service at her majesty's coronation, and he was appointed lord lieutenant of Cambridgeshire. His lordship m. first, Alice, daughter of Oliver Squyer, of Southly, near Portsmouth, and widow of Edward Myrffyn, of London, and of John Brigadine, of Southampton. By this lady he got a considerable fortune, and was enabled to purchase the manor of Kirtling. He had issue,

ROGER (Sir), his successor.

Thomas (Sir), m. first, Elizabeth, daughter of —— Colwell, and relict of Robert Rich, Esq., but had no issue. Sir Thomas m. secondly, Mrs. Bridgewater, and had a son, EDWARD.

Christian, m. to William, third Earl of Worcester.

Mary, m. to Henry, Lord Scroop, of Bolton.

His lordship espoused, secondly, Margaret, daughter of Richard Butler, Esq., of London, and widow of Sir David Brooke, Knt., Lord Chief Baron of the Exchequer; which lady survived him. He d. at his residence, called the Charter House, in the suburbs of London, 31st December, 1564, and was s. by his elder son,

SIR RICHARD NORTH, second Baron North, summoned to parliament from 30th September, 1566, to 24th October, 1597. This nobleman, in the time of his father, represented the county of Cambridge in parliament; and in the 18th of Elizabeth was one of the peers who sat upon the trial of Thomas, Duke of Norfolk. In a few years afterwards Queen Elizabeth honoured his lordship with a visit, at his seat in Cambridgeshire, where she was entertained, as Hollinshed relates, not in the least behind any of the best, for a frank house, a noble heart, and well ordered entertainment. In the 28th of the same reign, having accompanied the Earl of Leicester, general of the forces, sent to the assistance of the states, he was for his valour, made a banneret, and acquired reputation in the wars in the Netherlands. He was afterwards ambassador extraordinary from Queen Elizabeth to Charles IX.,

of France, was sworn of her majesty's privy council, and constituted treasurer of the household. His lordship m. Winifred, daughter of Robert, Lord Rich, of Leez, and widow of Sir Henry Dudley, by whom he had (with a daughter, Mary, who d. unmarried) two sons, namely,

JOHN (Sir), member of parliament for the county of Cambridge, m. Dorothy, daughter and co-heir of Sir Valentine Dale, LL.D., and had issue,

DUDLEY, successor to his grandfather.

John (Sir), K.B., gentleman usher of the privy chamber.

Roger, a naval officer of note, and engaged in making nautical discoveries.

Gilbert.

Elizabeth, m. to William, son and heir of Sir Jer. Horsey.

Mary, m. to Sir Francis Coningsby, of South Mymmes, Hertfordshire.

Sir John North d. in the life-time of his father, anno 1597.

Henry (Sir), a military man, who received the honour of knighthood from the Earl of Leicester, in the low countries. He was seated at Milden Hall, in Suffolk, in which he was s. by his elder son,

SIR ROGER NORTH, Knt., of Mildenhall, whose son and successor,

SIR HENRY NORTH, was created a baronet in 1660, and was s. by his son,

SIR HENRY NORTH, second baronet, who died A.D. in 1695; when the baronetcy expired, and the estates devolved upon his sisters as co-heirs, namely,

Thomasine, wife of Thomas Holland, Esq., son and heir of Sir John Holland, Bart., of Quiddenham, in Norfolk.

Dudley, m. to Sir Thomas Cullum, of Haslede, Suffolk.

Lord North d. 3rd December, 1600, and was s. by his grandson,

DUDLEY NORTH, third Baron North, who m. Frances, daughter and co-heir of Sir John Brocket, of Brocket Hall, in the county of Hertford, and dying in his eighty-fifth year, 16th July, 1666, was s. by his eldest son,

DUDLEY NORTH, fourth Baron North, K.B. This nobleman m. Anne, daughter and co-heir of Sir Charles Montagu, Knt., and niece of Henry, Earl of Manchester, by whom he had a numerous family; of which,

CHARLES, his successor, m. Catherine, daughter of William, Lord Grey, of Werke, widow of Sir Edward Mosely, Bart., and was summoned to parliament, in 1673, as LORD GREY, of *Rolleston.*

Francis (Sir), applying himself to the study of the laws, in the Middle Temple, became one of the great law luminaries of England. In 1672, he was appointed solicitor-general, and received the honour of knighthood. In 1673, he became attorney-general, and the next year was constituted Lord Chief Justice of the Court of Common Pleas. Upon the death of the Earl of Nottingham, in 1682, Sir Francis North was appointed LORD KEEPER OF THE GREAT SEAL, and created 27th September, 1683, BARON GUILFORD, of Guilford, in Surrey. His lordship *m.* Frances, second daughter and co-heir of Thomas Pope, Earl of Down, and dying in 1685, was *s.* by his son,

FRANCIS, second Baron Guilford, who *d.* in 1729, and was *s.* by his only son,

FRANCIS, third Baron Guilford, who inherited as seventh Baron North.

Dudley (Sir), *d.* in 1691, leaving two sons,
  Dudley, of Glenham, Suffolk.
  Roger.
John, D.D., clerk of the closet to King Charles II., Prebendary of Westminster, and Master of Trinity College, Cambridge, *d.* unmarried, in 1682.
Montagu, *d.* in 1710, leaving two sons and five daughters.
Roger, of the Middle Temple. This gentleman wrote an historical work, called, *Examen*, and the life of his brother, the Lord Keeper.
Mary, *m.* to Sir William Spring, Bart., of Packenham, in the county of Suffolk.
Anne, *m.* to Robert Foley, Esq., of Stourbridge, in Worcestershire.
Elizabeth, *m.* first, to Robert Wiseman, Knt., LL.D., Dean of the Arches, and secondly, to William, Earl of Yarmouth.
Christian, *m.* to Sir George Wenyeve, of Brettenham, in the county of Suffolk.
His lordship *d.* in 1677, and was *s.* by his eldest son,

CHARLES NORTH, Lord Grey, of Rolleston, as fifth BARON NORTH, who *d.* in 1690, and was *s.* by his eldest son,

WILLIAM NORTH, Lord Grey of Rolleston, and sixth BARON NORTH. This nobleman served under the great Duke of Marlborough, and lost his hand at the battle of BLENHEIM. His lordship *m.* Maria-Margaretta, daughter of Mons. Elmect, receiver-general to the States of Holland, but had no issue. He *d.* in 1734, when the BARONY OF GREY ROLLESTON became EXTINCT, while that of NORTH devolved upon his kinsman,

FRANCIS NORTH, third Baron Guilford, as seventh BARON NORTH (revert to Sir Francis North, second son of Dudley, fourth baron). This nobleman was created Earl of Guilford, in 1752, and the BARONY continued merged in the superior dignity, until the decease, in 1802, of

GEORGE-AUGUSTUS NORTH, third Earl of Guilford, and ninth LORD NORTH (son and successor of Frederick North, second Earl of Guilford, but better known as a statesman, by the title of LORD NORTH). This nobleman, *m.* first, Lady Maria-Frances-Mary Hobart, daughter of George, third Earl of Buckinghamshire, by whom he had one surviving daughter,

MARIA, *m.* to John, second Marquess of Bute. He espoused, secondly, Susan, daughter of the late Thomas Coutts, Esq., the Banker, and had two surviving daughters,
  SUSAN.
  GEORGIANA.
At his lordship's decease the Earldom of Guilford devolved upon his brother, Francis North, as fourth earl, while the BARONY OF NORTH, of *Kirtling*, fell into ABEYANCE, between his daughters, *Maria*, MARCHIONESS OF BUTE, and the *Ladies* SUSAN and GEORGIANA NORTH, as it still continues.

ARMS.—As. a lion passant, or. between three fleur-de-lis ar.

NORTH—BARONS GREY, OF ROLLESTON, IN THE COUNTY OF STAFFORD.

By Writ of Summons, dated 17th October, 1673, 25 Charles II.

Lineage.

The honourable
CHARLES NORTH, son and heir of Dudley, fourth Baron North, and brother of the Lord Keeper North, first Lord Guilford, having espoused Katherine, widow of Sir Edward Moseley, Bart., of Hough, in the county of Lancaster, and daughter of William Grey, of Chillingham, first LORD GREY, OF WERKE, was summoned to parliament in the life-time of his father, 17th October, 1673, as BARON GREY, of *Rolleston*, in the county of Stafford. His lordship *d.* in 1690, and was *s.* by his elder son,

WILLIAM NORTH, sixth Baron North, and second Lord Grey. This nobleman being bred to arms, served under the Duke of Marlborough, in all his campaigns, and had his right hand shot off at the celebrated battle of Blenheim. He was subsequently made lieutenant-general of the forces, and governor of Portsmouth. His lordship *m.* Maria-Margaretta, daughter of Mons. Elmet, receiver-general to the States of Holland; but dying in 1734, without issue, the Barony of North devolved upon his cousin, Frances, third Lord Guilford, and the BARONY OF GREY, OF ROLLESTON, became EXTINCT.

NORTHWODE — BARONS NORTHWODE.

By Writ of Summons, dated 8th January, 1313, 5 Edward II.

Lineage.

In the 42d Henry III., upon the death of REGINALD DE COBHAM, at that time sheriff of Kent, ROGER DE NORTHWODE, one of his executors, accounted to the exchequer, for the sums he had received during his sheriffalty. This Roger *d.* in the 14th of Edward I., whereupon his son and heir,

JOHN DE NORTHWODE, doing his homage, had livery of his lands. This John had summons to attend the king, to advise upon the affairs of the realm, in the 22d of Edward I. He had afterwards, in the same reign, a military summons, and served in the wars of Flanders. At the close of Edward I.'s time, he was sheriff of Kent, and in the beginning of Edward II.'s, we find him in the wars of Scotland, where he was more than once engaged. For his services on those different public occasions, he was summoned to parliament as a BARON, from 8th January, 1313, to 20th March, 1319. In which latter year he d. and was s. by (the son of his deceased son, John de Northwode, by Agnes, daughter of William de Grandison) his grandson,

ROGER DE NORTHWODE, second baron, summoned to parliament, 3d April, 1360. This nobleman served in the wars of Flanders and France, in the 14th and 16th of Edward III. His lordship m. Julian, one of the daughters of Sir Geffery de Say, (he had been in ward to Sir Geffery's widow, Idonea de Say,) and dying about the year 1361, was s. by his son,

SIR JOHN NORTHWODE, third baron, summoned to parliament from 1st June, 1363, to 20th January, 1376. This nobleman was in the French wars of King Edward III., and participated in the glory of that martial reign. He m. Joane, daughter of Robert Hart, of Feversham, in the county of Kent, and dying in 1379, was s. by his son,

ROGER NORTHWODE, fourth baron, but never summoned to parliament. He died s. p. and was s. by his brother,

WILLIAM NORTHWODE, fifth baron, never summoned to parliament. This nobleman (if he ever assumed the dignity) had issue,

    JOHN, his successor.
    Elizabeth, m. to Peter Cat, but of her descendants nothing is known.
    Eleanor, m. to John Adam, whose male descendant, (after five generations,)
        RICHARD ADAM, although married twice, appears to have had no issue. But his brother,
        ROGER ADAM, had five children, viz.—
            Richard.
            John.
            William.
            Bridget, m. to Adam Shepherd.
            Margery, m. to William Hawe.
            Anne.

This William, d. about the year 1406, and was s. by his son,

JOHN NORTHWODE, sixth baron, then ten years of age, who died s. p. in 1416, when the Barony of Northwode fell into ABEYANCE, and is now presumed to be vested in the descendants of the above Roger Adam.

ARMS.—Ermine, a cross ingrailed gules.

NORWICH — BARON NORWICH.

By Writ of Summons, dated 25th February, 1342, 16 Edward III.

Lineage.

GEOFFREY DE NORWICH, the first person of this name upon record, was involved in the baronial

contest with King John, and committed to prison in consequence. From him descended, it is presumed,

WALTER DE NORWICH, who, in the 5th of Edward II., was constituted one of the Barons of the Exchequer, and at the same time obtained a charter of free warren in all his demesne lands. In some years afterwards he was made treasurer of the exchequer, and had a grant of the manors of Dalham and Bradefield, with the advowson of the church of Dalham, in the county of Suffolk. To this learned judge, who d. in 2nd of Edward III., succeeded,

SIR JOHN DE NORWICH, Knt., who was in the wars of Flanders and Scotland, in the reign of Edward III., and was summoned to parliament as a BARON, from 25th February, 1342, to 3d April, 1360. His lordship had grants from the crown for his services, and licence to make castles of his houses at Metyngham, in Suffolk, and at Blackworth, and Lyng, in Norfolk. He d. in 1362, and was s. by his grandson,

JOHN DE NORWICH, second baron, but never summoned to parliament. This nobleman d. in 1374, without issue, when the BARONY OF NORWICH, became EXTINCT. His lordship's estates devolved upon his cousin, KATHERINE DE BREWS, daughter and heir of Thomas de Norwich, his grand-uncle, but that lady taking the veil at Dartford, William de Ufford, Earl of Suffolk, son and heir of Robert de Ufford, Earl of Suffolk, by Margery his wife, sister of Thomas de Norwich, father of the said Katherine, inherited as her heir.

ARMS.—Per pale gu. and az. a lion rampant, ermine.

Note.—From this family is said to have sprung that eminent one seated at Brampton, in the county of Northampton, of which Sir Erasmus Norwich, in the time of William III., m. Annabella, daughter of Thomas Savage, Earl Rivers.

O'BRYEN—VISCOUNT TADCASTER.

By Letters Patent, dated 19th December, 1714.

Lineage.

HENRY O'BRYEN, (descended from the celebrated Hibernian monarch Brian Boiroimhe,) eighth Earl of Thomond, in Ireland, was created a peer of Great Britain, by letters patent, dated 19th October, 1714, in the dignity of VISCOUNT TADCASTER. His lordship m. Lady Elizabeth Seymour, daughter of Charles, Duke of Somerset, but dying without issue in 1741, his Irish honours, with the VISCOUNTY OF TADCASTER, became EXTINCT.

ARMS.—Gu. three lions passant, guardant in pale, or. an ar.

O'BRYEN—BARON THOMOND.

By Letters Patent, dated 2nd October, 1801.

Lineage.

MURROUGH O'BRYEN, first Marquess of Thomond, in Ireland, (see Burke's Dictionary of the Peerage and Baronetage,) was created a peer of the united kingdom, by letters patent, dated 2nd October, 1801, as BARON THOMOND, *of Taplow, in the county of Bucks*. His lordship m. first, Mary, Countess of Orkney, and had several children, of whom one daughter alone survived, namely,

> MARY, who, succeeding her mother, became COUNTESS OF ORKNEY. Her ladyship m. the Hon. Thomas Fitz-Maurice.

The marquess espoused, secondly, Mary, daughter of John Palmer, Esq., of Torrington, in the county of Devon, and niece of Sir Joshua Reynolds, but had no issue. His lordship died in consequence of a fall from his horse, in 1808, when his Irish honours devolved upon his nephew, William O'Bryen, present Marquess of Thomond, while the BARONY OF THOMOND became EXTINCT.

ARMS.—Gu. three lions passant, guardant, in pale, or. and ar.

ODO—EARL OF KENT.

Creation of WILLIAM, *the Conqueror*, anno 1067.

Lineage.

ODO, *Bishop of Bayeux*, in Normandy, half brother of the CONQUEROR, having with "divers monks, and secular clerks," assisted at the battle of HASTINGS, "with their devout prayers and councils," had the whole county of Kent committed to his charge, after the victory, and was joined with William Fitz-Osborne, one of the principal generals, afterwards Earl of Hereford, in the superintendency of the military forces of the kingdom, as well in field as garrison. He was likewise a count palatine, and a JUSTICIARY OF ENGLAND; in the former capacity, he gave laws as a sovereign prince, having power over all other earls and great men, throughout the realm; and in the latter, he was the chief, immediately under the king, of all the courts of justice. In the *Lent* succeeding his coronation, King William having visited Normandy, Odo and Fitz-Osborne were constituted *custodes Angliæ*, or *regents*, during his absence, with authority to erect castles in all fit and proper places. Being thus seated in Kent, and so powerful that no man durst oppose him, he possessed himself of divers lordships, belonging to the Archbishopric of Canterbury; of which, when *Lanfranke* became archbishop, a complaint was made by that prelate to the king, who immediately ordered a convocation of the MEN OF KENT, versed in old customs and usages, to sit upon the matter; a meeting took place, accordingly, at PENENDEN HEATH, *Gaffray*, BISHOP OF CONSTANCE, presiding for the king, when judgment was given in favour of Lanfranke, viz.—"That he should enjoy the lands belonging to his church, as freely as the king himself did enjoy his own demesne lands." In 1074, ODO, and the Bishop of Constance, suppressed the rebellion of the Earls of Hereford and Norfolk; and in four years afterwards, being "*next to the king*" in authority, he was sent at the head of an army, to waste Northumberland, by reason that the men of those parts had risen in insurrection, and murdered WALCHER, *Bishop of Durham*. The Earl of Kent is accused of exercising great cruelty upon this occasion, and of despoiling the Church of Durham of

some rich ornaments, amongst which was a rare crosier of sapphire; certain it is, that his lordship was not proof against the seductions of unlimited power, and that he became, as most persons so invested have become, insolent, proud, and oppressive; the more so, it was alleged, because it had been foretold by certain soothsayers of Rome, that he was destined, at no remote period, to fill the papal chair, then the first throne in Christendom; and nothing short of that splendid dominion could now satisfy his high ambition. He purchased a magnificent palace at Rome, attached the senators to his interest by munificent gifts, and induced *Hugh*, EARL OF CHESTER, by promise of ample rewards, to accompany him with a chosen body of soldiers, into Italy. King William becoming, however, acquainted with the earl's proceedings, hastened back to England, and casually meeting his lordship at the head of this pompous retinue, in the Isle of Wight, upon his route to Normandy, assembled the nobles together, and in a passionate harangue impeached his conduct, concluding by a command that the guards should seize upon the delinquent; but no one daring to do so, on account of his episcopal character, the king himself arrested him; when Odo exclaimed, "That he was a clerk and a minister of God, and that he was amenable to the papal authority, by which alone he could be sentenced." To this the king replied, "I neither sentence any clerk or bishop, but my own earl, whom I made my vicegerent in my kingdom, resolving that he shall give an account of that his trust." Odo was immediately conveyed into Normandy, and during the remainder of the CONQUEROR'S reign, he was kept close prisoner in the Castle of Roan. He obtained his freedom, however, upon the accession of RUFUS, and was restored to his Earldom of Kent, but not to the high office of JUSTICIARY, which had been conferred upon William de Karilepho, Bishop of Durham. This latter circumstance, with the consequent diminution of his authority, kindling his wrath, induced him to fling off his allegiance to Rufus, his benefactor, and to espouse the cause of ROBERT *Curthose*. Hence raising the standard of rebellion in Kent, he wasted, with fire and sword, several towns belonging to the king, and to his great enemy, *Lanfranke*, Archbishop of Canterbury, but he was afterwards besieged by Rufus in Rochester Castle, and forced, upon surrendering, to relinquish ALL HIS HONOURS, and to abjure the kingdom for ever. Thence he repaired to Normandy, where being cordially received by *Curthose*, he had the entire government of the Dukedom committed to his care. He died at Palermo, in 1099, and was there interred. This very eminent personage is thus characterised by one of the old historians—"He was eloquent and magnanimous, courtly and (to speak according to the world) courageous; he was a great honourer of religious men; his clergy he stoutly defended, with his tongue and sword, and furnished his church with rich ornament, as his buildings, vestments, and plate of gold and silver, which he gave thereto, do testifie. In his youth, in regard, he was brother to the duke, he was advanced to the Bishoprick of BAYEUX, in which he sate more than fifty years.

His carnal affections being sometimes predominant, he begot a (natural) son, named JOHN, who was afterwards, by reason of his eloquence and ingenuity, of great esteem in the court of *King* HENRY I., and though he was a person sometimes addicted to secular levities, yet he had a great regard to ecclesiastick matters. The church of our lady, (at BAYEUX,) he built from the ground, and decked it with divers costly ornaments. In the church of St. Vigor, (sometime Bishop of Bayeux,) which is situate near the wall of that city, he placed monks, and constituted the religious and prudent ROBERT DE TUMBALENE, prior there, who, amongst the rest of his learned works, left a short clear and profound comment upon the CANTICLES; which monastery he made a cell to the Abbey of Dijon. He also sent young scholars to LIEGE, and other cities, where he knew the study of philosophy to flourish, and gave them large exhibitions for their support in learning. Of which so by him educated, were THOMAS, *Archbishop of York*, and SAMPSON, his brother, *Bishop of Worcester*; WILLIAM DE ROS, Abbot of FISCAMP, *in Normandy*; THURSTAN, Abbot of GLASTENBURY, and many others then living. So this Bishop ODO, though much entangled with worldly cares, yet he did many laudable things; and what he got indirectly, he bestowed upon the church and poor. Howbeit, at length leaving the world, he took a journey to ROME, with *Duke* ROBERT, his nephew, and died at PALERMO, in SICILY, and had a sepulture in the church of our lady there."

The Earl of Kent held after the conquest in England, by the gift of his brother, no less than FOUR HUNDRED AND THIRTY-NINE LORDSHIPS. In Kent, one hundred and eighty-four; in Essex, thirty-nine; in Oxfordshire, thirty-two; in Herefordshire, twenty-three; in Buckinghamshire, thirty; in Worcestershire, two; in Bedfordshire, eight; in Northamptonshire, twelve; in Nottinghamshire, five; in Norfolk, twenty-two; in Warwickshire, six, and in Lincolnshire, seventy-six.

ARMS.—Gu. a lion rampant ar. debruised with a crosier's staff gules.

OGLE—BARONS OGLE.

By Writ of Summons, dated 26th July, 1461, 1 Edward IV.

Lineage.

, This family, one of great antiquity in the county of Northumberland, assumed its surname from the Lordship of OGGIL, its principal seat, and

ROBERT OGLE, in the 15th Edward III., obtained licence to make a castle of his manor house there. In four years afterwards this Robert Ogle, upon the incursion of the Scots under the command of William Douglas, when they burnt Carlisle, Penrith, and other places, accompanied John de Kirkaby, then Bishop of Carlisle, in a charge which he made, upon a strong party of these bold invaders, and encountering their chief commander, wounded him in the side with his lance, being severely wounded himself; while the bishop was unhorsed, but gallantly recovering his saddle, escaped unhurt. Robert

Ogle m. Annabella, daughter and heir of Sir Robert Hephall, (by Cisily, daughter and heir of Sir Gilbert Chartney, Knt.,) and was *s.* by his son,

SIR ROBERT OGLE, who m. Helen, daughter and heir of Sir Robert Bertram, Knt.,[a] feudal Baron of Bothall, by whom he acquired a considerable accession of property, and had a son, ROBERT, who predeceased him, leaving a son, ROBERT. Sir Robert *d.* in the 36th Edward III., and was *s.* by his grandson,

SIR ROBERT OGLE. This feudal lord having been made prisoner by the Scots, in the 2d of Henry IV., obtained a grant from the king, of one hundred marks, towards the payment of his ransom; after which, in the 6th of the same reign, he served in the garrison of Berwick-upon-Tweed, under John Plantagenet, afterwards Duke of Bedford, then governor thereof. The next year, upon the death of David de Holgrave, the last husband of his grandmother, HELEN, he had livery, upon doing his homage, of the castle and manor of BOTHALL. Whereupon being thus possessed of that manor and castle, as also of the manor of Hephall, and the town of Lour-bottil, he entailed the same upon the heirs male of his body, upon condition that every such heir-male should bear the surname of Ogle, with the arms of Ogle and Bertram quarterly. He m. Joan, daughter and co-heir of Sir Alexander de Heton, Knt., and had livery of her property in the 19th of Richard II. He *d.* in 1409, and was *s.* by his eldest son,

. ROBERT OGLE, who forcibly possessed himself of the castle and manor of BOTHALL, which had been settled upon John, his brother, who bore the name of BERTRAM. Whereupon complaint being made in parliament, it was ordered that a writ should be sent to the sheriff of Northumberland, to require all those who then held that castle, to depart thence; and to command the said Robert to appear at Westminster by a certain day, to make answer to the king, for this misdemeanour. In the 5th of Henry V., he was constituted sheriff of Northumberland; and in the 2d of Henry VI., he was joined with *Henry*, Earl of Northumberland, and other great men, in those parts, to conduct James, King of Scotland, from Durham, into his own realm; that prince, being then, upon hostages

---

a ROBERT BERTRAM, temp. Henry II., certified his knights' fees to be three in number, by which service his son,

ROBERT BERTRAM, held the BARONY OF BOTHALL, in capite of the king.

From this Robert sprang.

ROBERT BERTRAM, feudal lord of Bothall, who, in the reign of Edward III., was sheriff of Northumberland, and sheriff of Newcastle, and was one of the chief northern barons who engaged the Scots at Durham, where he was so fortunate as personally to make William Douglas prisoner. He m. Margaret, daughter and co-heir of Constance, the wife of William Felton, and left at his decease, an only daughter and heiress.

HELEN BERTRAM, who m. Sir Robert Ogle, as in the text.

given, enlarged after an imprisonment of some years. He departed this life in the 15th of Henry VI., leaving issue,* by his wife, Maud, daughter of Sir Robert Grey, of Horton, in Northumberland, according to Collins, eight daughters, married to persons of the first rank in the county, and three sons, viz.

  ROBERT, his successor.

  John (Sir).

  William (Sir), from whom the OGLES of Kirkley, in the county of Northumberland, derive, and the OGLES of Worthy, in Hampshire, BARONETS (see *Burke's Dictionary of the Peerage and Baronetage*).

He was *s.* by his eldest son,

SIR ROBERT OGLE, who, in the 16th Henry VI., was made sheriff of Northumberland, and in the 38th of the same reign, was in a commission to treat regarding a truce with the Scots. In the 1st of Edward IV., he was made warden of the east marches, and in consideration of his good services, had a grant of the offices of steward and constable of ALNWICK, and other castles, in Northumberland. Shortly after this, he was summoned to parliament as a BARON (from 26th July, 1461, to 7th September, 1469), and in the same year, he obtained from the crown a grant in special title of the Lordship of Redisdale, and castle of Herbotel, then vested therein by the attainder of Sir William Talboys. In the 9d of Edward IV., his lordship was with the king in arms against the Lancastrians, and assisting at the siege of Bamburgh Castle, was made governor of that fortress upon its surrender. He *m.* Isabel, daughter and heir of Alexander de Kirkeby, of Kirkeby, in the county of Lancaster, eldest son of Sir Richard de Kirkeby, Knt., by whom he had issue,

  OWEN, his successor.

  Isabel, who *m.* first, Sir John Heron, of Chipchas, Knt., and secondly, John Wodrington.

His lordship *d.* in 1469, and was *s.* by his son,

OWEN OGLE, second baron, summoned to parliament from 15th November, 1482, to 15th September, 1485. This nobleman was in the battle of Stoke, 2d of Henry VII., on the part of the king against the Earl of Lincoln, and his adherents, and is the same that Polydore Virgil calls by mistake, George. In two years afterwards, he marched with the rest of the northern nobles, under Thomas, Earl of Surrey, to relieve NORHAM CASTLE, then besieged by the Scots. His lordship *m.* Eleanor, daughter of Sir William Hilton, Knt., and was *s.* by his only son,

RALPH OGLE, third baron, summoned to parliament from 17th October, 1509, to 28th November, 1511. This nobleman *m.* Margaret, daughter of Sir William Gascoigne, Knt., and had issue,

---

  * Dugdale enumerates his issue thus:—

  ROBERT, his successor.

  Margaret, *m.* to Sir Robert de Hasbottle, Knt.

  Anne, *m.* to Sir William Heron, Knt.

  Constance, *m.* to Sir John Milford, Knt.

  Joane, *m.* to —— Maners.

  ROBERT, his successor.

  William (Sir), *m.* Margaret, daughter of John Delaval, Esq., and had issue,

    James, of Cawsey Park.

    John, of Bedsyde.

  John.

  Anne, *m.* to Humphrey, son and heir of Sir William Lisle, Knt.

  Dorothy, *m.* first, to Sir Thomas Forster, and secondly, to Sir John Grey, of Horton, Knt.

  Margery, *m.* to George Harbottle, Esq.

His lordship *d.* in 1512, and was *s.* by his eldest son,

ROBERT OGLE, fourth baron, summoned to parliament from 23d November, 1514, to 3d November, 1529. This nobleman was in the vanguard of the English army at the battle of FLODDEN, where the King of Scotland sustained so signal a defeat, but continuing in the Scottish wars, he fell eventually at PAUNEERHAUGH, in 1529. His lordship *m.* Anne, daughter of Thomas, son and heir of George, Lord Lumley, by whom he had three sons, ROBERT, George, and John, and was *s.* by the eldest,

ROBERT OGLE, fifth baron, but never summoned to parliament. This nobleman *m.* first, Dorothy, daughter of Sir Henry Widderington, by whom he had issue,

  ROBERT, his successor.

  Margery, *m.* to Gregory Ogle, Esq., of Chapington, in Northumberland, (descended from Sir W. Ogle, brother of the first lord,) and had two sons,

    John.

    Robert.

His lordship espoused, secondly, Jane, daughter of Sir Cuthbert Ratcliffe, Knt., of Chartington, and had,

  CUTHBERT, successor to his brother.

  Thomas, *d. s. p.*

  Margaret, *m.* to Robert Wodrington, third son of Sir John Wodrington, Knt.

Lord Ogle fell at the battle of HALIDON, in 1544, and was *s.* by his eldest son,

ROBERT OGLE, sixth baron, summoned to parliament 14th August, 1553, to 5th November, 1558. His lordship *m.* Joan, daughter and heir of Sir Thomas Maleverer, Knt., of Allerton Maleverer, in the county of York, but dying *s. p.* in 1562, was *s.* by his half brother,

CUTHBERT OGLE, seventh baron, summoned to parliament from 11th January, 1563, to 17th October, 1601. This nobleman espoused Catherine, daughter and co-heir of Sir Reginald Carnaby, Knt., and had issue,

  Joane, *m.* to Edward Talbot, son of George, sixth Earl of Shrewsbury, and afterwards eighth Earl of Shrewsbury himself, but died *s. p.* in 1627.

  Catherine, *m.* to Sir Charles Cavendish, Knt., of Welbeck, in the county of Nottingham.

His lordship *d.* in 1597, and the BARONY OF OGLE fell into ABEYANCE between his two daughters, and so continued until the decease of JOANE, *Countess of Shrewsbury*, the elder, without issue, in 1627, when it was called out in favour of the younger;

CATHERINE CAVENDISH, relict of Sir Charles Cavendish, who obtained especial letters patent under the great seal, from King Charles I., dated 4th December, 1628, declaring her ladyship to be BARONESS OGLE, and ratifying the dignity to her heirs for ever. Her ladyship d. the next year, and was s. by her only surviving son,

SIR WILLIAM CAVENDISH, K.G., who had been created Baron Ogle, and Viscount Mansfield, in 1620. (For the particulars of this nobleman, afterwards so celebrated in the civil wars, as DUKE OF NEWCASTLE, refer to Cavendish, Baron Ogle, Duke of Newcastle, &c.)

His grace d. in 1676, and was s. by his only son,

HENRY CAVENDISH, second Duke of Newcastle, &c., and ninth BARON OGLE. This nobleman m. Frances, daughter of William, second son of Robert Pierpoint, Earl of Kingston, by whom he had a son, HENRY, who died s. p. in 1680, and five daughters, viz.

Elizabeth, m. first, to Christopher Monk, Duke of Albemarle, and secondly, to Ralph, Duke of Montagu, but d. issueless.

Frances, m. to John, second Earl of Breadalbane, and died s. p.

Margaret, m. to John Holles, Earl of Clare, afterwards created Duke of Newcastle, by whom she had an only daughter,

LADY HENRIETTA-CAVENDISH HOLLES, who m. Robert Harley, second Earl of Oxford, and left an only daughter,

LADY MARGARET CAVENDISH HARLEY, who espoused William Bentinck, second Duke of Portland, and was mother of

WILLIAM, third duke, father of William, present DUKE OF PORTLAND.

Catherine, m. to Thomas, sixth Earl of Thanet, and had five daughters, to survive, viz.

Catherine, m. to Edward, Viscount Sondes, heir apparent to the Earl of Rockingham.

Anne, m. to James, fifth Earl of Salisbury, and was great grandmother of James, the present MARQUESS OF SALISBURY.

Margaret, m. to Thomas Coke, Earl of Leicester, but died s. p.

Mary, m. to Anthony Grey, Earl of Harold, and secondly, to John, Earl of Gower.

Isabella, m. first, to Lord Nassau Paulett, and secondly, to Sir Francis Blake-Delaval, K.B.

Arabella, m. to Charles, Earl of Sunderland, and left an only daughter,

Frances, who m. Henry, fourth Earl of Carlisle.

His grace d. in 1691, when all his honours became extinct, except the BARONY OF OGLE, which fell into ABEYANCE, and still continues amongst the representatives of those who left issue.

ARMS.—Ar. a fesse between three crescents gu.

OLDCASTLE—BARON COBHAM.

By Writ of Summons, dated 8th January, 1313, 6 Edward II.

Lineage.

For an account of this nobleman, the celebrated LOLLARD leader, SIR JOHN OLDCASTLE, Baron Cobham, refer to Cobham, BARONS COBHAM.

ORREBY—BARON ORREBY.

By Writ of Summons, dated 4th March, 1309, 2 Edward II.

Lineage.

In the 22nd Henry II.

HERBERT DE ORREBY, (son of Alard de Orreby,) with Agnes, his wife, founded the priory of Hagneby, in the county of Lincoln. To this Herbert succeeded,

JOHN DE ORREBY, who d. in the 41st Henry III., and next after him we find

FULKE DE ORREBY, justice of Chester in the 44th Henry III., to whom the custody of several castles was then committed. This Fulke d. soon after, for the next year

THOMAS DE ORREBY was made justice of Chester upon his decease. This Thomas was s. by

JOHN DE ORREBY, who, in the 31st Edward I., was in the Scottish wars, and was summoned to parliament as a BARON in the 2nd, 3rd, and 4th of Edward II. His lordship d. in 1317 issueless, when the BARONY OF ORREBY became EXTINCT, and his lands were divided amongst his next heirs, namely, Edmund de Somervill, Alured de Sulney, and Robert de Willoughby.

ARMS.—Ermine, five chevronels g. on a canton, of the second a lion passant or.

PAGET—BARONS BURTON, EARLS OF UXBRIDGE.

Barony, } by Letters { 31st December, 1711.
Earldom, } Patent, { 19th October, 1714.

Lineage.

"The first mention I find," writes Sir William Dugdale, "of any bearing this name, who arrived to the dignity of the peerage, is

WILLIAM PAGET, a person endowed with excellent parts, as may seem from his ascent from so low a condition to those high preferments, whereunto, by sundry degrees, he attained; being son to ——— Paget, one of the serjeants at mace in the city of London, who was born near Wednesbury, in Staffordshire, of mean parentage, where there were some of that generation, till of late years, remaining." In the 23rd of Henry VIII. this William Paget, through his great abilities alone, obtained the appointment of clerk of the signet—in a few years afterwards he was made clerk of the council;

he next became clerk of the privy seal, and then clerk of the parliament, having the latter office conferred upon him for life. He subsequently received the honour of knighthood, was employed by *King Henry VIII.* upon several diplomatic occasions of high importance, and appointed one of his majesty's executors, and of the council to his son, by that monarch upon his death-bed. In the 2nd year of the new reign, (Edward VI.,) Sir William Paget had a grant in fee from the crown of EXETER HOUSE, (formerly belonging to the bishops of that see,) with a parcel of ground lying within the garden of the Middle Temple, adjoining thereto; which mansion he rebuilt for his own residence, and called it PAGET HOUSE. But it did not retain that designation for any length of time, it being afterwards called LEICESTER HOUSE, and then ESSEX HOUSE. In the 4th of Edward VI., Sir Edward was accredited ambassador extraordinary to the *Emperor* Charles V., and became so great a favourite with that monarch, that his imperial majesty was heard to say, " that Sir Edward Paget deserved to be a king as well as to represent one." Once, too, as the English ambassador came to court, the emperor observed, " Yonder is the man to whom I can deny nothing." At another time his majesty remarked, that England sent three sorts of ambassadors to him; the first was WOLSEY, whose great retinue promised much, but he did nothing; the second, Morisin, promised, and did much; the third, Paget, promised nothing, and did all. In the same year, Sir Edward being then a KNIGHT of the GARTER, was constituted comptroller of the king's household; made chancellor of the Duchy of Lancaster, and summoned to the House of Lords as BARON PAGET, *of Beaudesert, in the county of Stafford,* by writ, dated 23rd January, 1552: after which he was sent with the Earl of Bedford and Sir John Mason again to treat of peace with the French. Notwithstanding, however, these eminent services, he was accused by his enemies upon the fall of the PROTECTOR SOMERSET of divers offences, and committed to the Tower, deprived of the insignia of the Garter, and fined £6000, two of which were remitted, on condition that the other four were paid within a year. At the demise of King Edward his lordship espousing the cause of Mary, rode post with the Earl of Arundel to announce the event to her majesty, and that she had been proclaimed in the city of London; for which loyal proceeding he was ever afterwards highly esteemed by her majesty, and in the 3rd year of her reign was made lord privy seal. His lordship *m.* Anne, daughter and heir of Henry Preston, Esq., of the county of Lancaster, and had issue,

HENRY (Sir), his successor.
THOMAS, who succeeded as third lord.
Charles. This gentleman was attainted with his brother, Thomas, Lord Paget. Hollingshed relates that the Charles Paget was principal agent for the Roman Catholics, as it was proved on examination of the Earl of Northumberland's case, viz.: that in September, 1583, he came privately beyond sea to the Earl of Northumberland, at Pet-

wort, where the Lord Paget met him; and that on Throgmorton's being committed to the Tower, the Earl of Northumberland prevailed on the Lord Paget to quit the realm, and provided him a ship on the coast of Sussex, wherein he embarked.
Etheldreda, *m.* to Sir Christopher Allen, Knt.
Eleanor, *m.* first, to Jerome Palmer, Esq., and secondly, to Sir Rowland Clerk, Knt.
Grisild, *m.* first, to Sir William Waldegrave, and secondly, to Sir Thomas Rivet, Knt.
Joan, *m.* to Sir Thomas Kitson, Knt.
Dorothy, *m.* to Sir Thomas Willoughby, son of Sir Henry Willoughby, of Woollaton, in the county of Notts.
Anne, *m.* to Sir Henry Lee, Knt.

He *d.* in 1563, and was *s.* by his eldest son,
SIR HENRY PAGET, second baron, summoned to parliament 30th September, 1566. His lordship[*] *m.* Catherine, daughter of Sir Henry Lee, Knt., and had an only daughter,

ELIZABETH, *m.* to Sir Henry Lee, Knt. This lady left no issue; her uncle succeeded to the barony at her decease. But in this matter there is a good deal of confusion. Collins says, her ladyship *d.* 29th June, 1571, but Thomas Paget, the third baron, appears to have been summoned on the 4th of the previous April.

He *d.* in 1561, and was *s.* by his daughter,
ELIZABETH LEE, as Baroness Paget, at whose decease succeeded her uncle,
THOMAS PAGET, third baron, summoned to parliament from 4th April, 1571, to 6th January, 1581. This nobleman, being a zealous Roman Catholic, was obliged, in the reign of Elizabeth, to seek personal security in France, but he was attainted in parliament with his brother, Charles, as a wellwisher to the Queen of Scots; when the BARONY OF PAGET became FORFEITED, and his lands being confiscated, the Earl of Leicester got a grant of PAGET HOUSE. His lordship *m.* Nazaret, daughter of Sir Henry Newton, Knt., and left at his decease (anno 1589, at Brussels,) an only son,
WILLIAM PAGET, who was with the Earl of Essex in the memorable attack upon Cadiz, 39th Elizabeth, and being restored to the lands and honours forfeited by his father, was summoned to parliament as BARON PAGET from 5th November,

---

* William, Lord Paget, of Beaudesert, was seised in fee of the Baronies of Longden and Haywood, and of, and in the manors of Beaudesert, Longden, &c., and being so seised, by fine, 1st Mary, entailed the manors and baronies aforesaid, to him and the heirs male of his body issuing; and anno, 5th of Elizabeth, died, leaving Henry, his son and next heir male, which Henry entered into the baronies and lands aforesaid, by virtue of the aforesaid fine, and died thereof seised, 11th Elizabeth, leaving Elizabeth, his only daughter and heir; after whose death, Thomas Paget, brother and heir male of the said Henry, entered into the baronies and manors aforesaid, and was summoned to the parliament by virtue of the aforesaid fine.—COLLINS' PARLIAMENTARY PRECEDENTS.

1605, to 7th March, 1628. His lordship m. Lettice, daughter and co-heir of Henry Knolles, Esq., a younger son of Sir Henry Knolles, K.G., by whom he had issue,

WILLIAM, his successor.

Henry,
Thomas, } both d. unmarried.

Elizabeth, m. to Sir William Hicks, Bart., of Buckholt, Essex.

Dorothy, d. unmarried.

Catherine, m. to Sir Anthony Irby, Knt., of Boston, in the county of Lincoln, ancestor of the present LORD BOSTON.

Anne, m. first, to Sir Simon Harcourt, Knt., of Stanton Harcourt, in the county of Oxford, and secondly, to Sir William Waller, Knt., of Osterley Park, Middlesex, the celebrated parliamentary general.

He d. in 1629, and was s. by his eldest son,

WILLIAM PAGET, fifth baron, summoned to parliament from 13th April, 1639, to 8th May, 1661. His lordship was made a Knight of the Bath at the coronation of King Charles I. He m. Lady Frances Rich, daughter of Henry, Earl of Holland, and had issue,

WILLIAM, his successor.

Henry, who settled in Ireland, m. Miss Sandford, daughter of ⸺ Sandford, Esq., of Sandford, in the county of Salop, and had (with a daughter, Dorothy, who m. Sir Edward Irby, Bart.) a son,

THOMAS, a brigadier general in the army, who m. Mary, daughter and co-heir of Peter Whitcombe, Esq., of Great Braxted, in Essex, by whom he had an only daughter and heiress,

CAROLINE PAGET, who m. Sir Nicholas Bayley, Bart., and had a son,

HENRY BAYLEY, who inherited as ninth BARON PAGET. His lordship assumed the surname and arms of PAGET, and was created EARL OF UXBRIDGE. He was father of Henry-William, present MARQUESS OF ANGLESEY.

Thomas, d. unmarried.

Isabel, d. unmarried.

Lettice, m. to Richard Hampden, Esq., of Great Hampden, Bucks.

Elizabeth, d. unmarried.

Frances, m. to Rowland Hunt, Esq., of Boreaton, in the county of Salop.

Penelope, m. to Philip Foley, Esq., of Prestwood, Staffordshire.

Diana, m. to Sir Henry Ashurst, Bart.

Anne, d. unmarried.

His lordship d. in 1678, and was s. by his eldest son,

WILLIAM PAGET, sixth baron, summoned to parliament 6th March, 1679. This nobleman m. first, Frances, daughter of Francis Pierpoint, and grand-daughter of Robert, Earl of Kingston, by whom he had two sons,

William, who d. unmarried in his father's lifetime.

HENRY, successor to the title.

His lordship espoused, secondly, Isabella, daughter of Sir Anthony Irby, Knt., of Boston, by whom he had another son, William, who d. young. This nobleman, " the reputation of whose great abilities (says Banks) " will last as long as the memory of that celebrated peace of Carlowitz, concluded in 1698, shall remain in history," d. at an advanced age, 25th February, 1713, and was s. by his son,

HENRY PAGET, Baron Burton, (a dignity to which he had been raised in the life-time of his father, by letters patent, dated 31st December, 1711,) as seventh Baron Paget. His lordship was advanced to the EARLDOM OF UXBRIDGE on 19th October, 1714. He filled many high and important offices, but resigned all his employments in 1715. His lordship m. first, Mary, daughter and co-heir of Thomas Catesby, Esq., of Whiston, in Northamptonshire, and had a son,

THOMAS-CATESBY, Lord Paget. This nobleman, who was colonel of a regiment of foot, d. in the life-time of his father, anno 1742, leaving by his wife Lady Elizabeth Egerton, daughter of John, Earl of Bridgewater,

HENRY, who s. as second Earl of Uxbridge.

The earl espoused, secondly, Elizabeth, daughter of Sir Walter Bagot, Knt., but had no issue. He d. in 1743, and was s. by his grandson,

THOMAS-CATESBY PAGET, second Earl of Uxbridge. This nobleman d. unmarried in 1769, when the Barony of Paget devolved upon his kinsman, Henry Bayley, Esq., as ninth baron, (refer to issue of Henry, second son of fifth lord,) while the BARONY OF BURTON and EARLDOM OF UXBRIDGE became EXTINCT.

ARMS.—Sa. on a cross engrailed betw. four eagles displayed, ar. five lions passant of the first.

PARKER—BARONS MORLEY, BARONS MONTEAGLE.

Barony of Morley, } by Writ of Summons, { dated 29th Dec., 1299, 28 Edward I.

Barony of Monteagle, } { dated 23rd Nov., 1514, 6 Henry VIII.

Lineage.

ROBERT MORLEY, Baron Morley, (a dignity created by writ of Edward I., dated as above,) d. in 1442, leaving a daughter and heiress,

ALIANORE MORLEY, who m.

SIR WILLIAM LOVEL, second son of William, Lord Lovel, of Tichmersh; which William was summoned to parliament in right of his wife, as Lord Morley. He d. in 1476, and was s. by his son,

HENRY LOVEL, Lord Morley, but never summoned to parliament. This nobleman d. in 1489 issueless, when his sister,

ALICE LOVEL, became his heir. Her ladyship espoused, first,

SIR WILLIAM PARKER, standard bearer, and privy councillor to King Richard III., and secondly, Sir Edward Howard, second son of Thomas, Duke of Norfolk: by the latter she had no issue, but by the former she had a son,

SIR HENRY PARKER, who was summoned to parliament as BARON MORLEY from 15th April, 1593, to 28th October, 1555. This nobleman was one of the peers who signed the letter, 22nd HENRY VIII., to the Pope, regarding the king's divorce from Queen Katherine. His lordship m. Alice, daughter of Sir John St. John, of Bletsho, in the county of Bedford, and had an only son,

> HENRY, who was created a Knight of the Bath at the coronation of Queen Anne Boleyn, and d. in the 5th Edward VI., his father then living. He m. first, Grace, daughter of John Newport, Esq., and had issue,
>
>> HENRY, successor to his grandfather.
>>
>> Jane, m. to George Boleyn, Lord Rochford.
>>
>> ———, m. to Sir John Shelton, Knt.
>
> Sir Henry Morley m. secondly, Elizabeth, daughter and heir of Sir Philip Calthorpe, Knt., but had no issue.

In Walpole's Catalogue of Noble Authors, Lord Morley is mentioned as a voluminous writer, and Anthony Wood says, he was living, an ancient man, highly esteemed by the nobility, in the latter end of Henry VIII.'s reign. He d. in the time of Philip and Mary, anno 1556, and was s. by his grandson,

HENRY PARKER, Lord Morley, summoned to parliament from 20th January, 1558, to 8th May, 1572. This nobleman m. Lady Elisabeth Stanley, daughter of Edward, Earl of Derby, and had issue,

> EDWARD, his successor.
>
> Alice, m. to Sir Thomas Barington, Knt.
>
> Mary, m. to Sir Edward Leventhorpe, Knt.

His lordship was s. at his decease by his son,

EDWARD PARKER, Lord Morley, summoned to parliament from 26th January, 1581, to 5th April, 1614. This nobleman was one of the peers that sat in judgment upon Mary, Queen of Scots; on Philip, Earl of Arundel, and on Robert, Earl of Essex, all in the reign of Elisabeth; his lordship m. Elizabeth, only daughter and heiress of William Stanley, Baron Monteagle, and had issue,

> WILLIAM, his successor.
>
> Henry.
>
> Charles.
>
> Mary, m. to Thomas Abington, Esq., of Hinlip.
>
> Elizabeth, m. to Sir Alexander Barlow, of Barlow, in Lancashire.
>
> Frances, m. to Christopher Danby, Esq., of Leighton, in the county of York.

He d. in 1618, and was s. by his eldest son,

WILLIAM PARKER, who had been summoned to parliament in the life-time of his father, in right of his mother, as BARON MONTEAGLE, and was summoned as LORD MORLEY AND MONTEAGLE from 30th January, 1691, to 4th November in the same year. This is the nobleman to whom the very remarkable letter was addressed, by which the gunpowder-plot was fortunately discovered. It is said to have been written by his sister, Mary, wife of Thomas Abington, (or Habington,) of Hinlip, which Thomas had been cofferer to Queen Elizabeth. Abington was concerned in many projects for the release of Mary, Queen of Scotland, and contrived various places of concealment in his old

mansion at Hinlip. He was condemned to die for concealing Garnet and Oldcorn, the Jesuits, but was pardoned, at the intercession of his wife and Lord Monteagle.

Lord Morley and Monteagle m. Elizabeth, daughter of Sir Thomas Tresham, Knt., and had issue,

> HENRY, his successor.
>
> William.
>
> Charles.
>
> ' Frances, d. a nun.
>
> Katherine, m. to John Savage, Earl Rivers.
>
> Elizabeth, m. to Edward Cranfield, Esq.

His lordship d. in 1622, and was s. by his eldest son,

SIR HENRY PARKER, K.B., summoned to parliament as BARON MORLEY AND MONTEAGLE from 12th February, 1624, to 3rd November, 1639. His lordship m. Philippa, daughter and co-heir of Sir Philip Carrel, of Shipley, in Surrey, and dying in 1655, was s. by his only child,

THOMAS PARKER, summoned to parliament as BARON MORLEY AND MONTEAGLE from 8th May, 1661, to 19th May, 1685. His lordship m. Mary, daughter of Henry Martin, Esq., of Landsworth, in the county of Berks, but d. without issue, about the year 1686, when the BARONIES OF MORLEY AND MONTEAGLE fell into ABEYANCE between the issue of his two aunts, and so continue with their representatives. Those aunts were

> 1. KATHERINE, who m. John Savage, Earl of Rivers, and had issue,
>
>> THOMAS, who s. to the Earldom of Rivers, and was s. by his son,
>>
>>> RICHARD, Earl of Rivers, who d. in 1712, and was s. by his cousin,
>>>
>>>> JOHN SAVAGE, Earl of Rivers, with whose son,
>>>>
>>>>> JOHN, the earldom expired.
>>
>> John, died s. p.
>>
>> Richard.
>>
>> Elizabeth, m. to William, Lord Petre, but had no issue.
>>
>> Jane, m. first, to George, Lord Chandos, secondly, to Sir William Sidley, Bart., and thirdly, to GEORGE PITT, Esq., *of Strathfieldsay, in the county of Hants.* Her ladyship's great grandson by her last husband, GEORGE PITT, Esq., of Strathfieldsay, was created, in 1776, BARON RIVERS, *of Strathfieldsay,* and in 1802, BARON RIVERS, *of Sudley Castle,* with a special remainder. His lordship d. in 1803, and was s. by his son,
>>
>>> GEORGE PITT, second baron, at whose decease, in 1828, the first barony expired, but the second devolved, according to the limitation, upon his nephew,
>>>
>>>> HORACE - WILLIAM BECKFORD, Esq., as THIRD BARON; he d. in 1831, and was s. by his son,
>>>>
>>>>> GEORGE, present lord.
>>
>> Catherine, m. to Charles, brother of Sir William Sidley.

Mary, *m.* to William Killigrew, Esq.

Frances, *d.* young.

2. Elizabeth, *m.* to Edward Cranfield, Esq.

ARMS.—Az. betw. two bars, sa. charged with three bezants, a lion passant gules, in chief three bucks' heads caboshed of the second.

PARR—BARON PARR, OF KENDAL, EARL OF ESSEX, MARQUESS OF NORTHAMPTON.

Baker 11 41

Gr. ? 882

Barony,		1538.
Earldom,	by Letters Patent,	23rd December, 1543.
Marquisate,		16th February, 1557.

Marquisate revived, 13th January, 1559.

Lineage.

The family of PARR, although of knightly degree, appears not to have attained much celebrity until the reign of RICHARD II., when

SIR WILLIAM PARR *m.* Elizabeth de Roos, grand-daughter and heir of SIR THOMAS ROOS, *of Kendal,** and had livery of her inheritance. Upon

---

* The old feudal BARONS OF KENDAL descended, as set forth in the register of Cockersand Abbey, from IVO TAILBOYS, brother of Fulke, Earl of Anjou. The fourth in descent from whom,

WILLIAM DE LANCASTER, is presumed to have adopted that surname from being governor of Lancaster Castle. He *m.* Gundred, daughter of William, second Earl of Warren, and widow of Roger, Earl of Warwick, and was *s.* by his son,

WILLIAM DE LANCASTER, (called the *second*,) who was steward to King HENRY II. He *m.* Helewise de Stuteville, and left an only daughter and heir,

HELEWISE DE LANCASTER, who espoused Gilbert, son of Roger Fitz-Reinfred, and had (with three daughters) an only son, who adopting his mother's surname, *s.* to her estates as

WILLIAM DE LANCASTER (called the *third*). This feudal lord *d.* without issue, when the lands devolved upon his three sisters, as co-heirs, viz.

Alice, (the second,) *m.* to William de Lindsey, and her descendant,

 CHRISTIAN DE LINDSEY, *m.* Ingelram de Ghisnes, Lord of Courcy, in France, whose grandson,

  INGELRAM DE GHISNES, EARL OF BEDFORD, left an only daughter and heir,

   PHILIPPA, who died *s. p.*

Serota (the third,) *m.* —— Multon, and died *s. p.*

HELEWISE, (the eldest,) *m.* Peter de Brus, of Skelton, and had issue, Peter, who *d.* issueless, and four daughters, of whom the eldest,

 MARGARET, *m.* Robert de Roos, and her great grandson,

  SIR THOMAS DE ROOS, was *s.* in Kendal, and his other estates, by his grand-daughter,

   ELIZABETH DE ROOS, who *m.* as in the text, SIR WILLIAM PARR.

410

---

the accession of the Duke of Lancaster, as HENRY IV., Sir William Parr stood so high in the estimation of the new monarch, that he was deputed, with the Bishop of St. Asaph, to announce the revolution to the court of Spain. He *d.* in a few years afterwards, (6th Edward IV.,) being then seised of the fourth part of the manor of Kirby, in Kendal, in right of the heiress of Roos, and was *s.* by his eldest son, *= Agnes Crophull = Thomas* [?]

JOHN PARR, who *d.* within three years of his father, and was *s.* by his son, *= Alice Tunstall* [?]

SIR THOMAS PARR, who, taking part with Richard, Duke of York, was attainted in the parliament held at Coventry, 38th Henry VI.; he *d.* in the 4th Edward IV., and was *s.* by his son,

SIR WILLIAM PARR. This feudal lord appears to have enjoyed the favour of *King* EDWARD IV., and to have repaid it with great fidelity. In the 10th of that prince's reign Sir William was one of the commissioners appointed to adjust with JAMES III., of Scotland, some alleged violations of the truce then subsisting between the two kingdoms; and upon the return of *King* EDWARD, again to contest his right to the crown with MARGARET OF ANJOU, supported by the *king-maker*, EARL OF WARWICK, Sir William Parr met him at Northampton with a considerable force, and thence marched to BARNET FIELD, where the contest was decided in favour of his royal master. He was afterwards a knight banneret, and a KNIGHT of the GARTER. In the 22nd of the same reign he was constituted chief commissioner for exercising the office of CONSTABLE OF ENGLAND, and the same year he served in the left wing of the army, then sent into Scotland, under the command of Richard, Duke of Gloucester. Sir William *m.* Elizabeth, daughter of Henry, fifth Baron Fitz-Hugh, by whom (who *m.* secondly, Nicholas, Lord Vaux,) he had issue,

THOMAS, his successor.

WILLIAM, created LORD PARR, *of Horton.*

He was *s.* by his elder son,

SIR THOMAS PARR, who, upon the decease of his first cousin, *George*, seventh BARON FITZ-HUGH, in 1512, was found to be joint heir, with his aunt, *Alice*, (Fitz-Hugh) LADY FIENNES, to that nobleman's barony and lands. He *m.* Maud, daughter and co-heir of Sir Thomas Green, Knt., and had issue,

WILLIAM, his successor.

Anne, *m.* to William Herbert, EARL OF PEMBROKE, and her male descendant continues to the present time to inherit this earldom; but Philip, eighth Earl of Pembroke, leaving at his decease an only daughter,

 Lady CHARLOTTE HERBERT, who *m.* first, John, Lord Jeffries, and secondly, Thomas, Viscount Windsor, the co-heirship to the Barony of Fitz-Hugh, was thus severed from the Earldom of Pembroke. The representatives of her ladyship's two marriages are the present Earl of Pomfret, and the Marquess of Bute.

KATHERINE, *m.* first, to Edward Borough, secondly, to John Neville, Lord Latimer, thirdly, to *King* Henry VIII.. and fourthly, to Thomas, Lord Seymour, of Sudley, but died *s. p.*

The son, .

WILLIAM PARR, was brought to court by his sister, and rose rapidly into royal favour. He was first made one of the esquires of King Henry VIII.'s body, and he attended his royal master in the celebrated interview with FRANCIS, *King of France*, where he took part in the justing and feats of arms, being amongst the challengers on the English side. In the 30th of the same reign, he was advanced to the dignity of BARON PARR, of *Kendal*; but upon what day or month, the enrolment of his patent mentions not. He was summoned in the next year, and took his seat in parliament on the 28th April (1539). His lordship m. first, Lady Anne Bourchier, only daughter and heiress of Henry Bourchier, second Earl of Essex, (which marriage was dissolved by act of parliament, and the issue bastardised,) and soon after the elevation of his sister, Katherine, to the dignity of QUEEN CONSORT, he was created, being then a Knight of the Garter, by letters patent, dated 23d December, 1543, EARL OF ESSEX, with the precedency which the late Henry Bourchier, Earl of Essex, had enjoyed. His lordship was constituted by King Henry VIII., one of his executors, and upon the accession of his nephew, EDWARD VI., he was advanced to the MARQUISATE OF NORTHAMPTON, by letters patent, dated 16th February, 1547. In four years afterwards, he was made LORD GREAT CHAMBERLAIN OF ENGLAND, for life, and having about this time married, for his second wife, Elizabeth, daughter of George, Lord Cobham, he obtained in the 5th Edward VI., an especial act of parliament for annulling his marriage with the Lady Anne Bourchier, as also for ratifying his marriage with the said Elizabeth, and legitimating the children that might be born of that lady. Shortly after this his lordship was sent ambassador extraordinary to the King of France, to present to his majesty the order of the Garter, and to treat with him touching certain private affairs, being accompanied by the Bishop of Ely, and other distinguished personages. Before the close of this year he was one of the peers who sate upon the trial of the protector, Somerset. Espousing the cause of *Lady* JANE GREY, and joining the DUKE OF NORTHUMBERLAND, in proclaiming her QUEEN OF ENGLAND, upon the demise of *King* EDWARD, the marquess, on the total failure of the project, was committed to the Tower, and being afterwards arraigned, had sentence of death passed upon him, and ALL HIS HONOURS became FORFEITED. Notwithstanding which, execution was forborne, and before the close of the year, he was restored in blood by parliament, but not to his honours, so that he had no other title than William Parr, Esq., late Marquess of Northampton, and stood in no higher degree, until Queen Elizabeth ascended the throne, when her majesty was graciously pleased to create him, by letters patent, dated 13th January, 1559, MARQUESS OF NORTHAMPTON, to restore him to his lands, to make him one of her privy council, and to reinvest him with the order of the GARTER. His lordship

outliving his second wife, m. thirdly, Helen, daughter of Wolfangus Suavenburgh, but had no issue. The delight of this nobleman is said to have been music and poetry, and his exercise, war; though his skill in the field answered not his industry, nor his success, his skill. Yet King Edward called him, "his honest uncle;" and King Henry, "his integrity." His lordship *d.* in 1571, and was buried in the collegiate church at Warwick, where, about half a century before Sir William Dugdale wrote, his body, being dug up, was found perfect, the skin entire, dried to the bones; and the rosemary and bay lying in the coffin, fresh and green. His children by his first lady, having been illegitimated, and having none by his other wives, ALL HIS HONOURS, at his decease, became EXTINCT.

ARMS.—Ar. two bars, az. a border ingrailed sa.

PARR — BARON PARR, OF HORTON.

By Letters Patent, dated 23 December, 1543.

Lineage.

SIR WILLIAM PARR, of Horton, in the county of Northampton, uncle of William, Marquess of Northampton, and of QUEEN KATHERINE, last wife of King Henry VIII., having been constituted chamberlain to her majesty, was advanced to the peerage, by letters patent, dated 23d December, 1543, in the dignity of BARON PARR, of *Horton*. His lordship m. Mary, daughter of Sir William Salisbury, Knt., and had issue,

Maud, m. to Sir Ralph Lane.

Anne, m. to Sir John Digby, of Ketilby, in the county of Leicester.

Elizabeth, m. to Sir Nicholas Woodhall, Knt.

Mary, m. to Sir Thomas Tresham, Knt.

He *d.* in 1546, when the BARONY OF PARR, of *Horton*, became EXTINCT.

ARMS.—Same as PARR of Kendal.

PASTON—VISCOUNTS YARMOUTH, EARLS OF YARMOUTH.

Viscounty, } by Letters { 19th August, 1673.
Earldom, } Patent, { 30th July, 1679.

Lineage.

SIR ROBERT PASTON, Bart., of an ancient and "worshipful" family, in the county of Norfolk, having devoted his fortune and energies to the royal cause, during the civil wars, was elevated to the peerage by King Charles II., on 19th August, 1673, as *Baron Paston, of Paston*, and VISCOUNT YARMOUTH, both in the county of Norfolk. His lordship m. Rebecca, daughter of Sir Jasper Clayton, Knt., of London, and had issue,

WILLIAM, his successor.

Robert, m. Anne, daughter and co-heir of Philip Harbord, Esq.

Jasper, m. Lady Fairborn, widow of Sir Palmer Fairborn.

Thomas, a colonel in the army, drowned in 1693, leaving by his wife, Dorothy, daughter of Edward Darcy, Esq.

Robert, Captain, R.N.

Rebecca, m. to Admiral Sir Stafford Fairborn.

Margaret, m. to Hieronimo Alberto di Conti, a German.

The viscount was advanced to the EARLDOM OF YARMOUTH, 30th July, 1679. He was esteemed a man of refined taste and learning, and dying in 1682, was s. by his eldest son,

WILLIAM PASTON, second Earl of Yarmouth. This nobleman espoused, first, Charlotte-Jemima-Maria, natural daughter of *King* CHARLES II., by the Viscountess Shannon, wife of Francis Boyle, Viscount Shannon, and daughter of Sir William Killigrew, and had issue,

CHARLES, Lord Paston, a brigadier in the army, who predeceased him.

William, Captain, R.N., died before his father.

Charlotte, m. first, to Thomas Herne, Esq., of Heveringland, in Norfolk, and secondly, Major Weldron.

Rebecca, m. to Sir John Holland, of Quidenham, Bart.

His lordship m. secondly, Elizabeth, daughter of Lord North, and widow of Sir Robert Wiseman, but had no issue. He d. in 1732, when leaving no male issue, and the male line of his brothers having previously ceased, the BARONY, VISCOUNTY, and EARLDOM, became EXTINCT.

ARMS.—Ar. six fleur-de-lis (three, two, and one) and a chief indented or.

PATESHULL—BARON PATESHULL.

By Writ of Summons, dated 25th February, 1342, 16 Edward III.

Lineage.

In the time of *King* HENRY III.,

SIMON DE PATESHULL held the manor of Bletsho, in the county of Bedford, of the Barony of Bedford, by the service of one knight's fee. In the 17th of the same reign,

HUGH DE PATESHULL, uncle to Maud, wife of Nigel de Mowbray, gave to Hubert de Burgh, three hundred marks fine on behalf of the said Maud, that she might marry whom she thought fit, and enjoy her dowry.

To either of the above Simon, or Hugh, succeeded another,

SIMON DE PATESHULL, who m. Isabell, daughter and heir of John de Steingreve, and was s. by

SIR JOHN DE PATESHULL, who had summons to parliament as a BARON, on 25th February, 1342, but not afterwards. He d. in 1349, and was s. by his son,

SIR WILLIAM DE PATESHULL, never summoned to parliament, nor can he have been esteemed a baron, for his father had but one writ of summons, and there is no proof of sitting. The BARONY OF PATESHULL must therefore be considered as EXTINCT, at the decease of John, Lord Pateshull. William d. in 1366, when his estates devolved upon his sisters as co-heirs, viz.

Sybyl, m. to Roger de Beauchamp, and con-
412

veyed to him the manor of Bletsho, which manor was transferred by MARGARET, heiress of the Beauchamps, to her husband, Sir Oliver St. John.

Alice, m. to Thomas Wake, of Blysworth.

Mabel, m. to Walter de Fauconberg.

Katherine, m. to Sir Robert de Tudenham, Knt.

ARMS.—Ar. a fesse az. between three crescents, gules.

PAULET—DUKES OF BOLTON.

By Letters Patent, dated 9th April, 1689.

Lineage.

JOHN PAULET, fifth Marquess of Winchester, so celebrated in the civil wars, (see *Burke's Dictionary of the Peerage and Baronetage*,) left by his first wife, Jane, daughter of Thomas, Viscount Savage, an only son,

CHARLES PAULET, sixth Marquess of Winchester, who, for his zeal in promoting the revolution, was created DUKE OF BOLTON, by letters patent, dated 9th April, 1689. His grace m. first, Christiana, daughter of John, Lord Freshville, by whom he had one son, John, who d. in infancy. The duke espoused, secondly, Mary, one of the illegitimate daughters of Emanuel Scroop, Earl of Sunderland, by whom he acquired that considerable estate at Bolton, in Yorkshire, whence he derived the title of his dukedom : and had issue,

CHARLES, Marquess of Winchester.

William, who married twice, and left issue by both marriages.

Jane, m. to John, Earl of Bridgewater.

Mary, d. unmarried.

Elizabeth, m. to Toby Jenkins, Esq.

His grace d. 26th February, 1698-9, and was s. by his elder son,

CHARLES PAULET, second Duke, K.G., Lord Lieutenant of Ireland in 1777. His grace espoused first, Margaret, daughter of George, Lord Coventry, by whom he had no issue. He m. secondly, Frances, daughter of William Ramsden, Esq., of Byrom, in the county of York, and had

CHARLES, } successively DUKES OF BOLTON.
HENRY, }

Mary, m. first, to Charles O'Neal, Esq., and secondly, to Arthur Moore, Esq.

Frances, m. to John, Lord Mordaunt.

The duke wedded, thirdly, Henrietta Crofts, natural daughter of James Scot, Duke of Monmouth, by Eleanor, younger daughter of Sir Robert Needham, Knt., and had one son,

Nassau, who m. Isabella, daughter of Thomas, Earl of Thanet. Lord Nassau Paulet d. in 1741, leaving an only daughter,

Isabella, m. to John-James, third Earl of Egmont.

His grace d. 21st January, 1721-2, and was s. by his eldest son,

CHARLES PAULET, third Duke, K.G., Constable of the Tower of London. His grace m. first, Anne, only daughter and heir of John, Earl of Carberry, in Ireland, by whom he had no issue. He espoused, secondly, Lavinia Fenton, well known as an actress, in the character of Polly Peachum, by whom he had no issue after marriage, but had three sons previously. He d. in 1754, when the honours devolved upon his brother, .

HARRY PAULET, fourth duke, an officer in the army, and aid-de-camp to Lord Galway, in Portugal. His grace m. Catherine, daughter of Charles Parry, Esq., of Oakfield, in Berkshire, and had issue,

> CHARLES, } successively Dukes.
> HARRY, }
> Henrietta, m. to Sir Robert Colebrook, Bart.
> Catherine, m. first, to William Ashe, Esq., and secondly, to Adam Drummond, Esq.

The duke d. in 1758, and was s. by his elder son,

CHARLES PAULET, fifth duke,[*] at whose decease, unmarried, in 1765, the honours devolved upon his brother,

HARRY PAULET, sixth duke. This nobleman being bred to the sea service, attained the rank of admiral of the white. His grace m. first, in 1752, Henrietta, daughter of —— Nunn, Esq., of Eltham, by whom he had a daughter,

> Mary-Henrietta, m. to John, fifth Earl of Sandwich.

The duke espoused, secondly, Catherine, daughter of Robert Lowther, Esq., and sister of James, Earl of Lonsdale, by whom he had two daughters,

> Katherine, m. to Henry, Earl of Darlington, now Marquess of Cleveland, and d. in 1807.
> Amelia.

His grace d. 24th December, 1794, and after a considerable time consumed in establishing his right, the Marquisate of Winchester passed to George Paulet, Esq., of Amport, while the DUKEDOM OF BOLTON became EXTINCT.

ARMS.—Sa. three swords in pile, points in base ar. pomels and hilts or.

PAYNEL—BARON PAYNELL.

By Writ of Summons, dated 29th December, 1299, 28 Edward I.

Lineage.

SIR JOHN PAYNELL, of Drax, in the county of York, was summoned to parliament as a BARON, from 29th December, 1299, to 26th August, 1318. This nobleman is supposed to have died before 1326. No account is given of his issue, nor

---

* This nobleman entailed the major part of his great estates, should the male issue of his brothers fail, upon his natural daughter,

> JANE-MARY POWLETT, and that event taking place, the lady inherited. She m. in 1778, Thomas Orde, Esq., who assumed the name of POWLETT, and was created, in 1797, LORD BOLTON, of Bolton Castle, in the county of York. He d. in 1807, and was s. by his son,
>
> WILLIAM, present Lord Bolton.

does Dugdale in his Baronetage, take any notice of him; but in his Writs of Summons to Parliament, the name of "Johannes Paynell de Drax" occurs amongst the barons summoned to parliament, the 28th and 30th of Edward I., and the 11th and 19th of Edward II. The same name also occurs in the 30d, 33d, 34th, and 35th of Edward I., and in the 1st and 3d of Edward II., which is presumed, by Nicolas, to be the same person.

ARMS.—Two bars with an urle of martlets.

PECHE — BARON PECHE, OF BRUNNE.

By Writ of Summons, dated 29th December, 1299, 28 Edward I.

Lineage.

HAMON PECHE was sheriff of the county of Cambridge, from the 2d to the 19th year of King Henry II. He m. Alice, daughter of William Peverell, and one of the co-heirs of Pain Peverell, her brother, as part of the honour of BRUNNE, in the same shire. To this Hamon s. his son and heir,

GILBERT PECHE, who, in the 6th of Richard I., upon the collection of the scutage, then assessed for the king's redemption, paid £29. 1s. 8d., for the knights' fees of his parental inheritance, and two marks and a half for those of the honour of Brunne, which descended to him through his mother. He d. before the year 1217, and was s. by his son,

HAMON PECHE, who d. in 1241, in his pilgrimage to the Holy Land, and was s. by his eldest son,

GILBERT PECHE. This feudal lord d. in 1291, and was s. by his son,

GILBERT PECHE, who, having served in the wars of Gascony, 22d Edward I., was summoned to parliament as a BARON, from 29th December, 1299, to 3d November, 1306, and again 14th March, 1322. His lordship m. first, Maude de Hastings, by whom he had two sons, JOHN and EDMUND, neither of whom, however, were summoned to parliament, nor is any account given of their descendants. Lord Peche m. secondly, Joane, daughter of Simon de Grey, and to his children, by that lady, he left the greater part of his property, making King Edward I. heir to the rest of the barony. He d. in 1323.

ARMS.—Ar. a fesse betw. two chevronels, gules.

PECHE—BARON PECHE, OF WORM-LEIGHTON.

By Writ of Summons, dated 15th May, 1321, 14 Edward II.

Lineage.

This branch of the house of PECHE is said, by Dugdale, to have sprung from

ROBERT PECHE, Bishop of Coventry, in King Stephen's time—who is represented as having two sons,

> GEFFREY.
> Richard, Archdeacon of Coventry.

The elder,

GEOFFREY PECHE, *m.* Petronile, daughter, and eventually heir, of Richard Walsh, of Wormleighton, in the county of Warwick, and had a son,

RICHARD PECHE, who succeeded to the properties of his grandfather, the bishop, and his uncle the dean, as likewise to the manor of WORMLEIGHTON, through his mother, and was *s.* by his son,

SIR JOHN PECHE, of Wormleighton, who sided with *King* HENRY III. against the barons, and was summoned to parliament as BARON PECHE, from 15th May, 1321, to 22d January, 1336. His lordship was in the wars of Scotland, and was governor of Warwick Castle, in the 16th Edward II.; he was afterwards governor of Dover Castle, and warden of the Cinque Ports. He *d.* about the year 1339, leaving his grandson,

SIR JOHN PECHE, Knt., his heir. This feudal lord was never summoned to parliament, nor esteemed a baron, for we find him serving as one of the knights for the county of Warwick, in the parliament held at Westminster, in the 26th Edward III., and again in the 47th of the same reign. He *d.* in two years after, and was *s.* by his son,

SIR JOHN PECHE, (never summoned to parliament, nor esteemed a baron,) who attended, 9th Richard II., John, Duke of Lancaster, then bearing the title of King of Castile and Leon, into Spain, and is supposed to have died there in the same year, leaving two daughters, viz.

JOANE, who died *s. p.*

MARGARET, *m.* to Sir William de Montfort.

ARMS.—Gules a fesse betw. six cross crosslets ar. with a label of three points in chief.

PELHAM-HOLLES—DUKE OF NEWCASTLE.

See HOLLES-PELHAM, Barons Pelham, Earls of Clare, and Duke of Newcastle.

Note.—Thomas Pelham-Holles, Duke of Newcastle, died in 1768, not, as erroneously printed, 1761, in the article to which we refer.

PERCY—BARON EGREMONT.

By Letters Patent, dated 20th December, 1449.

Lineage.

SIR THOMAS PERCY, Knt., third son of Henry, second Earl of Northumberland, was created by King Edward VI., in consideration of his good services, BARON EGREMONT, *of Egremont Castle,* in Cumberland. His lordship fell at the battle of Northampton, in 1460, when the king was taken prisoner. He died, according to Dugdale, "without issue," when the BARONY OF EGREMONT became EXTINCT. Other authorities state, however, that he left a son, Sir John Percy, but who never assumed the title.

ARMS.—Same as Percy, Barons Percy, and Earls of Northumberland.

414

PERCY — BARONS PERCY, EARLS OF NORTHUMBERLAND, BARONS POYNINGS, BARONS PERCY, OF COCKERMOUTH, EARLS OF NORTHUMBERLAND.

Barony of Percy, by Writ of Summons, dated 6th February, 1299, 8 Edward II.
Earldom of Northumberland, by Charter of Creation, 16th July, 1377.
Restored, 11th November, 1414.
Again restored, 1470.
Barony of Poynings, by Writ of Summons, 23rd April, 1337, 11 Edward III.
Barony of Percy, of Cockermouth, &c., by Creation, 30th April, 1557.
Earldom of Northumberland, (New Creation,) 1st May, 1557.

Lineage.

The illustrious family of Percy is descended from one of the Norman chieftains (William de Percy) who accompanied William the Conqueror into England in 1066; and it derives its name from the village of Percy, near Villedieu. The family of Percy, of Normandy, deduced its pedigree from Geoffrey, (son of Mainfred, a Danish chieftain,) who assisted Rollo, in 912, in subjugating that principality, and acquired considerable possessions there.

WILLIAM DE PERCY, being high in favour with the victorious duke, obtained, according to Madox, in his "Baronia Anglica," a barony of thirty knights' fees from that monarch, in his new dominions, and thus became a feudal lord of the realm from the Conquest. This Lord William de Percy, who was distinguished amongst his contemporaries by the addition of Algernons, (William with the whiskers,) whence his posterity have constantly borne the name of Algernon, restored, or rather refounded, the famous Abbey of St. Hilda, in Yorkshire, of which his brother, Serlo de Percy, became first prior. Accompanying, however, Duke Robert, in the first crusade, 1096, he died at Mountjoy, near Jerusalem, the celebrated eminence, whence the pilgrims of the cross first viewed the Holy City, leaving four sons and two daughters, by his wife, Emma de Port, a lady of Saxon descent, whose lands were amongst those bestowed upon him by the Conqueror, and, according to an ancient writer, "he wedded hyr that was very heire to them, in discharging of his conscience." His lordship was *s.* in his feudal rights and possessions by his eldest son,

ALAN DE PERCY, second baron, surnamed the GREAT ALAN, who *m.* Emma, daughter of Gilbert de Gaunt; which Gilbert was son of Baldwin, Earl of Flanders, and nephew of Queen Maud, wife of William the Conqueror, and was *s.* by his eldest son,

WILLIAM DE PERCY, third baron; at whose decease, the eldest branch of the first race of Percys, from Normandy, became extinct in the male line, and their great inheritance devolved upon his lordship's two daughters, (by Alice de Tunbridge, daughter of Richard, Earl of Clare, who was usually styled De Tunbridge, from his castle of that name,) the Ladies Maud and Agnes de Percy, successively.

MAUDE DE PERCY, the senior, was second wife of William de Plesset, Earl of Warwick, by whom (who d. in the Holy Land, A. D. 1184) she had no issue. Her ladyship d. in 1204 or 5, and then the whole possessions of the Percys descended to the family of her sister,

AGNES DE PERCY, who m. Josceline, of Lovain, brother of Queen Adelicia, second wife of Henry I., and son of Godfrey Barbatus, Duke of Lower Lorrain, and Count of Brabant, who was descended from the emperor Charlemagne. Her ladyship, however, would only consent to this great alliance, upon condition that Josceline should adopt either the surname or arms of Percy; the former of which he accordingly assumed, and retained his own paternal coat, in order to perpetuate his claim to the principality of his father, should the elder line of the reigning duke at any period become extinct. The matter is thus stated in the great old pedigree at Sion House: "The ancient arms of Hainault this Lord Josceline retained, and gave his children the surname of Percie." Of this illustrious alliance there were several children, of whom,

HENRY DE PERCY, the eldest son, who appears to have died before his mother, m. Isabel, daughter of Adam de Brus, Lord of Skelton, with whom he had the manor of Levington, for which he and his heirs were to repair to Skelton Castle every Christmasday, and to lead the lady of the castle from her chamber to the chapel to mass, and thence to her chamber again, and after dining with her, to depart. This Henry left two sons,

WILLIAM, of whom presently.

Henry, ancestor of the Percys, of Hesset, Sussex.

RICHARD DE PERCY, the youngest son of Agnes and Josceline, got possession of the entire property of his aunt, Maud, Countess of Warwick, and even of a great proportion of that of his mother, and retained the same during the principal part of his life: at length, subsequently to infinite litigation, it was settled between him and his nephew, William de Percy, to whom the inheritance belonged, after a solemn hearing before the king in person, on the 6th July, 1234, (18th Henry III.) that the estates should be divided into equal portions between the parties during Richard's life; and that after his death, all the ancient patrimony of the Percy family should devolve upon his nephew, aforesaid; a small reservation having been made for Richard's son and heir, Henry de Percy. This Richard de Percy continued for the whole of his life at the head of the family, and enjoyed all its baronial rights. He was one of those powerful feudal lords who took up arms, in 1215, against John,

and having a principal hand in extorting the GREAT CHARTERS of English freedom, was chosen one of the twenty-five guardians to see the MAGNA CHARTA duly observed. He d. about 1244, and then his nephew,

WILLIAM DE PERCY, came into full possession of all those rights and properties which had been usurped at the decease of his mother; but did not live long to enjoy them, for he d. in 1245, and was s. by his son, (by his second wife, Elena, daughter of Ingelram de Balliol, by whom he obtained in dower, Dalton, afterwards called Dalton Percy, in the bishopric of Durham,)

HENRY DE PERCY, who m. Eleanor, daughter of John Plantagenet, Earl of Warren and Surrey; and dying in 1272, was s. by his only surviving son,

HENRY DE PERCY, ninth feudal lord, who was summoned to parliament from the 6th of February, 1299, (27th Edward I.) to 29th July, 1315, (8th Edward II.) This nobleman obtained, on the 19th November, 1309, from Anthony Beck, Bishop of Durham, by purchase, a grant of the Barony of Alnwick, in the county of Northumberland. His lordship was one of the great barons who subscribed, in 1301, the celebrated letter to Pope Boniface VIII., upon the attempt of his holiness to interpose in the affairs of the kingdom, intimating, "That their king was not to answer in judgment, for any rights of the crown of England, before any tribunal under heaven, &c., and that, by the help of God, they would resolutely, and with all their force, maintain against all men." He d. in 1315, and was s. by his eldest son,

HENRY DE PERCY, second Lord Percy, of Alnwick. This nobleman had a grant from the crown in the 2nd Edward III., of the reversion of the barony and castle of WARKWORTH, &c. He had summons to parliament from 1322 to the time of his death, the 26th February, 1351-2, when he was s. by his eldest son, (by Idonia, daughter of Robert, Lord Clifford,)

HENRY DE PERCY, third Lord Percy, of Alnwick; who, in the life-time of his father, had participated in the glories of Cressy, (26th August, 1346.) His lordship m. first, in her ladyship's fourteenth year, Lady Mary Plantagenet, daughter of Henry, Earl of Lancaster, which Henry was son of Edmund, Earl of Lancaster, Leicester, &c., second son of King Henry III.; by this alliance his lordship had two sons,

HENRY, his successor.

Thomas, created in 1397, *Earl of Worcester*; K.G., a very eminent warrior and statesman in the reigns of Edward III., Richard II., and Henry IV.

His lordship m. secondly, Joan, daughter and heiress of John de Orbey, of Lincolnshire, one of the barons in the reign of Edward III., by whom he left one daughter,

Mary, who m. John, Lord Ros, of Hamelake, but died s. p. in 1396.

He d. 17th June, 1368, and was s. by his elder son,

HENRY DE PERCY, fourth Lord Percy, of Alnwick, a distinguished military commander in the reign of Edward III., who, assisting as marshal of England at the coronation of King Richard II., was advanced, on the same day, 16th July, 1377, to the *Earldom of Northumberland*, with remainder to his heirs generally, and, like a barony in fee, transmissible, it would appear, to female as well as male heirs. His lordship m. first, Margaret, daughter of Ralph, Lord Nevill, of Raby, and had issue,

    HENRY (Sir), the renowned Hotspur, so celebrated in all our histories. He fought the famous battle of OTTERBOURN, near the Cheviot Hills, in Northumberland, (Chevy Chace,) where James, Earl of Douglas, was slain, and himself and his brother, Sir Ralph Percy, made prisoners. He m. Philippa, daughter of Edmund Mortimer, Earl of March, by Philippa, daughter and heir of Lionel Plantagenet, Duke of Clarence, and falling at the battle of Shrewsbury in 1403, left issue,

        HENRY, who s. as second Earl of Northumberland.

        Elisabeth, m. first, to John, Lord Clifford, and secondly, to Ralph, Earl of Westmorland.

    Thomas (Sir), m. Elisabeth, elder daughter and co-heir of David Strabolgi, Earl of Athol, by whom (who m. secondly, Sir Henry Scrope,) he had issue,

        Henry Percy, who left two daughters, viz.

            Elisabeth, m. first, to Thomas, Lord Burgh, and secondly, to Sir William Lucy.

            Margaret, m. first, to Henry, Lord Grey, of Codnor, and secondly, to Richard, Earl of Oxford.

    Ralph (Sir), m. Philippa, the other daughter and co-heir of David Strabolgi, Earl of Athol, but died s. p.

    Alan.

    Margaret.

The earl m. secondly, Maud, sister and heir of Anthony, Lord Lucy, which Anthony settled upon his lordship and his heirs the honour and castle of Cockermouth, with other great estates, on condition that her arms should be for ever quartered with those of the Percys. In the 7th year of Richard II. the earl having been elected one of the Knights of the Garter, the king bestowed upon him the robes of the order out of the royal wardrobe. In some years afterwards, however, being proclaimed a traitor, and his lands declared forfeited by King Richard, his lordship, in conjunction with his son, Sir Henry Percy, surnamed Hotspur, and Henry, Duke of Lancaster, accomplished the dethronement of that monarch, and placed the crown upon the head of Henry, Duke of Lancaster, under the title of Henry IV. Again dissatisfied with the government, the duke is charged with concerting the rebellion, in which his son, Hotspur, and his brother, the Earl of Worcester, engaged, in 1403, for transferring the sceptre to Mortimer, Earl of March, then a boy. Of these two eminent persons, Sir Henry Percy, the renowned Hotspur, fell, performing prodigies of valour, at Battle-field, near Shrewsbury, 21st July, 1403; and Thomas Percy, Earl of Worcester, was beheaded, after the battle, at Shrewsbury. The Earl of Northumberland fell subsequently, (20th February, 1407-8,) in arms

416

against the king, at Bramham Moor, near Haslewood, when his honours became forfeited under an attainder, but were restored, in 1414, to his grandson, (Hotspur's only son,)

HENRY DE PERCY, second Earl of Northumberland, who m. Lady Eleanor Nevil, daughter of Ralph, first Earl of Westmorland, and Joan de Beaufort, daughter of JOHN OF GAUNT, and aunt of King Henry V. Of this nobleman and his countess, and their issue, the following account is given in a very curious MS. preserved in the British Museum, and there said to be extracted "*Ex Registro Monasterij de Whitbye.*" "Henry Percy, the son of Sir Henry Percy, that was slayne at Shrewsbury, and of Elizabeth, the daughter of the Erle of Marche, after the death of his father and grauntsyre, was exiled into Scotland, in the time of King Henry V.: by the labour of Johanne, the Countess of Westmerland, (whose daughter, Alianor, he had wedded in coming into England,) he recovered the king's grace, and the county of Northumberland, so was the second Earl of Northumberland. And of this Alianor his wife, he begat IX sonnes and III daughters, whose names be Johanne, that is buried at Whitbye; Thomas (created) Lord Egremont; Katheyne Gray, of Ruthyn, (wife of Edmund, Lord Grey, afterwards Earl of Kent); Sir Raffe Percy; William Percy, a byshopp; Richard Percy; John, that dyed without issue; another John, (called by Vincent, in his MS. baronage in the herald's office, John Percy, senior, of Warkworth;) George Percy, clerk; Henry, that dyed without issue; besides the eldest sonne and successor, Henry, third Erle of Northumberland." His lordship, who was at the battle of AGINCOURT, was made lord high constable by King Henry VI., and fell at St. Albans, 23rd May, 1455, fighting under the banner of that monarch, and was s. by his eldest surviving son,

HENRY PERCY, third earl, who had m. Eleanor, daughter and sole heiress of Richard Poynings, who d. in the life-time of his father, Lord Poynings; by which marriage, the baronies of Poynings, Fitzpayne, and Bryan, came into the family of Percy; and Sir Henry Percy was summoned to parliament, while his father, the Earl of Northumberland, yet lived, (29th Henry VI.,) as Baron Poynings. His lordship fell leading the van of the Lancastrians, sword in hand, at the battle of Towton, on the 29th March, 1461, and his honours became subsequently forfeited, by an act of attainder, but were restored to his only son,

HENRY PERCY, fourth earl, K.G., who was confined in the Tower of London, from the death of his father until the 27th of October, 1469, when, being brought before Edward IV., at his palace of Westminster, he subscribed an oath of allegiance, and was restored to his freedom and dignity, although the reversal of his father's attainder does not appear upon the rolls of parliament. The king had previously created John, Lord Montague, Earl of Northumberland, but, upon the re-establishment of the rightful earl, Lord Montague was created Marquess of Montague. This Henry, fourth earl, fell a victim, in 1489, to the avarice of King Henry VII. In that year, parliament having granted the king a subsidy for carrying on the war in Bretagne, the Earl of Northumberland, as lord-lieutenant of his county, was empowered to enforce the same; but the tax causing a general commotion, his lordship wrote to inform the king of the discontent, and praying an abatement, to which Henry peremptorily replied, "that not a penny should be abated:" which message being delivered incautiously by the earl to the populace, who had assembled to complain of their grievances, they broke into his house, (supposing him to be the promoter of their sufferings,) Cocklodge, in Yorkshire, and murdered his lordship and some of his attendants, on the 28th April, 1489. The earl was s. by his eldest son,

HENRY-ALGERNON PERCY, fifth earl, K.G., ho m. Catherine, daughter and co-heiress of Sir Robert Spencer, Knt., of Spencer-Combe, Devon, by Eleanor, his wife, daughter, and at length co-heir, of Edmund Beaufort, Duke of Somerset, by whom he had issue,

    HENRY, his successor.

    Thomas (Sir), executed for Ask's conspiracy, 29th Henry VIII., leaving two sons,

        THOMAS, } successively Earls of North-
        HENRY, } umberland.

    Ingelram (Sir).*

    Margaret, m. to Henry Clifford, first Earl of Cumberland.

    Maud, m. to Lord Coniers.

His lordship d. in 1527, and was s. by his eldest son,

HENRY-ALGERNON PERCY, sixth earl, K.G. This nobleman m. Mary, daughter of George Talbot, Earl of Shrewsbury; but dying without issue, in 1537, and his brother, Sir Thomas Percy, having been previously attainted and executed, all the honours of the family became forfeited, and the Dukedom of Northumberland was conferred, by King Edward VI., upon John Dudley, Earl of Warwick; but that nobleman having forfeited his life and honours, by treason against Queen Mary, in 1553, her majesty was pleased to advance, by letters patent, dated 30th April, 1557,

THOMAS PERCY, son of the attainted Sir Thomas Percy, to the degree of a baron, by the titles of *Baron Percy, of Cockermouth; Baron Peynings, Lucy Bryan, and Fitz-Payne:* and on the day following, his lordship was created *Earl of Northumberland,* with remainder to Henry Percy, his brother, &c. This nobleman, having conspired against Queen Elizabeth, was beheaded at York, on the 22d August, 1572, (avowing the Pope's supremacy, affirming the realm to be in a state of schism, and those obedient to Elizabeth no better than heretics,) when his honours would have fallen under the attainder, but for the reversionary clause in favour of his brother,

---

* Sir Ingelram Percy. From this gentleman, JAMES PERCY, known as the trunk-maker, who, so pertinaciously claimed the honours of the house of Percy, about one hundred and fifty years ago, deduced his descent, (see his case in the Fourth Edition of *Burke's Dictionary of the Peerage and Baronetage*).

HENRY PERCY, who succeeded as eighth earl. His lordship m. Catherine, eldest daughter and co-heiress of John Neville, Lord Latimer, by whom he had eight sons and three daughters. The earl having been committed to the Tower, for participating in a supposed plot in favour of Mary, Queen of Scots, was found dead in his bed there, wounded by three bullets from a pistol, on the 21st of June, 1585, when he was s. by his eldest son,

HENRY PERCY, ninth earl, K.G. This nobleman, after every effort to involve him in the gunpowder plot proved in vain, was "cast" (says Osborne) "into the star chamber," by which he was sentenced to a fine of £30,000, with imprisonment in the Tower during his majesty's pleasure, and actually suffered several years' incarceration. His lordship m. Dorothy, sister of Queen Elizabeth's favourite, Essex, and widow of Sir Thomas Perrot, Knt., and dying 5th November, 1632, was s. by his eldest surviving son,

ALGERNON PERCY, tenth earl, K.G., who had been summoned to parliament in the life-time of his father, as *Baron Percy.* This nobleman took an active part during the civil wars, against King Charles I., but was entirely free of any participation in his murder. He subsequently promoted the restoration. His lordship d. on the 13th October, 1668, and was s. by his only son (by Lady Elizabeth Howard, second daughter of Theophilus, second Earl of Suffolk),

JOCELINE PERCY, eleventh earl. This nobleman m. Elizabeth, youngest daughter of Thomas Wriothesly, Earl of Southampton, Lord High Treasurer of England, by whom he left, at his decease, 21st of May, 1670, an only daughter,

    LADY ELIZABETH PERCY, who succeeded to the baronial honours of her ancestors, and was, in her own right, *Baroness Percy, Poynings, Fitz-Payne, Bryan, and Latimer.* Her ladyship m. first, when only fourteen years of age, (1679,) Henry Cavendish, Earl of Ogle, (son and heir of Henry, Duke of Newcastle,) who assumed the name of Percy; but his lordship died without issue, on the 1st November, 1680, and her ladyship m. in 1682, (thirdly, it is stated, but she appears to have been only contracted to Thomas Thynne, Esq., of Longleate, who was assassinated, 12th February, 1681-2,) Charles Seymour, Duke of Somerset, who also assumed, by preliminary engagement, the surname and arms of Percy, but from that stipulation he was released, when her grace attained majority. By this marriage, the duchess had thirteen children, the eldest surviving of whom,

    ALGERNON SEYMOUR, was summoned to parliament, in 1722, on the death of his mother, as *Baron Percy.* His lordship s. to the Dukedom of Somerset, in 1748, and was created *Baron Warkworth, of Warkworth Castle, in the county of Northumberland,* and *Earl of Northumberland,* on the 2nd October, 1749, with remainder to

        SIR HUGH SMITHSON, Bart., who

had married his grace's daughter, the Lady Elisabeth Seymour, and who succeeded to those honours upon the demise of the duke, in 1750, obtaining, in the same year, an act of parliament, to allow himself and his countess to assume the surname and arms of Percy. His lordship was installed a Knight of the Garter, in 1757; and created *Earl Percy*, and DUKE OF NORTHUMBERLAND, on the 18th October, 1766. His grace was grandfather to the present Duke of Northumberland.

Upon the decease of his lordship, (Joceline, eleventh earl,) ALL THE HONOURS of the Percys, save the baronies, became EXTINCT.

ARMS.—Quarterly, four grand quarters: first and fourth, or, a lion rampant, az. (being the ancient arms of the DUKE OF BRABANT AND LOVAIN;) second and third, gu. three lucies, or pikes, haurient, ar. for LUCY; second grand quarter, az. five fusils, in fesse, or. for PERCY; third, gu. on a saltier ar. a rose of the field, barbed and seeded ppr. for NEVILLE: fourth, quarterly, gu. and or. in the first quarter a mullet ar. for VERE.

Note.—NICOLAS, in his very clever SYNOPSIS, after recapitulating the descent of the BARONY OF PERCY, which has been the subject of considerable controversy, comes to the following conclusions:—

1st. That according to the fair deduction from modern decisions, the ancient BARONY OF PERCY, created by the writ of summons of 6th February, 27th Edward I., 1299, became EXTINCT on the death of Henry-Algernon, sixth earl, in 1537.

2nd. That the Barony of Percy, of Cockermouth and Petworth, with the Baronies of Poynings, Lucy, Bryan, and Fitzpayne, created by the patent of 30th April, 1557, became EXTINCT on the death of Joceline, eleventh earl, in 1670.

3rd. That Algernon Seymour, afterwards Duke of Somerset, and first Earl of Northumberland, was erroneously placed in the precedency of the ancient barony on being summoned to parliament in 1722.

4th. That Hugh Percy, grandson of the said Duke and Baron Percy, *jure matris*, and Hugh, the present Duke of Northumberland, were likewise erroneously placed in the precedency of the original barony.

5th. That the only Barony of Percy now vested in his Grace, Hugh, present Duke of Northumberland, is the barony in fee, created by the writ of summons, to his great grandfather, Algernon Seymour, in 1722.

PERCY- EARL OF WORCESTER.

Created 29th September, 1397.

Lineage.

SIR THOMAS PERCY, a younger brother of Henry, first Earl of Northumberland, having distin-

guished himself in the council and the camp, temp. Edward III., and Richard II., was created by the latter monarch EARL OF WORCESTER. Towards the end of Edward III.'s reign, Sir Thomas was the companion in arms of the heroic *Black* PRINCE; and he had a grant of one hundred marks per annum for life, out of the exchequer, for his good services, with a similar annuity for his especial services to the Black Prince. In the 1st of Richard II., he assisted at the coronation of that king, his brother, Henry, being then marshal of England. The next year, as admiral of the north seas, he was associated with Sir Hugh Calveley, Knt., and meeting with seven ships, and one man of war, laden with wine, brought them all into Bristol. He was subsequently employed with the Earl of Buckingham, to suppress *Jack Straw's* insurrection: and in the 10th of the same reign, he was made admiral of the fleet, for the great army of twenty thousand men then sent into Spain, with JOHN OF GAUNT, to establish that prince's right to the throne of CASTILE and LEON. In three years afterwards he was constituted Justice of South Wales, and subsequently VICE CHAMBERLAIN to the king. In the 18th, he was sent ambassador to France, being then steward of the king's household, and in a few years afterwards appointed admiral of the king's fleet for Ireland. Notwithstanding his lordship's high position in the estimation of King Richard, upon the deposition of that monarch, he seems to have made his ground good with the new king, for we find him deputed with the Bishop of Durham, to announce to the court of France, the revolution that placed the sceptre in the hand of Henry IV., and reconstituted soon after, steward of the household. Subsequently, however, joining his brother, the Earl of Northumberland, and his nephew, Hotspur, in an effort to restore the dethroned monarch, he was made prisoner at the battle of Shrewsbury, where his gallant nephew fell, and was beheaded immediately after, anno 1402. His lordship was a Knight of the Garter: he died without issue, when the Earldom of Worcester, became EXTINCT.

ARMS.—Same as Percy, Earls of Northumberland.

PHIPPS—BARON MULGRAVE.

By Letters Patent, dated 16th June, 1790.

Lineage.

CONSTANTINE JOHN PHIPPS, second Baron Mulgrave, of New Ross, in the peerage of Ireland, an enterprising naval officer, who made an effort to discover a north-west passage, was created a peer of Great Britain, by letters patent, dated 16th June, 1790, in the dignity of BARON MULGRAVE, *of Mulgrave, in the county of York.* His lordship m. in 1787, Anne-Elizabeth, youngest daughter of Nathaniel Cholmondeley, Esq., and had an only daughter,

ANNE-ELIZABETH-CHOLMONDELEY, who m. Lieutenant-General Sir John Murray, Bart.

Lord Mulgrave *d.* in 1790, and was *s.* in the Irish Peerage by his brother, HENRY, while the BARONY OF MULGRAVE, of *Mulgrave*, in the peerage of Great Britain, became EXTINCT.

ARMS.—Quarterly, first and fourth, sa. a trefoil, slipped, between eight mullets ar. for PHIPPS; second and third, paly of six ar. and as. over all a bend gu. for ANGLESEY.

PIERREPOINT—VISCOUNTS NEW-ARK, EARLS OF KINGSTON UPON HULL, MARQUESS OF DORCHESTER, DUKES OF KINGSTON UPON HULL.

Viscounty,		29th June, 1627.
Earldom,	by Letters	25th July, 1628.
Marquisate,	Patent,	25th March, 1644.
Dukedom,		30th July, 1715.

Lineage.

Although the family of PIERREPOINT did not attain the honours of the peerage until a period of comparatively recent date, yet were they persons of distinction ever since the conquest. In which eventful era,

ROBERT DE PIERREPOINT was of the retinue of William, Earl of Warren, and at the time of the general survey, held lands in Suffolk and Sussex, amounting to ten knights' fees, under that nobleman. The great grandson of this Robert, another

ROBERT DE PIERREPOINT, was a person of such extensive property, that being made prisoner fighting on the side of King Henry III., at the battle of Lewes, he was forced to give security for the payment of the then great sum of seven hundred marks for his ransom. He was, however, relieved from the obligation by the subsequent victory of the royalists at Evesham. He was *s.* by his son,

SIR HENRY DE PIERREPOINT, a person of great note at the period in which he lived. In the 8th of Edward I., Sir Henry having lost his seal, came into the Court of Chancery, then at Lincoln, upon Monday, the morrow of the Octaves of St. Michael, and made publication thereof; protesting that if any one should find it, and seal therewith, after that day, that the instrument sealed, ought not to be of any validity. He *m.* Annora, daughter of Michael, and sister and heir of Lionel de Manvers, whereby he acquired an extensive land property in the county of Nottingham, with the Lordship of Holme, now called HOLME-PIERREPOINT. Sir Henry *d.* about the 20th Edward I., and was *s.* by his elder son,

SIMON DE PIERREPOINT, who, in the 32d Edward I., was one of those that by special writ, bearing date upon the 8th day of June, had summons amongst the barons of the realm, to repair with all speed to the king, wheresoever he should then be in England, to treat of certain weighty affairs, relating to his and their honour; the sheriffs of every county having also command to cause two knights for each shire; as also two citizens, and two burgesses for each city and borough, to attend the king at the same time, "to advise and consent for themselves and the commonalty of their respective shires, cities, and boroughs, unto what the Earls, barons, and nobles, should at that time ordain." This Simon leaving a daughter (only), Sibilla, who *m.* Edmund Ufford, was *s.* by his brother,

ROBERT DE PIERREPOINT, a very eminent person in the reigns of Edward I. and Edward II., and distinguished in the wars of Scotland. He *m.* Sarah, daughter, and eventually heir, of Sir John Heriz, and was *s.* by his son,

SIR EDMUND DE PIERREPONT, from whom we pass to his lineal descendant,

SIR GEORGE PIERREPOINT, who, at the dissolution of the monasteries, in the reign of Henry VIII., purchased large manors in the county of Nottingham, part of the possessions of the Abbot and Convent of Welbeck; and others in Derbyshire, which had belonged to the Monastery of Newsted. He *d.* in the 6th Elizabeth, and was *s.* by his son,

SIR HENRY PIERREPOINT, who *m.* Frances, elder daughter of Sir William Cavendish, of Chatsworth, and sister of William, Earl of Devonshire; and was *s.* by his son,

ROBERT PIERREPOINT, who was advanced to the peerage by King Charles I., as BARON PIERREPOINT, *of Holme Pierrepoint*, in the county of Nottingham, and VISCOUNT NEWARK, by letters patent, dated 29th June, 1627, and the next year was created EARL OF KINGSTON-UPON-HULL. At the breaking out of the civil war, his lordship was one of the first and most zealous to espouse the royal cause, and he is said to have brought no less than four thousand men immediately to the standard of the king. He was soon after constituted lieutenant-general of all his majesty's forces, in the counties of Lincoln, Rutland, Huntingdon, Cambridge, and Norfolk; and was amongst the most popular of the cavalier commanders. His lordship became, therefore, an object of more than ordinary watchfulness to the parliamentarians, and was at length surprised and made prisoner, by Lord Willoughby, of Parham, at Gainsborough; whence he was despatched in an open boat towards Hull. But Sir Charles Cavendish, pursuing the boat and overtaking it, demanded the release of the earl, which being refused, his men fired, and; unhappily, killed Lord Kingston, and his servant, though they captured the boat and put the crew to the sword. This melancholy event occurred on the 30th July, 1643. His lordship bore so high a character for benevolence, hospitality, and liberality, that he was usually styled by the common people, "the good Earl of Kingston." He *m.* Gertrude, daughter and co-heir of Henry Talbot, third son of George, Earl of Shrewsbury, and had issue,

HENRY, Viscount Newark.

William, of Thoresby, m. Elizabeth, daughter and co-heir of Sir Thomas Harris, of Tong Castle, in Shropshire, and had

    Robert, who m. ——, daughter and co-heir of Sir John Evelyn, and had issue,

        Robert, } third and fourth Earls
        William, } of Kingston.

        Evelyn, fifth earl and first duke.

        Gertrude, m. to Charles, Viscount Newhaven.

        Gervase, created Baron Pierrepoint, of Hanslope.

        Frances, m. to Henry, Earl of Ogle.

        Grace, m. to Gilbert, Earl of Clare.

        Gertrude, m. to George, Marquess of Halifax.

This William was one of the leading members of the Commons, during the civil wars, he died after the restoration, in 1679.

Frances, m. Elisabeth, daughter and co-heir of Thomas Bray, Esq., of Eyam, in the county of Derby, and d. in 1687, leaving,

    Robert, who m. Anne, daughter of Robert Murray, Esq., and left,

        Francis, } died s. p.
        George, }

        William, whose sons died s. p.

        Jane, m. to Reverend Bernard Gilpin.

        Anne, m. to Thomas Newport, Lord Torrington.

    William.

    Henry.

    Frances, m. to William, son and heir of Lord Paget.

Robert, d. unmarried.

Gervase, d. unmarried, in Holland, anno 1679, bequeathing £10,000 to the first member of his family who should obtain the honour and title of a duke.

George, of Old Cotes, in Derbyshire, m. Miss Jones, sister of Sir Samuel Jones, of Corthen Hall, Notts, by whom he had two sons,

    Henry, } both d. unmarried.
    Samuel, }

    Frances, m. Philip Rolleston, Esq.

His lordship was s. by his eldest son,

HENRY PIERREPOINT, second Earl of Kingston. This nobleman remaining, like his father, most faithfully attached to the fortunes of King Charles I., was sworn of the privy council to that monarch, and created, 25th March, 1644, Marquess of Dorchester. His lordship m. first, Cecilia, daughter of Paul, Viscount Baynning, and had surviving issue,

    Anne, m. to John, Lord Ros, afterwards Earl of Rutland, from whom she was divorced.

    Grace, d. unmarried.

The earl espoused secondly, Lady Katherine Stanley, daughter of James, Earl of Derby, but had no surviving issue. His lordship, who was a man of learning, particularly in law and physic, died in 1680, when the Marquisate of Dorchester became extinct, but his other honours devolved

420

upon his grand nephew, (refer to descendants of William Pierrepoint, of Thoresby, second son of the first earl,)

ROBERT PIERREPOINT, third Earl of Kingston. This nobleman d. unmarried, while on his travels, in France, anno 1698, and was s. by his brother,

WILLIAM PIERREPOINT, fourth earl, who m. Anne, daughter of Robert, Lord Brooke, but dying without issue, in 1690, the honours devolved upon his brother,

EVELYN PIERREPOINT, fifth earl, who was advanced, on the 23d December, 1706, to the Marquisate of Dorchester, with remainder to his uncle, Gervase, Lord Pierrepoint, of Hanslope, and was created, on the 29th July, 1715, Duke of Kingston-upon-Hull. His grace was subsequently made a Knight of the Garter, and he was constituted, four different times, one of the lords justices, during his majesty's absence in his Hanoverian dominions. His grace m. first, Lady Mary Fielding, daughter of William, Earl of Denbigh, and had issue,

    William, Marquess of Dorchester, who d. in the duke's life-time, leaving

        Evelyn, who inherited as second duke.

        Frances, m. to Sydney, son of Sir Philip Meadows, Knt., and had, with other issue,

            Charles Meadows, Esq., who succeeding to the estates of his uncle, Evelyn, Duke of Kingston, in 1773, assumed the surname of Pierrepoint, and was elevated to the peerage as Baron Pierrepoint, Viscount Newark, and Earl Manvers. He d. in 1816, and was s. by his son,

                Charles, present Earl Manvers.

    Mary, m. to Edward Wortley-Montagu, Esq., and became celebrated as Lady Mary Wortley-Montagu.

    Frances, m. to John, Earl of Mar.

    Evelyn, m. to John, Lord Gower.

The duke espoused, secondly, Lady Isabella Bentinck, daughter of William, Earl of Portland, by whom he had,

    Carolina, m. to Thomas Brand, Esq.

    Anne, d. unmarried.

His grace d. in 1726, and was s. by his grandson,

EVELYN PIERREPOINT, second duke. This nobleman espoused Miss Chudleigh, one of the maids of honour to the Dowager, Princess of Wales, but the lady, so notorious as Duchess of Kingston, was afterwards convicted by her peers of bigamy. The trial took place in 1776, the Lord Chancellor Apsley officiating as high steward. His grace d. in 1773, when, leaving no issue, all his honours became extinct, while his estates devolved upon his nephew, (refer to issue of William, Marquess of Dorchester, son of the first duke,) Charles Meadows, Esq., who assumed the name of Pierrepoint, and was created Earl Manvers.

Arms.—Ar. semée of cinquifoils, gu. a lion rampant, sa.

PIERREPONT — BARON PIERRE-PONT, OF HANSLOPE.

By Letters Patent, dated 19th October, 1714.

Lineage.

GERVASE PIERREPONT, second son of the Hon. William Pierrepoint, second son of Robert, first Earl of Kingston, was created a peer of Ireland as Baron Pierrepont, of Ardglass, and of Great Britain, (19th October, 1714,) as BARON PIERRE-PONT, *of Hanslope, in the county of Bucks.* His lordship espoused Lucy, daughter of Sir John Pelham, Bart., of Loughton, in Sussex, but *d.* issueless in 1715, when all HIS HONOURS became EX-TINCT.

ARMS.—Same as the Earls and Dukes of Kingston.

PINKNEY—BARON PINKNEY.

By Writ of Summons, dated 6th February, 1299, 27 Edward I.

Lineage.

In the time of King Henry I.,

GILO DE PINCHENI gave certain lands lying at Wedon, in Northamptonshire, to the monks of St. Lucian, in France, who thereupon transplanted part of their convent to that place, and made it a cell to their monastery. To this Gilo succeeded his son,

RALPH DE PINCHENI, who was *s.* by his son,

GILBERT DE PINCHENI, who, in the 3rd, 5th, and 6th Henry II., was sheriff of the county of Berks: and upon the assessment in aid for marrying that king's daughter in six years subsequently, certified his knights' fees at fourteen and a half. He was *s.* by his son,

HENRY DE PINCHENI, who was *s.* by his son,

ROBERT DE PINCHENI, one of the barons who took up arms against King John, in consequence of which his lands were seized upon by the crown, and given to Waleran Tyes. But making his peace, they were restored to him, in the 1st year of Henry III. He was *s.* by his son,

HENRY DE PINCHENI, who *m.* Alice, sister and heir of Gerard de Lindesey, and dying in 1254, seised of the Barony of Wedon, in the county of Northampton, which he held of the king in capite by barony, besides lands in Bucks and Essex, was *s.* by his son,

HENRY DE PINCHENY. This baron had a military summons to attend the king against the Welsh, in the 42nd Henry III. He was *s.* at his decease by his son,

ROBERT DE PINCHENY, who, in the 10th Edward I., being in the king's service in Wales, had scutage of all his tenants by military service, in the counties of Northampton, Bucks, Bedford, Essex, Herts, Warwick, Oxford, Berks, Suffolk, Norfolk, and Somerset. He was afterwards in the wars of Gascoyne and dying about the year 1297, was *s.* by his brother,

HENRY DE PINKNEY, who was in the wars

of Scotland, in the 26th Edward I., and was summoned to parliament as a BARON, in the 25th, 27th, and 28th of the same reign. His lordship having no issue, made a surrender of his lands in 1301 to the king, and his heirs for ever. At his decease the BARONY OF PINKNEY became EXTINCT.

ARMS.—Or. four fusils in fesse, gu.

PIPARD—BARON PIPARD.

By Writ of Summons, dated 6th February, 1299, 27 Edward I.

Lineage.

RALPH PIPARD, said to be a younger son of Ralph Fitz-Nicholas, steward of the household to King Henry III., having distinguished himself in the Welsh and Scottish wars, temp. Edward I., was summoned to parliament as a BARON from 6th February, 1299, to 24th July, 1302. In the 30th Edward I. his lordship was made governor for life of Bolesover and Hareston Castles, in the county of Derby. Lord Pipard *d.* in 1309, leaving JOHN, his son and heir, but neither he nor any of his descendants were ever summoned to parliament, nor esteemed barons.

ARMS.—Ar. two bars gules on a canton, as. a cinquefoil, or.

PITT—BARONS CAMELFORD.

By Letters Patent, dated 5th January, 1784.

Lineage.

THOMAS PITT, Esq., of Boconnock, son and heir of Thomas, (elder son of Robert Pitt, brother of William, first Earl of Chatham,) was elevated to the peerage, 5th January, 1784, as BARON CAMELFORD, *of Boconnock, in the county of Cornwall.* His lordship *m.* Anne, daughter and coheiress of Pinkney Wilkinson, Esq., of Burnham, in Norfolk, and had issue,

THOMAS, his successor.

Anne, *m.* to William, Lord Grenville, uncle of the present Duke of Buckingham.

He *d.* in 1793, and was *s.* by his son,

THOMAS PITT, second baron, a post captain R.N. This nobleman fell in a duel with a gentleman of the name of Best, in 1804, and dying unmarried, the BARONY OF CAMELFORD became EXTINCT, while his estates devolved upon his sister, Anne, Lady Grenville.

ARMS.—Sa. fesse cheque, or. and as., between three besants of the second.

PLANTAGENET—EARLS OF CORNWALL.

Creation, 30th May, 1296.

Lineage.

JOHN PLANTAGENET, youngest son of *King Henry II.,* bore the title of EARL OF CORNWALL, (a dignity which had reverted to the crown upon the decease of Reginald de Dunstanvill, Earl of Cornwall, in 1175,) in the life-time of his elder brother,

King RICHARD L., but on succeeding that monarch, in 1199, as *King* JOHN, the EARLDOM OF CORNWALL merged in the crown, and so remained until it was conferred upon the same monarch's younger son,

RICHARD PLANTAGENET, who was made EARL OF POICTOU AND CORNWALL by his brother, King Henry III., on the 30th May, 1226. This prince acquired high reputation in the council and the field, and during the reign of his brother was one of the leading characters of Europe. In 1241 he was in the Holy Land, and then entered into a truce with the Soldan of Babylon, upon condition that the French prisoners there should be released; that Jerusalem, with all the parts adjacent, should be free from all molestation, and that other immunities should be granted to the christians. In 1252 the earl, journeying through France with a pompous retinue, viz., forty knights, all in rich liveries, five waggons, and fifty sumpter horses, (his lady and his son Henry being also with him,) the pope being then at Lyons, sent all his cardinals except one, besides a number of clerks, to meet the earl, and conduct him thither. And receiving the prince with great respect, feasted him at his own table. In 1255, upon a full meeting of the nobles in parliament assembled at Westminster, the king especially applied himself to the Earl of Cornwall in a formal speech for a large supply of money, viz., forty thousand pounds, the pope having also written to him letters for that purpose; but the prince appears not to have complied with the request. In about two years afterwards certain nobles of ALMAINE, having arrived in England, stated to the whole baronage, then met in full parliament, that, by the unanimous consent of the princes of the empire, the Earl of Cornwall was elected KING OF THE ROMANS; and those ambassadors were followed by the Archbishop of Cologne, and a numerous train of nobility, who came for the purpose of doing homage to the new monarch. Whereupon he gave them five hundred marks towards their travelling expenses, and presented the prelate with a rich mitre, adorned with precious stones. Soon after this the earl repaired to his new dominions, and was solemnly crowned king on ascension-day. In the contest which subsequently took place between the barons and *King* HENRY, he adhered with great fidelity to the latter, and commanded the main body of the royal army at the unfortunate battle of Lewes, where he was made prisoner. But he lived to see the termination of those troubles, and departing this life in 1272, at his manor of Berkhamstead, was buried in the abbey of Hales, which he had founded. The prince had married, first, the Lady Isabel Marshall, third daughter and co-heir of William, Earl of Pembroke, by whom he had four sons and a daughter, who all died young, except

    HENRY, who was taken prisoner with his father at the battle of Lewes, in which he had a principal command. Subsequently having embarked in the Crusade, and being at Viterbuin, in Italy, on his return he was barbarously murdered there in the church of St. Lawrence, at high mass, by

Guy, son of Simon Montfort, Earl of Leicester, the general of the baronial army, in revenge of his father's death, who had been slain at the battle of Evesham.

The King of Almaine espoused, secondly, Sanchia, third daughter and co-heir* of Raymond, Earl of Provence, by whom he had one surviving son,

    EDMUND, his successor.

He married thirdly, Beatrix, niece of Conrad, Archbishop of Cologne, but had no child by that lady. The prince was *s.* as Earl of Cornwall, by his son,

EDMUND PLANTAGENET, who accomplishing his full age, in the 55th Henry III., received the honour of knighthood, upon St. Edward's day, and was invested, soon after, with the title of EARL OF CORNWALL, by cincture, with the sword. In the 16th Edward I., he was made warden of England, during the king's absence in the wars of Scotland, and then marching into Wales, besieged Drosslan Castle, and demolished its walls. The next year, he was constituted sheriff for the county of Cornwall, in fee. His lordship m. Margaret, daughter of Richard de Clare, Earl of Gloucester, but dying without issue, his great inheritance devolved upon the king, as his next of kin and heir-at-law, while the EARLDOM OF CORNWALL became EXTINCT.

ARMS.—Same as the other Plantagenets.

PLANTAGENET—EARLS OF CHESTER, EARLS OF LEICESTER, EARL OF DERBY, EARL OF LINCOLN, DUKE OF LANCASTER.

Earldom of Chester, anno 1253.
Earldom of Leicester, 25th October, 1264.
Earldom of Derby, 16th March, 1337.
Earldom of Lincoln, 20th August, 1349.
Dukedom of Lancaster, 6th March, 1351.

Lineage.

EDMUND PLANTAGENET, surnamed *Crouchback*, younger son of *King* HENRY III., was born at London, in February 1245, and when he had attained his eighth year was solemnly invested by the pope, in the kingdom of Sicily and Apulia. About this time too, he was made EARL OF CHESTER. But neither of these honours turned out eventually of much value, for the real king of Sicily, *Conrad*, was then living; and the Earldom of Chester is said to have been transferred to the prince's elder brother, Edward, afterwards EDWARD I. He soon obtained, however, both possessions and dignities, for upon the forfeiture of Simon de Montfort, Earl of Leicester, the king, by letters patent, granted him the inheritance of the EARLDOM OF LEICESTER, as also the honour and stewardship of England; with the lands likewise of Nicolas de Segrave, an associate in the treason of Montfort. And the next ensuing year he had another grant from the crown of all the goods and chattels, whereof

---

* The other daughters and coheirs were,
    Margaret, *m.* to LEWIS IX., of France.
    Eleanor, *m.* to HENRY III., of England.
    Beatrix, *m.* to CHARLES, King of Sicily.

Robert de Ferrers, Earl of Derby, was possessed upon the day of the skirmish at Chesterfield. He subsequently had grants of the honour of Derby, with the castles, manors, and lands, of the said Robert de Ferrers; and the honour of Leicester, with all the lands of Simon de Montfort, late Earl of Leicester: to hold to himself and the heirs of his body. About the 54th Henry III., the earl went into the Holy Land, and returned within two years. In the reign of Edward I., he was in the Scottish wars and had the grants which he had received from his father confirmed, with additional castles, manors, and lands of great extent. In the 21st of that reign, he procured licence from the crown to make a castle of his house, in the parish of St. Clement's Danes, in the county of Middlesex, called the SAVOY. And founded the nunnery, called the *Minoresses*, without Aldgate, in the suburbs of London. He was afterwards in the Welsh wars; and then proceeded to France, being sent with the Earl of Lincoln, and twenty-six bannerets, into Gascony. He eventually invested Bordeaux, but not succeeding in its reduction, the disappointment affected him so severely, that it brought on a disease which terminated his life in the year 1296. The prince's remains were brought over to England, and honourably interred in Westminster Abbey. Upon his death-bed, he directed "that his body should not be buried 'till his debts were paid." This earl espoused first, AVELINE, (daughter of William de Fortibus, Earl of Albemarle,) COUNTESS OF HOLDERNESS, heir to her father, and by her mother, Countess of Devon and the Isle of Wight, but this great heiress died the following year, without issue. The prince *m.* secondly, Blanche, daughter of Robert, Earl of Artois, (third son of Lewis VIII., King of France,) and widow of *Henry*, KING OF NAVARRE, by whom he had surviving issue,

THOMAS, his successor.

HENRY, of whom hereafter, as restored Earl of Lancaster.

His highness was *s.* by his elder son,

THOMAS PLANTAGENET, Earl of Lancaster. who, in the 26th Edward I., doing his homage, being then esteemed of full age by the king, had livery of his lands, except the dowry of Blanche, his mother; and thereupon marched into Scotland, the king himself being in the expedition. The earl, who was hereditary sheriff of Lancashire, substituted *Richard de Hoghton*, his deputy in that office. For the remainder of this reign, the Earl of Lancaster was constantly employed in the wars of Scotland. In the 4th Edward II., having espoused Alice, only daughter and heiress of Henry de Lacy, Earl of Lincoln, he had livery of the Castle of Denbigh, and other lands of her inheritance; his homage for them being performed the ensuing year, in the presence of divers bishops, earls, and barons, and other of the king's council, in a certain chamber within the house of the Friars Preachers, in London. The earl is said to have borne the title of EARL OF LINCOLN, in right of this lady; after his decease, she married Eubold le Strange, who died *s. p.*, and thirdly, Hugh le Frenes; the which Eubold and Hugh, are deemed,

by many writers, to have been Earls of Lincoln. The said Alice styled herself Countess of Lincoln and Salisbury, and died issueless in 1348. In the 5th Edward II., the Earl of Lancaster joined the confederation against *Piers Gaveston*, and was made their general by those nobles and great personages, who had united for a redress of grievances. It is said, that his father-in-law, Henry de Lacy, Earl of Lincoln, had charged him upon his death-bed, to maintain the quarrel against Gaveston, and that thereupon he joined with the Earl of Warwick, and caused the FAVOURITE to be put to death. From this period, he was never fully restored to the confidence of the king, but was esteemed the great champion of the popular party, in whose cause he eventually laid down his life; for taking up arms against the Spencers, he was made prisoner in a skirmish at Boroughbridge, and being thence conveyed to Pontefract, was beheaded on a plain without the town, (where a beautiful church was afterwards erected, in honour of his memory,) in April, 1321. Dugdale details the events that immediately preceded the earl's untimely death, thus—"That being come to Boroughbridge, he there found Sir Andrew de Harcla, Warden of Carlisle, and the Marches, and Sir Simon Ward, Sheriff of Yorkshire, ready to encounter him. Where relating to Harcla his just quarrel to the Spencers, he (the earl) promised him, if he would favour his cause, to give him one of those five earldoms which he had in possession; and that Harcla refusing, he told him that he would soon repent it, and that he should die a shameful death (as it afterwards happened). Also, that Harcia, then causing his archers to shoot, the fight began, in which many of this earl's party being slain, he betook himself to chapel, refusing to yield to Harcla, and looking to the crucifix, said, ' Good Lord, I render myself to thee, and put myself into thy mercy.' Also, that they then took off his coat armor, and putting upon him one of his men's liveries, carried him by water to York, where they threw balls of dirt at him. Moreover, that from thence, they brought him back to the king at PONTEFRACT CASTLE, and there put him in a tower, towards the abby, which he had newly made. Likewise, that soon after, being brought into the hall, he had sentence of death, by these justices, viz:—*Aymer*, EARL OF PEMBROKE, *Edmund*, EARL OF KENT, *John de Bretaigne*, and *Sir Robert Malmethorpe*, who pronounced the judgment. Whereupon, saying, ' shall I die without answer?' A certain *Gascoigne* took him away, and put a pill'd broken hood on his head, and set him on a lean white jade, without a bridle; and that then he added, ' King of Heaven, have mercy on me, for the king of earth nous ad guarthi.' And that thus he was carried, some throwing pellots of dirt at him, (having a *Fryer-Preacher* for his confessor,) to an hill without the town, where he kneeled down towards the east, until one *Hugin de Muston* caused him to turn his face towards Scotland, and then a villain of London, cut off his head. After which, the prior and monks obtaining his body from the king, buried it on the right hand of the high altar. The day of his death was certainly upon the Monday next, preceding the *An-*

nunciation *of the Blessed Virgin.* Touching his merits," continues the same authority, " there happened afterwards very great disputes: some thinking it fit that he should be accounted a saint, because he was so charitable, and so much an honour of the religious; as also that he died in a just cause; but chiefly because his persecutors came within a short period to untimely ends. On the other side many there were who taxed him for adultery, in keeping of sundry women, notwithstanding he had a wife. Aspersing him likewise for cruelty, in putting to death some persons for small offences; and protecting some for punishment who were transgressors of the laws; alleging also, that he was chiefly swayed by one of his secretaries; and that he did not fight stoutly for justice, but fled, and was taken unarmed. Nevertheless many miracles were reported to have been afterwards wrought in the place where his corps was buried; much confluence of people coming thereto, in honour thereof, till the king, through the incitation of the Spencers, set guards to restrain them. Whereupon they flocked to the place where he suffered death; and so much the more eagerly, as endeavours had been used to restrain them, until a church was erected on the place where he suffered." ALL THE HONOURS of this prince became FORFEITED under his attainder: yet his brother and heir, (having himself no issue,)

HENRY PLANTAGENET, being a distinguished soldier in the Scottish wars, had livery of his lands in the 17th Edward II., and was restored to the dignity of EARL OF LEICESTER. This prince was subsequently one of the leaders in the great confederacy which overturned the power of the Spencers, and deposed King EDWARD II. Upon the accession of EDWARD III., the earl had the honour of girding him with the sword of knighthood, and as soon as the new monarch was crowned, he was appointed, the king being a minor, his guardian. After which, in the parliament begun at Westminster, the attainder against his brother being reversed, he was restored to all the lands of his father and brother, with the EARLDOMS OF LANCASTER AND LEICESTER, and the same year (1st Edward III.,) he was constituted CAPTAIN-GENERAL of all the king's forces in the marches of Scotland. The earl m. Maud, daughter and heiress of Sir Patrick Chaworth, Knt., and had issue,

HENRY, Earl of Derby, his successor.

Maud, m. first, to William de Burgh, Earl of Ulster, by whom she had an only daughter and heiress,

    ELIZABETH DE BURGH, m. to Lionel, Duke of Clarence.

The Lady Maud espoused, secondly, Ralph de Ufford, justice of Ireland, temp. Edward III., and brother of Robert, Earl of Suffolk, by whom she had an only daughter,

    MAUD, m. to Thomas, son of John de Vere, Earl of Oxford.

Blanch. m. to Thomas, Lord Wake, of Lydell, and d. issueless.

Eleanor, m. first, to John, son and heir of Henry, Earl of Buchan; and secondly, to Richard Fitz-Alan, Earl of Arundel.

Jane, m. to John, Lord Mowbray.

Isabel, prioress of Ambresbury.

His lordship d. in 1345, and was s. by his son,

HENRY PLANTAGENET, who, having distinguished himself in the life-time of his father in the Scottish wars, was made captain-general of all the king's forces there, had considerable grants from the crown, and was created EARL OF DERBY, (11th Edward III.) The next year he was with the king in the wars of Flanders, as he was in two years afterwards in the great naval engagement with the French, off Sluees. In the 18th Edward III. we find the prince again in the wars of Scotland, being then the king's lieutenant for the northern parts of England, and general of his army against the Scots; in which capacity he was authorised to treat of peace. After this, as EARL OF DERBY, (his father still alive,) he became one of the first and most successful captains of the age, reducing no less than fifty-six French cities and places of note to the dominion of the king of England, and taking immense treasure in gold. In the year of those great exploits his father died, so that he was prevented assisting the deceased earl's funeral. He had afterwards a chief command at the SIEGE OF CALAIS, bearing then the title of EARL OF LANCASTER, DERBY, and LEICESTER, and STEWARD OF ENGLAND; at which time he had, of his own retinue, eight hundred men at arms, and two thousand archers, with thirty banners, which cost him, in hospitality, a daily disbursement of one hundred pounds. In the 22nd Edward III., after having had previously for his brilliant services extensive grants from the crown, he was made the king's lieutenant in Flanders and France, and the next year was created, by letters patent, EARL OF LINCOLN, soon after which he was constituted the king's lieutenant and captain-general in POICTOU, made a KNIGHT OF THE GARTER, and created DUKE OF LANCASTER. To the latter high dignity he was raised in full parliament, and invested with power to have a CHANCERY in the county of Lancaster, and to enjoy all other liberties and royalties appertaining to a county palatine, in as ample a manner as the Earls of Chester did, in the county palatine of Chester. About this time, too, he was constituted admiral of the king's whole fleet westward. The same year, having obtained licence to go abroad to fight against the infidels, he was surprised in his journey, and forced to pay a large ransom for his liberty: which surprisal having occurred through the Duke of Brunswick's means, the English prince expressed his resentment in language so unmeasured, that the duke sent him a challenge; which being accepted, a day was appointed for the combat: but when it arrived, the Duke of Brunswick was so panic-struck, that he could not wield his shield, sword, or lance; while the Duke of Lancaster, with the most undaunted firmness, in vain awaited his attack. They were, however, afterwards reconciled, by the interference of the French monarch; and thus the English prince acquired great renown for personal valour, while his adversary was covered with disgrace. The close of this heroic nobleman's martial career, was quite as splendid as its opening, and after a most brilliant course of achievements, he d. in 1360, deeply lamented by all classes of his countrymen, including his gallant companions in arms. He lived in one of the most glorious periods of English history, and he was himself the FIRST actor in that splendid era. The prince espoused Isabel, daughter of Henry, Lord Beaumont, and left two daughters his co-heirs: viz.

> MAUD, m. first, to Ralph, son and heir of Ralph, Lord Stafford, and secondly, to William, Duke of Zealand, and died s. p.
>
> BLANCH, m. to JOHN of Gaunt, Earl of Richmond, fourth son of King EDWARD III.,

Which

JOHN (PLANTAGENET), styled of Gaunt, from the place of his birth, who had been created EARL OF RICHMOND, in 1342, was advanced to the DUKEDOM OF LANCASTER, by his father, King EDWARD III., in the 36th year of his reign. After the decease of his first wife, BLANCH, the great heiress of the Duke of Lancaster, he espoused Constance, elder daughter and co-heiress of Peter, KING OF CASTILE, and in her right assumed the title of King of Castile and Leon; in which regal dignity, as well as in those of Duke of Lancaster, Earl of Richmond, Derby, Lincoln, and Leicester, he had summons to parliament: he was likewise Duke of Aquitaine, and a Knight of the Garter. On the decease of Edward III., this prince was joined in the administration of affairs during the minority of his nephew, Richard II. He subsequently attempted the conquest of Spain, at the head of a fine army; and landing at the Groyne, advanced to Compostella, where he was met by John, King of Portugal, between whom and his eldest daughter, the Lady Philippa, a marriage was concluded. Thence he marched into Castile, and there ratified a treaty of peace, by which he abandoned his claim to the throne of Castile and Leon, in consideration of a large sum of money, and the marriage of Henry, PRINCE OF ASTURIAS, with his only daughter, by his second wife, the Lady Katherine Plantagenet. In the latter part of his life he dwelt in retirement, having incurred the displeasure of King Richard, by a motion which he had made in parliament, that his son, HENRY of Bolingbroke, should be declared heir to the crown. He d. at Ely House, Holborn, in 1399.

JOHN of Gaunt espoused, first, as already stated, Lady Blanch Plantagenet, the eventual heiress of the Duke of Lancaster, and had by her,

> HENRY, surnamed of BOLINGBROKE, who, having m. Mary, daughter and co-heir of Humphrey de Bohun, last Earl of Hereford, was created Earl of Hereford, 29th September, 1397.
>
> Philippa, m. to John, King of Portugal.
>
> Elizabeth, m. first, to John Holand, Earl of Huntingdon, and secondly, to Sir John Cornwall.

He m. secondly, Constance, elder daughter and co-heir of Peter of Castile, and by her had an only daughter,

> Katherine, m. to Henry, Prince of Asturias, afterwards, HENRY, the third King of Castile and Leon.

The duke m. thirdly, Catherine, daughter of Sir Payn Roet, alias Guen, King at Arms, and widow of Sir Otho de Swynford, Knt., by whom, before marriage, he had issue,

> JOHN DE BEAUFORT, Earl of Somerset, from whom the present ducal family of Beaufort derives.
>
> HENRY DE BEAUFORT, Cardinal of St. Eusebeus, and Bishop of Winchester.
>
> THOMAS DE BEAUFORT, Earl of Dorset, and Duke of Exeter.
>
> JOAN DE BEAUFORT, m. first, to Robert, Lord Ferrers, of Wemme, and secondly, to Ralph Neville, first Earl of Westmorland.

These children were legitimated by act of parliament, for all purposes, save succession to the throne, in the 20th of Richard II., and derived their surname from the castle of BEAUFORT, the place of their birth. JOHN of Gaunt was s. by his eldest son,

HENRY PLANTAGENET, surnamed of BOLINGBROKE, Earl of Hereford, who, upon the deposition of Richard II., was called to the throne as King HENRY IV., when his great inheritance, with the DUKEDOM OF LANCASTER, and the EARLDOMS OF HEREFORD, DERBY, LINCOLN, and LEICESTER, merged in the crown.

ARMS.—Gules, three lions passant, guardant or, a label of five points, with fleur-de-lis gules.

PLANTAGENET, surnamed DE BROTHERTON — EARL OF NORFOLK and EARL MARSHAL.

By Special Charter, dated 16th December, 1312.

Lineage.

THOMAS PLANTAGENET, eldest son of King Edward I., by his second wife, Margaret, daughter of Philip III., or the Hardy, of France, was born at Brotherton, in Yorkshire, anno 1301, whence the surname, "DE BROTHERTON," and before he had attained his thirteenth year, was advanced, by special charter of his half brother, King Edward II., (at the dying request of his predecessor,) dated 16th December, 1312, to all the honours which Roger le Bigod, some time Earl of Norfolk, and Marshal of England, did enjoy by the name of Earl, in the county of Norfolk, with all the castles, manors and lands, which the said Roger possessed in England, Ireland, and Wales, which had become vested in the crown, by the surrender of the said Roger. But in some years afterwards, the king seized upon the marshalship in the Court of King's Bench, because the Earl of Norfolk had failed to substitute some person on his behalf, to attend the justices of that court, upon their journey into Lancashire; he had, however, restitution of the high office, upon paying a fine of £100. This prince was repeatedly in the wars of Scotland, temp. Edward II. and Edward III., in the latter of which reigns he had a confirmation of the Earldom of Norfolk, and the office of earl marshal. He espoused first, Alice, daughter of Sir Roger Halys, Knt., of Harwich, by whom he had issue,

MARGARET, of whom hereafter.

Alice, m. to Edward de Montacute, and had a daughter,

JOAN, who m. William Ufford, Earl of Suffolk, and d. without male issue.

The prince espoused, secondly, Mary, daughter of William, Lord Roos, and widow of William le Brus, and had a son,

John, who became a monk at the Abbey of Ely.

Thomas of Brotherton d. in 1338, when the EARL-DOM OF NORFOLK became EXTINCT. But his elder daughter and co-heir, who eventually became sole heiress,

The LADY MARGARET PLANTAGENET, was created DUCHESS OF NORFOLK for life, by King Richard II., on the 29th September, 1397. Her grace, at the time styled Countess of Norfolk, claimed the office of earl marshal, at the coronation of that monarch, and prayed that she might execute the same by her deputy; but her claim was not allowed, owing to the want of sufficient time to investigate its merits, and the prior appointment for the occasion, of Henry, Lord Percy. This illustrious lady espoused, first, John, Lord Segrave, and had issue,

Anne, Abbess of Barking.

Elizabeth, m. John, Lord Mowbray (see Mowbray, Earl of Nottingham, and Duke of Norfolk).

The duchess m. secondly, Sir William Manny, K.G., and had an only surviving daughter,

Anne, m. to John Hastings, Earl of Pembroke.

Her grace d. in 1399, when the dignity became EXTINCT.

ARMS.—Gu. three lions passant quardant or. a label for difference.

PLANTAGENET — DUCHESS OF NORFOLK.

(Refer to PLANTAGENET, surnamed "De Brotherton," Earl of Norfolk).

PLANTAGENET — BARONS OF WOODSTOCK, EARLS OF KENT.

Barony, by Writ of Summons, dated 5th Aug., 1320, 14 Edward II.

Earldom, by Charter, dated in 1321.

Lineage.

EDMUND PLANTAGENET, surnamed of *Woodstock*, from the place of his birth, second son of King Edward I., was summoned to parliament, as "Edmundo de Wodestok," on the 5th August, 1320, about two years before he attained majority. He had previously been in the wars of Scotland, and had obtained considerable territorial grants from the crown. In the next year he was created EARL

496

OF KENT, and had a grant of the Castle of Okham, in the county of Rutland, and shrievalty of the county. About the same time he was constituted governor of the Castle of Tunbridge, in Kent; and upon the breaking out of the insurrection, under Thomas Plantagenet, Earl of Lancaster, he was commissioned by the king, to pursue that rebellious prince, and to lay siege to the castle of Pontifract. The Earl of Lancaster was subsequently made prisoner at Boroughbridge, and the Earl of Kent was one of those who condemned him to death. From this period, during the remainder of the reign of his brother, Edmund, of Woodstock, was constantly employed in the cabinet or the field. He was frequently accredited on embassies to the Court of France, and was in all the wars in Gascony and Scotland. But after the accession of his nephew, King Edward III., he was arrested and sentenced to death, for having conspired, with other nobles, to deliver his brother, the deposed Edward II., out of prison. Whereupon, by the management of Queen Isabel, and her paramour, Mortimer, he was beheaded at Winchester, (1390,) after he had remained upon the scaffold, from noon until five o'clock in the evening, waiting for an executioner; no one being willing to undertake the horrid office, till a malefactor from the Marshalsea was procured to perform it. The earl m. Margaret, daughter of John, Lord Wake, and sister and heiress of Thomas, Lord Wake, by whom he had issue,

EDMUND, } successively Earls of Kent.
JOHN, }

Margaret, m. to Amaneus, eldest son of Bernard, Lord de la Bretta, and died s. p.

JOANE, from her extraordinary beauty, styled "the Fair Maid of Kent," m. first, William Montacute, Earl of Salisbury, from whom she was divorced;* secondly, Sir Thomas Holland, K.G., and thirdly, the renowned hero, EDWARD, the Black Prince, by whom she was the mother of *King* Richard II.

The unfortunate earl's eldest son,

EDMUND PLANTAGENET was restored in blood and honours by parliament, the year in which his father suffered, and thus became *Baron Woodstock* and EARL OF KENT—but d. soon after in minority, unmarried, and was s. by his brother,

JOHN PLANTAGENET, third Earl of Kent, who m. Elisabeth, daughter of the Duke of Juliers, but died s. p. in 1352, when the EARLDOM OF KENT, and BARONIES OF WOODSTOCK AND WAKE, devolved upon his only surviving sister,

JOANE, the Fair Maid of Kent, who m. Sir Thomas Holland, Lord Holland, K.G. (see Holland, Earl of Kent).

---

* Collins, in explanation of the divorce, states, that the Earl of Salisbury had intended to have married her, had she not been previously contracted to Sir Thomas Holland; yet, during the absence of Sir Thomas, the Earl made a subsequent contract, and withheld the lady, until the Pope decided against him—when acquiescing, it was said, she was divorced.

PLANTAGENET—EARL OF CORN-WALL.

By Patent, anno 1398.

Lineage.

JOHN PLANTAGENET, second son of King Edward II., commonly called "John of Eltham," from the place of his birth, was created by patent, dated in 1327, EARL OF CORNWALL. This prince died unmarried in 1336, when the EARLDOM OF CORNWALL became EXTINCT.

ARMS.—Same as the other branches of the House of Plantagenet.

PLANTAGENET—DUKE OF CORN-WALL.

By Patent, dated in 1337.

Lineage.

EDWARD PLANTAGENET, the gallant *Black Prince*, eldest son of *King* EDWARD III., was advanced by patent, in 1337, to the dignity of DUKE OF CORNWALL, with the following limitation:—"Habend. et tenend. sibi et hæred. ac hæredii : suor. regum Angliæ filiis primogenitis, et ejusdem loci ducibus in regno Angliæ hæreditario ut predicitur successoris." He was subsequently created PRINCE OF WALES, and the dukedom merged in the principality. Since the dignity was so conferred upon Prince Edward, it has been vested in the HEIR APPARENT to the throne of England, who at his birth, or at the decease of an elder brother, becomes DUKE OF CORNWALL, and he is always created Prince of Wales. The Black Prince espoused his cousin, JOANE, commonly called the *Fair Maid of Kent*, daughter of Edmund, Earl of Kent, and widow of Sir Thomas Holland, by whom he left, at his decease, 8th July, 1376, his father, King Edward still living, an only surviving son,

    RICHARD, afterwards the unhappy KING RICHARD II.

PLANTAGENET — DUKE OF CLA-RENCE.

Created, 15th September, 1362.

Lineage.

GILBERT DE CLARE, Earl of Hertford and Gloucester, who fell at the battle of Bannockburn in 1313, leaving no issue, his titles became extinct, while his estates devolved upon his sisters, as co-heirs, of whom

    ELIZABETH DE CLARE, the youngest sister, had married JOHN DE BURGH, son of Richard, Earl of Ulster, and through this alliance the HONOUR OF CLARE came into the possession of the De Burghs. The heiress of Clare left a son,

        WILLIAM DE BURGH, *Earl of Ulster*, who m. Maud, sister of Henry Plantagenet, Duke of Lancaster, and left an only child and heiress,

        ELIZABETH DE BURGH, who espoused

LIONEL PLANTAGENET, third son of King Edward III., who became, *jure uxoris*, *Earl* of Ulster, and was created, 15th September, 1362, DUKE OF CLARENCE.[*] The prince was likewise a KNIGHT of the GARTER. He had an only child by the heiress of Ulster,

    PHILIPPA PLANTAGENET, who m. Edmund Mortimer, Earl of March, and had, with other issue,

        ROGER MORTIMER, Earl of March, who, in the parliament held 9th Richard II., was declared NEXT HEIR to the THRONE. This nobleman had, with other issue,

            EDMUND, his successor.

            Anne, who m. *Richard Plantagenet*, EARL OF CAMBRIDGE, younger son of Edmund, Duke of York, fifth son of Edward III., and had a son,

                RICHARD, Duke of York, who fell at Wakefield in 1460, leaving

                    EDWARD, Duke of York, who ascended the throne as EDWARD IV.

                    George, Duke of Clarence.

                    RICHARD, Duke of Gloucester, who ascended the throne as Richard III.

Lionel, Duke of Clarence, m. secondly, Violante, daughter of the Duke of Milan, but had no issue. He d. in 1368, when the DUKEDOM OF CLARENCE became EXTINCT.

ARMS.—Gu. Three lions passant guardant or.

PLANTAGENET — EARL OF CAM-BRIDGE, DUKES OF YORK, DUKE OF ALBE-MARLE.

Earldom, 13th November, 1362.
Dukedom, 6th August, 1385.
Dukedom of Albemarle, 29th September, 1397.

Lineage.

EDMUND PLANTAGENET, surnamed Langley, from the place of his birth, fifth son of King Edward III., was created by his father, on the 13th November, 1362, *Earl* OF CAMBRIDGE, and by his nephew, King Richard II., 6th August, 1385, DUKE OF YORK. This prince espoused, first, Isabel, daughter and co-heir of Peter, King of Castile and Leon, and sister of Constance, the wife of John of Gaunt, by whom he had issue,

    EDWARD, his successor in the Dukedom of York.

    RICHARD, of Conisburgh, who succeeded to the EARLDOM OF CAMBRIDGE. This prince

---

[*] The title of CLARENCE was derived from the honour of Clare.

was beheaded at Southampton for conspiring against Henry IV. in 1415, when the Earldom of Cambridge became forfeited. He had m. Anne,* sister and co-heir of Edward Mórtimer, Earl of March, son of Philippa, only daughter and heiress of Lionel, Duke of Clarence, second son of King Edward III., by whom he left an only son and a daughter, viz.

RICHARD, who succeeded his uncle as Duke of York.

Isabel, m. to Henry Bourchier, Earl of Essex.

Edmund, Duke of York, m. secondly, Joane, daughter of Thomas Holland, Earl of Kent, and sister and co-heir of Edmund, Earl of Kent, but had no issue. The Duke of York attained the highest reputation in the cabinet and the field, and after vainly endeavouring to sustain his imbecile nephew, Richard, upon the throne, he retired to his seat at Langley, upon the accession of Henry IV., and died there in 1402. The prince, who was a KNIGHT OF THE GARTER, was s. by his eldest son,

EDWARD PLANTAGENET, as second Duke of Yok, who had been created Duke of Albemarle, 29th September, 1397, and was restored to the Dukedom of York in 1405, which he had been previously rendered incapable of inheriting—he was also invested with the Garter. This gallant prince, who had become eminent in arms, fell at AZINCOURT in 1415, and his brother having been previously put to death, the Dukedom of York (the prince leaving no issue) devolved upon his nephew,

RICHARD PLANTAGENET, who was restored to the Earldom of Cambridge, and allowed to inherit as third Duke of York. This prince becoming afterwards one of the most powerful subjects of the period in which he lived, laid claim to the throne as the descendant of Lionel, Duke of Clarence, second son of Edward III., whereas the reigning monarch, Henry VI., sprang from John of Gaunt, Duke of Lancaster, third son of the same king, and thus originated the devastating war of the Roses. In his pretensions the duke was supported by the Nevils and other great families, but his ambitious projects all closed at the battle of Wakefield in 1460, where his party sustained a signal defeat, and he was himself slain. The prince had espoused Cicily, daughter of Ralph Nevil, Earl of Westmorland, and left issue,

EDWARD, his successor.

Edmund, said to have borne the title of Earl of Rutland. This prince at the age of twelve was barbarously murdered by Lord Clifford, after the battle of Wakefield.

George, Duke of Clarence, (see Plantagenet, Duke of Clarence.)

RICHARD, Duke of Gloucester, (afterwards King Richard III.)

Anne, m. first to Henry Holland, Duke of Exeter, and secondly, to Sir Thomas St. Leger, Knt., by whom she had a daughter,

---

* Through this alliance the house of York derived its right to the crown.

428

ANNE ST. LEGER, who m. Sir George Manners, ancestor of the present ducal house of Rutland.

Elizabeth, m. to John de la Pole, Duke of Suffolk.

Margaret, m. to Charles, Duke of Burgundy, but had no issue. This was the Duchess of Burgundy, so persevering in her hostility to Henry VII., and her zeal in the cause of York, who set up the pretended Plantagenets, Warbeck and Symnel.

Ursula.

Richard, Duke of York, was s. by his son,

EDWARD PLANTAGENET, fourth Duke of York, who, after various fortunes at the head of the Yorkists, finally established himself upon the throne as EDWARD IV., when the DUKEDOM OF YORK merged in the crown.

PLANTAGENET—EARLS OF BUCKINGHAM, DUKE OF GLOUCESTER.

Earldom, anno 1377.
Dukedom, 12th November, 1385.

Lineage.

THOMAS PLANTAGENET, born at Woodstock, 7th January, 1355, and thence surnamed "THOMAS OF WOODSTOCK," youngest son of King Edward III., espoused the Lady Alianore de Bohun, one of the daughters and co-heirs of Humphrey, last Earl of Hereford, Essex, and Northampton; and in consideration of that alliance was shortly afterwards made CONSTABLE OF ENGLAND (a dignity enjoyed for nearly two centuries by the Bohuns). At the coronation of his nephew, King Richard II., the prince was advanced to the EARLDOM OF BUCKINGHAM, with a grant of a thousand marks per annum, to be paid out of the exchequer, until provision of so much value should be made otherwise for him, and twenty pounds a year out of the issues of the county, whence he derived his title. From this period, he was constantly employed as a commander in foreign wars, until the 9th of the same reign, when, for his eminent services, he was created by patent, dated 12th November, 1385, DUKE OF GLOUCESTER. In that interim, he had been likewise sent into Essex, at the head of a large force, to suppress the insurrection of Jack Straw. The ceremony of his creation, as Duke of Gloucester, was performed at HOSELOW LODGE, in TIVIDALE, by girding with a sword, and putting a cap with a circle of gold, upon the prince's head; the parliament being then sitting at London, and assenting thereto. In two years afterwards, he was constituted JUSTICE OF CHESTER, but he subsequently forfeited the favour of the king, by his opposition to Robert de Vere, DUKE OF IRELAND, and his coalition with the lords who assembled in arms, at Haringey Park, to put an end to the power of that celebrated minion. After the disgrace and banishment of De Vere, the Duke of Gloucester obtained some immunities from the crown, but the king never pardoned the course he had pursued in that affair, and eventually it cost the duke his life. The

story of his destruction is thus told by Froissard—
" The king rode to Havering, in the county of
Essex, as it were on a hunting party, and came to
Plessy, where the duke then resided, about five
o'clock, the duke having just newly supped, who
hearing of his coming (with the duchess and his
children, met him in the court). The king hereupon being brought in, a table was spread for his
supper. Whereat being set, he told the duke, that
he would have him ride to London with him that
night; saying, that the Londoners were to be before
him on the morrow, as also his uncles of LANCAS-
TER and YORK, with divers others of the nobles;
and that he would be guided by their counsels,
wishing him to command his steward to follow
with his train. Hereupon the duke suspecting no
hurt, so soon as the king had supp't, got on horseback, accompanied with no more than seven servants, (three esquires and four yeomen,) taking the
way of Bondelay, to shun the common road to London; and riding fast, approached near Stratford, on
the river Thames. Being got thus far, and coming
near to the ambuscado* which was laid, the king
rode away a great pace, and left him somewhat behind.
Whereupon the earl marshal with his band, came
galloping after, and overtaking him, said: *I arrest
you in the king's name.* The duke therefore discerning that he was betrayed, call'd out aloud to the
king, but to no purpose, for the king rode on, and
took no notice of it. This was done about ten or
eleven o'clock in the night; whence he was forthwith carried into a barge, and so into a ship, which
lay in the Thames, wherein they conveyed him, the
next day, to Calais. Being thus brought thither,
he askt the earl marshal the cause thereof, saying:
*Methinks you hold me here as a prisoner; let me go
abroad, and let me see the fortress;* but the earl
marshal refused." Froissard concludes by stating:
" That the duke hereupon fearing his life, desired
to have a priest, who sang mass before him, that he
might be confessed; and so he had. When, soon
after dinner, having washed his hands, there came
into the chamber four men, who suddenly casting a
towel about his neck, strangled him." After this
violent death, the body of the prince was laid naked
in his bed, and it was rumoured that he died of a
palsy; the earl marshal going into deep mourning
for his lamented cousin. This account of the
duke's death is, however, according to Dugdale,
erroneous. "As appeareth" (saith that celebrated
antiquary) " by the deposition of John Hall, a servant to the earl marshal, then present, and in some
sort assisting in that most barbarous murder, viz.
' That in the month of September, 21st Richard
II., Thomas, Earl Marshal and Nottingham,
whom the deposition calls Duke of Norfolk,' (by
reason he was soon afterwards advanced to that
honour, as a reward for this bloody fact,) 'and one
John Colfox, his esquire, came in the night-time
to the chamber of the said Hall, in Calais; and that
Colfox calling him out of his bed, commanded him

* This plot to take away the life of the Duke of
Gloucester, was previously concerted with Thomas
Mowbray, Earl Marshal, and Earl of Nottingham,
Richard's great confidant

to come forthwith to his lord. Also, that when he
came, the Duke of Norfolk asked him, ' If he
heard nothing of the Duke of Gloucester;' and
that he answered, ' *He supposed him to be dead.*'
Whereupon the Duke of Norfolk replied, ' *No, he
is not; but the king hath given charge that he shall
be murthered;*' and farther said, ' that he himself,
with the Earl of Rutland,' (afterwards made Duke
of Aumarle,) ' had sent certain of their esquires and
yeomen, to be then there:' and likewise told him,
the said Hall, ' that he should also be present, in
his (Norfolk's) name;' but that Hall said, ' *No;*'
desiring that he might rather lose all he had, and
depart, rather than be present thereat; and that
the duke then replied, ' He should do so, or die for
it;' giving him a great knock on the pate.
" ' Moreover, that the said duke, with Colfox and
Hall, went to the church of Nostre Dame, in Calais,
where they found William Hampsterley and ......
Bradeston, (two esquires of the Duke of Norfolk,)
as also one William Serle, a yeoman of the chamber to the king; .... Faunceys, a yeoman of the
chamber to the Earl of Rutland; William Rogers
and William Dennys, yeomen of the said Duke of
Norfolk, and another yeoman of the Earl of Rutland's, called *Cock of the Chamber*, and that there it
was told to this Hall, that all the rest had made
oath, that they should not discover anything of
their purpose, causing him in like manner, to swear
upon the sacrament, in the presence of one Sir
William, a chaplain of St. George, in the church
of Nostre Dame, that he should keep counsel
therein. Furthermore, that after the oath thus
made, they went along with the Duke of Norfolk,
to a certain hostel, called Prince's Inn; and being
come thither, that the said duke sent Colfox,
Hampsterley, Bradeston, Serle, Faunceys, William
Roger, William Dennys, Cock of the Chamber,
and Hall, into a house within that inn, and
then departed from them, with some unknown
persons. Likewise, that so soon as they were come
into that house, there entered one John Lovetoft,
with divers other esquires, unknown, who brought
with him the Duke of Gloucester, and delivered
him to Serle and Faunceys, in an inner room of
the house, and said, ' Here are Serle and Faunceys;' and that they, thereupon, taking the duke
from Lovetoft, brought him to a chamber, and
said, ' They would speak with him;' adding, ' it
was the king's pleasure that he must suffer death.'
Whereunto he answered, ' *If it be so, it is welcome.*'
Also, that Serle and Faunceys, forthwith appointed a priest to confess him; and that being
done, made him lie down upon a bed, and laying a
feather-bed upon him, held it about his mouth till
he died, William Roger, William Dennys, and
Cock of the Chamber, holding down the sides of
it; and Colfox, Hampsterly and Bradeston, upon
their knees all the while, weeping and praying for
his soul, Hall himself keeping the door. Which
being done, he was attainted in the parliament,
held on Monday next, ensuing the feast of the Exaltation of the Holy Cross, of the same year.'" Of
those assassins, Hall, in the 1st of Henry IV., had
judgment in parliament, to be drawn from Tower
Hill to Tyburn, and there hanged and quartered;

and Serle being taken in Scotland, in the year 1404, had a similar sentence. The others, it is presumed, never returned into England. The Duke of Norfolk ended his days, and died of grief, in exile ; and Edward Plantagenet, Earl of Rutland, afterwards Duke of York, was slain at the battle of Azincourt. Thus the principal instigators and perpetrators of this foul deed, all met their deserts. The fate of the unhappy RICHARD, himself, is too well known, to require particularizing here. The death of the Duke of Gloucester occurred in 1397. He left issue,

HUMPHREY PLANTAGENET.

Anne Plantagenet, m. first, to Thomas, Earl of Stafford, by whom she had no issue ; and secondly, by virtue of the King's especial licence, (22d Richard II.,) to the said Thomas's brother, Edmund, Earl of Stafford, by whom she had a son,

Humphrey, created Duke of Buckingham.

Her ladyship espoused, thirdly, William Bourchier, Earl of Eu, in Normandy.

Joane, was designed to be the wife of Gilbert, Lord Talbot, but died unmarried.

Isabel, a nun.

The duke's son,

HUMPHREY PLANTAGENET, who was styled Earl of Buckingham, after the murder of his father, was conveyed to Ireland, by King Richard, and imprisoned in the Castle of Trim, where he remained until the accession of Henry IV., who purposed restoring him to all the honours, but he died upon his return to England, at Chester, in 1399.

ARMS.—Quarterly, France and England, a bordure ar.

Note.—*Thomas of Woodstock*, DUKE OF GLOUCESTER, was summoned to parliament in 1385, as Duke of Aumarle, but never afterwards by that title, nor did his above son, Humphrey, ever assume the dignity.

PLANTAGENET — EARL OF ALBEMARLE, DUKE OF CLARENCE.

Created, 9th July, 1411.

Lineage.

THOMAS PLANTAGENET, K.G., son of *King* HENRY IV., was created by his father, 9th July, 1411, *Earl of Albemarle* and DUKE OF CLARENCE. This martial and valiant prince being engaged in the wars of Henry V., fell at the battle of BAUGY in 1421, and dying without legitimate issue,* HIS HONOURS became EXTINCT.

* He had a natural son, SIR JOHN CLARENCE, called the "Bastard of Clarence," who accompanied the remains of his gallant father from Baugy to Canterbury for their interment. This Sir John Clarence had a grant of lands in Ireland from King Henry VI., and according to Camden, he bore for arms, "Party per chevron g. and az. two lions adverse saliant and gardant or. in the chief, and a fleur-de-lis, or. in base.

446

PLANTAGENET — EARL OF KENDALL, DUKE OF BEDFORD.

By Letters Patent, dated 6th May, 1414.

Lineage.

JOHN PLANTAGENET, third son of King Henry IV., by his first consort, the Lady Mary de Bohun, daughter and co-heir of Humphrey, Earl of Hereford, was created by his brother, *King* HENRY V., by letter patent, dated 6th May, 1414, EARL OF KENDALL and DUKE OF BEDFORD, being designated previously, "John de Lancaster." The achievements of this eminent person, form so prominent an era in the annals of the Plantagenets, and have been detailed so much at length by all our great historians, that it were idle to attempt more than a mere sketch of his most conspicuous actions, in a work of this description. His first public employment in the reign of his father, was that of CONSTABLE OF ENGLAND, and governor of the town and castle of Berwick-upon-Tweed. In the 3rd of Henry V., he was constituted lieutenant of the whole realm of England, the king himself being then in the wars of France, and the next year he was retained by indenture, to serve in those wars, being appointed general of the king's whole army, both by sea and land ; whereupon he set sail, and encountering the French near Southampton, achieved a great naval victory over them. In the year ensuing, the king making another expedition into France, the duke was again constituted lieutenant of the kingdom during his absence. In the 7th Henry V., with large reinforcements to the king in Normandy ; and the next year, assisted at the siege of Melon, which held out fourteen weeks and four days, before it surrendered. Upon the accession of HENRY VI., the duke was constituted chief counsellor and protector to the king, then an infant, and appointed at the same time REGENT OF FRANCE. But all his splendid achievements in "the land of the Gaul," great, glorious, and gallant as they were, lie for ever obscured, beneath one dark deed of inhumanity, his cruel, vindictive, and savage treatment, of the most undaunted of his foes—the enthusiastic Maid of Orleans, the renowned JOAN OF ARC.

The prince, who, with his other honours, had been invested with the Garter, espoused first, Anne, daughter of John, Duke of Burgundy, and secondly, Jacqueline, daughter of Peter, of Luxemburgh, Earl of St. Paul, but having no issue, the EARLDOM OF KENDALL and DUKEDOM OF BEDFORD became EXTINCT, at his decease in 1435. The duke's remains were interred in the Cathedral of *Notre Dame*, at Roan, under a plain tomb of black marble. He was deeply lamented by the English people. He had ever borne the character of one of the first captains of his age, and the greatest general of his line. His widow Jacqueline of Luxemburgh, espoused, secondly, Sir Richard Wideville, and had, with other issue, Elizabeth Wideville, who espoused, first, Sir John Grey, of Groby, and after his decease in the second battle of St. Albans, became QUEEN CONSORT of *King* EDWARD IV.

Lewis XI. of France, says Banks, being counselled to deface the Duke of Bedford's tomb, is said to have used the following generous expression:—

"What honour shall it be, either to us or you, to break this monument, and to rake out of the earth the bones of one, who, in his life-time, neither my father, nor any of your progenitors, with all their puissance, were ever once able to make fly one foot backwards; that by his strength or policy, kept them all out of the principal dominions of France, and out of this noble Duchy of Normandy. Wherefore I say, first, God save his soul, and let his body rest in quiet; which, when he was living, would have disquieted the proudest of us all; and as for his tomb, which, I assure you, is not so worthy as his acts deserve, I account it an honour to have him remain in my dominions."

ARMS.—France and England, a label per pale of five points, the first two erm. the other three az. charged with nine fleur-de-lis, or.

PLANTAGENET—DUKE OF GLOU-
CESTER.

Created, 26th September, 1414.

Lineage.

HUMPHREY PLANTAGENET, fourth son of King HENRY IV., by his first wife, the Lady Mary de Bohun, daughter and co-heiress of Humphrey, Earl of Hereford, Essex, and Northampton, Constable of England, was made a Knight of the Bath, at his father's coronation, along with his brothers, THOMAS, afterwards Duke of Clarence, and JOHN, Duke of Bedford. In the 1st of Henry V., he obtained with other grants, the CASTLE and LORDSHIP of PEMBROKE; shortly after which, being made DUKE OF GLOUCESTER, in the parliament held at Leicester, he had summons by that title, as well as by the title of EARL OF PEMBROKE, 26th September, 1414. In the 3rd of the same reign, the prince assisted at the siege of Harfleur, and he received soon after a dangerous wound, in the celebrated battle of AZINCOURT. During the remainder of the reign of his martial brother, the Duke of Gloucester was almost wholly engaged in the wars of France; and upon the accession of HENRY VI., he was constituted, as he had been twice before, upon temporary absences of the king, lieutenant of the realm. In this year it was, that he was involved in a serious dispute with William, Duke of Brabant, by reason of marrying that prince's wife, Jaqueline, Duchess of Hainault, who had come to England, upon some disagreement with her husband. The matter led to open hostilities, and a challenge to single combat passed between the two dukes, and was accepted; but that mode of deciding the affair was prevented by the Duke of Bedford, and the contest was finally terminated, by the Duke of Gloucester's bowing to the decision of the Pope, and withdrawing from the lady. He then espoused his concubine, Eleanor, daughter of Reginald, Lord Cobham; and in a few years afterwards, a complaint was made to parliament, against him, by one "Mistress Stokes and other bold women," because

he suffered Jaqueline, his wife, to be prisoner to the Duke of Burgundy, and for living himself with an adultress. In the 14th of Henry VI., he obtained a grant for life, of the Earldom of Flanders, which was held of the king in capite, in right of his crown of France; and he had numerous and most valuable grants of manors and lordships in England; he had also, an annuity of two thousand marks, out of the exchequer, during the king's pleasure. The duke incurring, however, the jealousy of MARGARET of Anjou, fell, at length, a victim to her machinations. Attending a parliament which had been called at St. Edmundsbury, he was arrested upon the second day of the session, by the Viscount Beaumont, Constable of England, accompanied by the Duke of Buckingham, and some others, and put in ward; all his servants being taken from him, and thirty-two of the chief of them sent to different prisons. The following night, the prince was found dead in his bed, supposed to have been either strangled or smothered; and his body was exhibited to the lords, as though he had died of apoplexy.

The duke, who received from the people the title of Good, and was called "the Father of his country," had, with his other honours, been invested with the Garter. He was a proficient in learning; wrote some tracts; laid the foundation of the Bodleian library, and built the divinity schools in the University of Oxford. The death of the prince happened in 1446, and as he left no issue, HIS HONOURS became EXTINCT.

ARMS.—Quarterly, France and England, a border, ar.

PLANTAGENET—DUKE OF GLOU-
CESTER.

Created in parliament, 1461.

Lineage.

RICHARD PLANTAGENET, brother of King Edward IV., was created, according to Dugdale, anno 1461, DUKE OF GLOUCESTER, but he was not summoned to parliament until the 10th August, 1469. He usurped the throne, upon the murder of his nephews, Edward V. and the Duke of York, in the Tower, under the title of RICHARD III.; he had previously governed the realm as Protector. Richard fell at BOSWORTH FIELD, 22nd August, 1485, and his rival Henry, Earl of Richmond, succeeded him, as Henry VII. When the Duke of Gloucester assumed the reins of government as king, the dukedom merged in the crown.

Note.—The body of King Richard was buried in the chapel of the monastery at Leicester, at the dissolution whereof, the place of his burial happened to fall into the bounds of a citizen's garden; which being afterwards purchased by Mr. Robert Kerrick, (some time Mayor of Leicester,) was by him covered with a handsome stone pillar, three feet high, with this inscription: "Here lies the body of Richard III., some time King of England." This he shewed me walking in his garden, 1612, (see Peck's Collection of Curious Historical Pieces, p. 85.)—BANKS.

PLANTAGENET — DUKE OF CLARENCE, EARLS OF WARWICK, AND SALISBURY.

Dukedom of Clarence,
Earldom of Warwick,
and Salisbury.
} by Letters Patent {
anno 1461.
25th March, 1472.

Lineage.

GEORGE PLANTAGENET, K. G., son of Richard, Duke of York, and brother of *King Edward IV.*, was created DUKE OF CLARENCE in 1461, and having married the Lady Isabel Nevil, daughter and co-heir of Richard Nevill, Earl of Salisbury, and Earl of Warwick, was advanced to those dignities by letters patent, dated 25th March, 1472. This unhappy prince was attainted of high treason, and suffered death, by being drowned in a butt of Malmsey, in the Tower, anno 1477, when all his honours became FORFEITED. *King Edward IV.*, assented of course to the execution, but he is said subsequently to have most deeply lamented having done so, and upon all occasions when the life of a condemned person was solicited, he used openly to exclaim, " Oh, unhappy brother, for whose life no man would make suit." The Duke of Clarence left issue,

    EDWARD, who, after his father's death, was entitled EARL OF WARWICK. This unhappy prince was born the child of adversity, and spent almost the whole of his melancholy life in prison. After the decease of his uncle, *King Edward IV.*, his other uncle, the Duke of Gloucester, had him removed to the Castle of Sheriff-Hutton, in Yorkshire, where he remained until the defeat of the Yorkists at Bosworth, placed him in the hands of Henry VII., by whose order he was transferred to the Tower of London, and there more closely confined than before, solely because he was the last male PLANTAGENET living. He was not allowed, however, a protracted existence, for being arraigned for high treason, and betrayed under a promise of pardon, into an acknowledgment of guilt, he was condemned, and executed upon Tower Hill, in 1499.

    MARGARET. This lady upon the atrocious murder of her brother, became the last member of the royal and illustrious house of PLANTAGENET (see Plantagenet, Countess of Salisbury).

ARMS.—Gu. three lions passant, guardant, or.

Note.—From the period that George Plantagenet, DUKE OF CLARENCE, lost his life in 1477, the DUKEDOM OF CLARENCE lay dormant, until revived in the person of His Royal Highness *Prince WILLIAM-HENRY* (Guelph), third son of *his Majesty King GEORGE III.*, who was created DUKE OF CLARENCE AND ST. ANDREWS, in the peerage of Great Britain, and EARL OF MUNSTER, in that of Ireland, on the 19th of May, 1789, ALL WHICH HONOURS merged in the crown, upon the accession of the duke in 1830, as

𝕶ing 𝖂illiam the 𝖋ourth.

PLANTAGENET — COUNTESS OF SALISBURY.

By Letters Patent, dated 14th October, 1513.

Lineage.

MARGARET PLANTAGENET, daughter of George, Duke of Clarence, and the Lady Isabel Nevil, eldest daughter, and eventually sole heir, of Richard, Earl of Warwick and Salisbury, son and heir of Alice, daughter and heir of Thomas Montacute, Earl of Salisbury, became the LAST OF THE PLANTAGENETS, upon the execution of her brother, EDWARD PLANTAGENET, called Earl of Warwick, by Henry VII. in 1499, and petitioned parliament, in the 5th of *King HENRY VIII.*, to be restored to the honours of her maternal family. Whereupon she was advanced to the dignity of COUNTESS OF SALISBURY on the 14th October, 1513; and obtained at the same time letters patent, establishing her in the castles, manors, and lands of Richard, late Earl of Salisbury, her grandfather, which had fallen to the crown by the attainder of her brother, Edward, called Earl of Warwick. Notwithstanding these substantial marks of royal favour, an opportunity in several years after was seized upon to destroy the only remaining branch of the Plantagenets in this illustrious lady; and at a period of life too, when, in the natural progress of events, her course was nearly closed. At the advanced age of seventy years, 31st Henry VIII., her ladyship was condemned to death, unheard by parliament, and beheaded on Tower Hill in two years afterwards, anno 1541, when her dignity, as COUNTESS OF SALISBURY, fell under the ATTAINDER. Her ladyship had espoused Sir Richard Pole, K. G., and had issue,

    HENRY, summoned to parliament as BARON MONTAGU (see Pole, Baron Montagu).

    Geffery (Sir), upon whose testimony his elder brother, Lord Montagu, was convicted of, and executed for, high treason. He received sentence of death himself, but did not suffer.

    Arthur, was charged, in the reign of Elizabeth, with projecting a scheme for the release of the Queen of Scots, and had judgment of death; but by reason of his near alliance to the crown no execution followed.

    REGINALD, in holy orders, was educated at Oxford, and obtained the Deanery of Exeter by the gift of King Henry VIII. He was abroad at the period that king abolished the papal authority in England, and not attending, when summoned to return, he was proclaimed a traitor, and divested of his deanery. He was afterwards, anno 1536, made a cardinal, and, as CARDINAL POLE, presided (one of three presidents) at the celebrated Council of Trent. When Queen Mary ascended the throne his eminence returned to England as legate from *Pope JULIUS III.*, and had his attainder reversed by special act of parliament. He was made, at the same time, ARCHBISHOP OF CANTERBURY, in which high episcopal dignity he continued until his death, which occurred on 17th November, 1558, being the very day upon which Queen Mary herself died: the tidings of that event are said to have broken the cardinal's heart, being at the time much weakened by a quartan ague. Whereupon his remains were interred in the cathedral at Canterbury. Few churchmen have borne so unblemished a reputation as this eminent prelate, and few have carried themselves with so much moderation and meekness. The friendship of such a man refutes in itself much of the obloquy which has been cast upon MARY by the eulogists of ELIZABETH, and goes far in the redemption of her character.

Ursula, m. to Henry, Lord Stafford.
With this noble lady expired the ROYAL and ILLUSTRIOUS HOUSE of PLANTAGENET.

PLANTAGENET–VISCOUNT L'ISLE.

By Letters Patent, dated 96th April, 1533.

Lineage.

ARTHUR PLANTAGENET, natural son of King Edward IV., by the Lady Elizabeth Lucy, having espoused Elizabeth, daughter of Edward Grey, first Viscount L'Isle of that family; sole heir of her niece, Elizabeth, Countess of Devon; and widow of Edmund Dudley, (see Grey, Viscounts L'Isle,) was created Viscount L'Isle, with limitation to his heirs male, by the said Elizabeth, by letters patent, dated 96th April, 1533, upon the surrender of that dignity by Charles Brandon,* afterwards Duke of Suffolk. His lordship had issue by the heiress of Grey,

> Bridget, m. to Sir William Carden, Knt.
> Frances, m. first, to John Basset, Esq., of Umberleigh, in the county of Devon, and secondly, to Thomas Monk, of Potheridge, in the same shire, from whom the celebrated General Monk is said to have descended.
> Elizabeth, m. to Sir Francis Jobson, Knt., Lieutenant of the Tower, and Master of the Jewel Office to Queen Elizabeth.

In the 34th of Henry VIII., Lord L'Isle was constituted Lieutenant of Calais, and some time after, incurring suspicion of being privy to a plot to deliver up the garrison to the French, he was recalled and committed to the Tower of London; but his innocence appearing manifest upon investigation, the king not only gave immediate orders for his release, but sent him a diamond ring, and a most

---

* Elizabeth Grey, only daughter and heiress of John, last Viscount L'Isle, of the Grey family, was contracted to Charles Brandon, who was created in consequence Viscount L'Isle, but the lady refusing, when she had attained maturity, to fulfil the engagement, the patent was cancelled. She afterwards espoused Henry Courtenay, Earl of Devon.

gracious message; which made such impression upon the sensitive nobleman, that he died the night following, 3d March, 1541, of excessive joy. His lordship was a Knight of the most noble order of the Garter. At his decease the VISCOUNTY OF L'ISLE became EXTINCT.

ARMS.—The coat of his lordship's father, King Edward IV., quartered with Ulster and Mortimer, under a baton.

PLANTAGENET — EARLS OF SURREY.

Refer to Warren, EARLS OF SURREY.

PLAYZ—BARON PLAYZ.

By Writ of Summons, dated 1297,
25 Edward I.

Lineage.

In the 17th of King John,
HUGH DE PLAYZ held seven knights' fees in the county of Sussex, and was one of the barons who took up arms against that prince. He m. first, Beatrix de Say, widow of Hugh de Nevill, but was divorced from that lady, and m. secondly, Philippa, one of the daughters and co-heirs of Richard de Montfichet, by whom he had his successor,

RICHARD DE PLAYZ, who, in the 53d of Henry III., as one of the nephews and heirs of Richard de Montfichet, paid his relief for a third part of the said Richard's lands. To this Richard de Playz, succeeded his son,

RALPH DE PLAYZ, who d. without issue, and was s. by his brother,

RICHARD DE PLAYZ, to whom succeeded,

GILES DE PLAYZ. This feudal lord had summons to attend the king on the affairs of the realm, in the 32d Edward I. He had afterwards a military summons to proceed to Gascony, and ultimately summons to parliament as a BARON, in the 25th of the same reign, but not afterwards. He d. in 1303, seised of the manor of Fulmere, in the county of Cambridge, and was s. by his son,

RICHARD DE PLAYZ, second baron, summoned to parliament from 20th November, 1317, to 14th March, 1322. This nobleman was s. by his son,

RICHARD DE PLAYZ, third baron, but never summoned to parliament. This nobleman was found, in the 8th Edward III., heir to John de Lancaster, of the county of Essex; he d. in 1359, and was s. by his son,

SIR JOHN DE PLAITZ, fourth baron, but never summoned to parliament, who d. in the 33rd Edward III., leaving an only daughter and heiress,

> MARGARET, who m. Sir John Howard, (his first wife,) by whom she had,
>> SIR JOHN HOWARD, whose daughter and heir,
>>> ELIZABETH HOWARD, m. John Vere, twelfth Earl of Oxford, in which dignity the BARONY OF

PLAITZ continued merged until the death of John, fourteenth Earl of Oxford, in 1526, when it fell into ABEYANCE between his three sisters and co-heirs, viz.

Dorothy, *m.* to John Nevil, Lord Latimer.

Elizabeth, *m.* to Sir Anthony Wingfield.

Ursula, *m.* first, to George Windsor, and secondly, to Sir Edward Knightly, but died *s. p.*

The BARONY OF PLAITZ, OR PLAITS, is now in ABEYANCE between Francis Dillon, Baron of the Holy Roman Empire, as representative of the said Elizabeth, Lady Wingfield, and the descendants and representatives of the above-mentioned Dorothy, Lady Latimer; of which his grace, the present Duke of Northumberland, is the eldest.

ARMS.—Party per pale, or. and gu., a lion passant, ar.

PLESSETS — EARL OF WARWICK, BARON PLESSETS.

Earldom, *jure uxoris*, temp. Henry III.
Barony, by Writ of Summons, dated 6th Feb., 1299, 27 Edward I.

Lineage.

The first of this family mentioned, is

JOHN DE PLESSETS, a domestic servant in the court of King Henry III., and a Norman by birth; who having served in the Welsh wars, was constituted governor of the castle of Devises, in Wiltshire, and warden of the forest of Chippenham, in the same shire. In the 24th of *King* HENRY's reign he was sheriff of Oxfordshire, and in two years afterwards he had a grant of the wardship and marriage of John Bisset; and likewise of the heirs of Nicholas Malesmaines. Certain it is that he enjoyed in a high degree the favour of his royal master, for upon the death of John Mareschal, who had married Margery, the sister and heir of Thomas de Newburgh, Earl of Warwick, the king sent his mandate to the Archbishop of York, the Bishop of Carlisle, and William de Cantilupe, requiring them that they should earnestly persuade this opulent widow to take John de Plessets for her second husband. Nay, so much did he desire the union, that upon Christmas-day in the same year, being then at Bourdeaux, he granted to John Plessets by patent, the marriage of this Margery, in case he could procure her consent; and if not, that then he should have the fine, which the lady would incur by marrying without the king's licence. This course of the king's, however, prevailed, and his FAVOURITE obtained the hand of MARGERY DE NEWBURGH, *Countess of Warwick*, and widow of John Mareschall, styled Earl of Warwick. De Plessets was subsequently constituted CONSTABLE OF THE TOWER of London, but not by the title of Earl of Warwick, nor did he assume that dignity for some time afterwards. He did, however, eventually assume it, for we find him so styled (31st Henry III.) by the king

in a licence granted him, to cut down oak timber in the forest of Dene; ever after which he is called EARL OF WARWICK. His lordship was appointed in four years afterwards one of the justices itinerant to sit at the Tower, for hearing and determining such pleas as concerned the city of London: and at the breaking out of the contest between Henry and the barons, he was constituted sheriff of the counties of Warwick and Leicester; but he lived not to see the issue of those troubles. His lordship *d.* in 1263; not having had issue by the Countess of Warwick, the Earldom of Warwick passed at her ladyship's decease to the heir at law (see Newburgh, Earls of Warwick). But he left, by a former wife, Christian, daughter and heir of Hugh de Sandford, a son and heir,

HUGH DE PLESSETS, who doing his homage, in the April ensuing, had livery of the manors of Oxenardton, Kedelinton, and Stuttesdon, in the county of Oxford, which were of his mother's inheritance; the two former being holden of the king by barony, for which manors in the 48th Henry III., he paid £100 for his relief. This feudal lord *m.* Isabel, daughter of John de Riparlis, and dying in 1291, was *s.* by his son,

HUGH DE PLESSETS, who being engaged in the Scottish wars, was summoned to parliament as a BARON on the 6th February, 1299, but having had no other writ, and none of his descendants being esteemed barons, Dugdale gives no further account of the family.

ARMS.—Six annulets gules, a chief cheque, or. and sa.

Note.—Hutchins, in his History of Dorsetshire, says, that ROBERT DE PLECY, OR PLESSETS, son of Sir Hugh, brother, or a near kinsman of John de Plessets, Earl of Warwick, in the 19th Edward I., held UPWINBORNE PLACY, in that county, which passed through several generations to

JOAN DE PLECY, an heiress, who *m.* Sir John Hamelyn, whose daughter, and eventual heiress,

EGIDIA HAMELYN, *m.* for her second husband, Robert Ashley, and conveyed to him the manor of Upwinborne-Plecy. The descendant of this marriage,

SIR ANTHONY ASHLEY, Knt., of Winborne, St. Giles, left an only daughter and heiress,

ANNE ASHLEY, who espoused Sir John Cooper, Bart., from which marriage the EXTANT EARLS OF SHAFTESBURY descend, and through which they inherit the manor of UPWINBORNE-PLECY.

PLUGENET—BARONS PLUGENET.

By Writ of Summons, dated 24th June, 1295, 23 Edward I.

Lineage.

In the beginning of HENRY II.'s reign,

HUGH DE PLUGENET had lands given him

in the county of Oxford, and in some years afterwards was owner of Lamburne, in Berkshire. He m. Sibell, daughter and co-heir of Josceus de Dinant, and had two sons, Alan and Josceus. To one of whom succeeded

SIR ALAN DE PLUGENET, who, after the battle of Evesham, in the 49th Henry III., was made governor of Dunster Castle, in the county of Somerset, and in three years, subsequently, obtained a grant from his maternal uncle, Robert Walrond, of certain manors in the counties of Wilts, Dorset, and Somerset, with the castle of Kilpeck, &c., in the county of Hereford, and at the death of the said Robert without issue, in the 1st Edward I., had livery of the same. This Sir Alan de Plugenet, distinguishing himself in the Welsh wars, and being esteemed a person of wisdom, and of military knowledge, was summoned to parliament as a BARON from 24th June, 1295, to 26th January, 1297. He d. in 1299, and was s. by his son,

SIR ALAN DE PLUGENET, second baron, K.B., summoned to parliament 19th December, 1311. This nobleman was constantly engaged in the wars of Scotland. He d. ————, leaving his sister,

JOAN DE BOHUN, heir to the BARONY OF PLUGENET, at whose decease s. p. in 1327, that dignity became EXTINCT.

ARMS.—Ermine, a bend engrailed gu.

POINTZ—BARONS POINTZ.

By Writ of Summons, dated 24th June, 1295, 23 Edward I.

Lineage.

This family, and that of CLIFFORD, is said to have sprung from a common ancestor, PONZ, whose grandson, WALTER, derived his surname from the place of his abode, CLIFFORD CASTLE, in the county of Hereford, and another of whose descendants was father of

OSBERT FITZ-PONZ, from whom sprang HUGH POINTZ, who, with his father, Nicholas Points, taking part with the revolted barons, had his lands, in the 17th John, in the counties of Somerset, Dorset, and Gloucester, seized by the crown, and given to Godfrey de Crancumbe. He was afterwards imprisoned in the castle of Bristol, but not strictly, as his friends had permission to visit him, and to supply him with necessaries. This Hugh wedded Helewise, daughter of William, and sister and co-heir of William Mallet, of Cory-Malet, in the county of Suffolk, and was s. by his son,

NICHOLAS POINTZ, who, residing in Gloucestershire, had military summons from the crown to march against the Welsh, in the 41st and 42nd of Henry III., but afterwards joined the other barons who took up arms against the king. He d. in the 1st Edward I., seised of the manor of CORY-MALET, in the county of Somerset, and several other estates. He was s. by his son,

HUGH POINTZ, who having been engaged in the wars of Wales, Gascony, and Scotland, was summoned to parliament as a BARON by King EDWARD I., on the 24th June, 1295. His lordship d.

in 1307, having had regular summonses to that year, and was s. by his son,

NICHOLAS POINTZ, second baron, summoned to parliament from 4th March, 1309, to 16th June, 1311. This nobleman was in the Scottish wars before and after his father's decease. He m. Elizabeth, daughter of Eudo de Zouche, by Millicent, daughter of William Cantilupe, Lord of Bergavenny, and co-heir of her brother, George; by whom he had the manor of Batecumbe, in free marriage. He d. in 1312, and was s. by his son,

HUGH POINTZ, third baron, K.B., summoned to parliament, from 20th November, 1317, to 24th February, 1343. This nobleman was s. by his son,

SIR NICHOLAS POINTZ, fourth baron, but never summoned to parliament. This nobleman m. Alianore, daughter of Sir John Erleigh, Knt., and had two daughters, viz.

AMICIA, m. to John Barry.

MARGARET, m. to John Newborough.

His lordship d. ————, when the BARONY OF POINTZ fell into ABEYANCE, between his daughters, as it still continues with their representatives.

ARMS.—Barry of eight or and gu.

Note.—From John Points, the younger brother of the last lord, descended a family of POINTS, which resided in Gloucestershire, when Sir William Dugdale wrote, but is now EXTINCT in the male line.

POLE — BARONS DE LA POLE, EARLS OF SUFFOLK, MARQUESS OF SUFFOLK, EARL OF PEMBROKE, DUKES OF SUFFOLK.

Barony, by Writ of Summons, dated 20th Jan., 1366, 39 Edward III.
Earldom of Suffolk, by Letters Patent, 6th August, 1385.
   Earldom of Pembroke, 21st February, 1443.
   Marquess, 14th September, 1444.
   Dukedom, 2nd June, 1448.

Lineage.

The founder of this family, which eventually attained such an exalted station, was

WILLIAM DE LA POLE, an opulent merchant, at Kingston-upon-Hull, who left two sons,

WILLIAM, of whom presently.

Richard, to whom King Edward III., in the 11th year of his reign, gave, "for his extraordinary merits," £1000 sterling, out of the exchequer. This Richard left a son and heir, WILLIAM, who m. Margaret, sister and heiress of John Peverel, of Castle Ashby, in the county of Northumberland, and had a son and heir,

    JOHN, who left, by Joane, his wife, sister and heiress of John, Lord Cobham, an only daughter and heiress,

      JOANE, who m. Reginald Braybroke, and had a daughter and heiress,

        JOANE BRAYBROKE, m. to Thomas Brooke, who became in her right, Lord Cobham.

The elder son,

WILLIAM DE LA POLE, was, like his father, a merchant, at Kingston-upon-Hull, and Mayor of that Borough. In the 10th year of King Edward III., this William contracted to furnish the army in Scotland, with wine, salt, and other provisions, but losing part of the cargo, in the transmission to Berwick-upon-Tweed, he had an allowance for the same in passing his accounts. In three years afterwards, being a person of great opulence, he was enabled to advance the sum of £1000, in gold, to the King, who then lay at Antwerp; for which important service, Edward being much in want, at the time, of supplies, he was constituted second baron of the exchequer, and advanced to the degree of banneret, with a grant out of the customs at Hull, for the better support of that rank. He was afterwards known as Sir William de la Pole, Senior. He m. Catherine, daughter of Sir John Norwich, and dying in the 40th of Edward III., possessed of extensive estates in the county of York, was s. by his son,

MICHAEL DE LA POLE, who, in the life-time of his father, had a grant in reversion, of £70 a year, to himself and his heirs, from Edward III., in consideration of that opulent person's services, whom the king denominated his "Beloved Merchant;" which annuity, William, his father, and Richard, his uncle, had previously enjoyed. This Michael de la Pole, despite of Walsingham's observation, "That as a merchant himself, and the son of a merchant, he was better versed in merchandize, than skilled in martial matters;" was an eminent soldier, and distinguished himself in the French wars, at the close of Edward III.'s reign; when he served immediately under the Black Prince. In the first year of Richard II., he accompanied John, Duke of Lancaster, then called King of Castile, in his voyage to sea; and the same year had the chief command of all the king's fleet to the northward; in which his own retinue were one hundred and forty men-at-arms, one hundred and forty archers, one banneret, eight knights, and a hundred and thirty esquires. In the next year, he was employed upon a mission to the Court of Rome; and in four years after, constituted CHANCELLOR, and keeper of the great seal—having had summons to parliament as a BARON, since the 39th of King Edward III. In the 8th of Richard II., his lordship procured licence to castellate his manor houses, at Wyngfield, Skernefield, and Huntingfield, in the county of Suffolk, and to impark all his woods and lands in the vicinity. And in the 9th of the same monarch, being still chancellor, he was created by letters patent, dated 6th August, 1385, EARL OF SUFFOLK, with a grant of a thousand marks per annum, to be received out of the king's exchequer. In the parliament held at this period, a dispute is recorded as having taken place between his lordship and Thomas Arundel, Bishop of Ely, in consequence of the king's having restored, at the earnest solicitation of that prelate, the temporalities to the Bishop of Norwich. The chancellor opposing the restoration, thus interrogated the

436

bishop, when he moved that measure:—"What is this, my lord, that you desire? Is it a small matter to part with those temporalities which yield the king more than a thousand pounds per annum? The king hath no more need of such advisers to his loss." To which the bishop answered, "What is that you say, Michael? I desire nothing of the king which is his own; but that which belongs to another, and which he unjustly detains, by thy wicked council, or such as thou art, which will never be for his advantage; (I think,) if thou beest so much concerned for the king's profit, why hast thou covetously taken from him a thousand marks per annum, since thou wast made an earl?"

After this, in the same year, we find the earl, notwithstanding his being lord chancellor, retained to serve the king, being a banneret, in his Scottish wars, for forty days, and obtaining a grant in consequence, to himself and his heirs male, of £500 per annum, lands, part of the possessions of William de Ufford, late Earl of Suffolk, deceased, viz., the Castle, Town, Manor, and Honour of Eye. In this year, too, he marched troops from all quarters, to London and its vicinity, in order to resist a menaced invasion of the French. But he was soon afterwards impeached by the Commons for divers misdemeanors and frauds, particularly for purchasing lands, while chancellor, "in deception of the king," and being found guilty, was sentenced to death and forfeiture. Upon the dissolution of parliament, however, he seems, through the protection of the king, to have set his foes for the moment at defiance, and to have relinquished the chancellorship only. But subsequently, the storm again gathering, he fled the kingdom with Robert de Vere, Duke of Ireland, and repairing to Calais, approached the castle, of which his brother, Edmund de la Pole, was captain, in the disguise of a Flemish poulterer, having shaved his head and beard; but it is said, that Edmund refused him admission without the previous permission of William de Beauchamp, the governor. "Brother," said the captain of the castle, "you must know that I dare not be false to the king of England for the sake of any kindred whatsoever; nor admit you in without the privity of William de Beauchamp, governor of this town." Whether this be true or false, certain it is that the earl never afterwards came back to England, but died at Paris, an outlaw, in 1388, his dignities having previously fallen under the outlawry. His lordship, who, amongst his other honours, had the Garter, was, like all the great nobles of the period, a benefactor to the church, having founded a Carthusian monastery, without the north gate, at Kingston-upon-Hull, and endowed it with lands of great value. He m. Katherine, daughter and heiress of Sir John Wingfield, Knt., and had issue,

MICHAEL (Sir).

Richard, died s. p.

Anne, m. to Gerard, son of Warine, Lord L'Isle.

Which

SIR MICHAEL DE LA POLE, in the 21st of Richard II., obtained the annulment of the judgment against his father; and upon the accession of

King Henry IV. was fully restored to the castle, manor,' and honour of Eye, with the other lands of the late lord, as also to the EARLDOM OF SUFFOLK, with a reversionary proviso, that those lands and honours should, in default of his male issue, devolve upon the male heir of his deceased father. This nobleman, who spent his time chiefly in the French wars, d. on the 14th September, 1415, at the siege of Harfleur. His lordship m. Lady Catherine de Stafford, daughter of Hugh, Earl of Stafford, and was s. by his eldest son,

MICHAEL DE LA POLE, as third Earl of Suffolk, but this gallant nobleman lost his life within a month of his accession to the title, at the celebrated battle of AGINCOURT, on the 25th October, 1415, leaving three daughters,

　Katherine, a nun.
　Elizabeth, m. to John de Foix, Earl of Kendal, and died s. p.
　Isabel, m. to Lord Morley, and died s. p.

At the decease of his lordship the Barony of De la Pole fell into ABEYANCE between those ladies, while the earldom devolved upon his brother,

WILLIAM DE LA POLE, fourth Earl of Suffolk, who, in the 6th of King Henry V., making proof of his age, had livery of his inheritance, his homage being respited. This nobleman was actively engaged in the glorious wars of that martial monarch, and attained the GARTER by his eminent services. Upon the death of King Henry his lordship was left in France with the Earl of Salisbury, to defend the castles and towns which had fallen to the English arms—and in the 1st year of King Henry VI., his two nieces, Elizabeth and Isabel, dying in minority without issue, and the other, Katherine, having taken the veil, his lordship inherited the entire property of his deceased brother, Earl Michael. About this period his lordship, in conjunction with the Earl of Salisbury, achieved a great victory over the French at Verneuil, and continued for several years afterwards to sustain the British banner upon the same soil. In the 6th of Henry VI. his lordship, with his companion in arms, Lord Salisbury, invested Orleans, and the latter nobleman being slain, the Earl of Suffolk was appointed captain of the siege, by the celebrated general, John Plantagenet, Duke of Bedford. In this affair he appears, however, to have been unfortunate, but he afterwards retrieved his reputation at Aumerle, which he carried, with its fortress, after no less than twenty-four assaults. In the 9th of the same reign he assisted at the solemn coronation of King Henry at Paris. In four years afterwards his lordship was deputed ambassador to Arras to treat of peace with the French, having licence to take with him gold, silver, plate, and jewels, to the value of two thousand pounds; and the next year was joined, in commission with the Duke of York, to proceed in the treaty. From this period the earl continued actively engaged as a military commander, or diplomatist, in the service of the crown, for which he was most amply compensated, by numerous and valuable grants, (amongst which was the reversion of the Earldom of Pembroke, should Humphrey Plantagenet, Duke of Gloucester and Earl of Pembroke, the king's uncle, die without

issue,) until the 23rd year of Henry's reign, when he was created MARQUESS OF SUFFOLK, (14th September, 1444,) by cincture with a sword, and putting a coronet of gold upon his head. This dignity was accompanied by a grant of £35 yearly out of the issues of the counties of Norfolk and Suffolk. Being at this period lord steward of the household, the marquess was sent into Sicily, to perform the solemnity of marriage with Margaret of Anjou, daughter of Regnier, titular king of Sicily, &c., and Duke of Anjou, as proxy for King Henry VI., and to conduct that celebrated woman into England. In the next year he was employed in negotiating peace with France, and he was soon after appointed lord chamberlain, and then LORD HIGH ADMIRAL OF ENGLAND. Upon the death of the Duke of Gloucester, in 1446, his lordship succeeded to the Earldom of Pembroke, and he was created DUKE OF SUFFOLK on the 2nd June, 1448. Which latter dignity is said to have been conferred upon him for advising the murder of the Duke of Gloucester; but be that as it may, his grace's prosperity endured not many years longer. For affairs becoming disastrous both at home and abroad, the popular voice became loud against him. He was charged with the loss of Anjou and Normandy—of causing the murder of the good Duke of Gloucester—of rapacity—and of the numerous other crimes which are generally attributed to an unsuccessful minister, in a season of calamity, by a disappointed people. Parliament soon after assembling, he was regularly impeached by the Commons, of high crimes and misdemeanors, and committed prisoner to the Tower; but released within a month, and restored to the king's favour. This act of royal clemency exciting, however, universal clamour, the king was obliged at length to banish him the realm; with the intention of recalling him, however, so soon as the storm had abated. But the unfortunate nobleman was doomed to immediate destruction, for after embarking at Ipswich for France, he was boarded by the captain of a ship of war belonging to the Duke of Exeter, then Constable of the Tower of London, called the Nicholas of the Tower, and being brought into Dover Road, was decapitated without further trial, on the side of the Cock Boat. It is recorded of this gallant personage that he served in the wars of France, full twenty-four years, seventeen of which were in uninterrupted succession without once visiting his native country. He was at one time made prisoner, whilst only a knight, and paid twenty thousand pounds for his ransom. His grace was fifteen years a member of the privy council, and thirty, one of the Knights of the Garter.

It is said that he first espoused, privately, the Countess of Hainault, and by her had a daughter, who married —— Barentine, but that afterwards taking to wife, Alice, daughter and heiress of Thomas Chaucer, grand-daughter of Geoffrey Chaucer, the poet, and of Sir John Philip, Knt., that daughter was proved a bastard.

All the Duke's honours, including the old BARONY OF DELAPOLE, which he inherited from his nieces, became FORFEITED under the attainder, but his eldest son,

JOHN DE LA POLE, having espoused the Lady Elizabeth Plantagenet, sister of King Edward IV. and King Richard III., was created DUKE OF SUFFOLK, by letters patent, dated 23d March, 1463. After which, in the 11th of the same reign, he was one of the lords then assembled in parliament, who recognised the title of Prince Edward, eldest son of that king, and made oath of fidelity to him. Upon the accession of King Henry VII., his grace was made Constable of Wallingford. The duke had issue,

> JOHN, who, by special charter, dated 13th March, 1467, was created EARL OF LINCOLN, and in the 2nd of Richard III., was appointed Lord Lieutenant of Ireland. After this, he was declared, by his uncle, the same monarch, heir apparent to the crown of England, in the event of the decease of his own son, Prince Edward. His lordship, in the next reign, having reared the standard of revolt, fell at the battle of Stoke, on the 16th June, 1487 (see De la Pole, Earl of Lincoln). and *Chapter*
> Edmund, who succeeded his father. *i 253*
> Humphrey, a priest.
> Edward, archdeacon of Richmond.
> Richard, of whom hereafter.
> Catherine, *m.* to William, Lord Stourton.
> Anne, a nun at Sion.
> Dorothy, *d.* unmarried.
> Elizabeth, *m.* Henry Lovel, Lord Morley.

His grace, who was a Knight of the Garter, *d.* in 1491, and was *s.* by his eldest surviving son,

EDMUND DE LA POLE, second Duke of Suffolk. We find this nobleman, although one of the last persons of rank remaining of the house of York, and of a family previously devoted to that cause, engaged in the beginning of Henry VII.'s reign, in that monarch's service; and so late as the 12th year, he was in arms with the Lords Essex and Mountjoy, against Lord Audley and the Cornish men, who suffered so memorable a defeat on Blackheath. But his grace being subjected to the ignominy of a public trial and condemnation (although immediately pardoned), for "killing an ordinary person in wrath," became so indignant that he immediately withdrew, without permission, to the court of his aunt, Margaret, Duchess of Burgundy, (sister of the Kings Edward IV. and Richard III.,) then the asylum for all the discontented spirits, who retained any feeling of attachment to the House of York, or had any cause of dissatisfaction with the existing order of things in England. He returned, however, soon after, and excusing himself to the king, assisted at the nuptials of Prince Arthur, with Katherine of Arragon. But he again departed for Flanders, accompanied by his brother, Richard, and remained in exile, until treacherously delivered up to the English monarch, by Philip, Duke of Burgundy, upon an express stipulation, however, that his life should not be endangered. On arriving in England, he was immediately committed to the Tower, where he remained a close prisoner until the 5th of Henry VIII., when that monarch caused the unfortunate Duke, solely from being a Yorkist, to be decapitated on Tower Hill, 30th April, 1513. His grace *m.* Margaret, daughter of Richard, Lord Scroope, and left an only daughter,

> Anne, who became a nun, in the convent of Minoresses, without Aldgate, in the suburbs of the city of London.

Notwithstanding the attainder of this duke, and the consequent forfeiture of his honours, the title, after his decease, was assumed by his brother,

RICHARD DA LA POLE, as third Duke of Suffolk, then living an exile in France. This gallant person commanded six thousand French at the siege of Therouena, when assaulted by King Henry VIII., and he fell at the battle of Pavia, in 1524, where his heroic conduct extorted the praise even of his foes; and the Duke of Bourbon honouring his remains with splendid obsequies, assisted in person, as one of the chief mourners. Thus terminated the male line of this gallant and highly gifted race; and the Dukedom of Suffolk passed by a new creation to King Henry VIII.'s brother-in-law, the celebrated Charles Brandon.

ARMS.—Ar. a fesse between three leopards' heads, or.

POLE—EARL OF LINCOLN.

By Special Charter, dated 13th March, 1467.

Lineage.

JOHN DE LA POLE, eldest son of John de la Pole, Duke of Suffolk, by the Lady Elizabeth Plantagenet, sister of Kings Edward IV. and Richard III., was created, in the 7th year of the former monarch, his father being then living, EARL OF LINCOLN. Upon the accession of his uncle, Richard, his lordship obtained several important grants of land from the crown, and was soon afterwards appointed lord-lieutenant of Ireland. Firmly attached to the house of York, the earl could ill brook the triumph of King Henry VII., and accordingly, upon the accession of that prince, removed to the court of his aunt, Margaret, Duchess of Burgundy, where he entered zealously into the affair of Lambert Simnell; in promotion of whose pretensions to the crown his lordship returned at the head of four thousand German soldiers, under the immediate command of Martin Swart, and having first landed in Ireland, and proclaimed the Pretender there, made a descent upon Lancashire, whence marching towards Newark-upon-Trent, in the county of Nottingham, he encountered the royal army at STOKE on the 16th June, 1487, where he sustained a signal defeat, and fell himself in the conflict. His lordship died, *s. p.*, when his honours became EXTINCT.

POLE—BARON MONTAGUE.

By Writ of Summons, dated 5th January, 1553, 24 Henry VIII.

Lineage.

The first of this family of whom any thing memorable occurs, is

SIR RICHARD POLE, Knt., (son of Sir Jeffrey Pole, Knt., of an ancient Welsh family,) who, being a valiant and expert commander, was first retained to serve *King* HENRY VII. in the wars of Scotland, and being a person highly accomplished, was made chief gentleman of the bed-chamber to Prince Arthur, and a Knight of the Garter. He *m.* the Lady Margaret Plantagenet, (afterwards Countess of Salisbury—see Plantagenet, Countess of Salisbury,) and had, with junior issue,[*] a son and heir,

HENRY POLE, who, in the 5th of Henry VIII., had special livery of the lands of his inheritance, and in eight years afterwards was restored to the king's favour by the title of LORD MONTAGU. But as to any creation, by patent or otherwise, nothing appears until the 24th of the same reign, when his lordship had summons to parliament as "Henrico Pole de Montagu." He attended King Henry in the celebrated interview with Francis, king of France, and was made a Knight of the Bath at the coronation of Anne Boleyn. But in a few years afterwards being charged, along with the Marquess of Exeter, by his own brother, Sir Jeffery Pole, with a design to elevate his youngest brother, Reginald, Dean of Exeter, to the throne, he was convicted of high treason before the Lord Audley, (lord chancellor,) acting as high steward of England, at Westminster, and was beheaded on Tower Hill on the 9th January, 1539, when the BARONY OF MONTAGU became FORFEITED. His lordship left by his wife, Jane, daughter of George Nevill, Lord Abergavenny, two daughters, his co-heirs, namely,

> Katherine, *m.* to Francis, second Earl of Huntingdon, represented now by the Marquess of Hastings.
>
> Winifred, *m.* first to Sir Thomas Hastings, a younger brother of the Earl of Huntingdon, and secondly, to Sir Thomas Barrington, of Barrington Hall, in Essex, from which latter union the present Sir Fitz-William Barrington, of Barrington Hall, descends.

In the first year of Philip and Mary, these ladies being restored in blood and honours, the BARONY OF MONTAGU was then placed in ABEYANCE, as it so continues to the present period.

ARMS.—Per pale or. and sa. a saltier engrailed counter changed.

POYNINGS — BARONS POYNINGS.

By Writ of Summons, dated 23rd April, 1337, 11 Edward III.

Lineage.

In the time of *King* HENRY II.,

ADAM DE POYNINGS, of Poynings, in the county of Sussex, was a benefactor to the monks of Lewes. This Adam left three sons, Adam, William, and John; from one of whom, it is presumed, descended

MICHAEL DE POYNINGS, who, in the 17th of John, adhered to the rebellious barons, and was *s.* by

THOMAS DE POYNINGS, who held ten

---

[*] For the particulars of the younger sons, amongst whom was the celebrated CARDINAL POLE, refer to PLANTAGENET, COUNTESS OF SALISBURY.

knights' fees in Poynings, and had issue, two sons, Michael and Lucas. The elder of whom,

MICHAEL DE POYNINGS, received summons upon the 8th June, 1294, (22nd Edward I.,) to attend the king, with other great men of the time, in order to advise touching the most important affairs of the realm; and he had military summons immediately after, to proceed in the expedition against France, which had been the result of that council. He was likewise actively engaged in the Scottish wars, both in the reign of Edward I. and in that of Edward II. He was *s.* by his son,

THOMAS DE POYNINGS, who was summoned to parliament, as a BARON, on the 23rd April, 1337. His lordship *m.* Agnes, one of the co-heirs of John, son of Bartholomew de Cryol, and was slain in the great sea fight with the French at Sluse, in 1339. He was *s.* by his elder son,

MICHAEL DE POYNINGS, second baron, summoned to parliament from 25th February, 1342, to 24th February, 1368. Upon the decease of the last lord, the king, by his letters patent, dated the 14th of the same month, acknowledging his great valour and eminent merits, and that he was slain in his service, received the homage of the present baron though then under age; and in recompence of those his father's sufferings, not only granted him livery of his lands, but the full benefit of his marriage, taking security for the payment of his relief. This Michael, Lord Poynings, participated in the glories of the martial reign of EDWARD III., and was amongst the heroes of CRESSY. His lordship *m.* Joane, widow of Sir John de Molyns, Knt., and *d.* in 1369; was *s.* by his son,

THOMAS DE POYNINGS, third baron, but never summoned to parliament. This nobleman *m.* Blanch de Mowbray, (who espoused, secondly, Sir John de Worthe, Knt.,) but *d.* without issue in 1375; was *s.* by his brother,

RICHARD POYNINGS, fourth baron, summoned to parliament from 7th January, 1383, to 3rd September, 1385. This nobleman *m.* Isabel, daughter and heir of Robert Grey, of Charlton-Grey, in the county of Somerset, who assumed the surname of FITZ-PAYNE, (see Fitz-Payne, Barons Fitz-Payne,) by his wife, Elizabeth, daughter and co-heir of Sir Guy de Bryan; which Isabel inherited eventually the estates of her maternal grandfather, as well as those of her father. Lord Poynings accompanied JOHN *of Gaunt* into Spain, and *d.* there in 1387; was *s.* by his son,

ROBERT DE POYNINGS, fifth baron, summoned to parliament from 25th August, 1404, to 13th January, 1445. This nobleman, who was in the French wars of Henry IV., Henry V., and Henry VI., fell at the siege of Orleans in 1446. His lordship had two sons, viz.

> RICHARD, who *m.* Alianore, daughter of Sir John Berkeley, of Beverstone, Knt., and dying before his father, left an only daughter and heir,
>
> > ELIZABETH DE POYNINGS, who *m.* Sir Henry Percy, son and heir of Henry, second EARL OF NORTHUMBERLAND.
>
> ROBERT, of Est Hall, Faukam-Aske, and Chelesfield (for whom and his descendants,

see POYNINGS, *Baron Poynings*, by letters patent).

Upon the decease of Robert, Lord Poynings, his grand-daughter, ELIZABETH, became heir to his estates and barony, and her husband,

SIR HENRY PERCY, was summoned to parliament as BARON POYNINGS, from 14th December, 1446, to 26th May, 1455, in which latter year his lordship succeeded to the EARLDOM of NORTH-UMBERLAND; and the BARONY OF POYNINGS, thenceforward shared the fortunes of the superior dignity. With the earldom, it was forfeited in 1408—restored in 1414—forfeited in 1461—restored 1471. On the death of Henry-Algernon, sixth Earl of Northumberland, issueless in 1537, the Barony of Poynings, with the Earldom, became EXTINCT, in consequence of the attainder of the Earl's brother, Sir Thomas Percy. On the 30th April, 1557, Thomas Percy, son and heir of the attainted Sir Thomas Percy, was created by *patent*, Baron Percy, of Cockermouth, and Petworth, BARON POYNINGS, &c. &c. with remainder, failing issue male, to his brother, Henry Percy, and his issue male; and he was shortly afterwards advanced to the dignity of *Earl of Northumberland*, with the same reversionary grant. This Henry Percy, the person in remainder, inherited the honours, and they remained vested in his descendants, until the demise of *Jocelin*, eleventh EARL OF NORTHUMBERLAND, without male issue, in 1670, when all the honours conferred by the patent, to Thomas Percy, including the BARONY OF POYNINGS, became EXTINCT.

ARMS.—Barry of six, or. and vert, a bend gules.

POYNINGS—BARON ST. JOHN, OF BASING.

By Writ of Summons, dated 29th December, 1299, 28 Edward I.

Lineage.

LUCAS DE POYNINGS, younger son of Thomas, first Lord Poynings, under the writ of Edward III., having m. in the 23d Edward III., Isabel, widow of Henry de Burghersh, daughter of Hugh de St. John, Lord St. John of Basing, (a barony created by writ in the 28th Edward I., see St. John,) and sister and co-heir of Edmund, Lord St. John, had an assignation of all the lands of her inheritance, and in some years afterwards, on the death of Margaret, the said Isabel's mother, he had a further assignation of the manors of Basing and Shireborne. This Lucas was in the wars of France, and had summons to parliament in his wife's barony (it is supposed) of ST. JOHN OF BASING, from 24th February, 1368, to 20th January, 1376. His lordship d. about the year 1385, and was s. by his son,

SIR THOMAS POYNINGS, Knt. who obtained licence in the 2d of Henry IV., by the title of LORD ST. JOHN, to go on a pilgrimage to Jerusalem, but was never summoned to parliament. His lordship had an only son,

HUGH, who d. in his father's life-time, leaving CONSTANCE, who m. John Paulet, and was grandmother of

SIR WILLIAM PAULET, first Marquess of Winchester, ancestor of the present marquess.

Alice, m. to John Orrell.

Joane, m. to Thomas Bonville.

Lord St. John d. about the 7th of Henry VI., when his grandchildren above-mentioned became his heirs, and the BARONY OF ST. JOHN, of *Basing*, fell into ABEYANCE amongst them, as it still continues with their descendants.

POYNINGS — BARON POYNINGS.

By Letters Patent, dated 30th January, 1545.

Lineage.

ROBERT DE POYNINGS, second son of Robert, fifth and last Lord Poynings, of the family, under the writ of Edward III., (see *Poynings*, BARONS POYNINGS, by summons,) was seised of the manors of East Hall, Faukam-Ayske, and Chellesfield, and was s. at his decease, 9th Edward IV., by his son,

SIR EDWARD POYNINGS, who, taking an active part in the revolution which placed HENRY VII. upon the throne, was sworn of the privy council to that monarch, and during the whole of the reign enjoyed the king's full confidence. He was one of the chief commanders sent in the 5th Henry VII., to the assistance of the *Emperor* MAXIMILIAN, against the French; and he was subsequently despatched at the head of a large force, to put down the supporters of *Perkyn Warbeck*, in Ireland; of which realm, Sir Edward (10th Edward VII.) was made DEPUTY in the absence of *Prince* HENRY, the king's younger son, then LIEUTENANT thereof. In ten years afterwards he was constituted Constable of Dover Castle, and was in the same office at Henry's decease. Sir Edward was the third of eighteen counsellors, bequeathed by the king to his successor; a privy council, in which it is said, there was not one lawyer, but a complete body of active and experienced men in their own orb. In the 1st of Henry VIII., being then a Knight of the Garter, and Comptroller of the King's Household, he was again made Constable of Dover Castle, and Warden of the Cinque Ports. In the 5th of the same reign, he was with the king at the siege of Therouene, at the head of six hundred chosen men in the body of the army, and upon the surrender of that place, he was left its governor, with a strong garrison. Sir Edward Poynings m. Elizabeth, daughter of Sir John Scott, but had no surviving issue. He had, however, by four concubines, three sons and four daughters, viz.

Thomas (Sir), of whom presently.

Adrian (Sir), Governor of Portsmouth, in 1561. Sir Adrian d. in the 13th Elizabeth, leaving three daughters, viz.

  Elizabeth, m. to Andrew Rogers, Esq.

  Mary, m. to Edward Moore, Esq.

  Anne, m. to George Moore, Esq.

Edward, slain at Boloin, in the 38th of Henry VIII.

Mary, m. to Thomas Clinton, Lord Clinton.

Margaret, *m.* to Edmund Barry, of Sennington, in the county of Kent.

———— *m.* to Sir Thomas Wilford, Knt.

Rose, *m.* to —— Leukenore.

Sir Edward *d.* in the 14th of Henry VIII. The eldest of the above illegitimate sons,

SIR THOMAS POYNINGS, Knt., was with *Charles Brandon*, DUKE OF SUFFOLK, at the siege of BURES, in the 36th Henry VIII., and was despatched with an account of the progress of the siege to the king, who was then before BOLOIN, at the head of a powerful army. Sir Thomas was graciously received, and, for his gallant services, elevated to the peerage, by letters patent, dated 30th January, 1545, as BARON POYNINGS, being at the same time appointed general of the king's whole army at Boloin; after which nothing further is recorded. His lordship *m.* Katherine, daughter and co-heir of John, Lord Marney, and widow of George Ratcliffe, Esq., but had no issue. By this lady he acquired considerable property in the county of Dorset, two parts of which he entailed upon his brothers, successively, and after them upon the children of his sisters. He *d.* in 1545, when the BARONY OF POYNINGS, became EXTINCT.

ARMS.—Same as the BARONS POYNINGS, by writ.

PULTENEY—EARL OF BATH.

By Letters Patent, dated 14th July, 1742.

Lineage.

The family of PULTENEY was founded by

ADAM DE CLIPSTONE, who acquired the manor of Pulteney, in Leicestershire, with his wife, Maud, daughter of John de Napton, and thence adopted the surname of PULTENEY. From this Adam lineally descended

SIR WILLIAM PULTENEY, one of the leading members of the House of Commons, temp. CHARLES II., and grandfather of

WILLIAM PULTENEY, Esq., a gentleman equally distinguished in parliament in the reigns of the two first sovereigns of the House of Brunswick. In 1714, Mr. Pulteney was appointed secretary of state, an office which he resigned in 1717. In 1723 he was made cofferer of the household, and sworn of the privy council; but he resigned again in 1725. In the reign of GEORGE II., he was leader of the opposition to the administration of Sir Robert Walpole, and so keenly was his eloquence felt by the court, that his name was erased in 1731 from the list of privy councillors. That proceeding having no other effect, however, than rendering Pulteney more popular, Sir Robert, at length, discovered that the only manner in which he could hope to triumph over so gifted a rival, was to cajole him into the acceptance of a peerage; and for that purpose the following letter was written to his royal master.

" Most Sacred,

" The violence of the fit of the stone, which has tormented me for some days, is now so far abated, that although it will not permit me to have the honour to wait on your majesty, yet is kind enough to enable me so far to obey your orders, as to write my sentiments concerning that troublesome man, Mr. Pulteney; and to point out (what I conceive to be) the most effectual method to make him perfectly quiet. Your majesty well knows, how, by the dint of his eloquence, he has so captivated the mob, and attained an unbounded popularity, that the most manifest wrong appears to be right, when adopted and urged by him. Hence it is, that he has become not only troublesome but dangerous. The inconsiderate multitude think he has not one object but the public good in view; although, if they would reflect a little, they would soon perceive, that spleen against those your majesty has honoured with your confidence, has greater weight with him than patriotism. Since, let any measure be proposed, however salutary, if he thinks it comes from me, it is sufficient for him to oppose it. Thus, Sir, you see the affairs of the most momentous concern are subject to the caprice of that popular man; and he has nothing to do, but to call it a ministerial project, and bellow out the word *favourite*, to half an hundred pens drawn against it, and a thousand mouths open to contradict it. Under these circumstances, he bears up against the ministry (and, let me add, against your majesty itself); and every useful scheme must be either abandoned, or, if it is carried in either house, the public are made to believe it is done by a corrupted majority. Since then things are thus circumstanced, it is become necessary for the public tranquillity, that he should be made quiet; and the only method to do that effectually, is to destroy his popularity, and ruin the good belief the people have in him.

" In order to do this, he must be invited to court; your majesty must condescend to speak to him in the most favourable and distinguished manner; you must make him believe that he is the only person upon whose opinion you can rely, and to whom your people look up for useful measures. As he has already several times refused to take the lead in the administration, unless it was totally modelled to his fancy, your majesty should close in with his advice, and give him leave to arrange the administration as he pleases, and put whom he chooses into office (there can be no danger in that, as you can dismiss him when you think fit); and when he has got thus far (to which his extreme self-love, and the high opinion he entertains of his own importance, will easily conduce), it will be necessary that your majesty should seem to have a great regard for his health; signifying to him, that your affairs will be ruined if he should die; that you want to have him constantly near you, to have his sage advice; and that, therefore, as he is much disordered in body, and something infirm, it will be necessary for his preservation, for him to quit the House of Commons, where malevolent tempers will be continually fretting him; and where, indeed, his presence will be needless, as no step will be taken but according to his advice; and that he will let you give him a distinguished mark of your approbation, by creating him a peer. This he may be brought to: for, if I know any thing of mankind, he has a love of honour and money; and, notwithstanding his great haughtiness and seeming contempt for honour, he may be won, if it be done with dexterity. For as the poet Fenton says, ' Flattery is an oil that softens the thoughtless fool.'

" If your majesty can once bring him to accept of a coronet, all will be over with him: the changing multitude will cease to have any confidence in him; and when you see that, your majesty may turn your back to him, dismiss him from his post, turn out his meddling partizans, and restore things to quiet: for them, if he complains, it will be of no avail; the bee will have lost his sting, and become an idle drone, whose buzzing nobody heeds.

" Your majesty will pardon me for the freedom with which I have given my sentiments and advice: which I should not have done, had not your majesty commanded it, and had I not been certain that your peace is much disturbed by the contrivance of that turbulent man. I shall only add, that I will dispose several whom I know to wish him well, to solicit for his establishment in power, that you may seem to yield to their entreaties, and the finesse be less liable to be discovered.

" I hope to have the honour to attend your majesty in a few days; which I will do privately, that my public presence may give him no umbrage."

     (Signed)   " ROBERT WALPOLE."

24th January, 1741.

In this scheme the king acquiesced, the bait took, and the pseudo-patriot, William Pulteney, having been restored to the privy council, was created by letters patent, dated 14th July, 1742, *Baron of Heydon, in the county of York, Viscount Pulteney, of Wrington, in Somersetshire;* and EARL OF BATH. His lordship *m.* Anne-Maria, daughter of John Gumley, Esq., of Isleworth, in the county of Middlesex, by whom he had a son, WILLIAM, *Viscount Pulteney,* who *d.* unmarried in the earl's life-time, anno 1763; he had likewise a daughter, who *d.* in 1741, at the age of fourteen. The earl *d.* in 1764, when, failing male issue, ALL HIS HONOURS became EXTINCT. His lordship's great estates devolved eventually upon his grand-niece, Henrietta-Laura Johnstone, who assumed the name of Pulteney, and was created COUNTESS OF BATH.

ARMS.—A fesse dancette gules in chief, three leopards' heads, sa.

PULTENEY — BARONESS BATH, COUNTESS OF BATH.

Barony, } by Letters { 23rd July, 1792.
Earldom, } Patent, { 26th October, 1803.

Lineage.

SIR WILLIAM JOHNSTONE, Bart., of Westerhall, in the county of Dumfries, *m.* Frances, daughter and heir of Henry Pulteney, Esq., next brother to William, Earl of Bath, (which lady was eventually heiress to his lordship's estates,) and had an only daughter,

HENRIETTA - LAURA JOHNSTONE, who succeeding to the great Pulteney fortune, assumed the surname and arms of PULTENEY, and was elevated to the peerage, 23rd July, 1792, as BARONESS BATH, with limitation of the dignity of Baron Bath to her issue male. Her ladyship was created

442

COUNTESS OF BATH, with a similar reversion of the Earldom of Bath, by letters patent, dated 26th October, 1803. She *m.* General Sir James Murray, Bart., who adopted likewise the name of PULTENEY, but had no issue. The countess *d.* in 1808, when the BARONY AND EARLDOM OF BATH both became EXTINCT.

ARMS.—A fesse dancette gules in chief, three leopards' heads, sa.

QUEROUALLE — DUCHESS OF PORTSMOUTH.

By Letters Patent, dated 19th August, 1673.

Lineage.

In the retinue of *Henrietta,* DUCHESS OF ORLEANS, sister of *King* CHARLES II., came to the court of St. James's, a French lady,

LOUISE RENEE DE PEUENCOVET DE QUEROUALLE, who, captivating the English monarch, CHARLES II., was mother, by his majesty, of a son, CHARLES LENNOX, DUKE OF RICHMOND, founder of the present noble house of Richmond, and was created for life, by letters patent, dated 19th August, 1673, *Baroness Petersfield, Countess of Fareham,* and DUCHESS OF PORTSMOUTH. Her ladyship being of a noble family in Britanny, Lewis XIV. conferred upon her the DUCHY OF AUBIGNY, a dignity still held by the Dukes of Richmond. The duchess, who enjoyed great influence during the life of her royal paramour, *d.* at an advanced age at Paris, in the year 1734.

ARMS.—Az. three bars, ar.

QUINCY—EARLS OF WINCHESTER.

By Creation of King John, about the year 1210.

Lineage.

In the reign of King Henry II.,

SAIER DE QUINCY had a grant from the crown, of the Manor of Bushby in the county of Northampton, formerly the property of Anselme de Conchis. He *m.* Maud de St. Liz, and had two sons,

    Robert, a soldier of the cross, and one of the companions in arms of LION-HEARTED RICHARD.

And

SAIER DE QUINCY, who was created EARL OF WINCHESTER, by King John. This nobleman was one of the lords present at Lincoln, when William, King of Scotland, did homage to the English monarch, and he subsequently obtained large grants and immunities from King John; when, however, the baronial war broke out, his lordship's pennant waved on the side of freedom, and he became so eminent amongst those sturdy chiefs, that he was chosen one of the celebrated twenty-five barons, appointed to enforce the observance of MAGNA CHARTA. Adhering to the same party, after the accession of Henry III., the Earl of Winchester had a principal command at the battle of Lincoln, and there being defeated, he was taken prisoner by the royalists. But submitting in the following October, he had restitution of all his lands; and proceeded soon after, in company with the Earls of Chester and Arundel, and others of the nobility, to the Holy Land, where he assisted at the siege of DAMIETA, anno 1919, and died in the same year, in his progress towards Jerusalem. His lordship m. Margaret, younger sister and co-heir of Robert Fitz-Parnell, Earl of Leicester, by which alliance he acquired a very considerable inheritance, and had issue,

> Robert, who d. in the Holy Land, leaving issue by his wife, Hawyse, daughter of Hugh Keveliok, Earl of Chester, an only daughter,
>> Margaret, m. to John de Lacie, Earl of Lincoln.
>
> ROGER, successor to the Earldom.
> Robert, m. Helene, daughter of Lewelyne, Prince of North Wales, and widow of John Scot, Earl of Huntingdon, by whom he left,
>> Anne, a nun.
>> Joane, m. to Humphrey de Bohun, the younger.
>> Margaret, m. to Baldwin Wake.

At the decease of the earl, his second son,
ROGER DE QUINCY, (his elder brother being still in the Holy Land,) had livery of his father's estates, and he subsequently succeeded to the EARLDOM OF WINCHESTER. This nobleman marrying Helen, eldest daughter and co-heir of Alan, Lord of Galloway, became, in her right, CONSTABLE OF SCOTLAND. By this lady he had issue,

> Margaret, m. to William de Ferrers, Earl of Derby, and brought to her husband the Manor and Barony of Groby.
> Elizabeth, m. to Alexander Comyn, Earl of Buchan, in Scotland.
> Ela, m. to Alan, Lord Zouch, of Ashby.

His lordship espoused, secondly, Maud, daughter of Humphrey de Bohun, Earl of Hereford, (widow of Anselme Mareschall, Earl of Pembroke,) and thirdly, Alianore, daughter of William de Ferrers, Earl of Derby, and widow of William de Vaux (this lady survived the Earl, and married, after his decease, Roger de Leybourne). Dugdale says, that the Earl had another daughter, but by which wife he could not discover, namely,

> Isabell, with whom a contract of marriage was made, by John, son of Hugh de Nevil, for his son, Hugh.

His lordship d. in 1264, when the EARLDOM OF WINCHESTER became EXTINCT, and his great landed possessions devolved upon his daughters, as co-heiresses.

ARMS.—Robert de Quincy—or a fesse gu. a file of eleven points, az.

> Roger de Quincy—gu. seven mascles, or three, three, and one.

RADCLYFFE — EARLS OF DERWENTWATER.

By Letters Patent, dated 7th March, 1688.

Lineage.

SIR FRANCIS RADCLYFFE, Baron of Dil-

ston, in the county of Northumberland, was elevated to the peerage, by King JAMES II., as Baron Tyndale, Viscount Radcliffe and Langley, and EARL OF DERWENTWATER.* His lordship m. Catherine, daughter and heir of Sir William Fenwick, of Meldon, in the county of Northumberland, and had issue,

> FRANCIS, Viscount Radcliffe, his successor.
> Edward, d. unmarried.
> Thomas, a military officer.
> William.
> Arthur.
> Anne, m. to Sir Philip Constable, Knt., of Flamborough, in Yorkshire.
> Catherine.
> Elisabeth.
> Mary.

His lordship d. in 1696, and was s. by his eldest son,
FRANCIS RADCLIFFE, second earl, who had married in his father's life-time, Mary Tudor, natural daughter of King Charles II., by Mrs. Davis, and had issue,

> JAMES, Viscount Radcliffe, his successor.
> Francis, died s. p.
> Charles, who became the second husband of CHARLOTTE-MARIA LIVINGSTON, Countess of Newburgh, in her own right, and had, with other issue,
>> JAMES-BARTHOLOMEW, who succeeded his mother, and became third Earl of Newburgh.
>> Mary, who m. in 1755, Francis Eyre, Esq., of Walworth Castle, in the county of Northampton, and had issue,
>>> FRANCIS EYRE, who inherited, as sixth Earl of Newburgh, and was father of the present EARL OF NEWBURGH.
> Mary-Tudor.

His lordship d. in April, 1705, and was s. by his eldest son,
JAMES RADCLIFFE, third earl. This nobleman, embarking with his brother, Charles Radcliffe, in the rising of 1715, to place the CHEVALIER

---

* Beyond Hay Castle, in Cumberland, the river DERWENT falls into the ocean, which rising in Barrodale, (a vale surrounded with crooked hills,) runs among the mountains called Derwent-Fells; wherein at Newlands, and some other places, some rich veins of copper (not without a mixture of gold and silver) were found; about which, there was a memorable trial, between Queen Elizabeth, and Thomas Percy, Earl of Northumberland, and Lord of the Manor; but in virtue of the royal prerogative, (there being veins of gold and silver,) it was determined in favour of the Queen. Through these mountains, the Derwent spreads itself into a spacious lake, wherein are three islands: one the seat of the family of Ratcliffe, Knt., temp. Henry V., who m. Margaret, daughter and heir of Sir John de Derwentwater, Knt.; another inhabited by miners, and the third supposed to be that, wherein Bede mentions St. Herbert to have led a hermit's life.—BANKE.

ST. GEORGE upon the throne, was made prisoner, sent to the Tower of London, and being soon afterwards found guilty of high treason, was beheaded on Tower Hill, 24th February, 1715-16, when ALL HIS HONOURS became FORFEITED. The earl had married Anne-Maria, daughter of Sir John Webb, Bart., by whom he had JOHN, *Viscount Radcliffe*, with another son, and a daughter, Mary, who *m.* ROBERT-JAMES, eighth *Lord Petre*. His lordship's brother,

CHARLES RADCLIFFE, who had married, as stated above, the Countess of Newburgh, was made prisoner at Preston, 14th November, 1715, and being transferred to London, was condemned for high treason, but effected his escape from Newgate, and retired into France. On the death of his nephew, JOHN, *Viscount Radcliffe*, in 1731, he assumed the title of EARL OF DERWENTWATER. Still adhering to the fortunes of the Stuarts, he embarked with his son, to join CHARLES-EDWARD, in 1745, but being made prisoner on board the Esperance privateer, by the Sheerness man-of-war, he was immediately committed to the Tower, and beheaded, under his former sentence, on the 8th December, 1746. The EARLDOM OF DERWENTWATER fell under the attainder of JAMES, the *third Earl;* if it had been, however, restored to the male heir of Charles Radcliffe, JAMES-BARTHOLOMEW, *third Earl of Newburgh*, it would have become EXTINCT, upon the decease of that nobleman's son and successor, ANTHONY-JAMES, *fourth Earl of Newburgh*, without male issue, in 1814, unless there remain some male descendants of Thomas, William, and Arthur, the younger sons of FRANCIS, the *first* EARL.

ARMS.—AZ. a bend ingrailed sa.

RAMSEY — EARL OF HOLDERNESSE.

By Letters Patent, dated 22nd January, 1621.

Lineage.

JAMES RAMSEY, of an ancient Scottish family, and one of the pages of honour to *King James* (VI.) I., having been mainly instrumental in saving the life of that monarch from the attempt of the *Ruthyns*, known as the "GOWRY CONSPIRACY," was rewarded with knighthood, the Earldom of Haddington in Scotland, and an augmentation to his arms, viz.: an arm holding a naked sword, with a crown in the middle thereof, and a heart at the point, with the motto, " *Hæc dextra vindex principis et patriæ.*" Upon the accession of his royal master to the THRONE OF THE TUDORS, his lordship accompanied him into England, and in some years afterwards, 22d January, 1621, was made a peer of the king's new dominions, by the titles of *Baron Kingston-upon-Hull*, and EARL OF HOLDERNESSE, with this especial addition to the honour, that annually on the 5th of August, (the thanksgiving day for the king's deliverance from the Earl of Gowry and his brother,) he and his heirs male should bear the sword of state before the king, in the solemnisation of that day's service. His lordship *m.* first, Lady Elizabeth Ratcliffe,

444

daughter of Robert, Earl of Sussex, by whom he had no surviving issue. He espoused, secondly, Martha, daughter of Mr. Alderman (Sir William) Cokain, of the city of London, but had no child. He *d.* in 1625, when ALL HIS HONOURS became EXTINCT.

ARMS.—Two coats per pale first sa. an arm issuing out of the sinister part of the escutcheon or. holding a sword erected ar. piercing a crown gules, and on the point a heart ppr.; secondly, or. an eagle displayed sa.

RATCLIFFE—BARONS FITZ-WALTER, VISCOUNTS FITZ-WALTER, EARLS OF SUSSEX.

Barony, { Originally, by Writ of Summons, dated 23rd June, 1295, 23 Edward I. { To the Ratcliffes, by Writ of Summons, dated 15th Sept., 1485, 1 Henry VII.

Viscounty, } by Letters { dated 18th July, 1525.
Earldom, } Patent, { dated 28th Dec., 1529.

Lineage.

In the 7th of King Henry V.,

SIR JOHN RATCLIFFE, Knt., Governor of Trounsak, in Aquitaine, had a thousand marks per annum allowed to him for the guard thereof, and in the 1st of Henry VI., being retained to serve the king, as seneschal of that duchy, had an assignation of four shillings per day for his own salary, and twenty marks a piece per annum for two hundred archers. In the 4th year of the same monarch, Sir John had a grant of the wardship of Ralph, Earl of Westmorland, in consideration of two thousand marks, then due to him by the king, for wages in his military capacity: and in seven years afterwards, he had an assignation of all the revenues of the crown, issuing out of the counties of Caernarvon and Merioneth, as also out of the lordships of Chirk, and Chirkland, to liquidate another arrear of service money, to the amount of £7099 13s. 1d. This eminent soldier, who was a Knight Banneret, and a KNIGHT OF THE GARTER, espoused ELIZABETH FITZ-WALTER, only daughter and heiress of Walter Fitz-Walter, last BARON FITZ-WALTER of that family, (revert to Fitz-Walter, Baron Fitz-Walter,) and was *s.* at his decease by his son,

SIR JOHN RATCLIFFE, who, in the 39th Henry VI., obtained a pardon of intrusion, for entering upon the lands of his inheritance without livery; and in the 1st of Henry VII., 15th September, 1485, was summoned to parliament, in right of his mother, as BARON FITZ-WALTER. In which year, being at that time steward of the king's household, he was joined in commission with Sir Reginald Bray, Knt., for exercising the office of chief justice of all the forests beyond Trent. And at the coronation of King Henry's consort, Queen Elizabeth, his lordship was associated with Jasper Tudor, Duke of Bedford, for performing the duties of High Steward of England. But afterwards implicated in the conspiracy in favour of PERKYN WARBECK, he was attainted of high treason, and being carried prisoner to Calais, whence he endeavoured to make his escape, by corrupting his keepers, he was there beheaded in the year 1495, when the BARONY OF FITZ-WALTER, became FORFEITED. Nevertheless his son and heir,

ROBERT RATCLIFFE, found much favour from King Henry VII., and was restored in blood and honours by act of parliament, in the 1st of Henry VIII., when he became second LORD FITZ-WALTER of the Ratcliffe family. In the 4th of the same reign, his lordship attended the king in the great expedition then made to Thérouenne, and Tournay; and in ten years afterwards, he commanded the van of the army sent into France, under the Earl of Surrey: for which eminent services he was created, by letters patent, dated 18th July, 1525, VISCOUNT FITZ-WALTER. His lordship was one of those peers, who, in four years afterwards, subscribed the articles against Cardinal Wolsey. He was subsequently made a Knight of the Garter, and elevated to the EARLDOM OF SUSSEX, on 28th December, 1529. The next year he subscribed the remonstrance of the peers to Pope Clement VII., regarding the king's divorce from Queen Katherine, and he was one of the nobles who attended HENRY into France, in 1532: after which he obtained an especial patent to himself, and his heirs male of the office of SEWER, at the time of dinner, upon the coronation-day of all future kings and queens of England, with a fee of twenty pounds per annum out of the exchequer; and was constituted LORD HIGH CHAMBERLAIN OF ENGLAND for life, upon the attainder of Thomas Cromwell, Earl of Essex. Besides all those honours, his lordship, in the spoliation of the church, was a considerable participator, having obtained from his royal master grants of the site of the abbey of Cleve, in Somersetshire, with its revenues; and of the college and chantry of Attleburgh, in Norfolk. The earl m. first, Elizabeth, daughter of Henry, Duke of Buckingham, and had issue,

HENRY, his successor.

George.

Humphrey (Sir), of Elnestow, in the county of Bedford, left issue,

    EDWARD, who inherited as fourth Earl of Sussex.

Frances, m. to Henry Cheeke, Esq.

His lordship espoused, secondly, Lady Margaret Stanley, daughter of Thomas, Earl of Derby, and had,

Anne, m. to Thomas, Lord Wharton.

Jane, m. to Anthony, Viscount Montague.

He m. thirdly, Mary, daughter of Sir John Arundel, of Lanherne, in Cornwall, and had an only son,

John (Sir), who died without issue.

His lordship d. in 1542, and was s. by his eldest son,

SIR HENRY RATCLIFFE, K.B., as third Lord Fitz-Walter, and second Earl of Sussex, who, in the 1st of Edward VI., upon the expedition then made into Scotland, had the command of sixteen hundred demi-lances; in which service, being unhorsed, he escaped very narrowly with his

life. At the demise of King Edward, the Earl of Sussex was amongst the first that declared for Queen Mary, and was in consequence constituted by that sovereign, soon after her accession, warden and chief justice itinerant of all the forests south of Trent. He was also made a KNIGHT OF THE GARTER. His lordship m. first, Lady Elizabeth Howard, daughter of Thomas, Duke of Norfolk, and had issue,

THOMAS, } successive Earls of Sussex.
HENRY,   }

Francis.

He espoused secondly, Anne, daughter of Sir Philip Calthorpe, Knt., by whom he had a son and daughter, viz.

Egremond, who, being a principal actor in the northern rebellion, was attainted and forced to fly the kingdom. He was afterwards put to death at Namurs, by Don John of Austria, for purposing to murder that prince.

Frances, m. to Sir Thomas Mildmay, Knt., of Mulsho, in the county of Essex, and had issue,

   Sir Thomas Mildmay, Bart., who d. in 1690.

   SIR HENRY MILDMAY, Knt., who, in 1640, claimed, by petition to the long parliament, in right of his mother, the BARONY OF FITZ-WALTER, but owing to the civil wars nothing was done at that time therein. Sir Henry m. Elizabeth, daughter of John Darcy, Esq., of Toleshurst Darcy, in the county of Essex, and dying in 1654, left three sons, viz.

     1. ROBERT, m. Mary, daughter and co-heir of Sir Thomas Edmonds, Knt., and had issue,

       Henry, died s. p.

       BENJAMIN, who was allowed the Barony of FITZ-WALTER, in 1669 (see Mildmay, Barons Fitz-Walter).

       Mary, m. to Henry Mildmay, Esq., of Graces, and had issue,

         Mary, m. to Charles Goodwin, Esq.

         Lucy, m. to Thomas Gardener, Esq.

         Elizabeth, m. to Edmund Waterson, Esq.

         Frances, m. to Christopher Fowler, Esq.

         Catherine, m. to Colonel Thomas Townshend.

     2. Henry, died s. p.

     3. Charles, m. to Martha, daughter and heiress of Sir Cranmer Harris, Knt., and left an only daughter,

       Mary, m. to Sir Charles Tyrrell, Bart., of Thornton.

The earl, being divorced from his second countess, obtained a special act of parliament in the 2nd and 3rd Philip and Mary, to debar her from jointure and dower. He d. 17th February, 1556, and was s. by his eldest son,

SIR THOMAS RATCLIFFE, fourth Lord Fitz-Walter, and third Earl of Sussex. This nobleman, in the life-time of his father, was deputed ambassador by Queen Mary to the Emperor Charles V. to treat of a marriage between herself and Prince Philip, the emperor's eldest son; and he proceeded afterwards to the court of Spain to the prince himself to obtain a ratification of the treaty. In the 2nd and 3rd of Philip and Mary, Sir Thomas Ratcliffe was constituted lord deputy of Ireland, and soon after his father's decease, his lordship was made chief justice of all the forests south of Trent. In the 4th and 5th of the same reign, the earl being then a Knight of the Garter, and captain of the pensioners, had his commission as deputy of Ireland renewed; which high office was confirmed to him upon the accession of Queen Elizabeth, with instructions to reduce the revenues of Ireland to the standard of England. In the 3rd of Elizabeth he was constituted LORD LIEUTENANT of the same kingdom, and in six years afterwards he had the honour of bearing the order of the Garter to the Emperor Maximilian. He was afterwards engaged in negotiating a matrimonial alliance between his royal mistress, and the *Archduke* CHARLES *of Austria*. In the 12th Elizabeth he was lord president of the north, and the next year, upon an incursion of the Scots, his lordship invaded Scotland and laid several of their towns and castles in ashes; amongst which were the castles of Anand and Caerlaveroc. He sate subsequently upon the trial of the Duke of Norfolk; and he was one of the commissioners (24th Elizabeth,) to treat regarding a marriage between her majesty and the Duke of Anjou. His lordship m. first, Lady Elizabeth Wriothesley, daughter of Thomas, Earl of Southampton, by whom he had two sons, Henry and Robert, who both d. young. He espoused, secondly,* Frances, daughter of Sir William Sidney, Knt., sister of Sir Henry Sidney, Knt., but had no issue.

This Thomas, Earl of Sussex, Sir Robert Naunton, in his Fragmenta Regalia, describes " as a goodly gentleman; of a brave noble nature, and constant to his friends and servants:" and goes on to state, " that there was such an antipathy in his nature to that of the Earl of Leicester's, that being together at court, and both in high employments, they grew to direct forwardness, and were in continual opposition; the one setting the watch and the other the sentinel, each on the other's actions and motions: for this Earl of Sussex was of great spirit, which backed with the queen's special favour, and supported by a great and antient inheritance, could not brook the other's empire: in so much as the queen, upon sundry occasions, had somewhat to do to appease and attain them, until death parted the competition, and left the place to Leicester." Upon his death-bed his lordship is said, by the same authority, thus to have addressed his friends: " I am now passing into another world, and I must leave

you to your fortunes, and the queen's grace and goodness; but beware of the gipsey, (meaning Leicester,) for he will be too hard for you all; you know not the beast so well as I do."—He d. in June, 1583, at his house of Bermondsey, in Southwark, and was buried at Boreham, in Sussex; but leaving no issue surviving, was s. by his brother,

HENRY RATCLIFFE, fifth Lord Fitz-Walter, and fourth Earl of Sussex, captain and chief governor of Portsmouth, and Knight of the Garter. His lordship m. Honora, daughter of Anthony Pound, Esq., of Hampshire, and dying 10th April, 1593, was s. by his only child,

ROBERT RATCLIFFE, sixth Lord Fitz-Walter, and fifth Earl of Sussex. This nobleman was with the Earl of Essex in the attack and sacking of the city of Cadis in the 39th Elizabeth, and was installed a Knight of the Garter the 19th of the ensuing reign (1621). His lordship m. first, Bridget, daughter of Sir Charles Morison, Knt., of Cashiobury, in the county of Hertford, and had issue,

> Henry, who m. Jane, daughter of Sir Michael Stanhope, Knt.
>
> Thomas.
>
> Elizabeth, m. to Sir John Ramsey, Knt., Viscount Hadington, afterwards Earl of Holderness.
>
> Honora.

All of whom, however, d. issueless before himself. The earl espoused, secondly, Frances, daughter of Hercules Meutas, Esq., of Hame, in the county of Essex, but had no issue. His lordship d. in 1629, when the BARONY OF FITZ-WALTER devolved upon the descendants of his aunt, by the half blood, Lady Frances Mildmay, (refer to issue of Henry, third Lord Fitz-Walter, and second Earl of Sussex, by his second marriage; and see MILDMAY, Lords Fitz-Walter,) and the other honours devolved upon (the son of Sir Humphrey Ratcliffe, of Elnestow; revert to issue of Robert, first Earl of Sussex,) his cousin,

SIR EDWARD RATCLIFFE, as sixth Viscount Fitz-Walter, and Earl of Sussex. This nobleman d. in 1641 without issue, when those honours became EXTINCT.

ARMS.—Ar. a bend ingrailed, sa.

RAYMOND — BARONS RAYMOND, OF ABBOT'S LANGLEY, IN THE COUNTY OF HERTFORD.

By Letters Patent, dated 15th January, 1731.

Lineage.

In the reign of *King* CHARLES II.,

SIR THOMAS RAYMOND, Knt., was one of the judges of the King's Bench, and his name is handed down to posterity by his law reports. His lordship was father of

ROBERT RAYMOND, another eminent lawyer, who became CHIEF JUSTICE of the KING'S BENCH, and was elevated to the peerage by letters patent, dated 15th January, 1731, in the dignity of LORD RAYMOND, BARON OF ABBOT'S LANGLEY, *in the county of Hertford*. His lordship m. Anne, daugh-

---

* This lady was foundress of Sydney-Sussex College, Cambridge, and d. 19th March, 1589, aged fifty-eight.

ter of Sir Edward Northey, attorney-general, temp. Queen Anne, and King George I., and dying in 1732, was s. by his only son,

ROBERT RAYMOND, second baron. This nobleman espoused Chetwynd, daughter and co-heir of Montagu, Viscount Blundell, in Ireland, but d. in 1753 without issue, when the BARONY OF RAYMOND became EXTINCT.

ARMS.—Sa. a chevron betw. three eagles displayed, ar. on a chief, or a rose between two fleurs-de-lis, gu.

REDVERS—EARLS OF DEVON.

See Courtenay, Earls of Devon.

RICH — BARONS RICH, OF LEEZE, IN THE COUNTY OF ESSEX, EARLS OF WARWICK, BARONS KENSINGTON, EARLS OF HOLLAND.

Barony of Rich,		16th Feb., 1547.
Earldom of Warwick,	by Letters Patent,	6th August, 1618.
Barony of Kensington,		8th March, 1622.
Earldom of Holland,		24th Sept., 1624.

Lineage.

The founder of this family,

RICHARD RICH, was an opulent mercer of London, who served the office of sheriff for that city, in 1441. He d. in 1469, leaving a son,

JOHN RICH, whose grandson,

RICHARD RICH, having studied law in the Middle Temple, was appointed, in the 21st Henry VIII., autumnal reader to that society. Shortly after which, he advanced through several eminent employments, to great wealth and high honours. In the 24th of the same king, he was constituted attorney-general for Wales, and in the next year, appointed the king's SOLICITOR-GENERAL. In the 27th, he had a grant of the office of chirographer to the Common Pleas; and about that time, visiting Sir Thomas More, Ex-Lord Chancellor, then a prisoner in the Tower, used his utmost exertions to persuade that great and eminent person to acknowledge the king's supremacy in spiritual affairs. In this year, too, he was appointed chancellor of the *Court of Augmentations*, a court formed to take cognizance of the revenues of the monasteries, which had considerably AUGMENTED the funds of the crown; and he had a grant of the scite of the Priory of Leeze, with the manor thereunto appertaining, in the county of Essex. Upon the accession of *King* EDWARD VI., being then a knight, he was elevated to the peerage, by letters patent, dated 16th February, 1547, (the fourth day before the coronation,) as BARON RICH, *of Leeze*, and constituted, on the 30th November following, LORD CHANCELLOR OF ENGLAND. But within five years, observing the dangers of the times, by the Duke of Somerset's fall, and other circumstances equally ominous, and having amassed a very large fortune, "like a discreet pilot," says Dugdale, "who seeing a storm at hand, gets his ship into harbour, he made suit to the king, by

reason of some bodily infirmities, that he might be discharged of his office, which being granted, the great seal was delivered to Thomas Goodrick, Bishop of Ely; after which, he (Lord Rich) lived many years, and at his own charge built the tower steeple at Rochford, in Essex." The cause of his lordship's resignation of the chancellorship is thus, however, more feasibly accounted for: "The Lord Rich being a fast friend to the great Duke of Somerset, then in the Tower, was endeavouring to serve him with the king; and for that purpose had written him notice of something designed against him by the council; and being in haste, directed the letter only ' to the duke,' bidding his servant carry it to the Tower, without giving him any particular directions ' to the Duke of Somerset.' The servant not knowing that his master was intimate with Somerset, but knowing that he was so with the Duke of Norfolk, (then also in the Tower,) gave the latter nobleman the letter by mistake. When the chancellor found out his error at night, fearful that Norfolk would discover him, he immediately repaired to the king, and desired to be discharged his office, feigning illness, which was merely to raise pity for himself, and prevent the malice of his enemies." The reputation of Lord Rich suffered deeply in the opinion of all honourable men, by the baseness of his conduct to Sir Thomas More. Upon the trial of the ex-chancellor, Rich was a witness against him, as to a pretended conversation in the Tower; and when he gave his evidence, Sir Thomas made answer: "If I were a man, my lord, that had no regard to my oath, I had no occasion to be here a criminal; and if this oath, Mr. Rich, you have taken, be true, then I pray I may never see God's face; which, were it otherwise, is an imprecation I would not be guilty of to gain the world." Sir Thomas then proceeded to charge him with being "light of tongue, a great gamester, and a person of no good, in the parish where they had lived together, or in the temple, where he was educated." After which, he went on to shew how unlikely it was, that he should "impart the secrets of his conscience to a man, of whom he always had so mean an opinion."

His lordship m. Elizabeth, sister of William Jenks, of London, grocer, and had issue, ROBERT, his successor, with three other sons, all of whom died issueless, and nine daughters, viz.

Margery, m. to Henry Pigot, Esq., of Abingdon.

Agnes, m. to Edmund Mordant, Esq.

Mary, m. to Sir Thomas Wrothe, Knt.

Dorothy, m. to Francis Barley, Esq.

Elizabeth, m. to Robert Peyton, Esq.

Winifride, m. first, to Sir Henry Dudley, Knt., and secondly, to Roger, Lord North.

Etheldreda, m. to Robert Drury, Esq.

Anne, m. to Thomas Pigot, Esq.

Frances, m. to John, Lord Darcy, of Chiche.

Lord Rich d. in 1568, and was s. by his eldest son,

ROBERT RICH, second baron. This nobleman was one of the peers upon the trial of the Duke of Norfolk, in the reign of Elizabeth, and was afterwards employed by her majesty, upon a diplomatic mission to France, as well as on some complicated affairs in Ireland. His lordship *m.* Elizabeth, daughter and heir of George Baldry, Esq., son and heir of Sir Thomas Baldry, Knt., of London, and had issue,

> Richard, *m.* to Katherine, daughter and co-heir of Sir Henry Knevit, Knt., and died *s. p.*, in the life-time of his father,
>
> ROBERT, his successor.
>
> Edwin (Sir), of Mulbarton, in Norfolk, *m.* Honora, daughter of Charles Worlick, Esq., and had issue,
>
> > Robert, who died *s. p.*
> >
> > Edwin (Sir), of Lincoln's Inn, died *s. p.*, in 1675.
> >
> > Richard, died *s. p.*
> >
> > Charles, created a baronet, by King Charles II., a dignity which expired with Lieutenant-General Sir Robert Rich, whose only daughter and heiress,
> >
> > > MARY-FRANCES RICH, *m.* the Reverend Charles Bostick, L.L.D., of Shirley House, Hants, who assumed the surname and arms of RICH, and was created a BARONET, in 1791. He *d.* in 1824, and was *s.* by his eldest son,
> > >
> > > > SIR CHARLES RICH, present Baronet.
>
> Frances, *m.* to Nathaniel Acton, Esq.
>
> Margaret.
>
> Honoria.

Frances, *m.* to Thomas Camock, Esq.

Elizabeth, *m.* to —— Castleton, Esq.

His lordship *d.* in 1581, and was *s.* by his eldest son,

ROBERT RICH, third baron. This nobleman, in the 40th of Elizabeth, was at the sacking of Cadiz, under the Earl of Essex, and was advanced by King James I., on the 6th August, 1618, to the EARLDOM OF WARWICK. His lordship *m.* first, Lady Penelope Devereux, daughter of Walter, Earl of Essex, and had issue,

> ROBERT, Lord Rich, his successor.
>
> HENRY (Sir), K.B., Captain of the King's Guard, who was elevated to the peerage, by letters patent, dated 8th March, 1622, as BARON KENSINGTON. His lordship was subsequently employed to negotiate a marriage between *Prince* CHARLES, (afterwards CHARLES I.,) and the Spanish Infanta; and when that treaty proved abortive, he was sent into France to sound the French Court, regarding a consort for the English Prince. He was advanced, on the 24th September, 1624, to the dignity of EARL OF HOLLAND, *in the county of Lincoln*, and installed shortly after, a KNIGHT of the GARTER. His lordship *m.* Isabel, daughter and heir of Sir Walter Cope, of Kensington, in the county of Middlesex, Knt., by whom he acquired the Manor and Mansion* of Kensington, and had issue,

---

* This ancient and venerable pile, situated beyond Kensington, on the road to Hammersmith, has since that period borne the name of HOLLAND-

> > ROBERT, second Earl of Holland, who succeeded as fifth EARL OF WARWICK.
> >
> > Charles.
> >
> > Henry.
> >
> > Cope, *m.* ——, and had a son,
> >
> > > COPE, whose son,
> > >
> > > > EDWARD, inherited eventually, the EARLDOMS OF WARWICK AND HOLLAND.

Lord Holland, after *King* CHARLES I. became a prisoner in the Isle of Wight, took up arms, with other loyal persons, to effect his restoration, but miscarrying at Kingston-upon-Thames, 7th July, 1648, he was pursued, made prisoner, and committed to the Tower, where he remained until after the execution of the king, when, being brought to trial with the Duke of Hamilton, the Earl of Norwich, Sir John Owen, &c., he was condemned to death, and executed by decapitation before the gates of Westminster Hall, 9th March, 1649.

> Charles (Sir), slain at the Isle of Rhee, in the expedition under the Duke of Buckingham.
>
> Lettice, *m.* first, to Sir George Carey, Knt., of Cockington, in the county of Devon, and secondly, to Sir Arthur Lake, Knt.
>
> Penelope, *m.* to Sir Gervase Clefton, Bart., of Clefton, in the county of Nottingham.
>
> Essex, *m.* to Sir Thomas Cheeke, Knt., of Pirgo, in Essex.
>
> Isabel, *m.* to Sir John Smythe, Knt.

The earl being divorced from his first countess, (who remarried Charles Blount, Earl of Devon,) espoused, secondly, Frances, widow of Sir George Paul, and daughter of Sir Christopher Wray, Knt., lord chief justice of the court of King's Bench, but had no other issue. His lordship *d.* in the same year in which he was advanced to the earldom, (anno 1618,) and was *s.* by his eldest son,

ROBERT RICH, second Earl of Warwick. This nobleman was a very distinguished personage in the time of the civil war. He was admiral for the long parliament—and during the usurpation enjoyed the full confidence of Cromwell. Lord Clarendon says, " That he was a man of a pleasant and companionable wit and conversation ; of an universal jolity; and such a licence in his words, and in his actions, that a man of less virtue could not be found out. But with all these faults he had great authority and credit with the people ; for by opening his doors, and spending a good part of his estate, of which he was very prodigal, upon them, and by being present with them at his devotions, and making himself merry with them, and at them, which they dispensed with, he became the head of that party, and got the style of *a goodly man.*" His lordship *m.* first, Frances, daughter of Sir William

---

HOUSE. It is now in the possession of the family of Fox, *Lords Holland;* having been purchased by Henry Fox, who thence assumed the title of HOLLAND, from William Edwardes, first Lord Kensington. See Robert Rich, second Earl of Holland, and fifth Earl of Warwick.

Hatton, alias Newport, Knt., (by Elizabeth, his wife, daughter and heir of Sir Francis Gundi, Knt., lord chief justice of the court of Common Pleas,) by whom he had issue,

ROBERT, *Lord Rich*, his successor.

CHARLES, who inherited as FOURTH EARL.

Henry,
Hatton, } both d. unmarried.

Anne, *m.* to Edward Montagu, second Earl of Manchester, the celebrated parliamentary general, distinguished by his victory over Prince Rupert, at Marston Moor.

Lucy, *m.* to John Robartes, Baron Robartes, of Truro, afterwards Earl of Radnor.

Frances, *m.* to Nicholas Leke, Earl of Scarsdale.

The earl espoused, secondly, Eleanor, daughter of Sir Edward Wortley, Knt., but had no other issue. He d. in 1658, and was *s.* by his eldest son,

ROBERT RICH, third Earl of Warwick, who was made a Knight of the Bath at the coronation of *King* CHARLES II. His lordship *m.* first, Lady Anne Cavendish, daughter of William, Earl of Devonshire, and had issue,

ROBERT, who *m.* in the life-time of his grandfather, Frances, youngest daughter of the *Protector* CROMWELL, and d. in about two months after, 16th February, 1657-8.

He *m.* secondly, Anne, daughter of Sir Thomas Cheeke, of Pargo, and had three daughters, viz.

Anne, *m.* to Sir John Barrington, Bart., of Barrington Hall, in the county of Essex.

Mary, *m.* to Sir Henry St. John. *r . Lydiard*

Essex, *m.* to the Hon. Daniel Finch, son of Heneage, Lord Finch, of Daventry, and eventually sixth Earl of Winchelsea.

The earl d. 29th May, 1659, when, leaving no male issue, the honours devolved upon his brother,

CHARLES RICH, fourth Earl of Warwick, who *m.* Lady Mary Boyle, daughter of Richard, first Earl of Cork, and had a son, CHARLES, *Lord Rich*, who espoused Lady Anne Cavendish, daughter of William, third Earl of Devonshire, but died *s. p.* in his father's life-time. The earl d. 24th August, 1673, when his estates, except Warwick House, in Holborn, passed to his sisters as co-heirs, and his honours devolved upon his kinsman, (refer to Robert, first Earl of Holland, second son of Robert, second Earl of Warwick,)

ROBERT RICH, second Earl of Holland, as fifth Earl of Warwick. This nobleman *m.* first, Elisabeth, daughter of Sir Arthur Ingram, Knt., by whom he had one surviving son,

Henry, LORD KENSINGTON, who *m.* Christiana, daughter of Andrew Riccard, Esq., and died *s. p.* in the life-time of his father. His widow *m.* John, Lord Berkeley, of Stratton.

The earl espoused, secondly, Lady Anne Montagu, daughter of Edward, Earl of Manchester, and had issue,

EDWARD, his successor.

Elizabeth, *m.* to Francis Edwardes, Esq., of Haverford West, whose only surviving son,

WILLIAM EDWARDES, Esq., inherited the family estates upon the decease of his cousin, *Edward-Henry Rich*, fourth EARL OF HOLLAND, and seventh EARL OF WARWICK, and was created a peer of Ireland in 1776, as BARON KENSINGTON.

His lordship d. in 1675, and was *s.* by his son,

EDWARD RICH, third Earl of Holland, and sixth Earl of Warwick. His lordship *m.* Charlotte, daughter of Sir Thomas Middleton, by whom (who espoused, secondly, the Right Hon. Joseph Addison,) he had an only son, his successor, at his decease in 1701,

EDWARD HENRY RICH, fourth Earl of Holland, and seventh Earl of Warwick, at whose decease, unmarried, in 1721, his fortune passed to his cousin, WILLIAM EDWARDES, Esq., (refer to Elisabeth, daughter of Robert, second Earl of Holland, and fifth Earl of Warwick,) while the honours reverted to his kinsman, (refer to Cope, youngest son of *Henry*, first EARL OF HOLLAND, second son of *Robert*, first Earl of Warwick,)

EDWARD RICH, Esq., fifth Earl of Holland, and eighth Earl of Warwick. This nobleman *m.* Miss Stanton, daughter of Samuel Stanton, Esq., of Lyme Regis, and had an only daughter, Catherine. His lordship d. in 1759, when ALL THE HONOURS of the Rich family became EXTINCT.

ARMS.—Gu. a chevron between three cross crosslets or.

RIPARIIS, OR RIVERS — BARON RIPARIIS.

By Writ of Summons, dated 6th February, 1299, 27 Edward I.

Lineage.

JOHN DE RIPARIIS was summoned to parliament, as a BARON, from 6th February, 1299, to 26th August, 1307. His lordship signed the celebrated letter to the pope, 29th Edward I., as " Johannes de Ripariis, Domine de Angre.". He d. in 1311, and was *s.* by his son,

JOHN DE RIPARIIS, second baron, summoned to parliament from 8th June, 1313, to 16th October, 1315, but neither himself nor his descendants had further summons, nor is there any thing more known about them.

ROBARTES — BARONS ROBARTES, OF TRURO, EARLS OF RADNOR.

Barony, } by Letters { 16th January, 1625.
Earldom, } Patent, { 23rd July, 1679.

Lineage.

RICHARD ROBARTES, Esq., of Truro, in Cornwall, had the honour of knighthood conferred upon him by *King* JAMES I., at Whitehall, in 1616, and was created a baronet in 1621. In four years afterwards he was advanced, through the influence of the favourite Buckingham,* to the peer-

---

* For which Sir Richard is said to have paid ten thousand pounds: and one of the charges brought

age, in the dignity of BARON ROBARTES, *of Truro*. His lordship *m.* Frances, daughter and co-heir of John Hender, Esq., of Botreaux Castle, in Cornwall, and had issue,

    JOHN, his successor.

    Mary, *m.* to William Rouse, Esq., of Halton, in Cornwall.

    Jane, *m.* to Charles, Lord Lambert, in Ireland.

His lordship *d.* in 1634, and was *s.* by his son,

JOHN ROBARTES, second baron. Although this nobleman fought under the parliamentary banner, he was favourably received by *King* CHARLES II., after the restoration; sworn of the privy council, appointed lord privy seal, and afterwards lord lieutenant of Ireland. In 1679, his lordship was advanced to the dignities of *Viscount Bodmin*, and EARL OF RADNOR (he was first created Earl of Falmouth, but the title was altered at the desire of the king). His lordship espoused, first, Lady Lucy Rich, daughter of Robert, Earl of Warwick, and had issue,

    ROBERT, *Viscount Bodmin*, a person of eminent talents, who died about the year 1681. In his embassy at the Court of Denmark. His lordship *m.* Sarah, daughter and heir of John Bodvile, Esq., of Bodvile Castle, in Carnarvonshire, and left issue,

        CHARLES BODVILE, successor to the honours.

        Russel, one of the tellers of the exchequer, *m.* Lady Mary Booth, daughter of Henry, Earl of Warrington, and had issue,

            HENRY, who succeeded as third EARL OF RADNOR.

            Mary, *m.* to —— Hunt, Esq., of Chester.

        Isabella, *m.* to Colonel Leigh, of Adlington, in the county of Chester.

        Sarah, *d.* unmarried.

        Lucy, *m.* to the Honourable George Booth, second son of George, first Lord Delamere.

        Essex, *d.* unmarried.

    Hender, M.P. for Bodmin, temp. Charles II. and James II., *d.* unmarried.

    John, *d.* young.

The earl *m.* secondly, Isabella, daughter of Sir John Smith, Knight of Kent, and had four other sons and five daughters, viz.

    Francis, M.P. in the reigns of Charles II. James II., William III., and Queen Anne. Mr. Robartes was a person of great learning, and vice-president of the Royal Society. He *m.* Anne, relict of Hugh Boscawen, Esq., and daughter of Wentworth, Earl of Kildare, by whom he had,

        JOHN, who succeeded as fourth EARL OF RADNOR.

    Francis, *m.* to Mary, daughter of William

---

against the Duke of Buckingham in parliament, anno 1696, was, " that, knowing him to be rich, he forced him to take that title of honour; and that, in consideration thereof, he paid ten thousand pounds to the duke's use."

Wallis, Esq., of Groveby, in Wiltshire, and died in 1734, leaving one son,

    John.

Mr. Robartes died at Chelsea, in February, 1717-18.

Henry, *m.* Miss Frances Coryton, and died *s. p.* Warwick.

Charles, *d.* unmarried.

Isabella, *m.* first, to John, Lord Moore, son and heir of the Earl of Drogheda, and secondly to Daniel Wycherley, Esq., of Shropshire.

Diana, *d.* unmarried.

Aranintha, *m.* to the Right Reverend (Bishop) Hopkins.

Olimpia.

Essex, *m.* to John Speccot, Esq., of Penhaile, in Cornwall.

The Earl of Radnor, was " a staunch presbyterian; sour and cynical; just in his administration, but vicious under the semblance of virtue; learned above any of his quality; but stiff, obstinate, proud, and jealous, and every way intracticable." He *d.* in 1685, and was *s.* by his grandson,

CHARLES-BODVILE ROBARTES, second earl, who *m.* Elizabeth, daughter and heir of Sir John Cutler, Knt., of the city of London, but died issueless in 1723, when his honours devolved upon his nephew,

HENRY ROBARTES, third earl, at whose decease, unmarried, at Paris in 1741, the honours passed to his cousin (refer to Francis, eldest son of the first EARL, by his second wife),

JOHN ROBARTES, Esq., as fourth earl. This nobleman *d.* in 1764, unmarried, when the EARLDOM OF RADNOR, *and minor honours*, became EXTINCT.

ARMS.—AZ. three estoiles of six points, and a chief waved, or.

ROBSART—BARON ROBSART.

Refer to BOURCHIER, *Barons Bourchier*, and *Earls of Essex*.

ELIZABETH BOURCHIER, *Baroness Bourchier*, *m.* for her second husband, Sir Lewis Robsart, K.G., who assumed the title, *jure uxoris*, of LORD BOURCHIER, but was summoned to parliament as LORD ROBSART.

ROLLE — BARON ROLLE, OF STEVENSTONE.

By *Letters Patent*, dated 8th January, 1748.

Lineage.

This family was originally of the county of Dorset, and the first of its members that removed into Devon, was

GEORGE ROLLE, a merchant of great opulence, and high reputation, in the city of London, who became an extensive purchaser of abbey lands. Besides which, he bought, temp. Henry VIII., the seat, manor, and large demesnes of STEVENSTONE, in Devonshire, from the *Moyles*, who had acquired the property by marriage with the heiress of the Stevenstones, the former lords. This George Rolle married thrice, and had no less than twenty children. By his second wife, Eleanor, second daughter of Henry Dacres, Esq., of London, merchant, he had (with two daughters) six sons, viz.

    JOHN, his successor.

    George, of whom presently.

    Christopher, d. unmarried.

    Henry, whose grandson, Henry Rolle, an eminent lawyer, became Lord Chief Justice, and one of the council of state, during the first years of the commonwealth, from 1648 to 1655.

    Robert.

    Maurice.

The second son,

GEORGE ROLLE, Esq., m. Margaret, daughter and heiress of Edmund Marrais, Esq., of Marrais, in Cornwall, and was s. by his son,

ANDREW ROLLE, Esq., of Marrais, whose son,

SIR JOHN ROLLE, inherited STEVENSTONE, and became chief of the family upon the failure of the male line of John Rolle, Esq., his great-uncle, in 1647. This gentleman, who was zealously attached to King CHARLES II., accompanied that monarch from Holland upon his restoration, and was made a Knight of the Bath, at the ensuing coronation. Sir John Rolle afterwards represented Devon in parliament, and was a leading member of the House of Commons. He m. Florence, daughter and co-heir of Dennis Rolle, Esq., and dying at an advanced age, in 1706, (the wealthiest commoner in England,) was s. by his grandson,

ROBERT ROLLE, Esq., M.P., who d. without issue in 1719, and was s. by his brother,

JOHN ROLLE, Esq., M.P. for the county of Devon. This gentleman is said to have been offered an EARLDOM by Queen Anne's last ministry, and to have declined it. He m. Isabella, daughter of Sir William Walter, Bart., of Sarsden, in Oxfordshire, and grand-daughter (maternally) of Robert, Earl of Ailesbury, by whom he had issue,

    HENRY, his successor.

    John, who assumed the surname of WALTER, upon inheriting the estates of his maternal uncle, represented the county of Devon in parliament, and d. in 1779.

    William, died s. p.

    Dennis, who eventually inherited the estates, and was father of

        JOHN ROLLE, in whom the title of Rolle was revived, and who is the present Lord Rolle.

Mr. Rolle d. 6th May, 1730, and was s. by his eldest son,

HENRY ROLLE, Esq., M.P. for the county of Devon, who was elevated to the peerage, 8th January, 1747-8, by the title of BARON ROLLE, of Stevenstone, in the county of Devon. His lordship d. unmarried, in 1750, when the dignity became EXTINCT.

ARMS.—Or. on a bar dancette, between three billets as. charged with as many lions rampant of the first, three bezants.

ROMARE—EARL OF LINCOLN.

Created in 1142.

Lineage.

The first of this name upon record,

GERALD DE ROMARE, feudal Lord of Bolingbroke, in Lincolnshire, m. Lucia, daughter of Algar, Earl of Chester, and widow of Two Tailboys; by whom (who espoused after his decease, Ranulph, Earl of Chester,) he had a son and successor,

WILLIAM DE ROMARE, Lord of Bolingbroke, who, in 1118, being governor of the garrison of Newmarch, in Normandy, stoutly resisted Hugh de Gournay, then in rebellion there; and remaining firm in his allegiance to King Henry I., was with that monarch at the battle of Brennevill, where a glorious victory was achieved over Lewis, King of France. But long after this, however, having laid claim, unsuccessfully, to those lands in England, of his mother's inheritance, which Ranulph, Earl of Chester, her last husband, had delivered up to the king, in exchange for the earldom, he returned to Normandy in great indignation, and rearing the standard of rebellion in favour of William, son of Robert Curthose, continued in open hostility for two years; but the king at length made him compensation, and restored him to the greater part of his right. Whereupon being honourably reconciled, Henry gave him in marriage a noble lady, viz., Maud, daughter of Richard de Redvers.

Upon the decease of Henry I., and the accession of Stephen, this eminent person espoused the cause of the new monarch, who appointed him one of his principal delegates to administer justice in Normandy; but he soon after went over to the Empress Maud, and joined his half brother, Ranulph, Earl of Chester, in the surprisal of the Castle of Lincoln (anno 1141). He had subsequently a command at the battle of Lincoln, so disastrous to the fortunes of Stephen, and the next year (1142) bore the title of EARL OF LINCOLN, in the grant by which he founded the Cistercian monastery at Revesby, in that county. His lordship had issue,

    William, who d. in his father's life-time (1152), leaving by Hawse, daughter of Stephen, Earl of Albemarle, a son,

        William.

    Hawye, m. to Gilbert de Gant (see Gant, Earls of Lincoln).

The earl was s. at his decease, by his grandson,

WILLIAM DE ROMARE, Lord of Bolingbroke, but this personage never assumed the title of Earl. In the 12th of Henry II., on the assessment of aid for marriage of the king's daughter, he certified his knights' fees de veteri feoffamento, to be thirty-two, and those de novo, twenty-five, a fourth and a third part. This feudal lord d. without issue, when the male line of the family ceased, but the earldom passed through the daughter of Earl William, to the house of Gant (see Gant, Earls of Lincoln).

ARMS.—Gules seven mascles and semée of crosslets or.

ROS, OR ROOS—BARONS ROS, OF HAMLAKE.

By Writ of Summons, dated 24th December, 1264, 49 Henry III.

Lineage.

The ancestor of this family, PETER, having in the reign of Henry I., assumed his surname from the Lordship of Ros, in Holderness, where he then resided, became

PETER DE ROS, or ROOS. This feudal baron m. Adeline, one of the sisters and co-heirs of the famous Walter Espec, Lord of the manor of Helmesley, called sometimes Helmeslac, but oftener *Hamlake*, in the North Riding of Yorkshire, and was s. at his decease, by his son,

ROBERT DE ROS, who, in the 3rd of Henry II., paid a thousand marks of silver to the king for livery of the lands inherited by his mother from her brother, Walter Espec. This Robert was a munificent benefactor to the knights templars. He m. Sybell de Valoines, (who, after his decease, wedded Ralph de Albini,) and dying sometime about the middle of the twelfth century, was s. by his son,

EVERARD DE ROS, a minor, and in ward to Ranulph de Glanvil. In the 12th of Henry II. this feudal lord held of the crown eight knights' fees, and in two years afterwards, upon collection of the aid for marrying the king's daughter, answered, one hundred and twelve shillings for those which were *de veteri feoffamento*, and thirty-one shillings and one penny for what he had *de novo*. He m. Rose, one of the daughters and co-heirs of William Trusbut, of Wartre, in Holderness, and had two sons. This Everard de Ros must have been a very considerable personage at the period. in which he lived, for we find him, in the year 1176, paying the then very large sum of £596 as a fine for his lands, and in four years subsequently £100 more to have possession of those which the Earl of Albemarle held. He d. soon after, and was s. by his elder son,

ROBERT DE ROS, of Furfan, who, in the 1st of Richard I., paid a thousand marks fine to the crown for livery of his lands. In the 8th of the same reign, being with the king in Normandy, he was committed to the custody of Hugh de Chaumont, for what offence appears not; with especial charge to the said Hugh, that he should keep him as safe as his own life: but Chaumont trusting William de Spiney with his prisoner, that person being corrupted, allowed him to escape out of the castle of Bonville: De Ros eventually gained nothing, however, by this escape, for Richard caused him nevertheless to pay twelve hundred marks for his freedom, while he had the false traitor Spiney hanged for his breach of faith. In the next reign, however, Robert de Ros found more favour, for upon the accession of King John, that monarch gave him the whole barony of his great grandmother's father, Walter Espec, to enjoy in as large and ample a manner as he, the said Walter, ever held it. Soon after which he was deputed, with the Bishop of Durham, and other great men,

to escort the king of Scotland into England, which monarch coming to Lincoln, swore fealty there to King John, upon the cross of Hubert, Archbishop of Canterbury, in the presence of all the people. About the 14th of King John's reign, Robert de Ros assumed the habit of a monk, whereupon the custody of all his lands, viz., *Works Castle*, in the county of Northumberland, with his whole barony, was committed to Philip de Ulcote, but he did not continue long a *recluse*, for we find him the very next year executing the office of sheriff for the county of Cumberland. At the commencement of the struggle between the barons and John, this feudal lord took part with the king, and obtained, in consequence, some grants from the crown; but he subsequently espoused the baronial cause, and was one of the celebrated TWENTY-FIVE appointed to enforce the observance of MAGNA CHARTA. In the reign of King Henry III. he seems, however, to have returned to his allegiance, and to have been in favour with that prince, for the year after the king's accession a precept was issued by the crown to the sheriff of Cumberland, ordering the restoration of certain manors granted by King John to De Ros.

Robert de Ros m. Isabel, daughter of William the Lion, king of Scotland, and had issue, two sons, WILLIAM, and Robert.

This feudal lord was the founder of the CASTLE OF HELMESLEY, otherwise HAMLAKE, in Yorkshire, and of the CASTLE OF WERKE, in Northumberland—the former of which he bequeathed to his elder son—the latter to the younger, with a barony in Scotland, to be held of the elder by military service. In his latter days he became a knight templar, to which order himself and his predecessors had ever been munificently liberal, and d. in that habit, anno 1227, was buried in the Temple church. He was s. in his barony by his elder son,

WILLIAM DE ROS, of Hamlake, who, upon giving security for the payment of £100 for his relief, had livery of his lands. This feudal lord, in the life-time of his father, was an active supporter of the baronial cause, and was made prisoner at the battle of Lincoln (1st Henry III.,) by the royalists, but soon after released and delivered up to his father upon bail. He was subsequently engaged in the wars of Gascony, and he had two military summonses in the 42nd Henry III., to march against the Scots and Welsh. By the deaths of his two great aunts, the sisters of his grandmother, Rose Trusbut, without issue, he became sole heir of the baronial estate of Trusbut and Watre. He m. Lucia, daughter of Reginald Fitz-Piers, of Blewleveny, in Wales, and d. in 1268, was s. by his son,

ROBERT DE ROS, who had m. in the lifetime of his father, Isabel, daughter and heiress of William de Albini, feudal Lord of Belvoir, by whom he acquired BELVOIR CASTLE, in the county of Lincoln, (see Daubeney, Barons Daubeney and Earl of Bridgewater,) and other extensive landed possessions. This great heiress was in ward to the king, and a mandate upon her marriage, bearing date at Windsor, 17th May, 1244, was directed to

Bernard de Savoy and Hugh Gifford, to deliver her to her husband, the said Robert: "but not," says Dugdale, "without a round composition, for it appears that both he and his wife, in the 32nd Henry III., were debtors to the king in no less than the sum of £3,295 13s. 4d., and a palfrey; of which sum the king was then pleased to accept by two hundred marks a year until it should be all paid." In the 42nd of the same reign he had two military summonses with his father, to march against the Scotch and Welsh—but afterwards rearing, with the other barons, the standard of revolt, he had a chief command at the battle of Lewes, so disastrous to the royalists, and to his custody, in the castle of Hereford, was especially committed the person of Prince Edward. He was at the same time summoned, as a BARON, to the parliament then called in the king's name by the victorious lords. But the fortune of war changing at the subsequent battle of Evesham, his lands were all seized by the crown, and held until redeemed by his lordship under "the *Dictum of Kenilworth*." In two years after this he must, however, have regained somewhat of royal favour, for he had then permission to raise a new embattled wall around the CASTLE OF BELVOIR. He d. in 1265, leaving issue by the "heiress of Belvoir,"

WILLIAM, his successor.
Robert.
Isabel, m. to Walter de Fauconberge.
His lordship was s. by his elder son,

WILLIAM DE ROS, second baron, summoned to parliament as "BARON ROS, of Hamlake," from 23rd June, 1295, to 6th October, 1315. This nobleman was one of the competitors for the crown of Scotland, in the 19th Edward I., through his grandmother, Isabel, daughter of William the Lion, King of Scotland. He was subsequently engaged in the wars of Gascony and Scotland; and discovering the intention of his kinsman, Robert de Ros, then Lord of Werke, to deliver up that castle to the Scots, he lost no time in apprising the king, who thereupon despatched him with a thousand men to defend that place, but the Scots attacking this force upon its march, cut it to pieces; when Edward himself advancing from Newcastle-upon-Tyne, soon obtained possession of the fort, and appointed Lord Ros its governor—allowing him, during his absence in Gascony, to nominate his brother, Robert, lieutenant. In a short time after, he had a grant of this castle, with its appurtenances, forfeited by the treason of his before mentioned kinsman; and for several subsequent years, his lordship was actively engaged in Scotland. In the 1st Edward II., he was constituted the king's lieutenant, between Berwick and the river Forth, and in six years afterwards, he was appointed warden of the west Marches of Scotland.

He m. Maude, one of the daughters and co-heirs of John de Veaux, who brought him the Manor of Feston, and lands in Boston, in the county of Lincoln—and had issue,

WILLIAM, his successor.
John, a very eminent person, temp. Edward II. and Edward III. In the former reign, he took an active part against the Spencers, and upon the accession of the latter

king, he was appointed steward of the household, and entrusted with a command in Scotland. He was likewise constituted one of the governors of the young monarch. In the 10th of the same reign, he was made admiral of the seas, from the river Thames, northwards; and the next year, he was with the king, in Gascony—as he was again in two years afterwards. He was summoned to parliament as BARON DE ROS, from 27th January, 1332, to 15th June, 1338, but dying in the latter year without issue, the BARONY became EXTINCT, while his property devolved upon his brother, William, Lord Ros, of Hamlake.

Anne, m. to Paine, son of Robert de Tibetot. His lordship d. in 1316, and was s. by his elder son,

WILLIAM DE ROS, third baron, summoned to parliament, from 20th November, 1317, to 12th September, 1342. This nobleman, in the 5th Edward II., was one of the commissioners appointed to negotiate peace with Robert Bruce, King of Scotland; about which time he came to an agreement with the king, regarding the Castle of Werke, which he then exchanged with the crown, for other lands. He was subsequently much engaged in the wars of Gascony and Scotland. His lordship m. Margery, elder sister, and co-heir of Giles de Badlesmere, of Ledes Castle, in Kent, a great feudal baron, by whom he had issue, WILLIAM, Thomas, Margaret, and Maud. He d. on 16th February, 1342, and was s. by his elder son,

WILLIAM DE ROS, fourth baron, summoned to parliament, from 25th November, 1350, to 20th November, 1351. This nobleman was one of the eminent martial characters, of the glorious reign of Edward III. He was at the memorable battle of CRESSY, a leader in the second brigade of the English army; he had a command at Newcastle-upon-Tyne, in the conflict, where David Bruce, King of Scotland, and many of his nobles, after sustaining a defeat, fell into the hands of the English; and he was subsequently (21st Edward III.) at the siege of Calais, with the Black Prince. His lordship m. Margaret, daughter of Ralph, Lord Nevill, (who espoused, after his decease, Henry, Lord Percy,) but dying in the Holy Land, in 1352, without issue, he was s. by his brother,

THOMAS DE ROS, fifth baron, summoned to parliament, from 24th August, 1362, to 3rd March, 1384. This nobleman was also engaged in the French wars, and is supposed to have shared the glory of Poictiers. His lordship m. Beatrix, daughter of Ralph, Earl of Stafford, and widow of Maurice Fitz-Morris, Earl of Desmond, by whom he had issue, JOHN, William, Thomas, Robert, Elizabeth, m. to Thomas, son and heir of Roger, Lord Clifford, and Margaret. He d. in 1384, and was s. by his eldest son,

JOHN DE ROS, sixth baron, summoned to parliament from 8th August, 1386, to 13th November, 1399. This nobleman was in the naval expedition in the 11th Richard II., under Richard, Earl of Arundel; and the next year he was joined with Henry, Earl of Northumberland, and Ralph, Lord

Nevill, in the government of Carlisle, and wardenship of the west Marches of Scotland. His lordship, who was not less distinguished for piety, than valour, died upon his pilgrimage to Jerusalem, at Paphos, in the Isle of Cyprus, anno 1393. He m. Mary, daughter of Henry de Percy, but having no issue, was s. by his brother,

THOMAS DE ROS, seventh baron, summoned to parliament, from 20th November, 1394, to 24th December, 1413. This nobleman was appointed LORD TREASURER of England, in the 4th Henry IV., and in the 6th he obtained, in consideration of his services, a grant from the crown, of one hundred marks per annum, for his life, to be paid out of the exchequer. In the 16th of the same reign, being then one of the king's council, and in such esteem that his residence near the court was deemed indispensable, he had the town of *Chyngilford*, in Essex, assigned him, for the abode of his servants and horses. It was about this period that his lordship preferred a complaint in parliament, against Robert Tirwhit, one of the Justices of the King's Bench, for withholding from him, and his tenants, of the Manor of Melton Roos, in the county of Lincoln, certain commonage of pasture and turbary, and with lying in wait for him, with five hundred men. To which charges, Mr. Justice Tirwhit pleading guilty in the presence of the king, and craving pardon, the case was referred to the Chief Justice, Sir William Gascoine, who determined that Tirwhit, attended by all his party, should meet Lord Ros, at the common in dispute, and bring with him two tons of Gascony wine, with two fat oxen, and twelve fat sheep, as provision for a dinner, to be then eaten by the assembled friends and adherents of the disputants, and that Tirwhit, in the presence of all, should make Lord Ros, a most submissive apology, tendering him, at the same time, five hundred marks, as a compensation. To which, it was also settled by the arbitrator, that the baron should reply: "At reverence of the king, who hath shewed himself to be a good and righteous lord: I will take nothing, but the oxen and sheep, for the dinner of those here collected." A free and open act of forgiveness was to follow this speech to Tirwhit and his partizans, and thus the matter terminated. His lordship m. Margaret, daughter of Sir John Arundel, and had issue, five sons, and three daughters. He d. at Belvoir, 1st September, 1414, and was s. by his eldest son,

JOHN DE ROS, eighth baron, but never summoned to parliament. His lordship was retained in the 4th Henry V., to serve the king in France, being then scarcely eighteen years of age. In two years afterwards he was with the Dukes of Exeter and Clarence at the siege of Roan, where he so gallantly distinguished himself, that he had a grant of the castle of Basqueville, in Normandy, to himself and his heirs male for ever. Continuing in those wars he fell within two years, anno 1421, at the fatal battle of BAUGIE, with his brother, William, the Duke of Clarence, and a great many of the flower of the English nobility. His lordship was s. by his next brother,

SIR THOMAS DE ROS, ninth baron, summoned to parliament 12th July, and 3rd August, 1429. This nobleman m. Alianor, daughter of Richard Beauchamp, Earl of Warwick, and was s. at his decease, in 1431, by his son,

THOMAS DE ROS, tenth baron, b. 9th September, 1427. During the minority of this nobleman, his great uncle, Sir Robert Ros, Knt., was deputed by the king to perform the office of Chamberlain to the Archbishop of Canterbury upon the day of his installation, which office belonged to the Lord Ros, in right of the tenure of a certain manor. His lordship, who was in ward to the crown, had, by especial favour, the livery of his lands in the 24th Henry VI. In the memorable contests commenced in that unhappy monarch's reign between the Houses of Lancaster and York, Lord Ros entered zealously into the cause of the former, and participated in its disasters, particularly at the battle of Towton-field: being with the king at York, when tidings of the defeat reached the unfortunate monarch, he fled with his royal master to Berwic, and was attainted in the 1st Edward IV., when his lands were confiscated, and BELVOIR CASTLE granted to the Lord Hastings, who eventually dismantled the splendid structure, which remained from that period little better than a heap of ruins until the reigns of Henry VIII. and Elizabeth, when its renovation was commenced, and completed by Thomas and Henry Manners, first and second Earls of Rutland. His lordship m. Philippa, daughter of John, Lord Tiptoft, and sister and co-heir of John, Earl of Worcester, and had issue,

> EDMUND.
>
> John, died s. p.
>
> Eleanor, m. to Sir Robert Manners, ancestor of the Earls and Dukes of Rutland.
>
> Isabel, m. to Thomas Grey, youngest son of Sir Ralph Grey, of Werke, but died s. p.
>
> Margaret, d. unmarried.

Lord Ros was summoned to parliament from the 2nd January, 1449, to 30th July, 1460. He was attainted 4th November, 1461, and d. in the same year. The BARONY OF ROS lay under the attainder until the complete triumph of the Lancastrians, by the accession of King Henry VII., when the elder son of the late lord,

EDMUND DE ROS, obtained (1st Henry VII.) an act of parliament, annulling and making entirely void, the act by which his father was attainted, and restoring to him all the estates and honours of the family. He was never, however, summoned to parliament. His lordship d. in 1508 unmarried, when the BARONY OF ROS fell into ABEYANCE between his sisters, and was, eventually, inherited by George Manners, the son and heir of Eleanor, Lady Manners, after her ladyship's decease.

Thus terminated the family of DE ROS, BARONS Ros, of Hamlake, but the barony has long survived its original possessors, and is now enjoyed by Lady Charlotte Fitz-Gerald, in whose favour it was called out of ABEYANCE in 1806, after being so situated for nearly a century and a quarter. Lady Charlotte assumed the additional surname of DE ROS.

ARMS.—Gu. three water budgets, ar.

ROS—BARON ROS, OF WERKE.

By Writ of Summons, dated 24th June, 1295,
23 Edward I.

Lineage.

ROBERT DE ROS, feudal Lord of Hamlake, who d. in 1227, conferred the castle and Barony of WERKE, in the county of Northumberland, which he held of the crown by the service of two knights' fees, upon his younger son, (see Ros, of Hamlake,)

ROBERT DE ROS, who, in the 21st Henry III., was constituted chief justice of the forest in the counties of Nottingham, Derby, York, Lancaster, Northumberland, and Cumberland, which office he held for several years afterwards. In the 39th of the same reign he made a temporary surrender of his CASTLE OF WERKE to the king, who was then advancing with an army upon Scotland, and deemed it impolitic to permit so strong a fort to remain in private hands. About this time charges were preferred against Robert de Ros, to whose care and guidance, with John de Baliol, the kingdom of Scotland, as well as its King, Alexander III., and the Queen Margaret, (daughter of the English monarch,) were committed, for arbitrary conduct in the discharge of his duty; for which he was, eventually, fined no less than one hundred thousand marks, but his innocence appearing afterwards manifest, the penalty was entirely remitted. In the 22nd Edward I. he had summons with other of the barons to repair to the king, to advise upon the affairs of the realm; and the next year he was summoned to parliament, on the 24th June, 1st October, and 2nd November, as " Roberto de Roos de Werke," but never afterwards. In a short time, subsequently, however, falling in love with a Scottish lady, he deserted to the Scots, having previously endeavoured to seduce from his allegiance, his kinsman, Lord Ros, of Hamlake. But that nobleman repairing to King Edward divulged the treason, and was forthwith despatched at the head of a thousand men to take possession of Werke, whither he was proceeding, when Robert de Ros, with a great body of Scots, surprised him at the village of Prestfen, and cut the whole English force to pieces. King Edward very shortly, however, most amply avenged himself at the battle of Dunbar, where no less than ten thousand and fifty-three Scotsmen fell; and WERKE coming into the possession of the crown, was conferred upon Lord Ros, of Hamlake.

Robert, Lord Ros, of Werke, m. Margaret, one of the four sisters and co-heirs of Petar de Brus, of Skelton, but regarding his heirs, the records differ. One inquisition says, that he had a son, WILLIAM, to whom his mother gave the castle of Kendal; while another asserts, that he had two daughters, heirs to their mother, viz.

Margaret, wife of John Salvain.

Isabel, m. to John de Knockther.

The BARONY expired under the treason of the baron.

ARMS.—Gu. three water budgets, sa.

ROS, OR ROOS—BARON ROS.

By Writ of Summons, dated 27th January, 1332,
6 Edward III.

Lineage.

See
ROS, LORD ROS, OF HAMLAKE.

John de Ros, second son of William de Ros, second Baron Ros, of Hamlake.

RUPERT — DUKE OF CUMBERLAND.

By Letters Patent, dated 24th June, 1644.

Lineage.

The Princess ELIZABETH, of England, daughter of King JAMES I., espoused Frederick V., Duke of Bavaria, elector palatine of the Rhine, and had, with other issue,

CHARLES LEWIS, successor to the dukedom of Bavaria.

RUPERT, count palatine of the Rhine, of whom presently.

Maurice, the companion in arms during the civil wars of his gallant brother, Rupert, known in English history as " Prince Maurice," d. unmarried in 1654.

Sophia, m. to Ernest-Augustus, Duke of Brunswick-Lunenburgh, elector of Hanover, and was mother of GEORGE-LEWIS, who ascended the British throne under the act of settlement, as GEORGE I.

The second son,

Prince RUPERT, coming into England in 1642, was elected a KNIGHT OF THE GARTER, and created by his uncle, King CHARLES I., 24th June, 1644, Baron of Kendal, in the county of Westmorland, Earl of Holderness, and DUKE OF CUMBERLAND. His highness, with his gallant brother, Prince MAURICE, was ever found amongst the most intrepid, enterprising, and indefatigable of the cavalier commanders; RUPERT, as general of the royal horse, and MAURICE, in command of some forces in the west. Indeed Rupert's fiery disposition appears frequently to have outrun his better judgment, and he has acquired the reputation of a bold and high-spirited officer, rather than of a cool and able commander. To his unbridled zeal the loss of MARSTON MOOR is to be attributed, and upon that the fate of the unhappy CHARLES mainly depended. In glancing at this sad page of English history, we find much to console us, and much to retrieve the character of the country, in the gallant bearing assumed by the gentlemen of England, and the thorough devotedness of her high-minded nobility. The foes of royalty may decry, with as much malignity as they please, the cause in which the cavaliers so nobly fought and bled; but they must concede to those chivalrous men, the meed at least of loyalty, the most enthusiastic fidelity, the most disinterested; and valour, the most heroic. Prince RUPERT retired into France when the royal cause became hopeless, but returned at the restoration, and subsequently filled some high official situations. In the different naval engagements with the Dutch, his highness was particularly signalized by his able conduct and his characteristic bravery. He d. unmarried in 1682, when the DUKEDOM OF CUMBERLAND, and minor honours, became EXTINCT.

ARMS.—Quarterly one and four sa. a lion rampant or. second and third paly bendy, ar. and as.

NOTE.—*Prince* RUPERT had by FRANCES, daughter and co-heir of Henry Bard, Viscount Bellamont, in Ireland, an illegitimate son, DUDLEY RUPERT, who was slain at the siege of Buda, a volunteer in the imperial army. His highness had likewise, by Mrs. Margaret Hughes, a daughter, RUPERTA, m. to Emanuel Scroope Howe, brother of Scroope, Viscount Howe, of Ireland.

RUSSELL—EARL OF ORFORD.

By Letters Patent, dated 7th May, 1697.

Lineage.

EDWARD RUSSELL, second son of the Hon. Edward Russell, fourth son of Francis, fourth Earl Bedford, being bred a naval officer, attained, after the revolution, the rank of admiral ; and in 1692, as commander of the fleet, achieved a splendid victory of the French under Monsieur de Tourville, off LA HOGUE, for which, and his other gallant services, he was created, on 7th May, 1697, BARON OF SHINGAY, *in the county of* Cambridge, (with remainder to the issue male of LETITIA, his eldest sister,) *Viscount Barfleur, in the Duchy of Normandy,* and EARL OF ORFORD, in the county of Suffolk. His lordship m. his cousin, Lady Margaret Russell, daughter of William, first Duke of Bedford, but d. issueless in 1727, when (his sister LETITIA having deceased previously without male issue) all HIS HONOURS became EXTINCT.

ARMS.—Ar. a lion rampant, gu. on a chief sa. three escallops of the field. A crescent for difference.

RUTHYN, OR RUTHVEN—EARL OF BRENTFORD.

By Letters Patent, dated 27th May, 1644.

Lineage.

PATRICK RUTHYN or RUTHVEN, Earl of Forth, in the peerage of Scotland, an eminent soldier in the wars of Sweden, Denmark, Russia, Poland, Prussia, and Germany, having drawn his sword in the cause of *King* CHARLES I., and distinguishing himself at *Edghill*, BRENTFORD, and *Newbury*, was made general of the king's army, and created a peer of England, by letters patent, dated 27th May, 1644, in the dignity of EARL OF BRENTFORD. His lordship d. at Dundee in 1651, leaving an only daughter, Lady Jane Ruthyn, (who m. James, Lord Forrester, of Scotland,) when the EARLDOM OF BRENTFORD became EXTINCT.

ARMS.—Paly of six ar. and gu. a crescent for difference.

456

RYTHRE—BARON RYTHRE.

By Writ of Summons, dated 29th December, 1299, 28 Edward I.

Lineage.

In the 25th Edward I.,
WILLIAM DE RYTHRE, having taken a part in the Scottish and French wars, was summoned to parliament, as a baron, by King Edward I., on 29th December, 1299, and he had writs from that period to 26th August, 1307. His lordship was s. by his son,

JOHN DE RYTHRE, second baron, but never summoned to parliament. In the 11th Edward II. he was governor of Skypton Castle, and in the 17th of the same reign, had a charter for free warren in all his demesne lands at Hazelwode, &c., and Adington, in Yorkshire. Neither himself nor any of his descendants having had summons to parliament, Dugdale gives no further account of the family. Modern genealogists try, however, to connect this old baronial house with the modern one of RYDER, but without a shadow of proof.

ARMS.—Az. three crescents or.

ST. AMAND—BARONS ST. AMAND.

By Writ of Summons, dated 29th December, 1299, (26 Ed. I.,) and 22nd March, 1313 (6 Ed. II.).

Lineage.

In the 6th year of HENRY III.,
ALMARIC DE ST. AMAND obtained a grant of two parts of the manor of Liskaret, in Cornwall, for his support in the king's service, and in nine years afterwards, being in the expedition then made into Wales, deported himself so gallantly, that the king remitted to him a debt, due by Walter de Verdon, his uncle, (whose heir he was,) which otherwise he should have paid to the exchequer by ten marks annually. The next year he had a grant of the manor of Bloxham, in Oxfordshire, and soon afterwards we find him governor of St. Briavil's Castle, in Gloucestershire, and warden of the forest of Dene, as also sheriff of Herefordshire, and governor of Hereford Castle. In the 21st of the same reign, he was again entrusted with the same important fortresses; and standing high in favour at court, he was one of the sponsors at the font when *Prince* EDWARD (son of Henry III.) was baptised, by *Otto,* the pope's legate. He was s. by his son,

RALPH DE ST. AMAND, who m. Asceline, daughter and co-heir of Robert de Albini, son of Robert de Albini, Baron of Caynho, in the county of Bedford, and paid in the 25th of Henry III., twenty-five pounds for his relief of one moiety of the lands of Joane de Beauchamp, another of the daughters and co-heirs of the said Robert Albini. This Ralph d. in five years afterwards, and was s. by his son,

ALMARIC DE ST. AMAND, for whose wardship, and the benefit of his marriage, Paulyne Peyvre, a great personage at that period, gave one thousand marks. In the 40th of Henry III., Almaric, however, made proof of his age, and had then livery of his lands: and the next year had a military summons to march against the Welsh. He d. in the 14th Edward I., and was s. by his eldest son,

GUY DE ST. AMAND, who d. issueless soon after, and was s. by his brother,

ALMARIC DE ST. AMAND. This feudal lord distinguished himself in the wars of France and Scotland, was summoned to parliament by King Edward I., as a baron, on the 29th December, 1299, and he had regular writs from that period to the 16th June, 1311. His lordship was at one time governor of Bordeaux. He d. without issue, in 1312, when the Barony of St. Amand became extinct, but his lands devolved upon his brother,

JOHN DE ST. AMAND, a professor of the canon law, and at that time called "*Magister Johannes de Sancto Amand*," who, doing his fealty, had livery of the deceased lord's lands, and was summoned to parliament as a baron, from 22d March, 1313, to 10th October, 1395. His lordship d. in 1326, and was s. by his son,

ALMARIC DE ST. AMAND, second baron, summoned to parliament from 8th January, 1371, to 22d August, 1381. This nobleman was in the Scottish and French wars, temp. Edward II. and Edward III. In the 31st of the latter king he was made Justice of Ireland, and had forty men at arms, with one hundred archers on horseback, assigned to attend him there, over and above the usual number of men at arms, which appertained to that high office. In the 47th Edward III., he was made steward of the forest of Rockingham, and governor of the castle. He d. in 1381, and was s. by his son,

ALMARIC DE ST. AMAND, third baron, summoned to parliament from 9th August, 1382, to 2d December, 1401. This nobleman, by indenture in the 8th of Richard II., was retained to serve the king in his wars of Scotland, and in the 1st of Henry IV., was made a Knight of the Bath, at the coronation of that monarch. He m. first, Ida ——, and had issue,

  Alianore, who m. Sir Gerard de Braybroke, Knt., and was mother of

    Gerard de Braybroke, who left issue,

      Elizabeth, who m. William de Beauchamp, afterwards summoned to parliament as Lord St. Amand.

    Maud, m. to John Babington.

    Alianore.

His lordship espoused, secondly, Alianore, heiress of the St. Elen family, and left a daughter,

  Ida, m. to Sir Thomas West, Knt., and died s. p. before the year 1426.

Lord St. Amand d. in 1403, leaving his younger daughter, Ida, and his grandson, Gerard de Braybroke, (son of his deceased elder daughter, Alianore,) his heirs; between whom the Barony of St. Amand fell into abeyance, and so continued until the year 1449, when it was called out in favour of Sir William de Beauchamp, husband of the deceased lord's great-granddaughter, Eliza-beth de Braybroke (refer to *Beauchamp*, Barons St. Amand).

Arms.—Or. frettée, sa. on a chief of the second, three besants.

ST. JOHN—BARONS ST. JOHN, OF STANTON ST. JOHN, IN THE COUNTY OF OXFORD.

By Writ of Summons, dated 24th December, 1264, 49 Henry III.

Lineage.

THOMAS DE ST. JOHN, of Stanton St. John, in the county of Oxford, was father of

ROGER DE ST. JOHN, who, in the 22d Henry II., was amerced one hundred and thirty-three pounds, six shillings and eightpence, for trespassing in the king's forests, in the county of Oxford. This Roger was s. by his son,

JOHN DE ST. JOHN, who was s. by his son,

ROGER DE ST. JOHN. This feudal lord having taken up arms with the barons against King Henry III., was summoned to parliament after the victory of those lords at Lewes, on the 24th December, 1264, and appointed governor of the castle of Oxford. He was slain, however, the following year, at Evesham, where his party sustained so signal a defeat. His lordship m. ——, sister of Richard de Luci, by whom he acquired a moiety of the lordship of Wolnestede, in the county of Surrey, and had an only son,

  John, who was never summoned to parliament, nor were his descendants.

The Barony of St. John, of Stanton, expired therefore with the first lord.

Arms.—Ar. on a chief gules, two mullets or, and a file of three points of the field.

ST. JOHN—BARONS ST. JOHN, OF BASING.

By Writ of Summons, dated 29th December, 1299, 28 Edward I.

Lineage.

At the time of the General Survey,

HUGH DE PORT held five lordships of the crown, in Hampshire, whereof Basing was one, and the head of the barony. He had also lands in the counties of Dorset and Cambridge. In the reign of Rufus, he took the cowl at Winchester, and was succeeded in his worldly affairs by his son,

HENRY DE PORT, Lord of Basing, who was s. by his son,

JOHN DE PORT, who, in the 12th of Henry II., contributed for his knights' fees (seven in number) to the assessment for marrying the king's daughter, fifty-seven marks. He was s. by his son,

ADAM DE PORT, Lord of Basing. This feudal baron was governor of the castle of Southampton, in the 15th of King John; and in the 22d Henry II., he was fined three hundred marks, for trespassing in the king's forests. In the 26th of the same reign, he gave a thousand marks to the king for livery of his wife's inheritance in Normandy; and that he might be restored to the king's favour, and do his homage. He *m.* Mabel, daughter of Reginald de Aurevalle, and grandchild and heir of Roger de St. John; and his posterity ever afterwards bore the surname of ST. JOHN. By this lady he had two sons, William and Robert. The elder,

WILLIAM DE ST. JOHN, assuming that surname, wrote himself *Willielmus de Sancto Johanne filius et hæres Adæ de Port*, and in the 15th John, gave five hundred marks to the king for livery of all the lands of *Adam de Port*, his father. The two following years he executed the sheriff's office for the county of Southampton: but was subsequently in arms with the other barons against the crown, and did not return to his allegiance until some time after the accession of HENRY III. He made his peace, however, effectually, for we find him in the 11th of that king, appointed governor of the islands of Guernsey and Jersey. He *m.* Godchild, daughter of N. Paganell, and was *s.* by his son,

RORERT DE ST. JOHN, who had a military summons, in the 42d Henry III., to oppose the incursions of the Welsh, and in three years afterwards, obtained a licence to fix a pale upon the bank of his moat, at BASING; as also to continue it so fortified, during the king's pleasure. In the 50th of the same reign, he was constituted governor of PORCHESTER CASTLE, and dying soon after, was *s.* by his son, (by his wife Agnes, daughter of William de Cantilupe,)

JOHN DE ST. JOHN, Lord of Basing, who succeeded likewise to the governorship of Porchester Castle. This baron acquired high military reputation in the wars of EDWARD I.; and in his capacity of lieutenant of Acquitaine, achieved some important conquests. In 1296, he took the city of Bayonne by assault, and its castle surrendered after a siege of eight days. Thence marching to BELLEGARD, at the time invested by the Earl of Arras, he was made prisoner, and conveyed to Paris; being, however, redeemed, (it was said, by *Alfonsus*, King of Gascony,) he was again in the wars of Gascony, as well as in those of Scotland: and was afterwards deputed ambassador to France, with John, Earl of Warren, and other persons of rank. He *m.* Alice, daughter of Reginald Fitz-Piers, and had issue,

    JOHN, his successor.

    William, who obtained from his father the castle of Beaumont, in Glamorganshire, and is considered the ancestor of the St. Johns of Bletshoe.

The elder son,

JOHN DE ST. JOHN, had been summoned to parliament as a BARON, in the life-time of his father, from 29th December, 1299, to 12th November, 1303, under the designation of "John de St. John, Junior," but afterwards as "St. John of Basing." This nobleman was eminent in the wars of Scotland, temp. Edward I. and Edward II. His lordship espoused Isabel, daughter of Hugh de Courtenay, and *d.* in 1329, was *s.* by his son,

458

HUGH DE ST. JOHN, second Baron St. John, of Basing, who *d.* in 1337, leaving,

    EDMUND, his successor.

    Margaret, *m.* to John de St. Philibert, and had a son, John, who *d.* in infancy.

    ISABEL, *m.* first, to Henry de Burgharsh, who died *s. p.*, and secondly, to Lucas de Poynings, who was summoned to parliament, it is presumed, "*jure uxoris*," 24th February, 1368.

His lordship was *s.* by his elder son,

EDMUND ST. JOHN, third Baron St. John, of Basing, who dying in minority, 21st Edward III., then a ward of the king, his sisters, MARGARET and ISABEL, became his heirs. The elder sister, Margaret, did not long survive, and her only issue, John de St. Philibert, dying an infant, the whole of the inheritance centered in the younger sister, Isabel, then married to her second husband, LUCAS DE POYNINGS, who in her right was summoned to parliament, and the BARONY OF ST JOHN, *of Basing*, was thus conveyed to the family of Poynings (see Poynings, Barons St. John).

ST. JOHN—BARONS ST. JOHN, OF LAGEHAM.

By Writ of Summons, dated 21st September, 1299, 27 Edward I.

Lineage.

In the 46th HENRY III.

ROGER DE ST. JOHN obtained licence to fortify his house at Lageham, in the county of Surrey, and so to hold the same, whilst himself and his heirs should continue loyal to the king; but within two years he joined the baronial standard, and, after the battle of Lewes, was one of the nine barons chosen to form the council of state. To this turbulent feudal lord succeeded,

JOHN DE ST. JOHN, who had summons to parliament as BARON ST. JOHN, *of Lageham*, from 21st September, 1299, to 6th October, 1315. This nobleman was actively engaged in the Scottish wars, temp., Edward I. and Edward II. His lordship *d.* in 1316, and was *s.* by his son,

JOHN DE ST. JOHN, second baron, summoned to parliament from 1st August, 1317, to 18th September, 1322. His lordship was in the expedition made into Scotland, 11th Edward II., and dying in 1322, was *s.* by his son,

JOHN DE ST. JOHN, third baron, summoned to parliament from 1st August, 1327, to 18th February, 1331. This nobleman *m.* Katherine, daughter of Geffrey de Say, and *d.* in 1349, was *s.* by his son,

ROGER DE ST. JOHN, fourth baron, who in the 25th Edward III., released to Sir Nicholas de Lovoyane, Knt., and Margaret, his wife, all his right in the manor of Lageham, and died shortly after, (in 1353,) issueless, leaving PETER DE ST. JOHN, *his kinsman*, his next heir: but none of the family were subsequently summoned to parliament.

ARMS.—Ermine, on a chief gules, two mullets or.

ST. JOHN — EARLS OF BOLING-BROKE.

By Letters Patent, dated 28th December, 1624.

Lineage.

SIR OLIVER ST. JOHN, of Penmark, in the county of Glamorgan, (of the family of St. John, of Stanton St. John,) *m.* Margaret,[*] daughter of Sir John de Beauchamp, and sister and heir of John, Lord Beauchamp, of Bletshoe, and was father of

SIR JOHN ST. JOHN, K.B., of Bletshoe, whose great grandson,

OLIVER ST. JOHN, was elevated to the peerage, in January, 1559, as BARON ST. JOHN, *of Bletshoe.* The grandson of this nobleman,

OLIVER ST. JOHN, fourth Lord St. John, of Bletshoe, was advanced, by letters patent, dated 28th December, 1624, to the dignity of EARL of BOLINGBROKE. His lordship *m.* Elisabeth, daughter and heir of William Paulet, grandson of St. George Paulet, a younger brother of William, first Marquess of Winchester, and had issue,

> OLIVER, *Lord St. John,* made Knight of the Bath, at the coronation of King Charles I. This nobleman fell, fighting under the royal banner, at Edgehill, 23rd October, 1624. He had *m.* Lady Arabella Egerton, daughter of John, first Earl of Bridgewater, and left four daughters, viz.
>
>> Frances, *m.* Sir William Beecher, Knt., of Howberry, in the county of Bedford.
>> Elisabeth, *m.* to George Bennett, Esq., of Cotsback, in Leicestershire.
>> Arabella, *m.* to Sir Edward Wyse, K.B., of Sydenham, Devon.
>> Dorothy, *m.* to Francis Carleton, Esq., of Apley Castle, Salop.
>
> PAULET (Sir), made Knight of the Bath, at the coronation of *King* CHARLES I.; *m.* Elisabeth, daughter and heir of Sir Rowland Vaughan, of the Spital, near Shoreditch, in the suburbs of London, and dying before his father, left,
>
>> OLIVER, } successively EARLS OF Bo-
>> PAULET, } LINGBROKE.
>
> Francis, *d.* unmarried.
> Anthony, *m.* ——, daughter of Kensham, Esq., of Tameford.
> Dorothy, *m.* to John Carey, Lord Rochford, eldest son of Henry, Earl of Dover.

His lordship *d.* in 1646, and was *s.* by his grandson,

OLIVER ST. JOHN, second Earl of Bolingbroke, and fifth Lord St. John, of Bletshoe. His lordship *m.* Lady Frances Cavendish, daughter of William, Duke of Newcastle, but dying *s. p.,* 18th March, 1687-8, was *s.* by his brother,

PAULET ST. JOHN, third Earl of Bolingbroke,

---

[*] This lady espoused, secondly, John Beaufort, Duke of Somerset, K.G., by whom she was mother of Lady MARGARET BEAUFORT, who *m.* Edward Tudor, Earl of Richmond, and had a son, *Henry,* EARL OF RICHMOND, who ascended the throne as HENRY VII. The Duchess of Somerset *m.* thirdly, *John,* VISCOUNT WELLES, K.G.

and sixth Lord St. John; of Bletshoe. This nobleman *d.* unmarried, 17th October, 1711, when the Barony of St. John, of Bletshoe, passed to the heir at law, Sir Andrew St. John, of Woodford, in the county of Northampton, and the EARLDOM OF BOLINGBROKE, became EXTINCT.

ARMS.—Ar. on a chief gules two mullets pierced or.

ST. JOHN — BARON TREGOZE, OF HIGHWORTH.

By Letters Patent, dated 21st May, 1626.

Lineage.

SIR OLIVER ST. JOHN, Baronet of Lydiard Tregose, was created Viscount Grandison, in the peerage of Ireland, temp. James I., first president of Munster, and afterwards constituted lord deputy of that kingdom. His lordship returned, in the 20th of the same monarch, and by his majesty's successor, was made a peer of England, 21st May, 1626, in the dignity of BARON TREGOZE, *of Highworth, in the county of Wilts.* His lordship *m.* Joan, daughter and heir of Henry Roydon, Esq., of Battersea, and widow of Sir William Holcroft, but had no issue. He *d.* in 1629, when the BARONY OF TREGOZE became EXTINCT.

ST. LIZ.—EARLS OF HUNTINGDON.

Creation of William the Conqueror.

Lineage.

The county which gave designation to this earldom was, according to Doctor Heylin, a thickly wooded forest, until the reign of the second Henry, when the timber was first cleared away; the chief town, from the celebrity of the forest as a chase, was called HUNTINGTOWN, which soon became abbreviated into Huntington, or Huntingdon. The Earldom of Huntingdon was conferred, by William the Conqueror, upon

WALTHEOF, (son of Syward, the Saxon Earl of Northumberland,) who had *m.* the daughter of that monarch's sister, by the mother's side, JUDITH. He was also Earl of Northampton, and of Northumberland: but conspiring against the Normans, he was beheaded, in 1075, at Winchester, leaving issue,

> Maud, *m.* first, to Simon de St. Liz, and secondly, to David, brother of Alexander, King of Scotland.
> Judith, *m.* first, to Ralph de Toney, and afterwards to Robert, fifth son of Richard de Tonbridge, ancestor of the Lords Fitz-Walter.

After the execution of Waltheof, King William offered Judith, his niece, the deceased earl's widow, in marriage to Simon St. Lis, a noble Norman, but the lady peremptorily rejected the alliance, owing, Dugdale says, to St. Lis's *halting in one leg:* which refusal so displeased the Conqueror, that he immediately seized upon the castle and honour of Huntingdon, which the countess held in dower, exposing herself and her daughters to a state of privation and obscurity in the Isle of Ely, and other places; while he bestowed upon the said Simon St. Liz the town of NORTHAMPTON, and the whole hundred of FALKSLEY, then valued at £40 per annum, to *provide shoes for his horses*. St. Liz thus disappointed in obtaining the hand of the Countess of Huntingdon, made his addresses, with greater success, to her elder daughter, the Lady Maud, who became his wife, when William conferred upon the said

SIMON DE ST. LIZ, the Earldoms of Huntingdon and Northampton. This nobleman built the castle of Northampton, as also the priory of St. Andrews there, about the 18th year of the Conqueror's reign, and was a liberal benefactor to the church. His lordship was a witness to King Henry I.'s laws in 1100, after which he made a voyage to the Holy Land, and *d.* in his return, at the Abbey of Charity, in France. He left issue,

> SIMON, who succeeded to the Earldom of Northampton, but was excluded from that of Huntingdon. He was, subsequently, however, restored.
>
> Waltheof, Abbot of Melrus, in Scotland.
>
> Maud, *m.* first, to Robert, son of Richard de Tonbridge, and secondly, to William de Albini, according to Dugdale; but Hornby, in his remarks upon Dugdale's errors, proves that such alliances, if not impossible, were very improbable.

Upon the death of Simon, Earl of Huntingdon and Northampton, his elder son, Simon, should have succeeded to both dignities, but it appears he only inherited the former. The Earldom of Huntingdon being assumed by

DAVID, son of Malcolm III., King of Scotland, who had married the deceased earl's widow, the Countess Maud, under the especial sanction of King Henry I. This nobleman succeeded to the Scottish throne, upon the decease of Alexander, his elder brother; and invading England, was met upon the border by King Stephen, when their differences were amicably adjusted; and

HENRY, son of the said David, King of Scotland, upon condition of swearing allegiance to Stephen, had the EARLDOM and HONOUR OF HUNTINGDON, with the borough of Doncaster and Carlisle as an augmentation thereto. Nay, he was in such high estimation with King Stephen, that upon that monarch's solemn celebration of the feast of Easter, he placed the Earl of Huntingdon on his right hand; which gave such displeasure to the nobility then present, that William Corbois, or Corbel, Archbishop of Canterbury, Ranulph, Earl of Chester, and several others, withdrew from court. He espoused Ada, sister of William, Earl of Warren and Surrey, and had issue,

> Malcolm, }
> William, } successively Kings of Scotland.
> David.
> Ada, *m.* to Floris, Earl of Holland.
> Margaret, *m.* to Conante Petit, Earl of Britanny. *aud wint B/ ~*

The earl *d.* in 1152, a little before his father, and upon his decease,

SIMON DE ST. LIZ, Earl of Northampton, was restored to the Earldom of Huntingdon. This
460

nobleman was a zealous supporter of King Stephen, against the Empress Maud, and continued ever opposed to any amicable adjustment of the contest. He *m.* Isabel, daughter of Robert, Earl of Leicester, and had issue,

> SIMON, who succeeded to the Earldom of Northampton, but not to *that* of Huntingdon. He was, however, restored, temp. Henry II.
>
> Amice.
>
> Hawyse.

His lordship[*] *d.* about the year 1154, and after his decease, King Henry II., in the first year of his reign, conferred in exchange for the counties of Northumberland, Cumberland, and Westmorland, (which the Scots had subjugated,) upon

MALCOLM, King of Scotland, son of Henry, Earl of Huntingdon, the Earldom of Huntingdon. This monarch died in 1165, *s. p.*, and was *s.* by his brother,

WILLIAM, King of Scotland, as Earl of Huntingdon. This monarch taking up arms in favour of Prince Henry, so exasperated King Henry II., that he immediately sent an army against him, and promised that the castle and earldom should be restored to the family of St. Lis, the rightful heirs; whereupon Simon St. Lis, Earl of Northampton, son and heir of Simon, last Earl of Huntingdon, of that family, levied troops, and appeared before the castle, when William, of Scotland, finding it untenable, made a surrender to St. Lis of that fortress, which the king of England ordered to be demolished, but, nevertheless,

SIMON DE ST. LIZ was restored to the EARLDOM OF HUNTINGDON, which he enjoyed for the remainder of his life. He *d.* in 1184, without issue, whereupon King Henry II. restored the earldom to King William, of Scotland, and that monarch transferred it to his younger brother, who thus became

DAVID, Earl of Huntingdon. This prince accompanied King Richard I. to the Holy Land, with five hundred men in his train; but upon his return, his fleet being scattered, his lordship was made prisoner by the Egyptians, and eventually redeemed by the Venetians. He espoused Maud, daughter of Hugh Kyvelioc, Earl of Chester, and had surviving issue,

> JOHN, surnamed Le Scot.
> Margaret, *m.* to Alan, of Galloway (see Baliol, feudal barons).
> Isabel, *m.* to Robert Bruce, of Annandale.
> Ada, *m.* to Henry de Hastings, Lord Hastings.
> Maud, *d.* unmarried.

His lordship *d.* in 1219, and was *s.* by his son,

JOHN LE SCOT, as Earl of Huntingdon, who, in right of his mother, became likewise Earl of Chester (see Scot, Earl of Chester). This

---

[*] This earl had a brother also called Simon de St. Liz, whose descendants settling at Seton, in the county of Rutland, assumed the surname of SETON. The heir female of this family *m.*, in the reign of Henry VI., Sir William Fielding, ancestor of the Fieldings, Earls of Denbigh.

nobleman d. in 1237, without issue, when the EARLDOM OF HUNTINGDON became EXTINCT, but his great possessions devolved upon his sisters as co-heirs.

ARMS.—Per pale, indented ar. and as.

ST. MAUR—BARONS ST. MAUR.

By Writ of Summons, dated 29th July, 1314, 8 Edward II.

Lineage.

The first of this family upon record,

MILO DE ST. MAUR, was involved in the baronial war against *King John*. The next is,

GEFFREY DE ST. MAUR, who m. the daughter and heir of William de Rughdou: and after him

LAURENCE DE ST. MAUR, who, in the 11th Edward I., obtained a grant for a weekly market at his manor of *Rode*, in the county of Somerset, and dying in the 24th of the same reign, was s. by his son,

NICHOLAS DE ST. MAUR. This feudal lord having been engaged in all the expeditions made into Scotland from the 27th to the 34th Edward I., was summoned to parliament as a BARON, in the 8th of the ensuing reign. His lordship espoused Elena, eldest daughter and co-heir of Alan le Zouche, Lord Zouche, of Ashby, in the county of Leicester, and dying in 1316, was s. by his elder son,

THOMAS DE ST. MAUR, second baron, but never summoned to parliament. This nobleman died s. p. and was s. by his brother,

SIR NICHOLAS DE ST. MAUR, third baron, summoned to parliament from 15th November, 1351, to 20th November, 1360. This nobleman was in the wars of France, temp. Edward III., first in the retinue of Maurice de Berkley, and afterwards in that of Thomas de Holand. His lordship m. Muriel, daughter and heir of James Lovel, only son of Sir Richard Lovel, Lord Lovel, of Kary, by whom he acquired the estates of Winfred-Eagle, in the county of Dorset, and of Castle Kary, in Somersetshire, with the BARONY OF LOVEL. He d. in 1361, and was s. by his elder son,

NICHOLAS DE ST. MAUR, fourth baron, who d. in the same year, under age, and was s. by his brother,

RICHARD DE ST. MAUR, fifth baron, summoned to parliament from 26th August, 1380, to 3d October, 1400. This nobleman was in the wars of France, in the 10th Richard II., in the retinue of Richard, Earl of Arundel, admiral of England. His lordship m. Ela, daughter and co-heir of Sir John St. Lo, Knt., and had issue,

RICHARD, his successor.

John (Sir), m. Margaret, daughter and heir of John Erleigh, and was s. by his son,

JOHN, who m. Elisabeth, daughter of Thomas, Lord Cobham, and left a son,

THOMAS, who d. in the beginning of Henry VII.'s reign. He m.

Philippa, daughter of Sir Edward Hungerford, and had a son,

JOHN, of Rode, in Somersetshire, who d. in his father's life-time, leaving

WILLIAM, whose only daughter and heiress,

JOANE, m. Sir Robert Drury, and died s. p.

Anne, m. to Robert Stawel, Esq., ancestor of the Lord Stawel.

Margaret, m. to William Bamfyld, and had a son,

SIR EDWARD BAMFYLD, who m. Elisabeth, daughter of Sir Michael Wadham, and had a daughter,

ELISABETH, who m. George Percival, Esq., ancestor of the Earls of Egremont.

Nicholas.

The baron d. in 1401, and was s. by his eldest son,

RICHARD DE ST. MAUR, sixth baron, summoned to parliament from 21st June, 1402, to 26th August, 1408. This nobleman went into Ireland with *Thomas*, DUKE OF SURREY, in the 22nd of Richard II., then lieutenant of that kingdom; and in the 4th of Henry III., he was in the wars of France. His lordship d. in 1409, leaving Mary, his wife, then *enciente*, who was afterwards delivered of a daughter,

ALICE ST. MAUR, born in the house of Thomas Creasy, citizen and mercer of London, in the parish of St. Lawrence, Cripplegate, in that city. This lady espoused

WILLIAM ZOUCHE, fifth BARON ZOUCHE, *of Haryngworth*, and the BARONY OF ST. MAUR continued vested in the Lords Zouche until the decease of

EDWARD, eleventh *Baron Zouche*, in 1625, when the Baronies of ZOUCHE *of Haryngworth*, of ST. MAUR, and of LOVEL OF KARY, fell into ABEYANCE between his lordship's two daughters and co-heirs, viz.

ELIZABETH, m. to Sir William Tate, of De la Pre, Northamptonshire, whose descendant in the fourth generation,

CATHERINE TATE, m. Charles Hedges, Esq., and was grandmother of SIR CECIL BISSHOPP, Bart.

Mary, m. to Thomas Leighton, Esq.

The BARONY OF ZOUCHE was,

however, called out in favour of SIR CECIL BISSHOPP, 27th August, 1815, and is now held by his daughter, HARRIET-ANNE, BARONESS ZOUCHE.

The BARONIES OF ST. MAUR, and OF LOVEL of Kary, fell into ABEYANCE, as stated above, upon the decease of Edward, eleventh BARON ZOUCHE, of Haryngworth, in 1625, between his daughters, ELIZABETH, wife of Sir William Tate, of De la Pre, in the county of Northampton, and MARY, wife of Thomas Leighton, Esq., as they still continue amongst the descendants of those ladies.

ARMS.—Az. two chevrons gu. in chief a file of three points az.*

ST. MAUR—BARON ST. MAUR.

By Writ of Summons, dated 20th November, 1317, 11 Edward II.

Lineage.

WILLIAM ST. MAUR, supposed to have been of the old baronial family of St. Maur, was summoned to parliament as a BARON from 20th November, 1317, to 14th March, 1322, but there is nothing further known of his lordship or his descendants.

ST. PHILIBERT—BARONS ST. PHILIBERT.

By Writ of Summons, dated 6th February, 1299, 27 Edward I.

Lineage.

NICHOLAS DE ST. PHILIBERT, in the 15th of John, was in the expedition then made in Poictou; and in the same reign

HUGH DE ST. PHILIBERT was in arms with the other barons against the crown, and did not return to his allegiance before the 1st of Henry III., when he had restitution of his lands. In the 10th of the latter king he was made governor of the island of Jersey. After this Hugh, came

ROGER DE ST. PHILIBERT, one of the rebellious barons made prisoner in 47th Henry III., at the battle of Northampton. And about the same time,

WILLIAM DE ST. PHILIBERT was also in the baronial ranks, and assisted in the defence of Dover Castle. But after the battle of Evesham, making his peace, and returning to his allegiance, he had restitution of his lands which had been seised, in the county of Northampton. The next of the family we find, is

HUGH DE ST. PHILIBERT, who, having been engaged in the French and Scottish wars, was summoned to parliament by King EDWARD I., as a

BARON, on the 6th February, 1299, but never afterwards. His lordship was s. by his son,

JOHN DE ST. PHILIBERT, who, like his predecessor, was in the French and Scottish wars: and in the 5th Edward III., was constituted Major of Bordeaux. He d. in two years afterwards, and was s. by his son,

JOHN DE ST. PHILIBERT, who, in the 21st Edward III., making proof of his age, and doing his homage, had livery of his lands, and was summoned to parliament 20th November, 1348, and 1st January, and 10th March, 1349. His lordship was in the wars of France, temp. Edward III., and d. in 1359. He m. Margaret, daughter of Hugh de St. John, and one of the co-heirs of her brother, Edmund de St. John, by whom he left a son,

JOHN DE ST. PHILIBERT, who d. in infancy, when the BARONY OF PHILIBERT, became EXTINCT.

ARMS.—Bendy of six, ar. and az.

ST. QUINTIN — BARON ST. QUINTIN.

By Writ of Summons, dated 8th June, 1294, 22 Edward I.

Lineage.

This family is said to have adopted its surname from the town of ST. QUINTIN, the capital of Lower Picardy.

SIR HERBERT DE ST. QUINTIN came into England with the Conqueror, and was grandfather of

SIR ROBERT DE ST. QUINTIN, who, in the time of Rufus, was one of the twelve knights, who divided, with Robert Fitz-Hamon, certain lands in Wales, which they had won by conquest, and there he erected the CASTLE OF ST. QUINTIN. The brother of this Sir Robert,

SIR HERBERT ST. QUINTIN, was father of

AMATELLUS ST. QUINTIN, who, in the reign of Richard I., was entitled BARON ST. QUINTIN, and was s. by his son,

HERBERT ST. QUINTIN, also styled Baron St. Quintin, who espoused Agnes, sister and co-heir of Anselm de Stutevill, and had five sons, of whom the three elder died s. p. WILLIAM, the fourth, carried on the line of the family, and Alexander is said to be ancestor of the baronets of the name. He had also two daughters, viz. Margery, m. to Sir William Rochfort, Knt., and Agnes, m. to Sir Fulke Constable, Knt., of Holmton. The fourth son,

WILLIAM ST. QUINTIN was ancestor of

HERBERT ST. QUINTIN, who was summoned to parliament, as BARON ST. QUINTIN, by King Edward I., on the 8th June, 1294.* This

---

* The modern family of SEYMOUR does not appear to have any connection whatever with the old BARONS ST. MAUR. They even bear totally different arms.

St. Maur.—"Ar. two chevrons gu. in chief of three points az."

Seymour.—"Gu. two wings conjoined in lure, or."

478

---

* Nicolas does not consider this writ a regular summons to parliament, nor the person summoned under it a BARON of the realm. Because "none of the higher temporal nobility, nor any of the spiritual peers, were included in it; nor was there any day fixed for the meeting." "It is also to be observed," continues the same authority, "that the

nobleman m. Margery, daughter and co-heir of Warine de Lisle, and left two daughters, viz.

 ELIZABETH, wife of John, Lord Grey, of Rotherfield, and died s. p.

 LORA, m. first, to Thomas, son of William de Poole, secondly, to John Clinton, and thirdly, to Sir Robert Grey, of Rotherfield, third brother of Lord Marmion—by the latter she had an only daughter and heir,

  ELIZABETH GREY, who m. Henry, Lord Fitz-Hugh, and her grandson,

   HENRY, Lord Fitz-Hugh, (see Fitz-Hugh,) left, with other issue,

    ELIZABETH FITZ-HUGH, who m. Sir William Parr, Knt., and had (with an elder son, William, created Lord Parr,) SIR THOMAS PARR, who left,

     WILLIAM PARR, Marquess of Northampton.

     ANNE PARR, m. to William Herbert, EARL OF PEMBROKE, from which period the titles of St. QUINTIN and MARMION have been numbered amongst the honours of the house of Pembroke.

     CATHERINE PARR, wife of Henry VIII.

ARMS.—Or. three chevrons gu. a chief barry of two, verry.

SANDYS — BARONS SANDYS, OF THE VINE.

By Writ of Summons, dated 3rd November, 1529, 21 Henry VIII.

Lineage.

Although this family did not attain the rank of

writ in question is the earliest on record, excepting that of 49th Henry III.; that the majority of the persons summoned in the 22nd Edward I. were never again summoned, excepting in the 25th of the same king; that several of the persons were not considered barons by tenure; and that of those who were barons by tenure, and summoned on those occasions, many were never included in any subsequent summons to parliament. The writ of the 22nd Edward I. has, however, on one occasion, (in the case of the barony of Ros,) been admitted as a writ of summons to parliament at the bar of the House of Lords; but the last 'General Report of the Lord's Committee, appointed to search for Matters touching the Dignity of a Peer of the Realm,' appears to confirm the objections here expressed." Yet under this, at least, doubtful writ, the extant EARLS OF PEMBROKE assume the dignity of BARONS OF ST. QUINTIN!

nobility until the time of HENRY VIII., yet we find it amongst the leading gentry of Hampshire at a much earlier period. In the 6th year of RICHARD II.,

SIR JOHN DE SANDYS, Knt., was sheriff of that county, and governor of Winchester Castle. And in the 12th HENRY IV. and 1st Henry VI.,

SIR WALTER SANDYS filled the same important offices. But the person who raised the family to the first grade in society, was

SIR WILLIAM SANDYS, an eminent soldier in the reigns of HENRY VII. and HENRY VIII. In the 7th of the former king he was in the expedition sent into Flanders, under the Earls of Derby, Shrewsbury, and other English noblemen, to aid the Emperor MAXIMILIAN against the French; and in five years afterwards he shared in the victory over the Cornishmen at Blackheath. In the 4th Henry VIII. he was sent, with other gallant persons from England, to assist FERDINAND, of Arragon, against the French; and he was subsequently, being at the time a KNIGHT OF THE GARTER, one of the commissioners deputed to make a palace before the castle gate at Guiennes, preparatory to the celebrated interview between HENRY VIII. and FRANCIS I. Upon the attainder of the Duke of Buckingham Sir William Sandys obtained a grant of the manors of Willesford and Stratton, in the county of Wilts, and in the 14th Henry VIII. he was treasurer of Calais: in which latter he led, in conjunction with Sir Richard Wingfield, the rear of the army sent under the command of the Earl of Surrey into France; and for his good services was summoned to parliament, as BARON SANDYS, from 3rd November, 1529, to 16th January, 1542. (Dugdale states from Stow, that six years previously he had been advanced to the degree of a baron of the realm at the king's royal palace of Bridewell, but that no patent of the creation is upon record.) He certainly bore the title of Lord Sandys long before the first of these summonses, and so designated, led the van of the army sent, under the Duke of Suffolk, into France, in the 15th Henry VIII., and in two years afterwards, as Lord Sandys, had a reversionary grant of the office of LORD CHAMBERLAIN, after the death of Charles, EARL OF WORCESTER. His lordship was in the train of WOLSEY, when the cardinal was deputed to complain to the king of France, of the sacking of Rome by the Duke of Bourbon. He subsequently subscribed the articles of impeachment against that celebrated prelate, and he signed the letter to Pope CLEMENT regarding Henry's divorce from Queen KATHERINE.

The principal seat of the Sandys family, anciently at the VINE, near Basingstoke, in Hampshire, had been alienated by an heiress to the family of BROCAS, but was recovered by this Lord Sandys, who rebuilt the manor-house there. His lordship m. Margery, only daughter and heir of John Bray, Esq., by whom he eventually acquired a considerable property, and dying in 1542, was s. by his only son,

THOMAS SANDYS, second baron, summoned to parliament from 14th June, 1543, to 5th November, 1556. This nobleman m. Elizabeth, daughter of George Manners, Lord Ros, and had issue,

HENRY, who m. Elizabeth, daughter of William Windsor, second Baron Windsor, and dying in the life-time of his father, left issue,

WILLIAM, successor to the title.

Thomas.

Margery, m. to Henry Carey, Esq., of Hamworthy, in the county of Dorset.

Walter (Sir).

His lordship was s. at his decease by his grandson,

WILLIAM SANDYS, third baron, summoned to parliament from 8th May, 1572, to 14th November, 1621. This nobleman was one of the peers who sate upon the trial of the Duke of Norfolk, and upon that of the unhappy Mary of Scotland, both in the reign of Elizabeth. Afterwards taking part, 43rd Elizabeth, with the Earl of Essex, in that nobleman's insurrection, he suffered imprisonment. His lordship m. first, Christian, daughter of ———— Anslow, Esq., and had a son, WILLIAM, his successor. He espoused, secondly, Catherine, called "the Fair Bridges," daughter of Edmund, Lord Chandos, by whom he had an only daughter,

ELIZABETH, who m. Sir Edwin Sandys, Knt., and had issue,

HENRY SANDYS, a colonel in the royal army during the civil wars—of whom hereafter, as successor to the fourth baron.

His lordship d. in 1623, and was s. by his son,

WILLIAM SANDYS, fourth baron, but never summoned to parliament. His lordship m. Alathea, eldest daughter and co-heir of John Panton, Esq., of Brinneskid, in the county of Denbigh, but d. without issue in 1629, when the barony devolved upon his nephew of the half blood,

COLONEL HENRY SANDYS, fifth baron, but owing to the civil wars never summoned to parliament. This nobleman, who was a brave and active cavalier officer, received a mortal wound in the fight at Bramdene, near Alresford, in Hants, 29th March, 1644, and d. the 6th April ensuing. His lordship m. Jane, daughter of Sir William Sandys, Knt., of Muserden, in the county of Gloucester, and had issue,

WILLIAM, } sixth and seventh barons.
HENRY, }

Miles, died s. p.

EDWIN, eighth baron.

Hester, m. to Humphrey Noy, Esq., son of William, Noy, Esq., attorney-general to King CHARLES I.

Alathea, m. to Francis Goston, Esq., of Alderidge, in the county of Southampton.

Mary, m. to Dr. Henry Savage, principal of Balliol College, Oxford.

Jane, m. to John Harris, Esq., of Old Woodstock, in the county of Oxford.

Margaret, m. to Sir John Mill, Bart., ancestor of the present Sir Charles Mill, Bart.

Margery, m. to Sir Edmund Fortescue, Bart., of Fallowfield, in the county of Devon.

Lord Sandys was s. by his eldest son,

WILLIAM SANDYS, sixth baron, summoned to parliament on 8th May, 1661. This nobleman m. Lady Mary Cecil, daughter of William, 2nd Earl of

Salisbury, but died s. p. in 1668. During the time of this lord, about the year 1654, the ancient family mansion of the VINE, erected by the first baron, in the reign of HENRY VIII., was either sold, or it passed by forfeiture or composition, to Choloner Chute, Esq., M. P. for Middlesex, in 1656. Lord Sandys was s. by his brother,

HENRY SANDYS, seventh baron, summoned to parliament from 6th March, 1678, to 21st March, 1680; at whose decease s. p. the title devolved upon his brother,

EDWYN SANDYS, eighth baron, but never summoned to parliament. This nobleman d. without issue about the year 1700, when his estates devolved upon his sisters, as co-heirs, (refer to issue of the fifth lord,) and the BARONY OF SANDYS, of the Vine, fell into ABEYANCE amongst those ladies, as it still continues with their representatives.

ARMS.—Ar. a cross raguly, sa.

SANDYS — BARONS SANDYS, OF OMBERSLEY.

By Letters Patent, dated 20th December, 1743.

Lineage.

This family of SANDYS, which does not appear any branch of the LORDS SANDYS, of the VINE, was originally seated at St. Bees, in Cumberland.

The Right Reverend EDWIN SANDYS, Archbishop of York, d. in 1588, leaving, with other issue,

SAMUEL SANDYS, Esq., his grace's eldest son, who inherited the manor of Ombersley, in Worcestershire, and served the office of sheriff for that county, temp. James I. From this gentleman lineally descended

SAMUEL SANDYS, Esq., who was elevated to the peerage by King GEORGE II., 20th December, 1743, as BARON SANDYS, OF OMBERSLEY, having previously filled the office of chancellor of the exchequer, and held other high and important situations. His lordship, after his elevation to the peerage, was made speaker of the House of Lords. He m. Letitia, daughter of Sir Thomas Tipping, Bart., of Wheatfield, in the county of Oxford, (by Anne, his wife, daughter, and eventually heir of Thomas Cheek, Esq., of Pyrgo, in Essex, by Letitia, daughter and heir of the Hon. Edward Russell, brother to William, first Duke of Bedford,) and had issue,

EDWIN, his successor.

Cheek, } both d. young.
Thomas, }

Martin, a colonel in the army, m. Mary, daughter of William Trumbull, Esq., son of Sir William Trumbull, secretary of state, temp. William III., by Mary, one of the daughters and co-heirs of Montagu, Viscount Blundell, in Ireland. Colonel Sandys had issue,

William.

Edward.

MARY, who m. in 1786, Arthur Hill, Marquess of Downshire, in Ireland, and was created in 1802, BARONESS

SANDYS, of Ombersley, with remainder to her second and younger sons by the marquess.

Colonel Sandys d. in 1768.
William, d. in 1749.
John, d. in 1758.
Henry, d. in 1737.
Letitia.
Anne, m. to Christopher Bethell, Esq.
Catherine, d. young.

His lordship d. in 1770, and was s. by his eldest son,

EDWIN SANDYS, second baron, who m. in 1769, Anna-Maria, daughter of James Colebrooke, Esq., and widow of Paine King, Esq., of Finchampsted-Abbey, in Northamptonshire, but died s. p. in 1797, when his estates devolved upon his sister, Mary, MARCHIONESS OF DOWNSHIRE, and the BARONY OF SANDYS, of Ombersley, became EXTINCT.

ARMS.—Or. a fesse dancette betw. three cross crosslets fitchée, gules.

SAUNDERSON—BARON SAUNDERSON, OF SAXEBY, VISCOUNT CASTLETON, EARL OF CASTLETON.

Barony,	by Letters Patent,	anno 1714.
Viscounty,		—— 1716.
Earldom,		—— 1720.

Lineage.

NICHOLAS SAUNDERSON, ESQ., was Sheriff of Lincolnshire, in the 34th Elizabeth, and he was afterwards created VISCOUNT CASTLETON, in the peerage of Ireland. He m. Winifred, daughter and heir of John Hultof, Esq., of Boston, in the county of Lincoln, and had issue,

NICHOLAS, his successor.
William (Sir), who wrote the History of Mary, Queen of Scots, King James, and Charles I.

His lordship was succeeded by his second son,

NICHOLAS SAUNDERSON, Viscount Castleton, in Ireland. This nobleman m. Frances, daughter of Sir George Manners, of Haddon, and his grandson,

JAMES SAUNDERSON, Viscount Castleton, in Ireland, was created a peer of England, in 1714, as BARON SAUNDERSON, of Saxby, in the county of Lincoln. In 1716, he was made VISCOUNT CASTLETON, of Sandbeck, in the county of York, and in 1720, EARL OF CASTLETON. His lordship d. without male issue, in 1723, when ALL HIS HONOURS became EXTINCT, and his great estate devolved, by will, upon Thomas Lumley, third Earl of Scarborough, (grandfather of the present earl,) who thereupon assumed, by act of parliament, the additional surname of "Saunderson."

ARMS.—Paley of Six ar. and az. over all a bend sa.

SAVAGE — VISCOUNTS SAVAGE, VISCOUNTS COLCHESTER, EARL RIVERS.

Viscounty of Savage,	by Letters Patent,	6th November, 1626.
Viscounty of Colchester,		5th July, 1621.
Earldom,		4th November, 1626.

Lineage.

Of this family, whose chief seat, for many generations, had been at the CASTLE OF FRODSHAM, in Cheshire, and partly at another house, more recently erected, at CLIFTON, on the opposite side of the river, called ROCK SAVAGE, was

SIR JOHN SAVAGE, one of the adherents of Henry, Earl of Richmond, who, by the victory of BOSWORTH, placed the crown on that nobleman's head, as HENRY VII. Sir John Savage was afterwards in the wars of France, and fell at the siege of BOLOINE. He was s. by his son,

SIR JOHN SAVAGE, Knt., who m. Elizabeth, daughter of Charles Somerset, the first Earl of Worcester, and was s. by another

SIR JOHN SAVAGE, Knt., who m. Lady Elizabeth Manners, daughter of Thomas, first Earl of Rutland, and had two sons, John and Thomas. The younger,

SIR THOMAS SAVAGE, Knt., was the nineteenth advanced to the rank of baronet, upon the institution of that order. He m. Elizabeth, eldest daughter, and eventually co-heir of Thomas, LORD DARCY, of Chiche; which Lord Darcy was created, on the 5th July, 1621, VISCOUNT COLCHESTER, and elevated, on the 4th November, 1626, to the dignity of EARL RIVERS, both honours to revert, in default of male issue, to his son-in-law, Sir Thomas Savage, and his heirs male, who was himself created, in two days afterwards, VISCOUNT SAVAGE, of Rock Savage, in the county of Chester. Lord Savage had issue by the Lady Elizabeth Darcy, seven sons and six daughters, viz.:

JOHN, his successor.
Thomas, m. Elizabeth, daughter and co-heir of William Whitmore, Esq., of Leighton, in Cheshire, and had issue,
    Darcy, who succeeded at Leighton, and left a daughter,
        BRIDGET SAVAGE, who m. Sir Thomas Mostyn.
    Elizabeth, m. to Marmaduke, Lord Langdale.
Francis.
William.
James.
Richard,
Charles, left a daughter,
    Mary Savage, who m. Jeremy Thoresby, of Leeds, and left two daughters,
        Elizabeth.
        Mary.
Jane, m. to John, Marquess of Winchester.
Dorothy, m. to Charles, Viscount Andover.
Elizabeth, m. to Sir John Thimbleby, Knt., of Irnham, in Lincolnshire.

Anne, *m.* to Robert, son and heir of Thomas, Lord Brudenell, afterwards Earl of Cardigan.

Catherine, a nun at Dunkirk.

Henrietta-Maria, *m.* to Ralph Sheldon, Esq., of Beoley.

His lordship *d.* in 1635, and was *s.* by his eldest son,

JOHN SAVAGE, second Viscount Savage, who succeeded his maternal grandfather in 1639, as VISCOUNT COLCHESTER, and EARL RIVERS. His lordship *m.* first, Catherine, daughter of William Parker, Lord Morley and Monteagle, and had issue,

THOMAS, his successor.

John, died *s. p.*

Richard, who *m.* ——, daughter and heir of —— Bridge, Esq., of Traford, and left a son,

JOHN, who inherited as FIFTH EARL.

Elizabeth, *m.* to William, Lord Petre.

Jane, *m.* first, to George, Lord Chandos, secondly, to Sir William Sidley, Bart., and thirdly, to George Pitt, Esq., of Strathfieldsaye, in Hampshire. By her last husband her ladyship left a son,

GEORGE PITT, Esq., of Strathfieldsaye, M.P. for the county of Hants, whose grandson,

GEORGE PITT, Esq., was created, in 1776, BARON RIVERS, *of Strathfieldsaye* (see Burke's Peerage and Baronetage).

Catherine, *m.* to Charles Sidley, Esq., brother of Sir William.

Mary, *m.* to Henry Killegrew, Esq., groom of the bed-chamber to James, Duke of York.

Frances, *d.* young.

The earl espoused, secondly, Mary, daughter of Thomas Ogle, Esq., of South Dissington, in Northumberland, and had one son,

Peter.

His lordship *d.* 10th October, 1654, and was *s.* by his eldest son,

THOMAS SAVAGE, third Earl Rivers, who became, in 1686, in right of his mother, heir of one moiety of the Baronies of Morley, Mounteagle, and Marshal. His lordship *m.* first, Elizabeth, natural daughter of Emanuel Scroope, Earl of Sunderland, (which lady, with her sisters, MARY, *Marchioness of Winchester*, and ARABELLA, wife of John Grubham Howe, Esq., eventually succeeded to the ancient inheritance of the Scroopes,) by whom he had issue,

THOMAS, *Lord Colchester*, who *m.* Lady Charlotte Stanley, daughter of Charles, Earl of Derby, and dying before his father, left an only daughter,

Charlotte, who *d.* unmarried.

RICHARD, his successor.

Elizabeth.

Annabella, *m.* to Sir Erasmus Norwich, of Brampton, in the county of Northampton, and died *s. p.*

The earl espoused, secondly, Lady Arabella Lindsey, daughter of Robert Bertie, Earl of Lindsey, but had no issue. He *d.* in 1694, and was *s.* by his only surviving son,

RICHARD SAVAGE, fourth Earl Rivers. This nobleman espoused Penelope, daughter of John Downes, Esq., of Wardley, in Lancashire, by whom he had surviving issue,

Bessey, *m.* first, to the Earl of Rochford, and secondly, to the Rev. Mr. Carter.

—— *m.* to James, Earl of Barrymore, in Ireland, and left an only daughter,

Penelope, who *m.* Major-General James Cholmondeley.

His lordship, who was an eminent soldier and statesman in the reigns of William III. and Queen Anne, *d.* in 1712, when his honours passed to his kinsman, (revert to Richard, third son of John, second Viscount Savage,)

JOHN SAVAGE, Esq., as fifth Earl Rivers, at whose decease unmarried, the VISCOUNTY OF SAVAGE, the VISCOUNTY OF COLCHESTER, and the EARLDOM OF RIVERS, became EXTINCT.

ARMS.—Ar. Six lions rampant (three, two and one) sa.

SAVAGE — COUNTESS OF RIVERS.

By Letters Patent, dated 21st April, 1641.

Lineage.

LADY ELIZABETH SAVAGE, daughter of Thomas Darcy, Lord Darcy, of Chiche, and EARL RIVERS, and widow of Thomas Savage, first VISCOUNT SAVAGE, *of Rock Savage*, was created on 21st April, 1641, COUNTESS OF RIVERS, *for life.* Her ladyship *d.* in 1650, when the title became of course, EXTINCT.

SAVILE—BARONS SAVILE, EARLS OF SUSSEX.

Barony, } by Letters { 21st July, 1628.
Earldom, } Patent, { 25th May, 1644.

Lineage.

The family of SAVILE is of great antiquity in the north of England.

In the reign of EDWARD III.,

SIR JOHN SAVILE, Knt., of Eland, in Yorkshire, was constituted escheator for the counties of Northumberland, Cumberland, and Westmorland: and in the next reign was sheriff of Yorkshire, and governor of the castle of York.

In the 2nd HENRY V.,

THOMAS SAVILE, of Thornhill, in the county of York, being at that time one of the esquires to Edward, Duke of York, was, in consideration of his good services, made forester of that prince's chase and park at Aryngden, in the same shire. From this Thomas, descended

SIR HENRY SAVILE, of Thornhill, K.B., temp. *King* HENRY VIII., who by ——, daughter and co-heir of Thomas Southell, Esq., of Southell, had a son and heir, EDWARD, an idiot. He had also, by a concubine, named Barkston, another son,

SIR ROBERT SAVILE, *alias* BARKSTON, Knt., who, in the 15th Elizabeth, served the office of sheriff for the county of Lincoln. He *m.* ——, sister of John, Lord Hussey, and widow of Sir Richard Thimelby; and was *s.* by his son,

SIR JOHN SAVILE, Knt., of Howley, in York shire, sheriff for Lincolnshire, in the 32nd Elizabeth, and member of parliament for the county of York, temp. *King* James I. and *King* Charles I. He was likewise high-steward for the honour of Pontefract; and was elevated to the peerage, by letters patent, dated 21st July, 1628, as Baron Savile, *of Pontefract.* His lordship was, subsequently, sworn of the privy council, and appointed comptroller of the household. Lord Savile *m.* first, Catherine, daughter of Lord Willoughby, of Parham, but had no issue. He espoused, secondly, Elisabeth, daughter of Sir Edward Carey, Knt., and had issue,

    Henry, who *m.* Helen, daughter and co-heir of William Ogelthorpe, Esq., and *d.* before his father, leaving a son,

        John, who *d.* also before Lord Savile.

    Edward, *m.* Anne, daughter and heir of Richard Tolson, Esq., of Cumberland, but died *s. p.*

    Thomas (Sir), who *s.* to the peerage.

    Robert, } *d.* unmarried.
    Edmund, }

    Catherine, *m.* to Sir Thomas Bland, of Kippax Park, in Yorkshire.

    Anne, *m.* to Piers Leigh, son and heir of Sir Piers Leigh, of Lime.

    Elisabeth, *m.* first, to Alveray Cooper, Esq., of Batley, in Yorkshire, and secondly, to Richard Banks, Esq.

    Frances, *m.* to the Rev. Thomas Bradley, D.D., rector of Castelford, in the county of York.

His lordship *d.* in 1630, and was *s.* by his eldest surviving son,

SIR THOMAS SAVILE, Knt., second Baron Savile. This nobleman was created Viscount Savile, of Castlebar, in the peerage of Ireland. His lordship was comptroller of the household, and attending *King* Charles I. at Oxford, was advanced, by letters patent, dated 25th May, 1644, to the dignity of Earl of Essex. During the whole of the civil wars he remained faithfully attached to the fortunes of his royal master, and his services merited fully the honours he received. His lordship *m.* first, Frances, daughter of Sir Michael Sondes, Knt., of Throwley, in Kent, and widow of Sir John Leveson, but had no issue. He espoused, secondly, Lady Anne Villiers, daughter of Christopher, Earl of Anglesey, and eventually sole heir of her brother, Charles, last Earl of Anglesey, of the family of Villiers. By this lady he had issue,

    James, Lord Savile, his successor.

    Frances, *m.* to Francis, Lord Brudenel, son and heir of Robert, Earl of Cardigan, by whom she had issue,

        George, third Earl of Cardigan.
        James.
        Mary, *m.* to Richard, Viscount Molineux, ancestor of the Earls of Sefton.
        Anne, *m.* first, to Sir Henry Belasyse, and secondly, to Charles Lenox, Duke of Richmond.
        Frances, *m.* first, to Charles Levingston,

second Earl of Newburgh, and secondly, to Richard, Lord Bellew.

His lordship *d.* in 1646, and was *s.* by his son,

JAMES SAVILE, second Earl of Sussex. This nobleman *m.* Anne, daughter of Robert Wake, a merchant at Antwerp, but dying without issue in 1671, the Earldom of Sussex, and the *minor honours,* became extinct, while his lordship's estates devolved upon his only sister, *Frances,* Lady Brudenel.

Arms.—Ar. on a bend, sa. three owls of the first, a crescent for difference.

SAVILE — VISCOUNTS HALIFAX, EARLS OF HALIFAX, MARQUESSES OF HALIFAX.

Viscounty,	} by Letters Patent.	{ 13th January, 1668.
Earldom,		{ 16th July, 1679.
Marquisate,		{ 22nd August, 1682.

Lineage.

The principal *legitimate* branch of the Savile family was represented by

SIR GEORGE SAVILE, Bart., of Thornhill, in the county of York, who *m.* Lady Mary Talbot, daughter of George, Earl of Shrewsbury, and was father of

SIR GEORGE SAVILE, Bart., who espoused Anne, daughter of Thomas, Lord Coventry, and was *s.* by his son,

SIR GEORGE SAVILE, Bart., of Thornhill, who, in consideration of his own and his father's eminent services during the civil wars, was elevated to the peerage by King Charles II., on 13th January, 1668, as *Baron Saville, of Eland, in the county of York,* and Viscount Halifax. In 1679, his lordship was created Earl of Halifax, and Marquess of Halifax, in 1682. He *m.* first, Lady Dorothy Spencer, daughter of Henry, Earl of Sunderland, and had issue,

    Henry, who *m.* Esther, daughter and co-heir of Charles de la Tour, Marquess of Gouvernet, in France, and died *s. p.*, in the time of his father.

    William, his successor.

    George, fell at the siege of Buda, in 1688, and *d.* unmarried.

    Anne, *m.* to John, Lord Vaughan.

His lordship espoused, secondly, Gertrude, daughter of William Pierrepoint, of Thoresby, second son of Robert, first Earl of Kingston, by whom he had an only daughter,

    Elizabeth, who *m.* Philip, eldest son of Philip Stanhope, Earl of Chesterfield.

The Marquess of Halifax was lord privy seal, and some time president of the council, temp. Charles II. He was esteemed a statesman of the first grade. Burnet characterizes him " as a man of great and ready wit; full of life, and very pleasant, but much turned to satire: his imagination was too hard for his judgment; and a severe jest took more with him than all arguments whatever. He let his wit run much on matters of religion, which got him the reputation of a confirmed atheist; but he denied

467

the charge; though he could not, as he said, *digest iron as an ostrich, or take into his belief things that would burst him.* Friendship and morality were great topics with him; and punctuality and justice more remarkable in his private dealings. In relation to the public, he went backwards and forwards, and changed sides so often, that, in the conclusion, no side would trust him."

His lordship d. in 1695, and was s. by his eldest surviving son,

WILLIAM SAVILE, second Marquess. This nobleman m. first, Elizabeth, daughter of Sir Samuel Grimston, Bart., of Goramby, in the county of Herts, and sister and heir of Sir Harbottle Grimston, by whom he had to survive, an only daughter,

ANNE, m. to *Charles*, third EARL OF AILESBURY.

His lordship espoused, secondly, Lady Mary Finch, daughter of Daniel, Earl of Nottingham, by Lady Essex Rich, daughter and co-heir of Richard, Earl of Warwick and Holland, and had, with two sons, who both died young, three daughters. viz.

Essex.
Dorothy, m. to Richard, Earl of Burlington.
Mary, m. to Sackville, Earl of Thanet.

The Marquess d. in 1700, when his estates devolved upon his daughters, as co-heirs, and ALL HIS HONOURS became EXTINCT.

ARMS.—Ar. a bend sa. three owls of the first.

SAY—BARONS SAY.

By Writ of Summons, dated 26th July, 1313,
7 Edward II.

Lineage.

The first member of the family of SAY mentioned by Sir William Dugdale, is

PICOT DE SAY, who, in the time of the CONQUEROR, was one of the principal persons in the county of Salop, under Roger de Montgomery, Earl of Shrewsbury. The next is

INGELRAM DE SAY, one of the staunchest adherents of *King* STEPHEN in his contest with the *Empress* Maud, and made prisoner with that monarch at the battle of Lincoln. After this gallant and faithful soldier, we come to

WILLIAM DE SAY, who m. Beatrix, the divorced wife of Hugh Talbot, and daughter of Geoffery de Mandeville, Earl of Essex, by whom he had issue,

William, who d. in the life-time of his father, leaving two daughters, viz.

Beatrix, who m. Geoffrey Fits-Piers, and from whom descended the Fits-Piers's, who subsequently succeeded to the Earldom of Essex.
Maud, m. to William de Bocland.
GEOFFREY.

The second son,

GEOFFREY DE SAY, was one of the barons chosen to proceed with William de Longchamp, Bishop of Ely, Chancellor of England, with the covenanted ransom of seventy thousand marks of

silver for the release of Richard I. He m. Lettice, sister, and at length heir, of Walkeline Maminot, and dying in 1214, was s. by his son,

GEOFFREY DE SAY, who, in the 16th John, paid four hundred marks to the king for livery of the lands of his inheritance both by father and mother. In the next year this Geoffrey was in arms with the other barons against the king, and was one of the TWENTY-FIVE appointed to enforce the observance of MAGNA CHARTA. His lands in the counties of Northampton, Cambridge, Essex, Herts, Norfolk, Suffolk, and Lincoln, were in consequence seized, and given to Peter de Crohim; but returning to his allegiance in the next reign he had full restitution, and on levying the scutage of Mongomery, 8th Henry III., answered for forty-two knights' fees. He m. Alice, daughter and co-heir of John de Cheyney, and d. in 1230 was s. by his son,

WILLIAM DE SAY, who, in the 44th Henry III., was constituted governor of the castle at Rochester, but being afterwards at the battle of Lewes, on the side of the king, he fled from the field on the defeat of the royalists. He d. in 1272, and was s. by his son,

WILLIAM DE SAY. This feudal lord had summons, with other great men, in the 22nd Edward II., to advise with the king upon the most important affairs of the realm; and he had subsequently a military summons to march into Gascony. He d. in 1295, and was s. by his son,

GEOFFREY DE SAY, then only fourteen years of age, whose wardship was given to William de Leyburne, in order that he might marry Idonea, daughter of the said William. In the 34th Edward III. he had livery of his lands upon doing his homage; and was in the expedition made at that period into Scotland. In the 7th of Edward II. he was summoned to parliament as a BARON, and thenceforward to the 14th of the same reign. His lordship m. Idonea de Leyburne, and d. in 1322, was s. by his son,

GEOFFREY DE SAY, second baron, who, making proof of his age, 19th Edward II., had livery of his lands, and was summoned to parliament from 25th February, 1342, to 15th July, 1353. In the 8th of Edward III. he obtained the king's charter for free warren in all his demesne lands within his lordships of Greenwich, Deptford, &c., and in two years afterwards he was constituted admiral of the king's fleet, from the mouth of the Thames westwards, in which service, besides himself then a banneret, he had of his retinue, four knights, twenty men at arms, and three archers. From this period Lord Say was constantly employed in the wars of France and Flanders, and deported himself with great gallantry. His lordship m. Maud, daughter of Guy de Beauchamp, Earl of Warwick, and had issue,

WILLIAM, his successor.

Idonea, who m. Sir John Clinton, Knt., of Mantoch, in the county of Warwick, third BARON CLINTON, and to this Idonea, ROBERT, present *Lord Clinton*, is elder co-heir.

Elizabeth, m. to Thomas de Aldone.

Joane, m. first, to Sir William Fienes, and her

grandson, JAMES FIENES, was summoned to parliament by King HENRY VI., as BARON SAY AND SELE, a dignity still extant. Joane Say espoused, secondly, Stephen de Valoines.

Lord Say d. in 1369, and was s. by his son,

WILLIAM DE SAY, third baron, summoned to parliament from 14th August, 1362, to 4th October, 1373. This nobleman was s. by his son,

JOHN DE SAY, fourth baron, who d. in minority, a ward to the king, in 1382, leaving his sister,

ELIZABETH DE SAY, his heir. This lady espoused, first, Sir John de Falvesley, who was summoned to parliament as a BARON, (see Falvesley,) and secondly, Sir William Heron, also summoned to parliament as a baron, (see Heron,) but d. without issue in 1399, leaving the descendants of her aunts, IDONEA, Lady Clinton, and JOANE, Lady Fienes, (refer to issue of second baron,) her heirs, amongst whose representatives the BARONY OF SAY has continued from that period to the present in ABEYANCE.

ARMS.—Quarterly or, and gu.

SCALES—BARONS SCALES.

By Writ of Summons, dated 6th February, 1299, 27 Edward I.

Lineage.

Of this name and family, (anciently written Eschalers and Scalers,) the first recorded is

HUGH DE SCALERS, who, in the time of King Stephen, was Lord of Berkhamsted, in the county of Essex. This feudal lord gave to the monks of Lewes, the churches of Withiall, Wadone, Ruthenalle, and Berkhamsted, by a deed sealed with the impression of an armed man, standing on his left foot, and putting his right on the step of a ladder, with his hands on the same, as if he were climbing—around which was the inscription—" Sigillum Hugonis de Scaleriis." This Hugh was s. by his son,

HENRY DE SCALERS, who, in the 19th Henry II., upon the assessment in aid, then levied for the marriage portion of the King's daughter, certified his knights' fees to be fifteen, for which he paid the sum of £10. 6s. 8d. Henry was s. by his son,

HUGH DE SCALERS, who was s. by his son, another

HENRY DE SCALERS. This feudal lord, making a journey to Jerusalem, died there, and was s. by his brother,

GEFFERY DE SCALERS, who d. in the 51st Henry III., and of this branch of the family, nothing further is known—we therefore turn to another : that founded by

STEPHEN DE SCALERS, nephew of Hugh, first Lord of Berkhamsted. To this Stephen, succeeded

WILLIAM DE SCALERS, who d. in the 9th of King John, and was s. by his son,

RICHARD DE SCALERS. In the 8th of Henry

III., upon the collection of the scutage of Montgomerie, this Richard was acquitted for his fifteen knights' fees, having been, as it seems, in that service. He died in seven years afterwards, leaving an only daughter and heiress,

 Lucia, who married Baldwin Fravill, which Baldwin had obtained the lady in ward, in consideration of two hundred marks paid to the crown.

Thus terminated another branch of the family. Of the same house, was

JOHN DE SCALES, Sheriff of Cambridgeshire and Huntingdonshire, in 1246 and 1259; but we proceed with the principal remaining branch,

ROBERT DE SCALES, who, in the 26th Henry III., paid a fine of £10 to the king, to be exempted from serving in the wars of Gascony, at that time. He d. in 1266, leaving two sons,

 William, who became a canon at Blackburgh, in the county of Norfolk.

And his heir,

ROBERT DE SCALES. This feudal lord, having distinguished himself in arms, both in Scotland and France, in the reign of Edward I. was summoned to parliament as BARON SCALES, by that monarch, from 6th February, 1299, to 22nd January, 1305, and dying in the latter year, was s. by his son,

ROBERT DE SCALES, second baron, summoned to parliament, from 3rd November, 1306, to 14th March, 1322. This nobleman, in the 34th Edward I., being made a Knight of the Bath, with Prince Edward and several others, attended him in the expedition made, at that time, into Scotland. His lordship m. Egelina, daughter of Hugh de Courtenay, and sister of Hugh, Earl of Devon, and d. in 1322, was s. by his son,

ROBERT DE SCALES, third baron, then in minority, for whose guardianship, his mother paid a fine of two hundred marks to the king. His lordship attained his majority in the 7th of Edward III., and in two years afterwards, we find him in the expedition made into Scotland, in the retinue of William de Ufford. He was again in Scotland the ensuing year, and in the 12th of the same reign, he attended the king into Flanders. From this period, until the 30th of Edward, he was almost unremittingly engaged in France. His lordship m. Catherine, sister and co-heir of William de Ufford, Earl of Suffolk, and had issue,

 ROGER, his successor.

 Margaret, m. to Sir Robert Howard, and had issue,

  Sir John Howard, who had a son,

   Sir John Howard, who dying in the life-time of his father, left a daughter,

    Elizabeth, sole heiress of her grandfather; this lady m. John de Vere, Earl of Oxford.

 Elizabeth, m. to Sir Roger de Felbrigg, and had issue,

  Sir Simon de Felbrigg, who m. Margaret, daughter and heiress of the Duke of Silesia, and left an only daughter and heiress,

Alana, m. Sir William Tyndal, of Dean, in the county of Northampton; grandfather of Sir William Tyndal, K.B., temp. Henry VII.

Lord Scales, who had summons to parliament, from 25th February, 1342, to 6th April, 1369, died in the latter year, and was s. by his son,

ROGER DE SCALES, fourth baron, summoned to parliament, from 26th December, 1375, to 3rd September, 1385. This nobleman was in the expedition made into France, in the 46th of Edward III.; and upon the breaking out of the insurrection under Jack Straw, temp. Richard II., his lordship was one of those eminent persons whom the insurgents seized, and compelled to march along with them. In the 5th of the same reign, Lord Scales, by an inquisition, was found to be one of the co-heirs to William de Ufford, Earl of Suffolk. His lordship m. Joane, daughter and heiress of Sir John de Northwode, and dying in 1386, was s. by his son,

ROBERT DE SCALES, fifth baron, summoned to parliament, from 30th November, 1396, to 3rd October, 1400. His lordship, at his accession to the dignity, was in his fourteenth year. In the first year of Henry IV., Lord Scales was one of the lords in parliament, that voted for the safe custody of the late King Richard II., and he embarked soon afterwards, in the expedition made into Aquitaine. His lordship m. Elizabeth, daughter of William, Lord Bardolf, by whom, (who m., after his decease, Sir Henry Percie, of Athol,) he had issue,

ROBERT, } successive Lords.
THOMAS, }

He d. in 1402, and was s. by his elder son,

ROBERT DE SCALES, 6th baron, but never summoned to parliament. This nobleman dying unmarried, in 1418, was s. by his brother,

THOMAS DE SCALES, seventh baron, summoned to parliament, from 13th January, 1445, to 9th October, 1459. This nobleman attained high military renown, in the reign of Henry V. and Henry VI. In 1436, upon the death of John Plantagenet, Duke of Bedford, the Normans rebelling, this Lord Scales was sent out with others, against them; when slaying many of the rebels, and destroying some of the towns and villages, the country was reduced to obedience. For this especial service, he obtained from the crown, a grant of £100 per annum, for life. In the 21st of Henry VI., his lordship was constituted one of the ambassadors then deputed to France, for the purpose of negotiating a peace. In the 28th of the same reign, we find Lord Scales in arms against Jack Cade; and in the subsequent conflicts between the Houses of York and Lancaster, he remained ever faithful to King Henry VI. His lordship m. Emma, daughter of John Whalesborough, and had issue,

THOMAS, who d. in his father's life-time.

Elizabeth, m. first, to Henry Bourchier, second son of Henry, Earl of Essex, who died s. p., and secondly, to Anthony, son and heir of Richard Widvile, Earl of Rivers, who was summoned to parliament in her right, as Lord Scales, but afterwards succeeded to the Earldom of Rivers—and was beheaded

470

in 1483—Lady Scales died previously, without issue.

Lord Scales, is said by Story, to have been murdered, on the 25th July, 1460, but Dugdale merely says, that he departed this life. After his lordship's decease, the second husband of Elizabeth, his only daughter and heiress, Anthony Widvile, was summoned to parliament, as Lord Scales, and upon the death of the said Elizabeth, without issue, the BARONY OF SCALES fell into ABEYANCE, between the descendants of Margaret, Lady Howard, and Elizabeth, Lady Felbrigg, (refer to issue of Robert, third baron,) as it still continues with their representatives.

The noble family of Scales resided for many generations, in great splendour and power, at the castle of Middleton, near Lynn, in the county of Norfolk.

ARMS.—Gu. six escallop shells ar, three, two, one.

SCHOMBERG — DUKES OF SCOMBERG.

By Letters Patent, dated 10th April, 1689.

Lineage.

JOHN MEINHARDT SCONBERG, or SCOMBERG, of an ancient and noble family in Germany, m. Anne, daughter of Edward Sutton, Lord Dudley, and was father of

FREDERICK SCOMBERG, a military officer of high reputation. This eminent person commenced his gallant career in the service of the States General; he was afterwards in Portugal, where he commanded the Portuguese army against the Spaniards, and in 1668, achieved by arms, the full recognition of the right of the House of Braganza to the crown of Portugal. We next find him in the service of France, and raised to the high military rank of marshal in that kingdom. In 1688, he accompanied the Prince of Orange into England, and when His Highness obtained the sceptre as William III., was elevated to the peerage, by letters patent, dated 10th April, 1689, as Baron Tayes, and Earl of Brentford, in the county of Middlesex, Marquess of Harwich, and DUKE OF SCOMBERG, all in remainder to his second surviving son, Charles, and his issue male; failure of which, to his eldest surviving son, Meinhardt, and his male descendants. His grace espoused, first, Johanna-Elizabetha, the daughter of his paternal uncle, and had issue,

Frederick, who resided in Germany.

MEINHARDT, who was created in the peerage of Ireland, in 1690-1, Baron of Tarragh, Earl of Bangor, and DUKE OF LEINSTER.

Otto, who fell at the siege of Valenciennes.

Henry, d. at Brussels.

CHARLES, successor to the honours, under the patent.

The duke m. secondly, Susanna, daughter of Count Anmale de Harcourt, in France, but had no issue. His grace, who, with his other honours, was a Knight of the Garter, fell at the BOYNE, in 1690, aged 84, and was buried at St. Patrick's, Dublin, with the following inscription—

"Underneath, lies the body of Frederick, Duke of Schomberg, slain at the battle of the Boyne, in the year 1690. The dean and chapter of this church, again and again besought the heirs of the duke, to cause some monument to be here erected to his memory. But when after many entreaties by letters and friends, they found they could not obtain their request, they themselves placed this stone; only that the indignant reader may know where the ashes of Schomberg are deposited.

"Thus did the fame only of his virtue obtain more for him from strangers, than nearness of blood from his own family."

His grace was *s.* according to the limitation by his son,

CHARLES SCOMBERG, second duke, who dying, unmarried, of a wound, received at the battle of Marsaglia, in Piedmont, anno 1693, was *s.* by his elder brother,

MEINHARDT SCOMBERG, Duke of Leinster, in Ireland, as third Duke of Scomberg. This nobleman *m.* Charlotte, daughter of Charles-Lewis, Elector Palatine, and had issue,

> Charles, Marquess of Harwich, Colonel of Horse, who *d.* in his father's life-time, anno 1713, *s. p.*
> Mary, *m.* to Count Dagenfieldt.
> Caroline, *d.* unmarried.
> Frederica, *m.* first, to Robert Darcy, Earl of Holderness ; and secondly, to Benjamin Mildmay, Earl Fitz-Walter, and *d.* in 1751.

His grace, who like his father was a military man of high reputation, died in 1719, when, for want of an heir male, ALL HIS HONOURS became EXTINCT.

ARMS.—Ar. an inescutcheon, *s.* surmounted by an escarbuncle of eight rays, or.

SCHULENBERG — DUCHESS OF KENDAL.

By Letters Patent, dated 30th April, 1719.

Lineage.

ERANGARD MELOSINE SCHULENBERG, a German lady, mistress to *King* George I., was created, in 1716, a peeress of Ireland, as Baroness of Dundalk, Countess and Marchioness of Dungannon, and Duchess of Munster. In 1719, her ladyship was enrolled amongst the nobility of Great Britain, in the dignities of Baroness Glastonbury, in the county of Somerset, Countess of Feversham, and DUCHESS OF KENDAL, *for life.* She was afterwards advanced to the rank of Princess of Eberstein, in the Germanic empire.

Her grace died in 1743, when ALL HER HONOURS became EXTINCT.

ARMS.—Quarterly ; first and fourth or. a lamb passant in fesse quartered gu. and ar. ensigned on its head with three standards of the second; second and third, ar. three eagles' legs couped at the thigh gu. And as a princess of the empire, in a shield surtout Jupiter, a lion rampant, lund, imperially crowned ppr.

SCHULENBERG — COUNTESS OF WALSINGHAM.

By Letters Patent, dated 7th April, 1722.

Lineage.

MELESINA DE SCHULENBERG, natural daughter of *King* GEORGE I., was elevated to the peerage of England, by letters patent, dated 7th April, 1722, as *Baroness of Aldborough, in the county of Suffolk*, and COUNTESS OF WALSINGHAM, both dignities *for life only.* Her ladyship *m.* Philip Stanhope, the celebrated EARL OF CHESTERFIELD, but died in 1776, without issue, when her honours became EXTINCT.

ARMS.—In a lozenge to coats quarterly ; first and fourth, or. a lamb passant in fesse, quartered, gules and ar. ensigned on the head with three standards of the second; second and third quarter, arg. three eagles' legs couped at the thigh, gules.

SCOT—EARL OF CHESTER.

By Inheritance, anno 1231.

Lineage.

The Lady

MAUD DE MESCHINES, eldest daughter of Hugh, (surnamed *Keveliok*,) third Earl of Chester, espoused David, Earl of Huntingdon, brother of William the Lion, King of Scotland, and had with four daughters, (see Meschines, Earls of Chester,) an only son,

JOHN LE SCOT, who, upon the demise of his uncle, in 1231, (his mother having died previously,) RANULPH de Meschines, (surnamed Blundevil,) fourth EARL OF CHESTER, without issue, succeeded to the whole Palatine of CHESTER, and became, in consequence, EARL of that county. This nobleman carried the sword, called *Curtana*, at the marriage of King Henry III., anno 1236; and Seldon, in his Titles of Honour, says, that his lordship then bore the express designation of "EARL PALATINE;" observing, that until the time of the second Henry he had never found "PALATINE" so applied. In the same year his lordship assumed the cross, but it is doubtful whether he ever set out for the Holy Land or not. He *d.* in 1244, by poison, suspected to have been administered by his wife, Helen, daughter of Llewellin, Prince of North Wales; and leaving no issue, the EARLDOM OF CHESTER was annexed to the crown for ever (in 1246) ; "*Ne tam praclara dominatio inter colos faminarum dividi contingeret ;*"—"Lest so fair a dominion should be divided amongst women :" the king bestowing upon the deceased lord's sisters other lands instead.

ARMS.—Or. three piles gu.

SCOTLAND, KINGS OF—EARLS OF HUNTINGDON.

See ST. LIZ, Earls of Huntingdon.

SCROPE — BARONS SCROPE, OF BOLTON, EARL OF SUNDERLAND.

Barony, by Writ of Summons, dated 8th January, 1371, 44 Edward III.

Earldom, by Letters Patent, dated 19th June, 1627.

Lineage.

In the 12th of Henry II., upon the aid levied for marrying the king's daughter,

ROBERT DE SCRUPE was one of the feudal barons required to make a return of his knights' fees, and he certified accordingly that he held three, *de veteri feoffamento* in the county of Gloucester. He was *s.* by his son and heir,

HENRY DES SCRUPES, (as the surname was then written,) who, in the 7th of King John, paid sixty marks for his relief ; and in the 2nd of Henry III., upon the collection of the scutage of that king's reign, paid six marks for those three knights' fees which he had by inheritance. He was *s.* by his son,

WILLIAM LE SCROPE, who, in the 24th Edward I., obtained a royal charter for free warren in all his demesne lands at EAST BOLTON, Little Bolton, Fencotes, and Parnswike, in the county of York. This William was *s.* by his son,

HENRY LE SCROPE, who was constituted one of the justices of the Common Pleas in the 2nd Edward II., and was summoned to parliament, *ex officio*, from the 8th to the 19th of the same reign ; between which periods he was advanced to the chief justiceship of the King's Bench. In the reign of Edward III. he was a second time placed on the bench of the Common Pleas, and he subsequently became chief of that court. His lordship *d.* about the year 1336, possessed of large estates in the counties of York and Hertford, and was *s.* by his eldest son,

SIR WILLIAM LE SCROPE, who was in the wars of Flanders and Scotland, temp. Edward III., and dying issueless in 1345, was *s.* by his brother,

SIR RICHARD LE SCROPE. This feudal lord was in the wars of France in the 33rd and 40th Edward III., and was constituted, in five years afterwards, treasurer of the exchequer ; having been summoned to parliament the year preceding, as a BARON, and from that period to the 3rd of Henry IV. In the 1st of RICHARD II. his lordship was made steward of the household, and the next year constituted the king's CHANCELLOR. Soon after this he had licence to encastellate his manor house at Bolton. In the 5th of the same reign he was a second time appointed CHANCELLOR, and likewise KEEPER OF THE GREAT SEAL, in parliament : " having," according to Walsingham, " not his fellow (of his degree,) in the whole realm, for prudence and integrity." His lordship was frequently included in commissions to treat of peace with the French and the Scotch ; and he deported himself with such integrity as chancellor, that he peremptorily refused to affix the great seal to a grant made by King Richard to one of his favourites ; telling the person, that the duty of his

office would not permit him to set the seal, committed to his keeping by the parliament, to all the king's indiscrete grants, until he had acquired a little more experience. In the same monarch's reign Lord Scrope had a memorable dispute with Sir Robert Grosvenor, Knt., touching the bearing of " az. a bend or." for his arms—which was tried, and eventually decided before *Thomas*, DUKE OF GLOUCESTER, then constable of England, when sentence was given in favour of his lordship, and a former judgment in favour of Grosvenor, for bearing the same arms, with a " bordure or." declared void ; by reason that such differences between strangers, and of one realm, were not deemed sufficient ; but intended merely for such as are of near alliance by consanguinity. His lordship had issue,

> ROGER, his successor.
>
> Richard, Archbishop of York, beheaded for conspiring against Henry IV.
>
> Stephen, Lord of Bentley, who *m.* Milicent, daughter and heir of Robert Tibetot, and left,
>> Stephen.
>> Margaret.

Lord Scrope, who was a noble benefactor to the church, *d.* in 1403, and was *s.* by his eldest son,

ROGER LE SCROPE, second Baron Scrope, of Bolton, summoned to parliament 20th October, and 23rd November, 1403. His lordship *m.* Margaret, one of the daughters and co-heirs of Robert, Lord Tiptoft, with whom he acquired the manor of Langor, Notts, and *d.* in 1404, was *s.* by his son,

RICHARD LE SCROPE, third baron, but never summoned to parliament. This nobleman, in the 7th HENRY V., attended the king in the expedition then made into France, but *d.* soon after, anno 1420, never having had summons to parliament. His lordship *m.* Lady Margaret Nevill, daughter of Ralph, Earl of Westmorland, and *d.* in 1420, was *s.* by his son,

SIR HENRY LE SCROPE, fourth baron, summoned to parliament from 3rd December, 1441, to 26th May, 1455, as LORD SCROPE, *of Bolton*. This nobleman, during his minority, accompanied John, Lord Scrope, of Upsal, in his embassy to the great master of the Order of St. John of Jerusalem ; and in the 18th Henry VI., making proof of his age, had livery of his lands. His lordship *m.* Elizabeth, daughter of John, Lord Scrope, of Masham and Upsal, by whom he had three sons, and was *s.*, at his decease in 1459, by the eldest,

JOHN LE SCROPE, fifth baron, summoned to parliament from 30th July, 1460, to 16th January, 1497. This nobleman espoused the cause of York, and during the reign of Edward IV. was a person of great influence and power. His lordship was a Knight of the Garter, and fought against the Lancastrians, as well as the Scots, particularly at NORHAM CASTLE, when that fortress was relieved by the Earl of Surrey, and the besiegers driven beyond the Scottish border. He *m.*ʳ Joane, daughter of William, Lord Fitz-Hugh, and was *s.* at his decease by his son,

SIR HENRY LE SCROPE, sixth baron, but never summoned to parliament. This nobleman *m.*

first, Elizabeth, daughter of Henry, Earl of Northumberland, by whom he had issue,

    HENRY, his successor.

    John, whose daughter,

        Margaret, m. Christopher Wyvill, Esq.

His lordship espoused, secondly, Alice, only daughter and heir of Thomas, Lord Scrope, of Upsal, and had an only daughter,

    Elizabeth, m. to Sir Gilbert Talbot, Knt.

He d. in 1506, and was s. by his elder son,

HENRY LE SCROPE, seventh baron, summoned to parliament from 23d November, 1514, to 9th August, 1529. This nobleman was at the battle of Flodden-field in the 5th of Henry VIII., and he was one of the peers, who, in the same reign, signed the celebrated letter to the pope regarding the divorce of Queen Katherine. His lordship m. Margaret, daughter of Thomas, Lord Dacre, and had issue,

    JOHN, his successor.

    ———, of Hamildon, in the county of Bucks.

    Anne, m. to John Vavasour, Esq., of Haslewood, in the county of York, from whom descended the *Extinct Baronets* Vavasour, of the same place, now represented by the Hon. Sir Edward Marmaduke Vavasour, who was created a baronet in 1828.

    Joane, m. to John, Lord Lumley.

    Elizabeth, m. to Sir Bryan Stapleton, Knt., of Carleton, in the county of York.

    Anne, m. to Thomas Rither, Esq., of Rither, in Yorkshire.

He d. about the year 1529, and was s. by his elder son,

JOHN LE SCROPE, eighth baron, summoned to parliament from 5th January, 1533, to 5th January, 1553. His lordship had livery of his lands in the 25th of Henry VIII., but in three years afterwards was involved in the conspiracy occasioned by the dissolution of the monasteries, called the PILGRIMAGE OF GRACE. He m. Catherine, eldest daughter of Henry, Earl of Cumberland, and had issue,

    HENRY, his successor.

    George.

    Edward.

    Thomas.

    Margaret, m. to Sir John Constable, Knt., of Burton Constable, in the county of York.

    Elizabeth, m. to Thomas Pudsey, Esq., of Bolton, in Craven.

    Alianore, m. to Richard Tempest, Esq., of Braswell.

    Catherine.

His lordship d. about the year 1554, and was s. by his eldest son,

HENRY LE SCROPE, ninth baron, summoned to parliament from 21st October, 1555, to 4th February, 1589. This nobleman, in the 5th Elizabeth, was constituted governor of the castle of Carlisle, and warden of the west marches towards Scotland. He was subsequently in arms against the insurgents under the Earls of Northumberland and Westmorland, and was made a KNIGHT OF THE GARTER. His lordship m. first, Margaret, daughter of Henry

Howard, Earl of Surrey, and sister of Thomas, Duke of Norfolk, by whom he had issue,

    THOMAS, his successor.

    Henry.

He espoused, secondly, Alianore, daughter of Edward, Lord North, and had an only daughter,

    Mary, m. to William Bowes, Esq., of Streatlam Castle, in the county of Durham, from whom descended,

        GEORGE BOWES, of Streatlam Castle, whose only daughter and heiress,

            MARY-ELEANOR BOWES, espoused JOHN, ninth *Earl of Strathmore*, and was mother of

                JOHN, tenth Earl of Strathmore, and

                THOMAS, present Earl.

            From this alliance the Earls of Strathmore have assumed the additional surname of Bowes.

His lordship d. in 1592, and was s. by his elder son,

THOMAS LE SCROPE, tenth baron, summoned to parliament from 19th February, 1593, to 6th October, 1610, who m. Philadelphia, daughter of Henry Carey, Lord Hunsdon, and dying about the year 1612, was s. by his only child,

EMANUEL LE SCROPE, eleventh baron, summoned to parliament from 5th April, 1614, to 17th May, 1625. This nobleman, in the reign of JAMES I., was president of the king's council in the north, and was created by *King* CHARLES I., 19th June, 1627, EARL OF SUNDERLAND. His lordship m. Lady Elizabeth Manners, daughter of John, Earl of Rutland, but had no issue.[a] He d. in 1627, when the EARLDOM OF SUNDERLAND became EXTINCT; and "the BARONY OF SCROPE OF BOLTON devolved (says Nicholas) on MARY, only daughter of HENRY, ninth Lord, who m. William Bowes, Esq., and it continued vested in her descendants until 1815, when the issue of all the other co-heirs having failed, the BARONY passed to Charles Jones, Esq., he being heir general of the body of Henry, the ninth baron, although he has never urged his claim to the dignity." Mr. Jones is likewise eldest co-heir of the Barony of Tiptoft, created by writ of Edward II., dated 10th March, 1308; and co-heir of one moiety of the Barony of Badlesmere.

ARMS.—Az. a bend. or.

---

[a] EMANUEL, EARL OF SUNDERLAND, and last Lord Scrope of Bolton, left three natural daughters, amongst whom the estates of the Scropes were divided, viz.

    MARY, m. first, to the Hon. Henry Carey, second son of Henry, Earl of Monmouth; and secondly, to Charles, Marquess of Winchester; which nobleman acquired the estate at Bolton, in the county of York, and was afterwards created Duke of Bolton.

    Annabella, m. to John Grubham Howe, Esq., ancestor of the Earls and Viscounts Howe. Mr. Howe obtained the manor of Langar, in Nottinghamshire, which came to the Scropes with the heiress of the Tiptofts.

    Elizabeth, m. to Thomas Savage, Earl Rivers.

SCROPE — BARONS SCROPE, OF MASHAM, AND UPSAL.

By Writ of Summons, dated 25th February, 1342, 16 Edward III.

Lineage.

Of the family of Scrope of Bolton, was

GEFFREY LE SCROPE, (brother, it is presumed, of the Chief Justice Scrope, temp. Edward III.) a great landed proprietor in the reign of EDWARD II., who obtained from that monarch licence to make a castle of his house at Clifton-upon-Yore, in the county of York, and had, at the same time, free warren in all his demesne lands at Clifton, and Parnewick, in Yorkshire, and at Whalton, in Northumberland. In the 17th of the same monarch he was constituted Chief Justice of the Court of King's Bench, as he was again in the 4th and 6th of Edward III., but being the next year sent abroad upon the king's affairs, he resigned his judicial office. He was afterwards in the wars of Flanders, and attained the rank of banneret. He m. Ivetta, daughter of William Rosse, of Igmanthorpe, and had issue,

> HENRY, his successor.
>
> John, m. Elizabeth, one of the daughters and co-heirs of David de Strabolgi, Earl of Athol, and widow of Sir Thomas Percy, Knt.

This learned and gallant person d. about the year 1340, and was s. by his elder son,

HENRY LE SCROPE, who, in the 5th Edward III., was in the wars of Scotland, and was summoned to parliament the next year as a BARON, and from that period to 15th Richard II. In the 19th of Edward III., his lordship was in the wars of France, and the next year he fought at the battle of Durham, where DAVID, King of Scotland, sustained so signal a defeat. He was afterwards one of the commissioners for arraying the county of York upon a menaced invasion by the French, and during the remainder of Edward III.'s reign, he was either actively engaged in the wars, or as a diplomatist. In the 2d of Richard II., being then a banneret, his lordship was sent ambassador, with others, to treat with Charles, KING OF NAVARRE, regarding a league between that prince and the King of England. He m. ——, and had issue,

> STEPHEN, his successor.
>
> WILLIAM, created Earl of Wiltshire.

His lordship d. in 1391, and was s. by his elder son,

SIR STEPHEN LE SCROPE, second baron, summoned to parliament from 23rd November, 1392, to 1st January, 1406. This nobleman received the honour of knighthood for his martial services in the life-time of his father, and distinguished himself both by sea and land. His lordship m. Margery, widow of John, son of Sir William de Huntingfield, Knt., and had issue,

> HENRY, his successor.
>
> John, of whom presently.
>
> Stephen, Archdeacon of Richmond.
>
> William.

He d. in 1406, possessed of large estates in the counties of Essex, Notts, Stafford, Lincoln, and York, and was s. by his eldest son,

SIR HENRY LE SCROPE, third baron, summoned to parliament from 26th August, 1406, to 26th September, 1414, as LORD SCROPE, of Masham. His lordship, in the 7th Henry IV., was employed in the embassy to Isabel, Queen of Denmark, and Eric, King of Denmark, to treat concerning the dowry of Philippa, the daughter of King Henry, then consort of the king of Denmark; and for a league between the two crowns. In four years after he was made treasurer of the king's exchequer, and the next year the king considering his great abilities, as also the necessity of his presence in parliament and council, assigned him, during his stay at Westminster, or London, the towns of Hamstede and Hendon, in the county of Middlesex, for lodging and entertainment of his servants and horses. In the reign of Henry V. Lord Scrope was appointed ambassador to treat of peace with the French. "But this great trust," says Dugdale, "he shamefully abused; for being a person in whom the king had so great a confidence, that nothing of private or public concernment was done without him; his gravity of countenance, modesty in his deportment, and religious discourse, being always such, that whatsoever he advised was held as an oracle; upon this his solemn embassy into France, (which none was thought so fit to manage as himself,) he treated privily with the king's enemies, (being in his heart totally theirs,) and conspired the king's destruction, upon promise of reward from the French: his confederates in this design being Richard, EARL OF CAMBRIDGE, (brother of the Duke of York,) and Sir Thomas Grey, a northern knight. But before this mischievous plot could be effected, (which was to have killed the king and all his brethren ere he went to sea; five ships being ready at Southampton to waft the king over into France,) it was discovered. Whereupon he had a speedy trial before Thomas, Duke of Clarence, and other peers, at Southampton, and being found guilty there lost his head, in August, 1415." His lordship had m. first, Philippa, daughter of Sir Guy de Brien, and secondly, Joane, Duchess of York, sister and co-heir of Edmund Holand, Earl of Kent, but had no issue. Upon his lordship's ATTAINDER, the BARONY OF SCROPE, of Masham, became FORFEITED; and his lands were seised, part of which, including Masham, the king conferred upon Henry, Lord Fitz-Hugh, for life. He was s. by his brother,

SIR JOHN LE SCROPE, who, upon the death of his brother, Stephen, archdeacon of Richmond, 2nd Henry VI., on doing his homage, had livery of his lands; and immediately, thereupon, by the consent of the lords in parliament, obtained a grant from the king, of the farms and rents of all those lordships which came to the crown by the attainder of Henry, Lord Scrope, his brother, to hold for four years. This Sir John Scrope wrote himself of Masham and Upsal, and was summoned to parliament as LORD SCROPE, of Masham and Upsal, from 7th January, 1426, to 26th May, 1455, having previously, according to Nicolas, (in 1421,) obtained a restoration of his brother's honours and inheritance. His lordship was afterwards in high favour at court, and constituted TREASURER OF THE KING'S EXCHEQUER. He m. Elisabeth, ———, and had issue,

John, who d. in the life-time of his father.
THOMAS, his successor.
Allanore.
Elizabeth, m. to Henry, Lord Scrope, of Bolton.

His lordship d. in 1455, and was s. by his eldest surviving son,

THOMAS LE SCROPE, fifth baron, summoned to parliament from 9th October, 1459, to 19th August, 1472. This nobleman m. ———, and had issue,

THOMAS, his successor.
Henry,
Ralph, } successively barons.
Geffery,
Alice, m. to James Strangways, Esq.
Mary, m. to Sir Christopher Danby, Knt.
Elizabeth, m. to Sir Ralph Fits-Randolph, Knt.

His lordship d. in 1475, and was s. by his eldest son,

THOMAS LE SCROPE, sixth baron, summoned to parliament from 15th November, 1482, to 12th August, 1492. His lordship m. Elizabeth, daughter and co-heir of John Nevil, MARQUESS OF MONTACUTE, by whom (who m. secondly, Sir Henry Wentworth) he had an only daughter, Alice, who m. Henry, LORD SCROPE, OF BOLTON, by whom she had a daughter, Elizabeth, m. to Sir Gilbert Talbot, Knt. His lordship d. in 1404, and the barony appears then to have devolved upon his daughter, ALICE, wife of Lord Scrope, of Bolton, but at her decease, in 1501, it reverted,* according to Nicolas, to her ladyship's uncle,

SIR HENRY LE SCROPE, seventh baron, summoned to parliament 28th November, 1511, and dying issueless, was s. by his brother,

RALPH LE SCROPE, eighth baron, but never summoned to parliament. This nobleman died in 1515, s. p., when the barony devolved upon his brother,

GEFFERY LE SCROPE, ninth baron, but never summoned to parliament. This nobleman dying like his two preceding brothers, issueless, (in 1517,) the BARONY OF SCROPE, OF MASHAM AND UPSAL, fell into ABEYANCE between his three sisters, (refer to daughters of Thomas, fifth baron,) as it still continues with their representatives.

ARMS.—Az. a bend or. in chief, a file of three points, ar.

SCROPE — EARL OF WILTSHIRE.

By Letters Patent, dated 29th September, 1397.

Lineage.

SIR WILLIAM LE SCROPE, second son of Henry, Baron Scrope, of Masham, was made seneschal of Aquitaine in the 6th Richard II., and after-

---

* Why it should so revert, while Lady Scrope, of Bolton's, daughter, Lady Talbot, and her descendants existed, is not explained.

---

wards constituted governor of the town and castle of Shirburgh. In the 16th of the same reign he was appointed vice-chamberlain of the household, and he purchased about that time from William de Montacute, Earl of Salisbury, the Isle of Man, with the crown thereof; it being then a right belonging to the lord of that island, to be crowned with a regal crown, and to bear the title of king. He was subsequently constituted lord chamberlain of the household, and was one of the ambassadors deputed to France to contract a marriage for King Richard, with Isabel, eldest daughter of Charles the Sixth, king of France. After this having large grants of confiscated lands from the crown, he was created, by letters patent, dated 29th September, 1397, EARL OF WILTSHIRE; and constituted justice of Chester, North Wales, and Flint, with a grant of the office of surveyor of all the forests within the principality of Chester. He was also made a Knight of the Garter. But as his rise to wealth, and advancement to honours were rapid and ill-advised, so his fall was sudden, although not unexpected; for on the accession of Henry, of Lancaster, to the throne, within little more than a twelvemonth, he was made prisoner in the castle of Bristol, and immediately beheaded, anno 1399, when the EARLDOM OF WILTSHIRE became FORFEITED. His lordship d. unmarried.

ARMS.—Az. a bend, or.

SEEZ—EARL OF DORSET.

Creation of WILLIAM, the Conqueror.

Lineage.

OSMUND DE SEEZ, a noble Norman, was made BISHOP OF SALISBURY, by King William, the Conqueror, and afterwards created EARL of the county of Dorset. This eminent prelate, who filled the high office of LORD CHANCELLOR of England, d. in 1099, and was buried at Old Sarum. In nearly three centuries and a half (1457) subsequently, he was canonised by Pope Calixtus, for the purity of his life, and the great services he had rendered to religion.

SEGRAVE—BARONS SEGRAVE.

By Writ of Summons, dated 24th December, 1264, 49 Henry III.

Lineage.

In the 19th year of Henry II.,

GILBERT DE SEGRAVE, Lord of Segrave, in the county of Leicester (whence he assumed his surname) held the fourth part of one knight's fee of William de Newburgh, Earl of Warwick, and in the 4th of Richard I., he was joint sheriff with Reginald Basset, for the counties of Warwick and Leicester, under Hugh de Novant, Bishop of Coventry; in which office he continued two whole years. He subsequently, 10th Richard I., gave four hundred marks to the king towards the support of his wars. This Gilbert was s. by his son,

STEPHEN DE SEGRAVE, who, in the 5th of King John, was Constable of the Tower of London, and remaining faithful to that monarch in his conflicts with the barons, obtained a grant (17th John) of the lands of Stephen de Gant, lying in the counties of Lincoln and Leicester; with the manor of Kintone, in the county of Warwick. In the 4th Henry III., he was made governor of Saubey Castle, Leicestershire, and the next year constituted sheriff of the counties of Essex and Hertford, and afterwards of Leicestershire. In the 8th of the same reign, he was governor of the castle at Hertford, and in two years after, one of the justices itinerant in the counties of Nottingham and Derby. About this period we find this successful person, whom Matthew Paris says, in his young days "from a *clerk* was made a *knight*," acquiring large landed property by purchase. In the 13th of Henry III., he bought the manor of Cotes, in the county of Derby, from the daughters and heirs of Stephen de Beauchamp, and he afterwards purchased from Ranulph, Earl of Chester and Lincoln, all the lands which that nobleman possessed at Mount Sorell, in the county of Leicester, without the castle; as also two carucates and a half lying at Segrave, which himself and his ancestors had previously held at the rent of fourteen shillings per annum. In the 16th Henry III., he obtained a grant of the custody of the castle and county of Northampton, as also of the counties of Bedford, Buckingham, Warwick, and Leicester, for the term of his life; taking the whole profit of all those shires for his support in that service; excepting the ancient farms, which had usually been paid into the exchequer. And, having been of the king's council for several years, as also chief Justice of the Common Pleas, he succeeded in the 16th of Henry III., Hubert de Burgh in the great office of JUSTICIARY OF ENGLAND, being at the same time constituted governor of Dover, Canterbury, Rochester, &c., and Constable of the Tower of London. After this we find him, however, opposed by the bishops and barons, and his manor-house at Segrave burnt to the ground by the populace, as well as another mansion in the county of Huntingdon. The king too, in this perilous crisis, deserted him, and cited him, along with Peter de Rupibus, Bishop of Winchester, and others who had been in power, to appear forthwith at court in order to answer any charge regarding the wasting of the public treasure, which might be preferred against them. Some of those persons, conscious of guilt, fled to sanctuary, and Stephen de Segrave sought an asylum in the abbey of Leicester, where he openly declared that he was and had been a priest, and that he resolved to shave his crown again to be a canon of that house. Nevertheless upon second thoughts, he braved the storm, and appeared at court, under the archbishop's protection; where the king called him a *wicked traitor*, and told him that it was under his advice he had displaced Hubert de Burgh from the office of Justiciary, and cast that eminent person into prison; nay, that had he gone the full length of his council, Hubert would have been hanged, and divers of the nobility banished. In twelve months subsequently, however, Stephen de Segrave made his peace by paying a thousand marks to the king, and he afterwards grew again into such favour, that in the

21st of Henry III., he was the means of reconciling the king with some of his most hostile barons. Subsequently he was made justice of Chester, and the king's chief councillor, and "being now," says Dugdale, "advanced in years, deported himself by experience of former times, with much more temper and moderation, than heretofore." This eminent person married two wives — first, Rohese, daughter of Thomas le Despenser, and secondly, Ida, sister of Henry de Hastings, with whom he had in frank-marriage, the manor of Bruneswaver, in the county of Warwick. Of Stephen de Segrave, so distinguished in the reign of Henry.III., Matthew Paris, thus speaks—"This Stephen, though come of no high parentage, was in his youth, of a clerk made a knight; and in his latter days, through his prudence and valour, so exalted, that he had the reputation of one of the chief men of the realm, managing the greatest affairs as he pleased. In doing whereof, he more minded his own profit, than the common good; yet for some good deeds, and making a discreet testament, he died with much honour." He departed this life, in 1241, and was s. by his son,

GILBERT DE SEGRAVE. This feudal lord having married Annabil, daughter and co-heir of Robert de Chaucumbe, obtained a grant, in the 15th Henry III., from Simon de Montfort, Lord of Leicester, of the whole town of Kegworth, in the county of Leicester, and in two years after, had a grant from the crown, of the manor of Newcastle-under-Lime, in the county of Stafford; being the same year constituted governor of Bolsover Castle. In the 26th Henry III., he was made justice of all the royal forests, south of Trent, and governor of Kenilworth Castle. In the 35th of the same reign, he was constituted one of the justices of *Oyer and Terminer*, in the city of London, to hear and determine all such causes, as had usually been tried before the Justice Itinerant, at the Tower of London. But in three years afterwards, being deputed, with Roger Bigod, Earl Marshal, on an embassy, was treacherously seized, (along with John de Plessets, Earl of Warwick, and divers others of the English nobility,) by the French, as he was returning, and died within a short period, of the severe treatment he had received in prison. His decease occurred somewhat about the year 1254, when he was s. by his son,

NICHOLAS DE SEGRAVE, who, in the 43rd Henry III., attended that monarch into France, but soon after espoused the cause of the barons, and became one of the most active leaders, in the ranks of those turbulent men. In the 47th of Henry's reign, he was amongst those who appeared openly in arms, and fortified Northampton; for which proceeding, his lands were seized by the crown. Upon the subsequent fall of Northampton to the royalists, Nicholas de Segrave fled to London, where the citizens having raised a large army for the barons, made him their general. At the head of this force, he marched with Gilbert de Clare, and Henry de Hastings, to the seige of Rochester, and thence to Lewes, at which place, the celebrated battle, so disastrous to the king, commenced, by a charge made by Segrave, at the head of the Londoners; in this, however, he was worsted by Prince Edward, who, flushed with success, pursued his advantage too far, and thus mainly contributed to the defeat which the royal arms sustained. The issue of this battle is well known. The king, prince Edward, and the chief of their adherents became prisoners to the rebels, who followed up their triumph, by immediately summoning a parliament in the king's name; to which Nicholas de Segrave was summoned as BARON SEGRAVE, on 24th December, 1964. But the tide soon ebbing, he was amongst the defeated at Evesham, where he was wounded and made prisoner. He was, however, admitted to the benefit of the Dictum de Kenilworth, and obtained a full pardon, with restoration of his lands, which had been seised. In four years afterwards, he attended Prince Edward to the Holy Land; and when that prince ascended the throne, he appears to have enjoyed a large share of royal favour. In the 4th year of Edward's reign, he was with the king in a campaign against the Welsh; and was subsequently employed in Scotland and Ireland; having had a second summons to parliament, on the 24th June, 1295. His lordship m. Maud de Lucy, by whom he had issue,

> JOHN, his successor.
>
> Nicholas, of Barton, summoned to parliament as "Nicholas de Segrave, jun.," from 24th June, 1295, to 26th January, 1297, and as "Nicholas de Segrave," from thence to 25th May, 1321. His lordship left an only daughter and heiress,
>
>> Maud, who m. Edmund de Bohun, in whose descendants and representatives this BARONY OF SEGRAVE is now vested (see Segrave, of Barton Segrave).
>
> Geffery, sheriff of the county of Leicester, 1st Edward II.
>
> Peter.
>
> Gilbert, Bishop of London.
>
> Annabil, m. to John de Plessets, son of Sir Hugh de Plessets, Knt.

His lordship d. in 1295, and was s. by his eldest son,

JOHN DE SEGRAVE, second baron, summoned to parliament from 26th August, 1296, to 6th May, 1325. This nobleman, in the life-time of his father, having been taken prisoner in the wars of Scotland, (9th Edward I.,) obtained from the king, in consideration of his services there, the grant of one hundred pounds towards the liquidation of his ransom. He was subsequently much engaged in the Scottish wars, and in the 24th of the same reign was constable of the English army in that country. The next year he was by indenture retained to serve Roger le Bigod, Earl of Norfolk, with six knights, himself accounted, as well in time of peace as in war, for the term of his whole life, in England, Wales, and Scotland; viz., in time of peace with six horses, so long as the earl should think fit, taking Bouche of Court for himself and his knights, and for his esquires, hay and oats; as also livery for six more horses, and wages for six grooms and their horses; likewise for himself two robes yearly, as well in time of peace as war, as for a banneret; and for his five knights, as for his other bachelors, viz., two yearly. Moreover, in time of war he was bound to bring with him his five knights with twenty horses; and in consideration thereof, to receive for himself and his company, with all those horses, forty shillings per day, but if he should bring no more than six horses, then thirty-two shillings: it being likewise agreed that the horses should be valued, to the end that a fair allowance might be made for any which should be lost in the service. For the performance of this covenant he had a grant of the manor of Lodene, in the county of Norfolk.

In the 26th of Edward I. his lordship was again in Scotland, and had a principal command at the battle of Faukirk. In three years after he obtained licence to make a castle at his manor house, of Bretteby, in the county of Derby, and he was next constituted governor of Berwick-upon-Tweed as also warden of Scotland. Subsequently we find him with King Edward at the celebrated siege of Caerlaverok. After the accession of Edward II., he was again made warden of Scotland, and within a short time, attending the king into that usual theatre of war, was amongst the worsted in the great defeat sustained by the English arms at Bannockburn, and was made prisoner by the Scots, who detained him for a year, until he was exchanged for Thomas de Moram, and other prisoners of that realm, who were incarcerated in London. His lordship eventually lost his life in Gascony, whither he was sent by the king, who had conceived some displeasure against him, for the escape of Roger Mortimer out of the Tower of London, under pretence of defending those parts, with Edmund, Earl of Kent, and others; where, being a great mortality, he d. anno 1325. His lordship m., in the life-time of his father, Christian, daughter of Sir Hugh de Plessets, Knt., by whom he had issue,

> STEPHEN, the companion in arms of his gallant father in the Scottish wars, but in the 12th of Edward II. one of the partisans of Thomas, Earl of Lancaster; yet submitting himself, he obtained his pardon, and, 16th Edward II., was made constable of the Tower of London. In the 18th of Edward he attended his father into Gascony, and there d. before him. He m. Alice de Arundel, and left issue,
>
>> JOHN, successor to his grandfather,
>> Stephen.
>
> John m. Julian, daughter and heir of John de Sandwic, and d. 23rd Edward III., left a daughter and heiress,
>
>> Mary.
>
> Eleanor.
>
> Margaret.
>
> Alice.
>
> Christian. ⟨*Sir M̃clun*⟩

The baron was s. by his grandson,

JOHN DE SEGRAVE, third baron, summoned to parliament from 29th November, 1336, to 15th November, 1351. This nobleman appears, like his predecessors, a distinguished personage in the field, during his comparatively short career; for he did not live beyond the age of thirty-eight. In the wars of France and Scotland, temp. Edward III., he took an active part, and was more than once retained to serve the king by indenture. His lordship made an illustrious alliance, in marrying the Lady MARGARET PLANTAGENET, daughter, and eventually sole heiress of Thomas de Brotherton, Earl of Norfolk, Marshal of England, younger son of King Edward I.: by this lady he left, at his decease in 1353, an only daughter and heiress,

Elizabeth, who espoused, John de Mowbray, fourth Baron Mowbray, and had issue,

JOHN, fifth Lord Mowbray, who was created Earl of Nottingham, but d. soon after in the flower of his youth, unmarried.

THOMAS, sixth Lord Mowbray, created after the decease of his brother, Earl of Nottingham, and Duke of Norfolk, Earl Marshal, and K.G. His grace m. twice, but had issue by his second wife, Elizabeth, daughter of John, Lord Strange, of Blackmere, only, viz.

THOMAS, who never bore the title of Duke of Norfolk, but was denominated simply, Earl Marshal; beheaded, 6th Henry IV., and d. without issue.

Thomas, restored to the Dukedom of Norfolk, succeeded in 1432 by his son,

JOHN, third Duke of Norfolk, d. in the 1st Henry IV., and was s. by his son,

JOHN, fourth Duke of Norfolk, left, at his decease, an only daughter,

ANNE, at whose decease, without issue, the Baronies of Mowbray and Segrave reverted to the descendants of the daughters of Thomas, first duke.

Margaret, m. to Sir Robert Howard, from whom the Howards, Dukes of Norfolk, derive.

Isabel, m. first, to Sir Henry Ferrers, Knt., by whom she had an only child, Elizabeth, m. to Edward Grey, second son of Reginald, Lord Grey, of Ruthyn. Her ladyship m. secondly, James, fifth Lord Berkeley, from whom the extant Earls of Berkeley derive.

Upon the decease, issueless, of Lady Anne Mowbray, only daughter and heiress of his Grace, John Mowbray, fourth and last Duke of Norfolk, of that family, the Barony of Segrave reverted to the descendants of the two daughters of Thomas Mowbray, first Duke of Norfolk, namely, Lady Margaret Howard, and Lady Isabel Berkeley, and fell into ABEYANCE amongst those, as it still continues.

The representatives of Lady Margaret Howard

478

are the present LORDS PETRE AND STOURTON, the representation having devolved, at the decease of Edward Howard, ninth Duke of Norfolk, upon his nieces, (the daughters and co-heiresses of Philip Howard, Esq., of Buckingham, in the county of Norfolk, his grace's brother,) namely,

Winifred, wife of William, fifteenth Lord Stourton, grandfather of the present LORD STOURTON.

Anne, wife of Robert-Edward, ninth Lord Petre, grandfather of the present LORD PETRE.

The representative of Lady Isabella Berkeley is the present EARL BERKELEY.

ARMS.—Sa. three garbs, ar. tied, gu.

SEGRAVE — BARON SEGRAVE, OF BARTON SEGRAVE, IN THE COUNTY OF NORTHAMPTON.

By Writ of Summons, dated 24th June, 1295, 23 Edward I.

Lineage.

NICHOLAS DE SEGRAVE, second son of Nicholas, Lord Segrave, being in the king's service in Gascony, was summoned to parliament as a BARON on the 24th June, 1295. His lordship was soon after in the wars of Scotland, and shared in the victory of Faulkirk. In the 33rd Edward I. Lord Segrave, whom Matthew Paris calls "one of the most worthy knights in this realm," being accused of treason by Sir John de Crombwell, Knight, challenged, in defence of his innocence, his accuser to single combat, according to the custom of the period; but the king not giving his consent to the duel, his lordship crossed the sea, for the purpose of meeting his antagonist without the realm. Having done so, however, unlicensed, he was taken into custody upon his return, and immediately brought to trial. The affair puzzled the judges, who were at a loss to come to a decision; however, after three days' consultation they declared that his lordship deserved death, and that all his goods should be confiscated: yet added, that in regard he departed not from England in any affront to the king, but to avenge his own quarrel, the king would do well to pardon him. Edward was much displeased at the boldness of the judges, who seemed to set bounds to his prerogative, and gave them a severe reprimand. But he, nevertheless, pardoned Segrave, and restored him to his possessions; several of the nobility having interceded for him, and entered into security for his future good conduct.

In the 1st Edward II. his lordship was constituted governor of the castle at Northampton, and marshal of England, and in four years after he obtained licence to make a castle of his manor house, at Barton Segrave.

Upon the grant of the marshalship to Lord Segrave, much animosity arose between him and William le Mareschall; which was allayed, however, by the king's interference. His lordship d. in 1322, leaving an only daughter and heiress,

MAUD SEGRAVE, who m. Edmund de Bohun, and in the representatives of this marriage, (if any exist,) the BARONY OF SEGRAVE, of Barton-Segrave, is now vested.

ARMS.—Sa. three garbs, ar. tied, gu.

SEYMOUR — VISCOUNTS BEAUCHAMP, OF HACHE, EARLS OF HERTFORD, DUKES OF SOMERSET, MARQUESSES OF HERTFORD, BARONS SEYMOUR, OF TROWBRIDGE.

Viscounty,		5th June, 1536.
Earldom,	by Letters	18th October, 1537.
Dukedom,	Patent,	16th February, 1547.
Marquisate,		3rd June, 1640.
Barony,		19th February, 1641.

Lineage.

Of this family, which derived its descent from Sir Roger Seymour, of Evenswinden, in the county of Wilts, Knt., who m. Cecilia, one of the sisters and co-heirs of John, Lord Beauchamp, of Hache, was

SIR JOHN SEYMOUR, of Wolf Hall, Wilts, who, in the 9th Henry VIII., being then one of the knights of the body to the king, obtained a grant of the constablewick of Bristol Castle, to himself, and Edward, his son, in as ample manner as Giles, Lord D'Aubeney, held the same. Sir John m. Elisabeth, daughter of Sir Henry Wentworth, of Nettlested, in the county of Suffolk, and had issue,

EDWARD, of whom presently.

HENRY (Sir), K.B., whose line is extinct.

THOMAS, created Baron Seymour, of Sudley.

JANE, who became QUEEN Consort of King HENRY VIII., and was mother of EDWARD VI.

Elisabeth, m. first, to Sir Anthony Oughtred, Knt., and secondly, to Gregory, Lord Cromwell.

Dorothy, m. first, to Sir Clement Smith, Knt., and secondly, to Thomas Laventhorpe, Esq.

The eldest son,

SIR EDWARD SEYMOUR, was one of the esquires of the body to King Henry VIII., and when his sister, Jane, (who had been maid of honour to the unhappy QUEEN Anne Boleyne,) became the wife of his royal master, his advancement to rank and influence was rapid and unrestricted. At the nuptials, (29th Henry VIII.,) he was elevated to the peerage, by the title of VISCOUNT BEAUCHAMP, of Hache, and appointed in two days afterwards captain of the Isle of Jersey. His father, Sir John Seymour, died the next year, when his lordship had livery of his lands; and he was created, by letters patent, dated 18th October, 1537, EARL OF HERTFORD, with remainder to his issue male thereafter to be begotten. He was next constituted LORD GREAT CHAMBERLAIN OF ENGLAND for life, and the same year he accompanied the Duke of Norfolk, lieutenant-general of the English army, consisting of twenty thousand men, into Scotland. His

lordship, during the remainder of the reign of his brother-in-law, was constantly engaged in the wars of France; and upon the decease of that monarch, he was chosen unanimously by the council, PROTECTOR to the young king, his nephew, EDWARD VI., and within a month constituted LORD TREASURER OF ENGLAND. Not previously being a baron of the realm, that dignity, under the title of BARON SEYMOUR, was conferred upon him on the 15th February, 1547, and he was created the next day DUKE OF SOMERSET, both honours in remainder to the heirs male of his body, by Anne, his second wife; failing which to "Sir Edward Seymour, son of the Earl of Hertford, by Katherine, his first wife, and the heirs male of Sir Edward Seymour, the son."* His grace was immediately after constituted EARL MARSHAL OF ENGLAND for life; and in the ensuing March he obtained a patent for the great office of PROTECTOR, and GOVERNOR of the king and realms. On the 3rd November following his grace had a special grant that he should sit alone, and be placed at all times (as well in the king's presence in parliament, as in his absence) upon the middle of the bench or stool, standing next on the right hand of the king's seat royal, in his parliament chamber. In the first year of the duke's administration he concluded a peace with France, directing then all his attention to bringing about a marriage between Mary, only daughter and heir of JAMES V., of Scotland, and his nephew, the English king. But the negotiation proving abortive, he subsequently invaded Scotland with a large army, and fought and won the

---

* This singular limitation is copied from the statement in page 49, of the Third General Report of the Lords Committee to search for Documents relative to the Dignity of a Peer of the Realm, to which is added, the following remark on the effect of the attainder of the said duke on the descendants of Sir Edward Seymour, his son:—"The attainder of the Duke of Somerset, his father, and forfeiture of his dignities, by act of parliament, of the 5th and 6th Edward VI., did not affect the dignity of the Duke of Somerset granted to Sir Edward Seymour, and the heirs-male of his body. By the terms of the grant, that dignity had vested, immediately after the patent passed the great seal, in Sir Edward Seymour, with limitation to the heirs male of his body, though the actual enjoyment of it by Sir Edward, and the heirs male of his body, was made to depend on the failure of heirs male of the body of his father by his second wife; and it is confidently affirmed, that on the extinction of the heirs male of the Duke of Somerset by his second wife, that dukedom would have devolved on the heirs male of Sir Edward Seymour, above-mentioned, even had not the act of restoration, in 1660, taken place, " because, so far as the said limitation was in question, it wanted no such act for its preservation." As the Barony of Seymour was granted with the same limitation, the preceding observations prove that it would have descended in a similar manner to the Dukedom of Somerset."—NICOLAS.

celebrated battle of MUSSELBURGH, chiefly by his own courage and conduct. Thus having traced the rise of this eminent person, it now remains for us briefly to narrate his fall. Exciting by his extraordinary prosperity the envy of his contemporaries, and incurring by his barbarous treatment of his brother, Lord Seymour, of Sudley, the hostility of the people, it required no great effort to hurl him from his giddy pre-eminence; and when he did fall the recollection of his having signed the death-warrant of his own brother, deprived him of much public sympathy. The moment he affixed his signature to that deed of fratricide his own doom was signed; and it was generally observed, that with his left hand he had cut off his right. Persons of his own rank designated him a blood-sucker and murderer, and declared aloud, that it was unfit that the king should remain under the protection of so ravenous a wolf. "Besides," (Sir William Dugdale writes,) "many well disposed minds conceived a very hard opinion of him, for causing a church near Strand bridge, and two bishop's houses, to be pulled down, to make a site for his new building, called SOMERSET HOUSE, in digging the foundation whereof the bones of many, who had been there buried, were cast up, and carried into the fields. And because the stones of that church and those houses were not sufficient for that work, the steeple, and most part of the church of St. John of Hierusalem, near Smithfield, were mined and overthrown with powder, and the stones carried thereto. So likewise the cloister on the north side of St. Paul's Cathedral, and the charnel house on the south side thereof, with the chapel, the tombes and monuments therein being all beaten down, the bones of the dead carried into Finsbury fields, and the stones converted to this building: and it was confidently affirmed, that for the same purpose he intended to have pulled down St. Margaret's church, at Westminster, but that the standing thereof was preserved by his fall." The duke's great rival and most bitter foe was John Dudley, Viscount L'Isle, afterwards Earl of Warwick and Duke of Northumberland. This nobleman, observing the gathering storm around the PROTECTOR, availed himself of it, and retired from court, accompanied by eighteen other influential members of the privy council. A course of proceedings ensued which compelled Somerset to remove the king from Hampton Court to Windsor, and finally terminated in placing the PROTECTOR himself at the mercy of his enemies. His grace was brought from Windsor, a prisoner, to London, and conducted on horseback through Holborn, between the Earls of Southampton and Huntingdon, followed by lords and gentlemen to the number of three hundred, all on horseback, to the Tower; where he was afterwards waited upon by certain lords of the council, who laid before him a list of twenty-eight articles of impeachment, to which they required his immediate answer. To these Somerset was induced to subscribe with his own hand an acknowledgment of guilt, and to offer at the same time to sue, upon his knees, to the king for pardon. This humble bearing saved his life; but he was stripped of his great offices of PROTECTOR, TREASURER, and MARSHAL, lost all his goods,

and nearly two thousand pounds in lands. Subsequently working by the most abject submission upon the feelings of the king, he was released from his imprisonment, his fines remitted, and his lands, save those which had been given away, restored. Within a short interval, too, he was feasted by the king, with a great shew of favour, and resworn of the privy council. A reconciliation was likewise effected between him and Dudley, who had become Earl of Warwick, and his grace's daughter was married to the earl's son and heir, Lord L'Isle. But this alliance was found to be no cement to the new-born friendship, nor was it sufficiently strong to preserve even the semblance of good feeling between the rival noblemen. Somerset was soon after accused of meditating the assassination of Warwick, who was then Duke of Northumberland, and being committed, with his duchess, to the Tower, was arraigned at Westminster Hall on the 1st December, 1551, before the Marquess of Winchester, then lord treasurer, as high steward for the occasion, and twenty-seven other peers, on five distinct charges, viz.

1. Of raising men in the northern parts of the realm.
2. Of assembling men to kill the Duke of Northumberland.
3. Of resisting his attachment.
4. Of killing the gens d'armes, and raising London.
5. Of assaulting the lords, and devising their deaths.

To which he pleaded not guilty, and was eventually acquitted of high treason, but convicted of felony, whereupon he had judgment to be hanged: a sentence, which most of our historians say, he might have avoided by praying the benefit of his clergy, but upon a closer inquiry it will be found, that he was thus condemned under a specific statute then in force, which made the conspiring the death of a privy councillor felony, without the benefit of clergy. After conviction he was detained nearly two months in prison, when he was at length brought to the scaffold on Tower Hill, 22nd January, 1552, and being attainted HIS HONOURS were supposed to have become FORFEITED. Amongst his grace's other dignities we had neglected to state that he was a KNIGHT OF THE GARTER. The duke's character differed entirely from that of his brother, Thomas, Lord Seymour, of Sudley. Dugdale says, "that Thomas was a person of great courage, courtly in fashion, in personage stately, in voice magnificent, but somewhat empty in matter. The duke greatest in favour with the people; Sudley most respected by the nobility; both highly esteemed by the king; both fortunate alike in their advancements; both ruined alike by their own vanity and folly. Both so well affected to the king, that the one might well be termed his sword, the other his target." His grace m. first, Katherine, daughter and co-heir of Sir William Filliol, of Woodlands, in the county of Dorset, and had issue,

EDWARD (Sir), of Berry Pomeroy, from whom descended Francis Seymour, created Lord Conway, ancestor of the extant Marquesses of Hertford; and Sir Edward Seymour, Bart., who succeeded as eighth Duke of

Somerset, and was grandfather of the present duke (see *Burke's Peerage and Baronetage.*)

John (Sir).

The duke espoused, secondly, Anne, daughter and heir of Sir Edward Stanhope, Knt., of Shelford, in the county of Notts, (by Elizabeth, his wife, great grand-daughter of William Bourchier, Earl of Ewe, in Normandy, by Anne, his wife, daughter, and at length sole heir, of Thomas, of Woodstock, Duke of Gloucester, youngest son of Edward III.) By this lady he had

> EDWARD, created Baron Beauchamp, of Hache, and Earl of Hertford.
>
> Anne, m. first, to John Dudley, commonly called Earl of Warwick, eldest son of John, Duke of Northumberland, and secondly, to Sir Edward Umpton, K.B.
>
> Margaret, } *d.* unmarried.
> Jane, }
>
> Mary, m. first, to Andrew Rogers, Esq., eldest son of Sir Richard Rogers, Knt., of Brianston, in the county of Dorset, and secondly, to Sir Henry Payton, Knt.
>
> Katherine, *d.* unmarried.
>
> Elizabeth, m. to Sir Richard Knightley, Knt.

The only son of the attainted duke, by his second wife,

SIR EDWARD SEYMOUR, upon whom the chief honours of his father were especially entailed, was created, by Queen Elizabeth, by letters patent, dated 13th January, 1559, BARON BEAUCHAMP, *of Hache*, and EARL OF HERTFORD. This nobleman incurred subsequently the displeasure of the queen, by marrying without her consent the Lady Catherine Grey, daughter of Henry, Duke of Suffolk, for which offence he had to pay a fine of five thousand pounds, and to endure nine years' incarceration; while the unhappy lady, being also committed to the Tower, was only released by death. The validity of this marriage was finally established at common law, by the verdict of a jury, of which John Digby, Esq., of Coleshill, was foreman. By this lady his lordship had three sons and one daughter, viz.

> 1. EDWARD, Lord *Beauchamp*, who, in the 6th of James I., obtained letters patent, that himself and the heirs male of his body, after the decease of his father, should be barons of parliament, and have place and voice therein. And also letters patent for the enjoyment of the Earldom of Hertford after his said father's decease. His lordship died however before that nobleman. He m. Honora, daughter of Sir Richard Rogers, of Bryanston, in the county of Dorset, and had issue,
>
>> Edward, who m. Anne, daughter of Robert, Earl of Dorset, and d. before his grandfather.
>>
>> WILLIAM (Sir), successor to his grandfather.
>>
>> FRANCIS (Sir), created 19th February, 1641, BARON SEYMOUR, *of Trowbridge*, in the county of Wilts. His lordship m. first, Frances, daughter and heir

of Sir Gilbert Prinne, of Allington, Wilts, and had issue,

>> FRANCIS, his successor.
>>
>> Frances, m. to Sir William Ducie.

Lord Seymour of Trowbridge espoused, secondly, Catherine, daughter of Sir Robert Lee, but had no issue. He d. in 1664, and was s. by his son,

>> CHARLES, second Lord Seymour, of Trowbridge, who m. first, Mary, daughter and sole heir of Thomas Smith, Esq., of Foley, by whom he had surviving issue,
>>
>>> Catherine, *d.* unmarried.
>>> Frances, m. to Sir George Hungerford, Bart.
>>
>> His lordship espoused, secondly, Elisabeth, daughter of William, Lord Allington, and had issue,
>>
>>> Francis.
>>> Charles.
>>
>> He *d.* in 1665, and was s. by his elder son,
>>
>>> FRANCIS, third Lord Trowbridge, who inherited as fifth DUKE OF SOMERSET.
>
> 2. Thomas, m. to Isabel, daughter of Edward Onley, Esq., of Catesby, in the county of Northampton, and died *s. p.*
> 3. Edward.
> 1. Catherine, who *d.* young.

The earl espoused, secondly, Frances, sister to Charles, Earl of Nottingham, and thirdly, Frances, daughter of Thomas, Viscount Howard of Bindon, but had issue by neither. He *d.* at an advanced age in 1621, and was s. by his grandson,

SIR WILLIAM SEYMOUR, second Earl of Hertford, who was created 3d June, 1640, MARQUESS OF HERTFORD. He had previously incurred the displeasure of *King JAMES I.*, by marrying without his majesty's consent, Arabella Stewart, for which himself and his wife were committed to the Tower; whence his lordship found means to escape, and passed beyond sea. But the unhappy lady remained a prisoner until her decease. The marquess, during the civil wars, continued faithfully attached to the royal cause, and upon the restoration of the monarchy was made a KNIGHT OF THE GARTER, and restored in 1660, by special act of parliament, to the DUKEDOM OF SOMERSET, with all the privileges as fully and amply, as though the attainder of the *Protector SOMERSET* had never occurred. The duke m. secondly, Lady Frances Devereux, daughter of Robert, Earl of Essex, and had issue,

> William, } who both *d.* unmarried.
> Robert, }
>
> Henry, who m. Mary, daughter of Arthur, Lord Capell, and dying in his father's lifetime, left
>
>> WILLIAM, successor to his grandfather.
>>
>> Elisabeth, who had a warrant from King Charles II., conferring upon her the rank and precedency of a duke's daughter. Her ladyship m. Thomas, Lord

Bruce, afterwards Earl of Ailsbury, to whom, as heir of her brother, the Duke of Somerset, she brought a considerable estate.

JOHN, who s. his nephew as Duke of Somerset. Arabella, d. unmarried.

Frances, m. first, to Richard, Viscount Molyneaux; secondly, to Thomas, Earl of Southampton, Lord Treasurer; and thirdly, to Conyers Darcy, son and heir of Conyers, Lord Darcy.

Mary, m. to Heneage, Earl of Winchelsea.

Jane, m. to Charles, Lord Clifford, of Lanesborough, son of Richard, Earl of Burlington.

His grace d. in 1660, and was s. by his grandson,

WILLIAM SEYMOUR, third Duke of Somerset. This nobleman d. in minority, unmarried, in 1671, when his estates devolved upon his sister, Lady Elizabeth Seymour, who m. Thomas, second Earl of Ailsbury, and his honours reverted to his uncle,

JOHN SEYMOUR, as fourth Duke of Somerset. His grace m. Sarah, daughter of Sir Edward Alston, Knt., but died s. p. in 1675, when the MARQUISATE OF HERTFORD became EXTINCT, but the other honours devolved upon his cousin (refer to Francis, third son of Edward, Lord Beauchamp, eldest son of Sir Edward Seymour, son and successor of the PROTECTOR).

FRANCIS SEYMOUR, third Lord Seymour, of Trowbridge, as fifth Duke of Somerset. This nobleman did not, however, long enjoy his elevation. In his travels in Italy visiting the church of the Augustinians, at Lerice, with some French gentlemen, his grace or one of his party was said to have insulted in the church some ladies of the family of Botti, for which supposed affront he was shot dead by Horatio Botti, husband to one of the ladies, at his inn door, (April, 1678,) when, dying unmarried, his honours devolved upon his brother,

CHARLES SEYMOUR, sixth Duke of Somerset. This nobleman was made a Knight of the Garter by King Charles II., and was of the privy council to King James II. He was subsequently, however, a promoter of the revolution, and in the reign of William, was constituted president of the council. His grace was one of the commissioners for the union with Scotland, temp. Queen Anne, and upon the accession of King George I., he was sworn of the privy council, and appointed master of the horse. His grace espoused, first, Lady JOCELINE PERCY, only daughter of Josceline, eleventh Earl of Northumberland, K.G., and the GREAT HEIRESS of the illustrious house of PERCY, by whom he had issue,

ALGERNON, his successor.

Percy, } d. unmarried.
Charles, }

Elizabeth, m. to Henry O'Brien, Earl of Thomond, and died s. p.

Catherine, m. to Sir William Wyndham, and her eldest son, Sir Charles Wyndham, succeeded his uncle, the Duke of Somerset, as Earl of Egremont.

Frances, d. unmarried.

4/52

Anne, m. to Peregrine Osborn, Marquess of Carmarthen, and afterwards Duke of Leeds. The duke m. secondly, Charlotte, daughter of Daniel, Earl of Winchelsea, and had two daughters,

Frances, m. to JOHN MANNERS, the celebrated Marquess of Granby, and was mother of Charles, fourth Duke of Rutland.

Charlotte, m. to Heneage Finch, Earl of Aylesford.

His grace d. in 1748, and was s. by his eldest son,

ALGERNON SEYMOUR, seventh Duke of Somerset, commonly called the Proud Duke of Somerset. This nobleman m. Frances, daughter of Henry, son of Thomas Thynne, Viscount Weymouth, by whom he had a son, GEORGE, who died in the life-time of his grandfather and father, and a daughter,

ELIZABETH, who m. Sir Hugh Smithson, Baronet, afterwards Duke of Northumberland.

Upon the decease of his mother, in 1722, his grace was summoned no parliament, as BARON PERCY; and he was created, 2nd October, 1749, Baron Warkworth, of Warkworth Castle, and Earl of Northumberland, with remainder, failing his own male issue, to his son-in-law, Sir Hugh Smithson, Baronet, and his male heirs, by the Lady Elizabeth, his wife; in default of which, the dignities of Baroness Warkworth and Countess of Northumberland, to the said Lady Elizabeth and her heirs male. He was further created the next day, Baron Cockermouth, and Earl of Egremont, both in the county of Cumberland, with remainder, failing his issue male, to his nephew, Sir Charles Wyndham, Baronet, by Katherine, his sister, and his issue male; failure of which, to Percy Wyndham, (who assumed the name of O'Bryen, and was created Earl of Thomond, in Ireland,) brother of the said Sir William Wyndham, and his issue male. *Charles*

The duke died in 1750, when the DUKEDOM OF SOMERSET devolved on Sir Edward Seymour, Baronet, (the descendant of Sir Edward Seymour, of Berry Pomeroy, elder son of the PROTECTOR Somerset, by his first wife,) as EIGHTH DUKE, the grandfather of Edward-Adolphus, present Duke of Somerset. The Earldoms of Northumberland and Egremont passed according to the patents, while the EARLDOM OF HEREFORD, VISCOUNTY OF BEAUCHAMP, and BARONY OF SEYMOUR, of Towbridge, became EXTINCT.

ARMS.—Quarterly, first and fourth or. on a pile gules between six fleur-de-lis, az. three lions of England, (being the coat of augmentation, granted by Henry VIII., on his marriage with Jane Seymour,) second and third gu. two wings conjoined in lure, tips downwards, or.

SEYMOUR—BARONS SEYMOUR, OF TROWBRIDGE.

By Letters Patent, dated 19th February, 1641.

Refer to SEYMOUR, *Viscounts Beauchamp of Hache, Dukes of Somerset, &c.*

SEYMOUR—BARON SEYMOUR, OF SUDLEY.

By Letters Patent, dated 16th February, 1547.

Lineage.

SIR THOMAS SEYMOUR, brother of the celebrated PROTECTOR Somerset, and of Jane Seymour, Queen Consort of Henry VIII., was elevated to the peerage by King Edward VI., 16th February, 1547, as BARON SEYMOUR, *of Sudley, in the county of Gloucester.* His lordship was lord high admiral of England, and a privy councillor. He espoused the QUEEN *Dowager,* Katherine (Parr), who d. in child-bed, in 2nd of Edward VI. His lordship, in the reign of his brother-in-law, had distinguished himself in arms, and was esteemed a person of lofty bearing, but turbulent, fierce, and ambitious. Conspiring against the power of his brother the PROTECTOR, and paying court to the *Lady* ELIZABETH, daughter of *King* HENRY VIII., with whom he was upon the point of contracting a private marriage, he was committed to the Tower by parliament, and condemned without any form of trial. The parliament was soon after dissolved, and his lordship was beheaded on the 6th day succeeding, under the warrant of his brother, the Duke of Somerset. Dying without issue, the BARONY OF SEYMOUR, *of Sudley,* would have become EXTINCT, had it not fallen under the ATTAINDER.

ARMS.—Same as Seymour, Viscounts Beauchamp of Hache, &c.

SHAUNDE—EARL OF BATH.

By Letters Patent, dated 6th January, 1485.

Lineage.

PHILIBERT DE SHAUNDE, a native of Brittany, having promoted the cause of the Earl of Richmond, was raised to the peerage of England, by that personage, after he had ascended the throne as Henry VII., in the dignity of EARL OF BATH, by letters patent, dated 6th January, 1485, but of his lordship or family nothing further is known.

ARMS.—Ar. on a cross sa. a leopard's head or.

SHEFFIELD—BARONS SHEFFIELD, OF BUTTERWICKE, IN THE COUNTY OF LINCOLN, EARLS OF MULGRAVE, MARQUESSES OF NORMANBY, DUKES OF NORMANBY, DUKES OF BUCKINGHAM.

Barony,		16th February, 1547.
Earldom,		7th February, 1626.
Marquisate,	by Letters	10th May, 1694.
Dukedom of Normanby,	Patent,	9th March, 1703.
Dukedom of Buckingham,		23rd March, 1703.

Lineage.

The family of Sheffield attained importance so early as the reign of Henry III., when

SIR ROBERT SHEFFIELD, Knt., flourished. He was s. by his son,

ROBERT SHEFFIELD, who m. Anne, daughter and co-heiress of Sir Simon Goure, and was s. by his son,

SIR ROBERT SHEFFIELD, who m. Genette, eldest daughter and co-heir of Alexander Lownde, of Butterwike, in the county of Lincoln, and thus became possessed of that lordship. From this Sir Robert descended

SIR ROBERT SHEFFIELD, who, in the 2nd of Henry VII., was one of the commanders in the royal army, against John, Earl of Lincoln, and his adherents, at the battle of Stoke. Sir Robert was afterwards speaker of the House of Commons, and recorder of London. He m. Helen, daughter and heiress of Sir John Delves, Knt., and was s. by his son,

SIR ROBERT SHEFFIELD, of Butterwike, who m. Margaret, daughter of Sir John Zouche, of Codnor, and left a son,

EDMUND SHEFFIELD, who was advanced to the peerage, on the 16th February, 1547, (two days before the coronation of King Edward VIth,) in the dignity of BARON SHEFFIELD, *of Butterwike, in the county of Lincoln.* The next year, his lordship having accompanied the Marquess of Northampton, to suppress the rebellion of Ket, in Norfolk, lost his life in the conflict. He had m. the lady Anne Vere, daughter of John, Earl of Oxford, and left issue,

JOHN, his successor.

Frances, m. to —— Metham, Esq.

Eleanor, m. to Denzel Holles, Esq., second son of Sir William Holles, Knt., of Houghton, in the county of Notts.

Elizabeth.

His lordship was s. by his son,

JOHN SHEFFIELD, second Baron Sheffield. This nobleman m. Douglas, daughter of William, Lord Howard, of Effingham, by whom (who espoused, secondly, Dudley, Earl of Leicester) he had issue,

EDMUND, his successor.

Elizabeth, m. to Thomas, Earl of Ormonde.

His lordship d. in 1569, and was s. by his son,

EDMUND SHEFFIELD, third baron. This nobleman distinguished himself in arms, in the reign of Queen Elizabeth, particularly in the celebrated defeat of the formidable ARMADA. He was subsequently made governor of the BRILL, and in the same reign, a Knight of the Garter. By King James I., his lordship was constituted president of the council, for the northern parts of the realm; and created by the succeeding monarch, on 7th February, 1626, EARL OF MULGRAVE. He m. first, Ursula, daughter of Sir Robert Tirwhit, of Ketilby, in the county of Lincoln, and had no less than fifteen children, of whom, Charles, d. unmarried, in the life-time of his father.

JOHN (Sir), m. Griseld, daughter of Sir Edmund Anderson, Chief Justice of the Court of Common Pleas, and dying in the lifetime of his father, left a son,

EDMUND, who s. his grandfather.

Margaret, m. to Walter Walsh, Esq., of Cas-the Hoel, in Ireland, and her second daughter and co-heiress,

  URSULA WALSH, espoused John Bryan, Esq., of Bawnmore, in the county of Kilkenny (his second wife). The only surviving child and heiress of this marriage,

    ELIZABETH BRYAN, marrying Oliver Grace, Esq., M.P. of Shanganah, in the Queen's county, a portion of the Sheffield property came, eventually, into the Grace family, and is at present enjoyed by

      Sir William Grace, Baronet.

Elizabeth, m. first, to Sir Edward Swift, Knt., and secondly, to Sir John Bourchier.

Mary, m. to Sir Ferdinand Fairfax.

Frances, m. to Sir Philip Fairfax.

Triphena, m. to George Verney, Esq.

His lordship espoused, secondly, Mariana, daughter of Sir William Urwyn, Knt., by whom he had three other sons and two daughters. He d. at eighty years of age, in 1646, and was s. by his grandson,

EDMUND SHEFFIELD, second Earl of Mulgrave, who m. Lady Elizabeth Cranfield, daughter of Lionel, Earl of Middlesex, and dying in 1658, was s. by his only son,

JOHN SHEFFIELD, third Earl of Mulgrave. This nobleman, who became one of the most eminent personages of the period in which he lived, first attained distinction in arms; being in the great sea fight at Sold-Bay, and afterwards captain of the Royal Catherine. In 1674, he was installed a Knight of the Garter, and soon after made gentleman of the bed-chamber to King Charles II. He was at the same time appointed colonel of the old Holland regiment, governor of Hull, and entrusted with the command of the forces sent to Tangier. In the 1st James II., his lordship was sworn of the privy council, and constituted LORD CHAMBERLAIN OF THE HOUSEHOLD. After the revolution, he was sworn of the new privy council, and created by King William, 10th May, 1694, MARQUESS OF NORMANBY, in the county of Lincoln. His lordship was further advanced, 2nd Queen Anne, 9th March, 1703, to the DUKEDOM OF NORMANBY, and created in a fortnight afterwards, DUKE OF BUCKINGHAM. The duke aspired to the fame of a man of letters, as well as a soldier and a statesman; and his literary productions have attained some popularity—but his abilities as a writer have been, of course, differently estimated.

Dryden (no great authority to be sure, when a nobleman is in question) says: "His thoughts are always just, his numbers harmonious, his words chosen, his expressions strong and manly, his verse flowing, and his turns as happy as they are easy." Walpole on the contrary thus characterises the noble scribe.

"The life of this peer takes up fourteen pages and a half, in folio, in the General Dictionary, where it has little pretensions to occupy a couple. But his pious relict was always purchasing places for him herself, and their son, in every suburb of

the temple of fame: a tenure, against which, above all others, quo warranto's are sure to take place. The author of the article in the Dictionary, calls the duke one of the most beautiful prose writers, and greatest poets of this age; which is also, he says, proved by the finest writers his contemporaries; certificates that have little weight, where the merit is not proved by the author's own works. It is certain, that his grace's compositions in prose have nothing extraordinary in them; his poetry is most indifferent; and the greatest part of both is already fallen into total neglect. It is said, that he wrote, in hopes of being confounded with his predecessor in the title; but he would more easily have been mistaken with the other Buckingham, if he had never written at all. He had a great deal of bravery, and understood a court. Queen Anne, who undoubtedly had no turn to gallantry, yet so far resembled her predecessor, Elizabeth, as not to dislike a little homage to her person. This duke was immediately rewarded, on her accession, for having made love to her before her marriage. Though attached to the house of Stewart and their principles, he maintained a dignity of honour in some points, independent of all connections; for he ridiculed King James's religion, though he attended him to his chapel; and warmly took the part of the Catalans against the Tory ministry, whom he had helped to introduce to the queen."

His grace m. first, Ursula, daughter of Colonel Stawel, and widow of the Earl of Conway, by whom he had no issue. He espoused, secondly, Catherine, daughter of Fulke Grevile, Lord Brooke, and widow of Baptist, Earl of Gainsborough, who also died issueless, in 1703-4; and the duke m. thirdly, Catherine, natural daughter of King James II., (by Catherine, daughter of Sir Charles Sidley, Baronet,) and widow of James, Earl of Anglesey, by whom he had three sons and a daughter, one of which, EDMUND, alone survived infancy.

His grace[*] died in 1721, and was s. by his son,

EDMUND SHEFFIELD, second Duke of Buckingham. This young nobleman served in 1734, as

---

[*] His grace left an illegitimate son, by a Mrs. Lambert, called,

  CHARLES HERBERT, who, at the decease of Edmund, the last duke, succeeded to a great part of the estates, including Normanby, in the county of Lincoln, and assumed by the will of his father, the surname of SHEFFIELD; he was created a baronet, in 1755, and the present Sir Robert Sheffield is his grandson and successor.

The family of Phipps, existing Earls of Mulgrave, were connected with the Sheffields, by William Phipps, Esq., grandfather of the present Earl Mulgrave, marrying Lady Catherine Annesley, only daughter and heiress of James, fourth Earl of Anglesey, by Catherine, natural daughter of King James II., which Catherine espoused, secondly, JOHN SHEFFIELD, Duke of Buckingham, and by him was mother of

Edmund, the last Duke of Buckingham, which Edmund was thus half brother to the said Lady Catherine Annesley, wife of William Phipps.

a volunteer, under the command of his uncle, the Duke of Berwick, in Germany, and was an aid-de-camp at the siege of Fort Kiel and Philipsburgh, where that eminent general lost his life. His grace died, however, the following year at Rome, of a rapid consumption, not having attained majority, and with him, the honours and male line of the DUCAL house of SHEFFIELD, EXPIRED.

ARMS.—Ar. a chevron between three garbs gules.

SHERARD — VISCOUNT SHERARD.

By Letters Patent, dated 31st October, 1718.

Lineage.

The Right Honourable
BENNET SHERARD, third Baron Harborough, in the peerage of Ireland, and first Lord Sherard in England, was created by letters patent, dated 31st October, 1718, VISCOUNT SHERARD, *of Stapleford, in the county of Leicester,* with remainder to his issue male, and advanced subsequently to the earldom of Harborough, with a special limitation. His lordship m. Mary, daughter of Sir Henry Calverley, Knt., of Ayerholme, in the bishoprick of Durham, but dying without surviving issue in 1732, when the English barony, and the earldom, and the Irish barony, devolved, according to the patent, upon Philip Sherard, Esq., ancestor of the present Earl of Harborough, but the VISCOUNTY OF SHERARD became EXTINCT.

ARMS.—Ar. a chevron, gu. between three torteauxes.

SIDLEY — COUNTESS OF DORCHESTER.

By Letters Patent, dated 2nd January, 1686.

Lineage.

CATHERINE SIDLEY, (only daughter of Sir Charles Sidley, Bart., of Southfield, in the county of Kent,) mistress of King JAMES II., was created by that monarch, 2nd January, 1686, *Baroness of Darlington, in the county of Durham,* and COUNTESS OF DORCHESTER, *for life.* By his majesty, her ladyship had an only surviving daughter,

Lady CATHERINE DARNLEY, who m. first, James Annesley, third Earl of Anglesey, by whom she had an only daughter,
    Lady CATHERINE ANNESLEY, who m. William Phipps, Esq., son of Sir Constantine Phipps, Knt., LORD CHANCELLOR OF IRELAND, and had a son,
        CONSTANTINE PHIPPS, who was created BARON MULGRAVE, in the peerage of Ireland : a dignity inherited by the present EARL MULGRAVE.

Her ladyship being divorced from Lord Anglesey, for cruelty and causeless ill-treatment on her husband's part, espoused secondly, John Sheffield, Duke of Buckingham, by whom she was mother of Edmund, second duke.

The countess, after the dissolution of her connec-

tion with the king, married Sir David Colyear, subsequently EARL OF PORTMORE, by whom she left one only surviving son, CHARLES, second *Earl of Portmore,* (the grandfather of the present earl). The conduct of this lady made so strong an impression upon the honourable mind of her father, Sir Charles Sidley, that he conceived ever after a rooted hatred to her royal paramour, and was a zealous promoter of the revolution. Being asked one day, why he appeared so warm against the king, who had created his daughter a countess, he replied, "it was from gratitude; for as his majesty had made his daughter *a countess,* it was but fit he should do all he could to make his daughter *a queen.*"

Her ladyship d. in 1692, when ALL HER HONOURS became as a matter of course EXTINCT.

SMITH—BARONS CARRINGTON.

By Letters Patent, dated 31st October, 1643.

Lineage.

This family deduced its line from
SIR MICHAEL CARINGTON, Knt., standard bearer to King RICHARD I. in the Holy Land, from whom descended
JOHN CARINGTON, who, in the beginning of HENRY IV.'s reign, having stoutly adhered to the deposed monarch, RICHARD II., was obliged to expatriate himself, and after residing some time abroad to assume for security the very general surname of SMITH. From this gentleman lineally sprang
JOHN SMITH, Esq., who being the lord treasurer's remembrancer in the exchequer, was constituted, in the 38th Henry VIII., second baron of that court. This learned person m. Anne, daughter and heir of John Harewell, Esq., of Wotton, in the county of Warwick, and from that union descended
SIR CHARLES SMITH, Knt., who, for his fidelity to King CHARLES I., was elevated to the peerage 31st October, 1643, as LORD CARRINGTON, *Baron of Wotton Waven,* in the county of Warwick, and was advanced on the 4th November following, to the dignity of Viscount Carrington, in the peerage of Ireland. His lordship m. Elisabeth, daughter of Sir John Carrill, Knt., of South Harting, in Sussex, and had issue,

FRANCIS, his successor.
Carrill.
John, who fell fighting under the royal banner at Ailesford in 1644.
Mary, m. to Sir George Wintour, Knt., of Huddington.
Lucy, } d. unmarried.
Anne, }
Margaret, m. to Sir Francis Hungate, Bart., of Huddleston, in Yorkshire.
Mary, d. unmarried.

Lord Carrington having occasion to visit France, and lodging at *Pontoise,* was there barbarously murdered by one of his own servants, on the 21st February, 1664, for the sake of his money and jewels; and his remains lieth interred in the church at that place, under a marble tomb erected to his memory. His lordship was *s.* by his eldest son,

FRANCIS SMITH, second Baron Carrington, and second viscount. This nobleman *m.* first, Juliana, daughter of Sir Thomas Walmesley, of Dunkenhalgh, in Lancashire, by whom he had an only son,

CHARLES, who *d.* in infancy.

His lordship espoused, secondly, Lady Anne Herbert, daughter of William, Marquess of Powis, but had no issue. He *d.* in 1705, when ALL HIS HONOURS became EXTINCT.

ARMS.—Ar. a cross, gu. between four peacocks, ar.

SOMERS—BARON SOMERS.

By Letters Patent, dated 2nd December, 1697.

Lineage.

JOHN SOMERS, the son of an eminent attorney in the city of Worcester, (John Somers, Esq., of Clifton-upon-Severn, in Worcestershire, by Catherine Severne, his wife,) having been brought up to the higher grade in the legal profession, acquired such reputation as an advocate, that he was engaged in the important case of the seven bishops, temp. JAMES II., and his speech upon that occasion will ever be regarded as one of the boldest, most impressive, and constitutional, delivered at the bar. After the revolution, Mr. Somers was appointed successively solicitor and attorney-general, and he received the usual honour of knighthood. In 1697 he was constituted LORD CHANCELLOR OF ENGLAND, and elevated to the peerage as LORD SOMERS, *Baron of Evesham,* in the county of Worcester. Of this great and learned personage, Walpole, in his Catalogue of Noble Authors, observes, " That all the traditional accounts of him, the historians of the last age, and its best authors, represent him as the most uncorrupt lawyer, and the honestest statesman: a master orator: a genius of the finest taste; and as a patriot of the noblest and most extensive views: as a man who dispensed blessings by his life, and planned them for posterity: at once the model of Addison, and the touchstone of Swift."

His lordship survived, however, his great mental powers, and *d.* in dotage, unmarried, anno 1716, when the BARONY OF SOMERS became EXTINCT, and his estates devolved upon his sisters as co-heirs, of whom,

MARY SOMERS, *m.* Charles Cocks, Esq., M.P. in 1692 for the city of Worcester, and had, with other issue,

Margaret Cocks, who *m.* Philip Yorke, afterwards LORD CHANCELLOR, AND EARL OF HARDWICKE.

And

JOHN COCKS, Esq., (successor to his father,) of Bruckmans, in the county of Hertford, M.P., who was *s.* by his son,

JOHN COCKS, Esq., at whose decease, unmarried, the estates reverted to his uncle,

JOHN COCKS, Esq., of Castleditch, whose eldest son and successor,

CHARLES COCKS, Esq., of Castleditch, M.P., was created a baronet in 1772, and elevated to the peerage as LORD SOMERS, *Baron of Evesham,* in 1784. His lordship *d.* in 1806, and was *s.* by his eldest son,

JOHN SOMERS COCKS, present *Earl of Somers.*

ARMS.—Vert, a fesse dancette, erm.

SOMERIE—BARON DUDLEY.

By Writ of Summons, dated 10th March, 1308, 1 Edward II.

Lineage.

In the reign of HENRY II.,

JOHN DE SOMERIE acquired the barony of DUDLEY, in Staffordshire, by marrying Hawyse, sister and heir of Gervase Paganell,* its former feudal lord, and was *s.* by his son,

RALPH DE SOMERIE, feudal lord of DUDLEY, who in the sixth of John, obtained from the crown, in exchange for the manor of Wolverhampton, (which was then granted to Hubert, Archbishop of Canterbury,) the manor of Swinford, and two other manors; which were thenceforth to be held by him and his heirs in fee; paying yearly to the exchequer by the hands of the sheriff of Staffordshire, the sum

* At the time of the GENERAL SURVEY,

RALPH PAGANELL possessed ten lordships in Devon, five in Somerset, fifteen in Lincoln, and the same number in Yorkshire. He was *s.* by his son,

FULK PAGANELL, who *m.* Beatrix, daughter and heir of William Fitz-Asculph, and thereby acquired the CASTLE OF DUDLEY, and other large estates in the county of Stafford. He was *s.* by his son and heir,

RALPH PAGANELL, *Lord of Dudley,* who was *s.* by his eldest son,

GERVASE PAGANELL, who adhering to the Empress Maud in 1138, against Stephen, held the castle of Dudley for that princess and her son. In the 19th Henry II., on the assessment in aid for marrying the king's daughter, he certified his knights' fees to be altogether fifty-six, and one third. In the 1st of Richard I., he was one of the barons who assisted at the coronation of that monarch. He *m.* Isabel, daughter of Robert, Earl of Leicester, widow of Simon St. Liz, Earl of Northampton, by whom he had issue,

Robert, who, it is presumed, died young.

HAWYSE, who became eventually sole heiress of the Paganells, and conveyed DUDLEY Castle and their other estates to her first husband, JOHN DE SOMERIE, as in the text. She espoused, secondly, Roger de Berkeley.

of £30., which was the ancient farm; and £5. more of increment, by equal payments at Michaelmas and Easter; performing to the king and his heirs the service of one knight's fee. He d. in 1210, and was s. by his son,

WILLIAM PERCEVAL DE SOMERIE, who by reason of his minority at his father's death, was in ward for his barony, which then consisted of ten knights' fees, and three parts. He d. in 1221, and was s. by his son,

NICHOLAS DE SOMERIE, at whose decease in 1226 issueless, the barony and lands reverted to his uncle,

ROGER DE SOMERIE, who performing his homage in the same year had livery thereof, but in four years afterwards those lands were seised by the crown, in consequence of their lord neglecting when summoned, to receive the honour of knighthood. This Roger de Somerie m. Nicola, daughter of William de Albini, second Earl of Arundel, and sister and co-heir of Hugh, fourth earl, by whom he acquired the manor of BARWE, in the county of Leicester. In the 37th HENRY III., he attended the king in an expedition into Gascony, and in the 41st and 42nd of the same reign, he had military summonses to march against the Welsh: after which, he began to make a castle of his manor house at DUDLEY, but was prohibited by the king to proceed therein, without his special licence; subsequently, however, adhering to the crown in the baronial war, he obtained the said licence, and he was afterwards made prisoner at the battle of LEWES, fighting under the royal banner. By his first wife, the co-heir of Albini, he had four daughters, viz.

JOANE, m. to John le Strange,
MABEL, m. to Walter de Sulcy,
MAUD, m. to Henry de Erdington,
MARGERY, m. first, to Ralph
Cromwell, of Tatshal, and secondly, to William Bifield.

} These ladies inherited their mother's estate.

Roger de Somerie espoused, secondly, Amabel, daughter and heir of Sir Robert de Chaucombe, Knt., and widow of Gilbert de Segrave, by whom he had issue,

ROGER, his successor.
John.
Margaret, m. to Ralph Basset, of Drayton.

He d. in 1272, and was s. by his elder son,

ROGER DE SOMERIE, who d. in 1290, and was s. by his son,

ROGER DE SOMERIE. This feudal lord died s. p., and was s. by his brother,

SIR JOHN DE SOMERIE, K.B., who, for his services in the Scottish wars, temp. Edward I. and Edward II., was summoned to parliament as a BARON* from 10th March, 1308, to 14th March,

---

*Although this barony is uniformly considered to be that of "DUDLEY," it appears very questionable if such is the proper designation. That antecedent to the latter part of the reign of EDWARD I., the tenure of the castle of Dudley constituted the family of SOMERIE, barons by tenure, can scarcely be doubted; but that such tenure did not establish a right in the possessor of the castle to demand a

1322. His lordship d. in the latter year, without issue, when his BARONY became EXTINCT, and his castles and lands devolved upon his sisters, as co-heirs, thus,

     MARGARET, m. to John de Sutton, had the CASTLE OF DUDLEY, with the manor of Leggenley, chase of Pensnet, and manor of New Synford-Regis, in the county of Stafford; as also the town of Dudley (see Sutton, Barons Dudley).

     JOANE, m. to Thomas Botetourt, eldest son and heir of John, Lord Botetourt, had the manors of Bradfield, Soleham, and Bastenden, in the county of Berks; with Rowley-Somery, and other lands in Staffordshire (see Botetourt, Barons Botetourt).

ARMS.—Or, two lioncels passant as.

STAFFORD — BARONS STAFFORD, EARLS OF STAFFORD, DUKES OF BUCKINGHAM, BARONS STAFFORD.

Barony, by Writ of Summons, dated 6th Feb., 1299, 27 Edward I.
Earldom, 5th March, 1351.
Dukedom, 14th September, 1444.
Barony, ———, 1547.

Lineage.

The first that assumed this surname,

ROBERT DE STAFFORD, possessed, at the time of the general survey, lordships in Suffolk, Gloucestershire, Lincolnshire, Warwickshire, and Staffordshire, in all one hundred and thirty-one—and Dugdale surmises, that the assumption of the surname of Stafford arose from his being governor of Stafford Castle, which had been erected by the Conqueror: for his name originally was DE TOENEI, and he is said to have been a younger son of Roger de Toenei, standard bearer of Normandy. Of this Robert de Stafford, who lived till Henry I.'s time, nothing further is known than his founding an AUGUSTINE PRIORY, at Stone, in Staffordshire, upon the spot where Enysan de Waltone, one of the companions of the Conqueror, had killed two nuns and a priest. He m. Avice de Clare, and was s. by his son,

NICHOLAS DE STAFFORD, who was sheriff of Staffordshire, temp. King Henry I. This feudal lord was s. by his son,

ROBERT DE STAFFORD, who was sheriff of Staffordshire from the second to the end of the sixth year, inclusive, of King Henry II.'s reign, and in six years afterwards paid towards the marriage portion of the king's daughter sixty marks

---

writ of summons to parliament, may be inferred from this fact, that John de Somerie, who was first summoned in 1308 (1st Edward II.) and who continued to be regularly summoned to 1322 (15th Edward II.) is never once designated as "DE DUDLEY," but is merely described as "Johanni de Somery."—NICOLAS.

for sixty knights' fees. This Robert performed a pilgrimage to Jerusalem, and d. about the year 1176, was s. by his son,

ROBERT DE STAFFORD, at whose decease, without issue, the feudal barony and lordships devolved upon his only sister and heiress,

MILISENT DE STAFFORD, who m. in the 5th Richard I. a Staffordshire gentleman of ancient family, named HERVEY BAGOT. This Hervey paying a fine of three hundred marks to the crown, had livery of his wife's inheritance, but in order to raise that sum he was obliged to sell the lordship of Drayton to the canons of St. Thomas, near Stafford. The son and heir of this Hervey, and Milisent, assuming his maternal surname, inherited the estates as

HERVEY DE STAFFORD. This feudal lord was with King Henry III. at the siege of Bitham Castle, in Lincolnshire, in the 5th of that monarch's reign. He m. Patronill, sister of William de Ferrers, Earl of Derby, and d. in 1237, was s. by his son,

HERVEY DE STAFFORD, who d. without issue in 1241, and was s. by his brother,

ROBERT DE STAFFORD, who, in the 25th Henry III., upon doing homage, and paying one hundred pounds for his relief, had livery of his lands. This feudal lord was in the wars of Gascony, 39th Henry III., and in four years afterwards he had a military summons to march against the Welsh. He m. Alice, one of the daughters and coheirs of Thomas Corbet, of Caus, in the county of Salop, and d. in 1282, was s. by his son,

NICHOLAS DE STAFFORD. This feudal lord, who was actively engaged against the Welsh, in the reign of King Edward I., was killed before Droselan Castle anno 1287, and was s. by his son,

EDMUND DE STAFFORD, who, having distinguished himself in the Scottish wars, was summoned to parliament, as a BARON, by King Edward I., on the 6th February, 1299—and he had regular summonses from that period until his decease. He m. Margaret, daughter of Ralph, Lord Basset, of Drayton, and had issue,

    RALPH, his successor.

    Richard, m. Maud, daughter and heir of Richard de Camville, of Clifton, and was called "Sir Richard Stafford, of Clifton, Knt." (see Staffords, of Clifton).

His lordship d. in 1308, and was s. by his elder son,

RALPH DE STAFFORD, second baron. This nobleman attaining majority in the 17th Edward II., and then doing his homage, had livery of his father's lands; and the next ensuing year, being made a knight by bathing, and other sacred ceremonies, had robes, &c., as a banneret, allowed him out of the king's wardrobe for the solemnity; after which he soon became a personage of celebrity in the wars of King Edward III. His lordship was first engaged in Scotland for some years, and he then embarked for Britanny, where he was made prisoner at the siege of Nantes. In the 19th Edward III. he was sent into Gascony, with Henry of Lancaster, Earl of Derby, and while that nobleman assaulted Berberath by land, Lord Stafford commanded the force which attacked it by sea. The next year he

was constituted seneschal of Aquitaine, when John, son and heir of Philip, king of France, coming to besiege Aguillon, where his lordship then resided, he stoutly defended that place against the whole power of the French, until King Edward came to his relief, and forced the enemy to raise the siege. After this, joining his troops with the army of King Edward, he had a principal command in the van of the English at the glorious battle of CRESSY. Upon the termination of this great conflict, his lordship being sent with Sir Reginald Cobham, and three heralds, to view the slain, reported the number to be eleven great princes, eighty bannerets, twelve hundred knights, and more than thirty thousand common soldiers. He was afterwards, when Calais surrendered, one of those appointed to take possession of that place for the king; and subsequently, his lordship was one of the ambassadors deputed to the Cardinals of Naples and Cleremont, to treat of peace between King Edward and Philip de Valois, then assuming the title of King of France. The next year he had licence to make castles of his manor houses, at Stafford and Nadeley; as also a grant from the king of £873, for his expenses in foreign service. About this time, his lordship was elected a KNIGHT of the GARTER, being one of the original members of that noble order. In the 24th Edward III., he was in commission with the Bishop of Durham, and the Lords Percy and Nevill, to treat with the nobles of Scotland, at York, for a firm and final peace between the two realms; for all which eminent services, he was created, on 5th March, 1351, EARL OF STAFFORD, and constituted lieutenant and captain-general of the Duchy of Aquitaine. His lordship m. Margaret, only daughter and heiress of Hugh de Audley, Baron Audley, and in right of his wife, EARL OF GLOUCESTER—by which alliance he acquired a considerable inheritance, and the BARONY OF AUDLEY is presumed to have merged in that of STAFFORD. He had issue,

    Ralph, who m. Maud, daughter of Henry, Earl of Derby, but died in the life-time of his father.

    HUGH, his successor.

    Beatrice, m. first, Maurice, son and heir of Maurice Fitz-Thomas, Earl of Desmond; secondly, Thomas, Lord Ros, of Hamelake; and thirdly, Sir Richard Burley, Knt.

    Joane, m. to John, son and heir of John Cheriton, Lord Powis.

    Elizabeth, m. to Fouke, son of Roger le Strange, of Whitchurch, in the county of Salop.

    Margaret, m. to Sir John Stafford, Knt.

His lordship d. in 1372, and was s. by his only surviving son,

HUGH DE STAFFORD, third Baron and second Earl of Stafford, who, following the steps of his noble father in those martial times, came very early into action, for at the age of seventeen he was in the wars of France, and again when he attained majority, being then in the retinue of the Black Prince. At the period he succeeded to the honours of his family, he was twenty-eight years of age, and he was subsequently, distinguished in all the wars of

Edward III., and in those at the beginning of King Richard II.'s time. In the 9th of the latter monarch, his lordship having obtained licence to travel, undertook a pilgrimage to the Holy Sepulchre, and in his return, died at Rhodes, in 1396, having had issue by his wife, the Lady Philippa Beauchamp, daughter of Thomas, Earl of Warwick.

> Ralph, who was murdered by John Holland, half-brother to King Richard II.

> THOMAS, WILLIAM, EDMUND, } successors alternately, to the honours of the family.

> Hugh (Sir), m. Elizabeth Bourchier, only daughter and heiress of Bartholomew, Lord Bourchier, and was summoned to parliament as BARON BOURCHIER. His lordship died s. p.

> Margaret, m. to Ralph, first Earl of Westmorland.

> Katherine, m. to Michael, son of Michael de la Pole.

> Joane, m. to Thomas Holland, Earl of Kent.

> Elizabeth, m. to John, Lord Ferrers, of Chartley.

The earl, who was a Knight of the Garter, was s. by his eldest surviving son,

THOMAS DE STAFFORD, fourth baron, and third Earl of Stafford, who in the 14th Richard II., making proof of his age, and doing his homage, had livery of his lands; and about the same time, upon the decease of Ralph, the last Lord Basset, of Drayton, was found to be one of his co-heirs.* His lordship was in the wars of France, in the 15th of Richard II., under the conduct of Thomas of Woodstock, Duke of Gloucester, whose daughter, the Lady Anne Plantagenet, he had married, but died without issue, when he was s. by his brother,

WILLIAM DE STAFFORD, fifth Baron, and fourth Earl of Stafford. This nobleman was but fourteen years of age when he came to the title, and in ward to the Duke of Gloucester. He died in three years after, and the honours devolved upon his next brother,

EDMUND DE STAFFORD, sixth Baron, and fifth Earl of Stafford, who, in the 22d of Richard II., by virtue of the king's special licence, married Anne, Countess of Stafford, widow of Thomas, third earl, his eldest brother (which marriage of the said Thomas and Anne had never been consummated, owing to the tender years of the earl). At the coronation of King Henry IV., this Edmund, Earl of Stafford, was made a Knight of the Bath, as was also Hugh, his younger brother. He was subsequently made a Knight of the Garter, but he was killed soon after, at the battle of Shrewsbury, fighting on the part of the king, anno 1403. His lordship left issue,

> HUMPHREY, his successor.

> Philippa, d. young.

---

* Thus, Margaret Basset, great aunt of the abovementioned Ralph, Lord Basset, was the wife of Edmund, first Lord Stafford, the earl's great-grandfather. For this inheritance he had a contest with the Shirleys.

Anne, m. first, to Edmund Mortimer, Earl of March, and secondly, to John Holland, Earl of Huntingdon.

The earl was s. by his son,

HUMPHREY DE STAFFORD, seventh Baron, and sixth Earl of Stafford, who, in the 2d of Henry VI., making proof of his age, had livery of his lands; as also of those which had descended to him by the death, without issue, of his uncle, Sir Hugh Stafford, Lord Bourchier. In the 6th of the same reign, his lordship obtained licence from the king to be absent from the realm of Ireland for ten years, but nevertheless to receive the revenue of all his castles, lordships, and lands there. From this period he served for several years in France, and was constituted, 19th of Henry VI., captain of the town of Calais, and tower of Risbanke; as also of the marches of Calais: in consequence of which services, and his near alliance in blood to the royal family, he was created, on the 14th September, 1444, DUKE OF BUCKINGHAM, with precedence before all dukes whatsoever, next to those of the blood royal; but a great dispute regarding this matter immediately arose between his grace, and Henry Beauchamp, Duke of Warwick, which required a special act of parliament to adjust, giving to the rival dukes precedency alternately, year about—the question was, however, finally set at rest by the death of the Duke of Warwick, issueless, in about two years after. In the 28th of Henry VI., the Duke of Buckingham was made constable of Dover Castle, and warden of the cinque ports; and in the 34th of the same reign, after the fatal battle of St. Albans, where the Duke of York being victorious, Humphrey, Earl of Stafford, his eldest son, lost his life: seeing what specious pretences were made by the Yorkists, to obtain the favour of the people, his grace, with the Duke of Somerset, made his way privately to Queen Margaret, and apprised her of the danger that impended. Continuing faithfully attached to the Lancastrian interest, the duke fell gallantly fighting under that banner at the battle of Northampton, on the 27th July, 1460. His grace, along with his other honours, was a Knight of the Garter. His wife was the Lady Anne Nevill, daughter of Ralph, first Earl of Westmorland, by whom he had, with other issue,

> HUMPHREY, Earl of Stafford, slain in the battle of St. Albans; leaving by Margaret, daughter and co-heir of Edmund, Duke of Somerset,

>> HENRY, who s. his grandfather.

> Henry (Sir), m. Margaret, Countess of Richmond, mother of King Henry VII.

> John, created Earl of Wiltshire (see Stafford, Earls of Wilts).

> Anne, m. first, to Aubrey de Vere, and secondly, to Sir Thomas Cobham, son of Reginald, Lord Cobham, of Sterborough.

> Joane, m. first, to William, Viscount Beaumont, and secondly, to Sir William Knevet, of Buckingham, in the county of Norfolk.

> Catherine, m. to John Talbot, Earl of Shrewsbury.

The duke was s. by his grandson,

HENRY DE STAFFORD, second Duke of Buckingham, who, being in ward to King Edward IV., was committed with Humphrey, his brother, to the tuition of Anne, Duchess of Exeter, the king's sister, with an assignation of five hundred marks per annum, for their maintenance. This nobleman was little heard of during the remainder of the reign of Edward IV., but being a main instrument in elevating Richard III. to the throne, he was made a Knight of the Garter, and CON-STABLE OF ENGLAND by that monarch; besides being promised the possession of the great inherit-ance of the Bohuns, Earl of Hereford, to which he pretended a right. But whether through disap-pointment at this promise not being afterwards fulfilled, or from a conscientious feeling, certain it is that he soon afterwards entered into a con-spiracy to place the Earl of Richmond upon the throne, and actually took up arms for the purpose; but the Courtenays and his other associates, not being able to second his movements, he found himself deserted, and was forced to seek an asylum at the house of an old servant, Humphrey Banaster, near Shrewsbury: by this servant he was, how-ever, betrayed and delivered up to his enemies, but the king refused to reward the betrayer, ob-serving " that he who could be untrue to so good a master, would be false to all other." The duke was beheaded soon after, in the market-place at Salisbury, anno 1483, without any arraignment, or legal proceeding. His grace had married Ca-therine, daughter of Richard Widville, Earl of Rivers, and left issue,

> EDWARD, his successor.
>
> Henry, created Earl of Wiltshire.
>
> Elizabeth, m. to Robert Ratcliffe, Lord Fitz-Walter.
>
> Anna, m. first, to Sir Walter Herbert, Knt., and secondly, to George, Earl of Hunting-don.

The earl was s. by his elder son,

EDWARD DE STAFFORD, who was restored, by King Henry VII., to the Dukedom of Bucking-ham, Earldom and Barony of Stafford, and all the other honours of his father. This nobleman was in arms against the Cornish-men, who rebelled in favour of Perkin Warbeck; and in the 24th Henry VII. he obtained several considerable grants. He was likewise made a Knight of the Garter, and LORD HIGH CONSTABLE OF ENGLAND. In the 2nd of Henry VIII. he had licence to impark a thousand acres of land at his lordship of Thornbury, in Gloucestershire, and was then in high favour with the king. But in some years afterwards, exciting the enmity of Wolsey, that ambitious prelate planned, and finally succeeded, in accomplishing his grace's ruin. It is stated that the offence given by the duke to the cardinal arose thus:—His grace upon some occasion holding a bason to the king, so soon as his majesty had washed Wolsey dipped his hands in the water, which appeared so derogatory to the rank of Buckingham, that he flung the con-tents of the ewer into the churchman's shoes; who, being highly incensed, menaced that he would stick upon the duke's skirts: a threat which his grace met by coming to court soon after richly dressed,

but without any skirts—and the king demanding the cause of so strange a fashion, the duke replied, that it was intended to prevent the cardinal's design. The duke, like his father, was doomed, however, to fall by domestic treason, for having discharged one Knevet, a steward, for oppressing his tenantry, that individual became a fit instrument in the hands of Wolsey to effect the object he had so much at heart. Knevet declared that the duke had contemplated the assassination of the king, in order that he might ascend the throne himself as next heir, if his ma-jesty died without issue; and upon this frivolous information one of the most illustrious noblemen in England was arraigned at Westminster, before Thomas, Duke of Norfolk, then sitting as LORD HIGH STEWARD OF ENGLAND for the occasion.

The duke pleaded his own cause, and sustained the character of an able and accomplished advocate, but to no purpose; he was found guilty, and sen-tenced to death. Upon which he addressed the high steward thus:—" My Lord of Norfolk, you have said as a traitor should be said to; but I was never any. I nothing malign you, for what you have done to me; but the eternal God forgive you my death. I shall never sue to the king for life, though he be a gracious prince; and more grace may come from him than I desire; and so I desire you and all my fellows to pray for me." The duke was executed by decapitation in pursuance of the judg-ment passed upon him, on Tower Hill, 17th May, 1521. When the emperor, Charles V., heard of the event, he is said to have exclaimed, " A butcher's dog has killed the finest buck in England."

His grace had married the Lady Alianore Percy, daughter of Henry, Earl of Northumberland, and left issue,

> HENRY, of whom presently.
>
> Elizabeth, m. to Thomas Howard, Duke of Norfolk.
>
> Katherine, m. to Ralph Nevill, Earl of West-morland.
>
> Mary, m. to George Nevill, Lord Bergavenny.

A bill of attainder followed the judgment and execution of the duke, and under that all his honours became FORFEITED. The fate of this illustrious house was marked by a more than ordi-nary degree of misfortune.

Edmund, Earl of Stafford, and his son, Humphrey, Duke of Buck-ingham, and his son, Humphrey, Earl of Staf-ford,	all fell in the de-solating war of the Roses.
Henry, second Duke of Buckingham, and his son, Edward, third and last Duke of Buckingham,	both beheaded and sacrificed to the feuds of party, and to private ma-lignity.

With the last duke sunk for ever the splendour, princely honours, and great wealth, of the ancient and renowned family of STAFFORD. Upon passing the bill of attainder against the duke, the parlia-ment enacted also a bill to restore in blood, but not in honours and lands, his grace's only son,

HENRY STAFFORD, to whom, however, the

king made immediate grants of manors in the county of Stafford and elsewhere, which had belonged to his father, and he obtained from the crown, in some years after, the CASTLE AND MANOR OF STAFFORD, with other of the estates of the deceased duke; but altogether producing only the annual income of £317. 13s. 1d. In the 1st of Edward VI., anno 1547, an act of parliament passed,[*] again restoring him in blood, and declaring, "that the said Henry, Lord Stafford, and the heirs male of his body coming, may be taken, and reputed as Lord Stafford, with a seat and voice in parliament as a baron; and further, that the said Henry be restored in blood as son and heir of Edward, late Duke of Buckingham, &c." His lordship m. Ursula, daughter of Sir Richard Pole, K.G., and Margaret Plantagenet, Countess of Salisbury, daughter of George, Duke of Clarence, and niece of Kings Edward IV. and Richard III., by whom he had issue,

    Edward, his successor.

    Richard, m. Mary, daughter of John Corbet, and had issue,

        ROGER, who claimed the barony upon the decease of Henry, fourth lord, in 1637, but was denied it on account of his poverty. He d. unmarried in 1640.

        Jane, who m. a joiner, and had a son a COBBLER, living at Newport, in Shropshire, in 1637—thus the great-great-grandson of Margaret Plantagenet, daughter and heiress of George, Duke of Clarence, sunk to the grade of a mender of old shoes.

    Walter.

    Dorothy, m. to Sir William Stafford, of Grafton, and from this lady, Mr. Richard Stafford Cooke, who claimed the ancient Barony of Stafford, derived descent. "But admitting this descent, (says Nicolas,) it is difficult to find any real claim which it affords to the Barony of Stafford. The ancient barony undoubtedly became FORFEITED on the attainder of Edward, Duke of Buckingham, in 1521, and which attainder has never been reversed. Henry Stafford, his son and heir, was created Baron Stafford de Novo, with an express limitation, to "the heirs male of his body coming," by act of parliament, 1st Edward VI., 1547, and which dignity became extinct on the termination of the male descendants of the said Henry, about the year 1640."

    Elizabeth, m. to Sir William Nevil, Knt., of Chebsey.

---

[*] Dugdale states, that he was restored in blood in 1529; but on a reference to the authorised collection of the statutes it appears, that, in the 14th and 15th Henry VIII., the act in question was passed, and which merely enabled the said Henry, and Ursula, his wife, and their heirs, to hold and enjoy certain estates, granted them by letters patent, dated 20th December, 1522.—NICOLAS.

This nobleman, who was esteemed for his learning and piety, d. in 1563, and was s. by his son,

EDWARD STAFFORD, second Baron Stafford, of the new creation, summoned to parliament in the 23d Elizabeth. His lordship m. Mary, daughter of Edward, Earl of Derby, and had issue,

    EDWARD, his successor.

    Ursula, m. to Walter Erdeswick, Esq.

    Dorothy, m. to ——Gervais of Chadsden.

He d. in 1603, and was s. by his son,

EDWARD STAFFORD, third baron. This nobleman m. Isabel, daughter of Thomas Forster, of Tonge, in Shropshire, whom Banks surmises to have been a chambermaid, from a paragraph in a letter of Rowland White, to Sir Robert Sydney, dated 23d November, 1595 (Sidney Papers): "My Lorde Stafford's sonne is basely married to his mother's chambermaid." His lordship had issue,

    EDWARD, b. in 1600, m. Anne, daughter of James Wilford, Esq., of Newnham-Hall, in the county of Essex, and d. in the lifetime of his father, leaving issue,

        HENRY, who s. his grandfather.

    Mary, m. to Sir William Howard, K.B., younger son of Thomas, Earl of Arundel (see HOWARD, Baron and Viscount Stafford).

The baron d. 25th September, 1625, and was s. by his grandson,

EDWARD STAFFORD, fourth baron, who d. unmarried in 1637, when the barony devolved upon his kinsman (revert to children of Henry Stafford, the restored baron in 1547).

    ROGER STAFFORD, b. at Malpas, in Cheshire, about the year 1572. "This unfortunate man (says Banks) in his youth went by the name of Fludd, or Floyde: for what reason, has not yet been explained: perhaps with the indignant pride, that the very name of Stafford should not be associated with the obscurity of such a lot! However, one Floyde, a servant of Mr. George Corbett, of Cowlesmore, near Lee, in Shropshire, his mother's brother, is recorded in a manuscript which was once part of the collections of the Stafford family: and it is not improbable, that this was some faithful servant, under whose roof he might have been reared, or found a shelter from misfortunes, when all his great alliances, with a cowardly and detestable selfishness might have forsaken him; and that he might have preferred the generous, though humble name of Floyde, to one that had brought him nothing but a keener memorial of his misfortunes." At the age of sixty-five he became, by the early death of Henry, Lord Stafford, (the great grandson of his father's elder brother,) in 1637, heir male of the family; and petitioned parliament accordingly, but eventually submitted his claim to the decision of King Charles, who decided "that the said Roger Stafford, having no part of the inheritance of the said Lord Stafford, nor any other lands or means whatsoever, should make a resignation of all claims and title to the said Barony of Stafford, for his majesty to dispose of as he should see fit. In obedience, and performance of which said order, the said Roger Stafford, who was never married, did by his deed enrolled, dated 7th December, 1639, grant and surrender unto his majesty the said Barony of Stafford, and the honour, name, and dignity of Lord Stafford. After which surrender, the king, by patent dated 12th September, 1640, created Sir William Howard, and Mary Stafford, his wife, Baron and Baroness Stafford, with remainder to the heirs *male* of their bodies, failure of which, to the heirs of their bodies, with such place or precedence, as Henry, Lord Stafford, brother of the said Mary, ought to have had as Baron Stafford.

With this unfortunate ROGER STAFFORD, who d. in 1640, the male line of the Staffords became EXTINCT, as did the BARONY OF STAFFORD, created in 1547.

ARMS.—Or. a chevron gules.

STAFFORD — BARON STAFFORD, OF CLIFTON.

By Writ of Summons, dated 8th January, 1371, 44 Edward III.

Lineage.

SIR RICHARD DE STAFFORD, younger son of Edmund, first Lord Stafford, (see Stafford, Barons and Earls Stafford,) having m. Maud, daughter and heiress of Richard de Camvile, of Clifton, in the county of Stafford, acquired that lordship, and was thence designated. Sir Richard Stafford distinguished himself in the French wars of King Edward III., and was seneschal of Gascony in that monarch's reign. He was s. at his decease by his son,

RICHARD DE STAFFORD, who, having been engaged in the French wars, was summoned to parliament, by King Edward III., as BARON STAFFORD, of Clifton, on the 8th January, 1371, and he had regular summons from that period to 20th October, 1379; he d. in 1381, leaving his son and heir,

EDMUND DE STAFFORD, in holy orders, who was afterwards Bishop of Exeter, and LORD KEEPER OF THE GREAT SEAL.

And another son,

SIR THOMAS STAFFORD, who came to possess the estate, and was s. by his son,

THOMAS STAFFORD, who d. issueless, leaving an only sister and heiress,

KATHERINE STAFFORD, who m. Sir John Arden, Knt., and left an only child,

MAUD ARDEN. This lady espoused Sir Thomas Stanley, and although none of the Staffords were summoned but Richard, the first lord, yet the BARONY still existed, and was conveyed to the family of her husband by this Maud, and continues vested in the representatives of that lady.

492

ARMS.—Same as Stafford, Earls Stafford, a crescent for difference.

STAFFORD — BARON STAFFORD, OF SUTHWYCK, EARL OF DEVON.

Barony, first by Writ of Summons, dated 26th July, 1461, and afterwards by Patent, dated 24th April, 1464.

Earldom, created 7th May, 1469.

Lineage.

This branch of the ancient house of Stafford sprang from

SIR JOHN STAFFORD, son of William Stafford, of Bromshull, in the county of Stafford, and descended from Hervey Bagot and Millicent Stafford (see Stafford, Lords Stafford, Dukes of Buckingham, &c.); which Sir John m. Margaret, youngest daughter of Ralph Stafford, first Earl of Stafford, and was s. by his son,

SIR HUMPHREY STAFFORD, a distinguished soldier in the martial reign of King Edward III., and one of the retinue of the BLACK PRINCE. He m. ——, daughter and heir of —— Greinvil, and was s. by his son,

SIR HUMPHREY STAFFORD, called "Humphrey with the silver hand," who m. Elizabeth, widow of Sir John Maltravers, of Hooke, in the county of Dorset, and daughter and heir of —— Dynham, by whom he had two sons,

HUMPHREY, his successor.

John, Bishop of Bath and Wells, and afterwards Archbishop of Canterbury, d. about the 30th Henry VI.

This Sir Humphrey was sheriff of the counties of Somerset and Dorset, in the reign of Henry IV., and dying in 1413, was s. by his elder son,

SIR HUMPHREY STAFFORD, who m. Elizabeth, daughter, and eventually sole heiress, of Sir John Maltravers, Knt., of Hooke, and had livery of the lands of her inheritance in the 8th Henry IV. By this lady he had issue,

John (Sir), m. Anne, daughter of William, Lord Botreaux, and dying in the life-time of his father, left a son,

HUMPHREY, who s. his grandfather.

William, m. to Katherine, daughter of Sir John Chidiock, and had a son,

HUMPHREY, of whom hereafter, as Lord Stafford, and Earl of Devon.

Alice, m. first, to Sir Edmund Cheney, of Brooke, in the county of Wilts, and had issue,

Elizabeth Cheney, m. Sir John Coleshill, Knt., and died s. p., 1st Richard III.

Anne Cheney, m. Sir John Willoughby, and had issue,

Sir Robert Willoughby, summoned to parliament as Lord Willoughby de Brooke.

Alice, Lady Cheney, espoused, secondly, Walter Talboys, by whom she had an only daughter,

Eleanor, who m. Thomas Strangeways, Esq., of Melbury, in the county of Dorset.

Sir Humphrey Stafford was s. at his decease by his grandson,

SIR HUMPHREY STAFFORD, who was slain, 30th Henry VI., in rencontre with the rebels under Jack Cade, at Seven Oaks, in the county of Kent, and was s. by his son,

HUMPHREY STAFFORD, appointed steward of the Duchy of Cornwall, in the 1st Henry IV., but d. the same year without issue, when the estates devolved upon his cousin, (refer to issue of William, son of Sir Humphrey Stafford, and Elizabeth, heiress of Maltravers,)

HUMPHREY STAFFORD, of Suthwyck, who was summoned to parliament as a BARON from 26th July, 1461, to 28th February, 1463. His lordship was created, by patent, dated 24th April, 1464, LORD STAFFORD, of Suthwyck, and advanced to the EARLDOM OF DEVON, 7th May, 1469; after the execution and attainder of Thomas Courtenay, Earl of Devon, who had been made prisoner at Towton Field. But this latter dignity he enjoyed only a few months: for being sent with eight hundred archers to assist the Earl of Pembroke in suppressing the northern rebellion under Sir John Conyers, he deserted the earl's banner owing to some personal slight, and caused the total defeat of that nobleman and his army; which conduct so irritated King Edward IV. that he immediately despatched letters to the sheriffs of Somerset and Devon, commanding them to seize Stafford wheresoever they should find him, and to put him to immediate death. His lordship was, in consequence, taken at a village called Brentmarsh, and thence conveyed to BRIDGEWATER, where his head was cut off on the 17th August, 1469. He had m. Isabel, daughter of Sir John Barre, Knt., but had no issue. All his honours fell, however, under the ATTAINDER; but his estates, comprising divers manors in the county of Dorset, by a feoffment made to John Stafford, Archbishop of Canterbury, Sir William Bonvill, and others, by Sir Humphrey Stafford with the silver hand, (which feoffers passed them to Katherine, late wife of William Stafford, Esq., to hold for life, with remainder to Sir Humphrey, son of the said William, and his lawful heirs; and in default of such issue, to the right heirs of Sir Humphrey with the silver hand,) descended to Elizabeth, wife of Sir John Colshill, in the county of Devon; Sir Robert Willoughby, son and heir of Anne Cheney, otherwise Willoughby, and Eleanor Strangeways, as heirs of Sir Humphrey Stafford with the silver hand (revert to issue of Alice, only daughter of Sir Humphrey Stafford, and Elizabeth, heiress of Sir John Maltravers).

Sir John Colshill dying without issue, 1st Richard I., the estates were then divided between the Willoughbys and Strangeways. From the Willoughbys, their dividend passed to the Paulets and the Blounts, and at length centred entirely in the former, who thereby became possessors of the manor of Hooke, in the county of Dorset.

ARMS.—Or, a chevron gu. within a bordure engrailed, sa.

STAFFORD — EARLS OF WILTSHIRE.

Created 5th January, 1470.
Revived in 1509.

Lineage.

LORD JOHN STAFFORD, youngest son of Humphrey, first Duke of Buckingham, was elevated to the peerage by King Edward IV., as EARL OF WILTSHIRE, and in three years afterwards was joined in commission with the Earl of Northumberland, and others, to treat with the ambassadors of James III., King of Scotland, for the adjustment of grievances complained of by both realms. His lordship m. Constance, daughter and heiress of Sir Henry Green, of Drayton, in the county of Northampton. The earl, who was remarkable for little more than his devotion to the House of York, by which he acquired the peerage and the garter, d. in 1473, and was s. by his only child,

EDWARD STAFFORD, second Earl of Wiltshire. This nobleman m. Margaret, one of the daughters and co-heirs of John Grey, second Viscount L'Isle, but d. without issue 24th March, 1499, when the earldom became EXTINCT. In some years afterwards the deceased lord's first cousin,

LORD HENRY STAFFORD, younger son of Henry, second Duke of Buckingham, was created by King Henry VIII., (in the first year of his reign 1509,) EARL OF WILTSHIRE. His lordship m. first, Margaret, Countess of Wilts, widow of the deceased lord, and secondly, Cecily, daughter and heiress of William Bonvile, Lord Harington, and widow of Thomas Grey, Marquess of Dorset, but d. without issue in 1523, when the EARLDOM OF WILTSHIRE became again EXTINCT.

ARMS.—See those of Stafford.

STAFFORD — BARON STAFFORD, OR BOURCHIER.

See *Bourchier*, BARONS BOURCHIER AND EARLS OF ESSEX.

Sir Hugh Stafford, Knt., married Elizabeth Bourchier, Baroness Bourchier, and in her right was summoned to parliament as a BARON. He d. however without issue.

STANHOPE—BARONS STANHOPE, OF HARRINGTON.

By Letters Patent, dated 4th May, 1605.

Lineage.

The family of STANHOPE was of great antiquity in the county of Nottingham, although it did not attain the dignity of the peerage, until comparatively modern times.

In the 48th Edward III.,

JOHN STANHOPE, of Rampton, served the office of escheator for Nottinghamshire, and the county of Derby, a public situation at that time little inferior to that of sheriff. From him descended another,

JOHN STANHOPE, who m. Elizabeth, daughter and heir of Steven Maulovel, (cousin and heir of Sir John Longvilliers, grandson to Thomas Longvilliers, Baron Longvilliers, temp. Edward III.,) and was s. by his son,

SIR RICHARD STANHOPE, Knt., who, in the 6th of Henry IV., was sheriff of the counties of Nottingham and Derby. From this Sir Richard descended,

SIR EDWARD STANHOPE, Knt., Constable of Sandale Castle, temp. Henry VII., whose second son,

SIR MICHAEL STANHOPE, Knt., obtained a grant, temp. Henry VIII., of the manor of Shelford, in the county of Nottingham, with its members, parcel of the possessions of the then dissolved monastery there, as also grants of lands in the counties of Lincoln and Derby. Sir Michael had a numerous family, of which the eldest son,

> SIR THOMAS STANHOPE, inherited Shelford, and was grandfather of Philip, first EARL of CHESTERFIELD.

And the third son,

SIR JOHN STANHOPE, Knt., of Harrington, in the county of Nottingham, having enjoyed high favour at the courts of ELIZABETH and JAMES I., was elevated to the peerage by the latter monarch, to whom he was vice-chamberlain, as BARON STANHOPE, of Harrington. His lordship m. Margaret, daughter and co-heir of Henry M'Williams, Esq., of Stanborne, in Essex, by whom he had issue,

> CHARLES, his successor.
> Elizabeth, m. to Sir Lionel Tollemache, Baronet, of Helmingham, ancestor of the present Countess of Dysart.
> Catherine, m. to Robert, Viscount Cholmley, of Kells, in Ireland, afterwards Earl of Leinster.

Lord Stanhope d. in 1620, and was s. by his son,

CHARLES STANHOPE, second baron. This nobleman lived abroad during the civil wars, temp. Charles I. He m. Dorothy Livingston, sister of James, Earl of Newburgh, but d. without issue, in 1677, when the BARONY OF STANHOPE, of Harrington, became EXTINCT.

Arms.—Quarterly, erm. and gules.

STANLEY—BARONS STANLEY.

By Writ of Summons, tested 15th January, 1456, 34 Henry VI.

Lineage.

This family, according to Dugdale, is " a branch of that, whose chief seat hath been for many ages at HOWTON, in Cheshire;" and it originally assumed its surname from the lordship of STANDLEIGH, in Staffordshire; which lordship was so called from the nature of the soil, it being rough and stoney, with divers craggy rocks around it. Standleigh was formerly possessed by the lords Aldelegh, or Audley, of Aldelegh, and was exchanged by Adam, the son of Lidulph de Aldelegh, with his cousin, William, son of his uncle, Adam de Aldelegh, which William became in consequence,

494

WILLIAM DE STANLEIGH, from whom descended,

SIR JOHN STANLEY, K.G., who m. Isabel, daughter and heiress of Sir Thomas Lathom, and acquired thereby the estates of Lathom and Knowesleys, in the county of Lancaster. Sir John was, subsequently, one of the most powerful personages in the kingdom. In the reign of Henry IV., he obtained, being then steward of the household, licence to fortify a house near Liverpool, which he had newly built, with embattled walls. He was afterwards lord deputy of Ireland. In 1399, he was lord justice and lord lieutenant of the same kingdom. In the first year of Henry V., being then constable of Windsor Castle, he was installed a Knight of the Garter, and was a second time constituted lord lieutenant of Ireland, for six years; in which government he died, on the 6th January, 1414. By the heiress of Lathom he left two sons,

> JOHN, his successor.
> Thomas, who m. Maud, daughter and heir of Sir John Arderne, of Elford, in the county of Stafford, and so long as his male line continued, Elford was their chief seat.

The elder son,

JOHN STANLEY, Esq., was made governor of Carnarvon Castle, and marrying Isabel, sister of Sir William Harrington, Knt., had a son,

SIR THOMAS STANLEY, Knt., who, in the 9th of Henry VI., was constituted lieutenant of Ireland, as his grandfather had been for six years, and he was subsequently made LORD CHAMBERLAIN TO THE KING. With King Henry, Sir Thomas was in high favour, and having been commissioned by that monarch, upon several occasions, to negotiate peace with his enemies, he was made a Knight of the Garter, and had summons to parliament as BARON STANLEY, by special writ, tested 15th January, 1456, but never afterwards. His lordship m. Joan, daughter and heir of Sir Robert Goushill, Knt., and had issue,

> THOMAS, his successor.
> William.
> John.
> Margaret, m. to Sir William Troubeck, Knt.
> Elizabeth, m. to Sir Richard Molineux, Knt.

His lordship d. in 1458-9, and was s. by his eldest son,

THOMAS STANLEY, second baron, summoned to parliament, from 30th July, 1460, to 9th December, 1482. This nobleman, who was steward of the household to King Edward IV., stood faithful to the interests of his son, Edward V., and incurred, in consequence, the jealousy of the PROTECTOR GLOUCESTER, from the moment that daring personage contemplated seizing upon the government. Lord Stanley was at the council, when Lord Hastings was arrested by order of the PROTECTOR, and then very narrowly escaped with his life, having received a violent blow on the head from a halbert. He was afterwards committed to prison, when the protector threw off the mask, and usurped the crown as Richard III., but released, lest his son, GEORGE, Lord Strange, should stir up the people to revolt. To ensure his support, the new monarch loaded his lordship then with honours;

constituting him lord steward of the household, CONSTABLE OF ENGLAND FOR LIFE, investing him with the Garter, &c.; but his having married for his second wife, MARGARET TUDOR, Countess of Richmond, and mother of Richard's rival, HENRY, Earl of Richmond, made him still an object of distrust to the usurper. So soon, therefore, as Richard was apprised of the Earl of Richmond's arrival in Britanny, and his projects regarding the English sceptre, Lord Stanley was commanded to discharge all his servants, and strictly prohibited holding any communication with his step-son. Subsequently he obtained permission to retire into the country, but was obliged to leave his son and heir, GEORGE, Lord Strange, as an hostage. This young nobleman, RICHARD afterwards threatened to put to death, should his father appear in arms on the part of RICHMOND, but the menace failed in keeping Lord Stanley from the field, who distinguished himself as one of the most active commanders at BOSWORTH, and when victory at length declared for LANCASTER, had the high honour of crowning upon the field of battle, his son-in-law and CHIEF, and proclaiming him KING OF ENGLAND, under the title of HENRY VII. His lordship was soon afterwards created EARL OF DERBY, and sworn of the privy council. He m. first, Lady Elizabeth Neville, daughter of Richard, Earl of Salisbury, and had issue,

GEORGE, who m. Joane, daughter and heir of John, LORD STRANGE, of Knokyn, and in her right was summoned to parliament, as Lord Strange. He died before his father, leaving

THOMAS, who s. as second EARL OF DERBY.

EDWARD, afterwards Lord Monteagle.
James, Bishop of Ely.
Margaret, m. to Sir John Osbaldeston.

His lordship espoused, secondly, as already stated, Margaret, Countess of Richmond, mother of the new king, but had no issue. He died in 1504, and from that period the BARONY OF STANLEY merged in the Earldom of Derby, until the decease of

FERDINANDO STANLEY, fifth Earl of Derby, and sixth BARON STANLEY, in 1595, when it fell into ABEYANCE, with the BARONY OF STRANGE, of Knokyn, amongst that nobleman's three daughters and co-heirs, viz.

ANNE, m. first, to Grey Bruges, Lord Chandos, and secondly, to Mervin, Earl of Castlehaven.

FRANCES, m. to Sir John Egerton, afterwards Earl of Bridgewater.

ELIZABETH, m. to Henry, Earl of Huntingdon. Both still continue with their representatives.

ARMS.—Az. on a bend ar. three bucks' heads, cabossed, or.

STANLEY—BARONS MONTEAGLE.

By Writ of Summons, dated 23rd November, 1514, 6 Henry VIII.

Lineage.

SIR EDWARD STANLEY, second son of

Thomas, first Earl of Derby, having commanded, in the 5th Henry VIII., the rear guard of the English army, at the battle of FLODDEN FIELD, and contributed, by extraordinary valour, at the head of a body of archers, to the total overthrow of the Scottish army, was the next year proclaimed LORD MONTEAGLE, by King HENRY, then holding his court at Eltham, in consideration of his gallant conduct, and in commemoration of having won an elevated position from the Scots; in which dignity he was summoned to parliament, from 23rd November, 1514, to 12th November, 1515. He was also made a KNIGHT of the GARTER.

"This nobleman's birth," says Banks, "his active childhood, and martial spirit, had brought him early to Henry VIII.'s notice and company, and his aspiring manhood to his service. The camp was his school, and his learning was a pike and sword. Whenever his majesty met him, his greeting was 'Ho, my soldier.' Twice did he and Sir John Wallop land, with only eight hundred men, in the heart of France; and four times did he and Sir Thomas Lovel save Calais; the first time by intelligence, the second by stratagem, the third by valour and resolution, the fourth by hardship, patience, and industry." His lordship m. Anne,[*] daughter and co-heir of Sir John Harrington, Knt., and had issue,

THOMAS, his successor.

Elizabeth, m. to Sir Thomas Langton, Knt., of Newton, in Lancashire.

He d. in 1523, and was s. by his son,

THOMAS STANLEY, second baron, summoned to parliament from 3rd November, 1529, to 23rd January, 1552. This nobleman was made a Knight of the Bath at the coronation of ANNE BOLEYN. His lordship m. Lady Mary Brandon, daughter of Charles, Duke of Suffolk, by whom he had issue,

WILLIAM (Sir), his successor.

Francis, } both d. young and issueless.
Charles, }

Elizabeth, m. to Richard Zouche, of Staffordel, in the county of Somerset.

Margaret, m. first, to William Sutton, and secondly, to John Tallard.

Anne, m. to Sir John Clifton, Knt., of Barrington, in Somersetshire.

Lord Monteagle espoused, secondly, Helen, daughter of Thomas Preston, Esq., of Levens, in Westmorland, but had no issue. He d. in 1560, and was s. by his son,

SIR WILLIAM STANLEY, third baron, summoned to parliament from 11th January, 1563, to 6th January, 1581. His lordship m. first, Anne, daughter of Sir James Leybourne, Knt., by whom he had an only child,

ELIZABETH, who m. Edward Parker, LORD MORLEY, and her son,

William Parker, was summoned to parliament as LORD MORLEY and MONT-

---

* Edmondson says he had a former wife, Elizabeth, daughter and heir of Thomas Vaughan, Esq., but had no issue.

EAGLE (see Parker, Barons Morley and Monteagle).

He wedded, secondly, Anne, daughter of Sir John Spencer, of Althorpe, in the county of Northampton, by whom (who espoused, after his lordship's decease, Henry, Lord Compton, and afterwards, Robert, Lord Buckhurst,) he had no issue. His lordship d. in 1561, when the BARONY OF MONTEAGLE devolved upon his only daughter and heiress, ELIZABETH STANLEY, who conveyed it to the family of her husband, *Edward Parker*, LORD MORLEY.

ARMS.—Ar. on a bend az. three bucks' heads caboshed or.; a crescent for difference.

STANLEY—BARONS STRANGE, OF KNOKYN.

Refer to Strange, Barons Strange, of Knokyn.

STAPLETON — BARONS STAPLE-TON.

By Writ of Summons, dated 8th January, 1313, 6 Edward II.

Lineage.

Of this family, which assumed its surname from the lordship of STAPLETON, upon the river Teys, in the Bishoprick of Durham, was,

NICHOLAS DE STAPLETON, who in the 17th of King John, was constituted governor of Middleham Castle, in the county of York, and from him descended,

MILES DE STAPLETON, who, having distinguished himself, temp. Edward I. and Edward II., in the wars of Gascony and Scotland, was summoned to parliament as a BARON, by the latter monarch, on the 8th January, 23nd May, and 6th July, 1313. His lordship m. Sibill, daughter and co-heir of John de Bella-Aqua, or Bellew, (by Laderina, his wife, fourth sister and co-heir of Peter, last Lord Bruce, of Skelton,) and was s. at his decease, in 1314, by his son,

NICHOLAS DE STAPLETON, second baron, summoned to parliament 25th February, 1342. This nobleman, in the time of Edward II., was involved in the insurrection of Thomas, Earl of Lancaster, and fined two thousand marks for saving his life; but the fine was remitted in 1st of Edward III. His lordship d. in 1343, and was s. by his son,

MILES STAPLETON, third baron, summoned to parliament in the 32nd Edward III. This nobleman was a person of great note at the period in in which he lived. He participated in many of the French campaigns of Edward III., and he marched under the banner of Philip of Navarre, to within nine leagues of Paris, when the French were obliged to enter into a truce. He was subsequently made a KNIGHT of the GARTER. His lordship m. Joane, daughter and heir of Oliver de Inghram, Baron Inghram, and widow of Roger le Strange, of Knokyn, and was s., at his decease, 47th Edward III., by his son,

THOMAS DE STAPLETON, fourth baron,

but never summoned to parliament. This nobleman died the same year he inherited, and leaving no issue, his sister,

ELIZABETH DE STAPLETON, wife of Thomas METHAM,

became his heir, and the BARONY OF STAPLETON has since been vested in her descendants.

ARMS.—Az. a lion rampant sa.

STAWEL—BARONS STAWEL, OF SOMERTON.

By Letters Patent, dated 15th January, 1683.

Lineage.

This family is said to have been of antiquity, but it arrived at no distinction until a period of comparatively modern date.

SIR JOHN STAWEL, K.B., m. Elizabeth, daughter of George Touchet, Lord Audley, and left a son,

SIR JOHN STAWEL, of Somerton, in the county of Somerset, who distinguished himself by his zeal in the royal cause during the civil wars. He was s. by his son,

RALPH STAWEL, Esq., who, in consideration of the sufferings of his father, and his own eminent services in the same cause, was elevated to the peerage by *King* CHARLES II., on the 15th January, 1683, as BARON STAWEL, *of Somerton*, in the county of Somerset. His lordship m. first, Anne, daughter of John Ryves, Esq., of Ranston, in the county of Dorset, and had an only son, JOHN, his successor. He m. secondly, Abigail, daughter of William Pitt, Esq., of Hartley Wespal, in the county of Stafford, by whom he had issue,

WILLIAM, } who succeeded successively to the
EDWARD, } title.

Elizabeth, m. to William Bromley, Esq., of Bagmton.

Catherine, m. to the Rev. William Higden, D.D.

Lucy.

Diana.

His lordship d. in 1689, and was s. by his eldest son,

JOHN STAWEL, second Baron Stawel, of Somerton. This nobleman m. Lady Margaret Cecil, daughter of James, Earl of Salisbury, by whom he left an only daughter, ——, who m. first, James Darcy, grandson of Conyers, Earl of Holdernesse, and secondly, John Barber, Esq., of Sunning Hill. His lordship d. at the early age of twenty-four, in 1692, and was s. by his half brother,

WILLIAM STAWEL, third baron, who m. Elizabeth, daughter of William Port, Esq., (by Elizabeth, his wife, daughter of William Forster, Esq., and sister of Sir Humphrey Forster, Bart.) By this alliance his lordship acquired the mansion and estate of Aldermaston, in Berkshire, (which had come to the Forsters by the heiress of Delamere, and to the Delameres through the heiress of Achard, which latter family obtained it by grant of HENRY I.) Lord Stawel had issue,

William, who d. unmarried in the life-time of his father, in February, 1739-40.

Charlotte, m. first, to Raise Hessel, Esq., and secondly, to Ralph Congreve, Esq., of Aldermaston.

His lordship d. in 1742, and was s. by his brother,

EDWARD STAWEL, fourth baron. This nobleman m. Mary, daughter and co-heir of Sir Hugh Stewkley, of Hinton Ampner, in the county of Hants, by whom he had issue,

Stewkley, who d. at Westminster school in the life-time of his father.

MARY, m. to Henry Bilson Legge, Esq. This lady having inherited the estates of her family, as sole heiress of her father, was created, in 1760, BARONESS STAWEL, of Somerton, with remainder to her heirs male by Mr. Legge (see Legge, Baroness Stawel). Her ladyship espoused, secondly, the Earl of Hillsborough.

His lordship d. in 1755, when the BARONY OF STAWELL, of Somerton, became EXTINCT.

ARMS.—Quarterly first and fourth gules, a cross of losenges, ar. for STAWEL; second and third sa. fusee, cheky ar. and az. between three bessants for PITT.

STRABOLGI—BARONS STRABOLGI.

By Writ of Summons, dated 14th March, 1329, 15 Edward II.

Lineage.

" Of this family," says Sir William Dugdale, " the first, touching whom I find mention, is

DAVID DE STRABOLGI, Earl of Athol, in Scotland, who, by Isabel, one of the co-heirs of Richard de Chilham, of Chilham Castle, in Kent, and Rosse de Dover, his wife, had issue,

JOHN DE STRABOLGI, Earl of Athol, who, in the 32nd Edward I., upon the death of Joane, widow of Richard de Dover, had livery of the manor of Leabes, in Kent, which descended to him through his mother. It is reported, (continues the same authority,) that, in 1366, King EDWARD I., being victorious in Scotland, taking much to heart the slaughter of John Comin, and the crowning of Robert de Brus, king of that realm, exercised a sharp revenge upon all whom he could discover to have had a hand therein; and that thereupon this John de Asceles (for so he is called,) fled the country; but being driven back from sea by contrary winds, was taken, carried to London, and sentenced to death in Westminster Hall. In respect, however, of his descent from royal blood, he was not drawn, as traitors usually are, but set on horseback, and hanged upon a gibbet fifty feet high, his head fixed on London bridge, and his body burnt to ashes." Being thus executed for treason, all his lands in Scotland were conferred by the crown upon Ralph Monthermer, EARL OF GLOUCESTER; but those lands were soon after recovered by purchase, and the recovery received the confirmation of the king, by the deceased nobleman's son and heir,

DAVID DE STRABOLGI, who, pursuing a different course to that of his father, and taking an active part in favour of the English interests, against Bruce, had a grant, from the crown, of the manor and honour of CHILHAM, and was summoned to parliament, as a BARON, by King Edward II., in the same year, 1329, and from that period to 3rd December, 1326. His lordship m. Joane, eldest sister and co-heir of John Comyn, of Badenagh, cousin, and one of the co-heirs of Adomare de Valence, Earl of Pembroke, and dying in 1327, was s. by his son,

DAVID DE STRABOLGI, (Earl of Athol,) second baron, summoned to parliament from 25th January, 1330, to 24th July, 1334. This nobleman, at the decease of his father, was but nineteen years of age, when Henry de Beaumont paid a thousand marks for his wardship and marriage: notwithstanding which, he stood in such fair esteem with the king, that in the 1st Edward III., although he had not then attained majority, he was allowed to do homage, and had livery of his lands. He subsequently inherited estates from his uncle, John Comyn; and lands also as one of the co-heirs of Adomare, Earl of Pembroke. His lordship, in the Scottish wars, was at one time engaged against the English monarch, and at another in his favour: he eventually, however, fell fighting under King Edward's (III.) banner. He m. Katherine Beaumont, and was s. in 1335 by his only son,

DAVID DE STRABOLGI, (Earl of Athol,) third baron, summoned to parliament from 20th January, 1366, to 6th April, 1369. This nobleman, at the decease of his father, was but three years of age. He was afterwards in the wars of France under the Black Prince. His lordship espoused Elizabeth, daughter of Henry, Lord Ferrers, of Groby, and had issue,

ELIZABETH, m. first, to Sir Thomas Percy, Knt., son of Henry, Lord Percy, by whom she had issue,

Henry Percy, who left two daughters, his heirs, viz.

Elizabeth, m. first, to Thomas, Lord Burgh, and secondly, to Sir William Lucy.

Margaret, m. first, to Henry, Lord Grey, of Cednor, and secondly, to Richard, Earl of Oxford.

Her ladyship espoused, secondly, Sir John Scrope, Knt.

PHILIPPA, m. first, to Sir Ralph Percy, brother of Sir Thomas, and secondly, to John Habham, Esq.

His lordship d. in 1369, when the BARONY OF STRABOLGI fell into ABEYANCE between his daughters, as it still continues with their representatives.

ARMS.—Paley of six, or. and sa.

STRANGE—BARONS STRANGE, OF KNOKYN.

By Writ of Summons, dated 29th December, 1299, 28 Edward I.

Lineage.

It is stated, that at JUSTS, held in the Peke of

Derbyshire, at CASTLE PEVERELL, where, amongst other persons of note, were present Oweyn, PRINCE OF WALES, and a son of the king of Scots, there were also two sons of the Duke of Bretaigne; the younger of them being named Guy, was called

GUY LE STRANGE, and from him that the several families of STRANGE subsequently descended. Taking that statement for granted, then we find that this Guy had three sons, all of whom possessed lands in Shropshire, temp. HENRY II. Those sons were,

1. GUY LE STRANGE, who had a grant from *King* HENRY II. to hold by the service of one knight's fee of the manors of Weston and Alvithele, in the county of Salop, and was sheriff of that shire from the 6th to the 11th of the same reign, and from the 17th to the 25th. He *d.* before the accession of King John, leaving

> RALPH LE STRANGE, his successor, who *d.* issueless, when his lands devolved upon his sisters as co-heirs.
> Margaret le Strange, *m.* to Thomas Noell.
> Joane le Strange, *m.* to Richard de Wapenburi.
> ————, *m.* to Griffin Fitz-Jervord.

2. HAMON LE STRANGE, Lord of Wrockwurdine, of whom nothing more can be said than that he gave his whole part of the common woods at Wombrugge, Salop, to the canons of that house, and died *s. p.*

And

3. JOHN LE STRANGE, who, in the 11th of *King* JOHN, possessed the lordships of Nesse and Chesewardine, in the county of Salop, which he held by grant of HENRY II. In the 18th of John he was sheriff of the counties of Salop and Stafford, and in the 3rd Henry III. he obtained the king's precept to the sheriff of Shropshire, for aid to rebuild part of his castle at KNOKYN, and to repair the rest of it. And, having been a liberal benefactor to the canons of Wombrugge, departed this life shortly after, when he was *s.* by his son,

JOHN LE STRANGE, a person of great note in his time. In the 16th John, his father then living, he was in the wars of Poictou; and in the 15th Henry III. he obtained a grant of the inheritance of the manor of WROCKWURDINE, for the yearly rent of £8, to be paid to the king, and his heirs and successors. In the 21st of the same reign he was appointed sheriff of the counties of Salop and Stafford; and constituted governor of the castle of Salop and Bruges. He was afterwards one of the barons marchers, and had command as such to reside in the marches, in order to resist the incursions of the Welsh. In the contest between HENRY III. and the barons, his lordship adhered with great fidelity to the king, and obtained for his loyalty a grant of the lands of Walter de Mucegros, which had been forfeited in that rebellion. He *m.* Amice ————, and had issue,

> JOHN, his successor.
> Hamon, of Ellesmere, which manor he gave to his brother, Roger.

408

> ROBERT, from whom descended the Stranges, of Blackmere (see *Strange*, BARONS STRANGE, *of Blackmere*).
> Roger, who obtained Ellesmere from his brother, Hamon.
> Avice, *m.* to Griffin de la Pole.

He *d.* in 1269, and was *s.* by his eldest son,

JOHN LE STRANGE, Lord of Knokyn. This feudal baron, in the time of his father, was deputy governor of Winchester Castle; and in the 48th HENRY III. he was constituted governor of the castle of Montgomery. He subsequently espoused the baronial cause, and after the triumph of the barons at Lewes, was reinstated in the governorship of Montgomery Castle. In the 3rd Edward I. he surrendered to his brother, Robert, his entire right in the manor of Wrockwurdine. His lordship *m.* Joane, one of the daughters and heirs of Roger de Someri, Baron of Dudley, and *d.* in 1276, when all his lands were seized upon by the crown, but in two years afterwards they were restored to his son and heir,

JOHN LE STRANGE, who, upon paying his relief, had livery thereof. This feudal lord, in the 14th Edward I., answered for three hundred marks to the king; which sums John, his grandfather, had borrowed from the Cheshire men, to maintain the wars of Wales. He was, subsequently, engaged in the wars of Gascony and Scotland, and, for his good services, was summoned to parliament as BARON STRANGE, *of Knokyn*, from 29th December, 1299, to 19th December, 1309, and likewise made a Knight of the Bath. His lordship *m.* Maud, daughter and heir of Roger D'Eiville, of Walton-D'Eyvill, in the county of Warwick, by whom he acquired that and other properties in the counties of Oxford and Cambridge, and had issue,

> JOHN, his successor.
> EUBOLO, who *m.* Alice de Laci, daughter and sole heir of Henry de Laci, Earl of Lincoln, and widow of Thomas Plantagenet, Earl of Lancaster. In right of this lady, Eubolo le Strange bore the title of EARL OF LINCOLN, but he died *s. p.*, and ALICE, his countess, surviving, espoused, thirdly, HUGO DE FRENES, who was also styled Earl of Lincoln, but he likewise died *s. p.* This great heiress *d.* in the 22nd Edward III., and was buried at Barling Abbey, with her second husband, Eubolo le Strange.
> Hamon, ancestor of the Le Stranges of Hunstanton, in the county of Norfolk.

His lordship *d.* in 1310, and was *s.* by his eldest son,

JOHN LE STRANGE, second baron, summoned to parliament, 13th June, 1311. This nobleman before and after his accession to the title, was in the Scottish wars. He *d.* the year after his father, and was *s.* by his elder son,

JOHN LE STRANGE, third baron, summoned to parliament 8th January and 26th July, 1313. His lordship *d.* in 1394, without issue, and was *s.* by his brother,

ROGER LE STRANGE, fourth baron, summoned to parliament from 25th February, 1342, to 10th March, 1349. This nobleman was made a Knight of the Bath, in the 20th Edward II., and in the reign of Edward III., was in the wars of Scotland and France. His lordship m. first, Joane, daughter and co-heir of Oliver de Ingham, by whom he had ROGER, his successor. He espoused, secondly, Maud ————, in whose right he held the manor of Middleton, in Cambridgeshire. His lordship d. in 1349, and was s. by his son,

ROGER LE STRANGE, fifth baron, summoned to parliament from 20th September, 1355, to 9th August, 1362. This nobleman was constantly engaged in the wars of Gascony and Britanny, temp. Edward III. and Richard II. His lordship m. Lady Aliva Fitz-Alan, daughter of Edmund, Earl of Arundel, and dying in 1382, was s. by his son,

JOHN LE STRANGE, sixth baron, summoned to parliament from 20th August, 1383, to 18th July, 1397. This nobleman, in the 10th of Richard II., was in the garrison of Berwick-upon-Tweed, and the next year in the Scottish wars. He m. Maud, daughter, and eventually co-heir of Sir John de Mohun, of Dunster, and dying about the year 1398, was s. by his son,

RICHARD LE STRANGE, seventh baron, summoned to parliament from 26th August, 1404, to 2nd January, 1449. This nobleman making proof of his age in the 5th of Henry IV., had livery of all his lands; Maud, his mother, being then dead. He was likewise, maternally, nephew and heir of Philippa, Duchess of York. His lordship m. first, Constance, daughter of ————, by whom he had no issue, and secondly, Elizabeth, daughter of Reginald, Lord Cobham, and dying in 1449, was s. by his only son,

JOHN LE STRANGE, eighth baron, summoned to parliament from 26th February, 1465, to 19th August, 1472. This nobleman espoused Jaquetta, daughter of Richard Wydeville, Earl Rivers, and sister-in-law of King EDWARD IV., by whom he left at his decease, in 1477, an only daughter and heiress,

JOHANNA LE STRANGE, who espoused

SIR GEORGE STANLEY, K.B. and K.G., eldest son of Sir Thomas Stanley, first Earl of Derby, and conveyed the BARONY OF STRANGE, of Knokyn, to the family of her husband, Sir George being summoned to parliament in that dignity, jure uxoris, from 15th November, 1482, to 16th January, 1497. This nobleman was sworn of the privy council, upon the accession of HENRY VII., and the next year he was one of the principal commanders who defeated John, Earl of Lincoln, and his adherents at STOKE. His lordship d. in 1497; his father, the Earl of Derby, then living, leaving issue,

    THOMAS, his successor.
    James.
    Jane, m. to Robert Sheffield, Esq.
    Elizabeth.

Lord Strange was s. by his eldest son,

THOMAS STANLEY, as tenth Baron Strange, who succeeded his grandfather as second EARL OF DERBY, in 1504; and the BARONY OF STRANGE, OF KNOKYN, merged in the superior dignity, until the decease of

FERDINANDO STANLEY, fifth Earl of Derby, and thirteenth BARON STRANGE, in 1594. This nobleman m. Alice, daughter of Sir John Spencer, of Althorpe, in the county of Northampton, and left three daughters, viz.

    ANNE, m. first, to Grey Bruges, fifth Lord Chandos, and secondly, to Mervin, Earl of Castlehaven.
    FRANCES, m. to Sir John Egerton, Knt., afterwards Earl of Bridgewater.
    ELIZABETH, m. to Henry Hastings, afterwards Earl of Huntingdon.

Amongst whom the BARONY OF STRANGE, OF KNOKYN, with that of STANLEY, fell into ABEYANCE, as both still continue with their representatives.

ARMS.—Gu. two lions ar. within a boarder ingrailed or.

STRANGE — BARON STRANGE, OF ELLESMERE.

By Writ of Summons, dated 24th June, 1295,
23 Edward I.

Lineage.

HAMON LE STRANGE, a younger son of the first John le Strange, of Knokyn, having stood firmly by King HENRY III., in his contest with Montfort, Earl of Leicester, was rewarded by a grant from the crown of the manors of Ellesmere and Stretton. The former of which he conferred upon his brother, (he died himself s. p.)

SIR ROGER LE STRANGE, who thus became of ELLESMERE, and served the office of sheriff for the county of York, in the 53d Henry III., and again in the 56th of the same monarch. In the 4th of Edward I., he obtained a confirmation of the grant made to him by his brother Hamon, of the castle and hundred of Ellesmere; and in some years afterwards he was made justice of all the forests south of Trent. In the 22d of the same reign, he had a military summons to march against the French, and he was summoned to parliament as a BARON from 24th June, 1295, to 26th August, 1295. His lordship m. Maud, widow of Roger de Mowbray, and one of the daughters and co-heirs of William Beauchamp, of Bedford. Dugdale states that he was living in 1303, but "that further he cannot say of him." It is presumed that he died s. p., when the BARONY became EXTINCT.

ARMS.—Same as Strange, of Knokyn.

STRANGE—BARONS STRANGE, OF BLACKMERE.

By Writ of Summons, dated 13th January, 1308,
2 Edward II.

Lineage.

This branch of the STRANGES sprang from

ROBERT LE STRANGE, brother of John le Strange, and uncle of John, BARON STRANGE, of Knokyn, who obtained from his said brother, all that feudal lord's right in the manor of Wrockwourdine, and marrying Alianore, sister and co-heir of William de Blancminster, alias Whitechurch, acquired the manor of Whitchurch, in Shropshire. He *d.* in the 4th of Edward I., and was *s.* by his elder son,

JOHN LE STRANGE, designated of BLACK-MERE, by reason that his manor house of White-church was situated close to a *Mere*, so called from the dark colour of its waters. This John *d.* unmarried soon after attaining majority, and was *s.* by his brother,

FULK LE STRANGE, who, having been engaged in the wars of Scotland and France, temp. Edward I. and Edward II., was summoned to parliament as BARON STRANGE, from 13th January, 1308, to 13th September, 1324. In the 12th of Edward II., his lordship obtained pardon for adhering to Thomas, Earl of Lancaster, and in four years afterwards he was constituted seneschal of the Duchy of Acquitaine. He *m.* Alianore, daughter and co-heir of John Giffard, of Brunsfield, and in her right acquired one third part of the manor of Thornhagh, in Nottinghamshire. His lordship *d.* in 1324, and was *s.* by his son,

JOHN LE STRANGE, second baron, summoned to parliament as BARON STRANGE, *of Blackmere*, from 6th September, 1330, to 20th April, 1343. This nobleman, in the 4th Edward III., was made governor of Conway Castle; he was afterwards in the wars of Scotland and France, and attained the high military rank of BANNERET. His lordship *m.* Ankaret, daughter of William Boteler, of Wemme, and sister and co-heir of Edward Boteler, *Clerk*, and dying in 1349, was *s.* by his elder son,

FULK LE STRANGE, third baron, who dying in minority issueless, was *s.* by his brother,

JOHN LE STRANGE, fourth baron, summoned to parliament 3d April, 1360. His lordship *m.* Lady Mary Fitz-Alan, daughter of Richard, Earl of Arundel, and had issue,

    JOHN, his successor.

    ANKARET, *m.* to Sir Richard Talbot.

He *d.* in 1361, and was *s.* by his son,

JOHN LE STRANGE, fifth baron. This nobleman *m.* Lady Isabel Beauchamp, daughter of Thomas, Earl of Warwick, and dying in minority, anno 1375, left an only daughter and heiress,

    ELIZABETH LE STRANGE, who espoused Thomas Mowbray, Earl of Nottingham, but *d.* issueless, 23d August, 1383.

Upon the decease of her ladyship, the estates and BARONY OF STRANGE, *of Blackmere*, reverted to her aunt, ANKARET, *Lady Talbot*, whose husband, Sir Richard Talbot, was summoned to parliament as LORD TALBOT, *of Blackmere*, and upon the death of his father, became fourth Baron Talbot (see Talbot, BARONS TALBOT).

ARMS.—Same as Strange, of Knokyn. ?

STRYVELIN—BARON STRYVELIN.

By Writ of Summons, dated 25th February, 1342, 16 Edward III.

Lineage.

In the 9th Edward III.,

SIR JOHN DE STRYVELIN was in the garrison of Edinburgh Castle, and in the 16th of the same monarch he was constituted one of the com-

missioners, with the Bishop of Durham, Ralph, Lord Nevill, and others, to treat of peace with the Scots. He was summoned to parliament as a BARON from 25th February, 1342, to 8th January, 1371; and he was in the famous expedition made into France in the 30th Edward III. His lordship *m.* Barbara, sister and co-heir of Adam de Swinburn, and left an only daughter and heir,

    CHRISTIAN DE STRYVELIN, who *m.* Sir John Middleton, Knt., of Belsay Castle, in the county of Northumberland, and from this union lineally descended,

        ROBERT MIDDLETON, Esq., of Belsay Castle, who was created a baronet in in 1662, and was great-great-grand-father, and *predecessor in the title* to the present

            SIR CHARLES - MILES - LAMBERT MONK (*olim Middleton*), Baronet, of Belsay Castle.

The time of Lord Stryvelin's decease is not exactly ascertained, but the BARONY must then have vested in his daughter, as it continues of course in her descendants.

ARMS.—Ar. on a chief gu. three round buckles or.

STUART—DUKE OF YORK.

By Letters Patent, dated 6th January, 1604.

Lineage.

His Majesty

    King JAMES I. espoused ANNE, daughter of FREDERICK II., *King of DENMARK*, and had surviving issue,

    HENRY-FREDERICK, *Prince of Wales.*

    Robert, who *d.* young.

    Charles, of whom presently.

    Elisabeth, *b.* in 1596, *m.* in 1613, to *Frederick*, COUNT PALATINE OF THE RHINE, and her daughter,

        SOPHIA espoused ERNEST AUGUSTUS, ELECTOR OF HANOVER. By the act of settlement this princess became heir to the crown of England, and her eldest son,

            GEORGE-LEWIS, in her right ascended the throne as GEORGE I.

The king's third son,

Prince CHARLES STUART, was created, by letters patent dated 6th January, 1604, DUKE OF YORK. Upon the decease of his elder brother, HENRY-FREDERICK, *Prince of Wales*, in 1612, his Royal Highness inherited the Dukedom of Cornwall, and was created PRINCE OF WALES. He succeeded his father on 27th March, 1625, as *King* CHARLES I., when the DUKEDOM OF YORK merged in the crown.

ARMS.—Royal arms of England.

STUART—DUKE OF YORK.

By Letters Patent, dated 27th January, 1643.

Lineage.

JAMES STUART, second son of *King* CHARLES

I., was declared Duke of York at his birth, and so created by letters patent, dated 27th January, 1643. His royal highness espoused, first, *Lady Anne Hyde*, eldest daughter of Edward, Earl of Clarendon, LORD HIGH CHANCELLOR of England, and had issue,

> Charles, } Dukes of Cam- } all of whom d.
> James, } bridge, } in infancy or
> Charles, Duke of Kendal, } childhood.
> Edgar, Duke of Cambridge, }

> Mary, espoused WILLIAM-HENRY, *Prince of Orange*, and ascended the British throne with her husband, at the revolution. Her majesty died *s. p.* in 1694.

> Anne, *m.* Prince George, *of Denmark*, and ascended the throne as *Queen* Anne; d. in 1714 without surviving issue.

The Duchess of York d. in 1671, and the duke wedded, secondly, in 1673, Mary Eleanor D'Este, daughter of Adolphus III., *Duke of Modena*. She was sister of Francis, Duke of Modena, and of Isabella, Princess of Parma and Placentea. Her mother was Laura Martinozzi, niece to Cardinal Mazarin, being daughter of *Count* Jerome Martinozzi, by that celebrated statesman's eldest sister, Margaret Mazarin. By this illustrious lady his royal highness had issue,

> Charles, Duke of Cambridge, who d. an infant.

> James-Francis-Edward, b. 10th June, 1688; his father being then king, he was declared Prince of Wales, and was baptised 15th October in the same year. The pope's nuncio held the prince at the baptismal font, in HIS HOLINESS's name, who was godfather, and the queen dowager godmother. This prince, upon the decease of his father in 1701, was proclaimed, by Louis XIV., at Paris, King of Great Britain, &c., and he endeavoured in 1715, to establish his right by arms. He was afterwards known as the Chevalier St. George. He m. in 1719, Clementina Sobieski, daughter of *Prince* James Sobieski, son of the King of Poland; by whom he had two surviving sons,

>> Charles-Edward, Duke of Albany, b. 20th December, 1780, the celebrated Chevalier who made so bold an attempt, in 1745, to regain the crown. He m. Ludovica, Princess of Stolberg, but died *s. p.*

>> Henry-Benedict, b. at Rome 26th February, 1725. This prince became a churchman, and having obtained a cardinal's hat, bore the designation of Cardinal York. His eminence d. in 1807, and with him expired the male line of the Royal House of Stuart.

The prince ascended the throne, as *King* James II., on the 6th February, 1685, when the Dukedom of York merged in the crown.

Arms.—Royal arms of England.

STUART—EARL OF CAMBRIDGE, DUKE OF GLOUCESTER.

By Letters Patent, dated 13th May, 1659.

Lineage.

His Majesty,

King CHARLES I., (called the *Martyr*,) espoused Henrietta-Maria de Bourbon, daughter of Henry IV., of France, and had surviving issue,

> Charles, *Prince of Wales*, who ascended the throne as Charles II.

> James, *Duke of York and Albany*, who ascended the throne as James II.

> Henry, of whom presently.

> Mary, *m.* to William of Nassau, Prince of Orange, and was mother of William III., of England. Her highness d. at London, of the small pox, in 1661.

> Elizabeth, d. in prison, of grief, in 1650.

> Anne, d. at three years of age, in 1637.

> Henrietta-Anna-Maria, *m.* to Philip, Duke of Orleans, in 1661, and d. in 1670.

The third son,

Prince HENRY STUART, b. at Oatlands 8th July, 1640, and thence denominated, "Henry of Oatlands," was created, by letters patent, dated 13th May, 1659, Earl of Cambridge and Duke of Gloucester. He was also elected a Knight of the Garter. His royal highness was in exile with his brother, Charles, during the usurpation, and returned to England when that prince was restored to the crown, but d. in 1660 unmarried, when all his honours became extinct.

Arms.—Royal arms of England.

STUART—DUKES OF CAMBRIDGE.

> By Letters Patent, { dated in 1661.
>   { —— 1663.
>   { —— 1667.
>   { —— 1677.

Lineage.

The following children of *James*, Duke of York, afterwards *King* James II., were created Dukes of Cambridge, viz.

> Charles Stuart, created in 1661, d. the same year, an infant, when the dukedom expired.

> James Stuart, created in 1663, d. in 1667, an infant, when the dukedom became extinct.

> Edgar Stuart, created in 1667, d. in 1671, an infant, when the dignity expired.

> Charles Stuart, created in 1677, d. the same year, an infant, when the honour became extinct.

Arms.—Royal arms of England.

STUART—DUKE OF KENDAL.

By Letters Patent, dated 1666.

Lineage.

CHARLES STUART, third son of *James*, Duke of York, (afterwards James II.,) was created DUKE OF KENDAL in 1666. He d. the next year, an infant, when the dignity became EXTINCT.

ARMS.—Royal arms of England.

STUART—EARL OF RICHMOND, DUKE OF RICHMOND.

Earldom, } by Letters { 6th October, 1613.
Dukedom, } Patent, { 17th May, 1623.

Lineage.

LODOVICK STUART, son of Esme, Duke of Lenox, in Scotland, was after his father's death brought from France, by *King JAMES VI.*, and put into possession of the estates and honours which had belonged to that nobleman. He had the lordship of Methven and Balquhidder. He was both high chamberlain and admiral of Scotland, and was sent, in 1601, ambassador to France. Upon King James's accession to the crown of England, his lordship was created, by letters patent, dated 6th October, 1613, *Baron Setrington, of Setrington, in the county of York*, and EARL OF RICHMOND. He was constituted master of the household, and first gentleman of the bedchamber; invested with the Garter, and appointed commissioner to the parliament in 1607, and advanced in 1623, to the dignities of *Earl of Newcastle*, and DUKE OF RICHMOND. His grace m. first, Sophia, daughter of William, Earl of Gowrie, in Scotland, secondly, Jean, daughter of Sir Matthew Campbell, of London, and thirdly, Frances, daughter of Thomas Howard, Viscount Bindon, and widow of Edward, Earl of Hertford, but d. without legitimate issue, in February, 1624, when his ENGLISH HONOURS became EXTINCT, while those of Scotland, devolved upon his brother, Esme Stuart, Lord D'Aubigny.

ARMS.—Quarterly, first and fourth, France, on a border gules. semée de fermaulx, or. : the second and third, or. a fesse chequy ar. and a border innrailed gules. an inescutcheon, ar. a salter ingrailed, between four cinquefoils, gu.

STUART — EARLS OF MARCH, DUKES OF RICHMOND, EARL OF LITCHFIELD.

Earldom of March, }
Dukedom, } by Letters { 7th June, 1619.
Earldom of } Patent, { 8th August, 1641.
Litchfield, } { 10th December, 1645.

Lineage.

LODOVICK STUART, Duke of Lennox, in Scotland, and Duke of Richmond, in England, died s. p., in 1624, when his English honours expired, while those of Scotland devolved upon his brother,

ESME STUART, Lord D'Aubigny, as third Duke of Lenox. This nobleman had been created by *King JAMES I.*, on the 7th June, 1619, *Baron Clifton, of Leighton Bromswold, in the county of Lincoln*, and EARL OF MARCH. His lordship m. Katherine, only daughter and heir of Sir Gervase

502

Clifton, Lord Clifton, of Leighton Bromswold, by writ of summons, dated 9th July, 1608, and had surviving issue,

  JAMES, his successor.

George, Lord D'Aubigny, who fell in the King's service, at the battle of Edgehill, 23rd October, 1642, leaving issue, by Frances, his wife, daughter of Theophilus, Earl of Suffolk,

  CHARLES, created Earl of Litchfield, and s. as sixth Duke of Lenox, and third Duke of Richmond.

  Catherine, who m. Henry O'Brien, Lord Ibrickan, son and heir apparent of Henry, seventh Earl of Thomond, and had an only daughter,

    KATHERINE O'BRIEN, who m. Edward Hyde, third Earl of Clarendon, and dying in the life-time of her mother, left

      EDWARD, who s. his grandmother.

      THEODOSIA, who m. Thomas Bligh, Esq., afterwards created Earl of Darnley. Her ladyship eventually inherited the BARONY OF CLIFTON, which had been conferred, by writ, upon her ancestor, Sir Gervase Clifton, and that dignity is now enjoyed by her descendants, the Blighs, Earls of Darnley.

Lodovick, canon of the cathedral of Notre Dame.

Bernard, commander of the king's troop of guards, in the civil wars, killed at Chester, in 1645.

John, general of horse, on the royal side, fell at the battle of Bramdene, in 1644.

Elizabeth, m. to Henry-Frederick Howard, Earl of Arundel.

Anne, m. to Archibald Douglas, Lord Angus, son and heir of William, first Marquess of Douglas.

Frances, m. to James Weston, Earl of Portland.

His grace d. in July, 1624, and was s. by his eldest son,

JAMES STUART, (fourth Duke of Lenox, in Scotland,) as second Earl of March. This nobleman was advanced, by letters patent, dated 8th August, 1641, to the DUKEDOM OF RICHMOND, with remainder in default of heirs male of his own body, to his brothers and their heirs male primogenitively. His grace was lord great chamberlain, and admiral of Scotland, lord steward of the household, warden of the cinque ports, gentleman of the bedchamber, and a Knight of the Garter. His grace m. Lady Mary Villiers, only daughter of George, Duke of Buckingham, and had issue,

  ESME, his successor.

  Mary, m. to Richard Butler, Earl of Arran.

The Duke of Richmond and Lenox adhered with unshaken fidelity to the king during the civil wars, and when money was raised upon loans to support the royal cause, he subscribed £40,000, "although there was not a man in England," says Duncan Stewart, "that offered more than £10,000, except Strafford, Lord Lieutenant of Ireland, who offered £20,000; and yet at the same time the duke had not the most considerable or profitable posts about the king, nor was his estate the greatest either; and when he was taken notice of by Sir Philip Warwick for his offer, he smilingly replied, 'I will serve the king in his person, though I carry but his cloak, as well and as cheerfully, as any in the greatest trust:' reflecting upon Hamilton. He paid his last duty to his master, *King* CHARLES, by putting him in his grave at Windsor." His grace *d.* in 1655, and was *s.* by his son,

ESME STUART, (fifth Duke of Lenox, in Scotland,) as third Earl of March, and second Duke of Richmond. This nobleman *d.* in his minority unmarried, anno 1660, and was *s.* by his first cousin,

CHARLES STUART, (sixth Duke of Lennox, in Scotland,) as fourth Earl of March, and third Duke of Richmond. This nobleman, in consideration of his father, *George*, LORD D'AUBIGNY'S, and his uncle, Bernard Stuart's, gallant services in the royal cause, had been created, by *King* CHARLES I., by letters patent, dated 10th December, 1645, Baron Stuart, of Newberry, in the county of Berks, and EARL OF LITCHFIELD. His grace espoused, first, Elizabeth, daughter of Richard Rogers, Esq., of Bryanston, in the county of Dorset. He *m.* secondly, Margaret, daughter of Lawrence, son and heir of Sir Robert Banaster, Bart., of Papenham, in Buckinghamshire; and thirdly, Frances, daughter of Walter Stuart, son of Walter, Lord Blantyre, but *d.* without issue at Elsenure, where he resided as ambassador-extraordinary from *King* CHARLES II. to the court of Denmark. Upon his lordship's decease the BARONY OF CLIFTON (that created by writ,) devolved upon his only sister, CATHERINE, *Lady Ibricken*, whose grand-daughter, and eventual representative, *Lady* THEODOSIA HYDE, espoused Thomas Bligh, Esq., afterwards Earl of Darnley, and conveyed the barony to the Bligh family. While ALL HIS OTHER HONOURS became EXTINCT, those of England certainly, but it appears that the extinction of the Dukedom of Lennox* is questioned, and the matter remains as yet undecided.

ARMS.—Same as Lodowick Stuart, Duke of Richmond.

---

* In 1829, *John Bligh*, EARL OF DARNLEY, presented a petition to the king, claiming the Dukedom of Lennox in the peerage of Scotland, as heir of line of Charles, sixth Duke of Lennox, and fourth Duke of Richmond, at whose death, in 1672, King Charles II. was served his grace's heir. As his majesty's (legitimate) issue became extinct in 1807 with the Cardinal York, and as that personage was the last heir male of the Stuarts, the Earl of Darnley put forward his claim as heir general, being descended from Catharine, sister of the duke mentioned above. The petition was referred to the House of Lords, and their lordships have not hitherto decided upon it.

SUDLEY—BARONS SUDLEY.

By Writ of Summons, dated 29th December, 1299,
28 Edward I.
By Letters Patent, dated 10th September, 1441.

Lineage.

HAROLD, according to Dugdale, the son of Ralph, Earl of Hereford, but, by other authorities, an illegitimate son of *King* HAROLD, possessed, at the time of the general survey, numerous lordships in England, amongst which was SUDLEY, in Gloucestershire, the chief place of his residence. He had two sons,

JOHN, his successor.
    Robert, who obtained of his father's lands
      EWYAS, in Herefordshire, and residing at
      the castle of Ewyas, assumed that surname.
The elder son succeeding to the family seat, adopted his designation therefrom, and became

JOHN DE SUDLEY. This feudal lord *m.* Grace, daughter of —— Tracy, Baron of Barnstaple, and had issue,

    RALPH, his successor.
    William, who adopted his mother's name of
      TRACY.
He was *s.* by his elder son,

RALPH DE SUDLEY, who, in the 12th Henry II., certified his knights' fees to be in number, four. He *m.* Emme, daughter of William de Beauchamp, of Elmley, and was *s.* by his son,

OTWELL DE SUDLEY. This feudal baron died *s. p.*, about the year 1195, and was *s.* by his brother,

RALPH DE SUDLEY, who, in the 10th Richard I., gave three hundred marks to the king for livery of his lands; in which sum sixty marks were included, which had been imposed upon his deceased brother, as a fine for the defect of a soldier, whom he ought to have maintained in Normandy. This Ralph was *s.* by his son, another

RALPH DE SUDLEY, who was *s.* by his son,

BARTHOLOMEW DE SUDLEY. This feudal lord was sheriff of Herefordshire, and governor of the castle of Hereford, in the latter end of the reign of HENRY III. He *m.* Joane, daughter of William de Beauchamp, of Elmley, and sister of William, first Earl of Warwick, and dying in 1274, was *s.* by his son,

JOHN DE SUDLEY, an eminent soldier in the reign of Edward I., and LORD CHAMBERLAIN to that king. He was in the French and Scottish wars, and had summons to parliament as a BARON, from 29th December, 1299, to 15th May, 1321. He *m.* a daughter of Lord Say, but died without issue in 1336, when another

JOHN DE SUDLEY was found to be his next heir. This John *m.* Eleanor, daughter of Robert, Lord Scales, and dying in 14th Edward III., left issue,

    JOHN, who *d.* young.
    Joane, *m.* to William Boteler, of Wemme, and
      had a son THOMAS, who obtained *Sudley*
      CASTLE.
    Margery, *m.* to Sir Robert Massey, Knt.

RALPH BOTELER, of Sudley Castle, descended from the above-mentioned THOMAS BOTELER, becoming a person of eminence, temp. Henry VI., was advanced to the dignity of BARON SUDLEY, on the 10th September, 1441. This nobleman, being a strenuous Lancastrian, excused himself from coming to parliament after the accession of Edward IV., by reason of his advanced age, and had so much favour shewn him, that he obtained letters patent of exemption from the duty during life. He was afterwards, however, attached and brought prisoner to London; when it is stated, that as he was departing from his seat, he cast a lingering look upon Sudley Castle, and exclaimed, " *Sudley Castle, thou art the traytor, not I.*" This castle he is said to have built out of the spoils he had obtained in the wars of France; he sold it eventually to the king. He m. Alice, daughter and heir of Sir William Delacourt, but leaving no issue, at his decease in 1473, the BARONY became EXTINCT, and his estates devolved upon his sisters as co-heirs, namely,

ELIZABETH, m. to Sir Henry Norbury.
JOANE, m. to Hamon Belknap, Esq.
ARMS.—SUDLEY, or. two bendlets, gu.
     BOTELER, gu. a fesse cheque, ar. and sa. betw. six cresslets or.

SUTTON—BARONS DUDLEY.

By Writ of Summons, dated 25th February, 1342, 16 Edward III.

Lineage.

Sir William Dugdale commences his account of the SUTTON family by the following observations: " In the time of Queen Elisabeth, when Ambrose Dudley, Earl of Warwick, and Robert, his brother, Earl of Leicester, (sons to John Dudley, some time Viscount L'Isle, Earl of Warwick, and lastly, Duke of Northumberland,) powerful men in their days, did flourish, the most learned and expert genealogists of that age, spared not their endeavours to magnifie this family, whence those great men did, by a younger son, derive their descent: some deducing it from *Sutton, of Sutton*, in Holderness; some from the *Suttons, of Sutton Madoc*, in Shropshire; but others from *Sutton, of Sutton-upon-Trent*, near *Newark*; whence the *Suttons*, of Arden, (near at hand,) are descended. Of which opinion was the right learned and judicious *Robert Glover*, then *Somerset Herald*; and *Henry Ferrers*, of Badsley-Clinton, in the county of Warwick, Esq., (a person likewise much versed in those studies,) all of them giving probable reasons for those their various conjectures. But, that these SUTTONS, *of Dudley*, did spring from Hugh de Sutton, most of them do agree."

This

HUGH DE SUTTON m. Elisabeth, daughter and heir of William Patrick, lord of the moiety of the Barony of Malpas, in the county of Chester, and was s. by his son,

RICHARD DE SUTTON, who espoused Isabel, only daughter and heir of *Rotheric*, the son of Griffin, and was s. by his son,

SIR JOHN DE SUTTON, Knt., who m. MARGARET, sister and co-heir of *John de Somerie*, LORD DUDLEY, by whom the Sutton family acquired the

404

CASTLE OF DUDLEY, and other considerable estates (refer to Someries, Baron Dudley). This Sir John Sutton passed away by deed, bearing date at Westminster, 19th October, in the 19th Edward II., all his right and title to the castle and manor of Dudley, with other lands, to Hugh le Despenser, son of Hugh, Earl of Winchester. But the grant thus made being extorted from him while in prison, and in fear of being put to death, it was cancelled upon the accession of EDWARD III., and the property restored. Sir John was s. by his son,

JOHN DE SUTTON, who was summoned to parliament as BARON SUTTON, OF DUDLEY, on the 25th February, 1342. His lordship m. Isabel, daughter of JOHN DE CHARLTON, *Lord of Powis*, and dying in 1359, was s. by his only son,

JOHN DE SUTTON, second baron, but never summoned to parliament. The wardship of this nobleman, he being in minority at his father's decease, was granted to *Richard*, EARL OF ARUNDEL, and sold by him to Sir Philip le Despenser, in the 5th Richard II., for three hundred and fifty marks. His lordship m. Elisabeth, daughter of Edward, Lord Stafford, and dying in 1376, was s. by his son,

JOHN DE SUTTON, third baron, but never summoned to parliament; d. in 1406, and was s. by his son,

JOHN DE SUTTON, fourth baron. This nobleman carried the standard at the solemn obsequies of the victorious HENRY V.; and, being also a knight in the 2nd HENRY VI., bore the title of BARON OF DUDLEY, at which time he was in the garrison of the CASTLE OF GHISNES, under its governor, *Humphrey*, DUKE OF GLOUCESTER, and continued there for some time. In the 6th of the same reign he was constituted lieutenant of Ireland for the term of two years; and for his good services was summoned to the parliament, then held at Reading, on the 15th February, 1440: in which year he was likewise appointed one of the commissioners to negotiate a truce with the Duke of Burgundy, or his ambassadors; and in the 27th of the same reign, being then one of the lords of the king's council, he was employed as ambassador to the same prince, to treat with him, and certain commissioners from the Flemings, touching *a freedom of trade* between England and the Low Countries. His lordship being a staunch Lancastrian, was made prisoner in two years after at Gloucester, by Richard, Duke of York, and sent to the castle of Ludlow. He was, subsequently, wounded at BLOXHEATH, and obtained from *King* HENRY VI., to whom he was treasurer, various grants of divers lordships, as also of the stewardship of Montgomery, Chirbury, &c. for life, to be executed either personally or by deputy. But, notwithstanding his fidelity to his royal master, he so far acquiesced in the rule of EDWARD IV., that he had a discharge from that prince of all the debts he owed the crown, and he afterwards obtained other immunities from the same king. Towards the latter end of Henry VI.'s reign, he was invested with the GARTER, and he had summons to parliament regularly from 18th of that king to the 22nd Edward IV. His lordship m. Elisabeth, daughter of Sir John Berkeley, of Beverstone, and widow of

Sir Edward Charlton, Knt., Lord Powis, by whom he had issue,

> EDMUND (Sir), who m. first, Joice, sister and co-heir of John Tiptoft, Earl of Worcester, and had, with other issue,
>
>> JOHN, who succeeded his grandfather.
>> Alianore, m. to Charles Somerset, Earl of Worcester.
>
> He m. secondly, Maud, daughter of Thomas, Lord Clifford, by whom he had,
>
>> Thomas, who m. ———, daughter and co-heir of Lancelot Threlkeld, of Yorworth, Esq.
>> Richard, in holy orders.
>> Joice, m. to William Middleton, Esq., of Stokeide, in the county of York.
>> Margaret, m. to Edward, Lord Powis.
>> Alice, m. to Sir John Ratcliffe, of Ordsale, Lancashire.
>> Dorothy, m. to Sir John Musgrave, Knt.

Sir Edward Sutton d. in the life-time of his father.

> John, who assumed the surname of DUDLEY, and became ancestor of the Dudleys, Earls of Warwick. He m. Elizabeth, one of the daughters and co-heirs of John Bramshot, Esq., of Bramshot, and was father of
>
>> EDMUND DUDLEY, the notorious minister of Henry VII. (see Dudley, Earls of Warwick).
>> William, Bishop of Durham.
>> Margaret, m. to George Longville, Esq., of Little Billing, in the county of Northumberland.

His lordship d. in 1452, and was s. by his grandson,

JOHN SUTTON, fifth baron, summoned to parliament from 9th December, 1483, to 1st September, 1487, who m. Cecilie, daughter of Sir William Willoughby, Knt., and dying in 1487, was s. by his son,

EDWARD SUTTON, sixth baron, summoned to parliament from 12th August, 1499, to 3rd November, 1529. This nobleman was elected a KNIGHT of the GARTER in the beginning of HENRY VIII.'s reign. He m. ———, and had issue,

> JOHN, his successor.
> Jane, m. to Thomas, Lord Dacre.
> Eleanor, m. to Charles Somerset, Earl of Worcestor, ancestor of the present Dukes of Beaufort.
> Catherine, m. to George Gresley.
> Elizabeth, m. to Sir John Huddleston, Knt.
> Joyce.

His lordship d. in 1530, and was s. by his son,

JOHN SUTTON, seventh baron, but never summoned to parliament. "It is reported," writes Dugdale, "by credible tradition, of this John, Lord Dudley, that, being a weak man of understanding, whereby he had exposed himself to some wants, and so became entangled in the usurer's bonds; John Dudley, then Viscount L'Isle, and Earl of Warwick, (afterwards Duke of Northumberland,) thirsting after DUDLEY CASTLE, (the chief seat of the family,) made those money merchants his instruments to work him out of it; which, by some

mortgage, being at length effected, this poor lord became exposed to the charity of his friends for subsistence; and spending the remainder of his life in visits amongst them, was commonly called Lord Quondam." His lordship espoused Lady Cicely Grey, daughter of Thomas, Marquess of Dorset, and had issue,

> EDWARD, his successor.
> George.
> Henry.
> Dorothy.
> Elizabeth.

He was s. at his decease by his eldest son,

SIR EDWARD SUTTON, eighth baron, summoned to parliament from 12th November, 1554, to 15th October, 1586. This nobleman, when Sir Edward Sutton, was in the expedition made into Scotland in the 1st Edward VI., and was appointed governor of Hume Castle upon the surrender of that fortress to the English. His lordship afterwards enjoyed so much favour from Queen MARY, that her majesty restored to him, by letters patent, DUDLEY CASTLE, and other lands of great value, which had vested in the crown, by the attainder of John Dudley, Duke of Northumberland. She constituted him likewise lieutenant of the castle of Hampnes, in Picardy, for life. Lord Dudley m. first, Catherine, daughter of John Brydges, Lord Chandos, of Sudley, by whom he had an only daughter,

> ANNE, m. to Thomas Wylmer, Esq., barrister at law.

He wedded, secondly, Lady Jane Stanley, daughter of Edward, Earl of Derby, by whom he had two sons,

> EDWARD, his successor.
> John, who m. ———, and left two daughters.

His lordship espoused, thirdly, Mary, daughter of William, Lord Howard, of Effingham, but had no issue. He d. in 1586, and was s. by his son,

EDWARD SUTTON, ninth baron, summoned to parliament from 19th February, 1593, to 3rd November, 1639. This nobleman m. Theodosia, daughter of Sir James Harrington, Knt., and had issue,

> FERDINANDO (Sir). This gentleman was made a Knight of the Bath at the creation of Henry, PRINCE OF WALES, in 1610. He m. Honora, daughter of Edward, Lord Beauchamp, eldest son of Edward, Earl of Hertford. Of this marriage, Mr. Porry writes, in a letter to Sir Ralph Winwood, dated London, 17th July, 1610, "Sir Ferdinando Dudley, heir to the Lord Dudley, was yesterday married to my Lord Beauchamp's only daughter, who hath £5000 in present to her marriage, and shall have £5000." Sir Ferdinando died before his father, leaving an only daughter and heir,
>
>> FRANCES, who succeeded her grandfather.
>
> Mary, m. to James, Earl Hume, in Scotland.
> Anne, m. to Meinhardt, Count Schomberg, and was mother of the celebrated
>
>> General FREDERICK, Duke of Schomberg, who fell at the Boyne in 1690.

Margaret, *m.* to Sir Miles Hobart, K.B.

Lord Dudley having lavished much of his property upon a concubine, and his children by her, and thus involved himself and the estates of the family so much in debt, was obliged, according to Dugdale, in order to extricate them, to bestow the hand of his grand-daughter and heiress, FRANCES SUTTON, upon HUMBLE WARD, the only son of William Ward, an opulent goldsmith in London, and jeweller to the queen.

His lordship *d.* in 1643, and was *s.* by his grand-daughter,

FRANCES WARD, (wife of the above-mentioned Sir Humble Ward, Knt., who was created by King CHARLES I., 23rd March, 1644, Lord Ward, of Birmingham,) as BARONESS DUDLEY. This lady had issue,

> EDWARD, who succeeded his father as LORD WARD, in 1670.
>
> William, who *m.* Anne, daughter and sole heir of Thomas Parkes, Esq., of Willingsworth, in the county of Stafford, by whom he acquired that and other estates, and had issue,
>
>> WILLIAM, his successor.
>>
>> Frances, *m.* to Robert Pigot, Esq., of Chetwynd, Salop.
>>
>> Jane, *m.* to Daniel Jevon, Esq.
>>
>> Rebecca, *d.* unmarried.
>
> Mr. Ward was *s.* by his son,
>
>> WILLIAM WARD, Esq., M.P. for the county of Stafford, temp. *Queen* ANNE and *King* GEORGE I. He *m.* Mary, daughter of the Hon. John Grey, of Enfield Hall, and had issue,
>>
>>> JOHN, of Sedgley Park, in the county of Stafford, who inherited the Barony of WARD at the decease of William, fifth baron, in 1740, and was grandfather of the present *John William Ward, Earl of Dudley.*
>
> Humble, *d.* young.
>
> Theodosia, *m.* to Sir Thomas Brereton, and secondly, to Charles Brereton.
>
> Honoria, *m.* to William Dilke, Esq., of Maxtock.
>
> Frances, *m.* to Sir William Noel, Bart., of Kirkley-Mallory, in the county of Leicester.

Her ladyship *d.* in 1697, and was *s.* by her eldest son,

EDWARD WARD, second Lord Ward, of Birmingham, as (eleventh successor to the Barony of Dudley, and) tenth BARON DUDLEY. His lordship *m.* Frances, daughter of Sir William Brereton, Bart., of Handford, in Cheshire, and sister and sole heir of Sir Thomas Brereton, by whom he had issue,

> John, who *d.* young.
>
> WILLIAM, *m.* Frances, daughter of Thomas Dilke, Esq., of Maxtock Castle, in the county of Warwick, and had issue,
>
>> EDWARD, who *s.* his grandfather.
>>
>> WILLIAM, successor to his brother.
>>
>> FRANCES, *m.* to William Lea, Esq., of Hales-Owen-Grange, in the county of Salop, and had issue,

506

FERDINANDO - DUDLEY LEA, of whom hereafter, as fourteenth BARON DUDLEY, upon the decease of William, thirteenth baron, in 1740.

William Lea, *d.* unmarried.

ANNE, *m.* to William Smith, Esq., of Ridgeacre, in the county of Salop.

Frances, *m.* to Walter Woodcock.

Mary, *m.* to —— Hervey, M.D., of Stourbridge.

Catherine, *m.* to Thomas Jardin, of Birmingham.

Elizabeth, *m.* to the Rev. Benjamin Briscoe.

The BARONY OF DUDLEY fell into ABEYANCE amongst these ladies at the decease of their brother.

Ferdinando, *d.* unmarried.

Catherine, *m.* to the Hon. John Grey, of Enfield Hall, and was mother of

> Harry Grey, third Earl of Stamford.

Humbletta, *m.* to Thomas Porter, Esq.

His lordship *d.* in 1701, and was *s.* by his grandson,

EDWARD WARD, eleventh Baron Dudley, and third Lord Ward. This nobleman *m.* Diana, daughter of Thomas Howard, Esq., of Ashford, in the county of Surrey, and dying in 1704, was *s.* by his posthumous son,

EDWARD WARD, twelfth Baron Dudley, and fourth Lord Ward; at whose decease unmarried in 1731, the honours reverted to his uncle,

WILLIAM WARD, thirteenth Baron Dudley, and fifth Lord Ward. This nobleman died, also unmarried, when the BARONY OF WARD, *of Birmingham,* passed to his kinsman, JOHN WARD, Esq., of Sedgeley Park, (refer to WILLIAM, second son of Frances Ward, Baroness Dudley,) and the BARONY OF DUDLEY devolved upon his nephew (revert to FRANCES, daughter of William Ward, eldest surviving son, of Edward, second Lord Ward, and tenth Baron Dudley),

FERDINANDO-DUDLEY LEA, Esq., as fourteenth BARON DUDLEY (15th in succession, one of the inheritors being a baroness). This nobleman died unmarried, in 1787, and his brother having pre-deceased him, also unmarried, the BARONY OF DUDLEY fell into ABEYANCE amongst his lordship's sisters, as it still continues with their descendants.

ARMS.—Of the SUTTONS—Ar. a cross patonce az. or. a lion rampant double queuée. vert.

Of the WARDS—Quarterly; first and fourth or. two lioncels passant az. for SOMERIE; two and three chequy or. and az. for WARD.

SUTTON—BARONS LEXINTON, OF ARAM.

By Letters Patent, dated 21st November, 1645.

Lineage.

ROBERT SUTTON, Esq., of Aram, in the

county of Nottingham, descended from a common ancestor, with the family of Sutton, Barons Dudley, was, in consideration of the eminent services he had rendered to the royal cause, during the civil war, elevated to the peerage, by letters patent, dated 21st November, 1645, as BARON LEXINTON,* *of Aram.* His lordship m. first, Elizabeth, daughter of Sir George Manners, of Haddon, in the county of Derby; secondly, ——, daughter of Sir Guy Palmes, of Ashwell, in the county of Rutland, and widow of Sir Thomas Browne, and thirdly, Mary, daughter of Sir Anthony St. Leger, Knt., by the latter of whom alone he had issue, viz.,

    ROBERT, his successor.

    Bridget, m. to John, eldest son of Conyers Darcy, son and heir-apparent of Conyers, Lord Darcy.

His lordship d. in 1668, and was s. by his son,

ROBERT SUTTON, second baron, who m. Margaret, daughter and heir of Sir Giles Hungerford, of Colston, in the county of Wilts, by whom he had issue,

    WILLIAM-GEORGE, who died in his father's life-time, anno 1713.

    Eleonora-Margareta.

    Bridget, m. to John Manners, third Duke of Rutland, and had issue,

        JOHN, *Marquess of Granby.*

        Robert, who assumed the surname of SUTTON, upon inheriting the LEXINTON estates. His lordship died s. p., in 1772, when those estates devolved upon his next brother,

        GEORGE, who then assumed the additional surname of SUTTON. Lord George Manners-Sutton m. first, in 1749, Diana, daughter of Thomas Chaplin, Esq., and had with other issue,

            John, who d. in 1826, leaving two sons,

               1. CHARLES, Archbishop of Canterbury, m. Mary, daughter of Thomas Thoroton, Esq., and left at his decease, in 1898, with other issue,

---

* LEXINTON.

This name is taken from Lexington, now called Laxton, in the county of Nottingham, which lordship

RICHARD LEXINTON held, in the reign of *King* JOHN, and was s. by

ROBERT LEXINTON, a learned judge, temp. Henry III., and justice itinerant for several northern counties. He was s. by his brother,

JOHN LEXINTON, who, in the reign of Henry III., was chief justice of all the forests north of Trent, and dying s. p., in the 41st of the same reign, was s. by another brother,

HENRY LEXINTON, Bishop of Lincoln, who d. the next year, leaving Richard Markham, and WILLIAM DE SUTTON, from whom the Lord Lexinton, of Aram, derived his heirs.

CHARLES MANNERS-SUTTON, *Speaker of the House of Commons.*

            2. Thomas, late Lord Chancellor of Ireland, created LORD MANNERS.

Lord George espoused, secondly, Mary, daughter of Joshua Peart, Esq., and had a daughter,

        Mary, m. to the Reverend Richard Lockwood, Prebendary of Peterborough.

Lord Lexinton, who had been envoy-extraordinary to the Court of Vienna, and was appointed ambassador-extraordinary to that of Spain, and for the treaty of Ryswick, d. in 1723, when the BARONY OF LEXINTON, *of Aram,* became EXTINCT, and the Sutton estates passed eventually to his nephew, *Lord* GEORGE MANNERS.

ARMS.—Ar. a canton sa.

SWILLINGTON — BARON SWILLINGTON.

By Writ of Summons, dated 3rd December, 1326, 20 Edward II.

Lineage.

Of this family, which assumed its surname from a lordship in the west riding of Yorkshire, was

ADAM DE SWILLINGTON, who, in the times of Edward I. and Edward II., was in the Scottish wars, and in the latter reign obtained charter for free warren, in all his demesne lands at SWILLINGTON, THORPE-PYRON, and THORPE o' the Hill, in the county of York, and was summoned to parliament as a BARON, 3rd December, 1326, but afterwards siding with the Earl of Lancaster against the Spencers, he was fined a thousand marks. On the accession of Edward I., however, matters being changed, that judgment was reversed by parliament, and his lordship marched again into Scotland. Moreover the next year he had another charter for free warren in his demesne lands, and had summons to parliament, to 5th March, 1328, but never afterwards; and nothing further is known of his lordship or his descendants.

ARMS.—Ar. a chevron sa.

SWYNNERTON — BARON SWYNNERTON.

By Writ of Summons, dated 23rd April, 1337, 11 Edward III.

Lineage.

Of this family, (one of great antiquity in the county of Stafford,) which derived its surname from the lordship of SWYNNERTON, many were knights, amongst whom was

SIR ROGER DE SWYNNERTON, who, in the 34th Edward I., had a charter for free warren in all his demesne lands, at his manor of Swynnerton, and for holding a market there. In the 4th Edward II. he was in the wars of Scotland, and in some years afterwards, he was constituted constable of the Tower of London. In the beginning of Edward III.'s reign, he had the rank of banneret, and was again in the wars of Scotland; when he was summoned to parliament as a BARON, on the 23rd April, 1337, but never afterwards, nor had any of his descendents a similar honour. His lordship left a son,

SIR THOMAS SWYNNERTON, Knt., who m. Matilda, daughter of Sir Robert Holland, and was s. by his son,

SIR ROBERT SWYNNERTON, Knt., who m. Elizabeth, daughter and heir of Sir Nicholas Beke, Knt., by whom he left an only daughter and heir,

    MAUD SWYNNERTON, who m. first, William Ipstone, by whom she had issue,

      William, who died *s. p.*

      Christiana, aged six, } *d.* in 1309.
      Alicia, aged three, }

    She espoused, secondly, Humphrey Peshall, and thirdly, Sir John Savage, of Clifton.

The last male heir of this family,

HUMPHREY SWINNERTON, of Swinnerton, left two daughters, his co-heirs, viz.,

    Margaret, m. to Henry Vernon, Esq., of Sudbury, in Derbyshire.

    Elizabeth, m. in 1552, to William, fourth son of Sir Anthony Fitz-Herbert, of Norbury, the celebrated judge of the Court of Common Pleas, temp. Henry VIII., and conveyed the manor of Swinnerton to her husband. The descendant of this lady,

      WILLIAM FITZ-HERBERT, of Swinnerton, upon the death of Sir John Fitz-Herbert, Knt., a distinguished cavalier commander, in 1649, became chief of the family, and inherited the principal seat, NORBURY,* from which time the estates of Swinnerton and Norbury have never been separated. From this William, we pass to his lineal descendant,

        THOMAS FITZ-HERBERT, Esq., twenty-fourth Lord of Norbury, and eighth of Swinnerton, b. in 1746, m. in 1778, to MARY-ANNE, youngest daughter of Walter Smythe, Esq., of Bambridge, in the county of Hants, and widow of Edward Weld, Esq., of Lulworth Castle, in the county of Dorset. (This lady, the *celebrated* MRS. FITZ-HERBERT, is still living, 1831). Mr. Fitz-Herbert died *s. p.*, in 1781, and was s. by his brother,

        BASIL FITZ-HERBERT, Esq., twen-

ty-fifth Lord of Norbury, and ninth Lord of Swinnerton, who m. Elizabeth, youngest daughter and co-heir of James Windsor Heneage, Esq., of Cadeby, in the county of Lincoln, and Gatcombe, Isle of Wight, and dying in 1797, was s. by his eldest son,

    THOMAS FITZ-HERBERT, Esq., twenty-sixth Lord of Norbury, and tenth Lord of Swinnerton; m. in 1809, Marian, daughter of John Palmer Chichester, Esq., of Arlington, in the county of Devon, and has a son and heir,

      CHARLES FITZ-HERBERT, b. 21st January, 1810.

ARMS.—Az. a cross flores sa.

Note.—Of this family was Sir Thomas Swinnerton, Lord Mayor of London, whose third son,

    THOMAS SWINNERTON, Esq., of Stanway Hall, in Essex, left an only daughter and heiress,

    THOMASINE SWINNERTON, m. William Dyer, Esq., who was created a BARONET, in 1678, and was great-great-grandfather, of the present

      SIR THOMAS RICHARD SWINNERTON DYER, Baronet.

SYDNEY — BARONS SYDNEY, OF PENSHURST, VISCOUNTS L'ISLE, EARLS LEICESTER.

Barony,	by Letters Patent,	13th May, 1603.
Viscounty,		4th May, 1605.
Earldom,		2nd August, 1618.

Lineage.

This family, anciently seated at Cranleigh, in Surrey, and at Kyngesham, in Sussex, derived its descent from

SIR WILLIAM SYDNEY, chamberlain to King Henry II., with which monarch he came into England from Anjou. From this Sir William lineally sprang,

SIR WILLIAM SYDNEY, who, in the 3rd Henry VIII., being then one of the esquires of the king's house, accompanied Thomas, Lord Darcy, into Spain, for the assistance of the Spaniard against the Moors; and when other persons of rank received the dignity of knighthood at the hands of King FERDINAND, excused himself from partaking thereof. The next year he was captain of one of the ships of war employed against the French, and came into action off the coast of Brest. In the 5th of the same reign Sir William (then a knight) was a chief commander at the battle of FLODDEN

---

* NORBURY came to the Fitz-Herberts, by grant of William, Prior of Tutbury, in 1195.

FIELD; and the next ensuing year he accompanied the Duke of Suffolk, the Marquess of Dorset, and other persons of distinction, to Paris, there to make proof of their skill in arms, against the DAUPHIN of France, and nine other select persons, whom he had chosen for his assistants at those solemn justs, there held in the month of November for all comers, being gentlemen of name and arms. The English noblemen and gentlemen landed at Calais, arrayed in green coats and hoods, that they might not be known. Sir William was subsequently one in the second band of the English at the justs held before the courts of HENRY VIII. and FRANCIS I. on the field of the Cloth of Gold. He was also chamberlain and steward to King Henry, and in the 15th of that monarch, accompanying the Duke of Suffolk into France, he shared in the glory then acquired by the English arms. After this, on the attainder of Sir Philip Vane, he had a grant of the honour of Penshurst, and manor of Enfield, with the park of Penshurst, and other manors and lands in Kent. Sir William m. Anne, daughter of Hugh Pagenham, Esq., and had issue,

> HENRY (Sir), his successor.
>
> Frances, m. to Thomas Ratcliffe, Earl of Sussex, whom she survived, and founded SYDNEY-SUSSEX COLLEGE, at Cambridge.
>
> ———, m. to Sir William Fitz-Williams, Knt.
>
> Mary, m. to Sir William Dormer, Knt.
>
> Lucy, m. to Sir James Harington, Knt.

He d. in the 7th of Edward VI., and was s. by his son,

SIR HENRY SYDNEY, who had been ambassador to France four years before, and the next year was constituted cup-bearer to the king for life. In the 2nd and 3rd Philip and Mary he was made vice-treasurer, and general governor of all the revenues of the crown in Ireland, and he was soon afterwards invested with the temporary government of that kingdom as lord justice, during the absence of the lord deputy, the Earl of Sussex. In the 2nd Elizabeth he was appointed lord president of Wales, and in the 5th sent upon a confidential mission into France. In 1564 (6th Elizabeth), he was made a KNIGHT of the GARTER, and in some years afterwards was thrice constituted by her majesty LORD DEPUTY OF IRELAND. This eminent person espoused Lady Mary Dudley, daughter of John, Earl of Northumberland, and sister of Robert, Earl of Leicester, by whom he had issue,

> PHILIP (Sir), a gentleman universally and almost enthusiastically admired for his great worth and extraordinary accomplishments. He was a soldier and a scholar, illustrious in letters and in arms, but more illustrious by his deeds of benevolence and humanity. He was mortally wounded in September, 1586, at the battle of Zutphen, in Guilderland, and d. on the 16th October following. Sir Philip Sydney m. Frances, daughter of Sir Francis Walsingham, and left an only daughter,
>
>> Elizabeth, m. to Roger, Earl of Rutland.
>
> ROBERT (Sir), of whom presently.

Thomas (Sir).

Mary, m. to Henry, Earl of Pembroke.

The second son,

SIR ROBERT SYDNEY succeeded as next heir male upon the death of his elder brother, Sir Philip. This gallant person, like his predecessors, acquired renown in arms, first under his uncle, Robert Dudley, Earl of Leicester, in the Netherlands, and afterwards with Sir Frances Vere, when he shared in the victory achieved at Turnholt, in Brabant, anno 1597. For these, upon the accession of King JAMES I., Sir Robert was elevated to the peerage as BARON SYDNEY, of Penshurst, in the county of Kent, by letters patent, dated 13th May, 1603, and upon the 24th July, in the same year, (it being the day of the king and queen's coronation,) he was appointed LORD CHAMBERLAIN to the queen. The next year he was created VISCOUNT L'ISLE. In 1616 he was installed a Knight of the Garter, and raised on 2nd August, 1618, to the EARLDOM OF LEICESTER, the ceremony of creation being performed in the hall of the bishop's palace at Salisbury. His lordship m. first, Barbara, daughter and heir of John Gammage, Esq., of Glamorganshire, and had issue,

> William (Sir), who d. unmarried before his father.
>
> ROBERT (Sir), made Knight of the Bath at the creation of Henry, Prince of Wales, succeeded his father.
>
> Mary, m. to Sir Robert Wroth, Knt.
>
> Catherine, m. to Sir Lewis Mansel, Knt.
>
> Philippa, m. to Sir John Hobart, Knt., eldest son of Sir Henry Hobart, Knt., Lord Chief Justice of the Common Pleas, from whom the Earls of Buckinghamshire descend.
>
> Barbara, m. to Sir Thomas Smith, afterwards made Viscount Strangford, in Ireland, ancestor of the present viscount.

His lordship espoused, secondly, Lady Smith, widow of Sir Thomas Smith, Knt.; he d. in 1626, and was s. by his eldest surviving son,

SIR ROBERT SYDNEY, K.B., second Earl of Leicester. This nobleman, who lived to the age of eighty years and eleven months, was esteemed of great learning, observation, and veracity. He m. Lady Dorothy Percy, daughter of Henry, Earl of Northumberland, and had issue,

> PHILIP, Viscount L'Isle, his successor.
>
> ALGERNON. The celebrated patriot, ALGERNON SYDNEY, who suffered death by decapitation on Tower Hill, 7th December, 1683, as a participator in the Rye House Plot: but his name will live so long as "the CAUSE for which Hampden bled in the field, and Sydney on the scaffold," shall be cherished by the free-born men of England. Of this eminent person Burnet writes, "he was too rough and boisterous in his temper to bear contradiction; he seemed to be a christian, but in a particular form of his own: for christianity he thought was to be like a divine philosophy of the mind, without all public worship, or any sign of a visible church. Still he was in all republican principles, and such an enemy to every thing

that looked liked monarchy, that he opposed Cromwell after he was made PROTECTOR: but he had studied the history of government in all its branches; had a knowledge of mankind, and of their tempers; and could insinuate himself into people that would hearken to his notions with a wonderful dexterity."

Robert, d. in 1674.

HENRY, created Earl of Romney.

Dorothy, m. first, to Henry, Earl of Sunderland, and secondly, to Robert Smyth, Esq.

Lucy, m. to Sir John Pelham, Bart.

Anne, m. to the Rev. Joseph Cart.

Elizabeth, m. to Philip, Viscount Strangford.

His lordship d. in 1677, and was s. by his eldest son,

PHILIP SYDNEY, third Earl of Leicester. This nobleman, in the life-time of his father, was a zealous republican, and during the usurpation, was all along of the protector's council, with a salary of £1000 a year. He had been from his youth, trained up a diplomatist, attending on his father to the states-general, and the courts of Denmark and France. His lordship espoused Lady Catherine Cecil, daughter of William, Earl of Salisbury, and had issue,

ROBERT, Viscount L'Isle, summoned to parliament in his father's life-time, as BARON SYDNEY, OF PENSHURST, anno 1689.

Dorothy, m. to Thomas Cheeke, Esq.

The Earl d. in March, 1697-8, and was s. by his son,

ROBERT SYDNEY, fourth Earl of Leicester. His lordship espoused Lady Elizabeth Egerton, daughter of John, Earl of Bridgewater, and had issue,

PHILIP, Viscount L'Isle.

JOHN, who succeeded as sixth earl.

Robert, who m. Mary, daughter of Sir Robert Reeve, Bart, and dying in 1698-9, left two daughters co-heirs, viz.

MARY, m. to Sir Brownlow Sherard, Bart.

ELIZABETH, m. to William Perry, Esq., of Wornington, in the county of Gloucester. This lady succeeded eventually as sole heiress to PENSHURST, and the other estates of the Sydneys. She claimed, in 1782, the BARONY OF SYDNEY, OF PENSHURST, under the presumption that Robert, Earl of Leicester, her grandfather, having been summoned in 1689, in the life-time of his father, in that nobleman's barony, a BARONY IN FEE had been created, but the claim was dismissed by the House of Lords. Mrs. Perry left an only daughter and heiress,

ELIZABETH-JANE-SYDNEY PERRY, who became the second wife of Sir Bysche Shelley, Bart., of Castle Goring, and had, with junior issue,

JOHN SHELLEY, who assumed the additional surname of SYDNEY, and having inherited the Sydney estates, and being created a baronet, is the present

SIR JOHN SHELLEY SYDNEY.

JOCELINE, who succeeded as seventh earl.

Elizabeth, m. to Sir Harcourt Masters.

Catherine, m. to William Parker, Esq.

His lordship d. in 1702, and was s. by his eldest son,

PHILIP SYDNEY, fifth earl, who m. Anne, daughter and co-heir of Sir Robert Reeve, of Thwaites, in Suffolk, but dying without surviving issue, in 1705, the honours devolved upon his brother,

JOHN SYDNEY, sixth Earl. This nobleman was constituted in 1717, warden of the cinque ports, and governor of Dover Castle; and upon the revival of the order of the Bath, he was elected one of the knights. His lordship d. unmarried, in 1737, and was s. by his only surviving brother,

JOCELYNE SYDNEY, seventh earl. This nobleman m. Elizabeth, daughter and heiress of —— Thomas, Esq., of Glamorganshire, with which lady his lordship had long pending disputes regarding misconduct, but he never obtained a divorce. He d. in 1743, when the estates devolved upon (the daughter of his brother, Col. Robert Sydney) his niece, ELIZABETH, who had married Robert Perry, Esq., and all the estates were conveyed by her daughter and heiress, ELIZABETH-JANE-SYDNEY PERRY to the SHELLEYS: while all the honours of the house of SYDNEY became EXTINCT; his lordship having deceased issueless.*

ARMS.—Or. a pheon az.

---

* By a trial at bar on a writ of right, at Westminster, 11th February, 1782, for Penshurst Place, park, and premises, in the county of Kent, it appeared that this Jocelyne, Earl of Leicester, never was divorced from his wife, the said Elizabeth Thomas; and that she had a child, a son, John Sydney, the demandant at the trial aforesaid; which John, therefore, in the eye of the law, was to be considered as a legitimate person, and as such, well entitled to the inheritance of the honours of the family. But with respect to the inheritance of the estates demanded by him, he failed to establish a better right than the tenant in possession. This (according to the statement at the trial) arose from his averment, that his father, Earl Jocelyne, was possessed thereof in fee, and not as tenant for life, which was the fact, as opened by the tenant; and further contended, that even had he been possessed thereof in fee, then by his will the earl had given them away to a third party. The event of this trial going to admit the legitimacy of the demandant, embraces an important question, as to the absolute extinction of the honours.—BANKS.

SYDNEY — VISCOUNT SYDNEY, EARL OF ROMNEY.

Viscounty, } by Letters { 9th April, 1689.
Earldom, } Patent,   { 25th April, 1694.

Lineage.

HENRY SYDNEY, youngest son of Robert, second Earl of Leicester, having contributed zealously to effect the REVOLUTION, was created, in the 1st of William and Mary, by letters patent, dated 9th April, 1689, *Baron Sydney, of Milton,* and VISCOUNT SYDNEY, *of Sheppey, both in the county of Kent,* and advanced 25th April, 1694, to the EARLDOM OF ROMNEY. His lordship held many lucrative employments under the crown, but dying unmarried, in 1704, ALL HIS HONOURS became EXTINCT.

ARMS.—Or. a pheon az. a crescent for difference.

TALBOT—BARONS TALBOT.

By Writ of Summons, dated 5th June, 1331,
4 Edward III.

Lineage.

The first mention of this family occurs in the *time* of the CONQUEROR, when we find RICHARD TALBOT witnessing a grant made by Walter Giffard, Earl of Buckingham, to certain monks in Normandy. The next of the name, is

GEOFFREY TALBOT, who, in the reign of HENRY I., held twenty knights' fees of the king: and was subsequently an active partisan of the *Empress* MAUD, against King Stephen. After this Geoffrey comes his (presumed) brother,

HUGH TALBOT, who, in the decline of life, assumed the cowl in the monastery of Beauveck, in Normandy, to which he had been a liberal benefactor, and was *s.* upon his retirement, by his eldest son,

RICHARD TALBOT, who, in the beginning of HENRY II.'s reign, obtained from the crown a grant of the lordship of LINTONE, in the county of Hereford, which Richard I. afterwards confirmed for two hundred marks. This Richard Talbot was *s.* by his son,

GILBERT TALBOT, who was *s.* by his son,

RICHARD TALBOT. This feudal lord *m.* Aliva, daughter of Alan Basset, of Wickombe, in the county of Buckingham, sister of Philip Basset, Justice of England, and widow of Dru Montacute. He was *s.* by his son,

GILBERT TALBOT, who, in the 45th Henry III., was constituted one of the justices itinerant for the county of Hereford, and in two years afterwards, upon the disturbance made by the Welsh, was ordered by the king to fortify MONMOUTH CASTLE, and other castles, of which he was then governor. He *m.* Guentian, daughter, and at length heiress of Rhese ap Griffiths, Prince of Wales. In consequence of which alliance, the TALBOTS, instead of their own arms, "*a bend of ten pieces, ar. and gu.,*" adopted those of the Princes of Wales, viz. "*a lion rampant or, in a field gu., with a border engrailed of the first.*" He *d.* in 1274, seised of the manors of LONGHOPE and REDLEY, in the county

of Gloucester, and the manors of ECCLESWELL and LINTONE, in Herefordshire; and was *s.* by his son,

RICHARD TALBOT. It was this feudal lord that adopted the arms of the Princes of Wales, which his descendants have since borne. In the 10th Edward I., he was in the expedition made into Wales, and in the 24th and 25th of the same reign, he was in the wars of Gascony; in which latter year, he was constituted governor of the castle of Cardiff. He had afterwards a military summons to prevent an invasion of the Scots, and he was a member of the great council or parliament, held at Lincoln, in the 29th Edward I., when with the other barons, he subscribed the letter to the pope, in which was asserted the King of England's right to the realm of Scotland. He *m.* the Lady Sarah Beauchamp, daughter of William, Earl of Warwick, and had issue,

> GILBERT, his successor.
>
> Richard, who *m.* Joane, daughter and coheir of Hugh de Mortimer, of RICHARD'S CASTLE, in the county of Hertford, and obtaining that seat, this branch of the Talbots was afterwards designated of "RICHARD'S CASTLE." He was *s.* by his son,
>
>> SIR JOHN TALBOT, of Richard's Castle, who was *s.* by his son,
>>
>>> JOHN Talbot, of Richard's Castle, who *d.* in the 19th Richard II., issueless, leaving his sisters his heirs, viz.
>>>
>>>> ELIZABETH, *m.* to Sir Warine Archdekne, Knt.
>>>>
>>>> PHILIPPA, *m.* to Sir Matthew Gournay, Knt.
>>>>
>>>> ELEANOR, unmarried.
>>>>
>>>> Amongst whom the estates were divided.

Lord Talbot *d.* in 1306, and was *s.* by his elder son,

GILBERT TALBOT, who was in the expedition made into Scotland, in the 26th Edward I.; and having been implicated in the murder of Piers Gaveston, obtained a pardon, in the 7th Edward II. In the 16th of the same reign, he was constituted governor of the town and castle of Gloucester, but being afterwards engaged in the insurrection of Thomas, Earl of Lancaster, against the power of the Spencers, he was compelled, in order to save his life and preserve his estates, to enter into a recognisance to pay £200, and also £2000 more, with one tun of wine. Upon the accession of EDWARD III., however, that obligation was cancelled. Moreover, being then a banneret, he became so active for the king in all his military affairs, that there was due to him, £116. 3*s.* 8*d.,* for the service of himself and his men-at-arms. In the 4th Edward III, he was constituted justice of South Wales, and he was summoned to parliament as a BARON, in the same year, and from that period to the 17th (1343). His lordship *m.* Anne, daughter of William Botelere, of Wemme, and dying in 1346, was *s.* by his son,

RICHARD TALBOT, second baron, summoned to parliament from 5th June, 1331, to 22nd October, 1355, as LORD TALBOT, *of Goderich Castle,* in the county of Hereford, the chief place of his abode.

This nobleman m. Elizabeth, daughter and co-heir of John Comyn, of Badenagh, by Joan, sister and co-heir of Aymer de Valence, Earl of Pembroke; and in her right, claiming (anno 1331) certain lands in Scotland, and adhering to Edward Baliol, who then preferred pretensions to the crown, would have entered that kingdom by land, but was prevented by King EDWARD III., whose sister, Joane, had been married to David Bruce, the son of Robert, King of Scotland. He invaded it, however, by sea, at the head of three hundred armed men, and soon after achieved a great victory over the Scots at GLEDDESMORE; but he was subsequently made prisoner, and had to pay two thousand marks for his redemption. In the 11th Edward III., his lordship was appointed governor of Berwick-upon-Tweed, as also justice there, and of all other the king's lands in Scotland. The same year being a BANNERET, he had an assignation of £900 of the tenth, then given in parliament, out of the city of Bristol, for his better support in the governorship of Berwick. In four years afterwards, he was again in the wars of Scotland, and subsequently (20th Edward III.) in the expedition made into France; at which latter period he laid the foundation of the priory of Flaneaford, within his lordship of Goderich Castle; and at this time too, he obtained from the king a grant for a PRISON at GODERICH CASTLE, for punishing malefactors. His lordship d. in 1356, and was s. by his elder son,

GILBERT TALBOT, third baron, summoned to parliament, from 14th August, 1362, to 8th August, 1366. This nobleman served under the BLACK PRINCE, in the wars of France; and in the 1st Richard II., he was in the king's fleet at sea, with Michael de la Pole, admiral for the north. His lordship m. first, Petronilla, daughter of James, Earl of Ormonde, by whom he had,

    RICHARD, who having m. Ankaret, sister and eventually sole heir of John, Baron Strange, of Blackmere, was summoned to parliament in the life-time of his father, from 3rd March, 1384, to 17th December, 1387, as LORD TALBOT, of Blackmere.

Lord Talbot espoused, secondly, Joane, daughter of Ralph, Earl of Stafford. He d. in 1387, and was s. by his son,

SIR RICHARD TALBOT, Lord Talbot, of Blackmere, as fourth Baron Talbot, summoned to parliament, in 1387, (the same writ in which he was also designated of "Blackmere,") as BARON TALBOT, of Goderich Castle, and from that period to 1393. His lordship was in the wars of Scotland, and attained the rank of banneret. In the 15th Richard II., he succeeded to the lands of the family of Hastings, Earls of Pembroke, derived through his great grandmother, Joane de Valence, sister and co-heir of Aymer, Earl of Pembroke, and wife of John Comyn, of Badenagh. By the heiress of Blackmere, he had four sons—

    GILBERT, his successor.
    JOHN, of whom hereafter, as successor to the barony.
    Richard, Archbishop of Dublin.
    Thomas, of Wrockwardine, in the county of Salop.

His lordship d. in 1396, and was s. by his elder son,

SIR GILBERT TALBOT, fifth baron, summoned to parliament, from 26th August, 1404, to October, 1417. This nobleman, as heir to the Earls of Pembroke, claimed to carry the great spurs at the coronation of HENRY V.; soon after which, he was constituted justice of Chester, and he was subsequently engaged in the French wars. In the 4th of the same reign, his lordship was appointed guardian and captain-general of the Marches of Normandy; and he was likewise a KNIGHT of the GARTER. He m. first, Joan, daughter of Thomas, of Woodstock, Duke of Gloucester, by whom he had no issue. His lordship espoused, secondly, Beatrix, illegitimate daughter of John I., King of Portugal, and widow of Thomas, Earl of Arundel, by whom he had a daughter, ANKARET. He d. in 1419, and was s. in the BARONIES OF TALBOT, and STRANGE, OF BLACKMERE, by his daughter,

ANKARET TALBOT, at whose decease, in minority, anno 1421, these honours reverted to her uncle,

SIR JOHN TALBOT, as sixth Baron Talbot, who having m. Maud de Nevill, eldest daughter and co-heir of Thomas, fifth Lord Furnival, had been summoned to parliament as LORD TALBOT, of Furnival, from 26th October, 1409, to 26th November, 1421. This is the renowned SIR JOHN TALBOT, one of the most illustrious characters in the whole range of English History. In 1412, he was appointed chief Justice of Ireland, and in two years afterwards, constituted LORD LIEUTENANT of the same kingdom. He subsequently distinguished himself in the wars of HENRY V., but his splendid reputation was acquired under the Regency, (John Plantagenet, Duke of) BEDFORD, temp. HENRY VI., when his name alone became terrible to the soldiers of France, owing to the numerous victories he had achieved. His lordship was attacked, however, by the MAID OF ORLEANS, near PATAY, in 1429, and his army being entirely routed, he became a prisoner to that enterprising and enthusiastic heroine. This defeat of Lord Talbot was followed by the loss of divers places of importance to the English. His lordship was detained in captivity, for no less than four years, but obtained at length his freedom, by the payment of a large sum of money, and the enlargement of Ambrose de Lore, an eminent captain of the French. Again taking the field, and again becoming renowned for his triumphs, he was created, in consideration of those eminent services, on the 20th May, 1442, EARL OF SHREWSBURY. After this, we find him reconstituted LORD LIEUTENANT OF IRELAND, and made a peer of that kingdom (anno 1446), as Earl of Waterford and Wexford; having at the same time the city of Waterford, with the castles, honour, land, and Barony of Dungarvan granted to him, and the heirs male of his body, and that he and they should thenceforth be stewards of Ireland. In a few weeks afterwards, his son, Sir John Talbot, was appointed LORD CHANCELLOR OF THAT KINGDOM. His lordship was now far advanced in life, but the English interests declining in France, he was once more induced to place himself at the head of the army there, and his courage and conduct restored for some time, at least, its glory. He was appointed LIEUTENANT of the DUCHY OF AQUITAINE, having under him, as captains of his men at arms and archers, his son, John Talbot, Viscount L'Isle, Sir John Hungerford, Lord Molines, Sir Roger Camoys, Sir John L'Isle, and John Beaufort, the BASTARD OF SOMERSET. Marching immediately to the place of his government, he took the city of BORDEAUX, and placed a garrison in it; whence proceeding to the relief of CHASTILLION, an engagement with the French army ensued, which terminated in the total defeat of the English, and the death of their gallant general, who was killed by a cannon ball. Thus fell, sword in hand, the immortal *John Talbot*, EARL OF SHREWSBURY, at the great age of *eighty*, on 20th July, 1453, after having won no less than forty pitched battles, or important rencounters. His remains were conveyed to England, and interred at Whitchurch, in the county of Salop; where a noble monument was erected in the south wall of the chancel, with this epitaph :

" Orate pro anima prænobilis domini, domini
": Johannis Talbot quondam Comitis Salopiæ, domini
" Furnivall, domini Verdon, domini Strange de
" Blackmere, et Mareschalli Franciæ, qui obiit in
" Bello apud Burdews, vij° julij, MCCCCLIII."

By the heiress of Furnivall, his lordship had issue,

    Thomas, who d. in France, in the life-time of his father.
    JOHN, his successor.
    Christopher (Sir).

The earl espoused, secondly, the Lady Margaret Beauchamp, daughter and co-heir of Richard, Earl of Warwick, and had,

    JOHN, created Baron and Viscount L'Isle, see that dignity.
    Humphrey (Sir), Marshal of Calais, died s. p. in 1492.
    Lewis (Sir), of Penyard, Herts.
    Joane, m. to James, first Lord Berkeley.

At the period of his lordship's advancement to the EARLDOM OF SHREWSBURY, the BARONY OF TALBOT, with those of STRANGE, *of Blackmere*, and FURNIVALL, merged in that dignity, and so continued until the decease of GILBERT TALBOT, seventh Earl of Shrewsbury, and twelfth BARON TALBOT, in 1826, when all three fell into ABEYANCE amongst his daughters and co-heirs, viz.

    Mary, m. to William, third Earl of Pembroke, and died s. p.
    Elizabeth, m. to Henry Grey, eighth Earl of Kent, and died s. p.
    ALATHEA, m. to Thomas Howard, who had been restored in 1603 to the EARLDOMS OF ARUNDEL AND SURREY, created earl marshal in 1621.

Upon the decease of Mary and Elizabeth, the two elder co-heirs, as stated above, *issueless*, the ABEYANCE of the BARONIES OF TALBOT, STRANGE, and FURNIVALL, terminated; and those dignities then vested in the third co-heir, ALATHEA, widow of *Thomas Howard*, EARL OF ARUNDEL, and

thenceforward they merged in the Earldom of Arundel, and Dukedom of Norfolk, until the decease of EDWARD HOWARD, ninth Duke of Norfolk, in 1777, without issue, when the BARONIES OF TALBOT, STRANGE, *of Blackmere*, and FURNIVALL, fell again into ABEYANCE between his grace's nieces, the two daughters and co-heirs of his brother, Philip Howard, Esq., namely,

    WINIFREDE HOWARD, who m. *William*, LORD STOURTON, and was grandmother of *William*, present LORD STOURTON.
    ANNE HOWARD, who m. Robert-Edward, Lord Petre, and was grandmother of *William-Francis*, present LORD PETRE.

These BARONIES remain still in abeyance between the LORDS STOURTON AND PETRE.

ARMS.—Gu. a lion rampant, or. with a border ingrailed of the second.

TALBOT — BARON L'ISLE, OF KINGSTON L'ISLE, IN THE COUNTY OF BERKS, VISCOUNT L'ISLE.

Barony,	} by Letters {	26th July, 1443.
Viscounty,	} Patent, {	30th October, 1452.

Lineage.

The Honourable
JOHN TALBOT, eldest son of John Talbot, the first and great Earl of Shrewsbury, by his second wife, the Lady Margaret Beauchamp, eldest daughter and co-heir of Richard, twelfth Earl of Warwick, and great grand-daughter of Warine, second Baron L'Isle, (see L'Isle, Barons L'Isle,) was created BARON L'ISLE, of Kingston L'Isle, in the county of Berks, by patent,* dated 26th July, 1443, limiting

* This, NICOLAS, in his Synopsis, terms one of the most extraordinary patents on record—and he proceeds. " The patent recites as a fact, that ' Warine de L'Isle, and his ancestors, by reason of the lordship and manor of Kingston L'Isle, had, from time whereof the memory of man was not to the contrary, the name and dignity of Baron and Lord L'Isle, and by that name had seat in parliament, &c. as other barons of the realm had ;' an assertion satisfactorily proved by the lords' committee on the dignity of a peer of the realm, in their third report, to have been entirely without foundation ; for not only had the said manor never been held in capite by the crown, but a period of above sixty years had elapsed, viz. from 23rd Edward I. to 31st Edward III., after writs of summons were generally issued, before the family of L'Isle, tenants of the manor of L'Isle, were ever summoned to parliament. Many arguments might be adduced to support the conclusion stated in the text relative to this dignity, but they are rendered useless, by the statement of the case in the report of the lords' committee just cited, page 191, et seq., and by the opinions of the great legal authorities, Coke and Blackstone. It is therefore sufficient to remark, that this singular creation probably arose from the powerful influence possessed by the Earl of Shrews-

the dignity to the said John, and his heirs, and assigns for ever, being tenants of the manor of Kingston L'Isle, and was advanced to the dignity of VISCOUNT L'ISLE on the 30th October, 1452. This nobleman, who served under his gallant father in France, was slain with that heroic personage at Chastillion, anno 1453. His lordship m. Joan, daughter and co-heir of Sir Thomas Chedder, of Chedder, in the county of Somerset, and widow of Richard Stafford, Esq., and had issue,

THOMAS, his successor.

Elizabeth; m. to Sir Edward Grey, (second son of Edward, Lord Ferrers, of Groby,) who was created Viscount L'Isle (see Grey, Viscount L'Isle).

Margaret, m. to Sir George Vere, Knt., and d. without issue.

The viscount was s. by his son,

THOMAS TALBOT, second Baron and Viscount L'Isle. This nobleman having a great contest with William, Lord Berkeley, of Berkeley Castle, concerning certain lands which he claimed in right of his grandmother, Margaret Beauchamp, Countess of Shrewsbury, lost his life by an arrow shot through the mouth, in a skirmish between the parties, at Wotton-under-Edge, in Gloucestershire, on the 20th March, 1469. His lordship m. Lady Margaret Herbert, daughter of William, Earl of Pembroke, but leaving no issue, his sisters became his co-heirs. The VISCOUNTY OF L'ISLE EXPIRED at his lordship's decease. "But," (says Nicolas,) "it is a very doubtful point into what state the BARONY then fell. In the third report of the lords' committee on the dignity of a peer of the realm, the case is most ably stated, and to it he (Nicolas) refers in support of the following conclusions: first, that the patent to John Talbot, in 1443, did not (though evidently intended so to do) affect the barony created by the writ to Gerard L'Isle, in 31st Edward III., and which, consequently, still remained in abeyance, but created a *new* barony, descendible according to the provisions of the patent: and secondly, with respect to the extremely difficult question, ' in whom is *that* barony now vested?' it is to be observed that, according to the high authority of Lord Chief Justice Coke and of Justice Blackstone, John Talbot, and his heirs, under the patent, had only a base or qualified fee in that dignity, and ' that the instant he or his heirs quitted the seigniory of this manor the dignity was at an end.' On the death of Thomas, second viscount, (continues Nicolas,) in 1469, without issue, his two sisters became his heirs, viz. Margaret, the wife of Sir George Vere, Knt., and Elizabeth,[*] Lady Grey, when it is presumed the BARONY OF L'ISLE became suspended, for although the said Elizabeth was possessed of the manor, she was not *sole* heir of John Talbot, her father, and consequently had not the two constituent qualifications necessary to entitle her to the dignity. On the

bury, in a reign, when more anomalies connected with dignities are to be found than under any preceding or subsequent monarch."—NICOLAS' SYNOPSIS.

[*] See Grey, Lord L'Isle.

514

death of her sister, Lady Vere, however, s. p., she appears to have become legally seised of the barony, as is recited in the patent granted to her husband."

ARMS.—Gules, a lion rampant, within a bordure ingrailed, or.

TALBOT—BARONS FURNIVAL.

See FURNIVAL; and TALBOT, *Barons* TALBOT.

TALBOT—DUKE OF SHREWSBURY.

By Letters Patent, dated 30th April, 1694.

Lineage.

CHARLES TALBOT, Lord Talbot, b. 24th July, 1660, s. his father as twelfth Earl of Shrewsbury, on the 16th March, 1667. In 1681, his lordship was constituted Lord Lieutenant and Custos Rotulorum of the county of Stafford; and he renounced the tenets of the church of Rome at the time that prosecutions were in such vigorous progress under the auspices of the *immaculate* OATES, against the unhappy persons charged with the fictitious popish plot. At the coronation of *King* JAMES II., the earl bore the *Curtance* or pointless sword; and the same year he was appointed colonel of the 6th regiment of horse: but disgusted with the proceedings of the court, he resigned soon after his military rank, and went over to the Prince of Orange, to whom he tendered his purse and sword; and Burnet states that Lord Shrewsbury was one of the nobles in whom the prince placed the most confidence, and by whose advice he was upon all occasions principally guided. Thus promoting the REVOLUTION, when that measure was accomplished by the elevation of WILLIAM and MARY to the throne, his lordship was immediately sworn of the privy council, and made principal secretary of state. In March, 1694, he was elected a KNIGHT OF THE GARTER, and the next month, created *Marquess of Alton*, and DUKE OF SHREWSBURY. In 1695 and 1697, his grace was one of the Lords Justices during the temporary absences of the king: and in 1699, he resigned the seals as secretary of state, but was constituted soon after, LORD CHAMBERLAIN of the household—an office which he subsequently held in the reign of *Queen* ANNE; and was afterwards (anno 1713) constituted by her majesty, LORD LIEUTENANT OF IRELAND. Upon the accession of *King* GEORGE I., the duke was made groom of the stole, and privy purse; and sworn a member of the new privy council. He was subsequently declared Lord Chamberlain of his majesty's household, while his duchess was appointed one of the ladies of the bedchamber to Caroline, Princess of Wales. His grace m. Adelhida, daughter of the Marquess of Paliotti, in Italy, descended maternally from Sir Robert Dudley, son of Robert Dudley, Earl of Leicester, the celebrated favourite of Queen Elizabeth, but d. without issue on the 1st of February, 1717-18, *Old Style*, when the honours he had inherited passed to the heir at law, and the *Marquisate of Alton*, and DUKEDOM OF SHREWSBURY, became EXTINCT.

ARMS.—Gu. a lion rampant, within a border ingrailed, or.

TALBOT—EARL TALBOT.

By Letters Patent, dated 10th March, 1761.

Lineage.

SIR GILBERT TALBOT, of Grafton, in the county of Worcester, K.G., third son of John, second Earl of Shrewsbury, m. first, Elizabeth, daughter of Henry, Lord Scrope, of Bolton, and had, with two daughters,

GILBERT (Sir), who left at his decease, in 1542, three daughters, his coheirs, viz.

MARGARET, m. to Sir Robert Newport, of Rushock, in Worcestershire.

ELIZABETH, m. to Sir John Lyttelton, of Frankley, ancestor to the Lords Lyttelton.

MARY, m. to Sir Thomas Astley, of Pateshull, in Staffordshire.

Humphrey (Sir), died s. p.

Sir Gilbert espoused, secondly, Ethelreda, daughter of Sir John Colton, of Landwade, in the county of Cambridge, and successively the widow of Thomas Barton, Esq., and of Sir Richard Gardiner, Lord Mayor of London, by which lady he had an only son,

SIR JOHN TALBOT, of Albrighton, in Shropshire, who eventually inherited the estates at Grafton. This gentleman m. first, Margaret, daughter and heir of Adam Troutbeck, Esq., of Mobberley, in Cheshire, and heir of her uncle, Sir William Troutbeck, by whom he had a son,

JOHN (Sir), his successor, whose grandson, GEORGE TALBOT, succeeded as seventh EARL OF SHREWSBURY.

Sir John Talbot espoused, secondly, Elizabeth, daughter of Walter Wrotesley, Esq., of Wrotesley, in Staffordshire, and was father of

JOHN TALBOT, Esq., of Salwarp, in Staffordshire, who m. Oliva, daughter and co-heir of Sir William Sherington, of Laycock, in Wilts, and was s. by his eldest son,

SHERINGTON TALBOT, Esq., of Salwarp and Laycock. This gentleman m. first, Elizabeth, daughter and co-heir of Sir Thomas Leighton, Knt., of Feckenham, in the county of Worcester (by Mary, his wife, daughter and co-heir of Edward, Lord Zouch, of Haringworth) by whom he had six sons, from none of which is there now any male issue. He m. secondly, Mary, daughter of John Washborn, Esq., of Wichenford, in Worcestershire, by whom he had three sons,

GEORGE, of Rudge, whose only daughter and heir, Catherine, m. Sir Clement Clarke, Bart., of Lawnde Abbey, Leicestershire.

William.

Francis, d. unmarried.

The second son,

WILLIAM TALBOT, Esq., of Sturton Castle, in the county of Stafford, m. Mary, daughter of Thomas Doughty, Esq., of Whittington, and had issue,

WILLIAM.

Catherine, m. first, to Walter Littleton, Esq. of Lichfield, and secondly, to the Right

Rev. Lancelot Blackburn, Archbishop of York.

Frances, m. to Samuel Jewkes, Esq., of Wolverley.

Mr. Talbot's only son,

WILLIAM TALBOT, having taken holy orders, was consecrated Bishop of Oxford, in 1689, translated to Salisbury, in 1715, and to the SEE OF DURHAM, in 1722. His lordship d. in 1730, leaving, by his second wife, Catherine, daughter of Mr. Alderman King, of the city of London,

CHARLES, of whom presently.

Edward, Archdeacon of Berkshire.

Sherington, major-general in the army.

Henry, a commissioner of the revenue.

Henrietta-Maria, m. to Dr. Charles Trimnel, Bishop of Winchester.

Catherine, m. to Exton Sayer, L.L.D.

The eldest son,

CHARLES TALBOT, having been bred to the bar, attained the highest honours of that learned profession. In 1717, he was appointed solicitor-general to George, Prince of Wales, and in 1726, he held the same office to King GEORGE I. In 1733, he was constituted LORD HIGH CHANCELLOR of Great Britain, sworn of the privy council, and elevated to the peerage, by letters patent, dated 5th December, in that year, as BARON TALBOT, of Hensol, in the county of Glamorgan. His lordship m. Cecil, daughter and heir of Charles Matthews, Esq., of Castle Menich, in Glamorganshire, and had surviving issue,

WILLIAM, his successor.

John, M.P. m. first, Henrietta-Maria, daughter and co-heir of Sir Matthew Decker, Bart., by whom he had no issue. He espoused, secondly, Catherine, eldest daughter of John, Viscount Chetwynd, in Ireland, by whom he had, with other issue,

JOHN CHETWYND, who s. his uncle in the Barony of Talbot, and was father of the present EARL TALBOT.

George, in holy orders, D.D. and Vicar of Guiting, in Gloucestershire, m. Anne, eldest daughter of Jacob, Viscount Folkstone.

His lordship d. in 1737, and was s. by his eldest son,

WILLIAM TALBOT, second Baron Talbot, of Hensol. This nobleman, upon the accession of King GEORGE III., was constituted Lord Steward of the household, sworn of the privy council, and created, by letters patent, dated 10th March, 1761, EARL TALBOT. His lordship officiated as Lord Steward at the coronation of his majesty. He m. Mary, only daughter and heir of Adam de Cardonnel, Esq., of Bedchampton Park, in the county of Southampton, secretary at war, temp. Queen Anne, and M.P. for Southampton, in the same reign, by whom he had one only surviving child,

Lady CECIL TALBOT, who m. George Rice, Esq., of Newton, M.P. for Carmarthen.

The earl having thus no male issue, was created, 17th October, 1780, Baron Dynevor, of Dynevor, in the county of Carmarthen, with remainder to his daughter and the heirs male of her body. His lordship d. in 1782, when the BARONY OF TALBOT passed to his nephew, John Chetwynd Talbot, Esq.

the BARONY OF DYNEVOR, devolved according to the limitation, and the EARLDOM OF TALBOT became EXTINCT.

ARMS.—Gu. a lion rampant, within a border ingrailed or. a crescent for difference.

TALBOYS—BARON TALBOYS.

By Writ of Summons, dated in 1529,
21 Henry VIII.

Lineage.

WILLIAM DE KYME, Baron Kyme, d. in 1338, without issue, when his estates, including the lordship of Kyme, in Lincolnshire, devolved upon his sister,

LUCIE DE KYME, who had married Gilbert de Umfranvill, Earl of Angus, and had issue,

GILBERT, Earl of Angus, whose only son,

ROBERT, died s. p. in his father's life-time.

Elizabeth, who m. Gilbert Burdon, and had a daughter and heir,

ELIZABETH BURDON.

ELIZABETH BURDON, inherited Kyme and the other lands through her mother, and espoused,

HENRY TALBOYS, from whom lineally descended,

SIR GEORGE TALBOYS, who m. Elizabeth, daughter of Sir William Gascoigne, and had with other issue,

GEORGE, of whom presently.

William, a priest.

Elizabeth, m. to Sir Christopher Willoughby.

Cecilia, m. first, to William Ingleby, Esq., of Ripley, in the county of York, and secondly, to John Torney, Esq.

Anne, m. first, to Sir Edward Dymoke, Knt., and secondly, to Sir Robert Carr.

Sir George was s. by his son,

GILBERT TALBOYS, of Kyme, who was summoned to parliament as BARON TALBOYS, of Kyme, by King HENRY VIII., in 1536. His lordship m. Elizabeth,* daughter of Sir John Blount, by whom (who m. secondly, Edward Clinton, first Earl of Lincoln), he had two sons, George and Robert, who both died in his life-time, issueless, and an only daughter,

ELIZABETH TALBOYS, who m. first, Thomas Wimbish, Esq., and secondly, Ambrose Dudley, Earl of Warwick, but had no issue. At the decease of his lordship, the barony devolved upon his daughter,

ELIZABETH WIMBISH, and her husband, Mr. Wimbish, claimed the dignity jure uxoris, when it was solemnly decided, in the presence of King HENRY VIII., "That no man, husband of a baroness, should use the title of her dignity, until he had a child by her, whereby he should become tenant by the courtesie of her barony." Her lady-

---

* This lady, after the death of her first husband, had an illegitimate child by King HENRY VIII., HENRY FITZROY, created DUKE OF RICHMOND.

516

ship, as stated above, espoused, secondly, the Earl of Warwick, but died s. p., when the BARONY OF TALBOYS became EXTINCT; while the estates passed to the heirs general, and in the division, the manor of KYME came to the Dymokes, of Scrivelsby, from whom, after a considerable time, it passed by sale to strangers.

ARMS.—Ar. a saltier gules, on a chief of the second, three escallop shells of the first.

TATSHALL—BARONS TATSHALL.

By Writ of Summons, dated 24th June, 1295,
23 Edward I.

Lineage.

Amongst the companions in arms of the Conqueror, were two staunch friends, and as Dugdale calls them, sworn brothers in war, but not otherwise allied,

EUDO and PINCO, upon whom, in requital of their gallant services, the royal Norman conferred large grants of land, whereof Tatshall, with the hamlet of Thorpe, and town of Kirksby, in the county of Lincoln, were a part. Eudo to hold his proportion of the king, and Pinco, his of St. Cuthbert, of Durham. The former,

EUDO, seated himself at Tatshall, and from him lineally descended,

ROBERT DE TATSHALL, who, in the 16th of Henry III., had custody of Bolesover Castle, and the next year, was governor of that of Lincoln. In four years afterwards, he had license to build a castle, at his manor of Tatshall. This feudal lord married first, Amabill, daughter and co-heir of William de Albini, Earl of Arundel and Sussex, with whom he acquired the castle and manor of Buckenham, in the county of Norfolk. He m. secondly, ———, daughter of John de Grey, and had with her the manor of Scondebury, in the county of Berks, held of the king by serjeanty, viz: the service of falconry. He d. in 1249, and was s. by his son,

ROBERT DE TATSHALL, who, in the 38th Henry III., upon levying the aid for making the king's eldest son knight, paid £50 for the twentyfive knights' fees, which he held, and in the 42nd of the same reign, received command to attend the king at Chester, well fitted with horse and arms, to oppose the incursions of the Welsh. In the course which this Robert adopted, between the barons and King Henry, he appears to have been particularly injudicious—for we find him at the battle of Lewes, defeated, under the royal banner—and the subsequent battle of Evesham, in a similar situation, under the baronial; the just recompense of deserting his colours. In the reign of Edward I., he became, however, eminently distinguished in the Welsh, Scotch, and French Wars, and was summoned to parliament as BARON TATSHALL, from 24th June, 1295, to 26th August, 1296. His lordship m. Joan, daughter and co-heir of Ralph Fitz-Ralph, feudal Lord of Middleham, in the county of York, by whom he acquired a considerable accession of property, and had issue,

ROBERT, his successor.

Emme, m. to Sir Osbert Cayly, and had issue,

    Sir Thomas Cayly, Baron of Buckenham, in right of his mother.

Joan, m. to Sir Robert Driby, and left a daughter and heiress,

    Alice, m. to Sir William Bernake, whose daughter, and the eventual heiress of her brother,

        Maud Bernake, m. Sir Ralph de Cromwell.

Isabel, m. to Sir John Orreby.

The baron d. in 1251, and was s. by his son,

ROBERT DE TATSHALL, second baron, summoned to parliament, from 6th February, 1299, to 13th September, 1302. This nobleman served in the Scotch and French wars, and dying in 1303, was s. by his son,

ROBERT DE TATSHALL, third baron, at whose decease, in minority, the BARONY fell into ABEYANCE, between

    Sir Thomas Cayly, son of Emme Tatshall, by Sir Osbert Cayly.

    Joan de Tatshall, wife of Sir Robert Driby.

    Isabel de Tatshall, wife of Sir John Orreby.

As it still continues with their descendants, while the estates passed thus:

    To Sir Thomas Cayly, the castle of Buckenham, with a fourth part of that manor, and half the parks thereunto belonging, and other lands in the county of Norfolk; from this Sir Thomas Cayly, descends the existing Baronets Cayly, of Brompton, in the county of York.

    To Lady Driby, the castle and manor of Tatshall, and other estates in the county of Lincoln.

    To Lady Orreby, the manor of Tybenham, and a part of the manor of Buckenham, with other lands in the county of Norfolk.

ARMS.—Chequée or and gu. a chief ermine.

THOMPSON—BARON HAVERSHAM.

By Letters Patent, dated 4th May, 1696.

Lineage.

SIR JOHN THOMPSON, Bart., a leading member of the House of Commons, and a zealous promoter of the revolution, was elevated to the peerage, on the 4th May, 1696, as BARON HAVERSHAM, of Haversham, in the county of Bucks. His lordship m. first, Lady Frances Wyndham, widow of Francis Wyndham, Esq., and daughter of Arthur Annesley, first Earl of Anglesey, by whom he had issue,

MAURICE, his successor.

George, who d. issueless.

Helen, m. to the Reverend Mr. Gregory, Rector of Tuddington, in the county of Bedford.

Elizabeth, m. to Joseph Grange, Esq.

Mary, m. to Arthur Annesley, fifth Earl of Anglesey.

Frances m. to Thomas Armstrong, Esq.

Martha, m. to Sir John Every, Bart.

Catherine, m. to —— White, General Attorney at Law,

Dorothy, m. to Captain Beckford, of the East India service.

Althamia, m. to Mr. Priaux, of Bristol.

Lord Haversham espoused, secondly, Martha, widow of Mr. Grahme, but had no other issue. He d. in 1709, and was s. by his elder son,

MAURICE THOMPSON, second baron. This nobleman, in the life-time of his father, served in the French war, and obtained distinction at the siege of Namur, where he was dangerously wounded. He was subsequently a colonel in the guards, and before his accession to the title, a member of the House of Commons. His lordship m. first, Elizabeth, daughter of John Smith, Esq., of Hertfordshire, by whom he had two daughters,

ELIZABETH, m. to John Carter, Esq.

Anne, m. to —— Reynolds, Esq., son of Richard, Bishop of London.

He m. secondly, Elizabeth, widow of William Green, Esq., and sister of Richard, Earl of Anglesey. His lordship d. in 1745, when the BARONY OF HAVERSHAM became EXTINCT.

ARMS.—Or. on a fesse dancette az. three stars ar. on a canton of the second, the sun in glory ppr.

THORPE—BARON THORPE.

By Writ of Summons, dated 16th July, 1381, 5 Richard II.

Lineage.

WILLIAM DE THORPE was summoned to parliament as a BARON, from 16th July, 1381, to 12th September, 1390. Nothing further, with any degree of accuracy, is known of this nobleman or his descendants. He is not mentioned at all by Dugdale.

THWENG—BARONS THWENG.

By Writ of Summons, dated 22nd February, 1307, 35 Edward I.

Lineage.

Of this family, anciently Lords of KIRTON CASTLE, in Yorkshire, was

SIR ROBERT DE THWENG, who, in the 22d of HENRY III., was deputed by the other barons to repair to Rome, and to lay at the foot of the pontifical throne, a complaint of the nobles of England, regarding some encroachment upon their ecclesiastical rights, by the holy see. He was s. by his son,

MARMADUKE DE THWENG. This feudal lord had a military summons to march into Scotland, 42nd Henry III., when the Scots had risen in rebellion against their king, the son-in-law of the English monarch. He m. one of the sisters and co-heirs of Duncan Darell, and left a son,

ROBERT DE THWENG, who was s. by his son,

MARMADUKE DE THWENG, who m. Lucia, one of the sisters and co-heirs of Peter de Brus, of Skelton (see Brice of Anandale), and acquired thereby considerable estates in the county of York.

517

In the 22nd of EDWARD I., this Marmaduke had summons amongst the other great men of that time, to repair with all speed to the king, and to afford him his advice touching the most important affairs of the realm. He had subsequently a military summons to march against the French. He was s. at his decease, by his elder son,

ROBERT DE THWENG. This feudal lord left an only daughter,

LUCY, who m. first, WILLIAM DE LATIMER, junr., but being divorced from him by sentence from the court of Rome, pronounced in the ecclesiastical consistory at York, she m. secondly, NICHOLAS DE MEINILL; thirdly, BARTHOLOMEW DE FANCORT, and fourthly, ROBERT DE EVERINGHAM.

He was s. at his decease, by his brother, as next heir male,

MARMADUKE DE THWENG, one of the most eminent soldiers of the period in which he lived, and being highly distinguished in the wars of Scotland, was summoned to parliament as a BARON from 22nd February, 1307, to 18th September, 1322. His lordship m. Isabel, daughter of William de Ros, of Igmanthorpe, in the county of York, and had issue,

WILLIAM, his successor.
Robert, } both priests.
Thomas, }
Lucia, m. to Sir Robert de Lumley, and her son,
    SIR MARMADUKE DE LUMLEY, assumed the arms of Thweng. His son,
      SIR RALPH DE LUMLEY, was summoned to parliament as BARON LUMLEY, by RICHARD II., but joining in the insurrection of Thomas Holand, Earl of Kent, temp. Henry IV., he fell in action: and being attainted, his honours expired. The attainder was, however, repealed in the reign of Edward IV. (see Lumley).
Margaret, m. to Sir Robert de Hilton, Knt.
Katherine, m. to Sir Ralph D'Aubenie.

His lordship d. in 1323, and was s. by his eldest son,

WILLIAM DE THWENG, second baron, summoned to parliament on the 30th December, 1324, but never afterwards. He m. Katherine, daughter of Thomas, Lord Furnival, of Hallamshire, but dying without issue in 1341, was s. by his brother,

ROBERT DE THWENG, who, doing homage in the same year, had livery of his lands. This baron was in holy orders, and d. of course, issueless (anno 1344), when he was s. by his brother,

THOMAS DE THWENG, also a clergyman. This baron being rector of the church at Lythum, founded a chantry of twelve priests and four clerks, in the parochial church there, to pray for the good estate of himself, and Henry, Lord Perci, and for the souls of their ancestors. Likewise for the souls of Robert de Thweng, and Maud, his wife; Marmaduke de Thweng, and Lucy, his wife, &c. &c. His lordship d. in 1374, when his estates devolved upon his sisters as co-heirs, and the BARONY OF

518

Thweng fell into ABEYANCE amongst those ladies, as it still continues with their representatives.

ARMS.—Or, a fesse gules.

TIBETOT—BARONS TIBETOT.

By Writ of Summons, dated 10th March, 1308,
1 Edward II.

Lineage.

In the 1st year of HENRY III.,

HENRY DE TIBETOT, being in arms for the king, had a grant in conjunction with Thomas Botterel, of the possessions lying in the counties of York and Lincoln, of Adam Painel, who fought on the other side; and dying in the 34th of the same reign, was s. by his son,

ROBERT DE TIBETOT, who, in the 50th of HENRY III., was made governor of the castle of Porchester, and having attended Prince EDWARD to the Holy Land, was high in favour, after he had ascended the throne, as EDWARD I., being then constituted governor of Nottingham Castle, justice of South Wales, and governor of the castles of Carmarthen and Cardigan. In the 13th of the same reign, he had a grant from John, the son of Gerard de Rodes, to himself, his wife, and his son, in fee, of the manors of Langar and Berneston, in Nottinghamshire. In the 20th, being then the king's lieutenant for Wales, he fought and defeated Rees ap Mereduth, in a great battle, wherein four thousand Welshmen were slain, and Rees himself having been made prisoner, was conveyed to York, and there executed. Robert de Tibetot was subsequently in the wars of Gascony and Scotland. He m. Eve, daughter of Pain de Chaworth, and had issue,

PAIN, his successor.
Hawyse, m. to John, son of Robert Fitz-Roger.
Eve, m. to Robert, son of Robert de Tatshall.

He d. in the 26th Edward I., and was s. by his son,

PAIN DE TIBETOT, who, serving in the Scottish wars, during the latter part of the reign of EDWARD I., was summoned to parliament as a BARON, upon the accession of EDWARD II. He was subsequently justice of the forests beyond Trent, and governor of the castle of Northampton. His lordship, who had made several campaigns into Scotland, fell eventually at the battle of STRIVELIN, anno 1314. He m. Agnes, daughter of William de Ros, of Hamlake, and was s. by his son,

SIR JOHN DE TIBETOT, second baron, summoned to parliament from 1st April, 1335, to 20th January, 1366. This nobleman was in the wars of France and Scotland, and was constituted governor of Berwick-upon-Tweed, in the 20th of Edward III. His lordship m. Margaret, daughter of Bartholomew, Lord Badlesmere, and co-heir of her brother, Giles, Lord Badlesmere, by whom he acquired a great accession of landed property, and had issue,

ROBERT, his successor. *and by 2nd s. he*
Pain (Sir), from whom the EARLS OF WORCESTER of this family descended.

He d. in 1367, and was s. by his elder son,

ROBERT DE TIBETOT, third baron, summoned to parliament from 24th February, 1368, to 8th January, 1371. His lordship m. Margaret, daughter of William Deincourt, Lord Deincourt, and had issue,

MARGARET, m. to Roger, second Lord Scrope, of Bolton.

MILICENT, m. to Stephen le Scrope, brother of the above Roger.

ELISABETH, m. to Philip le Despenser, the younger.

His lordship d. in 1372, when his lands devolved upon his daughters as co-heirs, and in the division thereof LANGAR fell to the eldest, and was conveyed by her to the SCROPES, whence it passed through an illegitimate daughter of Emanuel Scrope, Earl of Sunderland, to the family of HOWE. The BARONY OF TIBETOT, or TIPTOFT, fell into ABEYANCE amongst those ladies, as it still continues with their representatives.*

ARMS.—Ar. a saltier ingrailed, gules.

TIBETOT, OR TIPTOFT—BARONS TIBETOT, OR TIPTOFT, EARLS OF WORCESTER.

Barony, by Writ of Summons, dated 7th Jan., 1426, 4 Henry VI.

Earldom, by Letters Patent, 16th July, 1449.

Lineage. *by Eliot Aspun.*

SIR PAIN DE TIBETOT, younger son of John, second Lord Tibetot, m. Agnes, sister of Sir John Wrothe, Knt., and was s. by his son,

SIR JOHN DE TIPTOFT, who, in the 1st Henry IV., being retained in the service of that king, during his life, had, in consideration thereof, a grant of one hundred marks per annum, payable out of the issues of the county of Cambridge: and in six years afterwards, upon the attainder of Thomas Mowbray, Earl Marshal and Nottingham, had, in conjunction with Ralph de Rochfort, a grant from the king, of all the apparel pertaining to the body of that earl, and all his harness, for peace and war, as well for great horses called coursers, as saddles for tilts and tournaments. In the 8th of the same reign, upon the rebellion and forfeiture of Owen Glendower, he obtained all the lands of Rhese ap Griffith, (an adherent to Owen,) lying within the principality of South Wales, and the same year he was constituted chief butler of England. He was, subsequently, made treasurer of the household, and in the reign of Henry V. he was Seneschal of Acquitaine, president of the king's exchequer in Normandy, and treasurer of that duchy. In the 3rd Henry VI. he was appointed chief steward of the king's castles and lordships throughout Wales and the Marches, and the next year he had summons to parliament as a BARON. His lordship m. Joyce, second daughter and co-

heir of Edward Charlton, Lord Powys. (Dugdale says he bore the title of Lord Tiptoft and Powys, but he was never summoned by any other designation than that of "Johanni Tiptoft, Chr.") By this lady he acquired a considerable inheritance, and had issue,

JOHN, his successor.

Philippa, m. to Thomas, Lord Ros.

Joane, m. to Sir Edmund Inglethorpe.

Joyce, m. to Edmund, son and heir of John, Lord Dudley.

Lord Tiptoft d. in 1443, and was s. by his son,

JOHN DE TIPTOFT, second baron, who was created just as he had attained majority, 16th July, 1449, EARL OF WORCESTER. In 1457 his lordship was lord deputy of Ireland, and in the 1st Edward IV. he was constituted justice of North Wales for life. He was soon after made constable of the Tower of London, and the next year, being then treasurer of the exchequer, he assisted the king at the siege of Bamburgh Castle, held at the time by the Duke of Somerset, and other Lancastrians. His next great appointment was that of CHANCELLOR OF IRELAND, and in the 7th of the same reign being deputy of that kingdom to George, Duke of Clarence, he resided there for the protection of the realm. In three years afterwards he was constituted lieutenant of Ireland; as also constable of England, and again treasurer of the exchequer. At this time coming to Southampton, the king caused him to sit in judgment upon several of the Lancastrian party, who had then been made prisoners at sea, and the execution of twenty of those persons followed. Besides all this, it is further memorable of this nobleman, that having been bred a student at Baliol College, Oxford, and attained to an eminent degree in learning, he went to Jerusalem, and sojourned there for some time, whence he travelled into other countries, and returning through Italy, proceeded to Rome, for the express purpose of visiting the library at the Vatican. Here he made, it is said, so eloquent an oration to POPE Pius II., that it drew tears from the eyes of his Holiness. His lordship translated into English Publius Cornelius, and Cæius Flamínius; and wrote several learned Tracts, of which Bale makes mention. In Walpole's Royal and Noble Authors he is also noticed with high commendation. Being a staunch Yorkist, the earl, upon the temporary restoration of Henry VI., was placed in jeopardy, and forced to conceal himself from his enemies, but being at length found in the upper branches of a high tree, he was conveyed to London, and being adjudged to suffer death, was beheaded on Tower Hill, anno 1470, when ALL HIS HONOURS became forfeited. His lordship m. first, Cecily, daughter of Richard, Earl of Salisbury, and widow of Henry Beauchamp, Duke of Warwick, but had no issue. He espoused, secondly, Elizabeth, daughter of Robert Greyndour, by whom he had a son, John, who d. in infancy. He wedded thirdly, Elizabeth, daughter of Thomas Hopton, Esq., and widow of Sir Roger Corbet, Knt., of Morton Corbet, in the county of Salop, by whom he had an only son,

EDWARD DE TIPTOFT, who was restored in blood and honours by King EDWARD IV. when

---

* Margaret, Lady Scrope, is now represented by CHARLES JONES, Esq., the heir-general of her ladyship, and her husband, Roger, Lord Scrope.

he regained the crown, but dying unmarried in 1485, the EARLDOM OF WORCESTER became EXTINCT, while the BARONY OF TIPTOFT fell into ABEYANCE amongst his aunts, (see children of the first lord,) as it still continues with their representatives.

ARMS.—Ar. a saltier ingrailed, gu.

TONI—BARON TONI.

By Writ of Summons, dated 10th April, 1299, 27 Edward I.

Lineage.

The first of this family that came into England, was

RALPH DE TONI, son of Roger, standard bearer of Normandy, by Alice, daughter of William Fitz-Osborne. This Ralph was at the battle of Hastings, and he obtained from his successful chief, William the Conqueror, large grants of lands in different shires, of which Flamstead, in the county of Hertford, was the head of his barony. He inherited, at the decease of his father, the office of standard bearer, which was hereditary in the family. He m. Isabel, daughter of Simon de Montfort, and had issue,

Ralph, his successor.

Godechild, m. first, to Robert, Earl of Mellent, and secondly, to Baldwin, son of Eustace, Earl of Bolein.

Ralph de Toni d. in 1142, and was s. by his son,

RALPH DE TONI, who m. Judith, daughter of Waltheof, Earl of Huntingdon and Northumberland, and from this feudal lord, we pass to his descendant,

ROBERT DE TONI, who distinguished himself, temp. Edward I., in the wars of Scotland and Gascony, and had summons to parliament as BARON TONI, from 10th April, 1299, to 16th June, 1311. His lordship died issueless, about the latter year, when the BARONY became EXTINCT. His estates devolved upon his sister, Alice de Toni, who m. first, Thomas Leybourne; secondly, Guy de Beauchamp, Earl of Warwick, and thirdly, William Le Zouche, of Ashby, in the county of Leicester.

ARMS.—Ar. a maunch gu.

TOUCHET—BARONS AUDLEY, OF HELEIGH.

By Writ of Summons, dated 8th January, 1313, 14 Edward II.

Lineage.

The BARONY OF AUDLEY, was conferred, 8th January, 1318, by writ, upon

NICHOLAS DE ALDITHELEY or AUDLEY, and, at the decease of that nobleman's grandson,

NICHOLAS AUDLEY, the third baron, without issue, in 1399, it passed into the family of TOUCHET; the last lord's elder sister and co-heir,

JOANE AUDLEY, having married SIR JOHN TOUCHET, Knt., and her grandson,

520

JOHN TOUCHET, having, in consequence, been summoned to parliament, in the BARONY, on the 21st December, 1405. So far regarding this dignity, but although twice FORFEITED, in 1397, and in 1631, as it was fully restored by act of parliament, in 1678, and is at present enjoyed, it belongs to the EXTANT, more than the EXTINCT peerage.

TOUCHET—BARON TOUCHET.

By Writ of Summons, dated 29th December, 1299, 28 Edward I.

Lineage.

WILLIAM TOUCHET, supposed to have been a kinsman of the Lords Audley, was summoned to parliament as a BARON, from 29th December, 1299, to 3rd November, 1306, but of his lordship, nothing further is recorded.

TOWNSHEND — BARONESS OF GREENWICH.

By Letters Patent, dated 28th August, 1767.

Lineage.

JOHN CAMPBELL, second Duke of Argyll, b. 10th October, 1680, having, as LORD HIGH COMMISSIONER, given the royal assent, in the parliament of Scotland, to the introduction of the act of Union with England, on the 21st September, 1705, was created by Queen ANNE, on the 26th November, following, Baron Chatham, and EARL OF GREENWICH, in the peerage of England. In the next year, his grace made the campaign under the Duke of Marlborough, and distinguished himself at RAMELLIES, at the siege of Ostend, and in the attack of Menin; but his highest military reputation was acquired in 1708, at the battle of OUDENARD, where he commanded a division of the army, comprising twenty batallions, which was the first brought into action, and which maintained its ground, against a great disparity of numbers. Upon his return to England, he was sworn of the privy council, and he subsequently commanded-in-chief, as lieutenant-general, the English forces, under General Schuylemberg, at the attack of the city and citadel of Tournay. In 1710, the duke was installed a KNIGHT of the GARTER. In 1712, he was constituted commander-in-chief of all the land forces in Scotland, and captain of the company of foot, in Edinburgh Castle. Upon the death of Queen ANNE, his grace was one of the seven lords justices, in whom the government was vested, under the act of parliament, until the arrival of King GEORGE I., from Hanover. After which he was again appointed general and commander-in-chief of the forces in Scotland, and in that capacity, suppressed the rebellion of 1715, by his victory of DUMBLAIN, and his subsequent proceedings. For all these eminent services, he was advanced to a British dukedom, on the 30th April, 1718, as DUKE OF GREENWICH, and declared lord steward of the household. He was subsequently, master-general of the ordnance, field marshal, &c. &c.

His grace espoused, first, Mary, daughter of John Brown, Esq., and niece of Sir John Duncomb, Knt., (Lord Mayor of London, in 1708,) but had no issue. He m. secondly, Jane, daughter of Thomas Warburton, Esq., of Winnington, in Cheshire, and had five daughters, viz.

    CAROLINE, m. first, to Francis, Earl of Dalkeith, eldest son of Francis, Duke of Buccleugh, and secondly, to the Right Honourable Charles Townshend.

    Anne, m. to William Wentworth, Earl of Stafford, but died s. p.

    Jane, d. young.

    Elizabeth, m. to the Right Honourable James Stewart Mackenzie, brother of John, Earl of Bute.

    Mary, m. to Edward, VISCOUNT COKE, heir apparent of Thomas, Earl of Leicester, but d. without issue.

This illustrious nobleman, commonly called "THE GREAT DUKE OF ARGYLL," who was as conspicuous for patriotism and eloquence in parliament, as he had been for valour and conduct in the field, d. 4th October, 1743,* when his Scottish honours devolved upon his brother, and THOSE OF ENGLAND became EXTINCT.

His eldest daughter,

LADY CAROLINE, (Countess of Dalkeith,) then the wife of the Right Honourable JOHN TOWNSHEND, first Lord of the Treasury, and Chancellor of the Exchequer, was created, on the 26th August, 1767, a British peeress, as BARONESS GREENWICH, with the degree of BARON, in remainder to the heirs male of her body, by the said John Townshend. Her ladyship by her first husband, Lord Dalkeith, had no issue, but by the second had two sons and a daughter, viz.

    Thomas-Charles, } both predeceased their mother, issueless.
    William-John, }

    Anne, m. in 1779, to Richard Wilson, Esq., of Tyrone, in Ireland, and left a son.

The Countess of Dalkeith d. in 1794, when the BARONY OF GREENWICH became EXTINCT.

ARMS.—Quarterly, first and fourth, girony of eight pieces, or. and sa. for CAMPBELL; second and third, ar. a galley with her sails furled close, flag and pendants flying, and oars in action, all sa.

---

* To John, DUKE OF ARGYLL and GREENWICH, there is a fine monument in Westminster Abbey, by Roubiliac, on which is chiselled, the personification of History, employed in writing the following lines :

Britons, behold ! if patriot worth be dear,
A shrine that claims thy tributary tear.
Silent that tongue—admiring senates heard ;
Nerveless that arm—opposing legions fear'd.
Nor less, O Campbell, thine the power to please,
And give to grandeur all the grace of ease,
Long from thy life, let kindred heroes trace
Arts, which ennoble still the noblest race.
Others may owe their future fame to me,
I borrow immortality from thee.

TREGOZ—BARON TREGOZ.

By Writ of Summons, dated 6th February, 1299, 27 Edward I.

Lineage.

In the 5th year of King STEPHEN,

WILLIAM DE TREGOZ 'had the lands of William Peverel, of London, in farm ; and was s. by

GEOFFREY DE TREGOZ, who m. Annabil, daughter of Robert Gresley, by whom he had four daughters, and one son, his successor,

WILLIAM DE TREGOZ, who wedded —— daughter of Robert de Luci, (his guardian,) and dying in 1208, was s. by his son,

ROBERT DE TREGOZ. This feudal lord was sheriff of Wiltshire, in the 3rd of Richard I., and in three years afterwards, he was in an expedition then made into Normandy. He m. Sibel, daughter of Robert de Ewyss, and in the 7th of JOHN, upon collecting the scutage of that king's reign, answered thirty-eight marks for nineteen knights' fees, belonging to the honour of the said Robert de Ewyas. He was s. by his son,

ROBERT DE TREGOZ, who had a military summons to march against the Welsh, in the 42nd HENRY III., but joining the baronial banner in the same reign, he fell at the battle of Evesham, leaving a son,

JOHN TREGOZ, who doing his homage in the 52nd HENRY III., had livery of his lands; and had such favour from the king, notwithstanding his father's treason, that he was acquitted of fifty marks of the hundred pounds then due for his relief. After which, 10th Edward I., he attended the king in an expedition then made into Wales, and in the 22nd of the same reign, being in the campaign of Gascony, he had permission for his wife and family to reside in the castle of Devises, and to have fuel for their fires there. He was subsequently in the Scottish wars, and was summoned to parliament as a BARON on the 6th February and 10th April, 1299. His lordship m. —— and had issue,

    CLARICE, m, to Roger de la Warre, and left a son,

        JOHN DE LA WARRE,

    SYBIL, m. to Sir William de Grandison, Knt.

He died in 1300, seised of the castle of EWYAS-HAROLD, with its members in the marches of Wales, which he held by barony : the manor of Eton-Tregos, in the county of Hereford, and estates in the counties of Wilts, Salop, and Northampton. Upon his lordship's decease the BARONY OF TREGOZ fell into ABEYANCE, between his grandson John de la Warre, and his second daughter, Sybil de Grandison, as it still continues with their representatives.

ARMS.—Gules, two bars gemels, and in a chief, a lion passant, guardant, or.

TREGOZ—BARON TREGOZ.

By Writ of Summons, dated 22nd January, 1305, 33 Edward I.

Lineage.

HENRY TREGOZ, a distinguished soldier in

the Scottish wars, temp. Edward I. and Edward II., was summoned to parliament as a BARON, from 22nd January, 1305, to 14th March, 1322, but of this nobleman nothing more is known.

TREGOZ—BARON TREGOZ.

By Writ of Summons, dated 4th January, 1318, 11 Edward II.

Lineage.

THOMAS DE TREGOZ was summoned to parliament as a BARON, 4th January, 1318, and from 20th October, 1332, to 9th April, 1335, but nothing further is known of him.

TREVOR—(HAMPDEN) BARONS TREVOR, VISCOUNTS HAMPDEN.

Barony, } by Letters { 31st December, 1711.
Viscounty, } Patent, { 14th June, 1726.

Lineage.

RICHARD TREVOR, the representative of an ancient Welsh family, m. Matilda, daughter and heir of David ap Gruff, of Allington, by whom he had,

JOHN TREVOR, of Allington, who was s. by his eldest son,

JOHN TREVOR, of Allington, who m. Anne, daughter of Randal Broughton, Esq., of Broughton, in the county of Lancaster, and had four sons, John, Randal, David, and Edward. The eldest son,

JOHN TREVOR, was seated at Trevallin, in Denbighshire, and marrying Mary, daughter of Sir George Bruges, Knt., of London, had issue,

RICHARD (Sir), of Allington, m. Catherine, daughter of Roger Puleston, Esq., of Emrall, and left four daughters, his co-heirs, viz.

Magdalen, m. first, to Arthur Bagnall, Esq., of Staffordshire, and secondly, to —— Tyringham, Esq., of Tyringham, in the county of Bucks.

Mary, m. to Jever Lloyd, Esq., of Yale.

Dorothy, m. to Sir John Hanmer, Bart., of Hanmer, in the county of Flint.

Margaret, m. to John Griffith, Esq., of Lynn, in Carnarvonshire.

John (Sir), of whom presently.

Randulph, d. unmarried.

Sackville (Sir), a naval officer of high reputation, temp. James I.

Thomas (Sir), chief baron of the exchequer, temp. CHARLES I.

Winifred, m. to Edmund Puleston, Esq., of Allington.

The second son,

SIR JOHN TREVOR, Knt., of Trevallin, m. in 1673, Margaret, daughter of Hugh Trevannion, Esq., of Cornwall, and had issue,

JOHN (Sir), one of the principal secretaries of state, and a member of the privy council, in the reign of Charles II., m. Ruth, daughter of John Hampden, Esq., of Great

522

Hampden, in the county of Buckingham, and dying the year before his father, left issue,

JOHN, who s. his grandfather at Trevallin, m. Elizabeth, daughter of —— Clarke, Esq., and widow of John Morley, Esq., of Glynd, in the county of Sussex, by whom he had issue,

John Morley, of Glynd-Stanmerton, who d. 19th April, 1719.

Thomas, d. unmarried.

Elizabeth, m. to David Polhill, Esq., of Oxford, Kent.

Arabella, m. first, to Robert Heath, Esq., of Lewes, and secondly, to Brigadier-General Edward Montagu, only brother of George, Earl of Halifax.

THOMAS, of whom presently.

Richard.

Edward.

William.

Richard, M.D.

Anne, m. to Robert Weldon, Esq., of London.

Jane, m. to the Hon. Sir Francis Compton, fifth son of Spencer, Earl of Northampton.

Elizabeth, m. to William Masham, Esq., eldest son of Sir William Masham, Bart.

Sir John Trevor d. in 1673, and his eldest grandson, John Trevor, Esq., inherited Trevallin, while the next

THOMAS TREVOR, was brought up to the profession of the law, and having attained reputation at the bar, was made solicitor-general in 1692, when he received the honour of knighthood. In 1695, he became attorney-general, and on the accession of Queen Anne, was constituted Lord Chief Justice of the Court of Common Pleas, when he was elevated to the peerage, 31st December, 1711, as BARON TREVOR, of Bromham, in the county of Bedford. In 1726, he was appointed lord privy seal, and the next year he was declared one of the lords justices. On the accession of GEORGE II., he was again sworn lord privy seal, and in three years afterwards constituted president of the council. His lordship m. first, Elizabeth, daughter and co-heir of John Searle, Esq., of Finchley, in the county of Middlesex, by whom he had issue,

THOMAS, } successively Lords Trevor.
JOHN, }

Anne.

Laetitia, m. to Peter Cock, Esq., of Camberwell.

Elizabeth.

Lord Trevor espoused, secondly, Anne, daughter of Robert Weldon, Esq., and widow of Sir Robert Bernard, Bart., of Brampton, in the county of Huntingdon, and had,

ROBERT, who succeeded as fourth lord.

Richard, in holy orders, consecrated Bishop of St. David's in 1744, translated to the see of Durham in 1752, and d. unmarried, 9th June, 1771.

Edward d. young.

His lordship d. 19th June, 1730, and was s. by his eldest son,

THOMAS TREVOR, second baron. This nobleman m. Elizabeth, daughter of Timothy Burrel, Esq., of Cuckfield, in the county of Sussex, barrister at law; by whom he had an only daughter,

 ELIZABETH, m. to Charles, second Duke of Marlborough.

He d. 22d March, 1753, and was s. by his brother,

JOHN TREVOR, third baron, who had previously served in parliament for Woodstock, was a king's counsel, and one of the Welsh judges. His lordship m. Elizabeth, daughter of the celebrated SIR RICHARD STEEL, and left an only daughter, Diana, b. 10th June, 1744. He d. in 1764, and was s. by his half brother,

ROBERT TREVOR, fourth baron. This nobleman, in compliance with the testamentary injunction of John Hampden, Esq., of Great Hampden, assumed the surname and arms of HAMPDEN. His lordship was several years envoy-extraordinary to the states-general, and was constituted in 1746, one of the commissioners of the revenue in Ireland. In 1759, he was made joint post-master-general with the Earl of Besborough, which office he held until the year 1765, and was created, on the 14th June, 1776, VISCOUNT HAMPDEN. His lordship m. in 1743, Constantia, daughter of Peter Anthony de Huybert, Lord of Van Kruningen, of Holland, and had issue,

 THOMAS, his successor.

 John, who was appointed, 8th April, 1780, minister-plenipotentiary to the diet at Ratesston, and, 22d February, 1783, to the court of Sardinia. He succeeded to the honours, as third viscount.

 Maria Constantia, m. 25th May, 1764, to Henry Howard, twelfth Earl of Suffolk, and fifth Earl of Berkshire, by whom she had no surviving issue. Her ladyship d. in 1767.

 Anne, d. unmarried in 1760.

His lordship d. in 1783, and was s. by his elder son,

THOMAS TREVOR-HAMPDEN, second Viscount. This nobleman m. in 1768, Catherine, daughter of General David Graeme; but d. without issue, in 1824, when the honours devolved upon his brother,

JOHN TREVOR-HAMPDEN, as third viscount, b. 24th February, 1748-9. His lordship m. in 1773, Harriett, only daughter of the Rev. —— Burton, D.D, canon of Christ-church, but had no issue. He d. in the same year that he had inherited the honours, when ALL THOSE HONOURS became EXTINCT.

ARMS.—Quarterly, first and fourth ar. a saltier, gules, between four eagles displayed, az. for HAMPDEN: second and third, party p. bend, sinister, ermine and erminois, a lion rampant, or. for TREVOR.

TRUSSEL—BARON TRUSSEL.

By Writ of Summons, dated 25th February, 1342, 16 Edward III.

Lineage.

Of this very ancient Warwickshire family, was

RICHARD TRUSSEL, who fell at the battle of Evesham, 4th HENRY III.

As also

WILLIAM TRUSSEL, of Cublesdon, in the county of Stafford (which manor the Trussels acquired by Rosse, daughter and heir of William Pandolf, who had married into the family). This William was father of another

WILLIAM TRUSSEL, who m. Maud, daughter and heir of Warine Mainwaring, and from him descended

SIR WILLIAM TRUSSEL, who m. Bridget, daughter of William Kene (by Elizabeth, daughter of William Chicele, and niece of Henry Chicele, Archbishop of Canterbury, temp. Henry VI.) and was father of

SIR EDWARD TRUSSEL, whose daughter and heir,

 ELIZABETH TRUSSEL, espoused, in the time of Henry VIII., John Vere, Earl of Oxford.

But the principal branch of the family remaining, according to Dugdale, was that some time resident at Cublesdon; of which was

WILLIAM TRUSSEL, who, in the 22d of Edward I., received command to repair to the king, to consult upon the important affairs of the realm; and had subsequently a military summons to march into Gascony. He was s. by (his supposed nephew) another

WILLIAM TRUSSEL, who, in the 15th of Edward II., being one of the adherents of Thomas, Earl of Lancaster, was exiled in consequence; but returned in five years afterwards with Queen Isabel and Prince Edward, at the head of a considerable force, against the power of the Spencers; one of whom being brought afterwards to trial, had judgment passed upon him by this William, who was at that time in such estimation with the commons in convention assembled, as to be chosen their organ to pronounce the deposition of the unfortunate EDWARD II., which duty he executed in the following words:

 " Ego Will. Trussel, vice omnium de Terrâ
 Angliæ et totius parliamenti procurator,
 tibi Edwardo reddo homagium prius tibi
 factum et extunc diffido te, et privo omne
 potestate regia et dignitate, nequaquam
 tibi de cætero tanquam regi periturus."

Upon the accession of Edward III., he was constituted eschaetor-general on the south of Trent; but soon after, being opposed as strongly to the influence of Mortimer as he had previously been to that of the Spencers, he was again obliged to fly the kingdom, and to remain in exile until the favourite's fall; when, returning, he was reinvested with the eschaetorship. In the 13th of Edward III., he was admiral of the royal navy, from the mouth of the Thames westward; and in two years afterwards, being then a knight, he was in the expedition made into Flanders, and the same year in the Scottish campaign. In the 16th, being in the great expedition made into France, he was summoned to parliament as a BARON, and constituted admiral of all the fleet, from the mouth of the Thames to Berwick-upon-Tweed, his lordship's residence being then at Cublesdon. For the two following years he continued employed in the French campaigns, and two years afterwards he sate in judgment with Sir William Thorpe, chief justice of the Court of King's Bench, at the Tower of London, upon the Earls of Fife and Monteith, when the latter nobleman was hanged, drawn, and quartered, but the former spared. His lordship appears to have had but one summons to parliament, and the BARONY at his decease, became EXTINCT.

ARMS.—Ar. frettée gules on the joints bazantée.

Nots.—Besides the above, there was another

WILLIAM TRUSSEL, who, in the 27th Edward III., was at the battle of POICTIERS, in the immediate retinue of the BLACK PRINCE, and for his services, obtained from that gallant personage, a grant of forty pounds per annum for life, to be paid out of the exchequer at Chester. This William m. Idonea, sister of Edward de Boteler, and left an only daughter,

MARGARET TRUSSEL, who m. Fulk de Pembruge, and died s. p.

TUDOR—EARLS OF RICHMOND.

By Letters Patent, dated 23rd November, 1452.

Lineage.

SIR OWEN TUDOR descended from the PRINCESS OF WALES, espoused KATHERINE, widow of King HENRY V., and daughter of CHARLES VI., of France, by whom he had issue,

EDMUND, surnamed of HADHAM, having been born at that place, in the county of Bedford.

JASPER, created Earl of Pembroke.

Tacina, m. to Sir Reginald Grey, Lord Grey of Wilton.

The eldest son,

EDMUND TUDOR (of Hadham), was created by his half brother, King HENRY VI., on the 23rd November, 1452, EARL OF RICHMOND, with precedency of all other earls; and the same year he had a grant from the king, in fee, of the mansion-house of Baynard's Castle, in the city of London. He m. the Lady Margaret Beaufort,[e] daughter and heiress of John, Duke of Somerset, and great-grand-daughter of JOHN, of Gaunt,[†] by his last wife, Catherine Swineford, and had an only child,

e This illustrious lady outliving the Earl of Richmond, m. secondly, Henry, a younger son of Humphrey Stafford, Duke of Buckingham, and thirdly, Thomas, Lord Stanley, afterwards Earl of Derby: but had issue by neither. Her ladyship provided in her last WILL, dated 6th January, 1508, for two perpetual readerships in divinity, one at each of the universities; and she founded the school at Cambridge, called CHRIST'S COLLEGE; she also left provision for "a perpetual preacher of the word of God," in the same university. She lived to witness the coronation of her grandson, King HENRY VIII., and died on the 29th June, in the first year of that monarch's reign.

† It has recently been discovered, that in the original patent of legitimacy to the Beauforts, the children of this prince, born before wedlock, of his last wife, Catherine Swineford, (which, as it was ratified by parliament, parliament alone could alter,) the exception of inheritance to the crown does not occur; the words "excepta dignitate regali," being inserted only by the caution of Henry IV., in his confirmation ten years after. "Excerpta Historica."

HENRY, his successor.

He d. in 1456, and his remains were interred in the cathedral of St. David's, in Wales, with the following epitaph:

"Under this marble stone here inclosed, resteth the bones of the noble Lord, Edmund, Earl of Richmond, father and brother to kings; the which departed out of this world in the year of our Lord, 1456, the 3d of the month of November: on whose soul, almighty Jesus have mercy, Amen."

The earl was s. by his son,

HENRY TUDOR, second Earl of Richmond, then but fifteen weeks old. This noble infant being removed by his uncle, Jasper, EARL OF PEMBROKE, into Britanny, and thus remained there during the whole of EDWARD IV.'s reign, under the protection of Francis, DUKE OF PROVENCE, notwithstanding various efforts made by the English monarch to obtain possession of his person. At one time, Polydore Virgil relates, the duke confiding in the pledge of Edward, to marry the young earl to his daughter, Elizabeth, and thus unite for ever the red and white roses, had actually delivered him up to the English ambassadors, and that they had conveyed him to St. Malo's, on his way to England, but were detained by the earl's falling ill of a dangerous fever. In the interim, one John Chenlet, who had great influence in the ducal court, flew to the presence of the duke, and feelingly depicted the perils in which he had placed this last scion of Lancaster. To which his highness replied, "Hold thy peace, John, there is no such danger at all: for King EDWARD resolves to make him his son-in-law." But to this Chenlet instantly returned: "Believe me, most illustrious duke, he is already very near death; and if you permit him to be carried one step out of your dominions, no mortal man can preserve him from it." At which the duke, being not a little troubled, immediately despatched Peter Landoee, his third treasurer, to St. Malo's, with orders to bring the earl back. Peter, on hastening thither, is said to have detained the ambassadors with a long speech, while his servants conveyed the object of his care to a sanctuary in the city, whence he was soon after conducted in safety to his former residence. The subsequent contest between the EARL OF RICHMOND, and Crooked Backed RICHARD, our historians and our poets have so minutely detailed that it were idle to pursue the subject here: further than the simple fact, that the former having on the plains of Bosworth wrested the diadem from the brow of YORK, placed it on his own, and thus terminated the carnage of the ROSES. Upon the earl ascending the throne as HENRY VII., the EARLDOM OF RICHMOND merged in the crown.

ARMS.—Quarterly, France and England, in a border, az. eight martlets, or.

TUDOR — EARL OF PEMBROKE, DUKE OF BEDFORD.

Earldom, anno 1452.
Dukedom, 27th October. 1485.

Lineage.

JASPER TUDOR, surnamed of Hatfield, the

place of his birth, son of Sir Owen Tudor, by KATHERINE, Queen Dowager, of *King* HENRY V., was advanced by his half-brother, HENRY VI., in the parliament held at Reading, anno 1452, to the EARLDOM OF PEMBROKE, at the same time that his brother, EDMUND, *of Hadham*, was made Earl of Richmond. This nobleman being afterwards one of the main pillars of the cause of Lancaster, was attainted, and forced to fly when EDWARD IV. obtained the crown, and the Earldom of Pembroke was then conferred upon William Herbert, Lord Herbert, of Chepstow. Joining, subsequently, with the Earl of Warwick, he had a principal part in the temporary restoration of HENRY VI., and at that period he had the good fortune to find his nephew, HENRY, *Earl of Richmond*, in the custody of William Herbert's (Earl of Pembroke) widow, and presenting the boy to *King* HENRY, that monarch is said prophetically to have exclaimed— "This is he who shall quietly possess, what we and our adversaries do now contend for." The total overthrow of the Lancastrians at Barnet Field, and the re-establishment of EDWARD upon the throne again, however, broke down the fortunes of Jasper Tudor, and forced him, after some hair-breadth escapes, to seek an asylum for himself and his nephew, at the court of Britanny. Here, during the remainder of the reign of EDWARD IV., protection was afforded them, and here, in the reign of RICHARD III., they again unfurled the red banner, which soon afterwards waved in triumph on the field of BOSWORTH. Upon the accession of his nephew, as HENRY VII., Jasper Tudor was created DUKE OF BEDFORD at the Tower of London, on the 27th October, 1485. He was next sworn amongst the chief of the privy council, and constituted one of the commissioners to execute the duties of HIGH STEWARD OF ENGLAND at the king's coronation. His grace was afterwards appointed justice of South Wales, and LORD LIEUTENANT OF IRELAND for two years: he likewise obtained considerable grants from the crown: and was invested with the Garter. Upon the insurrection of the Earl of Lincoln in behalf of the *Pretender* SIMNELL, the Duke of Bedford was nominated joint commander with the Earl of Oxford, of the forces sent to oppose the Simnellites, and he ever enjoyed the entire confidence of the king. He m. Catherine, sixth and youngest daughter of Richard Wydeville, Earl Rivers, and widow of Henry, Duke of Buckingham, by whom (who *m.* after his decease Sir Richard Wingfield, K.G.) he had no issue.[*] He *d.* in 1405, when the DUKEDOM OF BEDFORD became EXTINCT.

ARMS.—Quarterly, France and England in a border, az. eight martlets, or.

TUDOR—DUKE OF YORK.

By Letters Patent, dated 1st November, 1491.

Lineage.

HENRY TUDOR, second son of *King* HENRY VII.

***

[*] He left an illegitimate daughter,
Helen, who *m.* William Gardiner, citizen of London, and was mother of the
STEPHEN GARDINER, *Bishop of Winchester*, so notorious in the reign of Mary.

was created on the 1st November, 1491, DUKE OF YORK, but upon the death of his elder brother, Arthur, he succeeded to the Dukedom of Cornwall, and was created Prince of Wales. His royal highness, subsequently, ascended the throne as HENRY VIII., when all his honours MERGED in the CROWN.

TUDOR—DUKE OF SOMERSET.

By Letters Patent, anno 1496.

Lineage.

EDMUND TUDOR, third son of *King* HENRY VII., was created, in 1496, DUKE OF SOMERSET. He *d.*, however, under five years of age, in 1499, when the DUKEDOM became EXTINCT.

TYES—BARON TYES.

By Writ of Summons, dated 6th February 1299, 27 Edward I.

Lineage.

In the time of *King* HENRY III.,
HENRY DE TYES held Shireburne, in Oxfordshire, by the grant of Richard, Earl of Cornwall, and was summoned to parliament as a BARON from 6th February, 1299, to 26th August, 1307. In the 28th Edward I., his lordship had free warren in all his demesne lands at Shireburne and Allerton, both in the county of Oxford. He *d.* in 1308, and was *s.* by his son,
HENRY DE TYES, second baron, summoned to parliament from 8th January, 1313, to 15th May, 1321. This nobleman was in the wars of Scotland, and for several years adhered faithfully to *King* EDWARD II., but afterwards joining in the insurrection of Thomas, Earl of Lancaster, he was taken prisoner at Boroughbridge, and being conveyed to London, was there beheaded for high treason, in 1321. His lordship *d.* without issue, leaving his sister,
ALICE DE TYES, who *m.* Warine de L'Isle, his heir, in whose descendants the BARONY of TYES is now vested.

ARMS.—Ar. a chevron, gu.

TYES—BARON TYES.

By Writ of Summons, dated 6th February, 1299, 27 Edward I.

Lineage.

In the 25th EDWARD I.,
WALTER DE TYES, in conjunction with Isabel, his wife, obtained numerous grants from the crown, lands in the counties of Bedford, York, Essex, and Bucks, and having served in the Scottish wars, had summons to parliament as a BARON from 6th February, 1299, to 26th August, 1307. In the 11th Edward II. his lordship was joint governor of the city of York, with Robert de Hasting. He *m.* Isabel de Steingrene, daughter of John de Stein-

grene, but died *s. p.*, in 1394, leaving MARGARET DE TYES, daughter of his brother, Roger, his heir, when the BARONY OF TYES became EXTINCT.

ARMS.—Ar. a chevron, gu.

UFFORD—BARONS UFFORD, EARLS OF SUFFOLK.

Barony, by Writ of Summons, dated 13th January, 1308, 2 Edward II.

Earldom, by Creation in Parliament, 16th March, 1337.

Lineage.

Of this family, says Sir William Dugdale, which afterwards arrived to great honour, I have not seen any thing memorable, until the 53rd Henry III., when Robert, a younger son of John de Peyton, of Peyton, in the county of Suffolk, assuming his surname from the lordship of Ufford, in that shire, became

ROBERT DE UFFORD. This Robert was JUSTICE OF IRELAND in the reign of Henry III., and again in the reign of Edward I. He *m.* Mary, widow of William de Say, and dying in the 26th of the latter king, was *s.* by his son,

SIR ROBERT DE UFFORD, Knt., who was summoned to parliament as a BARON from the 13th January, 1308, to 19th December, 1311. His lordship was in the expedition made into Scotland, in the 34th Edward I. He *m.* Cecily, one of the daughters and co-heirs of Sir Robert de Valoines, Knt., Lord of Walsham, and had issue,

ROBERT, his successor.

Ralph, Justice of Ireland in the reign of Edward III. (see Ufford, Barons Ufford).

Edmund (Sir), who, assuming the surname of Walsham, from his mother's lordship, became SIR EDMUND WALSHAM, and from him lineally descended

JOHN-JAMES-GARRETT WALSHAM, Esq., of Knill Court, in the county of Hereford, who was created a baronet on the 15th September, 1831 (*see Burke's Dictionary of the Peerage and Baronetage*).

He *d.* in 1316, and was *s.* by his eldest son,

ROBERT DE UFFORD, second baron, summoned to parliament from 27th January, 1332, to 14th January, 1337. This nobleman was in the wars of Gascony in the reign of Edward II., and he obtained, in the beginning of Edward III.'s reign, in requital of his eminent services, a grant for life of the town and castle of Orford, in the county of Suffolk, and soon after, further considerable territorial possessions, also by grant from the crown, in consideration of the personal danger he had incurred in arresting, by the king's command, MORTIMER, and some of his adherents, in the castle of Nottingham. In the 11th year of the same reign his lordship was solemnly advanced in the parliament then held, to the dignity of EARL OF SUFFOLK. Whereupon he was associated with William de Bohun, Earl of Northampton, and John Darcy, Steward of the King's Household, to treat with David Brus, of Scotland, touching a league of peace and amity. And the same year going beyond sea

536

on the king's service, had an assignation of £300 out of the exchequer, towards his expenses in that employment, which was in the wars of France; for it appears that he then accompanied the Earl of Derby, being with him at the battle of Cagant. After which time he was seldom out of some distinguished action. In the 12th Edward III., being in the expedition made into Flanders, he was the next year one of the marshals when King Edward besieged Cambray: and his lordship, within a few years, subsequently, was actively engaged in the wars of Britanny. In the 17th of this reign the Earl of Suffolk was deputed to the court of Rome, there to treat in the presence of his Holiness, touching an amicable peace and accord between the English monarch and Philip de Valois, and he marched the same year with Henry of Lancaster, Earl of Derby, to the relief of Loughmaban Castle, then besieged by the Scots. Soon after this he was made admiral of the king's whole fleet northward. For several years, subsequently, his lordship was with King Edward in France, and he was one of the persons presented by that monarch with harness and other accoutrements for the tournament at Canterbury, in the twenty-second year of his reign. In seven years afterwards we find the earl again in France, with the BLACK PRINCE; and at the celebrated BATTLE OF POICTIERS, fought and so gloriously won in the following year, his lordship achieved the highest military renown by his skill as a leader, and his personal courage at the head of his troops. He was, subsequently, elected a KNIGHT of the GARTER. His lordship *m.* Margaret, daughter of Sir John Norwich, and had issue,

ROBERT, summoned to parliament 25th February, 1342, *d.* in the life-time of his father,

WILLIAM, his successor.

Cecilie, *m.* to William, Lord Willoughby de Eresby.

Catherine, *m.* to Robert, Lord Scales.

Margaret, *m.* to William, Lord Ferrers, of Groby.

The earl's last testament bears date in 1368, and he *d.* in the following year. Amongst other bequests, he leaves to his son, William, " the sword, wherewith the king girt him, when he created him earl; as also his bed, with the eagle entire; and his summer vestment, powdered with leopards." His lordship was *s.* by his only surviving son,

WILLIAM DE UFFORD, second Earl of Suffolk, who had been summoned to parliament as a baron, in the life-time of his father, on the 4th December, 1364, and 20th January, 1366. This nobleman was in the French wars at the close of Edward III.'s reign, and in the beginning of that of Richard II. In the 50th of Edward he was constituted admiral of the king's whole fleet northward. At the breaking out of Jack Straw's insurrection, 4th Richard II., his lordship understanding that the common people contemplated forcing him into their ranks, and thus to represent him as one of their leaders, hastily arose from supper, and pursuing an unfrequented route, reached the king at St. Alban's, with a wallet over his shoulder, under the assumed character of servant to Sir Roger de Bois; but afterwards, being chosen by the Commons in parliament assembled, to represent to the lords certain matters of importance to the public welfare, the earl, while ascending the steps to their lordships' house, suddenly fell down dead, to the amazement and sorrow of all persons, rich and poor, on the 15th February, 1382. His lordship m. first, Joane, daughter of Edward de Montacute, and grand-daughter, maternally, of Thomas, of Brotherton, Earl of Norfolk, and secondly, Isabel, daughter of Thomas de Beauchamp, Earl of Warwick, and widow of John le Strange, of Blackmere, but having no issue, the EARLDOM OF SUFFOLK became EXTINCT, while the original BARONY OF UFFORD fell into ABEYANCE, between his sisters and heirs, (refer to children of Robert, first earl,) as it still continues amongst their representatives.

ARMS.—Sa. a cross ingrailed or.

UFFORD—BARON UFFORD.

By Writ of Summons, dated 3rd April, 1360, 34 Edward III.

Lineage.

RALPH DE UFFORD, brother of Robert, first Earl of Suffolk, having served in the wars of France and Flanders, in the martial reign of Edward III., obtained large grants of land from that monarch, in the counties of Berks and Dorset. Subsequently, (20th Edward III.,) being justice of Ireland, we are told, " he landed in that realm, with a great number of men-at-arms and archers." This distinguished person m. first, Maud, widow of William, Earl of Ulster, and sister of Henry Plantagenet, Earl of Lancaster, by whom he had an only daughter,

    MAUD, who m. Thomas de Vere, son of John de Vere, Earl of Oxford.

He m. secondly, Eve, daughter and heiress of John de Clavering, and widow of Thomas de Audeley, by whom he had issue,

    JOHN, of whom presently.
    Edmund (Sir), who inherited the estates of the family, upon the decease of his brother. Sir Edmund m. Sybil, daughter of Sir Robert Pierpont, and had issue,

        Robert (Sir), who m. Eleanor, daughter of Sir Thomas Felton, Knt., and left issue, three daughters, his co-heirs, viz.

            Ella, m. to Richard Bowes, Esq.
            Sybil, a nun at Barking.
            Joan, m. to William Bowes, Esq., brother of Richard, and left one daughter and heiress,

                Elizabeth, m. to Sir Thomas, son of William, Lord Dacres.

Ralph de Ufford d. in 1346, and was s. by his eldest son,

JOHN DE UFFORD, who was summoned to parliament as BARON UFFORD, on the 3rd April, 1360, but dying the following year, issueless, the dignity became EXTINCT, while his estates passed to his brother, Sir Edmund Ufford, Knt.

ARMS.—Sa. a cross ingrailed or.

UGHTRED—BARON UGHTRED.

By Writ of Summons, dated 30th April, 1343, 17 Edward III.

Lineage.

Of this family, which was of great antiquity in the county of York, was

ROBERT UGHTRED, who, in the 28th Edward I., obtained a charter for free warren, in all his demesne lands in that shire. He died in the 3rd of EDWARD II., and was s. by his son,

THOMAS UGHTRED, who became a person of great note in his time, and was celebrated in the Scottish wars, temp. Edward II. and Edward III. In the 10th of the latter reign, he was made admiral of the king's whole fleet to the northward, and for some years afterwards, he was again in the Scottish wars, when he attained the rank of banneret, and was constituted GOVERNOR OF PERTH. He was subsequently in the wars of Flanders, and had summons to parliament as a BARON, from 20th April, 1343, to 4th December, 1364. His lordship d. in 1365, leaving a son and heir,

SIR THOMAS UGHTRED, who was never summoned to parliament as a baron, nor were any of his descendants. Sir Thomas, like his father, was a military man, and became eminent likewise in the wars of Scotland. In the 50th Edward III., he was made constable and chamberlain of LOUGHMABAN CASTLE, and he was afterwards engaged in the wars of France. He d. in 3rd of HENRY IV., and was s. by his grandson,

THOMAS UGHTRED, who had married Margaret, daughter of Sir John Godard, Knt., but nothing further appears known of the family.

ARMS.—Gu. on a cross pattonce, or. five mullets of the field.

UMFRAVILL — BARONS UMFRAVILL, EARLS OF ANGUS.

Barony, by Writ of Summons, dated 24th June, 1295. Earldom, by Writ of Summons, dated 26th January, 1297, 23 and 25 Edward I.

Lineage.

In the 10th year of his reign, William the Conqueror granted the forest, valley, and lordship of Riddesdale, in the county of Northumberland, to his kinsman,

SIR ROBERT DE UMFRAVILL, Knt., otherwise, *Robert with the Beard*, Lord of Tours and Vian, to hold, by the service of defending that part of the country for ever, from enemies and wolves, with the sword which King William had by his side when he entered Northumberland. By this grant he had likewise, authority for holding, governing, exercising, hearing, and judging, in all the pleas of the crown, as well as others occurring within the precincts of Riddesdale. The next of this family mentioned is,

GILBERT DE UMFRAVILL, and after him,

ROBERT DE UMFRAVILL, who lived in the time of King Stephen. Next to him, but in what degree of relationship is unknown, came

ODONELL DE UMFRAVILL, of whom a monk of Tynemouth, in the reign of Henry III., grievously complained for his exactions upon his neighbours, towards repairing the roof of his castle at Prudhoe, of which he was feudal lord. This Odonell d. in 1182, and was s. by his son and heir,

ROBERT DE UMFRAVILL, who was s. by his son,

RICHARD DE UMFRAVILL. This feudal lord appears, in the 7th of Richard II., to have pledged his lands-of Turney, to Aaron, a Jew, for the sum of £22. 6s., which he then owed the Israelite. In the 5th of King John, his lordship obtained the right of preventing all persons from grazing, hunting, or cutting down timber, in the forest of Riddesdale; and in nine years afterwards, the times being then turbulent, he delivered up his four sons in hostage, with his castle of Prudhoe, as guarantee for his loyalty, upon the condition, that if he transgressed, the said castle became forfeited, and that he should himself be dealt with as a traitor; notwithstanding which, no sooner did the barons take up arms, than he appeared amongst them, when his lands were seized and granted to Hugh de Baliol. In the reign of King Henry III., however, he made his peace, and had restitution of the castle of Prudhoe, &c., but he was nevertheless far from enjoying the confidence of that monarch, as we find the king soon after issuing a precept to the sheriff of Northumberland, directing a jury of twelve knights to be empanneled, to inspect certain buildings at the castle of Herbótil, which this Richard de Umfravill was then erecting, and to demolish all that bore the appearance of fortifications. He d. in the 29th year of Henry III., according to Matthew Paris, " a famous baron, guardian and chief flower of the north, leaving his heir of tender years," which heir,

GILBERT DE UMFRAVILL, was committed to the guardianship of Simon de Montfort, Earl of Leicester, in consideration of ten thousand marks, paid by that nobleman to the king. This Gilbert attained majority, in the 43rd Henry III., and in six years subsequently, we find him in arms with the barons, but he made his peace prior to the battle of Evesham, and obtained then some immunities from the crown. In the 20th of Edward I., he was governor of the castle of Forfar, and the whole territory of Angus, in Scotland, and appears to have borne the title of Earl of Angus, according to Camden, in right of his wife. He was summoned to parliament, however, in three years afterwards, as BARON UMFRAVILL only, but in the 25th of the same reign, and from that period to the 1st Edward II., he had summons, as "Gilberto de Umfravill, Comiti de Anggos." But this dignity the English lawyers refused to acknowledge, (Angus not being within the kingdom of England,) until he had openly produced the king's writ in public court, by which he was called to parliament, under the title of EARL OF ANGUS. In the 27th Edward I., his lordship was constituted one of the king's commissioners for manning and fortifying the castles within the realm of Scotland, and to appoint wardens of the Marches. The next year he founded a chantry for two priests, to celebrate divine service

daily, in the chapel of our lady, within the castle of Prudhoe. The earl d. in 1308, and was s. by his eldest surviving son,

ROBERT DE UMFRAVILL, summoned to parliament, as second Earl of Angus, from 4th March, 1309, to 30th December, 1324. This nobleman distinguished himself in the life-time of his father, in the Scottish wars; and soon after his accession to the title, he was joined in commission with William, Lord Ros, of Hamlake, and Henry, Lord Beaumont, in the lieutenancy of Scotland. In the 11th Edward II., his lordship was appointed one of the commissioners, to treat with Robert de Brus and his partizans, for a truce between both realms. The earl m. first, Lucie, daughter of Philip, and eventually heiress of her brother, William de Kyme, by whom he had issue,

Elizabeth, m. Gilbert Burdon, and had an only daughter and heiress,

    ALIANORE, heiress to her uncle, Earl Gilbert, m. to Henry Talboys, from which marriage the Lord Talboys descended.

His lordship's second wife was named Alianore, but of what family is not mentioned; by this lady he had issue,

Robert (Sir), who d. issueless.

Thomas, m. Joane Rodam, and had,

  Thomas, who was father of

    Gilbert, died s. p., 9th Henry V.

    Elizabeth.

    Joane, m. to Sir Thomas Lambert.

    Margaret, m. to William Lodington.

    Agnes, m. to Thomas Hagerston, from which marriage the existing Baronets Hagerston, derive.

  Robert, K.G., temp. Henry IV., died s. p. 15th Henry VI.

Annore, m. to Stephen Waleys, son and heir of Sir Richard Waleys.

The earl d. in 1325, and was s. by his eldest son,

GILBERT DE UMFRAVILL, summoned to parliament as third Earl of Angus, from 27th January, 1332, to 26th August, 1380. This nobleman acquired great reputation in the Scottish wars, and was a chief commander at the battle of Durham, 20th Edward III., where David Brus, the Scottish monarch was totally defeated and made prisoner by the English. In the 25th Edward III., his lordship had permission, upon petition to the king and parliament, to transfer the prisoners, made within the liberty of Redesdale, whom he had the privilege of detaining, from his prison of Herbotil Castle, (then in a state of dilapidation,) to Prudhoe Castle, for the ensuing ten years. His lordship m. Maud, sister of Anthony de Lucy, and next heir of Joane, daughter and heir of the said Anthony, by whom he had an only son,

ROBERT (Sir), who m. Margaret, daughter of Henry, Lord Percy, and died in the life-time of his father, s. p.

The Earl d. in 1381, leaving Alianore, his niece, wife of Henry Talboys, his heir of the whole blood, and Thomas Umfravill, his brother of the half blood, his next male heir, but none of the family were ever subsequently summoned to parliament. The BARONY OF UMFRAVILL, created by the writ of 23rd Edward I., is, however, vested in the descendants and representatives of the said Thomas de Umfravill, of which the present Sir Carnaby Haggerston, Baronet, is one—(see children of Robert, second Earl of Angus, by his second wife).

ARMS.—Gu. a cinque-foil within an orle of cross crosslets, or.

UVEDALE—BARON UVEDALE.

By Writ of Summons, dated 27th January, 1332, 6 Edward III.

Lineage.

PETER DE UVEDALE was summoned to parliament as a BARON, from 27th January, 1332, to 22nd January, 1336; but Dugdale gives no account whatever of such a nobleman. He appears to have died issueless, when the BARONY OF UVEDALE became EXTINCT.

VALENCE—EARLS OF PEMBROKE.

Created, anno 1247.

Lineage.

WILLIAM DE VALENCE, son of Hugh de Brun, Earl of March, (on the confines of France and Poictou,) by Isabel, his wife, widow of King JOHN, derived his surname from the place of his birth, as the rest of his brothers did from theirs, and being so nearly allied to King HENRY III., (half brother, by the mother,) was brought into England, in 1247, with Guy de Lazinian, his elder brother, and Alice, his sister, in consequence of being oppressed by the king of France. Not many months after his arrival, he was made governor of Goderich Castle, and through the influence of the king, obtained the hand of JOANE, daughter and eventually heir of Warine de Monchensy, by Joane, his wife, second sister, and co-heir of Anselme Marshal, Earl of Pembroke. "Moreover," says Sir William Dugdale, " shortly after this, the king solemnising the festival of St. Edward's translation, in the church of Westminster, with great state, sitting on the royal throne, in a rich robe of Baudekyn, and the crown on his head, caused this William (with divers other young noblemen,) to be brought before him, and girt him with the sword of knighthood, and whilst he thus sate in his royal seat, casting his eye upon him, who penned down all particulars of the great solemnity, he called him nearer, and commanded him to sit upon the middle step, betwixt his chair and the floor, and said to him: ' Hast thou taken notice of all these things, and perfectly committed them to memory ?' He answered, ' Sir, I have so, deeming this famous ceremonial worthy to be recorded.' Whereupon the king replied ; ' I am fully satisfied that God Almighty, as a pledge of his further favours and benefits, hath vouchsafed to work one glorious miracle this morning, for which I give him thanks. I therefore intreat thee, and intreating require, that thou record these things exactly and fully, and write them in a book, lest that the memory of them should in time be lost.' And having so said

invited him with whom he had this discourse, to dinner that day, with three of his fellows; commanding likewise, that all other monks, who then came thither, with the whole convent of Westminster, should at this charge, be that day feasted at the public refectory there."

William de Valence had, subsequently, a grant from the crown, of the castle and honour of Hertford, as also another grant to himself and his lady, and to their issue, of all those debts which William de Lancaster did then owe to the Jews throughout the whole realm. "About this time," (writes Dugdale,) "this William de Valence, residing at Hertford Castle, rode to the Park at Hasthfel, belonging to the Bishop of Ely, and there hunting without any leave, went to the bishop's manor house, and readily finding nothing to drink but ordinary beer, broke open the buttery doors, and swearing and cursing the drink, and those who made it ; after all his company had drunk their fills, pulled the spigots out of the vessels, and let out the rest on the floor; and that a servant of the house hearing the noise, and coming to see what the matter was, they laughed him to scorn, and so departed."

In the 34th HENRY III., William de Valence was in the Holy Land, and in the 42nd had a military summons to march against the Welsh; but he was soon afterwards obliged to fly the kingdom, when the barons took up arms against the influence of himself and other foreigners; he came back, however, after an exile of only two years, under the protection of the king, but was not suffered to land by the barons, until he had sworn to observe the ordinances of Oxford. Nevertheless, the contest again breaking out, he had a chief command in the royal army, and with the prince, assaulted successfully the town of Northampton, when the whole baronial force was put to the rout, but soon rallying, owing to the junction of the Londoners, the battle of Lewes ensued, and victory deserted the regal banner. In this action, the king and his son became prisoners; but Valence, who then bore the title of EARL OF PEMBROKE, with the Earl of Warren, and others, escaped by flight, first, to Pevensey, and thence into France. His lands were, however, seized by the triumphant barons, and his lady, who was residing at Windsor Castle, ordered to retire immediately into some religious house. The battle of EVESHAM again, however, changing the fortune of war, and the power of the KING being re-established, the Earl of Pembroke, with the other staunch adherents of royalty, were restored to their possessions ; and his lordship had, subsequently, large grants from the crown. In the 18th EDWARD I., the earl, with Joane, his wife, presented a petition to parliament, setting forth, "that, whereas, upon the death of William de Monchensi, (brother to her, the said Joane,) they had obtained a bull from the pope directed to the Archbishop of Canterbury, touching the inheritance of the lands of the said William de Monchensi, thereby desiring, that the king would please to commit the tuition of Dionysia, the daughter of the said William, unto some person who might appear before the said archbishop, and such other judges as were named in the bull."

But it was answered, that the admission of that bull would tend to the diminution of the king's authority and power, by reason that such cases of hereditary succession ought not to be determined but in his own courts. Wherefore, in as much, as it did appear, that the object of the earl was to invalidate the sentence of the Bishop of Worcester, which had declared the said Dionysia to be legitimate, and his design to make her a bastard, in order that he might enjoy her estate, his lordship and his lady were prohibited to prosecute their appeal any farther. His lordship was afterwards engaged in the wars of France, and was slain there in 1296, when his remains were conveyed to England, and interred in Westminster Abbey, under a splendid monument. The earl had issue by the heiress of Minchensi, three sons and three daughters, viz.

John, who d. young.

William, killed by the Welsh in his father's life-time.

Aylmer, his successor.

Anne, m. first, to Maurice Fitz-Gerald, secondly, to Hugh de Baliol, and thirdly, to John de Avennes, but had no issue.

Isabel, m. to John de Hastings.

Joane, m. to John Comyn, feudal Lord of Badenagh, (son of John Comyn, and Mary, his wife, daughter of John Baliol,) and had issue,

    John Comyn, slain at Striveling in 1314, s. p.

    William Comyn, made prisoner in the same action, died s. p.

    Joane Comyn, m. to David de Strabolgi, Earl of Athol.

    Elizabeth Comyn, m. to Richard, Lord Talbot.

His lordship was s. by his only surviving son,

AYLMER DE VALENCE, second Earl of Pembroke. This nobleman was in the wars of Scotland, temp. Edward I., and obtained considerable grants from the crown, in that kingdom. His lordship being with King Edward at Burgh upon the Sands, immediately before the monarch's death, was one of those to whom the king recommended his son, and enjoyned him not to suffer Piers de Gaveston to come into England again. For which he was ever after much hated by Piers, "being called by him Joseph the Jew, in regard he was tall and pale of countenance." His lordship subsequently joined the coalition against the power of Gaveston, and assisted at the siege of Scarborough Castle, in which, upon its surrender, the FAVOURITE was made prisoner, and was soon afterwards beheaded, by orders of the Earl of Warwick, at Blackton Hill, near Warwick. In the 8th of Edward II., his lordship was constituted general of all the king's forces, from the river Trent, northwards, to Roxborough, and he obtained license to make a castle of his house at Bampton, in Oxfordshire. In two years afterwards he was again in the Scottish wars; but before the end of this year, being made prisoner in his journey towards the court of Rome, by John Moilley, a Burgundian, and sent to the emperor, he was constrained to give twenty thousand pounds of silver, for his ransom; by reason Moilley alleged,

530

that he himself having served the King of England, had not been paid his wages. After obtaining his liberty his lordship returned to the wars of Scotland, and for several subsequent years was engaged in that kingdom. In the 15th of Edward II., he was one of the lords who sate in judgment upon Thomas Plantagenet, Earl of Lancaster, and condemned that prince to death; "but this mercenary and time-serving act of infamy," it is said, was speedily atoned for by his own death, which occurred in two years after in France, where, attending Queen Isabel, he was murdered 27th June, 1323. His lordship m. first, Beatrix, daughter of Ralph de Nele, Constable of France; secondly, ——, daughter of the Earl of Barre; and thirdly, Mary,[*] daughter of Guy de Chastillion, Earl of St. Paul, but had no issue. His remains were conveyed into England, and buried in Westminster Abbey. Upon his lordship's decease, his estates passed to his sisters as co-heirs, and the EARLDOM OF PEMBROKE became EXTINCT.

ARMS.—Barry ar. and as. an orle of martlets gules.

VAUGHAN—BARONS VAUGHAN.

By Letters Patent, dated 25th October, 1643.

Lineage.

SIR JOHN VAUGHAN, Knt., son of Walter Vaughan, Esq., of Golden Grove, in Carmarthenshire, was created a peer of Ireland, in the 18th of JAMES I., and the next reign advanced to the dignity of Earl of Carberry, also in Ireland. His lordship m. first, Margaret, daughter of Sir Gilly Meyrick, Knt., by whom he had one surviving son, RICHARD, his successor, and a daughter, Mary, m. to Sir Francis Lloyd. He espoused, secondly, Jane, daughter of Sir Thomas Palmer, Knt., but had no issue. His lordship was s. at his decease by his son,

RICHARD VAUGHAN, second Earl of Carberry, who was made a Knight of the Bath, at the coronation of King CHARLES I., and was afterwards distinguished in the civil wars as a cavalier leader, being lieutenant-general for the counties of Carmarthen, Pembroke, and Cardigan; in which command, acting with great zeal and gallantry, he was rewarded with a peerage of England, on the 26th October, 1643, as BARON VAUGHAN, of Emlyn, in the county of Carmarthen; and he was constituted, after the restoration, lord president of the principality of Wales. His lordship m. first, Bridget, daughter and heir of Thomas Lloyd, Esq., of Llanlier, in the county of Cardigan, by whom he had no surviving issue. He espoused, secondly, Frances, daughter and co-heir of Sir John Altham, Knt., of Oxby, in Hertfordshire, by whom he had issue,

    Francis, who m. Lady Rachel Wriothesley, daughter of Thomas, Earl of Southampton, and died s. p. in the life-time of his father.

———

* This lady, who was great-granddaughter, maternally, of King HENRY III., founded, by grant from her cousin, Edward III., the college of Mary de Valence, in Cambridge, now called PEMBROKE HALL.

JOHN, his successor.
Altham.
Frances.
Althamia.

He wedded, thirdly, Lady Alice Egerton, daughter of John, Earl of Bridgewater, but had no issue. His lordship d. in 1687, and was s. by his eldest surviving son,

JOHN VAUGHAN, (third Earl of Carberry,) second Lord Vaughan. This nobleman was for some time governor of Jamaica. His lordship m. first, Mary, daughter of George Brown, Esq., of Green Castle, in the county of Carmarthen, but had no issue. He espoused, secondly, Lady Anne Montagu, daughter of George, Marquess of Halifax, and had an only daughter and heir,

    Lady ANNE VAUGHAN, who m. Charles Paulet, Marquess of Winchester, afterwards Duke of Bolton.

The earl d. in 1713, when (with his Irish honours) the BARONY OF VAUGHAN, of Emlyn, became EXTINCT.

ARMS.—Or, a lion rampant, gu.

VAUX — BARONS VAUX OF HARROWDEN.

By Letters Patent, dated 27th April, 1523.

Lineage.

The family of VAUX derived its surname from a district in Normandy, where it was originally seated. So early as the year 794 of the Christian era, a branch of the Vauxes is found in Provence, and then allied, by marriage, to most of the sovereign princes of Europe. They are mentioned in the records of that and subsequent periods, by the patronimic of Beaux, Baux, or Vaux, (B and V being used indiscriminately in the south of France,) and the ancient possessions of the Princes of Baux in that country, are still called, " Les Terres Baussenques," comprising Aix, Marseilles, &c.

In the year 1140, the Vauxes disputed the sovereignty of Provence with the house of Barcelona; and in 1173, they acquired the principality of Orange, by marriage with Tiburge, heiress of Orange. In 1214, William, PRINCE OF BAUX AND ORANGE, assumed the title of King of Arles and Vienne, which dignity was acknowledged, and confirmed to him by FREDERICK II.

In 1393, Raymond, King of Arles, Prince of Baux and Orange, left, by his first wife, Joane, Countess of Geneva, an only daughter, who married JOHN DE CHALONS, great chamberlain of France, and conveyed the titles and possessions of the house of Baux into that family, from which, by marriage with the heiress of Chalons, they came to the house of Nassau in 1530; and from this alliance the members of that house have since borne the title of PRINCES OF ORANGE.

* Bertram, second son of William, third Prince of Baux and Orange, went with Philip of Anjou, into Italy, when that prince ascended the throne of Naples. The son of this Bertram, another Bertram de Vaux, was Count of Montescasiosi, &c.,

and married Beatrix, daughter of Charles II., King of Naples and Sicily. His son, Francis de Vaux, espoused Margaret of Anjou, widow of Edward Baliol, King of Scotland, and grand-daughter of Philip of Anjou, Emperor of Constantinople, &c., in right of his wife, the daughter of Baldwin, Earl of Flanders, and Emperor of Constantinople. Upon this marriage, Francis de Vaux was created Duke of Andrea, in the kingdom of Naples, &c., and his descendants enjoyed the highest offices in the state, as the following inscription, translated from a monument erected in the year 1615, in the church of St. Clair, at Naples, fully attests.

" This monument is dedicated to the most illustrious family of Vaux, a potent race, decorated with the royal insignia, in the kingdom of Vienne and Arles, Princes of Orange, Counts of Geneva, and great rulers within the sovereignty of Provence, which they frequently subjugated to their dominion by force of arms. They were Emperors of Greece, Despots of Romania, Princes of Achaia, Premier Dukes of the kingdom of Naples, Princes of Tarento and Altamaro, Dukes of Andea, Ursino and Naro, Counts of Montescasiosi, Avellino, Saleto, Castro-Ugento, Nola, Alexana, and Acerraro, Great Constables, Justiciaries, High Chamberlains, and Stewards of that realm, under the kings of the house of Anjou, and Generals of the Papal armies. Hieronymus de Vaux has here deposited the bones of as many of his name and lineage as he has been able to collect, and out of piety to them has erected this monument to their memory. Videlicet to the memories of

    Antonia de Vaux, Queen of Sicily.
    Isabella de Vaux, Queen of Naples.
    Cecilia de Vaux, Countess of Savoy.
    Sibella de Vaux, Princess of Piedmont.
    Maria de Vaux, Dauphiness of Vienne.
    Isabella de Vaux, Despotisses of Servia."

The Prince of Joinville derived from Stephen de Vaux, who married the heiress of the Count de Joigny, in Champaigne, and assumed the name of Joinville, or Joignyville. His successors bore for arms, " ar. a bend gules" (nearly the same coat as the English Vauxes of Tryermayne, viz. ar. a bend chequy, or. and gu.) Of the house of Vaux, of Champaigne, was that celebrated Prince of Joinville, seneschal, or high steward of Champaigne, the companion and friend of Louis IX. of France, and author of a curious history of that monarch, translated by Colonel Johns: he d. in 1318.

The earliest account we have of the founders of the English branches of the Vauxes, is, that BERTRAND DE VAUX attended a tournament in the year 929, and was a favourite of ROBERT I., Duke of Normandy, grandfather of WILLIAM the Conqueror. The names of the descendants of this Bertram are traced through the Rolles Normand, written Baux, Vaux, Vaulx, and de Vallibus. At the time of the Norman conquest,

HAROLD DE VAUX, Lord of Vaux, in Normandy, having for religious purposes, conferred his seigory upon the abbey of the Holy Trinity, at Caen, (founded by Matilda, wife of WILLIAM the Conqueror,) came into England, accompanied by his three sons, viz.

1. HUBERT, who acquired the Barony of GIL-LESLAND, by grants of Ranulph de Meschines, upon whom the VICTORIOUS NORMAN had conferred the whole county of Cumberland. This Hubert was *s.* by his son,

> ROBERT DE VAUX, or VALLIBUS, who was founder of the prior of Pentney, in Normandy, and of the abbey of Lanercost, in Cumberland. He was sheriff of that shire, in the 21st of HENRY II., during which year the county, owing to the war, yielded no benefit to the king. He *m.* Ada, daughter and heir of William Engaine, and widow of Simon de Morville, and had two sons,
>
>> ROBERT DE VAUX, who died *s. p.*, and was *s.* by his brother,
>> RANULPH DE VAUX, who was *s.* by his son,
>>
>>> ROBERT DE VAUX, Governor of the castle of Carlisle, and of the county of Cumberland, temp. JOHN, and afterwards one of the barons in arms against that monarch. He was *s.* at his decease, by his son,
>>>
>>>> HUBERT DE VAUX, who left an only daughter and heiress,
>>>>
>>>>> MAUD DE VAUX, who *m.* Thomas de Multon, and conveyed the barony of Gillesland to that family. (See Multon.)

2. Ranulph, Lord Tryermayne, whose line terminated in an heiress,

> MABEL DE VAUX, who *m.* William Vaux, of Catterlen, a member of the branch founded by the youngest son.

3. Robert.

The youngest son,

ROBERT DE VAUX, seated himself in Normandy, and was *s.* by his son,

WILLIAM DE VAUX, who had three sons, ROBERT, Adam, and Oliver, *Prior of Pentney.* He was *s.* by the eldest,

ROBERT DE VAUX, who had several sons, of whom,

> ROBERT, (the eldest,) died *s. p.*
> JOHN (Sir), the second, was of Catterlen. Sir John Vaux's great-grandson and lineal descendant,
>
>> WILLIAM VAUX, OF CATTERLEN, *m.* MABEL VAUX, heiress of Tryermayne, and thus united two branches of the family. From this marriage descended,
>>
>>> JOHN VAUX, only son of John Vaux, of Catterlen and Tryermayne, whose daughter and heir,
>>>
>>>> JANE VAUX, *m.* in 1553, THOMAS BROUGHAM, Lord

of *Brougham*, the lineal ancestor of the present HENRY BROUGHAM, *Lord Brougham and Veux,*[*] LORD HIGH CHANCELLOR OF GREAT BRITAIN.

Philip, third son.
Oliver, fourth son.

The fourth son,

OLIVER DE VAUX, was one of the barons in arms against *King* JOHN. In the 13th of that monarch's reign, he paid five hundred marks, and five palfreys, for license to marry Petronill, widow of William de Longchamp, and daughter and heir of Guy de Croun,[†] feudal lord of Croun, by whom he had issue,

> Robert,
> William, } who both died *s. p.*
>
> JOHN, who succeeded to the estates, was steward of Acquitaine, in 1263, and had an allowance of £200 per annum, for his support in that office. He *d.* in 1286, leaving his two daughters, his heirs, viz.
>
>> Petronilla, *m.* to William de Nerford, who, in the division of the estates, had Therston and Shotestram, in the county of Norfolk; Wysete, in Suffolk, the moiety of a messuage in London, called Blaunch - Apleton, and other lands, amounting in all to twenty-five knights' fees.
>> Maud, *m.* to William de Ros, who had the manor of *Foston*, and other lands in Lincolnshire, with the moiety of the messuage in London, amounting to nineteen knight's fees.
>
> Roger.

The youngest son,

ROGER DE VAUX, was grandfather of

ROBERT VAUX, of Bodenham, in Cambridgeshire, whose son,

---

[*] Besides this, there is another and later alliance, between the VAUX and the BROUGHAM families.

> PETER BROUGHAM, about the beginning of the eighteenth century, married Elizabeth, daughter and heiress of Christopher Richmond, Esq., of Highhead Castle, in the county of Cumberland; which Christopher was grandson and heir of John Vaux, of Catterlen, through his mother, MABEL VAUX.

[†] GUY DE CROON, or CROUN, came in with the *Conqueror*, and held sixty-one lordships, all, or most of them in the county of Lincoln; FRISTON, in the district of Holland, being the head of his barony. He was *s.* by

> ALAN DE CROUN, who was father of
> MAURICE DE CROUN, living in 1181, and succeeded at his decease by his son,
> GUY DE CROUN, who accompanied RICHARD I. to the Holy Land. This feudal lord left at his decease an only daughter and heiress,
>
>> PATRONILLA DE CROUN, who *m.* first, William Longchamp, and secondly, (as in the text,) Oliver de Veux.

ELIAS VAUX, *m.* Elisabeth, daughter of Robert de Hastings, and was *s.* by his son,

WILLIAM VAUX, whose son,

WILLIAM VAUX, of Harwedon, or Harrowden, in the county of Northampton, *m.* Alianora, daughter of Sir Thomas Drakeston, Knt., of Welby, and was *s.* by his son,

SIR WILLIAM VAUX, of Harrowden, who *m.* Matilda, daughter of Sir Walter Lucy, Knt., and was *s.* by his son,

WILLIAM VAUX, of Harrowden, who, in the conflicts between York and Lancaster, fell under the banner of HENRY VI. at Tewkesbury, and his estates were alienated until the accession of *King* HENRY VII., when they were restored to his son and heir,

NICHOLAS VAUX, who, for his subsequent gallantry at the battle of *Stoke*, received the honour of knighthood. It is recorded of this Sir Nicholas Vaux, that at the marriage of *Prince* ARTHUR, 17th Henry VII., he wore a gown of purple velvet, adorned with pieces of gold, so thick and massive, that besides the silk and furs, it was valued at £1000; as also a collar of SS. weighing eight hundred pounds in nobles. Upon the accession of HENRY VIII. Sir Nicholas was made lieutenant of the castle of Guisnes, in Picardy, and in the 5th of the same reign he was at the siege of THEROUENE. He was, subsequently, one of the ambassadors to ratify the articles of peace with France, and growing so much in favour at court, he was advanced to the dignity of BARON VAUX, *of Harrowden*, on the 27th April, 1523, the solemnity of his creation taking place at the royal palace of Bridewell, in the suburbs of London. His lordship *m.* first, Elisabeth, daughter and heir of Henry, Lord Fitz-Hugh, and widow of Sir William Parr, Knt., by whom he had three daughters,

    Catherine, *m.* to Sir John Throckmorton, Knt., of Coughton, in the county of Warwick.

    Anne, *m.* to Sir Thomas Strange, of Hunston, in Norfolk.

    Alice, *m.* to Edward Sapcoate, of Elton.

Lord Vaux espoused, secondly, Anne, daughter of Thoms Green, Esq., of Green's Norton, in the county of Northampton, and had issue,

    THOMAS, his successor.

    William.

    Margaret, *m.* to Francis Pulteney, Esq., of Misterton, Leicestershire.

    Maud, *m.* to Sir John Fermor, of Eston, in the county of Northampton.

    Bridget, *m.* to Maurice Welsh, Esq., of Sudbury, in Gloucestershire.

His lordship *d.* in 1523, and was *s.* by his elder son,

THOMAS VAUX, second baron. This nobleman was one of those who attended Cardinal Wolsey in his splendid embassy to make peace between HENRY VIII., FRANCIS I., and the EMPEROR; and he was made a Knight of the Bath at the coronation of Anne Boleyne. He *m.* Elisabeth, daughter and heir of Sir Thomas Cheney, of Irtlingburgh, in Northamptonshire, and had issue,

    WILLIAM, his successor.

Nicholas.

    Anne, *m.* to Reginald Bray, of Stene, nephew of Edmund, Lord Bray.

His lordship *d.* in 1562, and was *s.* by his elder son,

WILLIAM VAUX, third baron. This nobleman *m.* first, Elizabeth, daughter of John Beaumont, Esq., of Grace Dieu, in the county of Leicester, and had issue,

    Henry, who *d.* in the life-time of his father.

    Aleanor, *m.* to Edward Brokesby, Esq., of Sholdby, in the county of Leicester.

    Elizabeth, a nun, at Caen, in Normandy.

    Anne.

His lordship espoused, secondly, Mary, daughter of John Tresham, Esq., of Rushton, in the county of Northampton, and had issue,

    GEORGE, who *m.* Elizabeth, daughter of Sir John Roper, Knt., of Welle Place, in Kent, afterwards created Lord Teynham, and dying in his father's life-time, left

        EDWARD, successor to his grandfather.

        William.

        Henry.

        Katherine, *m.* to Sir Henry Nevill, Knt., afterwards Lord Abergavenny, and had issue,

           John, } successively barons of
           George, } Abergavenny.

           Catherine, *m.* first, to Sir Robert Howard, Knt., son of Theophilus, Earl of Suffolk, and secondly, to Robert Berry, Esq., of Ludlow, in the county of Salop.

           Frances, *d.* unmarried.

           Elizabeth, *m.* to Thomas Stonor, Esq., of Oxfordshire.

    Mary, *m.* to Sir George Simeon, Knt.

    Joice.

    Edward.

    Ambrose (Sir).

    Muriel, *m.* to George Foulshurst.

    Catherine.

Lord Vaux, *d.* in 1595, and was *s.* by his grandson,

EDWARD VAUX, fourth baron. This nobleman *m.* Elizabeth, daughter of Thomas Howard, Earl of Suffolk, and widow of William, Earl of Banbury, by whom he had no legitimate issue. But two sons, born in the life-time of the lady's first husband, named Edward and Nicolas, were presumed to have been the issue of his lordship, and to those he devised his estates. Edward, the elder, died in minority, and through Nicholas and his descendants arose the celebrated contest for the Banbury peerage (see Knollys, Barons Knollys, and Earls of Banbury). Charles, the son of Nicholas, sold in 1694, the seat of Harrowden, which had been so many centuries in the Vaux family, to the Honourable Thomas Wentworth. Lord Vaux dying thus without issue in 1661, the BARONY OF VAUX, OF HARROWDEN, was supposed to have expired; but Banks, in his Stemmata Anglicana, cites the following monumental inscription, in the Church of Eye, Suffolk, to prove, that on the death of Edward, Baron Vaux, in 1661, the title devolved upon his brother, Henry, who, he conjectures to have been poor, and therefore, that he did not claim the dignity :—" Exit ultimus Baronu' de Harrowden, Henricus Vaux, Septemb. 20 Anno Dni. MDCLXIII.

ARMS.—Cheque, or. and gu. on a chevron, az. three roses, or.

VAVASOUR—BARON VAVASOUR.

By Writ of Summons, dated 6th February, 1299, 27 Edward I.

Lineage.

Of this family, which derived its surname from the high office of "King's Valvasour," (a dignity little inferior to the baronial,) and flourished for many ages in Yorkshire, was,

ROBERT LE VAVASOUR, who, in the 9th of King John, paid a fine of a thousand and two hundred marks, and two palfreys, that Maud, his daughter, widow of Theobald Walter, might be married to Fulke Fitz-Warine, an eminent baron, in those days. In the 31st of Henry III. he was sheriff of the counties of Nottingham and Derby, and so continued until the 39th of the same reign, having in the interim had the custody of the honour of Peverell committed to his charge. He m. Juliana, daughter of Gilbert de Ros, of Steeton, in Yorkshire, and was s. by, his son,

SIR JOHN LE VAVASOUR, who was s. by his son,

WILLIAM LE VAVASOUR, who, in the 18th Edward I., obtained license to make a castle of his manor house at Haslewood, in the county of York, and in three years afterwards was in an expedition made into Gascony. He was subsequently in the wars of Scotland, and had summons to parliament as a BARON, from 6th February, 1299, to 7th January, 1313. His lordship left three sons, ROBERT, Henry, and William, but none of these had summons to parliament. The youngest,

HENRY LE VAVASOUR, was the direct ancestor of Thomas Vavasour, Esq., of Haslewood, who was created a BARONET in 1628, which dignity EXPIRED with Sir Thomas Vavasour in 1826. The estates of the baronets devolved by will upon

The HONOURABLE

    EDWARD MARMADUKE STOURTON, who, changing his name to VAVASOUR, and being created a BARONET, is the present

    SIR EDWARD MARMADUKE VAVASOUR, of Haslewood, in the county of York.

ARMS.—Or on a fesse dancettée, sa.

Note.—Of this family it was remarked, that in twenty-one descents from Sir Mauger le Vavasour, temp. WILLIAM the Conqueror, not one of them had ever married an heir, or ever buried his wife.—BANKS.

VAVASOUR—BARON VAVASOUR.

By Writ of Summons, dated 26th July, 1313. 7 Edward II.

Lineage.

WALTER LE VAVASOUR, a distinguished

534

soldier in the Scottish wars, temp. Edward I., was summoned to parliament, by King EDWARD II., on 26th July, 1313, but not afterwards, nor were any of his family. His lordship's only daughter and heir,

    ELIZABETH LE VAVASOUR, m. Sir Thomas Strelly, of Nottinghamshire.

Upon the decease of Lord Vavasour, it is asserted that the BARONY OF VAVASOUR became vested in his daughter, and that it still exists in her descendants. " If, however," says Nicolas, " Walter le Vavasour was not immediately descended from William le Vavasour, the first baron of that family, and summoned in consequence of descent, this statement is probably incorrect, as it has been held that a single writ of summons, unaccompanied by a sitting in parliament, does not constitute a barony in fee."

ARMS.—Or a fesse dancettée, sa.

VERDON—BARONS VERDON.

By Writ of Summons, dated 24th June, 1295, 23 Edward I.

Lineage.

At the General Survey,

BERTRAM DE VERDON (of French extraction) possessed Farneham, in Buckinghamshire, since called Farneham-Royal, holding the same by grand serjeanty : viz. by the service of providing a glove upon the day of the king's coronation for his right hand ; and of supporting the monarch's right arm during the same ceremony, so long as he bore the royal sceptre. To this feudal lord succeeded,

NORMAN DE VERDON, who m. Lesceline, daughter of Geoffrey de Clinton, lord chamberlain and treasurer to King Henry I., and was s. by his son,

BERTRAM DE VERDON. This feudal lord was sheriff of Leicestershire, from the 16th to the 30th of King Henry II.'s reign, inclusive. He subsequently attended the lion-hearted RICHARD to the Holy Land, and was at the siege of Acon; which place upon its surrender was committed to his custody. This Bertram founded the abbey of Croxden, in the county of Stafford, anno 1176, and was otherwise a liberal benefactor to the church. He m. first, Maud, daughter of Robert de Ferrers, Earl of Derby, by whom he had no issue, and secondly, Rohese, but of what family is unknown. He d. at Joppa, in 1192, and was s. by his son,

THOMAS DE VERDON, who m. Eustacia, daughter of Gilbert Basset, and died in Ireland, anno 1199, without issue, when he was s. by his brother,

NICHOLAS DE VERDON, who in the 6th of John, paid to the king one hundred pounds, as also a courser and palfrey, for livery of those lands in Ireland, whereof his father died possessed. But in twelve years afterwards, taking part with the rebellious barons, all his lands were seized by special precepts from the crown, to the sheriffs of Warwick, Leicester, Stafford, Lincoln, Bucks, and Oxford, and placed in the custody of William de Cantilupe, during the king's pleasure. Submitting, however, to King Henry III., those lands were restored to him in the first year of that monarch, and he appears afterwards to have enjoyed the favour of the king. He died in 1231, leaving an only daughter and heiress,

ROHESE DE VERDON, who married Theobald de Butler, (a branch of the noble family of Butler, of Ireland,) but being so great an heiress, retained her maiden name after marriage, which her husband adopted. At the time of her father's decease, she appears to have been a widow. This lady, who founded the abbey of Grace Dieu, for Cistertian Monks, at Beldon, in Leicestershire, died in 1247, leaving issue,

    JOHN, her heir.

    Nicholas, who had the manor of Chinore, in Ireland, died *s. p.*

    Maud, *m.* to John Fitz-Alan, Earl of Arundel.

She was succeeded by her elder son,

JOHN DE VERDON (alias Butler). This great feudal lord, being one of the barons marchers, had orders, in the 44th Henry III., upon the incursions of the Welsh, to keep his residence upon the borders. After which he was one of the barons who adhered to the king, in the conflict between the crown and the nobles; and upon the triumph of the royal cause at Evesham, he was commissioned to raise forces in Worcestershire, for the purpose of attacking the only remaining hold of the barons, at Kenilworth. But these troubles being at length ended, John de Verdon was signed with the cross,[*] and accompanied Prince Edward to the Holy Land.

John de Verdon *m.* first, Margaret, daughter of Gilbert de Lacie, and heir to her grandfather, Walter de Lacie, by which alliance, the castle of Webbeley, in the county of Hereford, came into the Verdon family. He espoused, secondly, Alianore, whose surname is unknown, and dying in 1274, was *s.* by his son,

THEOBALD DE VERDON, who, in the 3rd Edward I., upon doing homage, had livery of his lands, paying £100 for his relief. At this period, he held the office of CONSTABLE OF IRELAND. For some years subsequently, this eminent person seems to have enjoyed the favour of the crown, and to have received several immunities; but in the 19th of Edward's reign, we find him arraigned for treason, and divers other misdemeanours, before the king and council, at Bergavenny, and condemned to imprisonment and confiscation; the king, however, taking into consideration the good services of his ancestors, and his own submission, freed him for a fine of five hundred marks; and he was soon after summoned to parliament as BARON VERDON. In the 29th of the same reign, (Edward I.,) his lordship was one of the barons in the parliament of Lincoln, who, by a public instrument, under their seals, sent to Pope Boniface VIII., asserted the right of King Edward, as supe-

rior lord of the whole realm of Scotland. Lord Verdon having had summons to parliament, to 3rd November, 1306, *d.* in 1309, and was *s.* by his only surviving son,

SIR THEOBALD DE VERDON, second baron, who, in the life-time of his father, had summons to parliament, as "Theobald de Verdon, Junior," from 29th December, 1299, to 22nd February, 1307, and afterwards, without the word "Junior," from 4th March, 1309, to 24th October, 1314. This nobleman, in the 6th Edward II., was constituted JUSTICE OF IRELAND, having likewise the lieutenancy of that realm, and the fee of £500 per annum, then granted to him. His lordship *m.* first, Maud, daughter of Edward Mortimer, Lord of Wigmore, by whom he had issue,

    Joane, *m.* to Thomas de Furnival, second Lord Furnival, and *d.* in 1334.

    Elizabeth, *m.* to Bartholomew de Burghersh.

    Margery, *m.* first, William le Blunt, secondly, Marcus Husse, and thirdly, John Crophull, by whom she had a son,

        Thomas Crophull, whose daughter and heiress,

        Agnes, *m.* to Sir Walter Devereux, Knt.

He espoused, secondly, Elizabeth, widow of John de Burgh, and daughter and eventually co-heir of Gilbert de Clare, Earl of Gloucester, by Jane Plantagenet, daughter of King Edward I., by whom he had an only daughter,

    Isabel, *m.* to Henry Ferrers, Lord Ferrers, of Groby, which Henry *d.* 17th Edward III., leaving by the said Isabel,

        William, Lord Ferrers.

        Philippa, *m.* to Guy de Beauchamp.

        Elizabeth, *m.* to —— de Assein.

Theobald, Lord Verdon, *d.* in 1316, when the BARONY OF VERDON fell into ABEYANCE amongst his daughters, and so continues with their representatives.

    ARMS.—Or. a fet gules.

VERDON—BARON VERDON.

By Writ of Summons, dated 27th January, 1332, 6 Edward III.

Lineage.

JOHN DE VERDON was summoned to parliament as a BARON, from 27th January, 1332, to 22nd January, 1336, and again on the 25th February, 1342, but never afterwards, and of his lordship nothing further is recorded.

VERE—EARLS OF OXFORD, MARQUESS OF DUBLIN, DUKE OF IRELAND.

Earldom, Creation of the Empress Maud, }anno
    and confirmed by Henry II. } 1135.
Marquisate, } Creations of { 1386.
Dukedom, } Richard II. { 1387.

Lineage.

The first mention of this noble and ancient family,

---

[*] Signed with the cross. Those persons who contemplated a voyage to the Holy Land, painted a cross upon their shoulders, as indicative of their profession.

(whose pedigree Leland deduces from Noah!!) is in the general survey of England, made by William the Conqueror, wherein,

ALBERIC DE VER, is stated to have possessed numerous lordships in the different shires, of which Chenisiton, (now Kensington,) in the county of Middlesex, was one, and Hedingham, in the county of Essex, where his castle was situated, and where he chiefly resided, another. This Alberic, m. Beatrix, daughter of Henry Castellan of Bourbourg, and niece maternally, (through Sibilla, his daughter and heiress,) of Manasses, Count of Ghisnes, by whom he had five sons, Alberic, Geoffrey, Roger, Robert, and William, and a daughter, Rohesia, m. first, to Pagan Beauchamp, and secondly, to Geoffery de Mandeville, Earl of Essex. Alberic de Ver, in the latter end of his days assumed the cowl, and died a monk; he was buried in the church of Colne Priory, which he founded, and was s. by his son,

ALBERIC DE VERE, who being in high favour with King Henry I., was constituted by that monarch LORD HIGH CHAMBERLAIN of England, to hold the same in fee, to himself and his heirs, with all dignities and liberties thereunto appertaining, as fully and honourably as Robert Malet, Lord of the honour of Eye, in Suffolk, who had then been banished and disinherited, has holden the said office. His lordship m. Adeliza, daughter of Gilbert de Clare, and had issue,

Aberic or Aubrey, his successor.
———, Canon of St. Osyth's, in Essex.
Robert, Lord of Twiwell, in the county of Northampton.
Adeliza, m. to Henry de Essex.
Juliana, m. to Hugh Bigod, Earl of Norfolk.

In the 5th year of King Stephen, when joint sheriff (with Richard Basset, then Justice of England,) of Surrey, Cambridge, Essex, and several other counties, his lordship was slain in a popular tumult at London, and was s. by his eldest son,

AUBREY DE VERE, who, for his fidelity to the Empress Maud, was confirmed by that princess in the LORD CHAMBERLAINSHIP, and all his father's great territorial possessions. He had likewise, other important grants with the Earldom of Cambridge, provided that dignity were not vested in the King of Scots, but if it were, then his lordship was to have his choice of the Earldoms of Oxford, Berkshire, Wiltshire, or Dorsetshire; all which grants being ratified by King Henry II., his lordship was created EARL OF OXFORD, with the usual grant to earls, of the third penny of the pleas of the county. In the 12th King Henry II., upon levying the aid for portioning the king's daughter, the Earl of Oxford certified his knights' fees to be in number twenty-eight, for which he paid £20; and in the 2nd year of King Richard I., he paid a fine of five hundred marks to the king, "for the sister of Walter de Bolebec to make a wife for his son." In four years afterwards, his lordship contributed £30. 2s. 6d., for the knights' fees he then held, towards the sum, at that time levied, for the ransom of the king. The earl m. first, Eufamia, daughter of Sir William de Cantilupe, by whom he had no issue, and secondly, Lucia, daughter and heiress of William de Abrincis, by whom he had,

AUBREY,
ROBERT, } successively Earls of Oxford.
William, Bishop of Hereford, anno 1198, d. in 1199.
Henry.
Adeliza.
Sarah.

His lordship d. in 1194, and was s. by his elder son,

AUBREY DE VERE, second Earl of Oxford, and Lord Great Chamberlain. This nobleman was sheriff of Essex and Herefordshire, from the 10th to the 15th of King John, inclusive—and was reputed one of the evil councillors of that monarch. His lordship d. in 1214, and having no issue, was s. by his brother,

ROBERT DE VERE, third Earl of Oxford, and Lord Great Chamberlain. This nobleman pursuing a different course from that of his deceased brother, was one of the celebrated twenty-five barons appointed to enforce the observance of MAGNA CHARTA. In the beginning of the reign of Henry III., having made his peace, his lordship appears, from a fine levied before him and others, to have been one of the judges in the Court of King's Bench. He m. Isabel, daughter of Hugh, and sister and heir of Walter de Bolebec, by whom he had issue,

HUGH, his successor.
Henry (Sir), of Great Addington, in the county of Northampton, whose grandson,
Richard Vere, m. Isabel, daughter of John Green, Esq., of Drayton, and heiress of her brother, whereby the manor of Drayton, in the county of Northampton, came into this branch of the Vere family, the male line of which terminated with
Sir Henry Vere, of Great Addington, Drayton, &c., who left by his wife, Isabel, daughter of Sir Thomas Tresham, four daughters, his co-heirs, viz.
Elizabeth, m. to John, Lord Mordaunt.
Anne, m. to Sir Humphrey Brown, Chief Justice of the Common Pleas, 34th Henry VIII.
Constance, m. to John Parr, Esq.
Etheldred, m. to John Brown, Esq.
Isabel, m. to Sir John Courtenay.

The earl d. in 1221, and was s. by his elder son,

HUGH DE VERE, fourth Earl of Oxford, and fifth Lord Great Chamberlain. In the 17th Henry III., this nobleman was solemnly knighted at Gloucester, the king at that time solemnizing the feast of Pentecost there. In 1245 his lordship's mother died, and he then, upon giving security for payment of his relief, namely, the sum of £100, and doing homage, had livery of the lands of her inheritance. In the 30th Henry III. he was one of the subscribing barons to the letter transmitted to the Pope, complaining of the exactions of his holiness upon this realm; and he sate in the parliament, 22nd Henry III., wherein the king was upbraided with his prodigal expenditure, and informed, that neither his treasurer nor chancellor, had the confidence of their lordships. The earl m. Hawise, daughter of Leyer de Quincy, Earl of Winchester, and had an only son, his successor, at his d. in 1263,

ROBERT DE VERE, fifth Earl of Oxford, and sixth Lord Great Chamberlain. This nobleman having arrayed himself under the banner of Montfort, Earl of Leicester, was amongst those who were surprised with young Hugh de Montfort, at Kenilworth, a few days before the battle of Evesham, and taken prisoner; but he made his peace soon after, under the "*Dictum of Kenilworth*," and we find him employed by King Edward I., against the Welsh, in the 14th of that monarch's reign. His lordship m. Alice, daughter and heiress of Gilbert, Lord Saundford,* Chamberlain in Fee, to Eleanor, Queen of Henry III., and had, with other issue,

> ROBERT, his successor.
> Alphonsus, m. Jane, daughter of Sir Richard Foliot, Knt., and had a son,
>> JOHN, who s. as seventh Earl of Oxford.
> Hugh, m. Dionysia de Monchensi, by whom he had no issue.
> Joane, m. to William de Warren.
> Lora, m. to Reginald de Argentein.

The earl d. in 1296, and was s. by his eldest son,

ROBERT DE VERE, sixth Earl of Oxford, and seventh Lord Great Chamberlain. This nobleman took part in the wars of Scotland, in the 24th and 27th of Edward I. His lordship m. Margaret, daughter of Roger Mortimer, Earl of March, but dying in 1331, without issue, his honours devolved upon his nephew,

JOHN DE VERE, as seventh Earl of Oxford, and eighth Lord Great Chamberlain. This nobleman who was a military personage of great renown, shared in all the glories of Edward III.'s martial reign. When he succeeded to the earldom, he had but just attained his eighteenth year—and very soon afterwards, we find him with the army in Scotland, where he appears to have been engaged for some years. In the 14th Edward III., he attended the king into Flanders. The next year he assisted "at the great feast and justing in London, which King Edward III. caused to be made, as it was said, for the love of the Countess of Salisbury. In the 16th year, he was again in the wars of France; to which service he brought forty men-at-arms, (him-

* This Gilbert inherited the manor of Hormede Magna, in the county of Herts, and held it by serjeanty of service, in the queen's chamber; which manor was conveyed by his heiress, Alice, to her husband, the Earl of Oxford—and sold by his successor, Edward Earl of Oxford, temp. Elizabeth, to Anthony Cage, citizen of London, whose representative, Daniel Cage, at the coronation of King James I., claimed the office of chamberlain to the queen; but the court for determining claims, came to no decision upon the case, because the Earl of Oxford held three manors by this office, and there was no proof that Ginges, was yet severed from the earldom.

self included,) one banneret, nine knights, twenty-nine esquires, and thirty archers on horseback, and had an allowance of fifty-six sacks of wool, for the wages of himself and his retinue. The next year he accompanied Henry de Lancaster, Earl of Derby, and divers other great personages, into Scotland, for raising the siege of Loughmaban Castle. And in the 18th, he was in Gascony, at the surrender of Bergerath; after which, proceeding to assault the castle of Pellegrue, he was taken prisoner in his tent, but soon after exchanged for the Viscount de Bonqueatyne—when he marched with the Earl of Derby, to Attveroche, then besieged by the French, and relieved it. "But about the feast of the Blessed Virgin," (writes Dugdale,) "returning out of Britanny, he was by tempest cast upon the coast of Connaught, in Ireland, where he and all his company suffered much misery from those barbarous people there, who pillaged them of all they had."

His lordship returned to France, soon after this event, and continued with little interruption, during the remainder of his life, actively and gallantly engaged in the wars in that country. He was one of the heroes of CRESSY, and he had a command upon the glorious field of POICTIERS. He eventually lost his life from fatigue, in the English army, encamped before the walls of Rheims, on the 14th January, 1306. The earl m. Maud, sister and heiress of Giles, Lord Badlesmere, and widow of Robert Fitz-Payn, by whom he had issue,

> THOMAS, his successor.
> AUBREY, who, upon the reversal of the attainder of his nephew, Robert, Duke of Ireland, succeeded as tenth Earl of Oxford (of this nobleman presently).
> John, died s. p.
> Margaret, m. first, to Henry, Lord Beaumont, and secondly, to Sir John Devereux, Knt.
> Isabel, m. first, to Sir John Courtney, Knt., and secondly, to Sir Oliver Denham.

His lordship, who left immense landed possessions in the counties of Hereford, Bedford, Leicester, Essex, Buckingham, Hertford, Dorset, Wilts, Suffolk, and Cambridge, was s. by his eldest son,

SIR THOMAS DE VERE, Knt., eighth Earl of Oxford, and ninth Lord Chamberlain. Of this nobleman little more is mentioned, than his being engaged in foreign warfare like his father, but not with the same renown. His lordship m. in the lifetime of the late earl, Maud, daughter of Sir Ralph de Ufford, and was s. at his decease, in 1371, by his only son,

ROBERT DE VERE, ninth Earl of Oxford, and tenth Lord Chamberlain. This nobleman doing homage, and making proof of his age, in the 6th of Richard II., had livery of his lands. His lordship becoming subsequently, the favourite of that weak and unfortunate prince, obtained large territorial grants from the crown, amongst which was the castle of Okeham, in Rutland, and was advanced to a new dignity in the peerage, by the title of MARQUESS OF DUBLIN, in which he had summons to parliament on the 8th August, 1396. Upon his elevation to the marquisate, his lordship obtained a grant of the land and domi-

·nion of Ireland, with all profits, revenues, and regalities, as amply as the king himself ought to enjoy the same, to hold by homage and allegiance. And in the next year, within a few months, he was created DUKE OF IRELAND. Those high honours and immunities exciting the jealousy of the nobles, and the favourite bearing his fortune imperiously, several of the great lords assembled at Haringhay House, near Highgate, in the county of Middlesex, and evinced open hostility to the royal minion. From thence, at the desire of the king, who became alarmed, they transferred their deliberations to Westminster, and in reply to an interrogatory put to them by the Bishop of Ely, then Lord Chancellor, they demanded that the king should dismiss the traitors that surrounded him, amongst whom they particularized " *Robert Vere, DUKE OF IRELAND.*" For the moment, however, Richard allayed this tumult by fair promises, but De Vere not considering himself safe, soon after effected his escape, in disguise, to the continent, accompanied by Michael de la Pole, Earl of Suffolk. He subsequently returned to England, at the head of four or five thousand men, and marching into Oxfordshire, was met at Radcote Bridge, on the river Isis, by the Earl of Derby and Duke of Gloucester, where his troops being surrounded, he could secure personal safety only by abandoning his sword, gauntlets, and armour, and thus swimming down the stream. In the pursuit, his grace's chariot having fallen into the hands of his foes, it is said that they discovered there letters from the king, calling upon him to hasten to London, and that the monarch would be ready to live or die for him. In a parliament soon after convened, through the influence of the nobles, the duke not appearing to a citation, was sentenced to banishment, and at the same time outlawed and attainted. He effected, however, again his escape to the continent, where, being wounded by a wild boar, while hunting, he died of the hurt, at Lovaine, anno 1392, in great distress and poverty; his English property being all confiscated, and his honours EXTINGUISHED, by the ATTAINDER.

His grace m. first, Lady Philippa De Courcy, daughter and co-heiress of Ingelram, Earl of Bedford, by his wife, the Princess Isabel, daughter of King Edward III., which noble lady, in the zenith of his prosperity, he repudiated, and m. secondly, one Lancerona, a joiner's daughter, who came out of Bohemia, with Anne, Queen consort of King Richard. He had issue, however, by neither; and upon his decease, the representation of the family reverted to his uncle,

AUBREY DE VERE, who, in the 16th Richard II., was, by consent of parliament, restored to all those lands which had been, by fine, entailed previously to the attainder of the deceased duke; having the Earldom of Oxford likewise restored to himself, and the heirs male of his body. His lordship in consequence, took his seat in the house of Peers, as tenth earl: but the office of Lord High Chamberlain, so long in the Vere family, was bestowed by the king, owing to the restored lord being infirm, upon John Holland, Earl of Huntendon, for life. The infirmities of his lordship

continuing, he had especial license to absent himself from the parliament held at Shrewsbury, in the 21st of Richard II.; in which the judgment passed ten years previously against his nephew, the Duke of Ireland, was revoked and annulled. The earl m. Alice, daughter of John, Lord Fitz-Walter, and had issue,

RICHARD, his successor.
John, d. unmarried.
Alice, m. to Sir John Fits-Lewes, Knt.

His lordship d. in 1400, and was s. by his elder son,

RICHARD DE VERE, eleventh Earl of Oxford. This nobleman was fourteen years of age, at the decease of his father, and had a grant of one hundred pounds a year out of his own lands for his maintenance during his minority. His lordship inherited very extensive estates in the counties of Essex, Kent, Cambridge, &c., and in the 8th of Henry IV., being then of full age, having assented, that Philippa, Duchess of Ireland, relict of the attainted duke, should enjoy her dower out of the entailed lands, the king, in compliance with an act of parliament, granted to his lordship and his heirs, all those lands and tenements, which, by the forfeiture of Duke Robert, came to the crown; excepting such as had been disposed of by himself, or King Richard II.

" About this time," says Dugdale, " or not long before, Maude, Countess of Oxford, widow of Earl Thomas, and mother of Robert, Duke of Ireland, still surviving, caused it to be divulged, that King Richard II. was alive; and that he would forthwith lay claim to his ancient honour; and procured *Harts* to be made of silver and gilt, (which were badges that king gave to his friends, souldiers, and servants) to be in the king's name distributed in the countrey, whereby the people might be the sooner allured to rise on his behalf; giving it further out, that he was privately kept in Scotland, till he could have a fit opportunity to come in with an army of French and Scots. Whereupon she was committed to prison, and her goods confiscated." This lady d. in 1422, leaving her cousin, Robert de Willoughby, her next heir. The Earl of Oxford m. Alice, daughter of Sir John Sergeant, Knt., of Cornwall, and had issue,

JOHN, his successor.
Robert, m. Joane, daughter of Sir Hugh Courtenay, and had issue,
    JOHN DE VERE, who m. Alice, daughter of Walter Keirington, and left a son, JOHN, who s. as fifteenth Earl of Oxford.

His lordship, who had been in the French wars, and was honoured with the garter, d. in 1417, and was s. by his elder son,

JOHN DE VERE, twelfth Earl of Oxford, then in his ninth year. In the 4th of Henry VI., his lordship had the honour of knighthood conferred upon him by that monarch, at Leicester, when the king himself received a similar honour at the hands of his uncle, the Duke of Bedford. In the 7th of the same reign, being still in ward, the earl had to pay a fine of £2000 for marrying Elizabeth, daughter of Sir John Howard, Knt., the younger, without license: but before the close of that year, having attained majority, and done homage, he had livery of his lands. In the 13th, his lordship obtained license to travel towards the Holy Land, with twelve persons of his company; and to take with him an hundred pounds in money, and to receive five hundred marks more by way of exchange. In the next year he went into Picardy for the relief of Calais, and the same year performing his homage, had livery of all those lands, which, by the death of Margaret, the wife of Sir John Howard, Knt., descended to her daughter, Elizabeth, Countess of Oxford, his lordship's consort. After this we find the earl joined in commission with John, Duke of Norfolk, and others, to treat with Charles de Valoys, or his ambassadors, touching a peace with France: and during the whole reign of Henry VI., being a staunch Lancastrian, always enjoying the confidence of the crown; but upon the accession of Edward IV., sharing the fate of his party, he was attainted in the first parliament of that monarch, with his eldest son, Aubrey, and beheaded on Tower Hill, anno 1461.

His lordship m. as already stated, Elizabeth, only daughter and heiress of Sir John Howard (uncle by the half blood of John Howard, first Duke of Norfolk) and heiress through her grandmother, Margaret, daughter of Sir John de Platz, to the Barony of Platz, by whom he had issue,

    Aubrey, beheaded with his father, 1st of Edward IV.

    JOHN, restored as thirteenth earl.

    George (Sir), m. Margaret, daughter and heiress of William Stafford, Esq., of Frome, and had issue,

        George, who d. in his father's life-time.

        JOHN, who inherited as fourteenth Earl of Oxford.

        Elizabeth, m. to Sir Anthony Wingfield.

        Margaret.

        Dorothy, m. to John Nevill, Lord Latimer.

        Ursula, m. first, to George Windsor, Esq., and secondly, to Sir Edmund Knightly.

    Richard (Sir).

    Thomas (Sir), died s. p. in 1489.

    Mary, a nun at Barking.

    Joane, m. to Sir William Norris, Knt., of Yatenden.

    Elizabeth, m. to William Bourchier, son and heir of Henry, Earl of Essex.

Upon the attainder and execution of John, twelfth Earl of Oxford, all the honours of the family expired, but his lordship's second, and eldest surviving son,

JOHN DE VERE, was restored as thirteenth Earl of Oxford, during the temporary triumph of the House of Lancaster, in the 10th of Edward IV., when he sate as Lord High Steward at the trial of John Tiptoft, Earl of Worcester, who was condemned and beheaded on Tower Hill. But his lordship, with Richard Nevill, the stout Earl of Warwick, being soon after totally routed by the Yorkists, at Barnet, and King Edward re-established upon the throne, himself and his two bro-

thers, Sir George, and Sir Thomas Vere, were attainted, but pardoned as to their lives. Subsequently escaping from prison, and ardently embarking in the cause of Henry, Earl of Richmond, he commanded the archers of the vanguard, at Bosworth field, and there mainly contributed, by his valour and skill, to the victory which terminated the bloody and procrastinated contest between the Houses of York and Lancaster. Upon the accession of this chief to the crown of England as Henry VII., his lordship was immediately restored to all his possessions, and sworn of the privy council: and at the coronation of the king, he was constituted one of the commissioners for executing the office of LORD HIGH STEWARD of England. The earl had besides large grants of confiscated property, and was made CONSTABLE of the Tower of London, and Lord HIGH ADMIRAL of England, Ireland, and the Duchy of Aquitaine. At the coronation of the Queen Consort, 3d Henry VII., his lordship was again one of the commissioners for executing the office of Lord High Steward, and he had subsequently a chief command in suppressing the rebellion of Lambert Simnell, and his partisans: as he had a few years afterwards in opposing Lord Audley, and the Cornish men, at Blackheath. Upon the accession of King Henry VIII., the Earl of Oxford was restored to the office of LORD GREAT CHAMBERLAIN of England, originally granted to his ancestor, Aubrey de Vere, by King Henry I., in which year he had the Constableship of the castle of Clare, in the county of Suffolk, confirmed to him for life; as also a grant and confirmation of the castle of Colchester, which Maud, the Empress, conferred upon his family. Of this distinguished personage, who was celebrated for his splendid hospitality, and was esteemed a gallant, learned, and religious man, and King Henry VIII., the following story is told.

The monarch visiting the earl's castle of Hedingham, was there sumptuously entertained by the princely noble; and at his departure his lordship's livery servants, ranged on both sides, made an avenue for the king: which attracting his highness's attention, he called out to the earl, and said, "My lord, I have heard much of your hospitality; but I see it is greater than the speech. These handsome gentlemen and yeomen, which I see on both sides of me, are surely your menial servants?" The earl smiled, and said, "It may please your grace, they were not for mine ease: they are most of them my retainers, that are come to do me service at such a time as this; and chiefly to see your grace." The king started a little, and rejoined, "By my faith, my lord, I thank you for my good cheer, but I may not endure to have my laws broken in my sight; my attorney must speak with you." It is added, that this affair cost his lordship eventually, no less than fifteen thousand marks, in the shape of compromise.

The earl m. first, Lady Margaret Nevill, daughter of Richard, Earl of Salisbury, by whom he had a son, John, who died young in the Tower of London, during his father's exile. His lordship espoused secondly, Elizabeth, daughter of Sir Richard Scroope, Knt., and widow of William, Viscount

Beaumont, but had no issue. The earl, who, with his other honours, was a Knight of the Garter, *d.* in 1513, and was *s.* by (the eldest surviving son of his deceased brother, Sir George Vere) his nephew,

JOHN DE VERE, as fourteenth Earl of Oxford, commonly called, "Little John of Campes," from his diminitive stature, and residence at Castle Campes, in Cambridgeshire. His lordship *m.* Lady Anne Howard, daughter of Thomas, Duke of Norfolk, but had no issue. He *d.* in 1526, when his sisters (refer to children of Sir George Vere, son of John, twelfth earl) became heirs to the ancient baronies* of the family, and those fell into ABEYANCE between them, as they still continue with their descendants; while the Earldom of Oxford passed to his cousin and heir-at-law (refer to descendants of the Hon. Robert Vere, second son of Richard, eleventh earl),

JOHN DE VERE, as fifteenth Earl of Oxford, and lord great chamberlain. This nobleman was a privy councillor in the reign of Henry VIII., and supported the measures of the court. His lordship signed the articles exhibited by the king against Cardinal Wolsey, and his name was to the letter addressed to the Pope (Clement VII.) by several of the nobility and divers churchmen, declaring that unless his Holiness sanctioned the king's divorce from Queen Katharine, the supremacy of the holy see within this realm would terminate.

The earl *m.* Elisabeth, daughter and heiress of Sir Edward Trussel, Knt., of Cubleadon, in the county of Stafford, by whom he had issue,

> JOHN, his successor,
> Aubrey, *m.* Margaret, daughter of John Spring, Esq., of Lanham, in the county of Suffolk, and had, with other issue,
>> HUGH, *m.* Eleanor, daughter of —— Walsh, Esq., and left a son,
>>> ROBERT, who *s.* as nineteenth Earl of Oxford.
>> Geffery, who *m.* Elisabeth, daughter of Sir John Hardkyn, of Colchester, and had, with other issue,
>>> Francis (Sir), some time Governor of Brill, in the Netherlands.
>>> HORATIO, the celebrated Lord Vere, of Tilbury (see that dignity).
>>> Frances, *m.* to Sir Robert Harcourt, Knt., ancestor of the extinct Earls of Harcourt.
> Elizabeth, *m.* to Thomas, Lord Darcy, of Chiche.
> Anne, *m.* to Edmund Sheffield, Lord Sheffield.
> Frances, *m.* to Henry, Earl of Surrey.

His lordship, who was a Knight of the Garter, *d.* in 1539, and was *s.* by his eldest son,

JOHN DE VERE, sixteenth Earl of Oxford, and lord great chamberlain, who, in the 32nd Henry VIII., had livery of those lands which descended to him from Elizabeth, his mother, sister and heir of John Trussel, Esq.; and in the 36th of the same monarch was in the expedition into France, when

Bulloigne was besieged and taken. His lordship *m.* first, Lady Dorothy Nevill, daughter of Ralph, Earl of Westmorland, by whom he had an only daughter,

> Katherine, *m.* to Edward, Lord Windsor.

The earl espoused, secondly, Margaret, daughter of John Golding, Esq., by whom he had issue,

EDWARD, his successor.

> Mary, *m.* to Peregrine Bertie, tenth Lord Willoughby de Eresby, by whom she had,
>> ROBERT, eleventh Lord Willoughby de Eresby, who claimed the Earldom of Oxford, and great chamberlainship, in right of his mother; but succeeded in the latter only. He was, however, created EARL OF LINDSAY. In this earldom, and the subsequent Dukedom of Ancaster, the Barony of Willoughby, and the chamberlainship continued until their extinction, in 1809, of those dignities, when the chamberlainship devolved jointly upon the last Duke of Ancaster's sisters and heirs,
>>> Priscilla, Lady Gwydyr.
>>> Georgiana, Marchioness Cholmondeley; and it is now vested in this lady, and her nephew, Peter, present Lord Willoughby de Eresby.

The earl *d.* in 1562, and was *s.* by his elder son,

EDWARD DE VERE, seventeenth Earl of Oxford, and lord great chamberlain. This nobleman was one of the peers appointed, 29th Elizabeth, to sit in judgment upon the unhappy Mary, Queen of Scotland, and his lordship had a command in the fleet equipped to oppose the Armada, in 1588. His lordship was one of the wits of the period in which he lived, and distinguished alike by his patriotism and chivalrous spirit. In the tournaments of Elizabeth's reign the Earl of Oxford was pre-eminently conspicuous, and upon two occasions he was honoured with a prize from her majesty's own hand, being conducted, armed by two ladies, into the presence chamber for the purpose of receiving the high reward. Walpole says, that he attained reputation as a poet, and was esteemed the first writer of comedy in his time. His lordship *m.* first, Anne, daughter of William Cecil, the celebrated Lord (Treasurer) Burghley, and had issue,

> Elizabeth, *m.* to William, Earl of Derby.
> Bridget, *m.* to Francis, Lord Norris, of Rycote.
> Susan, *m.* to Philip Herbert, Earl of Montgomery.

The earl *m.* secondly, Elizabeth, daughter of Thomas Trentham, Esq., of Roucester, in the county of Stafford, by whom he had an only child,

Henry, his successor.

This Lord Oxford was the first person who introduced perfumes and embroidered gloves into England, and presenting a pair of the latter to Queen Elisabeth, her majesty was so pleased with them, that she had her picture painted with those gloves on. His lordship lived to an advanced age, and dying in 1604, was *s.* by his son,

HENRY DE VERE, eighteenth Earl of Oxford, and lord great chamberlain, who m. Lady Diana Cecil, second daughter of William, Earl of Exeter, one of the greatest fortunes, and most celebrated beauties of the period, but had no issue. His lordship d. at the siege of Breda, in the Netherlands, where he had the command of a regiment, in 1625, when his honours devolved upon his cousin (refer to descendants of Aubrey, second son of John, fifteenth earl),

ROBERT DE VERE, as nineteenth Earl of Oxford. In the 2nd Charles I. there was great controversy between this Robert, and Robert Bertie, then Lord Willoughby de Eresby, in consequence of the latter claiming in right of his mother, Mary, daughter of John, sixteenth Earl of Oxford, and sister and heiress of Edward, seventeenth earl, the Earldom of Oxford, with the baronies in fee belonging to the family, and the great chamberlainship of England. The judges gave their opinion, however, in parliament, "that the earldom was well descended upon the heir male; but that the baronies having devolved upon heirs female, the three sisters of John, fourteenth earl, (refer to children of Sir George Vere, third son of the twelfth earl,) were then in ABEYANCE. As to the office of great chamberlain, it was also referred to the judges, then attending in parliament, to report, whether " that Robert, Earl of Oxford, who made the entail thereof, temp. Richard II., on the heir male, was at that time seised thereof or not, and admitting that he was, then whether such an office might be conveyed by way of limiting of uses." Upon this reference three* of the judges decided for the heir general, and two† for the heir male; five of their lordships only attending. Whereupon the Lord Willoughby was admitted on the 13th April, 13th Charles I., into the house, with his staff of office; and took his place above all the barons, according to the statute of 31st Henry VIII., and the next day, Robert de Vere took his seat as Earl of Oxford, next to the Earl of Arundel. His lordship m. a Dutch lady, Beatrix Van Hemmena, by whom he left at his decease, in 1632, (falling at the siege of Maestricht, where he commanded a regiment,) an only surviving child, his successor,

AUBREY DE VERE, twentieth Earl of Oxford. This nobleman, at the decease of his father, was but six years of age, and in ward to King Charles I. In 1648 he had command of a regiment of English infantry in the service of the states general. During the civil wars he espoused the royal cause, and suffered much in consequence, but after the restoration, he was sworn of the privy council, made a Knight of the Garter, and appointed lord lieutenant of the county of Essex.

His lordship m. first, Anne, daughter and co-heir of Paul, Viscount Bayning, by whom he had no issue. He espoused, secondly, Diana, daughter of George Kirke, Esq., one of the grooms of the bedchamber to King Charles I., by whom he had,

---

* Mr. Justice Doderidge.
Mr. Justice Yelverton.
Mr. Baron Trevor.
† The Lord Chief Justice Crew.
The Lord Chief Baron, Sir John Walter.

Charles, } both d. young.
Charlotte,

Diana, m. to Charles Beauclerk, (illegitimate son of King Charles II.,) DUKE OF ST. ALBANS. This lady became, eventually, sole heiress of her father, and representative of the noble family of De Vere, Earls of Oxford.

Mary, } both d. unmarried.
Henrietta,

The earl d. in 1702, (having acquiesced in the expulsion of the royal house, which he had previously so zealously upheld,) and leaving no male issue, the very ancient EARLDOM OF OXFORD, which had passed through twenty generations, became EXTINCT.

ARMS.—Quarterly, gules and or. In the first a mullett, ar.

VERE—BARON VERE.

By Writ of Summons, dated 21st September, 1299, 27 Edward I.

Lineage.

HUGH DE VERE, one of the younger sons of Robert, fifth Earl of Oxford, a military personage of high reputation, was summoned to parliament as a BARON from 27th September, 1299, to 3rd March, 1318. In the 28th Edward I. he was joined in an embassy to France with the Bishop of Gloucester, for negotiating peace between the two crowns: and the next year he was deputed to the court of Rome upon a mission of great importance. He was, subsequently, employed upon other diplomatic occasions, and was actively engaged in the Scottish wars. His lordship m. Dyonisia, daughter and heiress of William, son of Warine de Monchensy, which lady d. without issue, in 1313, when Adomare de Valence, son of the Lady Joane de Valence, was found to be her next heir. Lord Vere does not appear to have married a second time, and the BARONY became, therefore, at his decease EXTINCT.

VERE — BARON VERE, OF TILBURY, IN THE COUNTY OF ESSEX.

By Letters Patent, dated 25th July, 1625.

Lineage.

GEOFFREY DE VERE, third son of John, fifteenth Earl of Oxford, and brother of John, sixteenth earl, m. Elizabeth, daughter of Sir John Hardkyn, Knt., of Colchester, and had issue,

John, of Kisby Hall, in the county of Essex, m. Thomasine, daughter of —— Porter, Esq., and had two sons,

John, } who both died s. p.
Robert,

Francis (Sir). Of the exploits of this gallant person, an account appeared in 1657, under the title of " The Commentaries of Sir Francis Vere, being divers pieces of service, wherein he had command, written by himself," published by William Dillingham, D.D. Sir Francis m. Elizabeth Dent, daughter and co-heir of a citizen of London, by whom he had several children, all of whom, however, predeceased himself unmarried. He d. in 1608, and was interred at Westminster under a splendid monument.

Geoffrey, d. unmarried.

HORATIO, of whom presently.

Frances, m. to Sir Robert Harcourt, ancestor of the Earls of Harcourt.

The youngest son,

SIR HORATIO VERE, Knt., becoming one of the most eminent persons of the period in which he lived, was elevated to the peerage for his distinguished services, by King Charles I., in the dignity of BARON VERE, of Tilbury. The exploits of this gallant personage form a brilliant page in British History, and it would be in vain to attempt even to epitomise them here. He was so great a military officer that the first generals were proud of having served under him; and Clarendon, in mentioning Edward, Lord Conway, says, " he was bred up a soldier, in several commands under the particular care of Lord Vere." He also observes, that " Monk, Duke of Albemarle, had the reputation of a good foot officer, when he was in the Lord Vere's regiment, in Holland." Fuller in his " Worthies" thus characterises his lordship: " Horace, Lord Vere, had more meekness and as much valour as his brother; of an excellent temper: it being true of him what is said of the Caspian Sea, that it doth never ebb, nor flow, observing a constant tenor, neither elated or depressed with success. Both lived in war much honoured, and died in peace much lamented."

Lord Vere m. Mary, daughter of Sir John Tracy, Knt., of Tuddington, in the county of Gloucester, and had five daughters, his co-heirs, viz.

Elizabeth, m. to John Holles, second Earl of Clare, and had issue,

GILBERT, third Earl of Clare, whose son,

JOHN, fourth Earl of Clare, was created DUKE OF NEWCASTLE, K.G, and d. in 1711, leaving an only daughter and heiress,

Lady Henrietta Cavendish Holles, who m. Edward Harley, second Earl of Oxford, whose only daughter and heiress,

Lady Margaret Cavendish, m. William, second Duke of Portland. Upon the demise of John Holles, Duke of Newcastle, the honours of the Holles family expired, but they were revived in his grace's nephew, Thomas, Lord Pelham, from whom the extant Dukes of Newcastle derive.

Mary, m. to Sir Roger Townshend, Bart., of Raynham, in the county of Norfolk, from which marriage the extant Marquesses

Townshend derive. Her ladyship m. after the decease of Sir Roger, Mildmay Fane, second Earl of Westmorland, and had issue, VERE, who s. his half-brother, Charles, as fourth Earl of Westmorland.

Catherine, m. first, Oliver, son and heir of Sir John St. John, of Lydiard Tregose, and secondly, John, Lord Paulet.

Anne, m. to the celebrated parliamentary general, Sir Thomas Fairfax, Lord Fairfax, by whom she had an only daughter and heiress,

Mary, m. to George Villiers, second Duke of Buckingham.

Dorothy, m. to John Wolstenholm, Esq., eldest son of Sir John Wolstenholm, Bart., of Nostel, in the county of York, by whom she had no issue. Mr. Wolstenholm predeceased his father.

His lordship d. 2nd May, 1635, when the BARONY OF VERE, of Tilbury, became EXTINCT. Horatio, Lord Vere, was interred near his brother, Sir Francis, in Westminster Abbey.

ARMS.—See those of Vere, Earls of Oxford.

VESCI—BARONS VESCI.

By Writ of Summons, dated 29th December, 1264.

Lineage.

Amongst the most valiant of the Norman nobility in the train of the CONQUEROR, were

ROBERT DE VESCI, who possessed at the General Survey, the lordship of BADSBROCK, in Northamptonshire, with divers other estates in the counties of Warwick, Lincoln, and Leicester. And

YVO DE VESCI, upon whom King WILLIAM bestowed in marriage, ADA, only daughter and heiress of William Tyson, Lord of ALNWICK, in Northumberland, and MALTON, in Yorkshire, (which William's father, Gilbert Tyson, fell at Hastings, fighting under the Anglo-Saxon banner.) By this great heiress, Yvo had an only daughter and heir,

BEATRICE DE VESCI, who m. EUSTACE FITZ-JOAN,[*] Lord of Knaresborough, in Yorkshire, and had two sons.

---

* EUSTACE FITZ-JOHN, nephew and heir of Serlo de Burgh, (of the great family of BURGH,) the founder of Knaresborough Castle, in Yorkshire, and son of JOHN, called Monoculus, from having but one eye, is said by an historian of the period in which he lived, to have been " one of the chiefest peers of England," and of intimate familiarity with King HENRY I., as also a person of great wisdom and singular judgment in councils. He had immense grants from the crown, and was constituted governor of the castle of Bamburgh, in Northumberland, temp. Henry I., of which governorship however, he was deprived by King STEPHEN; but he subsequently enjoyed the favour of that monarch. He fell the ensuing reign, anno 1157, in an engagement with the Welsh, " a great and aged man, and of the chiefest English peers, most eminent for his wealth and wisdom." By his first wife, the heiress

WILLIAM, of whom presently.

Geoffrey.

The elder son of Beatrice, having inherited the great possessions of his mother's family, assumed its surname, and became

WILLIAM DE VESCI. This feudal lord was sheriff of Northumberland, from the 3rd to the 15th of HENRY II. inclusive, and he was subsequently sheriff of Lancashire. In the 19th of the same reign, upon levying the aid for marrying the king's daughter, he certified his knights' fees *De Veteri Feoffamento*, to be in number twenty, for which he paid seventeen pounds thirteen, and for his knights' fees, *De novo Feoffamento*, one pound eight and sixpence. In 1174, he joined Ranulph de Glanvil, Bernard Baliol, and Robert de Stutevil, in repelling an invasion of the Scots, and fought and won the great battle of ALNWICK, wherein the KING OF SCOTLAND himself was made prisoner, after his whole army had been routed. This William de Vesci espoused, Burga, sister of Robert de Stutevil, Lord of Knaresborough, by whom he acquired the town of Langton, and had two sons,

    EUSTACE, his successor.

    Warine, Lord of Knapton, whose only daughter and heiress,

        MARGERIE DE VESCI, espoused Gilbert de Aton, and his great grandson,

           GILBERT DE ATON, inherited eventually, all the lands of the Vescis (see Aton, Barons Aton).

He was *s.* at his decease in 1184, by the elder.

EUSTACE DE VESCI, who attaining majority in the 2nd RICHARD I., gave two thousand three hundred marks for livery of his lands, with liberty to marry whom he pleased. In the 14th *King* JOHN, when the first commotion arose amongst the barons, the KING hastening to London, summoned all the suspected lords thither, and forced each to give hostages for his peaceable demeanour. But this Eustace, one of the most suspected, refused to attend the summons, and fled into Scotland, when all his possessions in England were seized upon by the crown, and a special command issued to demolish his castle at Alnwick. But a reconciliation between the king and his turbulent nobles soon afterwards taking place through the influence of the Legate PANDULPH, Eustace had restitution of his estates. But this was a deceitful calm—the winds were only stilled, to rage with greater vio-

---

of Vesci, he had two sons, as in the text, and by Agnes, his second wife, daughter of William Fitz-Nigel, Baron of Halton, and constable of Chester, he left another son, called

    RICHARD FITZ-EUSTACE, Baron of Halton, and constable of Chester, who *m.* Albreda Lisours, half sister of Robert de Lacy, and had issue,

        JOHN, who becoming heir to his uncle the said Robert de Lacy, assumed the surname of LACY, and was ancestor of the EARLS OF LINCOLN, of that family (see Lacy, Earls of Lincoln).

        ROGER, surnamed Fitz-Richard, progenitor of the great families of Clavering (see Clavering).

lence—the baronial conflict ere long burst forth more furiously, and was only allayed by those concessions on the part of the crown, which have immortalised the plains of Runymede. The cause of this celebrated quarrel, in which, by the way the people had little or no *immediate* interest, was, doubtless, of long standing, and was based in the encroachment of the despot king upon the privileges of the despot noble; but the spark that ignited the flame, as is generally the case when oppression reaches its boundary, was personal injury; an affront inflicted by the tyrant JOHN upon this Eustace de Vesci. " Hearing," writes Sir William Dugdale, " that Eustace de Vesci had a very beautiful wife, but far distant from court, and studying how to accomplish his licentious desires towards her, sitting at table with her husband, and seeing a ring on his finger, he laid hold on it, and told him, that he had such another stone, which he resolved to set in gold, in that very form. And having thus got the ring, presently sent it to her, in her husband's name; by that token conjuring her, if ever she expected to see him alive, to come speedily to him. She, therefore, upon sight of the ring, gave credit to the messenger, and came with all expedition. But so it happened, that her husband casually riding out, met her on the road, and marvelling much to see her there, asked what the matter was? and when he understood how they were both deluded, resolved to find a common woman, and put her in apparel to personate his lady." The king afterwards boasting of the favours he had received to the injured husband himself, Eustace had the pleasure of undeceiving him, " whereat the king grew so enraged, that he threatened to kill him; Eustace, therefore, apprehending danger, hastened into the north, and in his passage, wasted some of the king's houses; divers of the nobles, whose wives the king had vitiated, accompanying him. And being grown strong by the confluence of their friends, and others, seised his castles, the Londoners adhering to them." When the tyrant was, subsequently, brought to submission, EUSTACE DE VESCI was one of the twenty-five celebrated barons appointed to enforce the observance of Magna Charta, but he was slain soon after, about 1216, by an arrow from the ramparts of BARNARD CASTLE, (belonging to Hugh de Baliol,) which he had commenced, or was about, besieging. He had *m.* the Scottish Princess, Margaret, daughter of WILLIAM, and sister of ALEXANDER, kings of Scotland, and was *s.* by his son,

WILLIAM DE VESCI, who, being in minority, was placed under the guardianship of William de Longespe, Earl of Salisbury. In the 10th Henry III. he obtained livery of all his lands, as well as of the castle of Alnwick (but the castle of Knaresborough had been alienated previously to the Stutevil's, Dugdale surmises, in the time of JOHN). After this we find no more of him until the 29th of the same reign, when he had a grant of five bucks and ten does, to be taken out of the king's forests at Northumberland, to stock his park at Alnwick, and he then paid to the king, upon collection of the aid for marrying his daughter, £12, for his twelve knights' fees in Northumberland. He m. first, Isabel, daughter of William Longespe, Earl of Salisbury, but had no issue. He espoused, secondly, Agnes, daughter of William de Ferrers, Earl of Derby, by whom he had two sons,[*] John and William, and dying in 1253, was s. by the elder,

JOHN DE VESCI, then in minority, and committed in ward, with Alnwick Castle to Peter de Savoy. This feudal lord was one of King HENRY III.'s chief commanders in the wars of Gascony, but afterwards joining with Montfort, Earl of Leicester, and the other barons, who had taken up arms to compel the king to observe the ordinances of Oxford, he was summoned to parliament as a BARON by those lords, when their power became dominant after the battle of Lewes, but he was afterwards made prisoner at Evesham, and forced to avail himself of the protection of the *Dictum de Kenilworth.* His lordship, subsequently, assumed the cross, and made a pilgrimage into the Holy Land. Upon his return, in the 2nd Edward I., he was constituted governor of Scarborough Castle, and in the 10th of the same reign was in the wars of Wales. This was the Sir John Vesci, who returning from the king of Arragon, brought over a great number of Gascoignes to King EDWARD to serve him in his Welsh wars. His lordship m. Mary, sister of Hugh de Lezinian, Earl of March and Engolesme; and secondly, Isabel de Beaumont, sister of Henry de Beaumont, and kinswoman of Queen Eleanor, but d. in 1289, without issue, when the great possessions of the family devolved upon his brother (then forty years of age),

WILLIAM DE VESCI, who was a person in great esteem with EDWARD I., and constituted by that monarch, in the 13th year of his reign, justice of the royal forests beyond Trent, and the next year one of the justices itinerant touching the pleas of the forests. After succeeding his brother he was made governor of Scarborough Castle, and the year ensuing, doing his homage, had livery of all those lands in Ireland, which were of the inheritance of Agnes, his mother, and he was made at the same time justice of that kingdom. But during his sojourn there, he was accused in open court, in the city of Dublin, in the presence of Gilbert de Clare, Earl of Gloucester, and others, of felony, and challenged to the combat by John Fitz-Thomas; for which he, subsequently, instituted a suit before the chief justice at Dublin against the said Fitz-Thomas on a charge of defamation, in saying, that he the said William de Vesci, had solicited him to a confederacy against the king: which charge being denied by Fitz-Thomas, and a schedule by him delivered into court, containing the words which he acknowledged, he was, thereupon, challenged

to the combat by this William, and he accepted the challenge. But the king being apprised of the proceedings, prohibited the battle, and ordered the combatants to appear before him at Westminster: to which place William de Vesci came accordingly, mounted upon his great horse covered, as also completely armed with lance, dagger, coat of mail, and other military equipments, and proffered himself to the fight: but Fitz-Thomas, although called, appeared not. The affair was afterwards brought before parliament, but dismissed, owing to some informality. It was finally submitted to the award of the king, but the ulterior proceedings are not recorded. In the 23rd Edward I. William de Vesci was again in the wars of Gascony, and he was summoned to parliament as a BARON on the 24th June, 1st October, and 2nd November, 1295. His lordship was one of the competitors for the crown of Scotland, through his grandmother, the Scottish Princess, MARGARET.[*] He m. Isabel, daughter of Adam de Periton, and widow of Robert de Welles, by whom he had an only son,

JOHN, who was justice of the forests south of Trent, and was in the wars of Gascony. He m. Clementina, a kinswoman of Queen Eleanor, but d. in the life-time of his father, issueless.

Upon the decease of his son, his lordship enfeoffed *Anthony Beke,* BISHOP OF DURHAM, in the CASTLE OF ALNWICK, and divers other lands, in trust for William, his bastard son, who inherited all his other estates. This trust the prelate is said to have basely betrayed, and to have alienated the inheritance, by disposing of it for ready money to William Percy; since which time the CASTLE OF ALNWICK, and those lands, have been held by the Percys and their representatives. His lordship d. in 1297, when all his great inheritance passed to his bastard son, WILLIAM, *de Kildare,* save the estates above-mentioned, in Northumberland; and the BARONY OF VESCI, became EXTINCT.

ARMS.—Or, a cross. ar.

VESCI—BARON VESCI.

By Writ of Summons, dated 8th January, 1313,
6 Edward II.

Lineage.

WILLIAM DE VESCI, of Kildare, natural son of *William,* LORD VESCI, who d. in 1297, having inherited all the Vesci estates, except the Castle of Alnwick, and the lands in Northumberland, of which he is said to have been defrauded by the celebrated Prelate, ANTHONY BEKE, was summoned to parliament as a BARON from the 8th January, 1313, to 29th July, 1314. His lordship died *s. p.* in the following year, when his estates reverted to the

---

[*] KIMBER, in his peerage of Ireland, says, that William had two other sons,

    THOMAS, ancestor of the Lords Knapton, (now Viscounts de Vesci,) in Ireland.

    Richard, from whom the Vescys, or Veseys, of Chimley, in Oxfordshire, descend.

But how came the ATONS to inherit the estates of the Vescis as heirs general, if these two male branches of the family were in existence?

[*] The legitimacy of this lady and her sisters, daughters of WILLIAM, *the Lion,* from whom other claimants arose, has been doubted by historians, from the fact of their claim being at once dismissed. Whereas had there been no flaw of this description, their pretensions were prior to those of either Baliol or Bruce, who had sprung from David, Earl of Huntingdon, brother of King William.

heirs general of his father, the said William, Lord Vesci, the family of ATON (see Aton, Barons de Aton) and the BARONY OF VESCI became EXTINCT.

ARMS.—Gu. a cross ar. with the mark of illegitimacy.

VILLIERS — BARONS WHADDON, VISCOUNTS VILLIERS, EARLS OF BUCKING-HAM, MARQUESSES OF BUCKINGHAM, DUKES OF BUCKINGHAM.

Viscounty,			August, 1616.
Earldom,	by Letters		5th January, 1617.
Marquisate,	Patent,		1st January, 1618.
Dukedom,			18th May, 1623.

Lineage.

This family, which is still extant, in the noble houses of Jersey and Clarendon, deduced its descent from the Villiers's Seigniours of Lile Adam, in Normandy: and the first of its members who came into England was amongst the companions in arms of the Conqueror.

SIR GEORGE VILLIERS, Knt., of Brokesby, in the county of Leicester, a person of eminent note, m. first, Audrey, daughter of William Sanders, Esq., of Harrington, in the county of Northampton, and had issue,

> William, created a baronet in 1619, a dignity which expired with his grandson, Sir William Villiers in 1711.
>
> Edward, from whom the present Earls of Jersey and Clarendon descend.
>
> Elizabeth, m. to John, Lord Butler, of Bramfield.
>
> Anne, m. to Sir William Washington, Knt., of Pakington, in the county of Lincoln.
>
> Frances.

Sir George Villiers m. secondly, Mary, daughter of Anthony Beaumont, Esq., of Glenfield, in the county of Leicester, which lady survived her husband, and was created Countess of Buckingham for life: by her he had issue,

> JOHN (Sir), created VISCOUNT PURBECK (see Villiers, Viscounts Purbeck).
>
> GEORGE, of whom presently.
>
> CHRISTOPHER, created Earl of Anglesey (see Villiers, Earls of Anglesey).
>
> Susan, m. to William Fielding, Earl of Denbigh.

Sir George, who was sheriff of the county of Leicester, in 1591, d. on the 4th of January, 1605. His second son by his last wife,

GEORGE VILLIERS, b. at Brokesby, 28th of August, 1599, received the first rudiments of his education at Billesden school, in Leicestershire, whence being removed at the age of thirteen, by his mother, he was sent into France, and there soon attained perfection in all polite accomplishments. Upon his return home, he came first to London as a suitor to the daughter of Sir Roger Ashton, one of the gentlemen of the bedchamber, and master of the robes to King James I., but was dissuaded from the connection by another courtier, Sir John Graham, one of the gentlemen of the privy chamber, who encouraged him to "seen fortune in

the court." Soon after this he attracted the attention of King James, and succeeded the favourite Carr, Earl of Somerset, as cup-bearer to his majesty (being, says Dugdale, of stature tall and comely, his comportment graceful, and of a most sweet disposition). From this period he rose rapidly in royal estimation, and the queen, through the influence of Abbot, Archbishop of Canterbury, an enemy of Somerset's, being induced also to protect him, his fortune was at once established. The first honour he received was that of knighthood, which was conferred in her majesty's bedchamber with the prince's rapier: he was then sworn a gentleman of the bedchamber (23d April, 1615) with an annual pension of £1000 payable out of the Court of Wards. The ensuing January he succeeded the Earl of Worcester, as master of the horse, and in a few months after was installed a KNIGHT OF THE GARTER. Before the close of the year (27th August, 1616) he was advanced to the peerage, by the title of BARON WHADDON, in the county of Bucks, the ceremony of creation being performed at Woodstock, the Lords Compton and Norris introducing the new peer, and Lord Carew carrying his robe: and he was very soon after created VISCOUNT VILLIERS. On the 5th of January, 1617, his lordship was created EARL OF BUCKINGHAM, with a special remainder, default of male issue, to his brothers, John and Christopher, and their male issue, and on the 1st of the same month, in the ensuing year, MARQUESS OF BUCKINGHAM. This last dignity was succeeded by his appointment to the great office of LORD HIGH ADMIRAL, and his being sworn of the privy council: and about this time his lordship was constituted Chief Justice in Eyre: master of the King's Bench office; High Steward of Westminster; Constable of Windsor Castle; and Chancellor of the University of Cambridge.

In 1623, the marquess was sent into Spain with Prince Charles, to accelerate the marriage then in contemplation between his royal highness and a Spanish princess. The journey, a very singular one, commenced on the 18th February, when the prince and marquess putting on false beards assumed the names of Thomas and John Smith, their sole attendant being Sir Richard Graham, master of the horse. Riding post to Canterbury, where they took fresh horses, they were stopped by the mayor, as suspicious persons, whereupon the marquess was constrained to take off his beard, and to satisfy Mr. Mayor, by stating that he was going in that private manner to survey the fleet, as Lord High Admiral. At Dover they found the prince's private secretary, Sir Francis Cottington, and Mr. Endymion Porter, who had provided a vessel for their use: on which they embarked, and landing at Boulogne, proceeded to Paris, and thence travelled through France to Madrid. During their sojourn in Paris, the marquess is said to have fallen in love with the Queen of France (Anne, of Austria, consort of Louis XIII.) Certain it is, that upon his return, RICHELIEU refused him permission to land in a French port. At Madrid, Buckingham was involved in a dispute with the Comte d'Olivares, and received some affronts for his haughty bearing, French garb, and great familiarity with the prince. His royal master continuing, however, to lavish favours upon him, sent out letters patent, dated the 18th of May, 1623, creating him DUKE OF BUCKINGHAM. The prince and duke, failing in the object of their journey, departed from Madrid on the 12th September, and arrived at Portsmouth in October, when his grace was made lord warden of the Cinque Ports, and steward of the manor of Hampton Court. The death of King James followed in about a year and half, but the influence of Buckingham experienced no diminution. His grace officiated as lord high steward at the coronation of the new king; and was soon after sent upon an embassy into Holland, where he purchased a rare collection of Arabic manuscripts, procured in remote countries by the industry and diligence of Erpinius, a famous linguist. Those valuable papers were presented to the University of Cambridge, for which he intended them, after the duke's death. His grace continued to bask in the same sunshine of royal favour, under King Charles, that he had so beneficially enjoyed in the last reign, but with the people he had become an object of great detestation. His influence was paramount, and to that influence was attributed all the grievances of the nation. The failure, too, of an expedition to the Isle of Rhee, for the relief of the Rochellers, completed his unpopularity. To recover the ground he had lost by this untoward enterprise his grace projected another expedition, and had repaired to Portsmouth in order to forward its sailing. Here, while passing through a lobby, after breakfasting with Sir Thomas Fryar, and other persons of distinction, he was stabbed to the heart with a pen-knife by one John Felton, a lieutenant in Sir John Ramsey's regiment, and died instantaneously. The assassination of the duke* took place on the 23rd August, 1628, when he had just completed his thirty-sixth year. His duchess was in the house, in an upper room, hardly out of bed, and the king and court at Sir Daniel Norton's, at Southwick, not much more than six miles off.

His grace had m. the Lady Katherine Manners, only daughter and heiress of Francis, sixth Earl of Rutland, and Baron De Ros, (which latter dignity she inherited at the decease of her father in 1639,) and had issue,

GEORGE, his successor.

---

*It is said, on the relation of Bishop Burnet, that the apparition of Sir George Villiers, his father, appeared to a man who had been formerly an old servant of the family, entreating him to go to the duke, and warn him, that some sad fatality would certainly happen to him, unless he did something to please the people, and remove their grievances. The old man, surprised at such a vision, was terrified; but on the same appearing a second, and a third time, he at last resolved to see the duke; and having obtained an interview, acquainted him with what had passed, and by a communication of certain events, touching a peculiar circumstance in the duke's life, convinced his grace so perfectly of what he had seen, that the duke exclaimed, "It must be true," for, excepting to himself and one person more, (who was not

Francis (posthumous), killed in a skirmish with the parliamentarians in 1648, and d. unmarried.

Mary, who, by letters patent, dated 31st August, 1628, had the title of Duchess of Buckingham limited to her in case of the failure of the male issue of her father; m. first, in 1634, Sir Charles Herbert, K.B., Lord Herbert, son of Philip, fourth Earl of Pembroke, who d. in a few weeks afterwards of the small pox, without co-habiting with his bride. Her ladyship espoused, secondly, Esme Stuart, Duke of Richmond and Lenox, and had an only son, Esme Stuart, Duke of Richmond and Lenox, who died s. p. Her grace m. thirdly, Thomas Howard, brother of Charles, Earl of Carlisle, but had no issue. She d. in 1685.

The duke was s. by his eldest son,

GEORGE VILLIERS, second Duke of Buckingham, and in right of his mother, Baron de Ros. This nobleman was very young at the time of his father's murder, and spent some years abroad after that event, travelling. He returned to England during the civil war, and had a command in the royal army at the battle of Worcester, 3rd September, 1651—from which unfortunate field, making his escape with difficulty, he reached London, and was thence enabled to make good his retreat to Holland. At the restoration of the monarchy his grace, with General Monk, rode uncovered before the king upon his public entry into London, and he was soon after made a Knight of the Garter. The Duke of Buckingham formed one of the unpopular administration of King Charles II., which was designated the Cabal, from the initial letters of the ministers' names. "But towards the latter end of that monarch's reign," says Banks, " by his strange conduct and unsteady temper, he sunk very low in the opinion of most people. He first seduced the wife of Francis Talbot, Earl of Shrewsbury, and then killed the earl in a duel."

Walpole, in his Catalogue of Noble Authors, observes, "when this extraordinary man, with the figure and genius of Alcibiades, could equally charm the Presbyterian Fairfax, and the dissolute Charles; when he alike ridiculed the witty king, and his solemn chancellor; when he plotted the ruin of his

likely to disclose it,) the same was not known to any one living. It is also related, that, the day after the duke's death, John Buckridge, Bishop of Ely, was pitched upon as the properest person to make known to the Countess of Denbigh the melancholy tidings of her brother's death, whom she tenderly loved; that hearing, when he came to wait upon her, she was at rest, he attended till she should awake of herself, which she did with the affrightment of a dream; her brother seeming to pass through a field with her in her coach, where hearing a sudden shout of the people, and asking the reason of it, was answered, "that it was for joy the Duke of Buckingham was dead." This dream she had scarce told her gentlewoman when the bishop entered the room to acquaint her with the mournful news.—BANKS.

country with a cabal of bad ministers, or equally unprincipled, supported its cause with bad patriots; one laments that such parts should be devoid of every virtue. But when Alcibiades turns chemist, when he is a real bubble, and a visionary miser, when ambition is but a frolic, when the worst designs are for the foolishest ends, contempt extinguishes all reflections on his character."

This nobleman, profligate as he was, held an elevated place amongst the great minds of his day, and as a wit was hardly equalled by any of his contemporaries. Of satirical quickness, his celebrated play upon Dryden's bombast is an extraordinary instance. Being at the first representation of one of the poet's tragedies, wherein a lover is made to say to his mistress,

" My wound is great, because it is so small,"
Buckingham cried out,

" Then 'twould be greater were it none at all."
The piece was instantly damned.

His grace was author of the " Rehearsal," a celebrated comedy, and of other plays, and of many distinguished works.

" He began life (says Banks), with all the advantages of fortune and person which a nobleman could covet; and afterwards, by favour of the king, had great opportunities of making himself as considerable as his father had been. But he miserably wasted his estate, forfeited his honour, damned his reputation, and, at the time of his death, is said to have wanted even the necessaries of life, and not to have had one friend in the world."

Pope[*] describes him as more famous for his vices than his misfortunes; that having been possessed of about £50,000 a year, and passed through many of the highest posts in the kingdom, he d. in 1687, at a remote inn in Yorkshire, reduced to the utmost misery.

His grace m. Mary, only daughter and heiress of Thomas, Lord Fairfax, the parliamentary general, and grand-daughter maternally of Horatio, Lord Vere, of Tilbury, but had no issue. He d. on the 16th April, 1687, and his sister MARY, to whom the dukedom of Buckingham was in remainder, provided she had outlived the male descendants of her father, having predeceased him, all the honours[†]

---

[*] " Behold what blessings, wealth to life can lend!
And see what comfort it affords our end—
In the worst inn's worst room, with mat half hung,
The floor of plaster, and the walls of dung;
On once a flock-bed, but repaired with straw;
With tape-tyed curtains never meant to draw;
The George and Garter dangling from that bed,
Where tawdry yellow strove with dirty red,
Great Villiers lies! 'alas, how changed from him,
That life of pleasure and that soul of whim!
Gallant and gay, in Clivedon's proud alcove,
The bow'r of wanton Shrewsbury and love;
Or just as gay at council, in a ring
Of mimick'd statesmen, and their merry king.
No wit to flatter, left of all his store;
No fool to laugh at, which he valued more—
There victor of his health, of fortune, friends,
And fame; this lord of useless thousands ends."

[†] The Earldom of Buckingham was subsequently,

---

which he had inherited from his father became EXTINCT, while the BARONY OF ROS, derived from his mother, fell into ABEYANCE between the heirs general of the sisters and heirs of George Manners, seventh Earl of Rutland.

ARMS.—Az. on a cross gules, five escallops or. a martlet for difference.

VILLIERS — COUNTESS OF BUCK-INGHAM.

By Letters Patent, dated 1st July, 1618.

Lineage.

MARY VILLIERS, daughter of Anthony Beaumont, Esq., of Glenfield, in the county of Leicester, widow of Sir George Villiers, of Brokesby, and mother of Sir George Villiers, Duke of Buckingham, was created COUNTESS OF BUCKINGHAM, for life, by letters patent, dated 1st July, 1618. Her ladyship d. in 1632, when the dignity EXPIRED, as a matter of course.

VILLIERS—BARON VILLIERS, OF STOKE, IN THE COUNTY OF BUCKS, VISCOUNT PURBECK.

By Letters Patent, dated 19th June, 1619.

Lineage.

SIR JOHN VILLIERS, Knt., elder brother of King James's celebrated favourite, George, Duke of Buckingham, (see Villiers, Dukes of Buckingham,) was elevated to the peerage, on 19th June, 1619, as Baron Villiers, of Stoke, in the county of Bucks, and VISCOUNT PURBECK, in the county of Dorset. His lordship m. first, Frances, daughter of the eminent Chief Justice (Sir Edward) Coke, a lady who eloped from him, in 1621, with Sir Robert Howard, and was subsequently sentenced, by the High Commission Court, to do penance in a white sheet, at the Savoy Church, in the Strand. After her misconduct, Lady Purbeck assumed the name of Wright, and gave birth, privately, to a son, who also bore that surname. She died in the king's garrison, at Oxford, in 1645, and was buried in St. Mary's Church.[a] His lordship espoused, secondly, Elizabeth, daughter of Sir William Slingsby, of Kippax, in the county of York, but had no issue. The viscount d. in 1657, when the Barony of Villiers, of Stoke, and the VISCOUNTY OF PURBECK, became EXTINCT.

ARMS.—Arg. on St. George's cross five escallops, or. a mullet for difference.

Note.—The son of Lord Purbeck's faithless wife, ROBERT WRIGHT, having married Elizabeth, daughter and heiress of Sir John Danvers, one of the regicide judges; obtained a patent from Cromwell, to assume the surname of his wife, in preference to that of Villiers, the latter name and family being so distinguished by hostility to the common-

---

but fruitlessly claimed, by the alleged descendant of his grace's uncle, Sir John Villiers—(see Villiers, Viscount Purbeck).

[a] Lyson's Magna Britannia.

wealth. In 1660, he levied a fine of his honours, and he is said to have destroyed the enrollment of the patent of peerage, disowning such an aristocratical appendage, as incompatible with patriotism. He eventually fled to France from his creditors, and d. there, in 1675, leaving issue,

ROBERT, of whom presently.

Edward, a captain in the army, m. Joan, daughter of —— Heming, and d. in 1691, leaving a son,

The REVEREND GEORGE VILLIERS, of Chargrove, in the county of Oxford, who claimed the Earldom of Buckingham, but no proceedings were adopted. He had issue,

GEORGE, who died. s. p. 29th June, 1774, when the male line of the family ceased.

Keth, m. to John Lewis, Dean of Ossory, and had issue,

VILLIERS WILLIAM LEWIS, who assumed the name of VILLIERS, in 1790, and m. Matilda, daughter of Lord St. John, of Bletsho.

The elder son,

ROBERT VILLIERS, claimed, in 1678, the dignities of *Baron Villiers, Viscount Purbeck,* and EARL OF BUCKINGHAM, as heir male of Sir John Villiers, Viscount Purbeck, and through him, heir to the Earldom of Buckingham, conferred upon Sir George Villiers, in 1617, which, upon the failure of that nobleman's male line, with his son, George, Duke of Buckingham, devolved, by special limitation, upon the male representative of his brother, the said John, Viscount Purbeck; but the House of Lords decided against him, upon the ground of his father's illegitimacy. Upon this occasion it was, that the house came to the celebrated resolution, "that no fine now levied, nor at any time hereafter to be levied to the king, can bar such title of honour, or the right of any person claiming such title under him that levied, or shall levy such fine;" thus confirming a similar decision in the case of the claim to the Barony of Grey de Ruthyn, 1st February, 1646. This Robert continued, however, to style himself Earl of Buckingham. He m. Margaret, daughter of Ulick de Burgh, Earl of St. Albans, and widow of Lord Muskerry, (who espoused, after his decease, Mr. Fielding, commonly called Beau Fielding,) and left a son,

JOHN VILLIERS, who likewise assumed the dignities of Viscount Purbeck, and Earl of Buckingham. This person became the associate of gamesters—and he cohabited, early in life, with the widow of —— Heneage, Esq., whom he afterwards married, and by whom he had two daughters. In 1790, he petitioned the king to be confirmed in the honours of his family, but died in three years afterwards. His unhappy daughters pursuing the course of their mother, sunk to the lowest state of dishonour. Upon the decease of this John Villiers, the representation of the family devolved upon

The REVEREND GEORGE VILLIERS, of Chargrove, in the county of Oxford, (revert to issue of Robert Wright, alias Danvers,)

548

who claimed the Earldom of Buckingham, but adopted no proceedings in furtherance thereof—and with his son and successor,

GEORGE VILLIERS, who d. in 1774, without issue, the male line of this assumed branch of the once great house of Villiers, EXPIRED.

VILLIERS—EARLS OF ANGLESEY.

By Letters Patent, dated 18th April, 1622.

Lineage.

CHRISTOPHER VILLIERS, youngest brother of George, first Duke of Buckingham, (see Villiers, Dukes of Buckingham,) was elevated to the peerage, on 18th April, 1623, as *Baron Villiers, of Daventry,* in the county of Northampton, and EARL OF ANGLESEY. His lordship m. Elizabeth, daughter of Thomas Sheldon, Esq., of Houiby, in the county of Leicester, and had issue,

CHARLES, his successor.

Anne, m. first, to Thomas, Viscount Savile, afterwards Earl of Sussex, and had,

JAMES, second Earl of Sussex, who died s. p., in 1761, when his honours expired.

Frances, m. Francis, Lord Brudenel, son and heir of Robert, Earl of Cardigan.

Her ladyship espoused, secondly, —— Barde, Esq., of Weston.

The earl, who was gentleman of the horse to King James I., d. in 1624, and was s. by his son,

CHARLES VILLIERS, second Earl of Anglesey, who m. Mary, daughter of Paul, Viscount Banning, and widow of William, Viscount Grandison, but dying without issue, in 1659, all his honours became EXTINCT; while his sister, Anne, Countess of Sussex, succeeded to the estates of the family. Thus terminated another branch of the great house of Villiers.

ARMS.—On a cross gules five escallops or. a mullet for difference.

VILLIERS — DUCHESS OF CLEVELAND.

See Fitz-Roy, Duke of Cleveland, and Southampton.

WAHULL—BARONS DE WAHULL.

By Writ of Summons, dated 28th January, 1297, 25 Edward I.

Lineage.

WALTER DE FLANDERS came into England with the CONQUEROR, and held, as a feudal lord, at the time of the general survey, considerable estates in the counties of Bedford and Northampton, of which WAHULL, (now Wedhull or Odhull,) in the former shire, was the head of his barony. To this Walter succeeded

WALTER DE WAHULL, whose son,

SIMON DE WAHULL, in the time of King HENRY I., or STEPHEN, with Sibyll, his wife, gave the church of Langford to the Knights Templars. He was s. by

WALTER DE WAHULL, who, in the 18th Henry II., upon the assessment of the aid for marrying the king's daughter, certified his knights' fees, de veteri feoffemento, to be twenty-seven, and those de novo, three. He was subsequently concerned in the insurrection of Robert, Earl of Leicester, and was made prisoner in a battle near St. Edmundsbury. He m. first, Albreda, widow of Guy de St. Walery, but had no issue. By Rosia, his second wife, he had, however, two daughters and two sons, Simon and John, and was s. by the elder,

SIMON DE WAHULL, who was fined, in the 22nd Henry II., ten marks for trespassing in the king's forests; and in the 2nd of RICHARD I., upon levying the scutage of Wales, paid £13. 10s. for his knights' fees: in the 6th of the same reign he paid £37 towards the sum levied for the king's redemption. This Simon gave to the nuns at Godston, into which convent his daughters, Mary and Cicely, had entered, a moiety of the church of Pateshill, in Northamptonshire. He d. in two years afterwards, when HENRY, ARCHBISHOP OF CANTERBURY paid £333. 6s. 8d. for the wardship of his heir, and benefit of his marriage, which heir was

JOHN DE WAHULL. This feudal lord d. in 1216, leaving his sisters his heirs, but the HONOUR OF WAHULL devolved upon the heir male of the family,

SAIHER DE WAHULL, who d. in 1250, and was s. by his son,

WALTER DE WAHULL, who, upon doing his homage, and giving security to pay £100 for his relief, had livery of the honour of Wahull, and the other lands of his inheritance. He m. Helewyse, daughter of Hugh de Vivon, and dying in 1269, was s. by his son,

JOHN DE WAHULL, who, attaining majority in the next year, and doing his homage, had livery of his lands. In the 22nd Edward I. he had a military summons to march into Gascony, and had subsequently a similar summons to proceed against the Welsh, but d. in two years afterwards, seised of the manor of Wahull, or Wodhull, which he held by the service of two knights' fees. He was s. by his son,

THOMAS DE WAHULL. This feudal lord was summoned to parliament, as a BARON,* on the 26th

---

* NICOLAS doubts if this WRIT constituted a parliamentary BARON, because it was only directed to the temporality. "The writ," he observes, "commands the persons to whom it is addressed to attend at Salisbury, on Sunday the feast of St. Matthew the Apostle next ensuing, viz., 21st September, 'nobiscum super dictis negotiis colloquium et tractatum specialiter habituri, vestrumque consilium impensuri; et hoc, sicut nos et honorem nostrum ac salvationem regni, nostri ac incolarum diligitis, nullatenus omittatis;' and it was directed to six earls and seventy-five barons, and to the judges; but not one of the bishops or abbots were included." He admits, however, that two subsequent writs in the same year supplied this omission, and he states, that the validity of the writ had never before been questioned, and that, in a special case brought before parliament, (that of Frescheville,) the slightest objection was not made.

January, 1297, 25th Edward I. He d. in 1304, seised of the Barony of Wahull, as also of the manor of Wahull, in the county of Bedford, and Pateshill, in Northamptonshire, leaving by his wife, Hawise, daughter of Henry Praers, an infant son and heir,

JOHN DE WAHULL, who, although possessing the honour of Wahull, had no similar summons to parliament, nor had any of his descendants. He d. in the 10th Edward III., leaving two sons,

JOHN (Sir), whose line terminated in heiresses,
 Elizabeth,
 Eleanor, } who both died s. p.
NICOLAS.

The second son, (or his son,) upon the termination of the line of the elder Sir John de Wahull, succeeded to the estates, and became

NICHOLAS DE WAHULL, of Wahull. He m. Margaret, daughter and heir of John Foxcote, Esq., and had issue,

THOMAS, his successor.
Richard.
Edith, m. to ———— Knesworth.
Margaret, m. to Simon Brown.

He d. in the 19th HENRY IV., and was s. by his elder son,

THOMAS DE WAHULL, who m. Elizabeth, sister and heir of Sir Thomas Chetwode, Knt., and had two sons, Thomas and William. He d. in the 9th of Henry V., and was s. by the elder,

THOMAS DE WAHULL, who m. Isabel, eldest daughter of Sir William Trussel, of Elmesthorp, and had issue,

JOHN.
Thomas.
Isabel, m. to ———— Bowden.

He was s. by his eldest son,

JOHN DE WAHULL, or WOODHULL. This gentleman m. Joan, daughter of Henry Etwell, of London, and had four sons, FULK, Thomas, William, and John; and three daughters, Elizabeth, Anne, and Mary. He was s. by his eldest son,

FULK WOODHULL, who espoused Anne, daughter and heir of William Newman, of Shenford, (by Margaret, his wife, one of the daughters and co-heirs of Thomas Lamport,) and had issue,

NICHOLAS, his successor.
Thomas.
Lawrence, of Molington, in the county of Warwick.
Mary, m. to Edward Cope, Esq., of Tower, in the county of Lincoln.
Jane, m. to William Bellingham, Esq.
Anne, m. to Richard Tresham, Esq., of Newton, in Northamptonshire.

Mr. Woodhull d. in the 24th Henry VII., and was s. by his eldest son,

SIR NICHOLAS WOODHULL, Knt. This gentleman wedded, first, Mary, daughter of Richard Raleigh, Esq., of Farnborough, in the county of Warwick, and had issue, ANTHONY and Joice. He m. secondly, Elizabeth, daughter and co-heir of Sir William Parr, Lord Parr, of Horton, and had,

 Fulk, who m. Alice, daughter of William Coles, of Leigh, and was ancestor of the Wedhulls, of Shenford.

Anne, m. to David Seamer, Esq.

Mary, m. to Richard Barnaby, Esq., of Watford, Northamptonshire.

Sir Nicholas d. in the 23rd HENRY VIII., and was s. by his eldest son,

ANTHONY WODEHULL, who, coming of age in the 31st of Henry VIII., had livery of his lands; but dying in two years after, left by Anne, his wife, daughter of Sir John Smith, an only daughter and heiress,

AGNES WODEHULL, who espoused, first, Richard Chetwode, Esq., and had a son and heir,

RICHARD CHETWODE, of whom presently.

She m. secondly, Sir George Calverley, Knt., and had two sons, who both predeceased her. Lady Calverley was s. at her decease, 18th Elizabeth, by her only son,

SIR RICHARD CHETWODE. This gentleman, in the time of JAMES I., preferred a claim to the BARONY OF WAHULL, or WODHULL, as possessor of the manor and castle of Odell (Wahull,) and his petition being referred to the Duke of Lenox, the Lord Howard, and the Earl of Nottingham, these noblemen returned the following certificate:—

" According to your majesty's direction, we have met and considered the petition of Sir Richard Chetwode, and find that the petition is true: and that before any usual calling of barons by writs, his ancestors were barons in their own right, and were summoned to serve the kings in their wars, with other barons; and were also summoned to parliament. And we conceive the discontinuance to have arisen from the lords of the honour dying at one year of age, and the troubles of the time ensuing: but still the title of baron was allowed in all the reigns by conveyances of their estates, and by pardon of alienation from the crown by the king's own officers, and £9 per annum, being the ancient fee for the castle guard of Rockingham, was constantly paid, and is paid to this day: so that, though there has been a disuse, yet the right so fully appearing, which cannot die, we have not seen or heard of any one so much to be regarded in grace, and in consideration of so many knights' fees, held from the very time of the Conquest, and by him held at this day; and a pedigree both on the father and mother's side, proved by authentic records from the time of the Conqueror, (which in such cases are very rare,) we hold him worthy the honour of a baron, if your majesty thinks meet.

  " Signed,   Lenox.
        Howard.
        Nottingham."

It appears, however, that notwithstanding so favourable a report, the king did not think fit to summon the petitioner in the ancient barony, but he offered to make him BARON OF WODHULL, by patent. This Sir Richard thought derogatory, and declined. Sir Richard Chetwode married twice, but had issue only by his first wife, Jane, daughter and co-heir of Sir William Drury, Knt., viz.

William, who d. in the life-time of his father.
RICHARD, d. also in the life-time of his father,

leaving issue by his wife Anne, daughter and heiress of Sir Valentine Knightley,

VALENTINE CHETWOOD, who m. Mary, daughter of Francis Shute, Esq., of Upton, in Leicestershire, and from him descended

 JOHN CHETWOOD, in holy orders, and D.D., whose son,

  KNIGHTLEY CHETWOOD, m. Hester, daughter and heir of Richard Brooking, Esq., of Totness, in the county of Devon, and was father of

   VALENTINE KNIGHTLEY CHETWOOD, who m. Henrietta-Maria, daughter of Sir Jonathan Copes, of Oxfordshire, and left the present

    JONATHAN CHETWOOD, Esq., of Woodbrook, in Ireland, who m. Margaret, daughter and co-heir of Laurence Clutterbuck, Esq., of Derryluskan, in the county of Tipperary.

ARMS.—Or, three crescents gules.

WAKE—BARONS WAKE.

By Writ of Summons, dated 1st October, 1295, 23 Edward I.

Lineage.

In the time of Henry I.,

HUGH WAC m. Emma, daughter and eventually heiress of Baldwin Fitz-Gilbert, by Adheldis, daughter of Richard de Rullos, which Baldwin was uncle of Gilbert de Gant, first Earl of Lincoln of that family. This Hugh Wac gave the lordship of Wilesford, in the county of Lincoln, to the monks of Bec, in Normandy, when it became a cell to that great abbey. He was s. by his son,

BALDWIN WAKE, who, in the 19th of Henry II., upon the assessment in aid of marrying the king's daughter, certified his knights' fees to be in number ten; and that they were bestowed upon his ancestor by King Henry I. This Baldwin was one of the barons who assisted at the coronation of King Richard I., upon the accession of that monarch. He d. in 1201, and was s. by his son,

BALDWIN WAKE, who m. Agnes, daughter of William de Humet, Constable of Normandy, by whom he acquired the manor of Wichendon. He d. in 1206, and was s. by his son,

BALDWIN WAKE. This feudal lord m. Isabel, daughter of William de Briwere, and dying about the year 1213, was s. by his son,

HUGH WAKE, who m. Joane, daughter and heiress of Nicholas de Stutevil, and upon the death of his uncle, William de Briwere, without issue, in 17th of Henry III., succeeded to his property. This Hugh d. in 1241, and was s. by his son,

BALDWIN WAKE. · This feudal lord, who took up arms with the barons in the reign of Henry III., was made prisoner at the storming of the castle of Northampton, in the 48th of that monarch's reign: but afterwards participated in the success of his party at Lewes. He was again, however, taken prisoner with young Simon de Montfort, at Kenilworth, but by some means or other effected his escape, and made head once more after the defeat of Evesham, with Robert Ferrers, Earl of Derby, under whom he fought at the battle of Chesterfield, but had the good fortune to escape with his life. He subsequently submitted to the king, and received a pardon, with restitution of his lands. He m. Hawise, daughter and co-heir of Robert de Quinci, and dying in 1282, was s. by his son,

JOHN WAKE, who was summoned to parliament as a BARON, on the 1st October, 1295, and from that period to the 29th December, 1299. This nobleman was engaged in the French and Scottish wars of King Edward I., and in the 27th of that monarch, his lordship was one of the commissioners assigned (with the Archbishop of York and others) to see to the fortification of the castles of Scotland, and guarding the marches. He d. in 1300, and was s. by his son,

JOHN WAKE, second baron, but never summoned to parliament. This nobleman survived his father but a short period, when dying issueless, he was s. by his brother,

THOMAS WAKE, third baron, summoned to parliament from 20th November, 1317, to 20th November, 1348. This nobleman taking part with Queen Isabel against the unfortunate Edward II., was appointed by that princess, acting in the name of the king, justice of all the forests south of Trent, and Constable of the Tower of London. Upon the accession of Edward III., his lordship was constituted governor of the Castle of Hertford, and he obtained license to make a castle of his manorhouse of Cotingham, in the county of York. He was subsequently a leading personage for seventeen years of the reign of King Edward; during which period he was constantly in the wars of Scotland, and once in those of France. He was also governor of Jersey and Guernsey, and constable of the Tower of London. His lordship m. Blanch, daughter of Henry Plantagenet, Earl of Lancaster, but d. in 1349, without issue, leaving his sister, Margaret, Countess of Kent, widow of Edmund of Woodstock, Earl of Kent, his heir, who carried the BARONY OF WAKE into the family of Plantagenet, whence it was conveyed by

    JOANE PLANTAGENET, the Fair Maid of Kent, the Countess's eventual heiress, into the family of her first husband, Sir Thomas Holland, Lord Holland, K.G.

    (See Plantagenet, Barons of Woodstock, and Earls of Kent.

    See likewise, Holland, Barons Holland, Earls of Kent, and Duke of Surrey.)

ARMS.—Or. two bars, gules; in chief three torteauxes.

Note.—From this old baronial family, the Wakes, Baronets of Clevedon, in the county of Somerset, claim descent.

WALCHER—EARL OF NORTHUMBERLAND, BISHOP OF DURHAM.

Upon the execution and attainder of WALTHEOF, EARL OF NORTHUMBERLAND, in 1075, (he was beheaded at Winchester, and the first so put to death after the Norman Conquest) WALCHER DE LORRAINE, Bishop of Durham, was entrusted with the government or earldom of the county of Northumberland. This prelate, by birth a Lorrainer, was a person of excellent endowments, greatly esteemed for his piety, integrity, and benevolence, but unhappily of so gentle a disposition, that he was unable to repress the arbitrary proceedings of his servants and soldiers: whereupon loud murmurs arose amongst the people, and a day was at length appointed for an amiable adjustment, when oppressors and oppressed assembled at a place called Gateshead, near Newcastle-upon-Tyne. But instead of acting peaceably, a violent turmoil commenced, in which the church, where the bishop sought safety, was set on fire, and the venerable prelate himself barbarously murdered, anno 1080.

ARMS.—Az. a cross between four lions rampant or.

Which still continue the arms of the Bishops of Durham.

WALEYS—BARON WALEYS.

By Writ of Summons, dated 15th May, 1321, 14 Edward II.

Lineage.

RICHARD WALEYS had summons to parliament as a BARON on the 15th May, 1321, but never afterwards. Of this nobleman, Dugdale gives no account, nor are there any particulars recorded of him. On his death it is presumed that the BARONY OF WALEYS became EXTINCT.

WALMODEN—COUNTESS OF YARMOUTH.

By Letters Patent, dated 4th April, 1740.

Lineage.

AMELIA SOPHIA DE WALMODEN, the presumed mistress of King George II., was elevated to the peerage by that monarch, by letters patent, dated 4th April, 1740, and conferring the dignity for life, under the titles of BARONESS AND COUNTESS OF YARMOUTH.

The field-marshal Count Walmoden (of Hanover) was generally deemed her ladyship's representative.

The countess d. in 1765, when her honours EXPIRED.

ARMS.—Or. three morions per pale, ar. and az. banded, gules.

WALPOLE—EARLS OF ORFORD.

By Letters Patent, dated 6th February, 1742.

Lineage.

This family is said to have been established in England before the Norman Conquest, and to have derived their surname from WALPOLE, in Norfolk, where they were enfeoffed of lands belonging to the see of Ely. The learned Camden states, "that the owner of Walpole gave both that, and Wisbish in the Isle of Ely, to the monastery of Ely, at the same time that he made his younger son, Alurn, a monk there."

The first of the Walpoles upon record, is

RICHARD DE WALPOL, from whom descended

HENRY DE WALPOL, who, in the baronial war, in the time of John, taking part against the crown, was made prisoner, and forced to pay an hundred pounds for his deliverance. In the last year of Henry III.'s reign, that monarch commands the sheriff of Lincoln to restore to him all those lands in the county, whereof he had been possessed when he fell from his allegiance to King John. This letter was dated at Oxford, the 29th of June, 1217, and sealed with the seal of William, Earl Marshal, styled the king's Justice, because (as the record says) the king had yet no seal. He was s. by

SIR JOHN DE WALPOL, who had been also involved in the baronial contest, and likewise returned to his allegiance in the reign of HENRY III. He had by Isabel, his wife, several sons, of whom

HENRY, was his successor.

RALPH was in holy orders, and became Bishop of Norwich, and subsequently of Ely; he obtained the archdeaconry of the latter place in 1971, and was elected Bishop of Norwich, 11th November, 1288: on his confirmation, John Peckham, Archbishop of Canterbury, addressed him in these memorable words:—
"My lord elect, there has an evil custom prevailed in the diocese of Norwich, of receiving the first fruits of the livings in your diocese, which proceeds from a spirit of covetousness, and is displeasing both to God and man. Let me therefore persuade you, if you have any concern for your soul's health, to lay aside this evil custom, which will thus tend to the public advantage:" to which he made reply, "I shall freely consent to what you have desired of me, and promise to do all, that is in my power, to prevent it." This took place at South-Malling, in Kent, after his return to England from waiting upon the king on the frontiers of Arragon, where he obtained the royal assent; and by patent, dated 7th February, the king recites, *that the church of Norwich, having elected this discreet man, Mr. Ralph de Walpol, Archdeacon of Ely, to the Bishopric of Norwich,* he confirms the said election, and commands John Peckham, Archbishop of

Canterbury, William de Redham, and Peter de Leycester, to deliver to him the temporalities, &c. Whereupon he was consecrated in the church of Canterbury on the 20th March ensuing. He sate in this see about ten years, and then upon the death of William de Luda, Bishop of Ely, was translated by the pope to that bishoprick. The convent of Ely had obtained the king's leave to proceed to an election, but could not agree amongst themselves; one part (the majority) made choice of JOHN SALMON, *their prior;* the other selected JOHN DE LANGTON, (then king's chancellor,) afterwards Bishop of Chichester; and, the election being thus in dispute, the merits were submitted to Robert Winchelsea, Archbishop of Canterbury, who, keeping the cause depending, an appeal was made to the pope, and both parties repaired to Rome, when his Holiness unwilling to set aside Salmon, sent the monks to a new election; but that proving equally unsatisfactory, the Pope, then to terminate the contest, translated Walpol to Ely, by a bull, bearing date 15th July, 1299, and made Salmon Bishop of Norwich. His lordship d. 20th March, 1301-2.

Sir John Walpol was s. by his eldest son,

SIR HENRY DE WALPOL, in the manors of Walpole and Houghton, who, in the 5th EDWARD I., is mentioned in a certain deed made by the prior and chapter of Ely, as having a mansion house in Ely. In the same reign he had military summonses to march into Flanders, and into Scotland. He m. Isabel, daughter of Sir Peter Fitz-Osbert, and heir to her brother, Sir Roger Fitz-Osbert (which lady, after his decease, espoused Sir Walter Jernegan, of Stoneham Jernegan, ancestor of the Jerninghams, Lords Stafford, and brought the lordship of Somerley-Town, and other lands, into that family). Sir Henry Walpol was s. by his son, another

SIR HENRY DE WALPOL, who, with Robert Baynard, was chosen knight of the shire for the county of Norfolk, in the parliament that met at Lincoln, in 9th Edward II., wherein it was ordered, that none should depart without the king's especial licence. In the 17th of the same reign he was returned into chancery amongst the knights, who (with other persons of note) were certified to *bear ancient arms from their ancestors.* This Sir Henry Walpol purchased divers lands in Walpole and Houghton, and dying soon after the 9th Edward III., was s. by his son,

HENRY DE WALPOL, who was returned one of the knights of the shire for the county of Norfolk, to the parliament summoned to meet at York, in the 7th Edward III., and was s. at his decease by his son,

HENRY WALPOL, Esq., a person of great note in the county of Norfolk, temp. HENRY VI. He m. Margaret, daughter of Sir Oliver le Grosse, Knt., of Costwick, in the county of Norfolk, and was s. by his eldest son,

HENRY WALPOLE, Esq., of Walpole and Houghton, who m. Margery, daughter of Sir John

Hardck, of Southaere, in Norfolk, and was *s.* by his son,

JOHN WALPOLE, Esq., of Houghton. This gentleman *m.* Elizabeth, daughter of Robert Shawe, Esq., of Derby, and was *s.* by his son,

THOMAS WALPOLE, Esq., who had a grant from William Fawkes, and others, of lands in Houghton, in the 1st Henry VII., and he had subsequently further grants of lands in the same reign. He *m.* first, Joane, daughter of William Cobb, Esq., of Sandringham, and secondly, Alice ———, but had issue by his first wife only, viz.

> John, who predeceased his father, leaving a widow, Anne Walpole, but no child.
> EDWARD, successor to his father.
> Henry, who *m.* Margaret, daughter and co-heir of —— Holtofte, of Whaplode, in Lincolnshire, Gent., and had issue,
> > THOMAS, of Whaplode, ancestor of the Walpoles, of Lincolnshire.
> > JOHN, an eminent lawyer, temp. Edward VI., M.P. for Lynn, in 1553; and called to the degree of serjeant at law, with seven others, in the following year: the feast upon which occasion was kept with the greatest splendour, in the Inner Temple Hall, 16th October, 1554, several officers being appointed for the management thereof; and each serjeant presented to the king and queen rings of the finest gold, of the value, besides the fashion, of £3. 6s. 8d. Serjeant Walpole *m.* Katherine, daughter of Edmund Knivet, Esq., of Ashwelworth, (by his wife, Jane, daughter, and eventually sole heir of Sir John Bourchier, Lord Berners,) by whom he left, at his decease, in 1557,
> > > WILLIAM, who *d.* issueless.
> > > Mary,
> > > Jane,
> > > Katherine, } co-heirs to their brother.
> > > Anne,
> Francis.
> Christopher, of Docking, in the county of Norfolk.
> Agnes, *m.* to William Russel.

Mr. Walpole *d.* 14th January, 1513-14, and was *s.* by his eldest surviving son,

EDWARD WALPOLE, Esq., who *m.* Lucy, daughter of Sir Terry Robsart, and heiress of her grandfather, the celebrated Sir John Robsart, K.B. and K.G., (in consequence of the decease of her brother, Sir John Robsart, and his daughter, Amie Robsart, wife of Sir Robert Dudley, afterwards Earl of Leicester, without issue,) by whom he had issue,

> JOHN, his successor.
> Richard, of Brakenash, in the county of Norfolk, who, by his wife, dated 26th March, 1566, left his whole estate to his younger brother,
> Terry, who *d.* in 1589, leaving issue by two wives.
> Elizabeth, *m.* to Martin Cobb, Esq., of Snetisham, in Norfolk.

Mr. Walpole *d.* in 1588-9, and was *s.* by his eldest son,

JOHN WALPOLE, Esq., who inherited the manor of Sidestern, in the county of Norfolk, and other lands, as heir of Amie Dudley (Robsart) the first wife of Robert Dudley, Earl of Leicester. Mr. Walpole *m.* Catherine, daughter and co-heir of William Calybut, Esq., of Coxforth, in the county of Norfolk, and had issue,

> Edward, who *d.* upon his travels in 1569.
> CALIBUT, successor to his father.
> Thomas.
> Catherine, *m.* to Philip Russel, Esq., of Burnhapthorp, in the county of Norfolk.
> Bona, *m.* to John Amyas, Esq., of Delpham, in the same county.
> Elizabeth, *m.* to Richard Bunting, Esq., of Southcreak, also in Norfolk.
> Bridget, *m.* to Henry Paynell, Esq., of Bellaugh, in the same shire.

Mr. Walpole *d.* in 1588, and was *s.* by his son,

CALIBUT WALPOLE, Esq. This gentleman *m.* Elizabeth, daughter of Edmund Bacon, Esq., of Hesset, in Suffolk, and had issue,

> ROBERT, his successor.
> John, of Southcreeke, *m.* Abigail, daughter and sole heir of Froximer Crocket, Esq., of Bromesthorpe, in Norfolk, and acquired thereby that estate. He left three daughters, his co-heirs, viz.
> > Elizabeth, *m.* to Edward Pepys, Esq., barrister-at-law, and conveyed to him a portion of Bromesthorp.
> > Bridget, *m.* to Francis Thoresby, Esq., of Gaywood, Norfolk.
> > Susan, *m.* to John Hare, Esq., of Snitterton, and conveyed to him a portion of Bromesthorp.
> Calibut, } both *d.* unmarried.
> Bacon,
> Elizabeth, *m.* in 1612, to Thomas Clifton, Esq., of Toftrees, in Norfolk.
> Anne, *m.* first, in 1614, to Thomas Pettus, Esq., son and heir of Sir Augustus Pettus, Knt., and brother of Sir Thomas Pettus, Bart., of Rackheath, and secondly, in 1619, to Sir Henry Hungate, Knt., of Bradenham, in Norfolk.

Mr. Walpole *d.* 4th May, 1646, and was *s.* by his eldest son,

ROBERT WALPOLE, Esq., who *m.* Susan, daughter of Sir Edward Barkham, Knt., Lord Mayor of London, 19th James I., and had issue,

> EDWARD, his successor.
> Elizabeth.

He *d.* in 1663, and was *s.* by his son,

SIR EDWARD WALPOLE, K.B., an eloquent and leading member of the parliament, which voted the restoration of King CHARLES II., and also of the long parliament, in both representing the borough of King's-Lynn. Sir Edward *m.* in 1649, Susan, second daughter and co-heir of Sir Robert Crane, Bart., of Chilton, in the county of Suffolk, and had surviving issue,

> ROBERT, his successor.
> Horatio, who *m.* Lady ANNE OSBORNE, daugh-

ter of Thomas, Duke of Leeds, and widow of Robert Coke, Esq., of Holkham, in Norfolk, but died *s. p.* in 1717.

Edward, Fellow of Trinity College, Cambridge, died in 1688, unmarried.

Anne, *m.* to Montfort Spelman, Esq., of Narborough, Norfolk, and died *s. p.* in 1691.

Dorothy, *d.* unmarried in 1694.

Mary, *m.* to John Wilson, Esq., of Leicestershire, and died *s. p.*

Elizabeth, *m.* in 1665, to James Frost, Esq., of Sandringham, Norfolk.

He *d.* in 1667, and was *s.* by his eldest son,

ROBERT WALPOLE, Esq., M.P. for Castle Rising, in the county of York, from the 1st William and Mary until his decease; deputy-lieutenant of the county of Norfolk, and colonel of its militia. He *m.* Mary, only daughter and heir of Sir Jeffery Burwell, Knt., of Rougham, in the county of Suffolk, and had surviving issue,

> ROBERT, his successor.
>
> HORATIO, *b.* in 1678. This gentleman, who was a diplomatist of the first grade, during the administration of his brother, was elevated to the peerage on the 4th June, 1756, as BARON WALPOLE, *of Walterton,* in the county of Norfolk. His lordship *m.* in 1720, Mary-Magdalen, daughter and co-heir of Peter Lombard, Esq., and dying in 1757, was *s.* by his eldest son,
>
> > HORATIO, second Baron Walpole, of Walterton, who succeeded his cousin, the celebrated *Horace Walpole,* fourth EARL OF ORFORD, in the Barony of Walpole; of Walpole, and was grandfather of the present EARL OF ORFORD.
>
> Galfridus, a naval officer, and member of parliament, temp. GEORGE I. This gentleman was treasurer of Greenwich Hospital, and afterwards (1711) joint post-master general. He *m.* Cornelia, daughter of Mr. Hays, of London, but died *s. p.* in 1726. His widow *m.* —— Kyrwood, Esq., of Herefordshire.
>
> Mary, *m.* to Sir Charles Turner, of Wareham, Norfolk.
>
> Dorothy, *m.* to Charles, Viscount Townshend (his lordship's second wife).
>
> Susan, *m.* to Anthony Hammond, Esq., of Wotton, in Norfolk.

Colonel Walpole *d.* in 1700, and was *s.* by his eldest son,

ROBERT WALPOLE, *b.* 26th August, 1674. This gentleman, who attained so much celebrity as MINISTER, temp. *King* GEORGE I. and King George II., was first returned to parliament by the borough of King's-Lynn, in 1700, and so long as he remained a commoner he sate for the same place, excepting one session: that in which he was a prisoner in the Tower, from 4th January, 1711-12, to the prorogation of the parliament on the 21st June following.

In June, 1705, Mr. Walpole was commissioned as one of the council in the affairs of the admiralty to the LORD HIGH ADMIRAL, *Prince* GEORGE OF DENMARK; and he was appointed secretary of war in two years afterwards. In January, 1709-10, he was made treasurer of the navy, but upon the change of

the ministry soon after he was removed from all his employments. Upon the accession of *King* GEORGE I. his eminent abilities were again enlisted on the side of the government. In 1714, five days after the new king's landing, he was made paymaster of the guards and garrisons at home, and of the forces abroad; and in the same year he was sworn of the privy council. In 1715 he was constituted FIRST LORD COMMISSIONER of the treasury, and chancellor of the exchequer; and the same year was chosen chairman of the committee of secrecy, appointed by the House of Commons, to inquire into the conduct of those evil ministers " that brought a reproach on the nation, by the unsuitable conclusion of a war, which was carried on at so vast an expense, and was attended with such unparalleled successes." The result of this impeachment of the Tory ministers of Anne, was the flight of Ormond and Bolingbroke, and the condemnation of *Harley,* EARL OF OXFORD, Prior, and some others, but the whole in the end escaped with impunity. In 1717 Mr. Walpole again withdrew with his friends from office, but in 1720 he returned, and was appointed paymaster-general. The next year he was placed in his former situation of first lord of the treasury, and chancellor of the exchequer: he was constituted one of the lords justices in 1723, and sworn sole secretary of state during the king's absence in Hanover, attended by the Lords Townshend and Carteret. In 1725 his majesty conferred upon him the honour of the Knighthood of the Bath, and he was in the same year again constituted one of the lords justices during another visit of the king to Hanover. In 1726 he was made a KNIGHT of the GARTER, and upon the accession of *King* GEORGE II., he was re-sworn of the privy council, and continued in his official employments of first lord of the treasury, and chancellor of the exchequer. At the coronation of the new monarch Sir Robert assisted as a privy counsellor, and as a Knight of the Garter, in the full habit and collar of the order. In 1740 he was again one of the lords justices, and the next year upon retiring from office he was elevated to the peerage by letters patent, dated 6th February, 1742, as *Baron of Houghton, Viscount Walpole,* in Norfolk, and EARL OF ORFORD, in the county of Suffolk. Thus have we simply enumerated the high offices and the high honours of this celebrated statesman. He ruled in what may be truly termed the *golden* age of governments—when the meshes of corruption had superseded the bonds of despotism; and Walpole's favourite maxim, that " every man had his price," was seldom found, we apprehend, delusive. His lordship rebuilt the ancient family seat at Houghton, and adorned it with a noble collection of pictures and statues. He *m.* first, Catherine, daughter of John Shorter, Esq., of Bybrook, in Kent, and had issue,

> ROBERT, his successor, who was created on the 10th June, 1723, LORD WALPOLE, *of Walpole,* in the county of Norfolk, with remainder to Edward and Horatio, his brothers, and in default of their heirs male, to his father, Sir Robert Walpole, and after him to the heirs male of Robert Walpole, Esq., Sir Robert's father,

Edward (Sir), installed a Knight of the Bath in 1753, M.P. for Lestwithiel, and afterwards for Great Yarmouth. On the appointment of the Duke of Devonshire to the lord lieutenantcy of Ireland, Sir Edward Walpole was made chief secretary, and sworn of the privy council of that kingdom. He was afterwards joint secretary of the treasury, and clerk of the pells. He d. unmarried.*

HORATIO, who inherited as fourth Earl of Orford.

Katherine, d. unmarried.

Mary, m. to George, Earl of Cholmondeley.

His lordship espoused, secondly, Maria, daughter and sole heir of Thomas Skerret, Esq., but by her had no issue. He d. in 1745, and was s. by his eldest son,

ROBERT WALPOLE, Lord Walpole, second Earl of Orford. This nobleman m. in 1724, Margaret, daughter and sole heir of Samuel Rolle, Esq., of Haynton, in the county of Devon, (which lady m. secondly, the Hon. Sewallis Shirley, and succeeded to the Barony of Clinton,) and dying in 1751, was s. by his only son,

GEORGE WALPOLE, third Earl of Orford. This nobleman disposed of the splendid collection of pictures made by his grandfather, Sir Robert Walpole, to the Empress of Russia. His lordship d. unmarried in 1791, when the honours reverted to his uncle, the celebrated

HORACE WALPOLE, as fourth Earl of Orford, b. in 1717. For this his youngest child, the Minister Walpole procured the places of usher of the receipt of the exchequer, comptroller of the great roll, and keeper of the foreign receipts. His lordship had for several years a seat in the House of Commons, but he was distinguished more in the literary than the political arena. Soon after returning from his travels, he purchased a villa at Twickenham, which he changed into a Gothic mansion, and there (the celebrated " Strawberry Hill,") he continued ever afterwards principally to reside. At that favourite retirement he established a private press, where he not only printed his own works, but many other curious compositions. From this press

---

* Sir Edward Walpole left three illegitimate daughters, viz.

    Laura, m. to the Hon. and Right Rev. Frederick Keppel, son of William-Anne, second Earl of Albemarle.

    Maria, m. first, James, second Earl Waldegrave, by whom she had issue,

        Elizabeth-Laura, m. to her cousin, George, fourth Earl of Waldegrave.

        Charlotte-Maria.

        Anna-Horatio.

    The countess espoused, secondly, H. R. H. WILLIAM-HENRY, Duke of Gloucester, and was mother of their royal highnesses,

        WILLIAM-FREDERICK, present Duke of Gloucester.

        Princess SOPHIA-MATILDA, of Gloucester.

    Charlotte, m. to Lionel, fourth Earl of Dysart.

---

first issued, " The Catalogue of Royal and Noble Authors," 1758, 2 vols, 12mo ; " Anecdotes of Painting," 1762 ; " Historic Doubts," 1768 ; " Mysterious Mother," 1768 ; " Miscellaneous Antiquities," 1772, 4to. His lordship d. unmarried 2nd March, 1797, when the BARONY OF WALPOLE, of Walpole, passed, according to the limitation, to his cousin, Horatio, second BARON WALPOLE, of Wolterton, (refer to second son of Robert Walpole, Esq., father of the first earl,) and the EARLDOM OF ORFORD, with the minor dignities, became EXTINCT.

ARMS.—Or. on a fesse between two chevrons, sa. three cross crosslets of the first.

WARD—BARONS DUDLEY.

Refer to Sutton, BARONS DUDLEY.

SIR HUMBLE WARD espoused FRANCES SUTTON, Baroness Dudley, and the Wards thus acquired that barony.

WARDE—BARONS DE LA WARDE.

By Writ of Summons, dated 29th December, 1299, 28 Edward I.

Lineage.

In the 31st year of King Edward I.

ROBERT DE LA WARDE was in the wars of Scotland, and again in the 34th, at which time he was steward of the king's household. He had been previously summoned to parliament as a BARON. His lordship was s. by his son,

SIMON DE LA WARDE, second baron, summoned to parliament from 30th December, 1324, to 24th July, 1334. This nobleman, who was governor of York, upon the insurrection of Thomas, Earl of Lancaster, in the 15th of Edward II., brought considerable forces to Boroughbridge in aid of the royal cause, where the earl received so signal a defeat, and being taken prisoner, was conveyed to Pontefract, and there beheaded. Lord De la Warde was subsequently constituted governor of Pontefract Castle, but of his lordship, or his posterity, nothing further is known.

ARMS.—Vairée ar. and sa.

WARREN—EARLS OF SURREY.

Creation of WILLIAM Rufus.

Lineage.

WILLIAM DE WARREN, Earl of Warren, in Normandy, a near relation of the CONQUEROR'S, came into England with that prince, and having distinguished himself at the battle of Hastings, obtained an immense portion of the public spoliation. He had large grants of lands in several counties, amongst which were the Barony of Lewes, in Sussex, and the manors of Carletune and Beningtun, in Lincolnshire. So extensive indeed were those grants, that his possessions resembled more the dominions of a sovereign prince, than the estates of a subject. He enjoyed too, in the highest degree, the confidence of the king, and was appointed joint-justice-general, with Richard de Benefactis, for administering justice throughout the whole realm. When citing some great disturbers of the public peace to appear before him and his colleague, and those refusing to attend, he took up arms, and defeating the rebels in a battle at FAGADUNE, he is said, for the purpose of striking terror, to have cut off the right foot of each of his prisoners. Of those rebels, Ralph Waher or Guader, Earl of Norfolk, and Roger, Earl of Hereford, were the ringleaders. His lordship was likewise highly esteemed by *King* WILLIAM *Rufus*, and was created by that monarch, EARL OF SURREY. He m. Gundred, daughter of the CONQUEROR, and had issue,

> WILLIAM, his successor.
> Raynald, one of the adherents of ROBERT *Curthose.*
> Edith, m. first, to Girard de Gornay, and secondly, to Drew de Monceux.
> ——— m. to Ernise de Colungis.

This potent noble built the castle of Holt; and founded the priory of Lewes, in Sussex. He resided principally at the castle of Lewes, and had besides Castle-Acre, in Norfolk, and noble castles at Coningsburg and Sandal. He died in July, 1089: and Dugdale gives the following curious account of his parting hour. "It is reported that this Earl William did violently detain certain lands from the monks of Ely; for which, being often admonished by the abbot, and not making restitution, he died miserably. And, though his death happened very far off the isle of Ely, the same night he died, the abbot lying quietly in his bed, and meditating on heavenly things, heard the soul of this earl, in its carriage away by the devil, cry out loudly, and with a known and distinct voice, *Lord have mercy on me: Lord have mercy on me.* And moreover, that the next day after, the abbot acquainted all the monks in chapter therewith. And likewise, that about four days after, there came a messenger to them from the wife of this earl, with one hundred shillings for the good of his soul, who told them, that he died the very hour that the abbot had heard the outcry. But that neither the abbot, nor any of the monks would receive it; not thinking it safe for them to take the money of a damned person." "If this part of the story, adds Dugdale, as to the abbot's hearing the noise, be no truer than the last, viz.—that his lady sent them one hundred shillings, I shall deem it to be a mere fiction, in regard the lady was certainly dead about three years before." The earl was s. by his elder son,

· WILLIAM DE WARREN, (Earl of Warren,) second Earl of Surrey. This nobleman joined Robert de Beleeme, Earl of Arundel and Shrewsbury, in favour of ROBERT *Curthose*, against HENRY I., and in consequence forfeited his English earldom and estates; but those were subsequently restored to him, and he was ever afterwards a good and faithful subject to *King* HENRY. His lordship m. Elizabeth, daughter of HUGH *the Great*, Earl of Vermandois, and widow of Robert, Earl of Mellant, by whom he had issue,

556

WILLIAM, his successor.
Reginald, who marrying Alice, daughter and heir of William de Wirmgay, became Lord of Wirmgay, in Norfolk. He founded the priory of Wirmgay, and left two daughters, viz.

> 1. BEATRIX DE WARREN, who m. first, Dodo Bardolf, Baron of Shelford, and left a son,
> > WILLIAM BARDOLF (see Bardolf).
> > She espoused, secondly, Hubert de Burgh, Earl of Kent.
> 2. Isabel.

Ralph.
Gundred, m. to Roger de Newburgh, Earl of Warwick.
Adeline, m. to Henry, son of David, King of Scots.

The earl d. in 1135, and was s. by his eldest son,

WILLIAM DE WARREN, (Earl of Warren,) third Earl of Surrey, who zealously espoused the cause of King Stephen, and had a chief command in the army of that monarch, in the battle fought at Lincoln, between him, and the adherents of the *Empress* MAUD. His lordship m. Ala, daughter of William Talvace, son of Robert de Beleeme, Earl of Shrewsbury, and had an only daughter and heir,

> ISABEL, who m. first, WILLIAM DE BLOIS, natural son of *King* STEPHEN, and secondly, HAMELINE PLANTAGENET, natural son of Geoffrey, Earl of Anjou, father of *King* HENRY II.

In the year 1147, the Earl of Warren and Surrey assumed the cross, and accompanied LEWIS, *King of France*, in an expedition against the Saracens: "an expedition," says Banks, "wherein the consecrated banner of the Christians fell into the hands of infidelity, and orthodox blood reeked in crimson sanctity on the Saracen's sword." From this unfortunate enterprise the earl never returned, but whether he fell in battle, or died in captivity, has not been ascertained. His only daughter, as stated above,

ISABEL DE WARREN, espoused, first,
WILLIAM DE BLOIS, Earl of Moreton, in Normandy, natural son of *King* STEPHEN, and this nobleman became, in consequence, EARL OF SURREY, having, by the grant of Henry, Duke of Normandy, upon the accord made between him and King Stephen, all those lands which Stephen held before he was king of England, as well in Normandy as in England, or elsewhere. Amongst these were the castle and town of Norwich, with the whole county of Norfolk, excepting what belonged to the churches, religious houses, and other earls, and, especially, excepting the *Tertium Denarium*, by reason whereof Hugh Bigot was Earl of Norfolk. He had also all the honour of Pevensey. This nobleman, who was of an unambitious disposition, and enjoyed the favour of HENRY II., accompanied that monarch to the siege of Thoulouse, and died there without issue in 1163. His widow, ISABEL, heiress of the Warrens, married, subsequently,

HAMELINE PLANTAGENET, natural brother to *King* HENRY II., who likewise obtained, *jure uxoris,* the EARLDOM OF SURREY, and assumed the surname and arms of WARREN. This nobleman bore one of the three swords at the second coronation of RICHARD I., and in the 6th of the same reign he was with that king in his army in Normandy. He *d.* in May, 1909, four years after the countess, and was *s.* by his son,

WILLIAM WARREN, *(Plantagenet,)* Earl of Warren and Surrey. In the contest between *King* JOHN and the barons, this nobleman sided at the commencement, and for a long time afterwards, with his royal kinsman, but eventually joined the banner of Lewis of France. On the death of *King* JOHN, however, he returned to his allegiance, and swore fealty to *King* HENRY III.; at the solemn nuptials of which monarch he had the honour of serving the king, at the banquet, with his royal cup in the Earl of Arundel's stead, who, being in minority, could not perform that office, as he had not been girt with the sword of knighthood. His lordship *m.* first, Lady Maud de Albini, daughter of the Earl of Arundel, but by her ladyship had no issue. He espoused, secondly, Maud, daughter of William Marshal, Earl of Pembroke, and widow of Hugh Bigot, Earl of Norfolk, by whom he had

    JOHN, his successor.

    Isabel, *m.* to Hugh de Albini, Earl of Arundel.

He *d.* in 1304, and was *s.* by his son,

    JOHN WARREN, *(Plantagenet,)* Earl of Warren and Surrey. This nobleman was but five years of age at the time of his father's decease, and was placed in ward with Peter de Savoy, the queen's brother. When he attained majority he attached himself zealously to HENRY III. in his conflicts with the barons, and maintained the cause of the king with his sword at the battle of LEWES. His lordship was a person of violent and imperious temper, and was often betrayed into acts of great intemperance; as in the instance of assaulting Sir Alan Zouch, and Roger, his son, in Westminster Hall, when he almost killed the one and wounded the other. And again, when EDWARD I. issued the first writs of Quo Warranto, his lordship being questioned as to the title of his possessions, exhibited to the justices an old sword, and unsheathing it, said, "Behold, my lords, here is my warranty, my ancestors coming into this land with WILLIAM the Bastard, did obtain their lands by the sword; and I am resolved with the sword to defend them, against whomsoever shall endeavour to dispossess me. For that king did not himself conquer the land, and subdue it, but our progenitors were sharers and assistants therein." The earl was constituted, by *King* EDWARD, general of all his forces on the north of Trent, for the better restraining the insolence of the Scots; whereupon he marched into Scotland, and so terrified the inhabitants that they immediately sued for peace, and gave hostages for their future good conduct. But the war soon after breaking out afresh, his lordship sustained a signal defeat at STRIVELIN, when his troops fled first to Berwick, and thence into England. The earl *m.* Alice, daughter of Hugh le Brun, Earl of March, and half sister by the mother of King HENRY III., and had issue,

    WILLIAM, who *m.* Joane, daughter of Robert de Vere, Earl of Oxford, and falling in a

tournament at Croydon, in his father's lifetime, left issue,

    JOHN, who *s.* his grandfather.

    ALICE, *m.* to Edmund Fitz-Alan, Earl of Arundel. This lady, upon the decease of her brother *s. p.,* inherited the great estates of the WARRENS, and conveyed them to the Fitz-Alans, and her son, RICHARD, Earl of Arundel, succeeded to their honours.

Alianore, *m.* first, to Henry, Lord Percy, and secondly, to the son of a Scottish earl.

Isabel, *m.* to John de Baliol, afterwards king of Scotland.

His lordship *d.* in 1304, and was *s.* by his grandson,

JOHN WARREN, *(Plantagenet,)* Earl of Warren and Surrey. This nobleman had the honour of knighthood conferred upon him, with two hundred other persons of distinction, in the 34th Edward I., when *Prince* EDWARD was also knighted with great solemnity. In the last year of *King* EDWARD his lordship was in the expedition made into Scotland, wherein that victorious prince died. In the 4th of the next reign he was again in Scotland, and so much in favour with the king, that he obtained a free grant of the castle and honour of PEKE, in Derbyshire, with the whole forest of HIGH PEKE, to hold during his life, in as full and ample manner as *William Peverel* anciently enjoyed the same, before it came to the kings of England by escheat. In the ensuing year we find his lordship, along with the Earl of Pembroke, besieging the *minion,* Piers Gaveston, in Scarborough Castle, and forcing him to surrender. He was, some years afterwards, one of those who invested the castle of Pontefract, at that time held by Thomas, Earl of Lancaster, and his adherents; and he subsequently sate in judgment upon, and condemned to death, that eminent Plantagenet. In the reign of Edward III. the earl appears constantly engaged in the wars of Scotland. His lordship *m.* first, Joane, daughter of the Earl of Barre, by whom he had no issue. In the life-time of this lady he cohabited publicly with MAUD DE NEREFORD,[*] a person of good family in Norfolk, but was at length obliged, by the Archbishop of Canterbury, to break off the connection. He obtained a divorce, however, from his countess, on the ground of a precontract with this Maud, yet he does not appear subsequently to have married her. His second wife was Isabel de Houland. He died in 1347, when, leaving no legitimate issue, his sister, ALICE, wife of EDMUND FITS-ALAN, eighth *Earl of Arundel,* became his heir, and conveyed the great estates of the WARRENS, (Plantagenets,) into the Fitz-Alan family. Her ladyship's son, Richard Fitz-Alan, ninth Earl of Arundel, is considered to have succeeded to the EARLDOM OF SURREY, and

---

[*] By Maud de Nereford he had two sons,

    JOHN DE WARREN.

    WILLIAM DE WARREN.

Upon whom he settled large estates. From JOHN, the Warrens, of Poynton, in Cheshire, are said to have descended.

so styled himself, but it is doubtful if he were ever formally invested with the dignity. He died in 1375, and was *s.* by his son and heir, RICHARD FIZ-ALAN, Earl of Arundel and Surrey, who was beheaded in 1397, when all his honours became FORFEITED (see Fitz-Alan, Earls of Arundel).

ARMS.—*Of the Warrens.*—Cheque, or an az.

Of Blois.—Gu. three pallets varry, on a chief, or. an eagle displayed gules, membered, az.

Of Plantagenet.—Semée of France, and a border of England. This coat was abandoned for that of Warren.

WATSON—BARONS ROCKINGHAM, EARLS OF ROCKINGHAM, BARONS OF MALTON, EARLS OF MALTON, MARQUESSES OF ROCKINGHAM.

Barony, } by Letters { 29th January, 1645.
Earldom, } Patent, { 19th October, 1714.
Barony of Malton, 28th May, 1728.
Earldom of Malton, 19th November, 1734.
Marquisate, 19th April, 1746.

Lineage.

Of the ancient family of WATSON, which flourished for several ages in the counties of Rutland, Northampton, and Cambridge, was

EDWARD WATSON, of Lydington, in Rutlandshire, who lived in 1460, and had fifteen children. The eldest of whom, his son and heir,

EDWARD WATSON, *d.* in 1530, leaving by his wife, Emma, daughter and co-heir of Anthony Smith, Esq., an only son,

EDWARD WATSON, Esq., of Rockingham Castle, in the county of Northampton, who *m.* Dorothy, eldest daughter of Sir Edward Montague, Knt., Lord Chief Justice of the King's Bench, and was *s.* by his son,

SIR EDWARD WATSON, who served the office of sheriff for Northamptonshire, in the 34th Elizabeth, and was knighted at the Charter House, in London, in May, 1603. He *m.* Anne, daughter of Kenelm Digby, Esq., of Stoke, in the county of Rutland, by whom he had issue,

.. LEWIS, his successor.

Edward, *d.* in 1658.

Anne, *m.* to Sir Charles Norwich, of Brampton, in the county of Northampton.

Emma, *m.* to John Grant, Esq.

Mary, *m.* to Sir Anthony Mayney, Knt., of Linton, in Kent.

Elizabeth, *m.* first, to Sir John Needham, of Litchborough, in Northamptonshire, and secondly, to Sir Edward Tyrell, Bart., of Thornton, in Buckinghamshire.

Sir Edward *d.* in 1616, and was *s.* by his elder son,

SIR LEWIS WATSON, Knt., who was created a BARONET on 23rd June, 1691. He was sheriff of Northamptonshire in the 9th Charles I., and in con-

558

sideration of his loyalty to that prince, for whom he garrisoned the castle of Rockingham, was advanced on 29th January, 1645, to the dignity of BARON ROCKINGHAM, *of Rockingham, in the county of Northampton.* His lordship *m.* first, Catharine, daughter of Peregrine Bertie, Lord Willoughby, of Eresby, but by that lady had no surviving issue. He espoused, secondly, Eleanor, daughter of Sir George Manners, of Haddon, in the county of Derby, Knt., and sister of John, Earl of Rutland, by whom he had one son and three daughters, viz.

EDWARD, his successor.

Grace, *m.* to Sir Edward Barkham, Bart., of Southouse, in Norfolk.

Frances, *m.* to Edward Dingley, Esq., of Charlton, in Worcestershire.

Eleanor, *m.* to Sir Charles Dymoke, Knt., of Scrivelby, in Lincolnshire, hereditary champion of England.

His lordship *d.* in 1653, and was *s.* by his son,

EDWARD WATSON, second Baron Rockingham, who espoused Lady ANNE WENTWORTH, daughter of the *celebrated* EARL OF STRAFFORD, by whom he had surviving issue,

LEWIS, his successor.

Thomas, who succeeded, upon the death of his uncle, William Wentworth, Earl of Strafford, in 1695, to the great bulk of that nobleman's estates, and assumed the additional surname of WENTWORTH. He was member of parliament for Higham Ferrers, and afterwards for Malton, in the reign of Queen Anne. He *m.* Alice, only daughter of Sir Thomas Proby, Bart., of Elton, in the county of Huntingdon, and dying in 1723, left an only child,

THOMAS WATSON-WENTWORTH, who was created 28th May, 1728, BARON OF MALTON, and advanced 19th November, 1734, to the dignities of *Baron of Wath and Harrowden, Viscount Higham, of Higham Ferrers,* and EARL OF MALTON. His lordship inherited the Barony of Rockingham at the decease of his cousin, in 1746.

Eleanor, *m.* to Thomas, Lord Leigh, of Stoneleigh, and *d.* in 1705.

Arabella, *m.* to Sir James Oxenden, Bart., of Dene, in Kent.

Anne, } both *d.* unmarried.
Margaret, }

His lordship *d.* in 1691, and was *s.* by his eldest son,

LEWIS WATSON, third baron. This nobleman, in his father's life-time, sate for Higham Ferrers, in the convention parliament, and was lord lieutenant and custos rot. for the county of Kent, temp. Queen Anne and George I. His lordship *m.* Catherine, younger daughter and co-heir of Sir George Sondes, of Lees Court, in the county of Kent, K.B., (afterwards created EARL OF FEVERSHAM,) and eventually heiress to her elder sister, Mary, wife of Lewis, Lord Duras. In consequence of this alliance Lord Rockingham, upon being advanced in the peerage by letters patent, dated 19th October, 1714, assumed two of the titles borne by his deceased father-in-law, namely, *Baron Throwley, and Viscount Sondes, of Lees Court,* both in the county of Kent. He was also created by the same patent, EARL OF ROCKINGHAM. His lordship had issue,

> EDWARD, *Viscount Sondes,* M.P. for New Romney, *m.* in 1709, Lady Catherine Tufton, eldest daughter and co-heir of Thomas, Earl of Thanet, and dying 21st March, 1721-2, left issue,
>
> > LEWIS, who succeeded his grandfather as Earl of Rockingham.
> >
> > THOMAS, who inherited the honours on the decease of his brother *s. p.*
> >
> > Edward, *d.* unmarried.
> >
> > Catherine, *m.* to Edward Southwell, Esq., of King's Weston, in the county of Gloucester, and had a son,
> >
> > > EDWARD SOUTHWELL, who succeeded, in 1776, to the Barony of DE CLIFFORD.
>
> George, *d.* in 1735.
>
> Mary, *m.* to Wray Saunderson, Esq., of Glentworth, in the county of Lincoln.
>
> Anne, *d.* young.
>
> Arabella, *m.* to Henry Furnese, Esq., son and heir of Sir Robert Furnese, Bart., of Waldershare, in Kent.
>
> Margaret, *m.* to Sir John Monson, Bart., of Burton, in the county of Lincoln, who was created, in 1728, BARON MONSON, and had,
>
> > JOHN, who *s.* to the BARONY OF MONSON, and was grandfather of
> >
> > > *Frederick John,* present LORD MONSON.
> >
> > LEWIS, who assumed the surname of WATSON, and was created, in 1760, BARON SONDES, *of Lees Court.* His lordship was grandfather of the present LORD SONDES.
>
> George, a brigadier general, died in 1777, *s. p.*

The earl *d.* in 1724, and was *s.* by his grandson,

LEWIS WATSON, second Earl of Rockingham. This nobleman espoused, Anne, daughter of Sir Henry Furnese, Bart., of Waldershare, but dying issueless in 1745, the honours devolved upon his only surviving brother,

THOMAS WATSON, third Earl of Rockingham, who *d.* in a few months afterwards, anno 1746, unmarried, and devised his estates to his cousin, the Hon. Lewis Monson, (refer to children of his aunt, Margaret,) upon condition, that he assume the surname and arms of WATSON. At the decease, thus, of this nobleman, ALL HIS HONOURS became EXTINCT, except the BARONY OF ROCKINGHAM, which passed to his kinsman, and next heir male (refer to Thomas, second son of Edward, second Baron Rockingham),

THOMAS WATSON-WENTWORTH, *Earl of Malton,* K.B., as fifth Baron Rockingham. His lordship was created on the 19th April, 1746, MARQUESS OF ROCKINGHAM. He *m.* Lady Mary Finch, fourth daughter of Daniel, Earl of Winchelsea and Nottingham, and had surviving issue,

> CHARLES, who was created, vitâ patris, 17th September, 1750, EARL OF MALTON, in the peerage of Ireland.
>
> Anne, *m.* in 1744, to William, Earl Fitz-William, and was mother of
>
> > *William,* present EARL FITZ-WILLIAM.
>
> Mary, *m.* in 1764, to John Milbanke, Esq., son of Sir Ralph Milbanke, Bart., of Halnaby Hall, and grand-uncle of the present Sir John Peniston Milbanke, Bart.
>
> Henrietta-Alicia, *m.* to Mr. Sturgeon.

This nobleman rebuilt the ancient family seat, WENTWORTH HOUSE, in a very splendid manner, and dying in 1750, was *s.* by his son,

CHARLES WATSON - WENTWORTH, Earl of Malton, as second Marquess of Rockingham. This nobleman, at the coronation of *King* GEORGE III., as deputy to the Duke of Norfolk, in his grace's capacity of lord of the manor of Worksop, presented to his majesty a right hand glove, before receiving the sceptre with the cross from the Archbishop of Canterbury, and after the king was enthroned, and whilst he received the homage of the peers spiritual and temporal, his lordship held the said sceptre, with the cross. He was elected KNIGHT of the GARTER in February, 1760, and installed in the May following. In 1765 he was appointed first lord of the treasury in the room of the Hon. George Grenville, and sworn of the privy council; but he held the reins of government then only a single year, and from that period was leader of a strong party opposed to the measures of administration, until restored in 1782, amidst almost the acclamations of the people. The marquess came again into office in his former post of FIRST LORD OF THE TREASURY, and chief of a government, which has since borne in history the title of "the Rockingham Administration," and of which CHARLES JAMES FOX and EDMUND BURKE formed a part. Under his lordship's auspices a pacific negotiation with the revolted states of America commenced, but he lived not to complete his patriotic projects. He was snatched from the hopes of a confiding people in the same year that he had returned to power, at the moment that he had reached the very summit of popularity. The marquess was esteemed for his purity, his principle, and his patriotism, but he was considered a man of no more than ordinary abilities, nor were his intellectual powers formed for any thing beyond the range of common conceptions. He *m.* Mary, daughter and heir of Thomas Bright, Esq., of Badsworth, in the county of York, but having no issue ALL HIS HONOURS at his decease became EXTINCT. His remains were interred in the Earl of Strafford's vault, in York Minster, about the 20th July, 1782, and the principal part of the WENTWORTH ESTATES, including Wentworth House and Malton, in the county of York, devolved upon his lordship's nephew, William, present Earl Fitz-William, who assumed the additional surname of "Wentworth."

ARMS.—Quarterly, first and fourth, ar. on a chevron ingrailed, az. between three martlets, sa. as many crescents, or. for WATSON. On a wreath, a Griffin passant, ar. beak, ducal collar, and fore legs, gules, for WENTWORTH.

WAYER, OR GUADER—EARL OF NORFOLK AND SUFFOLK.

Creation of WILLIAM the *Conqueror*.

Lineage.

RALPH DE WAYER, was constituted by WIL-
LIAM the *Conqueror*, EARL OF NORFOLK AND SUF-
FOLK. Some of our historians affirm, that this
nobleman was an Englishman by birth, born at
Norfolk; but others, that he was a native of
Britanny, which is the more probable, as he was
owner of the castle of GUADER, in that province.
Of this earl there is nothing memorable beyond his
treachery to his royal master, whom he sought to
destroy or expel; and to that end drew into his
plans, ROGER DE BRITOLIO, *Earl of Hereford*,
WALTHEOF, the great *Earl of Northumberland*, and
other persons of distinction. He espoused Emma,
sister of the Earl of Hereford, and he took the
opportunity of his wedding day to disclose to the
conspirators, when they were elated with wine, the
whole of his projects. As soon, however, as they
had recovered the effect of inebriation, the greater
number refused to participate, and the Earl of
Hereford alone joined him in openly resorting to
arms. The rebellion was quickly, however, suppressed by those stout and warlike prelates, ODO,
Bishop of Bayeux, and GEFFERY, *Bishop of Worcester*. The Earl of Norfolk privately deserted his
followers and fled into Britanny, leaving them to
their fate in their encampment at Cambridge: of
those, many were put to the sword, and more taken
prisoners. The castle of Norwich was subsequently
besieged, and his countess obliged to surrender, but
she was suffered to go beyond sea. In the end, this
turbulent person assumed the cross, and joined an
expedition under ROBERT *Curthose*, to Jerusalem,
against the Turks; where he afterwards became a
pilgrim, and died a great penitent.

He left issue, two sons and a daughter, viz.

    Ralph.

    Alan.

    Amicia, *m.* to Robert, Earl of Leicester, son
      of Robert, Earl of Mellant, and brought to
      him most part of the lands, which William
      Fitz-Osborne, her grandfather, held in Nor-
      mandy.

By the treason of Ralph de Wayer his EARLDOM
became FORFEITED.

ARMS.—Per pale, or. and sa. a bend varry.

WEDDERBURN — BARON LOUGH-BOROUGH, OF LOUGH-BOROUGH, IN THE COUNTY OF LEICES-TER.

By Letters Patent, dated 14th June, 1780.

Lineage.

ALEXANDER WEDDERBURN, eldest son of
Peter Wedderburn, of Chesterhall, North Britain,
(a lord of session, under the titulary designation of

LORD CHESTERHALL,*) having been brought up
to the English bar, and attaining high reputation
as a lawyer, was appointed solicitor-general in 1771,
attorney-general in 1778, and constituted lord chief
justice of the court of Common Pleas in 1780, when
he was elevated to the peerage as BARON LOUGH-
BOROUGH, *of Loughborough, in the county of Leicester*. In 1783 his lordship was appointed first
commissioner for keeping the great seal; and he
was constituted, 27th January, 1793, LORD HIGH
CHANCELLOR OF GREAT BRITAIN. In 1795 Lord
Loughborough, having no issue of his own, obtained a new patent, creating him Baron Loughborough, of Loughborough, in the county of Surrey,
with remainder to (his sister Janet's sons, by her
husband, Sir James Erskine, Bart.,) his nephews,
Sir James St. Clair Erskine, Bart., and John Erskine, Esq.; and he was advanced, in 1801, to the
Earldom of Rosslyn with a similar remaindership.
His lordship *m.* first, Betty-Anne, daughter and heir
of John Dawson, Esq., of Morby, in Yorkshire,
and secondly, Charlotte, daughter of William, Viscount Courtenay, but had no issue. The earl *d.*
3rd January, 1805, when the honours, created by the
patents of 1795 and 1801, devolved, according to the
limitation, upon his nephew, Sir James St. Clair
Erskine, Bart., and the BARONY OF LOUGHBO-
ROUGH, *in the county of Leicester*, became EX-
TINCT.

ARMS.—Ar. on a chevron between three roses
gules, barbed and seeded ppr. a fleur-de-lis, ar.

WELLES—BARONS WELLES.

By Writ of Summons, dated 6th February, 1299,
27 Edward I.

Lineage.

The first of this family mentioned by Sir William
Dugdale is

ADAM DE WELLES, who, in the 6th of
Richard I.,† paid ten marks for adhering to John,
Earl of Moreton, who at that time assumed more
authority, during his brother's captivity, than he
was afterwards able to justify. After this Adam
came

---

* In Scotland the JUDGES assume, upon being
raised to the bench, the designation of nobility, but
they are merely *titular* lords. In England a practice somewhat similar anciently prevailed, the
JUDGES being usually summoned to parliament
amongst the barons, *to give their advice*; but they
were not regarded as peers of the realm, nor did
the writ of summons constitute an hereditary peerage in the family of the person summoned. A
recurrence to this old custom at a period when
the peerage has become so overstocked with law
lords, might be found now a salutary adjunct to
reform.

† In *Camden*, RICHARD DE WELLES is stated to
have held the manor of Welles ever since the Conquest, by the service of being baker to the king.

WILLIAM DE WELLES, who, in the 9th of John, gave fifty marks for one knight's fee in Gremesby, in the county of Lincoln, and was *s.* by another

WILLIAM DE WELLES, who, in the 11th Edward I., obtained license for a weekly market and a yearly fair at his manor of Alfourd, in Lincolnshire. He *m.* Isabel de Vesci, and was *s.* by his son,

ADAM DE WELLES, who, in the 22nd EDWARD I., was in the wars of Gascony, and was summoned to parliament, as a BARON, on the 6th February, 1299, in which year he was made constable of Rockingham Castle, and warden of the forest. The next year he was in the wars of Scotland, and again in 1301 and 1302; and had regular summonses to parliament to the year of his decease, 1311, when he was *s.* by his son,

ROBERT DE WELLES, second baron, but never summoned to parliament. This nobleman *d.* in two years after he had attained majority, anno 1320, and leaving no issue, was *s.* by his brother,

ADAM DE WELLES, third baron, summoned to parliament from 20th July, 1332, to 20th April, 1343. This nobleman, at the period of his brother's death, was only sixteen years of age; he attained his majority in the 20th of Edward II., and doing his homage had livery of his lands. In the 7th EDWARD III. his lordship was in the wars of Scotland, and again in two years afterwards, at which latter period he was a knight. In the 16th of the same reign he was charged with ten men at arms, and ten archers for the king's service in France, and the like number in the next year. His lordship *d.* in 1345, and was *s.* by his son,

JOHN DE WELLES, fourth baron, summoned to parliament on the 15th December, 1357, and 20th November, 1360. The wardship of this nobleman, who was a minor at his father's decease, was granted to Margaret, widow of William, Lord Ros, of Hamlake. In the 22nd of Edward III., although still in minority, he caused his father's executors to purchase a rent of ten pounds per annum, from the monks of Bardney, for the behoof of the abbess and nuns of Grenefield, which monastery was founded by his ancestors; in consideration whereof they obliged themselves, and their successors, to find two fitting priests, to celebrate *masses, mattens, placebo, dirge,* and *commendation,* every day in the chapel of our lady, within that their monastery of Grenefield, for the health of the souls of his lordship's predecessors. His lordship had livery of his lands in the 29th of Edward III., and in four years afterwards he was in the wars of Gascony. He *d.* in 1361, and was *s.* by his son,

JOHN DE WELLES, fifth baron, summoned to parliament from 20th January, 1376, to 26th February, 1421. This nobleman served in the expedition made into Flanders, in the retinue of John, Duke of Lancaster, in the 27th of Edward III., and in the 1st of Richard II., was in the wars of France. The next year he was in the garrison of Berwick, under Henry Percy, Earl of Northumberland, its governor. His lordship subsequently obtained license to travel beyond sea,

and returning in the 8th of RICHARD II., had leave to go abroad again for the vindication of his honour, having received some affront from a knight in France. He seems to have come home solely to procure letters testimonial vouching for his credit and reputation. After this we find him in the Scottish wars; and in the 19th of the same reign, he was ambassador to Scotland, where during his sojourn, being at a banquet, where deeds of arms becoming the subject of conversation, his lordship exclaimed, *" Let words have no place; if ye know not the chivalry and valiant deeds of Englishmen; appoint me a day and place when ye list, and ye shall have experience."* This challenge was immediately accepted by David, Earl of Crawford, and London Bridge appointed as the place of combat. The battle was fought on St. George's day, and the Scottish earl was declared victor. Indeed he displayed such an extraordinary degree of prowess, that notwithstanding the spear was broken upon his helmet and visage, he remained so immovably fixed in his saddle, that the spectators cried out that in defiance of the laws of arms, he was bound thereto. Whereupon he dismounted, and got up again, and ran a second course; but in the third, Lord Welles was unhorsed and flung to the ground; on which Crawford dismounting, embraced him, that the people might understand that he had no animosity, and the earl subsequently visited his lordship with great courtesy until his recovery. Of this Lord Welles nothing further is known, than the period of his decease, anno 1421; although for eight years afterwards, summonses appear to have been regularly issued to his lordship. But there are other instances upon record, of summonses having been directed to barons after their deaths, probably from ignorance that the decease occurred. The case of Maurice, the fourth Lord Berkeley, is a remarkable instance; he *d.* in 1368, and summonses were addressed to him until 1380. Lord Welles was *s.* by (the son of his deceased eldest son, Eudo, by his wife, Maude, daughter of Ralph, Lord Greystock) his grandson,

SIR LEO DE WELLES, as sixth baron, summoned to parliament from 25th February, 1432, to 30th July, 1460. This nobleman received the honour of knighthood, in the 4th of Henry VI., from the Duke of Bedford at Leicester, with the young king himself, and divers other persons of rank. His lordship for several years after served with great honour in France, and was made LIEUTENANT OF IRELAND for seven years, in the 16th of the same reign. When the fatal feud between the Houses of York and Lancaster broke out, Lord Welles arrayed himself under the banner of the latter, and adhering to his colours with unbending fidelity, fell at the battle of TOWTON FIELD, on Palm Sunday, 1461. His lordship *m.* first, Joane, daughter and heir of Sir Robert Waterton, Knt., and had issue,

RICHARD (Sir), who *m.* Joane, daughter and heir of Robert, Lord Willoughby de Eresby, and was summoned to parliament in her right, as LORD WILLOUGHBY, from 26th May, 1455, to 28th February, 1460.

Alianore, m. to Thomas, Lord Hoo and Hastings (see that dignity).

Margaret, m. to Sir Thomas Dymoke, Knt.

Cecily, m. to Sir Robert Willoughby, son of Sir Thomas Willoughby, of Parham.

Catharine, m. to Sir Thomas de Launde, Knt., and had issue, two daughters, his co-heirs, viz.

> JOANE, m. to William Denton, Esq., and had a son,
>> JOHN DENTON.
> Margaret, m. to Thomas Berkeley, Esq., and had two sons,
>> William.
>> Maurice.

Lord Welles espoused, secondly, Margaret, sister and heir of Sir John Beauchamp, of Bletshoe, and widow of John Beaufort, Earl of Somerset (by whom she was mother of Margaret, Countess of Richmond, mother of King Henry VII.), and had another son,

> JOHN, created VISCOUNT WELLES (see that dignity).

An attainder followed his lordship's decease, under which the BARONY OF WELLES became forfeited: but his son,

SIR RICHARD WELLES, Lord Willoughby, had a grant in the 4th of Edward IV., through the king's especial favour, of all the goods, chattels, and moveables, whereof his father died possessed; and the next ensuing year had restitution of the manors of Welles, and other estates in the county of Lincoln, with lands in Northumberland. In three years afterwards (1468) his lordship obtained a full restitution in blood and honours. But this good fortune had a brief endurance, for the next year, Richard Nevill, the stout EARL OF WARWICK, taking up arms for the restoration of HENRY VI., made Sir Robert Welles, son and heir of Lord Willoughby and Welles, a brave and able commander, general of the Lancastrian forces. Whereupon Sir Robert drove Sir Thomas Burgh, a knight of the king's house, out of Lincolnshire, pulled down his dwelling, seized upon all his goods and chattels, and at the head of thirty thousand of the people, raised the standard of Lancaster, and cried King HENRY. Of this insurrection so soon as King EDWARD had intelligence, he summoned the Lord Willoughby and Welles to his presence, but that nobleman on arriving in London, with his brother-in-law, Sir John Dymoke, and learning that the king was highly incensed, fled to sanctuary at Westminster, and there determined to remain until his wrath was assuaged. The king hoping, however, to terminate the disturbance in Lincolnshire, without being obliged to take the field, sent for his lordship, and induced him to leave his asylum, upon a solemn promise of safety. He then required of Lord Welles, to command his son to lay down his arms, and in the interim marched at the head of what forces he could collect into Lincolnshire, taking Lord Welles, and Sir John Dymoke, with him. But when he arrived within two days' journey of Stamford, where his adversaries were stationed, he learned that Sir Robert Welles had refused to obey the injunctions of his father, which had been conveyed to him by letter, and becoming enraged at the refusal he caused, in violation of his royal promise, the heads of Lord Welles and Sir John Dymoke, to be forthwith cut off. In revenge of this act of treachery, Sir Robert Welles, without awaiting the coming up of Warwick, attacked the royal army, although superior in number to that which he commanded, but after a most gallant and obstinate struggle, his men at length deserting him, sustained a defeat, and being made prisoner, was immediately beheaded. The death of the father and his heroic son, took place almost at the same time in 1469, and they were both ATTAINTED after the restoration of Edward IV., in 1474. Lord Willoughby and Welles had issue, by the heiress of Willoughby,

> ROBERT (Sir), the gallant soldier whose fate we have just recorded. He died without issue, leaving a widow, Elizabeth, daughter of John Bourchier, Lord Berners. Her ladyship survived her husband but one year, when she bequeathed her body to be interred with his, in the church of the friars, at Doncaster.
> JOANE, m. to Richard Hastings, Esq., brother of William, Lord Hastings, chamberlain to King EDWARD IV.

To Sir Robert Welles, succeeded his only sister, the above mentioned

JOANE HASTINGS, whose husband,

SIR RICHARD HASTINGS, had so much favour from King EDWARD, that he obtained a special livery of all the castles, manors, lordships, and lands, whereof Richard, Lord Welles and Willoughby, and his son, Sir Robert Welles, died possessed,* and was summoned to parliament, as "Richardo Hastinges de Welles, Chl'r," on the 15th November, 1482, and 9th December, 1483. His lordship had an only son, ANTHONY, who predeceased him. He died himself in 1503, when, if his summons to parliament be deemed a continuation OF THE OLD BARONY OF WELLES, (but it must be recollected that the attainder was never reversed,) that barony fell into ABEYANCE, amongst the descendants of the daughters of LEO, the sixth Lord Welles; but if the summons be considered a new creation, the barony at his lordship's decease became then EXTINCT.

ARMS.—Gu. a lion rampant, double queveé, sa.

WELLES—VISCOUNT WELLES.

By Letters Patent, temp. HENRY VII.

Lineage.

JOHN WELLES, only child of Leo, sixth LORD WELLES, by his second wife, Margaret, Countess Dowager of Somerset, having taken up arms in

---

* In the act of attainder, special provision is made, that Richard Hastings, should enjoy certain manors that belonged to the said barons, in consideration of his having married Joane, sister and heir of Robert de Welles, and also of his loyalty and services.

behalf of his kinsman, HENRY, *of Richmond*,[*] was made constable of the castle of Rockingham, and steward of Rockingham Forest, after the accession of that personage to the throne as HENRY VII. He was also elevated to the peerage by letters patent, (but the date is not known,) as VISCOUNT WELLES, and was summoned to parliament in that dignity, on the 1st September, 1487. He was afterwards made a Knight of the Garter. His lordship *m.* the Lady Cicily Plantagenet, daughter of *King* EDWARD IV., and sister-in-law to *King* HENRY VII., by whom he had two daughters,

ELIZABETH, } who both died *s. p.*
ANNE, }

He died in 1489, when the VISCOUNTY OF WELLES became EXTINCT. His lordship's widow espoused Sir John Kyme, of Lincolnshire.

ARMS.—Or. a lion rampant, double quevée, sa. armed and langued, gu.

WENLOCK—BARON WENLOCK.

Created in 1461.

Lineage.

In the 17th HENRY VI.

JOHN WENLOK, or WENLOCK, was constituted escheator for the counties of Buckingham and Bedford; shortly after which, coming to court, he was made usher of the chamber to *Queen* MARGARET, when he had the title of esquire. He was next knighted, and appointed governor of Bamburgh Castle, in Northumberland. In the 28th of the same reign he was constituted CHAMBERLAIN to the queen, and he fought on the side of Lancaster at the first battle of St. Albans, when he was severely wounded. After this we find him advancing a sum of money, as a loan, to *King* HENRY VI., and subsequently chosen a KNIGHT OF THE GARTER. Notwithstanding these high honours, Sir John Wenlock joined, soon after, the standard of York, and fought under that banner at the battle of Towton-field, for which desertion he was rewarded, by *King* EDWARD IV., with a grant of the offices of chief butler of England, and steward of the castle and lordship of Berkhampsted, in Hertfordshire. He was also raised to the degree of a baron, as LORD WENLOCK, *of Wenlock*, in the county of Salop, and sworn of the privy council. In the first period of *King* EDWARD's reign his lordship was employed upon confidential embassies to the courts of Burgundy and France, and he was constituted lieutenant-governor of Calais, and the marches adjacent. But afterwards joining the Earl of Warwick, in the attempt to restore HENRY VI., he had a command at the battle of Tewkesbury, where he is said to have been slain by the Duke of Somerset, who furiously cleft his head with his battle-axe, for neglecting to come up in time, whereby the battle was lost, and the fate of the unhappy HENRY VI. decided for ever. His lord-

ship *m.* Elizabeth, daughter and co-heir of Sir John Drayton, but had no issue. He *d.* in 1471, when the BARONY OF WENLOCK became EXTINCT.

ARMS.—Ar. a chevron between three blackamoors' heads erased, sa.

Note.—The Barony of Wenlock has just now been conferred upon SIR ROBERT LAWLEY, Bart., whose ancestor, Thomas Lawley, inherited as next heir the estates of Lord Wenlock, at his lordship's decease in 1471.

WENTWORTH — BARONS WENTWORTH, OF WENTWORTH-WOODHOUSE, VISCOUNT WENTWORTH, BARONS RABY, EARLS OF STRAFFORD.

| Barony, Viscounty, Earldom, and Barony of Raby, Earldom, | by Letters Patent, | 20th July, 1628. 10th Dec., 1628. 12th January, 1640. 4th September, 1711. |

Lineage.

The surname of WENTWORTH is said by genealogists to have been derived in Saxon times, from the lordship of Wentworth, in the wapentake of STRAFFORD, in Yorkshire, where, at the time of the Conquest, lived

REGINALD DE WINTERWADE, (as the name was written in Domesday Book,) whose lineal descendant,

WILLIAM DE WYNTWORD, of Wyntword, *m.* in the time of HENRY III., Emma, daughter and heir of William Wodehous, of Wodehous, by whom he acquired that estate, and taking up his abode there, the family have since been designated the "Wentworths of Wentworth-Woodhouse." He was *s.* by his son,

WILLIAM DE WENTWORTH, of Wentworth-Woodhouse, who *m.* Beatrix, daughter of Gilbert Thakel, and had two sons,

WILLIAM, his successor.
RICHARD, Bishop of London, and CHANCELLOR OF ENGLAND, in 1338.

The elder son,

WILLIAM DE WENTWORTH, *m.* Dyonisia, daughter of Peter de Rotherfield, and had two sons,

WILLIAM, his successor.
John, *m.* ——, daughter and heir of —— Elmsall, of Elmsall, in Yorkshire, by whom he acquired that estate, and dying *s. p.* left it to his nephew, JOHN.

The elder son,

WILLIAM DE WENTWORTH, succeeded his father in 1295, and *m.* Isabel, daughter and co-heir of William Pollington, of Pollington, in the county of York, and had issue,

WILLIAM (Sir), his heir.
John, who inherited EMSALL, from his uncle, and marrying Joan, daughter of Richard de Teys, of Burgh-Walleys, in Yorkshire, was patriarch of the Barons and Viscounts Went-

---

[*] He was uncle by the half blood to Henry, Earl of Richmond, afterwards HENRY VII.

worth; the Knightly family, seated at Bretton, with divers other branches.

William de Wentworth was *s.* by his elder son,

SIR WILLIAM WENTWORTH, who *m.* Isabel (or Lucy), daughter and heir of Robert Hooton, of Hooton-Roberts, in Yorkshire, and was *s.* by his son,

SIR WILLIAM WENTWORTH, who espoused Lucy, daughter and co-heir of Walter, son and heir of Henry de Tynneslow, of Tynneslow, also in Yorkshire, and was *s.* by his son,

THOMAS WENTWORTH, who wedded Isabel, daughter of Sir William Fleming, Knt., of Waith. His grandson,

SIR THOMAS WENTWORTH, fought valiantly on the side of *King* HENRY VI., at the battle of HEXHAM, 3d April, 1463, when he was made prisoner with the Duke of Somerset and others. He *m.* Joan, daughter of Sir Richard Redman, Knt., of Harwood Tower, and was *s.* by his elder son,

WILLIAM WENTWORTH, Esq., who *m.* in the 39th of HENRY VI., Isabella, daughter of Sir Richard Fitz-Williams, of Aldwark, in Yorkshire, and sister of William, Earl of Southampton, by whom he had four sons, THOMAS, his successor, Ralph, George, and William, and a daughter, Elisabeth, who *m.* first, Thomas Lea, Esq., of Middleton, and secondly, Henry Arthington, Esq. Mr. Wentworth *d.* in 1477, and was *s.* by his eldest son,

SIR THOMAS WENTWORTH, who received the honour of knighthood for his bravery in the battle of Spurs. This gentleman, being a person of great opulence, went by the name of *Golden Thomas.* He paid a fine to be excused from being created a Knight of the Bath; and in 1523, he obtained a license from HENRY VIII., to wear his bonnet, and be covered in the royal presence, because he was infirm. He *m.* Beatrix, daughter of Sir Richard Woodrove, of Walley, Knt., and widow of John Drax, Esq., of Woodhall, and had issue,

    WILLIAM, his successor.

    Gervase.

    Michael, of Mendham, in Suffolk, comptroller to the queen, *m.* Isabel, daughter and heir of Percival Whitley, Esq., of Whitley, in the county of York, and was progenitor of the Wentworths of Wooley.

    Thomas, of Scorby, *m.* Grace, daughter of John Gascoigne, Esq., of Lasingcroft.

    Bryan.

    Elisabeth, *m.* to Ralph Durham, Esq.

    Isabel, *m.* to Nicholas Wombwell, Esq., of Thundercliffe, Yorkshire.

    Beatrice, *m.* to James Worrall, Esq., of Lower-slate, also in Yorkshire.

Sir Thomas *d.* in 1548, and was *s.* by his eldest son,

WILLIAM WENTWORTH, Esq., who *m.* Catherine, daughter of Ralph Beeston, Esq., of Beeston, and dying in 1549, was *s.* by his eldest son,

THOMAS WENTWORTH, Esq., High Sheriff of the county of York, in the 25th Elizabeth; *m.* Margaret, daughter and heir of Sir William Gas-

coigne,* Knt., of Gawthorpe, by which alliance he acquired the manor and seat of Gawthorpe, Cusworth, &c., and his descendants became co-heirs to the Baronies of Ferrers of Wemme, and Boteler of Wemme, then (and still) in ABEYANCE. He had issue,

    WILLIAM (Sir), his successor.

    Elisabeth, *m.* to Thomas Danby, Esq., of Farnley.

    Barbara, *d.* unmarried.

    Margaret, *m.* first, to Michael, son and heir of John, Lord Darcy, and secondly, to Jasper Blythman, Esq., of New Luthas.

    Catherine, *m.* to Thomas Gargrave, Esq., of Nestel-Priory, in Yorkshire.

Mr. Wentworth *d.* 14th February, 1586-7, possessed of lands in the county of York, to the amount of £6000 a-year, and was *s.* by his son,

SIR WILLIAM WENTWORTH, of Wentworth Woodhouse, Gawthorpe, &c. This gentleman was High Sheriff of Yorkshire, in the last year of Queen Elizabeth, and was created a BARONET on the 29th of June, 1611. He *m.* Anne, daughter and heir of Sir Robert Atkins, Knt., of Stowell, in the county of Gloucester, by whom he had three surviving sons, and three daughters, viz.

1. THOMAS, his successor.

2. William (Sir), of Ashby-Puerorum, in Lincolnshire. This gentleman was knighted by *King* Charles I., and fell at MARSTON-MOOR, fighting under the royal banner. Sir William Wentworth *m.* Elisabeth, daughter and co-heir of Thomas Savile, of Hasseldon Hall, in the county of York, and had with a daughter Anne, who *m.* Edward Skinner, Esq., of Thornton College, Lincolnshire, one surviving son,

    WILLIAM (Sir), High Sheriff of Yorkshire, in the 24th of CHARLES II.; *m.* Isabella, daughter of Sir Allan Appaley, Knt., treasurer of the household to James, Duke of York, and had issue,

      I. William, a military officer, *d.* unmarried, in 1693, while serving as captain of horse in Flanders.

      II. THOMAS, who succeeded his cousin, the Earl of Strafford, in the BARONY OF RABY.

      III. Peter, of Henbury, in Dorsetshire, *m.* Juliana, only daughter of Thomas Horde, Esq., of Cote, in

---

* MARY FERRERS, younger daughter and co-heir of Sir Robert Ferrers, Lord Ferrers, of Wemme, espoused

    RALPH NEVIL, a younger son of Ralph, Earl of Westmorland, and had a son,

      JOHN NEVIL, who *m.* Elisabeth, daughter and heir of Robert Newmarch, and left an only daughter and heiress,

        JOANE NEVIL, who *m.* SIR WILLIAM GASCOIGNE, and her daughter and heiress,

          MARGARET GASCOIGNE, espoused Thomas Wentworth, as in the text.

the county of Oxford, and had surviving issue,

WILLIAM, his successor, who m. Susanna, daughter of —— Slaughter, Esq., of Upper Slaughter Hall, in the county of Gloucester, and had two sons and three daughters,

FREDERICK-THOMAS, who succeeded to the EARLDOM OF STRAFFORD, at the death of his cousin, Thomas, second Earl of the second creation.

George.

Caroline.

Augusta.

Anne, m. to John Hatfield Kaye, Esq., of Hatfield Hall, Yorkshire.

Harriet, m. to Thomas, son and heir of Francis Arundel, Esq., of Stoke-Bruers Park, Northamptonshire.

IV. Paul, fell at the siege of Namur, in 1695, unmarried.

V. Allan, killed in storming the citadel at Liege, in 1702, and d. unmarried.

VI. Frances-Arabella, m. to Walter, Lord Bellew, of Ireland.

VII. Anne, m. to James Donolan, Esq., of Ireland.

VIII. Isabella, m. to Francis Arundel, Esq., of Stoke-Bruers Park.

IX. Elizabeth, m. to John, Lord Arundel, of Trerise.

3. George (Sir), of Wooley, M.P. for Pontefract, in 1640, but disabled from sitting on account of his loyalty to *King* CHARLES I., received the honour of knighthood, made general of the forces in Ireland, and sworn of the privy council of that kingdom. Sir George m. ——, daughter of Sir Francis Ruishe, Knt., of Sarre, in the Isle of Thanet, and left a son,

RUISHE WENTWORTH, of Sarre, who m. Susanna, sister of James Adye, Esq., of Barham, in Kent, and dying in 1695, left an only child and heir,

MARY, m. to Thomas, Lord Howard, of Effingham.

1. Mary, m. to Sir Richard Hooton, Knt., of Goldesburgh, in Yorkshire.

2. Anne, m. to Sir Gervase Savile, Bart., of Thornhill, also in the county of York.

3. Elizabeth, m. to James Dillon, Earl of Roscommon, the celebrated poet.

Sir William Wentworth d. in 1614, and was s. by his eldest son,

SIR THOMAS WENTWORTH, second baronet (b. 13th April, 1593), who became afterwards so conspicuous in the troubled times of the FIRST CHARLES. In the reign of JAMES I., Sir Thomas was member of parliament for the county of York, and also in the beginning of that of his suc-

cessor; but the latter monarch, soon after his accession, elevated him to the peerage, by letters patent, dated 22d July, 1628, as BARON WENTWORTH, of Wentworth-Woodhouse, and he was advanced on the 10th of the ensuing December, to the degree of VISCOUNT WENTWORTH. The next year his lordship was sworn of the privy council, made Lord Lieutenant of the county of York, and president of the north. In February, 1632-3, he was nominated Lord Deputy of Ireland; from which government he was recalled to command as lieutenant-general in the army then raised against the Scots. In 1640, he was created BARON RABY, *of Raby Castle*, in the bishopric of Durham, (with remainder, default his own male issue, to his younger brothers, and their issue male,) and EARL OF STRAFFORD. Soon after which he was made a KNIGHT OF THE GARTER, and constituted LORD LIEUTENANT OF IRELAND. About this period the republican and puritanical parties prevailing in parliament, Strafford became an object of their greatest distrust, and the destruction of his lordship was deemed indispensable to the accomplishment of their ulterior projects. An impeachment against him was therefore immediately voted by the commons, and Pym deputed to carry it up to the House of Lords. The earl was just entering to take his seat, when he was apprised of the prosecution, and ordered into custody. He was subsequently brought to trial on the 22d March, 1640-1, but his prosecutors were unable to establish their charges according to the laws of the land, and were therefore, after an investigation which lasted eighteen days, in which Strafford deported himself with a degree of firmness, moderation, and wisdom, that extorted admiration from his bitterest foes, obliged to resort to the very unusual and unconstitutional mode of proceeding by bill of attainder. So determined, however, were the commons to condemn him, that the bill was brought in and passed on the same day. It was read twice in the morning, and the third time in the afternoon; and carried by 204 voices, against 59. But in the lords, its progress was not so triumphant; and when it finally passed, forty-five peers only were present, of whom twenty-six voted in the affirmative. In the end, the unhappy nobleman was sacrificed to the clamour of the mob, and his own magnanimous consideration for the precarious position of his royal master. The populace goaded to frenzy, flocked around Whitehall, where the king resided, calling aloud for justice, and accompanying their savage vociferations with open and furious menaces. The queen and council were appalled: they advised CHARLES to sign the doom of the most faithful of his servants. Juxon, Bishop of London, alone had the fortitude to counsel the king not to act contrary to his conscience. But the earl hearing of his majesty's irresolution and anxiety, immediately addressed him, and with a devotion almost unparalleled, besought him for the sake of public peace, to put an end to his unfortunate, however blameless, life, and to quiet the tumultuous populace, by conceding the request for which they were so importunate (*see note at foot*). The king gave at last a most reluctant assent; and *Thomas*,

EARL OF STRAFFORD, the firmest prop of the monarchy, was thus, in the forty-ninth year of his age, consigned to the scaffold. He suffered death with his characteristic firmness upon Tower Hill, on the 12th May, 1641. His lordship is allowed to have possessed many amiable qualities—to have been endowed with great natural parts—to have had a cultivated understanding,—a brave and noble bearing; but he is accused of pride, arrogance, and ambition—and the epitaph, which Plutarch says that Sylla wrote for himself, is quoted as most appropriate to his tomb, "That no man did ever exceed him in doing good to his friends, or in doing mischief to his enemies; for his acts of both kinds were most notorious." As ruler of Ireland, he is designated, we fear too justly, by the title of a cruel, rapacious and vindictive tyrant. Amongst his bitterest foes was Sir Harry Vane, and he is said to have incurred the enmity of that celebrated person, by taking the title of Raby, from Raby Castle, then in possession of the knight. The earl m. first, Lady Margaret Clifford, daughter of Francis, Earl of Cumberland, which lady died s. p. He espoused, secondly, Lady Arabella Holles, daughter of John, Earl of Clare, by whom he had issue,

WILLIAM, his successor.

Anne, m. to Edward Watson, Earl of Rockingham, and had issue,

> LEWIS WATSON, third Earl of Rockingham.
>
> THOMAS WATSON, who assumed the name of WENTWORTH upon inheriting the estates of his maternal uncle.

Arabella, m. to John McCarthy, son of the Earl of Clancarty, in Ireland.

The earl wedded, thirdly, Elizabeth, daughter of Sir Godfrey Rhodes, Knt., of Great Houghton, in Yorkshire, by whom he had a son, Thomas, and a daughter, Mary, both of whom d. unmarried. His elder son,

WILLIAM WENTWORTH, was restored by patent, after the re-establishment of the monarchy, to all his father's honours, and was installed a Knight of the Garter. His lordship m. first, Lady Henrietta-Maria Stanley, daughter of James, Earl of Derby, and secondly, Henrietta, daughter of Frederick Charles de Roy de la Rochefoucauld, generalissimo of the forces of the king of Denmark, but d. without issue in 1695, when the greater part of his estates devolved upon his nephew, the Honourable Thomas Watson, son of Edward, Earl of Rockingham, and ALL HIS HONOURS became EXTINCT, save the BARONY OF RABY, which passed, according to the special limitation in the patent, to his kinsman (revert to issue of Sir William Wentworth, of Ashby Puerorum, second son of the first baronet),

THOMAS WENTWORTH, Esq., as third BARON RABY. This nobleman had in early life adopted the profession of arms, and served under WILLIAM III. in Flanders; where he acquired high reputation, particularly at the battles of Steinkirk and Landen. In the reign of Queen Anne he shared in several of the glorious campaigns of Marlborough, and was repeatedly ambassador to the courts of Berlin, Vienna, and the States General.

His lordship was advanced in consideration of his eminent services, by letters patent, dated 4th September, 1711, to the dignities of *Viscount Wentworth, of Wentworth Woodhouse, and of Stainborough*, and EARL OF STRAFFORD, with special remainder to his brother Peter. His lordship m. Anne, daughter and heir of Sir Henry Johnson, Knt., of Bradenham in the county of Bucks, by whom he had issue,

WILLIAM, his successor.

Anne, m. to the Right Honourable William Conolly, one of his majesty's privy council in Ireland.

Lucy, m. to Colonel Sir George Howard.

Henrietta, m. to Henry Vernon, Esq.

His lordship, who was a Knight of the most noble order of the Garter, d. in 1739, and was s. by his son,

WILLIAM WENTWORTH, second Earl of Strafford, of the new creation. This nobleman espoused Lady Anne Campbell, daughter of John, Duke of Argyll, but dying s. p. in 1791, the honours passed, according to the limitation, to his cousin (revert to issue of Sir William Wentworth, second son of Sir William, the first baronet),

FREDERICK - THOMAS WENTWORTH, Esq., as third Earl of Strafford. This nobleman d. at his seat, Henbury, in Dorsetshire, without issue, in 1799, when the BARONY OF RABY, the VISCOUNTY OF WENTWORTH, and EARLDOM OF STRAFFORD, became EXTINCT.

ARMS.—Sa. a chevron between three leopards' heads, or.

Note.—Last letter from Thomas, Earl of Strafford, to King Charles I.

"May it please your Sacred Majestye,

"It hath bin my greatest griefe in all these troubles, to be taken as a person which should endeavour to represent and set things amisse between your majesty and your people; and to give counsells tending to the disquiet of the three kingdomes.

"Most true it is, that this mine owne private condition considered, it hath beene a great maddnesse, since through your gracious favour I was so provided, as not to expect in any kind to mend my fortune, or please my mind, more, then by resting where your bounteous hands had placed me.

"Nay, it is most mightily mistaken, for unto your majesty it is well knowne, my poore and humble advises concluded still in this, that your majesty and your people could never bee happy, till there were a right understanding betwixt you and them: no other meanes to effect and settle this happinesse, but by the councell, and assent of parliament; or to prevent the growing evils upon this state, but by entirely putting your selfe in the last resort, upon the loyalty and good affections of your English subjects.

"Yet, such is my misfortune, this truth findeth little credit, the contrary seemeth generally to be believed, and myselfe reputed, as something of seperation betwixt you and your people; under a heavyer censure then which I am persuaded no gentleman can suffer.

"Now, I understand the minds of men are more incensed against me, notwithstanding your majesty hath declared, that in your princely opinion;. I am not guilty of treason, nor are you satisfyed in your conscience to passe the bill.

"This bringeth me into a very great streight, there is before me the ruine of my children and family, hitherto untouched, in all the branches of it with any foule crime. Here is before me the many ills, which may befall your sacred person, and the whole kingdome, should yourselfe and parliament part lesse satisfied one with the other, then is necessary for the preservation both of king and people. Here are before me the things most valued, most feared, by mortal man, *life or death.*

"To say, Sir, that there hath not beene a strife in me, were to make me lesse man, then God knoweth my infirmities give me. And to call a destruction upon myselfe and young children, (where the intentions of my heart, at least have beene innocent of this great offence,) may be believed, will find no easie consent from flesh and bloud.

"But with much sadnesse, I am come to a resolution, of that which I take to be most becoming in me, to looke upon that which is most principall in itselfe; which doubtlesse is the prosperity of your sacred person and the common-wealth, infinitely before any private man's interest.

"And therefore, in few words, as I put myselfe wholly upon the honour and justice of my peers, so clearly, as to beseech your majesty might have spared that declaration of yours on Saturday last, and entirely to have left me to their lordships: so now, to set your majesties conscience at liberty, I doe most humbly beseech your majesty, in prevention of mistakes which may happen by your refusall, to passe this bill; and by this meanes remove, (praysed be God,) I cannot say, this accursed, (but I confesse,) this unfortunate thing forth of the way, towards that blessed agreement, which God, I trust, shall ever establish betweene you and your subjects.

"Sir, my consent shall more acquit you herein to God, then all the world can doe besides. To a willing man there is no injury done. And as by God's grace I forgive all the world with a calmnesse and meeknesse of infinite contentment to my dislodging soule, so, Sir, to you can I give the life of this world, with all the cheerfulnesse imaginable; in the just acknowledgment of your exceeding favour. And only begge that in your goodnesse, you would vouchsafe to cast your gracious regard upon my poore Sonne, and his three sisters, lesse or more, and no otherwise, then as their (in present) unfortunate father, may hereafter appear more or lesse guilty of this death.

 "God long preserve your Majestye,
  "Your Majesties most faithful and
   "humble Subject and Servant,
    "STRAFFORD."

"*Tower,* 4th *May,* 1641."

WENTWORTH — MARQUESSES OF ROCKINGHAM.

Refer to WATSON, *Barons Rockingham, &c.*

The Honourable

THOMAS WATSON, second son of *Edward*

Watson, second *Lord* ROCKINGHAM, by *Lady* ANNE WENTWORTH, inherited the Wentworth estates upon the demise of his uncle, William, Earl of Strafford, in 1695, and assumed the additional surname of WENTWORTH; from this gentleman descended the Marquesses of Rockingham.

WENTWORTH — BARONS WENTWORTH, EARL OF CLEVELAND, VISCOUNT WENTWORTH, OF WELLESBOROUGH.

Barony, by Writ of Summons, dated 2nd Dec., 1529, 21 Henry VIII.

Earldom, } by Letters { 5th February, 1626.
Viscounty, } Patent, { 4th May, 1762.

Lineage.

This family, although of great antiquity in the county of York, did not attain the honour of the peerage until the time of HENRY VIII., when THOMAS WENTWORTH, Esq., son of Sir Richard Wentworth, Knt., of Nettlested, in the county of Suffolk, was summoned to parliament, by writ, as BARON WENTWORTH. His lordship m. Margaret, daughter of Sir Andrew Fortescue, Knt., by Anne, daughter and heir of Sir William Stonor, Knt., (by Anne, daughter and co-heir of John Nevil, Marquess of Montacute,) and had issue,

THOMAS, his successor.

Henry (Sir), m. Elizabeth, daughter of Sir Christopher Glenham.

Richard, m. to Margaret Roydon.

Anne, m. to Sir John Poley, of Bradley, in the county of Suffolk, Knt.

Cicily, m. to Sir Robert Wingfield, Knt.

Mary, m. to William Cavendish.

Margaret, m. first, to John, Lord Williams, secondly, to Sir William Darcy, and thirdly, to Sir John Crofts.

Joan, m. to Henry, Lord Cheney.

Dorothy, m. to Paul Wethypoole, Esq.

His lordship, who was lord chamberlain of the household, d. in 1551, and was s. by his eldest son,

THOMAS WENTWORTH, second baron, summoned to parliament from 23rd January, 1559, to 4th February, 1569. This nobleman, upon the demise of EDWARD VI., was one of the first who appeared for Queen Mary, and upon her majesty's accession his lordship was sworn of the privy council, and constituted deputy of Calais, and the marches thereof. In which high trust he continued until the surrender of that place, in the 5th of Mary, to the overwhelming force of the Duke of Guise, after being held by the English for upwards of two centuries. Lord Wentworth was subsequently tried by his peers on suspicion of cowardice or treachery, but honourably acquitted. In the reign of Elizabeth his lordship was one of the noblemen who sate in judgment upon the Duke of Norfolk, and upon *Mary,* QUEEN OF SCOTLAND. He m. Anne, daughter of Sir John Wentworth, Knt., of Gosfield, in the county of Essex, and had issue,

Thomas, who m. Elizabeth, daughter of William, Lord Burghley, but d. without issue in the life-time of his father.

HENRY, his successor.

Elizabeth, m. to William Hynde, Esq., son and heir of Sir Francis Hynde, Knt.

His lordship d. in 1590, and was s. by his son,

HENRY WENTWORTH, third baron, summoned to parliament 19th February, 1593. His lordship m. Anne, daughter of Sir Owen Hopton, Knt., and widow of Sir William Pope, Knt., by whom he had issue,

THOMAS, his successor.

Henry, major-general in the service of King CHARLES I., d. in 1644.

Jane, m. to Sir John Finet, Knt., of West Keele, in the county of Lincoln.

His lordship d. in 1594, and was s. by his elder son,

THOMAS WENTWORTH, fourth baron, who was created, 5th February, 1626, Baron Wentworth, of Nettlested, and EARL OF CLEVELAND. This nobleman was one of the most zealous supporters of the royal cause during the unhappy times of Charles I., and suffered much, including imprisonment in the Tower of London. He had the satisfaction, however, of witnessing the restoration of the monarchy, and headed a body of three hundred noblemen and gentlemen in the triumphal procession of CHARLES II. into London. His lordship m. first, Anne, daughter of Sir John Crofts, of Saxham, in the county of Suffolk, Knt., and had surviving issue,

THOMAS, who was summoned to parliament as Lord Wentworth, of Nettlested. His lordship m. Philadelphia, daughter of Sir Ferdinando Carey, Knt., and dying in his father's life-time left an only daughter,

HENRIETTA WENTWORTH, who succeeded her grandfather in the Barony of Wentworth.

ANNE, m. to John, Lord Lovelace, and succeeded her niece in the Barony of Wentworth.

The earl espoused, secondly, Catherine, daughter of Sir John Wentworth, Knt., of Gosfield Hall, in the county of Essex, and had an only child,

Catherine, who m. William Spencer, Esq., of Cople, in the county of Bedford, and d. issueless.

His lordship d. in 1667, when the EARLDOM OF CLEVELAND became EXTINCT, and the old Barony of Wentworth devolved upon his grand-daughter,

HENRIETTA WENTWORTH, as Baroness Wentworth. This lady resided at Toddington, in the county of Bedford, with the unfortunate Duke of Monmouth, whose attachment to her ladyship continued until his decease. Lady Wentworth survived his grace's execution but a few months, and her remains were interred under a costly monument at Toddington. Her ladyship d. in 1686, when the barony reverted to her aunt (refer to issue of the Earl of Cleveland),

Lady ANNE WENTWORTH, as Baroness Wentworth. This lady (as stated above,) m. John, Lord Lovelace, and had issue,

388

JOHN, who succeeded to the BARONY OF LOVELACE on the death of his father, and dying in the life-time of his mother, left, by his wife Margery, daughter and co-heir of Sir Edmund Pye, Bart., of Bradenham, in the county of Bucks, an only surviving child,

MARTHA LOVELACE, who succeeded her grandmother in the Barony of Wentworth. = Sir Hy Johnson — ?

Anne, d. unmarried.

Margaret, m. to Sir William Noel, Bart., of Kirby-Malory, in the county of Leicester, and had issue,

SIR THOMAS NOEL, Bart., who d. in 1688, s. p., and was s. by his brother,

SIR JOHN NOEL, Bart., who m. Mary, daughter and co-heir of Sir John Cloberry, of Winchester, Knt., and had two sons and a daughter, viz.

1. SIR CLOBERRY NOEL, Bart., who m. Elizabeth, daughter of Thomas Rowney, Esq., of Oxford, and had a son,

SIR EDWARD NOEL, who inherited the BARONY OF WENTWORTH on the decease of Martha Lovelace, LADY WENTWORTH, in 1745.

2. William Noel, one of the judges of the court of Common Pleas, m. Susanna, daughter of Sir Thomas Trollope, Bart., of Casewick, in the county of Lincoln, and had four daughters, his co-heirs, viz.

Susanna-Maria, m. to Thomas Hill, Esq., and was mother of

NOEL HILL, created, in 1784, BARON HILL.

Anne, d. unmarried.

Frances, m. to Bennet, third Earl of Harborough.

Elizabeth.

3. Anne Noel, who wedded Francis Mundy, Esq., of Markeaton, in the county of Derby, M.P. for Leicestershire, and had, with younger children,

WRIGHTSON MUNDY, Esq., of Markeaton, M.P. for Leicestershire ; m. Miss Anne Burdett, and was s. by his son,

FRANCIS NOEL CLARKE MUNDY, Esq., of Markeaton Hall. This gentleman was the author of the Descriptive Poems, Nudwood Forest, and the Fall of Nudwood. At his decease, in 1815, his bust, by Chantry, was placed in the county hall of Derby, by the magistrates of that shire. He was *s.* by his son,

THE PRESENT

FRANCIS MUNDY, Esq., of Markeaton Hall, M.P. for the county of Derby, who *m.* in 1800, Sarah, daughter of John L. Newton, Esq., Mickleover, in Derbyshire, and has issue,

William, *b.* in 1801.
Marian.
Louisa.
Emely.
Constance.

Anne, Lady Wentworth, *d.* in 1697, and was *s.* by her grand-daughter, (the barony being adjudged to her in parliament by descent, and confirmed in 1702,)

MARTHA LOVELACE, as Baroness Wentworth. This lady assisted at the coronation of Queen Anne, and walked in the procession, in her place, as a peeress. She *m.* Sir Henry Johnson, Knt., but *d.* without issue in 1745, when the BARONY OF WENTWORTH became vested in the family of Noel, and her ladyship's cousin, (refer to issue of Margaret, daughter of Lady Anne Wentworth, Baroness Wentworth,)

SIR EDWARD NOEL, Bart., of Kirby Malory, became BARON WENTWORTH. His lordship *m.* Judeth, daughter of William Lamb, Esq., of Farndish, in the county of Northampton, and had issue,

THOMAS, his successor.

Judeth, *m.* to Sir Ralph Milbanke, Bart. This lady and her husband assumed the additional surname of "NOEL" upon the decease of her brother, Thomas, Viscount Wentworth. She *d.* in 1822, leaving an only daughter and heiress, (Sir Ralph *d.* in 1825,)

ANNA-ISABELLA, *b.* 17th May, 1792, *m.* 2nd January, 1815, to the celebrated poet, *George*, LORD BYRON, and has an only child,

ADA BYRON.

Elizabeth, *m.* in 1777, to James-Bland Burges, Esq., (afterwards Sir James Lamb, Bart.,) but died *s. p.* in 1779.

Sophia-Susanna, *m.* in 1777, to Nathaniel, Lord Scarsdale, and dying 1782, left issue,

NATHANIEL CURZON, heir apparent to the Barony of Scarsdale.

William Curzon, killed at Waterloo.

Sophia-Caroline Curzon, *m.* in 1800, to Robert, Viscount Tamworth, who *d.* in 1824, issueless.

His lordship was advanced, by letters patent, dated 4th May, 1762, to the dignity of VISCOUNT WENTWORTH, *of Wellesborough, in the county of Leicester,* and dying in 1774, was *s.* by his son,

THOMAS NOEL, second Viscount Wentworth, and ninth successor to the Barony of Wentworth. His lordship died *s. p.* in 1815, when the VISCOUNTY became EXTINCT, but the BARONY OF WENTWORTH fell into ABEYANCE between his lordship's

sister, JUDETH, *Lady Milbanke*, and his nephew, the *Honourable* NATHANIEL CURZON, as it still continues between Lady Milbanke's only child,

ANNA-ISABELLA, Dowager LADY BYRON,

and

Mr. Curzon.

ARMS of the Wentworths. Sa. a chevron between three leopards' heads or. a crescent for difference.

WESTON—BARONS WESTON, OF NEYLAND, EARLS OF PORTLAND.

Barony, } by Letters { 13th April, 1628.
Earldom, } Patent, { 17th February, 1633.

Lineage.

RICHARD WESTON, one of the judges of the court of Common Pleas, temp. ELIZABETH, was father of

SIR HIEROME WESTON, Knt., of Boxwell, in Essex, whose son,

SIR RICHARD WESTON, Knt., was employed in the reign of JAMES I. as ambassador to Bohemia and subsequently to Brussels, to treat with the ambassadors of the emperor and king of Spain, regarding the restitution of the palatine. Soon after which he was constituted chancellor of the exchequer, and elevated to the peerage, on 13th April, 1628, as BARON WESTON, *of Neyland, in the county of Essex.* His lordship was subsequently made LORD TREASURER OF ENGLAND, invested with the GARTER, and created, 17th February, 1633, EARL OF PORTLAND. He *m.* first, Elizabeth, daughter of William Pincheon, Esq., of Writtle, in the county of Essex, by whom he had issue,

Richard, who *d.* unmarried in the earl's lifetime.

Elizabeth, *m.* to Sir John Netterville, Knt., son and heir of Viscount Netterville.

Mary, *m.* to Sir Walter Aston, Knt., son and heir of Lord Aston.

The earl espoused, secondly, Frances, daughter and co-heir of Nicholas Walgrave, Esq., of Boreley, in Essex, and had four sons and four daughters, viz.,

JEROME, his successor.

THOMAS, who succeeded his nephew as Earl of Portland.

Nicholas, died *s. p.*

Benjamin, who *m.* Elizabeth, daughter of Thomas Sheldon, Esq., of Hawley, in Leicestershire, and widow of Charles Villiers, Earl of Anglesey.

Anne, *m.* to Basil Fielding, son and heir of William, Earl of Denbigh.

Mary-Frances, *m.* to Philip Draycoote, Esq., of Paynsty, in the county of Stafford.

Catherine, *m.* to Richard White, Esq., of Halton, in Essex.

His lordship *d.* in 1634, and was *s.* by his eldest son,

JEROME WESTON, second Earl of Portland, who *m.* Lady Frances Stuart, daughter of Esme, Duke of Lennox, and had CHARLES, with three daughters, Henrietta, Mary, and Frances. His lordship d. 16th May, 1689, and was s. by his son,

CHARLES WESTON, third Earl of Portland. This nobleman, falling in the great naval engagement with the Dutch, 3rd June, 1655, and dying s. p., was s. by his uncle,

THOMAS WESTON, fourth Earl of Portland, who m. Anne, daughter of John, Lord Butler, of Bramfield, and widow of Mounjoy Blodnt, Earl of Newport, but dying without issue about the year 1688, his estates passed to his nieces, (the children of the second earl,) as co-heirs, while the HONOURS became EXTINCT.

ARMS.—Or. an eagle regardant and displayed, sa.

WHARTON—BARONS WHARTON, EARLS WHARTON, MARQUESSES OF MALMESBURY, AND OF WHARTON, DUKE OF WHARTON.

Barony, by Writ of Summons, dated 30th Jan., 1545, 36 Henry VIII.

Earldom,	} by Letters Patent,	{ 24th December, 1706.
Marquisate,		1st January, 1715.
Dukedom,		20th January, 1718.

Lineage.

Of this family, which derived its surname from "a fair lordship" situated upon the river EDEN, and was of great antiquity in the county of Westmorland, was

SIR THOMAS WHARTON, Knt., governor of the town and castle of Carlisle, who, in the 34th of HENRY VIII., assisted by Sir William Musgrave, at the head of only three hundred men, gallantly resisted an incursion of the Scots, put them to the rout, and made prisoners of the Earls of Cassilis and Glencairn, with several other personages of note. In two years after he marched into Scotland with the Lord Dacre, and had at the taking of Dumfries; for which, and other eminent services, he was summoned to parliament as BARON WHARTON, on the 30th January, 1545. In the 1st of PHILIP AND MARY, his lordship was constituted warden of the middle marches, and the next year he was made general warden of all the marches towards Scotland, and governor of Berwick. His lordship m. first, Eleanor, daughter of Bryan Stapleton, Esq., of Wighill, in the county of York, and had issue,

THOMAS, his successor.

Henry.

Joane, m. to William Penington, Esq., of Moncaster, in the county of Cumberland.

Anne, m. to Sir Richard Musgrave, Knt., of Harcla Castle, in Westmorland.

He wedded, secondly, Lady Anne Talbot, daughter of George, Earl of Shrewsbury, but had no other children. He d. in 1568, and was s. by his elder son,

THOMAS WHARTON, second baron, summoned to parliament from 2d April, 1571, to 6th

May, in the next year. His lordship espoused Lady Anne Devereux, daughter of Robert, Earl of Essex, and had issue,

PHILIP, his successor.

Mary, m. to —— Gower, Esq., of Stittenham, in Yorkshire.

Anne, m. to William Woolrich, Esq., of Sussex.

His lordship d. in 1572, and was s. by his son, then seventeen years of age,

PHILIP WHARTON, third baron, summoned to parliament, from 6th January, 1581, to 17th May, 1625. This nobleman m. Lady Frances Clifford, daughter of Henry, Earl of Cumberland, and had issue,

George (Sir), who m. Lady Anne Manners, daughter of John, Earl of Rutland. Sir George Wharton fell in a duel with his friend, Sir James Stuart, son of Lord Blantyr. In this unfortunate conflict both combatants were slain, and both interred in one grave at Islington, by the king's command, 10th November, 1609. Sir George d. without issue.

Thomas (Sir), m. Lady Philadelphia Carey, daughter of Robert, Earl of Monmouth, and dying before his father, left two sons,

PHILIP, successor to his grandfather.

Thomas.

Margaret, m. to Edward Wotton, Baron Wotton, of Maherley, in Kent.

Eleanor, m. to William Thwaytes, Esq., of Long Marston, in the county of York.

Frances, m. to Sir Richard Musgrave, K.B. and Baronet, of Edenhall, in Cumberland, ancestor of the present Sir Christopher Musgrave, Bart.

His lordship d. in 1625, and was s. by his grandson,

PHILIP WHARTON, fourth baron, summoned to parliament from 3d November, 1639, to 19th May, 1685. This nobleman, who attained majority in 1634, m. first, Elizabeth, daughter of Sir Rowland Wandesford, Knt., of Pickhay, in the county of York, and had an only daughter,

Elizabeth, who m. Robert Bertie, then Lord Willoughby de Eresby, afterwards third Earl of Lindsey, and is now represented by Peter-Robert Drummond-Burrell, LORD WILLOUGHBY DE ERESBY, son and heir of

Lady Priscilla Bertie, Lady Willoughby de Eresby, daughter of Peregrine, third Duke of Ancaster.

Georgiana - Charlotte, widow of George James, first Marquess of Cholmondeley, and second daughter of Peregrine, third Duke of Ancaster.

His lordship espoused, secondly, Jane, daughter of Arthur Goodwin, Esq., of Upper Winchendon, in the county of Bucks, and had two sons and four daughters, viz.

1. THOMAS, his successor.

2. Goodwin.

1. Anne, m. to William, only son of William Carr, Groom of the Bed-chamber to King James I.

2. Margaret, m. to Major Dunch, of Pusey, in Berkshire.

3. Mary, m. first, to William, son and heir of Edmund Thomas, Esq., of Wennoe, in the county of Glamorgan; and secondly, to Sir Charles Kemeys, Bart., of Kevanmably, in the same shire, M.P. for the county. Her ladyship's eldest daughter by her second husband,

    JANE KEMEYS, espoused Sir John Tynte, Bart., M.P. for Bridgwater, and was mother of

      SIR HALSEWELLE TYNTE, third baronet, who d. in 1730, s. p.

      SIR JOHN TYNTE, fourth baronet, in holy orders, d. unmarried in 1740.

      SIR CHARLES KEMEYS - TYNTE, fourth baronet, who, on the decease of his uncle, Sir Charles Kemeys, Bart., s. p., became representative of that ancient family, and inherited its great estates. Sir Charles Tynte represented the county of Somerset in parliament. He d. without issue, when the baronetcy expired, and his estates devolved upon his only sister's daughter, as under,

      JANE TYNTE, m. to Major Hassel, and left a daughter,

        JANE HASSEL, who inherited the estates of the Kemeys and Tynte families upon the death of her uncle, Sir Charles Kemeys Tynte. She m. Colonel Johnstone, of the Foot Guards, Groom of the Bed-chamber to *George*, PRINCE of Wales, afterwards GEORGE IV., who assumed, by sign manual, the surnames of KEMEYS-TYNTE. Colonel Tynte d. in 1807, and was s. by his only son, the *present*

        CHARLES KEMEYS KE-MEYS TYNTE, Esq., M.P. for Bridgwater, colonel of the Somerset Cavalry, who m. Anne, relict of Thomas Lewis, Esq., of St. Pierre, in the county of Monmouth, and had issue,

          1. CHARLES - JOHN, b. in 1800, m. Elizabeth, third daughter of Thomas Swinnerton, Esq., and has issue.

          2. Anne, m. to William Henry Cooper, Esq., only son of the Rev. Sir Wil-

liam Grey Cooper, Bart.

3. Jane.

4. Louisa.

5. Henrietta.

6. Anne.

4. Philadelphia, m. first, to Sir George Lockhart, Knt., of Carnwath, and secondly, to Captain John Ramsay.

Lord Wharton wedded, thirdly, Philadelphia, daughter of William Carr, already mentioned as groom of the bed-chamber to *King* JAMES I., and widow of Edward Popham, Esq., by whom he had a son, William, who d. unmarried. His lordship, who was a violent puritan, and an active parliamentary partisan, temp. Charles I., d. in 1695, and was s. by his eldest son,

THOMAS WHARTON, fifth baron. This nobleman, who was esteemed a profound and eloquent statesman, having devoted himself sealously to accomplish the revolution, was created by *Queen* ANNE, by letters patent, dated 24th December, 1706, *Viscount Winchenden*, in the county of Bucks, and EARL WHARTON, in Westmorland. His lordship was advanced, in 1715, to the dignities of MARQUESS OF MALMESBURY, in Wiltshire, and MARQUESS OF WHARTON; and he was at the same time made a peer of Ireland, as Baron Trim, Earl of Rathfarnham, and Marquess of Catherlogh. His lordship m. first, Anne, one of the two daughters and co-heirs of Sir Henry Lee, of Ditchley, in the county of Oxford, but by that lady had no issue. He espoused, secondly, Lucy, daughter of Adam Loftus, Lord Lisburn, in Ireland, and had,

    PHILIP, his successor.

    Jane, } both died s. p.
    Lucy, }

The marquess d. in 1715, and was s. by his only son,

PHILIP WHARTON, sixth baron, and second marquess, who was created DUKE OF WHARTON on the 20th January, 1718. Of this, the eccentric, witty, and gifted Lord Wharton, Walpole thus speaks: "With attachment to no party, though with talents to govern any, this lively man changed the free air of Westminster for the gloom of the escurial; the prospect of King George's garter for the Pretender's; and with indifference to all religion, the frolic lord, who had written the ballad on the Archbishop of Canterbury, died in the habit of a capuchin." After he had received a dukedom from GEORGE I. he became a strenuous opponent of the king's government, eventually espoused the tenets of the ancient church, and adopted the cause of the banished dynasty. In parliament his grace attained the reputation of an able and eloquent speaker; and his speeches against the ministers were delivered with much effect: in the instance of the South Sea affair Lord Stanhope was so excited by one of those tirades, that, in replying with extreme warmth, he burst a blood-vessel and died. Upon the bill of Pains and Penalties against Bishop Atterbury, his grace is accused of having deceived the minister by pretending to take part against the bishop, and having thus extorted from him, immediately prior to the third reading of the bill, the whole of his argument, came down to the House of Lords the next day, after a night of debauch without going to bed, and made one of the most masterly speeches in favour of the prelate, anticipating and answering all the arguments which could be adduced against him. His grace subsequently retired into Spain, openly adopted the colours of the chevalier, was a volunteer in the Spanish army before Gibraltar in 1727, and was attainted by parliament in the following year. The duke m. first, Miss Holmes, daughter of *Major General* HOLMES, and secondly, Miss O'Biern, maid of honour to the Queen of Spain, and daughter of Colonel O'Biern, an Irish officer, in the Spanish service, but had no issue. He retired at last into a Spanish monastery, and died there in 1731, when ALL HIS HONOURS, save the BARONY OF WHARTON, independently of the attainder, became EXTINCT; but were that act repealed the BARONY would then be vested in the present Marchioness Dowager Cholmondeley, Lord Willoughby de Eresby, and Charles Kemeys-Tynte, Esq., M.P., of Halswell House, in Somersetshire (refer to issue of the fourth baron).

ARMS.—Sa. a manch ar. within a border, or. an orle of lions gambs erased in saltier, gu. The border, &c., being an augmentation granted by Edward VI.

WIDDRINGTON — BARONS WIDDRINGTON.

By Letters Patent, dated 10th November, 1643.

Lineage.

SIR WILLIAM WIDDRINGTON, Bart., descended from a very ancient Northumbrian family, having raised a considerable force for the royal cause, and participated in the victories of the Duke of Newcastle, under whom he fought, was elevated to the peerage by *King* CHARLES I., by letters patent, dated 10th November, 1643, as BARON WIDDRINGTON, *of Blankney, in the county of Lincoln*. His lordship eventually fell, in the fight at Wigan Lane, when the Earl of Derby was defeated by Colonel Liburne, in August, 1651. Of this nobleman, Lord Clarendon observes, that "he was one of the most goodly persons of that age, being near the head higher than most tall men, of a very fair fortune; and one of the four of which King Charles made choice to be about the person of the prince, his son, as gentleman of the privy chamber. He was a man of great courage, but of some passion; by which he incurred the ill-will of many, who imputed it to an insolence of nature, which no one was further from in reality." His lordship m. Mary, daughter and sole heir of Anthony Thorold, Knt., of Blankney, in the county of Lincoln, and had surviving issue,

WILLIAM, his successor.

Edward, Captain of Dragoons, who fell at the battle of the Boyne. He m. Miss Horsley, daughter and co-heir of Sir John Horsley, Knt., and had issue,

Edward-Horsley (Sir), of Horsley, in Northumberland.

Theresa, m. to Sir William Wheeler, Bart., and was great great-grand-mother of the present SIR TREVOR WHEELER.

Ralph was engaged in the Dutch war, and lost his eyes therein.

Anthony, d. unmarried.

Roger, fell at the siege of Maestricht.

Mary, m. to Francis Crane, Esq., of Woodrising, in Norfolk.

Jane, m. to Sir Charles Stanley, K.B., grandson (through one of his younger sons) of William, Earl of Derby.

His lordship was s. by his eldest son,

WILLIAM WIDDRINGTON, second baron. This nobleman m. Elizabeth, daughter of Sir Peregrine Bertie, Knt., of Evedon, in the county of Lincoln, and grand-daughter of Robert, Earl of Lindsey, by whom he had four sons, WILLIAM, his successor, Henry, Roger, and Edward; and six daughters, viz.

Mary,
Elizabeth, } these ladies were all NUNS.
Dorothy, }

Anne, m. in 1689, to John Clavering, Esq., of Callaly, in the county of Northumberland, (a descendant of the Barons Clavering, see CLAVERING,) and of this marriage the present Edward Clavering, Esq., of Callaly, is the representative.

Catherine, m. to —— Southcote, Esq.

His lordship d. in 1676, and was s. by his eldest son,

WILLIAM WIDDRINGTON, third baron, who espoused Alathea, daughter and heir of Charles, Viscount Fairfax, and had issue, WILLIAM, his successor, Charles, and Peregrine, with two daughters, viz.

Mary.

Elizabeth, m. Marmaduke, fourth Lord Langdale.

His lordship d. in 1695, and was s. by his eldest son,

WILLIAM WIDDRINGTON, fourth baron. This nobleman, with his brothers, engaging in the rebellion of 1715, for the restoration of the Stuarts, they were all three made prisoners at Preston; and subsequently tried and convicted of high treason, 7th July, 1716. But in the next year, his lordship, with the Messrs. Widdrington, and several more, received a royal pardon, while his HONOURS became forfeited under the ATTAINDER. He m. first, Jane, daughter of Sir Thomas Tempest, of Stella, in the bishopric of Durham, and secondly, Mrs. Graham. He d. in 1743, leaving a son, Henry Widdrington, Esq., and two daughters, Alathea and Anne.

ARMS.—Quarterly, ar. and gu. a bend. sa.

WIDVILE OR WYDEVILE—BARONS RIVERS, EARLS RIVERS.

Barony, } by Letters { 29th May, 1448.
Earldom, } Patent,   { 24th May, 1466.

Lineage.

In the 37th of Edward III.,

RICHARD DE WYDVILL was constituted sheriff of Northamptonshire, and governor of the castle there; and again in two years after. In the 43d of the same reign, he was made escheator for the counties of Northampton and Rutland; and the year ensuing he was once more sheriff of North-amptonshire, and governor of Northampton Castle. To this Richard, succeeded

JOHN DE WYDEVILE, who, in the time of RICHARD II., filled the same offices in the counties of Northampton and Rutland. He was *s.* by

RICHARD DE WYDEVILE, who, in the 7th of HENRY IV., was likewise sheriff of Northamptonshire, and governor of its castle. In the 8th of HENRY V., being then one of the esquires of the body to that heroic prince, he was constituted seneschal of the Duchy of Normandy, and of the other parts of France under the dominion of the English monarch. In the 3d of Henry VI., he was governor of the Tower of London, and the next year he received the honour of knighthood from the king at Leicester. Soon after this, we find him lieutenant of Calais, under the Duke of Bedford, and residing there. From that period for several succeeding years, Sir Richard Wydevile was constantly engaged in the wars of France. In the interval he married, without licence, Jacqueline of Luxemburgh, daughter of Peter, Earl of St. Paul, and widow of his late commander, the king's uncle, John, Duke of Bedford; for which transgression, and for the livery of the castles, manors, and lands, constituting her grace's dower, he paid a fine of a thousand pounds. He served afterwards under Richard, Duke of York, and was elevated to the peerage, by letters patent, dated 29th May, 1448, as BARON RIVERS. His lordship was further rewarded by grants from the crown, amongst which was the manor of Westhall, in the county of Essex. He was made likewise a Knight of the Garter, and appointed seneschal of Acquitaine. In the contest between the Houses of York and Lancaster, Lord Rivers was a staunch supporter of the latter, until his daughter became QUEEN CONSORT of EDWARD IV., and then of course he veered to the new order of affairs. His Lancastrian predilections were forgotten by his royal son-in-law, and he was raised to high honours, and entrusted with high offices. His lordship was first made treasurer of the exchequer, and afterwards CONSTABLE OF ENGLAND, for life, with remainder to his son, Anthony, Lord Scales, also for life. He was likewise advanced in the peerage to the dignity of EARL RIVERS, by letters patent, dated 24th May, 1466; but the next year he was taken out of his manor-house of Grafton, by Robin of Ridsdale, at the head of the revolted Lancastrians, and carried to Northampton, where his head was cut off. STOW gives a different version of the manner of his lordship's death. He states that being defeated in a battle by Robin of Ridsdale, near Banbury, the earl flying from the field, was made prisoner in the forest of Dene, and conveyed to Northampton, where he was beheaded by order of the Duke of Clarence, and the Earl of Warwick, then in hostility to King EDWARD. By the Duchess Dowager of Bedford, his lordship had issue,

ANTHONY, his successor, who *m.* ELIZABETH, widow of Henry Bourchier, and only daugh-

ter and heiress of Thomas, Lord Scales, in whose right he was summoned to parliament as BARON SCALES, from 23d December, 1462, to the 23d of the ensuing February.

John, put to death with his father.

Lionel, Bishop of Salisbury.

Edward.

RICHARD, who succeeded his eldest brother in the honours of the family.

ELIZABETH, *m.* first, Sir John Grey, Lord Grey, of Groby, by whom she had issue,

    SIR THOMAS GREY, created MARQUESS OF DORSET.

    Sir Richard Grey, beheaded in the 1st year of Richard III.

Lord Grey fell in the second battle of St. Albans, fighting under the Lancastrian banner, and her ladyship espoused, secondly, *King* EDWARD IV., by whom she was mother of

EDWARD, Prince of Wales.	The unhappy children, supposed to have been murdered in the Tower, by the command of Richard III.
RICHARD, Duke of York.	

Elizabeth, *m.* to *King* HENRY VII.

Cecily, *m.* first, to John, Viscount Welles, and secondly, to Sir John Kyme.

Anne, *m.* to Thomas Howard, Duke of Norfolk.

Katherine, *m.* to William Courtenay, Earl of Devon.

Margaret, *m.* to Thomas Fitz-Alan, Earl of Arundel.

Anne, *m.* first, to William, Lord Bourchier, eldest son of Henry, Earl of Essex, secondly, to George Grey, Earl of Kent, and thirdly, to Sir Anthony Wingfield, Knt.

Jacquet, *m.* to John, Lord Strange, of Knokyn.

Mary, *m.* to William Herbert, Earl of Huntingdon.

Katherine, *m.* first, to Henry Stafford, Duke of Buckingham; secondly, to Jasper Tudor, Duke of Bedford; and thirdly, to Sir Richard Wingfield, K.G.

————, *m.* to Sir John Bromley, Knt., son of the renowned Sir John Bromley, who recovered the standard of Guyen, in the memorable battle of Corby, against the French.

The melancholy death of Lord Rivers occurred in 1469, and he was *s.* by his eldest son,

ANTHONY WIDVILE, Lord Scales, as second Earl Rivers. This nobleman, when Lord Scales, in the beginning of the reign of EDWARD IV., marched with the king into the north against the Lancastrians, and was one of the principal commanders at the siege of Alnwick Castle. He was soon afterwards made a Knight of the Garter, and he obtained a grant in tail of the Isle of Wight; his lordship about this period acquired great fame in a tournament at London, wherein he contested successfully with ANTHONY, the *Bastard of Burgundy,* brother of Charles, Duke of Burgundy. Dugdale thus details the combat: " Upon Thursday next after

Corpus Christi-day, the king being present, they ran together with sharp spears; and parted with equal honour. Likewise, the next day on horseback; at which time this Lord Scales's horse having a long sharp pike of steel on his chaffron, upon their coping together, it ran into the nose of the bastard's horse. Which making him to mount, he fell on his side, with his rider. Whereupon the Lord Scales rode about him, with his sword drawn, till the king commanded the marshal to help him up: no more being done that day. But the next day coming into the lists on foot, with pole axes, they fought valiantly, till the point of this lord's weapon entered the sight of the bastard's helm. Which being discerned by the king, he cast down his warder, to the end the marshal should sever them. Hereupon the bastard requiring, that he might go on, in the performance of his enterprise, and consultation being had with the Duke of Clarence, then constable, and the Duke of Norfolk, marshal, whether it might be allowed or not, they determined that if so, then by the law of arms, the bastard ought to be delivered to his adversary, in the same condition as he stood, when the king caused them to be severed, which, when the bastard understood, he relinquished his further challenge." During the temporary restoration of HENRY VI. Lord Scales fled with his brother-in-law, *King* EDWARD, into Holland, and returned with him before the close of the year, bearing the title of EARL RIVERS, his father and brother having been put to death in the interval. After the re-establishment of the power of Edward, his lordship was constituted governor of the town and castle of Calais, of the tower of Rysebank; as also of the castle of Guysnes, and the marches adjacent for seven years. He was likewise appointed captain general of the king's army, and of all his forces, both by sea and land. In the 13th Edward IV., upon the creation of *Prince* EDWARD to be Prince of Wales, and Earl of Chester, Lord Rivers, being made governor to him, obtained the office of chief butler of England. The fate of this accomplished and gallant nobleman, after the decease of EDWARD IV., marks the commencement of an era in our history. He was one of the first victims to the ambition of the *Crook-Backed* RICHARD; an ambition which not long after closed the dynasty of the PLANTAGENETS. His lordship, with his nephew, Sir Richard Grey, was treacherously seised by the Duke of Gloucester and his partisans, at Northampton, and some time afterwards beheaded in front of Pontefract Castle, where he had been confined, by order of the governor, Sir Richard Ratcliffe, without any form of trial, or being allowed to speak one word in his own vindication. Walpole assigns Lord Rivers a place in his noble authors, and observes " that though Caxton knew ' *none like to the Erle of Worcester*,' and thought that all learning in the nobility perished with Tiptoft, yet there flourished about the same period, a noble person, (Anthony, Earl Rivers,) by no means inferior to him in learning and politeness; in birth his equal, by alliance his superior, greater in feats of arms, and in pilgrimages more abundant." After the decease of his first wife, the HEIRESS OF SCALES, his lordship espoused, Mary, daughter and heir of Henry Fits-

Lewis, but had no legitimate issue.[*] His unhappy decease took place in 1483, when he was a. in all his honours, but the Barony of Scales, by his only surviving brother,

RICHARD WIDVILE, third Earl Rivers. This nobleman *d.* unmarried in 1491. By his testament bearing date, 20th February, 1490, his lordship directed his body to be buried in the Abbey of St. James's, in Northampton. He bequeathed to the parish church of Grafton all such cattle as he then had at Grafton, viz. two oxen, five kine, and two bullocks, to the intent that they should yearly keep an obit for his soul, and he appointed his nephew, Thomas, Marquess of Dorset, his heir, to whom he devised all his lands whatsoever; desiring that there might be as much underwood sold, in the woods of Grafton, as would purchase a bell, to be a tenor to the bells already there, for a remembrance of the last of his blood. Upon the decease of his lordship the BARONY AND EARLDOM OF RIVERS became EXTINCT.

ARMS.—Ar. a fesse, and canton gules.

WILINTON—BARONS WILINTON.

By Writ of Summons, dated 14th June, 1329,
3 Edward III.

Lineage.

In the 8th of HENRY III.

RALPH DE WILINTON was made governor of Bristol Castle, and had a grant of the wardenship of the forest, with that of the chase at Rainsham. In the 17th of the same reign he was governor of Devizes Castle, in Wiltshire, and in the 38th he was sheriff of Devonshire, and governor of the castle at Exeter. After this we find him in the ranks of the rebellious barons. He was *s.* by his son,

JOHN DE WILINTON, who, in the reign of EDWARD I., had several grants from the crown, but in that of Edward II., being involved in the Earl of Lancaster's insurrection, all his lands were seised by the crown. They were restored, however, by *King* EDWARD III., and by that monarch he was summoned to parliament as a BARON, from 14th June, 1329, to 15th November, 1338. His lordship was *s.* by his son,

SIR RALPH DE WILINTON, second baron, summoned to parliament on the 25th February, 1342, but never afterwards. This nobleman was in the wars of Scotland and France, and attained the high military rank of banneret. He *d.* without issue in 1348, when his uncle, REGINALD DE WYLINTON, became his heir; but of the family nothing further is known.

ARMS.—Gules a saltire varlée ar. and az.

WILLIAMS — BARON WILLIAMS, OF THAME.

By Writ of Summons, dated 2nd April, 1554,
1 Philip and Mary.

Lineage.

This nobleman descended from a common pro-

---

* The earl had an illegitimate daughter, Margaret, *m.* to Sir Robert Poynes, Knt.

genitor with the Sir Robert Williams, Knt., who assumed the name of CROMWELL, and was ancestor of the PROTECTOR.

The first person of this branch of the family, JOHN WILLIAMS, second son of Sir John Williams, of Burfield, in Berkshire, (by his wife, Elizabeth, daughter and co-heir of Richard More, Esq., of Burfield,) was a servant to *King* HENRY VIII., and had in the 18th of that monarch £10 per annum, granted to him, by patent, for the keeping of a greyhound. In some years afterwards he was clerk of the king's jewel office; and had interest enough to procure a patent for the office of master or treasurer of the same office. This, however, he was obliged to surrender, and to accept of a new patent jointly with Thomas Cromwell, then secretary of state. Having by these lucrative employments amassed considerable wealth, he purchased, in the 30th HENRY VIII., from Giles Heron, Esq., of Shakewell, in the county of Middlesex, the manors of Great and Little Ricott, in Oxfordshire. In the next year, being then a knight, he had a grant from the crown of the chief stewardship of the manors of Grafton and Hertwell, in the county of Northampton, with the keepership of the parks there: as also of the manors of Wytham, Weston on the Green, and Botley. And he was soon after constituted chief supervisor of all the swans within the river Thames, and all other waters in England, excepting those of the Duchy of Lancaster. Moreover, about this time he had a special patent for retaining ten persons, gentlemen and yeomen, in his household, and to give livery badges to them; and he had another grant of the office of treasurer of the court of augmentation. Upon the demise of EDWARD VI., Sir John Williams was one of the first who appeared in behalf of *Queen* MARY, and upon the accession of her majesty to the crown, was solemnly created LORD WILLIAMS, *of Thame*, at the palace of St. James's. He was summoned the next year in that dignity to parliament, but no patent of creation was ever enrolled. After which, upon surrendering his office of treasurer of the court of augmentations, he had in lieu thereof a grant of £390 per annum from the crown: and was constituted, on the marriage of the queen, lord chamberlain of the household to *King* PHILIP. Nor did his lordship enjoy less favour from *Queen* ELIZABETH, being, in the first year of her majesty's reign, appointed lord president of Wales. He subsequently resided as lord president in the castle of Ludlow. His lordship m. first, Elizabeth, widow of Andrew Edmonds, of Gressing Temple, in Essex, and daughter and co-heir of Thomas Bledlow, Esq. (son and heir of Thomas Bledlow, sheriff of the city of London, in 1472,) by whom he had issue,

> Henry, who m. Anne, daughter of Henry, Lord Stafford, and died issueless before his father.
> Francis, also predeceased his father, *s. p.*
> Isabel, m. to Sir Richard Wenman, Knt.
> Margery, m. to Sir Henry Norris, Knt., to whom she conveyed the manor of Ricott, or Rycote, in Oxfordshire, and Sir Henry was summoned to parliament from 8th May,

1572, to 24th October, 1597, as BARON NORRIS, *of Rycote*: their grandson,
> FRANCIS NORRIS, Lord Norris, of Rycote, was created, in 1620, Viscount Thame, and Earl of Berkshire.

He m. secondly, Margery, daughter of Thomas, Lord Wentworth, but had no issue. His lordship died in 1559, when his estates devolved upon his daughters, as co-heirs, and the BARONY OF WILLIAMS, *of Thame*, fell into ABEYANCE, between the same ladies, as it still continues with their representatives. Of Margery, the younger sister, the Earl of Abingdon is now heir general.

ARMS.—Ar. an organ pipe in bend sinister Saltierwise, surmounted of another dexter, between two crosses patée, ar.

WILLOUGHBY — BARONS WILLOUGHBY, OF PARHAM.

By Letters Patent, dated 16th February, 1547.

Lineage.

The family of Willoughby, by a pedigree drawn up in the time of ELIZABETH, appears to be descended from SIR JOHN DE WILLOUGHBY, a Norman knight, who had the lordship of Willoughby, in Lincolnshire, by gift of the CONQUEROR. From this successful soldier we pass to

SIR WILLIAM DE WILLOUGHBY, who, in the 54th of HENRY III., was signed with the cross, and accompanied *Prince* EDWARD into the Holy Land. He m. Alice, daughter of John, Lord Beke, of Eresby, and eldest co-heir of her brother Walter, Lord of Eresby, and had issue,

> ROBERT (Sir), his successor.
> Thomas, m. Margaret, sister and co-heir of Alun de Munby, and had a son, who, assuming the surname of his mother, became
>> William Munby. He died *s. p.*, and his estates were divided amongst his sisters.
> Margaret, m. to Walter, son of Sir Walter Hamby, Knt.

Sir William was *s.* by his elder son,

SIR ROBERT DE WILLOUGHBY, who inherited, in the 4th Edward II., as next heir, the estates of Anthony Bec, Bishop of Durham, and was summoned to parliament in three years afterwards as BARON WILLOUGHBY DE ERESBY. From this nobleman we pass to his great-great-grandson and lineal descendant,

WILLIAM WILLOUGHBY, fifth Baron Willoughby de Eresby, who m. first, Lucy, daughter of Roger, Lord Strange, of Knokyn, and had issue,

> ROBERT, his successor, and sixth Baron WILLOUGHBY DE ERESBY.
> Thomas (Sir), of whose descendants we are about to treat.

His lordship m. secondly, Joane, widow of Edward Plantagenet, Duke of York, and daughter of Thomas Holland, second Earl of Kent. He d. in 1409, and was succeeded in his title by his elder son, ROBERT; but we proceed with the younger,

WIL   WIL

SIR THOMAS WILLOUGHBY, of Parham, in the county of Suffolk; a gallant soldier, and one of the heroes of AGINCOURT. He m. Joane, daughter and heir of Sir Richard Fitz-Alan, Knt., (son of John Fitz-Alan, Lord Maltravers, second son of Sir Richard Fitz-Alan, third Earl of Arundel,) and was s. by his son,

SIR ROBERT WILLOUGHBY, who m. Cecilia, daughter of Leo, Lord Welles, and had issue,

ROBERT, } both knights.
Christopher, }

Margaret, m. to Thomas Skipwith, Esq., of Lincolnshire.

Sir Robert d. 30th May, 1465, and was s. by his elder son,

SIR ROBERT WILLOUGHBY, who died in minority, and was s. by his brother,

SIR CHRISTOPHER WILLOUGHBY, who was made a Knight of the Bath, 6th July, 1483, at the coronation of RICHARD III. In the next reign he raised forces to assist the king against the Earl of Lincoln, Lambert Simnel, and their adherents, and was afterwards at the battle of STOKE. He m. Margaret, daughter of Sir William Jenney, of Knotshall, in Suffolk, and had issue,

WILLIAM, who inherited the BARONY OF WILLOUGHBY de Eresby at the decease of JOANE WELLES in 1506, after the dignity had been out of the Willoughby family for half a century. His lordship became possessed also of the manors of Grimsby and Grimesthorp, with the greater part of the estates of the Lords Welles.

CHRISTOPHER, of whom presently.

George.

Thomas, from whom the extant WILLOUGHBYS, Lords Middleton, derive.

John,

Dorothy.

Catherine, m. to Sir John Heydon, Knt., of Baconsthorp, in the county of Norfolk.

Elizabeth, m. to William, Lord Eure.

The second son,

SIR CHRISTOPHER WILLOUGHBY, received the honour of knighthood for his valiant conduct at the siege of Tournay, temp. Henry VIII. He m. Elizabeth, daughter of Sir George Talboys, and sister of Gilbert, Lord Talboys, of Kyme, by whom he had issue,

WILLIAM, his successor.

Dorothy, m. to Ralph Hopton, Esq., of Wytham, in the county of Somerset.

Elizabeth, m. to Sir John Breuse, of Wenham, in Suffolk.

Anne, m. to Robert Hall, Esq., of Gretford, in Lincoln.

Sir Christopher was s. by his eldest son,

SIR WILLIAM WILLOUGHBY, Knt., who was elevated to the peerage, by letters patent, dated 16th February, 1547, in the dignity of LORD WILLOUGHBY, of Parham. His lordship having distinguished himself in the wars of HENRY VIII., was made lieutenant of Calais, and the adjacent marches, in the 4th of EDWARD VI., and he resided there during the remainder of that king's reign. He m. first, Elizabeth, daughter and heir of Sir Thomas

576

Heneage, Knt., by whom he acquired considerable estates, and had issue,

CHARLES, his successor.

Mary, m. to William Metham, Esq., of Bolington, in the county of Lincoln.

He wedded, secondly, Margaret, daughter of Robert Garnish, Esq., of Kenton, in Suffolk, and widow of Walter, first Viscount Hereford. His lordship d. in 1574, and was s. by his son,

CHARLES WILLOUGHBY, second Baron Willoughby, of Parham, who espoused Lady Margaret Clinton, daughter of Edward, first Earl of Lincoln, and had issue,

1. WILLIAM, who m. Elizabeth, daughter and heir of Sir Christopher Hilliard, Knt., of Wynstead, in Yorkshire, and, dying before his father, left, with other issue,

WILLIAM, successor to his grandfather.

Elizabeth, m. to Sir William Hickman, of Gainsborough, in Lincolnshire.

Catherine, m. to Joseph Godfrey, Esq., of Thorock, in the same shire.

Mary, m. to Sir William Booth, of Killingholm, also in Lincolnshire.

2. Ambrose (Sir), of Matson, in the county of Gloucester, m. Susan, daughter of —— Brooke, and left an only son,

EDWARD, who m. Rebecca, daughter of Henry Draper, Esq., and had surviving issue,

HENRY, who emigrated to Virginia, and died there in 1685, leaving

HENRY, who m. Elizabeth, daughter of William Pidgeon, Esq., of Stepney, in the county of Middlesex, and had, with other issue, 16 ℓ

HENRY, who s. as fifteenth lord.

William, who m. ——, daughter of —— Knockton, and left a son,

William, who died s. p.

FORTUNE, who m. Hannah, daughter of Thomas Barrow, and widow of Cook Pollet, Esq., of Swanscomb, in Kent, and left a son,

GEORGE, who s. as sixteenth BARON.

Richard, whose line ceased with his sons,

Sarah, m. to —— Birt.

Rebecca, m. to Richard Hull.

3. Edward, m. Elizabeth, daughter of Francis Manby, Esq., of Elsham, and widow of John Prescot, and had a son,

Edward, who d. young.

4. Charles, died s. p.

5. Thomas (Sir), m. Mary, daughter of —— Thorney, Esq., and had issue,

THOMAS, who succeeded as ELEVENTH LORD, under the supposition that the line of Sir Ambrose was extinct.

William, in holy orders in the church of Rome.

Mary, m. first, to Augustine Wingfield, and secondly, to —— Saul.

6. Catherine, m. to Sir John Savile, of Howley, in the county of York.

7. Margaret, m. to —— Erle, Esq., of Corpeey.

8. Anne, m. to Sir William Pelham, Knt., of Brokelsby, in Lincolnshire.

Charles, second Lord Willoughby, d. in 1603, and was s. by his grandson,

WILLIAM WILLOUGHBY, third Lord Willoughby, of Parham. This nobleman m. Lady Frances Manners, daughter of John, fourth Earl of Rutland, and had issue,

> HENRY,
> FRANCIS, } successively Lords Willoughby.
> WILLIAM,
>
> Frances, m. to Sir Bulstrode Whitlock, Knt., of Chilton, in the county of Wilts.
> Elizabeth, d. unmarried.

His lordship d. in 1617, and was s. by his eldest son,

HENRY WILLOUGHBY, fourth lord, at whose decease, in infancy, the title devolved upon his brother,

FRANCIS WILLOUGHBY, fifth lord, who m. Elizabeth, second daughter and co-heir of Edward Cecil, Viscount Wimbledon, and had surviving issue,

> Diana, m. to Heneage, second Earl of Winchelsea.
> Frances, m. to William, Lord Brereton, of the kingdom of Ireland.
> Elizabeth, m. to Roger Jones, Viscount Ranelagh.

This nobleman was drowned at Barbadoes, in 1666, and was s. by his brother,

WILLIAM WILLOUGHBY, sixth Baron Willoughby, of Parham. His lordship was governor of the Caribbee Islands, and d. at Barbadoes 10th April, 1673. He m. Anne, daughter of Sir Philip Carey, Knt., of Stanwell, in the county of Middlesex, and had, with other issue,

> GEORGE, his successor.
> JOHN, } who became successively Lords
> CHARLES, } Willoughby.
> Frances, m. first, to Sir John Harpur, Knt., of Swarkeston, in the county of Derby; secondly, to Charles Henry Kirkhoven, Baron Wotton, in England, and Earl of Bellamont, in Ireland; and thirdly, to Henry Heveningham, Esq., of Heveningham, in Suffolk.
> Anne, m. to Sir John Harpur, Bart., of Calke, in the county of Derby.
> Catherine, m. to Charles Cockain, third Viscount Cullen, in Ireland.

Lord Willoughby was s. by his eldest son,

GEORGE WILLOUGHBY, seventh baron, who m. Elizabeth, daughter and co-heir of Henry Fiennes, otherwise Clinton, Esq., by whom he had issue,

> JOHN, his successor.
> Anne, d. young.
> Elizabeth, m. to the Hon. James Bertie, second son of James, first Earl of Abingdon, and

was mother of Willoughby, third Earl of Abingdon.

His lordship d. in 1674, and was s. by his son,

JOHN WILLOUGHBY, eighth baron, who d. in 1678 unmarried, when the barony reverted to his uncle,

JOHN WILLOUGHBY, ninth baron. This nobleman died s. p. in 1678, and was s. by his brother,

CHARLES WILLOUGHBY, tenth baron, who m. Mary, daughter of Sir Beaumont Dixie, Bart., of Bosworth, in the county of Leicester, but died without issue in 1679, devising his estate to his niece, Elizabeth, wife of the Hon. James Bertie. Upon the decease of his lordship, the BARONY, by right, should have devolved upon the descendant of Sir Ambrose Willoughby, second son of Charles, the second lord; but that gentleman's grandson, Henry Willoughby, having emigrated to America, the second branch remained in ignorance of the failure of the elder, and putting in no claim to the title, it was presumed to have become likewise extinct: the BARONY OF WILLOUGHBY, of Parham, under these circumstances, was adjudged erroneously to the son and heir of Sir Thomas Willoughby, youngest son of the second lord, (refer to issue of Charles, second baron,) and he was summoned to parliament accordingly, 19th May, 1685, as

SIR THOMAS WILLOUGHBY, eleventh Baron Willoughby, of Parham. His lordship m. Eleanor, daughter of Hugh Whittle, Esq., of Horwath, in Lancashire, and had, with other issue,

> HUGH, his successor.
> Francis, m. to Eleanor, daughter of —— Rothwell, of Hay, in the county of Lancaster, and had issue,
>> Thomas, d. unmarried.
>> EDWARD, who s. his uncle as Lord Willoughby.
>> CHARLES, who s. his brother.

His lordship d. in 1692, and was s. by his eldest son,

HUGH WILLOUGHBY, twelfth baron. This nobleman m. first, Anne, daughter of Lawrence Halliwell, Esq., of Tockholes, in Lancashire, and had a son,

> Thomas, who d. young.

His lordship espoused, secondly, in 1692, Honora, widow of Sir William Egerton, and daughter of Sir Thomas Leigh, son and heir of Thomas, first Lord Leigh, but died s. p., in August, 1712, when he was s. by his nephew,

EDWARD WILLOUGHBY, thirteenth baron, who, when the honour devolved upon him, was abroad as a private soldier in the confederate army, under John, Duke of Marlborough. His lordship did not, however, enjoy the peerage long, for he d. in the next year, and was s. by his brother,

CHARLES WILLOUGHBY, fourteenth baron. This nobleman m. Hester, daughter of Henry Davenport, Esq., of Darcy Lever, in Lincolnshire, by whom he had, HUGH, his successor, and Ellen. He d. 19th July, 1715, and was s. by his son,

HUGH WILLOUGHBY, fifteenth baron. This nobleman was elected vice-president of the Royal Society in 1752, and president of the Society of Antiquaries in two years afterwards. His lordship was esteemed a man of abilities, but according to Cole's MSS. in the British Museum, he was a presbyterian of the most rigid class. " I have heard," (says Cole) " Mr. Coventry, of Magdalen College, Cambridge, declare that his conscience was so nice, that he could not bring himself to receive the sacrament in the church of England on his knees, without scruple, and thought it idolatry. He had a very small estate, and when he came to it, with the title, was in a very humble capacity in the army." He d. unmarried in 1765, when the BARONY was claimed by

HENRY WILLOUGHBY, representative of the elder branch, (refer to Sir Ambrose Willoughby, second son of the second lord,) and the house of Lords adjudged, in 1767, " That he had a right to the title, dignity, and peerage of Willoughby, of Parham; which was enjoyed, from the year 1680 to 1765, by the male line (now extinct,) of Sir Thomas Willoughby, youngest son of Charles, Lord Willoughby, of Parham, who were successively summoned to parliament by descent, in virtue of letters patent, bearing date 16th February, in the 1st year of Edward VI., and sat as heirs male of the body of Sir William, created Lord Willoughby, of Parham, by the said letters patent, contrary to the right and truth of the case; it now appearing, that Sir Ambrose Willoughby, the second son of the said Charles, (and elder brother of the said Thomas,) who was averred to have died without issue, left a son; and that Henry Willoughby, Esq., the claimant, is great-grandson and heir male of the body of such son, and consequently heir male of the said Sir William, who was created Lord Willoughby, of Parham, the male line of the elder son, Charles, Lord Willoughby, of Parham, having failed in or before the year 1680." Mr. Willoughby became, therefore, SIXTEENTH BARON WILLOUGHBY, of Parham, and took his seat in the House of Peers 25th April, 1767. His lordship m. Susannah, daughter of Robert Gresswell, Esq., of the county of Middlesex, by whom he had one surviving daughter, Elizabeth, who m. first, John Halsey, Esq., of Tower Hill, and secondly, Edward Argles, Esq. He d. 29th January, 1775, and was s. by his nephew,

GEORGE WILLOUGHBY, seventeenth baron, who d. issueless in 1779, when the BARONY OF WILLOUGHBY, OF PARHAM, became EXTINCT.

ARMS.—First and fourth or, frette az. second and third, sa. a cross engrailed or.

WILMOT — BARONS WILMOT, EARLS OF ROCHESTER.

Barony,   } by Letters { 29th June, 1643.
Earldom, } Patent, { 13th December, 1652.

Lineage.

The Honourable
HENRY WILMOT, only son of Charles, Viscount Wilmot, of Athlone, in the peerage of Ireland, was created a baron of England, by letters patent, of *King* CHARLES I., dated 29th June, 1643, as LORD WILMOT, *of Adderbury, in the county of Oxford.* He was at that time lieutenant of the
578

horse, in his majesty's armies throughout England and Wales, and attained high reputation, particularly at the battle of ROUNDWAY DOWNE. His lordship afterwards remained faithfully attached to *King* CHARLES II., during his exile, and was mainly instrumental in enabling his majesty to effect his escape after the fatal battle of Worcester. In consideration of these eminent services he was advanced by letters patent, dated at Paris, 13th December, 1652, to the EARLDOM OF ROCHESTER. His lordship m. Anne, daughter of Sir John St. John, Bart. of Lyddiard Tregos, in the county of Wilts, and dying at Dunkirk, in 1659, was s. by his only surviving child,

JOHN WILMOT, second Earl of Rochester. This is the nobleman who became so celebrated in the reign of Charles II., as the gifted, witty, but licentious companion of that merry monarch. His lordship, Walpole characterises as a poet, whom the muses inspired, but were ashamed to own, and who practised, without the least reserve, the secret which can make verses more read for their defects than for their merits. Lord Rochester's poems are truly described by the same author, as having more obscenity than wit, more wit than poetry, and more poetry than politeness. His lordship m. Elizabeth, daughter and heir of John Mallet, Esq., of Enmore, in the county of Somerset, and had issue,

> CHARLES, his successor.
>
> Anne, m. first, to Henry Bainton, Esq., and secondly, to Francis, son of Fulk Greville, Lord Broke.
>
> Elizabeth, m. to Edward Montagu, Earl of Sandwich.
>
> Mallet, m. to John Vaughan, first Viscount Lisburne, in Ireland, ancestor of the Earls of Lisburne.

The earl d. in 1680, and was s. by his son,

CHARLES WILMOT, third Earl of Rochester, who died unmarried, and in minority, the year after his father, when ALL HIS HONOURS became EXTINCT.

ARMS.—Arg. or a fesse, gu. between three eagles' heads erased, sa. as many eschallops, or.

WINDSORE—BARON WINDSORE.

By Writ of Summons, dated 22nd August, 1381, 5 Richard II.

Lineage.

At the time of the general survey
WALTER FITZ-OTHER possessed three lordships in Surrey, two in Hampshire, three in Bucks, and four in Middlesex; of which STANWELL, in the latter county, was the chief place of abode of himself and his descendants for several succeeding ages. Those lordships, manors, and lands, moreover, were held by his father, Sir Other, in the reign of EDWARD *the Confessor.* Walter Fitz-Other was warden of all the forests in Berkshire, and CASTELLAN OF WINDSORE in the time of WILLIAM *the Conqueror.* The name and family of his wife

are in doubt, as likewise the seniority of his three sons.*

WILLIAM, his successor.

Robert, Lord of Eston, afterwards called Estains, in Essex, in which he was *s.* by an only son,

William, who left a daughter, his heir,

Delicia, *m.* to Robert de Hastings.

Gerald, who bore the surname of FITZ-WALTER, and being successfully employed by *King* HENRY II., against the Welsh, was constituted governor of Pembroke Castle, and afterwards made president of the county of Pembroke. He *m.* Nesta, daughter of Rhese, Prince of Wales, and from their union sprang the Fitz-Geralds, DUKES OF LEINSTER, and other eminent families.

The eldest son,

WILLIAM, bore the surname of WINDSORE, and succeeded his father in his offices of warden of the forests of Berkshire, and CASTELLAN OF WINDSORE. The *Empress* MAUD confirmed to him, at Oxford, all the grants made to his ancestors of the custody of Windsore Castle, and of all lands, in as full a manner as they had enjoyed them in the time of her father, HENRY I. He assumed the designation of Windsore from his office, and left two sons,

WILLIAM, his successor.

Hugh de Windsore, lord of the manor of West Horsley, in the county of Surrey, which, by heirs female, devolved upon the Barons de Berners.

The elder son and heir,

SIR WILLIAM DE WINDSORE, was also a powerful baron in the reign of HENRY II., and in 1165, upon the assessment for a marriage portion for that monarch's daughter, he certified that he held sixteen knights' fees and a half *de veteri feoffamento*, and three and a half *de novo*, for which he afterwards paid £12 2s. 6d. In 1194 he attended the

---

* GERALD, who, in the Duke of Leinster's pedigree, is called the *eldest*, being placed *youngest* on the pedigree of the Earls of Kerry, and that disposition is supported by Segar, Dugdale, and Anstee, all eminent members of the Herald's College. These heralds maintain, that the appellation of *Fitz-Walter* was given to Gerald because he was the youngest son. LODGE, however, protests against such a conclusion, and says, " It deserves an inquiry, how the consequences of his being a younger son can be drawn from his having the appellation of Fitz-Walter? The custom of that age," he continues, " warrants the affirmation of the contrary ; and that the eldest son, especially, assumed for his surname the christian name of his father, with the addition of *Fitz*, &c. And this continued in use until surnames came to be fixed about the time of Edward I., and among many families until long after that time, younger sons being not so frequently known, or called by their fathers' christian name, as by that of his office or employment. For which reason the two brothers of Gerald are not called Fitz-Walter, but Windsore."

---

king in his expedition into Normandy, when he raised the siege of Vernuel, and beat the French in several skirmishes. Sir William de Windsore, it is supposed, eventually fell in that campaign. He left two sons, WALTER and William, and was *s.* by the elder,

WALTER DE WINDSORE, who had accompanied his father in the expedition into France. This baron having no male issue, divided, by virtue of a fine levied in the 9th Richard I., the whole barony of his father, with his brother, William de Windsore. He *d.* about the year 1205, leaving two daughters, his co-heirs, viz.

Christian, *m.* to Duncan Lascelles.

Gunnora, *m.* to Ralph de Hodseng.

In the division of the estates, as mentioned above, the deceased lord's brother, and the male representative of the family,

WILLIAM DE WINDSORE, had the lordships of Stanwell and Hakeburn, with other lands, &c., of considerable value: and in 1212 he paid into the exchequer one hundred pounds for livery of some part of the estates which was possessed by his nieces. He was *s.* by his son and heir,

WILLIAM DE WINDSORE, who died about the year 1275, and was *s.* by his elder son,

WILLIAM DE WINDSORE, of Stanwell, who *m.* Margaret, daughter of John Drokensford, and sister of Sir John Drokensford, Knt., and had issue, RICHARD, his successor, Walter, and a daughter, Margaret, who took the veil, and was a nun at Ankerwyke Monastery, near Staines. He was *s.* by his elder son,

SIR RICHARD DE WINDSORE, who, attaining majority in the 13th Edward I., had livery of the manor of Stanwell, in Middlesex, and of West Hakeburne, in Berkshire. In the 23rd and 25th of the same reign he was returned one of the knights for the county of Berks. In 1297 he had a military summons to march under Edmund, Earl of Lancaster, into Gascony, and he subsequently sate in parliament as one of the knights for the county of Middlesex. In the 17th Edward II., upon an inquisition in every county, returned into chancery, of such as inherited arms from their ancestors, Sir Richard de Windsore was named amongst those of the counties of Middlesex and Berks. He died in two years afterwards, seised of the manors of Stanwell, in Middlesex, and West Hakeburn, in Berkshire; as also the ward of the castle of Windsore. He left issue by his wife, Julian, daughter of Sir Nicholas Stapleton, of Hachilsay, in the county of York, William, rector of the church of Stanwell, and an elder son, his successor,

RICHARD DE WINDSORE, who served in parliament, temp. Edward III., for the counties of Middlesex and Berks. He *m.* first, Joane ——, by whom he had a daughter of the same name. He espoused, secondly, Julian, daughter and co-heir of James Mulynes, of the county of Southampton, and had two sons,

JAMES (Sir), his successor, ancestor of the Lords Montjoy, Earls of Plymouth, &c.

WILLIAM (Sir), of whom presently.

Richard de Windsore wedded, thirdly, Claricia, daughter of John Drokensford, and widow of John

York. He died in 1367, and was s. in his estates by his elder son, but we pass to the younger,

SIR WILLIAM DE WINDSORE, an eminent warrior and statesman, in the reigns of EDWARD III. and RICHARD II.; by the former monarch he was constituted LIEUTENANT OF IRELAND, and by the latter summoned to parliament as a BARON, from 22nd August, 1381, to 3rd March, 1384. His lordship m. about the year 1378, the famous and beautiful ALICE PERRERS,* but appears to have died without issue in 1384, as by the post-mortem inquisition taken before Nicholas Brembre, mayor of London, after enumerating his estates, it is stated, "that he died September 15th, 8th Richard II., leaving his three sisters his heirs, viz.

"Isabel, thirty-eight years of age, unmarried.
"Christian, thirty-four years of age, m. to Sir William Morieaux, Knt.
"Margery, aged thirty-two, m. to John Duket."

Upon his lordship's decease the BARONY OF WINDSORE became EXTINCT. Sir William Dugdale says, that Lord Windsore left daughters, but Collins considers those the issue of his wife, Alice, by another husband, and he quotes, in corroboration, a passage from her will; wherein styling herself widow of Sir William Windsore, she bequeaths to John, her younger son, her manor of Gaynes; and the residue of her goods, chattels, &c., to John and Joane, her children. This Joane married Robert Skerne, of Kingston-upon-Thames.

ARMS.—Gu. a saltier ar. between twelve crosslets or. with proper difference.

WINDSOR—BARONS MONTJOY.

By Letters Patent, dated 1st January, 1711.

Lineage.

WALTER BLOUNT, first Lord Montjoy, of Thurveston, in the county of Derby, and LORD TREASURER OF ENGLAND, had, with other issue,

JOHN BLOUNT, his eldest son, who predeceased him, leaving

EDWARD BLOUNT, second Lord Montjoy, which dignity became EXTINCT, with the EARLDOM OF DEVONSHIRE, upon the decease, without legitimate issue, of Charles Blount, eighth Baron Montjoy, and first Earl of Devonshire, in 1606.

Elizabeth, m. to ANDREWS WINDSOR, of the old baronial family of Windsor, who was summoned to parliament, as BARON WINDSOR, in 1529.

From the above Elizabeth Blount, and her husband, Andrews, Lord Windsor, lineally descended

THOMAS WINDSOR, sixth Baron Windsor, K.B., who died without issue in 1642, when the BARONY OF WINDSOR fell into ABEYANCE between his two sisters, viz.

Elizabeth, sen., m. to Dixie Hickman, Esq., and had issue,

THOMAS HICKMAN, who inherited his uncle's estates.

Elizabeth, jun., m. first, Andrew Windsor, and secondly, Sir James Ware.

---

* Of this celebrated woman, BARNES, in his history of the reign of King EDWARD III., states, "That being a person of extraordinary beauty, she was (49th Edward III.,) made Lady of the Sun, and rode from the Tower of London through Cheapside, accompanied with many lords, knights, and ladies; every lady leading a lord or knight, by his horse's bridle, till they came into West Smithfield; where presently began solemn justs, which held for seven days together. That she had been constantly misrepresented by most of our writers, (one taking it from another,) as being King EDWARD's concubine, but that it was improbable, from the reputation she had of being taken in marriage by so considerable a person as the Lord William Windsore; and that King EDWARD, who never else is said to have gone astray, even in the flower of his age, should, within five years of the queen's death, when he was very infirm, burn in flames. That the records wherein she is mentioned are not severe on her reputation, as appears from the charge against her, brought into parliament in the 1st Richard II., in these words:—

"Dame Alice Perrers was introduced before the lords, and by Sir Richard le Scrope, Knt., steward of the king's household, charged for pursuing of matters, contrary to orders taken two years before; namely, that no woman should, for any advantage, present any cause in the King's Court, on pain of losing all they had, and being banished the realm for ever. That, particularly, she had procured

580

Sir Nicholas Dagworth to be called from Ireland, whether he was sent; and that she also procured, from the king, restitution of lands and goods, to Richard Lyon, merchant of London, whereas the same lands, having been forfeited by him, had been given to the king's own sons. To all which the said Dame Alice replied, that she had not pursued any such thing for any advantage of her own. Whereupon divers officers, counsellors, and servants to King EDWARD III., being examined, proved that she made such pursuit; and that, in their conceits, for her own private gain. Then judgment was given by the lords against the said dame, that according to the order aforesaid, she should be banished, and forfeit all her goods and lands whatsoever."

Sir Robert Cotton, in his Abridgment of Records, makes this remark on the above judgment: "To say truth of the devil is counted commendable, and therefore surely the record against the said lady, being very long, proves no such heinous matter against her; only it sheweth, that the same dame was in such credit with EDWARD III., as she sat at his bed's head, when all of the council, and the privy chamber, stood waiting without doors; and that she moved those suits that they dared not; and these two suits, whereof she was condemned, seemed very honest; her mishap was, that she was friendly to many, but all were not so to her."

The effect of this conviction was, however, subsequently removed.

And it so remained until called out by the crown, 16th June, 1660, in favour of the above named

THOMAS HICKMAN, as seventh Baron Windsor, who thereupon assumed the additional surname of WINDSOR, and was created, 6th December, 1682, Earl of Plymouth. His lordship m. first, Anne, daughter of Sir William Savile, Bart., of Thornhill, in the county of York, by whom he had a son, OTHER, who predeceased the earl, leaving a son, OTHER, who inherited the honours. The earl espoused, secondly, Ursula, daughter and co-heir of Sir Thomas Widdrington, of Shirburn Grange, in the county of Northumberland, and had four sons and five daughters, the elder of whom,

THOMAS WINDSOR, having distinguished himself in the wars of Flanders, was created, by *King* WILLIAM III., a peer of Ireland, in the dignity of Viscount Windsor, and made a baron of the realm by *Queen* ANNE, on the 1st January, 1711, as LORD MONTJOY, *of the Isle of Wight.* His lordship m. Charlotte, widow of John Jeffries, second Baron Jeffries, of Wem, and only daughter and heir of Philip Herbert, Earl of Pembroke, by whom he had surviving issue, /

> HERBERT, his successor.
> Ursula, m. to John Wadman, Esq., of Imber, in the county of Wilts.
> Charlotte, m. to John Kent, Esq., of Salisbury.
> Catherine.
> Elizabeth.

He d. in 1738, and was s. by his son,

HERBERT WINDSOR, second Baron Montjoy, (and second Viscount Windsor). This nobleman m. Alice, sister and co-heir of Sir James Clavering, Bart., and left two daughters, his co-heirs, viz.

> Charlotte-Jane, m. to John, first Marquess of Bute, and was grandmother of the present marquess. Her ladyship d. in 1800.
> Alice-Elizabeth.

His lordship d. in 1758, when ALL HIS HONOURS, in default of male issue, became EXTINCT.

ARMS.—Gu. a saltire, ar. between twelve cross crosslets or, a crescent for difference.

WOTTON—BARONS WOTTON.

By Letters Patent, dated 13th May, 1603.

Lineage.

ROBERT WOTTON, of Bocton Malherbe, m. Anne, daughter and co-heir of Henry Belknap, and had two sons, viz.

> EDWARD (Sir).
> Nicholas, doctor of laws, who was of the privy council, and one of the executors to the will of *King* HENRY VIII., and was frequently accredited on diplomatic missions to the courts of France, Spain, and Germany. In the reign of EDWARD VI. he was one of the principal secretaries of state, as he was afterwards in the reigns of Mary and Elizabeth. He was a person of great learning, being versed in the Latin, French, Italian, and German languages. He d. 26th January,

1566, and was buried in the cathedral church at Canterbury, where a splendid monument was erected to his memory by his nephew, Thomas Wotton, Esq.

The elder son,

SIR EDWARD WOTTON, was a member of the privy council temp. HENRY VIII., and treasurer of the town and marches of Calais. He was likewise one of the executors to *King* HENRY, and named by that prince of the council to his son, *Prince* EDWARD: "being," says Dugdale, "of such great abilities, that he might have been lord chancellor of England, but that he modestly declined it." Sir Edward was s. by his son,

THOMAS WOTTON, Esq., who m. first, Elizabeth, daughter of John Rudstone, Esq., of Bocton Monchensy, and had issue,

> EDWARD, his successor.
> James, who received the honour of knighthood for his gallantry in the expedition to Cadiz, temp. Elizabeth.
> John.

He espoused, secondly, ———, daughter of Sir William Finch, of Eastwell, in Kent, and widow of —— Morton, and had another son,

> Henry, who was knighted by *King* JAMES I., and sent thrice ambassador to VENICE; once to the States General, twice to the court of Savoy, and upon several other equally important diplomatic missions. Sir Henry was subsequently appointed provost of Eton College.

The eldest son,

SIR EDWARD WOTTON, Knt., having been accredited as ambassador to the court of Portugal, was elevated to the peerage by *King* JAMES I., by letters patent, dated 13th May, 1603, as BARON WOTTON, *of Maherly, or Marley, in the county of Kent.* His lordship, like the other members of his family, was distinguished by great mental powers and superior attainments. He m. Heather, daughter and co-heir of Sir William Puckering, Knt., of Oswald Kirk, in the county of York, and was s. at his decease by his son,

THOMAS WOTTON, second baron. This nobleman m. Mary, daughter and co-heir of Sir Arthur Throckmorton, of Paulers Perry, in Northamptonshire, and had issue,

> Katherine, who m. first, Henry, Lord Stanhope, by whom, who predeceased his father, she was mother of
>> Philip, Earl of Chesterfield.
>> Mary, d. unmarried.
>> Katherine, m. to William, Lord Allington.
>
> Her ladyship espoused, secondly, JOHN POLIANDER KIRKHOVEN, Lord of Hemfleet, in Holland, and had a son,
>> CHARLES-HENRY KIRKHOVEN, who was created BARON WOTTON, *of Wotton.*
>
> She wedded, thirdly, Colonel Daniel O'Neile, one of the grooms of the bed-chamber to Charles II. Her ladyship was governess to the Princess of Orange, daughter of *King* CHARLES I., and attending her highness into Holland, sent over money, arms, and ammu-

nition, to his majesty's aid, for which service she was created, by CHARLES II., COUNTESS OF CHESTERFIELD for life.

Heather, m. to Baptist, Viscount Camden.

Margaret, m. to Sir John Tufton, Knt.

Anne, m. to Sir Edward Hales, Knt., of Tunstat, Kent.

His lordship d. in 1630, when the BARONY OF WOTTON, in default of male issue, became EXTINCT.

ARMS.—Ar. a saltier, sa.

WOTTON — COUNTESS OF CHESTERFIELD.

By Letters Patent, dated 29th May, 1660.

Lineage.

KATHERINE WOTTON, eldest daughter and co-heir of Thomas Wotton, second Lord Wotton, of Marley, was created, by King CHARLES II., COUNTESS OF CHESTERFIELD for life. Her ladyship d. in 1667, when the title became extinct (see Wotton, Barons Wotton).

WRIOTHESLEY — BARONS WRIOTHESLEY, EARLS OF SOUTHAMPTON, EARLS OF CHICHESTER.

Barony, Earldom, Earldom of Chichester, } by Letters Patent, { 1st January, 1544. 16th February, 1547. 3rd June, 1644.

Lineage.

Of this family the first mentioned,

JOHN WRYOTHSLEY, (commonly called Wrythe,) was faucon herald in the reign of EDWARD IV., and had letters patent for the office of Garter King at Arms, in the 1st of RICHARD III. He had two sons,

THOMAS, who was first a herald by the title of Walingford, and in the 20th HENRY VII. was constituted Garter King at Arms.

William, was also in the College of Arms as York Herald.

The younger son,

WILLIAM WRIOTHESLEY, York Herald, left a son,

THOMAS WRIOTHESLEY, who, in the 27th HENRY VIII., was made coroner and attorney in the court of Common Pleas; and in three years afterwards, being then one of the principal secretaries of state, was sent ambassador to treat of a marriage between his royal master and Christiana, second daughter of the King of Denmark. In the 32nd of the same reign, subsequently to his having had the honour of knighthood, he was made constable of the castle of Southampton. He was soon afterwards accredited one of the commissioners to treat with the Emperor, CHARLES V., and he was elevated to the peerage, by letters patent, dated

1st January, 1544, in the dignity of BARON WRIOTHESLEY, of Titchfield, in the county of Hants; which Titchfield being one of the monasteries then dissolved, he obtained by grant from the crown. Soon after this, upon the decease of Lord Audley, his lordship was constituted LORD CHANCELLOR OF ENGLAND, and the same year he was made a KNIGHT OF THE GARTER. He was subsequently appointed, by King HENRY, one of his executors, and named of the council to his son EDWARD VI. Three days before whose coronation he was created, by letters patent, dated 16th February, 1547, EARL OF SOUTHAMPTON. His lordship did not long, however, maintain his influence in this reign. Prior to the accession of the king he was opposed to the Duke of Somerset, and he had little chance, under the new order of affairs, of sustaining himself against so powerful a rival. The earl, in order that he might have the greater leisure to attend to public business, had, of his own authority, put the great seal into commission, and had empowered four lawyers, two of whom were canonists, to execute, in his absence, the duties of his high office. Complaints were made of this irregularity to the council, which, influenced by the PROTECTOR, readily seized the opportunity to depress his lordship. The judges were consulted upon the occasion, and gave it as their opinion, that the commission was illegal, and that the chancellor, by his presumption in granting it, had justly forfeited the great seal, and had even subjected himself to punishment. His lordship was immediately cited before the council, and, notwithstanding a most able defence, it was declared that he had forfeited the chancellorship, that a fine should be imposed upon him, and that he be confined to his own house during the king's pleasure. This eminent person was esteemed a man of learning, a good lawyer, and a most excellent chancellor. He was accustomed to observe, that "Force avead, but justice governed the world;" and that "he loved a bishop to satisfy his conscience, a lawyer to guide his judgment, a good family to keep up his interest, and an university to preserve his name."

He m. Jane, daughter and heir of William Cheney, Esq., and had issue,

HENRY, his successor.

Mary, m. first to William Shelly, Esq., of Michelgrove, Sussex, and secondly, to —— Lyster, son and heir of Sir Michael Lyster, Knt.

Elizabeth, m. to Thomas Ratcliffe, Earl of Sussex.

Katherine, m. to Thomas Cornwallis, Esq.

Mabel, m. to Sir Walter Sands, Knt.

Anne, m. to Sir Oliver Lawrence, Knt.

His lordship d. in 1550, and was s. by his son,

HENRY WRIOTHESLEY, second Earl of Southampton. This nobleman was a friend of Thomas, Duke of Norfolk, and involved himself in trouble by promoting the contemplated marriage of that nobleman with Mary, Queen of Scots, "to whom and her religion (says Dugdale), he stood not a little affected." He m. Mary, daughter of Anthony Brown, Viscount Montagu, and had issue,

HENRY, Lord Wriothesley.

Mary, m. to Thomas, Lord Arundel, of Wardour.

His lordship d. in 1581, and was s. by his son,

HENRY WRIOTHESLEY, third Earl of Southampton. This nobleman was the companion in arms of the Earl of Essex, and a participator in the treason by which that unhappy nobleman forfeited his life in the reign of Elizabeth. Lord Southampton was also tried, condemned, and attainted, but his life was spared; and upon the accession of *King James I.*, he was released from prison, restored in blood by act of parliament, and created by a new patent, date 21 July, 1603, Earl of Southampton, with the same rights, precedency and privileges that he had formerly enjoyed. He was also made a Knight of the Garter, and constituted captain of the Isle of Wight, and castle of Caresbroke. His lordship m. Elizabeth, daughter of John Vernon, Esq., of Hodnet, in the county of Derby, and dying in 1694, left issue,

Thomas, Lord Wriothesley.

Penelope, m. to William, Lord Spencer, of Wormleighton.

Anne, m. to Robert Wallop, Esq., of Furley, in the county of Southampton.

Elizabeth, m. to Sir Thomas Estcourt, Knt., one of the Masters in Chancery.

The earl was s. by his son,

THOMAS WRIOTHESLEY, fourth Earl of Southampton. This nobleman who was a staunch supporter of *King Charles I.*, was installed a Knight of the Garter at the restoration, and constituted Lord Treasurer of England. His lordship m. first, Rachel, daughter of Daniel de Massey, Baron de Rouvigny, in France, by whom he had two sons, who both died young, and three daughters, viz.

Elizabeth, m. to Edward Noel, eldest son of Baptist, Viscount Campden.

Rachsel, m. first, to Francis, son and heir of Richard, Earl of Carberry, in Ireland, and secondly, to the celebrated patriot, *William*, Lord Russell, so unjustly beheaded in 1683, son of William, fifth Earl of Bedford.

Magdalen, who d. young.

He wedded, secondly, Frances, daughter of Francis Leigh, Baron Dunsmore, which nobleman was created 3rd June, 1644, Earl of Chichester, with remainder, failing his own male issue, to his son-in-law, the Earl of Southampton and the heirs male of his body by his lordship's daughter, the said Frances Leigh. He died in 1653, and the honours of Lord Southampton, were then augmented by the Earldom of Chichester. By this lady, his lordship had four daughters,

Audrey, who d. unmarried.

Penelope, d. young.

Elizabeth, m. first, Joceline, Earl of Northumberland, and secondly, to Ralph, Lord Montagu, of Boughton.

Penelope, d. in infancy.

The earl espoused, thirdly, Frances, daughter of William, Duke of Somerset, and widow of Richard, Viscount Molineux, but had no issue. He died at Southampton House, "near Holburne, in the suburbs of London," 16th May, 1667, when all his

honours, including the Earldom of Chichester, became extinct.

Arms.—Az. a cross or. betw. four falcons closed, ar.

YELVERTON — VISCOUNTS LONGUEVILLE, EARLS OF SUSSEX.

Viscounty, } by Letters { 21st April, 1690.
Earldom, } Patent, { 26th September, 1717.

Lineage.

Of this family, one of great antiquity in the county of Norfolk, was

ANDREW YELVERTON, living in the reign of Edward II., who was father of

ROBERT YELVERTON, who was seated, temp. Edward III., at Rackheath, in the vicinity of Norwich, and marrying Cycely, daughter of Sir Thomas Bardolfe, left a son and heir,

JOHN YELVERTON, of Rackheath, who had, by his first wife, ———, a son and successor,

Robert, who died about the year 1420, leaving a son,

Thomas, of Rackheath, who died s. p. John Yelverton m. secondly, Elizabeth, daughter of John Read, of Rougham, in the county of Norfolk, and had a son,

SIR WILLIAM YELVERTON, a lawyer of great eminence, who was constituted one of the judges of the court of King's Bench in the 22nd Henry VI. This learned person appears to have stood equally well with the monarchs of both the Roses, as we find him not only continued in his judicial office by King Edward IV., but made a Knight of the Bath, in order to grace that prince's coronation; and upon the temporary restoration of *King Henry*, appointed by patent, dated 9th October, 1470, one of the judges of the court of Common Pleas. He m. Agnes, daughter of Sir Oliver le Gross, of Crostwick, in the county of Norfolk, Knt., and was s. by his son,

JOHN YELVERTON, Esq., of Rackheath, who m. Margery, daughter of William Morley, Esq., and had issue,

William (Sir), his successor.

Anne, m. to Thomas Farmey, Esq., of Helmingham.

He was s. by his son,

SIR WILLIAM YELVERTON, Knt., who was retained by indenture, anno 1474, to serve the king (Edward IV.) in person in his wars in France, with two men at arms, and four archers. He m. first, Anne, daughter of John Paston, Esq., of Paston Hall, in the county of Norfolk, by whom he had issue,

William, who died, in his father's life-time, s. p.

Anne, m. to Thomas Jermy, Esq., son of Sir John Jermy, Knt.

Margaret, m. to John Palgrave, Esq., of Norwood Barningham, in the county of Norfolk.

Eleanor, m. to John Conyers, Esq., son and heir of Sir Robert Conyers.

Sir William espoused, secondly, Eleanor, daughter of Sir Thomas Brewse, Knt., and had a son, his successor,

WILLIAM YELVERTON, Esq., of Rougham and Rackheath. This gentleman m. Catherine, daughter of John Raves, Esq., of the county of Essex, and had five sons, viz., WILLIAM, his successor, John, Nicholas, Edward, and Adam, and a daughter, Anne, m. to Matthew Canne, Esq., of Wessenham, in Norfolk. He was s. at his decease by his eldest son,

WILLIAM YELVERTON, Esq., of Rougham, who m. Margaret, daughter of ——— Garnond, of London, gentleman, and had two sons, WILLIAM and John, and three daughters, viz.

Mary, m. first, to William Baker, Esq., and secondly, to Henry Wayte, Esq.

Susan, m. first, to Edward Eston, Esq., of Reinham, in Norfolk, and secondly, to Edward Harvey, Esq.

Eleanor, m. to Richard Draper, Esq., of Marham, in the same county.

William Yelverton d. in the year 1541, and was s. by his elder son,

WILLIAM YELVERTON, Esq., of Rougham. This gentleman espoused, first, Anne, daughter and heir of Sir Henry Farmor, Knt., of East Barsham, in Norfolk, by whom he acquired a great increase to his landed possessions, and had issue,

HENRY, who inherited ROUGHAM, and the other estates of his father, as son and heir. He m. Bridget, daughter of Sir William Drury, of Hawsted, in Suffolk, Knt., and had issue,

WILLIAM, his successor, created a baronet in 1620. He m. Dionesse, daughter of Richard Stubbs, Esq., of Sedgeford, in Norfolk, and left

WILLIAM (Sir), second baronet, who m. Ursula, daughter of Sir Thomas Richardson, Knt., Speaker of the House of Commons, and afterwards Lord Chief Justice of the King's Bench, by whom he had, WILLIAM, and two daughters, Elizabeth and Ursula. He d. in 1648, and was s. by his son,

WILLIAM (Sir), third baronet, who died s. p. in 1649, when the baronetcy expired.

Henry (Sir), m. Alice, daughter and co-heir of the Right Rev. William Barlow, Bishop of Lincoln.

Margaret, m. to Thomas Tyrrell, Esq., of Gippinge, in the county of Suffolk.

William.

CHRISTOPHER, of whom presently.

Humphrey.

Launcelot.

Winifred, m. to Gwen Duckett, Esq., of Worthing, in Norfolk.

Anne, m. first, to Thomas Reade, Esq., of

Wishbyche, and secondly, to John Rawkins, Esq., of Essex.

Martha, m. first, to Thomas Fyncham, Esq., of Fyncham, in the county of Norfolk, and secondly, to John Higham, Esq., of Gifford, in Sussex.

Mr. Yelverton m. secondly, Jane, daughter of Edward Cocket, Esq., of Ampton, in Suffolk, by whom he had

Edward.

Charles.

William, m. to Grace, daughter of ——— Newport, Esq., of Buckingham.

Jane, m. first, to Edmund Lummer, Esq., of Manington, in Norfolk, and secondly, to John Dodge, Esq., of Wrotham, in Kent.

Chrysold, m. first, to Thomas le Strange, son and heir of Sir Nicholas le Strange, and secondly, to Sir Philip Woodhouse.

The third son of William Yelverton, by his first wife, Anne Fermor,

CHRISTOPHER YELVERTON, being bred to the bar, and called to the degree of serjeant at law, was constituted queen's serjeant in the 31st of Elizabeth. In some years afterwards he was chosen speaker of the House of Commons, and in the 44th of the same reign he was constituted one of the judges of the court of King's Bench. On the accession of King James his patent, as a judge, was renewed, and he was then made a knight. Sir Christopher m. Mary, daughter of Thomas Catesby, Esq., of Whiston, in the county of Northampton, and had issue,

HENRY, his successor.

Christopher (Sir).

Isabel, m. to Sir Edward Cope, of Cannon's Asby, in the county of Northampton.

Anne, m. first, to Thomas Sherland, Esq., of the county of Suffolk, and secondly, to Sir Edward Cocket, Knt., of Ampton, in the same shire.

Mary, m. to Sir William Gardiner, of Lagham, in Surrey.

Judith, m. to Edmund Abdy, Esq., of Lincoln's Inn.

His lordship d. in 1607, at Easton-Mauduit, a seat which he had purchased in Northamptonshire, and was s. by his elder son,

HENRY YELVERTON, Esq., of Easton-Mauduit. This gentleman having, like his father, adopted the profession of the law, was appointed SOLICITOR-GENERAL in 1613, and knighted about the same period. In 1617 Sir Henry Yelverton was made ATTORNEY-GENERAL; previously, however, he is said to have displeased the king by refusing to appear against the Earl of Somerset, at his trial for the murder of Sir Thomas Overbury, and in the October of the year in which he was advanced to the attorney-generalship we find him writing a letter to his royal master, complaining " of his unhappiness to fall under his majesty's displeasure, who had made him almost the wonder of his favour; that he conceived it to arise from some accident, befel in the late business of the marriage of Sir John Villiers; as also from a report, as if he had uttered some speeches to the dishonour of the Earl of

Buckingham." He pleaded his cause so successfully, however, that he very soon recovered any ground which he might have lost in JAMES'S opinion, but he was not so fortunate with the Duke of Buckingham, who seems, for a long time afterwards, to have regarded him with an evil eye. In 1620, principally through the machinations of that favoured nobleman, he was involved, with the lord mayor of London, and others, in a star-chamber prosecution, regarding the passing of certain clauses in a charter to the city of London, not authorised by the king's warrant; for this offence, although he made every submission, and that the charter was given up, he was adjudged to pay a fine of £4000, to be deprived of the office of attorney-general, and to be committed to the tower. He was subsequently prosecuted before parliament upon another account, and the House of Lords, 16th May, 1621, proceeded to sentence, and declare, "that the said Sir Henry Yelverton for his speeches, uttered here in court, which do touch the king's majesty's honour, shall be fined to the king in ten thousand marks, be imprisoned during pleasure, and make submission to the king: and for those which touched the Marquess of Buckingham, he should be fined five thousand marks, &c." Upon which Buckingham stood up, and did freely remit his portion of the fine; and the prince and the House agreed to move his majesty to mitigate the other part of the judgment. What proportion of the fine was ultimately forgiven is no where mentioned, but his misfortunes very soon afterwards terminated. The Duke of Buckingham visited him *incognito* in the Tower, and Sir Henry making a sufficient apology to his grace, he was presently set at liberty, and became again a practising barrister, until April, 1625, when a gentleman from the duke brought him a warrant from the king, appointing him one of the judges of the court of Common Pleas. In this situation he remained until his decease, on the 24th January, 1629-30, when his remains were interred in the parish church of Easton-Mauduit. Of this eminent person the following character is given by one of his own profession:

"Memorandum, That upon Sunday morning, being the 24th of January, 1629-30, died Sir Henry Yelverton, puisne judge of the Common Pleas, who before had been attorney-general to King James, and afterwards incurring his displeasure, was displeased and censured in the star-chamber. He then became a practiser again at the bar, from which he was advanced, by *King* CHARLES, to be a judge. He was a man of profound knowledge in the common laws, and ingenious and eloquent in expression; and for his life, of great integrity and piety, and his death universally bewailed." His lordship *m.* Margaret, daughter of Robert Beale, Esq., clerk of the council to Queen Elizabeth, and was *s.* by his eldest son,

SIR CHRISTOPHER YELVERTON, Knt., of Easton-Mauduit, who was created a baronet on the 30th June, 1641. He *m.* in 1630, Anne, youngest daughter of Sir William Twisden, Bart., of Roydon Hall, Kent, by whom he had issue,

    HENRY, his successor.

    Anne, *m.* first, to Robert, Earl of Man-

chester, and secondly, to Charles, Earl of Halifax.

Sir Christopher *d.* 4th December, 1654, and was *s.* by his son,

SIR HENRY YELVERTON, second baronet, member for Northamptonshire, in the parliament that voted the restoration of *King* CHARLES II. He *m.* Susan, BARONESS GREY DE RUTHYN, daughter and heiress of Charles Longueville, Lord Grey de Ruthyn, and great grand-daughter of Charles Grey, Earl of Kent (see Grey, Earl of Kent), by whom he had issue,

    CHARLES, his successor.

    Henry, heir to his brother.

    Christopher.

    Frances, *m.* to Francis, Viscount Hatton.

Sir Henry *d.* 28th January, 1676, and was *s.* by his eldest son,

SIR CHARLES YELVERTON, second baronet, who, upon the decease of his mother, 28th January, 1676, became BARON GREY DE RUTHYN. His lordship *d.* unmarried, of the small-pox, 17th May, 1679, and was *s.* by his brother,

SIR HENRY YELVERTON, as third baronet, and as Lord Grey de Ruthyn. This nobleman claimed, by inheritance from the Hastings, Earls of Pembroke, the right of carrying the golden spurs at the coronation of *King* JAMES II., and his claim being admitted, he bore them accordingly. His lordship *m.* Barbara, daughter of John Talbot, Esq., of Laycock, in the county of Wilts, and had, with other issue,

    TALBOT, his successor.

    Henry, *m.* ——, daughter of Major Carle, and had an only daughter, Barbara, who *d.* young.

    Barbara, *m.* to Reynolds Calthorpe, Esq., of Elvesham, in the county of Northampton.

His lordship was advanced to the dignity of VISCOUNT LONGUEVILLE on 21st April, 1690. He *d.* in 1704, and was *s.* by his elder son,

TALBOT YELVERTON, second Viscount Longueville, who was created, 26th September, 1717, EARL OF SUSSEX, with remainder, in default of his own male issue, to his brother, the Hon. Henry Yelverton, and the heirs male of his body. His lordship was appointed deputy earl-marshal of England in 1725, and he officiated as such at the coronation of *King* GEORGE II. He was made a Knight of the Bath upon the revival of that order, and subsequently sworn of the privy council. His lordship *m.* Lucy, daughter of Henry Pelham, Esq., of Lewes, in Sussex, clerk of the pells, and uncle of Thomas, Duke of Newcastle, by whom he had two sons,

    GEORGE-AUGUSTUS, } successively inheritors
    HENRY,   } of the honours.

The earl, who carried the golden spurs at the coronation of GEORGE I., died 27th October, 1730, and was *s.* by his elder son,

GEORGE-AUGUSTUS YELVERTON, second Earl of Sussex. This nobleman was one of the lords of the bed-chamber to *Frederick*, PRINCE OF WALES, and afterwards to his *Majesty*, *King* GEORGE III. He *d.* unmarried 8th January, 1758, and was *s.* by his brother,

HENRY YELVERTON, third Earl of Sussex. This nobleman m. first, Hester, daughter of John Hall, Esq., of Mansfield Woodhouse, Notts, and had an only surviving daughter,

> Lady BARBARA YELVERTON, who m. Edward Thoroton Gould, Esq., of Woodham-Mansfield, in the county of Notts, and dying in the life-time of her father, 9th April, 1781, left issue,
>> HENRY-EDWARD GOULD, who, upon the death of his grandfather, the Earl of Sussex, became LORD GREY DE RUTHYN, and assumed the surname of YELVERTON. He m. in 1809, Anna-Maria, daughter of William Kellam, Esq., and dying the next year, left an only daughter and heiress,
>>> BARBARA YELVERTON, Baroness Grey de Ruthyn, who m. 18th August, 1831, GEORGE, present Marquess of Hastings.
>> Barbara Gould, d. unmarried.
>> Mary Gould, m. to the Hon. and Rev. Frederick Powys, son of Lord Lilford.

The earl espoused, secondly, Mary, daughter of John Vaughan, Esq., of Bristol, but had no issue. He died in 1799, when the Barony of Grey de Ruthyn devolved upon his grandson, HENRY-EDWARD GOULD, Esq., who assumed the surname of YELVERTON, as stated above, and the VISCOUNTY OF LONGUEVILLE, with the EARLDOM OF SUSSEX, became EXTINCT.

ARMS.—Ar. three lions rampant, and a chief gules.

Note.— The family of YELVERTON, Viscounts Avonmore, in Ireland, is a branch of this family.

YORKE—BARON DOVER.

By Letters Patent, dated 11th September, 1788.

Lineage.

PHILIP YORKE, the first and eminent Earl of Hardwicke, LORD HIGH CHANCELLOR OF GREAT BRITAIN, m. Margaret, daughter of Charles Cocks, Esq., of the city of Worcester, and had five sons and two daughters (refer to Burke's Dictionary of the Peerage and Baronetage), of whom the third son,

SIR JOSEPH YORKE, K.B., having served as aid-de-camp to the Duke of Cumberland at the battle of Fontenoy, and subsequently attained the rank of a general officer, was elevated to the peerage on 11th September, 1788, as BARON DOVER, of Dover, in the county of Kent. His lordship m. the dowager Baroness de Boetzelier, a lady of Holland, but had no issue. Lord Dover was for many years ambassador at the Hague. He d. in 1792, when the barony became EXTINCT.

ARMS.—Ar. on a saltier az. a bezant: with the necessary difference as a junior branch of the house of Yorke.

ZOUCHE — BARON ZOUCHE, OF ASHBY, IN THE COUNTY OF LEICESTER.

By Writ of Summons, dated 26th January, 1297, 25 Edward I.

Lineage.

That the ZOUCHES branched from the Earls of Britanny is admitted by all genealogists, but they do not coincide in the exact line of descent.

WILLIAM LE ZUSCHE, in confirming to the monks of Swavesey, in Cambridgeshire, the grant made by his ancestors to the abbey St. Segius and Bachus, in Anjou, (to which the priory of Swavesey was a cell,) calls Roger la Zusche, his father, and Alan la Zusche, Earl of Britanny, his grandfather. This William d. in the 1st of JOHN, and was s. by his brother,

ROGER LE ZUSCHE, who, for his fidelity to King JOHN, had a grant, from that monarch, of the manors of Petersfield and Maple Durham, in the county of Southampton, part of the lands of Geffrey de Mandeville, one of the rebellious barons, then in arms. In the next reign he was sheriff of Devonshire, and had further grants from the crown. He m. Margaret ———, and had issue,

> ALAN, his successor.
> William, who left an only daughter.
>> Joice, who m. Robert Mortimer, of Richard's Castle, and had issue,
>>> HUGH MORTIMER, summoned to parliament as Lord Mortimer, of Richard's Castle.
>>> WILLIAM MORTIMER, who assumed the surname of ZOUCHE, and was summoned to parliament as LORD ZOUCHE, of Mortimer.

He was s. by his elder son,

SIR ALAN LE ZOUCHE, who, in the 26th of HENRY III., had a military summons to attend the king into France, and in ten years afterwards had the whole county of Chester, and all North Wales, placed under his government. In the 45th of the same reign he obtained a charter for a weekly market at Ashby la Zouche, in Leicestershire, and for two fairs in the year, at Swavesey. About the same time he was constituted warden of all the king's forests south of Trent, as also sheriff of Northamptonshire. In the 46th he was made justice itinerant for the counties of Southampton, Buckingham, and Northampton; and upon the arbitration made by Lewis, King of France, between HENRY III. and the barons, he was one of the sureties on behalf of the king. In three years afterwards he was constituted constable of the Tower of London, and governor of the castle at Northampton. Sir Alan Zouche was violently assaulted in Westminster Hall, in 1268, by John, Earl of Warren and Surrey, upon occasion of a dispute between them regarding some landed property, and with his son, Roger, who happened to be with him, severely wounded. He m. Elene, daughter and heir of Roger de Quinci, Earl of Winton, and had issue,

> ROGER, his successor.

Eudo, from whom the Zouches, Barons Zouch, of Harynworth (EXTANT) derive.

Alan le Zouche d. in 1269, and was s. by his elder son,

ROGER LE ZOUCHE, who m. Ela, daughter and co-heir of Stephen de Longespee, second son of William, Earl of Salisbury, and dying in 1285, was s. by his son,

ALAN LE ZOUCHE. This feudal lord having distinguished himself in the wars of Gascony and Scotland, temp. EDWARD I., was summoned to parliament by that monarch, as a BARON, on 26th January, 1297, and he had regular summonses from that period, until 7th Edward II., 26th November, 1313. In the 5th Edward II. his lordship was constituted governor of Rockingham Castle, in Northamptonshire, and steward of Rockingham forest. He d. in 1314, leaving three daughters, his co-heirs, viz.

> Elene, m. first, to Nicholas St. Maur, and secondly, to Alan de Charlton.
> Maud, m. to Robert de Holland.
> Elizabeth, a nun, at Brewode, in Staffordshire.

Amongst those ladies a partition was made, in the 8th of Edward III., of their father's lands, excepting the manor of ASHBY DE LA ZOUCHE, which the deceased lord gave to his kinsman, WILLIAM DE MORTIMER, whothereupon assumed the surname of ZOUCHE. Upon the decease of Lord Zouche the BARONY OF ZOUCHE, of Ashby, fell into ABEY-ANCE between his daughters, as it still continues with their representatives.

ARMS.—Gules ten bezants, or.

ZOUCHE — BARON ZOUCHE, OF MORTIMER.

By Writ of Summons, dated 26th December, 1323, 17 Edward II.

Lineage.

WILLIAM DE MORTIMER, younger son of Robert Mortimer, of Richard's Castle, by Joice, daughter and heir of William Zouche, having obtained the lordship of Ashby de la Zouch, from his kinsman Alan, Lord Zouche, of Ashby, assumed the surname of ZOUCHE; and was summoned to parliament as BARON ZOUCHE, of Mortimer, from 26th December, 1323, to 14th January, 1337. In the reign of Edward III., his lordship was made justice of all the forests, south of Trent, and constable of the Tower of London. He m. first, Alice de Tony, widow of Guy de Beauchamp, Earl of Warwick, and had a son, ALAN, his successor. He wedded, secondly, Alianore, daughter and heir of Gilbert de Clare, Earl of Gloucester, by whom he had a son, Hugh. His lordship d. and was s. by his son,

ALAN LE ZOUCH, one of the eminent warriors of the reign of Edward III., but never summoned to parliament. He was constantly engaged in the French and Scottish wars, and was in the celebrated battle of Cressy, shortly after which he died, and was s. by his son,

HUGH LE ZOUCHE, who left issue,

> HUGH, who died s. p.
> JOICE, who, upon the decease of her brother, inherited the estates. She m. Sir John Botetourt, of Wexly-Castle, and had a son,
>> JOHN BOTETOURT, who left a daughter and heir,
>>> JOICE BOTETOURT, who m. Sir Hugh Burnet, Knt., who died seised of the manor of Ashby de la Zouch, without issue. The manor came afterwards into the the possession of the Earls of Ormonde, and upon the attainder of John Butler, fifth Earl of Ormonde, and Earl of Wiltshire, fell to the crown. It was subsequently granted to William de Hastings, ancestor of the family of Hastings, Earls of Huntingdon.

ARMS.—Gu. ten bezants, or.

PEERAGES

OMITTED IN THEIR PROPER PLACES.

BACON — BARON VERULAM, VISCOUNT ST. ALBANS.

Barony, } by Letters { 11th July, 1618.
Viscounty, } Patent, { 27th January, 1621.

Lineage.

FRANCIS BACON, second son of Sir Nicholas Bacon, Lord Keeper in the reign of Elizabeth, having been brought up to the bar, was appointed queen's counsel in 1559; and soon after the accession of King James I., honoured with knighthood. In 1613, he was made attorney-general, and subsequently sworn of the privy council. In 1617, Sir Francis was constituted LORD KEEPER OF THE GREAT SEAL, and the next year he was entitled LORD HIGH CHANCELLOR of England. Within a few months afterwards, he was elevated to the peerage, 11th of July, 1618, in the dignity of BARON VERULAM, and created 27th January, 1621, VISCOUNT ST. ALBAN'S. His lordship was subsequently convicted of corruption in the exercise of his judicial functions, upon his own confession, and sentenced to pay a fine of £40,000, to be imprisoned during the king's pleasure, and to be ever afterwards incapacitated from holding office under the crown. Having in pursuance of this judgment, suffered a brief incarceration, and the fine being eventually remitted, his lordship withdrew into retirement, and devoted the remainder of his life to the most splendid literary labours. He m. Alice, daughter and co-heir of Benedict Barnham, Esq., an alderman of London, but died without issue, 9th April, 1626, when his honours became EXTINCT. The learned Bayle calls Lord St. Alban's one of the greatest geniuses of his age: Voltaire styles him the father of experimental philosophy, and Walpole terms him the prophet of arts, which Newton was sent afterwards to reveal. The latter author adds: "It would be impertinent to the reader to enter into any account of this amazing genius or his works; both will be universally admired as long as science exists. As long as ingratitude and adulation are despicable, so long shall we lament the depravity of this great man's heart! alas! that he, who could command immortal fame, should have stooped to the little ambition of power."

ARMS.—Gu. on a chief ar. two mullets sa. a crescent for difference.

508

BRAOSE — BARON BRAOSE, OF GOWER.

By Writ of Summons, dated 29th December, 1299, 28 Edward I.

Lineage.

WILLIAM DE BRAOSE came into England with the CONQUEROR, and held at the general survey considerable estates in the counties of Berks, Wilts, Surrey, Dorset, and Sussex. He was s. by his son,

PHILIP DE BRAOSE, who m. Berta, daughter of Milo de Gloucester, Earl of Hereford, and co-heir of her brother, William, Earl of Hereford, by whom he acquired Brecknock, with other extensive territorial possessions. He had two sons, William and Philip, and was s. by the elder,

WILLIAM DE BRAOSE, who likewise inherited the large estates of his mother. This feudal lord was a personage of great power and influence during the reigns of HENRY II. and RICHARD I., from the former of whom he obtained a grant of the "whole kingdom of Limeric, in Ireland," for the service of sixty knights' fees, to be held of the king and his younger son, JOHN. After the accession of the latter prince to the throne, as King JOHN, upon levying the scutage assessed subsequent to his coronation, De Braose accounted thirty marks for the scutage of John de Monmouth, and forty-five marks and a half for that of Adam de Port. In the next year he had a special charter from the king, dated at Faleise, granting to him and his heirs the privilege that no sheriff or other officer of the crown, should for the execution of their offices, lodge within the lands of his Honour of Braose, in Normandy; but that his own officers should give summons for all the pleas there, belonging to the king: as also that the king's justices itinerant, whensoever they were to come into the bailiwick of Faleise, should sit at Braose, and there hold plea of all matters belonging to the king, receiving entertainment for one day at the feudal lord's charge. His tenantry were also relieved by this charter from all "carriages and aid to the sheriff, or constables of Faleise;" and from all custom of victual whatsoever, which should be brought to or sold at that place. For several years after this period he appears to have enjoyed the favour of *King John*, and his power and possessions were augmented by divers grants from the crown. But in the 10th of the king's reign, when the kingdom laboured under an interdiction, and JOHN deemed it expedient to demand hostages from his barons to insure their allegiance, should the pope proceed to the length of absolving them from obedience to the crown, his officers who came upon the mission to the Baron de Braose, were met by MAUD, his wife, and peremptorily informed that she would not intrust any of her children to the king, who had so basely murdered his own nephew, *Prince* ARTHUR. De Braose rebuked her, however, for speaking thus, and said that if he had in any thing offended the king, he was ready to make satisfaction, according to the judgment of the court, and the barons his peers, upon an appointed day, and at any fixed place, without however giving hostages. This answer being communicated to the king, an order was immediately transmitted to seize upon the baron's person, but his lordship having notice thereof fled with his family into Ireland. This quarrel between De Braose and *King John*, is, however, differently related by other authorities. The monk of Lanthony states, that *King John* disinherited and banished him for his cruelty to the Welsh, in his war with *Gwenhwnwyn*, and that his wife Maud, and William, his son and heir, died prisoners in Corfe Castle. While another writer relates, " that this William de Braose, son of Philip de Braose, Lord of Buelt, held the lands of Brecknock and Went, for the whole time of *King* HENRY II., RICHARD I., and *King* JOHN, without any disturbance, until he took to wife the Lady Maud de St. Waleric; who, in revenge of Henry de Hereford, caused divers Welshmen to be murthered in the castle of Bergavenny, as they sate at meat: and that for this, and for some other pickt quarrel, *King* JOHN banished him and all his out of England. Likewise, that in his exile, *Maud*, his wife, with William, called *Gam*, his son, were taken and put in prison; where she died, the tenth year after her husband fought with Wenhunwyn, and slew three thousand Welsh." From these various relations, says Dugdale, it is no easy matter to discover what his demerits were; but what usage he had at last, take here from the credit of these two historians, who lived near that time. "This year, viz. anno 1210," quoth *Matthew* of WESTMINSTER, " the noble lady *Maud*, wife of *William de Braose*, with *William*, their son and heir, were miserably famished at Windsore, by the command of *King* JOHN; and William, her husband, escaping from Scorham, put himself into the habit of a beggar, and privately getting beyond sea, died soon after at Paris, where he had burial in the Abbey of St. Victor." And Matthew Paris, putting his death in anno 1212, (which differs a little in time,) says, " That he fled from Ireland to France, and dying at Ebule, his body was carried to Paris, and there honourably buried in the Abbey of St. Victor." "But after these great troubles in his later days," continues Dugdale, " I shall now say something of his pious works. Being by inheritance from his mother, Lord of Bergavenny, he gave to the monks of that priory, all the tithes of his castle there, viz. of

bread, wine, beer, cider; all manner of flesh, fish, salt, honey, wax, tallow; and in general, of whatsoever should be brought thither, and spent there: and moreover two marks of silver out of his lordship of Espines; and two marks of silver yearly out of his lands in England, as soon as God should enlarge them to forty pounds per annum: as also the toll on the market day, within the gates of that his castle. Which gift he so made to those monks of Bergavenny, conditionally, that the abbot and convent of *St. Vincenti*, in MAINE, (to which this priory of Bergavenny was a cell) should daily pray for the soul of him, the said William, and the soul of Maud, his wife."

This great, but unfortunate personage, had issue by his wife, Maud de St. Waleric,

William, who perished by starvation with his mother, at Windsor. He m. —— daughter of the Earl of Clare, with whom he had the town of Buckingham, in frank marriage, and left a son,

    JOHN, surnamed *Tadody*, of whom hereafter.

Giles, bishop of Hereford.

Reginald, who succeeded his brother, the bishop, in the representation of the family.

John (Sir), who had from his father the manor of Knylle or Knill, in the marches of Wales, and thence adopted the surname of KNILL. The lineal descendant of this Sir John de Knill, in the sixth degree.

    SIR JOHN DE KNILL, of Knill, was grandfather of

    WILLIAM KNILL, Esq., of Knill, who was *s.* by his son,

    JENKIN KNILL, Esq., of Knill, who m. Anne, daughter and co-heiress of Sir Richard Devereux, second son of William, Lord Ferrers, K.G., and dying in 1506, was *s.* by his eldest son,

    JOHN KNILL, Esq., of Knill, sheriff of the county of Radnor, in 1561. He m. Margery, daughter of Sir John Whittington, Knt. (who served the office of sheriff for Gloucestershire, temp. HENRY VII.) and was *s.* by his son,

    FRANCIS KNILL, Esq., of Knill, a Justice of the Peace for Herefordshire, temp. Elizabeth, m. Joane, daughter of Thomas Lewis, Esq., of Harpton Court, in Radnorshire, and dying in 1590, was *s.* by his only son,

    JOHN KNILL, Esq., of Knill, who d. unmarried, in 1609, when his estates devolved upon his sister and heiress,

    BARBARA KNILL, who conveyed them to her husband, John Walsham, Esq., of Prestaigne, by whose lineal descendant, SIR JOHN WALSHAM, Bart., they are still possessed.

Joane, m. to Richard, Lord Percy.

Loretta, m. to Robert Fitz-Parnell, Earl of Leicester.

Margaret, m. to Walter de Lacy.

Maud, m. to Griffith, Prince of South Wales.

Regarding his lands, it appears that in the 11th of

JOHN, the sheriff of Devon accounted for those in that shire, and the stock of cattle upon some other, was sold for the king's use; for in the next year, William de Nevill accounted for eighty-four pounds and five shillings, for three hundred and thirty-seven kine, which came from those lands, each cow then rated at five shillings. When the contest between John and the barons broke out, GILES DE BRAOSE, *Bishop of Hereford*, arraying himself under the baronial banner, was put in possession by the people, of Bergavenny, and the other castles of the deceased lord; and eventually, *King* JOHN, in the last year of his reign, his wrath being then assuaged, granted part of those lands to the bishop's younger brother and heir,

REGINALD DE BRAOSE, which grant was confirmed by *King* HENRY III., and he had livery of the castle and honour of Totness, with the honour of Barnstaple, having had previous possession of other estates. He m. Grecia, daughter of William de Brusre, and dying in 1221, was s. by his son,

WILLIAM DE BRAOSE. This feudal lord fell a victim to the jealousy of LEWELINE, *Prince of Wales*, who suspecting an intimacy between him and the princess, his wife, *King* HENRY's sister, invited him to an Easter feast, and treacherously cast him into prison at the conclusion of the banquet. He was soon afterwards put to death with the unfortunate princess. He had married Eve, daughter of Walter Mareschal, and sister of Richard, Earl of Pembroke, by whom he had four daughters, his co-heirs, viz.:

> ISABEL, m. first, to David, son of Leweline, Prince of Wales, and secondly, to Peter Fitz-Herbert.
> MAUD, m. to Roger, Lord Mortimer, of Wigmore.
> EVE, m. to William de Cantilupe.
> Eleanor, m. to Humphrey de Bohun.

The line of this branch thus terminating in heir-asses, we proceed with that founded by the Bishop of Hereford's nephew,

JOHN DE BRAOSE, surnamed *Tadody*, who had been privately nursed by a Welch woman, at *Gower*. This John had grants of lands from *King* HENRY III., and was also possessed of the Barony of Brambye, in Sussex, where he died in 1231, by a fall from his horse, his foot sticking in the stirrup. He m. Margaret, daughter of Leweline, Prince of Wales, by whom (who afterwards espoused Walter de Clifford) he had a son, his successor,

WILLIAM DE BRAOSE, who in the 41st HENRY III., when Leweline ap Griffin menaced the Marches of Wales with a great army, was commanded by the king to defend his own Marches about *Gower*, and the next year he had a military summons to attend the king at Chester. In two years afterwards, he was again in arms, under Roger de Mortimer, against the Welch; and he was subsequently one of the barons who became pledged for *King* HENRY, abiding the award of Lewis, King of France. He d. in 1290, and was s. by his son,

WILLIAM DE BRAOSE, who, in the 22nd of Edward I., had summons to attend the king with

other great men, to advise regarding the important affairs of the realm. And about the beginning of the ensuing September, was one of those who embarked at Portsmouth, with horse and arms, in the king's service, for Gascony. In the 28th and 29th of the same reign, he was in the wars of Scotland, and in the latter year he had summons to parliament as a BARON. In the 32nd, he was again in the Scottish wars, and then enjoyed so much favour, that the king not only confirmed to him and his heirs, the grant of Gower Land, made by King John to his ancestor, but granted that he and they should thenceforth enjoy all regal jurisdiction, liberties, and privileges there, in as ample a manner as Gilbert de Clare, son of Richard de Clare, sometime Earl of Gloucester, had in all his lands of Glamorgan. For several years afterwards, his lordship appears to have been constantly engaged upon the same theatre of war, and always eminently distinguished. In the 14th Edward II., being, according to Thomas, of Walsingham, "a person who had a large patrimony, but a great unthrift," his lordship put up for sale his noble territory of GOWER LAND, and absolutely sold it under the king's license, to the Earl of Hereford; but its contiguity to the lands of the younger SPENCER, (who was then high in royal favour, and the king's chamberlain,) attracting the attention of that minion, he forcibly possessed himself of the estate, and thus gave rise to the insurrection headed by Thomas Plantagenet, Earl of Lancaster. Lord Braose espoused Aliva, daughter of Thomas de Moulton, and had issue,

> ALIVA, m. to John de Mowbray.
> JOANE, m. to John de Bohun, of Midhurst.

His lordship, who had regular summons to parliament, to 10th September, 1325, died in that year, when the BARONY of BRAOSE, OF GOWER, fell into ABEYANCE between his daughters and co-heirs, and it so continues with their representatives.

ARMS.—Az. semée of cross croselets, gu. a lion rampant, or armed a langued gu.

BRAOSE—BARONS BRAOSE.

By Writ of Summons, dated 25th February, 1342, 16 Edward III.

Lineage.

SIR THOMAS DE BRAOSE, Knt., brother of William, Lord Braose, of Gower, having distinguished himself in the French and Scottish Wars of *King* EDWARD III., was summoned to parliament by that monarch as a BARON, from 26th February, 1342, to 15th July, 1358. His lordship m. Beatrix, daughter of Roger de Mortimer, and widow of Edward, son of Thomas, of Brotherton, Earl of Norfolk, and Earl Marshal of England, by whom he had issue,

> JOHN, his successor.
> Thomas (Sir).
> Joane.

He d. in 1361, and was s. by his elder son,

JOHN DE BRAOSE, second baron, who m. Elizabeth, daughter of Edward de Montague, but dying without issue, was s. by his brother,

SIR THOMAS DE BRAOSE, third baron, who died in his minority, unmarried, when the estates devolved upon his sister,

JOANE DE BRAOSE, who died issueless, when the BARONY OF BRAOSE became EXTINCT, and the estates passed to her cousin, Elizabeth, wife of Sir William Heron, Knt., the niece, through his sister, Beatrix, of the first baron.

ARMS.—Az. semée of cross crosslets, gu. a lion rampant, or armed and langued gu.

DEVEREUX—EARLS OF ESSEX.

By Letters Patent, dated 4th May, 1572.

Lineage.

WALTER DEVEREUX, second Viscount Hereford, was created on the 4th May, 1572, EARL OF ESSEX, in consideration of his descent from the family of BOURCHIER, which had previously held that earldom. His lordship being a military man of high reputation, was appointed, in the 19th Elizabeth, field marshal of the forces sent to suppress the rebellion of the Earls of Northumberland and Westmoreland; and he was afterwards employed in the wars of Ireland, with the title of Earl Marshal of that kingdom; he was also a Knight of the Garter. His lordship m. Lettice, daughter of Sir Francis Knolles, K.G., and had issue,

ROBERT, his successor.

Walter, killed before Roan.

Penelope, m. first, to Robert, Lord Rich, and secondly, to Charles Blount, Earl of Devon.

Dorothy, m. first, to Sir Thomas Perrot, Knt., and secondly, to Henry, Earl of Northumberland.

The earl d. at Dublin, on the 22nd September, 1576, but not without suspicion of having been poisoned, through the instigation of the infamous Robert Dudley, Earl of Leicester, who soon after repudiated his wife, Lady Douglas Howard, and espoused the widow of his lordship. Lord Essex was s. by his elder son,

ROBERT DEVEREUX, second Earl of Essex, the celebrated but unfortunate favourite of Queen ELIZABETH. His lordship was first brought to court, in 1585, by his step-father, the Earl of Leicester, and he subsequently attained the highest honours his sovereign could bestow. He was a privy councillor, a Knight of the Garter, master of the horse, earl marshal of England, and lord deputy of Ireland; he was likewise chancellor of the University of Cambridge. His ultimate fate is so conspicuous an event in history, that it would be impertinent to dwell at any length upon it here. His lordship having conspired against his royal mistress, and made a fruitless effort at insurrection, was taken prisoner, committed to the Tower, and thence, after being convicted by his peers of high treason, led to the scaffold, on the 25th February, 1600. The earl left issue by his wife, Frances, daughter and heir of Sir Francis Walsingham, and widow of Sir Philip Sidney, one son and two daughters, viz.:

ROBERT.

Frances, m. to William Seymour, Duke of Somerset.

Dorothy, m. first, to Sir Henry Shirley, Bart., of Stanton-Harold, and secondly, to William Stafford, Esq., of Blatherwick, in the County of Northampton.

His lordship's honours expired under the attainder, but his children being restored in blood, in 1603, his son,

ROBERT DEVEREUX, succeeded to the Earldom of Essex, and his late father's other dignities. This nobleman, who was installed a Knight of the Garter, in 1638, attached himself to the royal cause until 1642, when he accepted a commission in the parliament army, and afterwards distinguished himself as a parliamentary general. He d. on the 14th September, 1646, and was interred with national obsequies in Westminster Abbey, the two houses of parliament attending the funeral. His lordship espoused first, Lady Frances Howard, daughter of Thomas, Earl of Suffolk, from whom he was divorced, and that infamous woman m. afterwards, Sir Robert Carr, K.G., Earl of Somerset. The earl wedded secondly, Elizabeth, daughter of Sir William Paulet, of Eddington, in the county of Wilts, one of the natural sons of William, third Marquess of Winchester, and had a son, Robert, who died in infancy. His lordship leaving no issue, the EARLDOM OF ESSEX, at his decease, became EXTINCT, while his other honours passed according to their respective limitations. (See Viscount Hereford, Burke's Peerage and Baronetage.)

ARMS.—A fesse gules, in chief three torteauxes.

DUDLEY—BARON DENBIGH, EARL OF LEICESTER.

Barony,	by Letters	28th September,	1563.
Earldom,	Patent,	29th September,	

Lineage.

SIR ROBERT DUDLEY, a younger son of John, Duke of Northumberland, and brother of Lord Guilford Dudley, the unhappy husband of Lady Jane Grey, was appointed according to his biographist, Sir John Hayward, in the 5th of EDWARD VI., one of the six gentlemen in ordinary of the privy-chamber to that king; and Hayward adds, "that he was the true heir, both of his father's hate against persons of nobility, and cunning to dissemble the same; and afterwards for lust and cruelty, a monster of the court. And, as apt to hate, so a true executioner of his hate; yet rather by practice than by open dealing, as wanting rather courage than wit: and, that, after his entertainment into a place of so near service the king enjoyed his health not long." Upon the accession of MARY, Dudley was sent to the Tower with his father, and attainted; but, escaping the fate of that ambitious nobleman, he was soon afterwards restored, and made master of the ordnance. By QUEEN ELIZABETH he was at once taken into favour, raised to high rank, and invested with wealth and power. In the first year of her majesty's reign, he was made master of the horse, with a fee of one hundred marks per annum, and elected a KNIGHT of the most noble order of the GARTER. He was soon afterwards constituted Constable of Windsor Castle for life, and the queen subsequently proposed that he should become the husband of the beautiful but unfortunate MARY STUART, promising, in the event of the princess's assent, that she would, by authority of parliament, declare her heir to the crown of England, in case she died herself without issue. The alliance was marred, however, through the influence of France, although the FAVOURITE had been advanced the same year, that he might be deemed the more worthy of his royal bride, to the dignities of *Baron Denbigh* and EARL OF LEICESTER. But this proceeding of ELIZABETH has been considered as a mere experiment to enable herself to espouse Dudley with less dishonour, if he had been accepted by the Queen of Scots. In 1572 his lordship was one of the peers who sate upon the trial of the Duke of Norfolk, and he was appointed some years afterwards captain-general of an expedition sent into the Low Countries for the service of the United Provinces against the Spaniards; but in this enterprise, incurring, by his insolence, incapacity, and caprice, the displeasure of the Dutch, he was recalled, and constrained upon his return to humble himself to the queen, and with tears to beg of her majesty, " that, having sent him thither with honour, she would not receive him back with disgrace; and that whom she had raised from the dust, she would not bury alive!" He intended afterwards to retire to his Castle of Kenilworth, and commenced his journey thither, but died on the way at Cornbury Park, in Oxfordshire, on the 4th September, 1588. His lordship was a Knight of the Garter, and a Knight of St. Michael, a privy-counsellor, master of the horse, steward of the queen's household, constable of Windsor Castle, chancellor of the University of Oxford, justice in Eyre of all the forests south of Trent, and lieutenant and captain-general of the English forces in the Netherlands. " His death," says Rapin, " drew tears from the queen, who, nevertheless, ordered his goods to be sold at public sale for payment of the sums she had lent him. This infamous nobleman m. first the beautiful AMY ROBSART, daughter of Sir John Robsart, Knt.; and that unhappy lady he is accused but too justly of having murdered in the house of Forster, one of his tenants, at *Cumnor*, near Oxford. To this lone habitation she was removed, and there, after poison had proved inefficacious, she was strangled, and her corpse flung from a high staircase, that her death might appear to have been occasioned by the fall. He espoused, secondly, Douglas, daughter of William, Lord Howard, of Effingham, and widow of John, Lord Sheffield, by whom he had a son,

ROBERT (Sir).

Fearing that this latter alliance would cause a diminution of his influence with the queen, he tried by every means to repudiate her ladyship, and he subsequently attempted her life by poison, but unsuccessfully. His child by her, Sir Robert Dudley, he terms, in his will, his base son, but leaves him the principal part of his fortune. His third wife

was Lettice, daughter of Sir Francis Knollies, and widow of Walter, Earl of Essex; but by her he had no surviving issue. In the year 1575, Queen ELIZABETH paid the earl a visit at Kenilworth, and was there magnificently entertained by his lordship for 17 days, at the enormous expense of £60,000. About this period appeared a pamphlet, written with much force, entitled a Dialogue between a Scholar, a Gentleman, and a Lawyer, wherein the whole of Leicester's conduct was canvassed with great truth. The queen herself caused letters to be written from the privy-council, denying the charges, and vindicating the character of the FAVOURITE; but the book was not the less read nor credited.

Upon the decease of the earl, his HONOURS became EXTINCT. His son, Sir Robert Dudley, failing to establish his legitimacy, retired to Italy in disgust, and lived there the remainder of his life. (See Dudley, Duchess of Dudley.) Of Dudley, Walpole, in his Royal and Noble Authors, thus speaks: " Robert Dudley, called the natural son, probably the legitimate son of the great Earl of Leicester, having been deprived of his birthright, and never acknowledged as a peer of England, could not with propriety be classed among that order: yet he was too great an honour to his country to be omitted; and it is the duty of the meanest historian, and his felicity to have it in his power, to do justice to the memory of the deserving, which falls not within the compass of particulars to procure to the living. The author of those curious Lives of the Dudleys in the Biographia has already retrieved the fame of this extraordinary person from oblivion; and therefore I shall touch very few particulars of his story. He was educated under Sir Thomas Chaloner, the accomplished governor of Prince HENRY, and distinguished his youth by martial achievements, and by useful discoveries in the West Indies: but it was the house of Medici, those patrons of learning and talent, who fostered this enterprising spirit, and who were amply rewarded for their munificence by his projecting the free port of Leghorn. He flourished in their court, and in that of the emperor, who declared him Duke of Northumberland, a dukedom remarkably confirmed to his widow, whom CHARLES I. created Duchess of Dudley. Anthony Wood says, ' the duke was a complete gentleman in all suitable employments, an exact seaman, an excellent architect, mathematician, physician, chymist, and what not. He was a handsome, personable man, tall of stature, red-haired, and of admirable comport, and, above all, noted for riding the great horse, for tilting, and for his being the first of all that taught a dog to sit in order to catch partridges.' "

ARMS,—Or. a lion rampant, double quevée vert.

FITZ-ROY — EARL OF NORTHUMBERLAND, DUKE OF NORTHUMBERLAND.

Earldom,	{ by Letters	1st October, 1674.
Dukedom,	{ Patent,	6th April, 1683.

Lineage.

GEORGE FITZ-ROY, natural son of King

CHARLES II. by Barbara, Duchess of Cleveland, was created on the 1st October, 1674, *Baron of Pontefract, Viscount Falmouth*, and *Earl of Northumberland ;* and he was advanced, on the 6th April, 1683, to the DUKEDOM OF NORTHUMBERLAND. He was also invested with the Garter. His grace m. Katherine, daughter of Thomas Wheatley, Esq., of Brecknock, in the county of Berks, and widow of Thomas Lucy Esq., of Charlecote; but died *s. p.* in 1716, when all his honours became EXTINCT.

ARMS.—England, with a border componée, erm. and az.

FORTIBUS — EARLS OF ALBEMARLE.

Creation of the CONQUEROR.

Lineage.

ODO, Earl of Champaigne, having married ADELIZA, sister of the CONQUEROR, obtained from that monarch the Isle (as he calls it) of Holderness, and he had from the Archbishop of Roan, the city of Albemarle, upon the condition, that in all expeditions where that prelate went in person, he should be his standard-bearer with twelve knights. Holderness, at this period being a barren country, producing nought but oats, so soon as his wife brought him a son, ODO entreated the king to give him some land which would bear wheat, " whereby he might better nourish his nephew," the king granted him therefore the lordship of Bytham, in Lincolnshire. Others mentioning this gift to ODO, call it *Comitatum Holderness*, the county or Earldom of Holderness, which included a large portion of Yorkshire, upon the north-eastern side. Of this *Earl* ODO nothing further is known, than his joining Robert de Mowbray, Earl of Northumberland, and others, anno 1096, in a conspiracy to depose WILLIAM *Rufus*, and to place STEPHEN (afterwards king) upon the throne; for which conduct he suffered imprisonment. He *d.* in 1096, leaving a daughter, Judith, m. to Waltheof, Earl of Northumberland and Huntingdon, and a son, his successor,

STEPHEN, Earl of Albemarle, who, in the contest between WILLIAM *Rufus*, and his brother, ROBERT *Curthose*, remained faithful to the former; but that difference being adjusted, he embarked with *Curthose* for the Holy Land, and in the great victory achieved over the infidel near Antioch, had a principal command in the Christian army. He subsequently joined Hugh de Gornay in an unsuccessful attempt to depose HENRY I. in favour of ROBERT *Curthose*, and he made a similar effort afterwards for *Curthose's* son, *Prince* WILLIAM. In the last attempt some lost their lives, others were disinherited or imprisoned, but of the fate of the Earl of Albemarle nothing certain is known. He m. Hawise, daughter of Ralph de Mortimer, and had three sons and four daughters, viz.,

WILLIAM, surnamed *Le Grosse*, his successor.
Stephen.
Ingelram.

————, m. to the Vidam of Pynkeney. }
————, m. to the Vidam of Verberay. } All French and Normans.
————, m. to ‘Bertran de Brikebet. }
————, m. first, to William de Romare, and secondly, to Peter de Brus.

His successor,

WILLIAM, *Le Grosse*, third Earl of Albemarle, was a person of great note at the period in which he lived. In 1138 he was chief of those great nobles that gave battle to, and defeated, the Scots at NORTH ALLERTON, when DAVID, *King of Scotland*, had invaded the north with a mighty army, claiming Northumberland for his son *Henry*, in right of Maud, daughter and heir of Earl Waltheof. Upon this memorable occasion Thurston, Archbishop of York, caused a famous standard to be erected in the English camp, displaying the banners of St. Peter, St. John, of Beverley, and St. Wilfrid, of Rippin, with the sacred host. From which circumstance the ground whereon the battle was fought has ever since been termed STANDARD HILL. The Earl of Albemarle was rewarded for his gallantry with the Earldom of Yorkshire, and Robert de Ferrers with that of the county of Derby. His lordship, under the title of Earl of York, was subsequently with *King* STEPHEN at the battle of Lincoln, where that monarch sustained so signal a defeat. He m. Cicily, daughter of William Fitz-Duncan, (nephew of Malcolm, king of Scotland,) by Alice, daughter of Robert de Romely, Lord of the Honour of Skipton, in Craven, &c., by which marriage he enjoyed, as her inheritance, all that part of Yorkshire called Craven. By this lady he had two daughters,

HAWISE, who m. first, William de Mandeville, Earl of Essex, and secondly, William de Fortibus.

Amicia, m. to ———— Eston, by whom she had a son,

RANULPH, whose son,
JOHN, was father of
JOHN DE ESTON, or ASTON, who, as right heir after AVELINE DE FORTIBUS, claimed, in the 6th of EDWARD I., the EARLDOM OF ALBEMARLE, and had certain lands in Thornton to the value of £100 per annum, assigned to him to release his right therein.

WILLIAM, Le Grosse, died in 1179, and was succeeded in the Earldom of Albemarle by his son-in-law,

WILLIAM DE MANDEVILLE, Earl of Essex, who died *s. p.* in 1190; and HAWISE, his widow, marrying

WILLIAM DE FORTIBUS, he became, in her right, EARL OF ALBEMARLE, and *Lord of Holderness*. This William was constituted, by RICHARD I., one of the admirals of the fleet, in which that monarch soon afterwards sailed towards Jerusalem. His lordship died in 1194, leaving a son and heir, WILLIAM DE FORTIBUS, but in regard that HAWISE, the deceased lord's widow, was heir to the Earldom, and that she married

BALDWINE DE BERTUNE, Earl of the Isle of Wight, that William was postponed to Baldwine in the enjoyment of the Earldom of Albemarle, but Baldwine dying *s. p.* in 1912, the dignity then devolved upon the said

WILLIAM DE FORTIBUS, to whom *King John*, in the sixteenth year of his reign, confirmed all the lands which accrued to him by inheritance from his mother. The next year the earl, arraying himself on the side of the barons, was one of the celebrated TWENTY-FIVE chosen to enforce the observance of MAGNA CHARTA; but he subsequently deserted his party, and was, with *King John* in his expedition into the north, so marked by spoil and rapine. He was then constituted governor of the castles of Rockingham, in Northamptonshire, Saubey, in Leicestershire, and Bitham, in the county of Lincoln, with strict command to destroy all the houses, parks, and possessions of those barons who were in arms against the king. In the reign of HENRY III. his lordship fought at the battle of Lincoln under the royal banner, and shared largely in the spoils of victory. He was subsequently for and against the king by turns, and eventually died at sea, in his progress to the Holy Land. He *m.* Aveline, daughter and co-heir of Richard de Munfichet, a great baron in Essex, and was *s.* by his son,

WILLIAM DE FORTIBUS, Earl of Albemarle. This nobleman enjoyed the sheriffalty of Cumberland from the 41st of HENRY III. until the time of his decease. His lordship *m.* first, Christian, daughter and co-heir of Alan, of Galoway, but that lady died without issue. He espoused, secondly, ISABEL, daughter of Baldwine, EARL OF DEVON, by whom he had three sons, John, Thomas, and William, and one surviving daughter, AVELINE. The earl, journeying into France, died at Amiens in 1259, when the tuition of his two surviving sons, Thomas and William, was committed to their mother, Isabel, but these children appear to have lived only a short time, when the whole inheritance passed to the earl's daughter,

AVELINE DE FORTIBUS, whose wardship was granted by the king to Richard de Clare, Earl of Gloucester, for the whole term of fifteen years of her minority. This grant was, however, shortly after surrendered, and the king conferred the guardianship of the heiress to his eldest son, *Prince Edward*, who assigned the Castle and Barony of Skipton, in Craven, to Alexander, King of Scotland, during her minority, in consideration of the sum of £1500. This lady, independently of the great inheritance of the FORTIBUS family, became also heiress to her mother, Isabel, (who, upon the death of her brother, fifth Earl of Devon, styled herself Countess of Albemarle and Devon) and thus with both inheritances, she was heir to the EARLDOMS OF ALBEMARLE AND DEVON, to THE BARONY OF SKIPTON and THE SOVEREIGNTY OF THE ISLE OF WIGHT. Her ladyship espoused EDMUND PLANTAGENET, surnamed *Crouchback*, afterwards Duke of Lancaster; the king and queen and almost all the nobility of England attending at the wedding. She died, however, within a short time without issue, and her honours passed into other families.

ARMS.—Ar. a chief, gules.

GRENVILLE — BARON GLASTONBURY.

By Letters Patent, dated 20th October, 1797.

Lineage.

JAMES GRENVILLE, Esq. (son of the Right Honourable James Grenville, uncle to George, first Marquess of Buckingham, by Mary, daughter and heiress of James Smyth, Esq., of Harden, in the county of Herts), having been sworn of his majesty's most honourable privy council, and constituted one of the Lords of the treasury, in 1782, was elevated to the peerage on the 20th of October, 1797, as Baron Glastonbury, of Butley, in the county of Somerset, with remainder to his brother, General Grenville, who predeceased him in 1823, unmarried. His lordship *d.* without issue, in 1825, when the Barony of Glastonbury became EXTINCT.

ARMS.—Vert, on a cross arg. five torteauxes.

IPRE—EARL OF KENT.

Creation of King Stephen, anno 1141.

Lineage.

WILLIAM DE IPRE, said to be an illegitimate son of Philip, Earl of Ipre, in Flanders, having distinguished himself previously in arms, joined in 1137, the banner of King Stephen, then reared in Normandy against the Empress Maud, and continuing actively engaged in that prince's cause, was created by him in 1141, EARL OF KENT: in which year he commanded one of the divisions of King Stephen's army at the battle of Lincoln, where the king's forces experienced a signal defeat, and the monarch himself became a prisoner. The earl, however, effected his retreat, and recruiting his army, encountered, subsequently, the empress at Winchester, where he retrieved the fortunes of his royal master, and restored him to freedom and a crown. In the heat of these feuds his lordship is accused of burning the Abbey of Wherwell, in the county of Southampton, because the nuns had harboured some of the partisans of the empress, but after peace was restored, he made restitution by founding the Cistertian Abbey, at Borley, in Kent, anno 1144. Upon the death of King Stephen, the Earl of Kent, then a widower, departed from England, and assuming the cowl in the Abbey of Laon, in Flanders, died there about the year 1162. The earl *m.* ———— and had a son, who is said to have been cruelly murdered by the ministers of Theodoric, Earl of Flanders: in consequence of which, upon the decease of his lordship his EARLDOM OF KENT became EXTINCT; while his estates passed to his only sister, Matilde,[*] wife

[*] Hasted's History of Kent.

of Norman Fitz-Dering, ancestor of the Baronets Dering, of Surrenden Dering, in the county of Kent.

ARMS.—Girony of ten or. and az. an escutcheon gules. a Baton Sinister humettee ar.

LANE-FOX—BARON BINGLEY.

By Letters Patent, dated 13th May, 1762.

Lineage.

GEORGE FOX, Esq., who assumed the additional surname of LANE, M.P. for the city of York, having m. Harriot, only daughter and heiress of Robert Benson, Lord Bingley (see that title,) was advanced to the peerage, in the dignity of his deceased father-in-law, on the 13th May, 1762, when he was created BARON BINGLEY, of Bingley, in the county of York. By this lady, with whom he acquired £100,000, and £7,000 a year, he had an only son, ROBERT, who m. in 1761, Bridget, daughter of the Earl of Northington, but died in his lordship's life-time without issue. Lord Bingley d. in 1763, when the barony became EXTINCT.

ARMS.—First and fourth ar. a lion rampant gu. within a border sa.: on a canton of the first, a harp and crown, or. for LANE, second and third, a chevron between three foxes' heads erased gules, for FOX.

NORRIS—VISCOUNT THAME, EARL OF BERKSHIRE.

By Letters Patent, dated 28th January, 1680.

Lineage.

This family was one of consideration in King EDWARD III.'s time, and then of knightly degree. In the reign of HENRY VI.,

JOHN NORRIS was first, usher of the chamber, next, esquire of the body, and afterwards master of the wardrobe to that monarch. He was subsequently sheriff of the counties of Devon and Berks, and in the next reign (Edward IV.) he was continued in the post of esquire of the body to the king. He resided at Patenden, in Berkshire, and dying in the 6th of EDWARD IV., was interred at BRAY, in an aisle of that church, built at his own expense. He was s. by his son and heir,

SIR WILLIAM NORRIS, of Patenden, one of the knights of the body to King EDWARD IV. In the 2d of HENRY VII., this gentleman had a command in the royal army at the battle of STOKE; and in the 19th of the same reign he obtained a grant from the king of the custody of the manor of Langley, which manor was then in the crown by reason of the minority of EDWARD, son and heir of Isabel, late wife of George, Duke of Clarence; and he had the stewardship of several other manors in the county of Oxford, part of the property of the said EDWARD, and situated similarly during his minority. Sir William m. first, Isabel, daughter

and heir of Edmund Ingaldesthorp, and widow of John Nevil, Marquess of Montague, by whom he had three sons, who all died young, and three daughters, viz.

—— m. to Sir John Langford, of Bradfield.

Joane, m. to John Cheney, Esq., of Wodbey, in the county of Berks.

Elizabeth, m. to William Farmer, Esq., of Somerton, in the county of Oxford.

He wedded secondly, the Lady Jane de Vere, daughter of John, Earl of Oxford, and had a son,

SIR EDWARD NORRIS, Knt., who m. Fridiswide, daughter and co-heir of Francis, Viscount Lovel, by whom he had two sons,

JOHN, one of the esquires of the body to King HENRY VIII., m. Elizabeth, sister of Edmund, Lord Bray, but d. without legitimate issue, in the 6th of Elizabeth.

Henry.

The younger son,

HENRY NORRIS, who succeeded eventually to the estates and representation of the family, was made usher of the black rod, upon the resignation of Sir William Compton, Knt., in the 18th of HENRY VIII. He was also esquire of the body to the king, and one of the gentlemen of his privy chamber: but being afterwards involved in the fall of ANNE BOLEYN, he was committed to the Tower as one of her paramours. It is said, however, that the brutal HENRY felt some compunction in putting him to death, and offered him a pardon conditionally, that he would confess his guilt; but Norris resolutely replied, "That in his conscience, he thought the queen guiltless of the objected crime; but whether she were or not, he could not accuse her of any thing; and that he had rather undergo a thousand deaths, than betray the innocent." Upon the report of which declaration, the king cried out, "Hang him up, hang him up." He suffered death accordingly, and was attainted in parliament the same year. He had m. Mary, daughter of Thomas, Lord Dacre of the south, and left a daughter, Mary, m. first to Sir George Carew, Knt., and secondly, to Sir Arthur Champernon, Knt., and a son,

HENRY NORRIS, Esq., who resided at Wytham, in Berks, and received, in 1566, the honour of knighthood. In the 14th of Elizabeth, Sir Henry was sent ambassador into France, and in consideration of his good services upon that occasion, as well as the sufferings of his father, he was summoned to parliament, on the 8th May, 1572, as BARON NORRIS, of Rycote. His lordship espoused Margery, younger daughter and co-heir of John, BARON WILLIAMS, of Thame, (and one of the co-heirs of the said Barony of Williams,) by whom he acquired the lordship of Rycote, and had issue,

WILLIAM, Marshal of Berwick, who m. Elizabeth, daughter of Sir Richard Morrison, Knt., and dying in the life-time of his father, left an only son,

FRANCIS, who s. his grandfather.

John (Sir), a very eminent and gallant soldier, temp. Elizabeth, distinguished in the wars of the Low Countries, and in those of Ireland, in which latter kingdom he filled the office of president of the Council of Munster, and died there, unmarried.

Edward, Governor of Ostend, died s. p.

Henry, died of a wound received in action.

Thomas, President of Munster, and some time Justice of Ireland.

Maximilian, slain in Britanny.

His lordship d. in 1600, and was s. by his grandson,

FRANCIS NORRIS, second Baron Norris of Rycote, summoned to parliament, from 17th October, 1601, to 5th April, 1614. His lordship, at the creation of King James's son, Prince CHARLES, Duke of York, was made a Knight of the Bath, and some years afterwards, 29th January, 1620, advanced to the dignities of *Viscount Thame,* and EARL OF BERKSHIRE. His lordship m. Lady Bridget de Vere, daughter of Edward, Earl of Oxford, and had an only daughter and heiress,

ELIZABETH, who m. Sir William Wray, of Glentworth, in the county of Lincoln, one of the Grooms of the Bedchamber to King Charles I., and left an only daughter,

BRIDGET WRAY, who m. Edward, son of Edward, Earl of Dorset, and became, after his decease, second wife of *Montagu Bertie,* EARL OF LINDSEY, Lord Great Chamberlain of England: by the latter she had a son,

JAMES BERTIE, who in her right, inherited the BARONY OF NORRIS, *of Rycote.* He was afterwards created EARL OF ABINGDON — honours enjoyed by his descendant, Montagu, present EARL OF ABINGDON.

His lordship, who was a person of impetuous temperament, was at one time committed to the Fleet Prison, for a rude assault upon the Lord Scroop, in the House of Lords, while the peers were actually sitting, and the prince present. He died in 1620, from the effects of a wound which he had inflicted upon himself, with a cross-bow. The BARONY OF NORRIS, *of Rycote,* passed eventually, with his grand-daughter, into the family of BERTIE, and has since merged in the Earldom of Abingdon, while the VISCOUNTY OF THAME AND EARLDOM OF BERKSHIRE, became EXTINCT.

ARMS.—Quarterly—ar and gu. a fesse az., in the second and third quarters, a fret or.

SCOTT (FITZ-ROY)—DUKE OF MONMOUTH.

By Letters Patent, dated 14th February, 1663.

Lineage.

JAMES FITZ-ROY, natural son of *King CHARLES II.,* by Mrs. Lucy Walters, daughter of Richard Walters, Esq., of Haverford West, in the county of Pembroke, was elevated to the peerage, on the 14th February, 1663, in the dignities of

Baron Tyndale, *in the county of Northumberland, Viscount Doncaster,* and DUKE OF MONMOUTH, and afterwards invested with the garter. His grace was born at Rotterdam, and bore the name of *Crofts,* until his marriage with the celebrated heiress, Lady ANNE SCOTT, daughter and sole heir of Francis, second EARL of BUCCLEUCH, when he assumed that of SCOTT. By this lady he left two sons,

JAMES, Earl of Dalkeith, from whom the present Duke of Buccleuch, lineally descends.

Henry, created Earl of Deloraine, a title that became extinct in 1807.

The fate of the Duke of Monmouth, is an historical event, so well known, that it would be idle to enlarge upon it here—suffice it to state, that his grace, soon after the accession of King James II., took up arms to depose that monarch, and to establish his own right to the throne, as the legitimate son of King CHARLES II., (under the allegation, that the king had married his mother)—that he came to a pitched battle with the royal army, at SEDGEMORE, on the 6th July, 1685, and sustained a decisive overthrow—that he was soon afterwards made prisoner, and brought to the block, on the 15th of the same month, when the DUKEDOM OF MONMOUTH, and the minor honours became EXTINCT, under the attainder. Burnet characterises his grace, " as possessed of many good qualities, and of some that were bad; that he was soft and gentle, even to excess; and too easy to those who had credit with him; sincere and good-natured, and understood war well; but too much given to pleasure and to favourites." The duke had separated from his duchess, and lived with Henrietta, Lady Wentworth. Immediately prior to his execution, Rapin states, that Dr. Jennison and Dr. Hooper, the divines in attendance upon him, " tried, but in vain, to obtain satisfaction, regarding his connection with this lady, though he had a duchess of his own, and his pretending to be lawfully married to her before God; alleging that his first marriage was null, as being too young when he gave his consent. All the pains taken by the two doctors to convince him of the falsehood of this opinion were fruitless, nay, he chose rather to deprive himself of the communion, than own his engagements with that lady to be unlawful."

ARMS.—The royal arms of *King* CHARLES II., viz: quarterly, first and fourth, *France and England,* quarterly; second, *Scotland;* third *Ireland;* bruised, with a baton sinister, ar.

SONDES—EARL OF FEVERSHAM.

By Letters Patent, dated 8th April, 1676.

Lineage.

SIR GEORGE SONDES, Bart., of Lees Court, in the county of Kent, was elevated to the peerage, in consideration of the services he had rendered to King CHARLES I., by letters patent, dated 8th April 1676, in the dignities of *Baron Throwley, Vis-*

count *Sondes, of Lees Court*, and EARL OF FEVERSHAM, with remainder, failing his own male issue, to Lewis, Lord Duras, the husband of his elder daughter. His lordship *m.* first, Jane, daughter and heir of Sir Ralph Freeman, Knt., by whom he had three sons,

Freeman, who died young.

George, inhumanly murdered in his bed by his younger brother.

Freeman, who suffered death for the atrocious deed of fratricide.

The earl espoused, secondly, Mary, daughter of Sir William Villiers, of Brokesby, in the county of Leicester, Bart., and had two daughters,

Mary, *m.* to Lewis, Lord Duras, (see that dignity,) and died *s. p.*

Catherine *m.* to Lewis Watson, Lord Rockingham. This lady succeeded, on the decease of her sister issueless, to the entire fortune of her father.

His lordship *d.* in 1677, when his honours devolved, according to the limitation, upon his son-in-law, Lord Duras.

ARMS.—Ar. three blackmoor's heads couped ppr. between two chevronels, sa.

WHITWORTH—VISCOUNT WHITWORTH, EARL WHITWORTH.

| Viscounty, | By Letters | 14th June, 1813. |
| Earldom, | Patent, | 25th Nov., 1815. |

Lineage.

The WHITWORTHS, an ancient Staffordshire family, produced a nobleman of the kingdom of Ireland in the beginning of the last century, WHITWORTH, *Baron Whitworth, of Galway*, between whom and the eminent person of whom we are about to treat there are many points of singular similarity. Like his noble kinsman, (our English lord,) he was celebrated for the number and importance of his embassies, like him created Baron WHITWORTH, of Galway, and as if to complete the resemblance, died in the year 1725, (the last lord it will be seen died in 1825,) leaving no heir to his title. The brother of this Lord Whitworth, of Galway,

—— WHITWORTH, Esq., who was M.P. for Minehead, surveyor-general of woods and forests, and secretary of Barbadoes, settled at Leybourne, in Kent. His son,

SIR CHARLES WHITWORTH, Knt., M.P. for Minehead, *m.* in 1749, Miss Shelley, eldest daughter of Richard Shelley, Esq., commissioner of the Stamp Office, and had three sons and four daughters, the eldest of whom,

CHARLES WHITWORTH, Esq., was *b.* in 1754, and educated at Tunbridge school under the poet Cawthorne. Soon after he had completed his studies, Mr. Whitworth obtained a commission in

the guards. In 1776 he removed with his father to STANMORE, having joined that gentleman in obtaining an act of parliament to authorise the sale of Leybourne to James Hawley, Esq., M.D. and F.R.S., which seat is now the residence of Dr. Hawley's great grandson, Sir Joseph-Henry Hawley, Bart.

Mr. Whitworth's first diplomatic employment was at the court of Poland in 1786. Warsaw was then the centre of intrigues. A new partition of Poland happened to be in contemplation, and the generous effort for national independence, sealed then, as recently, the doom of this valiant and noble people. Mr. Whitworth was recalled from Poland in 1788, and accredited envoy extraordinary and plenipotentiary to the court of Russia. In 1793, when the English cabinet had embarked in the confederacy against France, it was deemed proper to invest the ambassador at St. Petersburgh with the Order of the Bath, to add to the dignity of his mission; and Sir Charles Whitworth from that moment assumed a conspicuous position in the field of European politics. Upon his return from this embassy he was created, 21st March, 1800, a peer of Ireland, by the title of Baron Whitworth, of Newport Pratt, in the county of Galway; and his lordship repaired soon after as plenipotentiary extraordinary, to Copenhagen. His next mission, having been previously sworn of the privy council, was in 1802, to the consular court of France, where his sojourn was but of brief duration. After numerous preliminary conferences with Talleyrand on the subject of the retention of Malta by the British government, Napoleon sent at length for the English ambassador, and a long and important interview ensued, unsatisfactory to both parties. A subsequent conference took place, when the FIRST CONSUL instead of healing, appears to have widened the breach, and his lordship's prompt and dignified repression of Napoleon's intemperate address before a full court, and all the foreign ambassadors, has been celebrated throughout Europe. He soon afterwards left Paris, and for the succeeding ten years remained in retirement. On the 2d March, 1813, Lord Whitworth was made a lord of the bedchamber, and created on the 14th June following, a peer of the united kingdom, as VISCOUNT WHITWORTH, *of Adbaston:* within two months after, he succeeded the Duke of Richmond, as VICEROY OF IRELAND, and he was advanced on the 25th November, 1815, to the dignities of BARON ADBASTON, and EARL WHITWORTH. He continued in the government of Ireland until 1817. His lordship *m.* 7th April, 1801, Arabella-Diana, eldest daughter and co-heir of Sir Charles Cope, Bart., of Brewern, in Oxfordshire, and widow of John-Frederick, third Duke of Dorset, but had no issue. He *d.* 12th May, 1825, when all his honours became EXTINCT, and his estates devolved upon his widow, the Duchess of Dorset, at whose decease in the August following, they passed to her two daughters and co-heirs,

MARY, Countess of Plymouth, and

ELIZABETH, Countess of Delaware.

PEERAGES,

EXTINCT, DORMANT, AND IN ABEYANCE,

ALPHABETICALLY, ACCORDING TO THE TITLE OF EACH DIGNITY.

D. Dukedom. M. Marquisate. E. Earldom. V. Viscounty. B. Barony.

Titles.	In the Family of	Period of Possession, Anno Domini.		Eventual Destination.
Albemarle, E.	Fortibus . .	from 1212 to	—	Extinct
Albemarle, D. . .	Plantagenet . .	1397	1399	Forfeited
Albemarle, E.	Plantagenet	1411	1421	Extinct
Albemarle, D. . .	Monk . .	1660	1668	Extinct
Aldeburgh, B.	Aldeburgh	1371	—	Abeyance
Allington, B.	Allington . .	1682	1691	Extinct
Ancaster and Kesteven, D.	Bertie	1715	1809	Extinct
Anglesey, E. . .	Villiers	1623	1659	Extinct
Anglesey, E.	Annesley	1661	1761	Extinct
Anson, B.	Anson	1747	1762	Extinct
Ap-Adam, B.	Ap-Adam	1299	—	Extinct
Archdekne, B. . .	Archdekne . .	1321	—	Abeyance
Archer, B.	Archer	1747	1778	Extinct
Argentine, B. . .	Argentine . .	1297	—	Extinct
Arundel, E.	Albini	1139	1243	{ Passed with Arundel Castle to the Fitz-Alans
Arundel, E.	Fitz-Alan	1243	1579	{ Conveyed by an heiress to the Howards
Arundel, B.	Arundel	1664	1768	Extinct
Ashburton, B.	Dunning	1782	1823	Extinct
Astley, B.	Astley	1295	1554	Forfeited
Astley, of Reading, B.	Astley . .	1644	1688	Extinct
Aton, B.	Aton	1324	—	
Audley, B.	Aldithley or Audley	1313	1392	{ Conveyed by an heiress to the family of Touchet
Audley, B. . .	Touchet	1405	1631	Forfeited
Audley, B.	Audley	1321	1591	Forfeited
Audley, of Walden, B.	Audley	1538	1544	Extinct
Aylesbury, E.	Bruce	1664	1747	Extinct
		B.		
Badlesmere, B. . .	Badlesmere . .	1309	1338	Abeyance
Baliol, B.	Baliol	1300	—	Extinct
Baliol, B. (Feudal) . .	Baliol			
Banbury, E.	Knollys	1626	1632	Dormant
Bardolf, B.	Bardolf	1299	1404	Forfeited
Basset, of Drayton, B.	Basset	1264	1390	Abeyance
Basset, of Sapcoats, B.	Basset	1264	1378	Abeyance
Basset, of Welden, B.	Basset	1299	—	Extinct
Bath, E. . .	Bourchier . .	1536	1654	Extinct
Bath, E.	Granville	1661	1711	Extinct
Bath, E.	Pulteney	1742	1764	Extinct
Bath, Bss. . .	Pulteney . .	1792	1808	Extinct
Bath, Css. . .	Pulteney	1803	1808	Extinct
Bavent, B.	Bavent	1313	1370	Abeyance
Bayning, V. . .	Bayning	1627	1638	Extinct

Titles.	In the Family of	Period of Possession.		Eventual Destination.
Bayning, Vis.	Bayning	from 1674 to 1698		Extinct
Beauchamp, B.	Beauchamp	1350	1360	Extinct
Beauchamp, of Bletsho, B.	Beauchamp	1363	—	
Beauchamp, of Hacche, B.	Beauchamp	1299	—	Abeyance
Beauchamp, V.	Seymour	1536	1552	Forfeited
Beauchamp, of Hache, B.	Seymour	1559	1750	Extinct
Beauchamp, of Kyderminster, B.	Beauchamp	1387	1490	Extinct
Beauchamp, of Powyk, B.	Beauchamp	1447	1496	Extinct
Beaumont, B.	Beaumont	1309	1507	Abeyance
Beaumont, V.	Beaumont	1440	1507	Extinct
Beaulieu, B.	Hussey Montagu	1762	1802	Extinct
Beaulieu, E.	Hussey Montagu	1784	1802	Extinct
Bedford, E.	Bellemont	1150	—	Extinct
Bedford, E.	Courcy	1366	1397	Extinct
Bedford, D.	Plantagenet	1414	1435	Extinct
Bedford, D.	Nevill	1469	1477	G. Nevill, Duke of Bedford, degraded by parliament
Bedford, D.	Tudor	1485	1495	Extinct
Beke, of Eresby, B.	Beke	1295	—	Abeyance
Belasyse, B.	Belasyse	1644	1692	Extinct
Belasyse, of Osgodby, Bss.	Belasyse	1674	1713	Extinct
Benhale, B.	Benhale	1360	—	Extinct
Berkeley, V.	Berkeley	1481	1492	Extinct
Berkeley, M.	Berkeley	1488	1492	Extinct
Berkeley, of Stratton. B.	Berkeley	1685	1773	Extinct
Berkshire,	Norris	1690	1690	Extinct
Berner, B.	Bourchier	1455	1743	Abeyance
Bertram, of Milford, B.	Bertram	1264	—	Abeyance
Berwick, D.	Fitz-James	1687	1695	Forfeited
Bindon, V.	Howard (Bindon)	1559	1691	Extinct
Bindon, E.	Howard	1706	1722	Extinct
Bingley, B.	Benson	1713	1730	Extinct
Bingley, B.	Lane-Fox	1762	1773	Extinct
Blount, B.	Blount	1296	—	Extinct
Blount, B.	Blount	1330	1337	Extinct
Bohun, of Midhurst, B.	Bohun	1363	—	Extinct
Bolingbroke, E.	St. John	1624	1711	Extinct
Bolton, D.	Paulet	1689	1794	Extinct
Bonvile, B.	Bonvile	1449	1554	Forfeited
Boteler, of Oversly and Wemme	Boteler	1295	—	Abeyance
Boteler, of Werington	Boteler	1295	—	Extinct
Botetourt, B.	Botetourt	1308	1406	Abeyance
Bourchier, B.	Bourchier	1342	1646	Abeyance
Brackley, V.	Egerton	1616	1829	Extinct
Brackley, M.	Egerton	1720	1803	Extinct
Bradeston, B.	Bradeston	1342	—	Extinct
Bradford, E.	Newport	1694	1762	Extinct
Braose, B.	Braose	1299	1322	Abeyance
Braose, B.	Braose	1342	—	Extinct
Bray, B.	Bray	1527	1557	Abeyance
Brecknock, E.	Butler	1660	1715	Forfeited
Brentford, E.	Ruthven, or Ruthyn	1644	1651	Extinct
Bridport, B.	Hood	1796	1814	Extinct
Bridport, V.	Hood	1801	1814	Extinct
Bridgewater, E.	D'Aubeney	1538	1548	Extinct
Bridgewater, E.	Egerton	1720	1803	Extinct
Bridgewater, D.	Egerton	1617	1829	Extinct
Bristol, E.	Digby	1622	1698	Extinct
Bruce, of Annandale, B.	Bruce	1295	1304	Extinct
Bruce, of Whorlton, B.	Bruce	1640	1747	Extinct
Bryan, B.	Bryan	1350	1456	Extinct
Buckingham, E.	Giffard	1066	1166	Extinct
Buckingham, E.	Plantagenet	1377	1400	Extinct

656

Titles.	In the Family of	Period of Possession.		Eventual Destination.
Buckingham, E.	Stafford	*from* 1400 to 1521		Forfeited
Buckingham, D.	Stafford	1441	1521	Forfeited
Buckingham, M.	Villiers	1618	1687	Extinct
Buckingham, D.	Villiers	1623	1687	Extinct
Buckingham, Cas.	Villiers	1618	1632	Extinct
Buckingham, D.	Sheffield	1703	1735	Extinct
Bulkeley, B.	Bulkeley	1784	1822	Extinct
Bulmer, B.	Bulmer	1342	——	Extinct
Burgh, or Borough, B.	Burgh	1487	——	Abeyance
Burghersh, B.	Burghhersh	1303	1369	{ Conveyed by an heiress to the family of Le Despencer.
Burlington, E.	Boyle	1664	1735	Extinct
Burnell, B.	Burnell	1311	1315	Extinct
Burnell, B.	Burnell	1350	1420	Abeyance
Burton, B.	Paget	1711	1769	Extinct
Butler, of Bramfield, B.	Butler	1628	1647	Extinct
Butler, of Lanthony, B.	Butler	1660	1715	Forfeited
Butler, of Lanthony, B.	Butler	1801	1820	Extinct
Butler, of More Park, B.	Butler	1679	1715	Forfeited
Butler, of Weston, B.	Butler	1673	1685	Extinct
Butler, of Weston, B.	Butler	1693	1759	Extinct.

C.

Titles.	In the Family of	Period of Possession.		Eventual Destination.
Cadogan, of Reading, B.	Cadogan	1716	1726	Extinct
Cadogan, E.	Cadogan	1718	1726	Extinct
Cailli, B.	Cailli	1309	1311	Extinct
Cambridge, E.	Avesnes	1340	——	Extinct
Cambridge, E.	Plantagenet	1362	1461	Merged in the crown
Cambridge, E.	Hamilton	1619	1651	Extinct
Cambridge, E.	Stuart	1659	1660	Extinct
Cambridge, D.	Stuart	1661	1661	Extinct
Cambridge, D.	Stuart	1663	1663	Extinct
Cambridge, D.	Stuart	1667	1671	Extinct
Cambridge, D.	Stuart	1677	1677	Extinct
Cambridge, D.	Guelph	1706	1727	Merged in the crown
Camelford, B.	Pitt	1784	1804	Extinct
Camois, B.	Camois	1264	1335	Extinct
Camois, B.	Camois	1383	——	Abeyance
Campden, V.	Noel	1628	1798	Extinct
Camville, B.	Camville	1295	——	Abeyance
Cantilupe, B.	Cantilupe	1299	——	Extinct
Capel, B.	Capel	1692	1696	Extinct
Carew, B.	Carew	1605	1629	Extinct
Carey, B.	Carey	1622	1661	Extinct
Carleton, B.	Boyle	1714	1725	Extinct
Carlisle, E.	Harcla	1322	1323	Forfeited
Carlton, B.	Carlton	1626	1631	Extinct
Carnarvon, E.	Dormer	1628	1709	Extinct
Carnarvon, E.	Brydges	1714	1789	Extinct
Carnarvon, M.	Brydges	1719	1789	Extinct
Carrington, B.	Smith	1643	1705	Extinct
Carteret, B.	Carteret	1681	1776	Extinct
Carteret, V.	Carteret	1714	1776	Extinct
Castleton, V.	Saunderson	1716	1723	Extinct
Castleton, E.	Saunderson	1720	1723	Extinct
Caversham, V.	Cadogan	1718	1726	Extinct
Cecil, of Putney, B.	Cecil	1625	1638	Extinct
Chandos, B.	Chandos	1337	——	Extinct
Chandos, B.	Brydges	1554	1789	Dormant
Chandos, D.	Brydges	1729	1789	Extinct
Chaworth, B.	Chaworth	1299	——	Extinct
Chedworth, B.	Howe	1741	1804	Extinct
Cheney, B.	Cheney	1487	1496	Extinct
Cheney, of Todington, B.	Cheney	1572	1587	Extinct

4 H

Titles.	In the Family of	Period of Possession.		Eventual Destination.
Cherleton, of Powys, B.	Cherleton	from 1313 to 1422		Abeyance
Chester, E.	Georbodus	1066	——	Passed to the family of Abrincis
Chester, E.	Abrincis	1070	1119	Passed to the family of Meschines
Chester, E.	Meschines	1119	——	Conveyed by an heiress to the family of Le Scot
Chester, E.	Le Scot	1231	1246	Annexed to the crown
Chester, E.	Plantagenet	1253	——	Supposed to have been transferred to the prince's elder brother, Edward, afterwards Edward I.
Chester, E.	De Montford	1264	1265	Forfeited
Chesterfield, Css.	Wotton	1660	1667	Extinct
Chichester, E.	Wriothesley	1644	1667	Extinct
Chichester, E.	Fitz-Roy	1674	1774	Extinct
Cholmondeley, B.	Cholmondeley	1645	1689	Extinct
Clare, B.	Clare	1066	1313	Extinct
Clare, E.	Holles	1624	1711	Extinct
Clare, E.	Holles (Pelham)	1714	1768	Extinct
Clare, of —— B.	Clare	1309	——	Extinct
Clarence, D.	Plantagenet	1362	1368	Extinct
Clarence, D.	Plantagenet	1411	1421	Extinct
Clarence, D.	Plantagenet	1461	1477	Forfeited
Clarence, D.	Guelph (see Plantagenet)	1789	1830	Merged in the crown
Clarendon, E.	Hyde	1661	1753	Extinct
Clavering, B.	Clavering	1295	1332	Extinct
Cleveland, E.	Wentworth	1626	1667	Extinct
Cleveland, Dss.	Villiers (Fitz-Roy)	1670	1774	Extinct
Clifford, B.	Clifford	1299	1461	Forfeited
Clifford, of Lanesborough, B.	Boyle	1644	1735	Extinct
Clifton, B.	Clifton	1376	——	Abeyance
Clinton, B.	Clinton	1330	1354	Extinct
Cobham, of Kent, B.	Cobham	1313	——	Extinct
Cobham, B.	Brooke	1645	1651	Extinct
Coke, V.	Coke	1744	1759	Extinct
Colepeper, B.	Colepeper	1644	1725	Extinct
Colchester, V.	Savage	1621	1728	Extinct
Collingwood, B.	Collingwood	1805	1810	Extinct
Columbers, B.	Columbers	1314	1342	Extinct
Colvill, B.	Colevill	1264	——	Abeyance
Conyers, B.	D'Arcy	1509	1778	Extinct
Conyngsby, B.	Conyngsby	1715	1761	Extinct
Conyngsby, E.	Conyngsby	1719	1761	Extinct
Conyngsby, Bss.	Conyngsby	1716	1761	Extinct
Conway, B.	Conway	1624	1683	Extinct
Conway, V.	Conway	1626	1683	Extinct
Conway, E.	Conway	1679	1683	Extinct
Corbet, B.	Corbet	1295	——	Extinct
Corbet, Vss.	Corbet	1679	1696	Extinct
Cornwall, E.	Moreton	1068	——	Forfeited
Cornwall, E.	Dunstanvill	1140	1175	
Cornwall, E.	Plantagenet	1226	1300	Extinct
Cornwall, E.	Gaveston	1308	1314	Extinct
Cornwall, E.	Plantagenet	1398	1336	Extinct
Cornwall, D.	Plantagenet	1337		
Cornwallis, M.	Cornwallis	1799	1823	Extinct
Cottington, B.	Cottington	1631	1683	Extinct
Coventry, E.	Villiers	1623	1687	Extinct
Coventry, B.	Coventry	1628	1719	Extinct
Cranfield, B.	Cranfield	1621	1674	Extinct
Craven, B.	Craven	1626	1697	Extinct
Craven, V.	Craven	1663	1697	Extinct
Craven, E.	Craven	1663	1697	Extinct

Titles.	In the Family of	Period of Possession.		Eventual Destination.
Craven, of Ryton, B.	Craven	from 1642 to 1650		Extinct
Creting, B.	Creting	1332	—	Extinct
Crew, B.	Crew	1661	1721	Extinct
Crofts, B.	Crofts	1658	1677	Extinct
Cromwell, B.	Cromwell	1308	1471	Abeyance
Cromwell, of Wimbledon, B.	Cromwell	1536	1540	Forfeited
Cromwell, B.	Cromwell	1540	—	Extinct
Cumberland, E.	Clifford	1525	1643	Extinct
Cumberland, D.	Rupert	1644	1682	Extinct
Cumberland, D.	Denmark, Prince of	1689	1708	Extinct
Cumberland, D.	Guelph	1708	1765	Extinct
Cumberland, D.	Guelph	1766	1790	Extinct.

D.

Titles.	In the Family of	Period of Possession.		Eventual Destination.
Dacre, of Gillesland, B.	Dacre	1482	1569	Abeyance
Dagworth, B.	Dagworth	1347	—	Extinct
D'Amorie	D'Amorie	1317	1404	Forfeited
Danby, E.	Danvers	1626	1643	Extinct
Danvers, B.	Danvers	1603	1643	Extinct
Darcy, B.	D'Arcy	1299	—	Abeyance
Darcy, B.	D'Arcy	1332	1418	Abeyance
Darcy, B., of Darcy	Darcy	1509	1538	Forfeited
Darcy, of Aston, B.	D'Arcy	1548	1635	Extinct
Darcy, of Chiche, B.	Darcy	1551	1639	Extinct
Darcy, B.	Darcy	1641	1778	Extinct
Darlington, Bss.	Sidley	1686	1717	Extinct
Darlington, Css.	Kilmanzegg	1722	1730	Extinct
Daubeney	Daubeney	1295	—	
Daubeney	Daubeney	1486	1548	Abeyance
Dauney, B.	Dauney	1327	—	Extinct
De Grey, M.	Grey	1740	1770	Extinct
Deincourt, B.	Deincourt	1299	1487	Forfeited
Deincourt, of Sutton, B.	Leke	1624	1736	Extinct
D'Ervill, B.	Dewill	1264	—	Extinct
De la Pole, B.	Pole (de la)	1366	1450	Forfeited
De la Mere	Booth	1661	1770	Extinct
Delaval, B.	Delaval	1786	1808	Extinct
Denbigh, B.	Dudley	1563	1568	Extinct
Denney, B.	Denney	1604	1660	Extinct
Derby, E.	Ferrers	1137	1265	{ Robert de Ferrers, eight Earl, dispossessed of the Earldom
Derby, E.	Plantagenet	1337	1399	Merged in the crown
Derwentwater, E.	Radcliffe	1688	1716	Attainted
Despencer, B.	Despencer	1264	1440	Attainted
Devereux, B.	Devereux	1384	1397	{ United with the Barony of Fitz-Walter
Devon, E.	Courtenay	1335	1461	Forfeited
•Devon, E.	Courtenay	1485	—	Dormant
Devon, E.	Stafford	1469	1469	Extinct
Devon, E.	Blount	1603	1606	Extinct
Digby, B.	Digby	1618	1686	Extinct
Dinan, B.	Dinan	1295	1509	Extinct
Doncaster, V.	Hay	1618	1660	Extinct
Dorchester, B.	Carlton	1628	1631	Extinct
Dorchester, M.	Pierrepont	1644	1680	Extinct
Dorchester, Css.	Sidley	1686	1692	Extinct
Dorchester, M.	Pierrepont	1706	1773	Extinct
Dorchester, E.	Damer	1792	1808	Extinct
Dorset, E.	Beaufort	1411	1426	Extinct
Dorset, E.	Beaufort	1441	1471	Forfeited
Dorset, M.	Beaufort	1442	1471	Forfeited
Dorset, M.	Grey	1475	1554	Forfeited

• The Earldom of Devon has recently been restored to the family of Courtenay.

Titles.	In the Family of	Period of Possession.		Eventual Destination.
Douglas, B. ..	.. Douglas	from 1786 to 1810		Extinct
Dover, E.	Carey	1628	1677	Extinct
Dover D. ..	.. Douglas	1708	1778	Extinct
Dover, B. ..	Yorke	1788	1799	Extinct
Dublin, M. ..	Vere	1386	1388	Forfeited
Dudley, B. ..	.. Somerie	1308	1322	Extinct
Dudley, B. ..	Sutton	1342	1697	{ Carried by an heiress to the Wards
Dudley, B. ..	Ward	1697	1740	Extinct
Dudley, Des. ..	.. Leigh	1644	1760	Extinct
Dunsmore, B. ..	.. Leigh ..	1698	1653	Extinct
Duras, B. ..	.. Duras	1673	1709	Extinct.

E.

Echingham, B. ..	Echingham	1311	——	Extinct
Effingham, E. ..	.. Howard	1731	1816	Extinct
Egremont, B. ..	Percy	1449	1460	Extinct
Ellesmere, B. ..	.. Egerton	1603	1889	Extinct
Engaine, B.	Engaine	1299	1367	Extinct
Edrington, B. ..	.. Edrington ..	1336	——	Extinct
Essex, E.	Mandeville	temp. Sept.		Extinct
Essex, E.	Fitz-Piers	1199	1227	{ Conveyed by an heiress to the Bohuns
Essex, E.	.. Bohun	1227	1372	Extinct
Essex, E.	Bourchier	1461	1539	Extinct
Essex, E. ..	.. Bromwell	1539	1540	Forfeited
Essex, E.	Parr	1543	1553	Forfeited
Essex, E.	Devereux	1572	1646	Extinct
Everingham, B. ..	Everingham ..	1309	1371	Abeyance
Eure, B.	.. Eure	1544	1698	Extinct
Exeter, D.	Holland	1397	1400	Forfeited
Exeter, D. ..	.. Beaufort	1416	1426	Extinct
Exeter, D. ..	.. Holland	1443	1461	Forfeited
Exeter, M. ..	.. Courtenay	1526	1536	Extinct.

F.

Falmouth, E.	Berkeley	1664	1665	Extinct
Falmouth, V. ..	Fitz-Roy	1674	1716	Extinct
Falversley, B. ..	.. Falversley	1383	1392	Extinct
Fanhope, B. ..	Cornwall	1436	1443	Extinct
Fauconberg, B. ..	.. Fauconberg ..	1295	1376	{ Conveyed by an heiress to the Nevills
Fauconberg, B. ..	Nevill	1429	1462	Abeyance
Fauconberg, of Yarum, B.	Belasyse	1627	1815	Extinct
Fauconberg, V. ..	.. Belasyse	1643	1815	Extinct
Fauconberg, E. ..	Belasyse	1689	1700	Extinct
Felton, B. ..	.. Felton	1313	——	Extinct
Ferrers, of Chartley, B.	Ferrers	1299	1449	{ Conveyed by an heiress to the family of Devereux
Ferrers, of Chartley, B.	Devereux	1461	1600	Forfeited
Ferrers, of Groby, B. ..	Ferrers	1297	——	{ Passed by marriage to the Greys
Ferrers, of Wemme, B.	Ferrers	1375	1410	Abeyance
Feversham, E.	Sondes	1676	1709	Extinct
Feversham, Css. ..	Schulemburgh ..	1719	1743	Extinct
Feversham, B. ..	.. Duncombe	1747	1763	Extinct
Fife, B.	Duff	1790	1809	Extinct
Finch, B. ..	.. Finch	1640	1680	Extinct
Fitz-Alan, B. ..	Fitz-Alan	1295	——	Abeyance
Fitz-Herbert, B. ..	.. Fitz-Herbert ..	1294	——	Extinct
Fitz-Hugh, B.	Fitz-Hugh	1321	1512	Abeyance
Fitz-John, B. ..	.. Fitz-John	1264	1296	Extinct
Fitz-Payne, B. ..	Fitz-Payne	1299	1354	Abeyance
Fitz-Reginald, B.	.. Fitz-Reginald ..	1294	——	Extinct
Fitz-Walter, B.	Fitz-Walter	1295	1432	Extinct

Titles.	In the Family of	Period of Possession.		Eventual Destination.
Fitz-Walter, B.	.. Ratcliffe	from 1485 to	——	
Fitz-Walter, V.	.. Ratcliffe	1525	1641	Extinct
Fitz-Walter, B.	.. Mildmay	1669	1753	Abeyance
Fitz-Walter, E.	Mildmay	1730	1753	Extinct
Fitz-Warine, B,	.. Fitz-Warine	1342	——	Extinct
Fitz-Warine, B.	Bourchier	1292	1636	Abeyance
Foliot, B.	.. Foliot	1295	——	Extinct
Freschville, B.	Freschville	1664	1682	Extinct
Freville, B.	.. Freville	1327	——	Extinct
Furnival, B.	Furnival	1295	1383	{ Conveyed by an heiress to the Nevills
Furnival, B.	.. Nevill	1383	——	{ Conveyed by an heiress to the Talbots
Furnival, B.	Talbot	1409	1666	Abeyance
Furnival, B.	.. Howard	——	1777	Abeyance.

G.

Titles.	In the Family of	Period of Possession.		Eventual Destination.
Gage, B.	Gage	1780	1791	Extinct
Gainsborough, E.	.. Noel	1682	1798	Extinct
Gant, B.	Gant	1295	1297	Extinct
Genevill, B.	Genevill	1299	——	Abeyance
Gerard, B.	Gerard	1603	1711	Extinct
Gerard, of Brandon, B.	Gerard,	1645	1702	Extinct
Ghisnes, B.	Ghisnes	1295	——	Extinct
Giffard, B.	Giffard	1295	1389	Abeyance
Glastonbury, B.	Grenville	1797	1826	Extinct
Gloucester, E.	Clare	——	1313	
Gloucester, E.	Audley	1337	1347	Extinct
Gloucester, D.	Plantagenet	1385	1399	Extinct
Gloucester, E.	Despencer	1397	1400	Attainder
Gloucester, D.	Plantagenet	1404	1446	Extinct
Gloucester, D.	Plantagenet	1461	1483	Merged in the crown
Godolphin, B.	.. Godolphin	1684	1766	Extinct
Godolphin, E.	.. Godolphin	1706	1766	Extinct
Godolphin, B.	.. Godolphin	1735	1785	Extinct
Goodrich, V.	Grey	1706	1741	Extinct
Gorges, B.	Gorges	1309	——	Extinct
Goring, B.	Goring	1644	1672	Extinct
Grandison, B.	.. Grandison	1299	——	Extinct
Grandison, B.	Grandison	1299	——	Dormant
Grantham, E.	.. Nassau	1698	1754	Extinct
Granville, B.	Granville	1702	1707	Extinct
Granville, E.	Carteret	1714	1766	Extinct
Greenwich, E.	Campbell	1705	1743	Extinct
Greenwich, D.	.. Campbell	1719	1743	Extinct
Greenwich, Bss.	Townshend	1767	1794	Extinct
Grendon, B.	Grendon	1299	——	Extinct
Gresley, B.	Gresley	1307	1347	Extinct
Grey, of Wilton, B.	Grey	1295	1604	Attainted
Grey, of Wilton, B.	Grey	1784	1814	Extinct
Grey, of Rotherfield, B.	Grey	1297	1487	Attainted
Grey, of Codnor, B.	Grey	1299	1496	Abeyance
Grey, of Groby, B.	Grey	1330	1554	Forfeited
Grey, of Powys, B.	Grey	1482	1552	{ Supposed to have fallen into Abeyance
Grey, of Werke, B.	Grey	1624	1706	Extinct
Grey, of Rolleston	North	1673	1734	Extinct
Greystock, B.	.. Greystock	1295	1569	Abeyance
Griffin, B.	Griffin	1688	1742	Extinct
Guildford, Css.	.. Boyle	1660	1673	Extinct
Guildford, E.	Maitland	1674	1682	Extinct.

H.

Titles.	In the Family of	Period of Possession.		Eventual Destination.
Hacche, B.	Hacche	1299	1306	Dormant
Halifax, V.	Savile	1668	1700	Extinct

Titles.	In the Family of	Period of Possession.		Eventual Destination.
Halifax, E.	.. Savile	.. from 1679 to 1700		Extinct
Halifax, M.	.. Savile	.. 1682	1700	Extinct
Halifax, B. ..	.. Montagu ..	.. 1700	1771	Extinct
Halifax, E.	.. Montagu ..	.. 1714	1715	Extinct
Halifax, E.	.. Montagu ..	.. 1715	1771	Extinct
Hampden, B. ..	Trevor (Hampden)	1776	1824	Extinct
Handlo, B. ..	.. Handlo	1342	1346	Extinct
Harcla, B.	.. Harcla ..	.. 1321	1323	Forfeited
Harcourt, B. ..	.. Harcourt ..	.. 1711	1830	Extinct
Harcourt, V. ..	.. Harcourt ..	.. 1721	1830	Extinct
Harcourt, E. ..	.. Harcourt ..	.. 1749	1830	Extinct
Harewood, B. ..	.. Lascelles ..	.. 1790	1795	Extinct
Harington, B. ..	.. Harington ..	.. 1394	1554	Forfeited
Harington of Exton, B.	Harington ..	.. 1603	1614	Extinct
Harold, E.	.. Grey	.. 1706	1741	Extinct
Hastang, B.	.. Hastang ..	.. 1311	1342	Abeyance
Hastings, B. ..	.. Hastings ..	.. 1264	——	Dormant
Hastings, of —— B. ..	Hastings ..	.. 1299	——	Extinct
Hastings, of Gressing Hall, B. ..	Hastings ..	.. 1342	——	Extinct
Hastings, of Loughborough, B.	Hastings ..	.. 1558	1558	Extinct
Hastings, of Loughborough, B. ..	Hastings ..	.. 1643	1666	Extinct
Hatton, B. ..	.. Hatton ..	.. 1642	1762	Extinct
Hatton, V. ..	.. Hatton ..	.. 1682	1762	Extinct
Hausted, B.	.. Hausted ..	.. 1332	——	Extinct
Haversham, B. ..	.. Thompson ..	.. 1696	1745	Extinct
Hay, of Sawley, B. ..	Hay	.. 1615	1660	Extinct
Heathfield, B. ..	.. Elliot ..	.. 1787	1813	Extinct
Henley, B.	.. Henley ..	.. 1760	1786	Extinct
Herbert, of Chepstow, B.	Herbert ..	.. 1461	——	Extinct
Herbert, of Chirbury, B.	Herbert ..	.. 1629	1691	Extinct
Herbert, of Chirbury, B.	Herbert ..	.. 1694	1738	Extinct
Herbert, of Chirbury, B.	Herbert ..	.. 1743	1801	Extinct
Hereford, E.	.. Bohun ..	.. 1199	1372	Extinct
Heron, B.	.. Heron ..	.. 1371	——	Extinct
Heron, B.	.. Heron ..	.. 1396	1404	Extinct
Hertford, E.	.. Clare ..	.. temp. Sept., 1313		Extinct
Hertford, E.	.. Seymour ..	.. 1537	1552	Forfeited
Hertford, E.	Seymour ..	.. 1559	1750	Extinct
Hervey, B.	.. Hervey ..	.. 1628	1642	Extinct
Hilton, B.	.. Hilton ..	.. 1295	——	Abeyance
Hilton, of —— B. ..	.. Hilton ..	.. 1332	——	Extinct
Hoese, B.	.. Hoese ..	.. 1295	——	Extinct
Holland, B. ..	.. Holland ..	.. 1314	1373	{ Conveyed by marriage to the family of Lovel, of Tichmarsh
Holland, B.	Holland ..	.. 1353	1407	Abeyance
Holland, B.	Rich ..	.. 1624	1756	Extinct
Holdernesse, E. ..	Ramsay ..	.. 1621	1625	Extinct
Holdernesse, E. ..	.. Darcy ..	.. 1682	1778	Extinct
Holles, of Ifield, B.	Holles ..	.. 1661	1694	Extinct
Hoo, B.	.. Hoo ..	.. 1447	1453	Extinct
Hopton, B.	.. Hopton ..	.. 1643	1652	Extinct
Houghton, B. ..	.. Holles ..	.. 1616	1711	Extinct
Houghton, B. ..	Walpole ..	.. 1749	1797	Extinct
Howard, B. ..	.. Howard ..	.. 1470	1777	Abeyance
Howard, of Bindon, V. ..	Howard ..	.. 1559	1619	Extinct
Howard, of Escrick, B. ..	Howard ..	.. 1628	1714	Extinct
Howard, of Castle Rising, B.	Howard ..	.. 1639	1777	Extinct
Howe, V.	.. Howe ..	.. 1782	1799	Extinct
Howe, E.	.. Howe ..	.. 1788	1799	Extinct
Hume, B.	.. Hume ..	.. 1604	1611	Extinct

Titles.	In the Family of	Period of Possession.		Eventual Destination.
Hume, B.	Hume (Campbell)	from 1776	to 1781	Extinct
Hungerford, B.	Hungerford	1426	—	Extinct
Hungerford, of Heytesbury, B.	Hungerford	1536	1541	Extinct
Hunsdon, B.	Carey	1559	1675	Extinct
Huntercombe, B.	Huntercombe	1295	1312	Extinct
Huntingdon, E.	St. Lis	1068	1237	Extinct
Huntingdon, E.	Clinton	1337	1354	Extinct
Huntingdon, E.	Holland	1387	1399	Forfeited
Huntingdon, E.	Holland	1417	1474	Extinct
Huntingdon, E.	Herbert	1479	—	Extinct
Huntingfield, B.	Huntingfield	1297	1377	{ Presumed to have fallen into Abeyance
Huntingfield, B.	Huntingfield	1362	—	Extinct
Hussey, B.	Hussey	1534	1537	Extinct
Hyde, of Hindon, B.	Hyde	1660	1753	Extinct
Hyde, of Wotton Basset, B.	Hyde	1681	1753	Extinct
Hyde, V.	Hyde	1681	1753	Extinct.

I.

Ingham, B.	Ingham	1328	1344	Abeyance
Ireland, D.	Vere	1387	1388	Forfeited
Jefferys, B.	Jefferys	1685	1703	Extinct
Jermyn, B.	Jermyn	1643	1703	Extinct
Jermyn, of Dover, B.	Jermyn	1685	1708	Extinct
Jervis, B.	Jervis	1797	1890	Extinct.

K.

Keith, B.	Keith	1801	1823	Extinct
Keith, V.	Keith	1814	1823	Extinct
Kendal, D.	Stuart	1666	1667	Extinct
Kendal, Dss.	Schulemberg	1719	1703	Extinct
Kent, E.	Odo	1067	1096	Extinct
Kent, E.	Ipre	1141	—	Extinct
Kent, E.	Burgh	1226	1243	Extinct
Kent, E.	Plantagenet	1321	1330	Forfeited
Kent, E.	Holland	—	1407	Extinct
Kent, E.	Nevill	1462	1463	Extinct
Kent, E.	Grey	1465	1741	Extinct
Kent, M.	Grey	1706	1741	Extinct
Kent, D.	Grey	1710	1741	Extinct
Kent, D.	Guelph	1799	1890	Extinct
Kensington, B.	Rich	1622	1759	Extinct
Keppel, V.	Keppel	1782	1786	Extinct
Ker, E.	Ker	1722	1804	Extinct
Kerdeston	Kerdeston	1332	—	Abeyance
Kingston, E.	Pierrepont	1628	1680	Extinct
Kingston, D.	Pierrepont	1715	1773	Extinct
Kirketon, B.	Kirketon	1362	1367	Extinct
Knollys, B.	Knollys	1603	1632	Dormant
Knovill, B.	Knovill	1295	—	Extinct
Knyvet	Knyvet	1607	1622	Extinct
Kyme, B.	Kyme	1295	—	Abeyance.

L.

La Mare, B.	Mare	1299	1313	Extinct
Lancaster, B.	Lancaster	1299	1334	Extinct
Lancaster, E.	Plantagenet	1267	1321	Forfeited
Lancaster, D.	Plantagenet	1351	1399	Merged in the crown
Langdale, B.	Langdale	1658	1777	Extinct
Lansdowne, B.	Granville	1711	1734	Extinct
Lascels, B.	Lascels	1295	1297	Abeyance
Latimer, B.	Latimer	1299	—	Abeyance
Latimer, of Braybrooke, B.	Latimer	1299	—	Extinct
Latimer, B.	Nevill	1432	1577	Abeyance

Titles.	In the Family of	Period of Possession.		Eventual Destination.
Lechmere, B.	Lechmere	from 1721 to 1727		Extinct
Leicester, E.	Beaumont	1103	1204	Extinct
Leicester, E.	Montfort	1206	1264	Forfeited
Leicester, E.	Plantagenet	1264	1321	Forfeited
Leicester, E.	Dudley	1563	1588	Extinct
Leicester, E.	Sydney	1618	1743	Extinct
Leicester, E.	Coke	1744	1759	Extinct
Leigh, B.	Leigh	1643	1786	Extinct
Lexington, B.	Sutton	1645	1723	Extinct
Ley, B.	Ley	1625	1679	Extinct
Leyburn, B.	Leyburn	1299	1309	Extinct
Leyburn, B.	Leyburn	1337	1348	Extinct
Ligonier, B.	Ligonier	1763	1770	Extinct
Ligonier, E.	Ligonier	1766	1770	Extinct
Lincoln, E.	Romare	1142	——	{ Conveyed by an heiress to the family of Gant
Lincoln, E.	Gant	temp. Hen. II., 1216		{ Gilbert de Gant, second Earl of Lincoln, was divested of his honours
Lincoln, E.	Meschines	1216	1231	Extinct
Lincoln, E.	Lacy	1232	1348	Extinct
Lincoln, E.	Plantagenet	1349	1399	Merged in the crown
Lincoln, E.	Pole	1467	1487	Extinct
Lincoln, E.	Brandon	1525	——	Extinct
Lindsey, M.	Bertie	1706	1809	Extinct
L'Isle, B.	L'Isle	1347	——	Abeyance
L'Isle, B.	Talbot	1443	——	
L'Isle, V.	Talbot	1452	1469	Extinct
L'Isle. B.	Grey	1475	——	
L'Isle, V.	Grey	1483	1512	Extinct
L'Isle, V.	Brandon	1513	——	Surrendered
L'Isle, V.	Plantagenet	1533	1541	Extinct
L'Isle, B.	Dudley	1541	1553	Forfeited
L'Isle, V.	Dudley	1542	1553	Forfeited
L'Isle, B.	Dudley	1561	1589	Extinct
L'Isle, V.	Sydney	1605	1743	Extinct
L'Isle, of Rugemont, B.	L'Isle	1311	1360	Presumed to be Extinct
Litchfield, E.	Stuart	1645	1672	Extinct
Litchfield, E	Lee	1674	1776	Extinct
Longueville, V	Yelverton	1690	1799	Extinct
Longvilliers, B.	Longvilliers	1342	1374	Extinct
Lonsdale, V.	Lowther	1696	1751	Extinct
Lonsdale, E.	Lowther	1784	1802	Extinct
L'Orti, B.	L'Orti	1299	——	Abeyance
Lovel, of Kary, B.	Lovel	1348	1351	Abeyance
Lovel, of Tichmersh, B.	Lovel	1299	1487	Forfeited
Lovel, V.	Lovel	1483	1487	Forfeited
Lovel, of Minster Lovel, B.	Lovel	1728	1759	Extinct
Lovelace, B.	Lovelace	1627	1736	Extinct
Lowther, B.	Lowther	1696	1751	Extinct
Lowther, B.	Lowther	1784	1802	Extinct
Lowther, V.	Lowther	1784	1802	Extinct
Lucas, B.	Lucas	1644	1705	Extinct
Lucy, of Egremont, B.	Lucy	1390	——	Extinct
Lumley, B.	Lumley	1384	——	Extinct
Lumley, B.	Lumley	1547	1609	Extinct
Luterel, B.	Luterel	1295	——	Extinct
Lyttleton, B	Lyttleton	1640	1645	Extinct
Lyttleton, B.	Lyttleton	1757	1779	Extinct.

M.

Macartney, B.	Macartney	1796	1806	Extinct
Macclesfield, E.	Gerard	1679	1702	Extinct
Malton, B.	Watson (Wentworth)	1728	1782	Extinct
Malton, E.	Watson (Wentworth)	1734	1782	Extinct

Titles.	In the Family of	Period of Possession.		Eventual Destination.
Maltravers, B.	Maltravers	from 1330 to	—	Annexed by act of parliament to the Earldom of Arundel
Maltravers, B.	Fitzalan			
Manny, B.	Manny	1347	1399	Extinct
Mansfield, V.	Cavendish	1690	1691	Extinct
Mansell, B.	Mansell	1711	1750	Extinct
March, E.	Mortimer	1328	1424	Extinct
March, E.	Plantagenet	1479	1483	Merged in the crown
March, E.	Stuart	1619	1672	Extinct
Marlborough, E.	Ley	1626	1679	Extinct
Marmion, B.	Marmion	temp. Wm. I.		
Marmion, B.	Marmion	1264	—	Extinct
Marmion, of Withington, B.	Marmion	1313	—	Abeyance
Marney, B.	Marney	1523	1525	Extinct
Marshal, B.	Marshal	1309	—	Abeyance
Masham, B.	Masham	1711	1776	Extinct
Mauduit, B.	Mauduit	1342	—	Extinct
Mauley, B.	Mauley	1295	1415	Abeyance
Meinill, B.	Meinill	1295	1299	Extinct
Meinill, B.	Meinill	1313	1322	Extinct
Meinill, B.	Meinill	1336	1778	Extinct
Melcombe, B.	Dodington	1761	1762	Extinct
Middlesex, E.	Cranfield	1622	1674	Extinct
Milbroke, B.	Cornwall	1442	1443	Extinct
Milton, B.	Damer	1762	1808	Extinct
Milton, V.	Damer	1792	1808	Extinct
Moels, B.	Moels	1299	1337	Abeyance
Mohun, B.	Mohun	1299	—	Extinct
Mohun, of Okehampton, B.	Mohun	1628	1712	Extinct
Molines, B.	Molines	1347	—	Extinct
Monmouth, E.	Carey	1626	1669	Extinct
Monmouth, D.	Scot (Fitz Roy)	1660	1685	Forfeited
Monmouth, E.	Mordaunt	1689	1814	Extinct
Montacute, B.	Montacute	1300	—	Conveyed by marriage to the Nevills
Montacute, B.	Nevill	—	—	Extinct
Montacute, B.	Pole	1533	1539	Forfeited
Montagu, B.	Nevill	1461	1471	Forfeited
Montagu, M.	Nevill	1470	1471	Forfeited
Montagu, V.	Brown	1554	1797	Extinct
Montagu, of —, B.	Montagu	1342	1361	Extinct
Montagu, of —, B.	Montagu	1357	—	Extinct
Montagu, of Boughton, B.	Montagu	1621	1749	Extinct
Montagu, E.	Montagu	1689	1749	Extinct
Montagu, M.	Montagu	1705	1749	Extinct
Montagu, of Boughton, B.	Montagu	1762	1772	Extinct
Montagu, D.	Montagu	1766	1790	Extinct
Montalt, B.	Montalt	1295	1329	Extinct
Monteagle, B.	Stanley	1514	—	Passed by marriage to the Parkers
Monteagle, B.	Parker	1605	1686	Abeyance
Montfort, B.	Montfort	1295	1367	Abeyance
Montgomery, B.	Montgomery	1342	—	Extinct
Monthermer, B.	Monthermer	1309	1471	Forfeited
Monthermer, B.	Monthermer	1337	—	Extinct
Montjoy, B.	Blount	1465	1606	Extinct
Montjoy, B.	Blount	1627	1681	Extinct
Montjoy, of the Isle of Wight, B.	Windsor	1711	1756	Extinct
Mordaunt, V.	Mordaunt	1659	1814	Extinct
Morley, B.	Morley	1299	1442	Conveyed by an heiress to the Lovels
Morley, B.	Lovel	1469	1469	Conveyed by an heiress to the Parkers

4 I

Titles.	In the Family of	Period of Possession.	Eventual Destination.
Morley, B.	Parker	from 1523 to 1686	Abeyance
Mortimer, B.	Mortimer	1295 1461	Merged in the crown
Mortimer, B. of Richard's Castle	Mortimer	1299 —	Abeyance
Mortimer, B., of Chirke	Mortimer	1307 —	Abeyance
Mulgrave, E.	Sheffield	1626 1735	Extinct
Mulgrave, E.	Phipps	1790 1792	Extinct
Multon, of Gillesland, B.	Multon	1307 1313	{ Conveyed by an heiress to the Dacres
Multon, of Egremont, B.	Multon	1297 1334	Abeyance
Munchensi, B.	Munchensi	1264 —	Extinct
Musgrave, B.	Musgrave	1350 —	Presumed to be Extinct.

N.

Titles.	In the Family of	Period of Possession.	Eventual Destination.
Nansladron, B.	Nansladron	1299 —	Extinct
Nereford, B.	Nereford	1297 —	Extinct
Nevill, of Raby, B.	Nevill	1294 1570	Forfeited
Nevill, of Essex, B.	Nevill	1336 1388	Extinct
Nevill, of ——, B.	Nevill	1342 —	Extinct
Newark, V.	Pierrepont	1627 1773	Extinct
Newcastle, E.	Stuart	1623 1694	Extinct
Newcastle, E.	Cavendish	1628 1691	Extinct
Newcastle, M.	Cavendish	1643 1691	Extinct
Newcastle, D.	Cavendish	1664 1691	Extinct
Newcastle, D.	Holles (Pelham)	1715 1768	Extinct
Newmarch, B.	Newmarch	1264 —	Extinct
Newport, E.	Blount	1628 1681	Extinct
Newport, B.	Newport	1642 1702	Extinct
Newport, V.	Newport	1675 1702	Extinct
Noel, of Ridlington, B.	Noel	1617 1798	Extinct
Noel, of Titchfield, B.	Noel	1681 1798	Extinct
Norfolk, E.	Wayher	1066 —	Forfeited
Norfolk, E.	Bigod	1140 1307	Extinct
Norfolk, E.	Plantagenet	1312 1338	Extinct
Norfolk, Des.	Plantagenet	1307 1399	Extinct
Norfolk, D.	Mowbray	1396 1475	Extinct
Norfolk, D.	Howard	1483 1572	Attainted
Normanby, M.	Sheffield	1694 1715	Extinct
Normanby, D.	Sheffield	1703 1735	Extinct
North, B.	North	1554 1802	Abeyance
Northampton, E.	St. Liz	1066 1184	Extinct
Northampton, E.	Bohun	1337 1372	Extinct
Northampton, M.	Parr	1557 1571	Extinct
Northampton, E.	Howard	1604 1614	Extinct
Northington, E.	Henly	1764 1786	Extinct
Northumberland, E.	Comyn	1068 1069	Extinct
Northumberland, E.	Copsi	1068 —	Extinct
Northumberland, E.	Cospatrick	1069 1070	Extinct
Northumberland, E.	Percy	1377 1461	Extinct
Northumberland, E.	Nevill	1464 1470	Resigned
Northumberland, D.	Dudley	1551 1552	Forfeited
Northumberland, E.	Percy	1557 1670	Extinct
Northumberland, E.	Fitz-Roy	1674 1716	Extinct
Northumberland, D.	Fitz-Roy	1683 1716	Extinct
Northwode, B.	Northwode	1313 1416	Abeyance
Norwich, B.	Norwich	1342 1374	Extinct
Norwich, E.	Denny	1626 1630	Extinct
Norwich, E.	Goring	1645 1672	Extinct
Norwich, E.	Howard	1672 1777	Extinct
Nottingham, E.	Mowbray	1383 1475	Extinct
Nottingham, E.	Berkeley	1483 1491	Extinct
Nottingham, E.	Fitz-Roy	1525 1536	Extinct
Nottingham, E.	Howard	1597 1681	Extinct.

610

Titles.	In the Family of	Period of Possession.		Eventual Destination.

O.

Ogle, B.	Ogle	from 1461 to 1597		Abeyance
Ogle, B.	Cavendish	1690	1691	Abeyance
Oldcastle, B.	Oldcastle	1409	—	Extinct
Orford, E.	Russell	1697	1727	Extinct
Orford, E.	Walpole	1742	1797	Extinct
Ormonde, D.	Butler	1681	1715	Forfeited
Orreby, B.	Orreby	1309	1317	Extinct
Oxford, E.	Vere	1155	1338	Forfeited
Oxford, E.	Vere	1392	1461	Forfeited
Oxford, E.	Vere	1464	1702	Extinct.

P.

Parr, of Kendal, B.	Parr	1538	1553	Forfeited
Parr, of Horton, B.	Parr	1543	1546	Extinct
Pateshull, B.	Pateshull	1342	1349	Extinct
Paynell, B.	Paynell	1299	—	Extinct
Peche, of Brunne, B.	Peche	1299	1323	Extinct
Peche, of Wormleighton, B.	Peche	1321	—	Abeyance
Pembroke, E.	Clare	1138	—	Conveyed by an heiress to the Marshals
Pembroke, E.	Marshal	1189	1245	Extinct
Pembroke, E.	Valence	1247	1323	Extinct
Pembroke, E.	Hastings	1339	1389	Extinct
Pembroke, E.	Pole	1446	1450	Forfeited
Pembroke, E.	Tudor	1452	1461	Forfeited
Pembroke, E.	Herbert	1468	—	Extinct
Pembroke, Mss.	Boleyn	1532	—	Extinct
Percy, B.	Percy	1299	1537	Extinct
Percy, B.	Percy	1643	1652	Extinct
Perth, B.	Drummond	1797	1800	Extinct
Peterborough, B.	Mordaunt	1628	1814	Extinct
Pierrepont, B.	Pierrepont	1627	1773	Extinct
Pinkney, B.	Pinkney	1299	—	Extinct
Pipard, B.	Pipard	1299	1309	Extinct
Playz, B.	Playz	1297	—	Abeyance
Plessets, B.	Plessets	1299	—	Extinct
Plugenet, B.	Plugenet	1295	1327	Extinct
Plymouth, E.	Fitz-Charles	1675	1680	Extinct
Points, B.	Pointz	1295	—	Abeyance
Portland, E.	Weston	1633	1688	Extinct
Portsmouth, Dss.	Queroualle	1673	1734	Extinct
Powys, B.	Herbert	1629	1748	Extinct
Powys, E.	Herbert	1674	1748	Extinct
Powis, M.	Herbert	1687	1748	Extinct
Powis, E.	Herbert	1743	1801	Extinct
Poynings, B.	Percy	1337	1670	Extinct
Poynings, B.	Poynings	1337	1670	Extinct
Poynings, B.	Poynings	1545	1547	Extinct
Purbeck, V.	Villiers	1619	1657	Extinct.

R.

Raby, B.	Wentworth	1640	1641	Forfeited
Raby, B.	Wentworth	1665	1799	Extinct
Radnor, E.	Robartes	1679	1764	Extinct
Ravensworth, B.	Liddell	1747	1749	Extinct
Raymond, B.	Raymond	1731	1753	Extinct
Rich, B.	Rich	1547	1759	Extinct
Richmond, E.	Alan or Fergaunt	temp. Wm. I.		Passed to the family of De Dreux
Richmond, E.	De Dreux	—	1390	Forfeited
Richmond, E.	Tudor	1452	1485	Merged in the crown
Richmond, D.	Fitz-Roy	1525	1536	Extinct
Richmond, E.	Stuart	1613	1694	Extinct.

611

Titles.	In the Family of	Period of Possession.		Eventual Destination.
Richmond, D.	Stuart	from 1623 to 1624		Extinct
Richmond, D.	Stuart	1641	1672	Extinct
Ripariis, B.	Repariis or Rivers	1299	——	Extinct
Rivers, B.	Widvile	1448	1491	Extinct
Rivers, E.	Widvile	1466	1491	Extinct
Rivers, E.	Savage	1626	1728	Extinct
Robartes, B.	Robartes	1625	1764	Extinct
Rochester, V.	Carr	1611	1645	Extinct
Rochester, E.	Wilmot	1652	1681	Extinct
Rochester, E.	Hyde	1682	1753	Extinct
Rochfort, V.	Boleyn	1525	——	Extinct
Rochfort, V.	Carey	1621	1677	Extinct
Rockingham, B.	Watson	1645	1782	Extinct
Rockingham, V.	Watson	1714	1782	Extinct
Rockingham, M.	Watson	1746	1782	Extinct
Rolle, B.	Rolle	1748	1750	Extinct
Romney, E.	Sydney	1694	1704	Extinct
Ros, of Hamlake, B.	Ros	1264	1509	Abeyance
Ros, of Wecke, B.	Ros	1296	——	Forfeited
Ros, B.	Ros	1332	1338	Extinct
Rythre, B.	Rythre	1299	——	Extinct.

S.

Titles.	In the Family of	Period of Possession.		Eventual Destination.
St. Albans, V.	Bacon	1621	1626	Extinct
St. Albans, E.	Burgh	1628	1650	Extinct
St. Albans, E.	Jermyn	1660	1683	Extinct
St. Amand, B.	St. Amand	1299	1312	Extinct
St. Amand, B.	Beauchamp	1313	1508	Abeyance
St. John, B.	St. John	1299	——	Presumed to be extinct
St. John, B.	St. John	1264	1265	Extinct
St. Maur, B.	St. Maur	1314	——	Abeyance
St. Maur, of B.	St. Maur	1317	——	Extinct
St. Philbert, B.	St. Philbert	1299	1359	Extinct
St. Vincent, E.	Jervis	1797	1823	Extinct
Salisbury, E.	D'Evereux	temp. Step.		{ Conveyed by an heiress to the family of Longespée
Salisbury, E.	Longespee	temp. Rich. I.		
Salisbury, E.	Montacute	1337	1400	Forfeited
Salisbury, E.	Montacute	1409	——	{ Conveyed by an heiress to the Nevills
Salisbury, E.	Nevil	1442	1471	Forfeited
Salisbury, E.	Plantagenet	1472	1477	Forfeited
Salisbury, Css.	Plantagenet	1513	1541	Forfeited
Sandys, B.	Sandys	1743	1797	Extinct
Sandys, of the Vine, B.	Sandys	1529	1700	Abeyance
Saunderson, B.	Saunderson	1714	1723	Extinct
Savage, Viscount	Savage	1626	1728	Extinct
Savile, B.	Savile	1626	1671	Extinct
Say, B.	Say	1313	——	Abeyance
Scales, B.	Scales	1299	——	{ Conveyed by an heiress to the Widviles
Scales, B.	Widvile	1462	1483	Abeyance
Scarsdale, E.	Seke	1645	1736	Extinct
Schomberg, D.	Schomberg	1689	1719	Extinct
Scrope, of Bolton, B.	Scrope	1371	——	Dormant
Scrope, of Masham, B.	Scrope	1342	1415	Forfeited
Scrope, of Masham, B.	Scrope	1421	1517	Abeyance
Seaforth, B.	Mackenzie	1797	1814	Extinct
Segrave, B.	Segrave	1264	——	Abeyance
Seymour, B.	Seymour	1547	1552	Forfeited
Seymour, of Sudley, B.	Seymour	1547	1549	Forfeited
Seymour, of Troubridge, B.	Seymour	1641	1750	Extinct
Sheffield, B.	Sheffield	1547	1775	Extinct
Sherard, V.	Sherard	1718	1739	Extinct
Shingay, B.	Russell	1697	1727	Extinct

612

Titles.	In the Family of	Period of Possession.		Eventual Destination.
Somers, B.	Somers	from 1697 to 1716		Extinct
Somerset, E.	Beaufort	1397	1471	Forfeited
Somerset, D.	Beaufort	1443	1444	Extinct
Somerset, D.	Beaufort	1448	1471	Forfeited
Somerset, D.	Tudor	1496	1499	Extinct
Somerset, D.	Fitz-Roy	1525	1536	Extinct
Somerset, D.	Seymour	1547	1552	Forfeited
Somerset, E.	Carr	1613	1645	Extinct
Southampton, E.	Fitz-William	1537	1543	Extinct
Southampton, E.	Wriothesley	1547	1667	Extinct
Southampton, Cas.	Villiers	1670	1774	Extinct
Southampton	Fitz-Roy	1674	1774	Extinct
Stafford, B.	Stafford	1299	1521	Forfeited
Stafford, E.	Stafford	1351	1521	Forfeited
Stafford B.	Stafford	1547	1640	Extinct
Stafford, V.	Howard	1640	1678	Forfeited
Stafford, Cas.	Howard	1688	1693	Extinct
Stafford, E.	Howard	1688	1762	Extinct
Stafford, of Clifton, B.	Stafford	1371	—	
Stafford, of Southwyck, B.	Stafford	1461	1469	Extinct
Stanhope, of Harrington, B.	Stanhope	1605	1675	Extinct
Stanley, B.	Stanley	1456	1594	Abeyance
Stapleton, B.	Stapleton	1313	—	Extinct
Stawell, B.	Stawell	1683	1755	Extinct
Stawell, B.	Legge	1760	1820	Extinct
Strabolgi, B.	Strobolgi	1329	1375	Abeyance
Strafford, E.	Wentworth	1640	1641	Forfeited
Strafford, E.	Wentworth	1665	1695	Extinct
Strafford, E.	Wentworth	1711	1799	Extinct
Strange, of Knokyn, B.	Strange	1299	1477	{ Conveyed by an heiress to the Stanleys
Strange, of Knokyn, B.	Stanley	1482	1594	Abeyance
Strange of Ellesmere, B.	Strange	1295	—	Extinct
Strange, of Blackmere, B.	Strange	1308	—	Extinct
Strivelyn, B.	Strivelyn	1371	—	Dormant
Sudley, B.	Sudley	1299	1473	Extinct
Suffolk, E.	Ufford	1337	1369	Extinct
Suffolk, E.	Pole	1385	1513	Forfeited
Suffolk, M.	Pole	1444	1513	Forfeited
Suffolk, D.	Pole	1448	1513	Forfeited
Suffolk, D.	Brandon	1514	1551	Extinct
Suffolk, D.	Grey	1551	1554	Forfeited
Sunderland, E.	Scrope	1627	1640	Extinct
Surrey, E.	Warren	temp. W. II.	—	{ Conveyed by an heiress to the Plantagenets
Surrey, E.	Plantagenet	1163	1347	{ Conveyed by an heiress to the Fitz-Alans
Surrey, E.	Fitz-Alan	1347	1397	Forfeited
Surrey, D	Holland	1397	1400	Extinct
Sussex, E.	Ratcliffe	1529	1641	Extinct
Sussex, E.	Savile	1644	1671	Extinct
Sussex, E.	Lennard	1674	1715	Extinct
Sussex, E.	Yelverton	1717	1799	Extinct
Swillington, B.	Swillington	1326	—	Extinct
Swynnerton, B.	Swynnerton	1337	—	Extinct
Sydney, of Penshurst, B.	Sydney	1603	1743	Extinct
Sydney, of Sheppey, V.	Sydney	1689	1704	Extinct.

T.

Tadcaster, D.	O'Bryen	1714	1741	Extinct
Talbot, B.	Talbot	1331	1777	Abeyance
Talbot, E.	Talbot	1761	1782	Extinct
Talboys, B.	Talboys	1529	—	Extinct
Tankerville, E.	Grey	1695	1701	Extinct
Tatshall, B.	Tatshall	1295	—	Abeyance

Titles.	In the Family of	Period of Possession.		Eventual Destination.
Thame, V.	Norris	from 1620 to 1690		Extinct
Thomond, B.	O'Bryen	1801	1808	Extinct
Thorpe, B.	Thorpe	1381	—	Extinct
Thweng, B.	Tweng	1307	1374	Abeyance
Tibetot, B.	Tibetot	1308	1372	Abeyance
Tibetot, B.	Tibetot	1426	1426	Abeyance
Toni, B.	Toni	1299	1311	Extinct
Torrington, E.	Herbert	1689	1716	Extinct
Torrington, B.	Newport	1716	1719	Extinct
Totness, E.	Carew	1626	1629	Extinct
Tregos, B.	Tregos	1299	1300	Abeyance
Tregos, B.	Tregos	1305	—	Extinct
Tregos, B.	Tregos	1318	—	Extinct
Trevor, B.	Trevor (Hampden)	1711	1824	Extinct
Trussel, B.	Trussel	1342	—	Extinct
Tunbridge, V.	Burgh	1624	1659	Extinct
Tyes, B.	Tyes	1299	1321	Dormant
Tyes, B. of	Tyes	1299	1324	Extinct.

U.

Ufford, B.	Ufford	1308	—	Extinct
Ufford, B.	Ufford	1360	1361	Extinct
Ughtred, B.	Ughtred	1343	—	Dormant
Umfraville, B.	Umfraville	1295	—	Dormant
Upper Ossory, B.	Fitz-Patrick	1794	1818	Extinct
Uvedale, B.	Uvedale	1332	—	Extinct.
Uxbridge, B.	Paget	1714	1769	Extinct.

V.

Valence, B.	Valence	1299	1323	Extinct
Vaughan, B.	Vaughan	1643	1713	Extinct
Vaux, of Harrowden, B.	Vaux	1523	1661	Extinct
Vavasour, B.	Vavasour	1313	—	Extinct
Verdon, B.	Verdon	1332	—	Extinct
Vere, B.	Vere	1299	—	Extinct
Vere, of Tilbury, B.	Vere	1625	1635	Extinct
Verulam, B.	Bacon	1618	1626	Extinct
Vesci, B.	Vesci	1264	1297	Extinct
Vesci, B.	Vesci	1313	1315	Extinct
Villiers, V.	Villiers	1616	1687	Extinct.

W.

Wahull, B.	Wahull	1297	—	Dormant
Wake, B.	Wake	1295	1407	Abeyance
Waleys, B.	Waleys	1321	—	Extinct
Wallingford, V.	Knollys	1616	1632	Dormant
Walpole, of Houghton, B.	Walpole	1742	1797	Extinct
Walsingham, Css.	Schulemberg	1722	1778	Extinct
Warren, E.	Mowbray	1451	1475	Extinct
Warren, E.	Plantagenet	1477	1483	Extinct
Warrington, E.	Booth	1690	1758	Extinct
Warwick, E.	Newburgh	1066	1242	{ Conveyed by an heiress to the Plessets
Warwick, E.	Plessets	1246	—	Passed to the Beauchamps
Warwick, E.	Beauchamp	1263	1445	Extinct
Warwick, D.	Beauchamp	1444	1445	Extinct
Warwick, Css.	Beauchamp	1445	1449	Extinct
Warwick, E.	Nevill	1449	1471	Forfeited
Warwick, E.	Plantagenet	1472	1477	Forfeited
Warwick, D.	Dudley	1547	1589	Extinct
Warwick, E.	Rich	1618	1759	Extinct
Welles, B.	Welles	1299	1461	Forfeited
Welles, B.	Welles	1468	1503	Presumed to be extinct
Welles, of B.	Welles	1487	1498	Extinct
Wenlock, B.	Wenlock	1461	1471	Extinct
Wentworth, B.	Wentworth	1529	—	Abeyance

614

Titles.	In the Family of	Period of Possession.		Eventual Destination.
Wentworth, of Wentworth Woodhouse, B.	Wentworth	from 1628 to 1695		Extinct
Wentworth, V.	Wentworth	1628	1799	Extinct
Weston, B.	Weston	1628	1688	Extinct
Westmoreland, E.	Nevill	1397	1570	Forfeited
Wharton, B.	Wharton	1545	1728	Forfeited
Wharton, E.	Wharton	1706	1728	Forfeited
Wharton, M.	Wharton	1715	1728	Forfeited
Wharton, D.	Wharton	1718	1728	Forfeited
Whitworth, V.	Whitworth	1813	1825	Extinct
Whitworth, E.	Whitworth	1815	1825	Extinct
Widdrington, B.	Widdrington	1643	1716	Forfeited
Willington, B.	Willington	1329	1348	Extinct
Williams, of Thame, B.	Williams	1554	1559	Abeyance
Willoughby, of Parham, B.	Willoughby	1547	1779	Extinct
Wilmington, B.	Compton	1728	1743	Extinct
Wilmington, E.	Compton	1730	1743	Extinct
Wilmot, B.	Wilmot	1643	1681	Extinct
Wiltshire, E.	Scrope	1397	1399	Forfeited
Wiltshire, E.	Butler	1449	1461	Extinct
Wiltshire, E.	Stafford	1470	1499	Extinct
Wiltshire, E.	Stafford	1509	1523	Extinct
Wiltshire, E.	Boleyn	1529	—	Extinct
Wimbledon, V.	Cecil	1626	1638	Extinct
Winchester, E.	Quincy	1210	1264	Extinct
Winchester, E.	Despencer	1322	1326	Extinct
Windsore, E.	Windsore	1361	1361	Extinct
Woodstock, B.	Plantagenet	1380	—	
Worcester, E.	Percy	1397	1402	Extinct
Worcester, E.	Beauchamp	1420	1431	Extinct
Worcester, E.	Tiptoft	1449	1470	Forfeited
Wotton, B.	Wotton (Kirkhoven)	1650	1602	Extinct.

Y.

Yarmouth, V.	Paston	1673	1732	Extinct
Yarmouth, E.	Paston	1699	1732	Extinct
Yarmouth, Css.	Walmoden	1740	1675	Extinct
York, D.	Plantagenet	1385	1461	Merged in the crown
York, D.	Tudor	1491	1509	Merged in the crown
York, D.	Stuart	1604	1625	Merged in the crown
York, D.	Stuart	1643	1685	Merged in the crown
York, D.	Guelph	1716	1728	Extinct
York, D.	Guelph	1760	1767	Extinct
York, D.	Guelph	1784	1826	Extinct.

Z.

Zouche, B.	Zouche	1299	1314	Abeyance
Zouche, of Mortimer, B.	Zouche	1323	—	Abeyance.

615

CHARTERS OF FREEDOM,

EXTORTED BY THE BARONS FROM KING JOHN.

𝕸𝖆𝖌𝖓𝖆 𝕮𝖍𝖆𝖗𝖙𝖆,

SIGNED AT RUNYMEDE, 15th June, 1215.

There are two copies of this celebrated charter in the COTTON Library, as old as the time of JOHN. One has still the broad seal, although some of the wax was melted by the flames which, consumed, on the 23d October, 1731, part of that valuable collection, and rendered a few letters of the charter illegible. Both charters appear to have been written by the same hand. That which is without a seal has two slits at the bottom, from which, doubtless, two seals were suspended.

RUNNEMEDE, or RUNYMEDE; that is, the MEAD OF COUNCIL, (so called from being the place where treaties concerning the peace of the kingdom had from early times been negociated,) is situated between Staines and Windsor. There both parties met on the 5th of June, and pitched their tents asunder in the meadow. On the King's side appeared the ARCHBISHOPS of Canterbury and Dublin, with the BISHOPS of London, Winchester, Lincoln, Bath, Worcester, Coventry, and Rochester; Pandulph, the Pope's Legate, and Almeric, Master of the Knights Templars in England; William Mareschall, Earl of Pembroke, the Earls of Salisbury, Warren, and Arundell; with the Barons Alan de Galoway, William Fitz-Gerald, Peter and Matthew Fitz-Herbert, Thomas and Alan Basset, Hugh de Nevil, Hubert de Burgh, Seneschal of Poictou, Robert de Roppeley, John Mareschall, and Philip de Albini. Upon the Baronial side there were so many as scarcely to be numbered. The chief was Robert Fitz-Walter, their General.

*** The paragraphs inserted between marks, thus [ ], are such clauses as were omitted in the Magna Charta of Henry III., and all the Charters that followed.

𝕵𝖔𝖍𝖓, 𝖇𝖞 𝖙𝖍𝖊 𝕲𝖗𝖆𝖈𝖊 𝖔𝖋 𝕲𝖔𝖉, 𝕶𝖎𝖓𝖌 𝖔𝖋 𝕰𝖓𝖌𝖑𝖆𝖓𝖉, 𝕷𝖔𝖗𝖉 𝖔𝖋 𝕴𝖗𝖊𝖑𝖆𝖓𝖉, 𝕯𝖚𝖐𝖊 𝖔𝖋 𝕹𝖔𝖗𝖒𝖆𝖓𝖉𝖞 𝖆𝖓𝖉 𝕬𝖖𝖚𝖎𝖙𝖆𝖎𝖓𝖊, 𝖆𝖓𝖉 𝕰𝖆𝖗𝖑 𝖔𝖋 𝕬𝖓𝖏𝖔𝖚: To the Archbishops, Bishops, Abbots, Earls, Barons, Justiciaries, Foresters, Sheriffs, Governors, Officers, and to all Bailiffs and others, his faithful subjects, greeting. Know ye that we, in the presence of God, and for the health of our soul, and the souls of our ancestors and heirs, to the honour of God, and the exaltation of holy church, and amendment of our kingdom, by the advice of our venerable fathers, Stephen, Archbishop of Canterbury, Primate of all England, and Cardinal of the holy Roman Church; Henry, Archbishop of Dublin: William, Bishop of London; Peter of Winchester, Jocelin of Bath and Glastonbury, Hugh of Lincoln, Walter of Worcester, William of Coventry, Benedict of Rochester, Bishops; and Master Pandulph, the Pope's Sub-Deacon and Servant, Brother Alymeric, Master of the Temple; and the noble persons, William Mareschall, Earl of Pembroke; William, Earl of Salisbury; William, Earl of Warren; William, Earl of Arundel; Alan de Galoway, Constable of Scotland; William Fitz-Gerald, Peter Fitz-Herbert, and Hubert de Burgh, Seneschal of Poictou, Hugo de Neville, Matthew Fitz-Herbert, Thomas Basset, Alan Basset, Philip de Albiney, Robert de Roppele, John Marescall, John Fitz-Hugh, and others, our liegemen, have, in the first place, granted to God, and by this our present charter confirmed for us and our heirs for ever:

I. That the Church of England shall be free,* and enjoy her whole rights and liberties inviolable. [And we will have them so to be observed, which appears from hence, that the freedom of elections, which is reckoned most necessary for the Church of England, of our own free will and pleasure we have granted and confirmed by our charter, and obtained the confirmation thereof from Pope Innocent the Third before the discord between us and our barons, which charter we shall observe, and do will it to be faithfully observed by our heirs for ever.]

II. We have also granted to all the freemen of our kingdom, for us and our heirs for ever, all the underwritten liberties, to have and to hold, them and their heirs, of us and our heirs:

III. If any of our earls or barons, or others who hold of us, in chief by military service, shall die, and at the same time of his death his heir is of full age, and owes a relief, he shall have his inheritance by the ancient relief, that is to say, the heir or heirs of an earl, for a whole earl's barony, by a hundred pounds; the heir or heirs of a baron, for a whole barony, by an hundred marks; the heir or heirs of a knight, for a whole knight's fee, by an hundred shillings at the most; and he that oweth less shall give less, according to the ancient customs of fees.

IV. But if the heir of any such be under age, and shall be in ward when he comes of age, he shall have his inheritance without relief, or without fine.

V. The warden of the land of such heir who shall be under age, shall take of the land of such heir, on reasonable issues, reasonable customs and reasonable services,† and that without destruction and waste of the men or things; and if we commit the guardianship of those lands to the sheriff or any other who is answerable to us for the issues of the land, and he make destruction and waste upon the ward-lands, we will compel him to give satisfaction, and the land shall be committed to two lawful and discreet tenants of that fee, who shall be answerable for the issues to us, or him to whom we shall assign. And if we give or sell the wardship of any such lands to any one, and he make destruction or waste upon them, he shall lose the wardship, which shall be committed to two lawful and discreet tenants of that fee, who shall, in like manner, be answerable to us, as hath been said.

VI. But the warden, so long as he hath the wardship of the land, shall keep up and maintain the houses, parks, warrens, ponds and mills, and other things pertaining to the land, out of the issues of the same land, and shall restore to the heir, when he comes of full age, his whole land stocked with ploughs and carriages, according as the time of wainage‡ shall require, and the issues of the land can reasonably bear.

VII. Heirs shall be married without disparagement§ (so as that, before

---

* *Free*—Freed from all *unjust* exactions and oppressions.
† *Issues*—Rents and profits issuing out of the lands or tenements of the ward.
Customs—Things due by custom or prescription, and appendant to the lands or tenements in ward; as advowsons, commons, stray, &c.: as also fines of tenants by copy of court roll.
Services—The drudgery and labour due from copyholders to their lords.
‡ *Wainage*—Implements of husbandry.
§ *Disparagement*—According to their rank.

marriage is contracted, those who are nearest to the heir in blood be made acquainted with it).

VIII. A widow, after the death of her husband, shall forthwith, and without any difficulty, have her marriage* and inheritance; nor shall she give any thing for her marriage, or her dower, or her inheritance, which her husband and she held at the day of his death; and she may remain in the capital messuage or mansion-house of her husband forty days after his death, within which term her dower shall be assigned.

IX. No widow shall be distrained† to marry herself, so long as she has a mind to live without a husband; but yet she shall give security that she will not marry without our assent, if she holds of us; or without the consent of the lord of whom she holds, if she holds of another.

X. Neither we nor our bailiffs‡ shall seize any land§ or rent for any debt, so long as there are chattels or debtors upon the premises sufficient to pay the debt. Nor shall the sureties of the debtor be distrained, so long as the principal debtor is sufficient for the payment of the debt.

XI. And if the principal debtor fail in the payment of the debt, having where-withal to discharge it, then the sureties shall answer the debt; and if they will, they shall have the lands and rents of the debtor until they be satisfied for the debts which they have paid for him, unless the principal debtor can shew himself acquitted thereof against the said sureties.

XII. [If any one have borrowed any thing of the Jews, more or less, and dies before the debt be satisfied, there shall be no interest paid for that debt, so long as the heir be under age, of whomsoever he may hold; and if the debt falls into our hands, we shall take only the chattel mentioned in the charter or instruments.]

XIII. [And if any one die indebted to the Jews, his wife shall have her dower, and pay nothing of that debt; and if the deceased left children under age, they shall have necessaries provided for them according to the tenement (or real estate) of the deceased, and of the residue the debt shall be paid, saving, however, the service of the lords. In like manner let it be to other persons than Jews.]

XIV. No scutage or aid shall be imposed in our kingdom, unless by the common council of our kingdom, except to redeem our person, and to make our eldest son a knight, and once to marry our eldest daughter; and for this there shall only be paid a reasonable aid.

XV. [In like manner it shall be, concerning the aids of the city of London; and] the city of London shall have all her ancient liberties and free customs; as well by land as by water.

XVI. Furthermore, we will and grant, that all other cities, and boroughs, and towns, and ports, shall have all their liberties and free customs; and shall have the common council of the kingdom concerning the assessment of their aids,‖ except in the three cases aforesaid.

XVII. [And for the assessing of scutages, we shall cause to be summoned, the archbishops, bishops, abbots, earls, and great barons of the realm, singly, by our letters.]

XVIII. [And furthermore, we will cause to be summoned, in general, by our

---

* *Marriage*—Liberty to marry where she will.
† *Distrained*—Compelled by seizing her goods.
‡ *Bailiffs*—In this place the sheriff and his under bailiffs are meant.
§ By the common law, the king for his debt, had execution of the body, lands and goods of the debtor; so that this is an act of grace, restraining the power the crown had possessed before.
‖ This is according to Dr. Brady's explanation, *they shall send their representatives or commissioners to the common council of the kingdom.*

619

sheriffs and bailiffs, all others who hold of us in chief, at a certain day, that is to say, forty days before their meeting, at least to a certain place, and in all letters of such summons, we will declare the cause of the summons.]

XIX. [And summons being thus made, the business shall proceed on the day appointed, according to the advice of such as are present, although all that were summoned come not.]

XX. We will not for the future grant to any one, that he may take the aid of his own free-tenants, unless to redeem his body, and to make his only son a knight, and once to marry his eldest daughter, and for this there shall be only paid a reasonable aid.

XXI. No man shall be distrained to perform more service for a knight's fee or other free tenements, than is due from thence.

XXII. Common pleas* shall not follow our court, but be holden in some certain place. Trials upon the writs of *Novel Desseisin*, and of *Mort d'Ancester*, and of *Durreine Presentment*,† shall be taken in their proper counties and after this manner. We, (or if we are out of the realm,) our chief justiciary shall send two justiciaries through every county, four times a year: who with the four knights chosen out of every shire, by the people, shall hold the said assizes in the county, on the day, and at the place appointed.

XXIII. And if any matters cannot be determined, on the day appointed to hold the assizes in each county, so many of the knights and freeholders, as have been at the assizes aforesaid, shall be appointed to decide them as is necessary, according as there is more or less business.

XXIV. A freeman‡ shall not be amerced for a small fault, but according to the degree of the fault; and for a great crime, in proportion to the heinousness of it: saving to him his contenement;§ and after the same manner, a merchant, saving him his merchandise.

XXV. And a villain shall be amerced after the same manner, saving to him his wainage,‖ if he falls under our mercy; and none of the aforesaid amerciaments¶ shall be assessed, but by the oath of honest men of the neighbourhood.

XXVI. Earls and barons shall not be amerced but by their peers,** and according to the quality of their offence.

---

* The king's court or palace was anciently the great or principal seat of judicature; but towards the close of King JOHN's reign, the jurisdiction of that court came to be divided, and common pleas referred to another court then erected. This new seat of justice was called the Bank, from being fixed at Westminster, where the justiciars were to sit, and not to follow the king's court.

† A writ of *Assize of Novel Disseisin* lies, where a tenant for ever, or for life, is put out or disseised of his lands or tenements, rents, common of pasture, common way, or of an office, toll, &c., that he may recover his right. A writ of *Mort d'Ancestor*, is that which lies, where any of a man's near relations die seised of lands, rents, or tenements, and after their deaths, a stranger seizes upon them. A writ of *Darreine Presentment*, lies, where a man and his ancestors have presented to a church, and after it is become void, a stranger presents thereto, whereby the person having right is disturbed. This article tended greatly to the ease of the jurors, and to the saving of charges to the parties concerned; for, before this statute, the writs of *Assize of Novel Disseisin*, &c., were returnable either before the king, or in the Court of Common Pleas, and to be taken there.

‡ By *Freemen* here, and in most places, must be understood *freeholders*, that is, those that held their lands of the king, or some other lord, by a stipulated relief.

§ *Contenementum* is to be understood of the means of a man's livelihood, as the arms of a soldier, the ploughs and carts of a husbandman, &c.

‖ *Wainage*—Carts, implements of husbandry, &c.

¶ *Amerciament* is derived from the French word *merci*, and signifies the pecuniary punishment of an offender against the king, or other lord, in his court, who is found to have offended, and to be at the mercy of the king or his lord.

** *Peers*—There are two orders of subjects, *Peers and Commoners*. The nobles have for their peers, all the peers of the realm; and the commoners are all deemed peers of each other.

XXVII. No ecclesiastical person shall be amerced for his lay tenement, but according to the proportion aforesaid, and not according to the value of his ecclesiastical benefice.

XXVIII. Neither a town nor any person, shall be distrained to make bridges over rivers, unless that anciently and of right they are bound to do it.

XXIX. No sheriff, constable,* coroners, or others, our bailiffs, shall hold pleas of the crown.

XXX. [All counties and heralds, wapentakes and trethings, shall stand at the old ferm, without any increase, except in our demesne lands.]

XXXI. If any one that holds of us a lay fee, dies, and the sheriff or our bailiff shew our letters patent of summons concerning the debt, due to us from the deceased; it shall be lawful for the sheriff or our bailiff, to attach and register the chattels of the deceased, found upon his lay fee, to the value of the debt, by the view of lawful men, so as nothing be removed until our whole debt be paid, and the rest shall be left to the executors, to fulfil the will of the deceased; and if there be nothing due from him to us, all the chattels shall remain to the deceased, saving to his wife and children their reasonable share.

XXXII. [If any freeman die intestate, his chattels shall be distributed by the hands of his nearest relations and friends, by view of the church, saving to every one his debts which the deceased owed.]

XXXIII. No constable or bailiff of ours, shall take corn or other chattels of any man, unless he presently give him money for it, or hath respite of payment from the seller.

XXXIV. No constable shall distrain any knight to give money for castle-guard, if he himself will do it in his own person, or by any other able man, in case he is hindered by any reasonable cause.

XXXV. And if we lead him or send him into the army, he shall be free from castle-guard, for the time he shall be in the army—by our command.

XXXVI. No sheriff or bailiff of ours or any other, shall take horses or carts of any, for carriage.

XXXVII. Neither we nor our officers or others, shall take any man's timber, for our castles or other uses unless by the consent of the owner of the timber.

XXXVIII. We will retain the lands of those convicted of felony, but one year and a day, and then they shall be delivered to the lords of the fee.

XXXIX. All wears for the time to come, shall be destroyed in the rivers of Thames and Medway, and throughout all England, except upon the sea coast.

XL. The writ which is called *Præcipe,*† for the future shall not be granted to any one of any tenement, whereby a freeman may lose his cause.

XLI. There shall be one measure of wine, and one of ale, through our whole realm, and one measure of corn; that is to say, the *London quarter,* and one breadth of dyed cloth, and *russett,* and *haberjects;*‡ that is to say, two ells within the list; and the weights shall be as measures.

---

* *Constable* is here taken for constable of a castle. They were men in ancient times of influence and authority; and for pleas of the crown, had the same power within their precincts, as the sheriff had within his bailiwick, before this act; and they commonly sealed with their portraiture on horseback. The territories of a castle regularly comprised a manor, so that every constable of a castle was constable of a manor.

† The writ called *Præcipe quod reddat,* from the first words in it, had several uses. It signified in general, an order from the king, or some court of justice, to put into possession one that complains of having been unjustly ousted. Apparently there were several abuses of this instrument.

‡ *Russets and Haberjects*—Species of coarse cloth.

621

XLII. From henceforward, nothing shall be given or taken for a writ of inquisition,* from him that desires an inquisition of life or limbs—but shall be granted gratis and not denied.

· XLIII. If any one hold of us, by fee-farm, or socage, or burgage,† and holds lands by another, of military service, we will not have the wardship of the heir or land, which belongs to another man's fee, by reason of what he holds of us, by fee-farm, socage, or burgage, unless the fee-farm is bound to perform military service.

XLIV. We will not have the wardship of an heir, nor of any land which he holds of another, by military service—by reason of any petit serjeantcy he holds of us, as by the service of giving us daggers, arrows, or the like.

XLV. No bailiff, for the future, shall put any man to his law,‡ upon his single accusation, without credible witnesses produced to prove it.

XLVI. No freeman shall be taken, or imprisoned, or disseised, or outlawed, or banished, or any ways destroyed; nor will we pass upon him, or commit him to prison, unless by the legal judgment of his peers, or by the law of the land.

XLVII. We will sell to no man, we will deny no man, or defer right nor justice.

XLVIII. All merchants§ shall have secure conduct, to go out of and to come into England, and to stay there, and to pass as well by land as by water, to buy and sell by the ancient and allowed customs, without any evil toils, except in time of war, or when they are of any nation in war with us.

XLIX. And if there be found any such in our land in the beginning of the war, they shall be attached, without damage to their bodies or goods, until it may be known unto us, or our chief justiciary, how our merchants be treated in the nation at war with us; and if ours be safe there, they shall be safe in our dominions.

L. [It shall be lawful, for the time to come, for any one to go out of the kingdom, and return safely and securely by land or by water, saving his allegiance to us, unless in time of war, by some short space, for the common benefit of the kingdom, except prisoners and outlaws, (according to the law of the land,) and people in war with us, and merchants who shall be in such condition as is above mentioned.]

LI. If any man holds of any escheat, as the honour of Wallingford, Nottingham, Boulogne, Lancaster, or of other escheats which are in our hands, and are baronies, and dies, his heir shall not give any other relief, or perform any other service to us, than he would to the baron, if the barony were in possession of the baron: we will hold it after the same manner the baron held it.

LII. [Those men who dwell without the forest, from henceforth shall not come before our justiciaries of the forest, upon common summons, but such as are impleaded or the pledges of any, for any that were attached for something concerning the forests.]

LIII. We will not make any justiciaries, constables, sheriffs, or bailiffs, but what are knowing in the law of the realm, and are disposed duly to observe it.

* *Inquisition*—This was a writ directed to the sheriff, to inquire whether a man sent to prison on suspicion of murder was so committed upon a reasonable ground of suspicion, or through malice and ill-will.

† *Fee Farm, Socage, and Burgage*—To hold in *Fee Farm*, is when there is some rent reserved by the lord upon the creation of the tenancy. In *Socage*, upon condition of ploughing the lord's lands, and doing other inferior offices of husbandry: and in *Burgage*, when the inhabitants of a Borough held their tenements of the king at a certain rent.

‡ *To his Law*, means to his oath.

§ By some old laws, foreign merchants were prohibited the kingdom, except in fair time, and their sojourn was then limited to forty days.

LIV. All barons who are founders of abbies, and have charters of the kings of England for the advowson, or are entitled to it by ancient tenure, may have the custody of them when void, as they ought to have.

LV. All woods that have been taken into the forests in our own time, shall forthwith be laid out again; and the like shall be done with the rivers that have been taken or fenced in by us during our reign.

LVI. All evil customs concerning forests, warrens, and forresters, warreners, sheriffs, and their officers, rivers and their keepers, shall forthwith be inquired into, in each county, by twelve knights of the same shire, chosen by the most creditable persons in the same county, and upon oath; and within forty days after the said inquest, be utterly abolished, so as never to be restored.

LVII. We will immediately give up all hostages and engagements delivered unto us by our English subjects as securities for their keeping the peace and yielding us faithful service.

LVIII. We will entirely remove from our bailiwicks the relations of Gerard de Athyes, so as that for the future they shall have no bailiwick in England. We will also remove Engelard de Cygony, Andrew, Peter, and Gyon de Canceles, Gyon de Cygony, Geoffry de Martyn, and his brothers, Phillip Mark, and his brothers, and his nephew, Geoffrey, and their whole retinue.

LIX. And as soon as peace is restored, we will send out of the kingdom all foreign soldiers, cross-bow-men, and stipendiaries, who are come with horses and arms, to the injury of our people.

LX. If any one hath been dispossessed or deprived by us, without the legal judgment of his peers, of his lands, castles, liberties, or rights, we will forthwith restore them to him; and if any dispute arises upon this head, let the matter be decided by the five-and-twenty barons hereafter mentioned, for the preservation of the peace.

LXI. As for all those things of which any person has, without the legal judgment of his peers, been dispossessed or deprived, either by King Henry, our father, or our brother King Richard, and which we have in our hands, or are possessed by others, and we are bound to warrant and make good, we shall have a respite till the term usually allowed the Croises, excepting those things about which there is a suit depending, or whereof an inquest hath been made by our order before we undertook the crusade; but when we return from our pilgrimage, or if we do not perform it, we will immediately cause full justice to be administered therein.

LXII. The same respite we shall have for disafforesting the forests which Henry, our father, or our brother, Richard, have afforested, and for the wardship of the lands which are in another's fee, in the same manner as we have hitherto enjoyed those wardships by reason of a fee held of us by knights' service; and for the abbies founded in any other fee than our own, in which the lord of the fee claims a right; and when we return from our pilgrimage, or if we should not perform it, we will immediately do full justice to all the complainants in his behalf.

LXIII. No man shall be taken or imprisoned upon the appeal of a woman for the death of any other man than her husband.

LXIV. All unjust and illegal fines, and all amerciaments imposed unjustly and contrary to the law of the land, shall be entirely forgiven, or else be left to the decision of the five-and-twenty barons, hereafter mentioned, for the preservation of the peace, or of the major part of them, together with the aforesaid Stephen, Archbishop of Canterbury, if he can be present, and others whom he shall think fit to take along with him; and if he cannot be present, the business shall, notwithstanding, go on without him: but so that if one or more of the afore-said five-and-twenty barons be plaintiffs in the same cause, they shall be set aside as to what concerns this particular affair, and others be chosen in their room out of the said five-and-twenty, and sworn by the rest to decide that matter.

LXV. If we have disseised or dispossessed the Welsh of any lands, liberties, or other things, without the legal judgment of their peers, they shall imme-diately be restored to them. And if any dispute arise upon this head, the matter shall be determined in the Marches by the judgment of their peers—for tene-ments in England, according to the law of England; for tenements in Wales, ac-cording to the law of Wales: the same shall the Welsh do to us and our subjects.

LXVI. As for all those things of which any Welshman hath without the legal judgment of his peers been disseised or deprived by King Henry, our father, or our brother, King Richard, and which we either have in our hands, or others are possessed of, and we are obliged to warrant, we shall have a respite till the time generally allowed the Croises, excepting those things about which a suit is depending, or whereof an inquest hath been made by our order before we under-took the crusade: but when we return, or if we stay at home, and do not per-form our pilgrimage, we will immediately do them full justice according to the law of the Welsh, and of the parts afore-mentioned.

LXVII. We will, without delay, dismiss the son of Lewelin, and all the Welsh hostages, and release them from the engagements they entered into with us for the preservation of the peace.

LXVIII. We shall treat with Alexander, King of Scots, concerning the re-storation of his sister and hostages, and his rights and liberties, in the same form and manner as we shall do the rest of our barons of England, unless, by the engagements which his father, William, late King of Scots, hath entered into with us, it ought to be otherwise, and this shall be left to the determination of his peers in our court.

LXIX. All the aforesaid customs and liberties which we have granted to be holden in our kingdom, as much as it belongs to us towards our people, all our subjects, as well clergy as laity, shall observe, as far as they are concerned, towards their dependants.

LXX. And whereas, for the honour of God and the amendment of our king-dom, and for quieting the discord that has arisen between us and our barons, we have granted all the things aforesaid. Willing to render them firm and lasting, we do give and grant our subjects the following security; namely, that the barons may chuse five-and-twenty barons of the kingdom, whom they think convenient, who shall take care with all their might to hold and observe, and cause to be observed, the peace and liberties we have granted them, and by this our present charter confirmed; so that, if our justiciary, our bailiffs, or any of our officers, shall in any case fail in the performance of them towards any person, or shall break through any of these articles of peace and security, and the offence is notified to four barons, chosen out of the five-and-twenty aforementioned, the said four barons shall repair to us, or our justiciary, if we are out of the realm, and, laying open the grievance, shall petition to have it redressed without delay. And if it is not redressed by us, if we should chance to be out of the realm, if it is not redressed by our justiciary, within forty days, reckoning from the time it hath been notified to us, or to our justiciary, if we should be out of the realm, the four barons aforesaid shall lay the cause before the rest and the five-and-twenty barons; and the said five-and-twenty barons, together with the community of the whole kingdom, shall distrain and distress us all the ways possible, namely, by seizing our castles, lands, and possessions in any other manner they can, till the grievance is redressed

624

according to their pleasure, saving harmless our own person, and the persons of our queen and children; and when it is redressed, they shall obey us as before.

LXXI. Any person whatsoever in the kingdom may swear that he will obey the orders of the five-and-twenty barons, aforesaid, in the execution of the premises, and that he will distress us jointly with them to the utmost of his power; and we give public and free liberty to any one that will swear to them, and never shall hinder any person from taking the same oath.

LXXII. As for all those of our subjects who will not of their own accord swear to join the five-and-twenty barons in distraining and distressing us, we will issue our order to make them take the same oath, as aforesaid.

LXXIII. And if any one of the five-and-twenty barons dies, or goes out of the kingdom, or is hindered any other way from putting the things aforesaid in execution, the rest of the said five-and-twenty barons may chuse another in his room, at their discretion, who shall be sworn in like manner as the rest.

LXXIV. In all things that are committed to the charge of these five-and-twenty barons, if, when they are all assembled together, they should happen to disagree about any matter, or some of them, when summoned, will not or cannot come, whatever is agreed upon or enjoined by the major part of those who are present, shall be reputed as firm and solid as if all the five-and-twenty had given their consent; and the foresaid five-and-twenty shall swear that all the premises they shall faithfully observe and cause with all their power to be observed.

LXXV. And we will not, by ourselves or others, procure any thing whereby any of their concessions and liberties be revoked or lessened; and if any such thing be obtained, let it be null and void; neither shall we ever make use of it, either by ourselves or any other.

LXXVI. And all the ill-will, anger, and malice that hath arisen between us and our subjects, of the clergy and laity, from the first breaking out of the dissension between us, we do fully remit and forgive. Moreover, all trespasses occasioned by the said dissension, from Easter, in the sixteenth year of our reign, till the restoration of peace and tranquillity, we hereby entirely remit to all, clergy as well as laity, and, as far as in us, do fully forgive.

LXXVII. We have, moreover, granted them our letters patent testimonial of Stephen, Lord Archbishop of Canterbury, Henry, Lord Archbishop of Dublin, and the bishops aforesaid, as also Master Pandulph for the Pope's security and concessions aforesaid.

LXXVIII. Wherefore, we will, and firmly enjoin, that the Church of England be free, and that all men in our kingdom have and hold all the aforesaid liberties, rights, and concessions, truly and peaceably, freely and quietly, fully and wholly, to themselves and their heirs, of us and our heirs, in all things and places, for ever, as is aforesaid.

LXXIX. It is also sworn, as well on our part as on the part of the barons, that all things aforesaid shall faithfully and sincerely be observed.

Given under our hand, in the presence of the witnesses above-named, and many others, in the meadow called Runymede, between Windsor and Stanes, in the 15th day of June, in the 17th year of our reign.

o - - - So as we are first acquainted therewith, or our justiciary if we should not be in England.

- - - o And in the same manner about administering justice, deforesting the forests, or letting them continue.

÷ Either in England or Wales.

∴ For ever.

Charter of Forests.

The FORESTS belonged originally to the crown, and the kings had at different periods granted parts and parcels of them to private individuals, who had grubbed them up, and made them arable and pasture: but yet all those parts retained the name of forest. These forests belonging to the king as his own demesnes, or as the sovereign lord, were a continual source of vexatious suits, as well against those who held them of the king, as against the neighbouring freemen, under pretence of the rights of the crown.

Every article of this charter clearly demonstrates how much the subject had been oppressed under pretence of preserving the Royal Forests.

John, by the Grace of God, King of England, &c.: Know ye, that for the honour of God and the health of our soul, and the souls of our ancestors and successors, and for the exaltation of Holy Church, and for the reformation of our kingdom, we have, of our free and good will, given and granted, for us and our heirs, these liberties hereafter specified, to be and observed in our kingdom of England for ever.

I. *Imprimis.* All the forests made by our grandfather, King Henry, shall be viewed by honest and lawful men; and if he turned any other than his own proper woods into forests, to the damage of him whose wood it was, it shall forthwith be laid out again and disaforested. And if he turned his own woods into forests, they shall remain so, saving the common of pasture to such as were formerly wont to have.

II. *Is the LII. and LV. of the great charter put into one chapter.*

III. The archbishops, bishops, abbots, earls, barons, knights, and free tenants, who have woods in any forests, shall have their woods as they had them at the time of the first coronation of our grandfather, King Henry, so as they shall be discharged for ever of all purprestures,* wastes, and assarts,† made in those woods, after that time, to the beginning of the second year of our coronation; and those who for the time to come shall make waste, purpresture, or assart in those woods, without our licence, shall answer for them.

IV. Our inspectors or viewers shall go through the forests to make a view, as it was wont to be at the time of the first coronation of our said grandfather, King Henry, and not otherwise.

---

* *Purprestures*—Encroachment upon the king's lands.
† *Wastes and Assarts*—Grubbing up wood, and making it arable, without licence.

V. The inquisition, or view for lawing* of dogs, which are kept within the forest, for the future shall be when the view is made, that is, every three years, and then shall be done by the view and testimony of lawful men, and not otherwise; and he whose dogs, at such time, shall be found unlawed, shall be fined three shillings; and for the future no ox shall be taken for lawing, and such lawing shall be according to the common assize, namely, the three claws of the dog's fore-foot shall be cut off, or the ball of the foot taken out. And, from henceforward, dogs shall not be lawed, unless in such places where they were wont to be lawed in the time of King Henry, our grandfather.

VI. No forester or *bedel*,† for the future, shall make any aleshots,‡ or collect sheaves of corn or oats, or other grain, or lambs or pigs, nor shall make any gathering whatsoever, but by the view and oath of twelve inspectors; and when they make their view, so many foresters shall be appointed to keep the forest as they shall reasonably keep sufficient.

VII. No swainmote, for the time to come, shall be holden in our kingdom oftener than thrice a year; that is to say, in the beginning of fifteen days before Michaelmas, when the agisters come to agist the demesne woods; and about the feast of St. Martin, when our agisters are to receive their pannage;§ and in these two swainmotes, the foresters, verderers, and agisters shall meet, and no other, by compulsion or distress; and the third swainmote shall be holden fifteen days before the feast of St. John the Baptist, concerning the fawning of our does; and at this swainmote shall meet the foresters and verderers, and no other shall be compelled to be there.

VIII. And furthermore, every forty days throughout the year, the verderers and foresters shall meet to view the attachments of the forests, as well of vert as venison,‖ by presentment of the foresters themselves; and they who committed the offences shall be forced to appear before them: but the aforesaid swainmotes shall be holden but in such counties as they were wont to be holden.

IX. Every freeman shall agist¶ his wood in the forest at his pleasure, and shall receive his pannage.

X. We grant, also, that every freeman may drive his hogs through our demesne roads freely and without impediment, and may agist them in his own woods or elsewhere, as he will; and if the hogs of any freeman shall remain one night in our forest, he shall not be troubled, so as to lose any thing for it.

XI. No man, for the time to come, shall lose life or limb for taking our venison; but if any one be seized and convicted of taking venison, he shall be grievously fined, if he hath wherewithal to pay; and if he hath not, he shall lie in our prison a year and a day; and if after that time he can find securities, he shall be released; if not, he shall abjure our realm of England.

XII. It shall be lawful for every archbishop, bishop, earl or baron, coming to us by our command, and passing through our forest, to take one or two deer by view of the forester, if present: if not, he shall cause a horn to be sounded, lest he should seem to steal them. Also, on their return it shall be lawful for them to do the same thing.

XIII. Every freeman, for the future, may erect a mill in his own wood, or

---

* *Lawing of Dogs*—Cutting off their claws, &c.
† *Bedel*—Bailiff of the forest.
‡ *Shall make any Ale-shots*—That is, taking ale-shots to execute the offender.
§ *Pannage*—Money for feeding hogs, with *mast* in the king's forests.
‖ *Vert as Venison*—That is, the offences which were committed in cutting wood or killing deer.
¶ *Agist*—Take in his neighbour's cattle to feed.

upon his own land, which he hath in the forest, or make a warren, or pond, a marl-pit, or ditch, or turn it into arable, without the covert in arable land, so as it be not to the detriment of his neighbour.

XIV. Every freeman may have in his woods, the avyries of hawks, of spar-hawks, falcons, eagles, and herons; and they shall likewise have the honey found in their woods.

XV. No forester, for the future, who is not a forester in fee, paying us rent for his office, shall take cheminage;* that is to say, for every cart two-pence, for half a year, and for the other half year, two-pence; and for a horse that carries bur-den, for half a year, a half-penny, and for the other half year, a half-penny; and then only, of those who come as buyer, out of their bailiwick, to buy under-wood, timber, bark, or charcoal, to carry it to sell in other places, where they will; and for the time to come, there shall be no cheminage taken, for any other cart or carriage horse, unless in those places where anciently it was wont, and ought to be taken; but they who carry wood, bark, or coal, upon their backs to sell, though they get their livelihood by it, shall for the future pay no cheminage for passage through the woods of other men. No cheminage shall be given to our foresters, but only in our woods.

XVI. All persons outlawed for offences committed in our forests, from the time of Henry, our father, until our first coronation, may reverse their out-lawries without impediment, but shall find pledges, that for the future they will not forfeit to us, in our forests.

XVII. No *castellan* or other person, shall hold pleas of the forest, whether concerning vert or venison; but every forester in fee shall attach pleas of the forest,† as well concerning vert as venison, and shall present the pleas or offences to the verderers of the several counties; and when they shall be enrolled and sealed under the seals of the verderers, they shall be presented to the chief forester, when he comes into those parts, to hold pleas of the forest, and shall be determined before him.

XVIII. And all the customs and liberties aforesaid, which we have granted to be holden in the kingdom; as much as belongs to us towards our vassels, all of our kingdom, as well laicks as clerks, shall observe as much as belongs to them, towards their vassals.

Note.—There is no original of this charter extant, nor any copy older than the 1st of Henry III.

---

* *Cheminage*—Fees for passing through the forest.
† May seize the body or goods of the offenders to make them appear.

THE

ROLL OF BATTEL ABBEY,*

FROM HOLINGSHED.

Thr Table containing the following names, was formerly suspended in the Abbey of Battel, in Sussex, with this inscription;

> Dicitur a bello, bellum locus hic, quia bello
> Angligenæ victi, sunt hic in morte relicti:
> Martyris in Christi festo cecidere Calixti:
> Sexagenus erat sextus millessimus annus
> Cum pereunt Angli, stella monstrante cometâ.

The authority of this celebrated document cannot, however, be much relied upon. "There are," says Sir William Dugdale, "great errors, or rather falsifications, in most of the copies of it; by attributing the derivation of many from the *French*, who were not all of such extraction, but merely *English*. For such hath been the subtilty of some monks of old, that, finding it acceptable unto most to be reputed descendants to those who were companions with Duke William in his expedition, therefore to gratify them, they inserted their names into that ancient catalogue."

Aumarle	Andevile	Bondevile	Breton·
Aincourt	Amouerduile	Brabason	Bluat and Baious
Audeley	Arcy and Akeny	Baskervile	Browne
Angilliam	Albeny	Bures	Beke
Argentoune	Aybeuare	Bounilaine	Bikard
Arundel	Amay	Bois	Banastre
Auenant	Aspermound	Botelere	Baloun
Abell	Amerenges.	Bourcher	Beauchampe
Arwerne		Brabaion	Bray and Bandy
Aunwers	Bertram	Berners	Bracy
Angers	Buttecourt	Braibuf	Boundes
Angenoun	Brebus and Byssy	Brand and Brouce	Bascoun
Archere	Bardolfe	Burgh	Broilem
Anuay	Basset and Bigot	Bushy	Brokeuy
Asperuile	Bohun	Banet	Burnell
Abbevile	Bailif	Blondell	Bellet

---

* Battel Abbey. William ordered the foundations of a monastery to be laid on the spot where he gained the victory over Harold; from which circumstance it was called Battel Abbey. As it was there he won the crown, he wished the new establishment to enjoy all the privileges of the royal chapel, and having obtained the consent of the metropolitan, and of the bishop of the diocese, declared it in a full assembly of prelates and barons, exempt "from all episcopal rule and exactions." It became in the language of later times *nullus diocesis*.

Beaudewin	Chaworth	Delaward	Fitz-Herbert
Beaumont	Cleremaus	Delaplanch	Fitz-Peres
Burdon	Clarell	Damnot	Fichet
Berteuilay	Chopis	Danway	Fitz-Rewes
Barre	Chaunduit	Deheuse	Fitz-Fitz
Busseuille	Chantelow	Deuile	Fitz-John
Blunt	Chamberay	Disard	Fleschampe.
Baupere	Cressy	Doiville	
Bevill	Curtenay	Durand	Gurnay
Berduedor	Conestable	Drury	Gresey
Brette	Cholmeley	Dabitott	Graunson
Barrett	Champney	Dunsterville	Gracy
Bonrett	Chawnos	Dunchamp	Georges
Bainard	Coiniville	Dambelton.	Gower
Barnivale	Champaine		Geugy
Bonett	Careuile	Estrange	Goband
Bary	Carbonelle	Estuteville	Gray
Brysn	Charles	Engaine	Gaunson
Bodin	Chareberge	Estriels	Golofre
Beteruille	Chawnes	Esturney.	Gobion
Bertin	Chaumont		Gressy
Berneuille	Caperoun	Ferrerers	Graunt
Bellew	Cheine	Folvile	Grelle
Beuery	Curson	Fitz-Water	Grenet
Bushell	Couille	Fitz-Marmaduke.	Gurry
Boranuile	Chalters	Fleues	Gurley
Browe	Cheines	Filberd	Grammori
Beleuere	Cateray	Fitz-Roger	Gernoun
Buffard	Cherecourt	Fauecourt	Grendon
Bonueier	Cammile	Ferrers	Gurdon
Botevile	Clerensy	Fitz-Philip	Guines
Bellire	Curly	Foliot	Griuel
Bastard	Cuily	Furaleueus	Greneuile
Brasard	Clineis	Fitz-Otes	Giateuile
Beelheime	Clifford.	Fitz-William	Giffard
Braine		Fitz-Roand	Gouerges
Brent	Denaville	Fitz-Pain	Gamages.
Braunch	Derwy	Fitz-Auger	
Belesur	Dive	Fitz-Aleyn	Hautasy
Blundell	Dispensere	Fitz-Rauf	Haunsard
Burdett	Daubeney	Fitz-Browne	Hastings
Bagott	Daniel	Fouke	Hanlay
Beauuise	Deuise and Dreull	Frevile	Haurell
Belemis	Devaus	Front de Bœf	Husee
Belsin	Davers	Facunburge	Hercy
Bernon	Dodingseis	Fors	Herloun
Boels	Darell	Frisell	Herne
Belefroun	Delaber	Fitz-Simon	Harecourt
Brutz	De la Pole	Fitz-Fouk	Henoure
Barchampe.	Delalinde	Folioll	Houell
	Delahill	Fitz-Thomas	Hamelin
Camois	Delaware	Fitz-Morice	Harewell
Camvile	Delsusche	Fitz-Hugh	Hardell
Chawent	Dakeny	Fitz-Hearis	Haket
Cauncy	Dauntre	Fitz-Waren	Hamound
Conderay	Desny	Fitz-Rainold	Harcord.
Colvile	Dabernoune	Flamvile	
Chamberlaine	Damry	Formay	Jarden
Chambernoun	Daueros	Fitz-Eustach	Jay
Comin	Dauonge	Fitz-Lawrence	Janiels
Columber	Duilby	Formibaud	Jercoruise
Cribett	Delasere	Frisound	Jaruile
Creuquere	Delahold	Fiaere	Jasperuile.
Corbine	Durange	Fitz-Robert	
Corbett	Delse	Furnivall	Kaunt
Chaundos	Delaund	Fitz-Geffrey	Karre

Karrowe
Keine
Kimaronne
Kiriell
Kancey
Kenelre.

Louensy
Lacy
Linnebey
Latomer.
Loveday
Lovell
Lemare
Leuetot
Lucy
Luny
Logeuile
Longespes
Louerace
Longechampe
Lascales
Louan
Leded
Luse
Loterell
Loruge
Longueuale
Loy
Lorancourt
Loious
Limers
Longepay
Laumale
Lane
Lovetot.

Mohant
Mowne
Maundeuile
Marmilon
Moribray
Morvile
Miriel
Maulay
Malebrauch
Malemaine
Mortimere
Mortimaine
Muse
Marteine
Mountbother
Mountsoler
Maleuile
Malet
Mourteney
Monfichet
Maleherbe
Mare
Musegros
Musarde
Moine
Montrauers
Merke
Murres
Morthule

Moncheneasy
Mallony
Marny
Mountagu
Mountford
Maule
Monthernon
Musett
Menevile
Manteuenant
Manse
Menpincoy
Maine
Mainard
Morell
Mainell
Malaluse
Memorous
Morreis
Morleian Maine
Malevere
Mandut
Mountmartem
Mantolet
Miners
Mauclerke
Maumchenell
Mouett
Meintenore
Meletak
Manuile
Mangisere
Maumasin
Mountlouel
Maurewarde
Momhaut
Meller
Mountgomerie
Manlay
Maularde
Menere
Martinaste
Mainwaring
Matelay
Malemis
Maleheire
Moren
Melun
Marceaus
Maiell
Morton.

Noers
Nevile
Newmarch
Norbet
Norice
Newborough
Neiremet
Neile
Normavile
Neofmarche
Nermitz
Nembruts.

Otevell

Olibef
Olifant
Olenel
Oisell
Olifard
Ounall
Orioll.

Pigot
Pery
Perepound
Pershale
Power
Painell
Peche and Pauey
Pevrell
Perot
Picard
Pinkenie
Pomeray
Pounce
Paveley
Palfrere
Plukenet
Phuars
Punchardoun
Pinchard
Placy
Pugoy
Patefine
Place
Pampilivun
Percelay
Perere and Pekeny
Poterell
Peukeny
Peccell
Pinell
Putrill
Petiuoll
Preaus
Pantolf
Peito
Penecord
Preuelirlegast
Percivale.

Quinci
Quintini.

Ros
Ridell
Rivers
Riuell
Rous
Rushell
Raband
Ronde
Rie
Rokell
Risers
Randiule
Roselin
Rastoke
Rinuili
Rougere

Rait
Ripere
Rigny
Richmonud
Rochford
Raimond.

Souch
Sheuile
Seucheus
Senclere
Sent Quintin
Sent Omere
Sent Amond
Sent Legere
Somervile
Sieward
Saunsouerre
Sanford
Sanctes
Sauay
Saulay
Sules
Sorell
Somerey
Sent John
Sent George
Sent Les
Seffe
Saluin
Say
Solers
Sent Albin
Sent Martin
Sourdemale
Seguin
Sent Barbe
Sent Vile
Suremounte
Soreglise
Sandvile
Sauncey
Sirewast
Sent Cheveroll
Sent More
Sent Scudemore.

Toget
Tercy
Tuchet
Tracy
Trousbut
Trainell
Taket
Trussell
Trison
Talbot
Touny
Traies
Tollemach
Tolous
Tanny
Touke
Tibtote
Turbevile
Turvile

Tomy and Tavernes	Vere	Vauuruile	Viuille
Trencheville	Vernoun	Veniels	Vancorde and
Trenchilion	Vessy	Verrere	Valenges.
Tankerville	Verdoune	Vachere	
Tirell	Valence	Vessay	Wardebois
Trivet	Verdeire	Vanay	Ward
Tolet	Vavasour	Vian	Wafre
Travers	Vendore	Vernoys	Wake
Tardeville	Verlay	Vrnall	Wareine
Tineville	Valenger	Vnket	Wate
Torell	Venables	Vrnaful	Watelin
Tortechappell	Venoure	Vasderoll	Watevil
Treverell	Vilan	Vaberon	Wely
Tenwis	Verland	Valingford	Werdonell
Totelles	Valers	Venecorde	Wespaile
	Veirny	Vallue	Wivell.

THE END.

LONDON:

HENRY BAYLIS, JOHNSON'S-COURT, FLEET-STREET.